Handbook
of
Public
Budgeting

PUBLIC ADMINISTRATION AND PUBLIC POLICY

A Comprehensive Publication Program

Executive Editor

JACK RABIN
Professor of Public Administration and Public Policy
Division of Public Affairs
The Capital College
The Pennsylvania State University--Harrisburg
Middletown, Pennsylvania

1. *Public Administration as a Developing Discipline (in two parts)*, Robert T. Golembiewski
2. *Comparative National Policies on Health Care*, Milton I. Roemer, M.D.
3. *Exclusionary Injustice: The Problem of Illegally Obtained Evidence*, Steven R. Schlesinger
4. *Personnel Management in Government: Politics and Process*, Jay M. Shafritz, Walter L. Balk, Albert C. Hyde, and David H. Rosenbloom
5. *Organization Development in Public Administration (in two parts)*, edited by Robert T. Golembiewski and William B. Eddy
6. *Public Administration: A Comparative Perspective, Second Edition, Revised and Expanded*, Ferrel Heady
7. *Approaches to Planned Change (in two parts)*, Robert T. Golembiewski
8. *Program Evaluation at HEW (in three parts)*, edited by James G. Abert
9. *The States and the Metropolis*, Patricia S. Florestano and Vincent L. Marando
10. *Personnel Management in Government: Politics and Process, Second Edition, Revised and Expanded*, Jay M. Shafritz, Albert C. Hyde, and David H. Rosenbloom
11. *Changing Bureaucracies: Understanding the Organization Before Selecting the Approach*, William A. Medina
12. *Handbook on Public Budgeting and Financial Management*, edited by Jack Rabin and Thomas D. Lynch
13. *Encyclopedia of Policy Studies*, edited by Stuart S. Nagel
14. *Public Administration and Law: Bench v. Bureau in the United States*, David H. Rosenbloom
15. *Handbook on Public Personnel Administration and Labor Relations*, edited by Jack Rabin, Thomas Vocino, W. Bartley Hildreth, and Gerald J. Miller
16. *Public Budgeting and Finance: Behavioral, Theoretical, and Technical Perspectives*, edited by Robert T. Golembiewski and Jack Rabin
17. *Organizational Behavior and Public Management*, Debra W. Stewart and G. David Garson
18. *The Politics of Terrorism: Second Edition, Revised and Expanded*, edited by Michael Stohl

46.   *Handbook of Public Budgeting,* edited by Jack Rabin

Additional Volumes in Preparation

Handbook of Organizational Consultation, edited by Robert T. Golembiewski

ANNALS OF PUBLIC ADMINISTRATION

1.   *Public Administration: History and Theory in Contemporary Perspective,* edited by Joseph A. Uveges, Jr.
2.   *Public Administration Education in Transition,* edited by Thomas Vocino and Richard Heimovics
3.   *Centenary Issues of the Pendleton Act of 1883,* edited by David H. Rosenbloom with the assistance of Mark A. Emmert
4.   *Intergovernmental Relations in the 1980s,* edited by Richard H. Leach
5.   *Criminal Justice Administration: Linking Practice and Research,* edited by William A. Jones, Jr.

Handbook
of
Public
Budgeting

edited by
Jack Rabin

Division of Public Affairs
The Capital College
The Pennsylvania State University–Harrisburg
Middletown, Pennsylvania

Marcel Dekker, Inc.   **New York • Basel • Hong Kong**

ISBN   0-8247-8592-4

This book is printed on acid-free paper.

MARCEL DEKKER, INC.
270 Madison Avenue, New York, New York 10016

Current printing (last digit):
10 9 8 7 6 5 4 3 2 1

 PRINTED IN THE UNITED STATES OF AMERICA

To my wife, Sandra, and my sons,
Daniel and Scott

Preface

Nearly ten years have passed since the publication of *The Handbook of Public Budgeting and Financial Management,* the first bibliographical treatise on the discipline. During that time a number of major developments have occurred.

First, two refereed journals were created, including *Public Budgeting and Financial Management* (Marcel Dekker, Inc.). Second, several textbooks were published as well as the only comprehensive public budgeting laboratory, the *Public Budgeting Laboratory* (Carl Vinson Institute of Government, University of Georgia). In addition, the Section on Public Budgeting and Financial Management of the American Society for Public Administration has established its own annual conference.

Moreover, a comprehensive, annotated bibliography of the field has appeared, *Public Budgeting and Financial Management* (Garland). These events, along with this edition and several related Handbooks under preparation, testify to the coming of age of this field.

This book is organized around two major themes: the budget process and budgeting fundamentals. Each chapter is a bibliographical treatise that will enable the reader to obtain an in-depth overview of each of the major subfields in this growing area.

In Unit I, The Budget Process, we present background theories, history, and ideas which serve as foundations for this area. Included here are such topics as basic theories, budget and culture, budget reforms, comparative government budgeting, teaching budgeting, and budget execution and management control.

In Unit II, Budgeting Fundamentals, we concentrate on basic applications, such as expenditure and revenue forecasting, accounting and auditing, taxation, expenditure control, computers, productivity measurement, the economic impact of budgeting, and capital investment.

Finally, in Unit III, Appendices, we submit a number of documents written by the U.S. Government Accounting Office, the Federal Reserve Bank, and the Congressional Budget Office. The three offices publish intensive research papers on subjects of interest; however, these items are rarely widely distributed. We present a few of those documents which we feel have had a direct impact on the subjects covered in this volume and also on the current practice and theory of public budgeting and financial management.

Much needs to be done, and we submit this volume as a stepping stone to the next decade during which much intellectual development must occur. For instance, we need a greater dialog and debate among practitioners and academicians who, even after decades, still rarely talk with one another. We have attempted to stimulate this debate through several conference panels on developments in budget theory as well as the ideas generated and discussed in this volume.

What is a budget? What is financial management? Where does one fit within the other? Why are we still wedded to the federal model, when so many transactions occur among the *eighty to ninety thousand* other governments in this country? What is our interface with economics, accounting, strategic management, and artificial intelligence?

It is up to you, our readers, to determine how well our endeavors have contributed to the advancement of knowledge. We encourage your comments, suggestions, and (above all) your criticisms.

Jack Rabin

Contents

UNIT III: APPENDICES

Contributors

Rosalyn Y. Carter *School of Public Administration, Florida Atlantic University, Fort Lauderdale, Florida*

Howard A. Frank *Department of Public Administration, Florida International University, North Miami, Florida*

George M. Guess *School of Public Administration and Urban Studies, Georgia State University, Atlanta, Georgia, and International Monetary Fund, Washington, D.C.*

Jean Harris *School of Business Administration, Pennsylvania State University–Harrisburg, Middletown, Pennsylvania*

W. Bartley Hildreth *Public Administration Institute, Louisiana State University, Baton Rouge, Louisiana*

Marc Holzer *National Center for Public Productivity, Rutgers University, Newark, New Jersey*

L. R. Jones *Department of Administrative Sciences, Naval Postgraduate School, Monterey, California*

William Earle Klay *School of Public Administration and Policy, Florida State University, Tallahassee, Florida*

Jerry McCaffery *Department of Administrative Sciences, Naval Postgraduate School, Monterey, California*

Gerald J. Miller *Department of Public Administration, Rutgers University, Newark, New Jersey*

Steven Parker *Department of Political Science, University of Nevada, Las Vegas, Nevada*

Joseph C. Pilegge *Department of Political Science, University of Alabama, Tuscaloosa, Alabama*

Irene S. Rubin *Public Administration Division, Northern Illinois University, DeKalb, Illinois*

Thomas A. Silvious *Applications Installations, Information Technologies, Inc., Richmond, Virginia*

John E. Stapleford *Department of Business and Economics, University of Delaware, Newark, Delaware*

Khi V. Thai *School of Public Administration, Florida Atlantic University, Fort Lauderdale, Florida*

Marcia Lynn Whicker *Department of Public Administration, Virginia Commonwealth University, Richmond, Virginia*

Aaron Wildavsky *Department of Political Science and Public Policy, University of California, Berkeley, California*

Unit One
THE BUDGET PROCESS

1

Budgeting:
Theory, Concepts, Methods, and Issues

Irene S. Rubin *Public Administration Division, Northern Illinois University, DeKalb, Illinois*

The function of a theory is to provide an orientation to a field, to state assumptions, to point to certain problems as of key significance, and to come up with some hypotheses about what causes what. In public administration, theory has the additional responsibility of culling practical problems and suggesting solutions. Budget theory in particular should be able to answer questions about why particular practices should be adopted, the importance of particular tasks, and the location of particular tasks in a larger process.

Budgeting does not currently have a theory in this sense. Writers on budgeting do not agree on common assumptions or recommendations. While there are some common questions that have long stirred interest in budgeters, there is no widely accepted set of linked hypotheses concerning cause and effect in budgeting. One paradigm—a set of hypotheses and a methodological approach—dominated the field for a while, but that dominance is now over.

Budget theory today is fragmented and incomplete. In some areas the field seems to be moving toward a consensus, while in others the level of disagreement is acute. Budget theory is in the process of being invented. Studying public budgeting is therefore exciting, but a little confusing. The purpose of this chapter is to organize and reduce the confusion by outlining some of the key assumptions, concepts, methodologies, and current issues.

BUDGET THEORIES AND ASSUMPTIONS

One function of a theory is to provide an overall orientation to a field. Of what is public budgeting a part? Why is it important? Who might want to study it, to find out what kinds of things? How is budgeting conceived?

At the broadest level, theory links public budgeting to the study of society. One reason to study budgeting is to learn about a society by looking at the way the government spends public funds, both in terms of the processes used and the priorities expressed. Budgeting varies enormously across time and across jurisdictions. It matters whether the public budgeting is being carried out in a capitalist, democratic, federal society, or in a socialist, authoritarian, national state. It matters whether the form of government is parliamentary or presidential. In the United States, state and local budgeting differs in significant ways from federal budgeting. The size of the budget, the scope and variety of functions performed by the public sector, the openness of the budget process, and the distribution of costs and benefits vary from society to society and from community to community.

Although in recent years observers have agreed that variations in budgeting from place to place and from time to time are significant, when the relationship of budgeting to society is examined for the United States, there has been little agreement as to what budgeting reveals about the society. Each theoretical school makes its own assumptions.

Neo-Marxists have argued that class interests dominate budgeting and allocation choices. Several different schools argue that government itself, as represented by the bureaucrats or agency heads, determine allocations, while some scholars have argued that interest groups dominate or even determine budgeting.*

The Neo-Marxists, who form only a loose kind of school, generally argue that government is controlled by capitalists, or those who own the means of production, and that they determine spending priorities to serve their own needs. Those needs include particular programs and funds that aid in the accumulation of capital. Social welfare programs in this theory are used to buy off opposition from the poor who would otherwise protest the system and possibly overturn it. Neo-Marxists call attention to military spending as enriching arms manufacturers, to increases in spending for economic development, much of which is a transfer payment from the average citizen to the relatively well-to-do, and to a variety of tax breaks that have benefited the well-to-do more than the poor. In a Neo-Marxian perspective, maintaining markets abroad has been the reason for both imperialism and wars, and preserving bond markets has been a major reason for much of state and local fiscal policy.

Neo-Marxists have usefully called attention to phenomena that might otherwise be ignored, but their models are still incomplete. Some, especially the older ones, tend to be

---

*One seminal Neo-Marxist work is that of James O'Connor, *The Fiscal Crisis of the State,* New York, St. Martin's, 1973. A second useful work in this school is Fred Block's "The ruling class does not rule: Notes on the Marxist theory of the state," *Socialist Revolution* 33 (May/June 1977) 6–27, reprinted in Thomas Ferguson and Joel Rogers, eds., *The Political Economy: Readings in the Politics and Economics of American Public Policy,* Armonk, N.Y., M. E. Sharpe, 1984. Both incrementalists and public choice theorists have often argued that the bureaucracy has disproportionate influence on spending levels. The key incrementalist study outlining the influence of the bureaucracy is Aaron Wildavsky's *The Politics of the Budgetary Process,* Boston, Little Brown, 1964. One of the seminal public choice studies that outline the importance of bureaucratic agencies in increasing expenditures is William Niskanen's *Bureaucracy and Representative Government,* Chicago, Aldine, 1970. Those who argue for interest-group determination of budget levels fall into a less cohesive or recognizable school. Some argue that the provision of pork to local districts drives much of the budget. See for example Morris Fiorina, *Congress: Keystone of the Washington Establishment,* New Haven, Conn., Yale University Press, 1977. Others argue that interest groups rather than geographic areas drive the budget. Much of this latter argument has gone on in the context of whether interest group pluralism works as billed. Opponents of interest group pluralism or what Lowi calls interest-group liberalism argue that the influence of interest groups is conditional, and sometimes, in some policy areas, is dominant. See Theodore Lowi, *The End of Liberalism,* 2nd ed., New York, W. W. Norton, 1979, and Michael Hayes, "The semi-sovereign pressure groups: A critique of current theory and an alternative typology," *Journal of Politics* 40 (February 1978), 134–161.

structural and deterministic, with little ability to explain variation over time and between geographic locations.* Studies looking for evidence of capitalist domination have found more variability than uniformity. Business groups sometimes do have disproportionate influence, but they are sometimes split, sometimes badly organized, and there are a variety of issues in which they have little interest. The Neo-Marxist model does not explain why one business group wins out over others, or when and why they sometimes lose. A theory that utilized differentiated interest groups would probably be more effective at capturing and describing business impact and would undoubtedly be better at outlining the impacts of other interests on the budget.

A second theoretical approach to linking budgeting and society is the public choice school. Individual theorists have taken widely varied positions, but what they share is the assumption that human behavior is based on individual economic rationality and the maximization of individual benefits, or what economists call utility. Their model of the ideal government is an extension of the marketplace where citizens can buy exactly the amount of services they want in the combinations they prefer. They deplore any departure from this model that provides people with more government services than they would choose on their own. They argue that a combination of majority voting and the ability of individuals and groups to share the cost of what they want with other taxpayers makes the costs of many benefits to individuals too cheap and inflates the demand for public goods and services. Government thus tends to overprovide services in comparison to a true market. In addition, the expansion of bureaucracy benefits the bureaucrats, so they always push for expansion, causing a second impetus to oversupply.

Public choice theorists emphasize the very important issue of the relationship between what the citizen taxpayers want government to do and spend and what it actually does and spends. There is no doubt that in a democracy this is a crucial linkage. This school emphasizes several mechanisms for achieving that linkage, including voting, suburbanization, and making budgeting, and especially taxation, more visible to the public.

The voting mechanism posits that citizens can choose among candidates those that best reflect their own spending priorities. Since there may be no candidate who matches their individual preferences, and those preferences may not be clearly stated, and candidates are chosen sometimes in primaries by less than a majority of voters, the level of control actually exerted by this mechanism may be tenuous.

The mechanism of suburbanization suggests that citizens choose their residences based on their preference for public service packages—they move to communities whose residents are people like themselves who want the same things from government and who are willing to pay similar amounts of taxes to get them. After a number of studies, however, it is not clear that people generally do this. The choice of where to live may be affected by many other factors, including cost of housing, proximity to work, closeness to relatives, and absence of crime.

The third mechanism, the openness of taxation, implies that the scope of government and the expense would be controlled if people clearly saw how much they were paying in taxes. People would then insist on receiving only those services most crucial to

*An excellent discussion of Neo-Marxist approaches to urban analysis is presented in M. Gottdiener and Joe Feagin, "The paradigm shift in urban sociology," *Urban Affairs Quarterly* 24 (December 1988), 163–187. The authors refer to some of these older models in passing, on the way to describing more current and dynamic models, that describe the urban outcomes as products of continuing struggles between capital and labor.

themselves, and would be unwilling to pay for more. The problem with this part of the theory (called fiscal illusion) is that obscured taxes are not just a plot hatched by government officials to expand government, but they are generally preferred by the public. The government is doing what the citizens want when it imposes taxes in less visible, small doses. This leaves the public choice theorists with the apparent contradiction that to bring about a tighter relationship between the public and government, government should go against the wishes of the public.

Despite some obvious strengths, public choice theory also has some weaknesses. This theory tends to be deterministic, and has difficulty explaining change over time. It postulates nearly continuous government growth, for example, although government growth has not been continuous, but jerky and stepwise. The theory cannot explain and does not deal with why government has not expanded further, taken on more functions, or why some functions have been added rather than others. On the one hand, public choice theorists see government as performing tasks the market has failed to perform, but on the other, they try to make government as much like a market as possible. They assume that all individuals, including bureaucrats and legislators, are interested only in maximizing their own utilities. A summary function of citizens' individual utilities should determine government spending, but the individual utilities of bureaucrats and legislators are viewed as narrow, self interested, and thwarting of the public will. The theory ignores the existence and importance of altruism and the existence of group goals that are different from individual goals. As one might expect, these theorists sometimes have difficulty figuring out how to aggregate individual utilities, since simple majorities may dominate minorities, and more complex voting patterns may contain contradictions.

The third major theory that relates budgeting to society is incrementalism, and its related theory of interest-group pluralism. Incrementalism argues that budgeting occurs virtually exclusively inside government; by inference, government is not directly controllable or controlled by society. Interest groups exist, but there are many interest groups, they represent a variety of interests, and none determines the outcomes. Writers in this school observed budgeting, and emphasized the process they saw, of agency request and legislative review, with stable actors over time, strategies of agency heads and responses by legislators, and norms worked out over time because the same actors remained in place and dealt with each other over time. The observers did not see the public, and so assumed they played little role; they did not see much of the interest groups, who often work behind the scenes, and so assumed they played little role.

The incrementalists watched too small a part of the public budgeting process, and at times just looked at the outcomes and tried to figure out what the process was that led to the outcomes. Their ability to perceive indirect effects, such as how politicians felt constrained by voters, was minimal. They did not observe the constraints that executive branch superiors put on budget requests, and they did not fully realize that the agency requests they saw were not the first step in the process. Consequently, they underestimated the relationship between the society and budgeting, and overestimated the autonomy of agencies in determining budgets.

Incrementalists saw budgeting as a formal process, based on bargaining and technical needs, but fairly devoid of policy concerns. Money had to be appropriated to run the agencies, the fiscal year had to begin, and divisive policy matters were decided elsewhere. As a result, the incrementalists did not envision the budget process as responding to perceived societal problems, emerging situations, or environmental changes. They assumed budgets would continue to be allocated pretty much the same way from year to year. Thus incrementalism was unable to theorize about changing budgets or budget process. As interest groups became more visible in the budget process, and consequently the process became less one of insiders working with each other developing their own norms of constraint, the theory could not cope.* As budgeting in Congress became more centralized, and the dominance of the agencies in determining outcomes clearly was reduced, the theory could not cope and became less descriptive. As entitlements became a more important part of the federal budget, the theory could not cope. It had no mechanism for explaining change other than major external events like a new president of a different party.

More recent theories of budgeting have not coalesced into a single school, but they have moved toward a common understanding of how budgeting relates to the society more broadly, and how seemingly technical internal decision making is influenced by actors who seldom seem to appear. The mechanisms for integrating budgets with the society are described in hierarchy theory[†], which focuses more on the executive branch, and by the macro-micro budget theorists,[‡] who focus more on Congress. The idea is similar in both cases.

Hierarchy theory says that the top levels of the executive branch make decisions about broad policy issues, and judge the environment, and pass that information down through the budget office to the agencies before they make their requests. Thus the identification of current problems and the selection of which ones will be addressed in the current budget are made early and frame the decisions of subordinates. Perceptions of interest group power may enter at this level or at the level of the budget office when it is judging requests from the agencies. The budget offices judge the requests based to some extent on knowledge of and performance of the agencies, and to some extent on the priorities given to them by the chief executive.

The macro-micro budgeting theory argues that bargaining still goes on over budget strategies, but broader policy issues are also explicitly dealt with and frame the choices and outcomes of the bargaining. On the congressional side, economic policies, priorities, spending ceilings, and assumptions about the growth of the economy are made by the budget committees, and to some extent guide or determine the decisions of the other committees as they work on parts of the budget.

The integration of budget policy and consideration of the environment and its constraints go on at federal, state, and local levels, regardless of the structure or degree of independence of the executive and legislative branches. At the city level, a city manager (chief executive) and the city council may meet at the beginning of the budget process,

---

*For a discussion of the inability of incrementalism to cope with these developments, written by a leading exponent of the theory, see Aaron Wildavsky, *The Politics of the Budgetary Process*, Boston, Little Brown, 1984, especially the preface and prologue to the fourth edition. Wildavsky later dropped his incrementalism in favor of more timely descriptions of the changes in budgeting.
†Hierarchy theory is the product of John Padgett. Key elements in the theory are outlined in "Hierarchy and ecological control in federal budgetary decision making," *American Journal of Sociology* 87 (1) 1981, 75–129.
‡See for example Lance LeLoup, "From micro budgeting to macro budgeting: Evolution in theory and practice," in Irene Rubin, ed., *New Directions in Budget Theory*, Albany, N.Y., SUNY Press, 1988. Actually both hierarchy and the macro-micro theories are intended to apply to both the legislative and the executive branches. I make the distinction here because of the expertise of the writers who originated each concept, and the greater organizational integrity of the executive branch so that the word hierarchy fits more naturally with the commonsense understanding of bureaucracy.

with the manager laying out the technical constraints and environmental problems, and the council laying out priorities, before the departments put in their budget requests. Both the manager's technical constraints and the council's priorities often appear in budget prefaces.

The current consensus is that budgeting is linked to the society and to the environment by both technical constraints and policy, and that interest groups are sometimes important in determining outcomes, although their role has not been well specified. Sometimes coalitions of interest groups form that approximate class boundaries, but there is no evidence of continuing class dominance. None of the deterministic models has survived well, and their inability to predict or explain change has been a major factor in their obsolescence. Current theory has drifted toward a consensus that allows for both direct and indirect influence of the environment over budgeting, and hence builds in the possibility of continuous change and adaptation.

The theories summarized above deal with why budgeting is important and provide an overall orientation to the field. Budget theory can also be helpful in explaining what budgeting is and how it operates. Much of this literature has taken the perspective that budgeting is decision making, and the task of theory is to describe the decision making that occurs during budgeting. Key issues have been how rational budgeting has been, how much effort has there been to get the best possible results, how much comparison of alternatives has there been, and what criteria are used to make decisions.

The theory has developed in a dialectical fashion. First, theory strongly emphasized rationality and getting the most from each dollar; then a second school grew up to refute the maximizers, arguing that very little rational decision making went on; the current literature argues for a variety of positions in between. Despite the emerging consensus on the middle ground, all three views continue to influence the literature.

The first position, characterized as the finance economists' position, emphasizes the need to allocate according to standards that will maximize the benefits to everyone. Among the standards often used is Pareto optimality, which means that budget increases should be allocated so that some individuals or groups are better off and none are worse off. This criteria would exclude any reallocation. Another standard that economists often allow is welfare economics, which means that government programs can make up for or change the market distribution of income to create greater equality. Under this standard, some reallocation would be acceptable.

Finance economists may disagree about the desirability of reallocation, but they generally agree that each new dollar of a public budget should be allocated to create the maximum of return in desired goods or services. This standard implies both efficiency and comparison of alternative spending choices, especially at the margins. So, to take a local example, the first hundred dollars of revenue we may wish to spend on roads, but the next hundred we may prefer to spend on public health. Once a minimum level of public health is achieved, we may wish to spend additional money on more roads. Presumably there is a limit, and the public would not desire more and more roads until they covered all available ground. Finance economists ask at the same time how much service will one more dollar provide, and how badly does the public want that additional service compared to what a dollar would provide in some other service area. Finance economists today often emphasize a variety of cost-benefit analysis techniques that combine analysis of how much a dollar will provide and compare projects in terms of the desirability to the community.

If finance economics is the thesis, incrementalism presented the theoretical opposite, or antithesis. Based on the theory of bounded rationality in decision making, incrementalism suggested that no one could make the comparisons necessary to make rational decisions. It would take too much time, and would require more information and more intelligence than people could normally bring to decision making. Moreover, the making of explicit choices between spending alternatives would sharpen controversy, increase the level of participation in budgeting, and generally slow it down if not stop it altogether. So rational decision making was neither possible nor desirable. Some of the incrementalists went further and argued that political decisions would be based on what projects benefited the voters in whose districts, and any attempt to impose other, supposedly more rational criteria on top of that crucial political choice would fail. Decision makers avoid comparisons by making across-the-board decisions, such as a 3% increase for all units, or a 2% productivity reduction across the board.

The current synthesis—synthesis may be too strong a word for the variety of positions—is part way between the two extremes. Without arguing that all projects are indeed subject to cost-benefit analysis, scholars no longer argue that budgets are reviewed by legislators concerned only with benefits for their districts*; similarly, while scholars do not argue that all expenditures are compared against each other to achieve the maximum benefit from each dollar of revenue, neither do they argue that all new spending decisions are made without examination or across the board.

Recent studies at the national level emphasize that while pork barrel distributive projects still exist, they are a small and shrinking portion of the budget.[†] One author argues that decisions to cut requests are not made all at the same time, in an across-the-board fashion, but in sequence, that requests are cut a bit, one at a time, and then added up to see if they come under the limit; if not, a second round of cuts is begun.[‡] Sometimes, across-the-board rules may begin a budget trimming process, but these estimates are then adjusted up or down on a case-by-case basis.

Arguments from the budget maximizers have always assumed that comparisons between programs would be fairly complete, even if only at the margins, and that programs that were found less worthy would be cut or eliminated. It has become increasingly evident that the structure of the budget and the type of expenditure limit the ability of budget trimmers to cut some programs; some are mandated, some have restricted funding, or matching funding, some programs actually generate revenue, and some are long term and contractual and cannot be readily adjusted except at fixed intervals. The decision about what kind of program to offer and whether to earmark money is also a budgetary decision; it locks a particular comparison of alternatives into the budget for a period of time. So comparisons do occur, but not necessarily annually, and some programs may be left out of the comparisons. The result is not rational budgeting in the sense of the finance economists, but neither is it the simple decision rules of the incrementalists.

The discussion to this point has summarized some of the key budgeting theories,

*Anton, one of the leading incrementalists for many years, had argued that the legislative budget review in Illinois in the 1960s was limited to their concern for the geographic distribution of projects. No more in-depth review took place. See Thomas Anton, *The Politics of State Expenditure in Illinois*, Urbana, University of Illinois Press, 1966.

[†]See R. Douglas Arnold, "The local roots of domestic policy," in Thomas Mann and Norman Ornstein, eds., *The New Congress*, Washington, D.C., American Enterprise Institute, 1981, 250–287.

[‡]John Padgett makes this argument in "Bounded rationality in budgetary research," *American Political Science Review* 74 (June 1980), 334–372.

suggested some of the assumptions they make concerning the relationship of budgeting to the broader society, and indicated that budget theory generally conceptualizes budgeting as a decision-making process. Each of the major historical theories has contributed some important truths, but has often been unable to explain change or has been too one-sided. Current budget theory accepts key themes from each major school, but also emphasizes the existence and meaning of change in budgeting, and has staked out, but not fully explored, a middle ground on the nature of budgetary decision making.

An understanding of budgeting requires not only an overview of the development of the broad theories, but also an understanding of the key concepts of budgeting.

BUDGET CONCEPTS

The most important of budget concepts is the concept of *budgeting* itself. What is a budget, and how does a public budget differ from that of a corporation or a family? "A budget links tasks to be performed to the amount of resources necessary to accomplish those tasks, ensuring that money will be available to wage war, provide housing, or maintain streets."* Budgets limit spending to the amount of income, ensuring balance and preventing overspending. Budgeting allocates scarce resources, and implies choice between potential objects of expenditure. The decision of what to spend the money on involves a process, in which individuals or groups are assigned parts of the decision, the parts are coordinated and timed, and resources are allocated.

In public budgeting, people and groups with different goals and points of view are always vying to get what they want out of government. There is often little consensus about what should be accomplished or for whom. In public budgeting, there is a separation between those who pay the bill, and those who make the decisions about how the money will be spent. The decisions makers are ultimately *accountable* to those who pay the bills. Budgets are an important link between taxpayers and public officials. Budgets tell citizens what their taxes are being spent on, and in a general way how well their money is being spent. If taxpayers do not approve the government's choices, they can, and sometimes do, refuse to approve additional taxes.

Public budgeting is both political and technical, influenced by interest groups and by agency heads. Budgeting has its routine parts, and its almost unpredictable and nonroutine parts. Public budgeting is *open to the environment,* in the sense that it is influenced by the economy, by public opinion, by other levels of government, by interest groups, by the press, and by politicians.

Budgeting is a decision-making process. That means that who makes the decisions, or parts of decisions, influences the distribution of power over outcomes. To get an accurate picture of who makes budget decisions, one needs to look across types of budgeting decisions. Some types of budget decisions, such as those setting limits on the growth of government or making tradeoffs between defense and social services, attract large coalitions of interest groups that approximate class interests, the rich, the middle classes, and the poor, or workers and owners. Other kinds of budget decisions attract specific narrow interest groups. The allocation of tax breaks often involves a single industry or company, sometimes even a single individual. Budget decisions involving the implementation of the budget normally involve no interest groups at all. An evaluation of the *distribution of budget-making power* must weigh these different types of decisions.

*Irene Rubin, *The Politics of Public Budgeting: Getting and Spending, Borrowing and Balancing,* New Jersey, Chatham House, 1990, chapter 1.

Budget processes vary, both between jurisdictions and across time. Some are more *open* to interest groups and the public than others. Some cities, for example, actively solicit public opinion about budget priorities, and keep citizens informed about budget choices; others virtually never solicit public opinion and seldom communicate about the budget except at tax increase time. Congress has sometimes organized budgeting decisions in a way that was open to interest groups, and sometimes locked up the decision making in privacy to keep the interest groups out.

Recent literature argues that when resources were relatively more plentiful and the decision had been made to expand spending, Congress reorganized itself to be more open to interest group and beneficiary demands. *There is a relationship between the allocation of decision-making power and budgetary outcomes.* Not only does this formulation begin to provide an explanation for changes over time, but it also suggests that budget process reflects societal conditions including the economy and public need, and that budget processes in turn influence both access of interest groups and spending levels.*

Descriptions of budget processes have not been simply a list of decisions, actors, and due dates, but descriptions of the shifting location of power. Discussion of budget process has often focused on the implications of these different arrangements. Two major dichotomies have been used to describe the shifts in location of power: *executive versus legislative,* and *top-down versus bottom-up.* Executive budgeting means that the chief executive and his staff have responsibility for putting together a budget proposal, and presenting it to the legislature for approval. Legislative budgeting means that the agencies make their proposals for spending directly to the legislature, without being evaluated first by the executive. Top-down budgeting means that budgeting is centralized, in either the executive branch or the legislative branch or both. An individual, a committee, or an office is responsible for setting overall targets, and evaluating requests in light of these targets. By contrast, bottom-up budgeting means there is no prior central policy control over the budget. Budgets are created as the aggregates of individual requests from agencies and from committees or subcommittees. The requests are put together with decision rules that avoid comparative consideration of the merits of programs.

There are positions between a pure executive and legislative budget. Even those that are considered executive budgets are in fact often in between the extremes of executive and legislative budgets. For example, most cities have executive budgets, but they are not pure types. Cities' budgets are normally drawn up by the mayor or manager, and his or her budget staff, and then approved by the council, which makes the process an executive budget. But the mayor may be a member of the council (the legislature), chosen by the council members to be mayor; the city manager, if there is one, is chosen by and may be fired by the city council. In effect, the manager is the staff of the council—the legislative branch. Where cities still budget with a legislative budget process, the finance committee of the council receives budget requests from the departments and holds hearings with each department, and makes recommendations to the council. Sometimes, however, the mayor sits in on these meetings, or actually makes the recommended cuts to the council, creating a hybrid that defies easy categorization. These examples suggest that for cities the budget process is often somewhere between the poles of the legislative executive distinction.

*See Allen Schick, "The distributive congress," in Allen Schick, ed., *Making Economic Policy in Congress,* Washington, D.C., American Enterprise Institute, 1983, and Charles Stewart III, *The Design of the Appropriation Process in the House of Representatives, 1865–1921,* Cambridge, Cambridge University Press, 1989.

Typically budgets are neither completely top-down nor completely bottom-up, but some combination of the two. Departments or agencies may have more or less freedom in putting together their budget proposals; chief executives sometimes give lots of advice in advance, and sometimes give very little. Sometimes top-down budget reviews are thorough and sometimes superficial.

The overall direction of change during this century has been toward more executive and more top-down budgeting. But at the national and state level, the degree of imbalance between the executive and legislative branches may have become too extreme, and there has been some motion back toward a more balanced division of budgeting power.*

Budget process describes not only who has power over budget decisions, but also how those decisions are actually made—how much information is provided, what kinds of decision rules are used, how much comparison there is between proposed expenditures.

The kind of information that is used for budget decision making is highly variable. Revenue projections may be the result of complex econometric models, modified by experience as the budget year commences or they may result from linear projection from previous years' experience plus an informed guess. Information about programs may be minimal or may include accounting data, performance evaluations, and other data. The budget format, which provides most of the data for the budget reviewers, is variable from jurisdiction to jurisdiction and from time to time. Sometimes information is presented one year and not in the following years, but still remains active in the minds of the decision makers. Sometimes extra information is made available when an issue is particularly salient or a key increase or decrease is being considered.

One of the ways that information about departments, agencies and programs is conveyed to decisions makers is through the budget request form that the agencies fill out. How do agencies *justify* their requests? Sometimes the information required is technical, almost arithmetical. For example, there are so many staff members, their salary is so much, their benefits cost so much, so many of them receive so much for longevity (the number of years they have been working in that position), and so many dollars are for salary increases. The agency is planning so many trips to such a place at so many dollars a trip. If there are no changes to the program or the way of managing it, a *constant services budget*, it will cost so many dollars for this agency next year. Budget justifications sometimes include descriptions of new programs requested or new equipment or staff needed. These may be justified in terms of workload data, community need, or future savings, or other arguments that agency heads think will be convincing.

In an executive budget process, this information from the agencies is collected, reviewed, altered, and put together in a recommended package for the legislature to review. The format of this proposal is also variable. One format is called a *line-item budget*. Expenditures are broken into accounting categories, and each line of the budget represents one such accounting category or item. For example, a budget request might include $2000 for travel, $500,000 for salaries, $25,000 for insurance, and $75,000 for office supplies. How detailed or general the line items are is highly variable even within jurisdictions that use primarily line-item budgets.

Line-item budgets seem almost deterministic. They tell little if anything about the cost or efficiency of programs provided (they provide the costs for departments and administrative units, not for the programs that the units provide). They provide almost no

*For a discussion of these trends see Irene Rubin, *The Politics of Public Budgeting: Getting and Spending, Borrowing and Balancing,* New Jersey, Chatham House, 1990, chapter 3.

information that might help decision makers choose which budget proposals to cut or which to increase. This format encourages budget officials to make cuts that are across the board, because they cannot make intelligent decisions between programs.

Straight line-item budgets that provide almost no other information are becoming relatively rare. Most public budgets today are in a program format, which emphasizes less the administrative unit of the department or agency and more the programs that each such unit provides, listing the costs for each one. While decision makers can still trim or increase budgets across the board if they choose, the allocational impacts of cutting one program or another are much more obvious, and the ability of decision makers to increase popular programs and decrease less popular ones is enhanced. *Program budgeting* makes it more obvious to the public what their tax dollars are buying, and whether their money is being spent for the programs they want. The level of controversy can be toned down or tuned up. With this budget format the policy decisions being made through the budget process are clearer to all the participants, and *tradeoffs* between programs are more obvious when they are being made.

Program budgets allow public officials to clearly choose between priorities and express them in the budget, but they do not provide a way of evaluating the relative efficiency or effectiveness of programs. Implicit in much of budgeting is that there is a technical component, requiring the administrators to get the most from each dollar and to put each additional dollar where it will get the maximum return of desired goods and services. This concept has led to the idea of a *performance budget,* in which program information is related in terms of the costs per unit of services delivered, and this information is included in the budget. Presumably decision makers would then allocate new or additional funds to those agencies operating at the peak of efficiency, and take funds away from those whose operations were less efficient or were decreasing the level of their efficiency.

Performance budgeting has had many difficulties, and while sometimes im-plemented has seldom worked as billed, and has often been modified. One problem with it is that it is easier to measure the costs per unit of service delivered in some programs than in others; second, for the concept to work, the quality of performance must be held constant, but we seldom measure the quality of service and program outputs over time; third, cost per unit of service delivered can vary independent of the agency's efforts, so an agency head may be held responsible for outcomes over which he or she has only limited control. Dollar losses due to fires, for example, depends on events and conditions over which the fire department has little control, such as the level of wind or rain, the number and age of wooden dwellings, how quickly a fire is called in, the time of day fires occur, and the existence of active arsonists. In addition, costs per unit of service delivered tend to go up, with everything else held constant, because inflation pushes up the costs of salaries and material. Even if employees work just as hard as they always have, unless they can continually introduce higher productivity, their programs will look worse. All these factors, plus a natural dislike of being continually evaluated, make performance budgeting difficult to sell and even harder to make work. The process of designing performance measures and maintaining records about them is time consuming, which creates both a reason and an excuse for agency heads and staff to slight the tasks.

Budget formats implicitly or explicitly define the range within which policy and allocational decisions will take place. Incremental budgets of the line item format provide comparisons between last year, this year, and the proposal for next year; this is about the only information that gives a clue that decision makers might latch onto. So they tend to focus on changes at the margins and what they mean. What is already in the budget is assumed to have been examined in previous years, and is at least in theory not examined further. But if budgets were formatted differently, they could focus attention not only on the differences between recent years, but also on some items from previous years that were once considered important but that now are less important than new proposed spending or program expansion. The format that allows for such reconsideration is called *zero-based budgeting*.

Zero-based budgeting in its full-blown form requires the agencies to put all their budget requests into decision packages, and rank order them in importance. A decision package is usually a program at a particular level of service and its associated cost. A department might have three programs and be able to offer them at three levels of service, good, fair, and poor. That would make nine decision units for the department to rank order. Then the rankings of the agencies are gathered and arranged according to criteria that make sense at a government-wide level. At the national level, a moderate level of defense might be the nation's top priority, but a vastly expanded defense department might be lower in priority than a program to house three-fourths of the homeless. The formation of such lists requires a conscious attention to the criteria that should be used to rank programs, including measures of public need, popularity, the dependence of people on the program (whether alternatives are available), and whether life is endangered by reducing the program. When a complete list of priorities is formed, the decision packages are funded in the order ranked; if the money runs out before the bottom of the list, those items are not funded. Items at the top may already be being performed, or they may be new or expanded programs. Money can be *reallocated* from the lower priorities to the higher ones.

Complete zero-based budgets of the form just described are relatively rare, in part because they assume a knowledge of program costs that may not be present, in part because they open the whole budget, much of which is not really likely to change, to such prioritization. As a result, simplified zero-base budgets, called *target-based budgets,* have been more widely used. Such budgets create a pool of money for reallocation by taking new money and a percent of existing funds. Agencies cut themselves by a given percent (presumably their lowest priority items) and propose what they would do with new money and why. These proposals are rank ordered and funded as far down the list as the money available allows. This procedure forces a clear statement of priorities, and links the goals of the governmental unit with the budget presented. It allows for some reallocation without creating unnecessary chaos or insecurity.

For many people the only part of budgetary decision making that is important is this question of how the process allocates money, who wins and who loses. Various budget formats provide at least partial answers to this question. In line-item formatting, with incremental budgeting, programs are never compared, and the existing set of priorities is largely maintained. Change is slow. To some extent, those who have, get, and those who have not yet made a successful claim have a very difficult if not impossible time getting heard. This pattern of budgeting pits those who have already gained budgetary power against new claims, and weighs heavily in favor of the old timers. In program budgeting, programs more explicitly compete against each other for new or additional money, but there is no mechanism for reallocation from one program to another as priorities or technology changes. Only in zero-based and target-based budgeting is competition between programs paired with a mechanism for reallocation. The potential rate of change is faster in any form of zero-based budgeting than in simple program budgeting, and both program and zero-based budgets provide for more change than incremental budgeting.

While some people are most concerned with allocation and particularly reallocation decisions, others are most concerned with the relationship of budgeting to outcomes. How does public spending achieve public goals? How tightly are the two linked? The idea of planning, of choosing goals and devising and funding programs to achieve those goals, is implicit in the more modern forms of budgeting. The planning may be more or less formal, and more or less encompassing, but the idea of an activist government defining and attempting to resolve problems through the budget is inherent in these budget formats. On the one hand they are defended as more rational and less wasteful; on the other, they allow for more public participation, more controversy, and more goal-directed change.

Planning programming budgeting systems was the most integrated and fullest statement of the linkage between planning and budgeting, but even when the full system is not adopted, budgets may state goals and link spending requests with those goals. Incrementalists implied that such goals could not be stated, because there would be so little agreement that a clear goals statement either would be impossible or would generate competing alternatives that would tear a community apart. At the local level, recent budget innovations suggest that this has not been that serious a problem; many of a city's competing goals are stated, and the programs in the budget that address each goal are listed, although often without the dollar amounts that might exacerbate controversy. Rather than suggest goallessness, these budgets suggest progress toward multiple goals, faster in some areas than others, and more in some years than others.

The emphasis on linking budgeting to goals has shown up in recent years with the linkage of *management by objectives* to budgets. Management by objectives (MBO) is a technique for specifying overall and intermediate goals and objectives, and getting employees to be responsible for the achievement of particular levels of achievement and particular tasks, so that the overall goal can be achieved. This kind of planning is formally linked to the reward system of employees. But it can and ultimately must also be linked to the budget to work; employees cannot promise to accomplish a particular level of work, and accept salary increments based on their success, unless they have sufficient resources in the budget to carry out that level of work. Thus MBO and budgets have been linked.

Underlying much of the discussion about budgets and allocations, planning and goals, is the question of *tradeoffs*. Many of the early budget theorists simply assumed that there were budget tradeoffs, because resources were limited, and money spent on one program or project could not be spent on another at the same time. Budgeting implied choices, and choices meant more of something equaled less of something else. But when the incrementalists went looking for such choices during the 1960s, they found instead relative stability of allocations, and they could not find allocation criteria, and often could not find programs, let alone a process that compared programs. They concluded that the limits of human intelligence and attention prevented budgeters from comparing all programs all the time, and the level of controversy that would be generated would be unacceptable, so that no comparison was in fact done.

The incrementalists gradually modified their position in two ways. One way was to argue that small incremental changes from year to year could accumulate over time to reflect changes in direction or priorities; the second way was to argue that allocational changes did occur at long intervals when some major external event occurred, like a major election that changed party and ideology or a war.

The idea of tradeoffs at the national level was obscured both by the theory that said changes and comparisons did not occur and that budgets were aggregates of the demands of individual agencies, and by the fact that for many of those years the federal government ran deficits. It appeared, for example, that the country could have both guns and butter, both military buildup and social programs at the same time. The budget total did not look fixed. Increased spending in one area correlated with increases in other areas, while the theory of tradeoffs suggested that there should be negative correlations. Even with deficits, total spending is limited, and tradeoffs have to occur, but with a model that required a negative correlation to prove the existence of tradeoffs, they were hard to find and prove.*

On the state and local levels, where revenue totals were more clearly fixed and deficits generally illegal, even when budgets were line item and incremental, tradeoffs were clearer. If one department is growing at 3% a year and another at 8% a year, within a few years the change in spending priorities is obvious. Thus after the urban riots of the 1960s, the federal and municipal response was to beef up local police departments. Over a period of years, relative spending on police departments with respect to other municipal departments was obvious.† When revenue sharing was eliminated in the mid 1980s, cities had to make explicit choices about which services would be maintained, or whether new revenue would have to be raised locally to replace the federal grant. There were clear issues of priorities and tradeoffs that observers could detect.

After the 1974 budget reform act in Congress, tradeoffs became more obvious at the federal level as well, not because the deficits were under better control, but because the budget process required an explicit guideline for each budget on how much to allocate to each major function in the budget. The early years of the Reagan presidency, with their emphasis on rapid military buildup and cutting back of social programs, made a dramatic statement about the existence of tradeoffs, but suggested that they are more acute and visible in some years than in others.

Tradeoffs are easier to see when they change, but they exist even in a stable and relatively unchanging budget. Any public budget reflects relative values placed on major categories of the budget. How much will be spent, relatively speaking, on prevention versus suppression in the fire department? Or on the State Department and negotiations versus the Defense Department and weapons? Or on covert operations versus overt operations? On attracting new businesses or maintaining existing ones? Even when these proportions do not change each year, they still represent tradeoffs (unless one drops the assumption of relative scarcity). Sometimes these tradeoffs are nested. For example, the first tradeoff may be between the operating and the capital budget. The next may be within the capital budget between water projects, street projects, and drainage projects. At the next level, within the streets capital budget, there may be a tradeoff between repair and replacement. Then the choices may be between concrete, brick, and blacktop streets, each of which are located in different parts of a city and have different wear characteristics. Within the operating budget there may be tradeoffs between salary and benefits, between regular wages and overtime, and between administrative staff and line employees.

The structure of the decision making brackets tradeoffs. That is, the decision-

---

*There has been an extensive literature on budget tradeoffs in recent years, but the results have been highly variable depending on the methodology used. For example, Bruce Russett, one of the key writers in this area, was unable to find major tradeoffs in his 1982 study of defense and domestic spending, "Defense expenditures and national well being," *American Journal of Political Science* 76 (December 1982), 767–777. But he argued that his lack of results does not mean that the tradeoffs do not occur. Rather, getting good data is a problem, and devising good theoretical specifications is difficult (p. 774).

†Susan Welch, "The impact of urban riots on urban expenditures," *American Journal of Political Science* 19 (November 1975), 741–760.

making process frames what the choices will be between, and what trades with what, and what does not trade with what. Generally, for example, cities do not trade off police and fire. The assumption is made that the city must have both. Rather, a category is devised called basic services, and basic services trade off against nonbasic services. What fits in basic and what fits in nonbasic may be variable, but what is often defined as basic is police, fire, streets, sanitation, and water; what is nonbasic is social services, planning and zoning, and other expenditures. Cities rather explicitly trade off capital and operating expenditures, but the federal government, which does not have a proper capital budget, cannot frame its tradeoffs in the same way. Decision makers reveal these tradeoffs in their conversations. Listening to them may help the quantitative modelers of tradeoffs specify their models more appropriately.

Viewing the budget in terms of tradeoffs emphasizes the policy aspect of budgeting, for example, the relative emphasis on regulation or on privatization, or on suppression and prevention. It also emphasizes, however, the narrower question of who benefits, who wins and who loses. The wins and losses may be viewed in terms of bureaucratic actors, and the winners ranked in terms of percentage of budget growth, but they may also be viewed in terms of class or interest groups. Looking at the allocation process in terms of the beneficiaries of government programs introduces several other budget concepts; equity, distribution, and redistribution.

Equity is a broad term that also applies to taxation, but in the context of spending choices it raises the topic of welfare economics. Does government have a role in making the distribution of income more equal than the market alone would create? Is the function of budget allocation more than getting the most out of every dollar and making services and programs efficient and effective? If so, how is this mission being carried out? Is the effect of spending (or taxing) to reallocate income from the rich to the poor? Or from the poor to the well to do? *Distribution* implies spending that does not affect the distribution of wealth, and *redistribution* suggests spending that does. Over the years, the word redistribution has picked up the connotation of taking money from the rich to give to the poor, but that leaves the reverse concept, taking from the poor to give to the rich, without its own word. Redistribution can be either up or down.

Distribution and redistribution have a second and related meaning in budgeting that suggests that some programs will create far more controversy than others. Distribution means that program beneficiaries are widespread, almost everyone benefits from a program, and there are few that define themselves as losers. Alternatively, it means that a few benefit, but that the losers either do not know that they are losers, or their loss is not politically salient to them. Redistribution means that some interests gain at the obvious expense of others.

Redistributive issues are highly contentious. It is much easier to maintain distributive and relatively peaceful politics when resources are reasonably plentiful. When money is particularly tight, what might have otherwise been defined as distributive may become redistributive and hence highly contentious. For example, as long as resources are reasonably plentiful, young people do not perceive programs to support the elderly as competitive with benefits to higher education, but with fiscal restraints and social services lumped together to compete for funding, the young may perceive themselves as in direct competition with the elderly. Then the young may be interested not only in what they themselves receive but also in what others receive.

If budget allocations restricted themselves to providing only goods and services that were widely desired and widely distributed, the public that pays the taxes would probably be quite content (assuming minimal waste, fraud, and abuse) that their priorities had been realized in the budget. They would be in essence buying services from the government that the government chose to provide and that were generally unavailable elsewhere or were much more expensive in the private sector. Even when goods and services are delivered to particular groups rather than to the population as a whole, most taxpayers accept this use of their money as long as they can get what they want from government at especially cheap prices. But when taxpayers perceive that their money is being spent on some other group instead of on themselves, they are likely to get angry at government.

The issue of allocation and reallocation thus raises the broader issue of *accountability*. Is government doing what the taxpayers want it to do? Do the priorities of the government, as reflected in the budget, reflect the priorities of the taxpayers? The idea of accountability in a democracy means that government is not a dictatorship, extracting taxes from the public and spending it at will; taxpayers are the ultimate bosses, and government's role is to serve, and to reflect the demands and desires of the taxpayers. The budget is one of the key vehicles for making government accountable to the people, by making the policy choices in the budget numbers clear. Government is also accountable to the public for spending tax money with as little waste as possible and without fraud or abuse.

Some public budgets provide more accountability than others, but overall they do a pretty good job of explaining how public money was spent and linking public priorities with public spending. There are a variety of techniques for achieving accountability, with some aimed more toward stating priorities and others more toward demonstrating that money was spent honestly and efficiently.

One of the key techniques for providing budgetary accountability is called *fund accounting*. It means that a budget is not one piggy bank, out of which expenditures come, but many smaller piggy banks, each of which has its own revenues and expenditures. Each piggy bank has its own purpose, and no one can spend more from any piggy bank than the piggy bank has in it (balance). These metaphorical piggy banks are called funds. These funds play several functions, but one of the most important of them is to see that money that has been earmarked for a particular purpose is indeed spent for that particular purpose and no other. The earmarked money is put into its own fund, and not mixed with other money for other purposes. If it is transferred to other funds, it leaves a paper trail describing how much money was transferred and for what purpose. If user fees are collected, for example, airport landing fees, these are put into a special account, which can be spent only on airports.

Inside a fund, money can be reasonably freely traded across categories of spending,* but transfers between funds are carefully monitored. That means that not all expenditures can in fact be traded off against all other expenditures. If a trust fund is set up for airports or highways, airport or highway spending is no longer competing with other expenditures for the same dollars. It has its own earmarked dollars that no other program can get. That means that a budget may be structured to make some tradeoffs easier and others more difficult or impossible to make in the short run. As a government sets up its fund structures it is often deciding also on what trades for what, and what may not be traded for what.

One key element of accountability is the completeness of the public record. If only some items are included in the budget, but others are decided on and paid for with tax

---

*There are often limits within funds, too, if specific legislation mandates spending on a particular program.

dollars, the budget may be very misleading. The more fragmented budgets are, that is, the more separate jurisdictions publish their own separate budgets, the harder it is for citizens to find out how their money is being spent. Especially at the local level where numerous units of government may perform one or two functions each, and not have the staff time or expertise to put together a budget that explains how much money was spent on what priority, *fragmentation reduces accountability*.

At all levels of government, when some functions are on budget and others are off budget (that is have separate budgets) it becomes confusing how money is being spent. On the other hand, when budgets are consolidated, they may contain many different kinds of programs and many different kinds of resources. These may not reasonably be added together. For example, a loan is not the same thing as a grant, since the loan should be returned over time, with interest. When a percentage is subtracted for expected defaults, the net cost of a loan program may be zero. A grant, by contrast, is money spent without expectation that it will come back. One cannot add grants and loans and expect the total to convey any meaning. How one can best report different types of resources in a public budget to maximize accountability is a problem yet to be fully worked out.

Accountability requires *financial control* during the budget implementation stage. The budget that is passed in full public view, and is the representative to the public of how public money is being spent, should be very similar to the budget that is actually implemented. There should be as few changes as possible, and those that are made should be technical, not policy laden. That means that cuts made during the year, as opposed to at budget time, should be across the board (such cuts minimize the policy implications); increases in revenue during the year should normally be either allocated according to a preset list of priorities, or put in an annual fund balance to be allocated as part of the following year's budget process. Departments and agencies must be prevented from seriously overspending their budgets, not only because such overspending presents the possibility of deficits, but also because it may change the priorities implicit in the budget that was legally approved.

One of the most fundamental concepts in budgeting is *balance*. Sometimes other goals of budgeting, such as trying to use public spending to stabilize the economy, seem to overrule balance and create deficits, but the concept of balance remains even during deficit budgeting. Balance means that total income has to match total outgo, with or without borrowing. If it has no concept of balance, if there is no attempt to match income and outgo, there is no budget. Balance means agreement over time between revenues and expenditures, not necessarily balance every minute or every week.

Balance can be defined more or less constrictively. For example, one could say that the budget had to be balanced when presented to the legislature. That is a fairly weak form of balance requirement, since the budget proposal is based on estimates of revenues and expenditures. To make a budget look balanced requires only a slightly higher estimate of revenue or a slightly lower estimate of expenditures. A more restrictive definition would require the budget to balance at the end of the year. Balance requirements can be more or less inclusive of the budget. That is, the requirement for balance may apply only to the operating budget, or even only to the general fund, or only to an enterprise fund. It may apply to any items on budget but not any items off budget. There may be in addition to the requirement for balance a restriction on the level of borrowing, or on the level of revenue. Some school districts have been borrowing by selling bonds to provide operating funds; under some laws they may be balancing their budgets—getting enough revenue to cover expenditures—while under other laws they would be operating with unbalanced budgets.

Throughout this essay, the idea has been emphasized that budgets and budgeting change. Some of this change is in response to changes in the environment, and some is in response to campaigns of *reform*. Reform means change in a direction advocated by some groups or individuals. It does not necessarily mean improvement. Over the years, major campaigns to reform budgeting have focused around increasing the power of the executive in forming and reviewing departments' and agencies' proposals, making decision making more open and accountable, making comparisons between programs more explicit and more rational, and changing the budget format and process to allow for at least some flexibility and possible reallocation. Current efforts at reform are focused on reducing the size of the federal deficit by strengthening the constraints on balance.

METHODOLOGY

Budgeting studies have used extremely varied methodology, and the methods used have often been linked at least loosely, with a set of issues or a broader intellectual approach to what is important about budgeting. Studies of budget process have normally been based on elite interviewing and participant observation. Studies of decision making have often been quantitatively modeled. The assumption seems to be, if there is a simple decision-making rule (because rationality is bounded), we ought to be able to model it quantitatively.

The resulting goodness of fit between the model and the real-world data has often been taken as confirmation that the original model was correct, even if several possible models could have produced the observed outcomes. More observation of decision making would save some of these models from trying to construct backward what decision making must have been like. The budgetary outcomes do not provide enough information on their own to allow useful modeling that is retroactively descriptive of decision making.

The tradeoffs literature has been highly quantitative, for example, using a variety of techniques including correlation and regression and time series analysis, but it tends to suffer from too little knowledge of how tradeoffs have been structured into the budget, and so often does not know where to look to see if tradeoffs occurred.

Surveys have also been a continuing part of budget studies, and are particularly useful to define changing practices at the state and local levels, where more qualitative work has difficulty generalizing. Multiple case studies have been used to combine qualitative aspects of both budget process and evaluation of innovation with generalizability. There has been little problem with the methodology in either of these two cases, and one expects these methods to continue to be used where this kind of information is needed.

For the future, more qualitative studies are needed, and studies of the variety and history of budgeting are required. These studies can usefully rely on time series data, where available, as well as more traditional historical techniques and comparative case studies. But the usefulness of the modeling approach is questionable until there is a better linkage between observational data and the assumptions of the models. This task may or may not be possible. As long as budget theory posited simple decision rules, relatively simple mathematics could model the outcomes, but with the demise of incrementalism and the potential substitution of more complex rules and tradeoffs, without assumptions of fixed revenue totals, the math may get out of control. Then the mathematics may dictate the model, and the models may become more unrealistic, and it is not clear what use an unrealistic mathematical model is.

ISSUES

Throughout this essay key issues have been highlighted. Some of them are the result of truncated lines of inquiry begun by a particular school of thought. Some of them reflect current consensus on where the field is going or needs to move. Some of them are questions that emerge from practice.

For example, the relationships among different business interests and their impact on budgets need further exploration. At the local level, during periods of growth, city boosters, including real estate interests, have often allied with bankers and savings and loans to provide the capital for growth, some of which is provided by cities in the form of infrastructure. But during periods of downturn, while additional spending might stimulate the economy or control the depth of the recession, the bankers have been interested in maintaining the balance between municipal revenues and municipal spending. They then become the policemen enforcing fiscal conservatism, in order to keep payments forthcoming on the loans they made, and to keep the city creditworthy. At this time the banks typically dominate and determine municipal fiscal policy. Banks play a role, though not necessarily the leading role, in the expansion phase, but often play the key role in the retrenchment phase, exaggerating the swings in the local economy. Why does this pattern occur? Why does the rescue of particular threatened business interests take precedence over either welfare or attempts to restore the economy at the local level? How was this pattern overcome at the federal level during the Great Depression, and is it reasserting itself now at the federal level?

Public choice theory postulates excessive public demands for government services, but provides no mechanism for the choice among demands, why some are successful and others not. And because the theory downplays the collectivity and predefines some functions as appropriately collective and others not, it cannot trace the pricking of the public conscience and the evolution of consensus that a widespread problem is a government responsibility and a right of citizenship. It is the elevation of beliefs that citizens are entitled to certain levels of health care or protection from the elements that has had the most impact on modern budgeting. How do entitlements evolve, how do they devolve, and over what period of time? What do they mean about the linkage between budgets and society, about class politics, about redistributive politics?

Hierarchy theory is supposed to tie budget process to changing environments, to be historically rooted, but to date the school has used data only from one period of time, and has assumed the policy input from the president. We have no good estimates of the impact of those policy constraints over time; what kind of policy statement has what level of impact on spending decisions; and how much of the budget is bottom up or top down over time, what determines the mix, and how does the mix influence the outcome. Does top-down budgeting ignore the technical and managerial constraints of budgeting? Do those come from the bottom up? How exactly do the technical and the policy aspects of budgeting merge? What would a successful merge look like, and what kinds of obstacles to a successful merge occur?

We have isolated some descriptors of budget processes, such as top-down and bottom-up budgeting, and macro and micro budgeting, but it is not clear that we have all the important descriptors tied down. Nor do we necessarily understand the impact of the various hybrids that have emerged combining the extremes of the Weberian ideal types.

Similarly, we have rejected the extremes of decision-making models that postulate either economic rationality or bounded rationality, but we have barely begun to map out the real territory that lies in between the extremes. Once we give up the idea of simple and stable decision rules, we open up the way to look at actual decisions, combinations of rules, varieties of determinants, and change over time and variation between places. Once we have mapped the variation, we can begin to try to explain it. Much more work needs to be done to link processes and decision making to outcomes. When and as this variation is mapped and the consequences more clearly understood, scholars can develop related sequences of cause and effect chains and create full budget theories that do more than provide a general orientation, key concepts, and key issues.

2

Political Dimensions of Federal Budgeting in the United States

Steven Parker *Department of Political Science, University of Nevada, Las Vegas, Nevada*

INTRODUCTION

This chapter will provide a discussion of scholarly literature relating to the political dimensions of budgeting at the national level of American government. Vast change has transformed much of this process in the last decade and thus the field is in a state of considerable flux. Recognizing this fact, we will begin with a treatment of the rise and fall of the theory known as incrementalism. This will be followed by an examination of the literature on executive and congressional budgeting. We will close with attention to the politics of the federal deficit.

INCREMENTALISM—THE POLITICS OF MICROBUDGETING

The paradigm known as incrementalism still commands a prominent place in any discussion of the politics of budgeting. As a general theory of budgeting, it reigned for decades and as such it is covered elsewhere in this volume. However, the current chapter needs to start with attention to it, since it is the very essence of politics.

For some analysts incrementalism remains the best way to explain the political reality of budgeting while for others it represents an old orthodoxy which must nonetheless be acknowledged before moving on to an examination of that which is more congruent with contemporary reality (Rubin, 1988a). For years, of course, the classic elaboration of this approach was to be found in the works of Richard Fenno (1966) and Aaron Wildavsky (1984, 1986). Over the course of two decades and four editions of his *Politics of the Budgetary Process* Wildavsky chronicled a system that was highly decentralized and relied on a "bottom-up" bargaining process. This process began with a base and focused primarily on the increments to it. During any given budget-negotiation cycle the great bulk of an agency's appropriation thus already enjoyed a consensus, and conflict was held to a minimum. Department heads were among the main actors and the rules of the game spelled out various strategies that they could employ. In the book's final, 1984, edition, however, Wildavsky warned readers that the system was changing because its central premises—predictability, limits, and collectivity—were no longer tenable.

Nonetheless, the last decade did give us a number of defenses of incrementalism. For example, Malachowski et al. (1987) argued that the old approach was still valid as long as certain modifications were made. The authors did this by updating Fenno's analysis with data from 1964–1984. These data focused on congressional changes of presidential spending requests, and they highlighted the significance of the concept of role flexibility. Specifically, the authors contended that the old roles (advocacy, guardianship, and appeals court) were not dead, but that their institutional homes had merely shifted. Thus, during the Carter and Reagan years the guardianship role was assumed by the executive branch while Congress took over appeals-court actions. Finally, the conclusion was presented that such a reinterpretation (stressing role flexibility and partisanship) made it premature to simply reject the incremental approach.

Accepting the validity of many of the model's criticisms, Pitsvada and Draper (1984) stated a similar position. Yes, there were problems, they noted, but when compared to other interpretations, it still represented the best way to see budgets. This was held to be so because five basic factors are operating to make incrementalist analysis even more useful: indexing, multiyear budgeting, continuing resolutions, baseline reviews, and agency use of incremental and decremental display formats. Explaining the logic of this argument, they point out that indexing, for example, makes a budget more incremental since each year a small adjustment is made to the base using some guide like the CPI. Similarly, baseline reviews provide a current services budget whose emphasis is on stability. The authors see these conclusions as beneficial to democratic theory since social needs and wants (at least in this country) seem to change only by increments.

Numerous interpretations of democratic theory rely upon the notions of bargaining and compromise, and it is thus noteworthy that just 2 years after the publication of the Pitsvada article, Jeremy Plant (1986) gave us a condensation and updating of Charles Lindblom's thoughts on the subject of budgeting. Here again we see the relevance of incrementalism because of the near-permanence of two constraints: man's limited intellectual ability and the fact of limited information. Their reality means that partisan mutual adjustment will continue to function as a mainstay of politics in general and as a mainstay of the budget process in particular. Comprehensive management and planning via the appropriations route would be too abstract for either the executive or legislative branches to accept.

In a very real sense, however, articles like these have, together, constituted no more than a minority, rear-guard action, since most of the last decade's scholarly attention to incrementalism has focused on its passage from the scence. Intellectual positions here spread across a continuum from those heralding its death or irrelevance to those contending that it has merely been supplemented by, or overlaid with, a new kind of politics. Three currents will be identified as the demise school, the base-adjustment school, and the new politics school of thought.

Demise

Let us begin with the position that incrementalism is dead. One of the most succinct statements of this view was provided by Lance LeLoup (1979) in a discussion of what he saw as incrementalism's analytical problems. His argument was essentially that the main phenomena selected for study are not the most appropriate ones. Specifically there are questions of (1) level of aggregation, (2) time and object of analysis, and (3) dependent and independent variables. The main burden of his argument is that the theory's choice of data in each of these areas (for example, agency-level aggregation and final appropriations) very nearly sets up a self-fulfilling prophesy. For example, if the aggregation does not distinguish between mandatory and controllable elements it will inevitably "discover" stability although such stability is not a result of budgetary bargaining. Because of problems such as these, hypotheses based on the theory are not falsifiable and thus the theory is not really "theory."

While the foregoing indictment is epistomological in nature, one by Bozeman and Straussman (1982) is essentially experiential. Written early in the Reagan era, it is based on the empirically verifiable fact that the administration had gone farther than any other in instituting a top-down budget process. Macrobudgeting sets priorities centrally and works within constraints set by an external environment. During this period, congressional spending resolutions and presidential taxation policy came to dominate the process. Bozeman and Straussman were thus arguing that the model no longer matched the reality: that incrementalism was ill-equipped to serve as a general theory of budgeting for the United States.

Regarding the concept of marcobudgeting, another article by LeLoup (1988a) is of relevance. In it he contends that incrementalism, or microbudgeting, tended to ignore the president's role in budgeting, while it was in fact central (and centralized) even in the paradigm's heyday—the 1950s and 1960s. To the extent that the Office of Management and Budget/Bureau of the Budget (OMB/BOB) was a subject of study it was conceived of as a mere bargaining agent, not as the packager of presidential priorities that it in fact was.

In other words, macrobudgeting has been with us for a long time, and it differs from microbudgeting in terms of the conceptualization of its key actors (authorization and appropriations committees versus budget committees), the dominant mode of legislation (individual bills versus budget resolutions), and its basic process (fragmented versus centralized).

Finally, Irene Rubin (1988a, 1989) has written on what she terms "the demise of incrementalism." The first of these two works is her introduction to a fine volume on budget theory. The subject is treated almost at once because much of the book is focused on the subject of new directions. As she puts it, "The need for a new budget theory became urgent with the demise of incrementalism." She explains this demise by arguing that the paradigm was at once too global, too narrow, and too difficult to prove or disprove. While the latter contention is reminiscent of LeLoup's 1979 analysis, the first point seemingly stands Lindblom on his head. The theory is too global because it was based on perceived characteristics of human nature—exactly the idea that was supposed to make muddling through inevitable. Her contention that it has been too narrow is an amplification of Bozeman and Straussman, that is, that it does not fit with observed reality.

Her 1989 article, which was an extended review of two books by Wildavsky, elaborates further on this last point. Thus, here we are presented with a catalogue of empirical failings. It cannot account for entitlement programs, explain top-down budgeting, or deal with cutbacks, interest groups, or the external environment.

Base Adjustment

One of the most important critiques of incrementalism has come from the work of Kamlet and Mowery (1980). These researchers have argued persuasively that the concept of the base is not fixed and that it has varied considerably at least since the days of the Kennedy administration. They show how OMB formulates the base in several different ways and how these vary significantly during the life of the planning period. For example, base may be defined as current estimates, as the cost of the ongoing level of activities, or as the mandatory budget. If the base is not stable but is indeed open to interpretation and negotiation then it is clear that the increment is not the sole focus of the process. Their analysis continues by pointing out that the selection of a definition can depend on at least three factors: the agency being considered, the context for use of the base, and the function it is intended to serve. If this is so, base is a highly volatile concept and one subject to the vaguaries of political and administrative discretion.

Another of their studies (Mowery, Kamlet, and Crecine, 1980) has provided an in-depth examination of the pre-Reagan administrations of Eisenhower, Kennedy, and Johnson. Here we see that incrementalism probably put too much emphasis on Congress rather than the presidency. Focusing on the relationship between the White House, OMB and the federal agencies, they show a linkage between fiscal and budgetary policies. The interdependence between domestic budgetary policy, defense budgetary policy, and fiscal policy makes it clear that presidents have been using a top-down approach for years and that the idea of an agency base has not been stable.

The New Politics

Finally, there is another group of scholars who also recognize that substantial change has taken place in budgeting. For them, however, this has altered the process not by making incrementalism irrelevant, but by adding new elements to the mix. As one of the fathers of the old orthodoxy, Aaron Wildavsky (1988) is fittingly found in this camp. He begins his *New Politics of the Budgetary Process* with a recognition of the reality of the changes that have occurred in the last two decades. He quickly adds, however, that they have not actually replaced anything: "rather the new has been layered onto the old." The operation of top-down rules, entitlements, federal credit, and changes at OMB are, for him, merely new additions to many of the old incremental verities. For example, the guardianship role identified by Fenno is still operative. It is just that today it is played primarily by the budget committees, not by the House Appropriations Committee. Yet he also recognizes that change runs deeper than this. Bowing to the evidence, he concedes that what makes the "new politics" new is precisely the fact of conflict over the base, and not just the increment.

If agreement about the base has eroded, then the fundamental hallmark of the new era is its loss of consensus. Regarding such a loss, he tells us that the central question concerns what has caused the budget process to become so "unsatisfactory." One of the reasons he offers concerns the growth of entitlement programs in conditions of growth, balance, and decline. The operation of backdoor spending through federal credit is another factor, and the subsidy activities of the Federal Financing Bank are detailed in chapter four.

Regarding the loss of consensus about the base, Donald Kettl (1989) has argued that three changes in the budget process have caused participants to focus on protecting themselves and their clientele groups rather than on expanding further. These three are as follows: changes in federal spending (indexing, budget-balancing), changes in federal taxation (where the use of trust funds, etc. has cut down on flexibility), and what he calls the "budgetary twilight zone" (government loan and tax expenditure activities). Thus, for example, indexing has plunged us into a fiscal ice age in which the benefits for some are assured while other agencies have to scramble all the harder to minimize damage to their bases. He dates this "politics of protection" from 1970, while he claims the preceding two decades were characterized by a "politics of expansion."

Similarly, Lee Sigelman (1986) has reexamined data from the American State Administrator Project and found that in none of the 4 years for which figures were available did a majority of high-ranking state administrators pursue budget increases in excess of 15%. In fact in every year a substantial number called for little or no agency expansion (the politics of protection). Clearly the idea of the bureaucrat as budget maximizer (Niskanen, 1971) is no longer descriptive of reality.

A thoughtful essay by Naomi Caiden (1983) is even more to the point. In "The politics of subtraction" she claims that the old rules invited incremental change but that the additional steps in today's process place the attention on conflict. Such conflict has generated new tactics, and she details the most significant ones: package splitting, leverage on essential matters, avoiding responsibility, negotiating alternatives, and brinksmanship. This, then, is another example of how the "new politics of the budgetary process" can be seen as an overlay—adding new dimensions to, rather than completely replacing, the old.

This section of the chapter has focused on the politics of incrementalism, examining defenses of the old orthodoxy and then three schools of thought regarding its current status. It is now time to turn our attention to research on how this, or some other, theory actually operates in the context of U.S. governmental institutions.

THE EXECUTIVE BRANCH

The President

Because ours is a system of separated institutions sharing power, it would be artificial to treat either the President or Congress in isolation. Like codependent spouses, the power of each is greatly affected by the power of the other. They interact constantly, and a sizeable body of literature has been produced focusing on budgetary relations between them. Basically there tend to be two overall positions: presidential dominance and congressional resurgence. Perhaps the best statement of the latter position is to be found in a book by James Sundquist (1981). He begins by tracing Congress's long-term loss of power during this century and then shifts to how it was reborn in the 1970s confrontations with Richard Nixon. While Sundquist considers many aspects of this confrontation, the one of greatest relevance to the current article is treated in a chapter entitled "To Regain the Power of the Purse." Here he recounts the executive excesses that led to the passage of the Congressional Budget and Impoundment Control Act of 1974. Writing in 1981, he noted that the law's centralizing effects established a strong counter to presidential dominance. The significant idea here is that of institutionalization, and a report card from the first several years after the book's publication does not invalidate its insight. He refers to a new orderliness and to the fact that Congress established its own decision-making capacity (with the budget committees) and its own source of independent information (the Congressional Budget Office). Such structural changes created a countervailing power that was previously absent.

A variation on this theme is also presented by Dennis Ippolito (1984), who claims that budget reform has not brought a basic realignment to the balance of power. Risking oversimplification, he writes that Congress' share of the spending power was not in danger earlier, and is not presently. Impoundment is no longer a problem, and presidential power has been further limited by the growth of uncontrollables.

The "congressional resurgence" position is, however, a minority phenomenon. Most authors who confront this question head-on tend to conclude that it is the President who dominates the budgetary process (LeLoup, 1977/1988b). However, such a view was not always accurate, and for an appreciation of the cyclical nature of budgetary power the reader is referred to a work by Pfiffner (1979). During the nineteenth century, Congress was dominant in budgetary matters, but inefficiencies and abuses led to calls for reform. An excellent case for the initiation of an executive budget process can be found in the Taft Commission's original report (1912). While its recommendations were initially rejected, many of them became part of the Budget and Accounting Act of 1921. A 50-year period of executive dominance followed, but then the cycle renewed itself in 1974 with Congress' reactions to executive budgetary "excesses."

One of the best-known spokesmen for the "presidential dominance" position is Howard Shuman (1984/1988). In both editions of his book he informs the reader that the budget is the nation's most important statement of its priorities and that it is initiated and orchestrated by the president. He then proceeds to show us exactly why and how this is so. Not unexpectedly, he begins with a discussion of the Budget and Accounting Act of 1921, which introduced the practice of executive budgeting.

He also takes an informal and extralegal approach, stressing what he sees as the main principles of executive budgeting. These he covers with labels such as rolling history, implied blackmail, sacred cows, the unofficial leak, and politics of the bureaucracy. He next includes a chapter on the "Reagan Revolution" where he focuses on how the President was able to convert the 1974 act to his own uses and pursue a four-point program: (1) to change fiscal and budget priorities and to reprogram resources from the civilian to the military sector; (2) to shift financial burdens to state and local governments; (3) to privatize numerous other government activities; and (4) to shift the tax burden from the wealthy.

A useful treatment of the development of executive domination is contained in a book by Louis Fisher (1975). After a brief review of nineteenth-century spending powers, he clearly chronicles the reform movement and the growth of central control inherent in the adoption of executive budgeting. One of the best-known case studies of a president's attempts to consolidate both general and budgetary powers is the study of the Nixon presidency done by Richard Nathan (1975).

Two general works on the subject of budgeting are also helpful because of the specific attention they devote to presidential budgetary power. Ippolito (1978) analyzes the Johnson, Nixon, Ford, and Carter presidencies and finds an interesting trend. Congress and the President appear to have used their budgetary powers to different ends, with presidents emphasizing military expenditures and Congress using its power on behalf of social programs.

While Ippolito looks at goals, LeLoup (1977/1988b) provides the reader with a concise typology of budgetary styles. The author examines the varying degrees of personal involvement that selected presidents have had in budgeting and presents the following set of categories: passive involvement, active involvement, and mixed involvement.

Discussing this typology, LeLoup accepts the widely held view of Eisenhower as essentially being passive and lacking in power. However, this interpretation has come under some attack. For an effective presentation of alternative evidence, the reader is referred to a fine analysis of Eisenhower's defense budget by Kinnard (1977). There one finds a picture of a strong president exercising power through the use of budget ceilings and active manipulation of the joint chiefs of staff.

Presidential budget power is also the subject of the book by Louis Fisher (1975), which was mentioned above. The focus of Fisher's work is the spending side—rather than the formulation and adoption side—of the budget process, and in it the author argues that Congress has been thoroughly unable to control executive spending decisions. Detailed attention is given to various tools of administative budgetary power: covert financing, impoundment, lump-sum appropriations, transfer of funds, reprogramming of funds, executive commitments, and timing of obligations. These vehicles enabled presidents and other executive-branch officials to get around congressional power by taking action after that branch's role was largely completed, that is, during the budget execution phase. Fisher (1972, 1974a,b) expanded this analysis with three shorter studies as well.

Today, of course, the subject of presidential budget power cannot be divorced from attention to Ronald Reagan's impact on it. This literature has boomed in recent years, and here we will consider a small sampling. Kamlet et al. (1988) use simulation for one type of assessment of his impact. They show that budget priorities were relatively stable from Eisenhower through Carter, but that with Reagan they changed dramatically. This was most striking with regard to increased defense spending and lowered domestic outlays. They base their comparison on what "would have been the case under pre-Reagan budget priorities."

Congressional scholar Allen Schick (1984) has focused not on substantive policy like this but on Reagan's impact on processes. He argues that although Reagan moved budgeting more toward a top-down approach he did not really give us new budget institutions. Instead, he pursued such ad hoc tactics of control as packaging the budget and aggressively working the Hill. Because of such facts the Reagan legacy will likely consist of four developments: 1) centralized budgeting; (2) multiyear budgeting; (3) a more comprehensive resource allocation process; and (4) a more active role for the president in the legislative process.

This fourth point has also been addressed by Robert Reischauer (1984) in a discursive essay on congressional budgeting. He concludes that neither house is capable of executing priority shifts or dealing with issues like retrenchment and deficit reduction without the cooperation and leadership of the president. He also suggests that this leadership is more important to the extent that the political parties have divided control of the two houses.

The effect of partisanship on presidential budgeting power during another era has been examined by Lowry et al. (1985) in a reanalysis of Fenno's original data. The authors proceed by using the concept of "presidential advocacy" and show that Congress plays its budgetary roles with greater or lesser degrees of strength depending on the partisanship of the executive branch.

Continuing with the concept of "presidential advocacy," several investigators have provided analyses of the Reagan years. LeLoup and Hancock (1988) use a chronological approach, dividing his administration into three time periods: 1981–1982, 1983–1986, and 1987–1988. During each of these periods three different elements of executive-legislative budgeting are considered:

1. Budgetary politics and issues—the extent to which conflict was based on ideological, economic or partisan differences.
2. Procedural changes—alterations in the budget process itself.
3. Policy results—the extent to which Reagan's budgets altered programs and priorities.

Assessments are then offered in each of these areas. For example, regarding policy, they conclude that "the Reagan revolution did not fail." The budgets achieved many of his goals: the growth in defense spending, the cut in discretionary domestic programs, and the shift in, or reduction of, the tax burden. In the area of procedures, however, they agree with Schick, concluding that the 1980s generated tremendous budgetary instability. They argue that such a condition resulted from three factors: (1) growing outlay inflexibility, (2) administration actions to limit congressional options, and (3) the increasing difficulty of making accurate economic and budget forecasts.

While the article just discussed analyzed three separate time periods, another study by one of the same authors focused exclusively on the early days of the Reagan administration (LeLoup, 1982). In this instance LeLoup assessed the impact of the 1981 budget battle on the overall budget process, emphasizing that it did three things. First, it resulted in the efforts of the entire committee system being set aside by a single vote. Further, it blurred the distinction between authorizing and appropriating committees, and finally it tended to weaken the overall committee system.

This theme of the reining in of decentralization is also taken up by Hartman (1982). In another early article he presents a preliminary conclusion about the increased power of the budget committees. Such a situation, of course, was not to remain unchanged.

A widely read, if somewhat undisciplined, account of the tension between centralization and decentralization, macro and micro, is provided by David Stockman (1986). This insider's narrative account of how he believes the Reagan Revolution failed takes its title from the author's diagnosis of the ills. It was a "triumph of politics" that thwarted the centralized working of the President's mandate and supply-side orthodoxy. Of course, this mildly self-serving portrayal focuses on the fact that it was Stockman's programming of the mandate that eventually was sacrificed to the winds of compromise, expediency, and failure. And it "failed" precisely for reasons having to do with microbudgeting politics—decentralization, vote trading, constituency service, interest-group activity, and the iron triangles of Theodore Lowi.

In the famous article by William Greider (1981) we learn of the ideologue's lament as he confronted the realities of power and pork via programs such as the fast-breeder nuclear reactor at Clinch River, Tennessee. This is a fine, journalistic account of the rough and tumble of microbudget politics set against the background of flawed macro-budget estimates.

Perhaps it is difficult for a true believer to accept the idea of compromise, but a fascinating cross-national study of defense budgeting by Michael Hobkirk (1984) concludes that it is inevitable here. This book-length, comparative analysis of budgetary institutions in the United States and Great Britain highlights the near impossibility of cleanly following a top-down approach in Washington. Hobkirk cites such factors as the ability of a service to take its case directly to Congress if it is dissatisfied with the priorities of the Secretary of Defense. In the absence of a tradition of party responsibility, neither the executive nor the legislative branches can eliminate the presence of in-terservice rivalries in the planning of defense expenditures. For Pitsvada and Draper

(1984), unlike Stockman, such evidence of the ongoing vitality of the iron triangles is a reassurance that democratic theory is still relevant.

The Office of Management and Budget (OMB)

For information about the OMB, there is no better place to start than with a book by Larry Berman (1979). Its first half is devoted to a history of the agency's predecessor, the Bureau of the Budget (BOB). Here we see an agency maturing in its sense of mission and analytical capability. In 1970, however, OMB was created as part of a Nixon reorganization, and it is doubtful that this change led to continued progress. Berman analyzes OMB's power decline in such areas as partisan politics, organizational requirements, and the growth of countervailing bodies, such as the Congressional Budget Office (CBO).

Another fine historical treatment is provided by Frederick Mosher (1984), who has traced the evolution of both the OMB and the General Accounting Office (GAO) in a book rich in contextual information. After sketching each agency in considerable detail, he gives the reader a final chapter that offers a systematic overview and analytical comparison. Here one learns, for example, that since World War II the OMB and GAO have been becoming more alike, with OMB moving away from an exclusively managerial concern and more toward finance, while the GAO has simultaneously developed more interest in management. In addition, both are essentially conservative agencies, staffed by generalists. Because both are seen as being reactors and counterpunchers, they are similarly viewed as enemies by interest groups and bureaucrats. In other words, they work for an agency with power.

Attempting to analyze just what kind of power the office has, Hugh Heclo (1975) concludes that it has too much political power and not enough analytical power. Throughout most of its history, its predecessor, the BOB, had been known for its "neutral competence." This impartial, nonpartisan expertise was the basis of its very real governmental authority. Richard Nixon "politicized" the OMB, turning its role away from neutral competence and toward political support for the president.

The reader can find this theme elaborated upon in two other articles (Berman, 1977, 1978), which document related facets of decline. In addition, Zeidenstein (1978) points out that the requirement that the director of the OMB be confirmed by the Senate is a direct consequence of the office's politicization.

Ultimately, assessments of the office's power must rest, of course, on the pivotal nature of its budget function, especially during the Reagan years (Benda and Levine, 1986). However, other factors have been shown to be contributory. Cooper and West (1988) focus on its central clearance of agency rules. While all rules must be submitted for review, the agencies are not bound to take OMB advice. Why do they usually comply, however? Cooper and West answer that OMB also has the power to review their budgets and "he who pays the fiddler calls the tune." Benda and Levine (1988) also relate its power to its responsibility for setting personnel ceilings—a function intimately tied to the budget process.

An indication of the extent to which OMB's decision-making process has changed over the years is provided by comparing two articles. Relying on data from the late 1960s, Bromiley and Crecine (1980) present a picture of the staff making budget decisions by balancing top-down and bottom-up approaches. In this model we see them relying both on agency-specific information and on aggregate economic and fiscal data. Hugh Heclo

(1984), on the other hand, provides us with an analysis of the Stockman era where a very different picture emerges. Not only do we see a decision process that became almost completely top-down, it was highly "personalized" as well. Decisions were made by Stockman after consultation with White House strategists. The OMB staff was then merely called upon to follow through on these choices rather than to independently analyze numerous policy options. Heclo writes that the political leadership believed that it knew exactly what to do and then simply oriented to the OMB staff as though it were a congressional office. David Mathiasen (1988) writes that other reasons for the agency's changed role include the 1982–1983 recession, the idea of "normal budget growth" coming under fire, and the concept of baselines.

This changed role, of course, raises the whole question of politicization again. Bruce Johnson (1984, 1989) is a former budget examiner who has provided first-hand accounts of the shift from neutral competence to advocacy. This shift involves three roles: formulating and enforcing the budget, negotiating with Congress, and practicing an advocacy mission with the media and interest groups. Wyszomirski (1982) reminds us that the trend did not start with Reagan. What she sees as a deinstitutionalization set in with Nixon and has continued ever since, with the office's leadership becoming ever more inexpert and partisan. Such a trend has sacrificed the organization's credibility.

Mosher and Stephenson (1982) are more skeptical of the charges of politicization. Relying on both interviews and the literature, they show that during the early Reagan years there was no increase in the number of the agency's political positions. Furthermore, they argue, OMB staff members have always had a predisposition to cut. Reagan's ideology merely provided them with an opportunity to "do what comes naturally" for budget examiners.

Agencies and Programs

The trend toward centralization that accelerated during the Reagan years had a major impact on the budgetary roles played by individual agencies and programs. Aaron Wildavsky (1988) has shown, however, that these roles have very diverse elements, combining "bottom-up, top-down and in-between" components. Indeed, while he gives a great deal of attention to subjects like reconciliation and sequestration, he still writes about the agency's role as featuring "the dance of the dollars."

Lance LeLoup (1977/1988b) also emphasizes many continuities when discussing agency advocacy during an era of retrenchment. One continuity involves the ongoing use of certain games and strategies. Several of these he labels as follows: calling out the troops, current fashion, the end run, and the foot in the door. Leonard Reed (1979) also compiled a number of these strategies and showed how they can be used to augment bureaucratic power. Several examples will suffice to convey the flavor of his approach:

The king's pawn opening—overstating what a program will cost.
The shortfall game—underestimating costs on "uncontrollables," shifting funds and making up the difference through supplemental appropriations.
The Washington Monument game—resisting cuts by threatening to eliminate essential programs.

A statement of general principles by Irene Rubin (1990) also sheds additional light on agency options. She claims that four characteristics of public budgeting help explain the politics of expenditures. These characteristics are multiple actors with different goals, decision making that is open to the environment, a separation between those who make spending decisions and those who pay taxes, and finally a budget process filled with constraints.

Regarding this last point, the Reagan years were, of course, a period of severe belt tightening for many federal agencies. The fact that some dealt with this phenomenon better than others is made clear in another book by Rubin (1985). Concerned with the shrinking federal government, it examines the effects of cutbacks on five different federal agencies: the Bureau of Health Planning, the Employment and Training Administration, the Urban Mass Transit Administration (UMTA), the Office of Personnel Management (OPM), and the Community Planning and Development Program. Among the five, those agencies with strong interest-group support were able to better resist the President and reverse cuts in funding levels. Remember David Stockman's lament? For example, UMTA had strong interest-group support and therefore cuts in its funding levels were reversed. In addition, the administration's proposed termination of operating subsidies was defeated. On the other hand, an agency like OPM with no real clientele was forced to take substantial cuts. The irony of Rubin's message is sobering. When it comes to retrenchment, agencies that have been colonized by their clientele groups are likely to be better off than their more professional counterparts that have held the interest groups at arm's length.

Joseph Wholey (1984) has also given us a comparative analysis of executive agency retrenchment. Like Rubin, he examined five agencies from 1981–1983 in order to observe the processes and impacts of cuts: the Food and Nutrition Service, the Employment and Training Administration, the Health Resources and Services Administration, the National Institute of Mental Health, and the Administration of Aging (AoA). His basic approach was to set out a list of OMB objectives and then determine the operational impact of each one on each of the five agencies. The objectives included items such as the reduction of spending, the reduction of agency staffing, and the combining of categorical programs into block grants.

Once this assessment was completed, Wholey, again like Rubin, examined whether programs enjoying broader political support were better able to resist retrenchment than those with weak political bases. For example, during a time of recession the Unemployment Insurance Program fared better than the Food Stamp Program. The constituency of the latter, we are reminded, is much less politically visible. Senior citizens also make a very active clientele, and thus AoA programs of nutrition and social services experienced only marginal cuts.

Numerous examinations of agency budgeting in the pre-Reagan era are also still useful. Many of them appropriately tended to focus on incrementalism. Evidence of administrative budgetary power was found by Wanat (1974). In his historical examination (1968–1972) of the Labor Department's budget process, he demonstrated that most of the incremental increases dealt with mandatory expenditures. Substantial changes did occur, however, in the discretionary area. Thus he clearly showed that not all of the budget was dealt with in an incremental fashion.

Padgett (1980) argued for a substitution of "serial judgment theory" in place of the Wildavsky/Lindblom approach. He argued that the latter is valid only if we confine our analysis to absolute dollar levels. When we shift to programmatic change, however, incrementalism simply becomes too rigid.

Less theoretical treatments of departmental budgetary power are also available. Korb (1977), for example, took an intradepartmental focus in his analysis of procedures at the Department of Defense. He analyzes three basic budgetary processes used there and clearly shows the critical nature of ceilings in generating compliance. The decentralized system is also examined in considerable detail, but the most valuable contribution of the study is its insistence on the fact that budgeting is an inherently political process.

On a related plane, Davis and Ripley (1967) examined interaction between executive agencies and the central budget staff. They conclude that agencies tend to see the budget staff as either hostile, neutral, or inclined to advocacy. The exact nature of each relationship will depend on such factors as presidential purposes, accessibility of information, past budgetary decisions, and the degree of need for support that both parties feel.

This agency/central budget staff relationship also has been treated by LeLoup and Moreland (1978). Theirs is a useful article for information on the amount of change that takes place in a budget before it ever gets to the Congress. Most studies focus on the changes that occur in the budget after it leaves the White House, but such analysis can tell only part of the story.

The statement made above about agency/congressional relations being the more usual focus of scholarly concern is perhaps best exemplified in a study done by Sharkansky (1965). Restricting himself to four agencies whose appropriations requests were heard by the same subcommittee allowed Sharkansky to introduce an element of control into his work. He analyzed the different ways in which the agenices dealt with the subcommittees—assertiveness, breaking of norms, use of promotional devices—and then sought to explain these strategies in terms of certain independent variables: public support, agency support, and the nature of the agency's programs. This last factor was found to be a critical element of agency power.

Today, of course, the politics of agency/congressional committee interaction frequently lack the urgency of Sharkansky's day. One reason for this is the fact that much of the discretion and uncertainty has been removed from the process by entitlement programs and indexation (Wildavsky, 1988). Currently 46% of the federal budget automatically goes to individuals and units of government meeting eligibility requirements established by statute. For a discussion of the magnitude and growth of this spending see Rivlin (1984).

Jeffrey Straussman (1988) has examined such programs not in terms of their aggregate impact on budget totals, but with an eye to their relationship to the political process. He presents entitlements as a type of rights-based budgeting and shows how the concept does not fit well with our traditional ideas about the appropriations process, since tradeoffs become impossible. This being so, he concludes that there are three broad lessons to be learned from studying the relationship between rights and budgets: (1) the need to extend our knowledge about the institutional character of the public budgeting process; (2) the need to further examine classic budgeting in rights-based environments; and (3) the impact of political change on rights-based budgeting.

One of the best studies of the politics of this subject is contained in a book by Kent Weaver (1988). His focus is indexation—the automatic adjustment of public policy outputs for inflation. This phenomenon, of course, involves officials' surrender of control over programs, and his study is an analysis of why they have been willing to do this. Three primary motivations are offered and discussed: credit claiming, good policy, and blame avoiding. The author then uses this framework in his treatment of a half-dozen indexing programs showing how decision makers weigh political costs and benefits.

The book concludes with an analysis of the consequences of indexation, consequences for the policy process, accountability, clientele groups, the economy, and the budget. Regarding the latter, both his case studies and overall data indicate that the combination of indexed and nonindexed programs increases federal deficits and that indexing tends to keep deficit-reduction plans off the agenda.

Another type of program change with direct political implications involves what is frequently called "off-budget budgeting" (Axelrod, 1989). What is at issue here is the question of federal credit programs. These are not included in the unified budget and thus do not come under the same micro and macro political controls.

Two book-length studies of this phenomenon are worth noting. The first, by Dennis Ippolito (1984), assesses the political and economic ramifications of a situation in which these credit programs can lay claims to funding without having to compete with direct spending. The book examines the sharp increase in loans and loan guarantees for housing, agriculture, education, and international affairs. There are also excellent case studies dealing with several big bailouts: Penn Central, Lockheed, New York City, and Chrysler Corporation. His central message is clear. Such programs provide well-defined and substantial benefits to important constituencies.

The second book, by Bennett and DiLorenzo (1983), is less satisfying because it is less measured. Where Ippolito factually cites the problems created by hidden spending, these authors adopt an almost shrill tone as they rail against off-budget enterprises (OBEs). The book is not so much an analysis of the budgetary implications of OBEs as it is an attempt to characterize their use in conspiratorial terms. Public office-holders at all levels of government are protrayed as either sinister manipulators or cowardly fools who turn to these devices as a way to subvert the public interest. The book is a thinly veiled attempt to make a morality play out of this aspect of public spending.

Case studies focus on New York State under Nelson Rockefeller and on numerous off-budget activities of local government. A separate chapter entitled "The Underground Federal Government" focuses on the loan guarantee and other functions of the Federal Financing Bank. Data are also presented on overall, guaranteed loan transactions of the federal goverment. Here the book is more factual and less alarmist, allowing the reader to compare the government's off-budget priorities.

CONGRESS

The Classic Appropriations Process

During the late 1970s and most of the 1980s the Congressional appropriations process was in a state of great flux. Buffeted by deficits, reforms, and mandatory cuts, it sought to identify a new modus operandi. However, prior to this period there was a more stable time. It was characterized by a "classic appropriations process," one that operated largely from the bottom up, and scholars documented it with a substantial body of literature. Among the numerous works extant, one of the best known and most influential is that of Richard Fenno (1966). Written more than two decades ago, it is still cited as the definitive work on the classic appropriations process in general, and on the functioning of the appropriations committees and subcommittees in particular. Beginning with the House Appropriations Committee, Fenno found its power manifest in protecting the power of the purse and serving as a "guardian" of the federal treasury. Such a mission was seen as "the essential bulwark of congressional power." What this meant in practice was a role orientation that urged committee members to examine agency budgets in great detail and make cuts wherever possible.

The role of the Senate Appropriations Committee, on the other hand, was that of an appeals court. Its deliberations were frequently concerned with agency requests for restoration of funds cut by the House, and Fenno found its record for the granting of such increases to be quite substantial.

Significant elaboration upon the Fenno thesis was provided by other sources (Horn, 1970; Fox, 1971), one of the best being a study of congressional budgeting for eight agencies (Thomas and Handberg, 1974). Comparing House and Senate actions on individual agencies over a 25-year period, the authors confirmed that the House Appropriations Committee in fact did reduce a greater proportion of agency requests than the Senate. However, they also found that highly constituency-oriented agencies were likely to receive favorable treatment from the appropriations committees of both houses.

The exercise of power through the cutting or restoring of funds characterized not only congressional-bureaucratic relations but also intracongressional relations. According to Fenno, the appropriations committees held a considerable amount of power over the substantive committees as well. These latter bodies frequently wanted higher appropriations for programs they backed, and this drive collided with the House Appropriations Committee's guardianship role. The result was a power confrontation—one that the Appropriations Committee could usually dominate.

The appropriations committees, of course, are divided into various subcommittees, and these are given considerable attention in the classic literature (Fenno, 1966; Horn, 1970; Polsby, 1971; Ripley, 1975). One of the most insightful studies was published by John Gist (1978). An analysis of Senate appropriations subcommittees, it clearly documented the existence of a prestige hierarchy among the subcommittees. The author hypothesized that this hierarchy was based on the degree of actual power that the subcommittees had over their appropriations; and power, in turn, was based on controllability. For example, the budgets examined by certain subcommittees contained high proportions of uncontrollable expenditures. This resulted in a low subcommittee power and prestige rating. It might be concluded, therefore, that there was a relationship between subcommittee power and budget controllability.

In a related study, Fenno (1962) claimed that the reason the appropriations committees functioned so effectively was that they were integrated so well. Such integration, in turn, was assured by five factors: consensus, the nature of the subject matter, the legislative orientation of committee members, the attractiveness of the committee for its members, and the stability of committee membership. Membership stability also was cited (Manley, 1970) as a key characteristic of the powerful Ways and Means Committee—another body intimately concerned with fiscal matters. Such factors, then, may be seen as bases of committee power.

Other works emphasized the impact of these and related variables. Joseph Harris (1964), for example, placed much emphasis on the fact that appropriations committee members tended to come from safe districts. This ensured them a long tenure and the chance to develop real budgetary expertise. Jeffrey Pressman (1966), in turn, took the logic one step further by highlighting the informal working relations that developed between these senior elected representatives and the budget officials in the executive branch. For the Ways and Means Committee, Catherine Rudder (1977) also showed that similar working relations existed between committee members, administrative officials, and the representatives of various affected interest groups.

A final condition for committee budgetary power during the classic period concerned staff resources (Schwengel, 1968; Ripley, 1975). An early recognition of the critical importance of this component may be found in the writing of Emmerich and McLean (1950). More than forty years ago, they raised questions about the training, role orientations, and ethics of individuals functioning in this key capacity.

Nelson Polsby (1971), one of Capitol Hill's most ardent defenders, wrote that although there are undoubtedly differences in the powers and processes of the Congress and the executive branch, these are outweighed by the similarities. For example, the budgetary decisions of both may be viewed not as reflecting differing levels of information and analysis but as responses to the demands of different groups. Thus, the fact that power is dispersed in Congress need not be a sign of weakness. Rather it may be a way of accommodating more and more groups and thus gaining more power. Such a theory is congruent with the work of David Truman (1951). In making classic budgetary allocations, therefore, both Congress and the President examined (1) what the agencies received last year, (2) external developments, (3) agency reputations for estimate accuracy, (4) previous programmatic commitments, and (5) interest group demands (Polsby, 1971).

One of the most thorough studies documenting congressional budget power during this period was that of Arnold Kanter (1972). He clearly showed the impact of congressional initiative on the defense budget during the 1960s. An uncritical examination of Congress's aggregate changes in proposed defense spending for that period would have made it appear that the legislative branch had minimal impact on the Pentagon. However, Kanter proceeded by breaking the sums down into expenditure categories and discovered that most congressional changes in the defense budget were concentrated in procurement and in RDT & E (research, development, testing, and evaluation). These two categories are of extreme policy significance, and Kanter demonstrated that, with regard to them, Congress was able to enforce compliance to its wishes. Such key programmatic power is overlooked when the analyst concentrates on aggregate figures.

A similar conclusion was reached by John Gist (1978) in his examination of the power prestige hierarchies of Senate subcommittees. One looking at modal changes in the executive budget made by the "average subcommittee" would have concluded that in general, Congress had little power. However, such an approach hid a great deal of useful data. Thus, Gist argued that our analyses must distinguish between the various subcommittees. Clearly, some were very powerful vis-à-vis the executive branch while others were largely passive.

The "Reformed" Appropriations Process

The stability of the classic period was not to last indefinitely. In the mid 1970s Congress moved into its confrontation with Richard Nixon, and then later, as Carter was replaced by Reagan, the deficits began to mount. The literature of this later era, an era through which we are still groping, has tended to take as its starting point the passage of the Congressional Budget and Impoundment Control Act of 1974.

A very well written article by Thomas Wander (1984) focuses on the forces that led to its adoption. Using March and Simon's (1958) concept of the "occasions for innovation," he examines the internal and external factors that together created a need for change. Adaptive reforms are those generated by external variables, and here he cites the state of the economy and the President's abuse of impoundment. While these were undoubtedly significant causes they were not alone. The law also sought to create ameliorative changes in response to the internal problems of widespread decentralization and committee conflict that had led to turf disputes. Thus, right from the start we see that the law was an attempt to solve two very divergent kinds of problems with a single legislative stroke. Other analyses of the causes leading to reform are provided by Lynch (1990), Penner and Abramson (1988), Schick (1980), and Pfiffner (1979).

That Congress tried to do too much with a single piece of legislation may be the reason for its difficulties, contradictions, and failures in the judgement of many who have studied it. One of its strongest critics has been Louis Fisher (1984, 1985), who has argued that the basic problem has been caused by the attempt to execute comprehensive budgeting via an institution based on decentralization and constituent service. This view sees it as doomed to inevitable failure from the beginning. Central to the reformed process is the passage of resolutions, and these, of course, are instruments of macroeconomic policy. However, Congress is designed so as to be able to best handle micropolicy. Cataloguing the resultant ills, Fisher notes that appropriations bills are now enacted in a less timely manner, that continuing resolutions have become more common, and that the deficits are larger than before the passage of the act.

A similar assessment is made by Kenneth Shepsle (1984), who argues that the law's objectives were sabotaged by excessive accommodation to existing power centers in the House. He documents this charge by citing a reluctance on the part of the House Budget Committee to challenge the turf of other committees. In addition there are what he calls the "adding machine function" and the "substitution effect," for example, the trimming of the budget by merely requiring that other levels of government take over certain expenditures.

Accommodation, however, is a relative concept and not necessarily positive or negative in and of itself. Interestingly, then, this same phenomenon is cited by Congressional scholar Allen Schick in his assessment in a book edited by Penner (1981). Noting that during the act's first 5 years the budget committees avoided explicit tradeoffs among functions, he merely reminds us that this is a disappointment only if the budget is to be seen as an outright contest over national priorities.

Five years later he gives us an even more measured critique (Schick, 1986). Yes, there have been shortcomings, but we must consider these in terms of the conditions under which the law must operate. Here he refers specifically to the nation's economic predicament during the 1970s and to the fact that congressional budgeting takes place within a presidential context. Examining the Ford, Carter, and Reagan presidencies, he outlines how the chief executive takes the budgetary lead and thus leaves Congress dependent on negotiations with him. Schick's reference to these two factors, of course, dovetails nicely with Wander's (1984) analysis of external factors, cited above. Regarding Wander's internal factors, he also notes that the act has had an impact on the role of party leaders, boosting their power.

The distinction between internal and external stresses is also made by Roger Davidson (1984), who uses it to separate reform from mere change. Here we learn that the law has been more successful (a generator of reform) in helping Congress deal with the external environment, one concerned with macroeconomics and presidential leadership. With regard to internal problems, however, the law's consolidative thrust has led to a danger of simply overloading the process—a process that has become a target for committee leaders in both chambers.

Again, though, we encounter the problem of relativity and elasticity of terms. The law has been effective in helping Congress deal with its external world, yet Hebert (1984) presents some interesting data regarding impoundment. This was, of course, prohibited and Congress was given the power to review rescissions and deferrals. However, his data indicate that presidents have been relatively free to exercise their deferral power and that even with rescissions they win most of the time.

Other scholars have taken a less evaluative approach to studying the law and have sought merely to assess its institutional impacts. Copeland (1984) for one examines four types of changes in the House of Representatives: (1) the provision of expertise via the CBO; (2) the generation of jurisdictional jealousies between the budget and other committees; (3) the fact that it has increased partisanship; and (4) the strengthening of bargaining power that it has given to those on the ideological extremes of both parties.

A similar type of analysis by Ellwood (1984) looks at the reform's impact on relations between the two chambers. Here the bottom line is found to be an increase in the power of the Senate, since the House need no longer be constitutionally first in the consideration of fiscal matters. He also demonstrates that the Senate tends to win more issues in conference than the House, due to the more stable membership on its Budget Committee and to its greater bipartisanship. He also has written (Ellwood, 1983) that the law's procedures have led to a shift from distributive to redistributive politics: from a politics designed to give something to everyone, to a politics of winners and losers.

During the reform period significant changes have also taken place in the nature and operations of congressional committees. These changes have produced a considerable new body of literature, but it is a literature best understood against the backdrop of the past. Before going further, it is worth noting that Bruce Oppenheimer (1983) has provided us with an excellent bibliographic essay synthesizing 15 years' worth of scholarly research on Congress and budgeting. He presents his material using a six-part framework: legislative actions or functions, legislative actors, the stages of policy making, legislative outputs, the influence of legislatures in different policy areas, and the differences among legislatures.

Above it was noted that more than two decades have passed since the publication of Richard Fenno's (1966) classic analysis of the congressional appropriations process. His work focused on the role orientations of the two appropriations committees. In the House the committee played the role of "guardian" of the federal treasury, while in the Senate the analogous role was that of "appeals court." Thus he noted that while the House frequently cut agency requests, Senate deliberations were concerned with their restoration.

The 1974 rules changes and the creation of the budget committees in each chamber, of course, altered these roles dramatically. An excellent analysis of this transformation was provided by Allen Schick (1980). He characterized the appropriations committees as having adopted the role of claimants, while the budget committees have taken on the role of guardian. This is so, he argues, since the act prohibits appropriations decisions until after the passage of the first budget resolution. Given the context, spending decisions during the 1970s were made, he believes, on the basis of silent accommodation.

Schick (1981) elaborated further on the idea of accommodation in another article assessing the act's first 5 years. Specifically, he writes that such a strategy deliberately avoided tradeoffs. Instead of prioritizing, the budget committees compartmentalized their spending decisions and avoided placing the functions in a zero-sum relationship to one another.

Obviously, however, this trend did not continue uninterrupted, changing quite dramatically in 1981 when Ronald Reagan managed to gain control of the congressional budgetary process. Lance LeLoup (1977/1984b) provides a broad overview of the change as it affected the Senate. Buttressing Schick, he first demonstrates, a "dominance of accommodation" during the 1970s. During this period the Senate Budget Committee ordinarily attempted to accept guidelines and guidance from the standing committees—in spite of occasional confrontations. However, during the early 1980s when the Republicans controlled the Senate there was a definite decline in accommodation. During this period the Senate Budget Committee was willing to engage in challenges to other standing committees, turf disputes, and the use of reconciliation packages to rewrite both authorization and appropriations bills. The shift from accommodation to confrontation, he concludes, can be at least partially attributed to the fact that Republicans enjoyed greater presidential leadership and sharper partisanship.

While both Reagan's leadership and Republican partisanship declined as the 1980s progressed, the best study of that later period finds that conflict was still central to congressional budgeting from 1982 to 1988. Penner and Abramson (1988) show how hostility marked relations between Republicans and Democrats, between members of Congress and the executive branch, and between senators and representatives, and how conflict even frequently boiled over among members of the same party. The fact that each year's cycle dealt with cutbacks generated both antagonisms and defensiveness. Each actor was very much on his own, the authors claim, each pursuing the blame game that goes with divided government.

Divided government has also meant that Congress's authorization committees continue to be active in the appropriations process. Such a conclusion was shown most effectively by Irene Rubin (1988b) in her study of procedures and outcomes relating to three programs: ACTION, the Federal Insecticide, Fungicide and Rodenticide Program (FIFRA), and the Department of Justice. She finds that in all three cases the authorization committees generated significant impacts on appropriations. Among other things, they affected floors and ceilings, engaged in earmarking, limited reprogramming and provided waivers.

The picture of Congress that emerges from the foregoing discussion of committees and budgeting is one of extreme flux overlaying a blend of centralization and decentralization. In fact, Auten, Bozeman, and Cline (1984) have also presented convincing evidence that top-down influences have been combining with bottom-up pressures to the appropriations process at least since 1956. Their work relies on a sequential model utilizing a "budget constraint" to show the top-down aspect.

On balance, Penner and Abramson (1988) conclude that today the process is malfunctioning—a condition that they characterize as "broken purse strings." However, they do not believe that the huge deficits were caused by this broken process. Instead, they argue, it has been the deficits themselves that have created the pressures emasculating the process.

Oversight

The next subject in this review of congressional budgeting power is that of oversight. Appropriations committees and subcommittees are ultimately involved in this process, and two distinctions drawn by Ogul (1976) help to explain their differing levels of commitment and involvement. First, there are manifest and latent functions to oversight. Latent functions are less immediately obvious and involve such things as constituent service. When they are present to buttress manifest functions, the effect is stronger oversight.

The other distinction involves what Ogul calls opportunity factors and conversion factors. Committees may exercise oversight if the opportunity factors, such as staff and information base, have been provided, but some conversion factor(s) will be necessary for these resources to be channeled into use.

An examination of appropriations politics by LeLoup (1984a) also contains implications for oversight. In this study of House Appropriations Committee-executive agency relationships we see the sources of conflict. These exist between the program-oriented goals of the agencies and the combination of economy-oversight goals of the Committee. The agencies want the Committee to think in broad, positive terms, while the Committee's own orientation leads it to adopt more particular and negative views regarding what may be unnecessary expenditures.

Such an orientation can easily result in misplaced oversight priorities, as Robert Art (1985) has argued. Relying on over 100 interviews with committee staffers, he has analyzed legislative treatment of the defense budget from 1975 to 1984. His conclusion is that both the authorization and appropriations committees are focusing too much attention on budgetary and programmatic oversight and not enough on policy oversight. The use of oversight for micromanagement purposes is questioned.

One of the classic treatments of oversight is that of Joseph Harris (1964). Years ago, he cataloged the types of actions that an appropriations committee or subcommittee could take to alter effectively the actions of an administrative agency. These include such actions as issuing reports, cutting appropriations to force compliance, and writing restrictions into the legislation itself. Silverman (1974) also emphasized the value of oversight as opposed to prospective policy analysis. Its advantages include the availability of a more diverse information base, a greater chance for legislative specialization, and better timing.

In addition to the committees, one other congressional agency is involved in the financial oversight function: the General Accounting Office (GAO). Because of its "watchdog" role, it is given a rather prominent place in the literature. To begin, two very useful books have been written by Mosher and by Brown. The study by Brown (1970) is somewhat dated but does cover the basics well: the agency's audit function, investigative activities, and legal work. The uniqueness of Brown's approach is that it proceeds by focusing on GAO interaction with a single executive agency, the Tennessee Valley Authority. Because of the extensive nature of our discussion of the appropriations process above, it is also relevant to note here that Brown includes in his work an examination of the kinds of services the GAO provides to appropriations committees and subcommittees.

Mosher's book (1979) is more ambitious. In the first half, it traces the evolution of the GAO from the role of voucher checker to that of program evaluator. Looking at a sweep of almost 60 years, the author refers to the different orientations as comprising a first, second, and third GAO. In an article on the same subject, Rourke (1978) presents a similar interpretation. He argues that the GAO has evolved through three separate roles. During its initial 30 years, it focused mainly on voucher audits. This was followed by a period in which the emphasis was on the auditing of managerial efficiency as well as legality. During the 1970s, however, attention shifted to program auditing as the agency moved into cost-benefit and cost-effectiveness analysis.

This reorientation also was noted by Marvin and Hedrick (1974), who described from the insider's angle how the GAO had moved into the field of program evaluation. In the process, they present examples of several such evaluations: social services for welfare recipients, the space shuttle, performance contracting, and the Neighborhood Youth Corps. We are, however, far from unanimity on the question of the desirability of this shift in orientation. Schick (1978), for one, believes that the GAO has gone too far and today is not paying enough attention to its original, and more basic, role.

Finally, another study by Mosher (1984) compares the GAO and OMB, and we see the two agencies beginning to develop similar orientations. However, the author seems to question whether the GAO has taken on too many oversight-related roles. A small sample includes its work as investigator, critic, evaluator, teacher, rule maker on financial matters, and ombudsman.

Whether one is in favor of, or in opposition to, this broadening of GAO scope, the fact remains that is has aided Congress in expanding its budgetary power. More information regarding program effectiveness and goal attainment is now available. However, this does not guarantee that it will be used. Like the CBO, the GAO is a power resource, not a power center.

An Electoral Connection?

Another way to examine the connection between politics and budgeting is to ask whether elections have an impact on the appropriations process. Perhaps the most extreme characterization of their linkage is a theory known as the political business cycle. It was developed by William Nordhaus (1975) and posits the existence of a cycle in a macroeconomic policy corresponding to the electoral cycle. A micro version of this hypothesis has been tested by Kiewiet and McCubbins (1985). The investigators employ an "electoral connection" model to examine appropriations decisions as the responses of reelection-seeking congressmen. Using data from the period 1948–1979, they discovered a pattern in which appropriations are indeed higher during election years. In this study officials thus appear to vote in ways that will maximize the probability of reelection.

This view is also presented in a nonquantitative way by former presidential economic advisor William Niskanen (1986). With echoes of David Stockman, he compares economists and politicians, informing the reader that the role of the policy advisor is to provide information on the potential effects of proposed programs. However, the interest of the politician is in reelection—something that concerns support or opposition to specific policies, rather than the effects of these policies or objective conditions. Shepsle and Weingast (1984) state further that this electoral connection politically distorts expenditure policies through two principles: (1) productive inefficiency—targeting expenditures to constituencies—and (2) the distributive tendency—gaining majority support by spreading expenditures broadly. Their evidence, however, is anecdotal.

Of course, not all analysts agree with such interpretations. Golden and Poterba (1980) examine public opinion polling and financial data frolm 1953–1978 and find no evidence for the existence of a political business cycle. Specifically, they assess the importance of electoral cycles and presidential popularity as a way of explaining macroeconomic policy, and find that neither fiscal, monetary, nor transfers policy has any statistically significant relationship to the electoral cycle.

Examining the period 1955–1981, Kamlet and Mowery (1987) are similarly unable to confirm any such relationship. A much more modest view of the electoral connection was published by Kiewiet (1983), who examined four dimensions of the ways in which people's economic views and concerns affect their votes: the incumbency-oriented hypothesis, the policy-oriented hypothesis, personal experience, and national assessments. Interestingly, he discovered that all four hypotheses were stronger during presidential than during congressional elections.

POLITICS OF THE FEDERAL DEFICIT

The purpose of this article has been to present an examination of scholarly literature on the politics of federal budgeting. Due to its very nature, the undertaking has been concerned with institutions and processes. However, one substantive problem has become so central to American politics in the late twentieth century that it cannot be divorced from elements of process. Here we refer to the problem of the federal budget deficit—a subject pregnant with politics. In fact, in a very well written book, James Savage (1988) assesses how the idea of balancing the budget has influenced American politics for 300 years. This book is a study of the history of the idea of balanced budgets as a symbol. Starting with colonial times and working forward through the Jeffersonians and Hamiltonians to the Keynesians and finally to the Reaganites, he shows how it has signified numerous virtues and a popular desire: to limit the ends and means of national government, to guard states' rights from encroachment, to control corruption, and to promote civic responsibility.

Assessments of the actual, as opposed to the symbolic, effects of deficits have been provided by scores of analysts. Among the more relevant for our purposes are the following. To begin with, Barth et al. (1984/1985) have argued quite convincingly that deciding whether deficits really do matter depends very much on one's assumptions and on the data. Empirical results purporting to show the economic effects of deficits are highly sensitive to the time period examined, the selection of dependent and independent variables, and the operational definition of the deficit that is used. However, most analyses of this subject tend to focus on the deficit's negative side. For example, Hoffman and Levy (1984/1985) examine its impact on credit, while Miner (1989), in a closely related way, looks at its effect on capital formation and the servicing of foreign creditors.

Given the fact that so many have written so ardently about the dangers of excessive debt, how is it that we have survived relatively unharmed? Paul Peterson (1986) argues that we have been able to incur huge deficits because the Federal Reserve Board's monetary policy has held down inflation.

To White and Wildavsky (1989) the deficit is intimately connected with conceptions of the public interest. Their study of the politics of debt during the Reagan years has resulted in a massive tome whose central theme is that the way in which we deal with the deficit will have a fundamental impact on the quality of our public life. Accordingly, they look at different ideas of the public interest and show how different political actors (in Congress, the executive branch, and among interest groups) have each sought to use the system to further their own goals.

As of this writing, of course, the most far-reaching action that has been taken to deal with the problem is the passage and implementation of the Balanced Budget and Emergency Deficit Control Act of 1985, popularly known as Gramm-Rudman-Hollings (GRH), a piece of legislation that White and Wildavsky describe as "budgetary terrorism." Their book includes a fascinating budgetary diary of events and actions leading up to passage of this act. A briefer treatment of how this bill became law can be found in LeLoup et al. (1987). The authors begin by tracing four aspects of congressional budgeting that led to GRH: (1) growing inflexibility caused by changes in budget composition, (2) the increasing vulnerability of budget totals to changes in aggregate economic performance, (3) large deficits, and (4) actions taken by the president to reduce congressional options. After dealing with these factors, they provide a case study of the political alignments and compromises that led to the 1985 passage. Included here is attention to the nature of the original bill, the type of opposition in the House, administration endorsement, and conference committee action.

Both LeLoup et al. (1987) and Havens (1986) also analyze the litigation surrounding GRH and the "fallback procedure." However, for the most effective overviews of the law's content the reader is referred to Rubin (1990) and Shuman (1988). Finally, for a positive assessment of its overall impact an article by Steven Sheffrin (1987) is recommended.

Of course, GRH is not the only policy option available for dealing with the deficit, and thus the last decade has witnessed a campaign to constitutionally mandate a balanced budget. An effective study of the politics surrounding this issue is provided by Robert Hartman (1982), who also gives the reader a good set of pros and cons. For a precise statement of opposition see Penner and Abramson (1988). John Hagen (1986) analyzes the possible consequences of such an amendment in terms of the judicial branch of government. He does this by looking at the issue in terms of how it might be administered by the courts. On balance, he concludes that the courts are not the most appropriate bodies for the making of budgets in a democracy. To buttress this point he focuses on three broad considerations: the institutional competence of courts, the issue of standing, and the trivialization of budget politics.

Nonetheless, support for the amendment strategy has been widespread. Starting with this as his premise, David Nice (1986) asks what kinds of states have actually supported it—as evidenced by state legislative passage of a resolution calling for the national constitutional requirement. As might be expected, he discovers that such states tend to have more conservative Republican and Democratic parties and more conservative voters, lower interparty competition, lower median income, and less metropolitan populations.

It is interesting to note that while Wildavsky views GRH as "budgetary terrorism" he is not opposed to other remedies. In an American Enterprise Institute (AEI) publication (Penner, 1981) he argues that constitutional expenditure limitation would be an effective policy. This prescription is repeated in his *New Politics of the Budgetary Process* (1988).

CONCLUSION

American scholars have produced a robust literature on the politics of national budgeting. Basic interpretations have focused on the replacement of the incrementalist theory with a paradigm combining elements of both top-down and bottom-up budgeting. While some dissent does exist, there appears to be a substantial consensus regarding the subject of presidential dominance, while Congress is viewed as having responded with aspects of both centralization and decentralization. Finally, it appears that solutions to the problem of the deficit will continue to plague scholars—just as they have plagued decision makers—for some time to come.

REFERENCES

Art, R. J. (1985). Congress and the Defense Budget: Enhancing policy oversight. *Political Science Quarterly* 100:227–248.

Axelrod, D. (1989). *A Budget Quartet*. St. Martin's Press, New York.

Auten, G., Bozeman, B., and Cline, R. (1984). A sequential model of congressional appropriations. *American Journal of Political Science* 28:503–523.

Barth, J., Iden, G., and Russek, F (1984/1985). Do federal deficits really matter? *Contemporary Policy Issues* 3:79–95.

Benda, Peter M. and Levine, Charles H. (1986). OMB and the central management problem: Is another reorganization the answer? *Public Administration Review* (Sept./Oct): 379–391.

Benda, P. M., and Levine, C. H. (1988). The assignment and institutionalization of functions at OMB: Lessons from two cases in work-force management. In *New Directions in Budget Theory*, I. Rubin (ed.), State University of New York Press, Albany, pp. 70–99.

Bennett, J. T., and DiLorenzo, T. J. (1983). *Underground Government: The Off-Budget Public Sector*. CATO Institute, Washington D.C.

Berman, L. (1977). The Office of Management and Budget that almost wasn't. *Political Science Quarterly* 92:281–303.

Berman, L. (1978). OMB and the hazards of presidential staff work. *Public Administration Review* 38:520–524.

Berman, L. (1979). *The Office of Management and Budget and the Presidency, 1921–1979*. Princeton University Press, Princeton, N.J.

Bozeman, B., and Straussman, J. D. (1982). Shrinking budgets and the shrinkage of budget theory. *Public Adminstration Review* (Nov./Dec.): 509–515.

Bromiley, P., and Crecine, J. P. (1980). Budget development in OMB: Aggregate influences of the problem and information environment. *Journal of Politics* 42:1031–1064.

Brown, R. E. (1970). *The GAO*. University of Tennessee Press, Knoxville.

Caiden, N. (1983). The politics of subtraction. In *Making Economic Policy in Congress*, A. Schick (ed.), American Enterprise Institute, Washington, D.C., pp. 100–130.

Cooper, J., and West, W. (1988). Presidential power and Republican government: The theory and practice of OMB review of agency rules. *Journal of Politics* 50, 4:864–895.

Copeland, G. W. (1984). Changes in the House of Representatives after the passage of the Budget Act of 1974. In *Congressional Budgeting*, W. Wander, F. T. Hebert, and G. W. Copeland (eds.), Johns Hopkins University Press, Baltimore, pp. 51–77.

Davidson, R. H. (1984). The congressional budget: How much change? How much reform? In *Congressional Budgeting*, W. Wander, F. T. Hebert, and G. W. Copeland (eds.), Johns Hopkins University Press, Baltimore, pp. 153–169.

Davis, J. W., and Ripley, R. B. (1967). The Bureau of the Budget and executive branch agencies: Notes of their interaction. *Journal of Politics* (November): 749–769.

Ellwood, J. W. (1983). Budget control in a redistributive environment. In *Making Economic Policy in Congress*, A. Schick (ed.), American Enterprise Institute, Washington, D.C., pp. 69–99.

Ellwood, J. W. (1984). Budget reforms and interchamber relations. In *Congressional Budgeting*, W. Wander, F. T. Hebert, and G. W. Copeland (eds.), Johns Hopkins University Press, Baltimore, pp. 100–132.

Emmerich, H., and McLean, J. (1950). Symposium on budget theory. *Public Administration Review* 10:20–31.

Fair, Ray (1978). The effect of economic events on votes for president. *The Review of Economics and Statistics*, LX, 2:159–173.

Fenno, R. (1962). The House Appropriations Committee as a political system: The problem of integration. *American Political Science Review* 56:310–324.

Fenno, R. F. (1966). *The Power of the Purse*. Little, Brown, Boston.

Fisher, L. (1974a). Congress, the executive and the budget. *Annals of the American Academy of Political and Social Science* (January): 102–113.

Fisher, L. (1974b). Reprogramming of funds by the Defense Department. *Journal of Politics* 36:77–102.

Fisher, L. (1975). *Presidential Spending Power*. Princeton University Press, Princeton, N.J.

Fisher, Louis (1984). The Budget Act of 1974. In *Congressional Budgeting*, W. Wander, F. T. Hebert, and G. W. Copeland (eds.), Johns Hopkins University Press, Baltimore, pp. 170–189.

Fisher, L. (1985). Ten years of the Budget Act: Still searching for controls. *Public Budgeting and Finance,* Autumn: 3–28.

Fox, D. M. (1971). Congress and U.S. Military Service budgets in the post-war period: A research note. *Midwest Journal of Political Science* 15:382–393.

Gist, J. R. (1978). Appropriations politics and expenditure control. *Journal of Politics* 40:163–178.

Golden, D. G. and Poterba, J. M. (1980). The price of popularity: The political business cycle reexamined. *American Journal of Political Science* 24, 4:696–714.

Greider, W. (1981). The education of David Stockman. *The Atlantic Monthly* (December): 27–54.

Hagan, J. P. (1986). Judicial enforcement of a balanced-budget amendment: Legal and institutional constraints. *Policy Studies Journal* 15:247–267.

Harris, J. P. (1964). *Congressional Control of Administration.* The Brookings Institution, Washington, D.C.

Hartman, R. W. (1982). Congress and budget-making. *Political Science Quarterly* 97:381–402.

Havens, H. S. (1986). Gramm-Rudman-Hollings: Origins and implementation. *Public Budgeting and Finance* (Autumn): 4–24.

Hebert, F. T. (1984). Congressional budgeting, 1977–1983: Continuity and change. In *Congressional Budgeting,* W. Wander, F. T. Hebert, and G. W. Copeland (eds.), Johns Hopkins University Press, Baltimore, pp. 31–50.

Heclo, H. (1975). OMB and the presidency: The problem of "neutral competence." *Public Interest* 38:80–98.

Heclo, H. (1984). Executive budget making. In *Federal Budget Policy in the 1980s,* G. B. Mills and J. L. Palmer (eds.), The Urban Institute, Washington, D.C., pp. 255–291.

Hobkirk, M. D. (1984). *The Politics of Defense Budgeting.* Macmillan, London.

Hoffman, R., and Levy, M. (1984/1985). Economic and budget issues for deficit policy. *Contemporary Policy Issues* 3:96–114.

Horn, S. (1970). *Unused Power: The Work of the Senate Committee on Appropriations.* The Brookings Institution, Washington, D.C.

Ippolito, D. S. (1978). *The Budget and National Politics.* Freeman, San Francisco.

Ippolito, D. S. (1984a). *Hidden Spending: The Politics of Federal Credit Programs.* University of North Carolina Press, Chapel Hill.

Ippolito, D. S. (1984b). Reform, Congress and the President. In *Congressional Budgeting,* W. Wander, F. T. Hebert, and G. W. Copeland (eds.), Johns Hopkins University Press, Baltimore, pp. 133–152.

Johnson, B. (1984). From analyst to negotiator: The OMB's new role. *Journal of Policy Analysis and Management* 3, 4:501–515.

Johnson, B. (1989). The OMB budget examiner and the congressional budget process. *Public Budgeting and Finance* 9, 1:5–14.

Kamlet, M. S., and Mowery, D. C. (1980). The budgetary base in federal resource allocation. *American Journal of Political Science* 24, 4:804–821.

Kamlet, M. S., and Mowery, D. C. (1987). Influences on executive and congressional budgetary priorities, 1955–1981. *American Political Science Review* 81, 1:155–178.

Kamlet, M. S., Mowery, D. C., and Su, T. T. (1988). Upsetting national priorities? The Reagan administration's budgetary strategy. *American Political Science Review* 82:1293–1307.

Kanter, A. (1972). Congress and the Defense budget: 1960–70. *American Political Science Review* 66:129–143.

Kettl, D. F. (1989). Expansion and protection in the budgetary process. *Public Administration Review* (May/June): 231–239.

Kiewiet, D. R. (1983). *Marcoeconomics and Micropolitics.* University of Chicago Press, Chicago.

Kiewiet, D. R., and McCubbins, M. D. (1985). Congressional appropriations and the electoral connection. *Journal of Politics* 47:59–82.

Kinnard, D. (1977). President Eisenhower and the Defense budget. *Journal of Politics* 39:596–623.

Korb, L. J. (1977). The budget process in the Department of Defense, 1947–77: The strengths and weaknesses of three systems. *Public Administration Review* 37:334–346.

LeLoup, L. (1979). The myth of incrementalism: Analytical choices in budgetary theory. *Polity* 10, 4:488–509.

LeLoup, L. (1982). After the blitz: Reagan and the U.S. congressional budget process. *Legislative Studies Quarterly* 7, 3:321–339.

LeLoup, L. (1984a). Appropriations politics in Congress: The House Appropriations Committee and executive agencies. *Public Budgeting and Finance* 4:78–98.

LeLoup, L. T. (1984b). The impact of budget reform on the Senate. In *Congressional Budgeting*, W. Wander, F. T. Hebert, and G. W. Copeland (eds.), Johns Hopkins University Press, Baltimore, pp. 78–99.

LeLoup, L. T., Graham, B. L., and Barwick, S. (1987). Deficit politics and constitutional government: The impact of Gramm-Rudman-Hollings. *Public Budgeting and Finance* 7:83–103.

LeLoup, L. (1988a). From microbudgeting to marcobudgeting: Evolution in theory and practice. In *New Directions in Budget Theory*, I. Rubin (ed.), State University of New York Press, Albany, pp. 19–42.

LeLoup, L. T. (1977/1988b). *Budgetary Politics*. King's Court Communications, Brunswick, Ohio.

LeLoup, L., and Hancock, J. (1988). Congress and the Reagan budgets. *Public Budgeting and Finance* 8, 3:30–54.

LeLoup, L. T., and Moreland, W. B. (1987). Agency strategies and executive review: The hidden politics of budgeting. *Public Administration Review* 38:232–239.

Lowery, D., Bookheimer, S., and Malachowski, J. (1985). Partisanship in the appropriations process: Fenno revisited. *American Politics Quarterly* 13, 2:188–199.

Lynch, T. D. (1990). *Public Budgeting in America*. Prentice-Hall, Englewood Cliffs, N.J.

Malachowski, J., Bookheimer, S., and Lowery, D. (1987). The theory of budgetary process in an era of changing budgetary roles FY48–FY84. *American Politics Quarterly*, 15, 3:325–354.

Manley, J. F. (1970). *The Politics of Finance: The House Committee on Ways and Means*. Little, Brown, Boston.

March, J., Simon, H. (1958). *Organizations*. John Wiley & Sons, New York.

Marvin, K. E., and Hedrick, J. L. (1974). GAO helps Congress evaluate programs. *Public Administration Review* 34:327–333.

Mathiasen, D. G. (1988). The evolution of the Office of Management and Budget under President Reagan. *Public Budgeting and Finance* 8, 3:3–14.

Mills, G. B., and Palmer, J. L. (eds.) (1984). *Federal Budget Policy in the 1980s*. The Urban Institute, Washington, D.C.

Miner, J. (1989). The Reagan deficit. *Public Budgeting and Finance* 9, 1:15–32.

Mosher, F. C. (1979). *The GAO: The Quest for Accountability in American Government*. Westview Press, Boulder, Colo.

Mosher, F. C. (1984). *A Tale of Two Agencies: A Comparative Analysis of the GAO and the OMB*. Louisiana State University Press, Baton Rouge.

Mosher, F., and Stephenson, M. O. (1982). The Office of Management and Budget in a changing scene. *Public Budgeting and Finance* (Winter): 23–41.

Mowery, D., Kamlet, M., and Crecine, J. (1980). Presidential management of budgetary and fiscal policymaking. *Political Science Quarterly* 95, 3:395–425.

Nathan R. P. (1975). *The Plot That Failed: Nixon and the Administrative Presidency*. New York.

Nice, D. C. (1986). State support for Constitutional balanced budget requirements. *Journal of Politics* 48:134–142.

Niskanen, W. A. (1971). *Bureaucracy and Representative Government*. Aldine Publishing, Chicago.

Niskanen, W. (1986). Economists and politicians. *Journal of Policy Analysis and Management* 5, 2:234–244.

Nordhaus, W. (1975). The political business cycle. *Review of Economic Studies* 42:169–189.

Ogul, M. S. (1976). *Congress Oversees the Bureaucracy: Studies in Legislative Supervision.* University of Pittsburgh Press, Pittsburgh.

Oppenheimer, B. I. (1983). How legislatures shape policy and budgets. *Legislative Studies Quarterly* 8, 4:551–597.

Padgett, J. F. (1980). Bounded rationally in budgetary research. *American Political Science Review* 74:354–371.

Penner, R. G. (ed.) (1981). *The Congressional Budget Process after Five Years.* American Enterprise Institute, Washington, D.C.

Penner, R. G., and Abramson, A. J. (1988). *Broken Purse Strings: Congressional Budgeting, 1974–1988.* Urban Institute Press, Washington, D.C.

Peterson, P. (1986). The new politics of deficits. *Political Science Quarterly* 100, 4:575–601.

Pfiffner, J. P. (1979). *The President, the Budget, and Congress: Impoundment and the 1974 Budget Act.* Westview Press, Boulder, Colo.

Pitsvada, B. T., and Draper, R. D. (1984). Making sense of the federal budget the old fashioned way—Incrementally. *Public Administration Review* (Sept./Oct.): 401–407.

Plant, J. F. (1986). Charles E. Lindbloom's "Decision-Making in Taxation and Expenditures." *Public Budgeting and Finance* (Summer): 76–86.

Polsby, N. W. (1971). *Congress and the Presidency.* Prentice-Hall, Englewood Cliffs, N.J.

Pressman, J. L. (1966). *House vs. Senate.* Yale University Press, New Haven, Conn.

Reed, L. (1979). The budget game and how to win it. *Washington Monthly* 10:24–33.

Reischauer, R. D. (1984). The congressional budget process. In *Federal Budget Policy in the 1980s,* G. B. Mills and J. L. Palmer (eds.), The Urban Institute, Washington, D.C., pp. 385–413.

Ripley, R. B. (1975). *Congress: Process and Policy.* Norton, New York.

Rivlin, A. (1984). *Economic Choices 1984.* The Brookings Institution, Washington, D.C.

Rourke, J. T. (1978). The GAO: An evolving role. *Public Administration Review* 38:453–457.

Rubin, I. S. (1985). *Shrinking the Federal Government.* Longman, NY.

Rubin, I. S. (1988a). *New Directions in Budgetary Theory.* State University of New York Press, Albany.

Rubin, I. S. (1988b). The authorization process: Implications for budget theory. In *New Directions in Budget Theory,* I. Rubin (ed.), State University of New York Press, Albany, pp. 124–147.

Rubin, I. (1989). Aaron Wildavsky and the demise of incrementalism. *Public Administration Review* 42:78–81.

Rubin, I. S. (1990). *The Politics of Public Budgeting.* Chatham House, Chatham, N.J.

Rudder, C. (1977). Committee reform and the revenue process. In *Congress Reconsidered,* L. C. Dodd and B. I. Oppenheimer (eds.), Praeger, New York.

Savage, J. D. (1988). *Balanced Budgets and American Politics.* Cornell University Press, Ithaca, N.Y.

Schick, A. (1980). *Congress and Money.* The Urban Institute, Washington, D.C.

Schick, A. (1981). The first five years of congressional budgeting. In *The Congressional Budget Process after Five Years,* R. G. Penner (ed.), American Enterprise Institute, Washington, D.C., pp. 3–34.

Schick, A. (ed.) (1983). *Making Economic Policy in Congress.* American Enterprise Institute, Washington, D.C.

Schick, A. (1984). The budget as an instrument of presidential policy. In *The Reagan Presidency and the Governing of America,* Salamon and Lund (eds.), The Urban Institute Press, Washington, D.C., pp. 91–125.

Schick, A. (1986). The evolution of congressional budgeting. In *Crisis in the Budget Process,* A. Schick (ed.), American Enterprise Institute, Washington, D.C., pp. 3–56.

Schwengel, F. (1968). Problems of inadequate information and staff resources in congress. In *Information Support, Program Budgeting and the Congress,* R. L. Chartrand, K. Janda, and M. Hugo (eds.), Spartan, New York, pp. 97–108.

Sharkansky, I. (1965). Four agencies and an appropriations subcommittee: A comparative study of budget strategies. *Midwest Journal of Political Science* 9:254–281.

Sheffrin, S. M. (1987). Fiscal policy tied to the mast: What has Gramm-Rudman wrought? *Contemporary Policy Issues* 5:44–56.

Shepsle, K. A. (1984). The congressional budget process: Diagnosis, prescription, prognosis. In *Congressional Budgeting,* W. Wander, F. T. Hebert, and G. W. Copeland (eds.), Johns Hopkins University Press, Baltimore, pp. 190–218.

Shuman, H. E. (1984/1988). *Politics and the Budget: The Struggle Between the President and the Congress.* Prentice-Hall, Englewood Cliffs, N.J.

Sigelman, L. (1986). The bureaucrat as budget maximizer: An assumption examined. *Public Budgeting and Finance* (Spring): 50–59.

Silverman, E. B. (1974). Public budgeting and public adminstration: Enter the legislature. *Public Finance Quarterly* 2:472–484.

Stockman, D. A. (1986). *The Triumph of Politics: How the Reagan Revolution Failed.* Harper & Row, New York.

Straussman, J. D. (1988). Rights-based budgeting. In *New Directions in Budget Theory,* I. Rubin (ed.), State University of New York Press, Albany, pp. 100–123.

Sundquist, J. L. (1981). *The Decline and Resurgence of Congress.* The Brookings Institution, Washington, D.C.

Taft Commission. (1912). Document No. 854, U.S. House of Representatives.

Thomas, R. D., and Handberg, R. B. (1974). Congressional budgeting for eight agencies, 1947–1972. *American Journal of Political Science* 18:179–187.

Truman, D. B. (1951). *The Governmental Process.* Knopf, New York.

Wanat, J. (1974). Base of budgetary incrementalism. *American Political Science Review* 68:1221–1228.

Wander, W. T. (1984). The politics of congressional budget reform. In *Congressional Budgeting,* W. T. Wander, F. T. Hebert, and G. W. Copeland (eds.), Johns Hopkins University Press, Baltimore, pp. 3–30.

Wander, W. T., Hebert, F. T., and Copeland, G. W. (1984). *Congressional Budgeting.* Johns Hopkins University Press, Baltimore.

Weaver, R. K. (1988). *Automatic Government: The Politics of Indexation.* The Brookings Institution, Washington, D.C.

White, J., and Wildavsky, A. (1989). *The Deficit and the Public Interest.* University of California Press, Berkeley.

Wholey, J. S. (1984). Executive agency retrenchment. In *Federal Budget Policy in the 1980s,* G. B. Mills and J. L. Palmer (eds.). The Urban Institute, Washington, D.C., pp. 295–332.

Wildavsky, A. (1981). Constitutional expenditure limitation and congressional budget reform. In *The Congressional Budget Process after Five Years,* R. G. Penner (ed.), American Enterprise Institute, Washington, D.C., pp. 87–100.

Wildavsky, A. (1975). *Budgeting: A Comparative Theory of Budgetary Processes.* Little, Brown, Boston.

Wildavsky, A. (1984). *The Politics of the Budgetary Process.* Little, Brown, Boston.

Wildavsky, A. (1986). *Budgeting: A Comparative Theory of Budgetary Processes.* Transaction Books, New Brunswick, N.J.

Wildavsky, A. (1988). *The New Politics of the Budgetary Process.* Scott, Foresman, Boston.

Wyszomirski, M. J. (1982). The de-institutionalization of presidential staff agencies. *Public Administration Review* (Sept./Oct.): 448–458.

3

Budgeting as a Cultural Phenomenon

Aaron Wildavsky *Department of Political Science and Public Policy, University of California, Berkeley, California*

A state of nature, as commonly conceived, is prior to society. There are individuals but they are presumably not connected to one another. Obviously, no society means no government and, hence, no budget. I reject this antisocial (worse still, this unbudgetary) view of the world. Without some sort of society, there can be no individuality. Budgets and social life imply one another. Ask how budgets ought to be made and you will hear also how social life ought to be lived.

Social organization requires social support. People have to be able to do things for other people. They have to be able to make demands in support of their way of life, and to hold each other accountable for things that go wrong. Mobilizing, allocating, and controlling resources is another expression for budgeting.

Budgets are promises. If agency proposals are approved, they will get the money the treasury promised them. Commitments made to certain classes of people—the elderly, the handicapped, the sick—will be kept no matter what. Different types of spending devices—annual appropriations, indefinite "no-year" entitlements, indexed entitlements—grade the degree of certainty that government promises will be kept. Making too many promises means that not all may be able to be kept to the same degree at the same time.

Budgets are social orders. A moral order regulating relations among people specifies commands and prohibitions. So does a budget. "There is no money" may not be the saddest sentence of them all, but it is one of the most conclusive. It is equivalent to the other great classes of prohibitions—there is no time, it is unnatural, and God forbids it (Douglas, 1975). Even the architecture of budgets, as in the family practice of providing envelopes for this or that expenditure, suggests an order of priorities. Students of the subject are used to ferreting out the implicit preferences of those who rule from the patterns of resource mobilization and resource allocation. Similarly, it should be possible to relate patterns of budgeting to regimes of rule through which political power is exercised in a society.

POLITICAL CULTURE

This comparison of political cultures is based on the proposition that what matters most to people is other people (Thompson et al., 1990; Douglas, 1982). Two questions are basic:

*This is a revised and updated version of "A cultural theory of budgeting," *International Journal of Public Administration*, 11(6):651–677 (1988).

Who am I—a member of a strong group that takes collective action or an individual able to transact freely with whomever I wish? What should I do? Should I do as I am told, being bound by numerous prescriptions, or should I do as I please, the only norm being the absence of physical coercion? The strength of commitment to the group or institution and the extent to which norms of everyday behavior are prescribed are the basic dimensions of political cultures from which other combinations are constructed.

The Primary Political Cultures

Group strength

		Weak	Strong
Number and variety of prescriptions	Many	Fatalism (apathetic regime)	Collectivism (hierarchial regime)
	Few	Individualism (market regime)	Egalitarianism (equitable regime)

Political culture provides motivation for the uses of resources. As soon as physical survival is assured, there is room to mobilize and allocate resources so as to do what matters most—support one's way of life. By invoking political culture, we bring back into budgeting the values and preferences that contain the differing motives for the particular use of resources in a given society.

Strong groups with numerous prescriptions combine to form a hierarchical regime. Strong group boundaries with few prescriptions form an equitable regime—a life of voluntary consent without inequality. By uniting few prescriptions with weak group boundaries and thereby encouraging endless new combinations, the bidding and bargaining of market regimes creates a self-regulating substitute for hierarchical authority. When boundaries are weak and prescriptions strong, so that decisions are made by people outside the group, such a controlled regime is fatalistic.

Just as an act is socially rational if it supports one's way of life, governmental budgeting is politically rational if it maintains the political regimes existing in that place and time. In regimes organized on a market basis, for instance, budgets reflect opportunity for gain by bidding and bargaining. Under hierarchical regimes in which the binding rules of social organization differentiate people and their activities by rank and status, budgets reflect that detailed division of labor. And when an equitable regime emphasizes equality of condition, budgets are devoted to (re)distributing equal shares.

My cultural hypothesis is that hierarchical regimes that strive to exert authority spend and tax high in order to maintain their rank and status. Market regimes, preferring to reduce the need for authority, spend and tax as little as possible. Equitable regimes spend as much as possible to redistribute resources, but their desire to reject authority leaves them unable to collect sufficient revenues.

When rich nations mimic the poor ones by coming close to repetitive budgeting—remaking the budget several times a year—or when poor ones achieve the certitude that used to be obtained only by the rich, governments have transcended their material conditions. When outside the grip of compulsion, governments make more or less of the circumstances in which they find themselves, the way is open for cultural explanations based not only on potential resources but also on what they prefer to do with them.

My task is not merely to set up models of rule in regimes but to relate them to budgetary behavior. Each regime, I hypothesize, is accompanied by a process of budgeting, not all the time but most of the time, not entirely but largely. The social relationships epitomized by these four regimes are supported by characteristic modes of budgetary behavior.

If social order and hence political regimes are congruent with budgetary processes, this symmetry should show up in the standard topics of the subject. Thus I shall deal with the form of budgeting, auditing, budgetary balance, and deficits (the distance between expenditure and revenue). I shall also examine the place of the budgetary base—agreed understandings on totals and items—among the political cultures. Finally, I shall provide a cultural explanation for the growth of government. It is best to begin with budgetary control because it shows power relationships most clearly: Is budgeting made from the top down or the bottom up? How is control exercised—by following the forms, or by producing the right results? How are errors detected and corrected? Is information avidly sought after or suppressed? How are sanctions and rewards applied?

FORMS OF BUDGETING

Every form of budgeting is supposed to produce results. The question is, what kind? Under the *exploitative budgeting* of apathetic regimes, the rulers seek to maximize the surplus of revenue over cost produced by the ruled. In the *productivity budgeting* of market regimes, it is the ability of money to make money, or to spend least for a given objective, that counts. The *redistributive budgeting* of equitable regimes aims at the redistribution of whatever goods there are. And the *procedural budgeting* of hierarchical regimes aims at the correct form. Who has the right to do what is as (or more) important than what is done.

Markets value autonomy; each unit, ideally, would be responsible for its own budget. Failure is to be unproductive and is punished by competitors bidding resources away. Success is performing well as measured by the productivity standards of the time. Reward is being able to use the gain for new and expanded enterprises, constructing ever-larger networks.

Social orders governed by hierarchical regimes penalize budgeters who disobey the rules (for limits on spending, for assessment of taxes, for transfers among categories). As long as officials allow the required forms, they expect to be protected. Suppose the economic or technical results, despite the good form, are unfortunate: Who pays the penalty? No one or everyone. Insofar as possible, the error will not be recognized, for otherwise procedure might not be accepted as perfect. If error has to be recognized, the blame will be shared throughout the hierarchy as a collective, so no one in particular is responsible, or it will be pinned upon deviants who ostensibly did not do the right thing. The offending parties will be subject to reeducation in the moral desirability of the rules, hopefully strengthening their attachment to the regime. Should that fail, should the offenders prove incorrigible, they will not receive promotion up the ladder and will lose the privileges that go with rank. Where the offender in an equity might be expelled, and in a market lose autonomy to invest resources, the deviant in a budgetary hierarchy suffers the worst fate—he is released from the rules on the grounds that he is out of his head.

When misfortune occurs, adherents of an egalitarian regime blame the system, the coercive hierarchies and inegalitarian markets that oppress the populace. Success is reducing disparities in reward and in status.

AUDITING AS A FUNCTION OF REGIME

Budgetary control requires budgetary information, and the quality of information depends on the degree of uncertainty perceived to be present in the situation. It is not information per se but the part of the budgetary process to which these competing cultures direct their members that is important. Markets and equities assess performance, the former's criterion being productivity of revenue and expenditure, the latter's equal assessment and distribution. Hierarchies are interested in outcomes, but it is not only the substance but the form that concerns them, for they care about maintaining the proper divisions of roles among the participants. Budget rituals, such as the rite of the exchecquer, with its minuet-like moves, reinforce the rightfulness of the regime by encapsulating its principles.

Hierarchies are interested both in budgetary promises (preaudit in modern parlance), so as to assess good legal intentions, and in retrodictions (postaudit), so as to determine whether there has been adherence to rules. Equities, being collectives, also care about pre- and postaudit but for a quite different purpose: they want assurance that egalitarian purposes and egalitarian results are being obtained. Market regimes could not care less about the past or future but only about present productivity, or the bottom line, as they call it.

Placing a high value on stability, hierarchies are, by their very structure, uncertainty-absorbing mechanisms. Uncertainty exists, of course, since knowledge of the future is woefully limited, but it is absorbed into the division of labor and its accompanying specialization: each level has to act as if it knew what it was doing. There has to be trust among levels, so each accepts the data provided by the others, provided only it is presented in the right way. Equities exist to oppose hierarchies and markets; they seek, in Marxist jargon, to "unmask" the power relationships underlying the unequal allocation of burdens and benefits.

It is market regimes that specialize in uncertainty. Their members are supposed to take risks in order to reap rewards. But social trust is in short supply. So market regimes accept uncertainty, judging expenditures by the degree to which objectives are achieved. Unlike hierarchies, budgetary procedures in markets are flexible but the demand for productivity is not. "What have you done for me lately?" is its perennial query. Where the equity insists on auditing for equality and the hierarchy on auditing for legality, the anarchy is in perpetual audit for results.

Budgetary boundaries are of three kinds—the total size of the enterprise in regard to the size of the economy, the balance between revenue and expenditure, and the demarcations among sources of income and items of spending. Let us begin with items of spending because the dividing lines are clear, written in, as it were, since mankind first learned to write.

Line-Item, Program, and Zero-Base Budgeting

The most prevalent modern form of expenditure budgeting is called line-item budgeting. Exactly. There are lines with sums attached and these lines separate items specifying the spending involved. The main criticism of this form is that the items are related to organizational needs, such as operations, maintenance, and personnel, rather than the broad purposes the spending is supposed to serve. Precisely. Line-item budgeting is the form par excellence of the hierarchy. The more lines there are, the finer the differentiation among them, the better they mirror the division of labor within the bureaucracy and, by extension, the roles and statuses the society is trying to maintain.

Program budgeting and zero-base budgeting, by contrast, reflect different social orders. By erasing lines of authority in favor of activities supporting broad objectives, program budgeting is designed to facilitate competition. The costs and benefits of alternative programs are arranged, and hopefully the most effective in terms of return is chosen. It is not the mix of resources that matters—any combination is acceptable—but only their effectiveness. Resources have no intrinsic merit, either in themselves or their forms, but only an instrumental value—the rate of return. It is no secret, indeed it is its avowed rationale, that program budgeting is based on economic models embodying market processes. Program budgeting is part of the rationale for a society of competitive individualism (programs compete instead of or in addition to people) whose political manifestation is in the market regime.

Similarly, if a society organized entirely on an egalitarian basis were to choose its form of budgeting, it would have to reject the line-item variety as redolent of hierarchy. Program budgeting would be anathema because it suggests that everything is negotiable through the common currency of market transactions. If an ideal form were devised for equities, it would have to be zero-base budgeting. For one thing, the zero-base approach, taking nothing for granted as if the budget were born yesterday, is perfectly suited for attacking existing relationships. All these, the product of social understandings reached over long periods of time, are, in concept, to be swept away. No base, no carryover of the dead hand of the past imposing its distinctions (read "line items") on the future, no social order. What could be better suited to an equity than a budgetary form presupposing that the world was to be made anew every year?

THE BUDGETARY BASE AS A
MANIFESTATION OF SOCIAL ORDER

If a budget both reflects and rationalizes a social order, as I contend, then the boundaries of budgeting should guard that order. This is the significance of the budgetary base, the largest part of the budget, the bulk of which is protected from serious scrutiny, so it remains unchallenged. Inside the base, excepting only small additions or subtractions, all is protected; outside the base, everything is up for grabs. On the stability of the budgetary base, therefore, rests the stability of the political pillars of society. An across-the-board attack on the budgetary base is equivalent to a revolution. Governments, therefore, seek to invest major sources of revenue and items of expenditures with some sort of sanctity. Each source or item becomes a minibudget with its own priorities. Breaching the budget is equivalent to opening up the boundaries of the social contract to renegotiation.

The base is nondiscretionary spending. It is a manifestation of social agreement on essentials. But if that is all there is, no more and no less, budgets would be predetermined. For there to be resource allocation, there must be discretionary income and expenditures, monies that might be raised or spent, or not, depending on circumstances. It is this slack, as resources in excess of immediate needs are called in the organizational literature, that has to be given relative ranking. These increments up or down are the stuff of ordinary budgetary dispute.

There is a regime, however, whose members lack discretionary income, and who, therefore, do not budget in the ordinary sense of acquiring or allocating resources. In apathetic regimes, the rules are not made by the people but for them. Just as there are no social boundaries for them to maintain, there are no boxes or niches or line items of revenue or expenditure. The culture is fatalistic; the people take what comes. The culture is timeless; there is no marked separation between the days and years, no past or future, only the present. There is no saving, no anticipation of tomorrow. The social experience necessary to make a budget, that is, to periodically relate income to outgo or to divide each into component parts, is missing.

From no real budgeting in apathetic regimes, we move to the flexible budgets of market regimes. Their form is to be formless: their rule is that all transactions among consenting adults are permissible. The base shifts with the next bargain. Budgetary totals may not shift much, but the programs that make them up do. Programs are in competition. The winners attract more discretionary resources. The budgetary process is extremely flexible—there are only a few general heads of taxing and spending, among which transfers are readily arranged—and experimental—new combinations are continuously being devised and discarded. Budgeting is like riding a roller coaster—fun if you stay on, awful if you fall off.

Boundaries make good budgets, I might say with apologies to Robert Frost, but lack of internal rules does not. Because the division of labor is suspect as elevating some people above others, and specialization is suspect because it suggests that some people know more than others, equities are ambiguous about role performance. Equities are for diminishing past distinctions, so they take on their political color by opposing the inequalities of the existing establishment, the usual alliance of hierarchies and markets. Because accumulation of resources is held suspect, economic development is held down. Thus the demand for equality leads to requirements for redistribution that are difficult to meet. The result is an all-or-nothing approach to budgeting in which no change alternates with radical change.

Hierarchy is the home of the budgetary base. Interaction in society establishes a base that is as well defined as its social structure. There ought to be and there are categories corresponding to a hierarchically organized list of priorities for taxing and spending. Very nice, providing only that social rigidity does not lead to rigor mortis of the budgetary process. Everything is dependent on mechanisms for evaluating revenues and expenditures so as to help make incremental adjustments. Each unit or status resists change. Absent adaptation, the economy runs down. Conflict accumulates. The budget becomes petrified.

When the budgetary base is widely accepted, conflict is limited both because there is an agreed starting point and because the increments are small. When the budgetary base is unacceptable, calculation becomes more complex and conflict rises. This is exactly what has happened in the United States federal government since the late 1970s. The president's budget is treated as "dead on arrival." Dispute immediately ensues over whether the base is last year's spending, the current services budget (the prior year adjusted for price changes), the Senate or House budget resolution, a continuing resolution (last year's appropriation plus some special provisions), on and on. Disputes over where to begin exacerbate those over where to end.

The growing dissensus over the federal budget is not reflected in disagreement over the desirability of budget balance, for everyone claims to want that; rather, the conflict occurs over whether budgets are to be balanced at higher or lower levels of taxing and spending. It is the size of government, involving as this does the kind of government, that is at issue.

BUDGETARY BALANCE

The Micawber principle—it is not the level of income and outgo but their relationship that matters—is essential to budgeting. It is important, therefore, in deriving the form of budgeting in each regime, to ask how expenditure and revenue are related to one another. Which regimes run deficits and surpluses? Which spend more than they take in or take in more than they spend? Which regimes are likely to have what kind of problems—too low revenues, too high expenditure, inability to vary either one?*

The potential expenditures and revenues of regimes exhibit a diversity so vast as to be unhandleable, but the number of ways in which governments can manage spending in relation to their management of resources is quite limited. The following possibilities exist:

1. Governments can manage neither their expenditures nor their revenues.
2. Governments can manage their expenditures but not their revenues.
3. Governments can manage their revenues but not their expenditures.
4. Governments can manage both their expenditures and their revenues.

These logical possibilities are drawn on the assumption that governments either can or cannot manage expenditures and revenues. But, of course, these are not all-or-nothing conditions: government may be able to manage a little or a lot. The significance of these all-or-nothing conditions is that they map out the various extremes that it is possible for governments to attain. There are two different ways in which governments may get the chance to choose: they can choose in one way if they have scope to manage their spending, and they can choose in another way if they have scope to manage their resources. If governments can manage both, they can also manage the overlap. Depending upon how they simultaneously mix increases or decreases in revenue and expenditures, they can vary the size of the balance or imbalance.

There are five strategies for relating revenues and expenditures so that these are kept within hailing distance of one another.

1. Do nothing.
2. Decrease spending.
3. Increase revenues.
4. Increase revenues and increase spending.
5. Decrease revenues and decrease spending.

My hypothesis is that the five alternative strategies generated by the ability or inability of governments to manage income and outgo are related to their cultures. Translated into political terms, this means that the essential relationships between revenue and expenditure vary with the kind of regime. The chart below predicts that fatalists will vary neither revenue nor expenditures. Their life is assumed to be beyond their control. Budget balance is achieved at very low levels.

*This section is adopted from joint work with Michael Thompson.

Table 1 Budgetary Strategies under Political Regimes

Culture: Fatalism
Regime: Apathy—cannot manage
  expenditure or revenue
Economic growth: Low
Strategy: Do nothing
Balance: Spending equals revenue
  at low levels
	Culture: Collectivism
	Regime: Hierarchy—can manage revenues
	  but not expenditures
	Economic growth: Medium
	Strategy: Maximize revenue
	Balance: Spending exceeds revenue at
	  high levels

Culture: Individualism
Regime: Market—can manage both
  expenditure and revenue at low levels
Economic growth: High
Strategy: Minimize expenditure and
  revenue
Balance: Deficit varies at low levels
	Culture: Eqalitarianism
	Regime: Equity—can manage expenditure
	  but not revenue
	Economic growth: Low
	Strategy: Minimize expenditure
	
	Balance: Spending exceeds revenue at
	  low levels

To understand budgeting by competitive individualists, it is necessary to go from private to public budgeting. In the private sphere, each competes with the other for goods, for credit, and for followers. Competition for resources increases spending. If their investments bear fruit, individualists are able to pay off; if not, competitors take their place. Both revenues and expenditures are high. At the governmental level, however, there is little desire for spending that does not directly benefit a particular entrepreneur. The state is kept poor as ostentation is reserved for rich individuals. Budget control assumes importance insofar as market regimes spend the minimum amount congruent with providing essential services. Consequently, very low spending is overtaken by even less revenue, so that deficits still arise. But these deficits have a different meaning, for they are revenue-led deficits designed to increase the size of the private sector.

Taxation, which involves getting some people to pay for others, is tricky. Since the benefits are collective but the costs are individual, market regimes find assessment difficult. Each participant has an incentive to pass the burden on to others. That is why market regimes are tempted to use tax farmers, individuals who bid for the right to collect a certain tax. Not only is this method congruent with individualism, but it avoids a direct determination of who should pay how much. Much the same can be said of consumption taxes. Alternatively, market regimes prefer "earmarked revenues" so that there is congruence between the cost and the benefit. For equities, earmarking is outrageous because it limits redistribution. Special funds would be acceptable, however, if they are explicitly devoted to redressing wrongs (to the poor, to nature) by redistribution. Equities obviously prefer steeply graduated income taxes and disfavor consumption taxes as repressive. In the name of equity, of course, they will use any tax. Hierarchies are ambivalent about earmarked taxes because segregation of funds is a principle of demarcation, but a jumble of funds resists central allocation. Hierarchies like all kinds of taxes because they need as much revenues as they can get.

The egalitarian collectives I call equities try to keep personal consumption to a minimum. Wealth is regarded as both a sign and a temptation to inequality. By abjuring wealth, they implicitly criticize the market regimes to which they are opposed and whose wealth they cannot, in any event, match, for equities find accumulation difficult. Lacking internal authority, they cannot make large revenue demands on members. Because accumulation of capital is a source of inequality, it is rejected. Whatever there is soon gets redistributed. Low levels of spending, avoidance of the conspicuous consumption of individualism, or of the public display that goes with hierarchical authority, justifies low levels of revenue.

A hierarchical regime is able to expand its revenues. Collective investment through forced saving enables past commitments to be made good in the future. Taxes, like other rules, are imposed from the top and punctiliously collected. But spending is not as easily controlled. Each role and status within the hierarchy has its prescribed duties, including the kinds of display that are required. New rules limiting display (sumptuary laws, as they are called) are not easily formulated or accepted because they upset prevailing distinctions. It is easier for hierarchies to raise money than to decrease spending. Hence their budgets are unbalanced, with high levels of expenditure being exceeded by even higher revenues.

The careful reader will observe that one of the available budgetary strategies— increase both revenues and expenditure—has not been attributed to any of the four regimes. Perhaps this strategy represents a logical possibility, though not an empirical actuality. But I think not. The reason for the omission is that heretofore I have considered only basic types (primary colors, if you will) and not the hybrid regimes that may be formed among them. In a social democracy composed of hierarchy and equity, for instance, the impulses toward equality of result are strengthened, thus leading to greater redistribution of income by the state. Social democracies, therefore, both tax and spend at maximal levels, thus fitting the fourth budgetary strategy.

How can hierarchies make sure that the public spends its money for collective purposes? How can equities make sure that goods are not used to create invidious distinctions? The solution to this dilemma (there is no telling what people will do with money) is to take it from the populace in cash and give it back in services. In this way the state can determine that income is used for what it considers good causes (the hierarchical preference), and it can also regulate the degree of display (the equity preference). In the seemingly simple act of shopping, for instance, the individual is likely to pay less for certain foods, because they are subsidized; pay more for others, because they are heavily taxed; and to pay a sales tax to boot, so that even experts find it difficult to calculate real prices. It is this sucking in and spitting out of resources that leads to the churning between taxation and expenditure that is so pronounced a feature of the modern welfare state. It might well be cheaper to calculate the gross effects of all these subsidies and sanctions (hence the complaints), but this is to miss the point or, rather, the objective, which is to increase state direction of private spending.

All Western nations are pluralist democracies. In these terms, that means they have elements of the three primary political cultures; they differ in the proportions of each, and it is the differing shapes of these hybrid regimes that create the kinds of imbalances experienced in recent decades. In the United States, as hierarchy becomes even weaker than it has been, the ever-strong market elements combine with a renascent egalitarianism to produce deficits fueled from rising social entitlements (the egalitarian contribution) and lower tax rates (a product of the market mentality). With stronger hierarchical and equitable political regimes—as in Sweden and the Netherlands—and weaker market forces, we find a combination of very high taxation and still higher expenditure. Where market forces are stronger and egalitarian elements weaker and hierarchy is still dominant (as in Germany, England, France, and Japan), spending, though still high, diminishes, and deficits are not quite so large. The difference between the administrations of Prime Minister Thatcher and President Reagan, both avowed adherents of market relationships, is that she was also part of a strong hierarchy, interested in balance among the whole and the parts. President Reagan, however, far less restrained by hierarchy, was able to pursue the goal of limited government in a more single-minded manner.

What, if anything, can I predict about budget imbalance in the future from this analysis? First I would have to know what the future balance of power among political cultures will be. This would be tantamount to understanding the sources and operation of social change in the world, and I make no such claim. Rather mine is an "as, if, and when" theory: when, as, or if various combinations of political cultures appear in the world, I predict patterns of expenditures, revenues, and deficits (rarely surpluses) that will be associated with them.

Balance in budgets depends on balance in society—a proposition in its general import at least as old as Aristotle. The budgets we get depend on the kind of people we are. We people in the Western world would not be experiencing unbalanced budgets unless we preferred political regimes that produce that outcome. If once we had something like balanced budgets and now we do not, this is not due to the conjurer's art (now you see it, now you don't) but because the balance among our ways of life has changed. As individualism has grown weaker and egalitarianism stronger, norms regulating budgetary behavior have been transformed from those justifying balance at low levels of spending to norms that encourage imbalance at higher levels of spending. How we choose to budget and how we like to live are different facets of the same question.

I have posed the question of balanced and unbalanced budgets in a different way: What sorts of people, organized into what ways of life, sharing which values, legitimating which social and political practices, would act so as to balance or unbalance their budgets? What combinations of political regimes lead to patterns of taxing and spending that produce (un)balanced budgets? Thus, the focus in budgetary theory changes from the resource position of nations to the ways in which they choose to make use of what they have.

WHY THE RICH MAY BE UNCERTAIN

The spur to cultural analysis was my inability in the first edition of *Budgeting* (Wildavsky, 1986a) to account for the coexistence of wealth with uncertainty. Why would nations with high per capita gross national products (GNPs), large amounts of resources, more than enough to get by, and the ability to withstand adversity for long periods of time, end up budgeting like banana republics? Why would these governments fail to fund all or most of their agencies by the end of the fiscal year? Why would their spending budget have to be redone several times a year? Why could agencies no longer count on receiving all the money specified in the budget? This is another way of asking why central control agencies felt it necessary to "claw back" funds previously allocated.

Wealth does provide protection against adversity. Redundancy of resources enables governments to fill in whatever is needed. Wealth is an advantage in gaining greater wealth, as it provides the wherewithal for a diversity of investments, some of which are bound to pay off. But wealth by itself is no certain barrier to its eventual dissipation.

Wealth itself does not guarantee it will grow faster than it is used. There is a strong element of preference here that I shall try to tap through political culture.

If market cultures were dominant, they would spend low, tax less, and invest all over the place. If hierarchies were dominant, they would tax high and spend higher, investing enough so that each generation could pay off its promise to the future, that is, to abide by the structured inequalities of the hierarchical way of life so each generation will be better off than the last. Should the typical alliance we call the establishment be formed between hierarchy and markets, the balance between them should assure moderate taxing and spending. Egalitarians, however, combine three tendencies leading to financial instability: (1) high spending in the service of equality of condition, (2) inability to collect revenues due to lack of authority, and (3) rejection of the authority exercised by others. When egalitarianism combines with hierarchy, the balance between them may be stable, the high taxing ability of the one supporting the redistributive proclivities of the other. But as the passion for equality grows, the phenomenon Scandinavians call "the scissors crisis" manifests itself: the rate of expenditure increase exceeds the rate of economic growth even in the best years. It is not the absolute decrease of revenues, however, but the rapid increase in spending, coupled with the resistance to reduction, that is responsible for the growing difficulty of responding to hard economic times. For it is the purpose of existing programs, especially entitlements, to keep individuals stable while government has to scramble to maintain itself. The budgetary instability of Western nations, far from being something imposed by external forces or a product of unfortunate circumstances, is built into the warp and woof of their public policies. Of course, they do not desire the collective consequences of the programs they have so willingly adopted. They do not want, but they may nevertheless get, the formula—the security of the citizen equals the insecurity of the government.

The United States has a little different problem, though the results are similar. It still spends and taxes considerably less than European social democracies. Therefore, it has more room to raise taxes or reduce spending. But the United States lacks one thing the social democracies possess—agreement on spending to support the welfare state. The inability to decide whether to raise taxes or to create a new tax, like the value-added tax, to reduce entitlements, to cut taxes to compel lower spending, or to increase spending and thereby insist on more taxes, leads to a continual stalemate. It is political conflict, not economic decline, that leads to the appearance of repetitive budgeting in the United States federal government.

The great question, I think, is not whether the budget will be balanced but how it will come closer to balance. Will there be a government of high taxes and substantial services or a government of low taxes and fewer services? The deep ideological dissensus that stultifies efforts to choose one or another solution, a conflict between Democratic party egalitarians and Republican hierarchists and individualists, has made agreement difficult. Why, then, was it possible to agree on deficit reduction amounting to something like $490 billion over 5 years in a law called OBRA (the Omnibus Budget Reconciliation Act of 1990)? The decline of the Cold War made it possible to reduce the defense budget further than in the past. And the replacement of a strong, economically conservative president, Ronald Reagan, with a hierarchically inclined social conservative, George Bush, disposed to compromise, made a big difference. And the desertion of the President by House of Representatives Republicans, dismayed at his disavowal of his "no-new-tax" pledge, made it necessary for the president to rely on Democratic majorities. Hence OBRA has a moderately progressive egalitarian cast.

GROWTH OF GOVERNMENT

The question of why government budgets grow may usefully be decomposed into several smaller queries:

1. Why does government spending in Western democracies grow in small steps or large leaps but hardly ever decline as a proportion of gross national product?
2. Why do government budgets in some nations grow faster than others? Why does the United States "lag behind" yet also gradually increase the size of government? Why do the other "Anglo-Saxon" democracies, such as Canada and Australia, fit the general trend of growth but still spend less than the Western European nations? Why do the Swiss spend so much less proportionately than the Swedes? If there is a "logic of industrialization," why does it not operate equally on all industrial nations?
3. Why is most of the growth of government budgets attributable to programs— pensions, health, education—that contain a significant redistributive component?

The rising proportion of national product spent through governments in the twentieth century, I contend, cannot primarily be explained by growing wealth or industrialization. Nor can it be attributed, as recent authors do, to the political changes that follow from modernization. On the contrary, the very wealth and technological capacity of these countries would make it possible, were they so inclined, to diminish the proportion of state activity in national economies.

Which political cultures (shared values legitimating social practices), I ask, would reject ever-greater governmental growth and which ones would perpetuate it? My hypothesis is that the size of government in any given society is a function (consequence, if you prefer) of its combination of political cultures. This cultural theory also explains the tendencies of political regimes to balance or unbalance their budgets.

The rise of equities, which view government as a force for equality against inegalitarian markets, has impelled the United States part way toward large government. European nations, which share strong hierarchies and moderate to strong egalitarianism, all have stepped up spending, and some (i.e., Sweden and the Netherlands), being more egalitarian, spend more than others (i.e., Switzerland). Canada is in between because while hierarchy remains strong, so do market relationships (Kudrle and Marmor, 1981; Lipset, 1968).

An empirical test of this cultural theory I have been propounding would have to include the reverse causal sequences to that postulated by the numerous camp followers of Wagner's law: increased equality would have to *precede* growth in proportion of public expenditure to national product. The rise of egalitarian regimes would lead to an increased desire for redistribution through government. Soon (say, in a generation) government spending on welfare and in total would rise significantly. Fortunately, Sam Peltzman has provided exactly the kind of test we require. Peltzman's Law, as I will call it, states that "reduced inequality of income stimulates growth of government" (Peltzman, 1980, p. 263). The greater the inequality between taxpayers in a prior period, Peltzman contends, the less inclined they are to support redistributive spending in a later period (Peltzman, 1980, pp. 285–286). Peltzman's Law may be broadened to say that cultural change precedes and dominates budgetary change: the size of the state today is a function of its political culture yesterday.

If cultural theory is superior to alternatives, expenditure should not merely have increased as a proportion of national product; its most egalitarian components should have gone up far more quickly and the least egalitarian (say, military spending) much more slowly. This, too, has taken place.

Looking at the programs that dominate budgets in Western nations from 1954 to 1980, Richard Rose finds that although the overall increase in the share of national product taken by government was 22%, the growth rates of major programs differed substantially from one another, and only economic infrastructure (i.e., roads and housing) increased at the average rate. Everywhere spending on defense fell as a proportion of national product, whereas income maintenance, education, health, and interest on the debt greatly increased. In the United States, for instance, spending on health rose 213%, whereas defense declined by 59% (Rose, 1985). Leaving out debt interest (which is a product of increasing deficits), programs concerned with income transfers, health (another form of equalizing income), and education (which tends, though not so strongly, in the same direction) have risen sharply.

Let us remind ourselves of what we wish to explain: (1) the continuous rise of public spending as a proportion of national product among industrial democracies; (2) the resistance to downward movement, that is, the absence of countervailing forces; and (3) despite the applicability of (1) and (2), the large difference in state spending that still separates the United States from other nations. In posing the grand question, I would associate myself with Harley Hinrichs's formulation (except that today his upper bound might well be doubled):

> A complex democratic industrialized state could function with a public sector, say, between 20 and 40 percent. The point where it settles within (or above) this range is most likely to be determined not by structural needs (which would demand, say only 20 percent) but by ideological commitments, toward a "welfare state" and/or toward the "security and defense" of an existing ideological system. (Hinrichs, 1966, pp. 9–10).

Since up to the present, "welfare" continues to dominate "warfare" spending in the democracies by more than two to one, it is to their "ideological systems," their values and practices, that I would look for explanations of the growth of government.

Spending could have increased absolutely by following the trend rate of increase in national product. Some programs could have gone beyond that rate if others were reduced by a similar amount. But that did not happen. More for one major program did not signify less for another. More for all is possible only if economic growth rises at the same rate, which did not happen, or if an implicit choice is made, not merely once but repeatedly, to increase the share government takes of national product. When movement toward equality of result is at stake—as in income maintenance, health, and education—one major program may be favored more than another, but all rise absolutely and relatively in regard to proportion of national income. It is this trend toward equalization—a steady increase in spending for redistributive programs—that is best explained by a cultural hypothesis.

Why has budgetary control in the West collapsed? The obvious answer—because governments and their constituents want to spend more—should not be ignored. On what do they want to spend? Largely, on egalitarian measures. We have come full circle in explaining the consequences of the rise of regimes favoring that budgetary outcome. The tendencies of political regimes to tax and spend in different ways are summarized in the following chart.

Table 2 Budgeting in Political Regimes

Culture	Individualism	Egalitarianism	Collectivism
Structure	Self-regulation	Voluntarism	Authority
Trust	Low	Low	High
Equality of:	Opportunity	Result	Law
Roles	Shifting	Ambiguous	Clear
Economic growth	High	Low	Medium
Regime	Market	Equity	Hierarchy
Power	Noncentralized	Shared	Centralized
Authority	Avoided	Rejected	Accepted
Blame	Internalized	Externalized (hidden hierarchies)	Collectivized (the system)
The good citizen	Competes	Reduces distinctions	Maintains distinctions
Private vs. public sectors	Minimal public, maximal private	Moderate public, minimal private	Maximal public, minimal private
Taxes	Very low	Very high	High
Collection	Low	Low	High
Process			
Criterion	Productivity	Redistribution	Procedural
Agreement on base	High on totals, low on items	Low on totals and items	High on totals and items
Procedures	Flexible	Rigid	Rigid
Spending	Low	Low	High
Responsibility	By program	By system	By position
Accounting	Results	Preaudit	Postaudit
Form	Program budgeting	Zero-budgeting	Line-item budgeting

BRINGING PREFERENCES BACK INTO BUDGETING

My aim has been to bring together various strands of thought about the relationship between cultures and budgets, expressed at different times and places (Wildavsky, 1982, 1985a, 1985b, 1985c, 1986a), into a single essay. I would like to end by stating what I conceive to be the advantages of taking a cultural approach to budgeting. First, a word about what cultural theory is not.

Cultural theory is not about the influence of ideas alone. Ideas are not disembodied, free to float anywhere, discarded like an old coat, any more than different arrays of taxes and expenditures may be rearranged at will. Always ideas are attached to the different kinds of social relations they justify, modify, or attack. Nor is this a theory of social determination in which a place in the social structure fixes one's position on budgets. Always, diverse sets of social relations are attached to ideas that legitimate or undermine them. No explanation, no legitimacy.

Cultural theory is a theory of multiequilibria; it does not provide optimum solutions. The reason is that the theory tells us in what sorts of direction adherents of a particular culture will want to go, say, toward greater or lesser equality. It does not tell us what instruments of policy, under the historical circumstances being studied, lead adherents of a particular culture to want to do. If egalitarians in the early days of the American republic thought that the central government was a source of inequality, and therefore wanted to limit it severely, and their spiritual (I should say, cultural) successors, liberal Democrats, want to use the central government to decrease inequality, they are both egalitarians but life has taught them different lessons.

Cultural theory is about how individuals who identify with rival cultures (sets of social relations and their accompanying rationalizations) seek to strengthen their preferred ways of life (assuming, of course, they have a choice) and to weaken others. Cultural theory, as I conceive it, is a form of functionalism, but the functions are performed for cultures not for societies.

The advantage of a cultural theory of budgeting is that it relates resource accumulation and resource allocation to many other aspects of life. Especially important is bringing people's preferences for the good life into budgeting. Thus we can hopefully give a more satisfactory answer to the perennial question of what difference it makes which way budgeting is carried on. For rational choice theorists, there is a suggestion: in addition to whatever participants are trying to get due to their local circumstances, they are also trying to act in a way that is globally rational, that is, to defend their way of life. Thus it is not sufficient to say that everyone is motivated by self-interest, because adherents of different ways of life define self-interest differently. Because cultural theory connects preferred ways of life to budgetary behavior, moreover, we are able to generate many falsifiable propositions. Cultural theory, in short, is a way to bring what different people want and why they want it into budgeting.

REFERENCES

Douglas, M. (1975). Environments at risk. In *Implicit Meanings*, Routledge & Kegan Paul, London, pp. 230–248.

Douglas, M. (1982). Cultural bias. In *In the Active Voice*, Routledge & Kegan Paul, London, pp. 183–254.

Hinrichs, H. H. (1966). *A General Theory of Tax Structure Change during Economic Development*. Harvard University Press, Cambridge, Mass.

Kudrle, R. T., and Marmor, T. (1981). The development of welfare states in North America. In Peter Flora and Arnold J. Heidenheimer (eds.), Transaction Books, New Brunswick, N.J., pp. 81–121.

Lipset, S. M. (1968). *Agrarian Socialism: The Cooperative Commonwealth Federation in Saskatchewan*. Anchor Books, Garden City, N.Y.

Peltzman, S. (1980). The growth of government. *Journal of Law and Economics* 23:209–287.

Rose, R. (1985). The programme approach to the growth of government. *British Journal of Political Science* 15:1–28.

Thompson, M., Ellis, R., and Wildavsky, A. (1990). *Cultural Theory*. Westview Press, Boulder, Colo.

Wildavsky, A. (1982). The budget as new social contract. *Journal of Contemporary Studies* 5:3–19.

Wildavsky, A. (1985a). Budgets as social orders. *Research in Urban Policy* 1:183–197.

Wildavsky, A. (1985b). A cultural theory of expenditure growth and (un)balanced budgets. *Journal of Public Economics* 28:349–357.

Wildavsky, A. (1985c). The logic of public sector growth. In *State and Market*, J.-E. Lane (ed.), Sage Publications, London, pp. 231–270.

Wildavsky, A. (1986a). *Budgeting: A Comparative Theory of Budgetary Processes*. Transaction Books, New Brunswick, N.J.

Wildavsky, A. (1986b). *A History of Taxation and Expenditure in the Western World* (with Carolyn Webber), Simon and Schuster, New York.

4

Budget Reforms

Joseph C. Pilegge   *Department of Political Science, University of Alabama, Tuscaloosa, Alabama*

Born in the turmoil of turn-of-the-century municipal reform movements, budgeting in the United States emerged as a key part of the "good-government" package of that period. During the near century since, no aspect of public administration has been more frequently subjected to the reformist zeal. Every change in the process or format of budgeting, however minor, has been labeled "reform." The literature on budgeting and financial management is filled with accounts of the aspirations and complications, the successes and failures of budgetary reform. It is the purpose of this chapter to explore this long-running phenomenon and its legacy.

INTRODUCTION: THE HISTORICAL RECORD

The idea and practice of an executive budget system came late to the United States. Usually associated with the development of representative political institutions, some have traced the roots of Britain's budgetary system back to the Magna Carta in 1215 (Burkhead, 1956). Although primarily concerned with the control of taxation rather than expenditures, rudimentary "budgets" appeared in Austria as early as 1766 and in France following the Revolution in 1789. But a national executive budget would not come into being in the United States until 1921.

Early Municipal Reform

Not only did budgeting come late to the United States, but unlike most subsequent budgetary reforms, it began at the lowest (local) level of government and gradually worked its way upward. At the time Congress decreed a national executive budget system, numerous municipalities and nearly one-half of the states already had put similar systems in place.

The innovation owed much to the existence of municipal corruption and its disclosure by the so-called "muckrakers," such as Lincoln Steffens and Ida M. Tarbell (Burkhead, 1956). Like its companion reforms in the areas of personnel management and administrative reorganization, the executive budget was designed to empower and thus hold accountable municipal executives who were, in financial matters, formally subordinate to powerful councils. Spearheaded by two influential reform groups and with strong support from the business community, budgeting was well established in most major American cities by the early 1920s (Lynch, 1990, p. 40). The New York Bureau of Municipal Research, founded in 1906, and the National Municipal League are usually credited with the groundwork necessary to establish the need for a municipal budget system.

Burkhead (1956) credits the New York Bureau with having had the greatest impact. Its work followed on the heels of the National Municipal League's first model municipal corporation act, which provided for a city budget process dominated by the mayor. In 1907, the New York Bureau's staff issued its first report entitled "Making a Municipal Budget" with specific recommendations for budgeting the city's health program (Buck, 1929, p. 13). Referring to the leadership of the Bureau, Waldo (1948, p. 32) described them as being "fired with the moral fervor of humanitarianism and secularized Christianity." Supportive of the new wave of scientific management, they "verged upon the ideas of a planned and managed society" and looked to the business organization and the "efficiency idea" as models for the conduct of public business.

If government was irresponsible, the corrective was to be found in executive leadership. And the budget was viewed as a formidable weapon in the arsenal of true executive power. In addition, the budget system would focus the spotlight of public attention on the city's political leadership, ending the long era of what the reformers described as "invisible government." Party bosses no longer would be able to divert public funds to private purposes without being held accountable (Cleveland and Buck, 1920).

Because budgeting was viewed by its advocates as well as its opponents as part of an overall plan to strengthen the executive, legislative hostility had to be overcome at all levels of government.

The Taft Commission

During most of the post-Civil War period, national government finances were characterized by annual budgetary surpluses. Beginning in 1894, however, the government experienced 6 consecutive years of deficits. In 1899, the deficit of $89 million was equal to 12.9% of expenditures.* (This compares with an average deficit/expenditure ratio of 14.8% for the 1977–1988 period.) Following a brief return to budget surpluses, deficits were again recorded in 3 of Theodore Roosevelt's 7 years in the presidency. Most importantly, deficits accrued during the first 2 years of the Taft administration, prompting the portly Ohio Republican to create the Commission on Economy and Efficiency, which produced in 1912 a report entitled "The Need for a National Budget."

The Commission's report, carrying the President's endorsement, fell on deaf ears in Congress. The procedures recommended, including systematic review by the president of estimates prepared by the agencies and the consolidation of those estimates into a single unified budget document to be presented to Congress, would not be adopted until a decade later. As Shuman (1988) has noted, there were political reasons going beyond mere executive-legislative conflict that led to the proposal's rejection.

Small budget surpluses in 1911 and 1912 had eased concerns about the deficit problem. Further, 1912 was an election year and Democrats controlled the House of Representatives where budget reform legislation would have to be initiated. Taft, of

Historical Statistics of the United States, 1789–1945. U.S. Department of Commerce, Bureau of the Census, Washington, D.C., 1949, pp. 296–299.

course, was defeated in his bid for reelection by the Democrat Woodrow Wilson, who had other reforms on his agenda. Undeterred, even in defeat, Taft unilaterally submitted a presidential budget to Congress for fiscal 1913. It was ignored.

The wheels of major budgetary reform had been set in motion, however. The so-called Taft Commission's recommendations would provide the basis for continuing discussion of the merits of an executive budget. Those recommendations, which would be incorporated in the Budget and Accounting Act of 1921, included the following: (1) the President, as the constitutional head of the executive branch, would submit to Congress, annually, a budget; (2) that budget would contain a budgetary message setting forth "the significance of the proposals to which attention is invited" as well as a summary financial statement to include an account of the revenues and expenditures for the last completed fiscal year, as well as (3) a summary of proposed expenditures, "classified by objects," and (4) a summary of proposed changes in legislation "to enable the administration to transact public business with greater economy and efficiency. . . ." The commission also recommended submission to Congress by the Treasury Department of a consolidated financial report showing revenues and expenditures, by departments, covering the past 5 years. It proposed that a uniform system of accounts be established under the President's authority and that the President clearly be responsible for recommending the content of appropriations bills.*

The Nineteenth Century

In the context of America's historical experience, the Taft Commission's recommendations represented a radical departure from "business as usual." While the conventional picture of earlier presidents being almost totally isolated from the budget process has been brought into question (Fisher, 1975), none could be said to have enjoyed the central role proposed in 1912. One of the earliest arguments in the running battle between president and Congress was over the question of presidential involvement in budget preparation (Chandler, 1987). Fisher has described the efforts of early presidents such as Jefferson, John Quincy Adams, Van Buren, and Tyler, usually acting through their Treasury secretaries, to influence the budgetary actions of Congress.

Granting the point that at least some nineteenth century presidents did seek to intervene, with varying degrees of success, in the budgetary process, the pre-1921 arrangements were clearly designed to enable Congress to exert control. The Constitution of 1787 says little about the subject, providing only that "no money shall be drawn from the Treasury but in consequence of appropriations made by law," and requiring the publication "from time to time" of an account of all receipts and expenditures (U.S. Constitution, art. 1, sec. 9).

From 1802 to 1865, control over both revenues and appropriations was concentrated in the House Committee on Ways and Means. This centralization within Congress enabled some presidents to influence appropriations through their role as leader of a political party. Otherwise, executive input was largely limited to the annual report of the Secretary of the Treasury, who also submitted to Congress at the outset of each session a Book of Estimates containing the expenditure requirements of the various departments and agencies, a function characterized by Burkhead (1956, p. 10) as "primarily clerical."

Such internal unity within the Congress broke down after the Civil War with the

---

*U.S. House of Representatives Document No. 854 (June 27, 1912), reprinted in Hyde and Shafritz (1978).

creation of a separate House Appropriations Committee. Before the end of the century, no fewer than 10 standing committees in the House and eight in the Senate had been given authority to recommend appropriations bills. The system of funding government operations at this time consisted essentially of agencies dealing more-or-less directly with particular committees of Congress. No one was responsible for formulating a coordinated budgetary program for the entire government (Selko, 1940). Agency spending officers submitted their needs to the particular congressional committee authorized to appropriate funds for that agency. Neither the agencies nor the individual committees were in a position to weigh the relative merits of these requests. Lacking any means of coordination or planning, it is not surprising that problems arose, including the much-criticized practice of incurring "coercive deficiencies."

This practice, common as well among state governments, broke down budgetary control. As Buck (1929, p. 486) described it, spending agencies were permitted to obligate themselves to expenditures in excess of their appropriations. Having done so, they then presented these claims to the legislature, which had no choice other than to provide the additional funds. Under this system of congressional finance, late nineteenth century presidents were largely limited to exhorting Congress toward fiscal prudence. Fortunately, most of the period was characterized by revenue surpluses, allowing nearly half of the Civil War debt to be paid off by 1884 (Kimmel, 1959).

But the age of innocence and of limited government was coming to a close. By the turn of the century the activities and accompanying expenditures of the federal government were expanding visibly. The first twentieth century president, Theodore Roosevelt, could openly discuss the responsibilities of an "affirmative kind" of administration. It would be left to his immediate successors, however, especially the otherwise phlegmatic Taft, to trigger the public debate that would lead ultimately to the adoption of an executive budget for the nation.

The Wilson-Harding Years

Taft, defeated for reelection in 1912, left office without having convinced Congress of the need for an executive budget. But the work of his commission in pointing out the deficiencies of the existing arrangements transformed budgeting into an "issue of national significance" (Burkhead, 1956, p. 21). Several factors had contributed to the deferral of action on the matter. First, of course, the fiscal needs of the government remained modest until the nation's entry into World War I. In addition, adoption of the sixteenth amendment and the subsequent enactment in 1913 of legislation imposing a national income tax promised relief on the revenue front. Within a year after the income tax went into effect, however, war broke out in Europe, with adverse consequences for the U.S. economy (Waltman, 1985, p. 32). Government revenues plummeted in the wake of a near-cessation of imports, a bank crisis, stock market failure, and drastic reductions in industrial production. Congress reacted with emergency revenue legislation focused mainly on raising excise taxes. Political attention again was riveted on the need for obtaining adequate revenues, rather than designing a method for rationalizing government expenditures. But that was a minor distraction compared with the advent of American involvement in the war.

Presiding over this sequence of events was Taft's successor, Woodrow Wilson, a reform-oriented executive whose long list of ideas for improving government did not include budgetary reform. Described as having only a "passing interest" in such matters, he relied heavily upon his Secretary of the Treasury William G. McAdoo (Waltman, 1985, p. 33). Also, Wilson was less committed than his predecessors to a balanced budget. In any event, no further action to establish a budget system would be taken until after the war. A single exception, largely the work of Congress and suggesting some support for greater executive involvement in the process, was the creation in 1916 of the Bureau of Efficiency, which was made directly responsible to the president (Selko, 1940, p. 101).

With bipartisan legislative support and Wilson's endorsement, Congress in 1920 passed a budget and accounting act embodying most of the recommendations of the Taft Commission. But Wilson surprisingly vetoed the measure, citing constitutionally based objections to a provision in the bill that exempted the chief accounting officer from the president's removal power. No further attempt at enactment of the legislation was made until after the election of 1920, which brought Warren Harding to the White House.

Harding, subsequently to be labeled the nation's least distinguished chief executive, signed a new Budget and Accounting Act into law within 3 months after assuming office and almost 1 year to the day from Wilson's veto of a virtually identical bill. Harding's campaign rhetoric had stressed the need for a "return to normalcy" and he apparently saw the budget bill as a vehicle for restoring a balanced federal budget and reducing the war-incurred national debt. Inadvertently, perhaps, he had simultaneously provided a major weapon in the development of the strong executive through the concentration of budget initiative in the hands of the president.

The Budget and Accounting Act

The Budget and Accounting Act of 1921 has been described by one historian of American public administration as "the watershed in the pursuit of executive budgetary efficiency" (Chandler, 1987, p. 361). The bill (42 Stat. 18, 1921) required the president to transmit to Congress annually "the Budget" and to assist him in this task created the Bureau of the Budget to be located in the Department of the Treasury. The Bureau (BOB), headed by a director appointed by and responsible to the president, was authorized to "assemble, correlate, revise, reduce, or increase" departmental budget estimates (Section 207). The act further required each department of the government to appoint a budget officer and to submit its spending estimates to the Bureau, thus ending the old practice of transmitting uncoordinated requests to Congress.

The legislation also created the General Accounting Office, to be headed by the Comptroller General of the United States, and transferred to the GAO the auditing functions previously carried out by the Treasury Department. The Comptroller General, appointed by the president to a 15-year nonrenewable term, was made subject to removal only by joint resolution of Congress (Section 303). It was this provision that had led Wilson to veto the earlier act. Along with reporting requirements, it was made clear that the government's principal auditing agency was accountable directly to Congress. As part of the budget reform, the House of Representatives in 1920 changed its rules to reduce to one the number of committees authorized to deal with appropriations. The Senate followed suit 2 years later (Neustadt, 1954).

The Bureau of the Budget

Located in the Treasury Department for the first two decades of its existence, the Bureau of the Budget was in fact directly responsible to the President from the outset (Buck,

1929, p. 295). This arrangement was formalized in 1939 when the Bureau was transferred to the newly created Executive Office of the President. At the outset, however, Harding had the good fortune to select as BOB's first director the energetic and capable Charles G. Dawes, a former Army general who later would become vice president under Coolidge. Dawes, committed to the notion that the Bureau was a presidential staff agency, was given wide discretion in dealing with administrative matters (Berman, 1979, p. 6). Obsessed with imposing efficiency and economy on departmental operations, he is credited with establishing the Bureau's key role and influence throughout the government (Buck, 1929, p. 450).

With his attention focused on the single task of reducing spending, however, Dawes neglected the broader issues of administrative management and reform (Berman, 1979, p. 7). Although the 1921 act clearly authorized the Bureau to concern itself with such matters (Section 209), neither Dawes nor his successors in the Coolidge and Hoover administrations showed much interest. Under Roosevelt, the Bureau would institutionalize its long-developing role as the clearing house for legislative requests, strengthening White House control over agency relationships with Congress (Neustadt, 1954).

It would fall to the report of Roosevelt's Committee on Administrative Management, the famous Brownlow Committee, to point out the Bureau's major failing as an instrument of administrative management (Berman, 1979, p. 12). Implementation of this report led to the creation of the Executive Office of the President (EOP) in 1939. As a first step in reorganization, the Bureau of the Budget was transferred from the Treasury Department to the EOP. Its newly expanded functions, elaborated in Executive Order 8248, gave high priority to "the development of improved plans of administrative management." Henceforth, in addition to its budgetary functions, the Bureau would be charged with advising the executive departments and agencies on improved administrative organization and practices.

As Berman (1979, p. 14) has noted, this "born-again Budget Bureau needed leadership of far greater vision and administrative ability than it had received since 1921." To this end, Roosevelt named Harold D. Smith as director, and it was he who created the "modern" Budget Bureau as "an indispensable presidential managerial staff." It was Smith's view that the budget reflects the President's program, and, when enacted, it becomes the work program of the government (H. D. Smith, 1945). In its new form and under new leadership, the Bureau was launched on a course, which it would follow to the present time, as the principal staff aide to the President. As Sorensen (1963, p. 29) would later note in discussing presidential decision making, "the official most often likely to loom largest in his thinking when he makes a key decision is not the Secretary of State or the Secretary of Defense but the Director of the Budget." More importantly, for our purposes, no important executive branch budget reform attempted over the next half century would stand a chance of succeeding without the active support of the BOB or, as it was later to be renamed, the Office of Management and Budget.

THE "MODERN" ERA

Adoption of the new executive budget system in 1921 was followed by a period of budgetary tranquillity that spanned nearly three decades. During that long period, the federal budget was "an immensely detailed document that provided surprisingly little information about the programs government carried out" (Pitsvada and Draper, 1989, p. 5). A traditional line-item format was employed in which an agency's request was broken down on the basis of things to be purchased and people to be employed, the "inputs" of the governmental process. The most significant portion of such a budget, then as now, focused on personnel costs. Separate lines spelled out in detail requests for funds with which to pay for supplies, equipment, utilities, and travel, among other items. This standard format also was found in most state and local jurisdictions, where it is still dominant (Daley, 1985; Friedman, 1975).

Allen Schick (1966), in a piece now regarded as a classic, linked the functions or purposes of budgeting to the forms of budgets. Drawing, in part, from the earlier work of Robert Anthony (1965), Schick posited three basic orientations of any budget system: control, management, and planning. While elements of each purpose are present in all budget types, one will typically predominate in any single system. Of the three, control was (and, I would argue, still is) primary. Control was the dominant aim of early line-item budgets with their hundreds—even thousands—of distinct items, each subject to individual scrutiny by reviewing authorities and ultimately incorporated into the language of appropriation bills.

The line-item or "object" classification was a product of an era in which legislators and the general public distrusted administrators (Burkhead, 1956, p. 128). By establishing detailed listings of things for which public funds were being spent and then linking each category of spending to a specific account, tight control could be exerted over the bureaucracy. That was the principal purpose of the system: to control expenditures at the agency and departmental levels and to hold public officials accountable after the fact through an extensive auditing process. This type of budget and accounting system, by detailing the objects of expenditure, greatly reduced the discretionary power of administrators (Schick, 1964).

Cursed by its critics as mindless, irrational, short-sighted, fragmented, and conservative (Wildavsky, 1981), it nevertheless fulfilled the need of legislative bodies to control public spending. In spite of its detractors, the structure and process of budgeting changed remarkably little until, with the distractions of the Great Depression and World War II out of the way, administrative reform movements resurfaced in the late 1940s. The ensuing 40-year period brought a succession of reforms, both structural and procedural, executive and legislative. It is these to which we now turn.

Performance Budgeting

Dissatisfaction with the standard line-item format appeared early. Lacking information regarding program goals or achievements, it was considered a poor instrument for relating public expenditures to public accomplishments. It might be interesting, even important, to know the salaries of clerk-typists in the engineering department, but that in itself was no clue as to what those employees were doing. Beyond providing year-to-year comparisons of costs and indicating the maximum amount of funds available, the budget was of limited usefulness to managers or policymakers in arriving at programmatic decisions. Nor was it helpful in explaining or justifying government programs to citizens.

Credit for introducing a performance-type budget into the federal government is usually awarded to the first Hoover Commission.* This report, issued in 1949, recommended that the "whole budgetary concept of the Federal Government should be refashioned by the adoption of a budget based on functions, activities, and projects" (p. 8). The idea was not new. Under a variety of different labels, performance budgeting had

*Commission on the Organization of the Executive Branch of the Government (1949).

appeared in several cities across the country prior to World War II. Indeed, the Taft Commission on Economy and Efficiency in 1912 had stressed the importance of presenting the budget in accordance with the subjects of work to be done (Burkhead, 1956, p. 134). While its adoption was not widespread, some federal agencies, notably the Department of Agriculture and the Tennessee Valley Authority, experimented with what was called "project" budgeting in the mid 1930s. A similar format was employed by the Department of the Navy in preparing its fiscal 1948 budget request. It was to these early efforts that the Hoover Commission looked in formulating its recommendations in 1949.

Under the traditional line-item or "object" budget, the legislative body provided funds to acquire the resources necessary to conduct the business of government. In short, the focus was on the amounts needed to pay for things: personnel, equipment, supplies, etc. Such a presentation revealed little about what was accomplished as a result of such expenditures. Policies, programs, and activities of the spending units of government were not incorporated into the budget document. The question of efficiency was not answerable based on the information available in the traditional budget. It should not be surprising, then, that the first major reform effort was directed toward the design of a budget format that would enable program managers, agency heads, elected officials, and citizens to gain some insight into the costs associated with the various activities of government. As the Hoover Commission report put it, "the all-important thing in budgeting is the work or service to be accomplished, and what that work or service will cost" (p. 8).

Performance budgeting, then, is an attempt to go beyond the dollars alone and the mere objects being bought and paid for, to look at the services being provided, the activities being carried out. Further, it seeks to attach cost figures to those programs and activities. Budgets take on a different appearance in response to the need to present information in a different context. Tied to cost-accounting techniques, performance budgets presented managers and policymakers with detailed breakdowns of the unit costs of agency outputs. Examples would include, at the local level of government, such things as the cost per mile of streets resurfaced, or the cost per ton of garbage collected. Such data made cost and performance comparisons possible across years or between one jurisdiction and another. A fully developed performance budget became, in effect, the work program for the budgeting unit. As such, it required more involvement on the part of program managers.

Congress, through the Budget and Accounting Procedures Act of 1950, provided for government-wide presentation of the national budget on a performance basis. Without using the term "performance budget," the Act specified that

> The Budget shall set forth in such form and detail as the President may determine—(a) functions and activities of the Government; (b) any other desirable classification of data; (c) a reconciliation of the summary of expenditures with proposed appropriations. (64 Stat. 832, Title I, Section 102)

Commenting on the innovation shortly thereafter, Seckler-Hudson (1953) pointed out that the new concept "basically means a focus of attention on the ends to be served by the government rather than the dollars to be spent." In constructing a performance budget, she added, the most important single task would be "the precise definition of the work to be done and a careful estimate of what that work would cost" (Seckler-Hudson, 1953, p. 5).

While performance budgeting suffered from indifference and neglect in Washington, it caught on in municipal governments across the country. Labeled "management budgeting" by the International City Management Association (ICMA, 1981, p. 103), the performance budget fit comfortably into a climate where increased attention was being focused on improving the efficiency of operations. It was also the case that many local government functions lent themselves to the kind of quantification demanded by the performance budget format. Activities such as solid waste collection, street maintenance, and fire protection have measureable outputs in terms of end results. Cost accounting enables these outputs (e.g., lane miles resurfaced) to be stated in terms of unit costs. Aggregating those costs produces a budget estimate of expenditures for that particular activity in a given year.

During this first wave of serious budgetary reform, many local governments adapted their financial presentations to the performance format, with or without cost-accounting techniques (Sherwood, 1954). Some, such as Los Angeles, received high marks (Eghtedari and Sherwood, 1960). Others got an "E" for effort, but were credited with doing less than might have been possible (Binford, 1972). Some, when placed under a more demanding microscope, were found to have fallen well short of providing accurate cost estimates of city services (Savas, 1979). Still, as an instrument for providing both managers and policymakers with detailed service performance-cost data, the performance budget represented a major step forward. Its usefulness is attested to by the relatively few cities that, having adopted it, later discarded the performance budget.

Program Budgeting

Performance budgeting, never fully accepted at the federal level of government, was swept aside in the early 1960s by a new development in budgetary technology: program budgeting. Entering the government by way of the Defense Department where it was hailed as an instant success, the Planning-Programming-Budgeting System (PPBS) was made mandatory for all federal agencies by President Johnson in 1965.* Like many budgetary reforms introduced into government, this one also had its roots in private industry. According to David Novick (1968), one of its earliest advocates, program budgeting actually made its governmental debut in 1942 when the War Production Board employed a version of it to assign priorities and control production of war materials. But it was the adoption of PPBS under the direction of Defense Secretary Robert McNamara that led to a decade of dominance of this approach throughout the 1960s.

The basic idea underlying program budgeting, including PPBS, is that budgetary decisions should be based on output categories (objectives and end products) rather than inputs (personnel and equipment costs). Charles J. Hitch, former Comptroller of the Defense Department and the man usually credited with installing PPBS there, described it as combining two management techniques: program forecasting and systems analysis. Program forecasting means focusing on goal-oriented programs rather than on expenditure objects and projecting both inputs and outputs into the future (Jones, 1969). Systems analysis seeks to study outputs by means of quantitative methods and a model where possible to enable policymakers to compare alternative courses of action.

Program budgeting goes beyond performance budgeting and its narrow concern with carrying out specific tasks efficiently. It asks, first of all, what the goals are of a government and its various agencies and institutions.

Program budgeting, especially as manifested in PPBS, was largely the contribution

---

*President Johnson's reasons for imposing PPBS on a government-wide scale remain unclear. On this point, see Golembiewski and Scott (1989).

of economists. It introduced into the budget-making process certain concepts previously ignored, except in rare and short-lived experiments. These included the systematic consideration of alternative means to accomplish a given task, the comparison at the margins of both program costs and benefits, and the idea of "tradeoffs" or substitutions in arriving at policy choices.

Basically there were five crucial elements involved in the program budgeting process:

1. A focus on the objectives or purposes of government. Once these fundamental objectives were identified, then all activities of the government—regardless of their organizational location—could be assigned to broad program categories (i.e., education, national security, health, etc.).
2. An across-the-board program structure, linking all the activities and their costs to those common programs. The total cost figures would then represent the "budget."
3. A multiyear program and financial plan. Employing an extended time horizon—usually 5 years—the future implications of present decisions could be projected, in terms of both costs and benefits.
4. Program analysis. At the heart of PPBS was the use of cost-benefit and cost-effectiveness studies to compare the various programs and projects being considered as alternative means to achieve a given objective or carry out a stated purpose.
5. Budget aggregation. Summing the total costs of program decisions resulted in the creation of the budget.

One of the claimed strengths of program budgeting—and, ultimately, one of its weaknesses—was that it pretended to ignore organizational boundaries. Because, as Novick (1979) put it, program structures rarely conform to either the appropriation structure or the organizational structure, corsswalks had to be created to convert program-based data into the necessary line-item, object-class, organizationally based budget. Neither Congress nor state legislatures exhibited a willingness to alter the traditional language of their appropriation bills to match the program format.

While budget theory may have no difficulty in abrogating agency and departmental jurisdictional boundaries, neither the bureaucracy nor the legislatures that oversee them are similarly inclined. In program budgeting, "organization gives way to program" (Novick, 1973). In the real world, it is usually the other way around. One of the most obvious revelations contained in program budgeting is the dispersed, overlapping, and sometimes conflicting organizational arrangements devised to house similar programs. The thought that immediately arises is, why shouldn't organization reflect program distributions? Why should public health programs be dispersed among more than 30 agencies, departments, boards, and commissions, as is the case in Alabama? In short, program budgeting encourages administrative reorganization. But few states—Kentucky and Washington come to mind—were willing to accompany the introduction of program budgeting with the restructuring of the executive branch of government. At the federal level, McNamara's success in using PPBS to overcome service boundary (and rivalry) problems in the Department of Defense was not matched elsewhere in the government. Instead, each department had its own program structure, and no coordinating authority emerged to integrate programs across organizational lines (Schick, 1973).

If performance budgeting was efficiency oriented, program budgeting fixed its sights on effectiveness. Given a set of agreed-upon goals, it presented policymakers with available alternatives, both in terms of objectives and the means by which to achieve them. Cost-benefit analysis (or cost-effectiveness analysis) was employed to cast alternative policy choices in quantitative terms. By displaying both the long-term benefits as well as the total costs of various proposals, this form of marginal analysis was intended to produce "new ways of thinking about policy making" (White, 1982).

Program budgeting, in its various manifestations, has its intellectual roots in economics and management science. Its underlying rationale is to improve rationality in the making of resource allocation decisions. In this, it adopts an anti-incrementalist posture. Unsurprisingly, its principal critics have been those political scientists. (Wildavsky, 1966, 1969; Gross, 1969; Lindblom, 1959, 1979) who viewed program budgeting as an attack on cherished principles of pluralist democracy and individualism. To the critics, bargaining is the essential element in policy making. Program budgeting, at least as practiced in PPBS, was seen as flawed by its omission of explicit consideration of political factors (Wildavsky, 1966). Schick (1966) suggested that PPBS took "an overly mechanistic view of the impact of form on behavior." He questioned the existence of "Budgetary Man" as a counterpart to the classical "Economic Man."

PPBS, nevertheless, shifted the thinking of budget officials from a concentration on the means of government to consideration of the ends and successfully introduced into the budgetary process both analysis and planning. The language and techniques of program analysis spread swiftly throughout the federal bureaucracy and filtered down to state and local governments as well. When the method was formally abandoned in 1971, it left behind a residue of disciplines and practices that continue, in some places to this day (Foster, 1985).

As an idea, program budgeting was both attractive and logical. It suggested that the government should plan what to do rather than blindly meander along (LeLoup, 1980). Still, by 1971, this innovation in budgeting had come to the end of its rope. The reasons for its demise have been catalogued by Allen Schick (1973). Imposed from above by the Bureau of the Budget, PPBS analysts remained outsiders, unable to penetrate the routines of agency budgeting. The Budget Bureau, itself, seemed less than enthusiastically committed to the reform. The new routines were imposed without accompanying increases in resources, and the centralizing tendencies associated with PPBS did not sit well with middle-level managers in the agencies. By highlighting duplication in service delivery functions and posing the threat of administrative reorganizations, the new system introduced additional conflict into the bureaucartic arena. Finally, like most budgetary reforms, PPBS was an instrument of executive branch origins. It was installed without taking into account congressional reactions. And that reaction, generally, was not favorable. What a bureaucrat wants from a budget may not be identical with what a legislator wants (Wanat, 1978, p. 105). In any event, Congress declined to alter its notions as to what it expected to find in a budget submission. Neither did the reform appear to result in noticeably different outcomes in Congressional budgetary decisions (Jernberg, 1969).

Management By Objectives

Although it was a product of the Kennedy-Johnson years, PPBS continued in use through the early days of the Nixon administration. In 1971, however, the technique was formally abandoned as a requirement for federal agencies. In its wake, reflecting a new emphasis on management at OMB, came another approach borrowed from the private sector: management by objectives (MBO). Conceptually, "the Nixon Administration sought to shift attention from problems of choice to problems of management" (Rose, 1977). By

1973, spurred by OMB deputy director Frederic V. Malek, management by objectives had been implemented widely throughout the federal government.

Reacting to one of the chronic complaints levied against PPBS—that it generated too much paperwork—management by objectives advocates in OMB played down the new system's manpower and paperwork requirements. The major federal agencies involved were allowed considerable discretion in defining objectives. It became, whatever the original intentions, a much less comprehensive approach than PPBS. With its primary focus on managerial aspects of program implementation, MBO placed less emphasis on long-range planning and program evaluation. Where PPBS tried to force the comparison of programs across organizational boundaries, MBO respected those jurisdictional lines. Where PPBS had had a centralizing, top-down orientation, MBO promised a more participative approach, with line managers heavily involved in the setting of agency objectives.

Operationally, management by objectives consists of a three-part cycle (Brady, 1973): First, managers and subordinates agree on a list of measureable, results-oriented objectives and link these to the departmental budget request. Second, milestones to be achieved en route to the objectives are established and periodic progress reviews are scheduled. These management conferences, scheduled bimonthly or quarterly throughout the year, assess the status of each objective and, if necessary, permit the objectives themselves to be changed to conform to new initiatives. Third, the results are evaluated, each manager submitting to the department head a year-end report describing successes and failures in meeting the objectives set earlier.

Like PPBS, management by objectives relied for success on the ability to clearly define goals and objectives. Like performance budgeting, it demanded an ability to measure performance against specific, quantifiable standards. Unlike its two predecessors, however, MBO failed to establish itself as an activity essential to budgeting. While a few agencies made an attempt to link MBO to the budget process, most were unable to make the connection. As Lynch (1990) explains, such linkage can be accomplished by using a matrix table juxtaposing agency objectives and budget activities. In this way, the amount of money needed to carry out a given objective during the budget year would be highlighted. Implementation of such a process encountered two related problems. First, since most programs have multiple objectives, it was difficult to isolate funds in mutually exclusive categories. Second, not all program activities were covered by MBO objectives. Worse, managers became fixated on identifying objectives, a process that became self-defeating since long lists of objectives were not accompanied by resources sufficient to carry out any but the first few (Wildavsky, 1984, p. 184).

Budgeting, it has been said, is a schizophrenic enterprise, trying simultaneously to accommodate both political choices and managerial decisions (McCaffery, 1976). The emphasis in PPBS was on the former, in MBO on the latter. Some saw the possibility that the two approaches could be combined into one that would offer more than either alone (DeWoolfson, 1975). It was not to be. When Richard Nixon flew west into temporary exile in California, management by objectives lost its champion in the White House. Gerald Ford, inheriting the whirlwind, undertook a "megamanagement" effort spanning a broad spectrum of administrative reforms in 1976. An avalanche of management improvement directives emanating from OMB buried management by objectives in its path (Rose, 1977). Instituted informally at the outset, MBO "evaporated" slowly and by 1979 remained viable only in scattered outposts of the federal government.

Zero-Base Budgeting

> Since government began, whenever politicians could find nothing better to do with
> their time and energy, and whenever they confronted the need to demonstrate concern
> for a public problem, they reorganized the public bureaucracy. (Peters, 1988, p. 17)

Or they reformed the budget process. The winding down of PPBS and management by objectives created only a momentary vacuum in budget styles. This time, the winds of change blew out of Texas and Georgia in the form of zero-base budgeting (ZBB). With a newly-elected President of the United States as its leading advocate, ZBB took hold in Washington in 1977. As with its predecessors, this budgetary innovation made its way to the nation's capital via the private sector and state and local government experiments (Pyhrr, 1973; Schick and Keith, 1976). At the time of its introduction into the federal government, an even dozen states already had taken steps to implement a similar process (U.S. Congress, Senate Committee on Government Operations, 1977).

Whatever else may have been claimed for this new approach—and much was claimed—it would, its advocates insisted, make possible the reallocation of funds from lower- to higher-level priorities and put an end to the much-condemned practice of incrementalism. It would, in President Jimmy Carter's words, make it possible to "plan and allocate resources more rationally" (Carter, 1977, p. 26). Scattered early reports from the field raised questions about the applicability of zero-base budgeting in state government (LaFaver, 1974; Scheiring, 1976). But Carter, as governor of Georgia, had been impressed by the technique and promised during the 1976 campaign that, if elected to the presidency, he would bring the reform to Washington with him. He was, and he did. Three months after his inauguration, the heads of executive branch departments were instructed to prepare their fiscal year 1979 budgets according to the zero-base format.

Developed in the private sector, notably for Texas Instruments, zero-base budgeting was sold to governments largely on the basis of the oldest promise contained in campaigns for budget reform. As a candidate for the presidency, Carter had declared the federal budget process to be "inefficient, chaotic, and uncontrollable." ZBB, he argued, would "reduce costs and make the federal government more efficient and effective" (Carter, 1977). This would be accomplished by improving the quality of budgetary information, involving line managers in the decision process, and emphasizing the kind of analysis that would shed greater light on the cost-effectiveness of programs.

Theoretically, zero-base budgeting drew on the insights of Verne B. Lewis (1952) and others who had argued that decision makers should consider more than a single recommended level of spending for various programs. In this sense, ZBB was a form of "alternative budgeting." It required managers to consider not only alternative levels of funding and service output, but alternative means for achieving objectives. In this, it shared some of the conceptual ground previously occupied by PPBS and management by objectives.

While not applied uniformly in every organization, ZBB basically involved a four-step process. First, organizational objectives were determined and "decision units" were defined. These were simply those units at which budgetary and programmatic decisions were made. Frequently, they were coterminous with existing organizational substructures, although they could be defined along broader program lines. Second, each decision unit was analyzed within the framework of a "decision package." This was the "building block" of the zero-base approach (Pyhrr, 1977). Each decision package consisted of a cluster of activities related to the accomplishment of the unit's objectives. At this point, managers were required to consider alternative means of achieving the objectives as well as different levels of services and resources. Also included at this stage of analysis were such factors as work loads, performance measures, and the costs and benefits associated with each level of service and expenditure. Ultimately, each activity contained in the package had to be considered in terms of reduced, current, and increased levels of effort and funding. In this way, managers presented higher-level decision makers with several choices to select from, rather than a single set of recommended figures. Based on such information, decision units could be compared with each other and decisions could be made to approve or disapprove competing claims on the budget. This ranking of decision packages constituted the third step in the process, frequently referred to as "prioritizing." Finally, at the highest level, the organization's budget request was formulated based on the funding needs associated with each adopted level of program activity.

A principal advantage claimed for ZBB was that it generated previously unavailable information that could be used in both managerial decision making and broader, higher-level policymaking. By offering decision makers multiple options it broke with the traditional "one best way" of presenting agency requests. To the extent that legislative bodies accepted the zero-base format—and acceptance was far from universal—it allowed them to view the probable consequences of providing different incremental levels of funding for various programs.

In the sense that budget formats determine how budgets are viewed, the information presented, and the kinds of questions asked, ZBB had an impact. Specifically, this approach shifted attention away from what is to be added to the current year program and focused upon increases to the minimum level of support (Lynch, 1990, p. 53). But an impact on the process is not the same thing as an impact on outcomes. On this point, ZBB produced its share of "rational skeptics." Even before the ink was dry on the FY 1979 federal budget, a study of ZBB's performance in Georgia raised pertinent questions as to whether it made a difference. Lauth (1978) found that, contrary to former Governor Carter's impression, ZBB had had relatively little impact on budgeting in Georgia. Its use in that state had failed to reduce incrementalism, reallocate budget shares, or change significantly the way in which agencies prepared their budgets. Schick (1978) rendered a similar verdict on federal ZBB, observing that it had "changed the terminology of budgeting, but little more."

Introduced by President Carter, zero-base budgeting departed Washington with him. The Reagan administration dropped the label, but decision units, variable funding level documentation, and priority rankings continued to be employed (Mikesell, 1986, p. 155). Indeed, in preparing the FY 1986 budget, the Reagan OMB literally zero-based (requested no funding) for several programs, including Amtrack and the Appalachian Regional Commission. Congress, as it had on several occasions with Carter, restored the funds.

Zero-base budgeting suffered from some of the same difficulties that had plagued its predecessors. It assumed an ability to clearly define the goals and objectives of each activity being budgeted, as well as the goals and objectives of the entire organization (Starling, 1979, p. 426). In addition, the process generated a massive amount of paperwork. In Georgia, there were 11,000 decision packages accompanied by 33 pages of instructions and 24 different forms. It was estimated that if the governor allotted 4 hours every day for 2 months he could spend about 1 minute on each decision package, not enough time to read it, let alone analyze it (Anthony, 1977).

Like PPBS and management by objectives, zero-base budgeting, to use Richard Rose's term, has "evaporated." Gone but not forgotten, it survives in pockets of the federal bureaucracy and, in altered form, in some 20 states. What all three of these executive branch budgetary reforms had in common was an emphasis on analysis. But analysis was either unwelcome or unnecessary.

The age of analysis may not be dead, but it is at least sleeping. Wildavsky (1989) has raised the question whether analysis has been driven from the field by "political dissensus." That is, when partisan and policy polarization have reached the levels currently seen in Congress, the nature of the important questions changes. V. O. Key (1940) had pondered whether analysis could inform the decision where the choice was between allocating marginal dollars to battleships or poor relief. He was skeptical. Wildavsky (1966, 1989) argued that such questions are too "aggregated" and too philosophical to be subjected to analysis. He added that when the critical questions center around the size of the deficit and the size of government and the parties cannot agree on either, stalemate results. "When size matters more than content, there is no need for analysis" (Wildavsky, 1989).

CONGRESSIONAL REFORMS

The budgetary reforms discussed thus far have been executive centered, technical, and geared toward improving the ways in which budgets are prepared. They have focused on the budget document itself, with minimal impact on the broader "process" by which spending decisions are finally arrived at. One often-cited cause of the failure of these reforms was their inability to alter significantly the way in which budgets were dealt with by the legislative branch of government. At the national level, Congress throughout most of the nation's history gave only sporadic attention to how it handled one of its principal responsibilities. The enactment of appropriation bills that confer legal authority on executive branch agencies to commit the government to certain expenditures has remained a largely haphazard process. Efforts to link revenues and expenditures were seldom attempted and short-lived.

Early Reforms

Prior to passage of the Budget and Accounting Act of 1921, congressional control of the budget process was sufficiently strong that little need for reform was evident. Agencies dealt directly with congressional committees, and presidential involvement was minor. The 1921 act, however, shifted the balance toward the executive. The Bureau of the Budget provided the President with staff expertise not available on Capitol Hill. The contrast "between executive management and congressional aimlessness" became clear (Starling, 1979, p. 417). The legislative branch, running contrary to the trend toward centralization of executive budget authority, maintained a decentralized approach to budget making. The arrangements, entrenched for more than a half century, are familiar. Authorization, revenue, and appropriation responsibilities were dispersed among separate committees in both houses. Nowhere did Congress attempt to pull the whole picture together (Lawton, 1953).

Periodically, in recognition of its deteriorating position, Congress would entertain proposals designed to remedy the situation. But it would be 1974 before serious reform of the legislative budget process would emerge. Before examining that still-in-place modification, a brief look at a few of the earlier efforts might set the stage.

Joint Committee on the Budget

In 1952, Senator John L. McClellan of Arkansas introduced a bill to create a joint committee of Congress to deal with the budget. The measure, which would have provided the committee with a staff of budget analysts to rival the executive branch's Budget Bureau, passed the Senate but was defeated in the House. The proposed committee would have included 14 members from the House and Senate Appropriations Committees. It was opposed in the House by the Chairman and ranking minority member of that body's Appropriations Committee, who contended that the proposed committee would encroach on the functions of their committee. After defeating the bill, the House added $500,000 to increase the staffs of the appropriations committees (Harris, 1952).

More than 50 years ago, A. E. Buck (1934) had recommended the consolidation of the appropriations committees in the two houses into a single joint committee on the budget. One supporting argument was that it would eliminate the need for duplicate hearings.

Inherent in the proposal for a joint legislative committee on the budget was the notion of a congressional counterpart to the Bureau of the Budget. Congress simply did not have access to the analytical data about the budget that was available to the executive branch (Wallace, 1959). As McClellan put it, Congress had "no authentic source of information to refute or contradict the claims of need and justification made by the spending agencies" (Harris, 1952). Proposals for correcting this imbalance usually centered on an expanded role for the General Accounting Office, a congressional agency. A more extreme suggestion would have transferred the Bureau of the Budget to Congress (Lawton, 1953). Questions of legislative interference in executive administration and the fear of possible partisan manipulation of congressional budget staff halted this reform in its tracks, at least temporarily.

The Legislative Budget

The provision for a so-called legislative budget has been called the least successful feature of the Legislative Reorganization Act of 1946 (Smithies, 1955). The act provided that the four congressional financial committees (House Ways and Means, Senate Finance, and House and Senate Appropriations) would recommend at the outset of each session the maximum limit on appropriations for the next fiscal year. The figure arrived at was to be based on consideration of the President's recommendations, including estimates of overall federal revenues and expenditures. If estimated receipts exceeded estimated expenditures, the act called for recommendations for reducing the national debt. If projected expenditures were greater than expected receipts, the concurrent resolution was to recommend an increase in the public debt sufficient to cover the expected deficit (Smithies, 1955, p. 93).

It was a noble attempt to make Congress take some responsibility for keeping revenues and expenditures in balance. But, as Smithies noted, it was doomed from the start. The antideficiency provision imposed no obligation on the Congress but affected only the President. There was no arrangement for recommending increases or decreases in taxation. The only way to eliminate a presidential deficit was through a reduction in spending. The attempt by Congress to impose a ceiling on appropriations was motivated by a zeal for retrenchment (Burkhead, 1956, p. 328). Efforts to implement the legislative budget in 1947 and 1948 failed and the process was abandoned.

This effort at reform revealed that Congress is in no position early in a session to set spending and revenue ceilings, a lesson that would have to be relearned 30 years later. As one observer noted, however, the ill-fated effort at reform reflected a congressional distaste for the system of considering the budget piecemeal. It showed "a desire for some means whereby Congress may at one time pass upon the total budget, revenues as well as expenditures" (Harris, 1952).

The Omnibus Bill

The Budget and Accounting Act of 1921 was designed, in part, to enable Congress to deal more effectively with the budget. It proved to be an elusive target. The President's budget, on arrival in Congress, was promptly divided into 12 or 15 parts and scattered among a like number of subcommittees in each house. (Since 1968, there have been 13 subcommittees and 13 appropriations bills in each chamber.) The Congress, therefore, never considered the budget as a whole or weighed the relative merits of all programs. Decisions made in the various subcommittees of the appropriations committees tended then, as now, to be relatively binding. Thus, the locus of power in budgetary matters was highly decentralized and the end product a fragmented whole.

One attempt to remedy this situation was the one-time use of something called the omnibus appropriation bill. This device, employed only in 1950, consolidated all appropriation bills into a single omnibus bill. The results were unsatisfactory and the experiment was not repeated.

There were numerous drawbacks to the omnibus approach. Most dissatisfaction arose from the fact that delay in the House of Representatives kept the bill from moving to the Senate until May 10, during a time when the fiscal year began on July 1. The Senate did not complete action until August 4, and subsequent conferences delayed signing by the President until September 6, 1950, 2 months after the start of the fiscal year (Burkhead, 1956, p. 330). In the apparent belief that the procedure conferred too much power on the chairmen of the appropriations committees, members of the House Appropriations Committee voted against their chairman and killed an effort to use the omnibus bill the following year. It was never revived.

Budget and Impoundment Act

As the size of government increased markedly in the years following mid-century, so did the federal budget. It grew in ways unanticipated by earlier reformers, not only in size but in complexity. The congressional budget process, however, remained decentralized, fragmented, and uncoordinated. Other problems, always lurking in the background, came to a head. Linda Smith (1977) identified four major factors that combined to produce the Congressional Budget and Impoundment Control Act of 1974, the single most comprehensive reform of the legislative budget process ever undertaken. The major problem and the one that triggered congressional action was that of impoundment (Pfiffner, 1979). This device, traceable back to the Jefferson administration, enabled the President to withhold spending authority already approved by Congress. Traditionally, it had been used only when further spending on a project was unnecessary because of cost savings, early completion, or where the need for economizing was shared by Congress and the President. The practice became controversial only when, beginning with the presidency of Franklin D. Roosevelt, appropriated funds were withheld from the spending agencies for budgetary or political purposes (Ippolito, 1978). Post-World War II impoundments by Truman, Eisenhower, and Kennedy were concentrated in the defense area. Lyndon Johnson extended the use of impoundments to curtail spending for domestic programs, although most were merely deferrals, the funds being released later.

The issue came to a boil during the Nixon administration when the President impounded upward of $20 billion in more than 100 programs, nearly all of them domestic and most involving grant-in-aid monies appropriated to assist state and local governments. The action, spread over a 4-year period, prompted more than 60 court cases as state and local public officials and interest groups sued the appropriate cabinet officers to obtain release of the funds (Axelrod, 1989). In all but a handful of cases, the plaintiffs were victorious. But Congress was not content to rely upon the courts to uphold the allocation of appropriated funds. The courts, in any event, had not addressed the issue of constitutionality but had relied upon language in the various statutes in ordering the funds released. Language severely restricting the President's impoundment authority would be included in the 1974 Budget Act.

In addition to impoundments, three other factors combined to prompt the 1974 reform legislation (L. L. Smith, 1977). First among these was the problem of "uncontrollable" spending. These were expenditure items locked into existing laws, which could not be changed merely as a result of the annual appropriations process. Entitlement programs such as Social Security and other trust-fund-based spending accounted for much of the total, which by 1970 had reached more than 50% of total federal outlays.

Another problem related to the increasing inability of Congress to pass appropriation bills by the beginning of the fiscal year. In each year between 1948 and 1974, Congress had failed to enact all 13 appropriation bills prior to the start of the fiscal year, in those days July 1 (Cranford, 1989, p. 67). As a result, most agences of the government were forced to operate under continuing resolutions for at least part of the year. These measures usually allow agencies to continue spending at levels provided in the preceding year, thus curtailing program improvements and playing havoc with agency planning.

A third problem contributing to the fragmentation and loss of control over the budget process was so-called backdoor spending. Closely related to, indeed the cause of, much of the "uncontrollability" problem, this form of off-budget financing accounted for more than $30 billion of federal spending by the early 1970s. Its principal forms included contract authority granted by the authorizing committees, which enabled some agencies to enter into contracts in advance of appropriations, thereby committing the government to pay the bills when they subsequently became due. In addition, some agencies were authorized to spend debt receipts as a result of selling their own bonds or by borrowing from the Treasury, all without action by the appropriations committees. Finally, certain agencies derive income from leases, rents, fees, or sale of government assets. These proprietary receipts (oil leases, grazing fees, military sales, etc.) show up as offsets to agency expenditures rather than income and outlays.

All of these matters, along with a general reassertiveness on the part of Congress in the wake of the Vietnam War and the Watergate scandals, combined to spur 2 years of study culminating in the Budget Act of 1974. In short, Congress was determined to discipline itself and retrieve budgetary powers ceded to the President during the previous half-century (Shuman, 1988).

Major Provisions of the 1974 Act

Structurally, procedurally, and politically, the 1974 act wrought changes in the way Congress deals with the budget. A political document, it reflects a host of compromises necessary to win acceptance. The act did not, for example, do away with any existing institutions, nor did it create something that might be called a congressional budget along the lines of the executive budget submitted by the President (Shuman, 1988, p. 217ff.). Essentially, and in summary form, the Act did the following:

1. It sharply curtailed the President's impoundment powers by creating procedures whereby Congress could block such measures. No longer could the executive, relying on OMB's apportionment power, unilaterally withhold from the agencies spending authority granted in congressional appropriation bills. Instead, the act prescribed two new procedures for presidents to follow in cases where the executive sought to delay or cancel authorized spending. Basically, the legislation (Title X) amended the Anti-Deficiency Acts of 1905 and 1950, which had conferred upon the President the power to limit or cancel spending under certain conditions. Henceforth, the executive would be required to notify Congress of any intent to impound funds or delay their use. Two new categories were established: deferrals and rescissions. In the case of the former, where the President wishes to delay the timing of obligations or reserve funds for future use, either house can block the action by passage of an "impound-ment resolution." This provision fell victim to a 1983 Supreme Court decision in an unrelated case that declared unconstitutional the one-house veto. With regard to a rescission, the effort to cancel spending authority altogether, both House and Senate must approve within 45 days after it is submitted or the President is forced to release the money. This provision has survived, and congressional approval has been granted sparingly. The usual practice employed to deny presidential rescission requests has been for Congress to refuse to vote on them, effectively killing them. During Ronald Reagan's second term, not a single rescission request was brought to a vote in Congress.

2. While the 1974 act did not abolish the existing taxing and spending committees of Congress, it did create a standing Committee on the Budget in each house, each with its own staff. In a move to provide Congress with more resources and expertise, the act also established the Congressional Budget Office, whose director is appointed by the Speaker of the House and the President pro tempore of the Senate. The principal function of the budget committees is to conduct hearings and present to their respective houses a budget resolution setting spending limits for about 20 functional categories (defense, agriculture, transportation, etc.) along with an aggregate total spending figure. This activity, taken early in the legislative phase of the process, is supposed to guide the future actions of the appropriations committees. It represents, to the extent that it is honored by subsequent actions, a congressional "budget." Initially, a second resolution, adopted 2 weeks prior to the start of the fiscal year, was designed to be binding and, in effect, to adjust differences created by appropriations actions taken after passage of the first resolution. However, the second resolution was subsequently abandoned and the first resolution has become the "binding" resolution (Shuman, 1988, p. 237). As for the Congressional Budget Office (CBO), its large professional staff was meant to serve Congress as a counterbalance to the analytical capacity available to the executive branch through OMB, the Council of Economic Advisers, and the Treasury Department (Ippolito, 1978). In addition to formulating a

congressional alternative to executive branch economic forecasts and budgetary proposals, CBO is also charged with providing the Budget Committees with information and assistance as requested. It also serves a similar function for the House Ways and Means and Senate Finance Committees as well as the appropriations committees in each house.

3. In addition to dealing with the impoundment problem and making internal structural changes, the Budget Act of 1974 altered the legislative budget process in substantial ways. First, it created a new fiscal year in an attempt to give Congress additional time to pass appropriations bills. The old fiscal year, which began on July 1 and ran through June 30 of the following year, was changed to an October 1–September 30 year. With an additional 3 months to consider the budget proposals, it was hoped— forlornly, as it turned out—that the appropriation bills would be enacted prior to the beginning of the fiscal year. In addition, the President was now required to submit something called the current services budget on November 10, prior to sending up his official budget request in January. The current services budget assumes no new programs or policy changes and simply estimates what it will cost next year to continue in place, with adjustments for inflation, those programs already authorized. Delivered to the Joint Economic Committee of Congress, it languishes there. Not taken seriously by OMB, which prepares it, or by members of Congress who prefer to await the arrival of "the real thing" in January, the current services budget remains an ornamental ritual lacking in impact. (Wildavsky, 1984; Shuman, 1988). The act set forth a rigid timetable designed to keep congressional budget action on a fixed track. The schedule has fallen into disuse as Congress, utilizing easily adopted rules, has repeatedly ignored or bypassed its self-imposed deadlines.

The Act in Operation

Any reform has to be judged on the basis of what it attempted to accomplish. While support for the 1974 legislation had many bases, some conflicting, it seems clear that most of the advocates of reform had certain changes in mind: to "rationalize" the congressional budget process by establishing fixed deadlines for completion of the various steps in order to produce appropriations bills "on time"; to enable Congress and its committees to view the budget in more comprehensive fashion, examining revenues and expenditures simultaneously; to curb the President's impoundment powers; to balance the budget—or at least move decisively in that direction; and to limit "uncontrollable" expenditures.

That Congress now takes a more unified approach to the budget is generally conceded. The work of the Congressional Budget Office has provided members of the budget and appropriations committees with revenue estimates and economic projections that provide an alternative view to similar estimates emanating from the executive branch. Budget resolutions enacted relatively early in the process set targets for spending by major category and establish, however briefly, an overall budget figure and deficit estimate that is frequently quite different from the President's projections. Congress now knows the probable fiscal consequences of its budgetary decisions. But balancing the budget has proved to be as elusive a goal as before reform. The deficit, as a percentage of budgetary outlays, averaged 6.5% in the 10 years preceding budget reform. In the decade following reform, the comparable figure was 16.2% (OMB, 1977–1989).

As for meeting deadlines and enacting appropriations bills by the beginning of the fiscal year, the record is not much improved over the prereform years. The first budget under the new rules (FY 1977) met all deadlines, and all 13 appropriations were passed prior to October 1. That performance was not repeated until 1988 (FY 1989). In the interim, legislative gridlock was the usual pattern. In 1980, 1981, and 1987, all the deadlines were missed. The bottom was reached in 1987 when, 2 days before Christmas, an omnibus continuing resolution containing all 13 joint House-Senate appropriations bills was finally signed into law. The huge package contained more than $600 billion in spending authority to cover the remaining three quarters of the 1988 fiscal year, which had begun nearly 3 months earlier.

The twin problems of "uncontrollable" spending and "backdoor" spending continued unabated after reform. The Office of Management and Budget had estimated that uncontrollables accounted for 70% of the budget in 1970. By 1988 the figure had reached 78%, fueled largely by fast-growing entitlement programs. In FY 1987, for example, entitlements, including Social Security, Medicare, and Medicaid, constituted 46% of the government's spending. Another 19% went to pay for contracts entered into in previous years, and 14% was devoted to paying interest on the debt. The 1974 bill required annual appropriations for new contract authority, but exempted from its provisions Social Security and most other trust fund, guaranteed loan, and insurance programs.

The act has had considerable effect in the area of restraining presidential use of the impoundment power. By subjecting proposed impoundments to congressional review and concurrence, the executive's discretionary use of this fiscal policy tool has been sharply curbed. Having appropriated the funds, Congress has not been inclined to revoke its action by allowing the President to withhold the money. Initially, the Ford administration, the first to be affected by the new law, interpreted the anti-impoundment provisions as a source of authority for withholding funds (Fisher, 1975, p. 200). Basing most of his requests for rescissions on policy grounds, President Ford encountered stiff opposition. Of some $9 billion of rescissions requested, 86% were rejected (LeLoup, 1980, p. 176). Later, President Reagan was similarly frustrated. Of $20 billion in rescissions requested between 1983 and 1988, Congress approved only 2%, or $400 million.

It was an obscure provision of the act, however, that eventually provoked the greatest controversy. As noted earlier, each house is required early in the session to adopt a budget resolution setting spending ceilings for each functional category of government as well as an aggregate spending level. To enforce those priorities and totals on the authorizing and appropriations committees, a process called reconciliation was provided. During the period between passage of the first budget resolution in May and the second resolution in September, the appropriations committees produce the spending bills. Since the amounts enacted had a tendency to exceed the totals specified in the first budget resolution, reconciliation was designed to instruct appropriations, authorizing, and revenue committees to take steps "reconciling" their actions with the budget resolution. In the early years of the new budget process, as one observer remarked, "reconciliation was hardly discussed, let alone attempted" (Collender, 1989, p. 39). The usual practice was for the second resolution to incorporate changes in spending or revenues resulting from actions taken since passage of the first resolution. This would change dramatically in 1981.

The Reagan administration, in office for little more than a month, saw in the reconciliation process an opportunity to dramatically alter numerous provisions of the fiscal year 1982 budget left behind by the recently departed Carter administration. Seizing on the reconciliation language in Section 304 of the Act, Reagan forces in the House and Senate contrived to use the device in concurrence with adoption of the first budget resolution. After lengthy and acrimonious debate in the two houses, administration supporters won the day. Reconciliation bills ordering spending cuts of $37.7 billion and $38.1 billion for fiscal 1982 passed the House and Senate, respectively. The actions of 15 House committees and 14 in the Senate were affected. After a month of conferences between the houses, a compromise bill was enacted mandating cuts of $35.2 billion in the fiscal 1982 budget and a reduction of $130.6 billion over 3 years (Cranford, 1989). Although the tactic was not successfully employed again, it shattered faith in a congressional process already plagued by internal problems. In a dramatic fashion, it demonstrated that a popular President, backed by astute strategists in Congress, could still dominate the budget process. Congressional budgeting would never be the same.

What had seemed like a good idea at the time of its passage, a reconciliation bill to ensure that actual spending and revenue policies stayed within adopted target figures, had been used to impose presidential policy priorities on the Congress. Since then, the reconciliation bill has become what one national publication called "an annual exercise in legislative lunacy." As a "must pass" bill, it has served as a vehicle for dozens of unrelated riders containing substantive legislation.

Within the Congress itself, the reform of 1974 had turned the world upside down. Where once the authorization and appropriations committees had dictated the budget, the new budget committees had come to dictate to them. After the debate of 1981, budget resolutions have given more discretion to the authorizing committees, more respect to the appropriations committees. But in the bleak budgetary environment of the late 1980s, the struggle to reduce the huge annual deficits turned Congress toward still another effort at reform.

Gramm-Rudman-Hollings

The principal failure of the 1974 Budget Act had been its inability to stem the flow of red ink in the federal budget. By the mid 1980s, a combination of tax reductions and increased outlays had produced annual deficits in excess of $200 billion. The budget process created in 1974 had been designed to revise congressional procedures to create a framework for more systematic consideration of federal fiscal policies and to enhance accountability in Congress for budget decisions (Collender, 1989, p. 14). Reducing the deficit and balancing the budget were secondary considerations. The Balanced Budget and Emergency Deficit Control Act of 1985, on the other hand, was almost single-minded in its focus on those matters. Known popularly as Gramm-Rudman-Hollings, in recognition of its principal authors in the Senate, this legislation, amended in 1987, built upon the 1974 act with the stated objective of reducing the annual deficit to zero by 1991 (later extended to 1993).

Specifically, Gramm-Rudman-Hollings (GRH) established a new five-stage process (Collender, 1989, p. 18–24), as follows.

Stage 1: The President's Budget

Submission of the President's budget initiates the congressional budget process. The 1985 legislation made two changes in presidential submission requirements. First, the date for presenting the budget to Congress was changed from 15 days after Congress convenes in January to no later than the first Monday after January 3, no matter when Congress convenes. This deadline has proved meaningless. When Congress fails to enact appropriations bills or continuing resolutions until December, the executive budget preparation cycle is delayed. If current-year spending distributions remain unknown well into the current fiscal year, planning for future years becomes unrealistic. Thus, when the massive continuing resolution covering fiscal 1988 spending was not completed until Christmas Eve, 1987, executive submission of the fiscal 1989 budget was delayed well into February. A second cause of delay occurs during a period of change in administrations. Since the process allows an incoming President to submit "budget updates," lawmakers will prefer to await those corrections before starting legislative review. In 1989, for example, outgoing President Reagan's budget request for fiscal 1990 arrived in January. However, congressional action was deferred until incoming President George Bush unveiled his budget on February 9.

A more serious alteration in the presidential role, however, is the GRH requirement that the executive budget must come in with a deficit no greater than that stipulated in the law for each fiscal year. Any combination of spending reductions or tax increases may be proposed to reach the target deficit figure. Congress, of course, is free to rearrange spending and revenue figures to arrive at its own version of the permissible deficit.

Stage 2: The Congressional Budget Resolution

Under the 1974 act, Congress was required to pass two budget resolutions, one in mid May, the second in mid September, the latter fixing the final, binding spending figures for the coming year. Under GRH, Congress enacts a single resolution each year, by April 15. The 1985 bill makes mandatory the inclusion in the budget resolution of reconciliation instructions. In other words, whenever changes in entitlements or taxes are required to meet the deficit targets, the appropriate authorizing committees are instructed to change laws within their jurisdictions to comply with the budget resolution. To conform with the deficit limit for the upcoming fiscal year, the congressional budget resolution can mandate any mix of spending reductions or revenue enhancements it considers appropriate.

Stage 3: Reconciliation

During the period between April 15 and June 15, committees ordered to make reconciliation changes must comply with those instructions. If they decline to do so, amendments to accomplish the same result can be offered during debate by other members.

Stage 4: Authorizations and Appropriations

During the period between April 15 and the beginning of the fiscal year on October 1, GRH assumes that action will be completed in both houses on all authorization and appropriation bills. Unlike budget resolutions, these actions represent actual commitments in the form of laws. As such, they are subject to presidential veto. The House is expected to complete its work on all appropriations bills by June 30, sending them on to the Senate. This deadline, like most of the others, has been repeatedly violated.

Stage 5: Sequestration

The most controversial mechanism in the GRH process is the provision for automatic spending cuts to go into effect when the President and Congress fail to agree on a spending plan that will meet the deficit ceiling prescribed in the law. As originally crafted, GRH assigned to the Comptroller General, who heads the General Accounting Office, responsibility for estimating the deficit and recommending spending reductions necessary to bring the deficit for the year down to the target level. This provision was challenged as unconstitutional by a dozen members of Congress led by Rep. Mike Synar (D-Okla.). In midsummer 1986, as Congress worked its way through the fiscal 1987 budget, the Supreme Court upheld a District Court ruling that the procedure violated the separation of powers concept. Writing for the 7-2 majority, Chief Justice Burger said that by "placing responsibility for execution (of the law) in the hands of an officer who is subject to removal only by itself, Congress in effect has retained control over the executive function. The Constitution does not admit such intrusion" (*Bowsher v. Synar, et al.,* Supreme Court of the United States, 7 July 1986).

The Court's ruling brought into play a backup provision included in the GRH bill. Under this provision, both houses of Congress had to enact a bill reducing spending to the targeted level and the President had to sign it. Vulnerable to delays and executive-legislative stalemate, the backup provision was replaced in 1987 by a new automatic sequestration process. In what has been called Gramm-Rudman-Hollings II, the director of OMB replaces the Comptroller General as they key figure in estimating the deficit and recommending where budget cuts will be required. The President then orders the reductions, without modification, to be made by the affected spending agencies.

The new procedure came into play on October 17, 1989. With the President and Congress unable to agree on how to meet the GRH-mandated deficit limit of $110 billion, the President ordered spending cuts of $16.1 billion for the 1990 fiscal year, then barely 2 weeks old. In accordance with terms of GRH, approximately one-half of the cuts were in defense spending and one-half came from domestic programs. With nearly two-thirds of government programs exempt from GRH cuts, the axe fell heavily on agencies with personnel-oriented budgets. But there was no panic. Most agency officials adopted a wait-and-see attitude, confident that a compromise would be worked out later.

THE FUTURE OF BUDGET REFORM

> The budget is a mythical beanbag. Congress votes mythical beans into it, and then tries
> to reach in and pull real beans out.—Will Rogers

Cynicism about the way governments finance their operations has provided a stimulus for and been a result of budget reform. Constantly disappointed by their efforts, reformers of the budget process reach back and try again. The latest reform, the Gramm-Rudman-Hollings effort to impose discipline on the budget process, provoked a tidal wave of skepticism. Rather than forcing budgetary actors to meet annual deficit targets, it quickly became "an excuse for accounting gimmickery and economic sophistry" (Gleckman, 1989). After witnessing the bookkeeping gymnastics and political brinksmanship associated with passage of the fiscal 1990 budget, one economist suggested that GRH be renamed the "Smoke and Mirrors Act" (Blinder, 1989).

Focusing reform efforts on the budget document and process may be aiming at the wrong target. If off-budget spending, the government's numerous credit activities, offsetting business-type revenues, and various forms of quasi-governmental spending mandated by statute are counted, probably more than one-half of public-purpose expenditure is not included in the budget. The federal budget, according to Michael Boskin (1982), is no longer a very comprehensive report or forecast of government involvement in the economy. Naomi Caiden (1987) has written that the federal budget has "lost credibility as a responsible document because of the quality of its figures." As for the annual budget process, about which so much fuss has been made, Caiden (1982) has declared it to be a "myth."

In spite of such concerns, or perhaps because of them, the calls for budget reform still echo across the fiscal landscape. Caiden (1981) has argued the case for yet another try at bringing the budget process into line with the nation's changing economic environment. Further, she suggests that the search for new approaches to budgeting is a task for each generation as it confronts changing economic and fiscal conditions.

The decade of the 1990s will undoubtedly see continued and renewed efforts at budgetary innovation. As in the past, most will likely be aimed at finding technical and procedural—not policy—solutions. Already on the table for discussion are such reforms as a 2-year federal budget cycle, multiple budgets to accommodate different categories of decisions, the incorporation of strategic planning techniques into a multiyear budgeting cycle, a single budget committee to replace the separate House and Senate committees, and—of course—an item veto for the President (McCaffery, 1985; McLain, 1981). All of these, along with such concepts as envelope budgeting, target-based budgeting, revenue budgeting, and others still in the gestation stage, can be expected to occupy the debate over managing the nation's finances into the twenty-first century.

REFERENCES

Anthony, R. N. (1965). *Planning and Control Systems: A Framework for Analysis.* Harvard University, Graduate School of Business Administration, Boston.

Anthony, R. N. (1977). Zero-base budgeting is a fraud. *The Wall Street Journal* (27 April), reprinted in Mikesell, John L., *Fiscal Administration*, 2nd ed., The Dorsey Press, Chicago (1986).

Axelrod, D. (1989). *A Budget Quartet: Critical Policy and Management Issues.* St. Martin's Press, New York.

Berman, L. (1979). *The Office of Management and Budget and the Presidency, 1921–1979.* Princeton University Press, Princeton, N.J.

Binford, C. W. (1972). Reflections on the performance budget: Past, present and future. *Governmental Finance* 1:30–32.

Blinder, A. S. (1989). Getting back to the spirit of Gramm-Rudman. *Business Week* 3131:16.

Boskin, M. J. (1982). Macroeconomic versus microeconomic issues in the federal budget. In *The Federal Budget: Economics and Politics*, Michael J. Boskin and Aaron Wildavsky (eds.), Institute for Contemporary Studies, San Francisco.

Brady, R. H. (1973). MBO goes to work in the public sector. *Harvard Business Review* 51:65–74.

Buck, A. E. (1929). *Public Budgeting.* Harper & Brothers, New York.

Buck, A. E. (1934). *The Budget in Governments of Today.* Macmillan, New York.

Burkhead, J. (1956). *Government Budgeting.* John Wiley & Sons, New York.

Caiden, N. (1981). Public budgeting amidst uncertainty and instability. *Public Budgeting and Finance* 1:6–19.

Caiden, N. (1982). The myth of the annual budget. *Public Administration Review* 42:516–523.

Caiden, N. (1987). Paradox, ambiguity, and enigma: The strange case of the executive budget and the U.S. Constitution. *Public Administration Review* 47:84–92.

Carter, J. (1977). Jimmy Carter tells why he will use zero-base budgeting. *Nation's Business* 65:24–26.

Chandler, R. C. (ed.). (1987). *A Centennial History of the American Administration State.* Free Press, New York.

Cleveland, F. A., and Buck, A. E. (1920). *The Budget and Responsible Government.* Macmillan, New York.

Collender, S. E. (1989). *The Guide to the Federal Budget: Fiscal 1990.* The Urban Institute Press, Washington, D.C.

Commission on Organization of the Executive Branch of Government. (1949). *Budgeting and Accounting.* U.S. Government Printing Office, Washington, D.C.

Cranford, J. (1989). *Budgeting for America.* Congressional Quarterly, Inc., Washington, D.C.

Daley, D. M. (1985). Control, management, and planning: A state-level replication of the Friedman Study of Budget Practices. *International Journal of Public Administration* 7:291–304.

DeWoolfson, B. H. (1975). Public sector MBO and PPB: Cross fertilization in management systems. *Public Administration Review* 35:387–395.

Eghtedari, A., and Sherwood, F. (1960). Performance budgeting: Has the theory worked? *Public Administration Review* 30:63–85.

Fisher, L. (1975). *Presidential Spending Power.* Princeton University Press, Princeton, N.J.

Foster, M. (ed.). (1985). *The Greener Side of Air Force Blue.* Air University, Maxwell Air Force Base, Ala.

Friedman, L. (1975). Control, management, and planning: An empirical examination. *Public Administration Review* 35:625–628.

Gleckman, H. (1989). The bottom line: Gramm-Rudman isn't working. *Business Week* 3099:36.

Golembiewski, R. T., and Scott, P. (1989). A micro-political perspective on rational budgeting: A conjectural footnote on the dissemination of PPBS. *Public Budgeting and Financial Management* 1:327–370.

Gross, B. M. (1969). The new systems budgeting. *Public Administration Review* 29:113–137.

Harris, J. P. (1952). Needed reforms in the federal budget system. *Public Administration Review* 12:242–250.

Hyde, A. C., and Shafritz, J. M. (eds.). (1978). *Government Budgeting: Theory, Process, Politics.* Moore Publishing, Oak Park, Ill.

ICMA. (1981). *Management Policies in Local Government Finance.* J. Richard Aronson and Eli Schwartz (eds.), International City Management Association, Washington, D.C.

Ippolito, D. S. (1978). *The Budget and National Politics.* W. H. Freeman, San Francisco.

Jernberg, J. E. (1969). Information change and congressional behavior: A caveat for PPB reformers. *Journal of Politics* 35:722–740.

Jones, R. H. (1969). Program budgeting: Fiscal facts and federal fancy. *Quarterly Journal of Economics and Business* 9:45–57.

Key, V. O. (1940). The lack of a budgetary theory. *American Political Science Review* 34:1137–1144.

Kimmel, L. H. (1959). *Federal Budget and Fiscal Policy, 1789–1958.* The Brookings Institution, Washington, D.C.

Kramer, F. A. (ed.). (1979). *Contemporary Approaches to Public Budgeting.* Winthrop Publishers, Cambridge, Mass.

LaFaver, J. D. (1974). Zero-base budgeting in New Mexico. *State Government* 47:108–112.

Lauth, T. P. (1978). Zero-base budgeting in Georgia state government: Myth and reality. *Public Administration Review* 38:420–428.

Lawton, F. J. (1953). Legislative-executive relationships in budgeting as viewed by the executive. *Public Administration Review* 13:169–176.

LeLoup, L. T. (1980). *Budgetary Politics,* 2nd ed. King's Court Communications, Brunswick, Ohio.

Lewis, V. B. (1952). Toward a theory of budgeting. *Public Administration Review* 12:42–54.

Lindblom, C. E. (1959). The science of muddling through. *Public Administration Review* 19:79–88.

Lindblom, C. E. (1979). Still muddling, not yet through. *Public Administration Review* 39:517–526.

Lynch, T. D. (1990). *Public Budgeting in America,* 3rd ed. Prentice-Hall, Englewood Cliffs, N.J.

McCaffery, J. (1976). MBO and the federal budgetary process. *Public Administration Review* 36:33–39.

McCaffery, J. (1985). Budget reform: The path to reform of process. *International Journal of Public Administration* 7:403–423.

McLain, L. F. (1981). How strategic planning can help put budgeting in perspective. *Governmental Finance* 10:35–40.

Mikesell, J. L. (1986). *Fiscal Administration: Analysis and Applications for the Public Sector*, 2nd ed. Dorsey Press, Chicago.

Neustadt, R. E. (1954), Presidency and legislation: The growth of central clearance. *American Political Science Review* 48:641–671.

Novick, D. (1968). The origin and history of program budgeting. In *Government Budgeting: Theory, Process, Politics*, A. C. Hyde and J. M. Shafritz (eds.), Moore Publishing, Oak Park, Ill.

Novick, D. (1973). *Current Practice in Program Budgeting (PPBS)*. The Rand Corp. Crane, Russak and Company, New York.

Novick, D. (1979). What program budgeting is and is not. In *Contemporary Approaches to Public Budgeting*, Fred A. Kramer (ed.), Winthrop Publishers, Cambridge, Mass.

Office of Management and Budget (1977–1989). *United States Budget in Brief*. (Annual.) U.S. Government Printing Office, Washington, D.C.

Peters, B. G. (1988). *Comparing Public Bureaucracies: Problems of Theory and Method*. University of Alabama Press, Tuscaloosa, Ala.

Pfiffner, J. P. (1979). *The President, the Budget, and Congress: Impoundment and the 1974 Budget Act*. Westview Press, Boulder, Colo.

Pitsvada, B. T., and Draper, F. D. (1989). Is it time for a new executive budget system? *Federal Management* 2:5–9.

Pyhrr, P. A. (1977). The zero-base approach to government budgeting. *Public Administration Review* 37:1–8.

Rose, R. (1977). Implementation and evaporation: The record of MBO. *Public Administration Review* 37:64–71.

Savage, J. D. (1988). *Balanced Budgets and American Politics*. Cornell University Press, Ithaca, N.Y.

Savas, E. S. (1979). How much do government services really cost? *Urban Affairs Quarterly* 15:23–42.

Scheiring, M. J. (1976). Zero-base budgeting in New Jersey. *State Government* 49:174–179.

Schick, A. (1964). Control patterns in state budget execution. *Public Administration Review* 24:97–106.

Schick, A. (1966). The road to PPB: The stages of budget reform. *Public Administration Review* 26:243–258.

Schick, A. (1973). A death in the bureaucracy: The demise of federal PPB. *Public Administration Review* 33:146–156.

Schick, A., and Keith, R. (1976). *Zero-Base Budgeting in the States*. Congressional Research Service, Washington, D.C.

Schick, A. (1978). The road from ZBB. *Public Administration Review* 38:177–180.

Seckler-Hudson, C. (1953). Performance budgeting in government. *Advanced Management* 18:4–9, 30–32.

Selko, D. T. (1940). *The Federal Financial System*. The Brookings Institution, Washington, D.C.

Sherwood, F. (1954). Some non-cost accounting approaches to performance budgeting. *Public Management* 36:9–12.

Shuman, H. E. (1988). *Politics and the Budget: The Struggle Between the President and the Congress*. Prentice-Hall, Englewood Cliffs, N.J.

Smith, H. D. (1945). *The Management of Your Government*. McGraw-Hill, New York.

Smith, L. L. (1977). The congressional budget process: Why it worked this time. *The Bureaucrat* 6:88–111.

Smithies, A. (1955). *The Budgetary Process in the United States*. McGraw-Hill, New York.

Sorensen, T. C. (1963). *Decision-Making in the White House*. Columbia University Press, New York.

Starling, G. (1979). *The Politics and Economics of Public Policy*. Dorsey Press, Homewood, Ill.

U.S. Bureau of the Census. (1949). *Historical Statistics of the United States, 1789–1945*. Department of Commerce, Washington, D.C.

U.S. Congress, Senate Committee on Government Operations. (1977). *Compendium of Materials on Zero-Base Budgeting in the States*. 95th Congress, First Session.

Waldo, D. (1948). *The Administrative State*. Ronald Press, New York.

Wallace, R. A. (1959). Congressional control of the budget. *Midwest Journal of Political Science* 3:151–167.

Waltman, J. L. (1985). *Political Origins of the U.S. Income Tax*. University Press of Mississippi, Jackson, Miss.

Wanat, J. (1978). *Introduction to Budgeting*. Duxbury Press, North Scituate, Mass.

White, M. J. (1982). The impact of management science on political decision making. In *Public Budgeting: Program Planning and Implementation,* F. J. Lyden and E. G. Miller (eds.), Prentice-Hall, Englewood, N.J.

Wildavsky, A. (1966). The political economy of efficiency: Cost-benefit analysis, systems analysis, and program budgeting. *Public Administration Review* 26:292–310.

Wildavsky, A. (1969). Rescuing policy analysis from PPBS. *Public Administration Review* 29:189–202.

Wildavsky, A. (1981). Budgetary reform in an age of big government. In *Contemporary Public Administration,* T. Vocino and J. Rabin (eds.), Harcourt Brace Jovanovich, New York.

Wildavsky, A. (1984). *The Politics of the Budgetary Process,* 4th ed. Little, Brown, Boston.

Wildavsky, A. (1989). The political economy of efficiency has not changed but the world has and so have I. *Public Budgeting and Financial Management* 1:43–53.

5

Comparative Government Budgeting

George M. Guess *School of Public Administration and Urban Studies, Georgia State University, Atlanta, Georgia, and International Monetary Fund, Washington, D. C.*

INTRODUCTION

The purpose of this chapter is to again examine the state of comparative public budgeting and suggest directions for future work. As an iterative process that should register constituent demands for public expenditure, subsidy, or tax expenditure, the budget process and its outcome as an approved and executed budget normally reflect the demands of powerful political constituents. To imagine, however, that changes in the structural mechanics of the process alone will change policy priorities is to expect the tail to wag the dog. The budget process may simply process demands generated elsewhere in the political system. Nevertheless, a budget process that consistently generates fiscal information, analysis, and policy priorities contrary to societal need will do so at the cost of ineffective policy results and inefficient expenditure patterns.

Hence, to compare formal budget structures and processes that have little connection with actual policy formulation or execution might be an interesting intellectual exercise. But analyses are needed that first link budgeting with both management practices and policy results, and then compare them to other systems. Such efforts can contribute to theory building by testing hypotheses cross-culturally, provide policy relevant lessons to practitioners, and enhance the role of the budget process in determination and implementation of better public policies.

To a large extent, the field of comparative public budgeting is advancing in narrow conceptual steps that tend to be severed from the larger need to guide and influence policymaking by providing useful information on fiscal and programmatic effects of alternative expenditures. This is due, in part, to the research difficulty of developing data to infer such linkages where institutionally none exists. But the insensitivity of policymakers to empirically backed recommendations for budgetary change is also due to the divergence between the need for political leaders to maximize their political fortunes in a few years and technocratic recommendations that may benefit the public welfare in many years without incumbent credit.

To suggest that the current crop of research questions is excessively narrow or technocratic is paradoxical given the fact that in the first edition of this book it was noted that the field of comparative government budgeting "is not a fertile source of tested hypotheses" (Guess, 1983, p. 161). Then it was also noted that *Public Administration Review* (International Budget Studies Section, 1950), the United Nations (1979), and the

U.S. General Accounting Office (1979) had all called for more comparative budgeting research. The paradox is that while more comparative hypotheses are being tested by researchers, the results of the research often do not penetrate the routines of government. Conversely, more individualized technical assistance missions and closed, face-to-face conferences seem to be producing more transfers of technology with efforts to link budgeting and policy results.

This chapter will reiterate the need for comparative research and suggest why we may be at an impasse if we expect more than gratuitous comparisons of tools and techniques that policymakers can either leave or take off the shelf. Most political cultures inhibit the production and free use of such information by budget practitioners or the public. Nevertheless, it will be demonstrated that international work continues in (1) refinement of comparative typologies, (2) case study research, and (3) comparative budgetary processes and practices. While comparative budgetary work continues in the United States focusing on states, local governments, and agencies, the emphasis of this chapter will be limited to international cases and comparative analysis.

Despite the need for further international comparative work (doctoral students, postdoctoral students, private consultants, and technical assistance missions provide most of the information), the difficulties of conducting comparative budgetary research, as well as policymaker tendencies to ignore its more valid and reliable results, will place real limits on substantive research in this area for the foreseeable future. These limitations will be examined in the final section of the chapter. Finally, it will be argued that the solution to the research constraint of distrust inherent in professionally weak and resource-poor governments is enhancement of political and financial support for comparative budgetary and policy research, training, and technology-sharing efforts.

CONSTRAINTS AND OPPORTUNITIES FOR COMPARATIVE RESEARCH

Despite the formidable constraints to the conduct of research and use of results, opportunities for improvement of budgetary and policy results may lie in more marginal informational exchanges among counterpart fiscal administrators. Comparative research is still needed to provide policy-relevant lessons tested in more than one setting. Such analyses provide receptive decision makers with more substantive and profound evidence that the technique they are about to employ or the expenditure they advocate will actually perform the expected results in a variety of conditions. Even without empirically grounded comparative research, policymakers often make gratuitous comparative statements that border on misrepresentation. The establishment of a quality in A by misrepresenting B is an example of the "fallacy of appositive proof" (Fischer, 1970, pp. 56–58). For example, a false comparison between the performance of zero-based budgeting (ZBB) in the U.S. government, and Dade County (Fla.) would allow one to conclude that alternatives analysis budgeting would not improve the efficiency and effectiveness of expenditures in Dade County. To prevent such false comparisons, comprehensive comparative budgetary research should be used to test the conditions that make for favorable and unfavorable ZBB results at the county level of government. This would produce results "not for the prescription of the single best budgeting system or blueprint of practices to be adopted by all countries" but for individual country reflection on their own practices "in the light of issues discussed and other countries experiences" [Organisation for Economic Co-Operation and Development (OECD), 1987, p. 7].

Currently, the field of budgeting is technocratically a science but prescriptively an art. The limitation on moving from art to science are practitioner-relevant propositions for solutions to budgetary problems that have been tested in comparative settings. For example, we are painfully aware of technical problems in classification of and establishment of costs (by object of expenditure or activity, by fixed, variable and semivariable category), establishment of nonpersonnel costs, prevention of budgetary games like shifting expenditures from operating to capital budgets, managing budget execution and interpreting variance analysis, preventing deceptive earmarking and off-budget shifts, and designing the best budget process for getting timely legislative-executive approval (Mikesell, 1986). We also know that the skills of accounting, auditing, planning, and management are all required for good fiscal administration and budgeting.

But public budgeting tends to lack established comparative principles that could serve as practitioner guidelines. Research tends to gloss over what is not known about the performance of tools and techniques in a variety of settings. It may be instructive to note the comparative example of the field of psychiatry as it attempts for the first time to indicate to its practitioners (including consultants, students, academics, and patients) which therapeutic techniques are most effective in treating which illnesses. In an effort not unlike this handbook, an American Psychiatric Association (APA) task-force report *(Treatments of Psychiatric Disorders)* will review various therapies tried and results obtained, present pertinent details from deviant cases, and then discuss which treatments might be considered effective under what circumstances (Alper, 1989, p. 26). With 450 varieties of psychotherapy, and over 200 recognized psychiatric disorders, authors of the report believe that psychiatry is enough of a science to warrant development of guidelines on which therapies are most effective.

Instructive for comparative budgetary research efforts to accomplish similar ends, opponents of the effort to raise diagnostic issues and synthesize results argue that psychiatry is still an art, largely based on treating individuals through interaction with the therapist. Clinical studies that are catalogued in the report are population-based and therefore more variable than medical maladies (Alper, 1989, p. 27). Opponents also fear that the report may be misused, depriving therapists of business, and producing litigation from patients that will now have an authoritative checklist of standards against which to measure psychiatric treatments. The APA-approved report will likely narrow the range of debate and stimulate discussion around finer points of controversy.

While such synthetic efforts are needed in comparative budgeting, the field is constrained by the opposite problem of application of techniques to group contexts (an iterative budget process influenced by groups of varying power). Comparative research presumes that individual and institutional forces can be isolated and measured. Variable influence can then be documented for specific conditions that should serve as a precedent for application elsewhere. But budgets are processed through competing institutions led by managers with personal agendas that often change jobs. Hence, institutional application would be limited by individual and chronological differences. Managers are keenly aware of these problems that derive largely from the need for administrative survival. Thus, managers may observe comparative results and pay lip service but implicitly conclude that "we are unique" and thus should not risk changes recommended by comparative research.

Similarly, policymakers may conclude personally that given managerial instability and their own tendencies to interfere (earmarks, reorganizations, budget transfers), any changes recommended to improve matters might make them worse. Hirschman (1989, p. 64) documents the "perverse effect" thesis that has been historically used by reactionaries and those whose power would be threatened to derail policy changes based on the presumption that coordinated actions by governmental institutions could improve social welfare. Opponents of "rational" (based on calculated costs and benefits) programs, such as minimum wage laws, maximum food prices, or budget processes that could improve policy effectiveness, challenge the "fallacy of composition" (Hirschman, 1989, p. 68) that groups and individuals behave similarly, and argue that groups are unable to weigh pros and cons. But clearly individuals are not always rational and groups irrational, leading always to perverse policy effects. Policy actions are often coordinated and achieve substantially desired results with benefits to social welfare. The question is, how can comparative knowledge be systematically developed and used to guide public resource allocation and to improve policy?

Current technical assistance efforts in "comparative budgeting" that capitalize on the dynamics of group-individual interaction may be the best way to stimulate valid comparisons of experiences and provide incentives for their application in new settings. It should also be noted that efforts producing comparative budgetary insights may flow not from any direct research in a field called "comparative public budgeting" but may derive from exchanges on related subjects of "fiscal administration" or "improvement of the administration of public resources." At the 1988 USAID-Price Waterhouse (USAID/PW) symposium on "Improving the Administration of Public Resources in Latin America," for example, the original 1979 GAO report (now in Spanish) calling for more research and training in public financial management was redistributed to participants from all Latin countries receiving U.S. foreign aid.

Working groups were initially afraid to reveal home-country problems in budget administration, such as failure to integrate accounting and budgeting systems, or difficulties in the evaluation of budget execution, such as absence of parameters for measuring performance. They were also reluctant to deal with the practice that evaluation and control should be done exclusively by the central budget office (USAID/PW, 1989, p. 9). But after several days of interaction between budget practitioners, observers, and USAID officials, recognition of common problems emerged and the "dirty laundry" came out. Evidence of weak data bases, formalistic and contradictory tax and financial management codes, and distrust among institutions often staffed by unprofessional appointees pointed to severe constraints for both operations and research. But the working group experience, including many solid recommendations, suggested that the way to generate information and its substantive use was not to encourage wider dissemination of more research and consultant reports. Rather, the most appropriate way to achieve results might be closed working group sessions among counterpart practitioners. Such sessions might also be logically prior to substantive research in contexts of high mutual distrust.

REVIEW OF COMPARATIVE BUDGETARY LITERATURE

Nevertheless, it was noted that by 1983 "a spate of international budgetary studies began to appear as never before in the history of comparative public administration" (Guess, 1989, p. 492). Despite the outpouring of mostly case studies, few advances have been made in theory, and many of the comparative studies remain formalistic and unlikely to be of use to consultants, budget practitioners, academics, or serious students. In this section, we review the strengths and weaknesses of efforts to (1) construct typologies and build theories, (2) produce case studies, and (3) perform comparative research of budget processes and expenditure results. In this brief review, we move beyond that examined in the first edition of this handbook, from approximately 1980 to the present.

Theories and Typologies

Since 1980, one finds fewer attempts by public administration scholars to develop new theories or typologies applicable to comparative budgetary analysis. Instead, greater emphasis has been placed on refinement of older "functionalist" perspectives. The current effort is to describe and compare the effect of functions, techniques or tools, and budget formats on expenditure efficiency and policy or program effectiveness. It should be stressed that such efforts are largely formalistic, and heavily reliant on the premise that the classical budget process, that is, general fund expenditures by agencies controlled by audits, is still extant and largely determines both expenditure and policy results. Efforts to build theory from such an obsolete conceptual base are unlikely to produce a relevant set of lessons for practitioners and scholars.

Without a guiding framework that can link budgetary inputs and outputs under varying conditions, policymakers and budget practitioners tend to make "seat-of-the-pants" judgments that may form significant patterns over time. Despite practitioner rejection of this possibility (they frequently suggest that case-by-case is reality and "patterns" fall into the realm of academic theory), policymakers tend to use unconscious models to guide their budgeting anyway. The classical framework is "functionalist" or the "tool orientation," which presumes better performance of specific methods and tools results in better budgetary performance. The "functional format emphasis" (Guess, 1983, pp. 173–178), for example, presumed that emphasis of budget formats (control, management, planning) would vary with sophistication of decision-maker needs and aspirations.

Comparative research could then uncover the actual determinants of functional format mixes in particular settings. The tendency to emphasize control over planning (object of expenditure format versus program or alternatives analysis format) would then be explicable by such demographic variables as the degree of "poverty and uncertainty" (Caiden and Wildavsky, 1974). For example, Wildavsky (1986, p. 16) argues that wealth and predictability enable budgets to be developed through guardian-spender conflict using incremental analysis from an agreed-upon base as an aid to calculation, with commitments kept by key actors. Conversely, poor countries engage in "repetitive budgeting" to compensate for distrust, lack of complex redundancy, or back-up duplication of resources. Poor countries paradoxically are more control-oriented, emphasizing cash-flow or revenue budgeting (like many U.S. cities), but spend substantial resources and time planning for the future (evident in the program budget formats in place in many poor countries).

As noted by Cutt (1983, p. 9), "Budgeting is a basic component of the public management cycle, and as part of that cycle, is linked formally or informally back to policy making . . . and forward through the stage of implementation of budgetary decisions. . . ." But at least two problems exist with current attempts to link demographic variables, such as poverty and uncertainty, to inputs and outputs of the budget process. First, it is a methodological long-shot from such broader, unspecified explanatory variables as "class influence," "regime accountability," and "organizational capability" (Guess, 1983, p. 178) to variations in budget processes and outputs. Despite skepticism of demographic and organizational approaches to budget research (Danziger, 1978), it is clear that some specification of the relationships between budgeting and the larger socioeconomic context is warranted. For example, it was recently noted that "Deficiency and disorder in managing government resources are vehicles which foster corruption, in turn fostering loss of confidence in democracy" (USAID/PW, 1989, p. 3). But the current fare of broad demographic variables cannot be rigorously linked to specific tools and processes that determine budgetary behavior in other than a general sense, that is, poor countries have poor management (inflexible controls), which produces poor budgets (inaccurate and incomprehensible), and poor policy results (more poverty). So what else is new?

The second problem relates to the inapplicability of solutions proposed based on use of broad demographic causal variables. Caiden (1985, p. 23), for instance, notes that "poverty and uncertainty appeared to result in a model of budgeting characterized by repetition and fragmentation, to which ideal prescriptions for reform seemed relatively inapplicable." From this analysis, the concept of "continuous budgeting" was proposed. Given that developing countries are subject to a high degree of uncertainty, annual budgets cannot incorporate reliable predictions. Hence, via continuous budgeting, annual budgeting should be deemphasized and departments allowed to request additions to annual spending rates at any time during the fiscal year.

But according to Goode (1984, p. 38) this "seems to retreat too far from the ideal of rational allocation of scarce resources among alternative uses. Continuous budgeting would repudiate comprehensive planning, would assign greater authority to the ministry of finance, and might well aggravate conflicts between the ministry of finance and spending departments." At the same time, proposals to enhance organizational "redundancy" as a cure for poverty to reduce budgetary fragmentation may only succeed in staffing up additional organizations that collude rather than compete. Such results would be unlikely to improve either budgeting or public policy effectiveness. Again, the causal variables that lead to these proposals are overbroad.

The classical model of comparative budgeting could then be summarized as a test of how far, why, and how successfully a budget system deviates from "incrementalism" or specialized analysis of parts of a budget to aid calculation and compensate for resource and time constraints. While Schick (1966, p. 50) suggested that all budget systems contain mixes of control, management, and planning functions, many comparativists presumed a normative evolution from control to planning as an important feature of development. This perspective also ignored the fragmentation of the general fund budget into varieties of specialized off-budget tools such as direct loans, some of which may contribute to or detract from control, and others of which may contribute to management or planning. As many wealthy countries suddenly began to budget repetitively out of cultural preference for egalitarianism (Wildvasky, 1986, p. 25), it became evident that the theoretical emphasis on reasons for deviations from incrementalism might not have been the appropriate overriding research questions for this field.

The academic obsession with confirming or rejecting alternative formats/decision processes to incrementalism largely continues to consume intellectual resources. While recognizing that incrementalism does not describe current budgeting in the United States or other wealthy nations, scholars such as Wildavsky still maintain that budget formats should not be reformed. "He argues that line item budgeting is a hardy perennial, the most adaptive form of budgeting, and that other forms of budgeting have been tried and failed" (Rubin, 1989, p. 79). Rubin suggests that the recognition that incrementalism is no longer descriptive with the argument that reforms are inappropriate is a contradiction.

However, it would seem that Wildavsky has always argued for formats that can be compared annually, provide comprehensive accounts of all expenditures, and lead to balance in the short run. Reforms that ignore these standards in favor of blue-sky planning would likely fail; reforms that link planning to rigorous accounting structures tend to succeed and would also limit the effects of poverty and uncertainty that derail any attempts to plan revenue and expenditures for the next year. For example, Wildavsky suggests that

> multiyear budgeting . . . a reform to enhance rational choice . . . would work well for certain parts of the budget like military procurements, which take years to complete. But benefits, salary and operating expense categories are ill-suited to long term budgeting. The size of these items is significantly influenced by external factors, such as inflation, that are difficult to predict. (1988, pp. 413–414)

Finally, the classical notion of budgeting is that the budget framework should produce a clear, comprehensive, annual specification of expenses and revenues and that incentives should be provided to direct individuals in agencies to work toward budgetary objectives and social interests (Mikesell, 1986, p. 140). Wolfson (1979, pp. 117–119) argues that program budget formats break up the tendency of "kleptocrats" (a unique synthesis of policymaking and kleptomaniac roles) to use the line-item format for self-promotion, and that it requires "enforced coordination" with others to identify budget choices. The question then is whether poor countries can gain more for budgetary results by stressing controls for incrementalism or by pushing for improvements in output information to feed back to policymakers. Both are normative emphases and need to be addressed by comparative researchers at the micro or "middle-range" level of utility for practitioners. The partial systems approach is needed to fill current information gaps "before we can subject general theoretical formulations to empirical confrontation" (LaPalombara, 1970, pp. 136–137).

Moving beyond the incrementalist debate then, the problems with current theories and typologies are more serious. We refer not to the expected charge that perspectives and typologies ignore the diversity of political cultures or misunderstand international differences. Such traditional charges are reflected, for instance, by Wildavsky's (1989) recent argument that new theories should include "ideological differences that affect management practice." Such charges ignore the real groundwork that needs to be done in many settings to improve information and reduce counterpart distrust. Such an emphasis would also move away from the practitioner need to develop workable processes and into the realm of high politics. This would likely reward endless debates on the effects of political culture on budgeting at the expense of deadlines. The problems of comparative budgeting are akin to those facing basic budget theory: their tenets and findings may have little to do with practice. The similarity of problems should not be surprising, for in a strict sense all social research is comparative in that cumulative advances in knowledge are made by application of associative evidence from other settings.

Two basic problems exist in budget theory, both of which relate to a formal-legal emphasis on tools and methods rather than on their substantive origins and impacts. First, which budget functions are the most critical to good budgeting? If this can be resolved, how do we know that better performance of those functions will lead to efficient expenditures and effective policies? The tendency toward "functional indispensability" in theory and practice, for example, is evident in the sacrosanct line-item format. But studies tend to examine the impacts of functional techniques, such as revenue estimation, as ends in themselves. This leads to "barefoot empiricism" or less theory and more method (Guess, 1983, p. 175). Similar to the problem of psychiatric theory and practice noted above, no theoretical guidance is available to indicate the conditions under which specific tools will lead to expected results. Further, better performance of specified functions may not aid in describing and comparing budget systems. Caiden (1985, p. 23) warns that use of normative models such as those leading to planning formats (program budgeting) may "divert attention from other salient features of the budget system." What this suggests is that a predominantly narrow functionalist emphasis tends to treat the budget system as a "static information system" (Caiden, 1985, p. 23), and this may be diverting attention from more important theoretical concerns.

Thus, the second problem is that theory has ignored the wider impact of tools and techniques on management issues and policy results. The budget process may not exclusively determine either efficient expenditures or effective policies. Conversely, the tools of fiscal administration require more than merely budgetary skills. This insight makes the debate over theoretical explanations of format reform even more marginal to real need. Such scholars as Salamon (1981) have recognized that policy actions are no longer described by discretion over direct or general fund budgetary expenditures. Federal action (as well as state-local and other-country public actions) now consist of multiple actions for problem-solving that may include such tools as loan guarantees, insurance, public enterprises, regulations, tax subsidies, and grants.

While such forms of action raise questions of policy coordination, management, and accountability (Salamon, 1981, p. 257), public administration theory has not responded. Research and theory stress agency budgeting and management accountability for control of their programs. But discretion over spending and use of Federal authority is now shared: managers are often held accountable for programs they do not control (1981, p. 259). According to Salamon (1989, p. 13), since public management has fundamentally changed with new forms of public action, new theories will be needed. "Instead of command and control, such theories will have to emphasize bargaining and persuasion. Instead of the clarification of directives, they will have to stress manipulation of incentives" (1989, p. 13). Since countries, states, and localities often use indirect forms of budgetary action, research is needed on the "political economies" (1989, p. 8) or the "distinctive network of organizational relationships" of each tool. If, with such common fiscal administration tools as grants and loans, the delegation of discretion over operation to nongovernmental third parties reflects the decline of direct government as an instrument of public action, then theories that debate agency efficiency with differing budget formats tend to be obsolete.

Case Studies

It was noted in the first edition that "case studies tend to stress single fiscal issues with marginal emphasis on budget processes" (Guess, 1983, p. 162). However, since that time, wider and more thorough studies of country budget processes have appeared (see for example Premchand and Burkhead, 1984). While in many cases, budget systems are recognized as "highly idiosyncratic" reflections of the "history, temperament, economic structure, and political institutions of a country" (Roberts, 1979, p. 18), other studies are formalistic, over-detailed, and of little use to either budget practitioners or policymakers. As indicated, comparative methods are often used even in case studies. Time-series data are often used, for example, to explain differences in budgeting or budget outcomes in single or multiple settings: both would be comparative. Similarly, competing institutional and demographic explanations might be used to explain differences in cross-sectional data. This also would be "comparative." The case studies reviewed here mostly employ comparative methods. It should also be evident that studies have evolved from emphases on budgetary reform (the incrementalist/rational comprehensive debate) and narrow formalistic analyses of budget rules and repertoires in earlier years, to more substantive comparisons of tools and techniques, with assessments of their wider policy implications. As in the case of comparative public administration generally, the field of comparative budgeting is being constructively fed from other disciplines such as economics and business (Guess, 1989, p. 493). This bodes well for the utility of future studies for decision makers as well as for the development of newer theories and methods.

As early as 1981, Premchand indicated skepticism of dichotomous distinctions between industrial and developing country budgeting. By then it was evident that, despite the inheritance by developing countries of industrial country budgetary systems, industrial countries often lacked budgetary stability, while poor countries in many instances demonstrated "functional complex redundancy" and other backup systems. The predominant theory of comparison (Caiden and Wildavsky, 1974) was already producing detailed answers to questionable inquiries for practitioners (Premchand, 1981, p. 17). Instead, Premchand recommended political actions to ensure better financial management. For example, he notes that efforts to control expenditures by agencies through constitutional limits will likely be self-defeating in that use of "escape mechanisms" will nullify their purpose and lead to the Latin American tendency toward executive "debudgetization" in response to legislative controls. He also suggests that the central problem of the 1980s would be to assure that budgets are implemented as formulated (1981, p. 24). That is, the reform issue has moved beyond traditional questions of "format" to the question of administrative and policy implications of efforts to control costs and expenditures.

A common cause stimulating budgetary case studies in the 1980s has been examination of public-sector responses to reduction of available resources. Budgetary inflexibility in the form of increasing uncontrollables for individual transfer payments, together with increased tax burdens, generated successful campaigns by many groups for limits on governmental activities. Many of the case studies of countries, states, and agencies examine how governments have responded to increasing fiscal constraints. Just as political repression often has a salutary effect on literary quality, fiscal scarcity may have had the same effect on generation of higher-quality comparative and case studies of budgeting.

In the United Kingdom as well as the United States and other industrial countries, the predominant ideological theme of the 1980s has been to cut public expenditures in order to cut borrowing, combat inflation, and generally reduce taxes. Public expenditures for such activities as "incomes policy" have been viewed as meddling with the free market and anathema to the passive notion of government as neutral referee. Ward (1982) documents the effect of the retreat from expenditure planning by Conservative government through strengthening of central Treasury controls on local government grants (paradoxically centralizing the public sector). Conservatives also replaced the system of allocating funds authorized by Parliament to departments for "volume plans" in constant prices. The new system imposes cash limits on volume plans with an allowance for inflation. If needed revenue exceeds the limits due to inflation, volume plans go unfulfilled. Such a system "makes effective planning virtually impossible and promotes long-term inefficiency in provision of public services" (1982, p. 41). What this suggests for practitioners is that changes in budgetary procedures that reflect an individualist economic ideology and politics may contribute more to budgetary instability in this industrialized country than any efforts to legislate "the passion for equality" (Wildavsky, 1986, p. 25).

At the same time, with reduction of central government financial support to local governments and increased public opposition to tax increases, ways must be found in the United Kingdom and elsewhere to improve the efficiency and effectiveness of public services. An interesting examination of the constraints and opportunities afforded by a tool that could lead to such results was conducted by Butt (1987) on the United Kingdom Local Government Finance Act of 1982. This provided for local municipal auditors to examine progress achieved toward "value for money" (VFM) or "securing economy, efficiency and effectiveness in the use of resources" (Butt, 1987, p. 5).

Most such audits are currently conducted on a consultancy basis by Price Water-house, U.K. For example, they found (applying VFM principles) that many budgets, such as those for water supply authorities, are "static" or not subject to dramatic changes in expenditures or revenues. They suggested that time could be better spent measuring ongoing productivity than stressing budgetary control of details. Auditors also recommended that annual budgeting be changed since the incentive has always been to spend year-end money on unnecessary projects. The budget process could encourage managers to benefit from savings by carrying forward unspent balances or allowing them to invest in items that could achieve greater productivity in the long term (1987, p. 9). However, Butt (1987) recognizes that the "ethos and culture of the public sector does not generally encourage a determined search for savings." With 60%–70% of all public sector costs in personnel, the obvious professional fear is that VFM audits could turn into a political search for overstaffing (1987, p. 10) by candidates seeking to capitalize on public support for a smaller public sector that will quickly produce more efficient and effective services.

In contrast with the "political economy" of tools approach used in the U.K. cases, many studies focus on formal-legal structures and overlook critical issues. Kunas (1982, p. 43), for example, describes Federal Republic of Germany budget reforms in 1969 that encouraged budgetary coordination, control, and planning. But after an extensively formalistic review of the budget process, no evidence of impact is cited. We learn, for example, that "Where the budget balance is disturbed or the whole economy takes a course different from that assumed during the preparation of the budget, prompt adaption of the fundamentals of the budget is called for" (1982, p. 52). We also learn that the budget balance is "disturbed when the foreseeable deficit is higher than authorized in the budget" (1982, p. 52). Such assertions hide more than they reveal and hardly form the basis for intelligent questions about the German budget process or its results. More importantly, with substantial available data on budget and policy activities in Germany, one could expect a more critical analysis of rules and repertoires.

By contrast, Korff (1983, p. 70) finds that budgetary rules and regulations in Germany "cannot substitute for an efficient financial policy by the elected government." Recognizing that the control and allocation functions of budgeting have taken second place to stabilization and growth, Korff questions whether the budget is even suitable for economic management (1983, p. 61). He finds the German budget unwieldy, with deficits caused by major expenditures for defense and social security (social transfer payments are also indexed to price increases). Thus, he argues that economic management has failed because of the inherent structure of the public budget in welfare states such as Germany. In addition to fixed and largely uncontrollable priorities, Korff notes that German budgets are much more detailed than budgets of other European countries with the exception of

Austria. While Parliament rarely concludes discussion of over 8000 items on time, it nevertheless "continues to insist on a detailed presentation of the budget" (1983, p. 65). The suggestion is that the system passively relies on budgetary control through general financial rules to make the hard choices that instead should be made by leaders actively demanding useful analytic information in specific policy areas.

Similarly, Barbieri and Monorchio (1982) examine the impact of the Italian budget process reform of 1978, which featured a new "financial law" to "guarantee overall coherence of spending in the public sector with economic conditions and national policy" (1982, p. 69), a new "multiyear budget," and a new "annual cash budget" (like the accrual method of accounting). Unfortunately, beyond a review of the legalities, the precise impact on "harmonization" of budgets is simply not evident from the case study. Further, a study of the Swedish budget process (Ysander and Robinson, 1982) notes that the high and growing degree of local government financial independence (45% of revenue from local taxes and only 25% from state grants, potentially reducing national leverage over local policies) is "one of the most striking features of the Swedish economy" (1982, p. 79). But how this came about or its budgetary implications are not spelled out. Ysander and Robinson also note that while the national government still classifies expenditures by ministries and agencies, state and local budgets have moved in the direction of "program budgeting" (1982, p. 81). But since most appropriations are still on an annual basis (1982, p. 81), it is unclear whether the format of programs and functions translates into incentives for comparing alternative means of attaining program objectives. Is this simply another case of form without incentive? Is this similar to the formal PPBS system (Planning-Programming-Budgeting System) of the Defense Department observed by Wildavsky (1988, p. 350) where each service is still not penalized for pushing its favorite program? Ysander makes no assessment of how program budgeting at the state and local level has worked.

By contrast, LeBlanc and Meys (1982) examine the Netherlands experience of attempting to control expenditures in the context of decreasing Dutch economic growth. It was found that methods such as PPB and ZBB made little difference to realistic cutbacks, while "multiyear budgeting" simply added to existing budget inflexibility (uncontrollables) by treating estimates to future funds as rights (1982, p. 60). Since in the Dutch political system the cabinet as a whole is responsible for size and composition of expenditures, the unlikelihood of consensus on cutbacks among 16 ministers makes it imperative that in the future the prime minister have greater authority over budgeting (1982, p. 64). The Netherlands case is interesting in that it demonstrates, among other items, how cutback principles get soiled in practice.

Due in part to the intellectual excitement of solving institutional puzzles in the complex, byzantine context of Latin American politics, case studies of public budgeting from this region are extremely realistic and intriguing. Formalistic studies ignoring political economy issues are quickly greeted with laughter if not contempt by practitioners. Given the formidable constraints to concerted institutional change (*gauchos,* for instance, gave little personal loyalty to institutions and fought instead for personal agendas or *personalismo*), they are of doubtful utility to most budget or policy practitioners. Nevertheless, such studies are read voraciously by senior administrators, almost as pulp, to find out what outsiders think is going on in the public sector. Such is the paradoxical theoretical value of practical comparative work!

An excellent example of the razor-sharp budgetary political economy work being done is that of Bird (1982) on Colombia. One could easily expect fiscal and political uncertainty to effect budgetary control of expenditures in a setting where 100,000 people have been killed (*La Violencia,* 1948–1951) and with the more individualized violence *(sicarios)* surrounding today's cocaine trade. Colombia has the highest murder rate in the world for a country not at war (10 people/day in Medellin) (Rosenberg, 1988, p. 22). In that much of this violence has been directed at the judicial system and in that expenditures require legal audits, one could expect certain constraints to coherent public budgeting and control.

Working backward from the recommendations, it becomes evident that the tight linkage of public budgeting and policymaking results means that reform of the latter system may be required before the former can function properly. The present budget system, a conventional product of a 1923 technical assistance mission, is now a public administration-dominated system that pursues control at the expense of efficiency (Bird, 1982, p. 88). Bird recommends that loosening of controls to end peculation, fraud, and political abuse could reduce the widespread earmarking and decentralization to escape controls that fragment policymaking. Excessive cross-checking and multiple signature requirements to compensate for distrust and fiscal uncertainty hamper the orderly execution of programs. Further, "the attempt to control everything, in addition to raising transaction costs substantially, results in a such a superficial level of control that nothing in fact is really controlled at all" (Bird, 1982, p. 93). Bird also found that a law artificially restricted revenue estimates to a 10% increase over the previous year. Given the tendency toward "repetitive budgeting" because of resource uncertainty, the restriction on the use of appropriate revenue estimation techniques simply exacerbates the attempt to realistically balance revenues and expenditures (also required by law).

Finally, instead of allowing "continuous budgeting" (Caiden and Wildavsky, 1974, p. 315), Bird recommends a limited number of revisions throughout the fiscal year subjected to the same scrutiny at the preparation stage as the initial budget (Bird, 1982, p. 95). He notes that many of the budgetary techniques in use serve the purposes of powerful interest groups that are far from the interests of society as a whole (1982, p. 97). In short, Bird indicates that for the budgetary process to serve developmental objectives, it must be converted from an obstacle to an opportunity by "incremental but substantive reforms" as those noted. This conclusion is reached by careful analysis of the impact of tools, such as revenue forecasting, and their current prohibition by law.

By 1983, more profound research began to appear on the impact of "radical changes" in the institutional and policy settings in which policymakers and budgeters had been working (Premchand, 1983, p. 5). For instance, Cutt (1983) compared Australian (state and commonwealth) experiences with attempts to modify the Westminister model (featuring executive secrecy about line-item negotiations between departments and treasury) in the 1970s. The 5-Year Rolling Programme (FYRP) budget required functional classifications in departments such as Defence and the Post Office.

But the marginal impact of the Australian program budgeting system is indicated by the fact that for the bulk of expenditures, supporting analysis emphasized financial accounting and extrapolation of line-items. Only for new starts did the budget system require "detailed analysis of a consequential nature, exploring questions of cost, benefit, or effectiveness and distributional implications" (Cutt, 1983, p. 15). Program analysis information was also internal to the treasury and the proposing department and not published in the budget papers for Parliament. Cutt also noted that while the functional classification concept was important, the categories were established by the treasury and had little operational meaning for the departments (1983, p. 16). Analysis was considered supplemental to that required by the traditional appropriation form. Though the practical benefits in the Australian institutional context are unclear, currently the commonwealth is debating whether to require parliamentary appropriation bills in program format. It was also noted that analysis varied widely in quality among departments (1983, p. 15), though no reasons are advanced for this variation. Nor is it evident whether departments actually based expenditure proposals on the results of comparisons of costs and benefits by function. From this largely formalistic analysis, one cannot conclude if program budgeting should be continued in Australia and tried in similar institutional settings.

In a similar formal-legal analysis of the impact of 1969 Malaysian PPBS reforms recommended by American consultants, Doh (1984) argues that "Under the stimulus of PPB, budget documents have become a more relevant source of information, the Treasury has become more development-oriented, the annual budget dialogue between the Treasury and the operating agencies has become more meaningful" (1984, p. 74). But if this PPB experience has been so successful, the question is why and how? Other than describing PPB procedures and Malaysian economic results, no empirical evidence is cited for such a causal connection.

By contrast, Doern (1983) examines the "political economy" of "envelope budgeting" in Canada. For instance, he ties "Neo-Conservative beliefs" that the government lacked discipline, spending was out of control, and excess spending was itself the "major cause of inflation and the growing economic malaise of the late 1970s and early 1980s" (1983, p. 39) to the new budget structure, which assigned blocks of expenditures to different cabinet committees with 5-year ceilings in 1979. The ministers produce "priority allocations" at high levels of aggregation expressed as 5-year percentage increases/ decreases for each envelope. If the targets are set and held, the system exercises control.

But the system could not tell cabinet committees what criteria should govern resource allocation or how to set priorities within an envelope. While each envelope was supposed to be a "supermarket of policy instruments" (Doern, 1983, p. 44), no evidence of incentives to generate or use alternative policy techniques is advanced. Further, a major purpose of the reform was to integrate policy and expenditure decision making to ensure full consideration of cost implications and ministerial responsibility. Nevertheless, a major failing of the system, as noted by the case study, was precisely its inability to relate policies to resources. Specifically, the artificially restrictive envelope structure encouraged budget practitioners to underestimate tax revenues, which provided "unexpected" extra revenues at the end of the fiscal year (1983, p. 39). This stimulated a scramble for funds, and allowed for additional expenditures without creating deficits.

Again, budgetary case studies continue to vary by quality of technique and tool analysis. Weaker ones place narrow emphasis on formal-legal structures, a problem noted with many comparative analyses by Bill and Hardgrave (1973, pp. 3–7). Yoingco and Guevara (1984, p. 112), for instance, describe performance review in the Philippines with the Management Audit and Improvement Program (MAIP). There, each ministry identifies performance indicators and defines target levels of accomplishment. But no indication is given on the problems leading to this system, how it functions, or whether its information is fed back into the preparation stage of the next fiscal year budget. That is, the entire political economy of the origins and impact of this tool is missing.

By contrast, more profound analyses treat rules and regulations largely as superstructure. According to Korff (1983, p. 70):

> The quality of budgeting is a foremost political problem that requires continual decisions in regard to actual claims, foresight on economic growth or decline, and a

balance between stability and inflationary trends. Effective budget regulations plan an important role, but they are comparable in the field of music to a fine quality piano which is of little use without a musician who is able and willing to play it.

It should be emphasized that the difference between the profound and superficial analysis may not be the quality of analyst alone. As will be indicated in the final section, the questions that can be effectively raised and answered depend substantially upon data availability on the public sector and budgeting in the host country. Such availability varies widely.

In addition to the impact of reforms on budgeting and policy, an emerging issue by 1983 was the cost and benefit of public-sector efforts to control budget deficits. Blondal (1983), for instance, describes a common fiscal policy attitude to balance the budget shared by all Icelandic political parties derived from the nineteenth century legacy of farming, which held that only balanced government and individual financial positions could be sound. Based on the strength of this cultural attitude, the Icelandic public sector has grown only 2.0% (the lowest among OECD countries, 1972–1980) and its deficits have been low (usually less than 1.0% of GNP and occasionally in surplus).

It is immediately evident that the Icelandic public sector is highly centralized (the central government accounts for 77% of revenues and expenditures), and that roughly 70% of the budget is uncontrollable (Blondal, 1983, p. 58). The Ministry of Finance keeps tight controls on requests for permanent staff additions, and also imposes spending limits on the agencies. At the same time, the rigidly centralized system designed to defensively guard against deficits tends to ignore the cost implications of the growing health and social security sectors. This state of affairs contrasts sharply with Irish budgetary behavior. There, efforts to control deficits through Department of Finance controls over departments were relaxed about 1958 as "departments were encouraged to think of themselves as development corporations" (Doyle, 1983, p. 75). Under this view, departments would not simply administer the country but develop it as well, with aggressive public expenditures. It is thus evident that achievement of improved budgetary balance will require "some reversal of decentralization of public expenditure control" (1983, p. 76).

In contrast to Irish revenue diversity (including access to the EEC budget for agricultural price supports), the entire Icelandic budget process and economy is driven by ad valorem revenues (imports and property). This revenue source is extremely responsive but can produce wide fluctuations in the budget position. Given the small size of the economy, the inflexibility of the budget process in the context of inflation (monetary policy accommodating increasing private sector wages) could become problematic when individual transfer payment increases clash with the cultural preference for balanced budgets.

By 1985, the bulk of national budgetary case studies clearly focused on political economy of budgeting and budget tools. Following in the "new realism" of Bird (1982) noted above, for example, Bailey (1984) traces (1) the legal and institutional bases of Mexican budgeting, specifically the influence of the revolution of 1910–1917, which gave rise to liberalism, nationalism, and socialism, (2) the rapid growth of the public sector with bureaucratic and technical problems encountered in the effort by President Lopez Portillo to introduce PPBS in 1977, and (3) the impact of the economic austerity program on both structures such as the Secretariat of Programming and Budget (SPP) and challenges to statist approaches to development caused by high inflation, low real growth rates, and regional public cynicism about central government in Mexico City.

A major technical problem with PPB, for instance, was reorganizing accounting data from traditional notions of branch, chapter, and item to PPB notions of program and subprogram (Bailey, 1984, p. 88). But even predictable implementation problems may have been less important than the evidence that better information alone could not have penetrated the bureaucratic labyrinths of SPP nor affected the priorities of other monoliths such as PEMEX in a vast public sector comprising 42% of gross domestic product (GDP) (1981) of which 46% was spent by nearly 700 "parastatals" (1984, p. 80). Only a thorough analysis of the political forces working on budget routines and repertoires, and probable economic impacts of particular techniques, can provide receptive policymakers with useful information. While the Bailey analysis provides such insights, it properly raises the question of the receptivity of decision makers to macroanalytic information where authoritarian internal routines provide disincentives to take risks.

Many of the case assessments of PPBS failure recount similar bureaucratic and technical problems in formulating program structures and implementing program (often accrual) accounting systems. But more recent cases, such as Dean (1986) on Sri Lanka, raise basic questions about the utility of PPB even for reformers. Following a substantive analysis of the technical origins and bureaucratic and political impacts of the PPBS tool in Sri Lanka, Dean questions whether PPBS is the most appropriate tool for bringing about reform in government financial management. He suggests (1986, p. 73) that PPB (1) encourages the myth that resource allocation decisions should be taken solely on efficiency criteria (rather than public service as the bottom line), (2) often cannot produce an evaluative criterion for efficiency because of shared costs and multiple outputs, (3) is oriented toward external review of departmental performance rather than to development of management information systems that could form the basis for such a departmental review, and (4) attempts to introduce common-format reporting for analytic areas that instead require in-depth investigation. Such findings take reformers far beyond the usual story of PPB derailment by legislative refusal to deal in line items and resistance to penetration of PPB paperwork by departments with their own agendas. The Sri Lanka case analysis of PPB weaknesses also coincides with more sophisticated discussions of the subject in the United States (Mikesell, 1986, pp. 151–152).

It was noted above that Caiden and Wildavsky (1974) recommended "continuous budgeting" or budgeting until departments needed extra funds from the Ministry of Finance, which could be anytime during the fiscal year. It was also noted that Goode (1984, p. 38) rejected this notion as moving too far away from the notion of a rational allocation of resources among alternative uses. Roe (1986) examines "continuous budgeting" in Kenya, which means that some activities such as salary payment obligations continue year-round. In Kenya, budgeting is a conflict between three perspectives on the function of the budget: as means for capital formation, service provision, and/or wage employment (1986, p. 96). Thus, the "budget" is a temporary compromise between interests with such perspectives that bridge gaps between official ceilings and the Development Plan; between operating ministry submissions (votes) and Treasury ceilings; and between published estimates and actual expenditures. Roe examines the unstable game between guardians (Treasury ceilings) and spenders (ministry votes) in the national effort to achieve expenditure control. While he notes that this effort is "not as glamorous as the rhetoric of planning and decentralization" (1986, p. 99), the impression is that increasing control can be achieved without damage to managerial flexibility or program results.

For instance, Roe suggests a useful measure of whether a project is underfunded might be the ratio of salaries and allowances to staff support costs. Personnel/support ratios greater than 4 : 1 indicate projects that are overfunded or should not have been in the first place (1986, pp. 100–101). While technically sound, the case illustrates the "budget as piano" syndrome suggested by Korff (1983, p. 70). Good budgeting requires attention to the willingness and ability of leaders to understand how the numbers produce effective policy results. Obsession with 4 : 1 ratios of personnel/support can demoralize a project staff that could temporarily require unplanned activity to achieve maximum service benefits. The budget process that demands year-round adherence to ceilings for programs of varying levels of cost-sharing and multiple objectives focuses greater attention to form rather than substance. Case studies that ignore this possibility also can provide misleading lessons to budget practitioners.

By 1988–1989, studies and conferences on budgeting widened to include the informal relationships between the budget process and fiscal administration. As noted above, studies on budgeting in Latin America had already expanded to include more substantive issues than the performance of formal-legal structures. Further, local academic interest in public budgeting as a subject for theoretical and empirical debate at the university level is expanding in such countries as Costa Rica (Arias, 1988). The U.S. foreign assistance program, finally recognizing that development depends on solid fiscal administration, is now attempting to encourage Latin nations to maintain linkages between planning and budgeting by inserting objectives from the operating plan in the annual budget. This has historically been done only by *convenio* or *consertacion* (interinstitutional treaties and agreements). It is now widely recognized that financial analysis of the budget is often superficial and does not lead to feedback of evaluative results to the budget process. The common failure to evaluate budget execution is due in part to bureaucratic turf wars, absence of parameters for measuring performance, and informational deficiencies on the true costs of services (USAID/PW, 1989, p. 9). Other related problems that are now being discussed together by counterparts in the region are the problem of earmarked revenues and nongermane budget legislative riders on appropriations *(colas presupuestarias)* (1989, p. 10).

As part of the overall U.S. effort, country studies offering analytic critiques of budget processes are now being performed on a more continuous basis. In recognition that information on revenues and expenditures form the basis of technical assistance in any policy area, the results of recent budgetary case studies are available to practitioners and academics with interests in specific problem areas. For example, an important finding by Johnson and Porras (1989, p. 17) is that presentation of the budget by the Guatemalan Ministry of Finance (DTP) in several detailed volumes amounting to over 4000 pages tends to overwhelm Congress and the public rather than to inform them of policies. The technical assistance team recommended specifically that the presentation be simplified and supported by greater technical analysis of program options (1989, p. 32).

Comparative Budgetary Processes and Practices

Though most of the empirical testing of international budgetary hypotheses has occurred since 1983, it cannot be said that the bulk of the work is explicitly comparative in the sense of comparing hypotheses in cross-cultural settings. While a spate of international budgetary case studies continues to pour from university researchers, international aid agencies, and private consultants, studies of comparative budgeting have been limited to a few high-quality efforts. The reasons for this paucity seem to be (1) the historical indifference of aid agencies to "research" that would produce lessons of less interest to budget practitioners than perhaps high politics system designers, and (2) the technical difficulty of conducting such research even where funding and moral support can be secured. It may be that the many high-quality case studies now being produced must be a logically prior step in the development of comparative budgetary theory and practical lessons. Ultimately, they may also form part of the informational base that will lead to increased interest in conducting comparative budgetary research.

Contemporary comparative research largely demonstrates the strengths and weaknesses of the cases cited above. That is, the more powerful field studies move beyond formal-legal structures to their origins and impacts on cross-cultural political and economic variables. Weaker studies, like the subject on which they focus, tend to become bogged down in the numbing prose of budget manuals, rules, procedures, and the legalities of formal routines, ignoring the potentially rich linkages between technical rules and their sociopolitical implications.

The motive force behind comparative budgetary research, of course, is to make theory more general and valid. "Because scholars were interested in developing and testing theories that would be applicable beyond the boundaries of a single society, the comparative method came into use in the social sciences" (Holt and Turner, 1970, p. 6). The difference between comparative cross-cultural research and research conducted within a single society is the "magnitude of certain types of problems that have to be faced" (1970, p. 6). Variables must be measured and value ascertained in different cultural contexts (1970, p. 14). This requirement is particularly important in budgeting.

Since budgets are the product of political conflict and the process consists of conflict resolution, how a society resolves its issues becomes important and, unless controlled for, could prove to be a methodological impediment to cross-cultural comparison. For instance, authoritarian cultural norms (in the United States and elsewhere) tend to produce a superficial consensus, where disagreement and hard challenges to official policies and procedures are viewed as impolite at best, subversive at worst. This kind of cultural consensus often includes disdain for outsiders (xenophobia) and fear of education (classical liberal norms as opposed to technical training), both of which feed back to superficial consensus. In order to gauge the effect of cultural differences at conflict resolution on expenditure patterns, one must construct an index of conflict resolution to permit valid comparison. This would apply to any important cross-cultural variable.

Given the intention of developing tested theory through comparative analysis, how have comparative budgetary efforts linked explanatory variables to budgetary behavior? It was noted above that most case studies have been largely atheoretic, and on the order of consultant reports. Those that used theory largely restricted themselves to single concepts, such as "continuous budgeting," and few attempts were made to compare practices in other cultures or systems. Nevertheless, a number of studies have used explanatory variables for comparative budgetary purposes, and the question is whether related field work tests these theories. That is, do the explanatory variables have utility for practitioners and academics? Or are they simply gratuitous ad hoc international comparisons for purposes of spicing up an otherwise mundane technocratic topic?

Since culture has been noted, it may be useful to begin with the concept as an explanatory variable. For example, Wildavsky's revised comparative work (1986) links the notion of "political cultures" to expected influences on budgetary outcomes. He defines political cultures as "regimes" identified by the "strengths of group boundaries" for actors such as government officials and political parties (1986, p. 337). His cultural theory is used to predict outcomes for (1) form of the budget, (2) degree of attack on the budgetary base, which is viewed as a "manifestation of social agreement on essentials" (1986, p. 339), and (3) proclivities toward balancing or unbalancing budgets.

The problem with use of cultural theory to predict statistical "central tendencies" is its elastic conceptual base. Wildavsky notes, for example, that the predictive value for cultural theory "depends upon social context for their realization" (1986, p. 333). If dependent on social context, what this suggests is that political culture may be a residual category, useful to identify stimuli when all other variables have been accounted for (Bill and Hardgrave, 1973, p. 114). Left this vague, it could also be either a cause or an effect of other variables. Since cultural regimes consist of some product of local groups and actors, the problem of sampling and definition of group composition that would permit precise classification also arises. That is, if the basic concept of the political culture is "orientation" (1973, p. 94), one must employ verbal responses and observed behavior patterns to gain empirical knowledge of this critical phenomenon. But the methodological problem remains of linking orientation to action.

Nevertheless, it is increasingly recognized that models of political and administrative behavior that ignore culture are incomplete (Inglehart, 1988, p. 1203). Important research with significant implications for budgeting is proceeding on the consequences for democratic development of cultural differences in interpersonal trust; that is, interpersonal trust is viewed as a prerequisite to the formation of secondary associations, which, in turn, are essential for effective political participation (1988, p. 1204). One could expect differences in conflict resolution styles and therefore in budget process and results. While the methodological problem remain (surveys still imply culture from attitudes, or behavior from orientation) and no in-depth field studies have been conducted, use of political culture as an explanatory variable is promising in that most current budgetary studies (e.g., rational choice) tend to analyze short-term fluctuations within programs and policies, taking cultural and institutional factors as constant. "But these factors are not constant, either cross-nationally or over time" (1988, p. 1229).

Other researchers continue to use "structures" and "functions" as explanatory variables. Despite considerable criticism leveled at this approach over the last several decades, like "political culture," these comparative tools are undergoing a renaissance in use and refinement. For example, LaPalombara (1970, p. 130) once noted that "once we have learned the important lesson of structural alternatives for functional performance and multifunctionality of similar structures, little remains of structure-functionalism that is useful to political science, and much remains that can be damaging to comparative research." It may be remembered that he had argued for a "partial systems" emphasis on decision making to direct attention to policy outputs and away from the inputs on which functionalism focused (1970, p. 143). Since that time, scholars have attempted to link the effects of organizational structures on budgetary outcomes and behavior. They have also examined the policy implications of differing budgetary functions across cultures, and this bodes well for both the development of cross-cultural theory and practical policy lessons.

Considerable research is now taking place, for example, on the linkage of budget outcomes and the structures of state enterprises (SOEs), also called government-sponsored enterprises (GSE) and parastatals. These are organizational structures created usually by special statutes, which permit them to engage in commercial-type activities (utilities, public transit, housing), to use their own revenues for operating expenses and capital investments, to borrow funds in capital markets, and to control their own assets (Axelrod, 1989, p. 2). It was noted earlier by Bailey (1984, p. 80) that Mexico has 700 "parastatals" or public enterprises and they constituted approximately 50% of total Mexican public expenditure. By contrast, Birch (1989, p. 8) finds that expenditures by the 12 Guatemalan public enterprises account for only 1.0% of GNP and only 27.9% of investment by the nonfinancial public sector.

What are the implications of this structural feature for budgetary control, policy coordination, and policy results? Axelrod (1989, pp. 8–10) cites field research indicating the multiple reasons for the existence of "off-budget" public enterprises: (1) market failure, such as for public housing, (2) the need to bypass expenditure and debt limitations of U.S. state and local governments, (3) the need to get around the red tape of traditional bureaucracy and enable fast, flexible policy responses, (4) to provide loan guarantees to the risk-averse private sector in areas such as small business, (5) to stimulate regional and economic development, (6) to rescue failed industries through creation of such enterprises as Conrail and Amtrak, and (7) to insulate policies and programs from political pressures. He suggests that in the United States and elsewhere, such enterprises often erode the unified budget concept, and make it difficult to develop coherent and comprehensive policies covering the entire public sector (1989, p. 13).

While simplistic calls for privatization or sale of state enterprises tend to ignore sunk costs and the need for public service as the "bottom line," Axelrod (1989, p. 26) recognizes that Congress and legislatures of other countries can achieve the same effect by conducting critical budget reviews of state enterprises focusing on program objectives and policy performance rather than merely on staffing controls, objects of expense, and details of operation. Thus, research is focusing on the "political economy" of public enterprise structural origins as well as its impact on budgetary outcomes and policy performance.

Similarly, Rubin (1988) explores fiscal and political causes of the variation in uses of municipal enterprises. Examining 133 cities in Illinois, she compares explanations for use of enterprise funds and finds that contrary to expectation, cities with revenue constraints do not use enterprises to expand services. Nor do reformed (council-manager, fiscally conservative in its propensity to underestimate revenue) cities prefer tax-supported services over enterprises. More reformed cities had more enterprise funds (1988, p. 546). Based on difficulties in explaining government variation in use of enterprise, she pointed to problems in specification of appropriate explanatory and dependent variables (1988, p. 546). The important feature is that comparative hypotheses and "structural" theories are being operationalized and tested in different cultural settings.

Still other comparative works appear that tend to ignore the "multifunctionality of similar structures" (LaPalombara, 1970, p. 130). For instance, OECD (1987, p. 7) compares practices and tools of its 19 members that limit total expenditure, monitor total expenditures during execution, and increase efficiency and effectiveness of expenditures. Recognizing that "international comparisons are fraught with difficulties in assessing relative performance" (1987, p. 10), the report simply describes "tools of the trade" used by senior public servants in member central budget offices. Consistent with this objective, the report describes formal roles and structures involved in budget decision making, the annual budget cycle, and indicates current reforms under discussion. The report reads like a government organization manual and provides few insights of use to one interested in how these tools perform. It should also be noted that apart from general comparisons of public enterprises and growth-composition of expenditure, no comparisons are made across country reports. In short, the report is more a collection of formal-legal case studies than the comparative analysis of budget structures billed at the outset.

In that functions are also performed by multiple structures, as noted, many despair of a functional research focus. But functions enable one to examine performance impact directly without concern for the labyrinths of bureaucratic structure and power. Functionalist analysis can point the way to reform based on field evidence of distributional impact. For example, how have such functions as efficiency and effectiveness of public spending been served by such programs as hiring freezes, civil servant censuses, voluntary retirement schemes, and use of economic analysis? Gray and Linn (1988, pp. 4–5) compare the functioning of such tools in Costa Rica, Botswanna, Chile, Thailand, Gambia, the Central African Republic, Ghana, Mexico, and Sri Lanka. They also examine the functioning of public enterprise "structures" and, consistent with Axelrod above (1989), note that "State-owned enterprises (SOEs) should be granted the autonomy to cover their costs through rational pricing, with managers held accountable for the quality of services and for financial viability of their enterprises" (Gray and Linn, 1988, p. 5).

Though structures and functions are not mutually exclusive concepts, rather than continue the debate over specification of concepts, it is probably more important that the research proceed to the cross-cultural origins and impacts of either structures or functions. For example, Seguiti (1986) compares the performance of the U.S. and Italian "functions" of legislative budget limits, implementation of program budget reforms, and strengthening of budgetary accountability. Along the way, he notes how similar "structures" perform these different functions in both cultures. For example, while the U.S. and Italian legislative decision processes are similar and produce similar results, such as transfer payments growing to be the largest expenditure categories, the U.S. legislative process fragments the budget into more pieces of legislation than the Italian system. Italy and other European nations classify expenditures by current and capital accounts, unlike the U.S. budget.

Similarly, Seguiti (1988) also notes the differences in the credit function between the two countries. While the U.S. "cash-based" accounting system does not provide legislators and decisionmakers with a measure of the cost of various credit programs (probability of default, net realizable value of assets), the Italian system also does not report accurate costs in that subsidy costs of revolving funds are not recorded in the budget (1988, p. 60). He suggests that better credit accounting alone cannot lead to reduction of government intervention "unless it is supported by political will" (1988, p. 65). In Italy, the absence of a strong and leading ideology of private entrepreneurship and less widespread awareness by the public of the need for efficient financial management in the public sector (1988, p. 65) constrain the use of the credit function to improve the efficiency and effectiveness of public expenditures. This contrasts with the United States, where both attitudes are present and political consensus is developing to curb government credit programs (1988, p. 66).

Recognizing that differences in U.S. and Italian budget processes reflect differences in the culture and philosophy of their respective peoples, Seguiti suggests that "The US system could be nourished and improved by the Italian experience as it relates to the structural composition and classification of the central government budget, especially in the comprehensive display of Italian budget figures and their fundamental distinction between operating and capital expenditures" (1986, p. 53). Thus, functional comparisons can serve the comparative purpose of raising the level of knowledge among respective policymakers, analysts, and citizens. It also "widens opportunities for improvements in the budget and legal structures within the countries" (1986, p. 53).

Use of functionalist comparisons is also useful where existing paradigms are conceptually limited and structural analysis is superficial. For example, Caiden (1985, p. 36) recognizes that "existing comparative models" do not describe budget systems in such countries as ASEAN, nor do these countries precisely exemplify the models. Focusing on such functions as coordinating mechanisms (auditing, cash monitoring, national planning, executive budgets), it is also evident that concepts such as "poverty and uncertainty that lead to fragmentation and repetition" (Caiden and Wildavsky, 1974) do not produce evidently useful policy prescriptions.

The problem in both comparative and case studies, again, lies in failure to link such functions to their political economy context. From the narrow functionalist analysis, Caiden is unable to answer basic questions, such as the potential effects of economic downturn on budget structures or policies (1985, p. 37). The apparent paradox of "self-sustaining subsystems" (1985, p. 36) or areas of stable priorities that reduce control and budget unity might be conceptually explained by use of broader functional concepts that included the political and economic utility of such islands of stability in ASEAN budgets.

Additionally, functional analysis of tools and techniques may be useful where structural analysis fails to account for the political economy of those items. For example, in the OECD review of its member expenditure control practices that focus on accounting structures, it is noted that in the Netherlands "revenues and expenditures have been budgeted and accounted for on a cash basis since the Government Account Act of 1976" (OECD, 1987, p. 40). But Axelrod (1988) explains the functional weaknesses of such legal rules for budgetary practice:

> One of the reasons the Netherlands dropped accrual accounting was the difficulty of accruing revenues. Some estimates on an accrued basis were so rosy that they led to additional expenditures. When actual revenues fell significantly short of accrued estimates, the government was forced to resort to increased deficit financing. (1988, p. 240)

In addition, several scholars have conducted exploratory budgetary studies using time as the principle explanatory variable (chronological comparisons). Bahl (1986), for example, notes the problems associated with attempting to compare fiscal centralization from 1974–1984 in industrialized countries. He compares OECD member revenue/expenditure shares and dependence on central government transfers, and finds that grant revenues to subnational governments have not been adequate (transfer revenues have increased less than in proportion to central government taxes) and that fiscal centralization is increasing (1986, p. 20). This suggests that subnational governmental budgets will experience increasing stress and that means must be found to increase the efficiency of expenditures (analytic or qualitative budget reforms) and the effectiveness of policies (privatization with accountability controls). Further comparative field research is needed to confirm or reject such findings within and across countries, and to compare the origins and impacts to tools used to respond to fiscal stress.

Finally, Sharkansky (1985) examines the impact of triple-digit inflation on changes in budget allocations for Israel, 1978–1984. Recognizing the substantial contribution of quasi-governmental authorities off-budget, he compares formal on-budget categories for operating and development (capital) budgets. While nominal budget totals increased by 21,700%, he found that most real-value shifts were incremental (or real nonincremental increases balanced out real nonincremental decreases). Other than debt service (which "won" under inflationary budgeting by increasing 95% in this period), most shifts were incremental. The "losers" were policymakers and budget officers that had to scramble continuously to guard resources from erosion (1985, p. 73). One could also argue that such actors won by "surviving" and that the real loser was the public welfare in loss of quality programs. Sharkansky notes indeed that inflation contributed to loss of quality control (1985, p. 73).

However, time-series comparative studies such as this need to be followed by in-depth analyses of such topics as ministry budgets, off-budget entities, and transfers between capital and operating categories. One is left with the uneasy impression that the real story is being told by other figures despite the assertion that this is "an important part if not all of the Israeli budget story" (Sharkansky, 1985, p. 66). Part of the problem is the assumption that time causes shifts in budgetary behavior. But the ordinate and abscissa can move together regardless of whether substantive or specious causality exists, such as variation in the occurrences of sun spots and stock market prices (Guess and Farnham, 1989, p. 57). For "time" to be a useful independent variable, secular trends, seasonal variations, cyclical variations, and irregular movements must have been controlled for. Sharkansky strongly suggests here that they have not. As Rubin (1988, p. 546) recognizes above, the choice of explanatory variables is critical to comprehensive explanation of budgetary behavior.

CONDUCTING COMPARATIVE BUDGETARY RESEARCH

More comprehensive cross-cultural tests of hypotheses pertaining to the origins and impacts of budgetary tools are needed. But even with additional funding, scholars must face a paucity of available data (much of which is simply unreliable or invalid) and byzantine organizational processes that often convert research efforts into the search for consistent rumors and anecdotes. Given the difficulty, for example, of tracing the determinants of expenditure origins beyond the insight that they are affected by "many factors" (Goode, 1984, p. 49) or the incidence of expenditures at a more disaggregate level than on prices, wages, profits, and land values (1984, p. 61), how should one proceed in the field to develop realistic hypotheses and gather data for testing?

Working with the financial support of the Fulbright Commission in Uruguay (1985), it was soon evident that my logically planned framework of (1) assessing political and economic factors affecting budget behavior, (2) describing how revenue forecasts and expenditure plans were converted into funded programs by the budget process, (3) evaluating the performance of the budget process, and (4) recommending improvements for the present system, faced severe constraints in practice that had little to do with available time or funding.

First, it was relatively easy to develop historical and contemporary evidence that the Uruguayan budget process was indeed subject to extreme fiscal and political uncertainty. While Uruguay is Latin America's most urban (85.0%) and most literate (96.3%) country [Inter-American Development Bank (IADB), 1987], gross domestic product (GDP) declined 9.5% in 1982 (IADB, 1987, p. 400), from one of Latin America's highest standards of living. A 10–12% GDP growth rate is considered necessary for simple maintenance of existing physical plant (Taylor, 1979, p. 279).

Beginning in the 1950s, Uruguayan policymakers harnessed national development to the livestock sector, subsidizing both the industry and urban consumers through price controls. As the industry was sheltered from real competition for 50 years, it became inefficient. Nationally, widening gaps between external-internal prices and real interest rates triggered capital flight. This led to tighter controls on the import of capital and intermediate goods, which caused severe reduction in domestic investment and growth. Policymakers then devalued the currency and the cycle began anew (World Bank, 1982, p. 1). With a population growth rate among the world's lowest (1.0%), 60% of government outlays for social welfare expenditures in 1980 (1982, p. 125), and a substantial public budgetary deficit (8.7% of GDP in 1982) (IADB, 1987, p. 400), the budget process was faced with substantial uncertainty.

But after gaining insight into the economic picture from the usual World Bank, IMF, IADB, and USAID sources, it was evident that political forces guiding the economy according to its own short-term laws needed to be described. While such forces could be measured indirectly by economic data in the long term, this would obviously not reflect the incentives of incumbent policymakers. Historically, the pattern of Uruguayan politics became relatively consistent by the 1930s as Colorado party boss and president Gabriel Terra established personal fiefdoms that ensured "the primacy of political over integrative policymaking" (Taylor, 1979, p. 282). An admirer of Benito Mussolini, Terra believed that an open political system would tend to preclude class struggle.

Thus, he encouraged "coparticipation" (apportionment of elective positions by means of quotas in the electoral law among parties offering candidates) at all levels of government, elected and appointed. As decisions now required negotiations and biparty support, this blurred lines of responsibility and responsiveness, and also damaged the authority of the presidency (Taylor, 1979, p. 282). "Since the state became a dispenser of patronage, efficiency became undesirable. As the systemic costs rose and interclass cleavages widened, ultimately there was a 'tyranny of all against all' " (1979, p. 282).

Following total discredit of both government policies and the civilian police force by the Tupamaros in the 1960s, the army assumed command of policymaking with links of varying scope and intensity between hard/soft line officer factions and civilian interest groups. Military command of politics after the *golpe* of 1973 (through the Institutional Acts that replaced most guarantees of the 1966 Constitution, and also eliminated party access to state resources) and of the economy (via confused attempts to deal with 71% inflation, 15% unemployment, an external debt of 71% of GDP, and low world prices for its principal exports of meat and wool) did not stimulate development. Eventually, the military regime extricated itself from the risks of making hard policy choices by encouraging acceptable candidates and national elections. They were also encouraged to withdraw to their barracks by their inability to translate militarization of administration into support by a clientistic base either within an existing party or new one. Gillespie (1985, p. 10) suggests that this is surprising "given the very large size of Uruguay's public sector and the number of posts to be filled. . . ."

Under the authoritarian regime *(regimen militar)*, "academic and scholarly analyses of economic issues and procedures have been denied publication, while leaders of all parties have been jailed and even murdered" (Taylor, 1979, p. 286). The primacy of politics over integrated policy that began in the 1920s–1930s deteriorated into contemporary budgetary "indifference (if not hostility) to statistical data" (1979, p. 278). According to Taylor, "each presidential term had allowed constitutionally for only one budget built alluvially on the expenditures of preceding generations. In effect, conventional contemporary budgeting criteria (for the Western-developed states) would have been radical restructuring for Uruguay" (1979, p. 279).

Such analyses indicated rather clearly that political and economic instability would create problems for coherent budgetary practices as well as research on those practices. For it was apparent that data and information produced during and after such events might also be suspect. This led to the second puzzle, how to accurately describe the budget process. This task was facilitated by working at the Presidential Office of Planning and Budgeting *(Planeamiento y Presupuesto)* by day, and teaching public budgeting to university students in Montevideo at the University of the Republic *(Universidad de la República)* by night (with U.S. cases on nonprofit budgeting and accounting translated into Spanish).

As in any complex budgetary policy system, understanding required accurate descriptions of all pertinent structures and functions involved in making, approving, executing, and auditing the budget. A review of the local literature in Spanish to gain some idea of which institutions performed which functions revealed nothing at the micro level of budget politics and policy. The budget process is treated as a "black box" in macro political economy analyses that generally note the complex constraints to development attendant on domestic political alliances to international economic forces (see for example Notaro, 1984). But analyses by local accountants, economists, and political scientists simply ignore the budget process as a worthy topic for discussion. This either implied that most actors in any budget process merely register dominant political preferences for allocation of resources, or that data were simply not available on such a sensitive subject. Either way, there was no local literature on the subject.

Nevertheless, it could be discerned from conversations with those at work that the Uruguayan budget is prepared and executed by an inflexible, centralized ("advanced corporatist") political system, which had recently turned civilian (President Julio Sanguinetti was elected in 1984). It was also evident that the President is trying to cut public sector expenditures, most notably the military budget, which commanded up to 33% of the budget. Thus, the budget process is largely controlled by the President through the Ministry of Finance *(Finanzas)* and Treasury *(Tesoro General)*. Treasury estimates tax collections *(recaudaciones)* for the fiscal year using regression techniques and other tools with substantial accuracy. The Ministry of Finance with assistance from the Office of Planning and Budgeting *(Presupuesto)* and Controller General *(Contaduría)* set expenditure ceilings *(topes)*. While the executive budget is constitutionally a 5-year budget (actually a plan, called *quinquenal*), an annual budget is prepared (explained as 1-year supplementals to the 5-year budget for consistency) since appropriations *(asignaciones)* are annual, not multiyear. The central administration requests funds *(pedidos y reclamas)* for its ministries *(incisos)* by line item.

Line items are called *rubros, programas,* and *articulos*. The executive budget is published in *Diario Oficial* as a lengthy administrative decree composed of *articulos*. This is consistent with Civil Law budgetary practice where each item is a matter of law rather than administrative management. In Illinois, Ervin (1988) notes that budgetary process at the local level depends on choice of state governing statute. Where the locality selected responsibility for budgeting as opposed to mere development of an appropriation ordinance, practitioners were more professional, relied upon information to a greater extent, and approached formal budgeting with increased attention and effort (1988, p. 48). In Uruguay, legalistic emphasis inhibits professional budgeting, evidenced nowhere more clearly than in the professional weakness of the *Oficina de Planeamiento y Presupuesto*. During the middle of budget preparation for FY 1986, for example, the entire office was ordered to move to a new location in the Office of the President (several weeks were spent boxing papers and hauling them to trucks, suggesting that their inputs were not terribly valuable anyway).

Programas are also like line items despite their planning connotations. The Constitution (Section XIV, Article 214, Chapter 1, 1966, pp. 69–70) requires expenditures and investments by each ministry to be in programs. Since expenditures are classified by departmental programs (requiring no alternatives analysis), this simply means by line item. Contrary to impressions, for a program budget system to be operationalized, the Constitution would have to be changed! As Taylor (1979) noted how radical even coherent budgeting based on real information would be, the idea of radically shifting from an incremental to a comprehensive program budget has little support!

While information may not penetrate the system to encourage rational change of budget priorities, the same cannot be said for monitoring budgetary execution. Uruguay is called "a nation of accountants" *(contadores),* suggesting that cash-flow considerations are paramount during the fiscal year. Note that the strict accounting principles are always applied to an approved deficit budget! Thus, information on transfers [*transferencias* between *incisos, rubros,* and *subrubros* (line-item accounts)], on increases *(aumentos y trasposiciones),* on decreases *(rebajas),* and on the quarterly status of appropriations *(asignacíon apertura y líquida)* are accurate and timely. The *Contadura* develops such reports as the annual *Balance de Ejecucíon Presupuestal,* which reports quarterly expenditures *(erogaciones por gastos y inversiones a nivel de inciso)* against appropriations, and the *Rendicíon de Cuentas* or executed annual budget.

By August 31, the executive budget *(quinquenal y pedidos asignaciones)* should be transferred to the *Asamblea General (Cámara)* for approval. A data problem exists here since the *Asamblea* was given a 10-year holiday by the military (1974–1984). What this suggests is that the *regimen militar* largely approved its own requests each year with only the International Monetary Fund (IMF) watching for excessive deficits and inflationary public expenditures. Nevertheless, by 1985, the *Asamblea* was back in business. The executive prepares a budget message containing its budget and requests for approval called the *Mensaje del Poder Ejectuvio A La Asamblea General.*

Unfortunately, even before 1973, the message provided only disaggregated information. It provides no discussion of the totals and no consistency of discussion (shifting from monetary to physical indicators of programmatic need such as number of employees and number of hectares of land). More importantly, no information is provided on differences between the amount requested and approved in past fiscal years. Comparing the *Balance de Ejecucíon* with the annual *Proyecto de Ley* might work if the core numbers were there. Investigation of a reference to studies *(estudios parlimentarios)* by the *Comisíon de Hacienda* in the legislature (Finance Committee) produced a few pages of large figures with no explanation of how they were arrived at. For future researchers in this country, each message in the *Diario de Sesiones de la Cámara de Senadores* runs over several volumes *(tomos)* and totals about 1000 pages. While the speeches were exciting around 1969–1973, the budgetary picture from these official sources, like Montevideo in winter, remains shrouded in fog.

With the realization that methodological and data problems were beginning to hamper my quest for the budgetary grail, I nevertheless formulated a demographic thesis based on Uruguayan political history. The shift from elected government to military rule (dissolution of the *Asamblea* by the President and military formation of the *Consejo de la Nacion* along the Brazilian model of military takeover in 1964) should be reflected in internal (management) and policy (external service) performance. As an irregular event affecting the flow of time, a *golpe* should have a significant impact on budgetary behavior. One might expect "repetitive budgeting" measurable by inter/intradepartmental *(inciso)* transfers. Comparing data from 1974–1984 with data from 1964–1974 should indicate significant differences in levels of transfers. Conversely, one might also expect to find strength of incremental practices, consistent with Sharkansky's (1985) findings on the effects of inflation on Israeli budgeting.

The demographic hypothesis attempted to assess budgetary performance (the third problem) in a data-weak context. That the hypothesis was superficially correct was indicated by a recent study (Oficina de Planeamiento y Presupuesto, 1985) revealing sectoral shifts in expenditures in 1972 and 1973. During those turbulent political years, spending for national defense and internal security increased from 11 to 16% (45%) and from 5 to 11% (120%) respectively. At the same time, expenditures for "others" (agriculture, industry, energy, and transport) diminished from 59 to 41% of the total budget (−30.5%). But this pattern could not be compared to shifts before 1970. Nor could the incidence of transfers be compared consistently to data before 1973. In stark terror at the realization that I was finished, I regained equanimity only through the restorative powers of a hot mug of yerba mate (Uruguay is the world's largest importer of yerba).

Many qualitative questions about the tools of the Uruguayan budget process simply could not be compared before and after the *golpe*. For example, how did the *golpe* affect rapidity of disbursement by Treasury of ministry payment orders? Was there evidence of an "accounting recognition" of payments that may never in fact be collected, as Bird (1982, p. 92) found in Colombia? How much of the immense paperwork required by the process (to the soothing background of military muzak at the Budget Office) is actually necessary? Did the *golpe* make a difference? Further, if major taxing and expenditure trends cannot be ascertained by reasonable search, how can the evolution of public sector activity be traced in the fashion of, for example, Bailey (1984) for Mexico? Finally, other than the obvious suggestion that informational quality be improved, few recommendations can be advanced (the fourth stage in my planned inquiry on the Uruguayan budget process) in a political culture that may be indifferent to qualitative information itself (Taylor, 1979). Neither the published executive budget nor the legislative *Mensaje* or *Proyecto de Ley* would suggest how to formulate any intelligent question beyond "what does it all mean?" These are drawing-room books, not meant to be read by critical minds.

SUMMARY AND CONCLUSION

In sum, more international case studies and comparative analyses of the political economies of budgetary tools and techniques need to be performed. Depending on the quality of data, a possible reflection of the openness of the political culture to learning and improvement, scholars need to test theories on the functioning of budgetary tools (off and on budget) for the public welfare. They need to ask critical questions and penetrate the often "numbing prose" and masses of bureaucratic regulations that offer little insight into real agendas and actual practices. They need assistance from host countries and international organizations.

However, where the data is insufficient for any level of scholarly work (other than development of trivial formal-legal decision sequences), scholars need to back off from their theories and hypotheses and concentrate on the development of low-cost data and information systems that could help both local practitioners and future researchers. Without the usual call for computers and management information systems that often freeze in illogical processes and into which few would willingly plug data, scholars and consultants should conduct information assessments on a documental and procedural basis. This could be done in a counterpart group format with the potential success of the USAID/Price Waterhouse experience noted above. What is the purpose of this document? How might our decisions be enhanced by better data? Such micro tasks should be considered for certain country contexts such as Uruguay. Such work would be clearly less glamorous than producing another tidy refeered article. But it should be remembered that such research successes often depended on the work of many local practitioners that developed incentive systems to gather and report important budgetary data regularly.

During my initial work at OPP in Uruguay, it was suggested to me that financial information was now (1985) less accurate than before the *golpe* of 1973, in part because the military buried much of the data and now gaps exist rendering time-series (even cross-sectional in some cases) comparisons difficult. Nevertheless, I was asked if other data might be collected by the Oficina de Planeamiento y Presupuesto (OPP) to improve expenditure efficiency (value for money). After the predictable recommendation that physical and financial indicators of expenditure performance be developed and information gathered continuously (for improved performance auditing and for better justification of requests), it was suggested that this had been tried. But institutional fragmentation *(Contaduría, Tesoro, Ministerios)* would prevent such a system from being operationalized.

This is a symptom of the larger problem of perceived inefficiency and politicization of the Uruguayan public sector historically. As in the United Kingdom, there is no serious basic management training for public officials (Butt, 1987, p. 7), particularly in the public budgeting area. Pay is low and workers are demoralized by the feeling that their efforts to rationalize the system go repeatedly unrewarded. This is a larger structural or political economy problem that cannot be resolved by more macrotheory or more gratuitous comparisons. The need is for development of incentive systems for use of relevant hard data in budgetary decision making.

It was recognized above (Dean, 1986), that the common-format reporting system used for line-item budgeting and also proposed by reformers in program budget systems is often ill-suited to in-depth investigations of productivity and budgetary behavior within departments. Researchers need to devise and recommend incentives for generating better budgetary information from which realistic questions can be asked about input-output relationships. Uruguay and similar advanced developing countries have high levels of technical skill and academic credentials. The major task for comparative budgetary research is to devise means by which this considerable professional energy is released to improve the efficiency of expenditures and the effectiveness of public policy.

REFERENCES

Alper, J. (1989). Health: Order on the couch. *Atlantic Monthly* 263:24–30.

Arias, R. (1988). *Presupuesto Publico, Guia Didactica de Texto Para El Estudio de la Asignatura*. Universidad Estatal a Distancia, San Jose, Costa Rica.

Axelrod, D. (1988). *Budgeting For Modern Government*. St. Martin's, New York.

Axelrod, D. (1989). *A Budget Quartet, Critical Policy and Management Issues*. St. Martin's, New York.

Bahl, R. (1986). The design of intergovernmental transfers in industrialized countries. *Public Budgeting and Finance* 6, 4:3–23.

Bailey, J. (1984). Public budgeting in Mexico, 1970–1982. *Public Budgeting and Finance* 4,1:76–90.

Barbieri, L., and Monorchio, A. (1982). The budget of Italy. *Public Budgeting and Finance* 2,3:65–74.

Bill, J. A., and Hardgrave, R. L., Jr. (1973). *Comparative Politics, The Quest for Theory*. Merrill, Columbus, Ohio.

Birch, M. (1989). Technical Memorandum #4, Public Enterprise Sector. Consultoria Para La Administracion Fiscal, Guatemala, C.A./Atlanta, Georgia State University.

Bird, R. M. (1982). Budgeting and expenditure control in Colombia. *Public Budgeting and Finance* 2,3:87–100.

Blondal, G. (1983). Balancing the budget: Budgeting practices and fiscal policy issues in Ireland. *Public Budgeting and Finance* 3,2:47–64.

Butt, H. A. (1987). Value for money: The experience of local government in the United Kingdom. *Public Budgeting and Finance* 7,4:5–12.

Caiden, N. J. (1985). Comparing budget systems: Budgeting in ASEAN countries. *Public Budgeting and Finance* 5,4:23–39.

Caiden, N. J., and Wildavsky, A. (1974). *Planning and Budgeting in Poor Countries*. John Wiley, New York.

Constitucion de la Republica Oriental del Uruguay. (1966). Asamblea General, Montevideo.

Cutt, J. (1983). The evolution of expenditure budgeting in Australia. *Public Budgeting and Finance* 3,2:7–28.

Danziger, J. N. (1978). *Making Budgets, Public Resource Allocation*. Sage, Beverly Hills, Calif.

Dean, P. N. (1986). Performance budgeting in Sri Lanka. *Public Budgeting and Finance* 6,2:63–76.

Doern, G. B. (1983). Canada's budgetary dilemmas: Tax and expenditure reform. *Public Budgeting and Finance* 3, 2:28–47.

Doh, J.-C. (1984). Budgeting as an instrument of development: The Malaysian experience. *Public Budgeting and Finance* 4,1:64–75.

Doyle, M. F. (1983). Management of the public finances in Ireland since 1961. *Public Budgeting and Finance* 3,2:64–79.

Ervin, O. L. (1988). Appropriating vs. budgeting: A comparison of municipal fiscal processes. *Public Budgeting and Finance* 8,4:45–54.

Fischer, D. H. (1970). *Historian's Fallacies, Toward a Logic of Historical Thought*. Harper and Row, New York.

Gillespie, C. (1985). Uruguay's transition from collegial military-technocratic rule. In *Transitions From Authoritarian Regimes, Volume II, Latin America*, G. O'Donnell, P. Schmitter, and L. Whitehead (eds.), Johns Hopkins, Baltimore.

Goode, R. (1984). *Government Finance in Developing Countries*. Brookings Institution, Washington, D.C.

Gray, C., and Linn, J. F. (1988). Improving public finance for development. *Finance and Development* 25,3:2–5.

Guess, G. M. (1983). Comparative government budgeting. In *Handbook on Public Budgeting and Financial Management*, J. Rabin and T. D. Lynch (eds.), Marcel Dekker, New York, pp. 161–191.

Guess, G. M. (1989). Comparative and international administration. In *Handbook on Public Administration*, J. Rabin, B. W. Hildreth, and G. J. Miller (eds.), Marcel Dekker, New York, pp. 477–497.

Guess, G. M., and Farnham, P. G. (1989). *Cases in Public Policy Analysis*. Longman, New York.

Hirschman, A. O. (1989). Reactionary rhetoric. *Atlantic Monthly* 263,5:63–70.

Holt, R. T., and Turner, J. E. (1970). *The Methodology of Comparative Research*. Free Press, New York.

Inglehart, R. (1988). The renaissance of political culture. *American Political Science Review* 82,4:1203–1231.

Inter-American Development Bank. (1987). Economic and Social Progress in Latin America, 1987
    Report, Special Section: Labor Force and Employment. IADB, Washington, D.C.
International Budget Studies Section. (1950). *Public Administration Review* 10,31–60.
Johnson, D., and Porras, J. (1989). Technical Memorandum #9, Analysis of the Budgeting
    System. Consultoria Para La Administracion Fiscal, Guatemala, C.A./Atlanta, Georgia State
    University.
Korff, H. C. (1983). Planning and budgeting in the Federal Republic of Germany. *Public Budgeting
    and Finance* 3, 4:57–71.
Kunas, S. (1982). The budget of the Federal Republic of Germany. *Public Budgeting and Finance*
    2,3:43–53.
LaPalombara, J. (1970). Parsimony and empiricism in comparative politics: An anti-scholastic
    view. In *The Methodology of Comparative Research*, R. T. Holt and J. E. Turner (eds.), Free
    Press, New York, pp. 123–151.
LeBlanc, L. J. C. M., and Meys, T. A. J. (1982). Flexibility and adjustment in public budgeting:
    The Netherlands experience. *Public Budgeting and Finance* 2,3:53–65.
Mikesell, J. L. (1986). *Fiscal Administration, Analysis and Applications for the Public Sector*.
    Dorsey, Chicago.
Notaro, J. (1984). *La Politica Economica En El Uruguay, 1968–1984*. Centro Interdisciplinario de
    Estudios Sobre El Desarrollo Uruguay, Montevideo.
Oficina de Planeamiento y Presupuesto. (1985). Clasificacion Sectoral Del Presupuesto Nacional y
    Participacion de Cada Sector En Todo Del Gasto Publico, 1970–1983. OPP, Montevideo.
Organisation for Economic Co-Operation and Development. (1987). *The Control and Management
    of Government Expenditure*. OECD, Paris.
Premchand, A. (1981). Government budget reforms: Agenda for the 1980s. *Public Budgeting and
    Finance* 1,3:16–25.
Premchand, A. (1983). Government budgeting: State of the art. *Public Budgeting and Finance*
    3,2:4–6.
Premchand, A., and Burkhead, J. (eds.). (1984). *Comparative International Budgeting and Fi-
    nance*. Transaction, New Brunswick, N.J.
Roberts, J. S. (1979). Financial Management in LDCs: Budgetary Practices at the Institutional
    Level. USAID, Washington, D.C.
Roe, E. M. (1986). The ceiling as base: National budgeting in Kenya. *Public Budgeting and
    Finance* 6,2:87–104.
Rosenberg, T. (1988). Columbia, Murder City. *Atlantic Monthly* 262,5:20–30.
Rubin, I. (1988). Municipal enterprises: Exploring budgetary and political implications. *Public
    Administration Review* 48,1:542–550.
Rubin, I. (1989). Aaron Wildavsky and the demise of incrementalism. *Public Administration
    Review* 49,1:78–81.
Salamon, L. M. (1981). Rethinking public management: Third-party government and the changing
    forms of government action. *Public Policy* 29,3:255–275.
Salamon, L. M. (ed.) (1989). *Beyond Privatization: The Tools of Government Action*. Urban
    Institute, Washington, D.C.
Schick, A. (1966). The road to PPB: The stages of budget reform. *Public Administration Review*
    26,4:243–258.
Seguiti, M. L. (1986). Toward comprehensive budgeting under fiscal limitations: A comparison of
    reforms in the U.S. and Italy. *Public Budgeting and Finance* 6,4:43–56.
Seguiti, M. L. (1988). An Italian perspective on U.S. federal credit reform. *Public Budgeting and
    Finance* 8,4:54–68.
Sharkansky, I. (1985). Who gets what amidst high inflation: Winners and losers in the Israeli budget
    process, 1978–84. *Public Budgeting and Finance* 5,4:64–75.
Taylor, P. B., Jr. (1979). Uruguay: The costs of inept political corporatism. In *Latin American
    Politics and Development*, H. J. Wiarda and H. F. Kline (eds.), Houghton Mifflin, Boston,
    pp. 262–280.

United Nations. (1979). *Strengthening Public Administration and Finance for Development in the 1980s: Issues and Approaches.* United Nations, New York.

U.S. Agency for International Development/Price Waterhouse. (1989). Improvements Needed in Managing Public Resources in Latin America. USAID/PW, Washington, D.C.

U.S. General Accounting Office. (1979). Training and Related Efforts Needed to Improve Financial Management in the Third World. GAO, Washington, D.C.

Ward, T. S. (1982). Budgetary practices in the United Kingdom. *Public Budgeting and Finance* 2,3:35–42.

Wildavsky, A. (1986). *Budgeting, A Comparative Theory of Budgetary Processes.* Transaction, New Brunswick, N.J.

Wildavsky, A. (1988). *The New Politics of the Budgetary Process.* Scott, Foresman, Glenview, Ill.

Wildavsky, A. (1989). Presentation on "Fifty Years of Budget Theory: From Line Items, PPBS, MBO, ZBB, to Performance Budgeting," 50th Annual Conference, American Society for Public Administration, April 11, Miami, Fla.

Wolfson, D. J. (1979). *Public Finance and Development Strategy.* Johns Hopkins, Baltimore.

World Bank. (1982). Economic Memorandum on Uruguay. World Bank, Washington, D.C.

Yoingco, A. Q., and Guevara, M. M. (1984). Budgetary practices and developments in the Philippines. *Public Budgeting and Finance* 4,2:99–115.

Ysander, B.-C., and Robinson, A. (1982). Establishing budgetary flexibility. *Public Budgeting and Finance* 2,3:21–34.

6

Teaching Budgeting: An Agenda for the 1990s

Jerry McCaffery *Department of Administrative Sciences, Naval Postgraduate School, Monterey, California*

The pedagogic deficit still appears to exist in the world of budgeting, but the ebb and flow of issues deny us the time to bemoan that fact. New problems confront teachers of budgeting and a new agenda must be created. This agenda ranges from what to do with the computer revolution, to coping with ethical behavior as teachers and practitioners of the art of budgeting, to preserving and expanding valued human resources in a situational context and providing them a mind set that will enable them to cope with a more complex budget environment, rather than simply letting them burn out and drop out of government service.

THE OLD PEDAGOGIC DEFICIT

The old deficit in teaching budgeting centered on the potential mismatch between what universities were teaching in professional master's degree programs and what governmental employers appeared to want (McCaffery, 1983; Grizzle, 1985). Surveys appear to show that employers want students to be competent in budget preparation-operating and capital, revenue forecasting, cost-benefit analysis, and accounting (Berne, 1985; MacManus, 1984). Grizzle (1985, p. 842) comments that while most courses covered budget preparation, fewer than a third "even mention expenditure forecasting skills or cost-benefit analysis." Moreover, only seven of 63 programs appeared to cover more than half the top 15 skills deemed important in the MacManus and Berne studies (Grizzle, 1985, p. 843). Particularly underprovided were training in cost-benefit analysis, cost-effectiveness analysis, fiscal impact analysis, cost-revenue analysis, financial condition evaluation, and tax administration. Skills and topics where provision appeared to match market desire focused on comparison of different budget system types [planning programming budgeting, zero-based budgeting (PPB,ZBB)], budget analysis including justification and performance indicators, and budget process (Grizzle, 1985, p. 842). This tends to support the earlier characterization of budget courses:

> In summary, we have persons whose theoretical base tends to be political science, teaching process-oriented, general courses whose model is usually the federal government, where the course is basically oriented around institutional description and defines budgeting as planning and is located in the executive branch. (McCaffery, 1983)

This profile tends to explain the underprovision of analytic tools later deemed essential in the Berne, MacManus, and Grizzle studies. Grizzle suggests that programs as a whole do seem to be out of step with practitioner preferences. She suggests that most of the skills being neglected are not "esoteric subjects which require long years of study to master" (Grizzle, 1985, p. 843), but rather that instructors should simply make the investment to master these subjects and teach them. She concludes that what seemed most lacking was an appreciation among instructors of the skills practitioners felt students needed.

McCaffery (1983, p. 204) suggested that budgeting was "too rich and complex an act to be summarized within the confines of a course or two," and that those who would train students for roles in the public sector ought to search for packages of courses crossing disciplinary lines to satisfy the intellectual skill requirements. This shifts the teaching burden from the individual to the curriculum. The problem with this approach is that curriculum building is not a simple task and that most schools have students for a limited time and have an array of other courses that they feel students also must take to become a well-rounded product. Time and opportunity costs limit this approach also.

As long as professional managers (Stillman, 1982) and students (Henry, 1979) continue to rank financial skills high among critical management skills, attention will continue to be focused on the teaching of budgeting. There is no reason to suppose these rankings have changed. In fact, with the continued problem of the federal deficit continuing to hold front-page attention, the turn of the economy and worsening of many state revenue situations into short-term deficits in 1990 and 1991, and the massive size and complexity of the savings and loan problem, the task and direction of teaching budgeting would seem to remain focused and on center stage. These additional complications in the world of budgeting have brought with them problems and opportunities. These both help and exacerbate the problem of teaching budgeting in the 1990s. Our agenda includes the personal computer as an analytic vehicle, ethics and budgeting, and, finally, equipping students intellectually to deal with an ambiguous and sometimes hostile world through a combination of situational and technical knowledge.

THE COMPUTER REVOLUTION IN GOVERNMENT

The personal computer is quickly becoming the analytic tool of choice in government, while academia appears to lag behind the power curve in addressing the preparation of students to cope with this brave new world. As a result, governments have undertaken huge training efforts. For example, Monterey County, Calif., and Dade County, Fla., two progressive but not untypical urban counties, have sophisticated training programs that utilize computer laboratories equal to and superior to many of the personal computer facilities available on most college campuses, and those facilities are busy every moment of the work day. The academic world lags behind for a variety of factors, including uncertainty about what to teach, who should teach it—computer experts or subject matter experts—division of opinion about career rewards for those who teach it—computer books no matter how intricate are not usually seen as respectable intellectually on many if not most campuses—and simple physical plant inadequacies. Even classroom design differs for computer instruction, with interactive instruction proceeding best in a room where all the computers face away from the wall in a U shape or double box, depending on the number of computers, so that the instructor can see the screens of all the students with whom he is working. Some universities simply do not have the money to establish computer laboratories, or when faced with the resource allocation question would rather put it directly into faculty research than what seems to be a peripheral area—personal computers. The point is that that area is not peripheral to government, and the solution is not to wait until high schools, vocational schools, and consultants train students in the use of these tools.

Why not let others train future administrators and simply wait a generation until those third graders who now write stories and play games on the computer become mid- and upper-level managers? There are many obvious reasons, but the most important is that society can simply not afford that solution, one that creates a split class of society in administration: those who understand computers and what they can do and those who do not. Computers enhance information provision, and if part of an organization's scarce resources is wasted debating the legitimacy of different approaches to information, then the cost of decisions is raised, and perhaps their timeliness and effectiveness are decreased.

Why not let others train future administrators in personal computer use? The real problem is one of thinking. Higher education in all its forms is about thinking; on-the-job training is about production within a specified environment. This involves thinking, but not of a higher order. Many computer uses in government are simple database uses, establishing client or user mailing lists. Police departments have all sorts of database uses. But the absence of a higher order of understanding of the full advantage of what the computer can do will prevent users from querying databases to tie different databases together—for example, the aggravated assault and drunken driving databases. If students are not taught to think about computers as decision aids, then they will treat them as thinking typewriters, using their graphics packages, arguing with the statistical tests that spreadsheet packages have irrespective of their validity in a particular case, and, in general, utilizing a set of tools unthinkingly. Moreover, since basic applications are generally stabilized and sophisticated, the products they produce look nice and are generally convincing when presented in policymaking sessions, no matter that the statistical procedure is the wrong one for the case, or the graph is anchored in the "wrong" year (either the one most persuasive to the presenter's case or simply one with no meaning at all). Higher education needs to address the thinking side of personal computer use. So pervasive have personal computers become, so convenient have software packages become, so persuasive appears their output that government workers everywhere are pulling down data, analyzing it, manipulating it, and arguing out decisions with it.

This proliferation of computer use has some negative outcomes. Computer output has a halo effect, just as typewritten documents must have had almost a century before. Now the typewriter is seen as a tool; no one in literate societies ascribes any magic to it. However, the same can not be said for computers. Moreover, so popular are personal computers that they now constitute a destabilizing force in the organization. Organizations have to be careful that a correct or official database is maintained at all times, because there are so many other numbers and reports being generated that seem official. Sometimes ordinary mainframe or system applications are bypassed because it is easier for the individual to work with the personal computer program he or she knows, and the official system begins to decay. Next the argument is heard that since no one seems to use the mainframe or official system, why do we invest so much in the way of resources in it? Then there is the variation where the analyst takes output from several computer information systems, picks out the key numbers, encoding them manually on a spreadsheet, and types them into a spreadsheet to produce yet another printout, when a more thoughtful approach might have combined the original programs into fewer programs or isolated the key numbers and allowed downloading or production of the last printout directly. One of my students observed a budget process where an analyst scanned about 11 program printouts for numbers, recorded them with pencil on a spreadsheet, and entered them into a computer to produce a budget. With the introduction of one new column in one of the printouts, he cut the number of programs necessary to three.

Then, of course, there is simple time inefficiency. Desktop publishing presents an unparalleled opportunity to fritter away time. Important reports should look good, but not all reports are important. Then, too, people in organizations still create whole tracking systems when the boss out of curiosity wanted the answer to one question that the system did not have. Even though he only wanted it that one day, a system gets created just in case he ever wants it again . . . and now with computers, that system can be produce an answer, graph it, and either deflate it for constant dollars, per capita trends, or present value and print it in a nice binder with several different type fonts and shades of grey.

The mission of higher education is to teach thinking, as well as some lower-order recognition skills. The personal computer revolution is outrunning higher education's ability and perhaps its interest to cope with this mission, and some disastrous consequences lurk in the shadows. This problem is particularly critical for the public sector. Where there is no market test, critical thinking is even more important. Without training in what to see and how to think about the data that personal computers so easily produce, government risks making decisions that are efficient but ineffective, quick but inequitable, and pretty but wrong.

THE COMPUTER REVOLUTION: THE ACADEMIC REACTION

In 1985 the National Association of Schools of Public Administration and Affairs (NASPAA) issued a curriculum report on the use of computers in classrooms. This report served as the starting point for the task force on teaching budgeting and financial management sponsored by the American Society for Public Administration (ASPA) section on Budgeting and Finance (SBFM). The NASPAA (1986) report stated that professionals working in government as general managers would be increasingly required:

To use computerized information systems in their daily work.
To find information of relevance to decision problems.
To retrieve that information and analyze it for the problem at hand.
To communicate the results of that analysis in written and graphic forms.
To communicate over electronic networks, both in their office and external to it.
To communicate their information to databases and other specialists outside their organization.

The NASPAA survey revealed that its schools were preparing to meet these challenges by offering a single course in computer literacy. Thus the report advocated that schools move beyond that single course and integrate teaching of computers into existing functional areas, and that furthermore they create information management as an additional core area in their programs. Moreover, programs were to establish computer labs and to expose students to problem-solving simulations, mainframe connections, and hands-on use of multiuser shared databases.

The SBFM (see Berne, 1985) task force made the following additional recommendations in July 1985:

1. All M.P.A. students should attain a basic proficiency in information management and data analysis.
2. Programs should consider requiring basic computer skills as an entrance prerequisite.
3. Instruction in information management and data analysis should be integrated directly into specialization courses.
4. Programs should provide access to minicomputers and mainframe computers to allow for sharing of hardware, software, and data resources.

The task force emphasized that information management and data analysis were important skills. In the areas of budgeting and financial management, the task force recommended that certain skills be treated as computerized skills. The nine members of the budgeting and financial management subgroup felt that certain skills or areas should be computerized. These were led by budget preparation, government financial accounting and reporting, expenditure forecasting, revenue forecasting, debt management, and capital investment decision-making.

The task force also found support for computerized training in cost-effectiveness analysis, present value concepts, and evaluation of financial condition.

Constraints

The task force recognized that there were a number of constraints to overcome in this effort. These included:

1. A tension in the teaching profession between generalists and specialists.
2. Difficulty in fitting the program in, in M.P.A. programs that are shorter than 2 years.
3. A tension between training for state and local jobs and for federal and international jobs. The report suggested that computer education may be of less importance to students interested in federal and international jobs.
4. Problems finding qualified people to teach. A shortage appeared to exist in the budgeting and financial teaching market, and adding computerization to it would only decrease the set of qualified people.
5. Computer facilities are required. These could be either mainframe or personal computers.
6. Reluctance to change, because change meant redirection of faculty resources, new positions, capital outlay money, and software money, all of which would be contested for by faculty who might believe in a more traditional use of the money.

Whatever these constraints, it was clear that a revolution was proceeding in the workplace and it could not be ignored.

THE COMPUTER REVOLUTION: WORKPLACE PROMISE AND TEACHING BURDEN

This revolution is affecting the way the work is done and who is doing it. It is as dramatic as the changeover from horses to airplanes as a mode of travel, in that it will make people think differently about the nature of work, organization structure, and even the physical nature of the workplace. While it affects all government functions, it perhaps has its most visible and influential impact on the budgeting and financial management functions.

For example, in Abilene, Tex., after the budget office has received the requests from the departments, budget teams consisting of budget officers and assistant city administrators review the requests. The financial data is then entered into a mainframe computer using a budget software package tailored for that purpose. Data are also entered into microcomputers using Lotus and the two sets of figures are checked against each other to ensure accuracy. "All the detailed line item breakdowns in the latter part of the budget are produced by the mainframe and downloaded into Wordstar to be compiled into reports, which are then printed by a laser printer" (Tobin, 1988).

The virtues of this system are:

1. The combined use of mainframe and micros acts as a check on data entry errors.
2. Lotus graphics ability is combined with the mainframe's superior capacity to produce the detailed line-item breakdowns for budget detail.
3. Once the data have been produced the mainframe can automatically enter them into the accounting system and use them for financial reporting for the next year.

This system combines budgeting, printing, graphics production, and the budgeting and accounting records systems.

Birmingham, Mich., uses a mini and micro system for budget control and tracking. It uses a minicomputer to store and manage data, but allows microcomputers to access the system to download data for analysis. Most of the data applications in the office are done with Lotus. In the budget area, the mini keeps track of each department's expenditures by month. These are then downloaded to a personal computer, which is used to produce reports that show expenditure by quarter over the preceding 2 years and their projected spending for the coming year. Departments then do their allotments based on their own work planning. In the quarterly budget reports, actual expenditures are compared with projected expenditures. A microcomputer is used to calculate the variance between the projected allotments and actual spending.

The budget process is ideal for a computer application, since most of the information stays the same and only one or two numbers change at a time. Done by hand, these changes would create a Herculean task. With the computer, their impact is much less. For example, the Monterey County budget officer (McCaffery, 1988b) said that he had at least 30 Lotus programs on his hard disk. These included:

Estimated salary savings (three spreadsheets)
Mid-year projections (two or three scenarios, thus two or three spreadsheets)
Tax anticipation notes and a cash flow analysis
A health program costout
County manager recommendations by department for the budget hearings, and for the final budget
A liability insurance workup
Salary by bargaining unit (8–10 different bargaining units mean 8–10 different memos of understanding and spreadsheets)
A spending limit spreadsheet calculating permissible spending growth according to state law
Welfare expenditures
Nonprogram revenues
Motor vehicle-in-lieu tax (three different categories)
Budget requests by department

Many of these involved more than one spreadsheet, since different iterations were done. Perhaps the major benefit for the last 3 years of transition to the mainframe computer was the ability of the personal computers and Lotus to track the diverse set of revenues the county has to deal with, tracking them by source, fund, department, and by budget unit. Future plans for the county included doing trend forecasting of fiscal solvency with standardized programs, analyzing the condition of counties of comparable size, and checking the state distribution of funds more closely to close the gap between notification of funds and receipt of funds. Hopes for the mainframe system included the ability to go get fiscal data, download it, massage it, and upload it back to the file, thus saving repeated data entry.

Whether done on a mainframe or a personal computer (PC), knowledge of spreadsheets was seen as vital in this office. The budget officer concluded his conversation by saying that being able to use a spreadsheet might well become a condition of employment in his office.

In general, computers are used most in public safety and general government administration. California cities appear to reflect this pattern. In a 1986 survey of data processing users done by the League of California Cites (1986) 240 cities reported using computer tools.

The following table shows the functional breakdown. This table summarizes a use index by counting number of pages devoted to computers by functions and number of uses per function for the major uses only. Note that there were over 110 pages in this locator section of the report.

Local Uses

Function	Number of pages	Number of uses
Police investigations	9	41
Fire protection	5	19
General accounting	8	8
Purchasing and inventory	4	11
Personnel	7	14
Budgeting and management	8	8

An examination of the budgeting and management function illustrated the range and variation of systems used and tasks performed. This gives the reader an idea of who does what in budgeting with computers.

Function	Cities	Mainframe	Mini	Micro
Expenditure forecasting	104	30	52	22
Revenue forecasting	99	27	50	22
Budget preparation	145	48	63	34
Program budget preparation	96	29	56	11
Program to line item	99	33	43	13
Budget monitoring system	144	48	80	16
Budgetary and financial analysis	96	26	52	18
Productivity measurement	18	4	10	4

In 1986 the system of choice was the minicomputer. A few cities used a mainframe and micros or a mini and micros, but not more than two or three in each function. Mainframes may be a historical relic in the sense that they were what was available prior to 1981, and 1981 is light years away in computer generations, but relatively close as government purchasing goes. Notice that budget monitoring is *not* a micro function; this is probably capacity related. Micros cannot handle the memory requirements. The same reason probably applies to converting line-item to program data: not only does the system have to handle a lot of data, the program itself is likely to be demanding.

In general, nationwide for microcomputers, word processing (42%) and spreadsheets and business graphics (30%) are the top two functional uses (Mulder, 1988). Database uses constituted 10% of use, and the rest was scattered among on-line services, desktop publishing, and project management according to a survey of cities. In the League of California Cities study the same pattern was reported.

Task	Number of cities	Micros
Word processing	165	94
Text editing	102	52
Spreadsheet	141	110
Charts/graphics	78	62
Statistical analysis	41	33

When office tasks are divided up into daily work, the microcomputer clearly dominates. Graphics and spreadsheet analysis are clearly microcomputer-dominated areas. Of 210 cities reporting that they used computers in the accounting function, only 22 reported using micros; these tended to be small, like Oroville, San Juan Bautista, Desert Hot Springs, or Mendota. The same pattern held for check preparing, check reconciliation, and payroll preparation.

A nationwide survey of cities over 50,000 in population reinforces this data. In city and county levels alone computers are used for some 450 different applications. (Northrop et al., 1990, p. 505), with cities over 50,000 averaging 84 applications. Managers said that cities experienced the most payoff in the areas of fiscal control and cost avoidance and better interaction with the public (Northrop et al., 1990, p. 512), but that payoffs were yet to be realized in nonfiscal areas. In an earlier study Kraemer and Northrop suggest city staffs rarely used computers for analysis (1989, p. 449) and argue that M.P.A. programs must train students to act in an environment that presumes computerization (Kraemer and Northrop, 1989, p. 450). In 1985, one-half of the 98 public management programs studied contained some computer training in from three to fourteen courses in their curricula (Kiel, 1986, p. 592).

While this is a good start, it is an effort that must continue and that must move more toward the teaching of the tools of analysis with personal computers. What the personal computer has done is to empower the individual and allow him or her to do things that were not within her grasp before—spreadsheet analysis, graphics, statistics. These skills and tools have become a supplement to the official systems. For example, when official numbers or legal requirements need to be met, like issuing checks or meeting payrolls, then official organizational systems take over, and these are different systems from the personal computer system and its users. One administrator said (McCaffery, 1988a), "I use spreadsheets all the time, but I do it as a check on the mainframe numbers. If I am going to be sent to jail [for a numerical error] it is Big Blue [affectionate reference to IBM mainframe computer] who is going to do it, not a pc." This is another way of emphasizing the reliability of the mainframe system, while at the same time pointing to the use of personal computers as personal analytic tools.

Thus at this point in time our observations include:

1. Official numbers seem to come from the big mainframe or minicomputers or even traditional bookkeeping machinery. Personal computers are used for independent analysis and preliminary argumentation. Personal computers are used as personal computers, what in another age would have been a slide rule . . . a tool to enhance personal productivity.
2. The major uses of this tool are for word processing and spreadsheets. Minor uses include database manipulation and statistical applications. These latter two take more expertise. Furthermore, most positions do not require these skills, whereas most positions require word processing and spreadsheet abilities, or can be usefully configured for their use.
3. While debate over who has the best or the leading spreadsheet continues, the idea of an electronic spreadsheet is firmly placed in the world of practitioners. To some extent, to know one spreadsheet is to know all spreadsheets and what they can add to instant analysis and complex and repetitive calculations. Academics no longer have to wait until the software market settles down in order to choose what to teach; this part is clear. The imperative is to teach a generic spreadsheet model, indicating the basic analytic uses, and let individuals learn local specific uses later.
4. Graphics are the newest tool. Judging from what appears on the desks of administrators, the ability to do arguments or justifications with graphs is a new tool, which has spread with the use of personal computers. Graphs are easy to understand and they convey complex arguments quickly. While spreadsheets are the tool, the real change seems to be to the use of graphics.
5. Sensitivity analysis—what-if analysis—is also a product of spreadsheet automation. In some cases tales are told of the board or council actually having a what-if case run while they deliberate (after all, once the spreadsheet is set up, the new numbers can be entered in the right cells and recalculated within seconds), but the most common use of what-if analysis seems to be in administrative settings, while graphics go forward to reviewing bodies.
6. The tools then associated with graphics also are important—tools like constant dollar conversion and choosing inflation indices with which to compare cost growth. When budget argument becomes a visual art, reviewers will have to start paying more attention to what year anchors a graph, because arguments about growth or decline can be biased depending upon what year the data series begins with. In all three of the units interviewed (McCaffery, 1988a) consumer price index comparisons were made for different purposes and put in graphics formats, to judge fare increases, to judge wage increases, and to evaluate contractual expenses. What used to be the tools of a specialist are now becoming tools that are used routinely.
7. Spreadsheet packages also have rudimentary statistical routines in them. They do not seem to be used much at this moment, but since they are available and since companies compete for sales, documentation is being written more and more

clearly, and since there is a subsidiary industry in explaining spreadsheet packages it may not be long before the smallest local government is doing regression analysis to predict cost growth. Availability and ease of access predict use. The risk to this is that inappropriate tools may be used to justify or sell services to budget reviewers who accept the argument because they can not judge the accuracy of the argument in the statistical model. They go along with it because it looks good.

8. Software is a way of thinking about problems. To get a spreadsheet to work requires a certain pattern of thought as well as data, and spreadsheets transfer the pattern of thought as well as the data from one person to another . . . in the cast of the template and in the data chosen to go into the template. On the positive side this transfer of knowledge about knowledge management is job enrichment, and downstream users and the organization will benefit. It is a freeing and an empowering process that has consequences for people and for organizations.

9. Clerical positions as clerical positions may be on the way out. John Peterson addressed this in commenting on an arbitrage rebate calculation under the Tax Reform Act of 1986, saying there is software available that "takes an extremely complicated concept and makes it so that any clerk can do the calculation" (Fiorda-lisi, 1988). In Monterey County I was told that there were no more clerical positions in the County Auditors Office and that the secretary in the data processing unit was now doing budgeting and spreadsheet managerial work analogous to what is normal-ly called the administrative assistant position range—what used to be a low-level professional position or the top of the series one could get to without a college education. It is clear that computer literacy empowers people; it is also clear that people can learn it on the job and that organizations are willing to invest training time to teach.

10. Top-level management positions may not change much, nor may mid-level manag-ers. Mid-level analysts may find themselves absorbing typing and data entry work that clerks used to do. Consensus among computer-literate mid-level people with whom I talked was that they were now doing what used to be done by a clerk/typist about half time for them, since there was no need to retype spreadsheets and manuscripts, and letters could be revised right up to the moment they were printed out. Organizations should become leaner at lower levels, and should not necessarily become larger at the middle level. In the end, an $800 computer is cheaper than a $12,000 clerk/typist.

11. Data entry and data security are problems. Privacy is an issue, when many workers are connected to private records. More important to the functioning of the organiza-tion is ensuring that the correct number is entered, if other people are going to depend on that number by downloading it and manipulating it. Making sure that it stays the right number is also a problem that has to be settled; the issue is who shall have the right to update the file and how the dates and time stamps should be put on the file to indicate which iteration this is. With the proliferation of personal computers everyone will have numbers. This is good to the extent that many people checking independently will keep the system correct and bad to the extent that many people entering the system may corrupt it. Arguments over the right numbers may make decision makers lose faith in the credibility of the system.

12. The great efficiency for the organization is entering data one time and permitting people to access and manipulate it within a custom-designed template—be it a simple spreadsheet run on an individual computer or a mainframe spreadsheet program. The efficiencies are simply staggering. For example, the Lawrence Town-

ship Volunteer Fire Department produces a report for the State Fire Marshall's office in 10 minutes on a PC—it used to take 3 or 4 hours (Ahern, 1988).

13. So pervasive is the mindset now for computers, that governments without computers are suspect; speaking of preparing reports for bond ratings, not only can governments prepare worry-free presentations quickly, but the fact that they have a computer "means their information is better and more timely" was the quote of a senior vice president at Standard and Poor's. Commenting that computers make it easier for governments to produce lists of new construction and tax base adjustments, she added that the rating agency had to be conservative if it did not have that information (Fiordalisi, 1988, p. 18.) . . . which I take to mean that all other things being equal, those without computers may be rated lower.

   It is also clear that those people who choose not to be computer literate or are so prevented are going to be out. With the widespread use of computers in schools, this should not be a problem, but both hardware and software change. Fortunately the software change trend lies in the direction of user simplicity, much as automotive engineering went to automatic transmissions and power steering, thus making it easier to shift and parallel park. Whether computer use will ever be as simple as running a toaster is debatable.

14. Individual isolation may be a problem; when the computer and the video screen take over for human interaction, what happens to corporate culture and corporate morale? It is possible that government could become the cottage industry of the next decade. When a professional can access a database, pull down the data, manipulate a report, and upload the analysis for someone else to read, where is the imperative for him or her to be stationed in a city, or county, or state, or federal office building as long as there are phone lines and modems? This is particularly true for staff positions where almost no public interaction is specified. For example, the government budget office of the future may have few clerks and many middle-level analysts who work at home and communicate electronically.

It may be that the next revolution in computers will be in small-sized, cheap, but powerful laptop computers, the kind that people will carry with them just as they used to bring their own pencil or pen to a job. They bring their computer; the organization provides the mainframe and the network that the person can access from a workstation at the office or at home. Meanwhile, there is a revolution occurring in government, not just at the local level. A recent study of federal budget analysts revealed that over half of the analysts polled thought that additional training in microcomputer technology and electronic spreadsheet usage would help them on the job. Computer instruction was their single highest priority item (Wright, 1989). The decline in price of personal computers and the increase in their capacity would seem to make this an irreversible process.

The academic community appears to be lagging behind this revolution in preparing students to cope with the ramifications of this revolution. However, there are sources for hope. Programs and instructors have begun to respond, and the dimensions of the field itself have become much more clear. For example, software has stabilized; while there are many spreadsheets, the concept of spreadsheet has stabilized, and what a budget analyst basically does with this spreadsheet can also be treated as stable. Hence it is deliverable knowledge.

What then are the obstacles for delivering that knowledge? Teaching analytic computer skills is a technology that must be developed before it can be taught. For most academics, it constitutes a third technology that must be learned, in addition to teaching and research, and for which the institutional reward structure is not yet clear. Professors learn research methodologies; often the statistical techniques and the software they are familiar with in research have little to do with predominant spreadsheet uses demanded in government. Consequently, research will also have to be done into how practitioners use computers for analysis. Until these tensions are resolved, agreement on what should be taught will lag behind what can be taught. Many academic uses look back to mainframe computer programs and techniques, while the most fruitful use of personal computers now seems to be in individual analysis and preparation of documents and graphs for policy argumentation. The academic profession will first have to recognize this discrepancy before it can react to it. This is a complex problem, but one the academic community cannot ignore.

FINANCIAL MANAGERS AND ETHICS

The inclusion of ethics material in financial management courses is an issue the academic community should not ignore. The reader who browses through any standard textbook on budgeting will find it rife with suggestions on how to behave in order to get budgets funded. Implicit or explicit, these are moral imperatives. All too often the classroom response is vague and evasive to simple questions about padding budgets or obscuring spending patterns to manipulate fund balances. This has not gone unnoticed.

One eloquent voice in this respect is Carol Lewis's: "Budget decision makers are trustees for the vulnerable, dependent, unorganized and politically inarticulate, those most liable to be overlooked in formulations of the public interest. Future generations are the most vulnerable and unrepresented of all" (Lewis, 1990, p. 4).

If this seems to make a positive case, Lewis also warns that the "twistings and turnings in the 1980's mirror political deadlock and ethical shortfall," and that tinkering with mechanisms has been substituted for political responsibility. She sees this as a purposeful choice, for when you "talk about process, you don't have to talk about tough choices" (Lewis, 1990, p. 6). Although willing to let the electorate and politicians shoulder a just portion of the blame, Lewis does not let public managers go unscathed. Padding may be commonplace, but it is still unethical, she notes, as are exaggerated promises and underestimated costs, substituting strategy for neutrality and accuracy, cutting corners rather than cutting budgets, and letting things slide when the going gets tough. Since the budget process depends on and rewards deceit, budgeting is in ethical deficit. Lewis's prescription is the restoration of a public trust among the elected, electors, and public managers founded on a notion of prudence. Individual judgments about the depth of the ethical deficit may vary, but the professorate in public budgeting and finance should and must come to grips with this issue. It is too important to be left to be done elsewhere.

It will not be an easy task. In a standard dictionary, ethics is defined as (1) a system of moral principles, (2) rules of conduct recognized in respect to a particular class of human actions or a particular group (the medical profession), (3) the moral principles of an individual, and (4) a philosophy dealing with values relating to human conduct, about the rightness and wrongness of certain actions and to the goodness or badness of the motives and ends of such actions.

Ethical is defined as pertaining to or dealing with morals or the principals of morality, pertaining to right and wrong in conduct.

Moral is defined as concerned with principles or rules of right conduct or the distinction between right and wrong. For example, moral obligations are founded on fundamental principles of right conduct rather than on legalities, enactment (of laws), or custom.

Morals and ethics refer to rules and standards of conduct and practice. Morals refers to generally accepted customs of conduct and right living in a society, and to the individual's practice in relation to these. Ethics now implies high standards of honest and honorable dealing and of methods used, especially in the professions or business (*Dictionary of the English Language*, Random House, 1987).

Although for most purposes ethical and moral can be treated as having almost identical meanings, more precise usage would seem to make moral a word to pertain to individual behavior and ethics to pertain to group behavior.

Moral behavior precedes ethical behavior in sequence of learning and hence time. Moral behavior is learned in the early stages of life and then applied in the later stages as the child assumes the roles and responsibilities of the adult life. Ethical behavior is a certain set of behaviors that pertain to certain roles. While the core behaviors may be the same, resting in fundamental moral principles, the range of what is considered ethical may be quite different. Two moral persons could have quite different sets of ethical behavior; for example, what is ethical behavior for a minister and a used car dealer could be quite different, though they both be moral men at heart. The difference is in the group they belong to; therefore ethical behavior is an acculturation to a group norm; hence we speak of the ethics of the medical profession. We do not speak of the ethics of the used car dealer profession. It would seem that in order for a group to have ethics there must be repetitive situations that arise with some frequency, complex enough so that they do not lend themselves to easy solutions, and complex enough so that they cannot become captured by laws or customary behavior. Thus the group has to be self-regulating in these grey areas beyond ready applicability of the law or regulations.

The point here is that a moral education for the young is not enough. When that person assumes an adult role in life, and in a profession, he or she is faced with choices that are more complex than those examples provided in his or her early training; hence the decisions to be made do not fit inside the previous moral framework and those people have to be socialized to the code of ethics of the profession they are joining: doctors learn not only a trade, but how doctors behave. When the behavior of lawyers passes the boundaries of what the community expects, a rash of lawyer jokes appears. Current jokes making the rounds are quite cruel. One asks: "Do you know why medical testing laboratories now use lawyers instead of rats? One, lawyers breed faster, so there are more of them. Two, lab personnel do not get as emotionally attached to them, and three, lawyers will do things rats will not." Some critics suggest that the public's appetite for lawyer jokes stems from its disappointment with the legal system. The recent plethora of government financial scandals has raised the issue of ethics for financial managers, and to some extent the savings and loan industry difficulties have led to suspicion of financial managers and the government people who regulated them.

FINANCIAL MANAGERS AND ETHICS

That ethics for administrators is a hot topic is both good and bad news. On the bad side lies a recognition that innate honesty, law, administrative rule, audits, and preaudit clearance procedures are no longer enough. On the positive side is the assumption that government administrators constitute a class of people who either have or can be taught a guidance mechanism so complex that it cannot be precisely spelled out in law or rules for an arena of administration so complicated that routine procedures are not enough. Lewis (1986) suggests that there is no single, viable rule universally applicable to all cases and that ethical decisions may become so complex that cross-pressuring may result in the inability to make decisions certain that one is right, or that they may result in dismissing the ethical aspects of decisions altogether.

However, the inescapable fact of life is that decisions have to be made. Lewis suggests that financial managers consider the following questions when faced with a troublesome decision:

1. Is it legal?
2. Is it effective?
3. Is it ethical?

Lewis also suggests asking who the issue effects, what their concerns or interests are, if everyone *can* live with the outcome, and if they *should have to* live with that outcome.

Especially for financial managers, Lewis suggests, the acid test may be whether they would like to read about their decision on the front page of their newspaper or have to explain it to their family.

Financial managers have an extra burden because their decisions involve money and the allocation of fiscal benefits or because they simply handle money and can be tempted to go astray.

FINANCIAL MANAGERS: AN EMPIRICAL VIEW

Academics are not the only ones concerned about ethics for government decision makers in the budgeting and finance area. At the 1989 Conference of the San Francisco Bay Area Federal Financial Managers Council, a highlight of the conference was a workshop on ethics. These were basically top-level middle managers, just below the senior executive service, holding a variety of budgeting and financial management positions for the federal government. Many of them served directly under political appointees in their regions. Questions about ethics were important to them. Over 90% of the group felt that media attention to the ethics of public officials had had a negative impact on confidence in the public sector. They did not feel that ethics laws overregulated the public sector (75% said laws did not). Over 90% said better leadership from top officials would help create a more ethical environment. Discussion later disclosed that they not only meant officials above their level, but themselves and people at their levels also had a responsibility to set the ethical tones. Slightly more than half the group felt that government officials should be held to a higher standard than their public sector counterparts.

They were asked to identify their areas of ethical concern (number of respondents: 32). Those responding "yes" to each area of concern were:

1. Appearance of impropriety, 69%.
2. Compliance, guidance, and enforcement, 41%.
3. Conflict of interest and financial disclosure, 40%.
4. Defense systems acquisition, 16%.
5. Ethics codes, 13%.

6. Financial management, 72%.
7. Information management, 3%.
8. Legislation and regulations, 16%.
9. Media relations, 0%.
10. Personnel management, 34%.
11. Postemployment restrictions, 16%.
12. Procurement and contracting, 47%.
13. Program management, 25%.
14. Public-private interface, 22%.
15. Recruitment and retention, 16%.
16. Resource allocation, 25%.
17. Service delivery, 25%.
18. Theories, concepts, and research, 3%.
19. Training and education, 3%.

Since the groups were groups of federal financial managers, their number one concern was financial management; had they been academics it might have been theories, concepts, and research about ethics. They were also not interested in media relations, training and education, and ethics codes.

They were concerned about the appearance of impropriety, conflict of interest and financial disclosure, and procurement and contracting. There were some group differences. The morning group was more concerned about personnel management, resource allocation, and service delivery, and the afternoon group was more concerned with defense systems acquisitions, and conflict of interest and financial disclosure. The differences reflected the agency and functional makeup of the individuals in the groups, with appearance of impropriety and financial management being the two leading categories. Later discussion disclosed that for most of the group, financial management included a multitude of activities, ranging from handling cash, to year-end spending, to misappropriation of funds and outright theft.

The groups were then subdivided and asked to discuss and report back a list of the top three to five ethical concerns facing them in their agencies and to suggest a start on an operational code of ethics. Not all of the groups reached consensus on this task. Results are reported for the groups that did.

Group I

Concerns

1. Data that is filtered or omitted to support a political decision.
2. Rationing of health care.
3. Actions based only on self interest.
4. Excessive nit-picking (raising details to stop or delay program implementation).

Operational Code

1. Set a good example.
2. Do what is morally correct.
3. Emphasize what can be done.
4. Standards should relate to people (e.g., rules for reduction in force appeared to safeguard individuals, but when reductions in force occurred, the rules were interpreted a different way than employees expected).

Group II

Concerns

1. Accuracy of management information (e.g., self-reporting of data by states—should it be accepted or to what extent should it be checked).
2. Political nepotism (the "good ol' boy" syndrome . . . in personnel selection and rewards).
3. Public image—the appearance of impropriety.
4. Spending excess resources rather than turning them back.
5. Handling directives from political appointees that are perceived to be unethical (or illegal).

Operational Code

1. Spend it like it is your own.
2. Check it out! (Find out about the request rather than blindly implementing it.)
3. Know the body of the law, regulations and policy that impact on your job (aids to help you check it out).
4. Raise the question (be a change agent).
5. Do not lie or bluff (but be careful about volunteering information).

Group III

Concerns

1. Relationships with service vendors (lunches, receptions, small gifts: do not accept them).
2. Employee retention of travel incentives.
3. Allowing outside groups to benefit from official actions.
4. Inconsistencies of ethics codes.
5. Poor ethical leadership

Operational Code

1. Do not accept favors (gifts, lunches, etc.).
2. Rather than travel incentives, ask the General Services Administration to negotiate lower rates (don't pick a higher-cost provider to get travel benefits).
3. Follow the standard government ethics code.

Group IV

Concerns

1. Conflict of interest.
2. Procurement fraud and bribery.
3. Misappropriation of funds.
4. Theft of government property.

Operational Code

1. Do not use office for personal gain.

2. Avoid gifts and gratuities.
3. Do not accept bribes.

Group V

Concerns

1. Acquisition practices.
2. Misuse of funds.
3. Favoritism (of organizations and people).
4. Misuse of government property (telephone, supplies).
5. Bribery.

Operational Code

1. No appearance of impropriety.
2. No favoritism—no acceptance of gifts.
3. Enforce required annual training in ethics.
4. No use of position for personal gain.

In this list of concerns and advisories, some were individual and some were collective. Some were obvious and some subtle, but taken together they constitute an inventory of a very complex horizon. Some dealt with issues up the chain of command, some down. Some dealt within the agency; others were external, between the agency and its clienteles. A consistent theme in the group was the appearance of impropriety. Also consistent was the difficulty of working with political appointees who came to government ignorant of the rules and regulations and ethical climate of government and impatient with "red tape" and, perhaps, with fiscal controls, although the point was made that sometimes they simply did not know and had to be told that what they wanted to do was illegal or skirted the edges of the ethical. Thus one person urged that political folks had to be made aware. Another said that they sometimes had to be urged to attack problems in program delivery and not by passing those problems on to another agency.

I closed the discussion by offering a very simplistic set of budget prescriptions:

1. Ask for what you need.
2. Spend what you must.
3. Follow legal directives and directions; object to others.
4. Operate frugally, but do the program.
5. Be a squeaky wheel when you should.
6. Protect yourself.

Unfortunately, the range of behaviors permitted by these injunctions is quite wide, and most ultimately invoke sophisticated judgments to implement. What comes through clearly in this discussion is the importance of the issue to real-life administrators. Lewis could be dismissed for painting too grim a picture—an ethical deficit?—or for dealing with something of a very transitory nature that will soon go away. When the administrators above still feel they have to include not taking bribes or stealing government property in an operational code, it becomes obvious that this is a fundamental problem that will not pass from the scene. Teachers of public budgeting and financial management are going to have to deal with teaching ethics for financial managers as a pedagogical issue. This will mean doing more than writing new chapters in standard textbooks and extending the final course lecture.

PROTECTING YOURSELF

Perhaps one of the most important gifts a teacher can give a student is a way of coping with the long-run frustrations of a career, a way that also helps that person do better for himself and for the society he or she serves. In this section, instead of offering more complexities for teachers of budgeting, we offer a partial solution.

Budgeting tends to be a world filled with closure, maybe as a derivative of spreadsheets, perhaps as a residual of the imperative to submit balanced budgets, in most jurisdictions. Technicians learn to make solid arguments involving numbers, and as they become more proficient their arguments become more complex and complete. Suddenly, they encounter turbulence; technical arguments are disregarded, even ignored. Some budget analysts simply give up on government at this point and seek other careers. There is a way to think around this problem, however.

Some years ago, I asked a group of 30 state and local administrators to write about how they decided how much to ask for (McCaffery, 1988a). Most of the essays captured budgeting in much the same way as the typical textbook, a series of steps that one proceeded through to arrive at a decision. The typical answer would include this list:

1. I determine what I am going to do—my purpose, mission.
2. I determine how much I am going to do—production goals, objectives.
3. I determine how I am going to do it—organizational structure, staff needs, other costs necessary to carry out the plan.
4. I determine cost assumptions—salary schedules, other cost factors.
5. Then I prepare budget justifications.

However, a minority of the group took a very different approach to the budget decision. Their solutions moved from numbers-dominated solutions to solutions that encompass both numbers and people in situations, for example, their relationship with their superior, long-term gaming strategies, even reference points set by other offices.

For example, one said, I take into account:

1. My project is the pet project of the administrators who will divide the amount allotted for the projects. Therefore, I can get most of what I can justify.
2. I try to find out how much (they) will likely be given (to divide).
3. I build a budget based on program needs, realizing that the person reviewing my budget believes everyone asks for more than they need—I know I'll be cut some, so I pad a little. I still need experience at calculating where he (the supervisor) will cut.
4. Once I have decided on the basic program and staffing needs, I don't make major changes—just adjust up and down as the process of budget approval is carried out between my project, my supervisor, the district's accounting, personnel, and purchasing departments, the district board, the Department of Training, and the City Council.
5. I realize that budget supplements are allowed and not too difficult to get, so if I can't get something I have to have or if conditions change rapidly, I know I can get more money later.

6. Because of the formula used to determine administrative costs, I know the majority of my program expenses must be justified as training and I plan the program and staffing to reflect this.

What is interesting here is the diagnosis of the process in a step-by-step isolation of key variables. These include the identification of the project as a pet project, an estimate of how much will be available, the felt necessity to pad a little, knowledge that the program itself is not vulnerable and that incremental adjustments up or down as the process continues will be enough, and the knowledge that if things go awry, a supplemental is available. This administrator seems comfortable in the process. Some may argue that this comes from the pet project syndrome; others may conclude that it rests on the administrator's analytic grasp of the budget process, his sense of the rules of the game, and confidence in his ability to operate to his best advantage with those rules.

Another administrator felt that projecting himself into the role of is superior was his most effective budget strategy.

> My approach to requesting either budget or disbursement authority is to project myself into the other person's position. I examine their environment, their pressures, their past experience, their constraints, their institutional culture and their philosophy, both personal and institutional. By that time I have already decided what I need. I then go through a process of building a case for all or part of what I need such that it will make sense to them from their point of view and is "approvable" within their environment.

The test of approvable is how they will feel defending the request:

"I try to make sure that I give them reasons they will feel comfortable using, if someone asks them why they approved my request."

In using this strategy, this administrator says he always tries to stick to the following principles:

1. Be honest with myself in determining what I need. I avoid the temptation to define what I need by what is safe to ask for.
2. Be honest with my request to them: I don't scheme, asking for two in order to get one.
3. Recognize their authority and responsibility: They have the right to say no.
4. Do not settle for a plain no: If the request is denied I ask for alternatives or a better way or acceptance of the consequences of saying no.

This is a situational approach to the budget decision. It takes sophistication and skill to implement, but it does allow for the joining of technical skills and interpersonal or situational, even political, factors in the calculus of the budget professional.

There is a danger to this approach. It comes close to defining what should be as what will go. That would vitiate the long tradition of progressive budget reformism and civil service neutrality wherein experts asked for what was necessary and politicians decided what to do based upon political calculations. In another guise this is the politics-administration dichotomy—an issue well argued for at least five decades, but not yet settled. The special case this chapter brings is that budgets dictate how programs are run. If the budget maker does not tell the political decision maker what the model program should be, then all that is left to compromise over is what cost people will accept, not what needs to be done. This ignores the price society may have to pay for not staffing its schools appropriately, not training its policemen right, or not adequately arming its military establishment. When the technicians give the politician what the technician thinks the politician wants to hear, many things can go wrong, and perhaps nothing stands a chance of going right.

But this is taking the approach to the extreme. Its value lies in looking at the budget situation as a network of events, some of which happen external to and superior to technical considerations. The simple injunction to view your budget or request as your superior would is one that most budgeteers never learn and many others forget. The higher the rank of the budgeteer the more the value the approach has, because the issues are greater, and probably less susceptible to technical analysis, and more likely to occur at the interface of politics and administration, where a contextual view is almost a prerequisite for success. Some seasoning of students into these intricate routines of budgeting will serve them well. There is no doubt but that those who go beyond a simple assumption that "right makes might" will enjoy public service more and be more successful in the world of budgeting. Young or inexperienced analysts are often dismayed when technical factors do not seem to count for as much as politics or situational factors. Those who learn to balance technical and situational considerations will last longer, do more good, and serve the public and themselves better. The trick is to keep this to a careful balancing of technical and interpersonal skills. As Figure 1 indicates, technicians learn over their career that

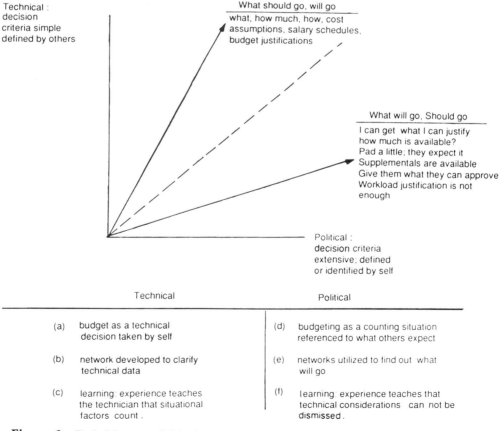

Figure 1 Technician or politician?

situational factors count in decisions; for the new budget analyst to have a technically correct decision reversed can threaten a career in public service. There is also little doubt but that more experienced administrators learn to inculcate politicians with expert values that rest on the acculturation to law and administrative practices in the subject matter area.

The approach of a few administrators to the budget decision as a situation rather than a decision has important implications for the practice and teaching of budgeting. This is not to denigrate analytic efforts. Rather, it is an attempt to situate them into a context where longer-term efforts will pay off for the individual and the jurisdiction.

CONCLUSION

Much remains to be done to cure the pedagogic deficit, and like the current federal deficit, the list of obligations seems to be increasing. They include more work on analysis, more with computers, more with ethics. Some of these are a melodies we may have forgotten, temporarily: ethics have always been important, we just forgot we had to face up to them in the budget course. The politics/administration dichotomy has been around awhile, we may just have forgotten we have to address it in the context of technical and situational behavior. While there are many causes for alarm in the picture, there are also some very hopeful signs that we are moving in the right directions.

REFERENCES

Ahern, C. (1988). Governments turn to desk-top publishing. *City and State* Feb. 15:25.

Berne, R. (1985). Core skills and skills concentrations. In *Working Papers on Graduate Curricula in Budgeting and Financial Management,* American Society for Public Administration, Section on Budgeting and Financial Management.

Fiordalisi, G. (1988). Paper flow staunched. *City and State* Feb. 15:18.

Grizzle, G. (1985). Essential skills for financial management: Are MPA students acquiring the necessary competencies? *Public Administration Review* Nov/Dec.:840–844.

Henry, N. (1979). The relevance question. In *Education for Public Service 1979,* G. Birkhead and J. Carroll (eds.), Syracuse University, Syracuse, N.Y.

Kraemer, K., and Northrop, A. (1989). Curriculum recommendations for public management education in computing: An update." *Public Administration Review* Sept./Oct.:447–453.

League of California Cities. (1986). *Data Processing in California Cities.* Sacramento, California, 1986. (These tables are taken from the application locator section in the report, pp. 128–238.)

Lewis, C. (1986). *Scruples and Scandals, A Handbook on Public Service Ethics for State and Local Government Officials.* University of Connecticut, Storrs, Conn.

Lewis, C. (1990). Public Budgeting: Unethical in Purpose, Product, and Promise. Presented at the Second Annual Conference of the Section on Budgeting and Financial Management of American Society for Public Administration, Washington, D.C., November.

MacManus, S. (1984). Budgetary Skills Needs of Different Types of Local Governments: A Market Survey. Paper presented at the American Society for Public Administration National Conference.

McCaffery, J. (1983). "Analyzing the pedagogic deficit in budgeting. In *Handbook on Public Budgeting and Financial Management,* J. Rabin and T. Lynch (eds.), Marcel Dekker, New York.

McCaffery, J. (1988a). The Computer Revolution Continues. Paper presented at the Region X annual conference of the American Society for Public Administration, October.

McCaffery, J. (1988b). *Budgetmaster.* J. McCaffery, Pacific Grove, Calif.

McCaffery, J. (1989). Strategies for achieving budgetary goals. In *Handbook of Public Administration*, J. Perry (ed.), Jossey-Bass, San Francisco, pp. 290–301.

Mulder, J. (1988). *City and State*, p. 18, from report of 81 respondents in 31 states, February.

NASPAA. (1985). Report: Special Issue. *Public Administration Review* 46:595–602.

Northrop, A., Kraemer, Dunkle, and King, (1990). Payoffs from computerization: Lessons over time. *Public Administration Review* Sept./Oct.:505–513.

Software Reference Guide. 1988. ICMA, Washington, D.C., pp. 231–232.

Stillman, R. (1982). Local public management in transition: A report on the current status of the profession. In *Municipal Yearbook*, ICMA, Washington, D.C.

Tobin, T. (1988). The budget as a communication tool. *MIS Report* 20:2.

Wright, D. (1989). Budget Analyst Training in Navy Type Commands. Thesis, Naval Postgraduate School.

7

Public Budget Execution and Management Control

L. R. Jones *Department of Administrative Sciences, Naval Postgraduate School, Monterey, California*

INTRODUCTION

The public budgeting cycle consists of the phases of budget formulation and execution. The formulation phase is subdivided into preparation of estimates by executive departments and agencies, review and negotiation between department budget officials and executive budget controllers, review and negotiation between departments and legislative oversight committees, enactment of budget appropriations by the legislature, approval or veto of appropriations by the elected executive, and legislative response to executive vetos if necessary. The execution phase of budgeting is comprised of the subcomponents of apportionment of appropriations, preaudit, spending (authorization of obligations, encumbrance, disbursement), monitoring and control of spending, financial reporting, financial and management audit, and evaluation of program implementation and policy outcomes.

The highly visible politics of budget formulation at times appears to mislead the public as to the importance of all of the phases of the budget process. While proposal, negotiation, and enactment are crucial in terms of determining the distribution of resources, efficiency and effectiveness are achieved or lost in the execution of budgets. Despite the importance and difficulty of negotiating the budget, perhaps the most challenging task in budgeting is to execute well so that the best program outcomes are achieved with some degree of efficiency and a genuine concern for the proper use of public funds. Budget execution skill is required to respond to inevitable contingencies that arise to complicate the implementation of programs in the manner planned and according to the promises made in budget formulation. Accountability must be maintained and at the same time uncertainty must be accommodated.

Budget execution typically is highly regulated to control what program managers may and may not do. Controllers are driven by the objective of insuring that budget

The views presented in this paper are those of the author and do not represent the position of the Naval Postgraduate School or the U.S. Navy. Please do not quote or reproduce without the written permission of the author.

The author wishes to acknowledge the assistance provided by Fred Thompson, Jerry McCaffery, Aaron Wildavsky, and others in drafting this chapter.

appropriations in total and by legally segregated account are not overspent by programs (Anthony and Young, 1984, Chaps. 7–9). However, controllers also must be concerned with underexecution. Department and agency budget officers and program managers do not want to underspend and thereby lose claim to resources in the following fiscal year. Central executive budget office controllers do not want programs to execute without good cause, so that money not used in the manner justified in budget formulation may be withdrawn from program managers. Executive controllers want to be able to withdraw funds from programs to protect the integrity of the appropriation process and to reallocate money to areas where it will be spent efficiently in response to client demand. For these reasons, budget execution typically is monitored and controlled carefully both by agency budget staff and central executive budget controllers. Execution also is often monitored closely by legislative oversight committees and their staffs out of a desire to insure that legislative will is implemented faithfully, and also to make sure that benefits are distributed to the clients targeted in the appropriation process (Anthony and Young, 1984, p. 288). Because the electoral fortunes of legislators are tied to some degree to the public perception that they are solving the problems and meeting the demands of their constituents, legislators have considerable interest in budget execution control.

Among the techniques used to control budget execution, variance analysis is probably the most familiar. Controllers and budget officials in government program offices monitor the differences between projected and actual revenues and expenses in total and by account. They monitor revenue and expense rates against allotment controls by quarter, month, week, day—temporal control generally is required by the allotment process. Other variables monitored are purpose of expense relative to budget proposal and appropriation rational, and location of revenues and expenses by unit and at times by geographical location. Monitoring of actual revenue and expense rates as well as program output and demand, where measurable, also is done to compare current spending to proposals made in the budget for the next year that are under negotiation at the same time as the fiscal year budget is expended. Comparisons are made to historical revenue and spending trends in some instances to better understand how current programs are performing. Budget execution monitoring and control is particularly important toward the end of the fiscal year for reasons stated above, to avoid both over- and underexpenditure relative to appropriation.

The purpose of the analysis of budget execution control provided in the following sections is to improve understanding of control dynamics, incentives, disincentives, and behavior of the various participants in the budget execution process. The analysis focuses most closely in this regard on the roles of the central executive budget office controller and the program manager. The other purpose served by this analysis is to ask whether there is cause to change the budget execution process as it operates in most public organizations and, if so, what directions change might take. The analysis delineates alternative types of control applied in executing budgets and the rational for employing these different methods. A distinction is drawn between budget execution control intended to influence the behavior and performance of managers of government programs from controls applied to affect independent private sector firms that contract to deliver goods or services to the public on behalf of government. The central theme of this analysis is that budget execution control system design should fit the objectives of control and the nature of the entity to be controlled (Anthony and Young, 1984, p. 20).

BUDGET EXECUTION CONTROL CHOICES

Research in public finance has paid considerable attention to budget formulation, but has tended to ignore budget execution (Simon et al., 1954; Shick, 1964, 1982). The reasons for this oversight are understandable: Government budgets are formulated in public, and the issues debated during this stage of the public spending process are dramatic and crucial. On the other hand, budgets are executed in private, and the issues raised in their execution are often mundane. Because of this selective attention, both observers and participants in the public spending process understand program analysis far better than controllership. Consequently, the conduct of program analysis has come to be guided by a fairly coherent set of professional standards. There is agreement on what is good analysis and what is good accounting practice. Although the design and operation of control systems can profoundly influence governmental performance, budget execution controllership is not guided by a coherent set of professional standards. Without appropriate performance standards, budget officers cannot be held accountable for performance of this function. Consequently, control systems are not designed to optimize the quality, quantity, and price of goods and services purchased with public money, but "to facilitate the controller's [other] work" (Anthony and Young, 1984, p. 21).

This situation is not due to the lack of positive theory. There is a rich theoretical literature on the design and operation of control systems. Rather, the problem is that the existing theoretical literature has not been organized so as to provide practical, normative standards to guide the conduct and evaluation of controllership. Part of the purpose of this study is specification of the standards that should govern budget execution controllership.

CONTROL IMPLICATIONS OF PUBLIC VERSUS
PRIVATE SUPPLY OF SERVICES

Control systems design and implementation is a problem encountered by planners and regulators as budget and financial controllers. The purpose of various types of control systems differ due to the details of their execution. However, all control systems designers face the same key choices: what, where, who, and when to control.

If the goal of financial controllership is the optimization of the quantity and mix of goods and services purchased with public monies, the choice of what and where to control is narrow. Financial controllers are primarily concerned with the operating behavior of service suppliers, the efficiency with which service suppliers produce goods and services, and the efficiency with which they use assets.

The choice of whom to subject to controls and when to execute those controls is not as easy. The control system designer has at least four options. First, the subject may be either an organization or an individual. Second, controls may be executed before or after the subject acts. The former may be identified as ex ante and the latter as ex post controls (Demski and Feltham, 1967). Ex ante controls are intended to prevent subjects from doing wrong things or to compel them to perform well. Necessarily they take the form of authoritative commands or rules that specify what the subject must do, may do, and must not do. Subjects are held responsible for complying with these commands, and the controller attempts to monitor and enforce compliance. In contrast, ex post controls are executed after the subject decides on and carries out a course of action and after some of the consequences of the subject's decisions are known. Since bad decisions cannot be undone after they are carried out, ex post controls are intended to motivate subjects to make good decisions. Subjects are held responsible for the consequences of decisions, and the controller attempts to monitor consequences and rewards or sanctions accordingly. The control system designer may choose between four distinct design alternatives: individual responsibility, ex ante or ex post, and organizational responsibility, ex ante or ex post. The significance of this choice, its relevance to financial controllership, and the economic logic that should guide it are explained subsequently.

PUBLIC GOODS AND SERVICES PRODUCTION OPTIONS AND CONTROL

The significance of budget control decisions is reflected in the debate over the merits of public production of goods and services versus privatization. Proponents argue that choices must be made between provision by rule-governed public monopolies and provision by competing private firms and conclude that the latter will usually be more efficient than the former. Since the choice the proponents of privatization pose resolves to a question of monopoly or competition, it may be inferred that provision by competing private firms will always be more efficient than provision by a public monopoly, except where production of the goods or service in question is characterized by decreasing costs.

The distinction drawn by proponents of privatization between provision by a public agency and provision by a private entity does not fully describe the range of choices available to the budget control systems designer or reflect all of the factors relevant to the choice. From the standpoint of public budget execution controllership, the distinction drawn between public and private provision is overly simplistic.

First, while it is true that most goods and services purchased with public money are produced by organizations and not individuals, effective control presumes individual responsibility and accountability. The public-private distinction ignores the financial controller's capacity to hold managers of public organizations within his jurisdiction directly responsible for their behavior. Consequently, the financial controller's capacity to influence directly the rewards and sanctions accruing to those individuals—salary, opportunities for advancement, and the like—are ignored. The financial controller cannot have this capacity where his relationship to the supplying organization is at "arm's length" and individual responsibility is veiled by the organization. The direct way in which an organization can be rewarded or punished is by increasing or reducing its budget appropriation or allotment, which may influence the individual manager's welfare only indirectly. The difference between holding individuals and organizations accountable, or between direct influence and indirect influence, is illustrated by an example. If the quality of services supplied by a public agency is unsatisfactory, the controller can recommend the dismissal of the agency manager. Where government has an arm's-length relationship with a service supplier and the relationship is unsatisfactory, all the controller can do is recommend termination of the relationship. The controller can punish the supplying organization, but cannot punish the manager responsible for the organization's failure— although his actions might very well lead the organization's board of directors to do so (Breton and Wintrobe, 1975; Williamson, 1964, 1975).

Unfortunately, punishing a monopoly such as an organization can be difficult. Consequently, where the supplying organization is a monopoly, the capacity to influence individual managers directly will have more utility, particularly if the controller can stimulate and exploit competition between alternative management teams. This can be verified by reference to the private sector, where natural monopolies produce intermediate products and where their existence usually inspires a process called vertical integration because of the benefits that result from substituting direct for indirect influence.

Second, the public-private distinction implies that responsibility can be vested in organizations only if the organization is private, and can be vested in individuals only if the organization is public. These implications are consistent with neither theory nor practice. For example, many state legislatures base their relationships with public entities such as universities or hospitals on self-denying ordinances that exempt managers from detailed oversight and direct control. Similarly, the managers of private entities supplying services to or for the government can, in certain instances, be held directly responsible for their behavior through legal constraints and threat of prosecution.

Most of the proponents of privatization implicitly presume that the services provided to or for government are homogeneous or fungible, which implies that the problem of identifying the most efficient supplying organization or management team resolves to a simple question of price search to reveal demand. In fact, many of the organizations supplying goods or services to or for government supply bundles of more or less heterogeneous products. Many of these products are hard to measure and costly to evaluate.

The most significant claim made by proponents of privatization is that control system design should depend on the cost and production behavior of goods or services. Unfortunately, they all too frequently fail to carry this claim to its logical conclusion. According to the economic theory of organization (Coase, 1937; Cheung, 1983; Holstrom, 1979; Mirlees, 1976), at least two factors are relevant to the choice of control system designs. The first is the ease with which the consequences of operating decisions can be monitored. The second is the desirability of interorganizational competition. According to this theory, where consequences are easily monitored, control should focus on the consequences of the subject's decisions. Where consequences are not easily monitored, control should focus on their content. Since consequences are easily monitored where entities produce homogeneous outputs or where a responsibility center within an entity performs fungible activities, the implication of this line of reasoning is that controllers should rely on ex post controls where homogeneous outputs are supplied and ex ante controls where each item supplied is, from the government "customer's" perspective, intrinsically unique.

Under this theory, interorganizational competition is desirable only where costs are constant or increasing as quantity of output (rate or volume) increases. Where costs decrease as output is increased, monopoly supply is appropriate. Since responsibility can be effectively vested in organizations only where customers or their agents are indifferent to the survival of one or more competing organizations, the implication of this conclusion is that controllers should vest responsibility in organizations only where interorganizational competition is possible and likely to be effective. Responsibility should be placed on individuals where competition is not present (Barton, 1982).

Each of the basic control system designs described above is widely employed in the public sector. The question is whether their use fully exploits the principle of comparative advantage; that is, is each appropriately employed? Before this question can be answered, it must be shown how these designs are used. This analysis concentrates on the use of ex ante controls. Generally, controllers should resort to ex ante controls only where the use of the goods or service purchased with public money is the least-worst alternative available. The logic of ex post control is widely understood and appreciated by policy analysts, but seldom by public sector budget officials. The logic of ex ante control is far less familiar to policy analysts.

PURPOSES OF EX POST BUDGET CONTROLS

Ex post financial controls are used to reveal demand. They are executed after operating decisions have been made, after asset acquisition and use decisions have been carried out and output levels monitored. Their subject may be either a free-standing organization, such as a private contractor or a quasi-independent public entity, or an individual manager subordinate to the controller, such as a responsibility center or program manager within a government agency.

In the first case, the structure of authority and responsibility within the organization is assumed to be an internal matter. The controller establishes a price schedule and specifies minimum service quality standards or a process whereby these standards are to be determined. This price or cost schedule may entail all sorts of complex arrangements, including rate, volume and mix adjustments, and default penalties. Where one organization can optimally supply the entire market, the controller may grant it a monopoly franchise, for example, in garbage collection for a small town or neighborhood. The significant characteristic of this approach is that a unit price cost schedule remains in effect for a specified time period (Goldberg, 1976; Thompson, 1984; Thompson and Fiske, 1978). This means that the government's financial liability will depend on the quantity of service provided and not on the costs incurred by the organizations supplying the service.

Where this budget control system design is employed, for example, where a municipality purchases gasoline at the spot-market price or where states commit themselves to pay free-standing organizations such as a university a fixed price for performing a specific service such as enrolling students or treating heart attacks, or where the Air Force buys F-16s for a fixed price, the controller must rely upon interorganizational competition to provide sufficient incentives to service suppliers to produce efficiently and make wise asset acquisition and use decisions. If interorganizational competition is effective, those organizations that don't produce cost-effectively will not survive.

However, even where the declining marginal cost of the service in question makes monopoly supply appropriate, ex post controls can still be employed. This is done in businesses and businesslike public sector enterprise organizations by holding managers responsible for optimizing a single criterion value, subject to a set of constraints (Anthony and Young, 1984). [The principal mechanism through which this control system design is employed at the federal level is the revolving fund (Bailey, 1967; Beckner, 1960).] For example, the manager is given the authority to make spending decisions to acquire and use assets, subject to output quality and quantity constraints determined by clients and is held responsible for minimizing costs. Large private sector firms produce comprehensive operating reports describing the performance of responsibility centers and programs, but their budgets seldom are very detailed. The logic of ex post control is that the purpose of the budget is to establish performance targets that are high enough to elicit from the organization's managers their best efforts. Such budgets might contain only a single number for each responsibility center—an output quota, a unit-cost standard, a profit, or a return-on-investment target.

Under this approach to budget control, the structure of authority and responsibility within the organization is of interest to the financial controller. The effectiveness of this design depends on the elaboration of well-defined objectives, accurate and timely reporting of performance in terms of objectives, and careful matching of spending authority and responsibility. Its effectiveness also depends upon the clarity with which individual reward schedules are communicated to responsibility center managers and the degree of competition between alternative management teams. Finally, under this approach, the financial liability of government depends upon the costs incurred in providing the service and not merely on the quantity or quality of the service provided.

EX ANTE CONTROL OBJECTIVES

In contrast to ex post budget controls, ex ante controls are demand-concealing. Their distinguishing attribute is that the controller retains the authority to make or exercise prior review of spending decisions. Ex ante financial controls are executed before public money is obligated or spent, and govern the service supplier's acquisition and use of assets. Examples of ex ante financial controls include not only object-of-expenditure appropriations, apportionments, targets, position controls, and fund and account controls that regulate spending by account and the kind of assets that can be acquired by governmental departments and agencies. Such controls also govern the behavior of private contracting entities that supply services to government or to clients on behalf of governments.

Execution of ex ante controls requires assessment of the consequences of asset acquisition decisions. This consideration may be implicit, as it is in the execution of the traditional line-item budget and basic-research contracts, or explicit, as in the execution of performance and program budgets and systems development contracts. It is often influenced by information on current and past performance, but the consideration of the consequences of spending decisions is always prospective in nature.

The logic of ex ante control is that constraining managerial discretion is the first purpose of budget execution. Since the degree of constraint will depend upon the detail of the spending plan, as well as the degree of compliance enforced by the controllers, these budgets need to be highly detailed. A department or agency budget must identify all asset acquisitions to be executed during the fiscal year and make it clear who is responsible for implementation.

Under ex ante budget control, service-supplying organizations must be guaranteed an allotment of funds in return for continuously providing a service for a specified period. The service provider will assume some responsibility for managing output levels or delivery schedules, service quality, or price to the government customer. Government is directly responsible for all legitimate costs incurred in the delivery of services, regardless of the actual quantity or quality of the services provided.

CONTROL OF GOVERNMENT LINE-ITEM BUDGETS AND ADMINISTERED CONTRACTS

The combination of ex ante control and individual responsibility is the budget execution control system familiar to public sector budget officers as the lump-sum or line-item annual budget appropriation. The combination of ex ante controls and organizational responsibility is the flexible-price, cost-plus, or administered contract. The ex ante/individual responsibility control system characterizes the majority of arm's-length contractual relationships entered into by the federal government and is also widely employed by state and local social service agencies to control the behavior of contractors.

If constraining managerial discretion were the sole function of this control system, it would be difficult to argue that they ever represented a least-worst alternative, let alone explain their widespread use. Consequently, this analysis will benefit from understanding in greater detail the purposes served by employing the flexible-price or administered contract (Peck and Scherer, 1962; Scherer, 1964; Fox, 1974) and then the lump-sum appropriation budget.

Policy analysts and economists appreciate the logic of interorganizational competition and recognize that it may be relied upon to provide incentives to service providers to achieve more efficient operations. However, unlike budget controllers, they seldom appreciate the difference in the role played by competition under a per-unit price schedule and a flexible-price contract. Under flexible-price contracts, where organizations are permitted to compete, they compete for the sole right to deliver a service. Competition, if it takes place at all, takes place prior to the production of the service in question. Economists refer to such a competitive regime as competition for the market, to distinguish it from competition in the market.

The purpose for granting a single supplier a monopoly franchise is straightforward. Because the supplier will produce the service for only one customer, in this case the government, no contracting organization would want to assume responsibility for providing a unique service without prior guarantee of reward. Further, it may be the case that only one organization is best qualified to provide a specialized service, so that the controller's first objective is identification of the most competent service supplier. This involves the evaluation of an array of proposals or bids submitted by organizations interested in supplying the service.

If budget controllers know what elected officials and their appointees want in the budget, and if potential service suppliers know how to meet these preferences, competitors' proposals can be satisfactorily evaluated on the basis of service quality attributes offered, promised delivery schedule, and price. In this case, a fixed-price contract is employed.

However, in many cases neither the budget controller nor the service supplier possesses sufficient knowledge of the value of service attributes or of costs and the production process prior to performance of the contract. Considerable experience is required to manage to a narrow range of outcomes. Where specialized goods or services are involved, no organization may have the requisite experience. Any organization that agrees to produce a unique good or service according to a specified schedule at a fixed price will assume a large financial risk. This risk can be shifted, but it can't be made to disappear. Since government can often bear such risks better than the supplying organization, and this is always the case where the federal government is concerned because of the size of the assets it commands and its ability to pool risks, the cost of the service to government will often be lower if government assumes all or a portion of the risk associated with acquisition of the good or service. Flexible pricing is one way for government to assume this risk. Further, the preferences of the controller's principals, the elected officials, may change during performance of a contract. Other fact-of-life changes may be made, to increase efficiency, that change attributes of the good or service. Under a fixed-price contract, it is difficult if not impossible to secure desired changes in goods or service attributes if they involve increased costs for the contracting organization.

Circumstance thus may dictate the use of flexible-price contracts. Unfortunately, once such a contract is signed, the normal incentives to least-cost production largely disappear. Decisions that affect cost, service quality, or price (i.e., asset acquisition and use decisions) must be made during performance of the contract. However, once the contract is signed, the service provider can no longer be trusted completely to make efficient choices. Consequently, to prevent bad decisions, service contractors must be denied some managerial discretion. This is precisely what ex ante controls do through the use of project budgets that detail the work to be performed, personnel, material and equipment to be used, input quality standards, and scheduled milestones. But ex ante controls are not merely intended to prevent bad things from happening; they also provide a basis for the enforcement of efficiency through bargaining and negotiations carried on during the performance of a contract.

This bargaining process is typically a repetitive two-party non-zero-sum game in which both parties have a common interest in reaching agreement but also have competing interests with respect to the content of agreements (Hofstede, 1967). In this game, the budget controller representing the "customer" tries to get as much of what he wants as he can at a given price, and the supplier tries to provide a given level of service for the highest possible price and profit. The relative bargaining power in a two-party non-zero-sum game largely depends on the quality and quantity of information available to each party. In particular, the budget controller's power is greatest where he knows the supplier's true cost schedule, but can withhold full information as to his preference or demand schedule (Breton and Wintrobe, 1975; Morgan, 1949; Myerson, 1979).

Using comprehensive ex ante controls under which changes can be made only with the prior approval of the other party or his agent, the party suggesting or initiating a change must necessarily reveal valuable information to the other. This can work to the advantage of the budget controller or the supplier, or both. For example, consider the following situation:

> . . . contracts and specifications are drawn for . . . a ship and agreed to. . . . The contractor discovers he can do the welding of some plates less expensively by another means. About that time the client decides that some room on the ship should be larger. . . . The contractor can plead that he cannot easily change the room size; however, if the client will permit the altered welding maybe a deal can be struck. (Stark and Varley, 1983, pp. 121–135)

When flexible-price contracting is appropriately employed, most change proposals are likely to be initiated by the service supplier, although this isn't always the case, for example, federal defense contracting. Prior to the performance of a contract, the controller may be somewhat uncertain about the policy and budget preferences of the elected officials he represents. Potential service suppliers may also be uncertain about their capacity to manage to fixed cost, quality, and schedule targets (Stark, 1983). Changes involving tradeoffs may tend to be more valuable to the service supplier than to the controller. In addition, competition for the market, together with flexible or cost-plus pricing, provides an incentive to potential service suppliers to promise more than they can deliver because contracts are awarded to the service suppliers who promise the most or promise equal amounts at lower costs. Consequently, very few contract winners make good on all their promises, especially where their managerial discretion is severely restricted by a full set of ex ante controls.

This fact will usually become evident to the contractor during performance of the contract. The contractor will also learn of the tradeoffs between cost, service quality, and delivery schedule and will eventually want or have to change his promises and plans. Under a full set of ex ante controls, such changes are contingent upon prior approval. To secure that approval the contractor must reveal information about his preferences, capabilities, and tradeoff possibilities. As a result, considerable power to enforce the preferences of elected officials rests with the budget execution controller.

A similar dynamic applies to line-item or lump-sum budget appropriations that have a comparative advantage for programs with decreasing costs and unique outputs. For example, lump-sum appropriations appear to be highly effective where substantial fixed facilities are required to provide services, when each problem, client, or task performed by the government service agency is in some sense unique, and when the most serious problems are supposed to be dealt with first. Many organizational units in government supply heterogeneous, hard-to-define, and nearly impossible-to-measure outputs, such as social service agencies or the U.S. Department of State (Thompson and Zumeta, 1981; Thompson, 1981).

Under the line-item appropriation budget, the controller retains the authority if not the ability to make most significant operating decisions. Presumably, controllers want as much information as possible on program alternatives, costs, and their consequences. The budget controller wants the service supplier to reveal a comprehensive menu of all possible actions and a cost or price list identifying the minimum cost for performing each action under almost all possible contingencies. However, there is no way to compel the manager of a government agency to reveal his unit's true production function even if he knows it. In most cases, he doesn't have this information. Consequently, the controller must settle for a practical approximation of this ideal. Here, the controller's authority provides a basis for the enforcement of efficiency through bargaining carried on during the execution of the budget. As a result, the policy preferences of elected officials may be approximated if not optimized. Over time, the supplying organization is compelled to address the "most important" problems and to resolve these problems at an agreed-upon cost.

The impetus for program change and innovation must come from the operating manager. The government responsibility center manager typically has an interest in increasing, if not maximizing, his budget. Otherwise he will be indifferent to circumstances in which low-priority problems drain resources from problems that are of greater importance to his executive branch superiors or to legislative sponsors. Here too, a full set of ex ante controls must be in place. At minimum this means that controllers must specify when, how, and where assets are to be employed and how much the subordinate can pay for them. In addition, money saved during the budget period from substituting less costly or more productive assets for more costly or less productive assets must revert to the treasury. Money lost in failed attempts to improve operations must be found elsewhere, and new initiatives requiring the acquisition of additional assets or reallocation of existing assets must be justified accordingly. These constraints are necessary not only because they prevent the manager from overstating asset requirements in high-priority areas to get resources for use elsewhere, thereby creating a precedent for higher levels of support in the lower-priority area, but also to force the subordinate manager to seek authorization to make changes in spending plans and, therefore, to reveal hidden preferences, capabilities, and tradeoff possibilities (Wildavsky and Hammann, 1965).

EFFECTIVENESS OF EX ANTE CONTROLS

Where a manager seeking to increase his budget is subject to tight ex ante controls, the controller can enforce efficiency during the budget period by requiring affirmative answers to the following questions: (1) Will a proposed change permit the same activity to be carried out at lower cost? (2) Will higher priority activities be carried out at the same cost? (3) Will proposed asset acquisitions or reallocations of savings support activities that have lower priority than those presently carried out? When operating managers are faced with these criteria, they respond appropriately. Controllers approve most changes in spending plans proposed by operating managers because only mutually advantageous changes will be proposed in most circumstances.

However, when line item or lump-sum appropriations have a comparative advantage, to say that ex ante controls are a necessary means of reinforcing the controllers' bargaining power should not imply that tight ex ante controls always must be administered by them. Under certain conditions, authority to spend money, transfer funds, fill positions, etc., may be delegated to subordinate managers. The threat of reimposition of ex ante controls will be sufficient to insure that the manager's behavior corresponds to the controllers' and elected officials' preferences. In order for such delegation to take place, the following conditions must be present: (1) reimposition of controls must be a credible threat; (2) the gain to the manager from delegation must more than offset the associated sacrifice in bargaining power; the manager of an agency in the stable backwaters of public policy has little to gain from relief from ex ante controls if the price of such relief is a change in business as usual; and (3) controllers must be confident that their monitoring procedures, including postaudit, will identify violations of "trust."

Clearly, all long-term relationships with private contractors and government goods and service suppliers rely to some degree on ex ante controls. Even the operation of fixed-price contracts requires prior specification of product quality standards and delivery schedules. But flexible-price, cost-plus type contracts and appropriated budgets require considerably higher levels of reliance on ex ante controls and also on monitoring and enforcing compliance. And the cost of tightly held budget execution control is high.

At the very least, adoption of one of the budget execution control systems described herein means that controllers must take steps to ensure that suppliers fairly and accurately recognize, record, and report their expenses. This, in turn, requires careful definition of costs and specification of appropriate account structures, accounting practices and internal controls, direct costing procedures, and the criteria to be used in allocating overheads. Still, accurate accounting does not guarantee efficiency. Even where the service supplier's financial and operational accounts completely and accurately present every relevant fact about the decisions made by its managers, they will not provide a basis for evaluating the soundness of those decisions. This is because cost accounts can show only what happened, not what might have happened. They do not show the range of asset acquisition choices and tradeoffs the supplier considered, let alone those that should have been considered but were not.

As noted, under line-item or lump-sum budgets and flexible-price contracts, asset acquisition decisions must be made by the contractor, but the contractor cannot be trusted completely to make them efficiently. Consequently, the contractor must be denied some discretion to make managerial decisions. The fundamental question is, how much must be denied? To what extent should government officials or their controller agents regulate, duplicate, or replace the contractor's managerial efforts?

This question must be addressed because oversight is costly both in terms of monitoring and reporting costs, and also because of the benefits sacrificed due to failure to exploit the contractor's managerial expertise. The controller and the government official will very seldom be more competent to make asset acquisition decisions than the contractor. The answer to this dilemma is that controllers and officials should do the minimum necessary, given the incentives faced by and the motivations of the contractor. However, at times, the minimum necessary is a great deal. This decision depends on circumstance and the controller's skill in exploiting the opportunities created by the contractors response to institutional constraints. In other words, all long-term relationships between government officials and contractors must rely on incentives, even those governed by lump-sum budgets and flexible-price contracts. The difference is that when these control system designs are employed, the incentives are deeply embedded in the process of budget/contract execution.

BUDGET EXECUTION CONTROL DYNAMICS IN THE "REAL WORLD"

Budget execution control should be matched to circumstances: increasing costs and homogeneous outputs imply one kind of design, while decreasing costs and heterogeneous outputs another. However, what we observe in practice is that this match is not always achieved. Controllers tend to rely on monopoly supply and ex ante controls (Thompson and Zumeta, 1981; Pitsvada, 1983; Draper and Pitsvada, 1981; Fisher, 1975). This combination cannot be appropriate for every service to which it is applied. Evidence can be marshaled to show that a variety of services might be performed satisfactorily by competing organizations, including in air traffic control (Poole, 1982), custodial services and building maintenance (Bennett and DiLorenzo, 1983; Blankart, 1979), day-care centers (Bennett and DiLorenzo, 1983), electrical power generation (Bennett and DiLorenzo, 1983), fire protection services (Poole, 1976; Smith, 1983), forest management (Hanke, 1982), management of grazing lands (Hanke, 1983), hospitals and health care services (Hanke, 1985, pp. 106–107), housing (Weicker, 1980), postal services (Hanke, 1985, p. 108), prisons and correctional facilities (Hanke, 1985, pp. 108–109), property assessment (Poole, 1980), refuse collection (Savas, 1977; Bennett and Johnson, 1979), security services (Hanke, 1985, pp. 109–110), ship and aircraft maintenance (Bennett and Johnson, 19 ; Bennett and DiLorenzo, 1983, p. 42), urban transit (Hanke, 1985, p. 110), and waste water treatment (Hanke, 1985, p. 110). Furthermore, even when controllers eschew monopoly supply, they frequently fail to fully exploit the benefits of competition. In New York City, for example, the municipal social services agency acquires child-care services for its clients from both public and private day-care centers. But public centers are subject to the full panoply of ex ante controls associated with lump-sum appropriation budgets, and private centers to those associated with flexible-price contracts.

To cite another example, Department of Defense (DoD) policy restricts the use of flexible-price contracts to situations characterized by considerable procurement risk (primarily R&D projects). In other contracts, the degree of incentive is supposed to be calibrated to the project's riskiness. The first ship in a multiship construction program is supposed to be constructed under a cost-plus-fixed-profit contract, while later editions are supposed to be built under fixed-price contracts on the assumption that experience permits the contractor to manage to a narrower range of cost outcomes and to assume a greater share of the risk burden. It may be observed that while DoD generally makes the proper transition from cost-plus to award-fee contracts as it moves from design to prototype development, it may not make the transition to a fixed-price contract for downstream production. To be consistent with the logic advanced here, selection of defense system production suppliers should be reduced to a question of cost and price search. Acquisition should be based upon fixed-price contracts, awarded by competitive bidding. Where production volume is sufficient, DoD should try to maintain long-term contractural relations with two or more producers, as multisourcing permits price search at each renegotiation of the relationship between the DoD and its suppliers. Nevertheless, winning a contract to develop a weapons system continues to be tantamount to winning subsequent production contracts in a high proportion of cases.

Finally, not only do controllers tend to subject government agencies and contractors to a wide array of ex ante controls, they often hold them to tight output, quality, and service delivery schedules. Performance targets that can be met all of the time are not very ambitious.

What accounts for mismatches between how budgets are controlled in practice and the approach advanced here? One explanation is ignorance of consequences on the part of the controllers and elected officials. Also, some of the empirical data required to employ the control criteria outlined here are often unavailable. The most critical gap in this knowledge is how costs vary with output. Definitions and measurements of service outputs and activities also are often inadequate. Insufficient effort has been made to correct this situation in most public organizations. Of the two tasks, getting knowledge about the shape of cost functions is the more difficult. But if we first answer the question, "Cost to do what?" this knowledge can be derived deductively in a manner similar to the methods used in cost accounting and conventional price theory. Cost and supply analysis can yield highly useful information about marginal and average costs. Finally, experimentation with funding and output levels will increase our knowledge of service supply and cost functions (Wildavsky, 1975; Larkey, 1979; Cothran, 1981).

The kind of information called for here requires a high level of analytical sophistication both in budget execution and system design, a skill that staff responsible for executing budgets may lack. Indeed, even if controllers had good information on cost and service supply functions, some might not know how to use it. Their experience tends to orient them to the administration of the traditional line-item, object-of-expenditure budget. Effective administration of a lump-sum or line-item appropriation requires no more than a modicum of arithmetical ability combined with a substantial amount of horse sense and bargaining savvy. However, matching control systems design to circumstances requires a practical understanding of applied microeconomics, and financial and managerial accounting. Controllers often fail to understand the ideas outlined here or how to implement alternatives to the line-item appropriations budget—where to exercise judgment and where to exercise specific decision rules. This is demonstrated by the persistent attempt of controllers to employ techniques devised for use within organizations, such as standard costs based on fully-distributed average historical costs, to establish per-unit prices for public organizations such as hospitals and universities.

BUDGET EXECUTION REFORM OBSTACLES

Ignorance of options and objectives is not a satisfactory explanation for controller decisions to resist reform. Ignorance can be corrected, and incompetence may be weeded out. If a better match between control system design and circumstances would have a substantial payoff, why hasn't this situation been corrected? One answer regarding the implementation of reform is as follows:

> A large part of the literature on budgeting in the United States is concerned with reform. The goals of the proposed reforms are couched in similar language—

economy, efficiency, improvement, or just better budgeting. The President, the Congress and its committees, administrative agencies, even the citizenry are all to gain by some change. However, any effective change in budgetary relationships must necessarily alter the outcomes of the budgetary process. Otherwise, why bother? Far from being a neutral matter of "better budgeting," proposed reforms inevitably contain important implications for the political system, that is, the "who gets what" of governmental decisions. (Wildavsky, 1961, pp. 183–190)

If the controllers and elected officials empowered to determine the methods used in executing budgets are rational, this quote implies that they have a strong interest in maintaining the status quo. To explain the persistent mismatch between budget execution control system designs and practice it is necessary to determine who benefits from the status quo and, therefore, who will oppose the adoption of a more appropriate type of control (Zimmerman, 1977). Members of Congress, state legislators, city council members, and any politician with a constituency worth cultivating would appear to lose as a result of the reforms proposed. As the collective holders of the power of the purse, legislators clearly have the authority to order budgets to be executed in almost any way they like, including the power to delegate this authority to controllers. Efficiency implies an exclusive concern with the supply of goods and services to the citizenry with some indifference as to the means used to supply the goods or even to the identity of the suppliers. However, legislators are frequently as concerned about where public money is spent and who gets it as they are with what it buys (Arnold, 1979; Ferejohn, 1974; Fiorina, 1977; Shepsle and Weingast, 1981). Line-item appropriations in general and object-of-expenditure budgets in particular are ideally suited to the satisfaction of legislative preferences with respect to how public money is spent, where it is spent, and who gets it.

It may be viewed as naive to claim that legislators are always individually or collectively devoted to maximizing the welfare of the citizenry at large. All too often legislators assert their prerogatives on behalf of palpably inefficient ends, such as opposition to closure of obsolete military bases. These actions may be frequent enough to persuade controllers and program managers that legislators aren't at all interested in efficiency. In fairness it may be observed that legislators have complex motives and that their actions and interests are no less complex. And legislators often reveal a respect for their own limited capacities to manage the delivery of goods and services. In many cases they are willing to delegate considerable authority to individuals who have the expertise they lack, both individually and collectively. Legislators usually withdraw this authority only when it is abused, and even then often reluctantly.* Indeed, many legislators appear to delegate far more authority to the budget controllers to experiment with alternative control system designs than the controllers want to use. Still, the power of the pork-barrel is strong in influencing legislators to retain a high degree of control over selected programs that provide benefits to their constituents. Reforms that appear to interfere with their ability to do this inevitably will be resisted individually and collectively.

Support for the claim that legislators are not entirely responsible for the excessive reliance on monopoly supply and ex ante controls is found in a comparison of the budget execution methods employed by council-manager and mayor-council municipalities. Despite the fact that under the former, controllers are directly subordinate to the legislative body, these municipalities are twice as likely to rely on competitive supply and either

---

*Note the protracted debate on presidential impoundment authority prior to the eventual enactment of the 1974 Congressional Budget and Impoundment Control Act (Fisher, 1975).

per-unit prices or fixed-price contracts as are their counterparts governed by a strong mayor and council. They are also more likely to rely on ex post internal controls. These findings hold even where region of the country, size and age of municipality, and per capita income are held constant. It also may be noted that council-manager municipalities appear to be generally more efficient than are mayor-council municipalities. Other things being equal, they tend to have lower taxes per capita, significantly lower tax rates, fewer employees, less debt, and higher bond ratings (Zimmerman, 1977).

BUDGET EXECUTION CONTROLLER PREFERENCES

The point of this discussion is not to deny that legislators have an interest in the status quo, but to suggest that this is by no means the whole story. Rather, to understand budget execution control system design and implementation we must also look to the controllers and to the incentives they face, to their interests, and to their preferences. As is the case with any control agents, budget controllers have considerable discretion in the exercise of their responsibilities (Mitnick, 1977). They have power to direct reform of control system design. But do they also have an interest in the status quo that predisposes them against reform?

Budget literature informs us that controllers are highly risk averse, particularly with respect to outlay estimates (Wildavsky, 1975; Larkey, 1979; Cothran, 1981). They are held to tight legal constraints that cause them to be risk averse. They behave as they do not because they are inherently cautious, although many of them are, but because of the incentives they face. Budget controllers are rewarded for their success in matching revenues and outlays. Fiscal balance tends to be their primary objective. This objective is reflected in a tendency to execute budgets so as to produce savings that may be appropriated when unanticipated problems arise, to shift fiscal responsibility to other levels of government, to the private sector, or to the future whenever possible, and to give greater emphasis to the certainty of outlay estimates than to the quality and/or quantity of service outputs.

Risk aversion may induce an excessive tolerance for technical inefficiency or slack. Slack is one means of economizing on the high costs and uncertainty of predicting the future and also the high cost of immediate response to changing conditions. Slack is not necessarily waste. But since elected officials hold them accountable for the accuracy of their fiscal plans, and because they are only partially responsible for avoiding inefficiency, it follows that controllers may tolerate excessive slack: more slack than would be justified by the goal of net benefit maximization and probably more than elected officials would prefer under some circumstances where constituent interests are threatened. Elected officials also show a tendency to defend their power and territory, and are not always free from pure ego defensiveness.

Similar logic applies to budget controller demands for operating information from program managers. Controllers benefit from better information but bear little if any of the cost of collecting it. As a result, controllers sometimes demand too much as well as the wrong kinds of information in budget preparation and execution. The program manager's surest justification for failure to meet the controllers' information demands is that data are not available. In some cases, in denying threatening information to the controllers, operating managers also may deny valuable information to themselves. However, program managers generally behave strategically in choosing what types of information to give to budget controllers.

Insofar as controllers are risk averse, the status quo is generally consistent with their preferences. Under both line-item budgets and flexible-price contracts, but especially under the former, annual outlays can be predicted with greater certainty, as can price, quantity or delivery schedule, and quality subject to some efficiency losses. Other things being equal, a truly risk-averse controller would prefer a solution to the service supply problem in which the program manager or contractor received a larger-than-optimal appropriation containing some slack that could be withdrawn without sacrificing valued outputs if unanticipated contingencies arose, and higher per-unit prices for lower output levels than would be optimal. Under certain circumstances such a pattern of outcomes would also be agreeable to the service supplier. However, this is possible *only under monopoly supply*. Thus, when competitive supply is appropriate, both the service supplier and the controller have an interest in the preservation of their tacit bargain and will oppose the shift to what the theory advanced here suggests is a more appropriate approach to budget execution control.

CONCLUSIONS

Improvements in budget execution control are both desirable and possible. This analysis explains why many of those responsible for designing and operating budget control systems oppose reform. If elected officials were entirely to blame for the frequent mismatch between budget execution control and practice, there would be little to do to improve control system design and implementation short of changing political institutions, which is not easy. Controllers, however, are responsible to elected officials. If the incentives that controllers face lead them to produce the wrong outcomes, the situation can be corrected by modifying these incentives. Such modifications could lead to increases in the quantity and quality of the goods and services purchased with public money, as well as a reduction in costs.

Ineffective or incompetent budget controllership is, perhaps, the most common managerial failure found in the public sector. This failure affects outcomes and achievements in every area of public policy. Controllers design, operate, and maintain budget control systems. The effectiveness of alternative budget control system designs depends upon the cost and production behavior of the good or service in question. But control strategies are seldom consciously or effectively matched to circumstances.

REFERENCES

Anthony, R., and Young, D. (1984). *Managerial Control in Non-Profit Organizations*. Irwin, Chapters 7–9.
Arnold, D. (1979). *Congress and the Bureaucracy*. Yale University Press, New Haven, Conn.
Bailey, M. (1967). Decentralization through internal prices. In *Defense Management*, S. Enke (ed.), Prentice-Hall, Englewood Cliffs, N.J., pp. 337–352.
Barton, D. P. (1982). Regulating a monopolist with unknown costs. *Econometrica* 50.
Beckner, N. V. (1960). Government efficiency and the military: Buyer-seller relationship. *Journal of Political Economy* 68.
Bennett, J., and DiLorenzo, T. (1983). Public employee labor unions and the privatization of "public services." *Journal of Labor Research* 4:43.
Bennett, J., and Johnson, M. (1979). Public v. private provision of collective goods and services. *Public Choice* 34:55–63.

Bennett, J., and Johnson, M. (19). *Better Government at Half the Price: Private Production of Public Services*. Caroline House, p. 52.

Blankart, C. B. (1979). Bureaucratic problems in public choice: Why do public goods still remain public? In *Public Choice and Public Finance*, R. Roskamp (ed.), Cujas, pp. 155–167.

Breton, A., and Wintrobe, R. (1975). The equilibrium size of a budget maximizing bureau. *Journal of Political Economy* 83:195–207.

Cheung, S. N. S. (1983). The contractual nature of the firm. *Journal of Law and Economics* 25.

Coase, R. (1937). The nature of the firm. *Economica* 4.

Cothran, D. (1981). Program flexibility and budget growth. *Western Political Quarterly* 34:593–610.

Demski, J., and Feltham, G. (1967). *Cost Determination*. Iowa State University Press, Ames.

Draper, F., and Pitsvada, P. T. (1981). Limitations in federal budget execution. *Government Accountants Journal* 30/3.

Ferejohn, J. (1974). *Pork Barrel Politics*. Stanford University Press, Stanford, Calif.

Fiorina, M. (1977). *Congress: Keystone of the Washington Establishment*. Yale University Press, New Haven, Conn.

Fisher, L. (1975). *Presidential Spending Power*. Princeton University Press, Princeton, N.J.

Fox, R. (1974). *Arming America: How the U.S. Buys Weapons*. Harvard University Press, Cambridge, Mass.

Goldberg, V. (1976). Regulation and administered contracts. *Bell Journal of Economics* 7:426–428.

Hanke, S. (1982). The privatization debate. *Cato Journal* 656.

Hanke, S. (1983). Land policy. In *Agenda 83*, R. Howill (ed.), Heritage Foundation, Washington, D.C., p. 65.

Hanke, S. (1985). Privatization: Theory, evidence, implementation. In *Control of Federal Spending*, Harris (ed.), Academy of Political Science.

Hofsted, G. H. (1967). *The Game of Budget Control*. Van Gorcum.

Holstrom, B. (1979). Moral hazard and observability. *Bell Journal of Economics* 10.

Larkey, P. (1979). *Evaluating Public Programs: The Impact of General Revenue Sharing on Municipal Government*. Princeton University Press, Princeton, N.J.

Meyerson, R. B. (1979). Incentives compatibility and the bargaining problem. *Econometrica* 47.

Mirlees, J. (1976). The optimal structure of incentives and authority within an organization. *Bell Journal of Economics* 7.

Mitnick, B. (1977). The theory of agency: The policing "paradox" and regulatory behavior. *Public Choice* 30.

Morgan, J. (1949). Bilateral monopoly and the competitive output. *Quarterly Journal of Economics* 63.

Peck, M., and Scherer, F. (1962). *The Weapons Acquisition Process: An Economic Analysis*. Harvard Business School, Cambridge, Mass.

Pitsvada, B. T. (1983). Flexibility in federal budget execution. *Public Budgeting and Finance* 3/2.

Poole, R. (1976). Fighting fires for profit. *Reason* May.

Poole, R. (1980). *Cutting Back City Hall*. University Books, p. 164.

Poole, R. (1982). Air traffic control: The private sector option. *Heritage Foundation Backgrounds* 216.

Savas, E. S. (1977). Policy analysis for local government. *Policy Analysis* 3:49–77.

Scherer, F. (1964). *The Weapons Acquisition Process: Economic Incentives*. Harvard Business School, Cambridge, Mass.

Shepsle, K., and Weingast, B. (1981). Political preferences for the pork barrel. *American Journal of Political Science* 25.

Shick, A. (1964). Control patterns in state budget executions. *Public Administration Review* 24:97–106.

Shick, A. (1982). Contemporary problems in financial control. In *Current Issues in Public Administration,* F. Lane (ed.), 2d ed., St. Martin's Press, New York, pp. 361–371.

Simon, H., et al. (1954). *Centralization vs. Decentralization in Organizing the Controller's Department.* The Controllership Foundation, New York.

Smith, R. G. (1983). Feet to the fire. *Reason* May:23–29.

Stark, R. (1983). On cost analysis for engineered construction. In *Auctions, Bidding, and Contracting,* R. Englebrecht-Wiggins, M. Shubik, and R. Stark (eds.), New York University Press, New York.

Stark, R., and Varley, T. (1983). Bidding, estimating, and engineered construction contracting. In *Auctions, Bidding, and Contracting,* R. Englebrecht-Wiggins, M. Shubik, and R. Stark (eds.), New York University Press, New York, pp. 121–135.

Thompson, F. (1981). Utility maximizing behavior in organized anarchies. *Public Choice* 36.

Thompson, F. (1984). How to stay within the budget using per-unit prices. *Journal of Policy Analysis and Management* 4/1.

Thompson, F., and Fiske, G. (1978). One more solution to the problem of higher education finance. *Policy Analysis* 3/4.

Thompson, F., and Zumeta, W. (1981). Controls and controls: A reexamination of control patterns in budget execution. *Policy Sciences* 13:25–50.

Weicker, J. (1980). *Housing.* American Enterprise Institute, Washington, D.C., p. 80.

Wildavsky, A. (1961). Political implications of budget reform. *Public Administration Review* 21:183–190.

Wildavsky, A. (1975). *Budgeting: A Comparative Theory of the Budgetary Process.* Little, Brown, Boston, pp. 118–119.

Wildavsky, A., and Hammann, A. (1956). Comprehensive versus incremental budgeting in the Department of Agriculture. *Administrative Sciences Quarterly* 10:321–346.

Williamson, O. (1964). *The Economics of Discretionary Behavior.* Prentice-Hall, Englewood Cliffs, N.J.

Williamson, O. (1975). *Markets and Hierarchies.* Free Press, New York.

Zimmerman, J. (1977). The municipal accounting maze: An analysis of political incentives. *Journal of Accounting Research* 21:107–144.

Unit Two
BUDGETING FUNDAMENTALS

8

Expenditure Forecasting

Howard A. Frank *Department of Public Administration, Florida International University, North Miami, Florida*

INTRODUCTION: THE DEMISE OF INCREMENTALISM, RISK AVERSION, AND FORECAST UTILITY

Migration Toward the Budget Constraint

Ultimately, any effort at budgeting entails intelligent conjectures regarding future expenditures. Such effort is not likely to be easy at any time, given the vicissitudes of both public policy and the economy. In the current era of fiscal stress, making estimates of future expenditures is likely to be even more difficult. The combination of a "tax rebellion" mindset and limited reserves at the local and state levels, and increasing talk of a balanced budget at the federal, suggests that significant underforecasts of expenditures will not be covered by large reserves or revenue "enhancements." Intentional underestimation of future costs, service levels, or inflation rates, which might have been viewed as legitimate tools with which to build a bureaucratic base in the past, must now be viewed from the administrative perspective as unacceptable and unwarranted.

This heightened concern for enhanced forecast accuracy in a nonincremental era is to be expected. The "Demise of Incrementalism" (Rubin, 1988, p. 3), brings with it the end of budgeting the status quo into the future with minor, marginal additions to the budgetary base. Fiscal restraint at all levels has imposed discipline on spending. Recent evidence (Lane and Westlund, 1987; Marlow and Manage, 1988) clearly indicates that previous models of local, state, and federal budgeting that viewed expenditures as a function of simple decision rules regarding budgetary markup and markdown from last year's base (Wagner, 1983), are inadequate. Aggregate expenditures in the current fiscal year are better explained by previous revenue receipts than by efforts at bureaucratic or interest-group budget maximization. Even incrementalism's leading exponent, Aaron Wildavsky, has had to admit that a top-down, constraint-driven approach to budgeting is the order of the day (Rubin, 1988; Wildavsky, 1989).

Elementary microeconomics gives us a diagrammatic shorthand for helping to explain what this suggests in terms of budgeting. In essence, all layers of government are being forced to budget closer to their respective revenue constraints. As shown in Fig. 1, this means that the federal government, thanks to the passage of Gramm-Rudman and a healthy dosage of fiscal realism, is trying to move toward a balanced budget. States and local governments, which have always had to pass balanced budgets, must now budget even more closely to their revenue limits.

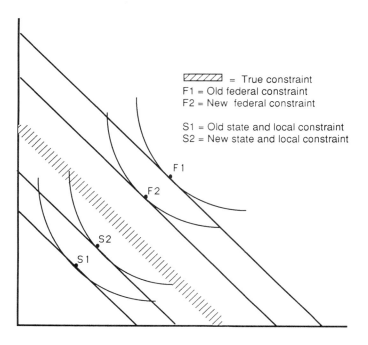

Figure 1 Budgeting closer to the true revenue constraint.

This migration toward the budget constraint is likely to be driven by political, normative, and technical factors. The weighting of each of these factors is likely to be different at the various levels of government. For example, at the federal level, the author will hypothesize that the greatest impediments toward more accurate expenditure forecasting are not as much technical as they are political and normative. Evidence presented later in this chapter will show that the federal government's annual outlay estimates are very accurate. It is in the out years that the budget estimates become inaccurate. This is not, in the author's judgment, a technical problem centering on estimation techniques or program costing, as much as it is a political and normative one. In essence, politicians have lacked the will to head toward a balanced budget. Perhaps more importantly, elected officials have made normative judgments to engage in overly optimistic economic forecasting, which ultimately leads to overestimation of revenue and underestimation of outlays, hence deficit spending, particularly in fiscal outyears.

The problems with state, and particularly local, government are quite different. These levels of government are bound by constitutional constraint to pass balanced budgets. Normatively, these governments have tended to understate revenue in an effort to restrain expenditures (Wildavsky, 1986; Bretschneider and Schroeder, 1988; Frank, 1988). The author will hypothesize that for state and local government (particularly the latter), limited technical ability and the tendency to overstate expenses may play a larger role in the kinds of forecasting methods deployed.

Risk Aversion and Innovation

Another factor inhibiting the move toward more accurate expenditure forecasting in government may be risk aversion on the part of actors in the budgeting process. At the federal level, use of more accurate cost estimates and realistic economic assumptions may mean more informed evaluation of policy tradeoffs, with decreased chance of implementing new programs, or increasing funding levels of old ones (Penner, 1982; Stockmann, 1987). At the local and state levels, the risk aversion takes on a different form. Fear of exceeding the budget constraint leads to a combination of understated revenue and overstated expenditures on the part of both elected officials and careerists (Wildavsky, 1986; Choate and Thompson, 1988). This in turn leads to a preference for forecasting techniques that project in accordance with desired up- or down-side bias, rather than in absolutely accurate terms. Risk aversion in any form retards innovation (Mahajan and Peterson, 1985; Kamm, 1987). As such, we might expect fear of and resistance to expenditure forecasting methods that estimate "truer," unbiased, numbers.

The Notion of Model Utility

The possible fear of unbiased forecasts that might preclude the implementation of new forecasting approaches or models relates to a larger domain, that being model utility. A particular forecasting model might forecast very accurately for a given budgeting situation. What use is the model, however, if the organization does not have sufficient data on hand to run it? What if the organization's staff cannot comprehend the model or its assumptions? Or what if the model forecasts well for a time frame of 6 months, but the organization needs accurate forecasts for 1 year out? Scott Armstrong (1985) has written that "Implementation is the Achilles heel of forecasting" (p. 49). This is because all too often, forecasting experts will try to implement a new forecasting model without taking into account the limits or needs of the organization or its personnel. These are critical variables in the forecast situation. Neglecting them will doom most efforts at enhancing forecast accuracy to failure before they start. Thus, the ultimate utility of a forecast model or approach is organizationally defined.

Chapter Overview

While there may be risk entailed in trying new techniques in expenditure forecasting, one might argue that in today's restrained fiscal environment, failure to experiment with new and potentially more accurate techniques carries with it risk as well. Moreover, as one acquires information about the various forecasting techniques available, the risk entailed in their possible implementation becomes reduced. The widespread availability of reasonably priced, user-friendly software (Beaumont, 1986) in the forecasting area suggests that many of the techniques to be discussed in this chapter are readily accessible for desk-top computer use.

This chapter is written with the intent of whetting the reader's appetite insofar as experimentation in this area is concerned. "Experimentation" must be stressed for two important reasons. First, research on state and local revenue and expenditure forecasting covering the past two decades (Bahl, 1980; Bretschneider and Gorr, 1987) has clearly shown that these governments have failed to try many of the forecasting techniques that have been used successfully in the private sector for inventory management and sales control for over 30 years. From the vantage of cost control for projects at the federal level, they may also be needed (Penner, 1982; Premchand; 1983). A second and possibly more important reason that trial and error will be needed in this area is that research on the nature of time-series data (Makridakis and Hibon, 1984) suggests that attempting to find "one best way" for forecasting in a given environment would be foolhardy. Every time series has its peculiarities, which must be catered to.

In essence then, the chapter stresses good forecasting practice, which is likely to be attained through an iterative process.

THE TECHNICAL SIDE OF FORECASTING

A Forecasting Continuum

One can think of the wide variety of forecasting methods and approaches available as lying on a continuum (Fig. 2) on which we move from nonmathematical, intuitive approaches to models that are quite simple mathematically, and still further to models that can be remarkably complex. Progressing along this continuum may or may not result in increased forecast accuracy. Perhaps more importantly, organizational needs and constraints may very well determine how far along this continuum an agency should and could move.

Qualitative and Accounting-Based Approaches

The adjective "qualitative" covers a great deal of turf in this category. What is common to all of these approaches is that human judgment, rather than mathematical computation, plays the decisive role in the forecast values.

Qualitative models assume that the forecast value for a time in the future is the same value as that time period in the past, with some possible modification. How that modification is arrived at might not be clear to an outsider observing the forecast process. The budgeter's forecast may be based on simple guesswork, or a well-thought-out process that takes many factors into account. Comparing the accuracy of this approach with that of more complex, quantitative approaches might be difficult, unless the forecaster could put his minding process on paper for future reference.

Another form of qualitative forecast is that of panel consensus or "expert opinion." Many forecasts of economic behavior are made this way. In situations for which there are few or no precedents, and hence historical cost data, these may be the only options available. For the state or local government considering the construction costs of a resource recovery facility that turns trash into electric power, or the federal budgeter who is trying to cost out the "Star Wars" initiative, these approaches may be the only options available.

Qualitative approaches to forecasting are frequently used in both the public and

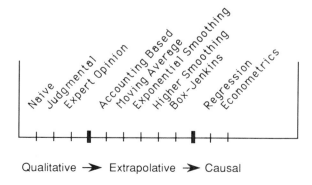

Figure 2 A forecasting methodology continuum.

private sector. These techniques have their pluses and minuses. On the plus side, it has been shown that individuals who have considerable experience with the forecast situation can deliver remarkably accurate predictions about its future behavior (Armstrong, 1984, 1985). Furthermore, for forecasts beyond 2 years, quantitative methods deliver such poor predictions (Wheelright and Makridakis, 1980; Mentzer and Cox, 1984; Armstrong, 1985) that the educated guesses of qualitative techniques become, by default, very good alternatives. On the negative side, qualitative forecasts are generally thought to be more time-consuming and expensive to implement than their quantitative counterparts (Bails and Peppers, 1982; Willis, 1987). And in head-to-head competition with quantitative methods, qualitative methods have generally been shown to be less accurate (Armstrong, 1985). This inaccuracy may be attributed in large part to psychological factors. Human beings change their operating assumptions too slowly relative to changes in their operating environment (Ascher, 1978). They also tend to be overly optimistic about future outcomes.

Moving further along the continuum, one finds accounting-based methods, which are sometimes referred to as identity-based approaches. These techniques are the most frequently used forecast models in government. An accounting- or identity-based forecast for a given time period is a function of the quantity of the object of expenditure being purchased, multiplied by its unit or average cost. For example, in a recently developed forecast manual for local governments, the Commonwealth of Massachusetts (1987) recommends expenditure categories (e.g., salaries, retirement, expenses, and debt service, etc.), and provides formulas for calculation the coming year's expense in those categories. Salary forecasts for the coming year are arrived at by multiplying the number of incumbents within a particular rank, times their average salary, with that product multiplied by the anticipated percentage salary increase. Retirement expenses are estimated as a fixed percentage of salaries. Expenses such as utilities and supplies are viewed as a function of last year's expenses within the category multiplied by the U.S. Department of Labor's price deflator reflecting inflation for the past year, as an estimate of inflation for the coming year. The amount set aside for debt service is determined by formulas driven by the amount of outstanding debt, interest rates, and retirement schedule.

This approach to expenditure forecasting has strengths and weaknesses. Its greatest strength lies in its simplicity—basic algebraic operations are generally all that are required for its use. Because of this, the approach lends itself nicely to implementation on electronic spreadsheet programs, which is an other strength. This approach also ties in with what is still the most frequently used budget approach—the line item. Last, but certainly not least, the accounting-based approach is likely to be reasonably accurate for many expense items, and very accurate for salaries and salary-related expenses such as unemployment and insurance, which are generally the largest component of any public budget (Scott, 1972). On the downside, this technique assumes a very static view of the nature of the operations for which it is used. Further, its accuracy is likely to be predicated on the proper disaggregation of expenditure categories. And lastly, the method's predictive ability is largely predicated on proper assumptions regarding the level of inflation. As we discuss below, governmental entities are notorious for underestimating inflation. They also tend to assume one inflation rate for all facets of their operations, which is quite misleading. These weaknesses greatly reduce this approach's accuracy for multiyear forecasting, which is an increasingly important tool in financial planning.

It is impossible to make a blanket statement about the forecast capability of naive and accounting-based techniques relative to some of the more complex methods along the forecast continuum. What can be said is that combinations of forecasting techniques are likely to yield substantial gains in forecast accuracy (Gupta and Wilton, 1987). Budgeters and other government officials should keep this in mind when contemplating their expenditure forecasts. Given the present state of forecast practice within the public sector, this suggests that budgeters should complement their current reliance on qualitative and accounting-based approaches with the extrapolative and causal approaches discussed below.

Extrapolative Approaches

These approaches, often referred to as time-series models, use mathematical formulas that weight previous values within a historical series in order to predict future values of that series. They range from the very simple to the very complex. Some approaches explicitly take into account the possible presence of trend or seasonality in a set of data; others do not. Virtually all extrapolative methods have been packaged in microcomputer software, which greatly facilitates their adoption. Time-series models have been used in the private sector for decades. Research on their strengths and weaknesses is voluminous.

The Moving Average

The model is as follows:

$$S_{t+1} = \frac{x_t + x_{t-1} + X_{t-N+1}}{N}$$

where S_{t+1} is the forecast value, x_t, x_{t-1}, and x_{t-N+1} are previous time periods in the series being forecast, and N equals the number of periods being forecast with.

The moving average is the simplest of extrapolative techniques. In effect, it operates by equally weighting the number of previous points in time that are being used to forecast the future value. If, for example, we were forecasting a value for June with a two-period moving average, June's forecasted value would be the April and May values summed and divided by two (alternatively, a weight of one-half of April's value added to one-half of May's value). If this were a three-period moving average, we would sum the values of March, April, and May, and then divide by three to arrive at the forecast value for June.

The decision as to how many past values to utilize in arriving at the forecast value is referred to as setting the length of the average. Brown (1963) points out that there are no hard and fast rules for fixing the length of the moving average. If the forecaster goes too far back in time, there is a good chance that irrelevant data will be taken into account, lessening accuracy and adding significantly to data requirements. On the other hand, if the length is kept too short, the model will overrespond to random shocks.

The moving average assumes that the series of data is stationary around a mean (Fig. 3)—that it has no significant trend or seasonality to it. This assumption is a deterrent to the model's effective use (Wheelright and Makridakis, 1980), in that the moving average will always lag the trend.

Empirical evidence indicates that the moving average, which weights all previous periods equally, will not forecast as well as other time-series techniques—such as exponential smoothing—which put greater weight on the most recent values.

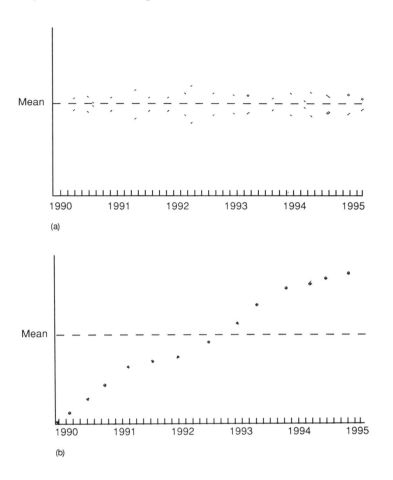

Figure 3 (a) Stationary series versus (b) nonstationary series.

Smoothing Techniques

The single-exponential smoothing model is

$$S_{t+1} = aY_t + (1\text{-}a)S_{t-1}$$

where S_{t+1} is the forecast value on period ahead, Y_t is the actual value in time period t, and a is the smoothing constant, which lies between zero and one.

In the words of its developer, Robert Brown, exponential smoothing is a "very special kind of weighted moving average" (1963, p. 13). In essence the model is a moving average of forecasts that have been corrected for observed error in the preceding forecast (Holt et al., 1960). For example, if one were attempting to forecast June expenditures in a given category, the forecast would be $F_{June} = F_{May} + a(A_{May} - F_{May})$ where A stands for the actual values and F symbolizes forecast values.

The "exponential" in exponential smoothing refers to the fact that past values' input into the current forecast die out exponentially, depending on the value of a, the smoothing constant. If this value is close to one, the previously forecast values rapidly lose their value in predicting current values. Contrariwise, if a is close to zero, past values maintain their predictive value for current forecasting over a longer period of time. Thinking of this in moving average terms, when the smoothing constant is higher, it signifies a moving average of short length, with a longer average implied if it is low (White et al., 1980). Computer programs routinely compute the value of the smoothing constant that minimizes forecast error.

This technique is robust to different types of data including moderate trend and seasonality (Gardner, 1985). Data requirements for the technique are minimal—a few values should be sufficient for initializing the series (Brown, 1963; Willis, 1987). This is an advantage over the moving average, which is thought to require more data.

Empirical comparison of extrapolation methods indicates that exponential smoothing is more accurate than the moving average (Gardner, 1985). In the M-Competition (described below), exponential smoothing was among the most accurate methods tested, and outperformed the Box-Jenkins model, which will be discussed shortly (Makridakis and Hibon, 1984; Hibon, 1984). This demonstrated level of accuracy, according to Gardner, suggests the technique "cannot be dismissed" (1985, p. 23) when searching for a forecast model.

The only discernible weaknesses of exponential smoothing are (1) it is thought to be a short-range technique (i.e., appropriate for forecasts of up to six periods); (2) the technique has no statistical or visual diagnostic tools to help the forecaster in determining model adequacy, as is the case with Box-Jenkins models (Wheelright and Makridakis, 1980; Gardner, 1985); and (3) the model may not be able to handle extreme trend or seasonality. Because of the last shortcoming, some will forecast with double-exponential smoothing, which, as its name implies, double smooths data to deal with increased trend. Another model that can deal with serious trend is Holt's two-parameter smoothing model, which finds a parameter for both the randomness of the data (i.e., adjusts for the correlation between points in time for the series) and possible trend. Still another variant of the single exponential smoothing model is the Winter's seasonal smoothing model, which has both trend and seasonal parameters. The trend and seasonal parameters in these derivatives will "turn off" if these factors are not present in the data being analyzed. This suggests that one might experiment with these approaches without fear of imposing nonexisting trend or seasonality on the data. Bails and Peppers (1982) and Willis (1987) give excellent descriptions of the implementation of these techniques.

Curve Fitting

Curve fitting is probably the most popular forecasting technique (Willis, 1987). It is found in many computer packages and pocket calculators. When state and local governments adopt quantitative forecasting methods for revenue and expenditures, curve fitting is the method of choice (Bretschneider and Gorr, 1987). Curve fitting is generally operationalized through the linear regression model:

$$y = a + bX$$

where y is the forecasted value for period X, a is the intercept, computed as the average of $Y - b$(the average of X), b is the slope parameter as calculated through least squares, and X is the period of the desired forecast, often referred to as the "time ticker."

If, for example, the calculated equation for a certain expense category was y = $100,000 + 1250X, and the analyst wished to forecast six periods out, our forecast here would be $100,000 + 1250(6) or $107,500.

Curve fitting's popularity may not be a good indicator of its accuracy. Hibon (1984) and Armstrong (1984, 1985), contend that when curve fitting against time is pitted against exponential smoothing or its derivatives, the latter generally prove to be more accurate. This is due to curve fitting's equal weighting of all previous points in a time series. This is contrary to the approach of the other techniques described here (save for the moving average), which is to give greater weight to the most recent points in a time series when forecasting.

Adaptive Filtering

All time-series approaches are based on the notion that future values can be obtained by fixing weights to the previous values in the series, then extrapolating into the future based on historical values. Ultimately, the techniques differ on how they assign these weights to past values. For example, in a three-period moving average, one arbitrarily assigns the weight of 0.33 to each of the three past values used in predicting the upcoming period's value. In exponential smoothing, the weights assigned to previous values are denoted by a, the smoothing constant. When exponential smoothing was developed 30 years ago, Brown (1963) suggested that the forecaster experiment with different values of a to find the best fit. Today, with the advent of sophisticated forecast software, the computer can find, within a few seconds, the value of a which minimizes forecast error.

Amalgamating the assignment of weights to previous values and the advent of sophisticated forecast software gives the framework for adaptive filtering, a term derived from communications engineering to describe the filtering of noise from the transmission of a message (Wheelright and Makridakis, 1980). In essence, this is an approach which operates through an interactive process, to find an optimal set of weights for previous values of the time series with which to forecast future values. The adaptive filtering model is as follows:

$$S_{t+1} = \sum_{i=1}^{N} w_i x_{t}, x_{t-1}, X_t-1 \ldots x_{t-k}$$

where S_{t+1} is the forecast for period $t + 1$; w_i are the weights to be assigned to the previous observations; X_t, X_{t-1}, X_{t-2}, etc. are the observed values in the previous time periods; and N is the number of weights.

The mathematical process whereby these weights are found is known as the method of steepest descent (Golder and Settle, 1976; Wheelright and Makridakis, 1980). For the model to operate, two assumptions must be met: (1) the series being operated on must be stationary (absent of trend) or made stationary through a process known as differencing, and (2) the sum of the weights must be unity.

In a manner akin to the moving average, adaptive filtering adjusts weights as new data update the series. This process is called a training iteration. The nature of the series and the training constant, k, determine the length of the training iteration. The value of k can be determined by the manager or the computer. The value normally chosen is somewhere around 1/N, where N is the number of weights. Twelve weights are generally used, since this should capture any seasonal pattern in the data, if it is present. Thus, the forecasts arrived at with the technique may be thought of as sophisticated 12-period moving averages.

Wheelright and Makridakis (1977, 1980) strongly support adaptive filtering. They believe that while its use may require forecasters to difference data (a procedure that computer programs will do with little effort), this is a far less painful procedure to implement than Box-Jenkins. Moreover, these authors claim that adaptive filtering will generally outperform Box-Jenkins in terms of forecast accuracy.

Box-Jenkins ARIMA Models

This model is represented as

$$Y_t = a + \phi_t y_{t-1} + e + \theta y_{t-p}$$

where Y_t is our predicted value, ϕ and θ are autoregressive and moving average terms with q as the highest lag, a is a possible trend component, and e is the error term, and the models being produced fit into the general ARIMA (p,d,q) (p,d,q)$_n$ format, with p representing the autoregressive parameters, d representing the times differencing is needed to achieve stationarity, and q being the moving average component, with the (p,d,q)$_n$ parameters representing possible seasonal components.

This is the most complex of the extrapolative methods described here, in terms of both mathematics and implementation. Mathematically, the Marquardt algorithm, which provides the solution for Box-Jenkins parameter estimation, is very time-consuming, even on mainframe computers (Pankratz, 1983). On microcomputers, a mathematical coprocessing chip is a virtual necessity if one wants to avoid blocks of 20–30 min or more for estimation. From the operational standpoint, this technique is highly interactive: An individual cannot obtain Box-Jenkins forecasts by simply pressing a button. A three-stage process, described below, is employed to derive parameter estimates and forecasts.

The technique's mathematical underpinnings have been documented for the better part of the century. Two British statisticians, George E. P. Box and Gwilym M. Jenkins, are credited with formalizing and popularizing the technique, and their work, *Time Series Analysis: Forecasting and Control* (1976), is considered the definitive work on the approach (McCleary and Hay, 1980; Pankratz, 1983).

Box and Jenkins have divided the world of time series into three basic types, the autoregressive, the moving average, and the mixed. In the autoregressive series, all previous points in time play some role in predicting future values. These are referred to as AR series, their parameters are designated as ϕ (phi), and they receive the p slot in the (p,d,q) designation often used to denote models. In a similar vein, another basic model is the moving average. These are referred to as MA series, their parameters are designated as θ (theta), and they receive the q slot in the (p,d,q) designation scheme. Moving average forecasts are based on values of the previous error terms (actual minus predicted values) for the previous points in the series. Lastly, there are mixed models, which have attributes of both building block models. They would have both p and q in their (p,d,q) classifications.

What is worth noting in this delineation is that an autoregressive series is one in which all past values have some contribution to make in predicting a future value. On the other hand, with a moving average series (or process, using Box-Jenkins jargon), after a certain number of prior values, generally two at most, previous values are no longer of any use in helping us predict future values. This is directly analogous to the length of a moving average, (Hoff, 1983; Vandaele, 1983). The autoregressive (AR) and moving average (MA) designations provide the bookends for the ARIMA acronym that is often used to describe this approach to modeling. The I stands for integrated, referring to the fact that computer programs that implement this technique translate the detrended and often transformed results of the forecast algorithm into the original metric of the series.

There are four assumptions that must be met to assure the proper operation of the model. The first is that the parameter values are constrained to less than unity. These conditions, known as stationarity in autoregressive models, and invertibility in moving average models, are to preclude the illogical situation in which greater weight is given to data points in the series that are further rather than closer in time to the forecast origin. This is consistent with what was said earlier in reference to the smoothing techniques and adaptive filtering—a "good" time-series model is thought to place the greatest emphasis on the most recent points in time when extrapolating into the future. A second fundamental assumption is that the values in the series must be stationary, or made stationary through differencing (Box and Jenkins, 1976; Hoff, 1983). A third assumption is that of homoscedasticity or constant variance of the data. To help assure that this assumption is met, many forecasters take the natural logarithms of the data being forecast (Vandaele, 1983).

A fourth and critical assumption, from an organizational standpoint, is that 50 data points is assumed to be the minimum number needed in a series in order to assure proper parameter estimation (Box and Jenkins, 1986). As we will discuss later in this chapter, data sufficiency is an important threshold concern in the adoption of a quantitative forecast model. Many agencies may have difficulty obtaining this long a series. One should note that this 50-point minimum may not be sufficient if seasonal factors are present. This hefty data requirement is a serious stumbling block in the adoption of this model.

Assuring that the first three of the assumptions are met is part of the iterative, three-step model-building process of the Box-Jenkins approach (Box and Jenkins, 1976; Wheelright and Makridakis, 1980), delineated as follows:

1. Model identification.
2. Model estimation and diagnostic check.
3. Forecasting.

In the model identification phase, the forecaster must postulate into which of the fundamental categories (e.g., autoregressive, moving average, or mixed) the series falls. This is done with the aid of examining autocorrelation and partial autocorrelation functions, which are diagrams of the data being correlated with lagged values of itself (Fig. 4).

Through examination of these two functions, the modeler can hopefully place the series into the correct category. Furthermore, the autocorrelation and partial autocorrelation function should enable the forecaster to choose an appropriate level of differencing, and, if warranted, seasonal parameters.

Assuming that the model type is correctly chosen, and that stationarity and seasonality have been dealt with, the modeler can estimate the parameters of the tentatively identified model. There are a number of diagnostic tools the forecast uses to check the adequacy of the model. Residuals of the model—actual minus predicted values—should be "white noise," or statistically equal to zero. Moreover, the residual autocorrelations or partial correlations should not sum to greater than an appropriate amount related to degree of freedom in the series (i.e., the series length). These residuals are in turn tested with a chi-square test or Q-test. Furthermore, the parameters identified should not be closely intercorrelated with one another. And lastly, the modeler should attempt to both add and remove parameters from the model, to see if there is any appreciable difference in results (Vandaele, 1983; Hoff, 1983).

If the model has not withstood this veritable barrage of diagnostics, the forecaster

```
(a) Degree of Regular Differencing = 1  Degree of Seasonal Differencing = 1

   Lag  Value  T-Value -1.0                      0.0                      +1.0
                        :----------------------------------------------------------:
     1  -0.52   -3.14   :         *****[*******|          ]                        :
     2   0.01    0.05   :              [        |          ]                        :
     3   0.11    0.54   :              [        |***       ]                        :
     4  -0.08   -0.38   :              [      **|          ]                        :
     5  -0.04   -0.18   :              [       *|          ]                        :
     6   0.07    0.31   :              [        |**        ]                        :
     7  -0.04   -0.18   :              [       *|          ]                        :
     8   0.06    0.28   :              [        |*         ]                        :
     9  -0.11   -0.53   :              [     ***|          ]                        :
    10   0.21    0.98   :              [        |*****      ]                        :
    11  -0.12   -0.54   :              [     ***|          ]                        :
    12  -0.18   -0.83   :              [    ****|          ]                        :
                        :----------------------------------------------------------:
                        [ ] = Estimated Two-Standard Error Limits

Box-Pierce Chi-Square Statistic with 12 Degrees of Freedom = 14.7  Probability = .26
```

```
(b)
    Degree of Regular Differencing = 1    Degree of Seasonal Differencing = 1

   Lag  Value  T-Value -1.0                      0.0                      +1.0
                        :----------------------------------------------------------:
     1  -0.52   -3.14   :         *****[*******|          ]                        :
     2  -0.36   -2.17   :            *[*******|          ]                        :
     3  -0.11   -0.66   :              [    ***|          ]                        :
     4  -0.08   -0.46   :              [     **|          ]                        :
     5  -0.13   -0.80   :              [    ***|          ]                        :
     6  -0.07   -0.45   :              [     **|          ]                        :
     7  -0.06   -0.38   :              [     **|          ]                        :
     8   0.05    0.29   :              [        |*         ]                        :
     9  -0.10   -0.57   :              [     **|          ]                        :
    10   0.17    1.00   :              [        |****      ]                        :
    11   0.13    0.79   :              [        |***       ]                        :
    12  -0.22   -1.32   :              [   *****|          ]                        :
                        :----------------------------------------------------------:
                        [ ] = Estimated Two-Standard Error Limits
```

Figure 4   Box-Jenkins analyses: (a) ARIMA identification autocorrelation, and (b) identification partial correlation functions.

must start from scratch and work with a newly identified tentative model. If the model appears to be satisfactory, one can attempt to forecast with it, which in the case of Box-Jenkins computer software means requesting the computer to forecast the desired number of periods from the origin. In addition to the standard measures of model adequacy that a forecaster would observe (e.g., mean absolute percentage error, mean square error), Box-Jenkins, unlike the other extrapolative techniques, generates percentage confidence intervals of the modeler's choice around the forecast values. Examining these values gives a fairly good idea as to the plausibility of the forecast.

The amount of time and degree of subjectivity entailed in the tripartite Box-Jenkins forecast process has opened it up to serious criticism. In the M-Competition, it took experts an average of an hour to identify a model and examine it for adequacy (Makridakis and Hibon, 1984). This, according to Lewandowski (1984), begs the question: How long should forecasting take for lay forecasters? The subjectivity problem is perhaps even more severe. McCleary and Hay (1980) declare that "ARIMA modeling has been called an *art* by many authors" (p. 91). Lusk and Neves (1984) and Armstrong (1985) have noted that interforecaster reliability in judging series is very low. Reinforcing this subjectivity are two other factors. The first is that the ostensibly objective diagnostic tools such as the autocorrelation and partial autocorrelation used for checking model adequacy are often misleading (Vandaele, 1983). The second and possibly more astonishing factor is that it appears to make little difference in forecast accuracy whether or not one operates with an entirely adequate model in the first place (Makridakis and Hibon, 1984).

Tolerating the time and subjectivity required of Box-Jenkins would be worthwhile if the technique delivered demonstrably superior forecast accuracy. Past research has suggested it does not. In reviewing 14 head-to-head competitions with exponential smoothing, Armstrong (1985) suggested that Box-Jenkins outperformed that much simpler technique only four times. In the M-Competition, the technique, which was the only model of the 24 compared that required user interaction, performed more poorly than most of the simpler techniques, even naive forecasting. This led Rudolf Lewandowski (1984) to write:

> Given the indisputable evidence provided by this comparison, the results clearly and most surprisingly demonstrate that the highly complex ARIMA-type Box-Jenkins method is in no way superior to other methods as far as forecasting accuracy is concerned. From the point of view of practical forecasting such a method is, therefore, of no value, no matter what academic experts say in its defense. (p. 247)

When Box-Jenkins was first popularized in the mid-1970s, it was all the rage in extrapolative techniques. Fifteen years of use and testing have shown that it has not lived up to its original billing. Mentzer and Cox (1984) noted extremely high dissatisfaction with the technique relative to other methods in their survey of sales forecasters. It is time-consuming and difficult to implement. It is not as accurate as many simpler techniques. From the author's vantage, one of its worst attributes could very well be that exposure to this technique could frustrate an individual attempting quantitative forecast methods for the first time. Such an experience could be traumatic, and lead to the abandonment of attempts at finding new and potentially more accurate forecast methods. From this standpoint alone, steering clear of Box-Jenkins would be advisable.

Causal Approaches

With naive or judgmental approaches, a predicted future value is based on conjecture. This prediction may be based on past experience with the phenomenon being forecast, comparison with similar situations, or simple guessing. While this approach may entail a reliance on numerical analysis of some sort, more likely than not, it will not. Identity-based approaches mirror the line items being forecast, in the sense that last year's expenditure in item X multiplied by an inflation factor is thought to be a good indicator of where next year's expenditures will lie. Extrapolative approaches have explicit mathematical relationships implied in their formulas in the sense that predicted values are seen as a function of weighted past values. Implicit in their use is the assumption of a steady state, one that allows the use of past values as sufficient for predicting future ones.

Causal approaches are different. As their name implies, they are based on efforts to find what "causes" the phenomenon being studied. For example, a budget analyst in a large city might try to predict police expenditures by examining their relationship to variables such as the unemployment rate, the percentage of population aged 20–34, the percentage of families on public assistance, total population, and per capita income. The underlying assumption to this approach is that if a causal theory of the phenomenon being forecast can be discovered, one should be able to make predictive statements—and hence forecast values—of the phenomenon. Furthermore, this approach allows the analyst to ask "what if" questions regarding changes in the environment. If police expenditures were related to the factors just mentioned, one could ask what an increase in the unemployment rate of 1%, and a 5% drop in the percentage of the population aged 20–34, would do to expenditures. Moreover, one could ask which of these variables was more important in predicting police expenditures.

The ability to test theories about the phenomenon being forecast is one of the great strengths of the causal approach. Its other great strength is that it tends to deliver more accurate forecasts over longer time horizons than either judgmental or extrapolative forecasting techniques. These strengths, however, come with a price. Causal approaches are more time-consuming and expensive to implement than simpler techniques along the forecasting methodology continuum. They also require more data and forecasting expertise for their successful operation. This suggests that certain organizations may not be able to use these approaches. In a similar vein, those organizations that can may have to weigh the benefits of enhanced accuracy and understanding to be gained from these approaches relative to the costs of their implementation.

The Linear Regression Model

Causal approaches to forecasting are undertaken with the linear regression model, which was originally developed in the 1820s by Gauss in Germany (Gujarati, 1978, p. 47), though Francis Galton is credited with having coined the term "regression" at the turn of the century. Galton used this term to refer to the tendency of short parents to have tall offspring and vice versa. In current parlance, we would refer to this as an example of regression to the mean. Today, we refer to regression as a process that tests if variation in a *dependent* variable can be predicted through knowledge of the mean or average value on one or more *independent* or *explanatory* variables. In the criminal justice example mentioned above, police expenditures would be the dependent variable, while the unemployment rate, percentage of population age 20–34, percentage of families on public assistance, total population, and per capita income would be the independent variables.

A process known as ordinary least squares (OLS) is used to estimate the relationship between the dependent and independent variables. This relationship is said to be a stochastic relationship as opposed to a deterministic one. This relates to the nature of social science as opposed to astronomical or scientific relationships. One can obtain solunar tables that will tell us when the sun will rise and set on June 10, 1995. One can also compute what the speed of an object dropped from an airplane at 20,000 ft will be when it reaches the 10,000-ft level. This is not the case with human behavior, which will always have a certain degree of unpredictability to it. The degree of relative predictability or unpredictability of the social phenomenon under examination is captured in the regression model. In our example, the crime rate, and hence police expenditures, is likely to be affected by the socioeconomic variables discussed. But the degree to which they impact such expenditures will always remain imprecise. Perhaps more importantly from the standpoint of forecasting, it is quite likely that our theories of how the environment is operating will not hold up very well over time. In our criminal justice example, the five independent variables in the model might have worked well in the past. Current demographic changes, however, suggest that the percentage of families with single parents might be a better predictor than the percentage of families on public assistance. The results of ordinary least squares estimation will help discover if that is the case.

The ordinary least squares process is dependent on the satisfaction of five underlying assumptions if it is to deliver unbiased results with the tightest possible confidence intervals around predicted values. Stated differently, certain assumptions must be met if this process is to deliver forecasts that are not persistently over or under actual values. They must also be met to assure precise forecasts. The degree of precision relates to the concept of a confidence interval around the estimates. The reader is referred to an introductory statistics text for a description of confidence intervals in general or to Montgomery and Peck (1982) for a discussion of how these intervals are constructed in regression. The nature of the assumptions to be met follows.

Linearity

The OLS model assumes that the variables being studied are linearly related to one another. Implied in this is the notion of constant proportionality in the relationship. Yet in daily life, this will not always be the case. We know that doubling our driving speed from 30 to 60 miles per hour will almost quintuple our braking distance. In this situation, it would be unreasonable to assume that braking distance and speed were linearly related. The relationship here would be curvilinear. The presence of nonlinearity does not preclude the use of least squares estimation. It does, however, call for a transformation of the dependent or one or more of the independent variables, using logarithms or some other metric. Many computer programs will actually find the transformation that best fits the data being modeled with.

Normal Distribution of the Data

The use of the regression model assumes a normal distribution of the data in all our variables. This was not an assumption of the model when it was first developed, but was subsequently added for a very good reason. If our data are not normally distributed, we cannot make statistical tests regarding the other assumptions of the model. Moreover, we cannot engage in the kinds of statistic tests described below used to determine the significance (predictive ability) of the entire regression model or its independent variables. As was the case with violation of the linearity assumptions, transformation of the data, particularly the logarithmic transformation, will tend to normalize the data. Almost all regression programs will give graphics that indicate the distribution of the data.

Absence of Multicollinearity

The causation of most social phenomena is likely to be complex. As such, most regression models will need more than one independent variable if they are to have good predictive value. The ordinary least squares model will accommodate multiple regressors (independent variables) very easily. In fact, one of its strengths is that it tells the forecaster what impact one independent variable has on the dependent variable, controlling for the presence of the other independent variables in the model. This control mechanism works well if the independent variables are not strongly correlated with (related to) one another. If they are, the mathematical underpinnings of ordinary least squares estimation begin to break down, and it becomes difficult to sort out the effects of the independent variables on the dependent variable. This problem is called multicollinearity or simply collinearity.

Some degree of multicollinearity is likely to be present in all multiple regression models. This is due to the nature of the variables that are frequently studied in the social sciences (Schroeder et al., 1986). The police expenditure model provides an example of this. The independent variables in this model, unemployment rate, percentage of population age 20–34, percentage of families on public assistance, total population, and per capita income, would probably show fairly strong correlations with one another. If the correlations between the independent variables are too strong, in either a positive or negative relationship, the model would have operational problems.

When serious multicollinearity is present, two difficulties occur with estimation. The first is that relationships between the independent and dependent variables, which in reality may be positive, may be estimated as negative, and vice versa. The second problem relates to inference about the variables in the model. In the presence of serious multicollinearity, there is a tendency to include variables in the model that would not be included in its absence. Either of these problems is likely to diminish the predictive ability of the forecast model.

Detecting multicollinearity is not easy. Any time independent variables correlate with one another at 0.50 or greater in absolute terms, one should suspect its presence. Typically, computer programs that perform regression generate other diagnostics for this problem (Gujarati, 1978; Montgomery and Peck, 1982; Agresti and Finlay, 1986).

Many forecasters respond to a perceived or actual multicollinearity problem by deleting independent variables from their model. This may result in seriously biasing the results of least squares estimation. The better solutions would be to create indices by combining some of the variables, or to mathematically combine variables with a process known as principal components analysis (Hanushek and Jackson, 1977).

Multicollinearity is a serious problem, which must be attended to if it is present in the regression model. If combining variables through indexing or principal components analysis does not solve the problem, estimation techniques other than ordinary least squares may need to be used for forecast purposes (Montgomery and Peck, 1982).

Absence of Heteroscedasticity

The errors in a regression model are the difference between actual values of the dependent variable and the values forecast by the regression model. If the mathematics of ordinary least squares are working properly, these errors should sum to zero. This suggests that the model is not predicting in a biased manner on either the up or down side, as the errors are canceling each other out. When this is the case, variance for the model is said to be constant. This condition is known as homoscedasticity.

There will be times when this condition is not present, and a fundamental assumption of ordinary least squares estimation is violated. This, not too surprisingly, is referred to as heteroscedasticity. Heteroscedasticity may occur for three reasons. The first is the "apples and oranges" nature of the data that are often used in regression analysis. Variables such as per capita income, years of education, and social status, cannot, a priori, be expected to have equal variance. This will in turn be reflected in unequal variance of the forecast values. Another cause that has an economic rationale is that many behaviors are not constant over the range of income levels. Given that personal income is frequently an independent variable in forecasting models, this cause is quite common. The third and final cause, which may be present if time-series rather than cross-sectional data are used, is change in recordkeeping procedures for the variables used.

If heteroscedasticity is present in the regression model, false inferences will be made with regard to its independent variables. As was the case with multicollinearity, this means variables will be retained in the model which should be excluded.

Detection of heteroscedasticity is not as difficult as multicollinearity. Modelers will often utilize scatterplots of the errors as a visual indicator of the problem. In the absence of heteroscedasticity, the residuals are "scattershot" or random in nature (Fig. 5). If heteroscedasticity is present, the errors take on some kind of pattern, generally a funnel or cigar. There are also quantitative measures that can be used to detect the presence of heteroscedasticity (Gujarati, 1978).

Mild cases of heteroscedasticity can be ameliorated through transformation, generally logarithmic, of the data. If this remedy does not work, procedures other than ordinary least squares must be used for estimation. Weighted least squares and maximum likelihood estimation are two commonly used alternative approaches (Hanushek and Jackson, 1977).

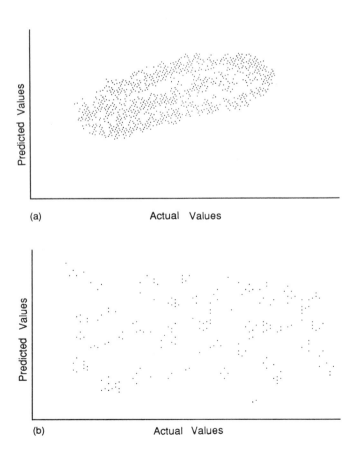

Figure 5 (a) Heteroscedastic and (b) homoscedoastic residual plots.

Absence of Autocorrelation

Most social and management science research using regression analysis is done using cross-sectional data: The researcher is working with data that represent a "snapshot" of one time period covering the variables of interest. Forecasting is different.

Generally, the forecaster will be working with time-series data, which may be of daily, weekly, monthly, quarterly, or annual periodicity. We know that with most economically related phenomena, what happens in the previous time period, or even further back, will have a significant impact on what happens in the immediate future. This relatedness across time periods is called *autocorrelation* or *serial correlation.*

The presence of autocorrelation is a serious threat to effective ordinary least squares estimation. When present, serial correlation will bias the estimation process. It will also lead the researcher to include variables in the model which would not be in its absence.

Autocorrelation can be detected through both graphics and statistical diagnostics. Scatterplots of the errors across time will appear as they do in Fig. 6, should autocorrelation be present. Computer packages that perform regression analysis routinely print out these plots. They also produce what is the known as the Durbin-Watson (D-W) statistic, which informs the forecaster of the presence of this condition.

Serial correlation is likely to be present in forecasting with time-series data. It may also be present if the forecaster has a problem with *misspecification*. This is the situation when the forecaster has excluded important independent variables from the model. Because of this, any forecaster who detects serial correlation must address the possibility that the diagnostics are giving a "false alarm" with regard to time sequence, and are instead indicating that the causal theory being tested is inadequate or inappropriate (Gujarati, 1978).

Assuming that the detected autocorrelation is caused by the time sequence of data, the modeler may need to either transform the data, or use alternatives to ordinary least square estimation. Details on how to deal with autocorrelation are provided in any econometrics or advanced regression textbook. Some regression programs will automatically correct for this condition, should it be detected.

Statistical Inference and Measures of Model Adequacy

When we hypothesize about possible relationships using the regression model, there are two questions that must be asked regarding its possible use. The first is whether the model has significant predictive ability. The second is whether or not the individual independent variables in the model are appropriate, or should be replaced with other variables, in a process often referred to as model building.

The first question is a macro question. A regression forecasting model represents a theory of how some phenomenon—in the current context, a public expenditure—can be explained by changes in independent variables. Until the forecaster collects data and runs the regression, this theory remains essentially untested. Thus, the first order of hand when ascertaining the worth of the model is to perform an F-test on it. This F-test states whether or not the model's predictive ability is significantly better than what would have been obtained by chance or haphazard guessing, without knowledge of the independent variables. The computer will normally print out the F-value along with its associated probability. Should this probability be low, generally less than 0.05, we can assume that the model has at least some "statistically significant" predictive ability.

The question of how well the model will predict is reflected in what is known as the

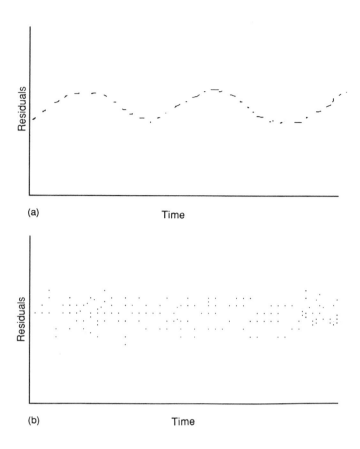

Figure 6 Residual plots showing (a) presence of serial correlation, and (b) absence of serial correlation.

multiple coefficient of determination, often referred to as R-squared. This coefficient has a range from zero to one, with the former suggesting no explanatory power and the latter indicating perfect explanatory power. While there are no absolutes in judging what a good R-squared should be, one generally expects forecasting models to have an R-squared of 0.80 or higher. This is an important measure to consider, as it is possible to have a "statistically significant" F-test and still have a model with low explanatory power. Some have criticized the R-squared measure in that it is always possible to increase it by adding new independent variables, even if these variables are not making significant contributions to explanatory power. The adjusted R-squared measure accounts for the number of independent variables in the model (Montgomery and Peck, 1982), and will deflate the R-squared measure to account for addition of insignificant variables.

The concern for inclusion of possible insignificant variables is the next concern for statistical inference in regression. The F-test discussed above may be thought of as the casting of the wide net in a statistical sense, in that it indicates if the model in general is worthwhile. In the multiple regression model, that is simply telling us that at least one of our independent variables has predictive value. It does not tell us which of the independent variables that may be. Nor does it tell us if the other explanatory variables have predictive power. For this, T- and F-tests on the individual independent variables must be conducted.

To clarify this, let us look at the hypothetical police expenditure model discussed earlier. In this model, we hypothesized that:

$$Y = a + b1(\text{unemployment rate}) + b2(\text{percentage of population between 20 and 34}) +$$
$$b3(\text{percentage of families on public assistance}) + b4(\text{total population}) +$$
$$b5(\text{per capita income})$$

where Y would be predicted police expenditures, a the constant, and b1 through b5 would be the *regression coefficients* indicating how change in their respective independent variables would affect police expenditures, controlling for the other independent variables in the model.

An overall F-test might suggest that the model has "statistically significant" power. The R-squared and adjusted R-squared may also suggest that the model has the potential for good predictive power. These indicators will not tell us which of our independent variables are truly helping in predicting police expenditures, however. We could find for example that the percentage of families on public assistance and percentage of population between 20 and 34 were not significant variables in helping predict police expenditures. This is the kind of information provided by the F- and T-tests on individual independent variables.

This information is important for three reasons. First, good social research practice tells us to aim for parsimony. We want to predict as much with as few variables as possible. Second, in the case of regression, keeping nonsignificant variables in the model makes for larger than necessary confidence levels in the predicted values. And lastly, by weeding out insignificant predictor variables, we can begin to refine the forecast model, hopefully leading to inclusion of new explanatory variables that might increase R-squared. This is very likely to be the case in much regression modeling, where one can expect to make many modifications of the base model before honing in on one that delivers maximum predictive power with the fewest variables and smallest confidence intervals around predicted values.

Econometric Modeling

The most sophisticated type of causal forecasting is the econometric model. Its use has generally been associated with the analysis of economic trends for the national economy, though such models have now been developed for states, regions, and large metropolitan areas. These models were first developed in the immediate post-World War II era, and have become increasingly sophisticated over time.

These models use the regression approach to forecasting, but generally do not use ordinary least squares estimation. This is due to the fact that econometric models are not, as the police expenditure model detailed above was, single-equation models. They are instead comprised of systems of equations that are solved simultaneously. In these simultaneous-equation models, the distinction between dependent and independent variables is replaced with the terms endogenous and exogenous variables. Endogenous variables are those whose values are computed within the econometric model. The values of exogenous variables come from outside data sources, judgment on the part of the forecaster, or even other econometric models.

The simultaneous solution of what may be hundreds of regression equations in these models allows for the calculation of feedback relationships between variables in the model, something that cannot be accomplished with a single equation approach. This accommodation of feedback relationships brings with it the violation of several of the assumptions discussed earlier; hence, ordinary least squares is generally not used in econometric estimation.

The use of econometric models is normally justified on two grounds. The first is that they allow for the testing of complex causal patterns in the phenomenon being studied. The second is that they are ostensibly more accurate than their simpler counter-parts. Very few would argue with the validity of the first contention. The alleged accuracy of econometric models relative to their simpler forecasting counterparts is another matter altogether. This is particularly true of short-range forecasts of 1 year or less. There is a growing body of literature that suggests that in time horizons of 1 year or less, Box-Jenkins or exponential smoothing models will forecast as least as well as, if not better than, their econometric counterparts (Nelson, 1972; Mahmoud, 1984). Even Nobel Laureate Lawrence Klein (1984), who has devoted much of his life to building econometric models, readily admits this.

Serious roadblocks exist for the building of econometric models at the local, regional, and state levels. It is clear that many of the agencies at these levels would not have the trained personnel needed to develop econometric models or comprehend models built for them (Bahl et al., 1977; Klay, 1983; Bretschneider and Gorr, 1987). Moreover, key socioeconomic data needed for the construction of these models are often unavailable for smaller cities and regions.

Econometric models at the subnational level have come under serious criticism. Most of these models are very sensitive to events in surrounding jurisdictions, leading to impaired predictive ability (Chang, 1979). They also tend to be overly simplistic in their formulations, with the general assumption being that most dependent variables are a function of personal income (Downs and Rocke, 1983). And lastly, analysis of the subnational models has shown that many suffer from serious multicollinearity while delivering low predictive ability as measured by R-squared (Duobinis, 1981).

The relative absence of econometric expenditure forecasting at the federal level may be attributed to the complexity of the task at hand—econometrically forecasting the thousands of expenditure items in many agencies would be a daunting, if not impossible, task. Moreover, experimentation by the Congressional Budget Office indicates that if seasonal factors are taken into account, methods such as the moving average and exponential smoothing do an excellent job in forecasting (Toulmin and Wright, 1983). If this is the case, engaging in the long and costly effort of developing econometric forecasting models for many federal expenditures might not be necessary.

The time, effort, and money needed to build and test an econometric model cannot be underestimated. Claudia DeVita Scott (1972) developed an econometric model for New Haven, Conn., in 1970. This model took 3½ man-years for its development. The computer programming took approximately 3 weeks. The cost of building the model was estimated to be $100,000. It was also estimated that annual upkeep of the model would be $12,000.

Obviously, the decision to construct an econometric model carries with it a large commitment in human and financial resources. For forecasts of 1 year or less, these models are no more accurate than simpler forecast models. Thus, unless one is interested in testing causal theory, or forecasting beyond a 1-year time horizon, simpler techniques along the forecast continuum should be exhaustively explored before the decision is made to build an econometric model.

Other Technical Aspects

The M-Competition

In 1982, Spyros Makridakis, one of the world's leading scholars in forecasting, sponsored a competition of time-series forecasting models in which nine experts in their respective techniques forecast with 1001 time series in an effort to compare the relative accuracy of the 24 methods or combinations thereof. The techniques ranged in complexity from naive forecasts to Box-Jenkins. The time horizons of the forecasts were from 1 to 18 months. The time series that were forecast came from a wide range of government, private, and educational activities. Some were economically sensitive series, and some were not.

This competition, which has come to be known as the M-Competition after its sponsor, produced some surprising results, which are of more than passing interest to anyone engaged in forecasting. These results apply to all forecasting approaches, in the sense that almost all forecasting entails work with time-series data either implicitly or explicitly, and the competition's findings directly relate to the nature of time series.

The two major findings of the competition, in the opinion of the sponsors (Makridakis and Hibon, 1984), were (1) the nature of the time series being forecast, in terms of trend, seasonality, and randomness, had more to do with forecast accuracy than the forecast technique being utilized, and (2) simple techniques tended to forecast as well as complex ones.

These two findings constitute a double-edged sword from the standpoint of the practicing forecaster. The first finding suggests that it is highly unlikely one will find a "workhorse" forecasting technique to handle all time series within an organization. Experimentation with a number of different techniques will probably be necessary to find the most accurate. This finding also suggests that there will be limited generalizability in research done in this area, since there is no assurance that techniques that forecast well in one organization will work well in another: The nature of the series rather than organizational attributes or functions should determine forecast accuracy.

If the need to experiment with limited hope for generalization within or between organizations is a bane, than the second finding, that simpler techniques forecast as well as complex ones, is a blessing. For the novice forecaster, techniques such as the moving average, single-exponential smoothing, and Holt are reasonably simple to understand. Techniques such as Bayesian forecasting, state space forecasting, and Box-Jenkins are not. The M-Competition findings suggest that one can experiment with simple, easily understood models, and not necessarily sacrifice forecast accuracy.

The M-Competition provided some other interesting findings. One of importance to model selection deal with the measure of accuracy used. The two primary forecast error measures are mean absolute percentage error (MAPE) and mean square error (MSE). The first measure, which is generally preferred by practitioners (Mentzer and Cox, 1984), sees accuracy in percentage terms, with the assumption that errors on the up or down side are to be equally penalized. The second measure, which is preferred by academics, tends to penalize larger errors more severely since it squares them. The rank ordering of the forecast methods tested often depended on which measure of accuracy was used. This suggests that for the experimenter in this area, the measure of forecast accuracy must be chosen with care. Armstrong (1985) details the various measures available to assess forecast accuracy, and the tradeoffs inherent in choosing one over the other.

As noted in the earlier discussion of time-series models, ARIMA did not perform well in the M-Competition, despite the fact that it was the only interactive method tested. The finding was also surprising in light of the technique's high regard in academic circles (Lewandowski, 1984). Another surprising finding was that models with built-in seasonal adjustment factors did not forecast as well as those without such factors, assuming that deseasonalized data were used with the nonseasonal models. This suggests that the seasonal parameters on some extrapolative models exaggerate seasonality at the expense of trend and randomness, thus reducing their overall accuracy.

The last finding of import to practitioners was the great increase in forecast accuracy derived from the simple averaging of forecasts. Various combinations of techniques were tried in the competition. In virtually all cases, the average forecast of the combinations was more accurate than that of the techniques used separately. Subsequent research by Mahmoud (1984), Schnaars (1986), and Guerts and Kelly (1986) has confirmed this. It was previously believed (Brandt and Bessler, 1983) that the combination of forecasting techniques could only work effectively if various weights were assigned to the forecasting models being combined to arrive at the lowest error forecast. Forecasters need not worry about finding an optimal combination—a simple average works very well.

Forecast Model Validation

Ultimately, any forecast model must be tested in practice to ascertain its true predictive ability. The best approach to this problem would be to decide upon the forecast model and see how well it works in future periods. This would be "best" from two standpoints. First, it would be the truest test of a model's performance. Second, and perhaps more important, there is considerable evidence to suggest that the use of a sample to estimate forecast ability may be misleading, in that pre- and postsample errors do not correlate well with one another (Makridakis, 1984). This means that a would-be forecaster could be lulled into a false sense of accuracy with a model that forecasts well with the sample, and subsequently falls apart when predictions are needed for budgetary purposes.

Unfortunately, most decision makers and forecasters do not have the time to pragmatically validate their forecast models. What most forecasters can do is split their sample into two parts. The first (earliest) part is what gets used for model estimation. The second (later) part of the data becomes a make-believe future. Predicted values derived from the first part of the sample are then compared with the values in the second part of the sample. This method of "holding out" data is a much more reliable indicator of future model performance than model building without such a procedure, in which "backcast" values are compared with the values in the entire data set (Armstrong, 1985). The "holding out" technique can be strengthened as follows. As future time periods become available, they are added to the second part of the sample. The earliest periods of the second portion of the sample then become the latest parts of the first sample. This successive updating of data helps assure that the model being fit approximates the ongoing reality it is being called upon to forecast.

Computerization

While it is possible for some of the simpler techniques, such as the moving average and exponential smoothing, to be done by hand, the more complex methods along the forecast continuum require computer implementation. The mathematical computations associated with advanced times-series and causal models would be overwhelming for even a single series, not to mention the dozens or hundreds that an analyst or budgeter might have to follow.

Fortunately, there are a considerable number of forecasting packages available today for desktop use. Their cost in relative terms is likely to be far less than the hardware on which they run. Most packages have the capacity to import data files that have been created in popular spreadsheet programs, a feature that should save much time in the forecasting effort. In fact, some forecasting programs have been developed as "add-ons" to spreadsheet programs. These low-cost additions may not have all the features of stand-alone forecasting software, but they may be adequate for the tasks in many public organizations.

C. D. Beaumont (1986) believes that many organizations will try to get the most for their computing dollar by purchasing general statistical software that has a forecasting component, as opposed to buying separate statistical and forecasting packages. While maximizing within a budget constraint is desirable, this approach will generally hurt the forecasting effort. Most broad-gauged statistical packages have limited forecasting method choices. Given the likely need for experimentation with several techniques prior to finding one or more that forecast accurately, it is important to consider the kinds of forecasting techniques that are available on prospective packages. And given the findings of the M-Competition, a package with several simpler techniques would be preferable to a package with only one or two complex methods.

Aside from differences in the techniques that they provide, another area in which these models differ is their degree of automation. Some packages are highly automated: They will tell the forecaster, with virtually no input, what technique forecasts most accurately, and then give the forecast results. Others are semiautomated, in that they provide statistical or graphical clues as to which models may be most appropriate, but require the modeler to execute the models in order to compare results. And finally, there are packages with virtually no automation, in the sense that finding the most accurate technique becomes a matter of trial and error on the part of the forecaster. From the author's vantage, the semiautomated packages may represent the best approach. The nonautomated packages may make the forecasting effort too tedious for practical application. At the other end of the spectrum, the totally automated packages, by virtue of their sophistication, may deprive the forecaster of important knowledge about the nature of the series being fit—for example, presence of trend or seasonality. From the standpoint of management and control, this may be as important as specific forecast values.

The most important part of any forecast software is its interpretability. As Beaumont (1986) writes, "Forecasting is a practical problem and thus it is crucial that the software chosen provides the analyst with results which are easy to interpret and understand" (p. 88). While this comprehensibility can be seen as a function of the software, it must also be viewed as a function of the ability of the forecaster. Knowledge of the underlying assumptions of a forecast model is critical if the model is to be understood in practice, or implemented in the first place.

A CONCERN FOR ORGANIZATIONAL UTILITY

Accuracy will always be the prime criterion for judging the value of a forecast (Klein, 1984; Mentzer and Cox, 1984). Management decisions are based on forecast values. Values that are well off the mark are of little use to management. An accurate forecast derived from a technique with which management is unfamiliar may, however, be of limited organizational utility. The implementation of a forecasting model must be seen as analogous to the implementation of any other operations research or management science tool. Forecasts take place in, and are utilized by, organizations and the people in them. Failure to take into account the needs and limits of organizations and their staff may very well doom implementation of new forecasting approaches and models before they begin.

Doktor, Schultz, and Slevin (1979) have written extensively on forecast implementation. They view a successful implementation as having three levels. The first or base level is that of technical validity. Here, the operations researcher or technical expert has developed an accurate model. The second level is that of organizational validity, which suggests that the model developed addressed the forecast problem at hand. The third level is that of organizational "correctness" (p. 14). This is the point at which the new forecasting technique contributes to the organization's effectiveness. Unfortunately, most efforts at moving beyond naive and judgmental techniques get stuck at the first level. Schultz (1984) has noted that there is a tendency on the part of most analysts to impose a solution on an organization's perceived forecast needs without paying sufficient attention to the users or their operating environment (pp. 44–46). According to Schultz and others, this unidirectional type of forecast model development will lead to user frustration and eventual abandonment of the model (Chambers et al., 1971; Bails and Peppers, 1982; Schultz and Slevin, 1983; Schultz, 1984).

The lack of concern for implementation has led to the recognition of a paradox. On the one hand, there is agreement that managers in both the public and private sectors have access to very sophisticated forecasting tools using desktop computers and readily available software (Klay, 1985; Makridakis, 1986). On the other hand, there is the growing recognition that lack of stakeholder input in the models to be considered, the framework in which they are to be deployed, and the specific criteria for their evaluation will lead to unsuccessful forecast model implementation (Armstrong, 1985).

This paradox is particularly cruel to small local governments and state agencies, which currently deploy the least sophisticated forecast methodologies. On face, these entities should benefit substantially from the newly available technologies. But given what we know about implementation difficulties in forecasting, the question raised is whether these organizations will be able to utilize the computer forecasting tools available to them.

There are two ways to address the question of model usability. The first is to see if support staff and decisionmakers comprehend the fundamental assumptions of a given model. Scott Armstrong (1985) contends that an analyst hoping to implement a given model should be readily able to explain the method, orally and in writing, to co-workers. It is only after this explanation that prospective users can make rational decisions regarding the benefits and costs of a forecast model, both personally and organizationally. In addition to ascertaining if basic assumptions are understood by the actors, key questions can be posited to which affirmative answers suggest enhanced probability of implementation (Armstrong, 1985, p. 318; Lawrence, 1983, p. 177). Among these questions are:

Has forecast accuracy been adequately defined prior to implementation?
Has the database been properly maintained prior to implementation?
Do the data for the model exist in the first place?
Is the model's cost perceived as being reasonable?

Would-be forecast utilizers should have in mind what a reasonable degree of accuracy is before they adopt a new forecast approach. This is particularly true with regard to multiyear forecasting. Forecasting beyond a year to 18 months is a difficult task for even the most sophisticated econometric models. At these horizons, double-digit percentage errors are the rule rather than the exception (Mentzer and Cox, 1984). A high degree of precision with such forecasts is as likely to be attributed to luck as it is to proper methodology or correct assumptions (Ascher, 1978).

As noted earlier, data availability has been a seriously neglected subject in forecast implementation (Bails and Pepper, 1982; Willis, 1987). Mikesell (1986) believes that lack of data is one of the primary inhibitors to attempts at adopting more advanced forecasting techniques at the state and local levels. The author's experience (Frank, 1988) with Florida local governments is probably generalizable to many jurisdictions and agencies: Data may be available, but not in time-series form. This raises the question, particularly in small organizations, of whether or not there are staff on hand who can sort through reports or accounting documents to put together time databases for extrapolative or causal models.

Wheelright and Makridakis (1980, pp. 27–28) have developed a model for assessing the costs of forecast model implementation as follows:

$$\frac{TC = d_1 + D_2 + S_1 + S_2 + r}{i}$$

where TC is total costs, d_1 is cost of model development, d_2 is cost of developing a working model, s_1 is storage cost of model, s_2 is storage cost of data, r is other variable costs of operation, and i is the number of items forecast with the same operation.

Obviously, the costs of developing a causal model will be much higher than for an extrapolative model. This is particularly the case if one is thinking in terms of developing an econometric model. On the other hand, with extrapolative models, existing computer software virtually precludes development costs. Development costs with extrapolative models would be limited to the trial and effort needed to find the most accurate technique and subsequent validation. The data and storage costs of a time-series approach may again be lower than those of the causal approaches. With the former, the only data needed are the series being forecast with—with the latter, a series is needed for the dependent variable and each independent variable.

Formulas have been developed (Armstrong, 1985; Mahmoud et al., 1986) that enable the forecaster, through the use of discounted cash flows, to assess the tradeoffs between forecast models that differ in accuracy, complexity, and cost. These formulas allow an analyst to measure the worth of enhanced forecasting in dollar terms, which may be a better bottom-line measure than mean absolute percentage error or similar measures of accuracy. Moreover, these formulas take into account the degree of uncontrollability inherent in the fiscal process at hand. If for example, 50–60 cents of a given budget dollar outlay is legislatively fixed for a coming fiscal year, increased accuracy in predicting such outlays may not be relevant unless changes are made in their enabling legislation. However, in future years, the uncontrollable portion of a budget may decrease. This would increase the relative worth of enhanced accuracy. But at the same time, given the nature of present value, these dollar enhancements in accuracy would be worth less than those that take place in earlier budget years. The formulas developed allow the forecaster to change assumptions regarding the degree of controllability and discount rate, thus allowing sensitivity analysis of the tradeoffs between techniques.

SOME GENERAL CONCERNS

Our discussion so far has centered on technical aspects of forecasting, and how these and the organizational aspects must be melded in order to produce relevant forecasts. There are general concepts related to the forecasting effort that are nontechnical in nature. They relate to forecasting as a planning tool. Accurate budgetary forecasting requires anticipation of significant changes in the operating environment. Not all of these changes can be anticipated—but changes in the price level and program coverage can be. Without anticipation of these changes, expenditure forecasting will be poor, regardless of its technical sophistication.

Changes in the Cost of Living

The cost of living does not stand still, and its general trend is upward. Government expenditures, particularly in long-range efforts that entail capital or research and development expense, tend to be underestimated. This may be attributed in part to the temptation to "lowball" future costs in order to make current outlays more palatable politically. But in part, this underestimation may result from a downplaying of inflationary impact. This underestimation is more serious than it would be for private sector planning in that government expenditures inflate faster than the general cost-of-living (Berne and Schramm, 1986). There are several explanations for this. The first and foremost is that government expenditures are very labor intensive. This makes them less amenable to gains in productivity through automation (Berne and Schramm, 1986). Another possible reason is a bureaucratic perception that the budget process rewards inefficiency rather than efficiency. This curbs innovations with the potential for lowering unit cost (Feller and Johnston, 1984). And finally, there is the public choice contention that government agencies can extract above-market prices for their goods and services through limited competition and elected official ignorance (Mehay and Gonzalez, 1987). For these reasons, government planners must operate on the assumption that even in times of moderate inflation, their costs are likely to inflate at a higher-than-market rate.

Until inflationary pressure picked up significantly in the 1970s, government officials tended to ignore the importance of inflation in their expenditure forecasting, using "the money of the day" (Premchand, 1983, p. 225) in their estimations. Those officials who did take it into account believed that the consumer price index (CPI) or implicit price deflator for state and local government would be sufficient for budgetary purposes. Using these measures could be misleading. If government expenditures inflate at greater than market rate, the CPI would understate price level change. The implicit price deflator is weak as an indicator in that it is undifferentiated by state or locale (Berne and Schramm, 1986).

Another deficiency with general measures of the price level is that they fail to account for the significant differences in inflationary pressures between various inputs such as land, labor, capital, and—in an era of heightened litigation and contracting out—legal and insurance expense. These differences can be reflected in significant inflation differentials between departments within a community. For example, in their study of Illinois municipalities from 1970 to 1976, Walzer and Stratton (1977) found that police and fire protection costs inflated at 5.2% annually, while libraries and parks and recreation inflated at about 2 percentage points less. We know that disaggregation of expenses is a critical component for expenditure forecast accuracy at all layers of government (Toulmin and Wright, 1983). These findings on differences in inflationary impact reinforce that point.

Construction of price indexes for communities or agencies is not a difficult task (Berne and Schramm, 1986). If agencies at all levels of government are to better estimate their long-term outlays, the development of such indices should be a high priority item.

Long-Range Expenditure Forecasting

In theory, expenditure forecasts more than one fiscal year out make eminent sense. Such forecasting allows political stakeholders and budget staff to see the fiscal implications of their current decisions. It helps both elected officials and administrative staff in anticipating fiscal problems, which, if left unattended, could become increasingly acute. As part of an overall financial plan, long-range expenditure forecasting at the state and local signals bond-rating agencies and other interested parties of the presence of significant and systematic financial planning (Boswell and Carpenter, 1986). It also helps the public in understanding the fiscal implications of government operations undertaken at current levels.

In practice, such forecasts are difficult to make and may be wildly inaccurate. There are three reasons for this. The first relates to the previous discussion of inflation. For both political and technical reasons, government agencies seriously understate it (Penner, 1982). The second is that no forecasting technique or staff, regardless of its sophistication, can cope with the unusually volatile economic conditions that have been experienced in the United States over the past 15 years or so. For example, very few economists expected the serious recessions of 1974–1975 (Klein, 1984) or 1981–1982 (Stockmann, 1987). Contrariwise, the economic disaster predicted after the stock market crash of October 1987 never materialized. Given the sensitivity of government outlays at all levels to changing economic conditions, this volatility will always be a serious stumbling block to high predictive accuracy for expenditures in the outyears. The third and final reason centers around political unwillingness to agree on baseline economic and policy assumptions upon which to build outyear forecasts. Paraphrasing from the old adage, "one man's assumptions are another man's commitments."

The Congressional Budget Office's (CBO) experience with long-range forecasts of current service outlays at the federal level sheds some light on the problems with long-range expenditure forecasting. The Current Services Budget, as called for by the Budget Reform Act of 1974, represents the budget baseline for the upcoming fiscal year, and assumes no change in policy for that year. The CBO's forecasts for current service outlays have shown no systematic up- or downside bias over its 15-year history (Howard, 1987; Plesko, 1988), which suggests freedom from partisan influence that might pressure the agency into making overly optimistic (e.g., underestimated) outlay estimates. The CBO has a highly trained staff with a budget of over 200 million dollars. Its forecasting methods are highly sophisticated.

Yet, with all this going in its favor, the Congressional Budget Office's Current Services forecasts seriously deteriorate in the outyears, and only a portion of the errors may be attributed to changes in policy. Table 1 shows the budget document year, the subsequent fiscal year's percentage error in outlays, and the error 3 fiscal years hence, in terms of current services outlays.

As one can see with these figures, the annual forecasts for expenditures are generally quite accurate. But the 1980–1981 recession wreaked havoc on the 3-year forecasts made in the latter Seventies. Even the FY 85 forecast for FY 88, which was not a recession year, had a double-digit forecast error. Evidence from the fiscal year 1981 underforecast of 48 billion dollars suggests that only 19 billion or about 40% could be

Table 1 Congressional Budget Office Outlay Forecasts Percentage Errors, 1 and 3-Year

Budget document year	Subsequent year error	Triannual error
1977	1.15 (FY 78)	19.77 (FY 80)
1978	−5.41 (FY 79)	−23.54 (FY 81)
1979	−8.73 (FY 80)	−16.80 (FY 82)
1980	−10.51 (FY 81)	−11.31 (FY 83)
1981	−11.04 (FY 82)	−15.26 (FY 84)
1982	−0.50 (FY 83)	−5.43 (FY 85)
1983	4.34 (FY 84)	6.28 (FY 86)
1984	−1.83 (FY 85)	6.71 (FY 87)
1985	2.24 (FY 86)	15.52 (FY 88)

Source: Plesko (1988).

attributed to policy changes from the previous fiscal year. Twenty-nine billion dollars came from forecast errors, and the lion's share of that error (20 billion) was attributable to inaccuracies in economic forecasts. Only 9 billion dollars could be attributed to poor estimation of direct program costs (Penner, 1982).

While one may argue that state and local expenditures are not as sensitive to economic up- and downturns as their federal counterpart, it can also be argued that few if any state or local entities can bring to bear the expertise or staff size that the federal government can and does bring its budgetary forecasting. Moreover, both the Office of Management and Budget and the Congressional Budget Office generate such forecasts. This appears to serve as a builtin system of checks and balances to preclude biased forecasting on either organization's part (Howard, 1987). Thus, the poor performance of the federal government in this area is likely to be an example of what would be the case in most government entities.

The relatively poor performance of federal outyear expenditure forecasting reinforces two points made earlier. The first is that at 2-year horizons or longer, even the most sophisticated causal approaches deliver forecasts with double-digit errors. This suggests that judgmental or extrapolative techniques become viable alternatives at such horizons (Wheelright and Makridakis, 1980). This is not because of innately superior ability at these forecast horizons. They become viable options based on cost effectiveness. Spending large sums on the development of causal models makes little sense if simpler techniques will perform as well, if not better.

The second point worth reiterating is that the successful implementation of any forecast endeavor—long- or short-range—implies more than forecast accuracy. A forecast must meet the needs of its organization if it is to be utilized. In the case of long-range expenditure forecasting, utility is likely to depend on all stakeholders agreeing to a realistic set of policy and economic assumptions, particularly with regard to the future rate of inflation (Penner, 1982). Gaining consensus on such policies is not likely to be easy. But without it, the forecasts are likely to be ignored, regardless of their potential accuracy. This makes for wasted budget staff time. It also dooms efforts at more rational analysis of the future impact of current budgetary decisions before they start.

Capital Expenditures

Capital expenditures are those that exceed certain organizationally defined dollar amounts, and have a usable life beyond 1 fiscal year. Streets, roads, and schools are the quintessential state and local capital expenditures. At the federal level, the capital expenditures that first come to mind are probably weapons systems, if only because of their checkered history of being completed behind schedule and over budget.

While such expenditures are intended to span many fiscal years, their impact on the annual budget cannot be neglected. Construction and acquisition costs of such projects may entail the service of debt, which includes repayment of principle and payment of interest. Some facilities, such as bridges or parks, may generate income. Virtually all capital facilities require some kind of maintenance. Completion of new facilities such as schools or libraries may require enhanced staffing in order to be opened. In short, capital expenditures are likely to have profound impacts on the cash flows of most public entities.

At the federal level, capital and operating expenditures are integrated into one budget. At the state and local levels, that is generally not the case. This raises the possibility of poor integration between capital and operating expenditures, with very negative results. The so-called infrastructure crisis has in part been attributed to this separation (Pagano, 1984), since many jurisdictions fail to account for maintenance of newly completed facilities in their future operating expenses. Stories of newly opened libraries and hospitals with empty floors and wings as a result of underestimated operating costs are not uncommon (McKinney, 1986). These incidents leave the public with the distinct impressions that either facility management was incompetent, or that the facilities were not needed in the first place.

Many of the difficulties inherent with capital expenditure forecasting may be eased if it is remembered that such expenditures are made in furtherance of operating programs. This ultimately means that the undertaking of capital expenditures must be linked to long-term assessment of service demands and responsibilities. If such assessments are made, the chances are lessened either that unneeded facilities will be built, or that the increased operational burden of new facilities will be understated.

The estimation of future demand for facilities is likely to entail many of the techniques discussed earlier. It is also likely to include different techniques, such as cohort analysis, simulation, and benefit-cost analysis (Steiss, 1989). Any assessment of need for a decade or two in the future is bound to have error. But the use of multiple techniques and assumptions, sometimes referred to as triangulation (Webb et al., 1981), may shed considerable light on what a useful forecast range for future demand would be. If two or more forecasting approaches yield reasonably similar results, one can have greater faith in the outcome.

Capital budgeting will undoubtedly entail considerable judgment, in that the setting of service priorities is not easily quantifiable. The assumption that such priorities will remain unchanged in the future may, however, be inappropriate. Careful attention should be paid to giving competing assumptions fair hearing in all stages of capital planning.

Likely Differences in Local, State, and Federal Approaches

All states save Connecticut and Vermont, and virtually all local governments, are constitutionally bound to pass balanced budgets. On the other hand, the federal government is not subject to such a constraint. From this one might infer that forecasting behavior at the state and local government might be different in approach than that undertaken at the federal level. One might hypothesize that the absence of a constraint at the federal level would lead to less concern for budgetary forecast accuracy than at the subnational levels. While on face this seems logical, in reality this is probably not the case.

For one thing, it is probably no longer realistic to view federal spending as unconstrained. The passage of the Gramm-Rudman Amendment has had a dampening effect on expenditure growth (Manage and Marlow, 1986). Furthermore, citizens are showing increased concern with the possible negative impact of the ever-increasing national debt. They are also unwilling to elect presidential candidates who want to raise taxes to fight the deficit. Taken as a whole, it would appear that Keynesian talk of "pump priming" is quite dead, and that federal expenditures as a percentage of gross national product are likely to remain at their 1989 level (22.2%) for the next 5 years (Congressional Budget Office, 1989).

From another vantage, one must ask what the impact of a budget constraint is in practical terms. Passing a balanced budget does not mean that 1 year hence the budget will actually end up in balance. With that in mind, the appropriate question is, "Which levels of government can best tolerate out-of-balance budgets at year end?" The federal government can borrow, but that path may not be as politically palatable as it once was. State governments run, on average, with reserves of less than 1% of general fund expenditure, a level that John Carnavale (1988) describes as "insufficient to hedge anyone's bets against the down side of a recession" (p. 45). On the other hand, local governments have traditionally been surplus builders (Downs and Smith, 1985; Wildavsky, 1986). The author's recent study (Frank, 1988) in Florida lent credence to this claim. In a random sample of 99 communities, the average general fund balance was two-thirds of a year's general fund expenditures.

Wildavsky's (1986) explanation of this local behavior relates to cities as being low persons on the intergovernmental fiscal totem poll, caught between inelastic revenue sources on the one hand, and rapidly burgeoning demands for labor-intensive, costly services on the other. In this environment, overstating anticipated expenses and understating anticipated revenue—in effect, trying to build a surplus—becomes a budgetary defense mechanism.

What this suggests is that risk-averse local officials may be afraid of adopting new forecast technologies that have potential for increased accuracy, but deliver a random amount of bias on the up- and downside. Work by Lauth (1986) at the state level, and Howard (1987) at the federal, indicates diminished credibility in the budget process for actors who persistently bias their expenditure forecasts downward. There is no similar evidence from work at the local level, and if anything, work by Bretschneider and Schroeder (1988) tends to reinforce Wildavsky's view of local budgeters as risk-averse surplus builders.

Local governments have experimented with new budget formats, performance measures, and computer enhancements in recent years (O'Toole and Marshall, 1987; Norris, 1988), but they have not seen fit to experiment with new forecasting techniques. In part this may be attributed to limited data and technical expertise. But in part it may reflect limited incentive to try methods that deliver a random amount of bias in their forecasts. As such, the author will speculate that local governments may not prove to be particularly fertile testing grounds for application of quantitative methods to expenditure forecasting.

EXPENDITURE FORECASTING: SOME EXAMPLES

This section describes examples of econometric, causal, and judgmental approaches used at the county, state, and federal levels, respectively. These examples are detailed in order to give the reader a feel for the subject matter detailed earlier in the chapter.

The Broward County Econometric Model

Broward County (Greater Fort Lauderdale), Fla., is a rapidly growing area comprised of 28 communities having a combined population of some 1.2 million. In 1983, officials of the county's Office of Planning and Office of Budget and Management Policy agreed to a joint effort in constructing this model. It was believed that the model would facilitate long-range planning of expenditures and capital outlays by providing forecasts on personal income and government revenue. It was also intended to provide fiscal impact assessment of changes in zoning and intergovernmental revenue.

The model consisted of a system of 81 simultaneous equations for 15 industrial sectors. Six equations in the model estimated personal income. The model was based on earlier work done by Glickman (1971, 1977) on regional econometric models developed for the Philadelphia Standard Metropolitan Statistical Area. The model's variable definitions are given in Table 2.

The econometric model used the exogenous variables to drive the endogenous information garnered on employment. Employment data in turn drove the wage rate variables. The final results of the econometric model were predicted values for personal income and governmental revenue.

The Broward County Econometric Model (BCEM) was completed (after 5 man-years of labor) and validated by 1984, with mixed results. The R-squared for all but four of the 77 endogenous variables was above 0.90. Yet when the model was used to predict values for years held out of the sample from which the model was built, mean absolute percentage error (MAPE) was unacceptably high. For 13 of the 77 endogenous variables, MAPE exceeded the 15.0% benchmark for accuracy that has been established for regional models. The model also suffered from serious problems with multicollinearity.

These problems, however, were not the reasons behind the model's fall into disuse. The demise of the BCEM was largely due to the failure to account for stakeholder needs at the time of its development. Decision makers in Broward wanted a predictive model for budgetary purposes. The model constructed treated Broward as an entire region, rather than 28 municipalities plus an unincorporated area for which the county had administrative responsibility. As such, its predicted values were of limited use to decision makers throughout the county, regardless of the model's accuracy or lack thereof. Those who built the model were out of touch with decision-maker needs, and decision makers had insufficient technical expertise to guide the forecasting staff toward the building of a model with greater utility.

State Approaches

There has been surprisingly little research done on forecasting of expenditures at the state level (Bahl et al., Liro, 1977; Bretschneider and Gorr, 1987). What little that has been done suggests that forecasting at this level is quite primitive, and seldom utilizes causal approaches. Judgmental and naive approaches are the standard techniques utilized. If and when quantitative approaches are used, regressing costs over time is the predominant technique.

Another shortfall with expenditure forecasting at this level is that it generally focuses on aggregated expenditures. This ignores a very useful "handle" for projecting costs. Nationwide, approximately 60% of the dollar cost of services rendered by state government can be linked to an identifiable client. Such services include education at all levels, public assistance, and prison and parole activities. Forecasting caseloads as

Table 2 Broward County Econometric Model Variables

Variable name	Variable definition
	Exogenous variables
AGE	Agricultural employment
AGW	Agricultural wages
ATE	Total number of employed
CONE	Construction employment
CONW	Construction wages
CONWR	Construction wage rate
EDE	Education employment
EDW	Education wages
ELE	Electrical employment
ELW	Electrical wages
ELWR	Electrical wage rate
FICA	Social insurance payments
FINE	Fines and forteitures
FIREE	Finance and real estate employment
FIREW	Finance and real estate wages
FIRWR	Finance and real estate wage rate
FPRIEW	Arming proprietor's income
GOVF	Federal intergovernmental revenue
GOVL	Local intergovernmental revenue
GOVT	Total intergovernmental revenue
HUMS	Human service revenue
INTR	Interest earning revenue
LIPERM	Licenses and permits
LOCE	Local governmental employment
MACHE	Machine employment
MACHW	Machine wages
MACHWR	Machine wage rates
MANUE	Manufacturing employment
MANUW	Manufacturing wages
MANUWR	Manufacturing wage rate
MEDE	Medical employment
MEDW	Medical wages
METER	Electrical water starts
MINE	Mining employment
MINW	Mining wages
MINWR	Mining wage rate
MREVO	Miscellaneous revenue other
MREVT	Miscellaneous revenue total
MFPRIEY	Nonfarming proprietor's income
NUMUN	Number of unemployed
OTHY	Other income
OUTLAY	Federal aid to local government
PHYS	Physical services revenue
PROPY	Property income
PYE	Personal income broward
REDW	Education wage gains since 1967
RELWR	Electrical wage rate
RETE	Retail employment

Table 2   Broward County Econometric Model Variables (continued)

Variable name	Variable definition
RETW	Retail wages
RETWR	Retail wage rate
RLOCW	Local government wages
RMANUWR	Manufacturing wage rate
RMEDW	Medical wages
RMCHWR	Machine wage rate
RNFPRIEY	Nonfarming proprietor's income
RPYB	Personal income
SALES	Taxable retail sales
SERE	Service employment
SERVO	Other services revenue
SERVT	Service revenue total
SERVW	Service wages
SERWR	Service wage rate
TAXO	Other tax revenues
TAXP	Property tax revenues
TAXT	Total tax revenues
TCUE	Transit, communications, utility employment
TCUW	Transit, communications, utility wages
TCUWR	Transit, communications, utility wage rate
TLF	Total labor force
TOT	Total revenues
TWB	Total wage bill
UNRATE	Local unemployment rate
WHOLE	Wholesale employment
SHOLWR	Wholesale wage rate
CPI	Consumer price index
GNP	Gross national product
POPR	Population—Broward
PRIME	Prime interest rate
PYUS	Personal income—United States
RGNP	Gross national product deflator
RPYUS	Personal income deflator
RUSMWR	U.S. minimum wage rate
USUN	U.S. unemployment rate

Source: Broward County Office

opposed to aggregated expenditures would allow decision makers to discern the differences in costs associated with policy and socioeconomic changes. Central budget agencies could mandate a common set of economic, social, and demographic assumptions upon which all agencies could forecast. This would deter program managers from overestimating current and future workloads in order to maximize budgets. And lastly, using this approach would force managers to look at unit costs in order to arrive at budgetary forecasts. This might in turn facilitate reviews that suggest how unit costs might be lowered or held constant.

In 1981, Thomas McCaleb and Charles Rockwood studied forecasting in 18 Florida agencies whose budgets accounted for 85% of total state general revenue expenditures.

The results of the survey, detailed in Table 3, were in the authors' words "surprising and disappointing" (McCaleb and Rockwood, 1986, p. 235).

McCaleb and Rockwood noted that budget size and institutional factors such as decentralized or nondecentralized administration had little to do with the type of forecasting employed. Economic Services, for example, which used judgmental forecasting, administered big-budget items such as AFDC (Aid to Families with Dependent Children) and Food Stamps. The authors also noted that personnel in the agencies often claimed that socioeconomic variables did not correlate well with their caseloads, that they often had little data with which to build more sophisticated models, or that appropriations had little to do with caseloads. From the authors' vantage, these factors were a convenient "rationale" (McCaleb and Rockwood, 1986, p. 235) rather than true impediments.

The extrapolative techniques used were remarkably simple. More often than not, time series were very short. With the exception of the community colleges, no effort was made to weight more recent data more heavily than earlier data. Seasonal factors were applied in few cases. The business cycle, which has been shown to significantly alter college and university enrollments, criminal activity, and community service demands, was ignored by all agencies.

Legislation passed in 1981 required formal estimating conferences for criminal justice, most phases of education (K–12 and community college enrollments), major programs in health and rehabilitative services (AFDC and Medicaid), transportation, and capital outlays. Staff of the affected agencies, the governor's office, and the legislature must agree on caseload and expenditure forecasts, which must be consistent with the statewide demographic and revenue consensus estimating process.

This legislation has served as a catalyst for change in the criminal justice and community college systems caseload and budgetary forecasting. Both of these agencies

Table 3 Florida Agency Forecast Methodologies

Forecast method	Agency	Program
No regular forecast	Criminal Justice	Courts
		State's attorneys
		Public Defenders
	Education	State university system
	Health	Aging and adult services
		Children, youth & families
		Public health
		Vocational rehabilitation
Judgment	Health	Economic services
Extrapolation	Criminal Justice	Probation
	Education	Community colleges
	Health	Medicaid
		Mental health
		Development services
Socioeconomic models	Criminal Justice	Prisons
		Parole
	Education	Public Schools
	Health	Children's medical services

Source: McCaleb and Rockwood (1986).

adopted cohort models for their workload forecasting. In the criminal justice budget, a regression model was used to estimate the "population at risk" (males between the ages of 18 and 29). Probability functions were then developed for the 14 length-of-service offense classes, which in turn were used to simulate actual release rates. This model has been modified in recent years to account for the elimination of parole and institution of flat-time sentencing. The community college system adopted a similar approach, using county-level graduation rates as the pool to which historical enrollment rates were applied. Evidence from McCaleb and Rockwood's follow-up study of 1986 suggests that caseload forecasting errors in these entities improved substantially as a result of the methodological changes. Criminal justice forecasting error went from an average of 10.0% to the 3.5% vicinity. Community college forecasting error stayed in the 5.0–6.0% vicinity, but the post-1981 environment was one of sharply dwindling enrollments, suggesting a more difficult forecasting task at hand.

The techniques adopted here were not particularly advanced, but they were effective. Their implementation shows that when there is a desire to move away from the judgmental/deterministic status quo that predominates in expenditure forecasting, previously perceived impediments such as data insufficiency can be overcome, often without much effort.

A Federal Example

No book chapter, much less a section thereof, could do justice to the complexity of federal budgeting and estimating. What seemed useful here was to detail the federal approach to a problem with which all levels of government must contend—the treatment of inflation. Specifically, we will look at a discussion of inflationary impact at the Department of Defense that was undertaken by the Congressional Budget Office (1986) on the problems inherent with defense inflation. As noted earlier, inflationary impact is likely to be higher on government expenditures than for expenditures at large. Moreover, the impact on inflation for defense expenditures, as for other governmental expenditures, is highly differentiated by object of expenditure.

The Department of Defense (DoD) has traditionally had problems with estimating the rate of inflation for its budget. Prior to 1982, Defense generally understated inflationary impact. In subsequent years, it has tended to overestimate inflation, and has reaped an "inflation dividend" in its budget. In addition to having problems with estimating inflationary impact. Defense has had difficulty in deciding how to budget for inflationary impact. For example, prior to 1970, DoD estimated costs in current dollars. When costs ran over budgeted amounts, supplemental appropriations were used to cover shortfalls. This was a messy procedure, which generally meant revisiting hard-fought policy decisions. Of late, DoD has attempted to differentiate between inflation funds and real (inflation-adjusted) costs, but accounting is not sophisticated enough to allow for this. Thus, while the department recognizes that it has been overappropriated for funding in recent fiscal years, it does not know if this money is still in the budget, or has been eliminated through reappropriations, transfers, and lapses.

Starting with basics, we do know that from 1972 to 1985, the Department of Defense's expenditures, as measured by the Bureau of Economic Analysis (BEA), have grown at a compound rate of 7.9% annually, whereas the gross national product (GNP) price index compounded at 6.4%. In part the higher rate for inflation could be attributed to increases in oil costs. But the major culprit behind the department's above-average inflation rate was major weapons systems, which are just over a quarter of the DoD's budget. These items inflated at 8.5% annually. In fact, beginning in 1983, the Office of Management and Budget allowed Defense to project major systems procurement costs to exceed the GNP deflator by a very significant 30%. As seen in Table 4, this pattern has been borne out historically, though in recent years, inflation for these expenditures has slown considerably.

This differential applies to most goods and services that the Pentagon acquires, but not to the same degree that impacts weapons systems. When fuel and compensation are taken out of consideration, DoD expenditures such as transportation, support, ammunition, and research and development inflated at 6.8% annually, just over the 6.4% figure for GNP.

In essence, this inflation differential suggests that the Pentagon faces many of the same problems that state and local governments face when they engage in the construction of capital projects such as schools and roads. Just as there may be few general contractors large enough to compete on bids for such projects in a given community or state, the Pentagon must often choose between a handful of contractors. Moreover, just as communities and states must often stay within their borders for contracts, the Pentagon is generally restricted to buy American, restricting its ability to seek out the lowest prices for parts and materials. And lastly, the Pentagon, like state and local agencies, must often purchase based on performance rather than price, which is bound to increase the costs of its weapons systems.

Defense planners tended to believe, as did most budgeters at the federal level, that the high inflation rates of the late 1970s and early 1980s would persist. They did not. In fact, defense expenditures for all categories in 1984 and 1985 were actually below the national inflation rate, with capital expenditures on weapons systems leading the fall. Of the nearly 1 trillion dollars spent on defense from 1983 to 1985, 30.2 billion was overbudgeted for inflation—the so-called "inflation dividend." The two major explanations for this were the possibility that DoD's indices for estimating inflation needed recalculation, and that the Reagan military buildup led to enhanced production, and hence greater supply and lower cost.

Putting aside the possible causes of this drop, the notion of attaching differentials to various components of the defense budget was viewed as dangerous in the sense that higher inflation factors could be self-fulfilling. In 1981, David Stockmann criticized the 30% differential for capital goods on these grounds. He also felt that allowing Defense to establish its own inflation factors instead of following OMB mandates in this area might

Table 4 Inflation Rates for Major DoD Systems Compared with GNP Inflation Rates

	1979	1980	1981	1982	1983	1984	1985	Average 1979–1985
Major systems	12.2	10.9	12.6	11.1	6.7	4.2	2.1	8.5
GNP	8.4	9.3	9.3	6.3	4.1	4.2	3.5	6.4
Major systems/ GNP	1.46	1.18	1.36	1.77	1.64	1.00	0.60	1.32

Source: Congressional Budget Office (1986, p. 31).

set a significant precedent that other agencies could adopt using similar rationale. The Congressional Budget Office has also stated this disagreement.

The absence of an agreed upon policy for treatment of inflation leaves DoD in a bind. If inflation picks up in the 1990s, capital expenditures may again inflate at a premium. This would leave Defense procurement for weapons systems subject to constant reprogramming in the face of budget cuts due to inflation, an action that reduces preparedness. It might also result in Congress violating a policy it set for itself in the 1950s but violated in the late 1970s and early 1980s—appropriating what it thought was "full funding" for weapons systems, and then finding that it had appropriated only half of what was needed for completion.

The Congressional Budget Office's 1986 recommendations for addressing this problem are exemplary for all levels of government. First, they suggested that DoD disaggregate its expenditures for the purposes of inflation index construction. Currently, Defense constructs an index for capital expenditures and another for all other areas such as operation and management, military construction, and minor procurement. The CBO recommended that Defense construct 10 indices for forecasting its inflation. The second, mentioned earlier, is that separate accounts be established for the nominal expenditures and inflation components for goods and service to be purchased. This would allow for the reallocation of funds from areas that were experiencing low inflation to those with higher rates. Unfortunately, Defense does not have the accounting structure to accommodate such an effort.

The critical nature of the inflation assumption for accurate long-term budgeting applies to all levels of government. The very real possibility that inflation assumptions may become self-fulfilling also holds for all governments. Nonetheless, inflation is a harsh reality that must be dealt with. Its over- or underestimation may have serious consequences. Disaggregation of expenditures and experimentation with various types of indices may be the best way of coming to grips estimating its impact.

CONCLUSION: THE NEED FOR EMPIRICAL COMPARISON

Limited Innovation

We know that when officials at all levels of government forecast expenditures, they generally utilize simpler naive and accounting based approaches. What we do not know is why that is the case? We could hypothesize three possible causes for the limited utilization of more advanced techniques along the forecast continuum:

1.   Simple techniques may forecast more accurately.
2.   Lack of forecasting training.
3.   Risk aversion.

Simple Techniques May Forecast More Accurately

Jerome McKinney (1986) contends, in his work on budgeting in public and nonprofit organizations, that "The sophisticated quantitative methods that have been devised to project expenditures have not been, to date, notably more successful than the manual, incremental, and piecemeal approaches which are still in wide use" (p. 168). McKinney believes that political factors are more easily taken into account with simpler techniques than with more complex, automated ones.

An offshoot of this is that from a management science perspective, the adoption of more advanced techniques may not yield accuracy that which make adoption worthwhile in terms of investment in learning new forecasting skills or purchasing computer enhancements. Here again is an empirical question that cries out for research. As noted earlier, cost-loss functions have been developed that address this question.

The nature of governmental expenditures may have something to do with the continued reliance on simpler techniques. Salaries are likely to make up the lion's share of most agency budgets. As noted earlier, deterministic techniques for salary forecasting that account for the number of incumbents in a particular job class, and multiply this by current salary plus an anticipated increment, will outperform most of the stochastic models discussed in this chapter (Scott, 1972). This suggests that the greatest forecast utility for the more complex models may lie in estimating nonpersonnel expenditures or inflation factors.

Lack of Forecasting Training

Forecasting is a neglected subject area in the public administration curriculum (Grizzle, 1985; National Task Force on Curriculum Reform, 1985). Finance officials with public administration backgrounds may not have knowledge of more advanced forecasting techniques. As noted earlier, those who are unfamiliar with a forecasting technique's assumptions and operations are unlikely to adopt it, regardless of its potential accuracy. Thus, lack of training in the forecasting area may preclude experimentation with methods that could enhance forecast accuracy.

Risk Aversion

As noted above, risk aversion may lead finance officials to prefer estimating approaches that deliver forecasts in line with up- or downside bias in order to "pad" budgets. Risk aversion may have another impact on the use of new forecasting technologies. Diffusion of new technology tends to be slower in the public sector than in the private sector (Feller and Johnston, 1984). In part, this is attributable to the self-selection of risk-averse individuals into public sector employment (Ukeles, 1982). Risk aversion and innovation do not mix (Kamm, 1987). It may very well be that forecasting techniques that have been used successfully in the private sector for decades have not been utilized in government because finance officials have been afraid to try them.

Concluding Thoughts

In the final analysis, no single forecasting method, be it naive, extrapolative, or causal, is likely to predict well for all expense items. Trying to find a bundle of techniques that delivers the highest degree of accuracy will require trial and error on the part of forecast experts who are trying to inform practice, and practitioners who are hoping to improve their accuracy. If this coalition is to succeed, however, forecasting experts may have to accept that in many instances, "simple may be better," not only in terms of accuracy, but also in terms of organizational relevance. Similarly, public finance officials may need to acquire a more advanced forecasting repertoire—and overcome their risk aversion to experiment with it!

It is the author's belief that today's fiscal realities are going to force experimentation in the expenditure forecasting area. Hopefully, forecast experts and practitioners can join forces in the search for enhanced accuracy, which has suffered from a serious lack of empirical investigation in the public sector for decades. The technical expertise of the experts, coupled with the strong concern for implementation of practitioners, could lead to the adoption of forecast methods that enhance accuracy, without overwhelming finance officials or those who rely on their work.

REFERENCES

Agresti, A., Finlay, B. (1986). *Statistical Methods for the Social Sciences,* 2nd ed. Dellen, San Francisco.

Armstrong, J. S. (1984). Forecasting by extrapolation: Conclusions from 25 years of research. *Interfaces* 6:52–66.

Armstrong, J. S. (1985). *Long Range Forecasting: From Crystal Ball to Computer,* 2nd ed. Wiley, New York.

Ascher, W. (1978). *Forecasting: An Appraisal for Policy-Makers and Planners.* Johns Hopkins, Baltimore.

Bahl, R. W. (1980). Revenue and expenditure forecasting by state and local governments. In *State and Local Government Finance and Financial Management,* J. E. Petersen, C. Spain, and M. Laffey (eds.), Government Finance Research Center, Washington, D.C., pp. 120–126.

Bahl, R., Cupoli, E. M., and Liro, J. (1977). Forecasting the local government budget. National Tax Association-Tax Institute of America. *Proceedings of the Seventeenth Annual Conference on Taxation.*

Bails, D. G., and Peppers, L. C. (1982). *Business Fluctuations: Forecasting Techniques and Applications.* Prentice-Hall, Englewood Cliffs, N.J.

Beaumont, C. D. (1986). Forecasting with micros: A cautionary tale. *Futures* 18:84–90.

Berne, R., and Schramm, R. (1986). *The Financial Analysis of Governments.* Prentice-Hall, Englewood Cliffs, N.J.

Boswell, C. R., and Carpenter, J. M. (1986). Long-range forecasting in Fort Worth. *Government Finance Review* 6:7–10.

Box, G., and Jenkins, G. (1976). *Time Series Analysis: Forecasting and Control,* 2nd ed. Holden Day, San Francisco.

Brandt, J. A., and Bessler, D. A. (1983). Price forecasting and evaluation: An application in agriculture. *Journal of Forecasting* 2:237–248.

Bretschneider, S., and Gorr, W. L. (1987). State and local government revenue forecasting. In *The Handbook of Forecasting: A Manager's Guide,* 2nd ed., S. Makridakis and S. Wheelright (eds.), Wiley, New York, pp. 118–134.

Bretschneider, S. and Schroeder, L. (1988). Evaluation of commercial economic forecasts for use in local government budgeting. *International Journal of Forecasting* 4:33–44.

Broward County Office of Planning. (1984). *Technical Documentation for the Broward County Econometric Model.* Fort Lauderdale, Florida.

Brown, R. G. (1963). *Smoothing, Forecasting, and Prediction of Discrete Time Series.* Prentice-Hall, Englewood Cliffs, N.J.

Carnavale, J. T. (1988). Recent trends in the finances of the state and local sector. *Public Budgeting and Finance* 8:33–48.

Chambers, J. C., Mullick, S. K., and Smith, D. D. (1971). How to choose the right forecasting techniques. *Harvard Business Review* 49:45–75.

Chang, S. (1979). An econometric forecasting model based on regional economic information system data: The case of Mobile, Alabama *Journal of Regional Science* 9:437–448.

Choate, G. M., and Thompson, F. (1988). Budget makers as agents: A preliminary investigation of discretionary behavior under state-contingent rewards. *Public Choice* 58:3–20.

Commonwealth of Massachusetts, Department of Revenue. (1987). *Forecasting FY 88–90 Revenue and Expenditures.* Boston.

Congressional Budget Office. (1986). *Budgeting for Defense Inflation.* Washington, D.C.

Congressional Budget Office. (1989). *The Economic and Budget Outlook: Fiscal Years 1990–1994.* Washington, D.C.

Doktor, R., Schultz, R. L., and Slevin, D. (eds.). (1979). *The Implementation of Management Science.* North-Holland, New York.

Downs, G. W., and Rocke, D. M. (1983). Municipal budget forecasting with multivariate ARMA models. *Journal of Forecasting* 2:377–388.

Downs, G. W., and Smith, R. A. (1985). Bias in the Formulation of Local Government Budget Problems. Paper delivered at the Annual Meeting of the American Political Science Association, New Orleans, 29 August–1 September.

Duobinis, S. F. (1981). An econometric model of the Chicago standard metropolitan area. *Journal of Regional Science* 21:293–320.

Feller, I., and Johnston, I. (1984). The innovation-productivity connection. In *Productivity and Public Policy,* M. Holzer and S. Nagel (eds.), Sage Publications, Beverly Hills, Calif., pp. 171–189.

Frank, H. A. (1988). *Model Utility Along the Forecast Continuum: A Case Study in Florida Local Government Revenue Forecasting.* Published doctoral dissertation. Florida State University, Tallahassee.

Gardner, E. S. (1985). Exponential smoothing: The state of the art. *Journal of Forecasting* 4:1–28.

Glickman, N. J. (1971). An econometric model of the Philadelphia region. *Journal of Regional Science* 10:15–32.

Glickman, N. J. (1977). Econometric model building at the regional level. *Regional Science of Urban Economics* 7:1–23.

Golder, E. R., and Settle, J. G. (1976). Monitoring schemes in short-term forecasting. *Operational Research Quarterly* 27:857–867.

Grizzle, G. (1985). Essential skills for financial management: Are MPA students acquiring the necessary competencies? *Public Administration Review* 45:840–844.

Guerts, M. D., and Kelly, J. P. (1986). Forecasting retail sales using alternative models. *International Journal of Forecasting* 2:261–272.

Gujarati, D. (1978). *Basic Econometrics.* McGraw-Hill, New York.

Gupta, S., and Wilton, P. C. (1987). Combination of forecasts: An extension. *Management Science* 33:356–372.

Hanushek, E., and Jackson, J. (1977). *Statistical Methods for Social Scientists.* Academic Press, New York.

Hibon, M. (1984). Naive, moving average, exponential smoothing and regression methods. In *The Forecasting Accuracy of Major Time Series Methods,* S. Makridakis, A. Andersen, R. Carbone, R. Fildes, M. Hibon, R. Lewandowski, J. Newton, E. Parzen, and R. Winkler (eds.), Wiley, Chichester, England, pp. 239–244.

Hoff, J. C. (1983). *A Practical Guide to Box-Jenkins Forecasting.* Lifetime Learning Publications, Belmont, Calif.

Holt, C. C., Mogdligiani, F., Muth, J. F., and Simon, H. A. (1960). *Planning, Production, Inventories, and Work Force.* Prentice-Hall, Englewood Cliffs, N.J.

Howard, J. (1987). Government economic projections: A comparison between CBO and OMB forecasts. *Public Budgeting and Finance* 4:14–25.

Kamm, J. B. (1987). *An Integrative Approach to Managing Innovation.* Lexington Books, Lexington, Mass.

Klay, W. E. (1983). Revenue forecasting: An administrative perspective. In *Handbook on Public Budgeting and Financial Management,* J. Rabin and T. Lynch (eds.), Marcel Dekker, New York, pp. 287–316.

Klay, W. E. (1985). The organizational dimension of budgetary forecasting: Suggestions from revenue forecasting in the states. *International Journal of Public Administration* 7:241–265.

Klein, L. R. (1984). The importance of the forecast. *Journal of Forecasting* 3:1–9.

Lane, J. E., and Westlund, A. (1987). Choice and constraint in budget-making. *Theory and Decision* 23:217–230.

Lauth, T. P. (1986). Mid-Year Appropriations in Georgia: Allocating the Surplus. Paper presented at the Southeast Conference on Public Administration, Pensacola, Fla., October 9–October 11.

Lawrence, M. J. (1983). An exploration of some practical issues in the use of quantitative forecasting models. *Journal of Forecasting* 2:169–181.

Lewandowski, R. (1984). Lewandowski's FORSYS Method. In *The Forecasting Accuracy of Major Time Series Methods,* S. Makridakis, A. Andersen, R. Fildes, M. Hibon, R. Lewandowski, J. Newton, E. Parzen, and R. Winkler (eds.), Wiley, Chichester, England, pp. 245–254.

Lusk, E. J. and Neves, J. S. (1984). A comparative ARIMA analysis of the III series of the Makridakis competition. *Journal of Forecasting* 3:329–332.

Mahajan, V., and Peterson, R. A. (1985). *Models for Innovation.* Sage Publications, Beverly Hills, Calif.

Mahmoud, E. (1984). Accuracy in forecasting: A survey. *Journal of Forecasting* 3:139–159.

Mahmoud, E., Goyal, S., and Shalchi, H. (1986). Loss-Cost Functions for Measuring the Accuracy of Sales Forecasting Methods. (Working Paper). University of Michigan, Flint.

Makridakis, S. (1984). The art and science of forecasting: An assessment and future direction. *Journal of Forecasting* 2:15–40.

Makridakis, S., and Hibon, M. (1984). Accuracy of forecasting: An empirical investigation. In *The Forecasting Accuracy of Major Time Series Methods,* S. Makridakis, A. Andersen, R. Fildes, M. Hibon, R. Lewandowski, J. Newton, E. Parzen, and R. Winkler (eds.), Wiley, Chichester, England, pp. 35–103.

Makridakis, S., and Wheelright, S. (1977). Adaptive filtering: an integrated autoregressive/moving average approach. *Operations Research Quarterly* 28: 425–437.

Marlow, M. L., and Manage, N. (1987). Expenditures and receipts: Testing for causality in state and local government finances. *Public Choice* 53:243–255.

McCaleb, T. S., and Rockwood, C. E. (1986). Forecasting caseloads for client-specific services in state government. *National Tax Journal* 39:234–241.

McCleary, R., and Hay, R. (1984). *Applied Time Series Analysis for the Social Sciences.* Sage Publications, Beverly Hills, Calif.

McKinney, J. B. (1986). *Effective Financial Management in Public and Nonprofit Agencies.* Quorum Books, New York.

Mehay, S., and Gonzalez, R. A. (1987). Outside information and the monopoly power of a public bureau: An empirical analysis. *Public Finance Quarterly* 15:61–75.

Mentzer, J. T., and Cox, J. E. (1984). Familiarity, application, and performance of sales forecasting techniques. *Journal of Forecasting* 3:27–36.

Mikesell, J. L. (1986). *Fiscal Administration: Analysis and Applications for the Public Sector,* 2nd ed. Dorsey Press, Chicago.

Montgomery, D., and Peck, E. (1982). *Introduction to Linear Regression Analysis.* Wiley, New York.

National Task Force on Curriculum Reform. (1985). Graduate curricula in budgeting and financial management: Recommendations for reform. *Public Budgeting and Finance* 5:3–22.

Nelson, C. R. (1972). The prediction performance of the FRB-MIT-PENN model of the U.S. economy. *American Economic Review* 62:902–917.

Norris, D. F. (1988). Microcomputers in financial management. *Public Budgeting and Finance.* 8:69–82.

O'Toole, D. E., and Marshall, J. (1987). Budgeting practices in local government: The state of the art. *Government Finance Review* 3:11–16.

Pagano, M. A. (1984). Notes on capital budgeting. *Public Budgeting and Finance* 4:31–40.

Pankratz, A. (1983). *Forecasting with Univariate Box-Jenkins Models: Concepts and Cases.* Wiley, New York.

Penner, R. G. (1982). Forecasting budget totals: Why can't we get it right? In *The Federal Budget: Economics and Politics,* A. Wildavsky, and M. Boskin (eds.), Institute for Contemporary Studies, San Francisco, pp. 89–110.

Plesko, G. A. (1988). The accuracy of government forecasts and budget projections. *National Tax Journal* 41:453–466.

Premchand, A. (1983). *Government Budgeting and Expenditure Controls: Theory and Practice.* International Monetary Fund, Washington, D.C.

Rubin, I. (1988). Introduction. In *New Directions in Budget Theory,* I. Rubin (ed.), State University of New York, Albany, pp. 3–14.

Schnaars, S. P. (1986). A comparison of extrapolation models on yearly sales forecasts. *International Journal of Forecasting* 2:71–95.

Schroeder, L. D., Sjoquist, D. L., and Stephan, P. E. (1986). *Understanding Regression Analysis: An Introductory Guide.* Sage Publications, Beverly Hills, Calif.

Schultz, R. L. (1984). The implementation of forecasting models. *Journal of Forecasting* 3:43–55.

Schultz, R. L. and Slevin, D. (1983). The implementation exchange: Science and affairs. *Interfaces* 13:36–38.

Scott, C. D. (1972). *Forecasting Local Government Spending.* The Urban Institute, Washington, D.C.

Steiss, A. W. (1989). *Financial Management in Public Organizations.* Brooks/Cole, Pacific Grove, Calif.

Stockman, D. (1987). *The Triumph of Politics: The Inside Story of the Reagan Revolution.* Avon Books, New York.

Toulmin, L. M., and Wright, G. E. (1983). Expenditure Forecasting. In *Handbook on Public Budgeting and Financial Management,* J. Rabin and T. Lynch (eds.), Marcel Dekker, New York, pp. 209–284.

Ukeles, J. (1982). *Doing More with Less: Turning Public Management Around,* AMACOM, New York.

Vandaele, W. (1983). *Applied Time Series and Box Jenkins Models.* Academic Press, New York.

Wagner, R. E. (1983). *Public Finance: Revenue and Expenditures in a Democratic Society.* Little, Brown, Boston.

Walzer, N., and Stratton, P. (1977). *Inflation and Municipal Expenditure Increases in Illinois.* Illinois Cities and Villages Municipal Problems Commission, Springfield.

Webb, E. J., Campbell, D. T., Schwartz, R. D., Sechrest, L., and Grove, J. B. (1981). *Nonreactive Measures in the Social Sciences,* 2nd ed. Houghton-Mifflin, Boston.

Wheelright, S. C., and Makridakis, S. (1980). *Forecasting Methods for Management,* 3rd ed. Wiley, New York.

White, M. J., Clayton, R., Myrtle, R., Siegel, G., and Rose, A. (eds.) (1980). *Managing Public Systems: Analytic Techniques for Public Administration.* Duxbury Press, North Scituate, Mass.

Wildavsky, A. (1986). *Budgeting: A Comparative Theory of Budgetary Processes,* 2nd ed. Transaction Books, New Brunswick, N.J.

Wildavsky, A. (1989). The political economy of efficiency has not changed but the world has and so have I. *Public Budgeting and Financial Management* 1:43–53.

Willis, R. E. (1987). *A Guide to Forecasting for Planners and Managers.* Prentice-Hall, Englewood Cliffs, N.J.

9

Revenue Forecasting: A Learning Perspective

William Earle Klay *School of Public Administration and Policy, Florida State University, Tallahassee, Florida*

Revenue forecasting sets the stage for budget deliberations. If a forecast offers the prospect for plentiful revenues, the ensuing debates and decisions are likely to be very different from those that are conducted under the expectation of revenue shortfalls. A forecast that anticipates ample revenues is music to the ears of those who wish to expand programs or cut tax rates. Conversely, a forecast of hard times to come may doom such plans, and be accompanied by intense battles over relatively small amounts of revenue. In short, it is revenue forecasting that establishes many of the basic parameters of expenditure deliberations and budget execution.

The life of the revenue forecaster is one of uncertainty, for a forecast is an effort to look at the future. Errors in the form of both under- and overestimations may have personal consequences. One forecaster, for example, resigned shortly after his projection of $7 million from a state's first sales tax ballooned into actual receipts of $22 million. When a sudden revenue shortfall became apparent in a state that had a better forecasting record than most, a senior legislator was heard to wonder whether the time had arrived to fire the forecasters and find some "better" ones. No jobs were lost in that instance, but it serves to illustrate that revenue forecasting is a complex process that can become politicized.

During this century, governments have become dependent upon income and sales taxes, as well as intergovernmental transfer payments, that are sensitive to economic fluctuations. The sensitivity of modern revenue structures to fluctuations in the economy has prompted a continuing effort to improve the quality, and particularly the accuracy, of revenue forecasts. Growth in the magnitude of government budgets has also heightened concern for accuracy. A 1% error in a projection of $50 million is $500,000, but a 1% error in a $5 billion projection is $50 million. If unexpected shortfalls occur, the continuity of government may be disrupted, while unanticipated surpluses may prompt taxpayer frustration.

Political and economic events have placed revenue forecasting on center stage in the deliberations of the federal government. Each assertion that cuts in tax rates will result in equal or greater revenues is a form of revenue forecast. Moreover, the deficit has made lawmakers more concerned than ever before about the revenue effects of changes in tax legislation (Vehoorn et al., 1988). Each proposed provision of the Tax Reform Act of 1986 had to be considered in the context of the revenue that it would produce or lose. In effect, a revenue forecast had to be done for each provision. Federal forecasters have had to develop new methodologies for "microforecasting," the projection of revenue impacts from specific changes in policy. These methodologies are often quite different from those for "macroforecasting," the projection of overall revenue receipts.

The world of the revenue forecaster, then, is one marked by uncertainty and a continuing demand for greater accuracy. The economy from which revenues are derived is complex and changes in ways that are difficult to fathom, yet the forecaster is expected to rise to the occasion through the application of increasingly sophisticated forecasting techniques, computer technology, and databases. Most of the literature about revenue forecasting is written by and for economists. Revenue forecasting, however, is not solely a matter for econometricians. Revenue forecasting is also a problem of administration in that it involves the design of organizational structures and processes that must cope with political pressures, with legislative-executive and interagency relationships, with specialist-generalist and person-machine "interfaces," and so on.

This chapter is written from the perspective of organizing to think about the future, for that is what revenue forecasters must do. Attention is first given to the nature and evolution of revenue forecasting. Particular attention is given to the methods of revenue forecasting, for these must be understood by those who wish to devise structures and processes in which to apply them. The presentation is primarily verbal to enable generalist administrators who lack a knowledge of econometrics to better understand the methodologies of revenue forecasting.

In most governments, revenue forecasting is the most highly developed form of forecasting activity. As such, revenue forecasting assumes an importance beyond that of establishing spending parameters. It is a source of information that can help to inform lawmakers about the nature of the jurisdiction which they serve. When lawmakers question forecasters about the nature of their economy and about possible trends therein, they are engaged in a process of learning. When the forecasters themselves critique the accuracy of their forecasts and the adequacy of their assumptions and models, they, too, are engaged in learning.

Such learning may lead to more enlightened policy. Knowledgeable policymakers should be able to fashion better tax policy, economic development policy, and so on. Some structures and processes of revenue forecasting are more conducive to learning than are others. This chapter, therefore, will look at ways to organize revenue forecasting to facilitate learning about important aspects of the policy environment.

NATURE AND EVOLUTION OF REVENUE FORECASTING

Bertrand de Jouvenel, in his seminal treatise on thinking about the future, observed that "the art of forecasting consists of passing from knowledge about present conditions to estimates of future conditions" (1967, p. 180). In making this passage, those who wish to forecast revenues are confronted by several problems common to forecasting in general. First, historical information must be gathered, because every forecast presupposes a search of the past to obtain knowledge. Then, methods must be developed and judgment applied to fashion a statement about the future.

The information needed and methods applied to public financial forecasts vary with the time horizon and purpose of the forecasts (Bretschneider and Gorr, 1987). Table 1 indicates how the time horizons of revenue forecasts vary with the purposes to which they are put. The most immediate form of revenue forecasting deals with projections of cash inflows to enable treasury managers to assure liquidity and invest cash surpluses wisely.

Forecasts are needed for the remainder of a budget year to enable budget managers to monitor likely receipts and adjust spending plans accordingly. Lawmakers and budget planners need longer-term forecasts with horizons of 1–2 years in order to develop new budgets. Finally, multiyear forecasts are needed to anticipate the revenue impacts of policy changes or new developments, and to assess the future fiscal health of a jurisdiction.

Forecasts, Projections, and Estimates

Forecasters differentiate between that which can be controlled and that which cannot. In this respect, revenue forecasting differs from expenditure forecasting. Policy changes can alter service levels during a budget year, so expenditure policy remains a variable. Tax policy, on the other hand, can rarely be changed in the midst of a budget year. Revenue policy is a given fact, and short-term forecasts result from forces that are largely beyond the forecaster's control.

Any forecast is confronted by uncertainty. It is customary among forecasters, therefore, to speak in terms of ranges of outcomes that reflect the possible consequences of different combinations of future events. In this regard, it is useful to distinguish between estimates, projections, forecasts, and predictions. Revenue analysts often use the term *estimates* to refer to possible future revenues, and this usage is likely to continue, though it lacks specificity and differs from usage in other disciplines. In demography, for example, an estimate refers not to a future population but to a past or present population at a time other than an official census count. The terms *projection* and *forecast* are preferable because they are more specific and are readily understood by forecasters in other fields.

A projection is essentially a statement, expressed either verbally or quantitatively, as to what is likely to happen if a given combination of assumed events should occur. A forecast, in turn, is a single projection, chosen from a series of possible projections, which the forecasters identify as being the most likely to occur. The forecast is the projection that is based on the set of assumptions that seemed to be most plausible at the time the series was made. The term *prediction* is not appropriate because it implies a statement of certainty about future events that obscures the conditional basis upon which each of the projections, including the forecast, are based. *Forecasting* is a useful term to describe the process of developing a series of projections and of making a forecast from this series.

Forecasters often shy away from identifying a projection as a forecast. The U.S. Bureau of the Census, for example, publishes several series of projections reflecting different sets of assumptions about fertility, mortality, and migration, but it resists identifying any one of these projections as an official forecast. The revenue forecaster is faced with a very different situation, however, because custom and political demands call for a single revenue forecast, rather than a range of possible future collections that would

Table 1 Purposes of Revenue Forecasts by Time Horizon

Purpose	Horizon
Cash flow planning	1 Day to several months
Budget execution	Remainder of current budget year
Budget preparation and authorization	1–2 Years ahead
Trend analysis, anticipation of fiscal health and policy impacts	Multiyear

reflect the uncertainties that actually exist about future events. The revenue forecaster is expected to "go on the line" in stating that a single set of assumed events is most likely to occur.

Assumption Management and Learning

Former Secretary of the Treasury William Simon was a notable exception to the public officials who demand a single forecast. He believed that the 5-year budget projections that resulted from the 1974 Congressional Budget and Impoundment Control Act should be done as series of projections rather than as single forecasts. "For many policy decisions," said Simon, "it is more important to know the range of possible results and their probabilities than it is to have a single estimate" (U.S. Congress, Joint Economic Committee, 1975, p. 9).

To understand revenue forecasting, one must first understand the importance of assumptions. A useful typology of four different types of budget projections, each based on a different set of assumptions, was suggested by Alice Rivlin (U.S. Congress, Joint Economic Committee, 1975) when she directed the Congressional Budget Office. The four types are (1) the existing form of "current services" projection that assumes no change in revenue or expenditure policies; (2) a "most desired" projection, which would assume that policies will be adopted to create a desirable outcome; (3) a "most feared" projection, which can reflect vulnerability to negative events or the continuation of adverse trends; and (4) a "most likely" projection, which would be a forecast based upon those assumptions about the economy and political process that the forecasters believe are most likely to occur.

Rivlin noted that it is very difficult for federal forecasters to produce "most likely" forecasts. The actions of the federal government affect the economy, and a "most likely" forecast that projects hard times ahead could adversely affect investor and consumer confidence, thereby creating a self-fulfilling prophecy. Consequently, even the current services projections often reflect optimistic long-range assumptions about the economy. Revenue forecasters in the states appear to place little reliance upon federal forecasts, and rely instead more upon private economic forecasting companies for information to guide the framing of their assumptions. State forecasters focus their energies toward producing "most likely" forecasts and believe that the inclinations of federal forecasters to be optimistic make the federal forecasts less reliable as sources of information.

A substantial amount of research into the accuracy of forecasting in general has generally concluded that the underlying assumptions of forecasters are far more important than the particular forecasting methods employed. Moreover, it is in the framing of assumptions that much of the learning takes place in revenue forecasting. Consequently, *the administration of revenue forecasting is essentially a process of assumption management.* Conflicts often occur about underlying assumptions and their consequences, and the administrator is challenged to find ways to shape deliberations to enhance learning rather than allow such differences of opinion to sidetrack the political process. The administrators of revenue forecasting must also assure that the assumptions are appropriate to the purpose of the forecast, that they do not become out of date, and that conflicting sets of assumptions do not create confusion in making or comparing revenue projections. In the last instance, the U.S. Office of Management and Budget instructs all federal agencies to forecast their future receipts using a common set of economic assumptions that are supplied by the budget agency itself. Comparability is achieved, enabling the OMB to assemble a total revenue forecast that is internally consistent. Many states also require similar uses of common sets of assumptions.

Elected officials often ask questions of revenue forecasters about the underlying assumptions of their forecasts. Table 2 presents a result of a survey of revenue forecasters in each of the 50 states (Klay and Zingale, 1980). It indicates that elected officials in the states are a bit more likely to question the assumptions made about the state economy than about the national economy, but both types of questions are very common. Note that elected officials in *every* state ask such questions. Not surprisingly, officials are much more likely to query about assumptions than methodologies. They also ask about the subjective feelings of confidence the forecasters have with respect to the accuracy of their forecasts.

This propensity of elected officials to ask questions about the underlying assumptions of revenue forecasts presents an opportunity for learning. Where elected officials are more prone to ask questions of forecasters, and to request a series of projections rather than a single forecast, the forecasters themselves seem to learn more about the workings of a state's economy. Moreover, where revenue forecasting is organized to promote deliberation, where elected officials ask for series of projections, and where they raise questions about a variety of matters including underlying assumptions, the elected officials themselves also seem to learn more (Klay, 1985). The benefits of such learning can extend well beyond the arena of revenue forecasting. It seems incumbent upon the administrators of revenue forecasting, therefore, to encourage such mutually educational interaction.

Brief History

Revenue forecasting is undoubtedly one of the older professions, but the emergence of sophisticated methods appears to be a twentieth century occurrence. An act of Congress in 1800, for example, required the Secretary of the Treasury to submit revenue forecasts to the Congress together with appropriate plans and analyses, but there is no evidence that this was ever done (Brundage, 1970, p. 6). Histories of revenue estimating are rare, but a brief account of the state of Pennsylvania's experience revealed that no forecasts of revenues were done there until the early 1920s when a budget process was finally established. In a neighboring state only two decades ago, it was reported that the state's forecasts were made by a single individual, late at night "after my wife and children have gone to bed" (Giovinazzo, 1971, p. 22). This individual, incidentally, had a good record of accuracy.

Table 2 Propensity of Elected Leaders in Each State to Ask Questions About Revenue Forecasts

Topic of questions	Very likely	Somewhat likely	Rarely	Never	N
Assumptions about national economy	39	8	3	0	50
Assumptions about state economy	45	3	2	0	50
Methodology used	20	15	15	0	50
Analysts' subjective feelings	22	20	8	0	50

In his landmark budgeting text, A. E. Buck (1929) identified three methods of estimating that were practiced at that time: (1) the automatic method of "rule of the penultimate year," (2) the method of averages, and (3) the method of direct valuation. The last is of no help in budget deliberations for it is not done until the beginning of a fiscal year, after all receipts of the previous year are known, and uses this information together with personal judgment to make a forecast for the year already underway.

The rule of the penultimate year began in nineteenth-century France and simply uses the amount of revenue collected during the previous year as a forecast of what will be received in the coming year. It is a method that treats the past as an exact model of the future, but as simple as it sounds, it is not without political overtones. Gupta (1967) reported that its application in nineteenth-century India was intended to shield the finance minister from criticism. It is inherently conservative in that it restricts growth in government expenditures. The use of penultimate year revenues as a forecast is apparently common among American local governments (Chang, 1979; Meltsner, 1971, Frank, 1988).

The method of averages is still widely used for several reasons. It is simple, understandable, and inherently conservative. The method of averages calculates the average dollar increase for the past few years (usually 3 or 5 years) and forecasts that revenues for the coming year will increase by this absolute average. An alternate method involves computing the average percentage increase per year. It is false to assume that the method of averages will eliminate the need for judgment in revenue forecasting. It is possible for average absolute increases and average percentage increases to yield different forecasts, and the choice between them is a matter of some judgment. Its conservative aspects have attracted the attention of some observers who wish to add greater discipline to federal budgeting. Rudolph Penner (1982), for example, proposed that long-range forecasts of the federal government should be based on the average experience of economic variables during the previous 5 years. Doing so, says Penner, would temper the tendency for optimistic assumptions in federal forecasts.

The simple techniques described by Buck will continue to be used, particularly for lesser revenue sources and in smaller jurisdictions that lack expertise in forecasting. Recent decades, however, have seen a rapid introduction of more sophisticated methods. The use of these newer, highly quantitative methods has coincided with the growing availability of computers. Herbert Simon (1973) pointed out that computers can assist administrators in two ways: as a source of historical data that can be rapidly retrieved, and as a tool to assist in developing models of complex processes involving intricate interrelationships. Revenue forecasters are now making extensive use of both attributes of computers. Microcomputer technology is having a profound effect on even local governments, and revenue forecasting has been found to be one of the most common uses of the new technology in such governments (Norris, 1988; Ostrowski et al., 1986). In no other area of public administration is the computer being put to such full use, and it is incumbent on those who are concerned with the impacts of computers to pay close attention to the administration of revenue forecasting.

Three Methods of Revenue Forecasting

Even though revenue forecasting is becoming increasingly sophisticated, it is probable that it will always reflect some combination of three distinct forecasting approaches (see Chambers et al., 1971).

Qualitative Methods

A forecasting process that uses only qualitative methods is one that, in its essence, relies solely upon human judgment. Qualitative methods are those that use the unique capacities of the human brain to perceive relationships and frame conjectures. Due to the highly quantitative nature of revenue collections and forecasts, the use of purely qualitative techniques to the exclusion of quantitative methods is both rare and questionable. On the other hand, revenue forecasting relies heavily upon human judgment. Under some conditions, judgment is an important factor in achieving forecast accuracy (Armstrong, 1983). Careful attention should be given to organizing the forecasting process to ensure that such judgment will be well informed and effectively expressed.

A survey of revenue forecasting activities in 33 states by the Public Policy Institute (1985) revealed that the states utilize several methods to improve the quality of judgment in revenue forecasting. In 17 of the states, for example, participants from the private sector are engaged in some sort of advisory role. These persons are not necessarily more knowledgeable than the states' own experts about either forecasting methods or the intricacies of the revenue bases. What they bring is a different perspective and knowledge about possible behaviors of key groups and actors in the private sector.

In the state of Delaware, for example, the official revenue forecasts are prepared by a body called the Governor's Economic and Financial Advisory Council. It is comprised of 20 members from both public and private organizations. The role of the council is to advise not only about revenue forecasts but about a wide range of financial and economic matters. In Hawaii, the Council of Revenues, a unique organization comprised of private citizens with relevant professional backgrounds, is responsible for preparing the official forecasts. In most states, private participation is limited to an advisory role.

A majority of the states have mechanisms to bring together persons from different organizations—the governors' offices, legislative staffs, departments of revenue, and so on—to enable their forecasts to benefit from various perspectives. If revenue forecasting involved nothing more than simple data collection and mathematical calculations, there would be no need for cooperative efforts. The existence of a wide variety of mechanisms to bring together persons of different perspectives attests to the fact that revenue forecasting requires the exercise of judgment. The administration of revenue forecasting, then, requires an understanding of the ways in which human judgment influences forecasts. It also requires the development of structures and procedures to ensure that the most relevant perspectives are introduced at the proper times.

Time-Series Trend Analysis

A time series is a set of chronologically ordered points of data, such as the amount of revenue that has been collected each day, week, month, quarter, or year for some historical period. The ready availability of such data on revenue collections has made time-series analysis very popular in revenue forecasting. In fact, the method of averages mentioned by Buck is a rudimentary example of time-series analysis. The attractiveness of time-series analysis lies in the fact that it enables the future of some variable to be forecast solely from a knowledge of the past behavior of the variable itself. Revenue forecasters may find themselves in situations in which the only historical data available are the revenue collections themselves. Time-series techniques can be used to develop a forecast about future yields from a single set of data about past yields.

Analysis of past yields is aided by plotting them on graphs. Harvey Henderson

(1978), a municipal finance director, recommended the use of semilogarithmic graphs because they reveal rates of changes in yields more clearly than arithmetic line graphs. According to Box and Jenkins (1976), there are three basic types of time-series methodologies: the moving average, the autoregressive, and the mixed techniques. Each of these approaches to time-series analysis can be applied using computation programs that can be readily purchased for personal computers. In fact, the easy availability of sophisticated time-series techniques may seduce persons who neither understand nor appreciate their subtleties and limitations.

The most basic moving average method simply computes a mean for yields in a fixed number of past years and uses the mean as the forecast. Other, more sophisticated methods begin with enabling the forecaster to weight some past years more than others, normally the more recent years. A particularly interesting form of moving average technique is exponential smoothing, which incorporates corrections for observed error in the preceding forecast (Brown, 1959). In moving-average techniques, past values eventually reach a point where they are no longer used.

In autoregressive techniques, all past values retain some contribution and much longer sets of historical data are typically needed. These techniques essentially apply the concept of regression, with lagged values of revenue yields being used to forecast subsequent ones. Several types of autoregressive techniques have been developed. Curve fitting, a method of choice among state and local forecasters (Bretschneider and Gorr, 1987), is generally operationalized through the linear regression model. For the most ambitious and best qualified of time series analysts, there exist techniques to combine the features of autoregressive models with moving average methods. The ARIMA (autoregressive integrated moving average) model of Box and Jenkins (1976) is probably the best known of these.

Time-series techniques are based upon an assumption that past patterns will continue in an uninterrupted fashion into the future, so these techniques tend to be of greater use in short-run revenue forecasts. The authors of a seminal treatise on long-range revenue forecasting cautioned that "in periods of little or no change, techniques based on simple time trends yield good results, yet change invalidates such projections precisely when that change calls for policy change" (McLoon et al., 1967, p. 14). The identification of turning points in an economy is perhaps the most difficult task in revenue forecasting. Unfortunately, time-series techniques are not well suited to identifying these points. The time-series methods are also of limited value in learning about the complex interactions of an economy, and are not very useful in framing alternative scenarios.

Causal Methods

The third category of revenue forecasting techniques, as the name implies, centers on causation. It deals not with the history of a single variable, as is the case with time series techniques, but with the historical interrelationships of two or more variables. The objective of causal methods in revenue forecasting is to utilize one or more predictor variables to forecast future tax yields directly, or indirectly by first forecasting the future tax base. A tax base is that portion of economic activity to which a tax applies. Causal methods are especially useful for policy purposes because they are the basis for constructing computer models to study the possible future implications of different sets of assumptions.

Causal modeling is becoming increasingly important in public administration, and it is in the development of revenue forecasts that causal modeling methods are first likely to be used by a government. Drawbacks to the use of causal methods include the fact that historical data must be gathered for each of the variables used to forecast tax bases or yields, and the costs of developing such methods can be considerable. Computer costs have decreased rapidly, however, and the use of computers in revenue forecasting is widespread. The section of this chapter that deals with the econometric revolution discusses the application of causal methods in some detail.

Multimethod Forecasting

King's (1979) survey of revenue forecasters in the states revealed that many of them preferred to make use of all three categories of forecasting methods—judgmental, time series, and causal—rather than place exclusive reliance upon one category. Other studies have shown that local governments often use a variety of methods (Bretschneider and Schroeder, 1985; Boswell and Carpenter, 1986). Any government is faced with a variety of forecasting needs. The best methods to forecast an income tax, for example, might be quite different from those best suited to forecast receipts from minor user fees.

It is often wise to use more than one method to forecast a single revenue source. In Idaho, for example, a composite approach combining both univariate time series and causal methods performed quite well with respect to accuracy (Fullerton, 1989). In Massachusetts, judgmental methods were more accurate than two separate causal econometric models over a period of several years (Public Policy Institute of New York, 1985). In fact, no causal model is free of judgment. McNown's (1986) study of several major econometric forecasting organizations revealed that judgement is a major factor in causal modeling. Reed's (1983) comparison of the performance of time-series and causal models suggests that each might be preferable for different forecasting horizons. He found that time-series methods were better for a single quarter ahead, but a causal model was better at forecasting revenues four quarters ahead. Bahari-Kashani (1983) found that a hybrid model using both a time-series model and an causal model performed well in forecasting the revenues of a large state.

One of the foremost scholars of forecasting, Spyros Makridakis (1987), conducted an extensive review of empirical studies of forecasting. He concluded that combining different forecasting methods substantially improves forecasting accuracy. Patterns and relationships change in an economy, and the process of comparing and combining forecasts made by different methods may help forecasters to recognize these changes. Mizrach and Santomero (1986), for the same reason, concluded that composite forecasting is especially useful when the structure of an economy is changing. When more than one forecasting technique is used, the forecaster should search for points of convergence and reasons for divergence. Doing so enables the forecaster to learn more about each forecasting method and the underlying dynamics of revenues. When different techniques yield similar results, policymakers may be justified in feeling more confident about the accuracy of their forecasts than when the opposite situation occurs.

THE ECONOMETRIC REVOLUTION

Revenue forecasting has been profoundly affected by the emergence of econometrics, the application of statistical procedures to economics, and by the emergence of computer technology, which has enabled econometricians to do computations that would have previously been impossible. Simple causal techniques, such as the use of a scattergram, are possible without computers, but econometrics today is highly dependent upon the computer. The age of econometrics began in the 1930s when Dutch economist Jan Tinbergen developed a number of equations to represent, or model, the workings of that nation's economy, and American efforts generally date from the 1950s.

The rapidity with which econometric forecasting found its way into the states was astounding. At the beginning of the 1970s, virtually no states were using econometric models to forecast revenues (Giovinazzo, 1971; Perry, 1971). A survey conducted by this writer at the end of that decade, however, revealed that 41 states were using computer-based models to forecast revenues. Cities such as Mobile, Ala. (Chang, 1976, 1979), as well as New Orleans, Dallas, and Winston-Salem, N.C., pioneered in the application of econometric techniques in local governments.

Econometric methods have become so widespread that many administrators of budget offices now find themselves in an awkward position. They often lack a knowledge of statistics and computer applications, yet they are officially responsible for revenue forecasts that are produced through the application of econometrics. If administrators are ignorant of the esoteric language of econometrics, they may fail to understand its underlying logic, its strengths, and its weaknesses. They could easily misuse econometric methods or fail to use them at all (Worthley and Heaphy, 1978). The purpose of this section, therefore, is to present, in mostly verbal terms, some basic information about econometrics as it applies to revenue forecasting.

Building a Model

Every forecast of a social system employs some kind of logical structure, or model (Pindyck and Rubinfeld, 1981). Building a formal model to forecast revenues forces participants to think about the relationships that underlie their forecasts. The expression of these relationships through mathematics forces the user to be explicit, as can be seen in the following relationship:

$$Y = f(X)$$

In the parlance of revenue forecasting, Y is the variable that is being forecast. It is the *dependent* variable, which is also called an *endogenous* variable, because it has been estimated by the model, and it can be either the revenue yield or a variable, such as retail sales, that is related to the base to which a tax will be applied. The statement merely says that Y is somehow dependent on (is a function of) the value of X, which is variously called the *explanatory, independent,* or *predictor* variable. The variables that are obtained from sources outside the model itself, such as information about past population estimates or inflation rates, are called *exogenous* variables. Thus, the process of developing a revenue forecasting model is to (1) develop a data history or time series for all variables, (2) develop a set of mathematical expressions that best explains the past relationships between these, and (3) devise a means of forecasting the future values of the explanatory variables.

Econometric models are causal models. Two general types of econometric models are used to forecast revenues—single-equation regression models, which may have one or more explanatory variables, and multiequation models. The latter incorporate several regression-type equations and allow forecasters to study the relationships between variables more fully. In some multiequation models the equations are solved sequentially, while in others the equations are computed in a simultaneous manner. The simultaneous approach allows for mutual interactions between variables. Most economists argue that the explanatory variables should be related both theoretically and statistically to that which is being forecast. The following equation, developed by Cupoli (1987) to forecast the sales tax for the city of Syracuse, N.Y., illustrates the use of popular, theoretically consistent, explanatory variables. It is a single equation used to forecast yield directly.

$$STR = RATE \times (-8,343,523,709 + 3,705,888.6CPI + 164,237.1RPCY + 16,457.6POP)$$

Where STR is the sales tax revenues, RATE the sales tax rate, CPI the consumer price index, RPCY the real per capita income, and POP the population.

This equation is a regression statement that says that, based on past relationships, the city's sales tax revenues (STR) can be forecast by multiplying the sales tax rate against the sum of a constant and three products. The constant is the Y intercept, and each of the three products is determined by multiplying exogenous variables by coefficients (often called "weights") that are determined primarily through regression analysis. Econometricians sometimes alter these coefficients when their judgement leads them to believe that alterations will increase future accuracy. The exogenous variables are the U.S. Consumer Price Index (CPI), the real per capita income for the county (RPCY), and the county population (POP). Data for the county and nation were used for exogenous variables, because no such data were available for the city itself. Data problems such as those encountered by Cupoli are common in developing causal models for local governments.

The explanatory variables used by Cupoli are commonly used in many jurisdictions (see Chang, 1976, 1979). Hambor et al., (1974), in their detailed presentation of a model developed for the state of Hawaii, relied heavily on state personal income, U.S. disposable income, and state population, although their study also revealed the usefulness of unique local variables such as tourism and sugar production. A study of models used for forecasting state general sales taxes concluded that "the dominant relationship specified in virtually all cases is that between yield and state personal income" (Adams, 1976, p. 15).

In order to see how well the model works as a forecasting tool, ex post (retrospective) estimates are normally done for each of several years in the past to see how closely the model would have forecast past dependent variables, such as revenues themselves, if the actual values of the explanatory variables had been known at that time. The difference between the actual and the estimated value is the error, also called a residual, and these differences are analyzed through the computation of a statistic, such as the standard error of the estimate, to develop an understanding as to how well the model fits the past relationships.

Ex post forecasting presents unique opportunities for learning about the nature and workings of an economy. Budgeters, however, are concerned mostly with ex ante forecasting, the development of projections into the future based on one or more possible future values for each of the explanatory variables. It is at this point that the importance of managing the process of assumption development becomes apparent.

Inaccuracy will occur when the model itself does not accurately reflect the most recent behavior of an economy. Long-term structural change in an economy may decrease the accuracy of a model that once performed well. Such changes rarely occur overnight, and a model that has forecast revenues well for several years is unlikely to suddenly become inaccurate. The more likely source of error from one budget year to the next is the use of inaccurate future values of the explanatory variables (Cupoli, 1987). A study of federal revenue forecasts, conducted by the Congressional Budget Office (1984), revealed that inaccuracies in aggregate revenue forecasts were primarily due to errors in economic assumptions.

The exogenous variables, the ones obtained from sources external to the model, are critical. For this reason, it is often wise to hold the number of exogenous variables to a relative few. The following guidelines, developed by the city of New Orleans, are especially appropriate to developing a model in a municipality or similar jurisdiction.

Explanatory Variables

Use as few explanatory variables as possible.

Project those variables as accurately as possible.

Estimate large revenue sources as a function of those variables, using binary variables (dummy variables) to deal with rate, policy, and formal changes.

Revenue Equations

Some justified theoretical relationship must exist between the revenue source being estimated and the explanatory variable.

In each equation, use as few explanatory variables as possible.

Adjust for autocorrelation (serial correlation of residuals over time, which may lead to unjustified levels of confidence in the model) when the adjustment yields an improved equation.

Using a Model: Interaction and Learning

Developing Assumptions

The future values of exogenous variables do not appear as a matter of course. They must be forecast. They may be forecast using time-series methods, such as extrapolation, but doing so reinforces the tendency of regression-based models to overlook recent events that may signal turning points in an economy. In some governments, the development of forecasts for exogenous variables involves complex interactions between key participants.

Lawrence Pierce (1971) described the process for developing underlying assumptions utilized by the so-called "troika" of the federal government—the Treasury, Office of Management and Budget, and Council of Economic Advisors. Individuals develop their own forecasts of key variables and then meet, often at great length, until a consensus is reached. The practice of bringing together knowledgeable persons from different parts of the government, in order to deliberate underlying assumptions, has become widespread in the states as well.

A survey by the Public Policy Institute of New York (1985) indicated that 17 of the 33 states studied used consensus methods in which members of different organizations in the executive and legislative branches meet together to deliberate such things as the future values of exogenous variables and resulting revenue yields. The state of Florida, with its Revenue Estimating Conference, has practiced consensus methods for many years.

Florida's conference was begun by a budget director who wanted to remove debates about the accuracy of competing forecasts from the floor of the legislature. He also wanted a process that was inclined to question and challenge the underlying assumptions upon which the forecasts of the state are based. The conference members include expert staff members of the Office of the Governor and the two houses of the legislature. The

Department of Revenue acts in an advisory capacity. Separate econometric models have been developed by the governor's staff and by legislative staff.

Ex post studies have indicated that these models represent the Florida economy well. The confidence that the participants have in their models leads them to spend most of their meeting time in developing the best possible projections of exogenous variables. Members regularly monitor actual events and compare them to assumed values, with some members emphasizing the monitoring of certain variables more than others. If actual values depart too far from the forecast, any member may call a meeting of the conference to update the forecast. The first day of regularly scheduled meetings is normally devoted to a discussion of national economic scenarios from econometric services and various other sources.

Members feel free to contribute information from any source, and they frequently discuss national and international events. As with the troika, satisficing prevails and the conference members discuss the values of the various assumptions until they feel comfortable that they have reached an overall consensus. They are concerned that these assumptions be logically consistant, however, and may chose to accept a single package of assumptions provided by a participant or a national econometric service. Although there are procedures for voting, a desire to obtain a consensus dominates, and discussion actually continues until a consensus scenario has been achieved.

States and localities are heavily dependent upon external sources of information about the national and regional economies of which they are a part. Most states subscribe to the services of one or more of the national econometric firms (King, 1979). These should not be accepted unquestioningly, for they are also prone to error, and local knowledge may be quite relevant. The construction of confidence intervals for forecasts is a helpful method to judge the confidence one should put into forecasts of either explanatory variables or revenues. Pindyk and Rubinfeld (1981) suggest a method for doing so that involves the insertion of values for an explanatory variable that are two standard deviations above and below the historic mean for that variable. The result is a crude approximation of a 95% confidence interval.

Learning Through Modeling

As is true of other types of forecasting, revenue forecasting is an effort to scan the environment and to learn from it. As such, revenue forecasting can be fashioned into an educational process that can enlighten officials about the subtleties and complexities of causal relationships in the jurisdiction's economy. The development of causal models apparently stimulates a great deal of learning. In a survey conducted by myself (Klay, 1985), respondents in 39 states said that their technical personnel who were engaged in causal model forecasting had learned more about the economies of their states. Moreover, respondents in 22 states said that these forecasters had learned a great deal.

Both technical and interpersonal factors seem to affect the degree to which forecasters learn from causal modeling. They seem to learn more in states that develop models of the state economy itself, and not merely models to forecast revenues directly. In addition, they seem to learn more where the state has also developed models to forecast future client populations. This suggests that more learning takes place in environments in which a variety of forecasts are developed, and that there may be transference of knowledge from one forecasting arena to another. Interestingly, forecasters seem to learn less where great credence is placed upon the values obtained from outside econometric firms. This suggests that there may be instances in which reliance upon such subscription services may reduce the propensity of forecasters to engage themselves in the process of investigation and questioning of underlying assumptions.

Interestingly, the forecasters seem to learn more in states where elected officials are also actively involved in inquiry. Where elected officials ask for a range of projections, especially, technical personnel were perceived to have learned more. Interactive factors seem to greatly affect the degree to which elected officials learn about their economies in the course of model development. Elected officials who ask questions about the state and national economies, who ask for ranges of projections, and who raise questions about forecast methodology seem to learn more. They also learn more in states that have engaged in special organizational efforts and consensus processes to forecast revenues. It seems, therefore, that organizational efforts to improve the quality of interaction may enhance learning by both elected officials and technical specialists. The development of causal models creates opportunities for such interaction.

SPECIAL PROBLEMS IN FORECASTING REVENUES

Income Taxes

In one way or another, most forecasts of income tax revenues depend on the concept of income elasticity. The term *elasticity* refers to the degree to which something changes in response to a change in something else. Revenue forecasters are concerned with the degree to which income tax yields change in response to changes in income. If an income tax is progressive, the elasticity coefficient may be quite high. This creates situations, especially during times of inflation, in which income tax yields grow more rapidly than income itself. Taxpayer resistance to such effects has prompted demands to adjust, or index, tax rates for inflation. Vosche and Williams (1987) show that such indexing can increase the accuracy of revenue forecasts. Indexing reduces the volatile effects of inflation on receipts.

The adoption of flatter rate schedules has affected the elasticity of state and federal income taxes. Using microsimulation models (which investigate the effects of changes in tax policy upon individual taxpayers), Galper and Pollock (1988) found that a reduction in elasticities had occurred in the income taxes of the federal government and several state governments as well. They reported that the elasticity of the federal individual income tax prior to the 1986 reforms was 1.95, but that it subsequently declined to 1.8. The latter figure, however, suggests that income tax revenues would still grow 1.8 times faster than taxable personal income. In a state that lacks a personal income tax, the adoption of even a flat-rate income tax can markedly improve the responsiveness of revenues to changes in per capita incomes (Carter, 1984).

Where local governments levy income taxes, forecasts of taxable income play a vital role. Forecasts for New York City have used projections of U.S. personal income, the city's inflation index, and its unemployment rate. New Orleans, on the other hand, has used U.S. personal income as a sole explanatory variable with good results. There are likely to be instances, however, in which local or state behavior deviates from national trends. In such situations local knowledge should be utilized. A forecasting model developed by Robb (1971) for Michigan emphasized the sensitivity of personal income and tax yields to major strikes in the auto industry. Ridgeway's (1974) study of the sensitivities of Nevada's revenues emphasized fluctuations in gambling activity.

Forecasting yields from corporate income taxes is more difficult than for individual income tax yields. A study by Giovinazzo (1971) found that corporate yields are some-times inelastic, suggesting that the accounting and business options that interstate corporations have may enable them to reduce taxable income in one state by shifting it elsewhere. In Hawaii, state personal income was used as a proxy for corporate profits, a decision that produced a reasonably good statistical fit.

Income tax forecasting in the federal government has undergone some substantial changes in the past decade. Originally, most attention was given to macroeconomic forecasting and to forecasting total revenue yields. The emergence of the concept of tax expenditures in the 1960s, the Gramm-Rudman-Hollings process, and the concern for revenue neutrality in the tax reforms of 1986 have prompted major new efforts to model the effects of changes in tax laws upon specific groups of taxpayers. Concern about the deficit, especially, has created a demand for highly detailed revenue forecasts. Such forecasts established the framework within which the House and Senate framed and debated the 1986 reforms.

Under federal statute, only the staff of the Congress's Joint Committee on Taxation (JCT) and the Office of Tax Analysis (OTA) of the Treasury have access to the most current base of data on taxpayers. Both organizations use large-scale simulation models to forecast the effects of specific changes in tax laws. The official forecasts for congressional debate are those of the JCT, and questions have invariably been raised about the extensive influence of their relatively closed forecasting process. (Vehorn et al., 1988). Not surprisingly, major efforts have been made to expand and improve the data base upon which these detailed forecasts are made. More economic and demographic data have been obtained from the Social Security Administration and the Bureau of the Census, and these have been combined with tax return data from the Internal Revenue Service.

It seems safe to predict that the detailed forecasting of income tax yields will continue. Increases in available computing capacity are prompting policymakers to request more and more detail from forecasters. This was the conclusion of a worldwide survey of econometric forecasting practices (Bodkin and Marwah, 1988).

Sales Taxes

Causal forecasts of sales tax yields are also highly dependent upon forecasts of personal income (Friedlander et al., 1973). Fullerton (1989), for example, developed a single-equation econometric model to forecast sales tax receipts in Idaho. His explanatory variables included measures of Idaho wage and salary disbursements—to indicate the level of disposable income and consumer sentiment in the state—and a personal consumption price deflator to measure retail price movements. He also used dummy variables (normally assigned values of either 0 or 1) for each quarter to adjust projections for seasonal variations in retail sales.

One of the earliest examples of causal modeling for consumption taxes was done in New York City (White and White, 1955). The authors encountered a common obstacle to forecasting in local governments, an absence of local data, so they chose to rely upon national income data. Fortunately, much more local data is available for large localities now than when White and White did their pioneering work. Consumer price indices and population estimates are generally available for large MSAs (metropolitan statistical areas), and these have been used by cities such as Dallas to forecast sales tax receipts.

Local peculiarities in consumption must be considered. Chang (1979) noted that

Vail, Colo., projects sales tax revenues from local population projections, the number of visitors to ski resorts, and the value of building permits. Time-series methods are also commonly employed to forecast sales tax revenues. The city of Oakland, Calif., has used *lagging*—predicting a future value of a variable from recent values of that same variable—to incorporate recent sales tax collections in addition to projected real per capita personal income and state unemployment rates.

When a government is heavily dependent upon sales taxes, a considerable degree of *disaggregation* is advisable. Florida (which has no personal income tax) makes separate forecasts of yields from consumer durables, autos, nondurables, and recreation, as well as from investments in farms, buildings, and business investment (Cooper et al., 1978; Huggins, 1975). Tennessee disaggregates according to 10 different categories of sources—food at home, food away from home, liquor, nondurables, durables, merchandise/services, lodging, utilities, automobiles, and manufacturing (Bohm and Craig, 1987). Disaggregation offers several advantages that may offset its higher costs. Inflation, for example, may have different effects on various types of sales. Disaggregation facilitates the monitoring of yields in each sales category, thereby allowing the forecaster to isolate more readily the source of a forecast error. Florida also conducts a monthly Consumer Sentiment Survey, which parallels the University of Michigan's national index of consumer sentiment, to gauge the financial situations and intentions of consumers.

The forecasting of taxes on the sale of services is a growing challenge for forecasters. For many years, there has been a trend in our society away from the purchase of goods and toward the purchase of services. As incomes increase, the proportion of income spent on the purchase of services also increases. To tap the revenue potential of the service sector, and to lessen the regressivity of sales taxation, many states are now looking at service taxes. The inclusion of services in a tax base can significantly affect the distribution of tax burden and yield (Blumenfeld, 1973). Moreover, Bohm and Craig (1987) have found that elasticities of tax yields vary considerably with the type of service being taxed. The purchase of some forms of services, amusement admissions for example, is much more discretionary than other forms of services such as those of a plumber. The predictability of services taxes, therefore, will vary greatly, depending upon the particular types of services that governments choose to tax.

Property Taxes

Even though real property taxes are considered to be relatively stable revenue sources, the forecasting of future yields is subject to several potential pitfalls. Cupoli (1987) has demonstrated that the forecasting of property tax yields involves both political and economic variables. The political variables include property tax rates, assessment ratios, and policies with respect to the exemption or favorable treatment of specific categories of properties. Each of these variables reflects policy decisions that may not be known at the time of the forecast. Relevant economic variables are those that have an impact upon market values.

Noting that residential property values are a function of both income and consumer demand, Cupoli's econometric model for long-range property value forecasts included measures of population size, real per capita income, and a housing price index. To forecast commercial property, he added a measure of interest rates as an indicator of profitability in the business sector. Bahl et al. (1979) developed a simpler model based on the average growth for any designated period of years:

$$\text{Yield} = (\text{base year} + \text{AYG})(\text{P})(\text{rate})$$

This equation allows the revenue yield to reflect average yearly growth (AYG) and millage rates, as well as inflation (P) where rapid increases in property values may occur. Hyclack (1976) found that three variables—real per capita income, population, and the area of the city—produced good results for South Bend, Ind. Inclusion of area allows annexations to be considered in an equation. The city of New Orleans has used assessed value, population, and millage rates as predictor variables. Once assessed value is known for the coming budget year, computation of expected property taxes is a straightforward task. Causal models, however, can be valuable tools to study the possible future effects of changes in both economic and political variables.

Intergovernmental Revenues and Miscellaneous Sources

Recipients of intergovernmental revenues are confronted with several forecasting problems. If an intergovernmental revenue is from an earmarked source, and not subject to policy changes, the task is essentially to identify the total amount likely to be collected by the donor government, and the relative competitiveness of the recipient government. On the other hand, qualitative forecasting (political prognostication) is needed to forecast receipts from donor governments where intergovernmental revenues are subject to frequent changes in policy.

Cupoli attempted to use econometric methods to forecast individual grant programs. He found that he could not do so very well and concluded that "it is not clear there is anything to be gained by econometrically forecasting those components of the budget that are largely determined by the political process" (1987, p. 195). He did find that the sum of all such programs tended to grow more regularly. It may, therefore, be advisable to forecast intergovernmental revenues in the aggregate.

There are instances, however, when forecasts must be made about revenues from particular intergovernmental programs. In many instances, the distribution of those revenues will be made according to one or more formulas. These formulas can be the basis for forecasts. Shaw (1982) used state distribution formulas as the basis of his efforts to forecast county receipts from a state-shared minerals severance tax. He developed projections of statewide coal production and of county portions of that production, as well as projections a county's portion of total state population. Once values have been forecast for each variable used in a distribution formula, a projection of receipts to the particular locality in question can be computed. Doing so is time-consuming, and it is likely that most recipient governments would choose to rely on simpler time-series methods tempered by political judgment.

Governments receive revenues from many different sources. Numerous agencies, for example, collect user fees. Generally speaking, the notion of selective attention applies to these revenue sources. Forecasters devote more time and effort to projecting the larger sources and those that tend to fluctuate widely from year to year. Causal methods are likely to be applied only to revenue sources of a high priority, while time-series methods or judgment alone tends to be used for the lesser sources. A division of labor is also employed in revenue forecasting. Typically, agencies that are responsible for collecting a source have a role to play in forecasting future receipts. State officials who administer federally funded programs are likely to have inside information regarding future levels of those federal funds. Collectors of specific user fees might also possess special knowledge about trends and events that will affect those fees.

Fiscal Impact Analysis

Fiscal impact analysis is a unique application of revenue and expenditure forecasting that is of particular importance to local governments. Also known as cost-revenue analysis, fiscal impact analysis is the application of one or more forecasting techniques to project probable revenues and costs, for each of several future years, that are expected from a new development or annexation (Levin, 1975). These projections, normally in current dollars, are done to alert policymakers as to whether new developments might place a net drain upon the fiscal resources of the government and, if so, for how long.

The long-range forecasting that is required for fiscal impact analysis can be greatly enhanced through the use of computer-assisted simulations. These simulations use causal models. One such simulation program is that developed by Woods and Dockson (1984) for communities of various sizes. On the expenditure side, their model allows projections to be developed for several economic, demographic, and service demand variables. On the revenue side, it allows revenue impacts to be projected by source, rather than merely in an aggregate fashion.

Shaw's (1982) study of the fiscal impacts of major new economic developments in energy producing localities illustrates the usefulness of fiscal impact analysis. He identified several factors of new developments that influence future revenues. These include direct and indirect effects on employment and business activity, sales and income effects, and impacts on property values induced by new populations with specified characteristics. New developments have varying effects on an economic base. Revenue forecasting for impact analysis requires projections to be made of the likely impacts of a development on the economic base.

Shaw's analysis of community impacts in Wyoming and West Virginia revealed that the total revenues generated by the developments were generally sufficient to meet increased demands over the long run, but negative impacts often occur as demands tend to mount before the new revenues become fully available. There are often jurisdictional mismatches between the sites of developments that enjoy the bulk of new revenues, especially property taxes, and other places that may be impacted with relatively little revenue benefit. Fiscal impact analysis, then, is a useful tool for state governments to employ to lessen such inequities and growing pains.

Unfortunately, the learning potential of long-range revenue forecasting and impact analysis is sometimes stifled by political forces. Danziger et al. (1982) studied the political uses of computer-based, fiscal impact models. They found that such models are often used as political tools, reinforcing the prevailing biases of the model users. Models can enhance the ability of officials to learn about policy alternatives, but it is apparently a common practice to restrict the exploration of alternatives. Whenever severe restrictions are placed on the alternative scenarios that are evaluated through such models, the capacity to learn from forecasting is diminished.

Monitoring and Revising

Revenue forecasts are inherently uncertain. It is necessary, therefore, to monitor receipts and to adjust forecasts when the margin of error is sufficient to warrant revisions. Much of the learning that takes place in revenue forecasting is accomplished through such monitoring. As events unfold, and these are compared with what was expected to occur, a deeper understanding of an economy and revenue behavior is likely to emerge. Monitoring and revision of forecasts are common practices, as is indicated in Table 3, which is based upon the survey of 33 states done by the Public Policy Institute of New York (1985).

As can be seen, no single time frame dominates for either the frequency of reevaluation or revision of state revenue forecasts. In nine states forecasts are reevaluated on an "as needed" basis, but in five states such reevaluations are done monthly. Most states reevaluate either quarterly or semiannually. Formal revisions are a bit less frequent than reevaluations. Only one state reported making monthly revisions, while those in the largest group revise forecasts only as needed. Ten do so on either a quarterly or semiannual basis. There is no reason to assume that the frequency of formal reevaluations or revisions is related to the quality of learning that takes place. It is likely, however, that those who monitor and revise with the intent of learning more about their economy and tax structure will have an edge in doing so.

POLITICAL AND ADMINISTRATIVE QUESTIONS

A Conservative Bias or a Contingency Reserve?

A tempting way to allow for the uncertainties of revenue forecasting is to intentionally underestimate revenues. This method has sometimes been called the "principle of conservatism" and has been recommended from time to time in major financial administration texts. Such underestimation, however, introduces a bias that is not politically neutral. Systematic underestimation works against those who wish to expand programs or provide immediate tax relief. It works in favor of those who wish to constrain expenditures or retain higher tax rates in the immediate future. Underestimation also causes year-end surpluses that can enhance the political capital of those who have influence over how such surpluses are spent. Revenue forecasting is an administrative function. It is difficult to justify the conduct of that function in a manner that biases the political process, especially when an alternative—contingency funds—is available.

A contingency reserve fund, commonly called a "rainy day" fund, is a fund used to hold monies in reserve until such time as revenue shortfalls occur. When they do, the fund is drawn upon to avoid the necessity of making budget cuts. The funding of rainy day funds varies among states and localities. Some states rely solely on specific legislative appropriations, but many use formulas to automatically transfer revenue surpluses when

Table 3 Frequency of Monitoring and Revision of State Revenue Forecasts, 33 States Responding

Frequency	Reevaluate forecast	Revise forecast
Monthly	5	1
Quarterly	8	5
Semiannually	8	5
Triannually		1
Annually		3
As needed	9	12

Data compiled from Public Policy Institute of New York (1985).

they occur. When automatic transfers are made, contingency funds operate in a counter-cyclical manner—putting money aside when times are good and drawing upon reserves when the economy takes a downswing.

A survey done in 1986 by the National Conference of State Legislatures (NCSL) revealed that more than half of the states had established contingency reserve funds. Many of these did so in response to the budget cutbacks they experienced during the recession of the early 1980s. Wolkoff's (1987) survey of the nation's largest cities found that 6 of 27 respondents had rainy-day funds, most of which were also established in response to that same recession. Somewhat curiously, he found that the cities that were most prone to cyclical fluations were not more likely to establish reserve funds.

Generally speaking, the magnitude of rainy-day funds should be related to the likely magnitude of the fiscal forecasting errors, including both revenue and expenditure forecasting errors, that a government is likely to experience. This seems to amount to about 5% in many cases. Vosche and Williams's (1987) calculations lead them to recommend a reserve of about 5% for the state of California. The NCSL recommends the use of rainy-day funds, funded in an amount equivalent to at least 5% of a state's budget. Wolkoff's survey of large cities also revealed that a maximum balance was about 5%. Contingency funds may be rarer in small localities, but it is interesting that a detailed study of several small governments revealed that they systematically underestimated their revenues by about 5% (Frank, 1988). Whether obtained through reserve funds or underestimation, 5% seems to be a common contingency goal. An exception is Rudolph Penner's (1982) suggestion that the federal government appropriate 2% of its budget for contingencies.

How Accurate Are the Forecasts?

Accuracy is the quality that is most desired of a revenue forecast. During the past decade, several independent studies have investigated patterns of accuracy in the federal, state, and local governments. These studies have revealed that patterns of error differ according to the level of government.

The federal government has frequently been accused of using overly optimistic economic assumptions, thereby overestimating future receipts. David Stockman (1986), former director of the Office of Management and Budget, raised eyebrows when he wrote in his memoir that unduly optimistic economic assumptions were purposely used as a strategy to justify the Reagan administration's 1981 package of tax reductions. Empirical studies, however, suggest that such use of assumptions is not the rule for short-term federal forecasts. The Congressional Budget Office (CBO) (1981) studied the Treasury Department's revenue forecasts over a 16-year period, 1963–1978, and found they had underestimated revenues in 10 years and overestimated them in 6 years. During those years, the mean annual percent error for the aggregate revenue estimate presented in the President's budget request was between 3 and 4%.

The most extensive study of federal forecasting performance is that of Kamlet et al. (1987), who studied federal forecasting over a period of 25 years. In spite of the growing sophistication of forecasting, they did not find that the accuracy of forecasts for such variables as GNP, inflation, or unemployment had increased over time. Short-run forecasts of both the executive and CBO, they concluded, are about as accurate as those of private forecasters and did not seem to have been sensitive to such political factors as the size of the deficit. The long-term forecasts of both branches, those for 2 or more years, tended to be consistently optimistic, and the executive slightly more so than the CBO. The degree of such optimism increased with both the forecast horizon and the degree of fiscal pressure.

At the state level, Cassidy et al. (1989) studied forecast error for revenue estimates applicable to the general fund budgets of 23 states from 1978 to 1987. Of 128 forecasts in their sample, 76 (59%) were underestimates, and the mean percent error was –0.51%. They concluded that state forecasting is unbiased and that such error as occurs is due largely to forecasters' inability to anticipate business trends and cycles.

This is the same conclusion reached by this writer and a colleague (Grizzle and Klay, 1986). We studied the accuracy of general sales tax forecasts in 28 states from FY 1981 through FY 1985. The mean and median errors were both +0.6%, while the median absolute error (disregarding plus and minus signs) was 3.3%. The range of error, however, was rather wide. When we excluded the most extreme errors (10% of errors), we found this truncated range to be from a 14% overestimate to a 9% underestimate. Many states do not do long-range revenue forecasting, and no study has been done of those that do. It is impossible to say whether states share with their federal counterparts an optimistic bias toward the long-term future.

Studies of local governments indicate that many of them have a conservative bias toward underestimation of revenues. Larkey and Smith's (1984) study of Pittsburgh and Bretschneider and Schroeder's (1985) study of Kansas City concluded that systematic underestimation was present. Rubin's (1987) study of revenue forecasts in 102 Illinois cities for FY 1986, however, revealed a considerable degree of accuracy in the forecasting of aggregate revenues. Some 45% forecasted accurately (within ± 2%), while 17% overestimated and 37% underestimated. She found that the tendency to underestimate was associated with the unpredictability of specific revenue sources; the more unpredictable the source, the greater was the tendency to underestimate it.

In a detailed study of revenue forecasting practices in Florida, Frank (1988) found that a random sample of 99 municipalities revealed a ratio of 0.92 of budgeted to actual revenues for FY 1986. After conducting intensive interviews in a dozen localities, he concluded that underestimates of about 8% for general fund sources were typical. Moreover, he found that underestimation was a common practice even in governments with substantial unspent balances. In Florida, at least, it appears that local forecasters heavily discount the costs of underestimation. In one rapidly growing municipality, the finance director expressed the hope that the resulting surpluses would lead to either property tax reductions or new capital facilities. In another community, a forecaster explained the reasoning for underestimation succinctly.

> If you underestimate revenue, you look like a saint, cause now you've got extra money to spend on something, and everybody's real happy that you underestimated. . . . There's smiles, and nobody thinks this guy did a bad estimate. If you come in too high, you're a villain. So, by that reward and punishment system, you are taught to underestimate. (Frank, 1988, p. 231)

The study of bias among revenue forecasters has been neglected and it is a fascinating topic. What is it that causes forecasters at different levels of government to behave differently? Why do states seem to strive to be accurate and to use reserve funds to cushion against uncertainty, while local forecasters are much more prone to underestimate? Why do federal forecasters seem to be consistently optimistic for the long-term future, but not much more so than other forecasters for the short term?

For state forecasts and short-term federal ones, it does not appear likely that the increasing sophistication of forecasting techniques will do much to increase overall accuracy. The federal government has invested heavily to improve the sophistication of its data bases and models, but the accuracy of its short-term economic forecasts did not improve during the period from 1962 to 1984; moreover, simple, single-equation models forecast aggregate revenues about as well as the complex federal models (Kamlet et al., 1987). The study by Grizzle and Klay found no significant correlation between measures of forecasting sophistication and accuracy. These findings concur with those of Makridakis (1987), whose survey of forecasts led him to conclude that simple techniques often forecast as well as complex ones. The one advantage that some complex models have is that they allow for microforecasting—the detailed projection of impacts from specific economic, demographic, and policy changes.

Does Fiscal Stress Affect Revenue Forecasting?

Fiscal stress places great pressures upon revenue forecasters. When a government's revenues do not keep pace with pressures for spending, the revenue forecasting function may come under close scrutiny. If the forecasts in stressed governments are optimistic, political pressures may be relieved temporarily. The consequences of shortfalls, however, are likely to be graver than in governments with abundant resources. How then do these countervailing sets of influences, for optimistic forecasts and for conservative forecasts, resolve themselves?

Caiden and Wildavsky's (1974) study of budgeting practices in very poor countries pointed out that overestimation of revenues was a common practice. Chapman (1982) found that the stresses of Proposition 13 in California had led to mixed behaviors. Stress tended to stimulate either underestimates or greater accuracy, but if underestimates lead to cuts in the budget, subsequent political pressures could lead to overestimates.

Rubin's (1987) study of 133 Illinois cities revealed differences in patterns of forecast error that were attributed to differences in fiscal stress. In cities that were not stressed, those in which revenues were growing well and that had relatively low property tax efforts, there was a tendency to underestimate revenues. Conversely, the cities that were stressed showed a tendency to overestimate revenues. Although she suggested that her findings confirmed those of Caiden and Wildavsky in a totally different setting, she also emphasized that there is much individuality among jurisdictions as to whether and how fiscal stress affects revenue forecasting.

One of the best studies of the relationships between fiscal stress and revenue forecasting was done by MacManus and Grothe (1986). They looked at 15 U.S. counties with populations over 100,000. Unlike other researchers who have looked only at patterns of accuracy, they looked at several behavioral responses. In the counties that were stressed, greater effort was given to develop and implement sophisticated revenue forecasting techniques. Such counties revised and updated their forecasts more frequently, hired more forecasters, and were more likely to do multiyear forecasts. In spite of these efforts, however, the forecasts of the fiscally healthy counties were still more accurate. They concluded that it is simply more difficult to forecast decline than economic stability and growth. If this is true, it may be that the observed tendency of stressed governments to overestimate is based upon something other than a calculated strategy. In summary, it does appear that fiscal stress affects the forecasting function, but the ways in which it does are complex, and no simplistic generalizations seem warranted.

Are There Special Problems in Forecasting Revenues in Developing Countries?

Forecasters in American local governments often complain of the lack of data available to them to use in forecasting. Their problems pale in comparison to those confronted by forecasters in many developing nations. One of the defining factors of a developed nation is its capacity to develop and utilize information. In developing nations, national revenue forecasts may be based upon rudimentary information. Moreover, much of their economy may be beyond the control of national policy.

Tandjung's (1987) study of revenue forecasting in Indonesia highlights some of the problems confronted by revenue forecasters in developing nations. He found that much of the data assembled since that nation gained its independence was of little use. Idiosyncratic personal rule, neglected development of the bureaucracy, cultural traits, and efforts to evade taxes undercut efforts to develop a reliable data base for economic measurement. National policymakers became dependent upon a bottom-up approach to revenue forecasting in which each of several agencies did forecasts of their own receipts. Some of these agencies maintained discipline but others had not.

Under such conditions, a central forecast can provide a base of comparison for agency forecasts. Inefficient tax administration in some countries has caused lags in the elasticities of taxes relative to rises in incomes. Tax administration might be more stringent if collecting agencies are required to explain differences between their collections and the projections of outside forecasters. Where data is lacking to develop reliable causal models, time-series techniques tempered by judgmental adjustments may be the most appropriate.

Global interdependence is one of the problems confronted by forecasters in developing nations. The economies, and the revenue forecasts, of developing nations are often greatly dependent upon international economic events over which they may have little control. National revenue forecasts in Indonesia, for example, require forecasts of the world supply and demand for oil. Other developing nations are similarly dependent upon shifts in world markets for various commodities. As the economies of the developed nations become increasingly intertwined, it is likely that the revenue forecasters in the developed nations will also be looking at international economic variables, especially for longer-term forecasts.

How Should Revenue Forecasting Be Organized?

Where should revenue forecasting be located in a government and who should be responsible for it? In the federal government, both the locus and the responsibility for revenue forecasting are divided. The Council of Economic Advisors (CEA) has responsibility for fundamental economic forecasts in the executive branch, but it is the Office of Tax Analysis (OTA) of the Treasury Department that prepares the revenue forecasts that underlie the President's budget recommendations. On the legislative side, staffs of the Joint Committee on Taxation (JCT) and the Congressional Budget Office (CBO) prepare separate revenue forecasts. The estimates of the JCT are the only official source of revenue estimates during congressional debate. The Gramm-Rudman-Hollings deficit reduction mechanism uses an average of CBO and executive forecasts for calculating probable deficits.

Table 4 shows the frequency of participation in revenue forecasting by members of the states' executive and legislative branches. It also shows the relative frequency of advisory participation by persons from the private sector. In 25 of the 33 responding

Table 4 Organizational Locus of Revenue Forecasting in the States, 33 States Responding

Participant	Official forecast	Other forecast(s)	Advisory role
Executive	25	3	
Legislature	2	18	
Joint executive/legislative	5		
Private sector	1		17

Data compiled from Public Policy Institute of New York (1985).

states, the "official" responsibility for revenue forecasts resides in the executive branch, most commonly within the central budget office. Only two of the states place official responsibility solely in the legislature, but six officially share responsibility jointly between the two branches. Note that in most states, revenue forecasting is done in both branches. When a legislature does not do the official forecast, it is likely to do its own.

The states, then, have adopted a pattern that resembles that of the federal government. Revenue forecasting is not the exclusive prerogative of either branch. The obvious consequence of this fact is that the revenue forecasters in each branch of government must somehow relate themselves and their forecasts to one another. In this regard, the states are a step ahead of the federal government. Although staff members of the two federal branches do interact somewhat, there is no formal procedure to bring the forecasters of the two branches together, and their forecasts typically compete for attention and acceptance.

In 17 of the 33 states that responded to the Public Policy Institute's survey (1985), efforts have been made to arrive at some sort of consensus among revenue forecasters. Where a consensus approach exists, underlying assumptions are likely to be questioned within the context of the forecasting process rather than on the floor of a legislature. It seems desirable for legislatures to continue to develop independent forecasting capacities, for doing so may improve accuracy (Bretschneider and Gore, 1987). Independent forecasts can be used to bring questionable underlying assumptions to light. The existence of competing forecasts without a means of arriving at consensus, however, invites partisan political argument over forecasts. Such argument is likely to be motivated more by political agendas than by a desire to improve accuracy.

It would be presumptuous and naive to suggest that there is a single structure or process that is best for revenue forecasting. The existing literature relative to revenue forecasting, however, does suggest several considerations. First, outmoded underlying assumptions are a common cause of forecast error (see Ascher, 1978), and administrative arrangements that encourage the questioning of underlying assumptions are therefore desirable. The existence of an independent forecast is likely to raise such questions. Surrounding the revenue forecasting process with secrecy, however, is likely to have the opposite effect.

Second, the forecasting function should be organized to assure close interaction between forecasters and several other groups of public officials. Close working relationships with the revenue collecting agency are needed to monitor receipts and develop useful data histories. Interaction with budget analysts is needed to keep the latter group aware of the degree of uncertainty and possible future constraints on expenditures. The most important set of interactions, though, is the set of those between forecasters and elected officials.

ORGANIZING FOR LEARNING

As discussed above, interactions between forecasters and elected officials can affect the knowledge of both groups about the workings of an economy. The results of this writer's research (Klay, 1985) into the factors affecting the knowledge of these two groups are summarized in Fig. 1. The knowledge of both forecasters and elected officials about the dynamics of their jurisdiction's economy is apparently related to the presence of active efforts to use computers to explore causal relations (modeling and simulation) as well as to the propensity of elected officials to ask questions about underlying assumptions.

There is slight evidence to indicate that organizational structure and process affects the accuracy of revenue forecasts. The work of Bretschneider et al. (1989) suggests that accuracy may improve slightly where forecasts are done by independent agencies and where interactive procedures exist to combine competing forecasts. Accuracy may suffer where too much reliance is placed upon outside advisors and where a single political party or ideology dominates. It may be that such dominance of perspective, or reliance upon outsiders, depresses the propensity of participants to raise questions about underlying assumptions. The reader should be aware, however, that the findings regarding relationships between organizational structure and process and forecast accuracy are very tenuous.

Fortunately, there is a great deal of overlap between some of these findings and those pertaining to the correlates of learning. The interactive, consensus-oriented processes that might contribute to greater accuracy also seem to enhance the knowledge of elected officials. There is doubt as to whether elaborate causal models contribute to forecast accuracy, for simpler methods typically forecast aggregate revenues as well. The advantages of detailed forecasting models pertain more to learning for policy development. Only detailed models allow forecasters to simulate the possible impacts of specific changes in tax laws or spending policies. In governments where such modeling and simulation activity is present, both forecasters and elected officials seem to learn more.

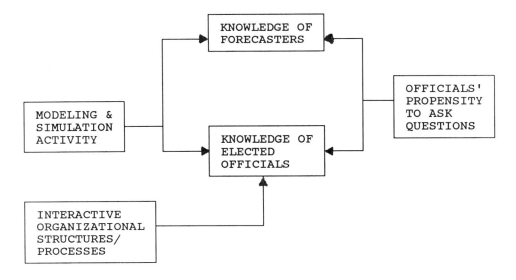

Figure 1   Factors affecting knowledge about economy.

The growing presence and capacity of computers offers increasing opportunities for learning. The cost of computer simulation runs has decreased markedly (Bodkin and Marwah, 1988). Moreover, new forms of computer-based simulations are now being developed to extend budgetary forecasting beyond the limits of econometrics. Chen's (1988) systems dynamics model of a state revenue process, for example, enables policymakers to study long-term interactions between public opinion and revenues. Forecasters would be wise to search for ways to use the potential of computers to enhance learning.

Revenue forecasting is important in two respects. It sets the parameters for budget deliberations. What is often overlooked, however, is that revenue forecasting is also a process of inquiry that can educate its participants. Revenue forecasting is often the only arena in which a government systematically explores aspects of its own future. When it is organized to enhance the knowledge of its elected officials, it may also promote improvements in the quality of a government's policies. Neglecting the potential of revenue forecasting to promote learning would be a waste.

REFERENCES

Adams, C. F., Jr. (1976). Forecasting Annual Tax Revenues: An Examination of Procedures Incorporating a Least Squares Estimating Methodology, Illustrated for a State General Sales Tax. Unpublished Ph.D. dissertation, State University of New York at Albany.

Armstrong, J. S. (1983). Relative accuracy of judgmental and extrapolative methods in forecasting annual earnings, *Journal of Forecasting* 2:437–447.

Ascher, W. (1978). *Forecasting: An Appraisal for Policy-Makers and Planners*. Johns Hopkins, Baltimore.

Bahari-Kashani, H. (1983). Revenue Forecasting in Washington State: The Development of a Model. Unpublished Ph.D. dissertation, Washington State University, Pullman.

Bahl, R., Schroeder, L., and Montrone, W. (1979). Forecasting municipal revenues and expenditures. ICMA Management Information Service Report, 11.

Blumenfeld, A. (1973). The Revenue and Equity Impacts of Adding Service Transactions to the Base of a Retail Sales Tax. Unpublished Ph.D. dissertation, University of Colorado.

Bodkin, R. G., and Marwah, K. (1988). Trends in macroeconomic modeling: The past quarter century. *Journal of Policy Modeling* 10:299–315.

Bohm, R. A., and Craig, E. D. (1987). The stability of revenues from state sales taxes. In *Proceedings of the Seventy-Ninth Annual Conference on Taxation, 1986*, S. J. Bowers (ed.), National Tax Association-Tax Institute of America, Columbus, Ohio.

Boswell, C. R., and Carpenter, J. M. (1986). Long range financial forecasting in Fort Worth. *Government Finance Review* 2:7–10.

Box, G. E. P., and Jenkins, G. M. (1976). *Time Series Analysis: Forecasting and Control*, 2nd ed. Holden-Day, San Francisco.

Bretschneider, S., and Gorr, W. (1987). State and local government revenue forecasting. In *The Handbook of Forecasting*, 2nd ed., S. Makridakis and S. Wheelright (eds.), John Wiley, New York, pp. 118–134.

Bretschneider, S., and Schroeder, L. (1985). Revenue forecasting, budget setting and risk, *Socio-Economic Planning Sciences* 19:431–439.

Bretschneider, S., Gorr, W., Grizzle, G., and Klay, W. E. (1989). Political and organizational influences on forecast performance: Forecasting receipts from state sales taxes. *International Journal of Forecasting*, Special Issue.

Brown, R. G. (1959). *Statistical Forecasting for Inventory Control*. McGraw-Hill, New York.

Brundage, P. F. (1970). *The Bureau of the Budget*. Praeger, New York.

Buck, A. E. (1929). *Public Budgeting*. Harper and Row, New York.

Caiden, N., and Wildavsky, A. (1974). *Planning and Budgeting in Poor Countries*. Wiley, New York.

Carter, S. R., Jr. (1984). Performance and Adequacy of a State Tax System: The Case of Tennessee. Unpublished Ph.D. dissertation, University of Tennessee, Knoxville.

Cassidy, G., Kamlet, M. S., and Nagin, D. S. (1989). An empirical examination of bias in revenue forecasts by state governments. *International Journal of Forecasting*, Special Issue.

Chambers, J. C., Mullick, S. K., and Smith, D. D. (1971). How to choose the right forecasting technique. *Harvard Business Review*, 49:45–74.

Chang, S. (1976). Forecasting revenues to municipal governments: The case of Mobile, Alabama. *Governmental Finance* 5:16–20.

Chang, S. (1979). Municipal revenue forecasting. *Growth and Change* 10:38–46.

Chapman, J. (1982). Fiscal stress and budget activity. *Public Budgeting and Finance* 2:83–87.

Chen, F. (1988). A simulation model of the Florida state funding system: A floritax system dynamics experiment. Paper presented to annual conference of the American Society for Public Administration, Portland, Ore.

Congressional Budget Office. (1981). *A Review of the Accuracy of Treasury Forecasts, 1963–1978*. U.S. Congress, Washington, D.C.

Congressional Budget Office. (1984). *An Analysis of Congressional Budget Estimates for Fiscal Years 1980–1982*. U.S. Congress, Washington, D.C.

Cooper, G. D., Huggins, J. A., and James, W. F. (1978). Simulations with the tax sector of a quarterly state econometric model. Mimeograph, Office of the Florida State Economist.

Cupoli, E. M. (1987). A Forecasting Model of Local Government Finances: A Case Study Approach—Syracuse, NY. Unpublished Ph.D. dissertation, Syracuse University, Syracuse, N.Y.

Danziger, J. N., Dutton, W. H., Kling, R., and Kramer, K. L. (1982). *Computers and Politics*. Columbia University Press, New York.

de Jouvenel, B. (1967). *The Art of Conjecture*. Basic Books, New York.

Frank, H. A. (1988). Model Utility along the Forecast Continuum: A Case Study in Florida Local Government Revenue Forecasting. Unpublished Ph.D. dissertation, Florida State University, Tallahassee.

Friedlander, A. F., Swanson, G. J., and Due, J. F. (1973). Estimating sales tax revenue changes in response to changes in personal income and sales tax rates. *National Tax Journal* 26:103–110.

Fullerton, T. M. (1989). A composite approach to forecasting state government revenues: Case study of the Idaho sales tax. *International Journal of Forecasting*, Special Issue.

Galper, H., and Pollock, S. H. (1988). Tax models in policy analysis at the state and local level. In *Proceedings of the Eightieth Annual Conference on Taxation, 1987*, F. D. Stocker (ed.), National Tax Association-Tax Institute of America, Pittsburgh, pp. 137–144.

Giovinazzo, V. J. (1971). State Revenue Estimating: An Econometric Approach Applied to Conditions in New Jersey. Unpublished Ph.D. dissertation, New York University, New York.

Grizzle, G., and Klay, W. E. (1986). Revenue forecasting in the states: New dimensions of budgetary forecasting. Paper presented to annual conference of the American Society for Public Administration, Anaheim, Calif.

Gupta, B. N. (1967). *Government Budgeting: With Special Reference to India*. Asia Publishing House, Bombay.

Hambor, J. C., Norman, M. R., and Russell, R. R. (1974). A tax revenue forecasting model for the state of Hawaii. *Public Finance Quarterly* 2:432–450.

Henderson, H. H. (1978). Revenue forecasting in a working perspective. *Governmental Finance* 7:11–15.

Huggins, J. A. (1975). An Annual Econometric Forecasting Model of the State of Florida. Unpublished Ph.D. dissertation, Florida State University, Tallahassee.

Hyclak, T. J. (1976). Projecting Local Government Revenue and Expenditure. Unpublished Ph.D. dissertation, University of Notre Dame, Notre Dame, Ind.

Kamlet, M. S., Mowery, D. C., and Su, T. (1987). Whom do you trust? An analysis of executive and congressional economic forecasts. *Journal of Policy Analysis and Management* 6:365–384.

King, R. L. (1979). Forecasting monthly tax revenue flows in the District of Columbia. Mimeograph, District of Columbia Department of Finance and Revenue.

Klay, W. E. (1985). The organizational dimension of budgetary forecasting: Suggestions from revenue forecasting in the states. *International Journal of Public Administration* 7:241–265.

Klay, W. E., and Zingale, J. A. (1980). Revenue estimating as seen from an administrative perspective. Paper presented to 35th Annual Conference of Revenue Estimating, National Association of Tax Administrators, Dearborn, Mich.

Larkey, P. D., and Smith, R. A. (1984). The misrepresentation of information in governmental budgeting. In *Advances in Information Processing in Organizations,* L. S. Sproull and P. D. Larkey (eds.), JAI Press, New York, pp. 63–93.

Levin, M. S. (1975). Cost-revenue impact analysis: State of the art. *Urban Land* 34:8–15.

MacManus, S. A., and Grothe, B. (1986). Revenue forecasting techniques and reactions to fiscal stress: Select U.S. counties. Paper presented to annual conference of the American Society for Public Administration, Anaheim, Calif.

Makridakis, S. (1987). The future of forecasting. In *The Handbook of Forecasting,* 2nd ed., S. Makridakis and S. Wheelwright (eds.), John Wiley, New York.

McLoon, E. P., Lupo, G. C., and Mushkin, S. J. (1967). *Long-Range Revenue Estimation.* George Washington University, Washington, D.C.

McNown, R. (1986). On the uses of econometric models: A guide for policy makers. *Policy Sciences* 19:359–380.

Meltsner, A. J. (1971). *The Politics of City Revenue.* University of California Press, Berkeley.

Mizrach, B., and Santomero, A. M. (1986). The stability of money demand and forecasting through changes in regimes. *Review of Economics and Statistics* 68:324–328.

National Conference of State Legislatures, (1986). Planning ahead for a rainy day: State budget stabilization funds. *Fiscal Letter* 8 (Jan/Feb).

Norris, D. F. (1988). Microcomputers in financial management: Case studies of eight American cities. *Public Budgeting and Finance* 8:69–82.

Ostrowski, J. W., Gardner, E. P., and Motawi, M. (1986). Microcomputers in public finance organizations: A survey of uses and trends, *Government Finance Review* 2:23–29.

Penner, R. (1982). Forecasting budget totals: Why can't we get it right? In *The Federal Budget: Economics and Politics,* M. J. Boskin and A. Wildavsky (eds.), Institute for Contemporary Studies, San Francisco.

Perry, W. A. (1971). A Computerized Model for Forecasting Revenue from Changes in the Iowa Individual Income Tax Provisions. Unpublished Ph.D. dissertation, University of Oklahoma, Norman.

Pierce, L. C. (1971). *The Politics of Fiscal Policy Formation.* Goodyear, Pacific Palisades, Calif.

Pindyck, R. S., and Rubinfeld, D. L. (1981). *Econometric Models and Economic Forecasts,* 2nd ed. McGraw-Hill, New York.

Public Policy Institute of New York. (1985). *An Analysis of State Revenue Forecasting Systems.* Albany, N.Y.

Reed, D. A. (1983). A Simultaneous Equations Tax Revenue Forecasting Model for the State of Indiana. Unpublished D.B.A. dissertation, Indiana University, Bloomington.

Ridgeway, T. R. (1974). The Responsiveness of Nevada State Tax Revenues to Changing Economic Conditions. Unpublished Ph.D. dissertation, University of Arizona, Tucson.

Robb, E. H. (1971). A Quarterly Econometric Model of Michigan. Unpublished Ph.D. dissertation, Michigan State University, East Lansing.

Rubin, I. S. (1987). Estimated and actual urban revenues: Exploring the gap. *Public Budgeting and Finance* 7:83–94.

Shaw, L. G. (1982). The Impact of Energy Facility Development on Local Government Revenues. Unpublished Ph.D. dissertation, West Virginia University, Morgantown.

Simon, H. A. (1973). Applying information technology to organization design. *Public Administration Review* 33:268–278.

Stockman, D. (1985). *The Triumph of Politics*. Harper and Row, New York.

Tandjung, I. (1987). The Estimation of Central Government Revenues in Indonesia. Unpublished Ph.D. dissertation, University of Illinois at Urbana-Champaign.

U.S. Congress, Joint Economic Committee (JEC). (1975). Five Year Budget Projections. Hearings Before Subcommittee on Priorities and Economy in Government.

Vehorn, C. L., McCool, T. J., and Jantscher, G. R. (1988). Revenue estimation: A more prominent part of tax policy. GAO Journal 2:64–71.

Vosche, J., and Williams, B. (1987). Optimal governmental budgeting contingency reserve funds. *Public Budgeting and Finance* 7:66–82.

White, M., and White, A. (1955). Model building approach to forecasting the New York City sales tax. *National Tax Journal,* 8:372–378.

Wolkoff, M. (1987). An evaluation of municipal rainy day funds. *Public Budgeting and Finance* 7:52–63.

Woods, M. D., and Dockson, G. A. (1984). A simulation model for community development planning. *Journal of the Community Development Society* 15:47–57.

Worthley, J. A., and Heaphy, J. J. (1978). Computer technology and public administration in state government. *The Bureaucrat* 7:32–37.

10

Governmental Accounting: An Overview

Khi V. Thai *School of Public Administration, Florida Atlantic University, Fort Lauderdale, Florida*

INTRODUCTION

Moneys collected and spent by governments must be recorded in a file, called the accounting system. Actions prior to revenue collections and cash disbursements, such as budget appropriations, apportionments, allotments, tax levies, and purchase orders, must also be accounted for. Without a good accounting system, accountability in budgeting cannot be preserved because taxpayers have no way to control the handling of public moneys by government officials. Unfortunately, in the field of public budgeting and financial management, the role of accounting is overlooked and there is a missing link between budget and accounting systems. In the federal government, for instance, budget and accounting systems are not prepared on the same basis: Programs, activities and organizational units are the basis of the budget, whereas objects of expenditure are the major focus of accounting. Therefore, Bowsher (1985, p. 177), the Comptroller General of the United States, recommended: "Budgeting and accounting should be on the same basis and use the same reporting categories so that meaningful management reports can be produced." In efforts to link budget and accounting systems, accounting should be treated as an integrated part of the budgetary process. This chapter will explain the importance of and trace the developments of governmental accounting and compare governmental accounting with business accounting; describe the accounting cycle; and explain the generally accepted accounting principles.

OVERVIEW OF GOVERNMENTAL ACCOUNTING

Governmental accounting is the art of analyzing, recording, summarizing, evaluating, and interpreting a governmental entity's financial activities and position, and communicating the results to those who are interested in government financial conditions.

Importance of Governmental Accounting

Governmental accounting is important for several reasons. First, it can provide policymakers and administrators with the reliable, relevant, and timely information they need to evaluate government performance and to set a course of future action. As an information system, accounting consists of a variety of functions ranging from data collection, processing, and control, to summarization, distribution, and interpretation (Buckley and Lightner, 1973, p. 4).

Second, every organization, whether private or governmental, has only a limited amount of resources at its disposal. The scarcity of public sector resources was widely felt recently with the tax revolt and spending ceiling movements. Every policy affecting future resources allocation necessarily involves either implicit or explicit comparison of the cost incurred or to be incurred with the benefits received or expected. Governmental accounting is a tool for the recording and forecasting of costs and benefits, and a prerequisite to effective budget execution.

Finally, accounting can provide policymakers, management, and interested citizens with a high level of confidence that government appropriations are not overspent and public resources are being used properly (Lodal, 1976). Sound accounting and reporting standards and procedures help assure that public resources be safeguarded.

Developments of Governmental Accounting

The origin of government accounting is sometimes traced to ancient governments. In the United States, the importance of accounting and reporting to governmental financial management and accountability was recognized in the U.S. Constitution: "A regular statement and account of the receipts and expenditures of all public money shall be published from time to time" (Article I, Section 9).

Tracing the development of governmental accounting in the United States is difficult because there is not a uniform accounting system. In Great Britain, France, and many other countries, local government accounting standards were set—or at least influenced—by the central or national government. In the United States, accounting systems and standards have evolved more or less independently at each level of governments, federal, state, and local. The Governmental Accounting Standards Board (GASB) and its predecessor, the National Council on Governmental Accounting (NCGA), have fostered accounting developments for state and local governments. The U.S. General Accounting Office (GAO) has played a leading role in setting accounting and auditing standards at the federal government level. However, accounting standards of the federal government and state and local governments have been brought closer together by each revision of statements of federal accounting standards. Moreover, since GAO was a prime mover in the establishment of GASB, this trend toward similarity is expected to continue (Hay, 1989, p. 663).

Developments in State and Local Governmental Accounting

The private sector is dominant in the American economy, and most citizens believe that less government is better. This was also true in the sphere of governmental accounting, which had not received much attention from researchers and accounting experts. The federal, state, and local governments did little before the turn of the twentieth century to improve recordkeeping and financial information, and they adopted business accounting. At the turn of this century, there were scandalous practices in the financial management of many cities, which resulted in a flurry of changes in accounting and reporting practices. The National Municipal League, which was established in 1894, suggested uniform municipal reporting formats. At the same time, the Census Bureau was interested in developing uniformity in city accounts and reports. In 1901, at the request of the Merchants' Club, Haskins and Sells, a private accounting firm, investigated the affairs of the city of Chicago and installed a completely new accounting system for that city.

The cities of Newton, Mass., and Baltimore, Md., published annual reports during 1901 and 1902 along lines suggested by the National Municipal League. In 1904, the state of New York passed legislation requiring uniform accounting and reporting; Massachusetts followed New York's action in 1906. Other states and cities enacted similar reforms in the period up to 1920, but the most important influence in government accounting developments in this period unquestionably was the formation in 1906 of the Bureau on Municipal Research, whose publications included what were essentially treaties on municipal accounting.

By the mid 1920s most major American cities had undergone a more or less thorough reform in governmental accounting. The pace of adoption of uniform accounting and reporting was accelerated in the 1920s by the passage of the Eighteenth Amendment and the corresponding loss of municipal revenue from taxes on the sale of alcoholic beverages, and by demands for more and expanded municipal programs.

Another significant development in governmental accounting came in 1934, with the emergence of the National Committee on Municipal Accounting under the auspices of the Municipal Finance Officers Association. Since then, numerous publications discussing proper and improved practice in municipal accounting and other areas of public budgeting and financial management have come from this Committee and the Municipal Finance Officers Association.

In 1951, the Committee, by then known as the National Committee on Governmental Accounting, published *Municipal Accounting and Auditing,* a compendium and revision of its major publications. This work became the "bible" of municipal accounting and has been the basis for the major modern textbooks in the field as well as for many state laws and guides relating to municipal accounting, reporting, and auditing. *Municipal Accounting and Auditing* was succeeded in 1968 by *Governmental Accounting, Auditing, and Financial Reporting* (GAAFR), often referred to as "the blue book" (Freeman et al., 1988, p. 24). The GAAFR principles are applicable not only to local but also to state governments. Some principles of GAAFR, however, were being criticized by many academicians, researchers, and practitioners. Thus, the National Council of Governmental Accounting (NCGA) revised the 1968 pronouncement of its predecessor, the National Committee on Governmental Accounting, in the late 1970s and early 1980s.

However, governmental accounting practices in state and local governments are still inadequate. As stated in the exposure draft report of the Governmental Accounting Standards Board Organization Committee (1981, p. 3), the levels of adherence to established accounting standards by state and local governments "have found to be relatively low." Many governmental accounting experts had made a similar observation. For example, the chairman and chief executive of Arthur Anderson and Co. asserted: "Financial reporting and accounting standards and the accounting systems and controls of many state and local governmental entities are deficient." The Public Finance Council of the Securities Industry Association also stated: "Uniform accounting practices do not exist." The above statements were made in February 1976 before the Senate Committee on Banking and Urban Affairs. Compliance with the generally accepted accounting principles (GAAP) has been so low that there is a saying, "GAAP isn't GAAP," that is, these principles are not generally accepted in governmental accounting practices (Hefferon, 1977, p. 44).

There were several reasons for the problem with GAAFR compliance. First, there did not exist a unique source of current state and local governmental accounting principles. Actually, before the establishment of the Governmental Accounting Standards

Board (GASB)* in 1984, accounting principles for state and local governments were derived from a number of sources:

1. The National Council on Governmental Accounting (NCGA) and its predecessors, the National Committee on Governmental Accounting and the National Committee on Municipal Accounting, promulgated accounting principles via its *Governmental Accounting, Auditing and Financial Reporting* (GAAFR), published in 1968, and revised and published several times in the 1980s. This publication, endorsed by the American Institute of Certified Public Accountants, has been considered a "bible" or "blue book" for state and local government accountants.

2. Pronouncements of the American Institute of Certified Public Accountants (AICPA) also set forth generally accepted accounting principles for state and local governments. One of those, *Audits of State and Local Government Units* (AICPA, 1980/1989), an industry audit guide, was prepared in 1974 by the AICPA Committee on State and Local Government Accounting and modified several times to make the guide consistent with and complimentary to NCGA's revised GAFRR and the General Accounting Office's revised accounting and audit standards and procedures.

3. Pronouncements of the Financial Accounting Standards Board (FASB) and its predecessors, the AICPA's Accounting Principles Board, and before that, the AICPA's Committee on Accounting Procedure, were endorsed by NCGA for governmental enterprise funds such as utilities and transportation systems.

4. The federal government requires that its grant programs to state and local governments be reported in accordance with certain accounting requirements. The accounting and reporting requirements are in some cases embodied in laws enacting grant programs, or in other cases set forth in circulars issued by the Office of Management and Budget.

5. Many states establish accounting and financial reporting practices for the state and its subgovernmental units including local governments.

The existence of multiple sources of accounting standards led to overlapping efforts, inconsistent conclusions, and thus the lack of compliance. Another major reason for the lack of accounting compliance was the lack of a nationwide mechanism enforcing governmental units to "prepare and publish financial reports in conformity with GAAP for issuance either to the general public or present and potential security holders" (GASBOC, 1981, p. 3). Why? First of all, many of the 80,000 state and local governmental units in the United States were not independently audited. Although many governmental auditors followed established standards as a matter of professional obligation, there was no enforcement mechanism to control the auditor's rules of professional conduct. Moreover, before 1980, bond-rating agencies did not require GAAP financial statements as a

---

*This organization has been the most influential group in the setting of standards for state and local governmental accounting and financial reporting. Its predecessor was the National Committee on Municipal Accounting, established in January 1934, and then reorganized in 1949 as the National Committee on Governmental Accounting, which was again reorganized in 1974 as the National Council on Governmental Accounting (NCGA). At the outset, NCGA worked under the auspices of the Municipal Finance Officers Association, then because autonomous with a broadly based membership. The NCGA ceased to exist when the Governmental Accounting Standards Board was established in 1984.

precondition to rating. Although since May 1980 Standard & Poor's Corporation, a major rating agency, has required, for its bond rating, certain criteria such as GAAP financial statements, the accrual basis of accounting, and the timely report, the impact of these requirements has been very limited in the existence of state-run or -sponsored municipal bond guarantee agencies such as municipal bond banks. Finally, the National Council of Governmental Accounting, a principal source of accounting standards for state and local governments, was perceived as an arm of another professional association, the Government Finance Officers Association, rather than as an independent body. It did not have the authority to enforce its pronouncements.

The third reason for the problem of compliance with generally accepted accounting principles (GAAP) was the distinctive environment of governmental accounting. State and local accountants are preoccupied with compliance with the various legal and contractual requirements, regulations, and restrictions that affect their financial management and accounting. A lack of legal compliance may jeopardize their careers. Meanwhile, there is no danger for them for not complying with GAAP. The importance of legal compliance is stated by GASB (1987, p. 33): "A governmental accounting system must make it possible both: (a) to present fairly and with full disclosure the financial position and results of financial operations of the funds and account groups of the governmental unit in conformity with generally accepted accounting principles, and (b) to determine and demonstrate compliance with finance-related legal and contractual provisions."

In addition to the lack of GAAP compliance, the governmental accounting standard-setting structure had certain shortcomings. First of all, although NCGA was the principal source of accounting standards for state and local governments, it consisted mostly of fiscal officers of governments and was not broadly representative of users of governmental financial reports. Second, NCGA was not independent or free of undue influence by any particular segment of its constituency. The NCGA was perceived as an arm of the Municipal Finance Officers Association, now renamed Government Finance Officers' Association. Third, NCGA had limited financial resources provided by the Government Finance Officers Association. Finally, it did not have enough manpower to deal with accounting problems as they emerged. The NCGA consisted of 21 volunteer members who served part-time and met periodically. Thus its members could not devote their efforts to a problem continuously without other intrusions and pressures. Moreover, they were likely to be faced with the dilemma of divided loyalties between the standard-setting board and their employers. Finally, as a part-time body, NCGA was not able to deal with the backlog of issues on a timely basis.

For the above reasons, a new governmental accounting standard-setting body was established in 1984. This new structure consists of three integrated parts: the existing Financial Accounting Foundation (FAF), the Governmental Accounting Standards Board (GASB), and the Governmental Accounting Standards Advisory Council (GASAC), as illustrated in Fig. 1.

The existing FAF, established in 1973, appoints, funds and oversees GASB and GASAC as it has done for the Financial Accounting Standards Advisory Council and the Financial Accounting Standards Board, a standard-setting body for the private sector accounting. In accordance with the structural agreement under which GASB was formed, the FAF board of trustees increased in membership from 12 to 15. The three new members would be governmental representatives.

The GASB consists of five members; the chairman is a full-timer, and the vice chairman and the three members are part-timers. The board members are appointed for

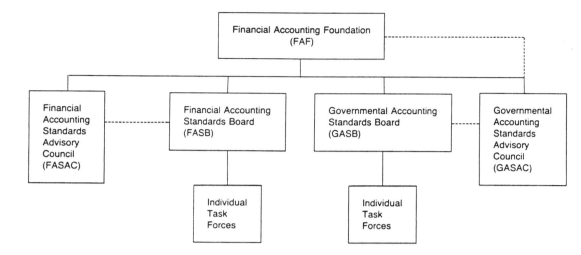

Figure 1   Governmental accounting standard-setting structures.

5-year terms by the FAF trustees after consulting with the national organizations of state, county, and municipal officials, and must be approved by GASAC. The mission of GASB is to establish or improve standards of accounting and reporting for state and local governments. GASB is staffed by a director of research, and technical and administrative staff members. Its first-year budget was $709,000 in operating expenses and $1,092,000 in operating revenues (Financial Accounting Foundation, 1985). Unlike its predecessor (NCGA), the new GASB is operated on a full-time basis, better staffed and financed.

The GASAC would consist of no fewer than 20 members nominated by various professional organizations representative of GASB's constituencies and appointed by FAF for 1-year terms but not more than four consecutive terms. The Advisory Council advises GASB on its technical agenda and helps it to establish project priorities, reviews and approves the FAF board of trustees' appointment for the GASB members, reviews GASB's operating budget prior to approval by the FAF board of trustees, and advises on selection of GASB task force members, and participates with the FAF board of trustees in structure review of GASB operations.

First appointments to both the GASB and GASAC were made in the spring of 1984. The Advisory Council held its first meeting in May 1984, and the GASB's first meeting was held a month later. Upon commencing operations, GASB issued Statement No. 1, "Authoritative Status of NCGA Pronouncements and AICPA Industry Audit Guide," in July 1984 to recommend that the currently effective pronouncements of the former NCGA and the AICPA would remain in force until replaced or modified. Moreover, an initial project agenda was established that was loaded with eight subjects reflecting current debatable issues in state and local governmental accounting. Since its establishment to the present, numerous statements and interpretations concerning critical accounting issues and concepts have been issued.

As required, the GASB was reviewed after its first 5 years of existence. The findings and recommendations of GASB review committee were included in the "Report of the Committee to Review Structure for Governmental Accounting Standards," published in early 1989. The review committee concluded that GASB has performed well and should continue to function under the Financial Accounting Foundation. It recommended several structure improvements. First, GASB should become a board of five full-time members, phased in over a period of 3 years, and the position of research director should be separate from that of board member. Second, GASAC's approval authority over FAF appointments should continue. Third, FAF should establish written criteria for GASB member selection, and one additional seat for a person with a government background should be added to the FAF board of trustees. Finally, the report also included recommendations concerning the jurisdictional dispute between GASB and the Financial Accounting Standards Board over certain "special entities," as will be explained in detail later in this chapter.

Developments in Federal Governmental Accounting

Although accounting systems have been a concern of the federal government and numerous statutes regarding accounting requirements have been issued since 1789, the development of federal accounting has lagged far behind the growth in complexity of federal governmental operations. Indeed, the federal government had done little before the close of World War II to improve its own recordkeeping, financial measurement reporting, and auditing. When the first U.S. Congress met in 1789, it was faced with the task of organizing the new government. One of the most perplexing problems of this task was controlling and accounting for public funds. Although the Act of September 2, 1789, established the Treasury Department in the executive branch, a very close relationship of this department with the Congress was ordered; the Treasury Secretary was required to report to the Congress in person or in writing all services relative to "finances." Despite the Congress's pledge to keep close touch with the Treasury Department, its controls were soon relaxed: the failure of the House of Representatives to entertain oral reports from the Treasury Secretary was followed by a gradual impairment of the Treasury Department's review mechanisms and procedures. Recognizing that its fiscal controls were gradually being weakened, the Congress repeatedly enacted correcting legislation including the Act of March 3, 1809 requiring public money to be accounted for in accordance with appropriations, and the Act of January 31, 1823 prohibiting the advance of public funds.

The most significant action of the Congress in accounting, however, was the enactment of the Budget and Accounting Act of 1921 establishing and authorizing the General Accounting Office (GAO) to audit and settle all public accounts, and to prescribe the forms, systems, and procedures for administrative appropriation and fund accounting (GAO, 1985a, pp. 1.3–1.6)

Although GAO was empowered to prescribe principles, standards, and related requirements for accounting, cooperating in the development and improvement of agency accounting and financial management systems, and reviewing and approving agency accounting systems, during the period from 1921 to the end of World War II GAO was primarily preoccupied with detailed auditing of individual vouchers. During this period, GAO's work "was characterized by a highly formal, legalistic review of each voucher, with approval for payment and the settlement of the affected accounts being dependent on the payment's conforming to an elaborate set of rules governing the use of public funds" (Havens, 1990, p. 2). The voucher audit focus utterly collapsed under the workload pressure of a growing government during the New Deal. Even with a staff of over 14,000 of whom most were auditing clerks, GAO could not keep up with the wave of vouchers. In its 1945 annual report, GAO reported a backlog of 35 million unaudited vouchers.

In coping with this problem, in 1947, after the end of World War II, a new approach to financial management and auditing was initiated: The executive departments and agencies would do their own voucher checking and accounting, and GAO would concentrate on prescribing accounting principles and standards and checking the adequacy of agency accounting and financial management systems. Consequently, the GAO staff shrank from almost 15,000 to about 6000 in 1953. The composition of staff has also changed from auditing clerks to professionals (Havens, 1990, pp. 4–5).

Also in 1947, a joint program for improving financial management was undertaken as an outgrowth of discussions between the Comptroller General, the Secretary of the Treasury, and the Director of the Bureau of the Budget (now the Office of Management and Budget). The most significant development in the federal accounting was the passage of the Budget and Accounting Procedures Act in 1950. The provisions of this act were based largely on the recommendations of the first Hoover Commission. The professional accounting consultants to this commission had been influenced strongly by the recommendations of NCGA (Hay, 1989, p. 663) and by the use, in private business, of accrual accounting. The 1950 act provides, among others, that:

The Comptroller General be responsible for prescribing the principles, standards, and related requirements for accounting for the guidance of the executive agencies.
Unified accounting and reporting systems be established in the Treasury Department to provide data on the financial operations and position of the government as a whole.
Adequate and effective agency accounting systems be established and maintained by the head of each agency to conform to principles and standards prescribed by GAO.

In compliance with the 1950 act, the General Accounting Office issued in 1952 the initial statements which "were in the form of (a) a general letter on the contribution of accounting to better management, and (b) Accounting Principles Memorandum No. 1 representing a comprehensive statement of broad principles and standards" (GAO, 1965, p. 2). These statements were supplemented in subsequent years by four additional accounting principles memorandums. In 1956, the Budget and Accounting Act of 1950 was amended (Public Law 84-863) to provide for use of accrual accounting, cost-based budgeting for internal operations and appropriation requests, and consistent classification.

In 1965, GAO issued a statement, "Accounting Principles and Standards for Federal Agencies," which replaced accounting principles memorandums issued beginning in 1952.

In 1972, the General Accounting Office issued a landmark document, *Governmental Auditing Standards: Standards for Audit of Governmental Organizations, Programs, Activities, and Functions,* known as the "Yellow Book," which has had significant influences not only on governmental auditing but also governmental accounting practices. This yellow book was significantly revised and issued in August 1989. The content of this document will be explored in detail in a later chapter, Governmental Auditing.

In 1978, the Congress passed a law (Public Law 95-595) to amend the Budget and Accounting Procedures Act of 1950. This amendment required that an annual report on an actuarial basis be provided by the Treasury Department to the Congress and General Accounting Office (GAO) and that GAO audit federal military and civil pension funds. A similar act, the District of Columbia Retirement Reform Act (Public Law 96-122), was also passed in 1979 to establish an actuarial basis for financing retirement benefits for police officers, firefighters, teachers, and judges of the District of Columbia.

Although GAO has set a goal of having all federal governmental accounting systems approved in the past several decades, this goal has not been reached yet. In 1982, the Congress passed the Federal Manager's Financial Integrity Act to strengthen internal control and accounting systems throughout the federal government and reduce fraud, waste, abuse, and misappropriation of federal funds. (For purposes of the act, the terms internal controls, internal accounting and administrative controls, and management controls are synonymous). The act also provided that the Office of Management and Budget prepare evaluation guidelines, in consultation with GAO, for use by agencies in determining whether their accounting systems are in compliance with GAO standards.

In order to make sure state and local governments are accountable for over $100 billion they receive in annual federal financial assistance, Congress passed the Single Audit Act in 1984 requiring an entity-wide audit of governments receiving $100,000 or more a year in federal financial assistance. This act forces state and local governments not only to meet the laws and regulations governing federal financial assistance programs but also to comply with GAAP. (See the chapter on Governmental Auditing for detailed information about the single audit.)

Despite those recent reform efforts, the federal government continues to be plagued by serious breakdowns in its financial management and accounting systems. In its various reports and testimonies, GAO (1984, 1985a, 1987a, 1988, 1989a, 1990) identified weaknesses and problems in federal financial management and accounting systems. In October 1989, OMB issued to each agency its critique of agency reporting under the Federal Managers' Financial Integrity Act, a list of 74 areas OMB has considered to be "high risk." Comptroller General Charles A. Bowsher stated: "Unless something more is done to correct the material deficiencies in management information and accounting systems, and material weaknesses in internal controls, *major issues of federal funds and the collateral fraud and abuse incidents will continue*" (GAO, 1990, p. 1).

Authoritative Sources of Governmental Accounting

According to GAO, there are three authoritative bodies for generally accepted accounting principles: the Governmental Accounting Standards Board (GASB), the Financial Accounting Standards Board (FASB), and the General Accounting Office (GAO, 1988, p. 2.1). GASB establishes accounting principles and financial reporting standards for state and local government entities. GAO establishes accounting principles and financial reporting standards for the federal government. FASB establishes accounting principles for nongovernment entities. In addition, some state and local governments and regulatory bodies also have established specific accounting principles. The American Institute of Certified Public Accountants cited another authoritative source of GAAP: *Preferred Accounting Practices for State Governments,* a research report issued in 1983 by the Council of State Government and NCGA. As stated by AICPA (1980/1989, p. 7), although having no official status and conflicting in some respects with current GAAP, this report represents the consensus views of the Project Committee, consisting of state financial officials and representatives of a number of public accounting firms. However, GASB (1987, p. xiv) does not formally cite it as an authoritative source of GAAP in the following GAAP hierarchy for state and local government accounting and financial reporting:

1.   Pronouncements of the Governmental Accounting Standards Board.
2.   Pronouncements of the Financial Accounting Standards Board.
3.   Pronouncements of bodies composed of expert accountants that follow a due process procedure, including broad distribution of proposed accounting principles for public

comment, for the intended of establishing accounting principles or describing existing practices that are generally accepted.
4. Practices or pronouncements that are widely recognized as being generally accepted because they represent prevalent practice in a particular industry or the knowledgeable application to specific circumstances of pronouncements that are generally accepted.
5. Other accounting literature.

Governmental Versus Business Accounting

Many governmental accounting observers believe that accounting for business and accounting for government are similar. A double-entry system of accounts applies to both governmental and commercial accounting. The accounting process is the same for both sectors: Documents form the basic record, transactions are recorded in journals of original entry and posted to general and subsidiary ledgers, trial balances are drawn to prove the equality of debits and credits, a chart of accounts is adopted to fit the organizational structure, and financial reports are prepared periodically and/or annually on the basis of information derived from the accounts. Moreover, with few exceptions, uniform accounting terms such as credit, debit, asset, liability, and equity, as will be explained later in this chapter, are used in both governmental and private sectors.

There are, however, major differences between governmental and business accounting. According to Freeman et al. (1988, pp. 12–13), governmental accounting and business accounting have different organizational objectives, sources of resources, and regulations and controls.

In addition, following are some, but not all, other principal differences between governmental and private accounting:

1. In governmental accounting, separate "funds" are required. Thus, the term "fund accounting" is used to mean accounting for governmental and other nonprofit organizations. The fundamentals of fund accounting will be discussed in depth later in this chapter. On the contrary, fund accounting is not used in the private sector.
2. In the private sector, the handling of fixed assets and depreciation is very clear: fixed assets must be recorded as assets on the balance sheet and are depreciated over their expected useful lives. In the government sector, fixed assets of a fund may or may not be recorded in that fund, and depreciation may or may not be recorded depending on the type of funds.
3. The term "transfer" is not used in business accounting. In governmental accounting, transfers are made frequently between funds. Such transfers often confuse the reader of the financial statements if they are not carefully disclosed.
4. Beside cash and accrual bases of accounting used in the private sector, governments also use encumbrance and modified accrual bases as will be explained later in this chapter.

GOVERNMENTAL ACCOUNTING EQUATION AND CYCLE

In order for governmental accounting to serve as a means of communication for budget decisions and fiscal accountability, it is important that certain fundamental conventions be established. These conventions are presented in the context of the accounting equation and cycle.

Accounting Equation

The accounting equation is the essence of double-entry accounting. It can be stated in several forms. The simplest one is given below:

$$\text{Assets} = \text{equities} \tag{1}$$

Assets are properties owned by a governmental unit or entity such as cash, taxes receivable, equipments, buildings and land. *Equities* represent rights to those properties. Equities may be divided into two principal types: creditor's equity and residual equity. The equities of creditors represent debts of a governmental unit or fund and are called *liabilities*. The residual equity implies the amount of assets that would be left after all debts or liabilities were paid, and are called the *fund balance*. To give recognition to the two basic types of equities, equation (1) is rewritten as follows:

$$\text{Assets} = \text{liabilities} + \text{fund balance} \tag{2}$$

"Liabilities" are customarily placed before "fund balance" in the accounting equation because creditors have preferential rights to the assets. The accounting equation is algebraic and all the rules of algebra apply. In the equation, any increase or decrease in one side must be followed by an increase or decrease of the same amount in the other side. Similarly, when an element in the equation is transferred to the other side of the equation, the sign of that element changes.

The fund balance or residual equity is sometimes given greater emphasis by transferring liabilities to the other side of the equation, yielding

$$\text{Assets} - \text{liabilities} = \text{fund balance} \tag{3}$$

All accounting transactions can be stated in terms of their effect on the three basic elements of the accounting equation.

Due to the complexity of the organizational operations, there are many transactions that affect the fund balance. These transactions consist of increases involving many different revenues, such as property taxes, licenses, and parking meter receipts, and decreases coming from many different expenditures, such as salaries and office supplies. If only the fund balance account were used to record these increases and decreases in fund balance, there would be confusion relative to the fund balance since the total would be constantly changing, and much useful, detailed information about revenues and expenditures would be lost. Therefore, it is desirable to record those increases or decreases in temporary accounts that facilitate analysis of the changes in the fund balance. These accounts are revenue and expenditure accounts.

Depending on the size of budget and the level of detailed information, one temporary account may be kept for revenues or expenditures. Thus, equation (2) can be expanded by the addition of revenues and expenditures as follows.

$$\text{Assets} = \text{liabilities} + \text{fund balance} + \text{revenues} - \text{expenditures} \tag{4}$$

However, by convention, no negative signs are used in accounting recording. In order to eliminate a negative sign in equation (4), the negative expenditure account is transferred to the left side of the equation to become positive as follows:

$$\text{Assets + expenditures = liabilities + revenue + fund balance} \qquad (5)$$

When recording a transaction, a governmental accountant or bookkeeper must know which accounts are affected by the transaction, and whether the accounts are increased or decreased. In accounting, the terms "debit" and "credit" are used to indicate "increase" or "decrease" in an account. Any debit of an account must be followed by a credit in the same amount of another account; and any credit of an account must be followed by a debit in the same amount of another account. This is basic double-entry accounting.

The accounting equation helps to identify debits or credits of accounts by following this rule: any increase in an account on the left of the accounting equation must be debited, and that increase must be followed (credited) by an increase of the same amount in an account in either side of the equation. In other words, debits are increases in assets and expenditure accounts, and decreases in liability, revenue, and fund balance accounts. Credits are decreases in assets and expenditure accounts, and increases in liability, revenue, and fund balance accounts.

Accounting Cycle

The accounting process is referred to as a cycle because the sequence is perpetually repeated. The accounting cycle consists of the sequence of events of the entire accounting process, from the initial recognition that a transaction should be recorded through the preparation of financial statements. Norvelle, 1989, p. 39)

To be more specific, an accounting cycle consists of the following steps (Fig. 2):

1. A transaction occurs and a source document is prepared or received.
2. The transaction is recorded in the journal or the book of original entry.
3. The journal entry is posted to the ledger.
4. A trial balance is prepared.

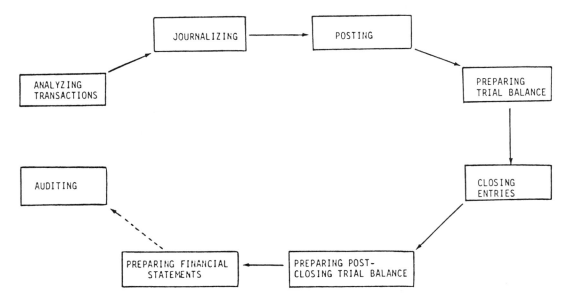

Figure 2   Basic phases in an accounting cycle.

5. Adjusting entries, if necessary, and closing entries are journalized and posted.
6. A postclosing trial balance is prepared.
7. Financial statements are prepared.

Transactions and Source Documents

A transaction is an economic event that affects the accounting equation. The effects of the event must be recorded in chronological order in a journal and in the proper accounts. The recording of every transaction is composed of an equal dollar amount of debit and credit. The evidence of a transaction is usually a business paper or an external document such as a vendor packing slip, shipping document, or a vendor invoice, and/or it may be an internal document such as a purchase requisition, a purchase order, a receiving report, or a check. The source document should provide all of the details of the transaction and must be kept in a file.

Journals: Books of Original Entry

The desirability of having a chronological and proper record of transactions led to the development of the journal, which is known as the book of original entry. Transactions are recorded first in the journal as they occur. *Journalizing* the transactions in a chronological order helps to simplify the task of later tracing some particular transaction. In order to facilitate the availability of information, most accounting systems make use of one or more journals. Following are some basic journals a governmental unit usually need:

Cash receipts journal: to record cash or checks received by the agency.
Cash disbursements journal: to record payments made by the agency.
Payroll journal: to record payroll checks paid by the agency.
Purchase journal: to record purchase orders issued by the agency.
General journal: to record all transactions that are not recorded in special journals.

The journals listed above, other than the general journal, are referred to as special journals. A typical journal (Fig. 3) contains the date, the titles of the accounts, the amounts of the debits and credits, the page number, and posting reference. In addition, explanatory comments generally follow the record of accounts and amounts.

Name of Government
General fund
General Journal
Fiscal year 19xx

Date	Account and explanation	Ref.	Debit	Credit
July 1	Cash	1	10,000	
	Taxes receivable - current property taxes 3		10,000	
	(To record collection of current year's property taxes)			
July 2	Expenditure	5	6,000	
	Vouchers payable	7		6,000
	(To record billings for materials and supplies)			

Figure 3 A typical journal form.

Name of Government
General Fund
General Ledgers
Fiscal year 19xx

Cash					Account No. 1

Date	Explanation	Ref.	Debit	Credit	Balance
	Opening balance				65,000
July 1		1	10,000		75,000

~~~~~~

Taxes Receivable					Account No. 3

Date	Explanation	Ref.	Debit	Credit	Balance
	Opening balance				150,000
July 1		3		10,000	140,000

~~~~~~

Figure 4   A typical ledger form.

Ledgers: Books of Final Entry

After being recorded in a journal, the transactions then are transferred or posted to a ledger at frequent and convenient intervals. *Posting* is the process of locating the specific account referred to in the journal and copying the amount of the debit or credit in the appropriate account. It can be performed manually or by the use of mechanical or electronic equipment, particularly computers. The *ledger* (Fig. 4) is composed of a number of accounts, which are (1) determined by the nature of the agency's operations, its volume of activities, and the extent of which details are needed, and (2) numbered to permit indexing and also for use as posting references in the journal. The order of the accounts in the ledger should agree with the order of the items in the balance sheets. A formally authorized order of accounts is referred to as the chart of accounts.

A ledger differs from a journal in many aspects. First, while *transactions* are a basic component for the journal, *accounts* are components for the ledger. Second, the ledger provides for the classification and summarization of data according to *function*, while the journal provides a detailed chronological history of the *financial events*. Third, while in the journal the individual transaction appears as a complete entity, in the ledger the individual transaction does not appear as a complete entity but it appears in different accounts. A governmental unit may need one or all of the following ledgers:

A *general ledger* consisting of every general ledger account in the governmental chart of accounts. Sometimes, a governmental unit maintains subsidiary ledgers for detailed records of revenues and expenditures in addition to the general ledger.

Operating ledgers for large governmental units. Revenues, appropriations, operating budgets, encumbrances, and expenditures can be recorded in operating ledgers consisting of a revenue ledger and a budget and expenditure ledger.

Name of Government
General Fund
Trial Balance
December 31, 19xx

	Debit	Credit
Cash	43,700	
Taxes Receivable -- Delinquent	42,100	
Taxes Receivable -- Current	18,300	
Vouchers Payable		16,500
Reserve for Encumbrances		23,000
Estimated Revenues	225,000	
Appropriations		215,000
Encumbrances	23,000	
Revenues		218,000
Expenditures	155,000	
Fund Balance		34,600
	-------	-------
	507,100	507,100

Figure 5   A trial balance form.

Payable ledgers and receivable ledgers. These ledgers can be added to record amounts for each individual or business to which the governmental unit owes money or that owes the government money.

Trial Balance

At the end of each accounting period, a summary of the ledger as set forth in the trial balance (Fig. 5) is prepared to determine that the mechanics of the recording and posting operations have been carried out accurately. The trial balance, where all general ledger accounts and their balances are listed, provides evidence that an equality of debits and credits exists in the ledger and can be transferred, without alteration, to the balance sheet and fund balance. The heading of the trial balance should identify completely the trial balance of a specific agency and ledger at a specific date. To prepare a trial balance, one must (1) "pencil foot," or write in small pencil figures, the total debits and the total credits of each account, (2) calculate the balance, the difference between the debit and credit totals in each account, and (3) list each account and its balance on the trial balance, which has two dollar columns—debit balances in the left column and credit balances in the right column. Total debits must equal total credits.

The mechanical equality of the account balances in the trial balance does not indicate the correctness of the accounting. The trial balance will still balance if a figure has been placed on the proper side but in the wrong account, if an incorrect amount has been recorded in a transaction, or if offsetting errors have been made.

Closing Entries

During the accounting period, a number of temporary accounts are employed in classifying and summarizing changes in the fund balance account. At the end of the fiscal period,* the balances in these accounts must be transferred into the fund balance account. This transferring process is called *closing*.

The following three steps are required to close the temporary accounts of a fund at the end of a period:

1. Obtain the balances of revenue and expenditure accounts from the trial balance, which is referred to now as the *preclosing trial balance*. This trial balance is the most convenient source of the balances of these temporary accounts.
2. Close the revenue accounts by debiting each revenue account and crediting the fund balance for the amount of the balance of each revenue account. The revenue accounts now have zero balances.
3. Close the expenditure accounts by crediting each expenditure account and debiting the fund balance for the amount of the balance of each expenditure account. The expenditure accounts are then closed because they have zero balances, but the closing entry becomes more complicated if there is an item or article ordered in one fiscal year but actually purchased in a preceding fiscal year, namely, an *encumbered expenditure*. The procedure for closing encumbrances is determined by the legal provisions of the government. Under the National Council on Governmental Accounting recommendations, the encumbrances should not be reported as expenditures or liabilities, but they should be reported as expenditures in the subsequent period in which the liability is incurred. Circumstances may occur with respect to legal provisions pertaining to closing entries for encumbrances:
    a. Where appropriations lapse at year end, even if encumbered, the closing entry should close everything pertaining to the appropriation. If an encumbered article is purchased in the year or years following the year of appropriation, the governmental unit may intend to honor the contract in progress at year end or cancel it. If the governmental unit intends to honor it, the appropriation for the fiscal year in which the article is purchased must contain authority for the expenditure.
    b. Where appropriations do not lapse at year end, or only unencumbered appropriations lapse, the closing entry should leave on the books the reserve for encumbrances account for subsequent year expenditures based on the encumbered appropriation authority carried over.

After being closed, the closing entries must be *journalized*. The entries are dated as of the last day of the accounting period, even though they are usually recorded at a later date. The account titles and amounts needed in journalizing the closing entries may be obtained from the ledger and fund balance. This process is applied to any adjustments due to errors.

Postclosing Trial Balance

After all of the temporary accounts have been closed, a trial balance, referred to as the *postclosing trial balance,* is prepared. The purpose of the postclosing trial balance is to assure that the ledger is in balance at the beginning of the new accounting cycle. The accounts and amounts of the postclosing trial balance should agree exactly with the accounts and amounts listed on the balance sheet at the end of the fiscal year.

*Accounting period may be daily, weekly, monthly, bimonthly, or semiannually, depending on the size of the organization and the information needs of management.

When these basic phases are completed, the accounting cycle begins again for the next fiscal year. The above accounting cycle does not include financial reporting. While many authors consider financial reporting as the final phase of the cycle (Buckley and Lightner, 1973, pp. 102–103; McCullers and Van Daniker, 1974, p. 2), some others do not (Niswanger and Fess, 1977, pp. 87–89; Granof, 1979, p. 58). Due to this reason and, particularly, its importance in the practices of public budgeting and financial management, financial reporting will be explored in a separate chapter.

GENERALLY ACCEPTED ACCOUNTING PRINCIPLES

As mentioned earlier, the federal government has its own accounting standards issued by the General Accounting Office; state and local governments follow the standards set forth by the Governmental Accounting Standards Board and its predecessor, the National Council on Governmental Accounting. Instead of analyzing these two sets of accounting standards in two separate sections of this chapter, the state and local government accounting principles will be focused. Wherever there is a difference between the two sets of standards, a remark is given.

The GASB's *Codification of Governmental Accounting and Financial Reporting Standards* presents 12 basic principles of governmental accounting and financial reporting, which are grouped into seven categories as follows:

Categories	Principles
Legal compliance and GAAP	1. Accounting and reporting capability
Fund accounting	2. Fund accounting systems
	3. Types of funds
	4. Number of funds
Fixed assets and long-term liabilities	5. Accounting for fixed assets and long-term liabilities
	6. Valuation of fixed assets
	7. Depreciation of fixed assets
Basis of accounting	8. Accrual basis in governmental accounting
Budget and budgetary accounting	9. Budgeting, budgetary control and budgetary reporting
Classification and terminology	10. Classification of accounts
	11. Common terminology and classification
Financial reporting	12. Interim and annual financial reports

These principles have been generally accepted by state and local governments, and accounting professions. After being established, the Governmental Accounting Standards Board (1987, p. xiii) immediately stated that

> all NCGA Statements and Interpretations heretofore issued and in effect at July 1984 are considered as being encompassed within the conventions, rules, and procedures referred to as "generally accepted accounting principles" and are continued in force until altered, amended, supplemented, revoked, or suspended by subsequent GASB pronouncement.

The first six categories of GAAP will be discussed in this section, and financial reporting, as mentioned earlier, will be explored in the chapter on Government Financial Reporting.

Accounting and Reporting Capabilities

> A governmental accounting system must make it possible both (a) to present fairly and with full disclosure the financial position and results of financial operations of the funds and account groups of the governmental unit in conformity with generally accepted accounting principles, and (b) to determine and demonstrate compliance with finance-related legal and contractual provisions.

Adherence to generally accepted accounting principles (GAAP) is essential to assuring that the same types of financial statements and disclosures, for the same categories and types of funds and account groups, are reported in the same measurement and classification. This makes it possible to compare financial data among governmental units.

Moreover, compliance with finance-related requirements is another important function of governmental accounting systems. This compliance is required even if legal provisions are archaic, useless, or even detrimental to good financial management. A variety of conflicts between legal requirements and GAAP may be encountered. For example, the cash basis of accounting may be the statutory requirement for an enterprise fund, whereas the accrual basis is essential to determining an enterprise's GAAP compliance. Conflicts between legal provisions and GAAP do not require maintaining two accounting systems. Rather, the accounting system is maintained on the legal compliance basis, but should include sufficient supplemental records such as schedules and/or narrative explanations to permit presentation of financial statements in conformity with GAAP (GASB, 1987, p. 41).

Table 1 Fund Structure in American Government

Fund classification	Types of funds	
	Federal government	State and local government
Governmental fund type	General fund	General fund
	Special funds	Special revenue funds
	Revolving funds	Debt service funds
	Management funds	Capital project funds
		Special assessment funds
		Trust funds (expendable— some)
Proprietary fund type		Enterprise funds
		Internal service funds
		Trust funds (nonexpendable— some)
Fiduciary fund type	Trust funds	Trust funds
	Deposit funds	Agency funds (no parallel to management fund; agency or expendable trust funds may serve this function)

Fund Structure

In terms of accounting, all state and local governmental units should be organized and operated on a fund basis.

Definition

"Fund" has two meanings. It may mean "resources" in one usage. Originally, "funds" meant "cash funds," which might be kept in separate cash boxes, drawers, or cigar boxes. Restrictions are placed on the use of cash in each drawer: some bills were paid from one drawer and others from another drawer. Since then, although the method of accounting has changed, funds are still used to segregate resources in accordance with the restrictions on their use.

In another usage, a

> fund is defined as a fiscal and accounting entity with a self-balancing set of accounts recording cash and other financial resources, together with all related liabilities and residual equities or balances, and changes therein, which are segregated for the purpose of carrying on specific activities or attaining certain objectives in accordance with special regulations, restrictions, or limitations. (GASB, 1987, p. 45).

Fund Establishment and Abolishment

A governmental fund may be established as a result of legal requirements, legislative action, or executive order. State or local statutes may require creation of certain funds, such as a fund to account for motor fuel taxes collected by the state and distributed to municipalities for local expenditures. Similarly, the legislature may create a fund to account for special items such as federal revenue-sharing receipts. Also, for administrative purposes, the operations of a major activity may be accounted for in a separate fund established by the executive. For example, a fund could be created to account for the operations of a central supply store.

Once established, a fund can be abolished by any authority as high as or higher than the one that created it. A fund that a local charter requires cannot be abolished by an executive or legislative action but only by revising the charter or amending state constitutional provisions.

Types of Funds

According to the GASB standards, all governmental operations are either governmental, proprietary, or fiduciary in nature. The most important governmental operations are those usually financed from taxes or other sources not directly related to the operations themselves. Proprietary operations are those similar to the operations of business organizations and are usually funded by direct charges against the persons who benefit from them. Finally, fiduciary operations are those undertaken by a government on behalf of, or in a fiduciary capacity for, some other person, group, or governmental agency. The structure of funds should be classified on these broad categories of governmental operations. However, the federal government accounting system is based on two fund types as required by agencies' operations and in accordance with those funds established by the Treasury Department: "(1) funds derived from general taxation and revenue powers and from business operations and (2) funds held by the government in the capacity of custodian or trustee" (GAO, 1987b, p. 57). Moreover, the federal fund is not strictly a fiscal and accounting entity with a self-balancing set of accounts, since the unified budget concept, adopted in fiscal year 1969, requires various federal budgets be presented within the framework of a single budget. Consequently, several problems have emerged. Because the budget's annual surplus or deficit has reflected the combined results of trust and nontrust revenues and expenditures, "this has led to two problems—a 'masking' of important budget trends and relationship, and a perceived misuse of trust fund receipts for financing other parts of the budget" (GAO, 1989c, p. 8). The current structure also is not organized in a way that facilitates tailoring budgetary decisions to the special needs of the government's business-type entities (GAO, 1989c, p. 10). Finally, it creates a bias against capital investment programs (GAO, 1989c, p. 12).

Governmental Fund Category

Four following types of governmental funds are recommended for state and local governments:

The *general fund* to account for all unrestricted resources not properly accounted for in another fund.

Special revenue funds, similar to special funds of the federal government, to account for the proceeds of specific revenue sources (other than special assessments), or to finance specified activities as required by law or administrative regulation (expendable funds or for major capital projects).

Debt service funds to account for the accumulation of resources for, and the payment of, interest and principal on general long-term debt.

Capital project funds to account for the receipt and disbursement of moneys segregated for the acquisition of major capital facilities (other than those financed by special assessment and enterprise funds).

Proprietary Fund Category

At the state and local levels, there are two types of proprietary funds: enterprise funds, and internal service funds.

Enterprise funds account for operations that are financed and operated in a manner similar to business enterprises, and for which preparation of an income statement is desirable.

Internal service funds account for operations similar to those accounted for in enterprise funds, but which provide goods or services exclusively for the benefit of departments of agencies within the municipality.

In the federal government, these two categories of funds—governmental and proprietary fund—are classified under "funds derived from general taxation and revenue powers and from business operations which include the following" (GAO, 1987, p. 57b):

General fund accounts consisting of (a) receipt accounts used to record collections not dedicated to specific purposes and (b) expenditure accounts used to record financial transactions arising under congressional appropriations or other authorizations to spend general revenues.

Special fund accounts consisting of separate receipt and expenditure accounts established to record receipts that are earmarked by law for a specific purpose but are not generated by a cycle of operations for which there is continuing authority to reuse such receipts.

Revolving fund accounts combining receipt and expenditure accounts established by law to finance a continuing cycle of operations, with receipts derived from such operations usually available in their entirety for use by the fund without further action by the Congress.

Management fund accounts combining receipt and expenditure accounts established by law to facilitate accounting for and administration of intragovernmental operations of an agency. Working funds, which are a type of management fund, may be established in connection with each of the foregoing account types to account for advances from other agencies.

Fiduciary Fund Category

At the state and local levels, there are *trust and agency funds,* which account for assets held by a governmental unit as trustee or agent for industrial, private organizations, and other governmental units. Trust funds consist of two types: *expendable* trust funds are ones whose resources may be expended (for example, pension funds), and *nonexpendable* trust funds are ones whose funds must be preserved intact (for example, governmental loan funds).

In the federal government, there are two similar fiduciary fund types: trust funds, and deposit funds that it holds in the capacity of custodian or trustee.

Trust fund accounts are accounts established to record receipts that are held in trust for use in carrying out specific purposes and programs in accordance with an agreement or statute. The assets of trust funds are frequently held over a period of time and may involve such transactions as investments in revenue-producing assets and the collection of revenue therefrom. In general, trust fund accounts consist of separate receipt and expenditure accounts. However, when the trust corpus is dedicated to a business-like operation, called a *trust-revolving fund,* a combined receipt and expenditure account is used.

Deposit fund accounts are expenditure accounts established to account for receipts (1) held in suspense temporarily and later refunded or paid into some other fund of the government or other entity or (2) held by the federal government as a banker or agent for others and paid out at the direction of the owner. Such funds are not available for paying salaries, grants, or other expenses of the federal government. Expenditures are often offset by receipts within this fund.

The above types of funds vary in accordance with whether their resources may be expended or preserved intact. A fund whose resources may be expended is referred to as an *expendable* fund. All governmental funds and some trust funds are classified as expendable and must receive additional revenues, which are expended during the year for any authorized fund expenditures. However, enterprise funds, internal service funds, and some trust funds, referred to as nonexpendable ones, must retain a portion of their resources at the end of each fiscal year in order to have capital to sustain their operations.

Account Groups

Besides the above three categories of funds, there is a fourth category of accounting entities, the *account groups,* to account for and control the government's general fixed assets and general long-term debt. In governmental accounting, fixed assets of all expendable funds (general fixed assets) and long-term liabilities of all expendable funds, except special assessment funds (general long-term liabilities), are aggregated and separately accounted for in two self-balancing groups of accounts. These account groups are referred to as the general fixed assets group of accounts and the general long-term debt group of accounts. They are not funds because they merely list assets and liabilities and do not require an appropriation or expenditure during the current accounting period. The types of fund and account groups recommended in GAAFR are summarized in Fig. 6.

In brief, there are different categories of funds. Each category reflects the need to account for separate operations and revenue sources earmarked for certain operations under legal restrictions. A governmental unit not only needs to establish and maintain funds required by law and sound financial management but also needs to establish an appropriate number of funds consistent with legal and operating requirements to avoid inflexibility, undue complexity, and inefficient financial administration caused by unnecessary funds.

Since each fund is considered an independent fiscal and accounting entity, it has a complete, self-balancing group of accounts. All general ledger accounts and subsidiary records are necessary to reflect compliance with legal provisions and to set forth the financial position and the results of financial operations of the fund. Moreover, amounts receivable from or payable to other funds should be recorded in the accounts of each fund and be presented separately in the financial statements until liquidated by payment or authorized interfund transfer.

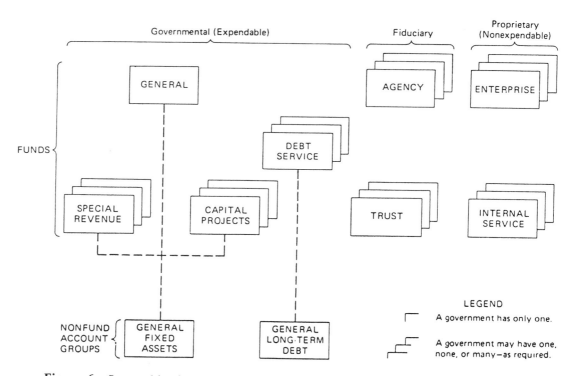

Figure 6 State and local government fund accounting structure. *Source:* Freeman, Shoulders, and Lynn, 1988.

Basis of Governmental Accounting

Basis of accounting relates to the timing of the measurement made, or, in other words, to when revenues, expenditures, expenses, and transfers are recognized in the accounts and reported in the financial statements of an agency. An accrual basis is required for the federal, state and local governments.

The 1956 amendments to the Budget and Accounting Procedures Act of 1950 prescribed the adoption of accrual accounting in all federal agencies as soon as possible. Although many efforts to transfer governmental accounting to the accrual basis were made, this accounting basis is not widely applied in the federal accounting systems. At the state and local government levels, too much emphasis is still given to cash basis of accounting. There are two reasons for the use of cash basis: cash accounting is the least complicated to use; and local and state statutes sometimes require that certain funds be on cash basis only.

In practice, governmental accounting systems must include data on "obligations" (encumbrance basis), "accrued expenditures or revenue" (accrual basis), "cash disbursements or receipts" (cash basis), and "actual or applied costs" (cost basis)—not just any one of these.

Encumbrance Basis

The first step in accounting is to record obligations. Encumbrances are purchase orders or other commitments for goods or services that have not yet been provided or rendered. In the case of personnel, a contract or a mere agreement to work constitutes the obligation. Once the agency makes commitments (called encumbrances), it is obligated to pay. As a result, an encumbrance reduces the amount of appropriations available for further commitments. When a commitment is involved, an entry is made to record the estimated amount of a proposed expenditure. The encumbrance basis of accounting is important because it provides administrators with information regarding the available or unencumbered appropriations balance so that they will not overspend their authorized budget.

Cash Basis

The cash basis of accounting is a basis of accounting under which transactions are recognized only when cash changes hands. The cash basis has two advantages: It is the least complicated to manage, and it serves as a means to control cash flow. However, the cash basis of accounting has more disadvantages than advantages for the following reasons:

It omits recognition of assets and liabilities not resulting in cash transactions. In other words, accounts receivable, accounts payable, and other accrued items are ignored.

It distorts the real revenues and expenditures of a budget due to its ignorance of accrued items.

It permits "manipulation" in budget execution by speeding up and/or slowing down cash collections and payments near the end of the fiscal period.

Accrual Basis Accounting

Accrual basis accounting recognizes transactions when they occur, regardless of the timing of related cash flows. Although it is more complicated than the cash basis accounting, accrual basis accounting avoids all the disadvantages of cash basis accounting mentioned above. Moreover, it enhances the relevance, neutrality, timeliness, completeness, and comparability of accounting measurements.

Modified Accrual Basis

The modified accrual basis is very complicated. As defined by GASB, revenues and other governmental financial resource increments (for example, bond issue proceeds) are recognized in the accounting period in which they become both "measurable and available to finance expenditures of the fiscal period" (GASB, 1987, p. 67). Most expenditures and transfers out are measurable and should be recognized when the related fund liability is incurred, except for (1) inventories of materials and supplies, which may be considered expenditures either when purchased or when used; (2) prepaid insurance and similar items, which need not be reported; (3) accumulated unpaid vacation, sick pay, and other employee benefit amounts, which need not be recognized in the current period, but for which larger-than-normal accumulations must be disclosed in the notes to the financial statements; (4) interest on special assessment indebtedness, which may be recorded when due rather than accrued, if approximately offset by interest earnings on special assessment levies; and (5) principal and interest on long-term debt, which are generally recognized when due.

At the time of this writing, a Measurement Focus and Accounting Basis Exposure Draft had been circulated with its response deadline on November 13, 1989. Due to a number of controversial issues, this exposure draft was revised. It is expected that when this handbook is published, a statement on measurement focus and basis of accounting would be issued by GASB.

The modified accrual basis is recommended for governmental funds and expendable trust funds, whereas the full accrual basis is applied to proprietary funds and nonexpendable trust funds. Specifically, the modified accrual or accrual basis of accounting should be used depending on the type of fund (GASB, 1987, p. 65) as follows:

Governmental fund revenues and expenditures should be recognized on the modified accrual basis. Revenues should be recognized in the accounting period in which they become available and measurable. Expenditures should be recognized in the accounting period in which the fund liability is incurred, if measurable, except for unmatured interest on general long-term debt and on special assessment indebtedness secured by interest-bearing special assessment levies, which should be recognized when due.

Proprietary fund revenues and expenses should be recognized on the accrual basis. Revenues should be recognized in the accounting period in which they are earned and become measurable; expenses should be recognized in the period incurred, if measurable.

Fiduciary fund revenues and expenses or expenditures (as appropriate) should be recognized on the basis consistent with the fund's accounting measurement objective. Nonexpendable trust and pension trust funds should be accounted for on the accrual basis. Expendable trust funds should be accounted for on the modified accrual basis. Agency fund assets and liabilities should be accounted for on the modified accrual basis.

Transfers should be recognized in the accounting period in which the interfund receivable and payable arise. There are two basic criteria for revenue and expenditure recognition: availability and measurability. When the revenues or expenditures are available and measurable, they should be recorded (accrual basis). On the contrary, when they are not available and measurable, the revenues or expenditures should not be recorded.

Cost Basis

The fifth type of accounting basis shifts from reporting the status of appropriation balances to the actual costs of providing goods and services. Resources used, regardless of when acquired, must be recorded. On this accounting basis, inventory and depreciation must be recorded. Inventory and depreciation may be kept on either a periodic or perpetual basis. This basis of accounting provides a relatively accurate picture of what resources are being consumed but may distort the cash flow picture. From a cash flow standpoint, it is of little immediate interest to know how long a police car, for example, will be of use, but it is important to know that the full bill for this car must be paid in its first year. Cost accounting is useful for budgeting in that it can identify the costs of goods or services.

The above accounting bases are not substitutes for one another. The encumbrance basis is valuable in ensuring that appropriations are not overspent or underspent. The accrual basis is essential for management purposes in that it shows the current status of assets and liabilities. The cash basis is important for determining the cash balance. The cost basis is important for identifying the resources consumed as distinguished from resources acquired and placed in inventory. The basis of accounting described above is summarized in Fig. 7.

Transaction	Encumbrance Basis	Accrual Basis	Cash Basis
	When order is placed	When materials are delivered	When bill is paid
Order for materials is placed.	Obligation is recorded as an undelivered order and a decrease to budgetary resources.		
Materials are received or constructively received.		This is recorded as a liability (accounts payable), as a charge to inventory, and as a decrease in undelivered orders.	
Payment is made for the materials.			Outlay is recorded as a reduction of a liability and a reduction to cash.
Materials are used or consumed.			

Figure 7   Illustration of accounting bases.

Budgets and Budgetary Accounting

As stated by GASB (1987, p. 73), "the accounting system should provide the basis for appropriate budgetary control." Thus, first of all, the basis used in a governmental unit's budgeting should be in conformity with the basis used in the accounting to assure that budget information is meaningful and not misleading. Preparation of the budget on a basis inconsistent with the accounting basis complicates financial management and reporting. At the federal level, the budget should be prepared on an accrual basis. At the state and local levels, budgets should be prepared, if practicable, in conformity with the basis recommended by GASB. Thus, the basis on which the budget is prepared will differ between funds using accrual basis and ones using cash basis. If there is a conflict between legal provisions and the generally accepted accounting principles (GAAP) concerning budgetary basis, GASB recommends that governmental units maintain the accounts and prepare budgetary reports on the legally prescribed budgetary basis to determine legal compliance and to maintain sufficient supplemental records that will permit presentation of financial statements on the basis of GAAP (GASB, 1987, p. 41).

Second, governmental fund accounting, often referred to as budgetary accounting, is recognized as a management control technique used to assist in controlling expenditures and enforcing revenue provisions. Because the annual budget is a legal compliance standard against which the operations of funds are evaluated, integration of budgetary accounts in fund accounting systems is "essential in general, special revenue and other annually budgeted governmental funds that have numerous types of revenues, expenditures and transfers" (GASB, 1987, p. 77).

Accounting for General Fixed Assets, Depreciation, and Long-Term Liability

A clear distinction (a) between fund fixed assets and general fixed assets and (b) between fund long-term liabilities and general long-term liabilities was made in GASB's *Codification of Governmental Accounting and Financial Reporting Standards*. All the fixed assets of a governmental unit should be accounted for through the general fixed assets account group except that fixed assets related to proprietary funds or trust funds should be accounted for through these funds. All the unmatured general-obligation long-term liabilities of a governmental unit should be accounted for through the general long-term debt account group, except that nonrecurrent liabilities of proprietary funds, special assessment funds, and trust funds should be accounted for through these funds.

The prime reasons for recording general fixed assets are accountability and control. Such assets are to be recorded at historical cost or estimated historical cost if the original cost is not available, or, in the case of gifts and contributions, at fair market value at the time received.

With respect to depreciation of fixed assets, governments are not required to depreciate general fixed assets, although depreciation is recognized in a proprietary fund and in those trust funds where expenses, net income, and/or capital maintenance are measured. The AICPA audit guide has renewed interest in depreciation of general fixed assets for two reasons: (1) the increasing trend in the number of governmental grants, both of federal to state and local, and of state to local, which allow depreciation as a reimbursable cost, and (2) the need to marshal all costs, including depreciation, for the purposes of evaluating the efficiency, economy, and effectiveness of programs (AICPA, 1980/1989, p. 17).

In the federal government, depreciation is required for (1) businesslike operations, such as revolving or industrial funds, and (2) activities that recover costs from reimbursements or users charges (GAO, 1987b, p. 35). Depreciation cost is equal to the cost of depreciable asset less the estimated future value, if significant.

Common Terminology and Classification of Accounts

Use of proper terminology and classification is essential throughout the financial process, in both business and governmental accounting. As mentioned elsewhere in this chapter, with few exceptions, uniform terminology is used in both fields. One of these exceptions is the inclusion in governmental accounting of the concept that "interfund transfers and proceeds of general long-term debt issues should be classified separately from fund revenues and expenditures or expenses" (GASB, 1987, p. 81). To avoid "double counting" when financial data are aggregated, interfund transfers should not be recorded as such unless they constitute revenues, expenditures, or expenses of the governmental unit as a whole. Similarly, general long-term debt proceeds, which provide revenues for a capital projects or debt service fund and which do not provide revenues in a true sense, should not be recorded as revenues. Explanations of the terms "revenues" and "expenditures" or "expenses" help to clarify the above requirement. "Revenues" means additions to assets that do not increase any liability, do not represent the recovery of an expenditure, do not represent the cancellation of certain liabilities with a corresponding increase in other liabilities or a decrease in assets, and do not represent contributions of fund capital in enterprise and internal service funds. "Expenditures" means costs of goods delivered or services rendered, whether or not paid for, including current operating "expenses," capital outlay, and provision for debt retirement. On the contrary, "expenses" are costs of goods or services consumed during an accounting period. In other words, "expenditures" are costs *incurred* (accrual basis), while "expenses" are costs *expired* (cost basis).

In governmental accounting, revenues and expenditures reflect the changes in the financial condition of a fund during the fiscal year. Since a governmental unit has many kinds of revenues and expenditures, it is useful, from both an internal and external management control as well as an accountability standpoint, to classify revenues and expenditures.

Generally, revenues are classified primarily by source, such as taxes, licenses and permits, intergovernmental revenues, charges for services, fines and forfeits, and miscellaneous in local governments. The classification helps to prepare and control the budget, to control revenue collection, and to prepare financial reports and statistics. Governmental units, however, may group revenues by organizational units, such as departments, bureaus, divisions, or other administrative agencies, depending on their organizational structure.

Expenditure classification, which is rather complicated, consists of the following types:

1. *Classification by organizational unit* is essential to responsibility accounting, as it corresponds with the governmental unit's organizational structure. This classification provides means for controlling expenditures and allocating administrative responsibilities.
2. *Classification by function or program* provides information on (a) the broad purposes or objectives of expenditures, such as general government, public safety, education, health and welfare, and (b) the functions of each broad purpose or objective, such as

police protection, fire protection, and correction under public safety. This classification allows (a) an accumulation of the expenditures in accordance with major functions within a governmental unit, and (b) a comparison of the "function" expenditures of a city, county, state, or country with another city, county, state, or country.

3. Each function or program consists of many activities that must be classified, that is, *classification by activity*. For example, the "police protection" function consists of such activities as police administration, crime control and investigation, traffic control, police training, and support services. The classification by activity allows the measurement of costs of governmental services and goods. Cost data are important for budget preparation and managerial control.

4. Expenditures are further classified on the basis of a fiscal period they are presumed to benefit. This is *classification by character,* which consists of (a) *current expenditures,* which benefit the *current* fiscal fiscal; (b) *capital outlays,* which are presumed to benefit both the present and future fiscal periods; (c) *debt service,* which involves expenditures made for past, present, and future benefits; and/or (d) *intergovernmental,* a fourth character classification, which is appropriate where one governmental unit transfers resources to another, such as when the federal government transfers "shared revenues" to state or local governments.
    The character classification provides policymakers, taxpayers, and other users with valuable information for appraising the cost of government during a fiscal period. Expenditures spent for debt retirement, for example, represent costs incurred by previous administrations, while capital outlays tend either to reduce the government cost in the future or to increase future benefits paid by current expenditures.

5. Expenditures are further classified by *object classes,* that is, according to the types of items purchased or services obtained, such as personal services, supplies, and other services and charges. ("Capital outlays" and "debt services" also are major objects of expenditure classifications.) This classification is essential to provide detailed information for administrative and reporting purposes. Each object class can be broken down into greater detail; "personal services," for example, can be divided into salaries, wages, and fringe benefits. GASB, however, recommends that excessively detailed object classifications be avoided because they complicate the accounting procedure and are of limited use in financial management (GASB, 1987, p. 87).

Chart of Accounts

To facilitate accounting work and the preparation of financial information, revenues and expenditures are classified, codified, and listed on a table called the chart of accounts. Being the heart of accounting systems, the chart of accounts provides a vehicle for controlling governmental assets and liabilities, and summarizing information in a useful and consistent manner. Variable accounting systems require consistent classification of revenues and expenditures throughout the accounting process. It is important that the chart of accounts be consistent with the budget structure so that information provided by accounting systems is useful to those who use financial reports, including internal management, elected officials, investors, and the public. Unfortunately, in many governments, there has been a missing link between budget and accounting data. Consequently, accounting data is not related to budget data (Bowsher, 1985, pp. 176–177), and many governments faced fiscal crisis because policymakers did not see developing fiscal problems in time to prevent fiscal crisis when they made budget decisions.

A sound chart of accounts should include the following elements:

Fund.
Nature of account or general ledger account (assets, liabilities, revenues, expenditures).
Organization.
Activities.
Objects of expenditure.
Source of revenue.
Programs and projects.

These elements must be codified to facilitate accounting consistency by a precise number of digits. The number of digits needed in the coding structure may vary depending on the size, complexity, and reporting needs of a government. For example, a government might assign one or two digits to a fund, two or three digits to object of expenditures. Figure 8 presents two coding samples.

CONCLUSION

In summary, governmental accounting is, in practice, as old as the government itself. Ironically, it has not received the interest of researchers and educators until recent years. Since governmental accounting has developed differently in federal, state, and local government systems, and since many authorities were involved in setting governmental accounting standards and procedures, it is not an easy task to analyze in a comprehensive

```
                                    Account Code — Simplified Structure

                                      1   -   711   -   11

Fund: General Fund                    1

Type of Account:
Expenditures for
Sanitation                                    711

Object of Expenditure:
Regular Salaries                                        11


                                    Account Code — Complex Structure

                                      01  - 700  - 10  - 01  - 101

Fund: General
      Fund                            01

Type of Account:
Expenditures                                  700

Organization:
Public Works Department                              10

Activity:  Sanitation                                      01

Object of Expenditure:
Regular Salaries                                                 101
```

Figure 8 Coding samples: simplified and complex structures.

way the developments, concepts, procedures, and principles of governmental accounting. This chapter has attempted to trace basic developments in accounting in all levels of government in the United States. This chapter has also attempted to compare and contrast different government accounting systems in the United States. Through this approach, the reader can follow basic governmental accounting concepts including fund accounting, basis of accounting, and accounting procedures.

As governmental accounting has recently become a matter of concern for practitioners, researchers, educators, and lawmakers, there remain many unsolved problems. Moreover, although there are generally accepted accounting principles for federal, state, and local governments, these principles are generally not followed by governmental agencies. Thus, even though governmental standards are set, compliance with these standards is another problem.

REFERENCES

AICPA. (1977). *Introduction to Local Government Accounting*. American Institute of Certified Public Accountants, New York.

AICPA. (1980/1989). *Audits of State and Local Governmental Units*. American Institute of Certified Public Accountants, New York.

Barden, H. G. (1975). The trouble with accounting research. *Journal of Accountancy* (January):58–65.

Bowsher, C. A. (1985). Sound financial management: A federal managers' perspective. *Public Administration Review* 45(1):176–84.

Buckley, J. W., and Lightner, K. M. (1973). *Accounting: An Information System*. Dickenson, Encino, Calif.

Burkhead, J. (1956). *Government Budgeting*. Wiley, New York.

Engstrom, J. H. (1979). Public sector accounting education status: Update and extension. *Accounting Review* 64(4):794–799.

Financial Accounting Foundation (1985). *Annual Report 1984*.

Fox, J. G. (1977). Education for governmental accountants. *Government Accountants Journal* 26(3):44–52.

Freeman, R. J., and Nuttall, D. M. (1978). The GAAFR restatement principles: An executive summary. *Governmental Finance* (May):2–13.

Freeman, R. J., Shoulders, C. D. and Lynn, E. S. (1988). *Fund Accounting: Theory and Practice*. Prentice-Hall, Englewood Cliffs, N.J.

General Accounting Office. (1965). *Accounting Principles and Standards for Federal Agencies*.

General Accounting Office. (1984). *Implementation of the Federal Managers' Financial Integrity Act: First Year*. GAO/OCG-84-3, August 24.

General Accounting Office. (1985a). *Policy and Procedures Manual for Guidance of Federal Agencies: Title 1, General Accounting Office*, February 13.

General Accounting Office. (1985b). *Financial Integrity Act: The Government Faces Serious Internal Control and Accounting Systems Problems*. GAO/AFMD-86-14, December 23.

General Accounting Office. (1987a). *Financial Integrity Act: Continuing Efforts Needed to Improve Internal Control and Accounting Systems*. GAO/AFMD-88-10, December 30.

General Accounting Office. (1987b). *Policy and Procedures Manual for Guidance of Federal Agencies: Title 2, Accounting*. August 31.

General Accounting Office. (1988). *Financial Management Issues*. GAO/OCG-89-7TR, November.

General Accounting Office. (1989a). *Financial Integrity Act: Inadequate Controls Result in Ineffective Federal Programs and Billions in Losses*. GAO/AFMD-90-10, November.

General Accounting Office. (1989b). *Federal Internal Control and Financial Management Systems Remain Weak and Obsolete: A Testimony.* GAO/T-AFMD-90-9, November 29.

General Accounting Office. (1989c). *Managing the Cost of Government: Proposals for Reforming Federal Budgeting Practices.* GAO/AFMD-90-1, October.

General Accounting Office. (1990). *Government Financial Vulnerability: Fourteen Areas Needing Special Review.* GAO/OCG-90-1, January 23.

Governmental Accounting Standards Board Organization Committee. (1981). *Exposure Draft Report.*

Granof, M. H. (1979). Governmental standard setting in perspective. *Journal of Accountancy* 43:56–63.

Gross, Jr., M. J., and Jablonsky, S. F. (1979). *Principles of Accounting and Financial Reporting for Nonprofit Organizations.* Wiley, New York.

Havens, H. S. (1990). *The Evolution of the General Accounting Office: From Voucher Audits to Program Evaluations.* GAO/OP-2-HP. January.

Hay, L. E. (1989). *Accounting for Governmental and Nonprofit Entities,* 8th ed. Richard Irwin, Homewood, Ill.

Kirk, D. J. (1979). The FASB: A progress report. *Government Accountants Journal* 28(3):17–23.

Lee, Jr., R. D., and Johnson, R. W. (1989). *Public Budgeting Systems,* 2nd ed. University Park Press, Baltimore.

Lodal, J. M. (1976). Improving local government financial information systems. *Government Accountants Journal* 26(3):18–29.

Lynch, T. D. (1989). *Public Budgeting in America.* Prentice-Hall, Englewood Cliffs, N.J.

McCullers, L. D., and Van Daniker, R. P. (1974). *Accounting and Budgetary Systems for Kentucky Municipalities.* University of Kentucky, Lexington.

Municipal Finance Officers Association. (1979). *Accounting Handbook for Small Cities and Other Governmental Units,* p. 16.

National Council on Governmental Accounting. (1988). *Governmental Accounting, Auditing and Financial Reporting.* Municipal Finance Officers Association, Chicago.

National Council on Governmental Accounting. (1979). *Statement 1—Governmental Accounting and Financial Reporting Principles.* Municipal Finance Officers Association, Chicago.

Niswanger, C. R., and Fess, P. E. (1977). *Accounting Principles,* 12th ed. South-Western, Cincinnati.

Norvelle, J. W. (1989). *Introduction to Fund Accounting.* Thoth Publishing, Tucson, Ariz.

Steinberg, H. I. (1979). A new look at governmental accounting. *Journal of Accountancy* (March):46–55.

Thai, K. V. (1985). Governmental accounting: recent developments and current issues. *International Journal of Public Administration,* 7(4):495–525.

White, R. H. (1975). Governmental accounting: Past, present and future. *Journal of Accountancy* (March):73–79.

Williams, J. M. (1978). Accounting, auditing and financial reporting. In *State and Local Government Finance and Financial Management: A Compendium of Current Research,* J. E. Petersen, C. L. Spain, and M. F. Laffey (eds.), Government Finance Research Center, Washington, D.C., pp. 86–94.

11

The Design of Taxes

Rosalyn Y. Carter   *School of Public Administration, Florida Atlantic University, Fort Lauderdale, Florida*

W. Bartley Hildreth   *Public Administration Institute, Louisiana State University, Baton Rouge, Louisiana*

INTRODUCTION

Governments must finance the provision of public goods and services. It is the power to tax that sets government apart from other types of organizations. While taxes are only one form of revenue for a governmental jurisdiction, taxes consistently generate great public debate and serve as the financial foundation for most government activity.

The purpose of this chapter is to demonstrate the diversity of tax structure designs. First, taxation is placed within the context of other revenue sources. Taxation as an economic concept then is explored in some detail. The remainder of the chapter is a review of major tax structures, namely, income, property, and consumption taxes. For each form of taxation, coverage is given on how each level of government implements the tax. The last section reviews the value-added tax as a major reform proposal.

SOURCES OF REVENUE

Governments raise revenues in a myriad of ways. The most common revenue source and the one with the greatest yield is taxation. Nontax revenue sources are growing in importance, however. One source of nontax revenue is user fees where recipients of a given public service pay all or part of the costs. A special type of current charge is penalty payments and forfeitures. By far not the least important, intergovernmental transfers are a primary source of revenue for many governments. A source of funds not covered here is government borrowing against future revenues to provide current goods and services.

Taxes

Taxes are governments' primary source of revenue. A tax is a required payment made to government. Governments compel payment of taxes to fund public goods and services. Taxes are also useful for other economic purposes. Tax policy effects the allocation of resources, the distribution of wealth, public choices, and stability of the economy on the macro level through the effect of fiscal and monetary policy on employment, prices, and growth.[1] Many different types of taxes are levied in numerous ways, dependent on the level and unit of government. This chapter explores the concept of taxation with particular emphasis on income, property, and consumption taxes.

User Fees

User fees are quid pro quo payments usually collected for some service provided, utility, or enterprise activity.[2] These benefit-based levies can be an effective component of a government's financing system. Areas experiencing extensive new residential and/or commercial development look at a benefit-based levy known as the impact fee. This up-front fee is designed to cover a proportionate share of the cost of increasing service system capacity to accommodate the growth.

When appropriately applied, user fees, in general, have several advantages over tax financing. First, when citizens pay directly for a service, they are more aware of what it costs to provide the service. Second, user fees provide local officials with a "market signal" that they can use to make more effective resource allocation decisions. Third, user fees can be used to control user behavior. Pricing helps ration services, thereby reducing excessive and wasteful service use. Fourth, user fees can improve overall financial equity because only those using the service must pay for it, and those using it the most, pay the most.

Penalty Payments and Forfeitures

A special form of revenue is penalty payments and forfeitures. *Penalties* are generally collected as result of some infraction. These include fines for felonies and misdemeanors, administrative fines for late payments, and fines for corporate wrongdoing in compliance with laws concerning restraints on trade or other prohibited activities such as pollution, false advertising and employee health and safety in the work place. *Forfeitures* are loss of property also for punitive reasons. Government takes possession of property acquired or used illegally. Subsequently, these assets are sold and the proceeds are kept by government. Both penalties and forfeitures are less revenue-generating oriented and more punitive in nature.

Interorganizational Transfers

Interorganizational transfers are revenues received by public organizations from other public organizations. These intergovernmental transfers come in two basic forms. One level of government may seek to influence the spending behavior of another, usually a lower-level unit, by providing funding for specified, targeted program(s). This is com-

---

[1] A more detailed discussion of tax policy as an economic tool can be found in Holcombe (1988) and Veseth (1984).

[2] See *Local Revenue Diversification: User Charges* (ACIR, 1987) and Bland (1989). For a discussion of the rationale and quantitative techniques for setting the correct level of user charges, see Senge (1986). A case study of user charge administration using Phoenix, Ariz., can be found in Flanagan and Perkins (1987). See Cory (1985) for a technical discussion of user charges as a method of rationing scarce public resources. Norris (1989) provides U.S. Supreme Court rulings on the constitutionality of federal user charges to industry for use of public infrastructure and other services provided by federal agencies.

monly known as a grant-in-aid. A second form of intergovernmental transfer comes as shared revenues from one unit of government to another. The donor government is usually a higher level of government and the receiving unit is a lower level of government.[3]

TAXATION

There are two parts to any tax, the *base* and the *rate*. The base refers to the body of wealth against which the tax is levied, for example, earned income or real property. It is important to identify the base precisely in order to collect tax. The administering government must identify precisely what is being taxed. Definition of the base is often harder than is readily apparent. Initially, the definition of the base is conceptual and abstract. For instance, most believe the base of the income tax is income. While this is true, a more precise definition of income is required to operationalize the tax. Income is generated in many ways, and precisely which types of income are subject to the tax must be clearly specified.

The most common tax bases in the United States are sales, income, and real property. Once the base has been determined and defined accurately, it must be measured to determine how much tax to collect. Measurement of the base can occur in three ways: (1) *ad valorem* (according to value) refers to the dollar value of the base; (2) *excise* is when the base is measured in terms of the number of units or by volume; and (3) the base can be grouped by classes according to some criteria such as with permits and licenses.

The rate refers to how much per base measurement is charged by the tax. Most rates are ad valorem in that a percentage of the base is charged. For example, in a 5% sales tax, retail sales is the base, and 5% of the dollar value of retail sales is collected. Some rates are levied against specific units as with excise taxes. In the case of the excise tax, a specific amount is levied against each unit of the base. The rates of both excise and ad valorem taxes can be set on a graduated scale so that the rate changes as the base changes.

Before we continue our discussion of tax rates, we must define two additional terms that can determine the actual rates paid by various tax payers. *Exemption* is actually an exclusion from the tax base. It refers to something that would ordinarily be a part of the tax base and therefore subject to the tax, but for some reason is specifically excluded. A good example is foodstuffs, which are exempted from the sales tax in many states. A *deduction* is an adjustment or reduction in the tax base for some special condition. For example, in the federal personal income tax, taxpayers may deduct charitable contributions from their taxable income.

In almost any tax policy, there are two rates: the *face* rate and the *effective* rate. The face rate, sometimes called the *nominal* rate, is the one that is found in formal statements of tax policy. These rates may or may not be applicable to all taxpayers. The degree of applicability depends on exemptions and deductions and other adjustments in the base. In contrast, the effective rate is the rate actually paid. This may vary from one taxpayer to another. The effective rate is determined by the taxpayer's tax liability divided by the unadjusted base, that is, the base without any deductions and exemptions. A taxpayer's liability is a function of the adjusted base (the base less the appropriate exemptions and deductions) and the rate. Therefore, the liability equals the adjusted base multiplied by the rate.

---

[3] An historical discussion of federal grant-in-aid programs and shared revenues with state and local governments can be found in Aronson (1985). For state and federal intergovernmental transfers see Aronson and Hilley (1986) and General Accounting Office (1990). A discussion of the loss of General Revenue Sharing and its impact on state and local governments can be found in Thai and Sullivan (1989).

An additional provision that can reduce tax liability is the *credit*. It is applied against the tax liability and is similar to exemptions and deductions in that it reduces the amount of tax owed. Because it is subtracted from the tax liability, it more directly affects how much tax is owed. Credits reduce tax liability dollar for dollar, whereas reductions in tax liability from exemptions and deductions vary, dependent upon the taxpayer's effective rate.

Reductions in tax liability, whether caused by exemptions, deductions, or credits, result in losses to the public treasury just as government expenditures result in a loss. These somewhat indirect expenses are called *tax expenditures*. They result from a policy choice not to collect a particular revenue for some reason. Tax expenditures are often an expedient indirect subsidy. By using tax expenditures, legislative bodies can provide more benefits than could be offered through more visible direct subsidies. However, tax expenditures are less controllable and more permanent than direct subsidies because they are less visible and indirect. And, what is more, tax expenditures should be perceived as public programs with substantial policy impacts that also affect the public purse and other policy choices by decreasing available resources.[4]

Tax *incidence* refers to who ultimately bears the burden of the tax. Just as the nominal rate of a tax may not be the rate actually paid, the *nominal* taxpayer (the individual defined by law as the taxpayer) may not be the individual who ultimately pays the tax bill. In many cases, the nominal taxpayer may be able to pass on, or *shift*, all or part of the tax liability to someone else. An example is that of landlords and the property tax. Part or all of the burden of the real property tax is passed on to tenants in their rent by the landlord (property owner), who is the nominal taxpayer.[5]

The revenue generated by a given tax policy is important, but equally as important is the stability of that revenue. Some types of taxes generate fairly stable revenue streams over the years, while others generate variable revenue streams. This phenomenon is known as *elasticity*. Here the concern is for the degree of sensitivity of tax yield or revenue generated to general economic activity. Income and sales taxes are relatively elastic or sensitive to economic conditions, meaning that revenues rise or fall in response to changes in the economy. The property tax, on the other hand, is relatively inelastic by comparison, and its revenues remain more stable for longer periods of time.

Types of Taxes

There are basically three ways to establish rate schedules for tax policy: progressive, proportional, and regressive. These terms describe the way the tax burden imposed on the taxpayer varies relative to the taxpayer's wealth.[6]

A *progressive* rate schedule is one where the rate increases (decreases) as the size of the base increases (decreases). As the simple example below illustrates, a progressive tax policy results in a greater liability for taxpayers with a larger base. Progressive tax policies appeal intuitively to our sense of fairness. One problem with progressive tax policies is that there may not be adequate monies at the higher end of the income distribution to allow for much progressivity without imposing a very high tax rate at the top.

Progressive taxation remains a controversial issue. Its proponents contend it is an effective policy tool for mitigating some inequities rising out of an unequal distribution of

---

[4] A more detailed discussion of the various types of tax exemptions, deductions, and credits, can be found in Pechman (1987, 1989).

[5] An economic and historical perspective of tax incidence is provided in Break (1974).

[6] See Holcombe (1988) and Veseth (1984).

Progressive Taxation

Base	$5000	$10000	$20000
Rate	10%	20%	30%
Tax	$500	$2000	$6000

wealth. This notion is based on two assumptions. First, government has a role in addressing issues of economic inequality. Second, progressive taxation can address these inequities. Generally, progressive tax policies have had a moderate effect on redistribution of wealth (see Pechman, 1989).

The rate schedule can instead be *proportional,* or flat rate. In this case, the nominal rate is the same for all taxpayers, but the liability still increases (decreases) as the size of the base increases (decreases). Therefore, in the case of an income tax, the rate would remain constant, but the base, and the tax liability, would change.

Proportional Taxation

Base	$5000	$10000	$20000
Rate	10%	10%	10%
Tax	$500	$1000	$2000

Finally, a *regressive* rate schedule is one where there is an inverse relationship between changes in the rate levied and the size of the base. In a regressive tax, the rate increases as the size of the base decrease, and conversely, the rate decreases as the size of the base increases. Therefore, the tax burden imposed on lower-income taxpayers is disproportionately greater than for higher-income households.

Regressive Taxation

Base	$5000	$10000	$20000
Rate	30%	20%	10%
Tax	$ 500	$2000	$2000

When trying to determine whether a given tax policy is progressive or regressive, it is insufficient to merely examine the rate schedule of the tax in question. A more comprehensive approach is required to ascertain how the total tax package impacts the taxpayer. This is a difficult task because the taxpayer faces numerous taxes from various levels of government. Second, definition of the base may be unclear. While the nominal base of tax policies can vary from real property, to retail sales, to income, etc., some economists argue that the actual base is always income since taxes are paid out of income.

Requirements of a Tax System

According to Adam Smith any good tax policy must pass four basic tests—both administrative and economic. They are equity, certainty, convenience, and economic.

Beginning with a discussion of *equity,* there is certainly a moral imperative to impose equitable tax policies. Equity is also a practical goal in that taxpayers will not tolerate an unfair tax policy for very long, no matter how efficient. In general, efficient unfair taxes are repealed or simply ignored. While there is universal agreement taxes should distribute their burdens equitably, there is almost universal disagreement as to what is meant by equity. Nonetheless, a good tax policy is one that distributes its burden across taxpayers according to some principle of equity. We shall examine several ways to approach the complicated question of equity later in this chapter.[7]

By *certainty,* we mean that tax policy should not be arbitrary. Rather, taxes should be imposed according to some set of rules. Taxpayers should know the rules and understand the tax consequences of their economic behavior.

Convenience implies that taxes should be levied in ways and at times that are easy for the taxpayer to pay. This not only means that the procedure for payment should be simple and clear, but also that taxes should come due at times when the taxpayer can logically pay them if possible. A common example is, taxes on crops should be due after the harvest rather than during planting season.

Economic has several meanings. First of all, government should not use too many resources for collecting the tax. In other words, the tax should be cost-efficient. Second, the tax should be *marketplace neutral,* that is, behavior in the marketplace should be distorted as little as possible because of the tax. If taxpayers change their economic activities in order to avoid the tax or minimize its impact, then resources may not be allocated to their most productive use in the market resulting in inefficiencies. Finally, taxes should promote economic efficiency. Instances where the market is efficient prior to imposing the tax require that the tax be marketplace neutral. In inefficient markets, the tax should encourage a more efficient allocation of resources.

Many of the required criteria conflict with each other. It is very difficult to design a tax policy that meets all of them. Convenient collection is often costly to administer, and such a tax may not be equitable. Taxes that redistribute income effectively or promote efficient allocation of resources may be costly and also unpopular.

Equity Criteria—Equal Sacrifice Principle

Taxes should be equitable. But what does equity mean? How is it defined? Many would answer the burden of the tax should be distributed equitably among taxpayers. How can that be accomplished? In response to this question, some economists subscribe to the *equal sacrifice principle* when developing tax systems to finance public goods and services. This concept dictates that taxpayers should be deprived of income to pay the tax according to some definition of equality. However, equity and equality may not necessarily be the same thing to all people. If we do assume that equality and equity are the same thing and the equal sacrifice principle is used to develop an equitable tax policy, then how will equal and sacrifice be defined? The equal sacrifice principle has three different definitions, and each implies a different type of tax policy to achieve equity (Holcombe, 1988; Veseth, 1984; and Pechman, 1989).

1. Equal Absolute Sacrifice

The simplest approach to the equal sacrifice principle holds that each taxpayer should pay the same amount to finance public goods and services. If the sacrifice is to be income forfeited to the tax (i.e., the base of the tax is income), then each taxpayer would pay equal amounts of income to the tax. The result would be a regressive tax. Both low-income and high-income taxpayers would lose equal amounts of income to the tax;

---

[7] See Holcombe (1988), Veseth (1984), Aronson (1985), and Pechman (1987, 1989).

however, they would lose different proportions of their income to the tax. The higher-income taxpayer would pay a smaller percentage of income to the tax than the lower-income taxpayer, meaning there would be an inverse relationship between the tax base, or income, and the tax burden. In the example below, each taxpayer sacrifices an equal amount of income to the tax. But as income increases, the proportion of income lost to the tax decreases. Consequently, equal absolute sacrifice can result in a regressive tax that places a disproportionately heavier burden on the poor. This example clearly illustrates how terms such as equity and equality must be carefully defined, and that the definitions have important implications for tax policy.

Equal Absolute Sacrifice

Taxpayer	Income	Tax	Tax burden
Low income	$ 5,000	$1,000	20%
Medium income	$10,000	$1,000	10%
High income	$20,000	$1,000	5%

Equal Proportional Sacrifice

A second approach to the equal sacrifice principle is that each taxpayer should sacrifice equal proportions of income to finance public goods and services. A tax system based on this notion would result in each taxpayer losing the same proportion of income to the tax but different dollar amounts to the tax. Therefore, high-income taxpayers would pay the same percentage as low-income taxpayers, and their tax burdens would be the same. The low-income taxpayer would sacrifice fewer income dollars to the tax than the higher-income taxpayer. In the example below, we see how a tax based on equal proportional sacrifice would impact taxpayers with varying levels of income. Each taxpayer bears the same tax burden, or loses the same proportion of income. However, as income rises, the actual amount paid also increases.

Equal Proportional Sacrifice

Taxpayer	Income	Tax	Tax burden
Low income	$ 5,000	$ 500	10%
Medium income	$10,000	$1,000	10%
High income	$20,000	$2,000	10%

Equal Marginal Sacrifice

The third and final approach to the equal sacrifice principle is based on the concept of the *marginal utility of income*.[8] Equal marginal sacrifice is based on the assumption that

[8] Equal marginal sacrifice also assumes that utility can be measured and that interpersonal comparisons of utility are possible. Many economists contest that assertion. Sacrifice theories assume that relative utilities are measurable and that the relations between income and utility are the same for all taxpayers. This has not been verified empirically. Economic theory has problems with equal marginal sacrifice. Many economists do not accept that utility can be measured and compared across individuals.

the marginal utility of income declines as income rises. The marginal utility of income refers to the value of the last dollar of income earned. Declining marginal utility of income means that each successive dollar of income earned is less valuable than the preceding dollar. Equal marginal sacrifice holds that each taxpayer should forfeit the same marginal utility when paying taxes. Consequently, taxpayers would pay varying amounts of income to the tax, and varying proportions of their income to the tax, but each taxpayer would sacrifice an equal marginal utility of income to tax. Generally speaking, the result is a progressive tax system[9] that would take a greater percentage of income for taxes from high-income taxpayers.

In the example below, taxpayers with various levels of income not only pay different amounts, but they bear unequal tax burdens, that is, they forfeit different proportions of their income to the tax. However, if the marginal utility of income is indeed falling, then they sacrifice equal marginal utility of income. This means that the loss of utility of income to the low-income family associated with a $50 tax bill is the same as the loss in utility of income to the high-income family with a tax bill of $2000. If the marginal utility of a dollar is indeed falling as an individual accumulates more dollars, such a tax system would demand that the rich pay more dollars and a greater proportion of income than their poorer counterparts to satisfy the notion of equal marginal sacrifice.

Equal Marginal Sacrifice

Taxpayer	Income	Tax	Tax burden
Low income	$ 5,000	$ 50	1%
Medium income	$10,000	$ 250	5%
High income	$20,000	$2,000	10%

Equity Criteria—Horizontal and Vertical Equity

Another method of examining equity in a tax policy is to consider the concepts of *horizontal* and *vertical* equity. Here we address the distribution of the tax burden across taxpayers in similar economic circumstances and dissimilar circumstances. The concept of horizontal equity means equal treatment for taxpayers in like situations. Vertical equity addresses the issue of treatment of taxpayers in different situations.

Horizontal Equity

How do we determine if taxpayers are in similar circumstances? Personal characteristics, such as income, wealth accumulation, and public goods and services received, can be used. The assumption here is that if taxpayers in similar circumstances carry different tax burdens then the tax system is arbitrary and intuitively unfair.

The issue of differential circumstances can be addressed through exemptions. Theoretically, personal exemptions are used to avoid taxing income that is inadequate to provide a subsistence level of support. In reality exemptions are not high enough to cover

---

[9] Actually, the type of tax system, progressive, proportional, or regressive, depends on the rate of decline of the marginal utility of income relative to the rise in income.

subsistence support. But some exemptions do relieve part of the tax burden for low-income taxpayers, and therefore add to the progressivity of the tax.[10]

Vertical Equity

Here the concern is that people in different circumstances will bear a different tax liability. Often vertical equity is measured by the relationship of average tax payments of households by income classes. The difference in tax burden should be proportionate to the variation in circumstances.

When horizontal equity and vertical equity are considered together, the two concepts can measure the fairness of a given tax policy. The results are useful because they are consistent with the common sense notion of equity. Taxes levied on the bases of equal sacrifice criteria should display both vertical and horizontal equity. This is intuitively appealing, but difficult to implement. The question of what constitutes similar circumstances and different circumstances remains. The answer is not always clear.

Ability to Pay or Benefits Received?

What is the basis of fairness? The debate centers on two measures: the *ability to pay* approach and the *benefits received* approach.

Ability to Pay

Adam Smith suggested that tax systems be based on the taxpayers' ability to pay. He suggested what he called a "degressive" tax system. In modern times, such a system is referred to as a progressive system. Smith's degressive tax system would impose a tax burden proportional to income beyond some basic exemption for necessities. The goal of the basic necessities exemption was to protect the poor from high tax burdens.

This concept of the ability to pay has had a major influence on the development of tax policy and has facilitated the acceptance of progressive taxation, since the ability to pay is assumed to increase as income increases. A tax policy that is not related to the ability to pay is inefficient for two reasons. People will have to sell assets to pay taxes or change their behavior to avoid the tax. The result could very well be a less efficient allocation of resources. According to the ability to pay, horizontal and vertical equity require similar taxes for the same ability to pay, and different taxes for differing ability to pay.

Should taxes be progressive, proportional, or regressive? Adam Smith said progressive. Other economists agree. However, some economists propose proportional or regressive taxes emerging from their views of equal sacrifice. How is the ability to pay measured? Should income be the measure or accumulation of wealth or the amount of public goods and services received? The answer is still subject to debate.

Benefits Received Approach

An early theory of taxation held before the mid-nineteenth century was that taxes should be distributed in accordance with benefits received in terms of public goods and services.

---

[10] See Kaplow (1989) for detailed examination of the concept of horizontal equity and a reconsideration of recent attempts to apply it to tax policy.

Proponents of this criteria usually seek to narrow the scope of government. Benefits received are assumed to be proportionate to the taxpayer's income, an assumption that may or may not be so. However, this principle has become the major rationale for proportional taxation. There are two basic criticisms of the benefits received approach: It promotes a restricted view of the role of government, and the assumption that government goods and services received are proportionate to income is without foundation.

INCOME TAXES

The income tax is a widely used tax in industrialized countries, and is often regarded as the fairest of taxes. It is a significant revenue generator in the United States with versions used at levels of government.

Most frequently, the rate schedules are established as percentages of income after exemptions and deductions. There are a number of benefits to an income tax. The base is sufficiently large to generate yields at relatively low rates. The income tax is a useful vehicle for implementing policy through tax expenditures. It is easy to administer and can be collected regularly throughout the fiscal year.

The income tax is a major part of the progressivity of the total tax system in the United States. It permits the imposition of a varied tax burden on individual level, and is capable of addressing both horizontal and vertical equity. The yield expands and contracts more rapidly than income. And it imposes less burden on consumption than other forms of taxation. It does reduce the incentive to work some, and its effect on savings is unclear.

Federal Personal Income Tax

All western industrialized countries tax personal income, though none rely on it as much as the United States. It is the most lucrative source of government revenue in the United States, accounting for almost half of federal revenues. With its graduated rate scale, the personal income tax is able to accommodate the ability-to-pay approach and the horizontal equity.

The federal government permanently adopted the personal income tax in 1913, and for the first 30 years or so it applied mainly to a few very-high-income taxpayers. The exemptions were so high that only a handful of incomes were large enough to pay even at the lowest rates. The exemptions were reduced during World War II to raise revenues. The rates were also raised at that time for the same reason. Since that time the rates have been reduced in 1964, 1981, and 1986. But the average tax paid by the average taxpayer remains high relative to pre-1940 liabilities (Pechman, 1987).

The combination of lower exemptions, higher effective rates, and higher incomes increases the yield. The yield of the personal income tax also rises with economic growth and inflation. In 1939, the total liability of the income tax equalled $1 billion or 1% of personal income. By the end of the 1980s, the total liability equalled $400 billion and 10% of personal income (Pechman, 1987).

Theoretically, the basic structure is somewhat simple, comprising only four steps. First, total all sources of income. Second, subtract all allowable deductions and exemptions to determine taxable income. Third, apply the appropriate rate to the balance of taxable income to determine the amount of tax. Finally, subtract allowable credits to determine taxes due.

Base—Adjusted Gross Income and Taxable Income

Adjusted gross income and *taxable income* are two important and separate concepts. Adjusted gross income is the closest approach in the law to the economist's definition of total income. There are important differences. Adjusted gross income equals total income from all taxable sources less some expenses incurred in earning that income, including expenses such as payments into self-employment and IRA accounts, and alimony. Generally, only money income is taxable, but some money income is excluded, such as interest on tax-exempt state and local securities; transfer payments including social security benefits for most workers, welfare payments, food stamps, and veterans' benefits; fringe benefits (employer contributions to pensions and health insurance are the most important); and income from savings through life insurance. Exclusion of nonmoney income means that items such as the following are not taxed: unrealized capital gains, in-kind fringe benefits, and imputed incomes such as rental value of owner-occupied homes.

Taxable income is computed by making two sets of deductions from adjusted gross income. The first set of deductions is related to personal and income expenditures that are allowed by law. These include charitable contributions, interest on home mortgages, state and local income and property taxes, some medical and dental expenses, some losses from casualty or theft, some employee business expenses, expenses related to investment income, and some miscellaneous expenses. The second set of deductions is the personal exemptions. They are deductions for the taxpayer, spouse, and other dependents. The dollar amount is adjusted periodically for inflation. Both of these adjustments, personal and income, erode the tax base or taxable income.

Tax Rates

The rates for the federal personal income tax are graduated by a bracket system. Even though the tax rates are graduated, much of the tax base is concentrated at the low levels. Income is divided into ranges and set into brackets. Different rates apply to the portion of the taxpayer's income falling into each bracket. The Tax Reform Act of 1986 nominally reduced the number of rates into two brackets: 15 and 28%. These rates became effective in tax year 1989. There were intermediate rate schedules for 1987 and 1988 in the transition period. There are four categories of taxpayers, and each category has its own rate schedule: married, filing jointly; married, filing separately; single head of household; and single.

Administration

The current system of withholding was implemented in 1943. It is based on the principle that taxes are due when the income is received. Taxes are withheld by employers so that payment is current for most wage and salary earners. For other types of income, the taxpayer estimates the taxes due and pays quarterly installments during the year the income is received. This withholding is the backbone of the payment system. There is no withholding on income other than wages and salaries. This results in serious under reporting and noncompliance. Clearly, a better system is needed. Final reconciliation between tax liability and prepayment through withholding and quarterly payments is done through filing an annual return. The taxpayer either pays the balance of what is owed, gets a refund of excess taxes paid, or credits the excess payments toward the next year's liability.

Economic Effects

There are three basic issues: stabilization of consumption expenditures, influence on the incentive to work, and effect on savings. Proponents of "supply-side" economics contend that reductions in the marginal rates motivate taxpayers to work and save more, resulting in economic growth. Their greater output will ultimately pay for the rate reductions by increasing the base. While some studies do show that tax policy generates some supply-side effects, the impact on rate reductions on economic growth tends to be exaggerated.

Stability and predictability in yield is an important criterion for tax policy. And equally as important is properly timed changes in tax yield which can help stabilize the economy. Tax policy can increase consumer demand in times of recession and decrease it in periods of expansion and inflation.

Progressive income tax yields fluctuate automatically with changes in income. And the response to changes in income is disproportionate. The withholding collection system only speeds the reaction more. Changes in tax rates have an almost immediate effect on yield and disposable income. Therefore, a progressive income tax can be a useful tool in promoting economic stability.[11]

Horizontal Equity

Horizontal equity requires that there be equal treatment for all income without regard to source. However, in reality, the system of exemptions and deductions results in different treatment for different types of income. Further complicating horizontal equity is a rate schedule that differentiates income based on its use and source. Two examples include the income tax credit on the earned income of low-income families, which helps to offset their tax burden, and the preferential treatment given the income derived from capital gains. The rationale for the latter is that irregular receipts should not be included as income. Income is also excluded from the tax base because of its use, such as deductions for expenses incurred in earning income, donations to charity, and medical expenses.

There is no economic reason for differential treatment of income based on use or source. These provisions erode the tax base and result in higher tax rates for all taxpayers. They also distort the efficient allocation of resources, placing a premium on earning/spending income in ways that get the special tax treatment. Further, there is a snowball effect. Those who do not derive benefits from the special treatment apply political pressure for more categories of special treatment. The distortions begin to take on their own momentum. Elimination of these provisions could result in one-third to one-fifth reduction in the tax base as compared with a more comprehensive approach. (See Pechman, 1989, for a more extensive discussion.)

State Income Tax

Successful administration of state income tax systems is new to the twentieth century. Prior unsuccessful attempts were due mainly to poor administration. Wisconsin was the

---

[11] See Aaron and Galper (1984) for a discussion of the federal personal income tax, tax reform and economic effects. The effects of the 1981 and 1986 laws are reviewed in Fullerton and Mackie (1989).

first state to succeed with state income tax in 1911, predating the Sixteenth Amendment bringing on a permanent federal income tax.

The income tax has been a lucrative revenue source for state governments. State income tax systems rank second only to the federal government in generation of revenue. Four factors account for their increasing status as a source of revenue: higher rates, a broadly defined base, effective administration incorporating a system of withholding, and high income elasticity.[12]

State administration of all revenues has generally improved during the decade of the 1980s. This is most particularly true of the income tax. In a number of states, the agencies responsible for the administration of the income tax have expanded their auditing and collections capacity. This was accomplished through the use of increased personnel, added computer technology, increased use of data tapes from the Internal Revenue Service, and attempts to influence taxpayer attitudes.

There are a number of differences in state and federal administration of the income tax. These differences include definition of taxable income, definition of interstate income, definition of residence, treatment of income splitting, dividends, credits, capital gains and allowed deductions. The definition of residence and origin of income, which is the primary difference, is a particularly important issue for states. It is only a concern for the federal government on foreign income.[13]

As early as 1920, the National Tax Association advanced the notion that the state of residence of the taxpayer should be the only factor that determines to what state taxes should be paid. This means that states would only tax income earned by residents of taxing state. Nonresidents would not be taxed on income earned in the taxing state. A second approach, pioneered by the state of Wisconsin, taxes all income generated within the state, by residents and nonresidents alike. Income earned by residents of the taxing state outside of its borders is not taxed.

Most states claim the right in their tax laws to tax all income earned by their residents wherever it is generated and all income generated in-state by nonresidents. However, in practice most states moderate their tax policies with credits and reciprocity agreements. Many states allow a credit for taxes paid to other states or exempt income taxed in another state through reciprocal agreements.[14]

Local Income Taxes

There are differences between local income taxes and the better known state and federal income taxes (see Hildreth, 1988). First, local income taxes generally are flat rate, not the progressive design of the federal income tax. Second, the administrative costs of the local tax is often higher than that found with broader-based state or federal income taxes. To get a desired scale of economies (and for policy reasons) some states such as Indiana, Maryland, and New York require local governments to "piggyback" the local income tax onto the state tax. This permits the state to collect the local tax, remitting tax proceeds back to the local jurisdiction after deduction of a collection fee. By doing so, local governments gain a progressive tax rate and a broader tax base in the process.

[12] For reviews of state tax trends, see Katz (1989), Inman (1989), Kolhauser (1988) and Gold (1987).

[13] For recent developments in state tax administration, see Snavely (1988).

[14] For a more lengthy discussion of state income taxes, see Aronson and Hilley (1986).

The tax base is the third point. Federal and state governments define taxable income broadly. Defining income broadly means to include wages, salary, tips, and commissions, as well as interest, dividends, rents, capital gains, and inheritances, for example. The simpler local government tax system—often termed a payroll, wage, or earnings tax— falls almost exclusively on an individual's wage and salary earnings. This means that individuals receiving income from investments or other nonwage sources are not taxed, allowing the tax burden to fall on those earning most of their income in wages and salaries.

A fourth difference is that the local tax version does not always require mandatory yearly filing by taxpayers. While always permitted (and even required in some individual tax situations), filing is less important when all employers have to withhold the tax from employees.

Business activities also fall under the local income tax with unincorporated businesses and professions always subject to the tax. In many applications, the tax is applied to corporate net profits attributable to activities within the jurisdiction. When adjacent localities do not impose a similar tax structure, the taxing locality may be at a business location disadvantage.

Local income tax liability may fall on all who live or work in the city, including nonresidents. Nonresidents are prone to claim discrimination in such situations. To the taxing jurisdiction, however, nonresidents benefit from many local services while working in the city. Even when both jurisdictions levy income taxes, their rates or bases may differ. To avoid double payment, the city of residence may provide a full or partial credit for related taxes paid elsewhere. In other cases, the city of residence may have the legal claim on the income of its residents, allowing a suburb to deprive a central city of revenue from commuters.

States can vary in the power they give local governments to tax.[15] For instance, most states grant the authority to levy a local income tax to only a few jurisdictions within a state. In Ohio and Pennsylvania, however, the local income tax is a general grant of tax authority, meaning that all governments of certain classes can levy the tax under specified conditions. Home-rule cities in states such as Texas appear to have the power to adopt the tax by charter amendment if, as in Texas, the tax is not prohibited by state law.

The local income tax is more prevalent for municipalities than counties or school districts. Counties in Maryland, Indiana, and Kentucky have the authority but vary greatly in their reliance on the tax. Georgia counties have the power to levy the tax but none have. School districts in Iowa, Ohio and Pennsylvania are the only ones with power to impose the tax.

PROPERTY TAXES

The property tax in the United States is a complex subject. It is not simply a tax; rather, it is actually 50 different taxes, and each comes with a plethora of local variations. We will review the major features that generally apply to property taxes in the following section.[16]

Historically, the property tax has been the most significant revenue source for

[15] See ACIR (1988).

[16] A general discussion of the property tax is found in Aronson and Hilley (1986).

government in the United States. It remains a primary source of revenue for local governments. The degree of reliance on the property tax varies by type of local government within and across the states. School districts are almost totally dependent on the property tax, whereas municipalities have been successful in developing alternate sources of revenues such as the income tax. Counties, townships, and single-purpose districts are also heavily reliant on the property tax. Persistence of the property tax reflects its reliability and the lack of alternatives for local governments. The base of the property tax is immobile, but the base of the sales tax or the income tax is vulnerable if taxpayers leave the jurisdiction to avoid the tax.

Levy Limits

Local governments are generally limited in their ability to levy the property tax. In some jurisdictions an affirmative vote of the citizens is required. This encourages officials to take to the voters special service levies. Separate property levies result, funding library operations, city police retirement, fire protection in a defined district, school salaries, school athletic departments, and many others. In this way, the voters either accept or reject a specific service increment: a "pick and choose" form of taxation. By earmarking revenue streams for particular purposes, citizens make the budget allocations, not elected officials. Issues perceived as more directly beneficial to voters are more likely to pass. A disadvantage is that when a service has an earmarked revenue source, the likely yearly spending rule is to spend all the amount collected, regardless of the efficiency or effectiveness of the service delivery. Competition among programs for scarce budget dollars is replaced by a monopoly over funds, with all the inefficiencies associated with such practices. A contrasting and more favorable perspective is that taxpayers gain more power over public policy when they can equate the cost of a service (using a separate millage, for instance) to the perceived service benefits derived from the tax.

Local governments with an interest in borrowing money in the credit market have to consider the affect their actions have on local credit quality—as reflected in the bond rating. Bond rating agencies tend to prefer the local property tax rather than a sales or local income tax. The reason is that a property tax represents steady tax revenues, except in the most severe economic downturn characterized by high property tax delinquencies. Bond rating agencies also watch ballot disapprovals as an expression of voter sentiment for levy changes even when the fiscal health and public services of the jurisdiction are not substantially at risk. This market assessment calls into question the indiscriminate use of the ballot box to test levy ideas; it underscores the need to ration the levies taken to the voting box.

Property Tax Base

There are basically two components to the property tax, real property and personal property. Real property includes land and improvements. Personal property can further be broken down to include tangible and intangible assets. Tangible assets includes physical items the individual owns, such as cars, boats, machinery, livestock, furnishings, etc. These are items the individual owns because of their intrinsic value. Intangible assets involve the individual taxpayer's legal property rights to valuable assets such as bank accounts, mortgages, stocks and bonds, and patents and copyrights. These assets the individual holds because they represent her/his right of ownership to something else. These are general definitions; there are, of course, numerous local variations.

Intangible property can be somewhat problematic depending on how assets are defined and what type of assets are included in the base. Some intangible assets are merely representative of real or personal property; others stand on their own separately. When intangible assets that are representative of real or personal property, such as mortgages, are included in the base, there is a problem of duplication. Some assets in the base are taxed twice, once on their own and again on the representation.

Some types of tangible personal property cannot be assessed because there is no acceptable method for determining ownership. An example is household goods. The most commonly taxed tangible personal property is commercial and industrial property. Usually this consists of machinery, equipment, and inventories.

The base upon which a real property tax is levied may be eroded as a result of exemptions. While the case for each tax base reduction rests on political acceptability, the equity of the property tax is reduced as a result. This can take the form of outright removal of property from consideration or property that is counted but later exempted. In far too many governments, no enumeration or tax value is calculated for property owned by governmental, religious, charitable, and education organizations. State constitutions may prohibit taxation of certain types of property, such as wealth held in the form of mutual funds, stocks, and other investment options. The lost revenues attributed to exemptions are unknown. In other jurisdictions the property may be exempt but it is subject to enumeration and valuation and then exempted.

Personal Property Tax

A property tax can also apply against tangible personal property, especially inventory and vehicles. While real property (land and immovable improvements, such as buildings) is generally the most widely known aspect of a property tax, personal property may be subject to taxation. Personal property usually includes livestock, household furniture, and business inventory (including automobile dealer inventories). The definition can also capture surface and subsurface oil and gas drilling equipment, and, in a more controversial manner, unextracted oil and gas reserves.

The assessment of inventory is fraught with problems due to the ease by which taxpayers can avoid taxes by underreporting stocks and moving goods and products out of the taxing site. In addition, inventories are inherently difficult to assess at fair market value due to differing accounting techniques employed by businesses. Thus, auditing of this difficult to administer tax is often ineffective, resulting in substantial lost revenues.

One application of an inventory tax is for property "in-the-ground"—such as unproduced (unextracted) oil and gas reserves. Yet when assessed, the value of the unextracted property is subject to market prices (such as oil prices), subjecting the taxing body to fluctuating revenue yields, as confirmed by Texas local governments in the 1980s.

Assessment

Probably the most serious issue plaguing the property tax is assessment. There are two basic problems, underassessment and inequity of individual assessments. As of the 1980 Census, the Census Bureau reports that on average real property is assessed at approximately 40% of market value. Underassessment is problematic because it results in higher tax rates levied against the base. If all property is equally underassessed, say at some uniform percentage of market value, then the only problem is unnecessarily high tax rates.

However, underassessment across the board usually results in unequal underassessment for individuals. So it can become an equity problem.

If underassessment is the generally accepted practice, the assessor's job is more difficult and the taxpayer has no way to determine if the assessment is fair or accurate. When full market value is the basis for assessment, the assessor has one concrete target for each parcel of property. Without such, by what standard does the assessor underassess? Underassessment easily gives way to unequal treatment. Moreover, the taxpayer has no way of knowing if her/his treatment is different from that received by others. However, if the practice is to assess at full market value, the taxpayer has a concrete basis of comparison.

Underassessment can bring on other problems. For example, a jurisdiction's total assessed value may be tied legislatively to other financial arrangements such as debt limitations or the basis for distribution of grant-in-aid funds. Many states provide tax breaks such as the exemption for owner-occupied residential housing. Underassessment increases the value of the exemption beyond the statutory dollar value.

By using the jurisdiction's total assessed value as the basis for other financial decisions, states encourage local officials to underassess and overassess. Localities may be encouraged to underassess to reduce their portion of the county property tax burden. Conversely, they may overassess to increase their portions of grants-in-aid or shared revenues, and to raise their debt limits.

There are two ways for states to resolve this problem. One is to stop using total assessed value as the basis for other financial decisions. The second is to require assessment at full market value.[17]

Reappraisal

When property is reappraised local governments may be limited in taking automatic advantage of increased appraisals, result in a "revenue neutral" approach. If reappraisal resulting in higher assessed values, existing millages are automatically "rolled back" to a level that will generate no more than collected under the prior levy at the prior assessment. This has been called a "truth in taxation" measure. To "roll forward" up to the prior levy, thereby capturing the increased assessment values, may require a supermajority (two-thirds) vote of the governing body.

Administration

The property tax collection process has historically been a local government function. Local governments were apportioned annual sums to collect in property taxes on behalf of the state treasury. During the Depression, property tax payments declined severely and many states relinquished their portion to relieve local governments. Since the Depression the percentage of state revenue attributable to the property tax has continued to decline. Alternative revenue sources have replaced the property tax, primarily sales and income taxes.

---

[17] Pillai (1987) presents results that show assessment reform can result in increased revenues to local governments due to an increase in the base. However, the increases can be accompanied by some shifting in the property tax burden to residential property owners from other classes of property owners.

The goals of property tax administration are fourfold: maximize revenues, uniform treatment of taxpayers, taxpayer compliance, and tax official compliance. Uniform treatment has far-reaching ramifications. Taxpayers who believe they are treated as their peers are more likely to disclose and more willing to pay. This is true irrespective of the tax policy. Greater taxpayer compliance protects the revenue stream, and serves to ease the administrative tasks of collection, auditing, and investigation. Not only is uniformity important to efficient administration and protection of revenues, but it also underlies the equity of the tax systems.

Across the 50 states, there are two schools of thought regarding administration of the property tax and the role of the states, centralized and decentralized administration. Decentralized administration is by far the more traditional model. Supporters argue that property values are best understood by local officials, who will better serve the interests of the local community. In many states using this model, local officials resist professionalism and centralization in an effort to protect their traditional roles. Such systems are often highly political.

During the 1930s, as the states withdrew from the property tax arena, the general wisdom was that local officials would be more capable of evaluating local property. Over the years, however, the evidence shows that this has not been the case. Local control of the property tax has resulted in poor administration and deterioration of assessment and equity.

A few states have moved assessment to the state level. Others have moved to encourage professional training for local assessors. States may also mandate that standards regarding assessment be met by local assessors.

Centralized administration, including close supervision of local officials by the state, tends to be supported by larger property taxpayers. It is argued that uniformity and more streamlined administration occurs with the centralized approach, and that centralized systems are more equitable. In such systems, the discretion of local assessors and other officials is limited by state monitoring and legal requirements, resulting in more uniform treatment across taxpayers.

Recent studies of assessment review and appeals systems have shown that uniform treatment and equity may be enhanced through centralized administration and increased professionalism.[18] In addition, increased services to taxpayers, facilitating their participation in administration, helped to curb assessment problems. Increased taxpayer knowledge of and easy access to the system is central to improving equity. Indeed, it may not be decentralization that is problematic; rather, politicization is possibly the culprit. Local control can be retained if political discretion is held in check by taxpayer involvement and uniform standards.[19]

Economic Effects

Incidence

There are two approaches used to evaluate the incidence of the property tax (see Aronson and Hilley, 1986). The first approach treats the property tax as two separate taxes, a tax on land and tax on improvements. The burden of the tax on land is born by the owner exclu-

---

[18] See Alexander (1985) and Landretti (1988) for discussions of increased use of computer technology in property tax administration.

[19] See Pops (1985).

sively, while the tax on improvements is shifted to consumers in the form of higher prices for goods. The result here is a tax that is regressive across some income groups, primarily those with incomes below $30,000.

Adherents to the second approach argue that the burden of the tax is born by the property owners, falling on the income they derive from owning the property. The property tax is perceived as a tax on capital income paid by the owners of capital. Here the result is a progressively distributed tax burden.

Which approach yields the correct assessment of property tax incidence? The answer to that question is difficult. Both approaches rest on assumptions which are questionable. And as yet, there are no empirical answers.[20]

Equity

The base of the property tax is the gross value of the property, not the property owners' income. All taxes levied against things share this trait. The rate of the property tax is typically *ad valorem,* that is, proportional. Equity can be defined in many ways; however, one definition of equity is tax liability should be proportionate across income groups. If this definition is accepted, then the property tax is problematic in relation to equity.[21]

CONSUMPTION TAXES

A consumption tax is levied on a taxpayer's expenditures for goods and services rather than on that person's income or property. Various types of consumption taxes are in use today. On the state and local levels, retail sales taxes are employed. At all levels of American government, excise taxes are used to generate revenues based on the consumption of such items as alcohol, tobacco, and petroleum products. A later section of the chapter examines a third tax form, the value-added tax.

General Sales Taxes

The most widely used of the consumption taxes is the general sales tax. Its initial development was somewhat slow at state level due to the success of excise taxes.[22] There was also the dual fear of out-migration to nonsales tax states and taxing interstate commerce. The latter was brought on by the Supreme Court's broad interpretation of constitutional protection of interstate commerce.[23]

States started to look to the sales tax during the Great Depression. A new revenue source was needed that was insensitive to economic downturns. The property tax was collapsing and there did not appear to be any competition for retail sales as a base coming from the federal government. Congress had demonstrated that it was unwilling to levy a federal sales tax.

---

[20] See Harmon (1989) for results showing that for states with property tax rates that exceed the national average and where the property tax base is primarily residential, the burden is distributed proportionately.

[21] Additional equity problems are generated by tax revolt measures such as California's Proposition 13; see Wiseman (1989).

[22] For a general discussion of the sales tax see Aronson and Hilley (1986) and ACIR (1989).

[23] All interstate transactions that are not to be taxed by the states include sales by in state merchants to out-of-state taxpayers, and sales by out-of-state merchants to in-state taxpayers.

Almost all states use the sales tax and in half the states, local governments use it as well. In Louisiana, for example, even school districts levy a sales tax.

Sales Tax Base

Generally the sales tax is levied against nongrocery and nonpharmacy physical goods at the point of retail sale. By focusing the tax base on retail sales, two important problems are avoided. Manufacturers are not put at a competitive disadvantage, and the complications with interstate commerce are reduced.

Specific exemptions in a retail sales tax base narrow the focus even more. These exemptions represent political and technical concerns. Some states, Florida and Massachusetts, for example, have recently made an effort to extend general sales tax to service activity in the economy as service becomes more and more a part of the economy. There is strong political resistance, but this is an area to watch in the near future. Services are a logical inclusion, and by excluding them from the sales tax, the state is missing a large part of consumer spending.

When local governments have the authority to impose varying tax levels (up to a state statutory limit), the aggregate tax rate will vary within county boundaries and throughout the state, resulting in significant tax overlap. Besides the complexity for vendors who must collect the tax, sales tax differentials can influence sales and, therefore, tax collections. "Jurisdiction shopping" can occur especially by higher income groups and for large durable purchases, such as furniture and appliances. Most sales taxes are actually a sales tax on purchases within the jurisdiction and a use tax on purchases outside the jurisdiction but subsequently brought into the jurisdiction. The base of a local sales (and use) tax is subject to erosion as a result of decisions made by the local governing body, the state or the Federal government. For example, the state imposes uniformity by permitting certain exemptions against both state and local sales tax bases. In some cases, local governments may further erode the base by granting additional exemptions.

Actions by the federal government influence state and local sales taxes. In 1985, Federal law was changed to exempt federal food stamps from state and local sales taxes. Federal income tax reform in 1986 eliminated the deduction on federal income tax returns for state and local sales taxes paid. Of course, this only affects those who itemize their federal taxes. The loss of deductibility should make taxpayers more conscious of the higher economic burden associated with the sales tax relative to other taxes, resulting in a resistance to higher, or even current, sales tax levels. Not only has the incentive to utilize the sales tax weakened, but an incentive exists to shift the tax burden away from the sales tax and to those areas where federal tax law lessens the economic burden, such as toward more property and income taxes, which remain deductible. Where those tax instruments are greatly restricted, outright prohibited reliance upon the sales tax continues despite the federal tax code disincentives.

Vendors Compensation

Jurisdictions levying a sales tax generally provide the vendor with a means to recoup the expenses of collecting and remitting the tax to the taxing jurisdiction. Once the total tax amount due is calculated, vendors are generally allowed to keep part of the tax due, usually a percentage of the total tax due. This method of compensation assumes that collection costs increase in the same manner as total sales, termed a variable cost in accounting terminology. Instead, the vendor's tax collection costs may represent a fixed cost but the vendor receives a variable benefit—vendor compensation.

A vendor's compensation system based upon a percentage of collections has flaws. An approach used in some places is to decrease the compensation rate as tax liability increases. This approach permits smaller (in tax dollars collected) vendors to receive compensation for their tax collection role while restricting the larger vendors from receiving an inequitable return for the same role.

Administration

Local governments have significant latitude in maximizing the yield of the constrained sales tax since they retain control over enforcement and collections. The search for tax efficiencies often turns to the consolidation of sales tax collection systems either county-wide or at the state level. The purpose of such efficiencies is to reduce the amount of the gross tax proceeds that must go for administration; local services are financed from the net. To dismiss efficiency moves in a perfunctory manner may indicate the lack of interest in maximizing dollars for use by direct local services.[24]

The collection costs as a percentage of sales tax revenue varies by jurisdiction. For example, countywide collection costs as a percentage of total collections may range from less than 1% to 10%. As the total cost of collections increases, other administrative arrangements may save taxpayers money. For example, the state may be able to collect the local sales tax at a lower cost and with more effective auditing capability, as is required in many states.

Inefficient local collection practices are codified by statute and contract. For example, the Sheriff of Jefferson Parish, Louisiana—the major suburban county adjacent to New Orleans—collects the tax and charges 11% of the gross to the parish governing body and 9.5% to the school district, all according to state law. In such a situation officials have made explicit allocation choices: more for administrative overhead and less for the direct local services explicitly called for by the levy.

Equity

The most severe complaint is the regressivity of the sales tax. While the rate is usually a flat rate tax—a proportional rate—a percentage of retail sales, as a percentage of income, the poor forfeit a higher percentage than the wealthy. The degree of regressivity is contingent on the coverage of the tax. Exemptions for food, drugs, and other necessities mitigates the regressivity. However, these exemptions are a clear example of how two requirements of tax policy conflict. The exemptions that are an attempt to make the tax more equitable, complicate administration of the tax.

Many economists who sympathize with the goal to moderate regressivity suggest elimination of all exemptions and the provision of an income tax credit for purchases of necessities by low income households. This solution is only useful to a state that imposes an income tax. This approach would improve horizontal equity, reduce compliance costs, and increase revenues.

---

[24] See Martin (1987) for description of the first interstate compact to coordinate enforcement of sales and use taxes.

For a majority of taxpayers, the differences in tax burden associated with the sales tax result from differences in consumption patterns related to factors other than income. Equity arguments concerning the sales tax burden must be considered in light of the total tax burden. Regressivity or progressivity of a given tax should only be significant in terms of the equity of the total tax system borne by the taxpayer. The sacrifice argument assumes summation of sacrifices imposed by all taxes in whole tax system. There are decisive and practical reasons that explain the use of regressive taxes by local governments. States have more latitude, but choices on progression are still limited by migration possibilities. The federal government has the greatest freedom to impose progression. The key issue is the incidence on individuals of total taxes from all three levels. Incidence assumptions can determine the degree of progressivity.

There remain two major questions regarding progression. Does Congress determine progression of federal taxes after considering evidence of incidence of state and local taxes? And can Congress adjust the progression of federal taxes to fit 50 different tax systems? Does Congress use federal taxes as instrument to secure the desired total incidence? Given the evidence, that would be hard to prove. Such a system would be difficult for the federal government to design and implement. The scale of federal progression needed for states relying primarily on the sales tax would not be at all suitable for states relying primarily on the income tax. Congress could, of course, address some hypothetical average state. If that was the case, taxpayers in states with the greatest deviations from the hypothetical average would get the most imperfect adjustments.

Excise Taxes

In contrast to the general sales tax, certain taxes are levied on specific commodities or services and are often called excise taxes. Federal excise taxes date back to the beginning of the republic starting with an excise tax on distilled spirits in 1791. An elaborate excise tax system that included taxes on liquor, carriages, snuff, sugar, and other activities was used to pay the Revolutionary War debt. The early pattern was to impose the taxes to finance wars and then to repeal them after the crisis. Along the way, however, many became permanent parts of the federal revenue system. Congress has expanded the scope of excise taxes over the last several decades, either to fund targeted programs or to promote various social goals. Recent examples of social goals pursued through excise taxes include the "gas guzzler" tax on fuel-inefficient vehicles and the tax on hazardous chemical substances.

There are three basic forms of excise taxes, although not mutually exclusive. User fee-oriented taxes are those where users pay for benefits received. Examples include a motor fuels tax to fund the highway infrastructure and room taxes on hotel and motel occupancy. The second form is sumptuary or "sin" taxes. They impose a price on those with poor health habits, like smokers and drinkers. The third form is regulatory or privilege taxes, where the government permits specific economic activity, especially a monopoly, in return for payment of tax. An example of this form of tax is a local government gross receipts public utility tax. Each form of taxation will be briefly reviewed by looking at one example.

Motor Fuels Tax

Motor fuel taxes are used to finance roads, highways, and public transit, since those who use the transportation infrastructure pay for the service. This is most visibly evident in the

Interstate Highway System. In the 1950s, federal excise taxes on gasoline and other related goods were earmarked for the Highway Trust Fund. It continues to fund the large federally funded highway system, but when federal gasoline taxes were recently increased, some tax proceeds were diverted instead to general purposes.

Most states prohibit local governments from separately adopting this tax; instead, the state agrees to share its tax proceeds with local governments for specific purposes. In states where there is local tax authority, county governments are the most frequent taxing jurisdiction.

Alcoholic Beverage Tax

Taxes on alcoholic beverages have a long history in America, with the Whiskey Rebellion of 1794 being an early indicator of the political ramifications of such taxation. These taxes are considered a form of "sin" tax since they may be designed, in part, to discourage the consumption of items that impose social costs—as in accidents caused by drunk drivers. Some form of the alcoholic beverage tax is found at each level of government, although less frequently at the local level. Often, a local beer tax is "piggybacked" on a similar state tax. The state takes a collection fee off the top, remitting the remaining amount to the appropriate taxing authority.

Privilege Tax

As a way to allow public utilities (e.g., gas, electric, cable television, and telephone) to utilize public right-of-way, governments grant franchises, but at the price of a tax on that privilege. Needless to say, a franchise is a valuable asset to a public utility and, as a result, government extracts a price. Privilege taxes usually are structured as a percentage of gross receipts. Utilities are permitted to pass the tax on to the customer, thus making the tax regressive given the necessity of such services to households. At the same time, however, this scheme makes the tax easy to administer since the firm, not the government, handles collection expenses.[25]

Equity and Economic Effects

The equity and economic effects of excise taxes depend on the design of each particular tax structure. Three points need to be made. One concerns the equity effect. An analysis by the Congressional Budget Office (1990) of increased federal taxation on tobacco, alcoholic beverages, and motor fuels relative to family *incomes* shows that the burden would fall more on lower-income families than other families. The study reveals that when measured relative to total annual family *expenditures*, however, the results for lower-income families are similar to those for other families. Second, excise taxes may help offset social costs associated with their consumption and encourage certain behavior such as the conservation of oil. Third, high tax rates relative to surrounding jurisdictions can lead to location-driven consumption, that is, purchases in the lower tax area.

VALUE-ADDED TAX

The value-added tax (VAT) is often suggested as an option for tax reform in the United States. Widespread use in European countries coupled with recent adoption in Canada

---

[25] See Bland (1989) for a comprehensive review of local taxes.

focuses attention on the VAT as a possible tax reform. Advocates of VAT adoption in the United States see it as a means to provide relief from existing taxes, especially federal income taxes and the payroll tax, and/or increasing federal deficits (Pechman, 1989). Does the VAT necessarily hold the same promise for the United States as for Europe and Canada? Such a question warrants thorough examination. However, we will first define the VAT, and discuss various forms of the VAT. Secondly, we will discuss alternative modes of implementation. Finally, we will adress the question, is the VAT a serious contender for tax reform in the United States?[26]

What Is The VAT?

The VAT is for all practical purposes a sales tax on the value added. The value added for any producer is the difference between sales and the value of materials, supplies, and labor inputs for goods produced. It differs from the sales tax in that it is collected at each stage of the production process rather than at the end point of retail sale. The simplified example below illustrates the basic operation of the VAT.[27]

Producer A makes a profit of $10 on good A.
Producer B buys all of Producer A's output and produces good B valued at $30.
Producer C buys all of Producer B's output and produces goods sold retail for $60.

The value added by Producers A, B, and C, respectively is $10, $20, and $30, for a total value added of $60. Should government impose a VAT at a rate of ten percent, government will collect $6 in revenue. Producer A will pay $1, Producer B will pay $2, and Producer C will pay $3. At each stage in the production process, government collects ten percent of the value added. For the consumer, the effect is to raise the price of the good by $6. Government could generate the same revenue by levying a ten percent retail sales tax at the final point of sale to be collected by Producer C. The VAT can be very similar to the retail sales tax from the consumer's perspective. It does differ in its administration for government and collection for other taxpayers throughout the production process.[28]

Implementing the VAT

Two major implementation questions must be addressed when impelmenting a VAT: methods of collection and definition of the base. Collection is simply an administrative/enforcement issue. Whereas, definition of the base affects rate setting, distribution of the tax burden and, ultimately the efficiency and equity of the tax.

First we will address collection. There are basically two methods: the *invoice* method and the *subtraction* method. The invoice method is by far the most popular. It is used in all European countries imposing the VAT and it is the method suggested in most serious reform proposals in the United States. The subtraction method is the simplest and most direct.[29]

[26] Aaron (1981) provides an excellent summary background on the VAT and its implementation in Europe as compared with proposed implementation in the United States.
[27] This three producer example is a variation of one used by Aaron (1981). It is modified and repeated to illustrate various changes in the VAT.
[28] For a comparison of the VAT and the retail sales tax, see Pechman (1987) and Aaron and Galper (1985).
[29] See Aaron and Galper (1985) for a clear discussion of the subtraction method.

In a system using the invoice method, the VAT is collected by each producer on all sales. The tax is then rolled into the price of the good paid by the buyer at the next stage. Producers receive a credit for taxes they pay their suppliers if they can document the taxes have been paid. The assumption here is that an automatic audit trail is created as buyers insist all previously paid taxes are recorded. Using our three producer example: Producer A would pay a tax of $1; Producer B would pay a gross tax of $3 but would receive a credit of $1 for the tax paid by Producer A; Producer C would pay a gross tax of $6 with a credit of $3 for taxes paid by A and B. Government has generated revenue of $10 or ten percent of the value added (Aaron, 1981).

A second more complex issue is determination of the base. Here several important questions arise: what is done with international trade, and exempt goods and/or variable rates? International trade complicates imposition of the VAT because treatment of imports may necessarily differ from treatment of exports. Most countries currently use the *destination principle*. Goods for export are exempt or all taxes paid are rebated at the point of export. Imports, on the other hand are taxed fully. No credits are given for taxes paid in other countries, thereby maintaining imported goods on the same plane with goods produced domestically (Aaron, 1981).

The most efficient VAT would be one with a proportional rate, i.e., a single rate applied against all goods. Not only is this more efficient, but it simplifies administration as well. Economic efficiency and administrative ease notwithstanding, the question of equity looms over the VAT. Pechman (1989, 1987) argues the adoption of the VAT in the United States would be regressive. Regressivity can be mitigated somewhat through exemptions for necessities, or application of differential rates. Differential rates, including zero rates for some goods (exemption) is a potential administrative nightmare.

A VAT for the United States

Should a VAT be adopted in the United States? Such a step is not likely to yield the same experience as in Europe.[30] There are several major differences to consider.

The administrative apparatus for the VAT does not exist in the United States. In most European countries, the VAT replaced an old regressive tax, the *gross turnover taxes,* which operated very similarly to the VAT. Consequently, the administrative system required was already in place. Further, taxpayers were already accustomed to paying taxes in the required fashion. So there was little start up costs and not much need in tax payer education, two benefits which will not be realized in the United States.

The gross turnover tax was also an inefficient tax. There was no credit to producers for taxes paid at previous stages. Needless to say, such a system served as an incentive for vertical mergers which may not have been otherwise justified (Aaron, 1981). Using the earlier example, Producer A would pay a tax of $1; Producer B would pay a tax of $3, and would receive no credit for taxes paid by A; and Producer C would pay taxes of $6, and also be given no credit for previous taxes paid. The total revenue generated to government would be $10 as opposed to $6. However, through a merger, Producer ABC would only incur a liability of $6 under the tax (Aaron, 1981). In Europe, the VAT replaced inefficient taxes, such is not the case in the United States.

Another major difference with implementation in Europe is the governmental system. Most countries adopting the VAT are unitary systems. The expectations being the

---

[30] Aaron (1981) provides an extensive discussion on the European experience with the VAT and the implications for adoption in the United States.

Federal Republic of Germany (prior to unification) and most recently Canada. While the German national government shared revenues with local governments, the formula used was a source of conflict (Aaron, 1981). On the other hand, implementation in Canada, will be interesting to watch.

CONCLUSION

As this chapter has demonstrated, tax structure design is complicated and has real economic implications. To levy a tax is to impose an economic burden. Therefore, taxation and its design deserve deliberate decisions with clearly defined purposes and scope. Tax policy, however, accumulates over time. Compounding the situation is the cumulative tax burden arising from taxes levied by overlapping taxing jurisdictions. Plus, governments use relative tax positions for competitive advantage in the drive for economic development. As a result, from time to time, governments turn to tax reform and comprehensive revenue system reform. This comprehensive approach is warranted given the increased emphasis on non-tax revenue sources due, in part, to voter reluctance to increase taxes. Together, these considerations illustrate the need for deliberate decisions regarding tax design in particular, and the revenue system in general.

NOTE

Sections of Local Income Taxes, Property Taxes, General Sales Taxes and Excise Taxes (pp. 285–295) are from W. Bartley Hildreth (1988) and are reprinted by permission of Louisiana State University Press from *Louisiana's Fiscal Alternatives: Finding Permanent Solutions to Recurring Budget Crises,* edited by James A. Richardson. Copyright © 1988 by Louisiana State University Press.

REFERENCES

Aaron, H. J. (1981). Introduction and summary. In H. J. Aaron, (Ed.), *The Value-Added Tax: Lessons from Europe.* Washington, D.C.: The Brookings Institution.

Aaron, H. J. and Galper, H. (1984). Reforming the tax system. In Alice Rivlin (Ed.), *Economic Choices: 1984* (pp. 87–117). Washington, D.C.: The Brookings Institution.

Aaron, H. J., and Galper, H. (1985). *Assessing Tax Reform.* Washington, D.C.: The Brookings Institution.

Advisory Commission on Intergovernmental Relations. (1987). *Local Revenue Diversification: User Charges.* Washington, D.C.: Advisory Commission on Intergovernmental Relations.

Advisory Commission on Intergovernmental Relations. (1988). *Local Revenue Diversification: Local Income Taxes.* Washington, D.C.: Advisory Commission on Intergovernmental Relations.

Advisory Commission on Intergovernmental Relations. (1989). *Local Revenue Diversification: Local Sales Taxes.* Washington, D.C.: Advisory Commission on Intergovernmental Relations.

Alexander, J. T. (1985). Cost-effective solutions using small computers for property tax efforts. *Property Tax Journal, 4*(1): 17–24.

Aronson, J. R. (1985). *Public Finance.* New York: McGraw-Hill.

Aronson, J. R. and Hilley, J. L. (1986). *Financing State and Local Governments,* 4th ed. Washington, D.C.: The Brookings Institution.

Bland, R. L. (1989). *A Revenue Guide for Local Government.* Washington, D.C.: International City Management Association.

Break, G. F. (1974). The incidence and economic effects of taxation. In Alan S. Blinder and Robert M. Solow (Eds.), *The Economics of Public Finance* (pp. 119–237). Washington, D.C.: The Brookings Institution.

Congressional Budget Office (1990). *Federal Taxation of Tobacco, Alcoholic Beverages, and Motor Fuels.* Washington, D.C.: Congressional Budget Office.

Cory, D. (1985). Congestion costs and quality adjusted user fees: A methodological note. *Land Economics, 61*(4): 452–455.

Flanagan, J. A., and Perkins, S. J. (1987). Annual user fee review program of the City of Phoenix, Arizona. *Government Finance Review, 3*(3): 13–18.

Fullerton, D., and Mackie, J. B. (1989). Economic efficiency in recent tax reform history: Policy reversals or consistent improvements. *National Tax Journal, 42*(1): 1–13.

General Accounting Office (1990). *Federal-State-Local Relations: Trends of the Past Decade and Emerging Issues.* Washington, D.C.: General Accounting Office.

Gold, S. D. (1987). Developments in state finances, 1983 to 1987. *Public Budgeting and Finance, 7*(1): 5–23.

Harmon, O. R. (1989). A new view of the incidence of the property tax: The case of New Jersey. *Public Finance Quarterly, 17*(3):323–348.

Hildreth, W. B. (1988). State and local fiscal relations in Louisiana. In J. A. Richardson (Ed.), *Louisiana's Fiscal Alternatives: Finding Permanent Solutions to Recurring Budget Crises* (pp. 74–104). Baton Rouge, LA: Louisiana State University Press.

Holcombe, R. G. (1988). *Public Finance.* Reston, VA: Reston Publishing.

Inman, R. P. (1989). The local decision to tax: Evidence from large U.S. cities. *Regional Science & Urban Economics, 19*(1): 455–491.

Kaplow, L. (1989). Horizontal equity: Measures in search of a principle. *National Tax Journal, 42*(2):139–154.

Katz, J. (1990). Mission impossible. *Governing, 3*(9): 28–33.

Kolhauser, R. (1988). The growth in state taxes: A review of the 1971–87 period. *Illinois Business Review, 45*(3):9–13.

Landretti, G. J. (1988). The role of automation in the pursuit of full value: A case study. *Property Tax Journal, 7*(1): 101–127.

Martin, S. W. (1987). The Great Lakes Interstate Sales Compact: An innovative approach to tax enforcement. *Government Finance Review, 3*(1): 15–17.

Norris, J. E. (1989). The assessment of user fees to recover generic regulatory costs. *Public Utilities Fortnightly, 123*(13): 42–45.

Pechman, J. A. (1987). *Federal Tax Policy,* 5th ed. Washington, D.C.: The Brookings Institution.

Pechman, J. A. (1989). *Tax Reform, the Rich and the Poor,* 2nd ed. Washington, D.C.: The Brookings Institution.

Pillai, V. (1987). Property tax assessment reform: A source of local revenue windfall or fiscal retrenchment? *American Journal of Economics and Sociology, 46*(3): 341–353.

Pops, G. M. (1985). An overview of property assessment review and appeal systems: Goals, variables, and issues. *Property Tax Journal, 4*(2): 105–128.

Senge, S. V. (1986). Local government user charges and cost-volume-profit analysis. *Public Budgeting and Finance, 6*(3): 92–105.

Snavely, K. (1988). Innovations in state tax administration. *Public Administration Review, 48*(5): 903–909.

Thai, K. V., and Sullivan, D. (1989). The impact of termination of General Revenue Sharing on New England local government finance. *Public Administration Review, 49*(1): 61–67.

Veseth, M. (1984). *Public Finance.* Reston, VA: Reston Publishing Company.

Wiseman, M. (1989). Proposition 13 and Effective Property Tax Rates. *Public Finance Quarterly, 17*(4): 391–408.

12

Tax Expenditure Control

Jean Harris   *School of Business Administration, Pennsylvania State University–Harrisburg, Middletown, Pennsylvania*

INTRODUCTION

Billions of dollars of indirect, constructive spending occur each year via tax provisions. Unlike direct spending, indirect spending accomplished via tax provisions is exempt from the scrutiny of a systematic and traditional control process and remains hidden from public view in the technical jargon of tax codes.

In a speech delivered in 1967, Surrey coined the term "tax expenditures" to describe spending implemented by way of tax provision (Forman, 1986). Offering further explanation, Surrey and McDaniel write:

> The term "tax expenditures" refers to the fact that many of the provisions of the U.S. tax laws are intended, not as necessary structural parts of a normative tax, but rather as tax incentives or hardship relief provisions. These provisions are thus really spending measures. (Surrey and McDaniel, 1980, pp. 123–124)

By normative tax is meant a set of criteria for defining a model tax; for example, a model income tax. Other terms used to describe the tax expenditure concept are backdoor spending, hidden spending, off-budget spending, silent spending, and tax subsidy.

A manifest example of a tax expenditure is an energy credit. Noncohesive public incentives to encourage energy conservation could be structured as a direct expenditure, such as a grant, or as a tax expenditure, such as an energy credit. To the representatives of a governmental entity, grants represent an allocation of benefits financed as a direct expenditure of a resource, revenue at present in existence, whereas tax expenditures represent an allocation of benefits financed via indirect expenditure of a resource, revenue potentially collectable in the future. While an energy credit clearly is a tax expenditure, one may question whether a tax deduction for dependents within a family is intended as a subsidy (tax expenditure) or as an adjustment made to increase the degree of progressivity of the tax structure. Because the definition of income is open to debate, classification of tax expenditures may be more a matter of placement on a continuum than a division between dichotomous categories (Pomp, 1988).

Similar economic effects result in relationship to direct expenditures and to tax expenditures. But consideration of the most basic control features indicates a difference with reference to accountability for these two spending mechanisms. Basic control includes such procedures as projection of costs, an institutionalized competition for resource appropriation, periodic authorization of spending, and monitoring of spending.

The monitoring of spending includes maintenance of cost information, public distribution of cost information, and comprehensive examination of efficiency or effectiveness either alone or in combination of selected expenditures (via operational auditing). Each of these basic control procedures is much stronger for direct expenditures than for tax expenditures.

Increases in either tax expenditures or direct expenditures ultimately result in higher taxes or less services. Direct expenditures reduce the stock of public revenues on hand at present by increasing disbursements, outflows. In contrast, tax expenditures reduce the flow of public revenues potentially on hand by reducing collections, inflows in the future. Direct expenditures and tax expenditures when adopted share two attributes: (1) each provides a benefit, and (2) each reduces public revenues. Thus, it is this sharing of these two attributes, in particular, that supports the characterization of tax expenditures as a form of spending equivalent to that of direct expenditures.

A tax expenditure represents two separate constructive transactions (between taxpayer and governmental entity) offset and then reported as one net transaction. From the perspective of the governmental entity, the first transaction, A, is the collection of an economically imposed tax, and the second transaction, B, is a resource disbursement affected via tax provision. Because the parties to both transactions are the same, it is easy to affect an offset. The result is one net transaction, C, between taxpayer and taxing agency, representing the reported receipt of a net amount of revenue. If transactions A and B were reported as two separate transactions, however, a distinct record for collection and another for disbursement would exist. Instead, this one net transaction, C, represents collection of the economically imposed tax (transaction A) reduced by a resource disbursement (transaction B). Recording the net transaction, C, obscures both the economically imposed tax and the resource disbursement, and thereby impairs the exercise of control over the collections function (tax policy) and the disbursements function (budget policy) of the governmental entity.

McDaniel (1979a) provides a comprehensive listing of the various forms tax expenditures may take as follows:

1. Departures from a normative tax base, such as exclusions, exemptions, deductions, and credits.
2. Departure from normal rate structures, such as the granting of preferential rates on capital gains.
3. Departure from rules defining taxable units, such as the rule that corporations and their shareholders are separate entities.
4. Departure from normal accounting period rules, such as the authorization of accelerated depreciation.
5. Departures from normal international tax rules, such as exclusion of income earned abroad.

Although tax expenditures are sometimes described as a form of silent spending, this description is a misnomer because what is silent (i.e., observed) is not the spending *per se* but the recorded trail of transactions as found in the traditional financial control system. Surrey and McDaniel observe,

> . . . it is being increasingly recognized that unless attention is paid to tax expenditures,
> a country does not have either its tax policy or its budget policy under full control.
> (Surrey and McDaniel, 1980, p. 124)

Some argue that tax expenditure controls lack the simplicity of traditional controls. But the offsetting of collections and disbursements (1) violates the most basic principle of financial control (segregation of collections and disbursements) and (2) converts two simple and separate transactions into a single complex net transaction. Segregating collections from disbursements contributes to the reliability of information pertaining to collections and to disbursements. Conversely, offsetting collections and disbursements impairs the reliability of such information and, as a consequence, makes planning and monitoring more difficult than is necessary. Additionally, failing to equate tax expenditures with direct expenditures severely weakens the control activated by expenditures competing for resources. If the revenue system were not used to affect spending, traditional controls would suffice; with spending being implemented through the revenue system, nontraditional controls are necessary because the alternative to this situation is no control.

This chapter focuses on the development of control procedures for tax expenditures. Two separate but related questions merit consideration with reference to the tax expenditures. First, what kinds of control procedures are appropriate for a tax expenditure control system? Second, how desirable are individual items of tax expenditure? The latter question lies outside the scope of concern in this chapter. In considering tax expenditure control, acceptance of the tax expenditure concept and disclosure of tax expenditure costs are necessary but not sufficient conditions for tax expenditure control. The net transaction nature of tax expenditures, the magnitude of expenditures, and the weakness of existing controls create the need for stronger tax expenditure control systems.

The second question centers on the desirability of individual items of tax expenditure. Such a question relates not to the design of control systems but to their application. System design and application are related because a control system must ensure that information is relevant to the evaluation of individual items of tax expenditure. However, as stated previously, the evaluation of specific, individual items of tax expenditure is outside the scope of this present chapter.

CONTROL CONSIDERATIONS

The objective of tax expenditure control is to incorporate tax expenditure costs into policy analysis as a form of spending. As typical of control systems (Maciariello, 1984), a comprehensive tax expenditure control system encompassing planning, implementation, and monitoring would operate to affect (1) formulation of expectations inherent in planning allocation, (2) implementation of the allocation of resources, and (3) monitoring of performance resulting from resource allocation.

The practical motivation for tax expenditure control is that tax expenditures represent a significant amount of spending, which has the effect of transferring and allocating public resources. Tax expenditure may not be reported at the state and local levels. And even when reported, systematic monitoring of tax expenditures is uncommon. Although comprehensive examination to evaluate effectiveness or efficiency either alone or in combination (via operational auditing) is routine for direct expenditures, such examination is exceedingly rare for tax expenditures. Thus, tax expenditures, being exempt from the kinds of controls applicable to direct spending, are far more likely to escape annual review than direct expenditures. Because almost all tax expenditures are entitlements, it is extremely difficult to fix total costs in advance. Because the monitoring of tax expenditures is sporadic, excessive costs may be incurred for years before a control concern arises. Aside from being a weakly controlled form of spending, there are certain other characteristics of tax expenditures that intensify the need for them to be controlled.

Magnitude and Growth

The magnitude of federal tax expenditures is substantial, and they are increasing more rapidly than direct expenditures (Gregory and Morberg, 1990; Benker, 1985; Vasche, 1987). Estimated federal tax expenditures for 1991 are representative of 41% of direct federal spending (Gregory and Morberg, 1990). From 1978 throughout 1986 federal tax expenditures increased on average 16% each year, while each year direct expenditures increased on average 11% (Gregory and Morberg, 1990). Although federal tax reform in 1986 reduced tax expenditures, federal tax expenditures from 1988 to 1991 are estimated to be increasing faster than direct spending (Gregory and Morberg, 1990). This same trend of rapid tax expenditure growth was observed during the 1970s (Manvel, 1979; Noto, 1981).

At the state level tax expenditures are also substantial and increasing more rapidly than direct expenditures (Gregory and Morberg, 1990). In 1988, Michigan's tax expenditures were 49% of direct expenditures, and from 1982 throughout 1988 they increased on average 7.4% each year while direct expenditures increased on average each year by 6.7% (Gregory and Morberg, 1990). Vasche (1987) reports California's 1987–1988 tax expenditures were 45% of direct expenditures, and that for this same period tax expenditures increased by 8% as compared to a 3% increase for direct expenditures. For a discussion of the magnitude of passive tax expenditures, expenditures passed on to states by automatic incorporation of federal tax policy into state tax law, see Hildred and Pinto (1986).

Costs Ignored

Tax expenditures are often advocated as a means of introducing individual choice and administrative efficiency. Decision making is decentralized. Each taxpayer decides whether to pursue beneficial behavior, and benefits are promptly disbursed through tax filings. Structuring spending as a tax expenditure avoids the cost of creating or expanding administrative agencies to administer a direct expenditure program. But the tax expenditure solution is not without costs (Elkin, 1989). Absent control, the effect of tax expenditure policy may be obscured but not avoided. The emphasis on administrative efficiency often ignores other costs, such as windfall benefits, impaired administrative effectiveness, distorted tax and budget analyses, and unintended consequences.

Windfall Benefits

When tax expenditures are offered as incentives to alter taxpayer behavior, many taxpayers receive a windfall benefit for action they would have taken anyway in the absence of incentive. For example, if two-thirds of the taxpayers claiming an energy credit would have taken action to conserve energy without a tax incentive, the incentive only motivated one-third of the beneficiaries, and the remaining two-thirds received a windfall benefit. Windfall benefits are a special concern in the design of industrial development expenditures in particular.[1]

[1] For additional literature evaluating industrial development incentives, see Baum (1987), Bosworth (1984), Fisher (1985), Grady (1987), Gregory and Morberg (1990), Helms (1985), Jacobs (1979), Ledebur and Hamilton (1986), Lind and Elder (1986), McGuire (1986), M. McIntyre (1981), McIntyre and Tipps (1985), Papke and Papke (1986), Plaut and Pluta (1983), Peretz (1986, 1988), Pomp (1985a), Regan (1988), and Stephenson and Hewett (1985).

Impaired Administration

The primary function of a revenue agency is collection of revenue, not the administration of social programs. The effectiveness of having a support (staff) agency administer operational (line) programs such as child care, energy conservation, and industrial development is open to question. Tax agency personnel may be unaware of specific program goals, and unable to evaluate program efficiency or effectiveness. Public policy objectives such as antidiscrimination rules that apply to direct spending may not apply to tax expenditures. Although such costs are not measurable with any degree of precision nor perhaps even immediately apparent, long-term administrative effectiveness costs may attach to a tax agency administering operational programs.

Distorted Tax Analyses

The failure to separate collections (tax) and disbursement (budget) distorts the analyses of both tax and budget policies. Tax liability is reduced by a spending offset and thus does not provide a true measurement of tax in an economic sense. Additionally, budgets exclude indirect tax expenditures and thus do not provide a true measurement of total spending. This lack of reliability distorts the analyses of both tax and budget policies.

Whether tax expenditures distort tax equity depends on the definition given to the term tax. If one adopts the popular definition of tax (Benker, 1985) as net obligation (economic tax less resource disbursement), then tax expenditures potentially can affect tax equity. Tax expenditures, and tax incentives in particular, are not elements of a normative, theoretical concept of income. Yet these incentives may alter significantly the net obligation (economic tax less resource disbursement) of taxpayers in similar economic circumstances. Tax expenditures may be targeted to benefit taxpayers with the same income quite differently. Thus, the principle of horizontal equity, treating taxpayers in the same economic circumstances equally, appears to be violated because separate spending and tax transactions are combined in one net transaction. Besides this discrepancy, the principle of vertical equity, treating taxpayers in dissimilar economic circumstances fairly, may appear to be violated. A progressive tax system is considered fair on the basis of the theory of diminishing marginal utility of income. Tax expenditures may operate in such a fashion as to appear to be altering the nature of a progressive tax system. Within the framework of a progressive tax structure, tax expenditures have an upside-down affect because they increase the amount of spending directed to taxpayers with higher incomes. In the extreme, tax expenditures could operate to produce a progressive tax structure if based upon an economic tax (tax obligation before offset), but a regressive tax structure if based upon a net obligation tax (obligation after offset).

If one accepts the idea that tax expenditures are a form of spending and adopts the definition of economic tax as the gross obligation before offsetting resource disbursements (McDaniel, 1985), tax equity is not affected by tax expenditures any more than it is affected by direct spending, but resource distribution equity may be affected seriously. McDaniel (1985) argues that the problem is not the actual distortion of horizontal equity or vertical equity, but the distorted analysis of tax and budget issues resulting from failing to separate the net obligation into economically imposed tax and into resource disbursement for purposes of analysis.

Failure to distinguish between economic tax and resource disbursement has significant implications for revenue neutral tax reform. The argument for reform is that repeal of tax expenditures combined with reduction in the rate of economic tax will leave taxpayers in the same revenue neutral position. But the result of such reform may be to protect the benefit of tax expenditure spending for current beneficiaries via incorporation into the economic tax.

Distorted Spending Analysis

If tax expenditures are excluded from a total spending concept, spending analysis is distorted. No distributional accounting is available reporting who benefitted from tax expenditures and to what extent (Leonard, 1986). If fiscal crisis requires a reduction in spending or an increase in economically imposed tax, constructive spending (which occurs via tax provision) often is treated as an element of taxation protected from reduced spending (Thuronyi, 1988). The result is that substantial amounts of constructive spending are excluded from consideration when pending deficits mandate action. Consequently, if some stakeholders receive benefits from direct expenditures and other from tax expenditures, then the stakeholders receiving benefits from direct expenditures will bear a disproportionate share of the cost of deficit management.

Unintended Consequences

Tax expenditures are a form of subsidy to which qualifying taxpayers are entitled. If authorizing legislation is drafted with less than extreme caution, tax expenditure provisions may be claimed by more parties than anticipated and for unexpected purposes (e.g., industrial development bonds). Even if tax expenditures operate as intended, economic behavior may be distorted (e.g., overbuilding of commercial real estate).

THEORIES OF TAX EXPENDITURE USE AND REPORTING

Most of the literature about the subject at present focuses on amplifying the concept of tax expenditures, debating the concept or applying the concept in the evaluation of particular items of tax expenditure. Two issues that have received much less attention are (1) why tax expenditures are used as a financing mechanism and (2) what provokes control.

Tax Expenditures

Wildavsky (1979a) describes the tax expenditure mechanism as an "end run" around normal allocation procedures, and contends that use of it does not result from an ignorance of economics. Senator Russell Long, in referring to tax expenditures, states "I have never been confused about it. I've always known that what we were doing was giving government money away" (Surrey and McDaniel, 1976, p. 716).

Political scientists offer several explanations about why incentive or hardship relief programs are administered by a treasury department, a support (staff) department, rather than by operating (line) departments such as commerce, education, agriculture, etc., which were established to provide services to the public. Moreover, political scientists offer some explanations about the motivations for tax expenditure reporting.

Hansen (1983) constructs a general theory to explain tax expenditure spending. The core of this theory posits that tax expenditures are encouraged by two significant advantages: (1) benefits will be highly visible to beneficiaries but virtually invisible to nonbeneficiaries, and (2) costs will be obscured both for beneficiaries and for nonbeneficiaries.

King (1984), Schick (1986), and Steinmo (1986) contribute to a social benefit theory by pointing up the desirability of using tax expenditures for intrusion into the private sector. Social benefit theory posits that mature democratic governments assume the primary role of redistributing income and purchasing services rather than providing services (Schick, 1986). Schick (1986) argues that this changed role has been accompanied by a shift from administrative budgeting, designed to exercise control over cash receipts and disbursements, to transfer budgeting. In the case of transfer budgeting, public and private sector boundaries are blurred, and the primary purpose is to influence beneficiary behavior. Accordingly, tax expenditures are beneficial mechanisms because they enable government to influence private sector behaviors by supporting private sector endeavors in a nonintrusive manner. Thus, tax expenditures are viewed as serving a unique function rather than merely substituting for direct expenditures.

Tax expenditures and direct expenditures are viewed as substitutes for each other because either may be used to transfer resources. However, the substitute nature of tax expenditures and direct expenditures may not extend to administration. The view that tax expenditures and direct expenditures are distinct instruments of fiscal administration is supported by observations of the magnitude and pattern of growth for tax expenditures and for direct expenditures. Schick (1986) discusses the relationships between growth in indirect expenditures, such as tax expenditures, and growth in direct expenditures and transfer spending. Schick defines transfer spending as, "spending to influence the behavior of households, firms, and other private recipients of public funds," (Schick, 1986, p. 6). He observes that both direct expenditures and tax expenditures grew rapidly in the postwar years and are both subject to reduction in times of budgetary stress. Thus, tax expenditures seem to serve a unique function. King (1984), Schick (1986), and Steinmo (1986) recognize the tendencies for democratic governments to transfer benefits from the public sector to private sector through tax expenditures, and to finance traditional public services through direct expenditures. King (1984) grouped United States tax and direct expenditures into 18 categories in relationship to their function with reference to budget. He found weak reliance on tax expenditures in military categories, moderate reliance in social welfare and product promotion categories, and strong reliance in intergovernmental fiscal assistance categories. Thus, tax expenditures seem to be more adaptable to transfer functions rather than to service functions.

Havemann (1977) and Surrey and McDaniel (1980) suggest an individual political benefit theory. Independent of the possible provision of social benefit, tax expenditures may provide an individual political power benefit to tax committee members. Operational issues can become tax issues when drafted as tax expenditures. Thus, tax committee members may exercise power over operational programs and appropriations by advocating tax expenditures (Havemann, 1977; Surrey and McDaniel, 1980).

Tax Expenditure Reporting

Tax expenditures are a target of control because tax expenditures are at the core of distributive policies concerning "who gets what." Havemann (1977) documents, without exploring, the intensely partisan nature of national debate on reporting with Democrats strongly favoring reporting and Republicans strongly opposed to it. Possible explanations for the partisan nature of debate include (1) Republicans are ideologically drawn to tax expenditures as a way of operating government without creating large administrative agencies; (2) the least entrenched tax expenditures (i.e., investment stimuli) have been associated with a Republican agenda; and (3) a larger proportion of Republican agenda spending is advocated in the form of tax expenditures. Thus Republicans may be less supportive of tax expenditure disclosure and control. At the state level, where prolonged deficit spending is more difficult, party does not appear to affect the desirability of control (Harris, 1990).

Schick's (1986) analysis lays the foundation for an explanation of motivations for tax expenditure reporting that is dependent on budgetary stress caused by fully utilizing revenue capacity. Schick (1986) contends that budgetary stress due to attempts at reducing the growth in direct spending has led to similar stress in relationship to reducing indirect expenditures. He views the production of reports as a response to this budgetary stress aimed at reducing indirect expenditures such as tax expenditures. Benker (1985) also views reporting as a means of increasing options in times of fiscal need. She writes that reporting can, "provide lawmakers with budget flexibility during economic downturns," (Benker, 1985, p. 25).

Both Benker (1985) and Schick (1986) cite high budgetary stress as a possible motivation for tax expenditure reporting. However, they attribute this stress to different sources. Schick (1986) views this stress as a result of excessive growth in transfer spending, whereas Benker (1985) suggests that this stress develops from poor economic conditions.

Schick's (1986) and Benker's (1985) observations may characterize the first stage in a creating a control concern. Excessive growth in transfer spending combined with poor economic conditions may result in a robust resistance to new taxes followed by a strong demand for maintenance of traditional government services. In time, resistance to taxes, combined with demand for services, may contribute to the development of control systems for tax expenditures. From an accountability perspective, neither direct expenditure nor tax expenditure control is synonymous with expenditure reduction. Expenditure control provides relevant and reliable financial cost-related information to draw on for planning, for implementing, and for monitoring resource allocations. Such information is useful because it contributes to the reduction of uncertainty in decision making. However, depending upon the circumstances and issues, financial costs may or may not be a priority factor for policymakers.

TAX EXPENDITURE REPORTING

Tax expenditure reporting is intended to meet a need for cost information. The need for cost information arises because revenue is a scarce resource, as is especially apparent in times of budgetary stress. Without cost information, tax expenditures could escape public oversight entirely. Reporting is the most basic control over tax expenditures because it is essential for other, potentially stronger controls to function.

Reporting Objectives

The primary objective of tax expenditure reporting is to facilitate tax expenditure control. Reporting contributes to the achievement of control in a number of ways (Benker, 1985). Reporting promotes acceptance of the tax expenditure concept. Such acceptance is at the core of initiating tax expenditure controls. Additionally, reporting promotes understanding about a tax system. The systematic analysis of tax provisions results in a cataloging of tax expenditure provisions, which prompts consideration of the normative, theoretical nature of a tax, and original legislative intent. Reporting also may provide helpful information for making decisions when a change in fiscal circumstances merits rapid adjustment.

The literature on tax expenditure reporting supports the conclusion that reporting serves many functions relating to the evaluation of public policies in general and tax policies in particular. Furthermore, utility is not limited to a single objective because reporting serves as a general source of information contributing to the achievement of multiple objectives.

As a case in point, reporting provides tax expenditure cost (spending) estimates relevant to the basic aspects of control: namely, formulation of expectations in planning resource allocations, implementation of resource allocations, and monitoring of resource allocations. This information is relevant to (1) evaluating proposed and existing tax provisions in terms of revenue foregone, and (2) evaluating direct and indirect tax expenditures as alternative means of financing. Because the control problem results from offsetting collections and disbursements, one control objective should be to produce information that separates the economic tax and resource allocation components of the combined net transaction. Although reporting does not provide information about the economic tax obligation, reporting should facilitate the production of such information.

Information availability alone will not result in the achievement of effective control. Relevant and reliable information is useful in forming expectations, and then monitoring performance after the allocation of resources. Because effective control requires the production of and also the consideration of relevant and reliable information, reporting, therefore, may be viewed as one important aspect of a control system.

Arguments against Reporting

The central aspect of the tax expenditure concept is that tax expenditures represent an allocation of benefit. Vickery (1947) discussed the idea that a reduction in taxable income constituted a subsidy to taxpayers. McKenna (1963) wrote a seminal paper about disclosing the opportunity cost of involved in granting tax preferences. Wolfman noted that "tax support of science resembles a direct federal expenditure" (Wolfman, 1965, p. 171).

Surrey, as Assistant Secretary for Tax Policy in the U.S. Treasury Department, was the most influential person in gaining acceptance for the tax expenditure concept among policy makers in the United States and abroad. Among Surrey's achievements are the introduction in 1967 of the tax expenditure concept at the U.S. Treasury Department (Forman, 1986), overseeing research that produced in 1968 the first tax expenditure budget for the United States (Forman, 1986; Wolfman, 1984), and promoting the adoption in 1974 of the tax expenditure budget in the annual budget (Wolfman, 1984). In addition, he led the academic debate concerning the validity of the tax expenditure concept (Andrews, 1972; Bittker, 1969a, 1969b; Blum, 1975; Surrey and Hellmuth, 1969), and authored or co-authored the three most comprehensive books on the subject of tax expenditures (Surrey, 1973; McDaniel and Surrey, 1985; Surrey and McDaniel, 1985). Griswold (1984) lists a complete bibliography of Surrey's works.

The problem with tax expenditures is an absence of control. No one has argued that spending via tax provisions should be free of control, because it is an insupportable argument. Instead, argument has focused on the feasibility of extending control mechanisms, such as disclosure and review, to tax expenditures.

Surrey describes tax expenditure as

. . . deliberate departures from accepted concepts of net income . . . through various special exemptions, deductions and credits . . . to affect the private economy in ways that are usually accomplished by expenditures in effect to produce an expenditure system described in tax language. (Surrey and Hellmuth, 1969, p. 528)

Surrey's reference to "accepted concepts of net income" introduces the idea of a normative tax. Bittker also discusses the idea of a normative tax by referring to "a generally acceptable model, or set of principles" (Bittker, 1969a, p. 247), and "a standard or set of criteria for a 'proper' or 'correct' tax structure" (Bittker, 1969b, p. 528). The Haig-Simons definition of income is referenced as such a model criterion (Bittker, 1969a). The concept of normative tax is at the heart of the debate over the identification of tax expenditures.[2]

When the tax expenditure concept originally was advanced, Surrey and Hellmuth debated with Bittker the merits of the general concept (Bittker, 1969a, 1969b; Surrey and Hellmuth, 1969). Many later discussions of the tax expenditure concept are grounded in Bittker's (1969b) two major criticisms, impossibility of identification and estimation. Bittker's (1969a) criticisms strike at two basic tax expenditure assumptions, the existence of a normative tax and the ability to measure tax expenditures. Thus Bittker (1969a) challenges the relevance of tax expenditure estimates by contending that expenditures cannot be identified in the absence of an accepted normative standard, and the reliability of tax expenditure estimates by contending that their costs cannot be measured.

Identification (Relevance)

Bittker (1969b) argues that tax expenditures cannot be identified because there is no agreement on the norms (standard provisions) that a normative (model) tax would include. Thus, in the absence of agreement on the norms of a normative tax, departure from the norm such as tax expenditures, cannot be identified. Bittker's (1969a, 1969b) concern with defining normative tax was shared by Andrews (1972) and Blum (1975). The Committee on Fiscal Affairs of the Organization for Economic Co-operation or OECD (1984) also identified conceptual difficulty in defining a normative tax structure as the primary obstacle to adoption of reporting by OECD countries.

Surrey and Hellmuth respond that the purpose of tax expenditures is not to "show deviations from an 'ideal tax base,' " but "to represent the cost of special tax provisions . . . to allow decisions which make the most effective use of all budgetary resources" (Surrey and Hellmuth, 1969, p. 530). As the discussion of this issue continued it became apparent that Surrey and McDaniel were arguing for a more adaptable view of normative tax than that view offered by Bittker. Surrey and McDaniel write:

The tax expenditure concept posits that an income tax is composed of two distinct elements. The first element consists of structural provisions necessary to implement a normal income tax, such as the definition of net income, the specification of accounting rules, the determination of the rate schedules and exemption levels, and the application of the tax to international transactions. These provisions compose the revenue-raising aspects of the tax. The second element consists of the special preferences found in every income tax. These provisions, often called tax incentives or tax subsidies, are departures from the normal tax structure and are designed to favor a particular industry, activity, or class of persons. (Surrey and McDaniel, 1985, p. 3)

[2] For additional discussion on normative income tax models, see Andrews (1972), Blum (1975), M. McIntyre (1980), Pomp (1988), Richardson (1989), Surrey and McDaniel (1985), and Thuronyi (1988).

The New York State Department of Taxation and Finance (1988) draws on the work of Surrey and McDaniel (1985) to identify five elements of a normative tax: tax base, accounting methods, tax unit, tax rate schedule, and realization of income.

The Congressional Budget Act of 1974 defines tax expenditures from a normative tax perspective as

> revenue losses attributable to provisions of the Federal tax laws which allow a special exclusion, exemption, deduction from gross income or which provide a special credit, a preferential rate of tax, or a deferral of liability. (Special Analysis G, 1989, p. 347)

In 1983 the Office of Management and Budget (OMB) introduced two changes that caused its tax expenditure report to differ from the Congressional Budget Office (CBO) report, although widespread classification agreement still exists (Special Analysis G, 1989). First, OMB adopted a reference tax law definition of tax expenditures that resulted in the exclusion of 13 items of tax expenditure listed by the CBO from items of tax expenditure listed by the OMB. Ture (1981) sets forth the arguments for the OMB's restricted definition of tax expenditures, whereas McDaniel and Surrey (1982) respond by defending the CBO's broader definition. The reference tax law definition may be viewed as a refinement of the normative tax approach. Under the reference tax law definition, tax expenditures are "deviations from general rules that could be compared to the subsidy and transfer programs on the outlay side of the budget" (Special Analysis G, 1989, p. 348). General deviation from a normative, comprehensive standard are excluded from tax expenditure classification. For example, accelerated cost recovery system (ACRS) depreciation was excluded from tax expenditure classification by OMB based on the view that it is a general deviation rather than a deviation from a general rule. However, Thuronyi (1988) offers a general rule explanation for ACRS. Second, OMB implemented outlay equivalent cost, as a second method of measuring expenditure costs. Outlay equivalent cost is the cost of the direct expenditure that would be required to provide the same benefit to beneficiaries directly (McDaniel and Surrey, 1982). For additional discussion of CBO and OMB differences see Richardson (1988) and Sheppard (1984).

The debate over the need to define a normative tax reflects the most basic question, How may one identify tax expenditures? M. McIntyre (1980) and Thuronyi (1988) proposed identification approaches which avoid the concept of normative tax. Three proposed approaches to identification are:

1. *Normative*—costs are estimated for tax provisions that are departures from a normative model (Andrews, 1972; Bittker, 1969a, 1969b; Blum, 1975; Surrey, 1973; Surrey and Hellmuth, 1969; Surrey and McDaniel, 1985).
2. *Structural*—costs are estimated for all structural provisions that could possibly be considered as tax expenditures (M. McIntyre, 1980).
3. *Substitute*—costs are estimated for tax provisions for which a direct expenditure could achieve the same objective with no loss of efficiency (Fiekowsky, 1980; Thuronyi, 1988).

Each approach as listed immediately above reflects a different emphasis. The normative approach emphasizes the logic of tax theory, the structural approach emphasizes the decision maker's need for revenue cost, and the substitute emphasizes the need for service costs. All three approaches include subjective elements. For an extensive discussion of definitional problems see Thuronyi (1988).

Although tax expenditure identification has been debated at length in academic literature, McDaniel reports that the first decade of national tax expenditure reporting in the United States reveals "remarkably little controversy over the items that have been included in tax expenditure lists" (McDaniel, 1979a, p. 589). At the federal level the CBO and OMB produced virtually identical lists until 1983 and continue to reflect general agreement.

Measurement (Reliability)

Bittker's (1969b) second criticism is that tax expenditures cannot be measured because no adjustment is made for the behavioral responses of taxpayers. Consider the repeal of consumer interest deduction. The deduction for consumer interest is being phased out; however, the deduction for home mortgage interest remains. The behavioral response of taxpayers is to capture the same benefit by pursuing an alternative strategy of increasing borrowings in the form of home equity loans. Consequently, the estimated amount of revenue lost to the treasury from permitting consumer interest deduction does not represent the revenue the treasury will gain from a repeal of the same deduction. Other forms of secondary effects merit mention, such as structural, functional, and investment effects.

Structural effects result from alternative provisions being afforded by the tax structure. Assume mortgage interest is the taxpayer's only item of itemized deduction. If the taxpayer did not itemize home interest expense as a deduction, the taxpayer would be entitled to a standard deduction. Thus, if the home interest deduction were repealed and the taxpayer claimed a standard deduction, the revenue gain to the treasury would be reduced by benefits resulting from the standard deduction.

Functional effects result from alternative resources being required to meet the same objective. If taxpayers were not entitled to a home interest deduction, perhaps a direct expenditure program would be funded to meet the objective of encouraging housing production and home ownership. The cost of the alternative direct expenditure program would reduce the gain to the treasury from repeal of the home mortgage interest expense deduction.

Investment effects result when the tax expenditure is intended as an investment to stimulate economic growth which in turn generates more revenue. Thus, one may argue that some "tax expenditures" may actually be "tax generators" when the secondary investment effect is considered. For example, if the home interest deduction were intended to stimulate housing construction and did so, the benefit of revenue generated from additional tax collections on construction industry income could be viewed as reducing the tax expenditures cost of the deduction. The theoretical potential of new revenues exceeding tax expenditure cost is probably rare because more taxpayers tend to benefit from a tax expenditure than respond to it. For example, every new homeowner receives the benefit of mortgage interest deduction, but perhaps the deduction only influences the home purchase decision for two-thirds of new homeowners. For the other one-third of new homeowners the mortgage interest deduction is a windfall benefit.

Surrey and Hellmuth (1969), in responding to the exclusion of interactive effects from the measurement of tax expenditures, question why differing methodological standards should apply to tax expenditures and direct expenditures. The same procedure, excluding interactive effects, is used to estimate direct expenditures. They explain that secondary interactive effects reflecting beneficiary behavior are not incorporated into either tax expenditures or direct expenditure analysis. McDaniel (1979c) argues that the problems of estimation are no different for tax expenditures than for direct expenditures. A change in either type of expenditure may trigger secondary interactive effects, increasing or decreasing another expenditure. Additionally, the estimation of tax and direct expenditures depends on assumptions pertaining to future economic conditions and behaviors of those taxpayers affected by programs. McDaniel (1979c) concludes that methodological limitations do not invalidate the concept of estimating direct expenditures or tax expenditures.

Given the impossibility of incorporating into cost estimation the numerous potential secondary effects, assuming that no changes in taxpayer behavior result from a change of tax provision makes sense, the complication of secondary effects may be more of a problem of interpretation than of measurement. In using tax expenditure estimates, it is important to understand that because of secondary interactive effects the estimates do not represent the amount of revenue that is expected to result from repeal of a provision. Moreover, the almost certain occurrence of some secondary effects means that tax expenditures cannot be added together to produce a meaningful total measure of foregone revenues. However, the addition of tax expenditures may produce meaningful comparisons of the relative growth and distribution of tax expenditures by functional categories, tax, etc.

Tax expenditure identification and computation issues underscore degrees of difference between tax expenditures and direct expenditures. There is less consensus about what constitutes a tax expenditure than a direct expenditure, and less precision in measuring their costs than in measuring costs for direct expenditures, as almost all tax expenditures are entitlements. This lack of consensus and precision exists because tax expenditures are a logical construct and not an historical reporting of a past transaction or event (Thuronyi, 1988). Despite inherent differences between tax expenditures and direct expenditures, the tax expenditure concept remains operative. A continuing interest in the amount of resources allocated by way of tax provisions is evidenced by the increasing number of governmental entities that are investing resources to estimate and report tax expenditures.

Right to Income

The tax expenditure concept has been criticized as representing the idea that all income belongs to the government. Kristol (1974) makes this argument as follows:

> So they (tax expenditure reporting advocates) come quickly to refer to all exemptions and allowances in our tax laws as "tax subsidies" or even "tax expenditures." But note what happens when you make this assumption and start using such terms. You are implicitly asserting that all income covered by the general provisions of the tax laws belongs of right to the government, and that what the government decides, by exemption or qualification, not to collect in taxes constitutes a subsidy. Whereas a subsidy used to mean a governmental expenditure for a certain purpose, it now acquires a quite another meaning—i.e., a generous decision by government not to take your money. (Kristol, 1974, p. 15)

The State of New York Legislative Commission on Public-Private Cooperation (LCPPC) (1987) advances three counterarguments.

1. The right of individuals to income is inherent in the concept of net income. Surrey and McDaniel make exactly this same point when they write, "including all items of

gross income and subtracting the costs of producing that income . . . does not in any way assert that all income belongs to the government" (Surrey and McDaniel, 1976, p. 687).

2. A function of government is to set tax rate schedules. According to Surrey and McDaniel, the tax expenditure concept does not dictate adoption of a 100% rate necessary to support the argument that all income belongs to the government (Surrey and McDaniel, 1976).

3. Tax expenditures are a form of subsidy that has the effect of altering the amount of tax paid by nonbeneficiaries. Senator Edward Kennedy writes, "the amount of tax expenditure is a measure of how much more taxes the average citizen has to pay, because others pay too little" (Kennedy, 1976).

Review Is Adequate

There are three components to the argument that review is adequate, each of which is discussed by Benker (1985).

1. The review of each individual tax provision is subject to extensive examination and debate prior to adoption.

2. Most major tax expenditures are enshrined through massive public support in tax codes. The revenue loss from expenditures for which repeal is politically feasible is so marginal as to not justify the cost of review.

3. Tax expenditures, especially industrial development expenditures, are in reality investments to enhance the competitive position of states in attracting business. Additional scrutiny could create the image of a negative business climate.

The merit of each of these arguments is doubtful. Exhaustive examination of any expenditure on an individual basis and at only at one point in time does not assure comparative review as part of a total package of tax expenditures and direct expenditures, nor the ongoing oversight involved in monitoring these following their adoption. No systematic procedures or inherent characteristics justify excluding tax expenditure from the periodic competition for resources applied to direct expenditures.

Repeal of tax expenditures is not the primary objective of reporting, no more than repeal of direct expenditures is the primary objective of direct expenditure reporting. The objective of reporting is to facilitate the management of public resources. Gregory and Morberg explain that

> Examining only the direct spending side considerably distorts the view of winners and losers in the competition for public dollars, while also restricting the range of options available to decision-makers for resolving public issues. (Gregory and Morberg, 1990, p. 5)

For example, the amount of federal direct expenditure funding for housing in 1990 was 17.7 billion dollars. However, the amount of federal tax expenditure for housing was 72.2 billion dollars. Eighty percent of federal support for housing is distributed via tax expenditures. Relying only on information for direct expenditure dollar amounts provides an extremely distorted accounting of the extent of public financial support for housing. Whether support should be provided and at what levels are two questions separate from investigation into whether complete cost information should be available for a complete accounting.

For those tax expenditures that are viewed as investments the investment nature of the expenditure does not justify the absence of disclosure. Direct expenditure investments are disclosed. In fact, the need for information about the cost of investments is fundamental to producing an evaluation of return. Without measurements of costs, an investment cannot be evaluated by customary standards of accounting in relationship to return. The public relations effect of industrial development expenditures (investment) does not justify exempting tax expenditure investment from cost evaluation any more than it justifies exempting direct expenditure investment from cost evaluation.

Adverse Consequences

A final set of arguments against tax expenditure reporting predicts that various adverse consequences will result from this practice. Such consequences include a pejorative perception of provisions classified as tax expenditure, the elimination of tax expenditures, and increases in direct spending to replace tax expenditures (State of New York LCPPC, 1987). Tax expenditures have been reported at the federal level for over twenty years, absent the occurrence of predicted consequences. Tax expenditure reporting does not assume that tax expenditures have no merit and should be terminated any more than direct expenditure reporting assumes direct expenditures have no merit and should be terminated. Tax expenditure classification is the beginning of a control process to subject tax expenditures to periodic, institutionalized scrutiny.

Arguments for Control and Reporting

The basic argument for reporting tax expenditures is the argument for control over tax and budget policy. A utilitarian argument for tax expenditure reporting is advanced in a report by the State of New York Department of Taxation and Finance.

> The real question for tax expenditure reporting is whether such reports can be useful to policy makers. Tax expenditure reporting should be viewed as a practical, not philosophical matter. The structure of a state's tax system is a critical policy concern. The reporting of the revenue implications of the provisions of that system is a necessary element in any informed policy discussion. (New York State Department of Taxation and Finance, 1987, p. 7)

The core aspect of the tax expenditure concept is that tax expenditures represent an allocation of benefit. Absent the recognition of this concept, three standard controls are avoided by using the tax expenditure vehicle to encourage desired behaviors or relieve hardships.

1. Avoided is the disclosure of the amount of public support for programs implemented via tax provision. Lack of disclosure contributes to a lack of understanding resulting from lack of information for the identification of beneficiaries, distributional impacts, and estimates of effective tax rate.
2. Avoided is the periodic scrutiny characteristic of programs funded via direct expenditure. Accordingly, tax expenditures do not compete with direct expenditures and are seldom held to the same standards of scrutiny.
3. Avoided is the traditional control of separating responsibilities for revenue collections and disbursements. Legislative tax committees may dominate legislation designed to collect and to disburse resources.

The Committee on Fiscal Affairs of the OECD (1984) study listed three arguments in favor of reporting and tax expenditure oversight:

1. Tax expenditures are a route for governments to pursue policies and should be subject to the same evaluation and control procedures that are applied to government subsidies provided by direct expenditures.
2. A review of government policies in any area will be more effective if all the different methods of government intervention . . . are taken into account and if similar budgetary techniques are used to evaluate the cost of tax and direct expenditures.
3. Control of government expenditure will stand less chance of success if tax expenditures can be easily substituted for direct expenditures (Committee on Fiscal Affairs of the OECD, 1984, p. 10).

Given acceptance of the tax expenditure concept, reporting is fundamental to tax expenditure control. By itself, reporting constitutes one form of control, disclosure. Although disclosure alone is a weak control, it is essential to the institution of stronger controls such as periodic scrutiny, and to the integration of direct expenditure and tax expenditure control processes. However, by itself reporting can provide educational information about the extent of spending via tax provision, foster public discussion on tax system design, and provide information to facilitate cost-benefit analyses of tax expenditure programs.

Extent of Tax Expenditure Reporting

The tax expenditure concept has gained wide acceptance. The United States and most European countries have adopted some form of tax expenditure reporting. Following a slow but steady trend, over a third of the states in the United States have adopted periodic reporting of tax expenditures. Municipalities have joined the trend, by focusing on recording property tax abatements. The implementation of reporting forces consideration of (1) technical questions such as choice of tax expenditure definition, measurement method, time coverage, and data collection, and (2) report design questions relating to the classification and analysis of information.

National Level

West Germany was the first country to adopt tax expenditure reporting and published its first report in 1966 (McDaniel, 1980). Benker (1985) lists nine countries that report tax expenditure reports: Austria, Australia, Canada, France, West Germany, Japan, Spain, the United Kingdom, and the United States. In a 1983 study, the Committee on Fiscal Affairs of the OECD (1984) described these reports and reviewed multinational use and implementation of reporting.

Among countries that report tax expenditures, Canada has adopted the most extensive structure for integrating control of tax expenditures and direct expenditures in a budget system (Doern, 1983; Elkin, 1989; McCaffery, 1984; Schick, 1986). In the Canadian system, cabinet committees (departments) are assigned responsibility for managing an envelope (portfolio) of resources that includes both tax expenditures and direct expenditures. Tax expenditure increases are charged to the envelope, reducing the resources available for direct expenditure. Reductions in tax expenditures are added to the envelope if the tax expenditure is judged equivalent to a direct expenditure. Otherwise, reductions in tax expenditures are added to general revenues. All changes to envelopes must be approved by the minister of finance and the minister responsible for the affected operating policy.

The first tax expenditure report for the United States was prepared in 1967 under the direction of Surrey, and was included in the *Annual Report of the Secretary of the Treasury for Fiscal 1968*. In 1974 Congress passed the Congressional Budget Act, which mandated the Congressional Budget Office (CBO) to publish an annual report of tax expenditures for individual and corporate income taxes. The actual tax expenditure estimates are prepared by the staff of the Joint Committee on Taxation for the CBO. The same 1974 law required the executive Office of Management and Budget (OMB) to include a tax expenditure analysis with the President's *Annual Budget*. This analysis has been published annually since 1976 as "Special Analysis, Section G" of the President's *Annual Budget*. For additional discussion on the history of reporting in the United States see Benker (1985), Edwards (1988), and Forman (1986).

State Level

In 1971, California became the first state to adopt tax expenditure reporting, and issued its first report in 1976. Since 1980, the number of states publishing periodic reports has increased from 4 to 21. Of the 21 states that issue periodic reports, 4 states initiated reporting prior to 1980, 9 states initiated reporting between 1980 and 1985, and 8 states initiated reporting after 1985. Some states report annually and others report biennially. Eleven states have issued at least five reports, and an additional five states have issued three or four reports. Table 1 shows the states that have adopted tax expenditure reporting.

Table 1 States That Report Tax Expenditures[a]

State	Frequency	First report	State agency that prepares report
Arizona	Annual	1982	Ariz. Dept. of Revenue
California	Annual	1976	Legislative Analysts
Delaware	Quadrennial	1987	Division of Revenue
Hawaii	Annual	1982	Tax & Research Planning
Louisiana	Annual	1983	Dept. of Revenue and Taxation
Maine	Biennial	1983	Dept. of Finance
Maryland	Annual	1977	Dept. of Budget and Fiscal Planning
Massachusetts	Annual	1984	Dept. of Revenue
Michigan	Annual	1980	Dept. of Treasury
Minnesota	Biennial	1985	Minn. Dept. of Revenue
Mississippi	Annual	1986	Center for Policy Research and Planning
Montana	Annual	1988	Dept. of Revenue
Nebraska	Biennal	1979	Dept. of Revenue
New York	Annual	1990	Dept. of Taxation and Finance
Ohio	Biennial	1988	Dept. of Taxation
Pennsylvania	Annual	1988	Office of the Budget
South Carolina	Annual	1989	S.C. Tax Commission
Texas	Biennial	1981	Tex. State Comptroller
Virginia	Annual	1989	Virginia Dept. of Revenue
Washington	Biennial	1984	Wash. State Dept. of Revenue
Wisconsin	Biennial	1975	Dept. of Revenue

[a]Arkansas, Indiana, Missouri, and North Carolina have issued special, non-periodic reports. Alabama and Kentucky have prepared reports for internal use only. *Sources:* Benker (1985), Edwards (1988), Harris (1990), and New York State (1988). See Gold and Nesbary (1986) or Harris (1990) for specific report titles and addresses of preparing agencies.

Tax expenditure reporting at the state government level has been the subject of four studies [Benker, 1985; Gold and Nesbary, 1986; Harris, 1990; State of New York Legislative Commission on Public-Private Cooperation (LCPPC), 1987]. Except for Harris, the authors of these studies were associated with organizations concerned with promotion of reporting standards. Benker (1985) prepared the first study for the National Association of State Budget Officers. This study included analysis of a survey made in 1984 of executive and legislative budget offices by the Advisory Commission on Intergovernmental Affairs. Gold and Nesbary (1986) of the National Conference of State Legislatures (NCSL) analyzed data obtained from a separate 1984 survey of state legislative fiscal officers. The New York LCPPC report (1987) was made for the New York State Assembly, and subsequently summarized by Edwards (1988) for the Government Finance Officers Associations. Harris's (1990) study was a dissertation research project.

Both the NCSL and New York LCPPC addressed the issue of what processes and report content should characterize tax expenditure reports. Each of these groups recommended model reporting programs. Recommended models share some common attributes, but unique attributes of each are not in conflict.

At the state government level, tax expenditures reporting differs in three ways from reporting at the federal government level (Gold and Nesbary, 1986). First, the general concept is broader than that adopted at the federal government level. Second, state tax expenditure analyses exclude more items of expenditure from estimation than federal tax expenditure analyses. And third, state tax expenditures are estimated using one rather than two methods of estimation.

Gold and Nesbary (1986) explain that the tax expenditure concept tends to be more complicated or broader at the state level because state analysts extend the concept to more types of taxes. The extension of the concept to sales taxes and other taxes is necessary because state governments rely less on income taxes than the federal government. However, the extension to other taxes is complicated because there is less general agreement on normative tax structure of other taxes (Hedgespeth and Moynihan, 1984). For example, Gold and Nesbary (1986) indicate that if a sales tax is viewed as a consumption tax, the exemption of services represents a tax expenditure, but if the sales tax is viewed as a tax on personal property, the exemption of services does not represent a tax expenditure.

State tax expenditure analyses may exclude more items from estimation than federal tax expenditure analyses. Some states exclude the effect of any provision required by the state's constitution or any provision adopted for conformity with federal tax structure (Gold and Nesbary, 1986). These tax expenditures may be viewed either as part of a modified normative structure or practically beyond change. Furthermore, some states impose threshold values on expenditure estimates before reporting or restrict reporting to expenditures adopted after a base year (Benker, 1985). The imposition of threshold values restricts the use of scarce analytical resources to significant tax expenditures, and reporting on expenditures adopted after a base year shifts the focus to the recently adopted, less entrenched tax expenditures.

State tax expenditures are estimated using the revenue foregone method of measurement (Gold and Nesbary, 1986). In contrast, the OMB at the federal level uses both the revenue foregone and outlay equivalence measurement methods. Each of these methods will be discussed later in this chapter.

There has been a steady interest in tax expenditure reporting at the state level for the past 15 years. Organizations concerned with fiscal policy control have sponsored studies to describe state-level reporting and proposed model reports. These studies establish that (1) reporting as conducted by states differs from reporting as conducted by the federal government, and (2) reporting as conducted by states is a highly diverse, rather than uniform, activity among them.

Local and Municipal Level

At the municipal level, interest has centered on the recording and uniform reporting of property tax abatements. Martin (1989) defines a tax abatement as a temporary reduction in tax for a limited time period during which economic development is expected to occur. A 1986 survey of local governments found 25% of cities and 42% of counties report information on tax abatements and cancellations, a subset of tax expenditures (Ingram and Robbins, 1987). The Government Finance Officers' Association (GFOA) has supported research calling for issuance of governmental accounting standards on the recording and reporting of tax abatements. The GFOA published a research report by Regan (1988) arguing for the issuance of tax expenditure reports for economic development incentives including tax abatements. Uniformity of reporting is an issue because numerous political subdivisions within a state may abate taxes. Local decisions to abate taxes, especially property taxes, may effect obligations of the state to finance services or evaluations at the state level concerning financing of local economic development. Additionally, the GFOA sponsored a research report by Martin (1989) recommending an accounting model for incorporating property tax abatements into conventional accounting records.

The initial concern of the GFOA is recording and reporting of tax abatements for economic development purposes. Regan (1988) advocates legislation requiring localities in New York State to record the value of abatements and provide a report to each affected jurisdiction (city, state, or county). Hughes and Motekat (1988) report that four out of seven presenters at a 1988 hearing on future governmental accounting issues encouraged the addition of tax expenditure recording and reporting standards to the agenda of the Governmental Accounting Standards Board (GASB). Martin (1989) reproduces correspondence asking that GASB address tax expenditure recording and reporting.

Literature on the extent of tax expenditure reporting supports the conclusion that the tax expenditure concept has broad applicability and has gained widespread acceptance. The tax expenditure concept has been adapted to a variety of taxes, and reporting has been adopted by multiple levels of government.

Implementation of Tax Expenditure Reporting

The implementation of reporting forces report preparers to consider questions of computation and presentation. Definition, measurement method, time coverage, and data collection are issues that affect the computation of tax expenditures. These issues are relevant to control because of their potential to affect the interpretation of information. The absence of uniformity related to these matters makes it is extremely difficult to compare tax expenditure reports issued by different entities. Besides this difficulty, changes over time, particularly improvements in data collection, affect the reliability of time series analyses.

Definition

As previously discussed, tax expenditures may be defined as (1) departures from a normative tax, (2) items represented by structural components such as exemptions, deductions, credits, etc., or (3) costs for which a direct expenditure alternative may substitute. In practice, the application of these differences has not produced widespread disagreement on tax expenditure classification. Basic definitional approaches may be modified by source of expenditure, statute or constitutional provision, amount of expenditure, date of expenditure adoption, etc. These modifications do produce different listings.

Measurement Method

Three distinct theoretical methods exist for measuring tax expenditures. These methods are known as the (1) revenue foregone, (2) revenue gain, and (3) outlay equivalence methods. (Committee on Fiscal Affairs of the OECD, 1984). Most reporters use the revenue foregone method, while the Office of Management and Budget (OMB) uses both the outlay equivalence and revenue forgone methods. The object of measurement differs with each measurement method.

The revenue foregone method is designed to measure the amount by which tax revenues are reduced because of the existence of a particular provision. It is an after-the-fact measure of the cost of a given provision. The foregone amount is the difference in revenue based on a comparison of existing legislation including the provision of interest and the same legislation without the provision of interest. Taxpayer behavior is accepted as observed for the period under consideration. No secondary interactive effects are considered.

The revenue gain method is designed to measure the amount by which tax revenues would increase if a given provision were repealed. In theory, use of this method requires consideration of secondary effects such as changes in taxpayer behavior, changes in the level of economic activity, and interactions among taxes. The difficulty of taking secondary effects into consideration is substantial. No reporters are known to use this method in actual practice.

The outlay equivalence method is designed to measure in pretax dollars the direct expenditure that would be required to achieve the same after-tax dollar benefit if a tax expenditure were replaced by a corresponding direct expenditure program. The outlay equivalence method differs in perspective and objective from the revenue foregone and revenue gain methods (Schick, 1986). The revenue foregone and revenue gain methods assume the perspective of a government entity with a revenue management objective, while the outlay equivalence method assumes the perspective of a citizen beneficiary (taxpayer) with a benefit (financial management) objective. Leonard (1986) discusses the relationship between management objective and measurement method. For additional discussions of measurement methods see Committee on Fiscal Affairs of the OECD (1984), Gold and Nesbary (1986), McDaniel and Surrey (1982, 1985), Richardson (1989), and Schick (1986).

Time Coverage

In preparing tax expenditure reports, one basic decision is whether to estimate historical tax expenditures, forecast current and future tax expenditures, or do both. Three approaches are discussed in a report prepared by the New York State Department of Taxation and Finance (1988). The three approaches are application of (1) historical data to historical tax law, (2) historical data to current tax law, and (3) trended data to current tax law. The first approach provides the most statistically correct estimates, but may not be relevant to current and future years. The second approach provides for the estimation of new tax expenditures, but requires the assumption that taxpayers behave the same under old and new tax laws, which weakens the reliability of data. The third approach matches current data to current law. However, it is a technically complex, expensive approach, which by trending estimates increases the uncertainty associated with final estimates. All three approaches are used and may provide meaningful information about the relative magnitude of various tax expenditures.

Data Collection

Regardless of other production consideration, unless quality data can be obtained the reliability of reports will be impaired. The New York Department of Taxation and Finance (1988) classifies data sources by degree of reliability. The most reliable source for developing estimates is data from tax returns filed with reporting entity, followed by aggregate data such as Statistics on Income, federal estimates of tax expenditures, and self-constructed estimates from nontax data. The federal government and some states maintain databases developed from actual returns for statistical and reporting purposes. If not available, developing databases is a expensive endeavor. A return database, however, will not provide all the information one needs for estimating tax expenditures. For example, state returns may not provide specific information on benefits that flow through from federal provisions. Moreover, estimates of the costs of exemptions, particularly sales tax exemptions, may be extremely unreliable because of the lack of quality data.

Definition, measurement method, time coverage, and data collection are issues to resolve in producing tax expenditure reports. Decisions related to these issues affect the interpretation of reports. Thus it is important that users understand the choices and their resultant implications.

Utility of Tax Expenditure Reporting

The tax expenditure literature presents reporting as a tool to aid in control of fiscal resources. The absolute magnitude of tax expenditures and growth in tax expenditures justify a concern for oversight control. However, few states have developed any form of institutionalized tax expenditure oversight process. Precisely how control may be achieved has not received as much attention as explaining the control problem. However, certain control objectives are discussed.

Improved Debate

The general overall objective of tax expenditure reporting is to contribute to an increased awareness of tax expenditure cost stimulating control over tax expenditures. Davenport (1980) argues that one of the primary benefits of the tax expenditure concept and reporting is improvement in the quality of debate, generating pressure on legislators to justify their actions. Casual observation reveals that a perspective on policy discussions that was once limited to academic journals is appearing in more common forums. Organizations such as Common Cause have developed criteria for evaluating tax expenditures (Benker, 1985). Discussion of the desirability of a specific direct expenditure program to rescue the savings and loan industry versus an alternative tax expenditure program appeared in *Newsweek* (Reibstein and Friday, 1989). Arguments for eliminating mortgage interest deductions on second homes to obtain financing to meet public housing needs appeared in a regional newspaper, *Roanoke Times & World News* (London, 1990).

Improved Management

Four control objectives are related to the management of tax and spending policies. From the inception of reporting, cost comparison and revenue comparison were mentioned as objectives (Surrey and Hellmuth, 1969; Surrey, 1972). The earliest and most frequently mentioned objectives, cost comparison and revenue comparison, may be regarded as primary objectives. The first of these objectives, comparison of direct expenditure costs with indirect tax expenditure costs, is advocated as a means of encouraging adoption of the most cost beneficial means for administering social programs (Benker, 1985; McDaniel, 1979b; Surrey and Hellmuth, 1969; Wolfman, 1965). A second objective is to protect revenue bases from erosion (Benker, 1985; Gold and Nesbary, 1986; Regan, 1988; Surrey, 1972) by considering revenues foregone from tax expenditures. Erosion of revenue bases from increases in tax expenditures may have the same effect on public deficits as increases in direct expenditures (Richardson, 1989). A third objective is to achieve an equitable distribution of exchange by considering the distribution of economic tax and tax expenditures (McDaniel, 1985; Surrey, 1972; Weinberg, 1987). A fourth objective is to contribute to designing tax incentives that operate in the most cost-beneficial manner (Regan, 1988). Given the recent and limited discussion by reporting advocates of distributional impact and efficient design of tax incentives these objectives appear peripheral.

Policy Impact

The impact of tax expenditure information on policymakers is a subject that has not attracted much attention. Advocates of reporting, while supporting greater institutionalization of tax expenditure oversight, seem to assume (1) that cost/benefit comparisons are central to decision making and (2) that tax expenditure report information will be used as a management tool in preparing economic cost/benefit comparisons to guide fiscal decisions. Neither of these assumptions has been verified. The subject of policy impact may have been deferred until time has given policymakers the opportunity to accumulate experience in using such information. Perhaps the subject has been avoided rather than deferred because policy impact is difficult to capture (Peltz, 1978; Weiss, 1979).

Assessments of the utility of tax expenditure reporting tends to be based on personal accounts. Praising reporting, M. McIntyre makes this observation:

> It has induced Congress to alter its procedures for scrutinizing tax subsidies, now called tax expenditures, and it has focused public attention on the indefensible consequences that often result when Congress uses special deductions, exemptions and other tax mechanisms to achieve its spending goals. (McIntyre, 1980, p. 79)

Salamone describes the Minnesota Tax Expenditure Report as "a key tax reference document used in tax committee discussions" (Salamone, 1989, p. 32). California's Governor Deukemejian is a critic of reporting. In 1984, he recommended its termination, stating, "the report seems to have little impact, since a number of tax expenditures have been adopted over the last decade" (Benker, 1985, p. 44). However, California continues to report tax expenditures, and also has initiated the operational auditing of tax expenditures.

A few published references to tax expenditure report utility are inconsistent with the rational objectives advanced by reporting proponents. R. McIntyre (1981) observes that the availability of tax expenditure analyses has supported the evaluation and adoption of new tax benefits on spending grounds, while fairness and administrability have been ignored. Pomp (1988) reports that tax expenditures data have been used by legislators to show the value of tax benefits enacted on behalf of their constituency and by special interest groups to show need for additional tax benefits.

R. McIntyre (1981), Richardson, (1988), Surrey and McDaniel (1980), and Thuronyi (1988) compiled case analyses of the influence of reporting on specific federal tax reform. Except for the Surrey and McDaniel (1980) case report, each of the cited cases question whether report information has a significant impact on policy making. Thuronyi observes, "institutional problems aside, evidence also indicates that Congress has not taken the tax expenditure concept fully to heart" (Thuronyi, 1988, p. 1171). Harris (1990) conducted the only systematic study of tax expenditure report use by state legislators. She found over 75% of legislators who serve on tax committees view reports positively and consider report information when discussing tax policy. Leonard (1986) discusses the limitations of informational reporting as a control mechanism.

Aggregate Analyses

Much of the literature on tax expenditure reporting centers on conceptual arguments about what is a tax expenditure or on arguments for adopting reporting. The informational content of reports has received much less attention.

Empirical analyses of report information in the aggregate are rare except for the evaluation of individual tax expenditures. King (1984) identifies policies supported by federal tax expenditures. Noto (1981) and Weinberg (1987) estimate the distributional impact of federal tax expenditures; Joulfaian (1985) estimates the distributional impact of Massachusetts tax expenditures. Hildred and Pinto (1986) estimate the impact of federal tax expenditures on state revenues. The nonadditiveness of tax expenditure estimates resulting from the disregard of secondary effects is a major obstacle to aggregate studies. Other obstacles are the lack of comparability among state reports, lack of comparability over time because of changing estimation models and classifications, and the absence of data disclosure except by tax.

OTHER CONTROLS

Aside from tax expenditure reporting, a number of other procedures have been proposed to strengthen control. These may be described as report oversight, structural integration, design of legislation, and disclosure controls.

Report Oversight

Report oversight control includes such procedures as (1) preissuance and postissuance reviews and (2) extension of reporting to include report analysis and the comprehensive evaluation of selected expenditures (operational auditing).

Although report production is common, preissuance and postissuance review of report information is rare. Preissuance review refers to the review of report information prior to distribution by an agency external to the preparing agency. Such review may contribute to report quality by ensuring consideration of completeness, reliability, and relevance of report information.

Postissuance review refers to legislative review of report information after its distribution. At the state level, it is the exception rather than the rule to find responsibility assigned for reviewing tax expenditure costs. Absent the adoption of a review process, review is sporadic.

When postissuance reviews are undertaken, the analysis that some reports contain seems useful. A tax expenditure report may be nothing more than a catalog of tax expenditures with cost estimates attached. However, state reports are starting to aggregate and to classify data in ways to facilitate analysis (Noto, 1981; State of New York LCPPC, 1987). For example, expenditure data may be disclosed by government function such as agriculture, education, etc., and include graphic displays. The Tax Expenditure Appendix of the Executive Budget for fiscal year 1987–1988 for Michigan shows that 90% of the support for commerce is in the form of tax expenditure. Considering only direct expenditures one could conclude minimal public support for the commerce function. Some state reports estimate the effect of recent tax expenditure repeals and adoptions. Other reports list tax expenditures that are scheduled to terminate in the next few years. A few states show the distribution impact of some tax expenditures by income groups. It is evident that an effort is being made to improve the presentation of report information.

Canada, California, and Nebraska have undertaken analyses to evaluate either alone or together the effectiveness and the efficiency of selected tax expenditures. This is a form of operational auditing. Some of the issues associated with such an analysis include determination of (1) criteria for selecting expenditures to review (Pomp, 1988) and (2) criteria and procedures to apply in evaluating selected tax expenditures (Benker, 1985; Elkin, 1989; McDaniel, 1979b). This is a promising control procedure because it permits the comprehensive analysis of a limited number of tax expenditures where strong justification for evaluation exists. The New York State Department of Taxation and Finance (1988) discusses the difficulties in evaluation tax expenditures. Elkin (1989) describes the Canadian approach to tax expenditure auditing.

Structural Integration

Structural integration controls include appropriations process integration and accounting. When postissuance review does occur, it is usually initiated and limited to tax committee review. Because tax expenditures are regarded primarily as tax provisions rather than spending provisions, the spending aspect of tax expenditures may escape spending controls. As previously mentioned, Canada has a system that explicitly submits tax expenditures to spending control. Additionally, at present Michigan is investigating ways of integrating the tax expenditure and appropriation processes. Whereas it may be unproductive to include all tax expenditures in an appropriations process, it is difficult to justify exclusion of provisions intended solely as direct expenditure substitutes from such a process (Andrews, 1972). Leonard (1986), McDaniel (1980), McDaniel and Surrey (1982), and M. McIntyre (1988) advocate integrating tax expenditures into the appropriations process, thereby activating competition for resources as a control over both tax and direct expenditures.

The State of Michigan has issued tax expenditure reports since 1980. In a recent report to the Michigan legislature, Gregory and Morberg (1990), writing for the House Fiscal Agency, argue for stronger process integration controls. They contend that revenues are persistently insufficient to fund current programs creating a structural deficit.

Based on their analysis, Michigan faces structural deficits because (1) economy-wide shifts from manufacturing to services reduce the revenue base, (2) the United States Government continues to pursue policies of disinvestment in states, (3) public demand for services such as prisons and health care has increased significantly, and (4) the rate of increase in tax expenditures is larger than the rate of increase in direct expenditures. Of these factors, the state legislature has the most direct influence over increases in tax expenditures. Gregory and Morberg (1990) conclude that (1) structural deficits justify stronger tax expenditure control and (2) stronger tax expenditure control requires consideration of integrating the direct and tax expenditures control processes.

At the local level it has been proposed that the traditional accounting system incorporate tax expenditure transactions. The major local tax is often a property tax, which structurally may be quite simple in comparison to an income tax. For example, the base is the assessed value of property with a statutory rate applied. If taxes are abated, as an incentive to undertake a particular action, the revenue gain cost is easy to estimate because of fewer secondary interactive effects.

Hughes and Motekat (1988) outline how recording of tax expenditures could be incorporated into an accounting system. They suggest recording the gross revenue before allowance for tax expenditures and then recording the expenditure as a deduction from revenue. In a research report to GFOA, Martin (1989) recommends a similar accounting model for recording property tax abatements. The proposed treatment is analogous to the recording of tuition waivers by universities (*Audits of Colleges and Universities*, 1975) and charity and insurance allowances by hospitals (*Hospital Audit Guide*, 1985). The advancement of proposals to incorporate reporting of tax abatements into the traditional accounting system reflects acceptance of the tax expenditure concept and confidence in the measurement of tax abatements.

The accounting treatment proposed by Hughes and Motekat (1988) and Martin (1989) may not be adequate. Consider (1) Schick's (1986) argument that cash receipt and disbursement controls applicable to administrative budgeting are inappropriate for transfer budgeting and (2) McDaniel's (1985) arguments that tax subsidies and direct subsidies at present are analyzed quite differently absent theoretical justification. Schick cautions:

> Merely placing nonconventional transactions in the budget might be little more than a bookkeeping change; it might not significantly improve the capacity of government to control the allocation of resources through nonconventional financing instruments. (Schick, 1986, p. 17)

The challenge is to create effective controls for nonconventional spending.

Design of Legislation

Controls over the design of legislation include procedures that limit the loss of revenue from tax expenditures. Examples of such controls are (1) restricting the amount of benefit that all taxpayers can receive by requiring advance application for a benefit received from such tax expenditures as venture capital credits, (2) restricting the amount of benefit that any single taxpayer can receive by restricting benefits to a maximum dollar amount, (3) restricting the class of taxpayers eligible for benefits, and (4) sunsetting benefits by specifying a termination date for the authorizing tax provision. Sunsetting is intended to force a periodic review of the applicable tax expenditure.

Disclosure

Aside from tax expenditure reporting, two disclosure tools are fiscal notes and specific identification. A number of state legislatures now require that proposed legislation be reviewed for its potential impact on revenue and that fiscal notes be attached to proposed legislation estimating the impact of the legislation on revenue. Thus a fiscal note requirement compels the estimation and disclosure of tax expenditure costs prior to adoption of the expenditure provision. Specific identification of corporate beneficiaries has been advocated as a disclosure control by Pomp (1988). This proposal equates the treatment of direct expenditures and tax expenditures. The beneficiaries of much public spending are a matter of public record. Pomp (1989) argues that specific identification would stimulate public interest in tax expenditure control by giving a reality to statistics.

CONCLUSION

Aside from reporting, governmental entities have little experience with tax expenditure control procedures. McDaniel described tax expenditure reports as providing an "analytic tool to be used by practical legislators and government policy officials responsible for real budget and tax policy decisions" (McDaniel, 1979a, p. 589). Discussing the use of the federal tax expenditure budget or report, McDaniel (1979c) recommends regular review of tax expenditure programs, coordination of tax expenditure programs with direct expenditure programs, and automatic termination or sunsetting of tax expenditures. The National Conference of State Legislatures (Gold and Nesbary, 1986) suggests submission of a tax expenditure report with the direct expenditure budget, assignment of review responsibilities to a specific committee, automatic termination of new tax expenditures, and review and disposal of the tax expenditure report in a manner analogous to the direct expenditure budget. Pomp (1988) emphasizes the need for the state to institutionalize periodic comprehensive reviews of selected tax expenditures including the examination and disclosure of beneficiaries. Surrey and McDaniel (Surrey and McDaniel, 1980; McDaniel and Surrey, 1982) advocate dividing the tax expenditure report into functions in a manner similar to the direct expenditure budget. Each of these recommendations assumes the availability of the most fundamental control tool, tax expenditure report information.

The institutionalization of tax expenditure oversight has been neglected at the federal level and haphazard at the state level (Pomp, 1989; Richardson, 1989). Sunsetting, automatic termination of expenditures by states, though not customary, is common. Some states have put limits on a few types of tax expenditures. A few states have assigned review responsibilities to specific legislative committees. But for the most part, coordination of tax expenditure programs with direct expenditure programs, limiting the overall amount of tax expenditures, coordination between tax committee and other substantive committees, increased involvement of spending committees, and treatment of the tax expenditure reports in a manner analogous to the direct expenditure budget have not occurred.

When one looks at the history of direct expenditure controls over a period of more than a century, tax expenditure controls are quite new as innovations. The rapid acceptance and extension of such innovation is perhaps more surprising than the incompleteness of control systems at this point in time. In less than 25 years, most industrial countries and over one-third of the states in the United States have adopted tax expenditure reporting.

Additionally, a few governmental entities have integrated a direct expenditure control process with a tax expenditure control process or have initiated operational auditing of tax expenditures. As budgetary stress intensifies, it is likely that more attention will be given to tax expenditure control systems.

REFERENCES

Andrews, W. D. (1972). Personal deductions in an ideal income Tax. *Harvard Law Rev.*, *86:*309–385.

Audits of Colleges and Universities (2d ed.) (1975). American Institute of CPAs, New York, NY.

Baum, D. N. (1987). The economic effect of state and local business incentives. *Land Econ.*, *63:*348–360.

Baumbusch, P. L. (1981). Surrey and tax expenditures: Further comments. *Tax Notes, 12:*500–502.

Benker, K. M. (1985). *Tax Expenditure Reporting: Closing The Loophole In State Budget Oversight*. National Association of State Budget Officers, Washington, DC.

Benker, K. M. (1986). Tax expenditure reporting: Closing The loophole in state budget oversight. *Natl. Tax J.*, *39:*403–417.

Bennett, J. T., and DiLorenzo T. J. (1983). *Underground Government: The Off-Budget Public Sector*. Cato Institute, Wash., DC.

Bezdek, R. H., and Zampelli, E. M. (1986). State and local government tax expenditures relating to the federal government. *Natl. Tax J.*, *39:*533–538.

Bittker, B. I. (1969a). Accounting for federal "tax subsidies" in the national budget. *Natl. Tax J.*, *22:*244–261.

Bittker, B. I. (1969b). The tax expenditure budget—A reply to professors Surrey and Hellmuth. *Natl. Tax J., 22:*538–542.

Blum, W. J. (1975). Book review. *J. Corp. Tax.*, *1:*486–490.

Blum, W. J. (1979). The tax expenditure approach seen through anthropological eyes. *Tax Notes*, *8:*699–701.

Blum, W. J., McClennen, L., and Pedrick, W. H. (1978). The tax expenditure approach and funeral expense. *Tax Notes, 7:*327–329.

Bobrow, D. B., and Dryzek, J. S. (1987). *Policy Analysis by Design*. University of Pittsburgh Press, Pittsburgh, PA.

Bosworth, B. P. (1984). *Tax Incentives and Economic Growth*. The Bookings Institution, Washington, DC.

Brannon, G. M. (1979). Brannon cuts tax expenditures by $14 billion! *Tax Notes, 8:*171–173.

Brannon, G. M. (1980). Tax expenditures and income distribution: A theoretical analysis of the upside-down subsidy argument. In H. J. Aarons and M. J. Boskins (eds.), *The Economics of Taxation*, The Brookings Institution, Washington, DC, pp. 87–98.

Break, G. F. (1985). The tax expenditure budget—The need for a fuller accounting. *Natl. Tax J.*, *38:* 261–265.

Brennan, G., and Buchanan, J. (1980). *The Power To Tax*. Cambridge University Press, Cambridge, UK.

Committee on Fiscal Affairs of Organization for Economic Co-operation and Development. (1984). *Tax Expenditures*. OECD, Paris, France.

Davenport, C. (1980). Tax expenditure analysis as a tool for policymakers. *Tax Notes, 11:*1051–1054.

Doern, G. B. (1983). Canada's budgetary dilemmas: Tax and expenditure reform. *Public Budgeting & Finance, 3:*28–46.

Dermer, J. D., and Lucas, R. G. (1986). The illusion of management control, *Accounting, Organization and Society, 11:*471–482.

Dermer, J. (1987). *Managerial Control and Organizational Thrashing: A Public Service Perspective*, Volume I. Second Interdisciplinary Perspective On Accounting Conference, University of Manchester, Manchester, UK.

Dermer, J. (1988). Control and organizational order. *Accounting, Organization and Society*, *13*:25–36.

Dreyfus, D. A. (1977). The limitations of policy research in congressional decision making. In C. Weiss (ed.), *Using Social Research in Public Policy Making*, D. C. Heath, Lexington, MA.

Driessen, P. A. (1987). A qualification concerning The efficiency of tax expenditures. *J. Public Econ.*, *33*:126–131.

Dunn, W. N. (1981). *Public Policy Analysis: An Introduction*. Prentice-Hall, Englewood Cliffs, NJ.

Ebel, R. D. (1986). The role of research in formulating tax policy. In S. D. Gold (ed.), *Reforming State Tax Systems*, National Conference of State Legislatures, Denver, CO, pp. 56–66.

Edwards, K. K. (1988). Reporting for tax expenditures and tax abatements. *Govt. Financial Rev.*, *4*:13–17.

Elkin, B. (1989). Auditing tax expenditures or spending through the tax system. *Int. J. Govt. Auditing, 10*:7–16.

Feldstein, M. (1980). A contribution to the theory of tax expenditures: The case of charitable giving. In H. J. Aarons and M. J. Boskins (eds.), *The Economics of Taxation*, The Brookings Institution, Washington, DC, pp. 99–122.

Feller, I., King, M. R., Menzel, D. C., O'Conner, R. E., Wissel, P. A., and Ingersoll, R. (1979). Scientific and technological information in state legislatures. *Am. Behav. Scientist, 22*:417–436.

Fenno, R. F. (1966). *The Power of The Purse*. Little, Brown, Boston.

Fiekowsky, S. (1980). The relation of tax expenditures to the distribution of the "fiscal burden." *Can. Taxation, 2*:213–216.

Fisher, P. S. (1985). Corporate tax incentives: The american version of industrial policy. *J. Econ. Issues, 19*:1–19.

Forman, J. B. (1986). Origins of the tax expenditure budget. *Tax Notes, 30*:537–545.

Freeman, R. A. (1983). *Tax Loopholes: The Legend and the Reality*. American Enterprise Institute-Hover Policy Study, Washington, DC.

Gold, S. D. (ed.) (1986). *Reforming State Tax Systems*. National Conference of State Legislatures, Denver, CO.

Gold, S. D., ed. (1988). *The Unfinished Agenda for State Tax Reform*. National Conference of State Legislatures, Denver, CO.

Gold, S. D., and Nesbary, D. (1986). State tax expenditure review mechanisms. *Tax Notes, 30*:883–891.

Grady, D. O. (1987). State economic development incentives: Why do states compete?" *State Local Govt. Rev., 19*:86–94.

Green, A. (1984). The role of evaluation in legislative decision making. *Public Admin. Rev., 44*:265–267.

Gregory, W. C., and Morberg, J. T. (1990). *Silent Spending*. House Fiscal Agency, Lansing, MI.

Griswold, E. N. (1984). Statesman, scholar, mentor. In Memoriam: Stanley S. Surrey. *Harvard Law Rev. 98*:329–350.

Halperin on Sunset for Tax Expenditures. (1979). *Tax Notes, 8*:788.

Hamm, K. E., and Robertson, R. D. (1981). Factors influencing the adoption of new methods of legislative oversight in the U.S. states. *Legis. Stud. Q., 6*:133–150.

Hansen, S. (1983). *The Politics of Taxation*. Praeger, New York, NY.

Harris, J. E. (1990). Tax Expenditures: Report Utilization by State Policy Makers. Ph.D. dissertation, Virginia Polytechnic Institute and State University.

Harstad, P. F. (1981). Committee eyes budgetary constraints on tax expenditures. *Tax Notes, 23*:1487–1488.

Harstad, P. F. (1981). Tax expenditures called "The Spending of The 1980s." *Tax Notes, 13:*1532–1534.

Havemann, J. (1977). Tax expenditures—Spending money without expenditures. *Natl. J., 9:*1908–1911.

Hayes, D. C. (1983). Accounting for accounting: A story about managerial accounting. *Accounting, Organization and Society, 8:*241–249.

Hedgespeth, G., and Moynihan E. (1984). Special Problems in Developing a State Tax Expenditure Budget. Proc. 52d Annual Meeting of National Association of Tax Administrators, pp. 123–129.

Helms, L. J. (1985). The effect of state and local taxes on economic growth: A time series-cross section approach. *Rev. Econ. Stat., 67:*574–582.

Hildred, W. M., and Pinto, J. V. (1986). Passive tax expenditures: Estimates of states' revenue losses attributable to federal tax expenditures. *J. Econ. Issues, 20:*941–952.

Hopwood, A. G. (1987). The archeology of accounting systems. *Accounting, Organization and Society, 12:*207–254.

Hospital Audit Guide (6th ed.). (1985). American Institute of CPAs, New York, NY.

Hughes, J. W. (1981). The tax expenditure concept: Its interpretation and measurement plus an evaluation. *Natl. Public Accountant, 26:*22–25.

Hughes, J. W., and Motekat J. (1988). Tax expenditures for local governments, *Public Budgeting & Finance, 8:*68–73.

Ingram, R. W., and Robbins, W. A. (1987). *Financial Reporting Practices of Local Governments.* Government Accounting Standards Board (Research Report), Stamford, CT.

Ingram, R. W., Robbins, W. A., and Stone, M. S. (1988). Financial reporting practices of local governments: An overview. *Govt. Financial Rev., 4:*17–21.

Jacobs, J. (1979). Biding for Business: Corporate Auctions and The 50 Disunited States. Public Interest Research Group, Washington, DC.

Jones, C. O. (1977). *An Introduction to the Study of Public Policy.* Duxbury Press, N. Scituate, MA.

Joulfaian, D. (1985). Revenue estimation and progressivity: The case of the Massachusetts income tax. *Natl. Tax J., 38:*415–419.

Kettl, D. F. (1988). *Government by Proxy (Mis?) Managing Federal Programs.* Congressional Quarterly Press, Washington, DC.

Kennedy, E. M. (1976). [Letter to the editor.] Senator Kennedy on the concept of tax expenditures. *Washington Post,* May 2.

Kennedy, E. M. (1979). Kennedy on Tax Expenditures and the Budget Concept. *Tax Notes, 8:*84.

King, R. F. (1984). Tax expenditures and systematic public policy: An essay on the political economy of the federal tax code. *Public Budgeting & Finance, 4:*14–31.

Kristol, I. (1974). Taxes, poverty, and equality. *Public Interest, 33:*15.

Ledebur, L. C., and Hamilton W. W. (1986). The failure of tax concessions as economic development incentives. In S. D. Gold (ed.), *Reforming State Tax Systems,* National Conference of State Legislatures, Denver, CO, pp. 101–118.

Lees, J. D. (1977). Legislative oversight: A review article on a neglected area of research. *Legis. Studies Q., 2:*193–207.

Leonard, H. B. (1986). *Checks Unbalanced.* Basic Books, New York.

Lind, N. S., and Elder, E. H. (1986). Who pays? Who benefits? The case of the incentive package offered to the Diamond-Star automotive plant. *Govt. Financial Rev., 2:*19–23.

London, J. W. (1990). Stop subsidizing the rich. *Roanoke Times and World News,* p. 9(A), January 8.

Lowe, T., and Machin, J. L. J. (1983). *New Perspectives In Management Control.* St. Martin's Press, New York.

Maciariello, J. A. (1984). *Management Control Systems.* Prentice-Hall, Englewood Cliffs, NJ.

Malan, R. M., Jr., Martin, S. W., and Regan, E. V. (1988). The cost of tax incentives. *Govt. Financial Rev., 4*:3.

Manvel, A. D. (1979). Tax expenditures continue to grow. *Tax Notes, 8*:206–207.

Markus, M. L., and Pfeffer, J. (1983). Power and the design and implementation of accounting and control systems. *Accounting, Organization and Society, 8*:205–218.

Martin, S. W. (1989). *Accounting and Reporting for Property Tax Abatements.* Grand Valley State University, Grand Rapids, MI.

McCaffery, J. (1984). Canada's envelope budget: A strategic management system. *Public Admin. Rev., 44*:316–323.

McDaniel, P. R. (1979a). The tax expenditure concept: Theory and practical effects. *Tax Notes, 8*:587–592.

McDaniel, P. R. (1979b). Evaluation of particular tax expenditures. *Tax Notes, 8*:619–625.

McDaniel, P. R. (1979c). Institutional procedures for congressional review of tax expenditures. *Tax Notes, 8*:659–664.

McDaniel, P. R. (1980). Federal spending limitations. *Tax Notes, 10*:475–479.

McDaniel, P. R. (1985). Identification of the "tax" in effective tax rates," "tax reform" and "tax equity." *Natl. Tax J., 38*:273–279.

McDaniel, P. R. (1988). The impact of the tax expenditure concept on tax reform. In N. W. Brooks (ed.), *The Quest for Tax Reform,* Carswell, Toronto, pp. 387–396.

McDaniel, P. R., and Surrey S. S. (1982). Tax expenditures: How to identify them; How to control them. *Tax Notes, 14*:595–625.

McDaniel, P. R., and Surrey, S. S. (eds.) (1985). *International Aspects of Tax Expenditures: A Comparative Study.* Kluwer Law and Taxation Publishers, Seventer, The Netherlands.

McGuire, T. J. (1986). Interstate tax differentials, tax competition, and tax policy. *Natl. Tax J., 39*:367–373.

McIntyre, M. J. (1976). The Sunset Bill: A periodic review for tax expenditures. *Tax Notes, 4*:3–6, 9.

McIntyre, M. J. (1980). A solution to the problem of defining a tax expenditure. *U.C. Davis Law Rev., 14*:79–103.

McIntyre, M. J. (1981). Tax incentives for investment: A review of a study of studies. *Tax Notes, 12*:491–492.

McIntyre, R. (1981). Lessons for tax reformers from the history of the energy tax incentives in the windfall profits tax act of 1980. *Boston College Law Rev., 22*:705–746.

McIntyre, R. S., and Tipps, D. C. (1985). Exploring the investment-incentive myth. *Challenge 28:* 47–52.

McKenna, J. P. (1963). Tax loopholes: A procedural proposal. *Natl. Tax J., 16*:63–67.

New York State, Department of Taxation and Finance (1988). *Issues In State Tax Expenditure Reporting: A Discussion Paper.* Office of Tax Policy Analysis, Albany, NY.

Noto, N. A. (1981). Tax expenditures: The link between economic intent and the distribution of benefits among high, middle, and low income groups. In *Studies in Taxation, Public Finance and Related Subjects* (A Compendium, volume 5), Fund for Public Policy Research, Washington, DC.

Oversight Subcommittee Hearings Initiate Tax Expenditure Review. (1979). *Tax Notes, 8*:389–390.

Papke, J. A., and Papke, L. E. (1986). Measuring differential state-local tax liabilities and their implications for business investment location. *Natl. Tax J., 39*:357–366.

Peltz, D. C. (1978). Some expanded perspectives on use of social science in public policy. In M. J. Yinger and S. J. Cutler (eds.), *Major Social Issues,* The Free Press, New York, pp. 346–357.

PENTAD on Employee Benefit Plans After TEFRA (1982). *Tax Notes, 17*:147–148.

Peretz, P. (1986). The market for industry: Where angels fear to tread. *Policy Studies Rev., 5*:624–633.

Peretz, P. (1988). Modelling the provision of industrial development incentives. In R. Hula (ed.), *Market Based Public Policy,* Macmillan, London, pp. 150–180.

Plant, J. F. (ed.) (1986). Charles E. Lindblom's "decision-making in taxation and expenditures." *Public Budgeting & Finance, 6*:76–86.

Plaut, T. R., and Pluta, J. E. (1983). Business climate, taxes and expenditures, and state industrial growth in the United States. *Southern Econ. J. 50*: 99–119.

Pomp, R. (1985a). A New York perspective on tax incentives: The role of tax incentives in attracting and retaining business. *Multistate Tax Commission Rev. 1985*: 1–9.

Pomp, R. (1985b). The role of tax incentives in attracting and retaining existing business. *Tax Notes, 29*:521.

Pomp, R. (1986). Simplicity and complexity in the context of a state tax system. In S. D. Gold (ed.), *Reforming State Tax Systems*, National Conference of State Legislatures, Denver, CO, pp. 119–142.

Pomp, R. (1988). State tax expenditure budgets—And beyond. In S. D. Gold (ed.), *The Unfinished Agenda for State Tax Reform*, National Conference of State Legislators, Denver, CO, pp. 65–81.

Pomp, R. (1989). Discussion: State tax expenditures—And beyond. In F. Stocker (ed.), *1988 Proceedings*, National Tax Association—Tax Institute of America, Columbus, OH, pp. 33–36.

Premchand, A. (1983). *Government Budgeting and Expenditure Controls*. International Monetary Fund, Washington, DC.

Regan, E. V. (1988). *Government, Inc. Creating Accountability for Economic Development* (Monograph of Government Finance Research Center). Government Financial Officers Association, Washington, DC.

Reibstein, L., and Friday, C. (1989). The smart money in S & L's. *Newsweek 113*: 40.

Richardson, A. J. (1987). Accounting as a legitimating institution. *Accounting, Organization and Society, 12*:341–355.

Richardson, P. (1988). *The Effects of Tax Reform on Tax Expenditures*. Congressional Budget Office, Washington, DC.

Richardson, P. (1989). Tax expenditures and tax reform: The federal experience. In F. Stocker (ed.), *1988 Proceedings*, National Tax Association—Tax Institute of America, Columbus, OH, pp. 23–28.

Rogers, C. A. (1987). Expenditure taxes, income taxes, and time-inconsistency. *J. Public Econ., 32*:215–230.

Rogers, J. M. (1988). *The Impact of Policy Analysis*. University of Pittsburgh Press, Pittsburgh, PA.

Rosenbloom, D. H. (1987). Constitutional perspectives on public policy evaluation. *Policy Studies J., 16*:233–241.

Rosenthal, A. (1981a). Legislative behavior and legislative oversight. *Legislative Studies Q., 6*:115–131.

Rosenthal, A. (1981b). *Legislative Life*. Harper & Row, New York, NY.

Ross, S. G. (1985). A perspective on international tax policy. *Tax Notes, 26*:701–706.

Salamone, D. (1989). Minnesota's experience with tax expenditure reporting. In F. Stocker (ed.), *1988 Proceedings*, National Tax Association—Tax Institute of America, Columbus, OH, pp. 28–33.

Schick, A. (1986). Controlling nonconventional expenditures: Tax expenditures and loans. *Public Budgeting & Finance, 6*:3–19.

Sheppard, L. A. (1984). Tax expenditure budget revisited. *Tax Notes, 22*:557–558.

Shoup, C. (1975). Surrey's pathways to tax reform—A review article. *J. Finance, 30*:1329.

Simon, H. A. (1976). *Administrative Behavior: A Study of Decision-Making Processes in Administrative Organizations* (3rd ed.). Free Press, New York.

Special Analysis G: The Fiscal 1990 Tax Expenditure Budget. (1989). *Tax Notes, 42*:347–376.

State of New York Legislative Commission on Public-Private Cooperation (LCPPC). (1987). *Tax Expenditure Reporting Requirements: An Effective Way to Monitor "Back Door" Spending*. State of New York, Albany, NY.

Steinmo, S. (1986). So what's wrong with tax expenditures? A reevaluation based on Swedish experience. *Public Budgeting & Finance, 6*:27–44.

Stephenson, S. C., and Hewett, R. S., (1985). Strategies for states in fiscal competition. *Natl. Tax J., 38*:219–226.

Surrey, S. S. (1972). Tax subsidies as a device for implementing government policy. *Tax Adviser, 3*:196–204.

Surrey, S. S. (1973). *Pathways to Tax Reform*. Harvard University Press, Cambridge, MA.

Surrey, S. S. (1980). Our Troubled Tax Policy: False Routes and Proper Paths to Change. Taxation with Representation Fund, Washington, D.C., 1980. Speech to 73rd annual meeting of National Tax Association, New Orleans, LA.

Surrey, S. S., and Hellmuth, W. F. (1969). The tax expenditure budget—response to Professor Bittker. *Natl. Tax J., 22*:528–537.

Surrey, S. S., and McDaniel, P. R. (1976). The tax expenditure concept and the Budget Reform Act of 1974. *Boston College Ind. Commercial Law Rev., 17*:679–738.

Surrey, S. S., and McDaniel, P. R. (1980). The tax expenditure concept and the legislative process. In H. J. Aarons and M. J. Boskins (eds.), *The Economics of Taxation*, The Brookings Institution, Washington, DC, pp. 123–144.

Surrey, S. S., and McDaniel, P. R. (1985). *Tax Expenditures*. Harvard University Press, Cambridge, MA.

Tax Expenditure Series Draws Comment. (1979). *Tax Notes, 8*:740.

The CBO on the Tax Expenditure Concept. (Oct. 26, 1981). *Tax Notes, 13*:1011–1013.

Thuronyi, V. (1988). Tax expenditures: A reassessment. *Duke Law J. 1988*: 1155–1206.

Ture, N. B., and Sanden, K. B. (1977). *The Effects of Tax Policy on Capital Formation*. Financial Executive Research Foundation, New York.

Ture's Unreleased Testimony on Tax Expenditures. (1981). *Tax Notes, 13*:1535–1539.

U.S. Senate, Committee on the Budget, 95th Congress, 2d Session. (1978). Tax Expenditures: Relationships to Spending Programs and Background Material on Individual Provisions. Government Printing Office (Committee Print), Washington, DC.

Vasche, J. D. (1987). Tax expenditure reporting—A comment. *Natl. Tax J., 40*:255–257.

Webber, D. J. (1983). Obstacles to the utilization of systematic policy analysis. *Knowledge: Creation, Diffusion, Utilization, 4*:534–560.

Webber, D. J. (1984). Political conditions motivating legislators' use of policy information. *Policy Studies Rev., 4*:110–118.

Webber, D. J. (1987). Legislators' use of policy information. *Am. Behav. Scientist, 30*:612–631.

Weinberg, D. H. (1987). The distributional implications of tax expenditures and comprehensive income taxation. *Natl. Tax J., 40*:237–253.

Weiss, C. H. (1979). The many meanings of research utilization. *Public Admin. Rev., 39*:426–431.

Weiss, C. H. (1987). Congressional committee staffs (do, do not) use analysis. In M. Bulmer (ed.), *Social Science Research and Government*, Cambridge University Press, Cambridge, UK, pp. 94–113.

Wildavsky, A. (1979a). *How To Limit Government Spending*. University of California Press, Berkley.

Wildavsky, A. (1979b). *The Politics of the Budgetary Process* (3rd ed.). Little, Brown, Boston.

Wissel, P., O'Connor, R., and King, M. (1976). The hunting of the legislative snark: Information searches and reforms in U.S. state legislatures. *Legis. Studies Q., 1*:251–267.

Wolfman, B. (1965). Federal tax policy and the support of science. *Univ. PA Law Rev., 114*:171–186.

Wolfman, B. (1984). Statesman, scholar, mentor. In Memoriam: Stanley S. Surrey. *Harvard Law Rev., 98*:343–345.

Wolfman, B. (1985). Tax expenditures: From idea to ideology, *Harvard Law Rev., 99*:491–498.

Zwier, R. (1979). The search for information: Specialists and nonspecialists in the U.S. House of Representatives. *Legis. Studies Q., 4*:31–42.

13

Governmental Auditing

Khi V. Thai *School of Public Administration, Florida Atlantic University, Fort Lauderdale, Florida*

INTRODUCTION

In managing government programs, officials and employees must render a full account of their activities to the public. While not only always specified by law, this accountability concept is inherent in the governing process. The requirement for accountability has led to increased demand for more information about government programs and services. As stated by the General Accounting Office (1988, p. 1.3), policymakers and private citizens want and need to know not only whether government funds are handled properly and in compliance with laws and regulations, but also whether governments achieve the purposes for which programs were authorized and funded, and whether these programs are administered economically and efficiently.

Thus, a sound financial management should include "thoughtful budgeting, appropriate accounting, meaningful financial reporting, and timely audits by qualified auditors" (Freeman et al., 1988, p. 2). A typical reader of government financial statements or reports issued by management has no opportunity to assess the credibility of these statements or reports. Auditing provides an expert's independent, professional judgment on the matters covered in the audit report and adds credibility to properly prepared statements or reduces credibility of improperly prepared ones. "Auditing is a process of accumulating and evaluating evidence to formulate an independent, professional opinion or other judgment about assertions made by management" (Freeman et al., 1988, p. 898).

Schlosser classified auditing in the United States into three branches: (1) "internal" or business auditing, which is performed by independent auditors within a profit organization; (2) governmental auditing, which is practiced by governments of all levels; and (3) independent auditing, which is provided by certified public accountants to the above branches. After classifying auditing as described above, Schlosser (1986, pp. 1–10) stated, "Governmental auditing is the most comprehensive of the three branches of auditing."

Not only is it the most comprehensive but governmental auditing also is the most important of the three branches, as it involves the largest manpower and workload. In the federal government alone, the Department of Health and Human Services, with the second largest auditing staff in the federal government, has a workload of more than 1000 installations, about 550 state agencies, more than 10,000 units of local governments, and about 85 intermediaries and 10,000 hospitals and extended-care facilities under the Medicaid program (Scantlebury, 1986, p. 9–7).

As it is normally performed only after annual financial statements or reports are prepared, auditing is considered by some accounting experts as the last stage of an accounting cycle. However, since the scope of government auditing has been expanded from financial and legal compliance to economy and efficiency, and program results, auditing is not necessarily carried out at the end of each accounting cycle but can be performed at any time as management wishes or law requires.

This chapter will provide an overview of governmental auditing, and explore audit procedures and standards in federal as well as state and local governments.

OVERVIEW OF GOVERNMENTAL AUDITING

Evolution of Governmental Auditing

The idea of auditing is as old as organized governments. The evolution of governmental auditing can be traced from two perspectives: authoritative sources and scope of governmental auditing.

Authoritative Sources of Auditing

In the United States, in the early days of the Revolution, accounts were examined by various committees of the Congress itself. As the volume of auditing increased, these committees had to employ persons who were not delegates to the Congress. Later a Superintendent of Finance was appointed, and delegates ceased examining accounts entirely. When the first Congress met in 1789, it was faced with the task of organizing the new government. One of its most perplexing problems was accounting for and controlling public funds. The Act of September 2, 1789, establishing the Treasury Department, created five key officers, including the Secretary of the Treasury, a Treasurer, a Registrar, an Auditor, and a Comptroller, and required their appointments be approved by the Senate. The Secretary was required to plan for the improvement and management of the revenue and to estimate public receipts and expenditures. The Treasurer had the duties of receiving, keeping, and properly disbursing the public funds and rendering accounts to the Comptroller. The Registrar was charged with accounting and related custodial duties. The Comptroller supervised the adjustment and preservation of accounts, countersigned warrants, prosecuted delinquent revenue officers, and collected debts due the United States, but his principal duty was deciding the lawfulness and justice of claims and accounts. Finally, the Auditor was responsible for examining the accounts and certifying the balances to the Comptroller for decision.

To secure more adequate fiscal controls, the Congress added, in 1817, additional auditors and comptrollers to the Treasury Department and established, in 1836, the Office of Auditors of the Treasury for the Post Office Department. In 1894, the Dockery Act abolished all added comptrollers, except the Comptroller of the Treasury, and assigned the Treasury Department's six auditors to examine the accounts of designated departments and to certify balances in the accounts, subject to appeal to the Comptroller.

During the debate on the Act of 1789, James Madison observed that the Comptroller's duty partook strongly of the judicial character and that there might be strong reasons why such an officer should be responsible to the public, instead of serving at the pleasure of the executive branch. However, the Comptroller remained within the executive branch until 1921 when the Budget and Accounting Act was enacted. Under this act, James Madison's idea of making the Comptroller responsible to the public was realized by creating the General Accounting Office (GAO) under the direction of the Comptroller General. The act shifted audit responsibilities from the executive branch to the legislative branch. Both GAO and the Comptroller General have been expressly recognized by the Congress (in, for example, the Reorganization Act of 1945, and the Accounting and Auditing Act of 1950) as an agency in the legislative branch or an auditing agent of the Congress.

The GAO was granted authority to audit and settle all public accounts; to settle and adjust all claims by and against the Federal government; to prescribe the forms, systems, and procedures for administrative appropriation and fund accounting; and to certify balances in the accounts. Since its creation, the auditing authority of GAO was expanded to government corporations, nonappropriated activities (such as restaurants, concessions, canteens, vending machine operations and other revenue-producing activities), Postal Office, and funds contributed solely by the U.S. government to international organizations. GAO is also an authoritative auditing-standard-setting body of the federal government. Auditing standards for state and local governments have evolved in directions different from the federal auditing standards. While GAO, a governmental agency, has the authority to issue auditing standards for federal agencies, audit standards and requirements for state and local governments come from three different sources:

1. Federal government requirements. The GAO, the Office of Management and Budget (OMB), and other federal agencies have issued various audit standards, guidelines, and circulars and other publications that contain important standards and guidance for audits of specific federal assistance programs. As required by the Single Audit Act of 1984 and the OMB Circular A-110, the GAO audit standards have to be followed by state and local governments that receive federal financial assistance. Moreover, these standards are generally applicable to and recommended for use by local government auditors and public accountants in state and local government audit practice. State and local audit organizations including AICPA, the Institute of Internal Auditors, and the American Evaluation Association (formerly the Evaluation Research Society) have officially adopted these audit standards.

2. State government requirements. In some circumstances, state agencies prescribe accounting systems, financial reports, and audit guidelines and regulations relating to governmental entities within their jurisdiction. As mentioned in a previous chapter on governmental accounting, if there are conflicts between these guidelines and GAAP/GAAS, guidelines established by states do not supersede generally accepted accounting principles issued by the Governmental Accounting Standards Board or generally accepted auditing standards issued by AICPA and federal agencies; rather, a governmental entity should comply with both.

3. AICPA auditing standards, interpretations and guidelines. In most state governments and some large local governments, there is an independent auditor or auditing office. In some other large local governmental units and a majority of small local governments where a full-time auditor is not necessary, auditing service is usually contracted to public accountants, preferably certified public accountants (CPAs). Due to this practice, AICPA Statements on Auditing Standards (SASs) and related interpretations have had great impacts on the audits of financial statements of state and local governments.

The American Institute of Certified Public Accountants (AICPA) has been one of three sources of audit standards and requirements for state and local governments. In

1939, AICPA created the Committee on Auditing Procedure "to examine into auditing procedure and other related questions" (AICPA, 1988, p. 731). This Committee was authorized to prepare Statements of Auditing Procedure (now Statements of Auditing Standards) to guide independent auditors in the exercise of their judgment in the application of auditing procedures. The first Statement under the title of "Extensions of Auditing Procedure" was issued on September 19, 1939, and the "Codification of Statements on Auditing Procedure" was issued in 1951 with its latest version issued in 1988. The name of the Committee on Auditing Procedure was changed to the Auditing Standards and Procedures in 1972, and to the Auditing Standards Board in 1978. Also, the name of the AICPA auditing statements was changed from Statement on Auditing *Procedure* to Statement on Auditing *Standard*. From 1939 to 1972, 54 Statements on Auditing Procedure were issued, and since 1972 to the time of this writing, 63 Statements on Auditing Standards have been issued. As mentioned above, independent auditors have been significantly involved in state and local government auditing. AICPA has to modify its auditing standards whenever a change in accounting, financial reporting, and auditing standards made by the Governmental Accounting Standards Board, GAO, and other federal agencies. For example, in 1987, Statement no. 52 on Auditing Standard, "Omnibus Statement on Auditing Standards—1987," was issued to amend Statement no. 5 (July 1975) to recognize statements and interpretations issued by the Governmental Accounting Standards Board for statements of state and local governments, among other emerging accounting issues within the private sector.

In addition to its auditing statements, AICPA also issued in 1974 an audit guide, entitled *Audits of State and Local Governmental Units* (with its fifth revision published in 1989). This publication contained financial and compliance audit standards and procedures, which were adopted by the Governmental Accounting Standards Board (formerly the National Council on Governmental Accounting), the U.S. General Accounting Office, and other federal agencies.

Scope of Governmental Auditing

Evolution of governmental auditing also has been significant in its scope. Indeed, the scope of governmental auditing has been broadened with the passage of time. Since the formative days of the federal government, financial audits were the single auditing objective, which was to assure that:

Expenditures are not unreasonable and extravagant.
Vouchers and payrolls are mathematically accurate.
Sufficient budget is available.
There is compliance with financial and legal requirements.

However, financial audits have two significant limitations. First of all, this type of control does not assure efficiency and effectiveness in governmental operations. For example, this audit assures that the price of office supplies purchased by an agency is recorded accurately, but it does not assure that the supplies were actually needed. Similarly, this audit assures that payrolls are correctly prepared and paid, but it does not assure that employees on the payrolls performed efficiently.

Moreover, governments do not operate on the basis of profit making. The lack of profit measurement coupled with limitations of the above audit objective has led to a need for audits of economy and efficiency. Thus, the concept of economy and efficiency audits was endorsed in the Budget and Accounting Act of 1921. Section 312 of this Act stated:

> The Comptroller General shall investigate, at the seat of government or elsewhere, all matters relating to the receipt, disbursement, and application of public funds, and shall make to the President when requested by him, and to Congress at the beginning of each regular session, a report in writing of the work of the General Accounting Office. . . . In such regular report, or in special reports at any time when Congress is in session, he shall make recommendations looking to greater economy or efficiency in public expenditures.

The Legislative Reorganization Act of 1946 reasserted this scope of auditing by directing GAO to analyze expenditures of government agencies to determine whether public funds were *economically and efficiently* administered.

In 1949, GAO initiated what it called "a comprehensive audit program" (GAO, 1985, p. 7). This program recognized that the accounting and *internal control* procedures of each agency are the basic points of effective management control over the government's financial operations. This comprehensive audit program was adopted in the Accounting and Auditing Act of 1950. This act required federal agencies to maintain adequate systems of accounting and internal control, and authorized GAO to evaluate federal agencies' accounting and internal control systems.

Despite the 1950 act's requirement, federal agencies' accounting and internal control systems were not adequately designed and maintained. For this reason and in an effort to reduce budget deficits by controlling waste, fraud, and inefficiency, the Federal Managers' Financial Integrity Act was passed in 1982. The act requires the federal department and agency managers to evaluate whether internal control systems have weaknesses that can lead to fraud, waste, and abuse in government operations. The act also requires federal managers to report annually to the President and the Congress on their internal control systems and plans to correct identified weaknesses. Agencies submitted their first reports on December 31, 1983, and thereafter by December 31 of each year. Moreover, since fiscal year 1986, OMB has also summarized government-wide implementation of the Financial Integrity Act in its annual management reports that accompany the President's budget.

Despite the serious efforts of federal agencies to comply with the Financial Integrity Act, problems continue to plague the federal government's internal control and financial management systems. According to a most recent report, GAO (1990) found that no mechanism now exists to ensure that federal agencies take corrective action.

In the Legislative Reorganization Act of 1970, the Congress again broadened the scope of auditing by authorizing GAO to review and analyze the *results* of government programs and activities, and to make cost-benefit studies on a self-initiated basis, when ordered by either house of Congress or when requested by an appropriate congressional committee. Section 204 of the Act stated:

> The Comptroller General shall review and evaluate the results of Government programs and activities carried on under existing law when ordered by either House of Congress, or upon his own initiative, or when requested by any committee of the House of Representatives or the Senate, or any joint committee of the two Houses, having jurisdiction over such programs or activities.

In implementing this act and previous acts relating to auditing, the General Accounting Office (GAO) issued in 1972 "Standards for Audit of Governmental Organizations, Programs, Activities, and Functions," which was revised in 1981. In 1988, this publication was again revised and issued under a new title, *Government Audit Standards*. This publication formally prescribed audit standards and procedures (Fig. 1) that cover not only financial operations but also program economy and efficiency, as well as program results. The GAO auditing standards also have changed the scope of auditing in state and local governments, as mentioned earlier in this chapter.

Another auditing development was the single audit concept. The rapid expansion of federal grants to and contracts with state and local governments, universities, hospitals, and other nonprofit organizations has led to a major audit problem: in many instances, the same accounting systems and transactions were subjected to numerous reviews and tests, and frequently the recipient organization was audited by various federal audit agencies and independent public accountants. Thus, after having been experimented with for 5 years, the single-audit approach—that is, one audit can satisfy the major aspects of many audits done of an organization—was required by Congress by the Single Audit Act of 1984.

The purpose of the single audit is:

To improve the financial management of state and local governments with respect to Federal financial assistance programs.

To establish uniform requirements for audits of federal financial assistance provided to state and local governments.

To promote the efficient and effective use of audit resources.

To ensure that the federal government rely upon and use audit work in its financial aid programs.

Annual single audits are required for state and local governments that receive a total amount of federal financial assistance of either $100,000 or more in any of its fiscal years, or $25,000 or more, but less than $100,000 in any fiscal year, if it elects to implement the Single Audit Act requirements in lieu of separate financial and compliance audit requirements of the federal financial assistance programs.

If a governmental unit receives less than $25,000 in any fiscal year, it is exempt from the audit requirements of the Single Audit Act and all other federal audit requirements. Moreover, biennial audits may be accepted for governmental units that have policies calling for audits less frequent than annual.

A cognizant agency, which usually is a major grantor, is assigned by the OMB Director for any city, village, or country that wants a single audit. The single audit will cover financial and compliance, the entire operations of a state or local government, or, at the option of that government, departments, agencies, or establishments that received, expended, or otherwise administered federal financial assistance during the year. Public hospitals and public colleges and universities may be excluded from state and local audits.

The single audit does not limit the authority of federal agencies to make, or contract for, audits and evaluations of federal financial assistance programs, or the authority of any federal agency inspector general or other federal audit official. Moreover, it does not prohibit any state or local government or subrecipient from carrying out additional audits.

The audit report, prepared at the completion of the single audit, serves many needs of state and local governments, as well as meeting the requirements of the Single Audit Act. The audit report has to state that the audit was made in accordance with the provisions of the OMB Circular A-128, "Audits of State and Local Government." This Circular requires the auditor to comment on at least:

Financial statements and on a schedule of federal assistance showing the total expenditures for each federal assistance program.

The study and evaluation of internal control systems. The auditor identifies the controls that were evaluated, the controls that were not evaluated, and the material weaknesses as a result of the evaluation.

Compliance containing a statement of positive assurance with respect to those items tested for compliance, negative assurance on those items not tested, a summary of all instances of noncompliance, and an identification of total amounts questioned as a result of noncompliance.

The costs of single audits are charged to federal assistance programs. State and local governments should follow the federal procurement standards prescribed by Attachment P of OMB Circular A-102, "Uniform Requirements for Grants to State and Local Governments." These standards provide that federal grant recipients should consider whether it would be more economical to purchase the services from private accounting firms or to enter into intergovernmental agreements for audit services.

Classifications of Audits

The expanded scope of auditing traced in the preceding section covers two basic types of auditing: financial and performance audits. These types of audits will be explored in detail in the remaining part of this chapter. In addition, there are several other classifications of audits.

Pre-Audits and Postaudits

On the basis of when the examination is made, audits may be classified as pre-audit and postaudit. A pre-audit is an examination of financial transactions prior to their completion. This is an integral part of internal financial management control. The pre-audit achieves the most traditional purpose of auditing: detection and protection of fraud and accounting errors. On the contrary, a postaudit is conducted after transactions and events have occurred.

Internal and External Audits

Audits may be classified as internal and external on the basis of the relationship of the auditor and the agency being audited. Internal auditing is "an independent appraisal activity within the organization for the review of operations as a service to management. It is management control which functions by measuring and evaluating the effectiveness of other controls" (NCGA, 1980, p. 86). Internal audits are conducted by employees of the agency being audited. Internal auditors or audit agencies within a governmental unit may be subject to administrative direction from persons involved in the government management process (GAO, 1988, p. 3.8).

On the contrary, external auditing is performed by nongovernment organizations (e.g., public accounting firms or consulting firms) and government agencies (e.g., U.S. General Accounting Office, and state/local audit and evaluation offices), which are independent of the agency being audited. There are three groups of external auditors:

1. Independent auditors elected by the people or appointed by the legislative body. This is the case of the federal government with the Comptroller General of the United

States, and most states and few municipalities. They are responsible directly to the people or the legislative body. Election of auditors works well in some jurisdictions, but in some others, auditors with minimal qualifications are elected to the office.
2.   Officials of a governmental unit other than the one being audited, namely, the auditee. In some states, state audit agencies are responsible for auditing their local governmental units.
3.   Independent public accountants and auditors. Most local governments and a few federal agencies and state governments have their audits performed by this group of external auditors. How does a governmental unit select an external auditor? This question will be addressed later in the next section.

The internal and external audits are similar in scope, standards, and procedures, as will be discussed later in this chapter. Moreover, both audits provide the same benefits: constructive recommendations supported by unbiased and relevant information.

Selection of Auditors

As mentioned earlier, governmental audits may be conducted by governmental audit agencies or nongovernmental audit organizations. Attention has to be given to selection of auditors or audit organizations. It is important that a sound procurement practice be followed when contracting for audit services. Many governments attempt to select an auditor by competitive bidding. The American Institute of Certified Public Accountants and the National Committee on Governmental Accounting (1968, p. 129), in a "Joint Statement on Competitive Bidding for Audit Services in Governmental Agencies," issued in 1955 and revised in 1961, considered competitive bidding as inappropriate:

> Competitive bidding . . . is not an effective procedure in arranging for an independent audit. It is not effective for the simple reason that an audit is not something which can be covered by rigid specifications. An audit is a professional service requiring professional independence, skill, and judgment. An independent auditor should have as much latitude as he may find necessary to be assured that the records are in order and that the system of accounts is functioning properly. . . .
>
> This statement is not intended to challenge the right of government officials to obtain some estimate of their auditing expenses. Once a governmental agency has decided to engage an independent auditor, it ought to discuss the engagement with the auditor it believes to be the best qualified to render the most satisfactory service. After the independent auditor has surveyed the fiscal records and identified the principal problems, it should be possible to develop an understanding on the scope of his audit and on the length of time which will be required for its completion. The independent auditor should then be in a position, if required, to give an estimate of the cost of the service which is not likely to be exceeded unless he encounters unforeseen problems.
>
> This approach to the selection of an auditor, reflecting a legitimate concern for costs is perfectly reasonable and acceptable. But no one gains—indeed, everyone is likely to lose—when auditors are selected by competitive bidding on the basis of the lowest possible price.
>
> It would be in the best interest of all concerned for political subdivisions employing a certified public accountant or a firm of certified public accountants to do so in the same way in which they would select an attorney, doctor, or other professional advisor—choose the one in whom they have the most confidence, discuss the work to be done, and agree on the basis for the fee.

In 1968, the National Committee on Governmental Accounting (1968, p. 128) endorsed the above position by stating that auditors should be selected only on the basis of professional competence and experience. This will not only mean that the auditor should be a certified public accountant authorized to practice in the jurisdiction being audited, but that he should have appropriate experience in the audit of governmental units and a demonstrated high level of attainment in such a professional practice. There must be a clear recognition on the part of both public officials concerned and independent accountants that auditing services are truly professional in nature. This being the case, the audit services should be compensated on the basis of professional fees agreed upon in advance of the engagement and not on the basis of competitive bids. . . .

Selection of independent public auditors by competitive bidding has decreased significantly in local government since the issuance of the above joint statement. This decline, however, was reversed by the insistence of several federal agencies, and many state and local governments, on securing audit services on the basis of competitive biddings.

The National Intergovernmental Audit Forum, an organization of federal, state and local government audit executives, recommended:

Governmental agencies . . . contracting for audits by other than government employed auditors, should be encouraged to engage public accountants by competitive negotiations that take into consideration such factors as the experience, plans, qualifications and price of the offeror. The weights to be assigned to each factor should be tailored to the particular tasks to be performed. (NCGA, 1980, p. 90)

After an auditor has been selected, in order to avoid any misunderstanding of the nature, scope, or other aspects of audit services, a contract should be in written form and should specify among other things:

The type and purpose of the audit.
The exact objects to be audited (such as departments, and funds).
The period the audit is to cover.
Approximate beginning and completion dates and the date of delivery of the report and the number of copies of the report.
The terms of compensation and reimbursement of the auditor's expenses.
The place at which the audit work will be done.

The GAO auditing standards are built on two types: *financial audits,* including financial statements and financial related audits, and *performance audits,* consisting of economy and efficiency and program results. Provision for such a broad audit scope does not imply that all audits should be of such an extensive scope. Indeed, as stated by GAO (1987, p. 2–6), "Audits may have a combination of financial and performance audit objectives, or may have objectives limited to only some aspects of one audit type."

This statement highlights the importance of a clear understanding of the audit scope by all interested parties. This takes on added importance when an auditor is engaged to perform the audits. The engagement agreement between a governmental unit and the auditor should specify the scope of the work to be done as defined in the standards, to avoid misunderstandings.

Few governmental audits can be extended into all important aspects of an agency's operations. Rather, an audit focuses on one primary aspect of the comprehensive audit to meet a specific need of policymakers, managers, other governments, investors, and the public, while other aspects of the audit receive secondary attention.

As each type of audit can be performed separately, audit contracts should specify which types of audits are to be covered and the auditor's report should indicate which type is audited. Today, financial audits are most widely carried out in state and local governmental units.

Quality of Nongovernmental Auditors

The audit quality of private firms has been a matter of concern in the federal government. In late 1985 and early 1986, the Subcommittee on Legislation and National Security of the House Committee on Government Operations conducted hearings to review the quality of audits of federal assistance programs performed by nonfederal auditors, and the General Accounting Office issued two reports on CPA audit quality of those programs. In a 1985 report, GAO found that one-third of the governmental audits performed by certified public accountants did not satisfactorily comply with standards. The following are frequent deficiencies identified by regional offices of federal inspectors generals (GAO, 1985):

Auditors' reports do not include a statement on internal control, compliance with generally accepted auditing standards, and/or applicable laws and regulations.

Some auditors' reports include statements on internal controls but fail to identify the entity's significant controls or, having identified the controls, do not identify the controls that were evaluated, the controls not evaluated, the reasons why they were not evaluated, and any material weaknesses identified.

Auditors' reports do not adequately describe the scope of audit work performed or the agency guidance followed in the conduct of the audit.

Auditors fail to report, or inadequately report, findings of noncompliance with laws and regulations.

Auditors opine on financial statements that contain unexplained inaccuracies, such as accounts not in balance, incorrect accounts, incorrect adjusting entries, improper reporting formats, missing schedules, and missing information.

In a hearing conducted on March 19, 1986, of the House Subcommittee on Legislation and National Security, Charles A. Bowsher, U.S. comptroller general, made the following recommendations:

Strengthen enforcement efforts through positive enforcement programs and referral of substandard audits to disciplinary bodies, which should act promptly and decisively.

Broaden continuing professional education requirements to include a specified level of governmental accounting and auditing for practitioners performing these audits.

Require that governmental audits be included in peer reviews.

Place greater emphasis on governmental accounting and auditing in the Uniform CPA Examination.

Include governmental audits in accounting firms' internal reviews of their audit quality.

Seek an expansion of college curriculum to include greater attention to the nature and performance of governmental accounting and auditing (*Journal of Accountancy,* June 1986, p. 55).

In its most recent study, GAO (1989, p. 1) concluded:

CPAs complied with auditing standards in 35 of the 40 audits we reviewed. In particular, we found in these audits sufficient evidence of studies and evaluations of internal controls over federal expenditures and testing of compliance with laws and regulations. Failure to meet these two audit requirements was the predominant problem CPAs had in conducting governmental audits, according to our 1986 review of CPA audit quality, which included both single audits done under Office of Management and Budget (OMB) Circular A-102 prior to the passage of the act and grant audits.

AUDIT STANDARDS

As mentioned above, despite various authoritative sources of auditing, two sets of audit standards are widely recognized: the AICPA standards and the GAO standards. The AICPA standards are recognized as being appropriate for financial audits, but insufficient for the broader scope of governmental auditing. The GAO auditing standards cover not only financial audits, but also audits of economy and efficiency and program results. The two standards are both effective because the AICPA standards are recognized and incorporated into the GAO audit standards. The GASB recognized both standards in its Statement no. 1. In its revised audit standards for state and local governmental units, the American Institute of Certified Public Accountants, in turn, endorsed the GAO audit standards.

In addition the above two sets of audit standards, the following audit guides contain useful information for certain types of auditing:

Audits of State and Local Governmental Units as revised in 1989, published by AICPA, useful to state and municipal auditing.
AICPA Statement of Position 89-6, "Auditors' Report in Audits of State and Local Governmental Units," issued on August 11, 1989, amending the *Audits of State and Local Governmental Units*.
Statement on Auditing Standards no. 3, "Compliance Auditing Applicable to Governmental Entities and Other Recipients of Governmental Financial Assistance," issued in April 1989.
"Auditing Governmental Organizations," a chapter in *Governmental Accounting, Auditing, and Financial Reporting* published by the Municipal (now Government) Finance Officers Association in 1968 with its last revised version published in 1988, also useful to state and municipal auditing.
OMB Circular A-102 (and Attachments A through P thereto), "Uniform Requirements for Assistance to State and Local Governments", January 1981.
OMB Circular 123, "Internal Control Systems," August 1983.
OMB Circular no. A-128, "Audits of State and Local Governments," April 12, 1985.
OMB Notice, "Questions and Answers on the Single Audit Process of OMB Circular 128 'Single Audits of State and Local Governments,' " November 13, 1987.
OMB, *Internal Control Guidelines* (Washington, DC, 1983).

Moreover, several state governments and state CPA societies prescribe audit procedures applicable to governmental units within those states. Specific accounting, auditing, and/or reporting requirements are also imposed on large federal programs.

In auditing practices, audit standards must be distinguished from audit procedures. "Standards deal with quality, while procedures are the actual work that is performed" (Freeman et al., 1988, p. 904). Standards are to be followed by auditors and audit organizations when required by law, regulation, agreement or contract, or policy. They pertain to the auditor's professional qualifications, the quality of audit effort, and the characteristics of professional and meaningful audit reports.

Basic Premises

The GAO (1988, pp. 1.4–1.6) highlights the objectives of the auditing standards in 10 basic premises:

1. The term "audit" includes both financial and performance audits as described earlier in this chapter.
2. Public officials have the responsibility to apply resources efficiently, economically, and effectively to achieve the purposes for which the resources were furnished. This responsibility applies to all resources, whether entrusted to public officials by their own constituency or by other levels of government.
3. Public officials are accountable both to the public and to other levels and other branches of government for the resources provided to carry out government programs and services. Consequently, they should provide appropriate reports to those to whom they are accountable.
4. Public officials are responsible for establishing and maintaining an effective internal control system to ensure that appropriate goals and objectives are met, resources are safeguarded, laws and regulations are followed, and reliable data are obtained, maintained, and fairly disclosed.
5. Public officials are responsible for complying with applicable laws and regulations. That responsibility encompasses identifying the requirements with which the entity and the official must comply and implementing systems designed to achieve compliance with those requirements.
6. Financial auditing is an important part of the accountability process since it provides an independent opinion on whether an entity's financial statements present fairly the results of financial operations, and whether other financial information is presented in conformity with established or stated criteria. Performance auditing also is an important part of the accountability process because it provides an independent view of the extent to which government officials are faithfully, efficiently, and effectively carrying out their responsibilities.
7. Unless legal restrictions or ethical considerations prevent it, auditees or audit organizations should make audit reports available to the public and to other levels of government that have supplied resources.
8. Different levels of government share common interests in many programs. In many government financial assistance programs, the interests of individual government often cannot be isolated because the resources applied have been commingled. Therefore, audits of financial assistance programs having common interests and shared funding should, to the extent practicable, be designed to satisfy the common accountability interests of each contributing government.
9. Cooperation by federal, state, and local governments in auditing programs of common interest will minimize duplication of audit effort and benefit all concerned, intergovernmental operations.
10. Auditors may rely on the work of others to the extent feasible once they satisfy themselves as to the other's independence, capability, and performance by appropriate tests of their work or by other acceptable methods.

General Audit Standards

The *general audit standards* relate to the qualifications of the staff, the independence of audit organizations or individual auditors, the exercise of due professional care in conducting the audit and in preparing related reports, and the presence of quality control. They apply to all audit organizations, both government and nongovernment, conducting governmental audits. These general audit standards are set forth in the GAO's *Government Audit Standards* as follows.

Qualifications

"The staff assigned to conduct the audit should collectively possess adequate professional proficiency for the tasks required" (Standard no. 1). The audit staff should have interdisciplinary knowledge and skills (including such areas as accounting, statistics, law, engineering, social science, public administration, economics, and actuarial science) necessary for the audit to be conducted. Moreover, the audit staff should maintain professional proficiency through strictly required continuing education and training.

Independence

"In all matters relating to the audit work, the audit organization and the individual auditors, whether government or public, should be free from personal and external impairments to independence, should be organizationally independent, and should maintain an independent attitude and appearance" (Standard no. 2). The auditor and the audit organization are responsible for maintaining independence so that opinions, conclusions, judgments, and recommendations will be impartial and will be viewed as impartial by knowledgeable third parties. The audit organization has to establish policies and procedures in place to help determine if auditors have any personal impairments that bias the audit. These impairments include, but are limited to, official, professional, personal, or financial relationships; preconceived ideas toward individuals, groups, organizations, or objectives of a particular program; and financial interest, direct or substantially indirect, in the audited entity or program. Moreover, some external factors that may interfere with an auditor's ability to perform independent and objective opinions and conclusions include interference external to the audit organization in assignment, appointment, and promotion of audit personnel; restrictions on funds or other resources provided to the audit organization; and influences that jeopardize the auditor's continued employment for reasons other than competency. For government audits, auditors should be sufficiently removed from political pressures to ensure that they can conduct their audits objectively and report their findings, opinions, and conclusions objectively without fear of political repercussion.

Due Professional Care

"Due professional care should be used in conducting the audit and in preparing related reports" (Standard no. 3). Auditors and audit organizations should follow all applicable standards in conducting governmental audits. Auditors should use sound professional judgment in determining applicable standards that are to be followed. Exercising due professional care means using sound judgment in considering:

The scope, methodology, tests and procedures for the audit.
What is necessary to achieve the audit objectives.
Materiality and/or significance of matters to which the tests, procedures, and methodology are applied.
Effectiveness and/or efficiency of internal controls.

Cost versus benefits of the audit.
Reporting time-frames.

Due professional care also includes followup on known findings and recommendations from previous audits. Management of an audited governmental entity is responsible for prompt and appropriate corrective actions. The audit report should disclose the status of known but incorrect significant findings and recommendations from prior audits that affect the current audit objective.

Quality Control

"Audit organizations conducting government audits should have an appropriate internal quality control system in place and participate in an external quality control review program" (Standard no. 4). This standard requires that audit organizations adopt and follow applicable audit standards, policies, and procedures. Moreover, they should have an external quality control review at least once every 3 years by an organization (such as AICPA, GAO, National State Auditors Association, Intergovernmental Audit Forum, or the Institute of Internal Auditors) that is not affiliated with the organization being reviewed.

Field Work Standards

The general audit standards explained above apply to all types of governmental audits. In conducting auditing work, auditors have to follow necessary standards, depending on the types of audits. Currently, governmental auditing consists of two basic types: financial audits and performance audits. *Financial audits* include financial statement and financial related audits. *Financial statement audits* are to ascertain (1) whether the agency's financial statements of an audited entity present fairly the financial position, results of operations, and cash flows or changes in financial position in accordance with generally accepted accounting principles, and (2) whether the entity has complied laws and regulations for those transactions and events that may have the material effect on the financial statements.

Financial related audits include determining (1) whether financial reports and related items, such as elements, accounts, or funds, are fairly presented, (2) whether financial information is presented in accordance with established or stated criteria, and (3) whether the entity has adhered to specific financial compliance requirements. (GAO, 1988, p. 2.3). Financial related audits may cover the following items: segments of financial statements; financial information (e.g., statement of revenue and expenses, statements of cash receipts and disbursements, statement of fixed assets); reports and schedules of financial matters (e.g., expenditures for specific programs or services, budget requests, and variances between estimated and actual financial performance); contracts (e.g., bid proposals, contract pricing, compliance with contract terms); grants; internal control systems and structure over accounting, financial reporting, and transaction processing; computer-based systems; financial systems (e.g., payroll systems); and fraud.

Performance audits include economy and efficiency, and program audits. *Economy and efficiency audits* determine (1) whether the entity is acquiring, protecting, and using its resources (such as personnel, property, and space) economically and efficiently, (2) the causes of inefficiencies or uneconomical practices, and (3) whether the entity has complied with laws and regulations concerning matters of economy and efficiency. (GAO, 1988, p. 2.3). Technically, economy deals with cost savings, whereas efficiency implies benefit maximizing. In examining economy and efficiency, auditors should, for example, consider whether the audited entity has followed sound procurement practices; acquired the appropriate type, quality, and amount of resources at the lowest cost; properly protected and maintained its resources; avoided duplication of effort by employees and work that serves little or no purpose; complied with laws and regulations that could significantly affect the acquisition, protection, and use of the entity's resources; and had an adequate system for measuring performance on economy and efficiency.

Program audits, as defined by GAO (1988, p. 2.3), are "determining (1) the extent to which the desired results or benefits established by the legislature or other authorizing body are being achieved, (2) the effectiveness of organizations, programs, activities, or functions, and (3) whether the entity has complied with laws and regulations applicable to the program." In reviewing a new or ongoing program, auditors may assess, for example, whether its objectives are proper, suitable and relevant; the extent to which it achieves a desired level of program results; whether it complements, duplicates, overlaps, or conflicts with other related programs; and compliance with laws and regulations applicable to the program, as well as the adequacy of management's system for measuring and reporting effectiveness. The auditors may also identify factors inhibiting satisfactory performance and ways of making programs work better.

Field Work Standards for Financial Audits

The GAO field work standards for financial audits are summarized as follows (GAO, 1988, pp. A.2–A.3):

A. Relationship to AICPA Standards

1. The standards of field work for government financial audits incorporate the AICPA standards of field work for financial audits, and prescribe supplemental standards of field work needed to satisfy the unique needs of government financial audits.

2. The field work standards of the AICPA and the [GAO] supplemental standards [in chapter 4 of GAO's *Government Auditing Standards]* apply to both financial statement audits and financial related audits.

B. Planning:

1. Supplemental planning field work standards for government financial audits are:

   a. Audit Requirements for all Government Levels: Planning should include consideration of the audit requirements of all levels of government.

   b. Legal and Regulatory Requirements: A test should be made of compliance with applicable laws and regulations.

      (1) In determining compliance with laws and regulations:

      (a) The auditor should design audit steps and procedures to provide reasonable assurance of detecting errors, irregularities, and illegal acts that could have a direct and material effect on the financial statement amounts or the results of financial related audits.

(b) The auditor should also be aware of the possibility of illegal acts which could have an indirect and material effect on the financial statements or results of financial related audits.

C. Evidence (Working papers)

1. The AICPA field work standards and this statement [GAO's *Government Audit Standards*] require that: A record of the auditors' work be retained in the form of working papers.

2. Supplemental working paper requirements for financial audits are that working papers should:

a. Contain a written audit program cross-referenced to the working papers.

b. Contain the objective, scope, methodology and results of the audit.

c. Contain sufficient information so that supplementary oral explanations are not required.

d. Be legible with adequate indexing and cross-referencing, and include summaries and lead schedules, as appropriate.

e. Restrict information included to matters that are materially important and relevant to the objectives of the audit.

f. Contain evidence of supervisory reviews of the work conducted.

D. Internal Control

1. The AICPA field work standards and this statement [GAO's *Government Auditing Standards*] require that: A sufficient understanding of the internal control structure is to be obtained to plan the audit and to determine the nature, timing, and extent of tests to be performed.

Field Work Standards for Performance Audits

The GAO field work standards for performance audits are summarized as follows (GAO, 1988, p. A.5):

A. Planning: Work is to be adequately planned.

B. Supervision: Staff are to be properly supervised.

C. Legal and Regulatory Requirements: An assessment is to be made of compliance with applicable requirements of laws and regulations when necessary to satisfy the audit objectives.

1. Where an assessment of compliance with laws and regulations is required: Auditors should design the audit to provide reasonable assurance of detecting abuse or illegal acts that could significantly affect the audit objectives.

2. In all performance audits: Auditors should be alert to situations or transactions that could be indicative of abuse or illegal acts.

D. Internal Control: An assessment should be made of applicable internal controls when necessary to satisfy the audit objectives.

E. Evidence: Sufficient, competent, and relevant evidence is to be obtained to afford a reasonable basis for the auditors' judgments and conclusions regarding the organization, program, activity, or function under audit. A record of the auditors' work is to be retained in the form of working papers. Working papers may include tapes, films, and discs.

Audit Report Standards

At the completion of an audit, the auditor has to write and submit an audit report. The reporting standards vary with the types of audits.

Reporting Standards for Financial Audits

The GAO reporting standards for financial audits are summarized as follows (GAO, 1988, pp. A.4–A.5):

A. Relationship to AICPA Standards

1. The standards of reporting for government financial audits incorporate the AICPA standards of reporting for financial audits; and prescribes supplemental standards of reporting needed to satisfy the unique needs of governmental financial audits.

2. The reporting standards of the AICPA and the [GAO] supplemental standards [in chapter 5 of GAO's *Government Auditing Standards*] apply to both financial statement audits and financial related audits.

B. Supplemental reporting standards for government financial audits are:

1. Statement on Auditing Standards: A statement should be included in the auditors' report that the audit was made in accordance with generally accepted government auditing standards. (AICPA standards require that public accountants state that the audit was made in accordance with generally accepted auditing standards. In conducting government audits, public accountants should also state that their audits were conducted in accordance with the standards set forth in chapters 3, 4, and 5 [of GAO's *Government Auditing Standards*]).

2. Report on Compliance: The auditors should prepare a written report on their tests of compliance with applicable laws and regulations. This report, which may be included in either the report on the financial audit or a separate report, should contain a statement of positive assurance on those items which were tested for compliance and negative assurance on those items not tested. It should include all material instances of

noncompliance, and all instances or indications of illegal acts which could result in criminal prosecution.

3. Report on Internal Controls: The auditors should prepare a written report on their understanding of the entity's internal control structure and the assessment of control risk made as part of a financial statement audit, or a financial related audit. This report may be included in either the auditor's report on the financial audit or a separate report. The auditor's report should include as a minimum: (a) the scope of the auditor's work in obtaining an understanding of the internal control structure and in assessing the control risk, (b) the entity's significant internal controls or control structure including the controls established to ensure compliance with laws and regulations that have a material impact on the financial statements and the results of the financial related audit, and (c) the reportable conditions, including the identification of material weaknesses, identified as a result of the auditors' work in understanding and assessing the control risk.

4. Reporting on Financial Related Audits: Written audit reports are to be prepared giving the results of each financial related audit.

5. Privileged and Confidential Information: If certain information is prohibited from general disclosure, the report should state the nature of the information omitted and the requirement that makes the omission necessary.

6. Report Distribution: Written audit reports are to be submitted by the audit organization to the appropriate officials of the organization audited and to the appropriate officials of the organizations requiring or arranging for the audits, including external funding organizations, unless legal restrictions, ethical considerations, or other arrangements prevent it. Copies of the reports should also be sent to other officials who have legal oversight authority or who may be responsible for taking action and to others authorized to receive such reports. Unless restricted by law or regulation, copies should be made available for public inspection.

Reporting Standards for Performance Audits

The GAO reporting standards for performance audits are summarized as follows (GAO, 1988, pp. A.5–A.6):

A. Form: Written audit reports are to be prepared communicating the results of each government audit.

B. Timeliness: Reports are to be issued promptly so as to make the information available for timely use by management and legislative officials, and by other interested parties.

C. Report Contents

1. Objectives, Scope, and Methodology: The report should include a statement of the audit objectives and a description of the audit scope and methodology.

2. Audit Findings and Conclusions: The report should include a full discussion of the audit findings, and where applicable, the auditor's conclusions.

3. Cause and Recommendations: The report should include the cause of problem areas noted in the audit, and recommendations for actions to correct the problem areas and to improve operations, when called for by the audit objectives.

4. Statement on Auditing Standards: The report should include a statement that the audit was made in accordance with generally accepted government auditing standards and disclose when applicable standards were not followed.

5. Internal Controls: The report should identify the significant internal controls that were assessed, the scope of the auditor's assessment work, and any significant weaknesses found during the audit.

6. Compliance With Laws and Regulations: The report should include all significant instances of noncompliance and abuse and all indications or instances of illegal acts that could result in criminal prosecution that were found during or in connection with the audit.

7. Views of Responsible Officials: The report should include the pertinent views of responsible officials of the organization, program, activity, or function audited concerning the auditors' findings, conclusions, and recommendations, and what corrective action is planned.

8. Noteworthy Accomplishments: The report should include as description of any significant noteworthy accomplishments, particularly when management improvements in one area may be applicable elsewhere.

9. Issues Needing Further Study: The report should include a listing of any significant issues needing further study and consideration.

10. Privileged and Confidential Information: The report should include a statement about any pertinent information that was omitted because it is deemed privileged or confidential. The nature of such information should be described, and the basis under which it is withheld should be stated.

D. Report Presentation: The report should be complete, accurate, objective, and convincing, and be as clear and concise as the subject matter permits.

E. Report Distribution: Written audit reports are to be submitted by the audit organization to the appropriate officials of the organization audited, and to the appropriate officials of the organizations requiring or arranging for the audits, including external funding organizations, unless legal restrictions, ethical considerations, or other arrangements prevent it. Copies of the reports should also be sent to other officials who may be responsible for taking action on audit findings and recommendations and to others authorized to receive such reports. Unless restricted by law or regulation, copies should be available for public inspection.

PERFORMANCE AUDITING PRACTICES

Due to its relative simplicity compared with performance audits, financial audit process is not described in this chapter. Because GAO recognizes and incorporates the AICPA financial audit standards in its standards, the reader should read the AICPA audit guide, *Audits of State and Local Governmental Units* (with its most recent revised version published in 1989), on how to plan and to conduct financial audits. Preliminary steps in financial audits are familiarization with the nature of the audited organization, its internal control system, and the legal and contractual provisions governing the budget execution. These provisions include restrictions regarding the provision and disbursement of revenues and the control of budget and funds. Moreover, the auditor should be thoroughly familiar with the auditing guidelines applicable to the governmental unit being audited, namely, the auditee.

Audit Process

Performance audits are more time-consuming and complicated than financial audits. A sound performance audit should adhere to the following phases as recommended by GAO (1976, p. 2.11):

1. Survey.
2. Review.
3. Report including recommendations, where appropriate.

Survey Phase

The survey phase of an audit encompasses gathering general working information, studying legislation, and testing management controls.

Gathering General Working Information

An auditor should obtain general working information on all important aspects of the agency being audited or a segment thereof in as short a time as possible. This kind of information will enable the auditor to start organizing the audit work and make plans for preliminary testing and detailed review of controls and activities. Gathering general working information should be done through initial contacts with agency officials who are informed about the general plans and the nature of the audit. Discussions with these officials may lead to obtaining valuable information or identifying troublesome areas.

Some of the sources from which general working information may be readily obtained include:

Legislative reference files of the General Accounting Office or of the agency being audited.

Budget data submitted to the legislative body.

Printed hearings of legislative committees on authorizations and appropriations or on agency activities and related reports.

Reports prepared by the agency being audited, other governmental agencies, outside consultants, universities, or research organizations.

Reorganization plans.

Historical and informational pamphlets about the agency or its programs.

Agency internal audit, inspection, or other internal reports.

Agency procedural manuals, policy procurement directories, or regulations.

Through initial contacts with agency officials and examination of printed documents, general information such as the following can be compiled:

History, background, and purposes of the activities or programs being examined.

Organization of the agency such as division of duties and responsibilities; principal delegations of authority; nature, size, and location of field offices; number of employees.

Types, cost, and location of the assets.

Other financial data such as cost of operations by periods, year-by-year records of income from revenue-producing operations, borrowing authority and operations, if any.

The general working information is used in planning succeeding phases of the audit and as a source of reference in carrying out the detailed examination work.

Studying Legislation

The pertinent laws and legislative history should be carefully studied to ascertain congressional intent as to:

The purpose, scope, and objectives of the activity or program being examined.

The manner in which they are to be conducted and financed.

The nature and extent of the agency's authority and responsibility.

Limited Testing of Management Controls

The policies established to govern agency activities under examination should be analyzed for conformity with applicable laws and congressional intent and their appropriateness for carrying out authorized activities or programs in an effective, efficient, and economical manner.

The auditor also obtains practical working information on how the agency's system of controls *actually* works by testing the effectiveness and usefulness of controls over specific work activities. This information is useful in identifying possible management weaknesses and other matters on which the expenditure of additional time and effort will be warranted during the review phase.

At completion of the survey phase, the auditor is able to clearly identify important issues and problems to be examined in more depth. Survey information is used to establish specific review objectives, estimate staffing requirements, schedule work at specific locations, prepare work programs, and establish target dates for completion of the review and reporting phases.

Review Phase

This phase consists of the detailed examination or evaluation of specific activities or operations to the extent necessary to achieve the approved objectives of the assignment in accordance with out prescribed auditing standards.

Detailed examination or evaluation work includes exploring and developing all pertinent and significant information necessary to properly consider, support, and present our findings, conclusions, and recommendations.

Report Phase

The results of the audit work should be promptly communicated, either orally or in writing, to the Congress, appropriate congressional committees, or agency officials as a basis for action, where necessary, and for information purposes. Except in very unusual circumstances, some type of external communication should follow every review performed.

Relationship between Audit Phases

A close relationship exists between all phases of work performed on an audit assignment. The manner and extent to which these phases are carried out and the interrelationships between them vary between assignments, depending on the objectives established in each case, whether the audit is being made for the first time or is a recurring or followup assignment, and the significance of the activities or programs to be examined. For example, more survey work would normally be performed on an initial assignment than one involving activities that have been previously reviewed. In the latter cases, some updating of general information will be required, but complete new surveys should not be necessary.

In all assignments, the nature and objectives of the reporting should be established as soon as possible and all audit work performed so as to meet those requirements adequately and promptly.

Some Underlying Principles

Some basic principles underlying the nature of our audit work are summarized below.

Prerequisites for Evaluations of Agency Operations

The starting point in a performance audit is to find out how the agency itself conducts its work and makes its decisions. Without this knowledge, the effectiveness of the agency's methods, policies, or procedures cannot be satisfactorily evaluated.

Emphasis on Opportunities for Improvement

In planning and conducting audits, emphasis should be given to those aspects of agency operations and activities in which opportunities for improvement appear to exist. Thus, auditors need to examine subjects or problems of known or anticipated congressional interest such as management weaknesses like ineffectiveness, inefficiency, waste and extravagance, improper expenditures, and failure to comply with laws or congressional intent. In their reports, auditors also should give recognition to (1) audit work resulting in favorable findings, (2) work sufficiently intensive to enable the reporting of no significant findings, and (3) general reviews that reveal no indications of weakness warranting closer examination.

Identification of Individuals Responsible for Deficiencies

In developing audit findings and identifying related management weaknesses, auditors should try, to the extent applicable, to determine the specific individuals or organizational unit responsible for the deficiency for use as appropriate in obtaining corrective action. Although it is not necessary to disclose in audit reports the names of employees immediately responsible for the actions or operations being criticized, it is desirable to communicate this information to top agency officials orally or in the letter transmitting copies of the report to the agency head. On request, or when deemed desirable, such information should also be disclosed to responsible legislators.

Actions Against Accountable Officers

Although auditors are not empowered to direct changes in agency policies, procedures, and functions, they do possess the power to refuse credit to accountable officers for payments made illegally or improperly from appropriated funds. With this power, they are thus responsible for taking actions against the accountable officer or his surety to enforce recovery of money illegally or improperly paid out.

Violations of Criminal Laws

In performing auditing, auditors may encounter violations of criminal laws that warrant the attention of federal agencies having criminal law enforcement responsibilities. The responsibility for investigating violations of federal criminal laws is vested in the Federal Bureau of Investigation (FBI), except in certain specialized areas where the responsibility is assigned to other agencies. The more important types of federal criminal law violations that may be encountered in audit work and that are subject to referral to the FBI are fraud, false claims, conflict of interest, perjury, bribery, and theft or embezzlement of government funds or property. It is necessary to promptly furnish to the appropriate criminal law enforcement agency all information concerning suspected criminal law violations arising in auditing.

Detection and Prevention of Fraud

The detection of fraud is not a primary reason for an audit. However, the possibilities of fraud in governmental programs and activities should be given full consideration in this type of audit, and any indications of fraud should be investigated to the point where a determination can be made to refer it to the proper criminal law enforcement agency.

CONCLUDING REMARKS

Audit reports, which are the end products of auditing, contain valuable information about the operations of the agency being audited, and particularly audit recommendations. The usefulness of auditing depends on the effectiveness of actions taken on audit recommendations. Where operating officials disagree with the auditor's recommendations, a mechanism should be established to reconcile the differences or to call for a decision at a higher management level.

Primary responsibility for action and followup on audit recommendations rests with management. However, reporting a finding, observation, or recommendation does not mean the end of an auditor's concern with the matter. From time to time he/she should ascertain whether his/her recommendations have received serious management consideration and whether satisfactory corrective action has been taken.

REFERENCES

American Institute of Certified Public Accountants. (1989). *Audits of State and Local Governmental Units*. AICPA, New York.

Auditing Standards Board. (1988). *Codification of Statements on Auditing Standards*. American Institute of Certified Public Accountants, New York.

Auditing Standards Board. (1989). *Statement on Auditing Standards No. 63, Compliance Auditing*

Applicable to Governmental Entities and Other Recipients of Governmental Financial Assistance. American Institute of Certified Public Accountants, New York.

Freeman, R. J., Shoulders, C. D., and Lynn, S. L. (1988). *Fund Accounting: Theory and Practice*, 3rd ed. Prentice-Hall, Englewood Cliffs, NJ.

General Accounting Office. (1972, 1981). *Standards for Audit of Governmental Organizations, Programs, Activities, and Functions*. U.S. Government Printing Office, Washington, DC.

General Accounting Office. (1974). *Comprehensive Audit Manual*. U.S. Government Printing Office, Washington, DC.

General Accounting Office. (1980). *Guidelines for Financial and Compliance Audits of Federally Assisted Programs*. U.S. Government Printing Office, Washington, DC.

General Accounting Office. (1985). *Inspectors General Find Significant Problems*. U.S. Government Printing Office, Washington, DC.

General Accounting Office. (1988). *Government Audit Standards*. U.S. Government Printing Office, Washington, DC.

General Accounting Office. (1989). *Single Audit Act: Single Audit Quality Has Improved but Some Implementation Problems Remain*. U.S. Government Printing Office, Washington, DC.

General Accounting Office. (1990). *Government Financial Vulnerability: Fourteen Areas Needing Special Review*. U.S. Government Printing Office, Washington, DC.

Government Finance Officers Association. (1968, 1980, 1988). *Governmental Accounting, Auditing and Financial Reporting*. Government Finance Officers Association, Chicago.

Office of Management and Budget. (1985). *Circular A-128, Audits of State and Local Government*. OMB, Washington, DC.

Scantlebury, D. L. (1986). Federal government auditing. In J. A. Cashin, P. D. Neuworth and J. F. Levy (eds.), *Cashin's Handbook for Auditors*, McGraw-Hill, New York.

Schlosser, R. E. (1986). The field of auditing. In J. A. Cashin, P. D. Neuworth and J. F. Levy (eds.), *Cashin's Handbook for Auditors*, McGraw-Hill, New York.

14

Budgets, Financial Management, and Computers in Government

Marcia Lynn Whicker *Department of Public Administration, Virginia Commonwealth University, Richmond, Virginia*

Thomas A. Silvious *Applications Installations, Information Technologies, Inc., Richmond, Virginia*

COMPUTERS IN SOCIETY AND GOVERNMENT

Well into a period dominated by a technology powerful enough to have a major epoch named after it, computers have revolutionized the way government does business and business deals with government. Thus, the computer or information era follows the industrial era and the agricultural era before it. In each instance, a powerful technology and breakthrough in scientific information fundamentally reorganized production.

In the agricultural era, new knowledge about seeds and planting cycles, domestication of animals, and development of the plow provided an alternative to hunting and gathering as well as relief from constant close proximity to subsistence existence, allowing the development of cities and modern culture. In the industrial era, harnessing mechical energy in the form of turbines and engines, along with standardization in the organization of production, provided relief from physical back-breaking drudgery plus great expansion of the material wealth of society.

And in the information era, the interface of electronic circuitry with digitized sequential streams of data has expanded the analytic power of mankind to allow the achievement of tasks previously impossible, from statistical analysis of mind-numbing masses of information to efficient projections of future outcomes. Nowhere in government has the computerization of work had a greater impact than in the area of finance and budgeting, an area blessed and beset with huge amounts of numeric information.

Computers process, manipulate, massage, analyze, and create information at unbelieveable speeds with unerring accuracy, and information is essential to the management of large organizations (Rademacher and Gibson, 1983; Stevens, 1986). In short, computers have fundamentally altered the flow of life blood of bureaucracies. First introduced as payroll management tools in many organizations, the use of computers expanded to include budgeting, forecasting, and financial planning. Money and computers, then, have always had a somewhat happy, if at times, tentative marriage.

GENERATIONS OF COMPUTERS

Paralleling a biology metaphor, computers are often called "generational," depending upon the time when they were developed and the technology upon which they were based (Koffman, 1985; Mano, 1982). Unlike many complex biological species, computers have progressed through several generations in a very short time. Five generations of computers have been developed in just five decades.

Use of the computer for budgeting and finance functions has shifted with each generational advance in hardware. Computers were particularly introduced for large-scale financial functions when third-generation mainframes became widespread. With the introduction of fourth-generation microcomputers, even small organizations and agencies have been able to use computer-assisted software to handle budgetary and financial information more efficiently.

First Generation

First-generation computers used vacuum tubes (Bartee, 1972). Unlike the relays they replaced, vacuum tubes had no moving components. Vacuum tubes used grids and electricity to act as switches. Invented by Lee DeForest in 1906, the vacuum tube remains the easiest current-controlling device to understand. Vacuum tubes were large, expensive, and often burned out when the computer was operating. Computers using vacuum tubes, on the other hand, performed faster than their relay counterparts. Their operating speeds were clocked in milliseconds (one-thousandths of a second).

Input to these first generation computers was accomplished with punched cards. Internal storage consisted of magnetic drums. By the late 1950s, first generation computers were being used by many large firms. Then came the transistor.

Second Generation

The development of the transistor allowed the creation of components of computers that were smaller, less expensive, more reliable, and cooler in operation. The transistor is an electronic component that acts as a switch in response to voltage changes. Transistors replaced vacuum tubes as switching devices in computers. They are solid-state devices that embody the best qualities of vacuum tubes without the power consumption and heat dissipation. They are made from a semiconductor material, such as silicon, and operate at speeds fast enough to be measured in microseconds (one-millionths of a second). Second-generation computers were based on transistor technology and allowed the computer industry to grow exponentially, as the costs of individual computers dropped significantly. The second generation was short-lived, however. By 1965, a new generation was in the market.

Third Generation

IBM released their 360-series computers in 1965. These were the first computers that could be classified as *mainframe computers*—large systems designed primarily for institutional computing needs. IBM advertised them as being "third generation" computers. Their emphasis on this phrase led to the term being used for all computers built in the same timeframe. The most important feature of this new generation was the integrated circuit (IC).

The integrated circuit is a device in which many transistors and other electronic components can be housed. In this configuration, an electronic circuit that performs a specified function can be contained in a small silicon crystal that is totally enclosed in a plastic case, with leads from the sides that allow connection to other such circuits. The ease with which these IC "chips" can be interchanged allows for effective modular design, troubleshooting, and maintenance of complex digital (or analog) circuits. Further encapsulation of specific-function circuits is possible by assembling these chips on printed circuit boards, thus creating larger circuits that can be simply plugged in to existing hardware.

IC chips are classified in size by their *gate complexity*. That is, they are broken down into four groups based on the number of basic logic units, or *gates*, contained inside a single chip. Each of these gates represents a decision point based on the presence or absence of voltages at their inputs. The voltages constitute information flows with substantive meaning. The four designations for IC size are as follows:

SSI: A *small-scale integration device* has a complexity of 10 gates or less. These were the first ICs developed and were used in third generation computers.

MSI: Medium-scale integration devices have complexities of from 10 to 100 gates. These have become handy to use for elementary logic functions.

LSI: Large-scale integration devices have more than 100 gates and are used for microprocessors, calculator chips, and large memory units.

VLSI: Very-large-scale integration devices have thousands of gates in them and are used in larger computers, as well as for microprocessors.

Fourth Generation

The development of LSI technology led to the development of many of the computers still in use today. In the late 1970s and early 1980s, computers that bridged the gap between third-generation computers using SSI and MSI technology and fourth-generation computers employing VLSI size circuits were manufactured. The use of LSI technology also allowed computers to become smaller. Minicomputers—computers smaller than mainframes but larger than the currently popular desktop computers—were developed as a result. Minicomputers have basically the same components as mainframe computers, but operate at slower speeds and have less memory. These minicomputers offer a less expensive alternative to mainframe computers for smaller business with large computing needs.

Fourth-generation computers use VLSI circuitry. The advent of these computers increased computing power and speed, allowing them to operate at speeds measured in *nanoseconds* (billionths of seconds). The division between third and fourth generations is often blurred, since they differ in the scale of technology rather than in fundamental principles. The early 1980s saw the beginning of an almost new industry with the development of the microcomputer. These computers were small enough to fit on a desktop, and soon became ubiquitous in government, business, and education. VLSI circuits allowed all the logic necessary for a basic computer to fit on one IC chip. These chips, called *microprocessors,* were developed as the basis for the desktop microcomputer.

Several categories of standard high-level computer programs have been created for microcomputers and have contributed to their widespread use. These programs have been developed to be *user-friendly,* that is, they were developed with the noncomputer scientist in mind. Some categories of microcomputer software are:

Word Processing: Word processing packages allow rapid creation of text and have editing facilities that far exceed even programmable typewriters. Since microcomputers have nonvolatile memory (e.g., data will remain stored in memory even when the power is off), blocks of text can be easily manipulated, edited, and retrieved. Unlike programmable typewriters, where revisions must be reentered at a new work session, microcomputers allow multiple copies of old text or copies of recently edited text to be retrieved at separate work sessions.

Spreadsheets: Spreadsheets are multipurpose packages primarily used for analyzing numerical information, usually in columns. Businesses use spreadsheets to keep budgeting, accounting, and project data, in varying degrees of detail. Spreadsheets can also be used to easily generate tables and graphs of these data.

Databases: Database management packages allow businesses and other organizations to maintain and easily update large amounts of data, including client mailing lists, personnel records, and inventory. These packages are used for quick access to specific items within large databases. They employ the most efficient searching techniques available to pull out subsets of items for specific uses or updating.

Statistical software: Typically found on larger systems, statistical software has been developed for microcomputers. Statistical packages are designed to handle complex calculations on numerical data. Statistical analyses performed by these packages permit the user to examine trends using descriptive statistics, as well as to predict future outcomes from current databases.

Graphics: Microcomputer graphics packages permit users to display data in a variety of visual forms, including pie charts, bar graphs, and scatterplots. Graphics also includes the video display of computer games and other nontextual information.

Communications: Microcomputers have the unique feature of being able to be used both as a single-user computer and as a terminal to a larger multiuser computer. The latter is accomplished through the use of communications software. This capability provides the user with access to computer information sources, that is, "bulletin boards," large computers at work and other places, and large networks.

It is important to note that these types of software are available for computers of all sizes. They were not widely available for computers of all sizes. They were not widely available to smaller organizations and individuals without mainframe access, however, until the development of fourth-generation microcomputers.

Fifth Generation

Several projects are currently underway to develop and improve fifth-generation computers (Institute for New Generation Computer Technology, 1984). Unlike third and fourth generations, which differ from each other primarily in the scale of technology employed, fifth-generation projects are attempting to develop computers based on new principles (Ishikawa, 1986; Karin and Smith, 1987). In earlier generations, even the most high-powered, fast computer could perform only one instruction at a time. The goal of fifth-generation projects is to overcome this limitation through *parallel processing,* allowing various parts of a complex program to be processed simultaneously. Machines that employ this technology have been created that have passed the one billion instructions per second barrier (BIPS).

Some fifth-generation computers are also called *supercomputers*. The term supercomputer, however, has been used throughout the history of computers to describe the most powerful computer available at the time. Today, supercomputers are the machines that have broken the BIPS barrier. Today's supecomputers are 10 times faster than the fastest available mainframe. Some supercomputers, such as the CRAY-2, are so fast and powerful that their central processors that make the calculations must be cooled with liquid nitrogen! These machines are very expensive, and are used for very large-scale projects, such the creation of robots, artificial intelligence applications including voice recognition and vision systems, and physics experiments. As their costs are reduced and the technology becomes more widespread, they may be used for finance functions as well.

COMPUTER HARDWARE AND MAJOR COMPONENTS

Like all complex systems, computers consist of four basic parts—inputs, outputs, a unit that converts inputs to outputs, and a storage unit. These *hardware components* differ from the logical instructions that tell the computer what calculations to make (Lee, 1982; Sloan, 1976; Wells, 1976).

Computer software is the sets of logical instructions that direct the computer to make various calculations. Software differs from hardware in that the logical instructions can be modified and rewritten as computing tasks change. Examples of software include many operating systems, compilers, programming languages, and other software packages such as statistical software discussed above. Much software is hardware dependent. That is, the instructions one machine understands are in many cases different from those understood by another machine. Not only is this true for different sizes of computers, but also for different brands of computers. This makes it very important for hardware in any particular office or agency to be compatible, so that the same software runs on the various micros and the micros are capable of being networked into the mainframe in larger offices.

The basic hardware components in any computer system are described next.

The Central Processor Unit

The central processor unit (CPU) is the heart of the computer, handling electrical impulses that control all processes. All instructions to the computer, regardless of how they are entered, are processed in the CPU. CPUs, like all computer components, are *digital*, driven by whether an electrical voltage is present or absent.

The major component of the CPU is called the *arithmetic logic unit*, or ALU. The ALU is a digital circuit that performs addition, subtraction, multiplication, and division. It accepts its input from and sends its output to temporary storage units called *registers*. The CPU has many registers. Data in the form of electrical impulses travel between the registers and the ALU on *buses*. Buses are cables consisting of many small wires. Each wire of the bus has the capability of carrying one electrical impulse at a time. Transmission of data over the bus wires is regulated by a clock. For each clock tick, all of the wires in the bus are set simultaneously. Depending on the information being transmitted, some of the bus wires may receive voltages and some may not. The pattern these digital "on–off" transmissions take during one clock tick represents a single piece of information. This piece of information may be either data or an *instruction*.

An instruction is a directive to the CPU to perform a very specific task. Instructions are given in the most minute detail possible. For example, in order to add two numbers, the CPU would need to receive instructions for where to find the first number, where to find the second number, and instructions to add them together, and an instruction directing where to store the answer. The numbers to be retrieved may be in one of several locations, including one of several registers in the CPU or a storage space outside the CPU. The results of an instruction can either be stored in a register or storage space outside the CPU, or be output to a peripheral device (e.g., a printer, screen, tape, or disk). The number of wires in a bus is a multiple of 8.

As instructions are executed, part of the CPU controls the sequencing of the instructions so that they are executed in the proper order. This part is called the *control unit*. The control unit consists of a register called the *program counter,* which maintains the location of the next instruction to be processed. Two other components of the CPU involved in this control are decoders and multiplexers. A *decoder* is a circuit that takes two inputs, a substantive input and a selector. The selector determines across which of the wires in the bus the substantive input will travel. A *multiplexer* (MUX) does exactly the opposite of the decoder: it selects which of the many inputs from the bus will be sent to a output. While the decoder has one input with many outputs, the multiplexer has many inputs with one output. These two devices are, in essence, CPU traffic controllers. An additional CPU component, a *shift register,* or shifter, moves a series of pieces of digital information either to the left or the right to facilitate arithmetic calculations and logical operations.

The electrical activity within the CPU generates heat as a byproduct. The amount of traffic the CPU handles determines how it is cooled. The smallest CPUs, such as those found in microcomputers, do not generate much excess heat and can be cooled with air and a small fan. Larger CPUs must be cooled with either water or refrigerant running in pipes through the CPU. The largest of supercomputers are cooled with liquid nitrogen, a powerful coolant that occurs in liquid form only at extremely cold temperatures.

Main Memory

Since there are a limited number of registers in the CPU, a computer needs additional storage space. This space must be very close to the CPU to allow a sufficiently fast instruction flow so that CPU time is not wasted. This storage is called *main memory*. When a computer is in operation, an entire program is loaded into main memory at once before execution of the program begins. There are two types of main memory: *read only memory* (ROM) and *random access memory* (RAM). ROM is usually associated with firmware, as it contains nonreplaceable instructions. Information in RAM can be freely accessed or replaced. While RAM is volatile (its contents are lost when power is turned off), ROM is not.

Memory consists of a collection of storage registers. These registers are made of flip-flops. A *flip-flop* consists of logic gates connected in such a way that it can hold or discharge an electrical impulse. The impulse that the flip-flop can hold is a bit. There is a one-to-one correspondence between flip-flops and bits, so that there is a physical flip-flop for each bit of information. Each register in main memory has eight flip-flops. The information stored in each register—that is, eight bits—is a *byte*. A byte is the smallest unit of memory available. Bytes of memory are usually grouped in twos. A pair of bytes is called a *word*.

There are many prefixes attached to the word "byte" to denote how many bytes of memory are grouped together. The term *kilobyte* refers to 1024 bytes of memory. The term *megabyte* refers to 1024 kilobytes, or 1,048,576 bytes. In the vernacular, kilobyte is sometimes shortened to simply "K", and megabyte is often shortened to "meg." Sometimes people describe a kilobyte as consisting of a thousand bits, and a megabyte as consisting of a million bits, although technically, these rounded-off numbers are incorrect.

Each byte of memory has a unique address. The CPU must know from an instruction which address contains the needed information. In most cases items are stored in memory in pairs of bytes or words. More rarely, specific bytes are stored individually. The address of a byte in memory is placed in a separate special register within the CPU called the *memory address register* (MAR). The information contained in memory at this address is transferred to another special register in the CPU called the *memory buffer register* (MBR). Information transfer, as a result, from memory to the MBR is called *retrieval,* or a *read* operation. By contrast, transfers in the opposite direction, from the MBR to the memory address in the MAR, is called *storage,* or a *write* operation.

The CPU, main memory, and registers associated with each comprise the guts of the computer. In mainframe computers, the CPU, main memory, and the CPU cooling apparatus are housed in one box. *Peripheral devices*—secondary memory, communications equipment, terminals, and printers—are housed separately. In smaller computers, some peripherals, excluding input and output devices, are housed in the same box as the CPU and main memory. Without peripheral devices, the computer's guts would be rendered useless.

Secondary Memory

Read and write operations are not confined to main memory. Main memory is used for execution. More permanent storage of information must take place elsewhere. Devices designed for such storage are referred to collectively as *secondary memory.* Examples of these devices include disks and magnetic tape drives. *Disks* are the major form of secondary memory used today, and take many shapes. A disk is a round device coated with a film that is capable of storing magnetic spots. Information stored on disks can be accessed directly by a *read/write head,* much like a stylus on a record player that can be moved to the appropriate song without playing all the preceding songs.

In large computer systems, many disks are stacked on top of one another to form cylinders called *disk packs.* A *disk drive* contains the read/write head and a mechanism to rotate the disk pack it holds. Some disk packs can be removed from their disk drives, making the disk pack portable. Many disk packs, however, are permanently installed in their disk drives and cannot be removed. These are called *fixed drives.* Smaller computers, particularly microcomputers, can have small versions of fixed disks, often called *hard disks.* Common sizes of microcomputer hard disks are 20, 30, and 40 megabytes. With improving technology, many new microcomputers contain hard disks with much larger capacity including 80 and 120 megabytes, and even larger.

Most microcomputer software, however, is stored on thin, portable, singular *floppy disks.* Typically, floppy disks are enclosed in a square plastic sheath and come in two sizes—5¼ inches square, and 3½ inches square. These floppies, as they are often called, have a hole in the middle, and a small exposed section with which the read/write head comes in contact. Practically all microcomputers are equipped with at least one and often two floppy disk drives. These disk drives have a slot, into which the floppy disk to be used is inserted. Once the floppy disk is properly inserted, a two-position latch called the door must be closed into a locked position for the read/write head to access the information contained on the disk.

Older floppy disks are *single-sided,* so that information may be stored on only one side of the disk. Newer floppies are *double-sided,* allowing information to be stored on both sides of the floppy (diskette). Floppies, or diskettes as they are sometimes called, also differ in how compactly the information is stored, and hence how much information can be stored on a single diskette. Density refers to the number of tracks capable of storing information grooved on a diskette's surface. *Single-density* diskettes contain 24 tracks per inch (TPI) of storage space, while *double-density* diskettes have 48 TPI of storage. Even more compact *high-density* diskettes have 96 TPI.

The total amount of information that can be stored on a diskette is a function of both the number of usable sides and its density. A single-sided, single-density disk, rapidly becoming a thing of the past, can store 90 kilobytes of information. A single-sided, double-density disk can hold 180 K, while a double-sided, double-density disk may contain up to 360 K. High-density diskettes are much rarer than the commonly used double-sided, double-density floppies. These very compact disks require a high-density disk drive, found only on IBM PC-AT class microcomputers, and can hold up to 1.2 megabytes. Portable computers and laptops typically use 3½ inch disks, which also come in double density and high density versions.

Today, tape drives are used primarily for backup and long-term storage, although in earlier days they were the main means of magnetic storage. Made from the same material as audio tapes, computer tapes range in size from compact cassettes for microcomputers to larger nine-track reel-to-reel tapes used on minicomputers and mainframes. Tapes are useful, but have some disadvantages. Information on them must be accessed sequentially. Unlike disks, which allow access to specific memory locations without processing other information, retrieving data from a tape requires passing over all the information stored before it. Human operators must mount tapes on tape drives for them to be used, unlike fixed disks where the stored information is continuously and instantly available. Tapes also break with frequent or incorrect use. Two major advantages of tapes are that they are relatively inexpensive, and they are portable from one computer to another. Yet another advantage of tapes is the long-term storage they provide, allowing fixed disk space to be used for more important or frequently accessed data.

Input Devices

Input devices are necessary to enter information into the computer so that it can be processed by the CPU (Hohenstein, 1980). Early mainframe computers used *card readers* to transfer information from punched cards to the CPU. The 80-column format of the punched cards is still used today in some data storage and is called "card image." Early computers used a seven-dot code for representing characters on computer tape called the *American Standard Code for Information Interchange* (ASCII), a generic code whose use is continued to the present day.

Advances in electronics led to the development of the electronic keyboard as an input device. Ironically, linking computer use to typing caused more widespread use of computers initially among middle management and secretaries. Since many executives were not used to typing, they proved less adept at using this new and powerful technology. Across time, the stigma attached to computers due to the typing that keyboard input requires has abated, and computer illiteracy is now viewed as a major managerial weakness, especially in finance and budgeting.

The further development of keyboards as input devices was an incentive to computer hardware manufacturers to create a number of different types of devices using the keyboard. Many of these "workstations" could be attached to the same computer, and came to be known as *terminals*. Terminals consisted of a keyboard that was attached to a complimentary output device, usually a printer or, more commonly used today, a television-type screen. Advances in keyboard design allow terminal keyboards to have special keys not ordinarily included on a typewriter keyboard. These keys are usually arranged around the traditional typing keys, either on the left, above, or to the right.

These special keys include *function keys,* or keys that perform specific redefinable operations, such as listing files or getting help while using a popular software package. Other keys can form a *number pad* for rapid numerical input. The *break* key is often used to interrupt the computer during the execution of a command.

Several keys deal with cursor control. Four keys with arrows on them are called the *cursor movement* keys. They move the *cursor,* a highlighted space on the screen showing the user where on the screen the next typed character will appear. A key equivalent to a carriage control on a typewriter is the *enter,* or *return* key. When the user hits this key, the cursor moves to the next line, and the information on the preceding line is sent to the computer.

Other keys move the cursor rapidly across blocks of lines. These are the *Home, End, PgUp,* and *PgDn* keys. The exact function of these keys may vary across different types and brands of computers. The Home key may move the cursor rapidly to the top of the screen, while the End key may move it quickly to the bottom of the screen. In some computers, the Home key quickly moves the cursor to the *command line.* In some software packages, the command line is a special line on the screen where commands to the CPU may be submitted. PgUp refers to the "page up" key, causing the cursor to scroll upward (backward) toward the beginning of the file or manuscript. Similarly, PgDn is the "page down" key that moves the cursor downward (forward) toward the end of the material on which the user is working.

Some keys on the keyboard can be used to expand the number of symbols that can be input from that particular type of keyboard. Such keys include the *control, alternate, shift,* and *escape* keys. To type a symbol that can be accessed through the use of these keys, the user must type the desired character while holding down the specialized key. For example, on many systems an end-of-file character (EOF) designating the end of the current input stream is represented by a "control D" sequence. This means the user must type the D key while holding down the control key (usually marked with the letters "Ctrl"). There are numerous other combinations of keys specific to each computer and software packages. Users may find out about these by reading their operating system and software manuals.

Less commonly used than keyboards, *mark sensing* devices may also be employed to enter data into computers. The blanks filled in with number 2 pencils on standardized tests, such as the SATs, GREs, and LSATs, are read by an *optical scanner,* which recognizes the marks by the magnetic properties of the pencil lead. Optical scanners are expensive and are typically used by larger institutions, such as corporations and universities. As their cost declines and the technology improves, other mark sensing devices are being adapted to aid the blind in reading ordinary printed materials.

Some input devices are either light or touch sensitive. A *light pen* reads specially coated tags, and may be used in inventory systems and libraries. Light pens can also read information from a terminal screen, by pointing the light at the portion of the display to be used for input.

A *mouse* is another commonly used input device. It consists of a plastic case enclosing a ball protruding slightly from a hole in the bottom. "Dragging" the mouse means moving it around on the desk top in front of the computer screen or on a specially prepared felt pad. Dragging causes an arrow on the screen to move in response. Moving the mouse on the desktop to the right, for example, moves the arrow to the right on the screen. A mouse also has from one to three keys at the top used in making choices. In many software packages, menus offering the user an array of choices are displayed using *icons*, graphic symbols of the choices. Items are selected from the menu by dragging the mouse to position the arrow by the desired icon, then clicking the key on top to make the selection.

Some terminals have touch-sensitive screens. As menus appear, the user simply points to and touches the desired choice. This type of input is especially useful for children first using computers in elementary educational software, as well as for consumer-oriented exhibitions using computers.

Output Devices

Input and output devices are usually complementary, used in pairs (Eadie, 1982). For example, terminals usually consist of a keyboard for input, paired with a screen for output. Major output devices used today include printers, plotters, and various types of graphics equipment, which produce printed output or *hardcopy*. Other output devices are based on character displays, and include screens. The formal name for screens used to display output electronically is *cathode ray tube*, or CRT. CRTs are typically paired with keyboards to make a terminal, and may be either *monochrome*, displaying characters in only one color (typically green or amber), or *color*, using multiple colors.

While some simple graphics packages may be used with a monochrome monitor, more sophisticated packages require a color monitor to be used maximally. To display characters on the screen, data is passed to an *electron gun*, which fires electrons toward the screen. The electrons pass through two sets of *deflection plates* (actually two passive electronic components called capacitors) that deflect the electron to the proper horizontal and vertical position on the screen. The screen is coated with a phosphor, a material that emits light where the electron beam strikes the surface.

For a color monitor, three different electron guns are used to fire electrons onto the screen; the coating on the screen, however, is separated into *picture elements* or "pixels." These pixels are arranged as triangles of three dots, each dot corresponding to one of three basic colors—red, blue, and green. The intensity with which electrons are fired at these *triads* determines what color emits from the pixel when it is lighted. Depending on the capabilities of the hardware supporting the CRT and the number of pixels on the screen, called the *resolution*, a multitude of colors is possible. Improvements in monitor resolution and character definition have allowed graphics and image processing software to become much more sophisticated.

CRTs allow *interactive processing*, so that the user of the terminal communicates with the computer by typing commands, instructions, or data on a keyboard while the computer's responses are displayed on the screen. By contrast, *batch processing* requires that all instructions and data be submitted simultaneously. The user is totally removed from the computing process, and must wait for the output. By analogy, interactive processing resembles making a telephone call, while batch processing is like mailing a letter and waiting for a response. Interactive processing is particularly useful in data entry and inquiry, program development, word processing, message communications, and graphics. Despite controversy over the health hazards of long-term use of CRTs, no significant radiation is emitted. The greatest difficulty from extended CRT use is eye-strain, which may be reduced by a soft filter placed in front of the CRT screen to alleviate glare.

Printers are also a widely used output device, for several reasons. Hardcopy is easier to read than output on the screen in many circumstances. Printed copy provides a permanent record, and protects against loss of programs or data due to equipment failures. Further, large amounts of data or instructions can be scanned much more quickly in hardcopy form than by scrolling through it on the screen. Payroll checks, customer bills, mailing labels, and certain records require printed output.

The selection of a suitable printer may greatly affect the level of satisfaction individuals and organizations develop for their computer operations. Printers differ on several dimensions, including printing quality, speed, cost, and special capabilities. Only some printers produce *letter-quality printing,* often a requisite for printers used extensively for text processing. Some business applications may make speed the top priority in printer selection, while other applications may require special capabilities, like graphics or plotting functions.

Impact printers that utilized a device or mechanism to print one or more characters on the paper at a time by physically impacting the paper were the first type of printer to dominate the market. Impact printers may be subdivided into *dot matrix* printers, which strike the paper with different combinations of metal pins, and *character printers,* which use hammer mechanisms like those in typewriter, producing images by striking carbon ribbon against paper. The characters formed with a dot matrix printer consist of arrangements of tiny printed dots. This type of printer is typically faster than a character printer, but only recently have dot matrix printers begun to approach near-letter-quality output. With character printers, the letters are formed by continuous ink and are considered letter-quality. Character printers have often operated at slower speeds than dot matrix printers, however.

Both types of imact printers are electromechanical devices, and have the disadvantages of being both noisy and subject to frequent breakdowns. Impact printers that print an entire line at one time are called *line printers,* and operate at relatively fast speeds, when compared to *serial printers* that print less than a line at one time. Line printers can print entire lines of up to 120 characters at speeds approaching 1000 lines per minute. An entire line is transferred to the printer at electronic speeds, and the characters on the line are stored in a *buffer* until the entire line is assembled.

A buffer is a section of memory that is set aside to collect data to be treated as a single data item. All the characters for the line in the buffer are then printed with one mechanical operation. The paper is fed through the printer with one mechanical operation. The paper is fed through the printer at a uniform speed so that it has advanced by the time the next line is assembled and ready to be printed. These mechanical operations ultimately limit the printer speed. Compared to dot-matrix printers, which are commonly attached to microcomputers for home use, line printers are much more expensive and are typically used in institutional settings for high-volume, multiuser output.

Even faster than line printers are *nonimpact* printers, which come in several varieties. Speeds approaching thousands of lines per minute may be achieved with *electrostatic* printers. This type of printer is particularly suitable when multiple copies are not required. They require special paper coated with electrical conductive material. Printing occurs when the special paper is charged with electrodes to produce characters made of small dot patterns. *Electrothermal printers* operate similarly, but use heated rods and heat-sensitive paper instead of electrodes and electrically conductive paper. *Laser printers* may also be characterized as nonimpact printers, and are increasingly common. These printers project a light image onto photosensitive paper, which is then developed by a process similar to that used for normal photographs. Emulating the technology used in Xerox-type machines, *xerographic printers* typically use 8 ½ by 11 plain paper, and are frequently used in offices.

Communications Devices

A *data communications processor* is a specialized input/output (I/O) processor designed to communicate directly with data communications networks. It may distribute and collect data from many remote terminals connected through telephone and other communications lines. Data communications processors allow a computer to intersperse servicing fragments of the demands of different users, thereby appearing to be servicing many users at once. They are used to increase efficiency in *time-sharing* environments, where multiple users make demands on a system at once. The task of a data communications processor is to transmit and collect digital information from each terminal, to determine whether the information is data or control, and to respond to requests for preestablished procedures. The data communications processor also has the standard I/O processor tasks of communicating with the CPU and with memory.

Data communications processors and standard I/O processors differ from each other in how they communicate with I/O devices. Standard I/O processors have a common I/O bus consisting of many data and control lines to communicate with peripherals. The use of multiple control lines allows rapid transmission of information. Data communications processors communicate with each terminal with a single pair of wires, and both data and control information are transmitted serially. As a result of serial processing, transmission rates are much slower.

Telephone lines, or other public or private communications facilities, connect the remote terminals to the data communications processor. A converter is needed for the digital computer information, since telephone lines were originally designed for voice communications, not digital signals. A modulator-demodulator, or *modem,* is the most common device used to translate analog (voice) signals to digital (data) signals and back. A signal is translated by the modem on the originator's side, is sent over the telephone lines and is converted back to digital format on the receiver's side by a second modem. Modems come in all sizes and shapes, and may be installed internally to the computer, or connected externally via a cable. Internal modems are less obtrusive and do not take up extra space. External modems have the advantage of being easily portable from one computer to another.

There are many parameters that must be synchronized between two modems to allow them to understand each other. If these parameters are not set correctly, the data will be converted from digital to analog in one format, but converted back to digital in another format, making it undecipherable. One of these parameters is the speed of transmission, or *baud rate.* It is measured in *bits per second.* Commonly used baud rates include 300, 1200, and 2400 bits per second (bps) for smaller computers. Larger computer systems use modems with baud rates of from 9600 bps to 192,000 bps. Modems that communicate over telephone wires, however, are restricted to the 9600 bps speed.

Another important communications parameter is *parity*. Depending on the type of code being sent (e.g., ASCII), a word of data will have an extra bit attached to it that is used for error checking of the data. The *parity bit* is used to determine if the word that is translated back into digital format has been converted incorrectly. There are different kinds of parity used in error detection. Parity can be set to either *even* or *odd*. It can also be ignored. Once parity is set, it remains fixed until it is reset. Modems communicating with each other must be set to the same parity. With even parity, the parity bit is set to make all transmitted words contain an even number of ones, whereas with odd parity the parity bit will be set to make all words have an odd number of ones. With even parity, error checking consists of verifying that every transmitted word has an even number of ones. Similarly, with odd parity, all words are checked for an odd number of ones.

There are other bits that are attached to transmitted words. *Start bits* and *stop bits* are added to the words to mark clearly the beginning and ending of each word, since all the words come over the telephone line in a constant stream. *Data bits*, then, are the bits that actually represent the data item being transmitted.

The mode of operation is another parameter that needs to be synchronized to maximize effective communication between digital devices. *Simplex* is a mode of operation in which data is transmitted and received in one direction only. It is not normally used for data communication, because the receiver cannot respond to the transmitter. Such communication is generally used for radio and television broadcasts. Conversely, *duplex* is a mode of communication in which parties at both ends can send and receive traffic simultaneously. Duplex transmissions can occur in two forms—half duplex and full duplex.

Half duplex operation allows transmission of traffic in both directions; however, only one side can transmit at one time. It is analogous to a radio conversation, in which the party on the receiving end must wait for a signal from the transmitter that the message is complete before transmitting a response. *Full duplex* operation is more commonly used in digital-to-analog and analog-to-digital communication such as in the case of modems. This mode of communication is analogous to a telephone conversation, in which both parties of the conversation are free to send and receive messages at will, without waiting for one side to finish. Fittingly, many applications of modems using this type of communication occur over telephone lines.

OPERATING SYSTEMS AND USER INTERFACES

An *operating system* (OS) is a program that serves as a manager of computer system use (Calingaert, 1982; Coffman, 1973). When a user turns on a microcomputer or gives a password for access to a larger computer, the operating system's user interface provides tha initial contact with the CPU (Davis, 1977; Sayers, 1971). The OS, however, in most circumstances does not perform the final tasks requested by the user. Rather, it calls upon software packages, which perform most user tasks. The OS acts like a traffic policeman who directs traffic requests to the CPU, while specialized software packages are analogous to the vehicles on the road that actually move the drivers (users) and passengers (clients) from one destination to another.

Operating systems vary greatly among all sizes and brands of computers, and typically are hardware dependent in that they can only run on one type of computer architecture (Deitel, 1984; Tannenbaum, 1987). A computer's architecture is determined by the type of processor or processors in the CPU. One example of a leading hardware-dependent operating system today is Microsoft Corporation's disk operating system (DOS) used on many IBM and IBM clone microcomputers. This operating system can be used on many brands of computers, but all must have the same microprocessing hardware. When machines can run the same operating system, they are called compatible, and they also have the capacity then to run the same applications software. Another operating system growing in popularity in UNIX, a portable OS capable of running on many different types of machines with different types of architecture.

Operating systems engage in several crucial resource allocation functions, including the ones described next.

Job Control

This function involves managing and sequencing jobs in multiuser systems as different demands are placed upon the system. The operating system's job is to manage the various stages of execution of all processes handled by the computer, deciding which process the CPU will execute at what time interval. Included in this function is a procedure for handling interruptions in program execution and unplanned system halts called "crashes." Multiuser systems require *job control language* to deal with commands between users and the CPU. The operating system also handles the powering up of the system, doing a validity check as the computer is activated. In microcomputers, this is called "booting the sytem."

Memory Management

Since all processes that are run on a computer require some sort of storage, memory management is a second OS function, including secondary memory or disk storage. Typically in most multiuser systems, systems programmers who maintain the operating system implement quotas on the amount of secondary storage each user is allowed, often allocated by tracks of memory or megabytes. In single-user microcomputers, the amount of storage is constrained by the size of the storage devices used.

Since disk storage is limited, the OS must make optimal use of it, both by effective placement of data within files as well as by managing file systems. There are three basic ways of storing data within files: a simple sequence of bytes (the approached used by UNIX); storing data in fixed-length records (used by the CP/M OS); and the indexed-sequential access method (ISAM), an approach used on many mainframes. This involves storing data in hierarchically arranged blocks.

Systems of files can be arranged either sequentially or hierarchically, and information about files is kept in a *directory,* which in many OSs is itself a file. The file information contained in a directory includes the location, size, type, security, ownership, and last modification of the file. Sequentially arranged files are kept in one master directory. Hierarchical file systems use a master directory called a *root directory,* and *subdirectories*. Files are accessed by following a unique *path* through the hierarchical file structure. A path can be specified by either an absolute path name or a relative path name. With an absolute path name, all directories from the root to the file must be specified as the file's name. With a relative path name, only directories between the current directory (the user's position in the file hierarchy) and the needed path must be specified.

Input/Output Control

The OS also controls the flow of data between the CPU and memory and the peripherals. Peripherals hooked to the same computer do not have to be made by the same manufacturer, but must be compatible with each other, so that the data sent back and forth will be interpreted correctly. Any computer may have multiple peripherals attached to it.

While the CPU may transmit signals to a device at one speed, the peripheral may operate at a slower speed, something called asynchronous operation. Different CPU and peripheral speeds are particularly evident in electromechanical devices, where speed is hampered by mechanical moving parts. Because of slower peripheral speeds relative to the CPU, the OS must often store signals for the peripheral until the device is ready to receive them.

For CPUs to compensate for the slowness of peripherals, input and output are often transmitted through *buffers*. A buffer is a temporary storage area between the peripheral and the CPU in which information is collected. When the buffer is full, the information is transmitted collectively to its destinations. Buffers may be located in the peripherals, in main memory, or on disks.

Diagnostic Error Processing

Errors can occur anywhere at any time and are an inevitable part of computing. A good operating system must diagnose the source and type of error if it is to be corrected swiftly. Error-checking circuits combined with error-checking software constantly monitor a system, and checking circuits are also built into peripherals. These circuits and associated software are responsible for flagging errors and branching to the appropriate recovery routine. The recovery routine will generate error messages for the user or system operator, and attempt to restore normal system functioning.

In some extreme cases errors will require shutting down the system. (In the case of microcomputers, this involves turning the computer off, waiting at least 30 seconds to avoid a power surge jolt to the circuitry, and turning it back on again to reboot.) Should a system shutdown occur, buffers that are filled for input will need to be saved by the OS so that users will not lose input. The procedure a user must follow to recover data varies across systems.

Processing Support

The OS must provide supervisory routines to keep track of system usage, a function called processing support. The typical OS has routines for keeping track of time used, for testing and debugging software, for statistics on resource utilization, and for keeping status information accessible to running software. Status information is also kept on current users, executing jobs, number of active terminals, number of jobs printed, etc.

SECURITY

Protecting a computer system from espionage and sabotage is a complex task provided by the operating system, as well as procedures for physical protection. The amount of security an OS must provide depends on from whom and/or what the system is to be protected.

The most basic type of security is user authentication, usually through passwords. Each user must give his or her unique password to gain access to the system. After receiving an issued password, users may typically change it to something of their own liking. Novice users tend to use their own names as passwords, but such passwords are easy for intruders to guess. To guard against intruders who may try to guess a password for a specific user, many systems will invalidate a password if a set number of incorrect attempts at the password occurs. Some systems also require users to frequently change their passwords, to lessen the time that an intruder has to crack a password, and to serve as a method for identifying defunct accounts.

Aside from passwords, security includes levels of user access to specific files in the file system. Access to files is generally divided into three categories—access by owner, access by a specific group of users to which the owner belongs, and access by everyone on the system. Further, these categories of privileges extend to individual processes. As a rule, the OS's default is to allow as little privilege as possible, unless intructed otherwise.

Other principles of security are simplicity, uniformity, and acceptability. If the system is simple and uniform, it will be much easier to implement blanket security procedures. Simplicity and uniformity also make a security system more acceptable to users and increase the likelihood that security procedures will be followed. Nor should security become so complex it is a burden to the OS. In a well-designed system, security can be achieved without relying on obsurity to fool the intruder, and such an approach makes the security system simpler. The designers should assume an intruder will know how the system works, and avoid concentration on making the security system obscure. In general, a security system should provide protection for all files in the system without discouraging use.

HUMAN INTERFACES

The OS may run a program that allows users to communicate easily with the computer, called a *user interface*. User interfaces come in a variety of forms. Generally, the user interface will generate a prompt, which is a cue to the user that the computer is ready for input from the keyboard. This signals the user to type in a command for the OS to execute.

The simplest user interface is the command interpreter for the disk operating system (DOS), used on IBM microcomputers and compatibles. When the user types a command, the interface searches the disk for a program with that command's name. In DOS, the command program may reside in a separate file, called an external command, or the command may be a procedure in the file COMMAND.COM on the OS disk, called an internal command. In general, DOS recognizes whether or not a command is external or internal, which expedites processing. The COPY command is an example of an internal command. DOS looks through COMMAND.COM to find the procedure to copy a file and execute it. By contrast, if the request were to format a diskette and the FORMAT command were given, DOS would look on the DOS diskette for FORMAT.COM, since it is an external command.

Microsoft's version of DOS (MS-DOS), which is used on IBM microcomputers and compatibles, is the most prevalent operating system for microcomputers. Other microcomputers operating sytems with similar interfaces are the CP/M operating system found on Commodores, and Apple Computer's own disk operating system, commonly called Apple DOS. An interface that is very complex yet simple to use on microcomputers is the user interface to the Apple Macintosh series of computers, which is executed by dragging and clicking a mouse.

On minicomputers, the operating systems become more complex, as do the user interfaces. An operating system found on many minicomputers, but also gaining popularity for use on microcomputers, is the UNIX operating system, which has an interface of a command interpreting program called a *shell*. It is a program run by UNIX for the sole purpose of executing other programs, including other shells, a unique feature of UNIX.

There are two basic versions of UNIX. The first was developed by AT&T in the late 1960s. This version is System V, and the user interface to it is called the *Bourne* shell, after its originator. Since FCC regulations initially prohibited AT&T from marketing UNIX, it was given to universities for research. The University of California at Berkeley subsequently developed a second version of UNIX, called 4.0 BSD (Berkeley Software Distribution). Its user interface is called the C shell. While the two UNIX shells are basically similar, there are subtle syntactic and semantic differences between the two. In many operating systems today, manufacturers have combined the two versions to provide the advantages of both.

Versions of UNIX developed for microcomputers are increasingly popular due to their inherent communications abilities. Xenix, MINIX, and Ultrix are brands of UNIX-based operating systems that run on microcomputers. As in the case of larger computers, which handle multiple user interfaces, microcomputers can be configured for two different OSs and their associated interfaces. Depending on need, users may switch between operating systems. In many cases, one of the UNIX-based OSs may be installed as a second operating system on microcomputers, in addition to DOS.

Other than UNIX, there is a variety of OSs for minicomputers. Among the more commonly used are VMS on Digital Equipment VAX computers, VM on IBM minicomputers, and Unisys on Sperry computers. While UNIX is a portable OS that will run on many different brands of computers, VMS, VM, and Unisys are designed for only one brand of computer. Each of these has its own user interface.

The most complex user interfaces occur in mainframe operating systems. Usually, business users of mainframes may avoid interfacing directly with the OS by logging into an applications program designed for them. Others who must interact with the mainframe may need to know more about computing to use the interface effectively. For example, many IBM mainframes running VM or MVS operating systems will run the Customer Information and Control System (CICS) program for business users. At the same time, other user interfaces to the OS can be running, including the time-sharing option (TSO). In this configurations, end users (users running software others have written) will be doing their work in CICS, while systems administrators and operators will be using TSO.

Other user interfaces combine command interpretation with other applications, such as text editing. Older interfaces like ROSCOE and WYLBUR are interactive text editors that allow the user to submit batch jobs to the OS for execution. On IBM machines running the virtual machine OS (VM), the conversational monitoring system (CMS) provides the user with menu-driven access to applications. Meanwhile, the operating system provides users with the appearance of having the entire machine to themselves, when in fact they are sharing the resources with many others.

THE PROCESS OF COMPUTERIZATION AND SYSTEM UPGRADES

Adopting new computer applications and system upgrades typically involves introducing new applications or operating systems onto a mainframe or minicomputer, or upgrading a computer network that allows distributed processing from physically separate workspaces with linkages to a mainframe. Sometimes the installation of an entirely new computer or system is involved. Generally, this process involves several steps:

1. *Preliminary study.* A preliminary study conducted by technicians and consultants is developed, assessing the needs for greater computing resources, the hardware and software options available, and the costs of various options. Ideally, concern at this stage is directed toward employee training needs and system security, but these issues are often omitted, creating problems later.
2. *System design.* System design includes an identification of various issues, including:

    What functions will be addressed through "batch" noninteractive processing versus those that require "on-line" interaction between the user and the program?
    How many "workstations" are needed and what security provisions should be provided at each?
    Should workstations be "dumb terminals" that function only as access points to a larger mainframe or minicomputer, or should they be stand-alone microcomputers that are networked in through hardwiring or through modems using the phone lines into a larger computer and/or local area network (LAN).
    Should one large computer, likely a mainframe for larger governments, handle all the computing needs of the jurisdiction, or should a smaller computer, likely a minicomputer, dedicated solely to finance and budgeting functions be purchased?
    What financial management and budgeting software packages should be purchased? Should different packages be purchased for accounting, planning, and budgeting, or should an integrated financial management package be used?
    What is the "system environment" in which the new software applications will be expected to function (IBM, UNIX, VAX, etc.)? How will the software interact with the operating system on the larger computer?
    What type of commications software, if any, is needed to make the new applications accessible (software to allow networking into the larger computer and data bases on it)?
    What procedures have been developed for backing up crucial data files and how physically will the backups occur?
    How will the new system or applications be serviced, and how easy and financially costly will future upgrades and expansions be?

3. *System test.* This phase is crucial since it may uncover impacts unanticipated in the preliminary study. At this stage, presumably such impacts can be better addressed and controlled than once the system is fully operational and the organization is dependent upon it. Debugging of errors and handling glitches in software-to-hardware or software-to-operating system interfaces should occur. Old systems or applications should remain in use until unanticipated impacts and glitches are resolved.
4. *Full system installation.* After the system is tested, it is ready to be installed. Temporary downtime and user inconvenience should be minimized. For this reason, depending on the size of the installation, it may occur at night, or over a weekend or during a scheduled holiday.
5. *Audit and evaluation.* Audit and evaluation make up a frequently neglected step of

system or application adoption. After a reasonable period, the new installation should be systematically reviewed by managers to ascertain if it is improving productivity and addressing needs as initially envisioned. With periodic evaluations, problems not caught in the preliminary study or test can be identified, as well as desirable expansions and upgrades.

SPREADSHEET CAPABILITIES AND FEATURES

Spreadsheets are software packages designed to permit easy manipulation of columns of data. These are commonly used for budgetary planning, and in smaller government jurisdictions may be the only software used. Across time, spreadsheets have been adapted to perform additional functions such as graphic presentations of data and elementary statistical analyses.

While some integrated spreadsheet packages are sufficiently broad that they include word processing utilities, spreadsheets were created primarily to manipulate numerical data. Among the applications spreadsheets can handle are financial projections, budgets, sales projections, inventories, tax accounting, profit planning, production records, and research and development.

How does one package meet all these various user needs? Typically, spreadsheets are not subdivided into individual programs such that each is dedicated to one of the above tasks, but rather are designed for the single purpose of manipulating tabular data. A software spreadsheet is an electronic implementation of a "paper and pencil" spreadsheet. It consists of rows and columns of initially blank cells that the user can fill with data. The spreadsheet user decides how the columns and rows of the matrix can be filled with data to accomplish a particular task.

For example, in a spreadsheet used for budgeting, columns may contain data representing budget requests, last year's allocations, and current allocations or appropriations. As additional information about budgetary decisions is acquired, budgetary analysts may easily insert the data into the appropriate cells for display and analysis. Totals for various columns and rows are automatically recalculated to include the newly added data. Spreadsheets then relieve the analyst of laborious lengthy tabulations of accounting and financial data previously done by hand calculator, and often the source of numerous errors.

The recalculation feature of spreadsheets allows managers to quickly see the change in revenue as a result of a modification of costs. Such rapid responses to proposed changes increase the ability of managers to predict organizational efficiency and performance. Managers may also examine the consequences of other resource allocation decisions quickly and effectively by not only looking at how production and sales figures are altered when one or more inputs are changed, but also seeing the shifts on displays generated with presentation graphics.

Just as word processing packages and desktop publishing have revolutionized text processing in offices and classrooms, spreadsheets have greatly facilitated numerical recordkeeping for a wide array of organizations. Spreadsheets have greatly eased the pain of maintaining tax, budget, checking, cash flow, and dispersement records for such organizations, as well as for individuals.

The versatility of spreadsheets has extended their utility beyond the easy entry and maintenance of financial, production, and sales data. Among these other uses are creating and updating mailing lists, constructing and keeping files of client data, and maintaining a personal notebook with reminders of appointments and things to be done. Several features of this genre of software that have made it a powerful, analytical tool, as described next.

A Matrix of Named Cells

A spreadsheet, as noted above, is a matrix of cells. Each cell has a unique identification label that specify the row and column of the cell's location. Many spreadsheets denote rows with numbers and columns with letters in sequence. Some newer spreadsheets have adopted numbers to designate both rows and columns, following a convention used in matrix algebra. In other case, at a glance a user is oriented to the positions of cells in the spreadsheet by their row and column addresses.

Moving around the Window

Larger spreadsheets can contain as many as 256 columns and 2048 rows. If a spreadsheet this large were to be printed on paper, it would be over 21 feet high and almost twice as wide! Since a monitor's screen cannot display that much information simultaneously, users must examine portions of the spreadsheet through a *window*. Individual cells within the window are highlighted through the use of two different cursors. A cell will appear on the screen in *reverse video*—a display where the normal background and letter colors are reversed—denoting the *cell pointer*. At the top of the window display, the row and column identification of the highlighted cell appears, followed by its contents. The *standard cursor* appears on the same line at the top of the window, and marks the position on the screen where keyboard input will be entered. As soon as the user depresses the enter key, the newly recorded information typed at the standard cursor at the top of the window is displayed in the highlighted cell within the spreadsheet matrix.

The cell pointer can be expanded to encompass more than one cell. The group of cells highlighted by the expansion is called a *range*. How this expansion is achieved varies across spreadsheets. In the popular spreadsheet Lotus 1-2-3, two methods may be employed: a user may either issue Lotus commands, or "anchor" the cell pointer at a cell of origin and use the cursor movement keys to define the range. If a range is specified and a group of cells is highlighted, only the cell of origin is displayed at the top of the window by the standard cursor.

Marking a range of cells is a very versatile feature of spreadsheet software. Once a range has been defined, it can be copied, moved, deleted, converted to a different numerical format (e.g., decimal to dollar notation), manipulated with mathematical formulas, given a name for future reference, or used as data for a graph. When a range is no longer needed, it can be eliminated without changing the contents of its cells.

Entering Commands

An easy way to manipulate ranges of cells, as well as to use the many other tools a spreadsheet offers, is to make use of the package's command set. Although the set of commands a spreadsheet will recognize varies from package to package, many of the data manipulation commands are the same. Typical commands that spreadsheets recognize include Copy, Move, Delete, File, Print, and Graph. These and other commands are normally enclosed in a menu, from which the user may select an option. In Lotus 1-2-3 and Twin, the menus are displayed by typing the forward slash character (/) and the command sets are the same, but in Lotus the menu appears at the top of the window, whereas in Twin the menu appears at the bottom.

When a menu is displayed in the window, the leftmost menu option will be highlighted. The user may then select the desired option by typing either the first letter of a command in the menu or by moving the *menu pointer* to highlight the desired option and depressing the carriage return key. As a command from the menu is highlighted by the menu pointer, a description of the command is given on the line beneath the menu in the window display. The description may either specify in greater detail the nature of the command, or may list *subcommands* that are related to that option. These subcommands form a second menu if the option under which they are displayed is selected.

For example, in Lotus, typing the forward slash produces the second menu to be displayed vertically downward from that title rather than horizontally as in many packages. While still depressing the mouse button, the user may select an option from that vertical menu by positioning the mouse so that the desired option is highlighted. Once the option has been highlighted, letting go of the mouse button will select the option, execute the command, and hide the pull-down menu from which it was selected.

Entering the Data

Using the commands a spreadsheet offers does no good if there are no data on which to operate. Entering data into a spreadsheet is fairly straightforward; the user simply moves the cell pointer to the desired cell, types the information for that cell and moves the cell pointer away. When the spreadsheet is invoked, it is automatically in *data entry mode*—that is, cell contents can be typed immediately. Typing the forward slash as in Lotus or the equivalent will shift the spreadsheet from data entry mode to *command mode,* at which point commands may be given.

Spreadsheets can handle many types of data. Character data may represent row and column descriptions (labels), identification data such as names, or empirical data such as letter grades. Numerical data may take the form of integers, decimal numbers, or identification data such as Social Security numbers. Numbers may be either positive or negative, and may be entered as mathematical expressions. For example, the number -6 may be entered into a cell, or the expression $-2*3$, to produce the same result in the cell. Similarly, entering the expression $2\char`^8$ (2 raised to the eighth power) in a cell is equivalent to typing the number 256.

Once the required data have been entered into the spreadsheet, it can be shaped and formated to convey extra visual meaning. Personal style and required emphases determine whether labels are to be right justified, left justified, or centered, as well as the degree of precision and format for displaying numbers. Choosing the right format for data simplifies manipulation and improves understanding of the figures displayed.

Presentation Features

The presentation features of spreadsheets are not standardized, and are a major source of competition among packages. Part of the reason that presentation features vary widely is that office needs for visual aids in reports and meetings also vary widely. Offices typically select the spreadsheets that will most closely fulfill their presentation needs.

Presentation capabilities largely include the ability to generate bar graphs, pie charts, scatterplots, and trendlines, as well as the ability to calculate and display relative frequencies and other descriptive statistics. The degree of sophistication with which a spreadsheet handles these tasks determines the market for the package. A typical high-end package—one that can handle high-volume use—is expected to have the highest quality of presentation graphics and the ability to calculate many different descriptive statistics about the data.

Other Extras

The appeal of a particular spreadsheet may be enhanced by the integration of other types of software as options within the package itself. The package Symphony is a good example of software that integrates the spreadsheet features of Lotus 1-2-3 with word processing, communications and graphics. Further, a spreadsheet may be preferable if it can interface with other separate software packages. How well different genres of software allow sharing of data is often important enough to influence a purchaser's decision on which package to buy. An office manager may buy Lotus 1-2-3 for company spreadsheet users to take advantage of sharing data between 1-2-3 and other popular packages such as WordPerfect and dBase III+.

SPECIFIC SPREADSHEETS

The various spreadsheets available may be evaluated by several criteria, including ease of learning and use, error handling, performance, versatility, memory requirements, and price. Spreadsheet users may also consider whether or not the software takes advantage of a *math coprocessor*—a chip that facilitates faster computations.

Lotus 1-2-3, written by Lotus Development Corporation, is a spreadsheet often accompanied by *HAL,* a "NATURAL" language program designed to save time, employ simpler macros, and enhance program power. Lotus is commonly used on IBM PCs and compatible microcomputers. Although HAL does not make learning Lotus any easier, it does make using Lotus more convenient. The macros that HAL allows users to write are more complicated but more powerful than those normally written using 1-2-3. This combination package also ranks high in other criteria used to evaluate spreadsheets, especially in performance, versatility, and error handling.

In terms of performance, Lotus 1-2-3 calculates formulas and mathmatical expressions more quickly by using a math coprocessor to help with multiplications. Because of this, Lotus peforms exponentiation far more quickly than many other packages. Lotus is also an very versatile spreadsheet. The 1-2-3/HAL combination, however, cannot edit a data model larger than available RAM, allow files to be locked on multiuser systems, allow user-defined functions, or concatenate strings. Only in conjunction with HAL will 1-2-3 link to separate data models or list statistical dependencies. On the other hand, the 1-2-3/HAL combination leads the industry in its ability to recognize errors and prevent the loss of data. Managers and nontechnical users can become productive quite quickly with Lotus.

The *Smart Spreadsheet,* written by Innovative Software, is a competitor to Lotus 1-2-3 and is also commonly used on IBM machines. Some versions of Smart will also run on UNIX operating systems. While it has the capability to outperform Lotus in math computations and it offers more features, it is not nearly as easy to use, nor does it handle errors as well. For example, Smart recalculates the values in the spreadsheet faster than Lotus in multiplication, addition, exponentiation, and division. Further, Smart allows sorting in ascending or descending order while the user is still using the worksheet, whereas Lotus does not. Also, Smart does operations on inverted matrices and calcuates matrix determinants, procedures necessary for calculating many statistics. Lotus does not perform any matrix operations.

By contrast with 1-2-3, the Smart Spreadsheet can edit data models larger than available RAM and concatenate strings. Smart, however, is harder to use than Lotus. Formating ranges of cells, sorting data, and changing column widths are examples of tasks that are more difficult to accomplish with Smart than Lotus. Also, Smart's error messages do not give recovery instructions that are as clear as those given by 1-2-3. Despite these shortcomings, the Smart Spreadsheet is one of the mose widely used and powerful of the various packages available. Users concerned about real-time calculations and extensive statistical forecasting would benefit from Smart.

Another major competitor in the spreadsheet market is *Excel*, manufactured by Microsoft Corp. Versions of Excel are available not only for IBM and IBM-compatible microcomputers, but also for the Apple Macintosh. In fact, Excel is by far the leading spreadsheet available for the Macintosh. While Excel can outperform and has more features than Lotus, it requires more hardware, since Excel was designed to run on state-of-the-art equipment. Lotus, since its introduction in 1982, has not changed in basic design. While it has been updated to keep abreast of machine development, it was never intended to capitalize on state-of-the-art hardware advances.

Excel is easier to learn and use than Lotus, mostly because the Macintosh's menuing system allows users to become productive very quickly. Like Smart, Excel can link other spreadsheets to the one in current use. Also like Smart, Excel has more functions available than does Lotus. While Lotus 1-2-3 is the spreadsheet of choice for MS-DOS environment, Excel seems to be the preferred spreadsheet package used on the Macintosh.

On larger, multiuser systems, *20/20* is a powerful spreadsheet package that is available for VAX/VMS and UNIX systems. It has many popular features found in single-user oriented software such as Lotus. 20/20 takes advantage, however, of the larger computer's power and versatility to make a spreadsheet that can outperform the single-user software. If 20/20 is being used from a terminal on a minicomputer or mainframe, the terminal should be either a terminal suited for graphics, such as those made by Tektronix, Inc., or a terminal that has enhanced capabilities for handling text, such as the Digital Equipment Corporation's (DEC) VT100 family of terminals.

In addition to the spreadsheets discussed above, there are many others avaialble to users. Among them are SuperCalc, VisiCalc, Quattro, Multiplan, VP-Planner and PFS:Professional Plan. Choosing a spreadsheet package, like choosing a word processor or database software, is a function of what equipment the intended users have, what skills the users have, and what goals they intend to accomplish. While spreadsheets are general, multipurpose programs often used for financial data, accounting software has been developed to more easily handle the specialized functions needed for manipulating accounts. The next section will describe criteria for selecting accounting software.

ACCOUNTING SOFTWARE

Features and Capabilities

A sound accounting system is crucial to the execution and implementation phase of the budget cycle. Without such a system, managers have little support for making crucial allocative and other financial decisions. Prior to the revolution in computer technology, most agencies kept books laboriously, by hand. Many accounting conventions, such as posting and referring to ledger accounts as "T-accounts," stem from those pre-computerized days. Not only did more errors creep into financial records, typically to be discovered later and tracked down through tedious back-checking, but also financial reports were not as frequent nor as timely.

With the dissemination of third-generation computers, large organizations became leaders in computerizing financial records and accounting systems. Typically, three decades ago, the finance and accounting departments were the most computerized departments in their organizations. Lacking access to mainframes, such advantages were rarely available to smaller businesses, local governments, and nonprofit organizations. More recently, microcomputers have allowed the development and spread of integrated accounting programs, bringing the advantages of computerized accounting systems to small as well as large organizations.

Criteria for Evaluating Accounting Packages

Many of the same criteria used to evaluate spreadsheets also apply to integrated accounting packages, including ease of installation, learning and use; error handling; versatility; and power. Additionally, users of accounting packages are concerned about security of financial data and auditing, as well as documentation and reliability. Since timely and accurate financial information is important to management, the reporting features of integrated accounting packages are an important criterion in package selection.

Standard reporting features include balance sheet, income statement, and cash flow information. Most packages permit aging of current accounts payable and a listing of bills due, as well as reports on the age and status of accounts receivable. These reports expedite cash management by facilitating the collections process and allowing managers to delay disbursements until payments are due.

While such reports in earlier times were provided only on a systemmatic basis, often quarterly or monthly, integrated accounting packages allow these reports to be generated easily as management needs the information. The value of the reports depends upon how current the information they contain is, which in turn depends upon frequent and current data entry to update the financial and accounting data base. How easily the package allows updating and the input of additional data, then, becomes an additional concern to users of automated accounting systems.

More than in the selection of other types of software, vendor support is important in the selection of accounting packages. While some vendors provide support free of charge, others may require a subscription fee as well as a charge for responding to specific requests. Accounting package users should also consider whether or not they will need customized services at some future point, and if so, whether the vendor provides them.

SPECIFIC ACCOUNTING PACKAGES

Solomon III is produced by TLB, Inc., for IBM and IBM-compatible microcomputers. This package is accompanied by easily followed learning materials. It also has good help screens, making the package easy to learn, although the help screens must be installed separately from the program. It has powerful accounts receivable and accounts payable functions, although the accounts receivable functions are not as easy to use as the accounts payable functions. Its general ledger functions and general reference manual are also excellent. Solomon III performs well in identifying errors and preventing data loss. Despite these advantages, it is difficult to print balance sheets and income statements using Solomon. The package remains, however, one of the better ones available.

M.A.S. 90 was written by the State of the Art, Inc. This package can run on either MS-DOS or UNIX operating systems. One of its strengths is the ease of learning and using ending adjusting entry functions. While Solomon III does not permit users to view reports on their screens without printing them out, M.A.S. permits users to view most but not all of the reports on their CRTs to determine if a printed version is needed. M.A.S. also has a good custom report writer. It does not have a tutorial, however, nor does it have help menus. Its performance is slow, and posting transactions as well as inputing prior balances is difficult. M.A.S. does print tickets for shipping and makes cash forecasts by due date, but does not allow users to override system-generated due dates on invoices.

Macola was developed by a company bearing the same name. It is rich in features, and is designed for use in larger companies. The package is versatile, allowing users to chose from various modules including general ledger, accounts receivable, and accounts payable modules. There is no accompanying tutorial and the manual is difficult to use, making the package harder to learn than some others. Nor is error handling as good as in some other packages. Nonetheless, Macola is fast and has nice reports. It lacks a predefined balance sheet and income statement format.

Accpac is one of the better accounting packages, excelling in performance and reporting. It has good documentation, and features windowing menus that layer on top of each other to make it ease to see the current location in the menu system. Accpac runs on IBM and compatible computers. Accpac produces information readable by the SuperCalc spreadsheet. While the financial report writer is difficult to learn, it is one of the most flexible. The package contains complete on-line help. Its purchase initially was accompanied by a 30-day money-back guarantee, an unprecedented offer in the software industry.

Other packages on the market include Platinum, Realworld Accounting, Cyma Professional, and IBM Business Adviser. HARMONY, EasyBusiness Systems, BPI Enterprise Series, and Libra are further options for organizations considering computerization of their accounting systems. While such a conversion may initially be time-consuming, expensive, and tedious, the rewards of greater power, more frequent and accurate reports, and customized financial modules make the effort worthwhile to budget and financial officers, as well as general management.

OTHER TYPES OF FINANCIAL AND BUDGETING SOFTWARE

An explosion in information technology has led to a proliferation of software for all types of computers and all types of financial functions, many of which are specialized to a particular level of government and type of agency. The International City Management Association (Ulrich, 1990) regularly publishes a software reference guide with reviews of various specific software packages, along with names and addresses of vendors. Also listed are specific tasks each package will perform, and the system requirements (operating system and hardware requirements) for its intallation and operation. In some instances, price ranges are given. This reference would provide a good starting point for any government considering the purchase of new software applications. Some of the functions for which software packages are available include:

1. *Capital financing and planning.* Packages here provide budgeting and cash flow tools for tracing municipal debt; for calculating bond prices, management, and refinancing; and for calculating the time value of money, rates of return, and life cycle net worth of capital projects. Among them are DebtBASE, Micro-MuniPrograms, BBLease, BondCalc II, FinCAP, MINIBOND, MunEase, ReFunder, BEST BID, TRUERATE, ZMATH, LC2M Life Cycle Cost Analysis, and ROCS (Rebate Output Calculation System).

2. *Cash and investment management.* Treasury information and management functions include examination of investment values and alternatives, cash flow analysis, tracking pooled investments by funds, and portfolio analysis and management. Packages include Public Treasury RESOURCE, Cash and Investment Management, CASHCALC, Portfolio Management, MAXBACK Investment and Cash Management System, Investment Manager, (Portfolio Tracking System), and GATEWAY.

3. *Comprehensive accounting.* Numerous systems are available here for fund accounting, payroll, report generation, purchase order systems, and other accounting related functions. Packages include Municipal System, ACS Municipal Accounting, PC-FUND, municiPAL, IFAS, AlphaBARS Fund Accounting, Governmental Fund Accounting, Civic Systems, FundSense, Governmental Financial System (GOV-SYS), Integrity Fund Accounting System, CSI Cititech Software Solutions, Municipal Operations Manager (MOM), GMS (Government Management System), Custom Municipal Software, GIFTS (Governmental Integrated Financial Tracking System), Data West Municipal Management, Response Financial information Management System, FUND IV, BUCS (Budgetary Control System), Municipal Finance Management, WOS Fund Accounting, GMS Financial Management System, C-Fast, T-Fast, MIP Fund Accounting System, Fund Accounting System, FundBalance Financial System, Financial Management Systems, Moore Comprehensive Accounting Systems, Fund Accounting System, Fund Accounting-Payroll and Advanced Utility Billing, Government Accounting System, MRS (Municipal Reporting System), ONLINE FAMIS, Fund Accounting Manager, RTSS Comprehensive Accounting Software, Budgetary Accounting System, Citi-Pak, Springbrook Software Fund Accounting, Total Financial Software, BANNER Financial Management System, MUNIS Municipal Information System, Administrators—Accountant and Paymaster, DPC Fund Accounting and Payroll, MacFIscal, and Willaimson Law Book NY State Municipal Accounting.

4. *Financial analysis and forecasting.* Functions performed here including monitoring budget balances by program activity, object, and line item, analyzing fund balances, forcasting revenues and expenses, and performing fiscal impact analysis. Packages include Economic Analysis, Budget Tracker, GovRatio, RevEx, FundTools Version 2, Performance Advisor, and FISCALS-Fiscal Analysis System.

5. *Fixed assets.* These packages track the value, status, and progress of fixed assets. Available programs include Fixed Assets, Fixed Asset Tracking, AlphaBARS Fixed Assets, Governmental Fixed Assets, Civic Systems Fixed Assets, FACS (Fixed Assets Control System), GGMS Fixed Assets Inventory, Capital Asset Manager, Fixed Asset Accounting and Control System (FAACS), Fixed Assets Manager, and Fixed Asset Accounting.

6. *Payroll:* These packages maintain payroll including deductions, withholding, and benefits across various pay periods and tax tables. They include PAYMATE Governmental Payroll System, Civic Systems Payroll, CHIPS (Comprehensive

Integrated Payroll System), Super P/R Payroll System, Job Cost Payroll System, Payroll Planner, and Payroll.

7. *Tax Assessment, Billing*. Packages here calculate real estate and personal property taxes as well as special assessments. Ownership and valuation information is stored and used. Applications include ACS Property Tax System, ACS Sales Tax System, Governmental Appraisal, Property Tax Assessment and Billing System, Property Tax Collection and Delinquency System, Civic Systems Special Assessment, Univers, Property Taxes, Tax Assessment and Billing, Property Tax-11, Property Tax Manager, COMPASS (Comprehensive Assessment Administration System), GYRO Property Tax Valuation Assistance, Appraisal System, Ultra, Sigma Property Information System, Personal Property Tax System, Real Estate Tax System, and Tax Assessment.

8. *Miscellaneous*. Miscellaneous functions and the associated packages include:

Accounts receivable (Miscellaneous Accounts Receivable System and Receivables Manager).
Auditing (Auditing Performance System for Fund Accounting FASTIG).
Budget preparation (Budget Preparation System and Budget Advisor).
Business licenses management (Business License System).
Cash receipt accounting (Cash Register System, Remittance Accounting, Manatron CIMS, and Receipts Manager).
General ledger accounting (Integrity General Ledger System and Super G/L General Ledger System).
Risk management (Risk Management Program).
Special improvement district (Service District and Special Improvement District/ Maintenance District Management).

Software available for finance-linked functions includes:

9. *Economic development*. These packages manage trade promotion efforts, provide assistance to economic development organizations and chambers of commerce, and examine real estate development issues, especially for low-income housing.

10. *Complaint tracking*. Packages here help track citizen requests for service and complaints.

11. *General management:* Work and resource allocation as well as survey database manipulation are among general management functions assisted by applications software.

12. *Management tools*. Expert system support, evaluation of alternatives, and policy and goal percentaging can also be assisted with applications software.

13. *Project management*. Fully integrated project management, including schedules, pay requests, cash flow forecasts, job costs and estimates, and financial summaries are included in project management software.

14. *Planning:* Computerized fiscal impact analysis and simulations are available to assist planning efforts.

OBSTACLES TO EXPANDED COMPUTER APPLICATIONS IN GOVERNMENT

Powerful technologies also paradoxically produce their own backlash. New technologies require new skills, and as they change rapidly, constant learning. New technologies also redefine what is good. Computer illiterate management is rapidly becoming inefficient and even ineffective management. Despite this, obstacles to the full harnassing of computer power remain (Worthley, 1986).

Personal Problems

The single greatest obstacle to full exploitation of computers both in general government management and in budgeting-related activities is personnel-related issues, including recruitment, training, retention, redeployment and resistance problems (Worthley, 1986). Hardware and software acquisition, by comparison, are comparatively easier, facilitated by various vendors eager to assist new system purchases and installations.

While with small systems in local government and nonprofit organizations, existing personnel may be trained to fulfill new job demands generated by new computer upgrades, larger systems in large local governments, state governments, and federal agencies require technical operators, programmers, and systems operators. Rarely does government employment match the salaries these specialized personnel may garner in the private sector. Thus, newly graduated employees with little job experience may work for government long enough to acquire on-the-job training in various computer applications and then move to the private sector for salary increases, making retention of specialized computer employees difficult.

Training personnel in computer applications is also a recurring problem. Undertraining has applied to both computer specialists, who may not be sufficiently versed in the organizational goals and missions of the agency for which they work, as well as nonspecialist on-line users, who may not fully understand the capabilities and limits of the system they are accessing.

Coupled with and in part resulting from undertraining, employee resistance to new computer applications and upgrades has been an additional problem in many agencies. Resistance ranges from the most typical form of nonuse of the system, resulting in a decline in productivity, to inputing inaccurate data and actual sabotage of equipment. Further, new applications may indicate that personnel need redeployment into different functions and work environments, an additional source of resistance at times.

Security

Inadequate security provides another major obstacle to full harnessing of computer power. Periodically, hackers break into supposed secure computers, proving that no computer or database is immune from this problem. When security is breached through unauthorized access and use, data may be manipulated or lost. In finance, computerized embezzlements occur less frequently than traditional paper and pencil embezzlements and thefts, but the average dollar loss associated with each incidence has increased greatly. Laws protecting the privacy of individuals may also be undercut when security is inadequate.

Operational Failures

A computerized budgeting and financial management system that "crashes" frequently and unexpectedly will be frustrating to users. Delays and downtime will undermine system usage. Crucial to overcoming this problem is the maintenance of adequate backup systems to protect users from information loss.

Data Excess

Data pollution or excess may also undermine computer usage. Reports that generate too much information or information in forms that are not relevant to user needs will quickly be ignored. This problem may occur when a standard financial management software package is purchased that is not customized and is not well suited to the needs of the purchasing agency or jurisdiction.

As expansion of the role of computers continues, these obstacles need to be addressed so that the full power of this technology may be harnessed for the public good. To err is to be human. To be fast, efficient, and productive is to be computerized. While even with finance and budgeting the explosion of information technologies is too great for any single person to track, computer illiteracy is an increasingly unforgiveable sin. So let the expansion of this productivity-enhancing tool begin.

REFERENCES

Bartee, T. C. (1972). *Digital Computer Fundamentals*. McGraw-Hill, New York.

Calingaert, P. (1982). *Operating System Elements*. Prentice-Hall, Englewood Cliffs, NJ.

Coffman, E. G., Jr., and Denning, P. J. (1973). *Operating Systems Theory*. Prentice-Hall, Englewood Cliffs, NJ.

Davis, W. S. (1977). *Operating Systems*. Prentice-Hall, Englewood Cliffs, NJ.

Deitel, H. M. (1984). *An Introduction to Operating Systems*, rev. 1st ed. Addison-Wesley, Reading, MA.

Eadie, D. (1982). *A User's Guide to Computer Peripherals*. Prentice-Hall, Englewood Cliffs, NJ.

Hohenstein, L. (1980). *Computer Peripherals for Minicomputers, Microprocessors, and Personal Computers*. McGraw-Hill, New York.

Institute for New Generation Computer Technology. (1984). *Fifth Generation Computer Systems*. North-Holland, Amsterdam.

Ishikawa, A. (1986). *Future Computer and Information Systems*. Praeger, New York.

Karin, S., and Smith, N. P. (1987). *The Supercomputer Era*. Harcourt Brace Jovanovich, Boston.

Koffman, E. B. (1985). *Problem Solving and Structured Programming in Pascal*, 2nd ed. Addison-Wesley. Reading, MA.

Lee, G. (1982). *From Hardware to Software*. MacMillan, London.

Mano, M. M. (1982). *Computer System Architecture*. Prentice-Hall, Englewood Cliffs, NJ.

Rademacher, R. A., and Gibson, H. L. (1983). *An Introduction to Computers and Information Systems*. South-Western Publishing, Cincinnati.

Sayers, A. P. (ed.) (1971). *Operating Systems Survey*. Auerbach, Surrey, England.

Sloan, M. E. (1976). *Computer Hardware and Organization: An Introduction*. Science Research Associates, Chicago.

Stevens, R. (1986). *Understanding Computers*. Oxford University Press, Oxford, England.

Tannenbaum, A. S. (1987). *Operating Systems: Design and Implementation*. Prentice-Hall, Englewood Cliffs, NJ.

Ulrich, C. (ed.) (1990). *Software Reference Guide 1990*. Research and Information Services, International City Management Association, Washington, DC.

Wells, M. 1976. *Computer Systems Hardware*. Cambridge University Press, Cambridge.

Worthley, J. A. 1986. Computer technology and productivity improvement. In M. Holzer and A. Halachmi (eds.), *Strategic Issues in Public Sector Productivity: The Best of Public Productivity Review, 1975–1985*, Jossey-Bass, San Francisco, pp. 205–213.

15

Productivity Measurement

Marc Holzer *National Center for Public Productivity, Rutgers University, Newark, New Jersey*

INTRODUCTION

A productive society is dependent upon productive government. But the production of government services is no simple task. The many parts to the public sector productivity "puzzle" include budgeting and financial management; planning and management; measurement and evaluation; motivation and supervision; decision making and policymaking. No part of the puzzle is more important than the fiscal piece, and no government can remain fiscally sound if it is inefficient and ineffective. This chapter will present an overview of productivity management, with particular attention to the measurement concerns that must precede budgetary decisions on resource allocation.

The concepts of productivity and budgeting have always been linked. For instance, the century-old reform clamor to expunge corruption and partisan appointments, which lay at the origin of civil service, was intended to insulate the management process from politics, so that public servants might efficiently carry out their policy-implementing responsibilities. In the intervening century improvements in public and fiscal administration have had one ultimate objective—improved productivity.

Despite this progress, a chronic obstacle to systematic productivity improvement has been the contradiction between expectations and perceptions of performance. Despite a century of improvement in the delivery of government services, the public is frustrated, angry, and still demands that government personnel be smarter and work harder. Business and citizen groups, and their media surrogates, still demand greater "productivity," "efficiency," "effectiveness," and "economy." As in the nineteenth century, those demands are still reinforced by occasional and dramatic failings ranging from fiscal mismanagement to project mismanagement. And pressures for productivity are likely to increase in frequency and intensity through the final years of the twentieth century as desires for personal resources (or personal "productivity") conflict with demands for social investments (or societal "productivity") in health, welfare, education, and public safety services. Both contradictions have only one solution—for public agencies to improve their capacities to be productive, to apply those capacities to the efficient and effective delivery of services, and to convince the public that such actions are occurring.

Unfortunately, however, the public distrusts their public organizations. Elected officials and candidates for elective office have much to gain by criticizing the bureaucracy's image of low productivity, and by suggesting simplistic solutions. They have little to gain during their short terms of office by investing in sophisticated productivity programs that are likely to pay back only over long terms. Thus, despite the political rhetoric of "efficiency and effectiveness," we have seen serious productivity efforts undersupported and even eliminated.

The National Commission on Productivity and Quality of Work Life was established under President Nixon, reduced to a "National Center" with tenuous funding under President Ford, and finally dropped under President Carter. President Reagan's staff quickly eliminated the local, state, and federal productivity assistance programs in the Office of Personnel Management. They then gave license to the voluntary "Grace Commission" (formerly known as the "President's Private Sector Survey on Cost Control") to ceaselessly attack the competency of federal employees by developing overstated possibilities for savings from "quick and dirty" analyses by corporate executives on loan to the Commission (the great bulk of those savings, however, turned out to be a function of public policy as defined by the Congress and the President, rather than public and personnel administration as managed by the bureaucracy). Finally, the Reagan administration redefined productivity as efficiency, virtually without regard to effectiveness or outcomes. At the local level, simplistic solutions to productivity included California's Proposition Thirteen and other tax revolt initiatives, the ideological assumptions of which were that:

Government is bloated, consuming too many resources.
A leaner public sector will be more efficient, somehow generating the same services with fewer resources.
Output to input ratios will improve as a smaller workforce (e.g., lesser inputs) produces services (e.g., same outputs) at the same quantitative and qualitative levels.
The loss of personnel will somehow be compensated for with better planning, management, automation, procedures simplification, etc.

In reality, however, the investments necessary to accomplish those tasks were lacking and the workforce became demoralized.

A more recent variation on this cutback theme has been the thrust toward privatization, that public sector services should be shifted (not merely contracted out) to the private sector as a means of producing the same services at lower costs, especially lower personnel costs. The results are a shift of some employees to the private sector (usually at lower salaries and benefits and under a less advantageous personnel system) outplacement of some displaced employees to other agencies of government, and the loss of employment in more than a few cases. And there is no guarantee that services will be delivered with the public sector's inherent considerations for equity.

For the forseeable future government will be under tremendous fiscal pressure as a function of a lack of confidence, the myth of privatization, and declining tax receipts. Such fiscal pressures demand productivity—and productive planning-budgeting-management decisions depend as much upon measurement as upon any other piece of the productivity puzzle.

Can we measure public sector productivity? The short answer is "yes." There is a great deal of research that demonstrates that measurement of public services is conceptually sound and feasible. In fact, the field is fairly well developed.

Productivity measurement is not new. Concerns with public sector productivity measurement have been as constant as concerns with high taxes, corruption, or incompetence. Measurement is implicit in questions from all parts of the political spectrum, in discussions among business people and union people, in analyses by reporters and academicians: "Is crime up?" "Are the streets cleaner?" "What benefits will a new building produce?" "Is the air quality better?" "How well are our children doing in school?"

Productivity measurement is continually evolving. A century ago efficiency was paramount. But we have since added effectiveness, impact, and performance to our measurement agendas (Epstein, 1988; Hatry, 1979). And productivity measurement is an important part of the most recent emphases on quality, such as total quality management (Milakovich, 1991).

Despite a long history and a broadening conceptual base, productivity measurement is misunderstood. The concept suffers from casual but misleading myths: that outputs and outcomes cannot be measured in the public sector; that managerial risks outweigh rewards; that data is not readily available; that the effort will be too complicated to use.

Our objective within this chapter is to clarify the relationship between measurement and productivity improvement. Initially, that linkage can be visualized in a simple, symmetrical context (causal factors, Fig. 1) in which "quantity" and "quality" represent the two major dimensions of an organization's output. As this diagram suggests, the results of human and technological efforts must be measured along the two dimensions of quantity ("How many clients are served?" "How many units of service are delivered?") and quality ("Are the services delivered to certain standards?" "What is the effor rate?")

An equally simple systems view (management system concept, Fig. 2) of productivity improvement emphasizes the importance of feedback. Although feedback can be subjective, the implicit need for objective data is underscored within that loop. Resource allocation decisions, that is, budgets, are inextricably linked to the feedback: "Are taxpayers satisfied with the service?" "Do clients have a favorable view of an agency's actions?"

In a more sophisticated systems overview (an overview of productivity, Fig. 3), an expanded view of measurement is portrayed as central to the productivity improvement

Figure 1   Causal factors affecting productivity change.

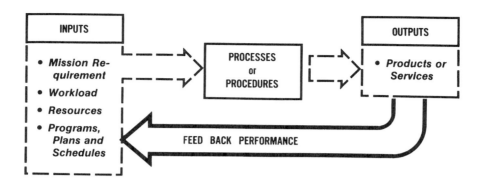

Figure 2   Management system concept: a model.

process. In this view, "output" is a narrow term, which may limit views of productivity improvement. If managers are to make better decisions as to resource allocation and reallocation, then they will need not only measures of outputs (how much of a service is provided, such as checks issued or hospital days provided) but of "outcomes" (what the service results in, such as improvements in a client's quality of life or ability to maintain employment). This overview also argues that we must measure the production of "internal" services (such as maintenance, training and auditing) as well as those "external" services that are produced for clients. Such internal services are necessary prerequisites to the production of external outputs and outcomes. A productive agency must therefore monitor and improve productivity at all three stages: internal services, external services, and outcomes.

Such data is useful to internal decision makers (i.e., managers), external actors, such as elected officials, clients, advocate groups, and the press; these are the actors who often make choices based upon feedback about a program's outputs or outcomes. Yet much of that feedback is "soft," based upon critical successes or failures, rumors, personal experiences, etc. As the "objective" arrow in Fig. 3 suggests, productivity measurement offers an opportunity to develop and present "hard" data instead. Such data can help defend or expand a program, rather than suffering from relatively subjective, political decisions. Particularly important in proving evidence of progress are timely data that reflect cost savings, additional services, independent evaluations of service levels, client satisfaction, and reductions in waiting or processing times.

As the figures above indicate, measurement is only part of a broader productivity program. For example, in one approach to productivity improvement, the measurement "cycle" (analyze–measure–analyze . . .) is just one of "five steps to improving productivity" (Table 1). Although the four other steps might be dismissed casually as "common sense," they (as well as the other elements of this list) are the "shoals" upon which productivity programs often come to grief.

In another of many comprehensive alternatives ("productivity improvement steps," Table 2), measurement (step six) is apparently only one of 10 necessary steps. The need for measurement is, however, implicit in many of the other steps, such as "goals and objectives" in step 1, "large backlogs, slipping deadlines, high turnover, or many complaints" in step 3, the need for "data" in step 7, or "measurable" success in step 10.

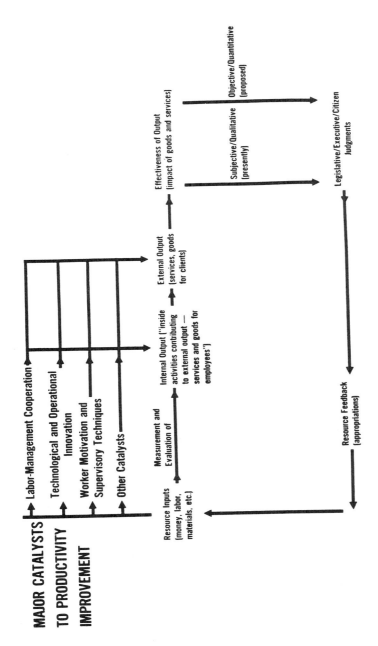

Figure 3 An overview of productivity

Table 1 Five Steps to Improving Productivity

1. Make goals and purposes clear.
2. Rate performance of managers. Do they:
    Provide clear directions?
    Give employees work that uses their skills, challenges their ability and intelligence?
    Ensure that work groups are harmonious?
    Provide promotional opportunities, interesting work?
    Give workers a voice in decisions that affect them?
    Create an environment that workers feel part of?
3. Involve people in looking for opportunities.
    What barriers and obstacles need to be overcome?
    What tasks can be done more efficiently?
    What might be dropped? Shortened? Simplified?
    Are employees unhappy about too much/little work?
    Can performance appraisal system be of use?
4. Analyze, measure, analyze.
    Analyze objectives, problems, opportunities.
    Decide what ought to be measured.
    Define output/input measures.
    Establish data collection system.
    Analyze validity and usefulness.
5. Choose ripe opportunities.
    "People" Approaches
    Procedural approaches
    Environmental approaches
    Capital investments/budget considerations

Source: *Managers Guide for Improving Productivity* (1980).

PRODUCTIVITY AS A RATIO

Productivity is the ratio of outputs and outcomes (work done, products distributed, services rendered, impact achieved) to inputs (labor, capital, materials, space, energy, time, etc.). Productivity *improvement* has to do with favorable changes in that ratio. Thus, in developing and utilizing productivity measures, it is important to recognize the differences between various ratios of improvement (see Fig. 4).

1. *Inputs decline, outputs/outcomes remain constant.* This ratio represents a cutback management situation in which management is forced to respond productively. For example, faced with a cutback in staff, a state mental health facility may reorganize, allowing for the same level of services with more efficient use of remaining staff.
2. *Inputs remain constant, outputs/outcomes improve.* Many critics advocate this case. They often expect "quick fixes" based on limited perspectives or critiques by groups external to the agency. For example, they might propose that each social services worker increase applications processed by 25%. This might be a reasonable goal, but only in the long run as better management of inputs improves outputs. Still, without the capacity to invest in better management, and to provide adequate services to more applicants, this case is less reasonable than case 3.

Table 2 Productivity Improvement Steps

Step 1. Clarify goals and obtain support. Productivity programs must agree upon, and have commitments to, reasonable goals and objectives, adequate staff and resource support, and organizational visibility. The full cooperation of top management and elected officials is a prerequisite to success.

Step 2. Locate models. As productivity is an increasing priority of government, existing projects can suggest successful paths and ways to avoid potential mistakes. Models are available from computer networks, the professional literature, and at conferences.

Step 3. Identify promising areas. As a means of building a successful track record, new productivity programs might select as targets those functions continually faced with large backlogs, slipping deadlines, high turnover, or many complaints. Because personnel are the largest expenditure for most public agencies, improved morale, training, or working conditions might offer a high payoff. Organizations might also target functions where new techniques, procedures, or emerging technologies seem to offer promising paybacks.

Step 4. Build a team. Productivity programs are much more liely to succeed as bottom-up, rather than top-down or externally directed, entities. Productivity project teams should include middle management, supervisors, employees and union representatives. They might also include consultants, clients, and representatives of advocacy groups. If employees are involved in looking for opportunities, then they are likely to suggest which barriers or obstacles need to be overcome; what tasks can be done more efficiently, dropped or simplified; which workloads are unrealistically high or low.

Step 5. Plan the project. Team members should agree on a specific statement of scope, objectives, tasks, responsibilities, and time frames. This agreement should be detailed as a project management plan, which should then be updated and discussed on a regular basis.

Step 6. Collect program data. Potentially relevant information should be defined broadly, and might include reviews of existing data bases, interviews, budgets, and studies by consultants or client groups. A measurement system should be developed to collect data on a regular basis, and all data should be supplied to the team for regular analysis. The validity and usefulness of such information should be constantly monitored.

Step 7. Modify project plans. Based upon continuing team discussions of alternative approaches and data, realistic decisions must be made about program problems, opportunities, modifications, and priorities. For instance, could a problem best be solved through the more intensive use of technology, improved training, better supervision, or improved incentives?

Step 8. Expect problems. Projects are more likely to succeed if they openly confront, and then discuss, potential misunderstandings, misconceptions, slippages, resource shortages, client and employee resistance, etc. Any such problem, if unaddressed, can cause a project to fail.

Step 9. Implement improvement actions. Implementation should be phased in on a modest basis and without great fanfare. Those projects that are highly touted but then do not deliver as expected are more likely to embarrass top management (and political supporters), with predictable consequences. Those that adopt a low profile are less likely to threaten key actors, especially middle management and labor.

Step 10. Evaluate and publicize results. Measurable success, rather than vague claims, is important. Elected officials, the press, and citizen groups are more likely to accept claims of success if they are backed up by hard data. "Softer" feedback can then support such claims. Particularly important in providing evidence of progress are timely data that reflect cost savings, additional services, independent evaluations of service levels, client satisfaction, and reductions in waiting or processing times.

Source: Holzer (1988a).

1. SAME OUTPUT/OUTCOMES

LESS INPUT

2. MORE OUTPUT/OUTCOMES

SAME INPUT

3. MUCH MORE OUTPUT/OUTCOMES

MUCH LESS INPUT

4. MUCH MORE OUTPUT/OUTCOMES

MORE INPUT

5. LESS OUTPUT

MUCH LESS INPUT

Figure 4   How is productivity improved?

3. *In this case inputs decline substantially, outputs/outcomes improve substantially.* Some elected officials and private sector critics advocate this scenario. It is, however, almost always based upon unreasonable and naive assumptions, for example, that waste is of enormous proportions.

4. *Inputs increase moderately, outputs/outcomes improve substantially.* This is a more likely case, as it allows for continued modest investments in improved productive capacity. But in the short run, a true productivity program is more likely to experience temporarily decreasing productivity—constant outputs while inputs increased modestly to allow for improved internal capacities, which will then increase outputs at a later stage. For example, in a state correctional facility investments in training, buildings, and equipment may be necessary in year 1 prior to improved correctional services in year 2.

5. *Inputs decline substantially, outputs/outcomes decline less rapidly.* Although the output to input ratio is apparently increasing, drastic cutbacks in resources often result in cutbacks in services that fall most heavily on those citizens least likely to have alternatives. In a situation of deep cutbacks a municipal college, for example, may be forced to cut psychological counseling services to students—most of whom are unlikely to be able to purchase such services privately and will therefore be less likely to graduate.

Although multiple measures of public sector services cannot usually be aggregated as productivity "indices," (analogous to the bottom line of profit in the private sector), it is possible to measure public sector performance:

1. If service quality is to be maintained or improved, a measurement program must be oriented to effectiveness, rather than just quantity or efficiency.
2. Management's uses of productivity measures are often in the budgeting and fiscal area: estimating resource requirements, justifying budgets, reducing costs, reallocating resources, investing increased resources, and improving benefit-cost linkages.
3. A measurement program, which requires substantial expertise and careful planning, should ask and begin to answer the following questions:

In terms of program performance:

How much of a service is provided?
How efficiently are resources used?
How effectively is a service provided?

In terms of effectiveness indicators for performance:

What is the intended purpose of the service?
What are the unintended impacts of the service?
How effective is the service in prevention of problems before they arise?
Is the service adequate?
Is the service accessible?
Are clients satisfied with services?
Are services distributed equitably?
Is a product durable?
To what extent is a service provided to clients with dignity?

In terms of desirable characteristics of performance measures:

Is a service significant?
Is the service appropriate to the problem being addressed?
Is performance quantifiable?
Are services readily available?
Are services delivered in a timely manner?
Are services delivered in a relatively straightforward manner?
Is a measure of performance valid?
Is a measure acceptable?
Is performance measured completely?
Are measures accurate?
Are measures reliable?

In terms of management's uses of productivity measures, are measures used to help:

Set goals?
Estimate resource requirements?
Develop budget justifications?
Reduce costs?
Develop organization improvement strategies?
Control operations?
Reallocate resources?
Hold individuals or organizational units accountable?
Motivate employees to improve performance?
Compare agencies or subunits to similar entities or to past levels of achievement?

Predict periods of work overload or underload?
Link increased resources to policy outcomes or to systemwide problems?
Improve benefit-cost linkages?
Develop more sophisticated capacities for measurement?

In terms of data collection:

Are existing records analyzed?
Are clients surveyed?
Are taxpayers surveyed?
Are services rated by professional or trained observers?
Are special data collection techniques utilized?

In terms of the analysis of productivity data:

Are before versus after comparisons made?
Are measures displayed in a time series?
Are comparisons made with other areas, jurisdictions, or client groups?
Are comparisons made with targets?

A CASE IN POINT

Nowhere has the application of these criteria been clearer and more successful than in the Department of Sanitation (DOS) (Holzer, 1988). As a function of a program which evolved incrementally, the DOS was able to claim, for example (Mayor's Management Report, 83–94):

More than a 50% improvement in refuse collection productivity, from an index of 63.2 in
    FY 80 to a level of 97.4 in FY 87;
An improvement in street cleanliness of similar dimensions, from a low of 53% of streets
    rated acceptably clean in 1980 to a high of 74.0 so rated for FY 86, and an
    "almost-as-good" rating of 72.8 for FY '87 (a drop that the DOS attributes to
    exceptionally poor winter weather).
Reductions in night collections, missed collections, and crew collection size.
Increases in equipment availability and reliability, abandoned vehicle removal, and
    enforcement of Health and Administrative Code regulations.
Advances in waste disposal, recycling, and resource recovery.

A major characteristic of the new (i.e., since 1978) productivity improvement system in DOS included measurement, as well as labor-management cooperation, technological innovations, and management actions.

Solid waste collection is perhaps one of the easiest public sector functions to measure and track over time. But that ease of application applies only to a narrow set of functions such as tons of refuse collected, households serviced, employees, labor hours, and cost of the entire operation. Ratios can then be calculated between those factors, such as cost per ton of refuse collected ($/ton collected), or tons collected per crew collection hour (National Commission on Productivity, 8). DOS has, however, developed a much more sophisticated management information system (MIS), in part with help from the Mayor's Office of Operations). The Mayor's Management Report (83–94), which is issued semiannually, includes a wide range of data (see figures attached): cleanliness ratings of streets based upon observations (initially as "Project Scorecard" by an outside group, and now under the Office of Operations), refuse collection productivity based upon an index, data differentiating collections by time of day, figures as to timeliness of collection, enforcement data regarding summons issued per day by sanitation enforcement agents, recycling data regarding tons of various materials picked up, information on absence control and overtime, figures on capital commitments and expense reductions, etc. These figures are useful at the top management and policy levels, and are scrutinized by the media and interest groups.

Data of a different, more sophisticated, order is also utilized for productivity management purposes at the many intermediate steps which contribute to the Department's outputs. In the Bureau of Motor Equipment (BME), for instance, profit center reports calculate input "costs," output "value" (representing what the city could have paid to the private sector if tasks had been contracted out), "profit" as the difference between costs and value, and a "productivity factor" (ratio of output to input). BME's claim that its profit centers are cost-effective and competitive with the private sector is based upon "bottom line" data (Contino, 1984, pp. 12–13), the methodology and substance of which have been confirmed by the Office of the City Comptroller. Within BME, eight shops as an aggregate have, since their inception, been operating with a productivity factor of 1.47, which means that every dollar invested by the city produced $1.47 worth of products or services. Given the amount of investment, the net result was an annual "profit" of $3,737,000 for 1986, and a cumulative "profit" of $18,320,000 from March 1981 through the end of calendar 1986. Such data can also be broken out on a quarterly basis to clarify the short-term results of organizational changes. BME claims that (Contino, 1984, pp. 13–14)

> The figures . . . prove the theory that when employees have a say in running their jobs and operations and when they are given an accurate MIS to track their accomplishments (in this case the "profit center" MIS), productivity will improve. From the first "quarter" to the next three "quarters" combined, the eight profit centers improved productivity from 1.21 to 1.50—a gain of 24%—and increased profits from $1.15 million/year to $2.4 million/year—a gain of 109.3%.

Data can also help diagnose organizational problems. Quarterly data on the passenger car shop showed an apparent drop of 10% in productivity. Examination and discussion of that data with labor brought to the surface the worker's reservations about beating industry-wide standards; work accomplished was often omitted from daily work sheets so as not to increase expectations. Dropping the requirement to list the actual time to do a job corrected that problem, and productivity increased sharply. A "loss" in the Motor Room was diagnosed partially as an accounting problem and partially as a productivity problem, both of which were subsequently corrected with the cooperation of labor.

THE MEASUREMENT LITERATURE

The development of expertise in productivity measurement can be accelerated through attention to the literature. Extensive published analyses are available to "fill out" the menus above. *Public Sector Productivity* (Holzer and Halachmi, 1988), for example, is a resource guide that lists hundreds of books, articles, journals, and other sources of measurement knowledge in just the last decade.

The beginning of the 1980s was marked by the publication of the *Productivity*

Improvement Handbook for State and Local Government (Washnis, 1980), encompassing 1492 pages of tools and techniques. Of the four chapters devoted to productivity measurement, one dealt specifically with "Evolution of Budgeting and Control Systems," and another with "Audit Approaches to Productivity Measurement." A more recent publication, the *Public Productivity Handbook* (Holzer, 1991, also in this Marcel Dekker series), includes analyses of measurement, performance, outcomes, and evaluation.

That the momentum for measurement has advanced significantly is evidenced not only by these handbooks, but by a critical mass of research. Perhaps the most important and sustained effort has been by Harry Hatry and his colleagues at the Urban Institute. *Measuring the Effectiveness of Basic Municipal Services* (Hatry et al., 1974) "provides an overview of a system of procedures by which local governments can obtain regular feedback on how well they are serving their citizens with respect to the basic services they can provide." *How Effective Are Your Community Services?* (Hatry et al., 1977) "raises issues in nine functional areas that should make department heads and other local officials sensitive to the needs of the citizens they serve, and gives officials some new ways to think about their role in the delivery of essential services." *Efficiency Measurement for Local Government Services* (Hatry et al., 1979) "seeks to measure the efficiency of local government services in water supply, police apprehension of criminals, central purchasing and group residential care for children. Stressing the difficulty of efficiency measurement, it recommends that the basis for any evaluations should be made on the *quality* and *difficulty* of the incoming workload." *Applied Program Evaluation in Local Government* (Poister, et al., 1979) is intended to help cities develop data collection and analytical abilities so that they can conduct more such work on an in-house basis. *Performance Measurement: A Guide for Local Elected Officials* (Urban Institute, 1980) is an "overview of the what, how and cost of performance." *Measuring Performance in Human Service Systems* (Budde, 1980) concentrates on how agencies can improve their professionalism and service, cut their costs, and perform more effectively. The *Productivity Measurement Handbook* (Christopher, 1986) contains proved techniques for productivity measurement of white collar operations. *Performance and Credibility* (Wholey et al., 1986) focuses on four leadership functions essential to improving the performance and credibility of public and nonprofit organizations: establishing organizational and program performance objectives; assessing performance by monitoring outcome-oriented indicators; stimulating improvement in efficiency, productivity, and cost-effectiveness; and communicating the value of an organization's goals and activities in a credible way. *Strategic Issues in Public Sector Productivity* (Holzer and Halachmi, 1986) examines productivity improvement problems and possibilities along five dimensions: productivity improvement concepts; measurement issues; labor-management cooperation; federal, state, and local approaches; and computer applications. *Productivity Measurement and Management* (Halachmi and Holzer, 1987) reviews problems and possibilities regarding productivity measurement and management at different levels of government, and offers guidelines for measuring productivity in complex jobs which produce intangible outcomes. This symposium demonstrates how management science technologies can be used successfully to measure policy impact and accomplishments. *Promoting Productivity in the Public Sector* (Kelly, 1988) provides an interdisciplinary policy studies perspective, emphasizing the theoretical issues involved in the politics of measuring public sector performance, as well as giving empirical assessments of how selected policy, program and strategic factors are related to productivity improvement efforts. *Using Performance Measurement in Local Government* (Epstein, 1988) is written to "help public officials, students, and concerned citizens understand public service performance measurement and its value to the community. It emphasizes the many ways public officials can use measurement for the benefit of government and community."

The dialogue on public sector productivity measurement has continued quarterly since 1975 through the *Public Productivity and Management Review* (PPMR, formerly *Public Productivity Review*), which emphasizes implementation of organizational goals and objectives; measurement of levels of efficiency and effectiveness; cooperation between management, labor, and clients; and recognition of the fiscal, legal, political, and technological constraints to productivity enhancement. For example, the PPMR published measurement-related research on "Governmental Efficiency" (Rabin, 1990), in which Miller argues that "efficiency, equity and parsimony dictate government financial innovations, [and] that efficiency is (a) basic beliefs underlying public financial management" (Miller, 1990, p. 333).

AN OPTIMISTIC PERSPECTIVE

The New York City Sanitation Case is not unique. The substantial research and experience with public sector productivity measurement programs in scores of federal, state, and local agencies is sufficient to dispel misconceptions that executives care little about operational efficiency and effectiveness. Many managers and executives are professionally committed to productivity improvement through measurement. Their commitments are at least as strong as those of transient policymakers, and their innovations are at least as promising and sophisticated as those proposed by their sometimes condescending corporate critics.

Such productivity programs promise to benefit all interested parties in a win-win relationship. Employees will benefit from more equitable distribution of workload, clearer indications of their progress, and sometimes by earning more money. Managers and executives will benefit from an improved capacity to control workload and work levels, and to produce services, as anticipated. Elected officials will benefit from efficiently and effectively operated services, which the public expects and appreciates. Clients will benefit from improved services and reduced frustrations. And, as the "bottom line," the general public will benefit from more efficient and effective uses of tax dollars.

REFERENCES

Budde, J. F. (1979). *Measuring Performance in Human Service Systems: Planning, Organization, and Control*. Amacom, New York.

Christopher, W. F. (1986). *Productivity Measurement Handbook*, 2nd ed. Productivity Press, Cambridge, MA.

Contino, R. (1984). Productivity Gains through Labor-Management Cooperation—NYC Department of Sanitation, Bureau of Motor Equipment. New York City Department of Sanitation, New York, July.

Epstein, P. D. (1988). *Using Performance Measurement in Local Government: A Guide to Improving Decisions, Performance, and Accountability*. National Civic League Press, New York.

Halachmi, A., and Holzer, M. (eds.) (1987). Productivity measurement and management. *Public Productivity Review, 44*. Jossey-Bass, San Francisco.

Hatry, H. P., et al. (1979). *Efficiency Measurement for Local Government Services*. The Urban Institute, Washington, DC.

Hatry, H. P., et al. (1977). *How Effective Are Your Community Services?* The Urban Institute, Washington, DC.

Hatry, H., P., et al. (1974). *Measuring the Effectiveness of Basic Municipal Services.* The Urban Institute, Washington, DC.

Holzer, M. (1988a). Focus: Productivity improvement in New York State—The science and art of capacity building. In *Managing New York State,* Number 1, 1988. Albany, New York: Governor's Office of Employee Relations. [The 10 steps contained in this article are based, in part, on Holzer et. al., *Managing for Productivity,* including previous work by Constance Zalk.]

Holzer, M. (1988b). Productivity in, Garbage out: Sanitation gains in New York. *Public Productivity Rev., 11*(3):29–36.

Holzer, M. (ed.) (1991). *Public Productivity Handbook.* Marcel Dekker, New York.

Holzer, M., and Halachmi, A. (eds.) (1986). *Strategic Issues in Public Sector Productivity: The Best of the Public Productivity Review, 1975–1986.* Jossey-Bass, San Francisco.

Holzer, M., and Halachmi, A. (1988). *Public Sector Productivity.* Garland Press, New York.

Kelly, R. M. (ed.) (1988). *Promoting Productivity in the Public Sector: Problems, Strategies and Prospects.* St. Martin's Press, New York.

Managers Guide for Improving Productivity. (1980). Office of Intergovernmental Personnel Programs, United States Office of Personnel Management, Washington, DC.

Mayor's Management Report. Office of Operations, City of New York, semiannual publication.

Milakovich, M. E. (1991). Total quality management for public service productivity improvement. In M. Holzer (ed.), *Public Productivity Handbook,* Marcel Dekker, New York.

Miller, G. J. (1990). Efficiency as a competing principle in public financial management. *Public Productivity Manage. Rev., XIII*(4):331–351.

Poister, T. H., McDavid, J. C., Magoun, A. H. (1979). *Applied Program Evaluation in Local Government.* Lexington Books, Lexington, MA.

Rabin, J. (ed.) (1990). Governmental efficiency. Symposium in *Public Productivity Manage. Rev. XIII*(4):331–396.

Urban Institute. (1980). *Performance Measurement: A Guide for Local Elected Officials.* The Urban Institute, Washington, DC.

Washnis, G. J. (ed.) (1980). *Productivity Improvement Handbook for State and Local Government.* John Wiley and Sons, New York.

Wholey, J. S. (1987). Organizational excellence. In *Stimulating Quality and Communicating Value.* D.C. Heath, Lexington, MA.

16
Economic Impact of Budgeting

John E. Stapleford   *Department of Business and Economics, University of Delaware, Newark, Delaware*

INTRODUCTION

Like an elephant in a petunia patch, government budgets have become so immense that the slightest shifting is bound to make an impression on the whole economy. In real (inflation-adjusted) dollars government expenditures have risen from approximately 7% of gross national product (GNP) at the turn of the century to 10.4% in 1929, 23.1% in 1950, and finally 37.3% in 1987 (Musgrave and Musgrave, 1978). Government expenditures were 45.3% of 1987 national income. With indirect economic effects taken into account, the 1987 proportions rise to 61.7% of GNP and 72.9% of national income (Stern, 1975). Twenty-five years ago nearly one out of every nine dollars of the average middle class family's income went to taxes; today the same family pays at least nearly one dollar out of every four (Bell and Gabler, 1976).

As the above statistics demonstrate, the public sector has become a dominant component of the American economy. For this reason it is essential that individuals involved with the formulation of government budgets understand the likely economic impacts of potential budgetary alternatives. Changes in revenues and expenditures cannot be made solely on the basis of individual public program objectives because there may be significant associated economic consequences: consequences that might even run counter to the desired program objectives. The purpose of this chapter is to review various theories concerning the manner by which public budgeting may impact the U.S. economy.

Initial subsections are devoted to tracing the theoretical developments in economic thinking from the pre-Keynesian stance advocating limited government intervention, through the Keynesian revolution advocating an active economic role for the government sector as critical in spurring aggregate demand. The monetarist view provides a different perspective, focusing on government's ability to impact money and credit markets while abstaining from inflationary expenditure policies. The discussion of the public choice school, while not bringing us full circle to the pre-Keynesian position, outlines arguments for strict budget rules.

Next, four budget models are presented. This section centers on the models' practicality, countercyclical features, inflationary bias, and uses as a fiscal tool to impact aggregate demand.

The preceding looks at budget impacts from a national accounts perspective. Later sections of the chapter describe how impacts of individualized budget acts may be estimated. Topics addressed include intergovernmental aid, investment programs, and transfer programs.

The chapter closes by reviewing research in the health field and in family structure, which documents the pathological impacts stemming from economic changes. Thus, we must think of impacts beyond the economic, some on the order of life and death, when considering the federal budget.

THEORETICAL DEVELOPMENTS

Pre-Keynesian Economics

It can be and has been demonstrated repeatedly by economists that both individuals and societies benefit from voluntary exchange. In any situation where individuals' preferences differ, voluntary exchange allows reallocation of products and resources, resulting in a more preferred position for each individual. Whether it is Huck Finn trading a small tick to Tom Sawyer for a recently fallen tooth, or Bolivia trading bauxite to Peru for crude petroleum, each party to voluntary exchange may separate feeling wealthier than before. If, in addition to differences in preferences, individuals or nations differ in their productivity across a range of products, the potential gains from voluntary exchange increase even further.

Because they regarded voluntary exchange as superior to centrally directed allocation, pre-Keynesian economists generally advocated a limited role for government. Government's primary function was to maintain conditions conducive to voluntary exchange. This entailed protection for citizens from foreign coercion (national defense) and the protection of one citizen from coercion from another citizen (administration of justice). In addition, government should facilitate commerce by maintenance of such items as a standard currency and a system of weights and measures, and government should erect and maintain those public "institutions and those public works, which, though they may be in the highest degree advantages to . . . society, are, however, of such a nature, that the profit could never repay the expense to any individual or small number of individuals" (Smith, 1976).

The public finance focus of pre-Keynesian economists fell mainly upon issues of allocative or economic efficiency. Economic efficiency refers to the allocation of scarce resources among alternative uses in such a way as to maximize the satisfaction (or benefits) received by members of a society. Economic theory asserts that a reallocation of resources should be made so long as the incremental or marginal social benefits gained will exceed the incremental or marginal social costs of the change, where social costs represent the benefits foregone by removing resources for their next best alternative use. To the extent that net social benefits can be obtained by shifting resources from the private to the public sector, such a shifting will move society closer toward the objective of economic efficiency.

To operationalize the marginal social benefit and marginal social cost allocation principle requires quantification of benefits and costs. Pre-Keynesian economists looked toward price signals in a voluntary market system to accomplish this measurement task. In a voluntary market system, under conditions of perfect competition, market prices will represent a state of equality between the marginal social benefits of output and the marginal social costs of production. The closer a capitalistic economy reflected the conditions of perfect competition in its individual markets, argued pre-Keynesian economists, the greater would be the level of economic efficiency achieved. Subsequently, the greater the level of economic efficiency, the higher would be the levels of output, income, and employment enjoyed by the society.

To achieve high levels of output, income, and employment, pre-Keynesian economists concentrated on the issue of the efficient allocation of society's resources within and between the private and public sectors. If uninhibited by government, the voluntary market system would produce a self-regulating or self-equilibrating economic system that would automatically tend toward high levels of output and income and toward full employment. Exogenous shocks may temporarily move the economy away from full employment, but the market system would quickly adjust and full-employment general equilibrium (a steady state among all markets) would soon be restored.

Backed by the dire economic experiences of the Great Depression, John Maynard Keynes challenged the classical economists' position with the General Theory of Employment, Interest and Money (1936). Keynes rejected the classical assertion that perfectly competitive markets will always tend toward a full employment equilibrium. The challenge was successful and the resulting Keynesian theory, to be explained in the next section, dramatically altered legislators' behavior toward budgeting and economic policy.

The Keynesian Revolution

In contrast to the classical economists, Keynes argued that an economy will not necessarily come into equilibrium at full employment nor at high levels of output and income. Keynes applied the individual market concepts of supply and demand to the economy as a whole and asserted that aggregate demand could be equal to aggregate supply at any level of economic performance. Keynes thereby altered the focus of public policy economics from economic efficiency to the relative performance of economic aggregates, that is, output, income, and employment, over time.

The aggregate supply or output potential of an economy at any time is primarily determined by its available resources (land, labor, and capital), technology, and entrepreneurial spirit. When these elements of production are completely utilized, actual gross national product, or the market value of all final goods and services in the economy, is equal to potential GNP. Achievement of potential GNP is necessarily accompanied by full employment and a high level of income flowing to those possessing the various elements which enter into production.

Keynes considered the aggregate supply of an economy as given and therefore considered the achievement of potential GNP to depend on aggregate demand. If aggregate demand was insufficient, equilibrium would occur below full employment and actual GNP would fall short of potential. If aggregate demand was excessive, equilibrium would occur above full employment and actual GNP would exceed potential due to an inflationary increase in prices as the demand for goods and services exceeds the capability of supply to fully respond. As Keynes saw it, the economic and budgetary role of government was to "fine-tune" the national economy: stimulating aggregate demand when actual GNP was below potential and reducing aggregate demand when actual GNP exceeded potential. Thereby government could assure the maintenance of full employment, high income, and stable prices.

The methods Keynes advocated for government to utilize to alter aggregate demand derived from his understanding of aggregate demand. Aggregate demand is defined as the sum of the expenditures made by households, businesses, government, and foreigners. Specifically, the components of aggregate demand are consumption (C), investment (I), government spending (G), exports (X), and imports (M). Consumption is simply expenditures made for consumer goods and services. Investment is spending by businesses on plant and equipment (physical capital). Government spending on goods and services complements consumption. To achieve a full accounting of demand expenditures, adjustment must be made for foreign spending on domestic goods (exports) and domestic spending of foreign goods (imports). The sum of these components of aggregate demand is labeled national income (Y) and is represented by the equation $Y = C + I + G + (X - M)$.

According to Keynes, consumption is directly related to the level of disposable income in an economy, where disposable income is the amount of income people have to spend or save after personal taxes have been paid on the total income received. Keynes further observed that while the level of consumption directly depends on the level of disposable income, consumption does not increase as fast as disposable income. At lower levels of disposable income households have a propensity to consume more than their income allows, while as higher levels of income are achieved households have an increasing propensity to save from income.

Figure 1 shows the simple relationship between consumption and disposable income for a society. The 45-degree line represents what would occur if households used all their money on consumption at any particular level of disposable income. The Keynesian consumption relationship, or consumption function, is labeled C and shows that at low levels of income (left of DI), households spend more money than they receive, while they spend a decreasing proportion of what they receive at higher levels of income (right of DI). The area between the consumption function and the 45-degree line shows the amount households are saving or depleting their savings. The slope of the consumption function indicates the change in consumption resulting from a change in disposable income. This slope relationship is referred to as the marginal propensity to consume (MPC) of the households in the economy.

Keynes acknowledged that realized investment would have to equal realized savings, but unlike the classical economists he did not believe that changes in savings would be the primary determinant of private investment demand. To classical economists an increase in savings by household would lower the interest rate and the lower interest rate would induce businesspersons to increase investment. While acknowledging that changes

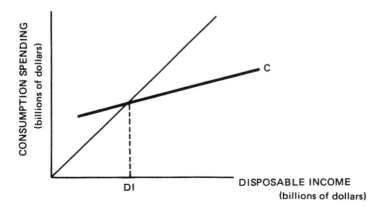

Figure 1   The Keynesian consumption function.

in savings and the interest rate influenced investment, Keynes saw businesspersons' expectations of profits as the primary determinant of investment. Investment demand could therefore be independent of any particular level of savings.

Assuming investment demand is an independent constant dollar amount, it can be added to the consumption function to give a more accurate description of aggregate demand (Fig. 2). Since disposable income is directly related to GNP, we can replace disposable income on the horizontal axis with real (inflation-adjusted) GNP. The 45-degree line now represents aggregate supply, or the amount of final goods and services that can and will be produced at various levels of aggregate expenditures. The equilibrium point where aggregate demand (C + I) and aggregate supply intersect (point N) determines actual GNP for the economy.

Referring to Fig. 2, it can be seen that an increase (decrease) in aggregate demand, whether from a change in net investment or real consumption, will cause a magnified increase (decrease) in actual GNP. For example, an increase in aggregate demand (C + I) of $100 billion in Fig. 2 results in a $500 billion increase in actual GNP. The principle of the multiplier explains why an increase in aggregate demand will lead to an even larger increase in actual or equilibrium GNP.

The multiplier is the amount by which a change in aggregate demand is multiplied to produce the ultimate change in actual GNP. Numerically the multiplier is the ratio of the change in GNP to the original change in aggregate demand. In our example, the multiplier would be 5, or $500 billion divided by $100 billion. The explanation of the multiplier is based on the concept that one person's spending is another person's income. In other words, suppose our $100 billion increase in aggregate demand arose form the construction of new steel plants in the United States. The $100 billion spent on construction accrues as wages and profits to construction workers, owners of construction firms, and workers and owners of companies producing construction supplies. These individuals will not hold their income but, according to their marginal propensity to consume, will spend a portion of the money on consumer goods. Their spending represents an additional boost to aggregate demand. For example, if the marginal propensity to consume (MPC) is

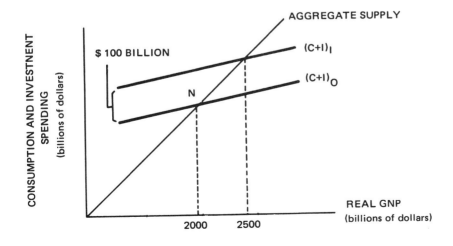

Figure 2   The Keynesian multiplier.

0.8, $20 billion will go into savings and consumption expenditures will rise by $80 billion.

The $80 billion spent on consumer goods now accrues to retailers, workers, and owners in various parts of the consumer goods industry. These individuals will in turn save a portion of this income and spend the remainder, according to the MPC. As Table 1 shows, these rounds of spending will continue until infinity or until the amounts involved are infinitesimal. The cumulative addition to GNP after all the rounds of spending are exhausted is $500 billion or five times the initial increases in aggregate demand. These rounds of spending represent a geometric progression and the multiplier may be approximated by dividing (1 – MPC) into 1.

$$\text{Multiplier} = 1 / (1 - \text{MPC})$$

Aggregate demand, aggregate supply, and the multiplier are the very basic concepts on which the Keynesian theory of income determination is founded. We are now sufficiently prepared to examine how Keynesian economics would direct budgetary policy in order to achieve the objectives of potential GNP, high income, full employment, and stable prices.

Neo-Keynesian Fiscal Policy

The budget, as Jesse Burkehead (1965) points out, "is not passive and is properly regarded as a tool of fiscal policy, that is, as an instrument for consciously influencing the economic life of a nation." Specifically, the economic goal of neo-Keynesian fiscal policy has been to bring actual GNP into equilibrium at potential GNP, which will concurrently ensure full employment, high income, and minimum inflation. Under the influence of Keynesian theory, fiscal policy has come to mean deliberate government utilization of public spending and financing in the development and stabilization of the economy.

Table 1. The Multiplier as Rounds of Spending (Billions of Dollars)

Spending round	Increment to income	Increment to consumption (MPC = 0.8)	Increment to savings (1−MPC = 0.2)
1	100	80	20
2	80	64	16
3	64	51.20	12.80
4	51.20	40.96	10.24
5	40.96	32.77	8.19
6	32.77	26.21	6.56
7	26.21	20.97	5.24
8	20.97	16.78	4.19
9	16.78	13.42	3.36
10	13.42	10.74	2.68
•	•	•	•
•	•	•	•
•	•	•	•
11 through infinity	53.69	42.95	10.74
Cumulative total	500.00	400.00	100.00

In the Keynesian schema government spending on goods and services is a component of aggregate demand. Changes in government spending will therefore produce direct changes in aggregate demand and through a multiplier will change actual GNP. Alternatively, changes in government taxes or debt will have a more indirect impact upon aggregate demand and actual GNP by changing the amount of disposable income in the economy. The actual fiscal policies enacted will depend on whether the national economy is in a recessionary or inflationary stage of the business cycle.

During recession, neo-Keynesian theory calls for expansionary fiscal policies to close the gap between actual and potential GNP (Fig. 3a). Expansionary fiscal policies include increased government spending and/or decreased taxes. Increased government spending would directly raise aggregate demand, while lower taxes would stimulate consumption (and ultimately investment) through an increase in disposable income. If the federal budget is initially in balance, however, expansionary fiscal policy would also require deficit spending through an increase in government debt.

During inflation, when actual GNP exceeds potential GNP, neo-Keynesian theory calls for contractionary fiscal policies (Fig. 3b). Contractionary fiscal policies include decreased government spending and/or increased taxes. Decreased government spending would directly lower aggregate demand, while higher taxes would dampen consumption (and ultimately investment) through a decrease in disposable income. If the federal budget is initially in balance, contractionary fiscal policies may require the accumulation of a revenue surplus.

Government spending, taxing, and borrowing compose the basic discretionary fiscal policy tools of our nation. Under the mandate of the Employment Act of 1946 to "promote free competitive enterprise . . . the general welfare (and) maximum employment, production and purchasing power," Congress and the federal government have utilized these fiscal tools with increasing frequency. Since a majority of congressmen and presidents covet reelection, the fiscal actions most frequently taken have been increased government spending, tax cuts, and substantial borrowing with concomitant growth in the federal debt. While there have been some notable successes, primarily in the early 1960s, the overall performance of neo-Keynesian fiscal policy has been mixed. After a succession of prolonged periods of simultaneously high inflation and high unemployment (stagflation) during the 1970s, few economists would heartily echo President Nixon's assertion that "we are all Keynesians now."

Counter-Keynesians: The Monetarists

Since as long ago as the sixteenth century when Spanish imports of gold and silver from the New World caused inflation throughout Europe, economists have recognized that the supply of money is an important determinant of an economy's performance. Just how important, however, is a matter of considerable contention.

Monetary policy is defined as deliberate government actions taken to alter the money supply and/or interest rates. Today, most governments around the world consciously engage in some form of monetary policy. In the United States, monetary policy is primarily a function of the Federal Reserve System's Board of Governors and Open Market Committee. The Federal Reserve System (the Fed) is this nation's central bank, and member banks of the Fed comprise over 40% of all the nations's commercial banks and hold over 75% of all commercial bank deposits. The seven members of the Fed's Board of Governors are appointed by the president to 14-year terms and, in addition, one

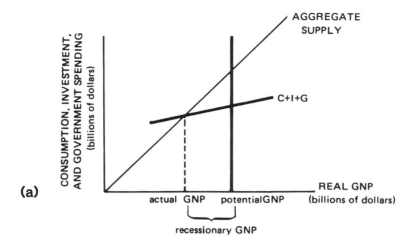

(a)

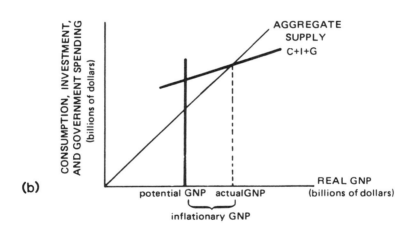

(b)

Figure 3   Recessionary and inflationary gaps.

member of the board is appointed by the president to a 4-year term as chairman. The board members also hold seats on the Open Market Committee, together with five presidents of the 12 district federal reserve banks. Given the length of their appointments, the board is able to formulate the nation's monetary policies unfettered, hypothetically, by the ever changing winds of politics.

The main monetary policy tools of the Fed are the required reserve ratio, the discount rate, and open market operations. The required reserve ratio is the minimum percentage of its deposit liabilities that each member bank of the Fed must keep on reserve. The required reserve protects the member banks against runs on deposits and, more importantly, from the perspectives of monetary policy, it constrains the banks' ability to "create money" by lending deposits to investors. An increase (decrease) in the required reserve ratio will cause a decrease (increase) in lending activity and deposits throughout the banking system and ultimately tends to cause the nation's money supply to fall (rise). Similarly, an increase (decrease) in the discount rate, the interest rate charged to member banks for loans from the federal reserve banks, will decrease (increase) lending activity, deposits, and, ultimately, the money supply. Finally, the Fed can impact the money supply through its open market activities. When the Fed sells (buys) U.S. government securities in the open market, banks' reserves and/or deposits will decrease (increase) by the purchase amount and the money supply will fall (rise).

Neo-Keynesians see monetary policy as a complement to fiscal policy and believe monetary policies should be continually adjusted in order to maintain the economy at potential GNP. Neo-Keynesians contend that changes in the money supply lead directly to changes in the interest rate and, all other things being equal, to changes in investment. During a recession, for example, easy money policy—an increase in the money supply— will reduce the interest rate, causing a rise in investment and therefore a rise in aggregate demand. Inflation is no threat according to the neo-Keynesian school. The decline in interest accompanying an "easy money" increase in the money supply will encourage people to hold larger real cash balances and thus will decrease the velocity at which money circulates through the economy. The decline in velocity will offset the increase in the money supply and prevent price inflation arising from "too many dollars chasing too few goods."

Neo-Keynesians would complement fiscal policies with discretionary monetary policies during recovery periods as well. In other words, the money supply would be reduced, causing the general rate of interest to rise, and choking off inflation, through declines in investment, aggregate demand, and actual GNP. Make no mistake, however, neo-Keynesian theory places monetary policy in a secondary role. To neo-Keynesians demand creates its own supply. Aggregate demand is the determinant of actual GNP. While investment is an important component of aggregate demand, changes in interest rates have but a minor impact compared with businessmen's expectations of profits. You can't "push on a string," claim neo-Keynesians, and they advocate expansionary fiscal policies as the most effective and least costly mechanism for maintaining full-employment GNP.

Monetarists, a school of economists lead by Nobel laureate Milton Friedman, view the world quite differently from the neo-Keynesians. To monetarists the national economy is inherently stable, and precarious swings in the business cycle, particularly since World War II, are primarily attributable to erratic changes in the nation's money supply. Monetarists contend that the velocity with which money circulates is rather stable, so that changes in the money supply translate directly into changes in the general level of prices. Neo-Keynesian-based budgetary policies have consequently not succeeded in maintaining full employment but they have produced stagflation (high inflation and high unemployment).

Under the influence of neo-Keynesian theory the Fed has concentrated upon controlling interest rates rather than the money supply. The Fed has failed, say monetarists, as roller coaster fluctuations in interest rates and prices evidence. Monetarists believe the real interest rate is determined by the market interaction of business investors and savers, and it is not significantly affected by changes in the money supply. Since interest represents compensation to savers for foregone consumption, the market interest rate will always contain an inflation premium as savers seek to avoid any decline in real compensation. An increase in the money supply leads to an increase in prices, inflation, and the market interest rate, while the real interest rate and real investment remain stable.

Although the higher prices accompanying increased inflation will initially stimulate private spending and investment as wages and profits appear to rise, households soon find real purchasing power declining and firms find real profits squeezed by rising costs. Economic stagnation then occurs, calling forth a host of expansionary neo-Keynesian fiscal policies.

Besides neo-Keynesian-encouraged utilization of discretionary policies, monetarists contend that expansionary fiscal policies have contributed to money supply and price instability. Borrowing from the private sector to finance deficit federal expenditures may reduce funds available for private investment and deter expansion in economic activity. Instead, the U.S. Treasury may sell bonds to the Fed in return for cash or credit based on an expansion of the money supply through increased printing of Federal Reserve notes. Since the late 1940s, federal budget deficits have, in fact, been continually accompanied by an increase in the Fed's holding of government securities. Growth in government spending has not been purely a matter of fiscal policy; the fiscal illusion of something for nothing has come at the expense of sound money supply management and price stability.

Despite the neo-Keynesian faith in an almost infinitely elastic real aggregate supply of goods and services, real output in the United States has grown almost 3% per annum over the past four decades. "Inflation is a monetary phenomenon," assert Friedman and Friedman (1980), adding, "there is no example in history of a substantial inflation that lasted for more than a brief time that was not accompanied by a roughly corresponding rapid increase in the quantity of money." The cure, according to Friedman, as well as other monetarists, is to abandon attempts to fine-tune the economy with discretionary monetary policies and direct the Fed to expand the money supply at a steady rate in accordance with real economic growth. In the long run, predict monetarists, the result will be minimization of inflation, dampening of the business cycle, and an end to the stagflation relationship.

Counter-Keynesians: The Public Choice View

Additional criticisms of neo-Keynesian policies have come from the public choice school of economists. Public choice economics focuses on collective decision making in nonmarket or political settings. Public choice theory leans heavily on pre-Keynesian economics and therefore gives considerable attention to issues of allocative (economic) efficiency and individual behavior in response to price and nonprice signals. James Buchanan, founder of the Center for Study of Public Choice, and Richard Wagner (1977) comment:

> A central confusion in the whole Keynesian argument [lies] in its failure to bring policy alternatives down to the level of choices confronted by individual citizens, or confronted for them by their political representatives, and, in turn, to predict the effects of these alternatives on the utilities of individuals.

As public choice proponents see it, rational politicians have little trouble accepting the neo-Keynesian call for using the federal budget as the primary tool for maintaining high employment and output. Rational politicians seeking to maximize votes are given only good news by neo-Keynesian economists. Not only could and should expenditures be increased without raising taxes, such deficit spending is for the good of the whole economy. "Easy budgets," especially during recessionary periods, represent sound financial and economic policy. If inflation threatens, the burden of raising interest rates could and should be shifted off the shoulders of the legislators and the back of the nonelected Federal Reserve System.

With the neo-Keynesian blank check in hand, it is no wonder, say public choice economists, that the past two decades has been characterized by increasing resort to deficit budgets and expansion of the public debt (particularly when state and local government debt is included). Putting aside the neo-Keynesian palliative that this debt is just something we owe to ourselves, debt financing allows the current generation of taxpayers to increase consumption at the expense of next generation taxpayers. Efficient use of resources requires citizens to simultaneously weigh the costs and benefits when making decisions concerning public sector goods and services. Debt financing separates costs from benefits in time and encourages increased allocation of resources to government. Rational politicians will continuously expand government programs that confer benefits on the special interest groups essential to their reelection, while costs are pushed into the future.

To the extent that government productivity falls short of private sector productivity, overallocation of resources to the public sector as a result of debt financing will decrease real economic growth. Combined with growth in the money supply due to both expansionary neo-Keynesian monetary policies and deficit financing through Federal Reserve purchases of government securities, falling productivity means inflation. Inflation confuses the allocation signals in the price system and compounds economic inefficiencies.

Inflation has toppled emperors in ancient Rome, kings and empires in Europe, and dictators in South America and Africa. Hyperinflation helped lead to communism in Russia and Nazism in Germany. Lord Keynes claimed there is no surer means of overturning the existing basis of society than to debauch the currency. Among its many consequences, inflation

- Increases the uncertainty and thereby the costs of market transactions
- Redistributes wealth arbitrarily from net debtors (such as government) to net creditors
- Reduces the balance of trade by decreasing exports and facilitating imports
- Encourages the transfer of resources from productive activities into inflation avoidance activities
- Decreases investment as businesspersons seek additional compensation for uncertainty related to price instability
- Arbitrarily "taxes" anyone on fixed incomes
- Creates net income transfers to government as progressive tax rate structures increase personal and corporate tax revenues faster than inflation

Most important, persistent government-bred inflation causes unemployment because, as Friedrich Hayek (1979) observed,

> employment does not depend on aggregate demand. Employment depends on resources being adjusted to the distribution of expenditures. So you cannot in the long run control employment by just spending more money. That leads in the short term only to a temporary misdirection of resources and remains effective only so long as you accelerate inflation—it is only when prices come in higher than expected that all the misdirected resources can still be employed where they are. But the allocation to profitable uses is postponed. As a consequence you have an ever-increasing backlog of misapplied resources—misapplied because the price system has not been allowed to operate as the guide to where these resources should be used.

In other words, full employment is not a goal that can be attained in the long run through applications of neo-Keynesian policies by rational politicians. As practiced, neo-Keynesian policies will disrupt interrelations among the components that make up the economic order, leading to increasing inefficiency in industry, culminating in higher unemployment, and more government interference.

Nor can the neo-Keynesians escape public choice criticism through resort to balanced budget increases in government spending. Neo-Keynesian theory contends that an increase in government spending financed by an equal-sized tax hike will raise actual GNP because citizens pay taxes out of both consumption funds and savings. The additional government spending will exceed the foregone private consumption by a multiplier of this foregone savings. Such a thesis, note public choice proponents, unfortunately fails to recognize that increases in the marginal tax rates on wages, dividends, and interest create disincentives for individuals to increase productivity, assume risk, invest, and engage in legal economic activities. Regarding the latter, estimates are that the underground or hidden economy in the United States presently is equivalent to at least 15% of the legally recorded GNP, with associated federal tax losses of at least $50 billion in 1979 (Joint Economic Committee, 1980).

As with the monetarists, the public choice advocates see no painless cure for years of neo-Keynesian indulgence. High unemployment must be endured over the short run in order to eliminate inflation-based distortion of price signals and to achieve an economically efficient reallocation of resources in the long run. This was, in fact, the policy pursued by the Reagan administration which brought on the 1981–1982 recession. Budgets are not made by angels but by ordinary politicians who are continously pressured to respond through spending to the demands of their individual constituencies. The neo-Keynesian "blank check" must be removed and government must concentrate once again on balancing its own budget rather than purportedly balancing the economy. Public choice economists favor the adoption of a constitutional amendment requiring a balanced federal budget except during periods of national emergency as declared by a two-thirds vote of each house in Congress. Such a constitutional rule would protect politicians from relentless constituency pressures. More important, the balanced budget rule would prevent shifting of the real costs of new programs onto future generations; the benefits of increased spending would have to be weighed against the full costs, and the neo-Keynesian illusion of "something for nothing" would be disposed.

BUDGET MODELS

Since 1930 the federal government has incurred budget deficits in fifty of the fiscal years. This performance, not unsurprisingly, has led to an ever increasing public debt. Such behavior invites a questioning whether the federal budget should be balanced frequently, occasionally, or not at all. Four models of a budget policies have been proposed: annually balanced budget, cyclically balanced budget, functional finance, and the full-employment balanced budget.

The annually balanced budget views the federal sector as similar to a household entity. Sustained spending on credit eventually brings ruin to the imprudent household. Likewise it is argued that monetizing yearly budget deficits will bring about ruinous inflation and destroy the nation's credit. The solution is a balanced budget.

Unfortunately, this budget model would accentuate business cycles instead of performing as a countercyclical tool. During recessionary periods, tax revenues would be falling and tax rates would have to be increased and/or spending reduced to bring the budget in balance. This would have the effect of further dampening consumption and investment, thus plunging a recession into a depression. In more fortunate economic times tax revenues would increase along with spending. This would impact aggregate demand to the extent of producing an inflationary spiral.

The cyclically balanced budget theoretically is the ideal government tool to impact the economy through changes in aggregate demand. During recessionary periods government deficit spending is practiced in order to bring aggregate demand toward full employment levels. When boom times occur, surpluses are accumulated to offset previous deficits and dampen aggregate demand in an attempt to escape an inflationary spiral.

However grand this budget model appears in theory, it has a serious shortcoming in practice. The business cycle is a recurrent phenomenon, though not periodic. The lessons of the past provide only a rough guide as to the length and amplitude of any given cycle. Thus it is impossible to forecast the length of the budget period and formulate a realistic taxing and expenditure program that would be in balance.

Functional finance views the budget as a nonentity. This model sees government as pursuing fiscal measures to effect full employment and economic growth while perpetuating a noninflationary environment. While political leaders might disagree with the characterization, the budget process has been following this logic for the past 50 years. The success of the application is in increasing doubt, given seemingly unmanageable inflationary conditions and the ever-growing federal debt.

The full-employment balanced budget is an attempt to formulate a cyclically balanced budget. Expenditure levels would be set based on merits of the public projects. Revenues to fund such expenditure levels would be derived by setting tax rates that would yield a surplus given full-employment conditions.

The countercyclical nature of the budget is theoretically irrefutable. During recessions, expenditures would enhance aggregate demand while tax rates would be low, a budget deficit being produced. During boom periods revenues would exceed expenditures, furnishing a surplus and dampening an inflationary aggregate demand.

Due to the fixed nature of this budget, full employment is not a theoretical certainty. In essence, the fiscal role of government follows a long-term plan and is not allowed to engage in discretionary fiscal policy. The countercyclical nature of this budget model, although apparent, may not operate at a magnitude necessary to "spend our way out of a recession" or curb hyperinflation.

DISAGGREGATE IMPACTS

Intergovernmental Aid

Discussion of fiscal and monetary policy naturally focuses on aggregate budgetary issues such as changes in the size of expenditures and revenues relative to national income. While such issues certainly have a bearing on macroeconomic performance, changes in the disaggregation of expenditures and revenues across budgetary line items also will effect macroeconomic performance and more particularly may alter the spatial variation of economic performance across the nation.

Aggregate statistics do not reveal that since the last world war there has been a significant fiscal shift within the public sector. Between 1950 and the present the number of federal employees per capita has declined by about 5%, while the state-local number has more than doubled. The level of state-local purchases has increased at compound rate of 9.7% per annum compared with 7.8% per annum for federal purchases. Since the mid

1960s state-local governments have assumed a major role in direct resource utilization by the public sector.

Certainly, intergovernmental aid trends must be an important explanatory factor of state-local government growth. As Table 2 indicates, despite decreases during the Reagan years intergovernmental aid has become a critical revenue source at both the state and local levels. From 19.8% of state and 38.6% of local own-source general revenues in 1940, intergovernmental aid became equal to 37.9% of state and 78.8% percent of local own-source general revenues in 1980, and under the Reagan administration declined to 32.4% and 61.5%, respectively, in 1987. While state aid to local government is nearly four times the amount of federal aid, the gap is closing. Between 1950 and 1970 state aid to locals increased 9.17% per annum as federal aid increased 13.4% per annum. From 1970 through 1980 the state aid growth rate climbed to an average rate of 12.2% while the federal aid rate was an astounding 30.3% per annum. During the 1980s the state aid growth rate moderated to 7.7% while federal aid actually decreased by 1.1% per annum.

Regardless of the macroeconomic policies pursued by the federal government, $120 billion of federal intergovernmental aid is certain to impact the locational efficiency of economic activity in the United States. There is a variety of sound reasons why federal grants might be given to noncentralized governments. First, a major source of state-local fiscal distress is the relatively income-inelastic structures of their tax systems. A "fiscal mismatch" arises as own-source property and sales tax revenues in slow-growth economic areas dwindle while demand for social services and economic development subsidies soars. Federal transfers from fiscally strong to fiscally weak jurisdictions may help equalize fiscal effort and ease fiscal distress. Second, the federal government may consider certain public services to be so essential that state-local provision is encouraged through grant subsidies. Third, jurisdictional boundaries often do not coincide with the spatial disbribution of benefit incidence from essential nonfederal public services. In the absence of federal subsidies a suboptimal quantity would be produced of any state-local public service characterized by significant benefit spillovers.

Theory and statistical evidence indicate that the form in which federal grants are given to state-local governments significantly alters the impact on the subsequent expenditures by those governments. Matching grants increase the recipient government's

Table 2. Intergovernmental Aid as a Percentage of Own-Source Revenues for State and Local Governments

	To states		To local governments	
Year	From federal government	From local governments	From federal government	From state governments
1987	30.1	2.2	7.7	53.8
1980	36.5	1.4	16.3	62.5
1970	33.5	1.7	5.1	52.4
1960	31.0	1.8	2.6	41.6
1950	25.7	1.7	2.6	44.0
1940	18.2	1.6	5.6	33.0

Source: U.S. Dept. of Commerce, Bureau of the Census, *Historical Statistics of the U.S. Colonial Times to 1970,* and *Governmental Finances,* series GF, Number 5, annual.

income while they simultaneously reduce the price of the target service relative to other public goods. Since nonmatching grants, such as revenue sharing, provide only an income effect, nonmatching grants stimulate less spending per grant dollar than matching grants. Although nonmatching grants do not call for as great a state-local spending effort as matching grants, nonmatching grant money seems to "stick where it hits." McGuire (1979) estimates, for example, that on the average $0.85 out of every nonmatching grant dollar is spent producing services while only $0.15 goes toward state-local tax relief.

Investment Programs

As Dupuit (1952) recognized in 1844, each fiscal act on the part of government amounts to some sort of redistribution, which leaves the affected parties in altered economic conditions. While Dupuit's concept is correct, a conventional treatment of fiscal impact analyses centers on examination of the effects of capital investment programs and income transfers. Investment programs receive attention due to the economic multiplier effects generated. Transfer programs provoke inquiry in that this activity represents an act on the part of government to alter the distributive shares stemming from the market system.

Investment outlays account for over one-fifth of total federal expenditures in 1989. Of an estimated $1137 billion budget for fiscal year 1989, approximately $282 billion was classified as funding for investment-type programs. Sample programs include the Department of Transportation, Federal Highway Administration ($13.7 billion); Education, Training and Employment Programs, including the Job Training Partnership Act ($26.7 billion); and Department of Housing and Urban Development, Community Development ($6.3 billion) (Budget of the United States, 1990, Office of Management and Budget).

Tools to Evaluate and Estimate Impacts

Investment programs produce primary and induced impacts. Primary impacts may be evaluated using cost-benefit models. Export base and input-output analyses are two models commonly used to estimate rippling effects through the economy.

Cost Benefit Analysis

Cost-benefit analysis takes on a variety of forms depending on the nature of the project. For example, the U.S. Army Corps of Engineers is charged with maintaining the nation's waterways. This entails improvements to harbors, such as building breakwaters and dredging. Impacts are evaluated using a benefit-cost model focusing on transport savings. Costs are taken as required budget outlays for initial and periodic improvements, while benefits relate to the cost savings enjoyed by carriers and shippers. This model implicitly assumes a competitive environment in which cost savings ultimately sift down to consumers.

Highway development uses capital and recurrent costs of improvement, which are identical to the Corps' evaluation framework. The benefit framework is expanded to include not only effects on vehicle operating costs, but to extending benefit estimates to consider values of travel time saved, accident avoidance, and noise avoidance.

Recreation investments have been evaluated by constructing demand curves from travel cost data. Travel costs borne by those at the recreation site serve as a proxy for an admission fee. As such, these participants are thought to value the recreational experience at least as much as travel costs incurred, which become the estimate of benefits.

Cost-benefit analysis is used as an evaluation tool. If all the relevant effects of investment programs can be placed in a common numeric (dollars), then the model may be employed to rank alternative investment opportunities on the basis of their net benefits.

Export-Base and Input-Output Analyses

Once an investment occurs, the economic impacts may be estimated using export-base multipliers or more elaborate input-output relationships. Using export-base logic, the initial investments from the federal level are viewed as an exogenous shock to the state and/or local economic system. Since in national income accounting a dollar invested by definition creates a dollar in income, this influx of funds creates increased consumption opportunities. The full impact of the initial investment is dependent on consumption propensities and the degree of self-sufficiency of the region. If the initial incomes totally circulate within the region, impacts are enhanced. Typically, consumption is partially directed at goods and services imported into the region, and thus income leakages occur, which dampen the multiplier effect.

Input-output analysis uses production requirements to estimate direct and indirect impacts from an initial investment. For example, an investment in highway development requires direct inputs from fabricated metals, transportation equipment, stone, clay, glass, etc. In turn these sectors have input requirements from primary metals, fabricated metals, and mining sectors. These rounds of inter-industry spending constitute the indirect economic effects. In addition, labor is used and paid by each of these industries. The economic impacts which result from workers subsequently spending their wages constitute induced economic effects. The greater the proportions of input requirements and consumer spending that are satisfied from sources within a region, the greater the final impact of an investment project upon that region's economy.

Export-base and input-output force an appreciation of the dramatic economic impacts stemming from public works programs. It should come as no surprise that the federal budgetary process is rife with logrolling in order to gain these economic plums for state and local constituencies.

Transfer Programs

Transfer programs constitute an intention by government to alter the distribution of income. This amounts to a recognition of market failure, where personal economic rewards may depend on such diverse factors as education and training, innate ability, health, family background, racial group, religion, and, as Jencks et al. (1979) contend, just plain luck.

Moreover, a free labor market system discourages equality of results. Equality would imply that each economic unit's marginal product was equal. Given the differences in the above-cited factors, anticipated equal outcomes is not a reasonable expectation. Attempts at redressing imperfections stemming from the market take the form of transfer programs.

Social welfare expenditures were approximately $500 billion for 1987. The largest segment of this amount came from programs administered through the Social Security Administration, particularly Medicare ($288.5 billion) and Medicaid ($27.6 billion). Direct-income transfers were affected through Food Stamps ($12.4 billion), housing assistance ($11.1 billion), Supplemental Security Income (SSI) ($10.8 billion), and Aid to Families with Dependent Children (AFDC) ($7.4 billion) (U.S. Social Security Administration, 1989).

The impacts of direct-transfer programs form a contentious area. One line of argument focuses on the dulling of incentives because of redistribution. First, recipients are discouraged from productive pursuits due to government-guaranteed subsistence. Second, taxpayers funding such programs may perceive leisure as more attractive than work, at the margin, since increased transfer payments may require increased tax revenues. Over time, it is contended, the goal of distribution supersedes the goal of productivity, with the result that a shrinking pie permits less and less to be divided.

Another viewpoint sees the market system as filled with imperfections. Rewards are seen as being based on chance, family background, sex, etc., and surely not on competitive forces providing for efficient economic outcomes. Thus direct transfers act to redress the consequences wrought by an imperfect system. The inequitable distribution of income is made more equitable.

The macroimpacts stemming from redistribution are varied and to some extent indeterminate in regard to the direction of the change. The act of a transfer requires redistribution where such redistribution affects interpersonal consumption habits. Those parties taxed to accommodate the transfer probably would have spent the funds on a different basket of goods and services than the poorer recipients of the transfer. This difference in demand articulation poses effects on the entire supply network, ranging from breakfast-cereal producers to pleasure-boat manufacturers. As might be expected, certain sectors benefit from increased demand while others suffer.

Redistribution has a negative impact on savings. Those taxed have the financial capacity to engage in saving reduced. Recipients must, in some cases, use entire incomes for the necessities of life. Saving, in and of itself, is somewhat uninteresting. However, the stock of savings provides investment funds. Thus, if all income goes toward consumption in the present, no surplus is allowed to accumulate. This being the case, no new or replacement investment is allowed to occur and eventually the capital stock and productive capacity of the nation deteriorate.

IMPACTS BEYOND THE ECONOMIC

Testimony by M. Harvey Brenner (1979) before the Joint Economic Committee, Congress of the United States, places the issue of impacts in a perspective transcending the economic. Brenner's research has focused on time series: correlating mortality, selected pathological indices of cardiovascular disease, cirrhosis, suicide rate, homicide rate, imprisonment rate, and mental hospital admission rate to national economic indices of per capita income, unemployment rate, and inflation rate. His findings indicate that abrupt economic changes are stress provoking, with undesirable changes such as unemployment and income loss substantially more generative of pathology.

With respect to families, it is apparent that a change in family structure can reduce (divorce, separation, death of a wage earner, out of wedlock birth) or increase (remarriage) the economic well-being of persons in a family. Causation does, however, flow in the opposite direction—that is, changes in economic conditions, particularly labor market conditions, can cause changes in family structure. Families in which the husband encountered employment problems are more likely to experience separation and divorce, and children of unemployed fathers are three times as likely to be abused as children of employed fathers (Schiller, 1989).

The magnitude of the federal budget ($1.3 trillion, 1990 estimate), together with state and local government budgets, has significant effects on income and employment. A budget promoting allocative efficiency and economic stabilization simultaneously promotes income gains and a move toward full employment. An ideal budget would enhance incentives to production, aid development of capital and capital spending, and reward employment-generating enterprise, while effecting transfers that, while not dulling incentives, provide for the economically deprived. This budget would presumably be the work of angels, not political office holders.

REFERENCES

Bell, M., and Gabler, R. L. (1976). Government growth: An intergovernmental concern. *Intergovernmental Perspectives*. 4:9.

Brenner, H. M. (1979). Influence of the Social Environment on Psychopathology: The Historic Perspective. Submitted as a Prepared Statement Before the Joint Economic Committee, Congress of the United States, Washington, D.C.

Buchanan, J. M., and Wagner, R. E. (1977). *Democracy in Deficit: The Political Legacy of Lord Keynes*. Academic, New York, p. 34.

Burkhead, J. (1965). *Government Budgeting*. John Wiley & Sons, New York, pp. 59–60.

Friedman, M., and Friedman, R. (1980). *Free to Choose*. Harcourt Brace Jovanovich, New York, pp. 254–255.

Hayek, F. A. (1979). As quoted in Lawrence Minard, Wave of the Past? Or Wave of the Future? *Forbes* 10:49.

Joint Economic Committee (1980). *Hearings on the Underground Economy*. Government Printing Office, Washington, D.C.

Keynes, J. M. (1920). *The Economic Consequences of the Peace*. Harcourt Brace Jovanovich, New York, p. 236.

McGuire, M. C. (1979). The analysis of federal grants into price and income components. In *Fiscal Federalism and Grants-in-aid*, P. Mieszkowski and W. H. Oakland (Eds.). The Urban Institute, Washington, D.C.

Musgrave, R. A., and Musgrave, P. B. (1978). *Public Finance in Theory and Practice*. McGraw-Hill, New York, p. 132.

Office of Management and Budget, Executive Office of the President (1988). *The Budget of the United States Government, Fiscal Year 1989*. Government Printing Office, Washington, D.C.

Schiller, B. R. (1989). *The Economics of Poverty and Discrimination*. Prentice-Hall, Englewood Cliffs, New Jersey, p. 50.

Smith, A. (1976). *An Inquiry Into the Nature and Causes of the Wealth of Nations*, Book V. University of Chicago Press, p. 244.

Stern, I. (1975). Industry effects of government expenditures, U.S. Department of Commerce, Bureau of Economic Analysis. In *Survey of Current Business* 55:5.

ADDITIONAL READINGS

Clawson, M., and Knetsch, J. (1966). *Economics of Outdoor Recreation*. Johns Hopkins University Press, Baltimore.

Dupuit, J. (1952). On the measurement of the utility of public works. In the English translation, *International Economic Papers* 2:83–110.

Heggie, I. G. (1972). *Transport Engineering Economics*. McGraw-Hill, London.

Jencks, C., Bartlett, S., et al. (179). *Who Gets Ahead?: The Determinants of Economic Success in America*. Basic Books, New York.

Keynes, J. M. (1936). *The General Theory of Employment, Interest and Money*, 1964 Ed. Harcourt, Brace and World, New York.

Musgrave, R. A., and Musgrave, P. B. (1989). *Public Finance in Theory and Practice, 5th Ed.*, McGraw-Hill, New York.

Water Resources Council (1979). Procedures for Evaluation of national Economic Development (NED) Benefits and Costs in Water Resources Planning (Level C); Final Rule. Washington D. C., *Federal Register 44, 242*.

17

Capital Investment and Budgeting

Gerald J. Miller   *Department of Public Administration, Rutgers University, Newark, New Jersey*

Capital investment drives all other financial management decisions in a public organization. Capital investments drive the operating budget because it is these investments that prompt the hiring of employees and the scheduling of maintenance and other routine expenditures (Crecine, 1969). Capital investments drive productivity in that purchases of equipment and facilities become the primary source for improvements in efficiency and effectiveness (Swiss, 1991). Capital investments determine the direction community development or redevelopment will take, and they set the balance among forces in maintaining the economic base. Investments also create a community's competitive position among rival residential and industrial locations, affecting future growth in governmental revenues (Schneider, 1989; Pagano and Moore, 1985). Indeed, the controversies engendered by capital investment decisions go far in shaping what communities will be (Adams, 1988).

SIGNIFICANCE OF THIS STUDY

This study seeks to fill a void. Capital investment and budgeting suffer from neglect, researchers now realize, despite nearly five decades of concern nationwide with the physical structure, the built environment, of communities. As one researcher put it (Adams, 1988, p. 6),

> For all the concern about the infrastructure problem that is now being expressed by policy makers and policy analysts, little that has been written moves beyond surveying the deteriorating conditions of public facilities and calling for more public investment. We have little information about how public officials go about making investment decisions, and even less about how their decisions affect their communities.

The lack of knowledge exists in all aspects of capital investment and budgetary decision making, leading us in this chapter to try to outline what we know as well as to pose questions suitable to finding answers to those things we do not know.

CAPITAL INVESTMENT AS STRATEGY

A systematic guide to capital investment eludes researchers and official decision makers alike because there seem to be at least three contradictory explanations for the decisions that should or could be made. The first characterizes investment as the measured, *planned* response to the goals of the organization and community. The second reveals capital decisions as the community's *reaction* to what private markets demand or to what rival locations threaten. The third suggests that capital investments are *opportunistic,* that is, necessarily, nearly random and unrelated to a given purpose. Thus, while we seek to outline what we know and what we do not know about capital investment, we face the three opposed views of choice from the very start.

In all three, however, there are strategic elements, and we may overcome contradiction by viewing capital investments as *strategic* decisions that top managers and elected decision makers must make. Ordinarily, we would use strategy in defining the organization's method of coping with the future through various devices—frameworks, techniques, and plans—either to bend the course of future events to their advantage, to eliminate competitive threats to organization survival, or to exploit opportunities for increasing organization wealth and security.

Instead of speaking in terms of an *organization,* however, we often refer to the focus of strategy as the *public interest,* whether the interest is that of the citizenry in a locality, in a state, or in the nation as a whole. Planning the future, eliminating competitive threats, or exploiting opportunities for the public interest—the community—emerges as strategy and as the focus of capital investments.

Let us illustrate the strategic nature of planned, reactive, and opportunistic capital investments. First, planning incorporates community interests in such a way that a strategic vision of the future comprehends all points of view. This strategic vision becomes the future, almost as a self-fulfilling prophecy, in the form of infrastructure projects and programs that are put in place to anticipate and guide change. Yet those spearheading the consensual forces and those whose analyses inform it sway the process in their own interests.

The second, reactive, explanation for investment is a strategy of responding to rival communities and deterring their triumph at one's own expense. Such strategies for investment involve creating a mix of community enhancements that turn one's own disadvantages to advantages. For instance, communities without industry create outstanding school systems to entice families to live in what then becomes an even more attractive bedroom community. Such communities also become irresistible to services industries at such time as the community decides to diversify, using its highly educated residential population as a labor force attraction.

The final method is that related to opportunism, each investment exploit of which is only coincidentally related to any other. Individual interests, by implication, get wedded to each other and are rationalized in retrospect.

Each of these types of capital investment strategies has an internal logic of its own, and these logics[1] may be called linear, nonlinear, and opportunistic logics, respectively.

Linear Logic

If those who have reviewed large bodies of research could erect a monumental image of strategic management, they would create optimization. Strategy, as such, follows a "linear" logic in which plans precede action. This variation appears to dominate thinking in strategy, since the major review of work in not-for-profit organizations (Wortman,

[1]"Think of a logic as simply a line of argument that is shaped around several basic ideas or principles" (Gilbert et al., 1988, p. 5).

1979) and a set of pictures of its use in organizations outside business (Bryson and Roering, 1988) echo linear logic by characterizing what they find studied and practiced as synopticism rather than as competition or a forceful search for advantage (MacMillan, 1978, 1983; Freeman, 1984; Zald, 1970).

Nonlinear Logic

Ironically, just as many tout optimization, the private sector gives heed to strategy's ancient meaning. Popular business organization writers often define strategic effort as instilling organization loyalty and parrying threat (Neuhauser, 1988). This "tribal warrior" concept (Ramsey, 1987) conforms to what is meant by the Greek verb *stratego*, "to plan the destruction of one's enemies through effective use of resources" (O'Toole, 1985; Evered, 1983). The reference has also been reversed. Even Clausewitz (1956, p. 121) argues that "it would be better, instead of comparing [War] with any Art, to liken it to business competition, which is also a conflict of human interests and activities. . . ."

The military operation connotation comes from Luttwak (1987; Summers, 1987), one of the modern teachers on strategy in war who conceptualizes the logic of strategy as paradox. He contrasts the logic of strategy with linear logic. Linear logic, military style, follows the Latin dictum *si vis pacem, para pacem*, or "if you want peace, prepare for peace." In actuality, war follows a paradoxical logic: *si vis pacem, para bellum*, or "if you want peace, prepare for war."

According to Luttwak (p. 4), "In war deterrence is all. . . . To be ready to attack is evidence of peaceful intent, but to prepare defenses is aggressive or at least provocative."

Strategy in war is the reversal of opposites. Luttwak continues,

> [On the battlefield] a bad road can be good precisely because it is bad and may therefore be less strongly held or even left unguarded by the enemy. . . . a paradoxical preference for inconvenient times and directions, preparations visibly and deliberately left incomplete, approaches seemingly too dangerous for combat at night and in bad weather, is a common aspect of tactical ingenuity.

If private sector strategists resemble ancient and modern military ones, they see strategy as nonlinear in its logic and use deception and paradox (e.g., Quinn and Cameron, 1988).

Opportunism

Beyond apparently linear logic in the public sector and the nonlinear logic of the private sector, one other exists in Wildavsky's "strategy" for budgeters (1988). His budgetary person is more opportunistic, following neither linear nor nonlinear logic. As if constructing a redoubt, the budgeter builds confidence, finds allies, and shows results. Events occur as if they were assaults on the budgetary base; electoral defeat of mentors in Congress, economic catastrophe for programs or revenues, and changes of allies with issues force ever more ingenious defenses. These same types of events—electoral selection (like natural selection), economic change, or issue mutation—provide opportunities that can be exploited (Wildavsky, 1988, pp. 100–119).

This form of strategy resembles the emergent strategy that many have found most appropriate for or characteristic of public sector managers. That is, "the function of emergent strategies would seem to be most compatible with the adhocracy configuration, in which many people—operating personnel, experts and advisors of all kinds, managers at all levels—are potentially involved in the establishment of precedents and, so, the strategies" (Mintzberg and McHugh, 1985, p. 162). To Ring and Perry (1985, p. 282), the point is imperative:

> Given previous arguments regarding policy ambiguity, open and intense influence processes and coalition instability, public organizations can be characterized as low on deliberate strategy and high on emergent and unrealized strategy. If this characterization is correct, any manager who is unable, for instance, to relinquish intended strategies in order to pursue emergent strategies is likely to fail.

Something more complex than linear and nonlinear logics—opportunism perhaps—must be used in describing public sector strategy.

Complex, Serial Combinations of "Logics"

Despite reviews and popular writing, research indicates additional, far more complex, combinations of concepts in the actual, observed use of strategy. Consider the work by Alfred Chandler (1962). In a survey of American business history, from the canals, to the railroads, on into the industrial revolution and to modern-day developments, he posed the theory that the structure of modern organization emerges from the strategy the business pursues as it defines and capitalizes on opportunities. The pattern of industry development was (1) accumulation of resources, (2) rationalization of the use of those resources, (3) expansion into markets to accumulate more, and (4) "re-rationalization" of the use of these resources and on and on *ad infinitum*. Thus, strategy—often horizontal mergers to accumulate, vertical mergers to rationalize, for example—led to structure; in this case, he hypothesized structural decentralization followed by centralization.

In the next three major sections, we focus attention on capital investment strategies that follow the three logics. In the first, we concentrate on the capital programming approach, one incorporating cost-benefit analysis and following the linear logic. The second section takes up nonlinear strategies in which competition and, to some extent, deterrence take hold. In the third section, we illustrate cases of investments that follow an opportunistic logic. Finally, we reflect on situations in which the three logics may exist in some serial fashion.

THE PLANNING OR LINEAR APPROACH TO STRATEGIC CAPITAL PROJECT CHOICES

Decisions involving what capital investments to make, when to make them, and how much to spend on them create great conflict. For reducing conflict, reformers—planners—plot and follow what amounts to a linear strategy. Recall that a linear strategy is one in which plans precede action. In this section, we explore linear strategy implied in capital programming and the other procedures involved in reformed capital budgeting,[2] with detailed attention given linear strategy's primary tool, the process of cost-benefit analysis. The programming approach, in following a linear logic, is based on optimization of resources; therefore, we end the section with a discussion of this logic and its assumptions.

[2]Many textbook accounts will parallel the discussion here; however, this section rests on the fine presentations in Vogt (1975, 1977) as well as those in Wacht (1987) and Gordon and Pinches (1984). See also Moak and Killian (1964), Steiss (1975), and the references in Bozeman (1984).

Background

Beginning with the Burnham plan of the City of Chicago, modern city planning has connected the city plan with the capital budget through capital improvements programming—CIP (Schultz, 1989; Scott, 1969). The city plan is a guide to the physical development of a jurisdiction. It is long range, covering a period longer than a year, and the plan is comprehensive. The entire geographical area comes within the plan's purview, and the plan includes transportation, housing, land use, utility systems and recreation elements, attempting to interrelate them in a meaningful way. A *capital project,* or capital improvement project, is any major nonrecurring expenditure or any expenditure for physical facilities. A *capital improvements program* (CIP) is a schedule of capital improvement projects for several years, showing estimated costs and sources of financing. The most commonly used period for a CIP is the period used for comprehensive land use planning with plans of varying generality from 5 to 20 years. A *capital budget* is a list of projects in the CIP, along with costs and financing sources. *Capital budgeting* refers to the whole process of analyses and decisions involved in moving from capital projects to a CIP to a capital budget. Often the first year of capital budget is included in the capital improvements section of the annual operating budget for the upcoming fiscal year.

According to an authoritative survey (Beal and Hollander, 1979), the plan and capital improvements relate in three ways. First, the plan may act as a growth management tool and the CIP may be the yoke for development. For example, development permits may await the completion of infrastructure projects.

Second, the planning function may be made to relate internally to finance by organization means. Urban planning and financial planning are often organized as a single department.

Third, subdivision regulation forces allocation of costs of public facilities between homeowner and government. Developers are required to install some facilities before the city government accepts responsibility for the development through extension of services.

Justification

The need for capital budgeting rests on the accepted fact that public funds are limited. Almost without question, available financial resources fall short of the amount needed to fund what decision makers believe is necessary to cope with all future events. Priority setting being a necessity, the capital program and budget offer an approach that is valued for its perceived rationality.

That is, capital budgeting isolates, for analysis and priority setting, the costly and nonrecurring expenditures from which the community receives long-lived benefits. More specifically, capital budgeting provides a systematic way to prevent unplanned project needs; avoid project duplication; coordinate projects; provide time for technical project design; allow orderly project acquisition; establish priorities; and formulate long-range financial plans. For example (Vogt, 1977), a new park might require land purchase, site development, and new facility construction over several years before the park is open to the public. The benefits of the new park could last for decades or centuries. To pay for the park in 1 year could be too costly, much less failing to recognize the intergenerational benefits, which might suggest that the park be paid for over many years. Therefore, the park is a prime capital project, which, through the CIP and later the capital budget, receives the study needed to manage the project systematically, efficiently, and equitably.

Thus, according to Vogt (1977), the capital improvement program exists for reasons that suit managers. First, because of size and durability, capital projects have a permanent impact on the community, suggesting the need for careful planning. A multiyear capital program provides time for such long-term planning. Second, the nature and permanence of capital projects usually require special expertise at each stage of management, again necessitating a multiyear planning process. Third, it is much easier to reverse an operating decision once made than to eliminate a capital project once finished. Mistakes are more costly and long lasting; a multiyear programming period allows details to be worked out and decisions reviewed several times before actually constructing the project. Fourth, because capital expenditures are generally easier to postpone than operating costs, a mechanism to restore this imbalance is needed. A capital program provides the high profile that enables managers to assert the equally important capital investment expenditure. Fifth, capital costs tend not to be constant from year to year. A capital programming approach helps to level the peaks and valleys of capital expenditures.

Planning the Capital Program

The capital program emerges from the overall plan and planning policies of the community. Ideally, capital projects fulfill long-term operating objectives, and exist as part of an overall plan for service delivery, economic growth, community betterment, or even redistribution of wealth.[3] Within already accepted and well-developed policy directives, general plans, and centralized coordination, capital projects implement land use plans and policies and comply with projected population densities and commercial or industrial uses.

[3]The overall plan, as well as the capital budget, represents communitywide interests. That is, capital programming is a complicated process whose outcomes have far-reaching impacts, not only for the departments involved, but for the community as a whole. The process produces considerable involvement from various actors trying to influence capital programming. Following Vogt (1977) and Moak and Hillhouse (1975), the actors should include department heads, central budget staff and chief administrative officer, the governing body, and the taxpayers as a whole.

Estimating capital requirements generally begins with a call from the central budget staff for estimates and by distributing forms. The estimates may be developed under various instructions. The central authority may or may not place a ceiling on the departmental requests. A ceiling forces the department to realistically set priorities for projects and makes the budget staff's work easier. On the other hand, such an approach tends to stifle imagination and innovation through the initial negative approach of an estimated ceiling. The establishment of a ceiling inhibits the department in transmitting overall capital needs, which may heighten awareness at central levels within the organization.

Capital budget requests generally originate with department heads or their staff. At this level, review of the budget is fairly parochial. Department heads have a unique view of the organization in that their view will be from the prospective of their departmental expertise. There will be a tendency to think of these projects as the most important and projects of other departments as less important.

Capital projects are also often submitted with no expenditure ceiling specified. Consequently, more projects are submitted than can be funded. Prioritization is necessary to achieve the required cutbacks.

Prioritization is frequently achieved by scheduling. Scheduling helps alleviate waste by insuring construction of facilities required initially, that is, before primary construction. For example, sewers will be scheduled for construction prior to building a street so that it will not be necessary to cut new pavement during sewer construction.

A danger of prioritization by scheduling is that rarely are projects completely eliminated. More often they are postponed and placed further down the schedule. As projects stay on the schedule for several years there can be a maturation effect; they may become bona fide projects with funding, even though they logically do not have a high priority.

Prioritization requires review to insure that the project relates to the overall goals and policies of the jurisdiction. "Projects must be weighed in light of their contribution to programs which, in themselves, are not of equal rank. We emphasize that the project contribution-to-the-program approach, rather than the departmental or functional approach, should dominate thinking" at this level, say Moak and Hillhouse (1975: p. 200).

A key element of strong capital programming and the one element most often missing is a strong central budget authority. A strong central budget authority in this context not only monitors and reviews the budget, but also coordinates the overall planning process. This requires strong centralized planning and well-articulated organizational policies. Utilizing planning tools, such as cost-benefit analysis, a strong central budget authority can balance one type of project against another to achieve the overall plans, goals, and priorities of the community. With a strong central coordinating body and centralized planning, it is impossible to evaluate objectively the need for a new water treatment plant versus the need for a new arterial thoroughfare or a new park. Each of these projects is so different that without central planning they cannot be compared to each other.

A central budget authority promotes a *trickle-down* effect rather than a *percolate-up* type budget. The trickle-down budget relies on major policy and program decisions made at a centralized level with department heads asked to submit specific budget proposals in support of these policy decisions. A percolate-up budget, on the other hand, utilizes recommendations formulated by the operating agencies and forwarded to a centralized budget staff. The budget staff has to pick and choose among the various alternatives, which lack a central theme.

The central executive must act as adjudicator between the various department heads and the central budget authority. He or she makes sure the budget as submitted reflects his or her own understanding of policy directives and objectively judges the adequacy of the various proposals and their contribution to the overall mission of the organization. The chief executive must insure proper decisions among competing priorities and that the programs submitted are properly integrated into the overall function of the organization. Objectivity is necessary to formulate good, sound recommendations but is often impaired by anticipated political responses. The desire for a good "batting average," unfortunately, may outweigh the staff's special responsibility to bring objectivity to the process.

The role of the governing body is to set policy. The legislators must judge the capital budget and its consistency with their policies. At this level, objectivity often breaks down due to the politically expedient or pet project that one or more legislators may be supporting, not necessarily because of its overall importance, but because of a localized importance, especially if ward policies are involved.

The legislative body should hold public hearings to obtain citizen input on the various proposals. However, according to authorities on the matter (Moak and Hillhouse, 1975, p. 112),

> the legislative body should not be brought into the capital programming process prior to completion of the executive budget. Compromises in this direction tend to invite persistent legislative attempts to influence decisions all along the way with a resultant in the weakening of the executive's responsibility for budget formulation. Since they have the final decision, legislators should wait for the legislative review stage, at which point their voices will be heard.

The legislature's function is to establish the upper level of capital outlays consistent with overall fiscal policy. The legislature resolves conflicts that might exist between an expert's view and those of laypersons. Legislators also assess opposing viewpoints of citizens and citizens groups and furnish political leadership on major investments and capital decisions.

The citizens and taxpayers at large are also actors in this process. They view the capital budget as an important investment of their tax dollar and want personally some of the benefits of such investment. They will push for one particular project or another, which may or may not have a priority in the context of the overall plan but which is nevertheless important to the individual citizen or group. Pressure is frequently exerted by these individuals or groups.

Project Selection and Scheduling with Cost-Benefit Analysis

The selection of projects rests on analysis, and the analysis usually follows an investment theory. A primary project selection method advanced by economists and endorsed by professional managers[4] is one utilizing cost-benefit comparisons with projects having the best return on investment being funded. Generally, these comparisons are made on the basis of two calculations, net present value (NPV) and/or internal rate of return (IRR), the subjects of this section.

Rationale and Method of Cost-Benefit Analysis

One of the reasons a government exists is to act as agency of last resort. Government usually gets asked to do those things everyone else is either unwilling or unable to do. Formally, therefore, one of the major concerns of government policymakers has to do with compensating for what markets fail to provide or which markets leave as a consequence of what they do provide. For the purpose of description here, we call government action to remedy market failures, the provision of public goods. This chapter describes the way governments make choices in coping with market failure. First, we reintroduce the fiscal allocation role of government and briefly explain how governments fulfill it. Second, we explain how market failure occurs. Third, we discuss the decision-making process that is used to determine the proper amounts of public goods that should be produced by governments. Finally, we discuss the relatively new concept of "nonmarket failures" and the contributions of economic reasoning to the financial management of government agencies.

Fiscal Functions of Government

Regardless of the forces government fiscal policies are meant to loosen or harness in the name of "doing those things no one else will do," there are certain goods that few will produce—often leaving it to government to provide some things everyone needs. For instance, national defense, the classic case, is a commodity that is too expensive, too complicated, and, in general, too hazardous to society to leave for each citizen to provide for him or herself.

The last reason—hazardous—may be the most important reason for not having an "every-man-for-himself" situation. That is, if everyone had the responsibility to look out for herself, we would have lost the very reason for having a nation in the first place, the acknowledgment that we are one and want to act together to protect and further our collective interest.

In any case, we find government as provider of last resort when "market failure" occurs. Market failure strikes when the normal processes of the giant auction we call the economy does not work efficiently, specifically when rationing is either not feasible or not desirable (Stiglitz, 1988; Musgrave and Musgrave, 1980).

Rationing is not feasible when no one can be excluded from use of a product or service. Fire services to a complex of abutting apartments may not be feasible since containing a fire in one gives benefits to all. Since no one is excluded, all except the one who pays become free riders. No price system for rationing makes sense.

[4]The authoritative guide to local capital budgeting is the so-called "green book" (Aronson and Schwartz, 1987). Written by economists, its discussion of capital budgeting is completely given over to a discussion of cost-benefit analysis.

Rationing may also be undesirable, even though feasible. For instance, an uncrowded bridge could be paid for with a toll device forcing drivers to pay as they entered. Because the bridge is uncrowded, the toll may actually decrease traffic, however.

In both cases, rationing through normal market mechanisms does not work as it would otherwise. Other methods must be used to decide allocation: how much each apartment dweller should pay for fire protection and how big a bridge to build.

Government's allocation functions relate to the provision of public goods. Generally, the problem is to decide how much and what type of public goods to provide. Decision makers need some sort of mechanism for deciding these questions, and, luckily, they have not just one but three mechanisms: the Pareto criterion (Pareto, 1906), the Kaldor criterion (Kaldor, 1939), and the mechanism in place that allows us to invoke these criteria.

Pareto Criterion

Named after the nineteenth century economist, the criterion guides selection of a policy by favoring those in which at least one person is better off and no person is worse off as a result of the policy.

What policies have such an unambiguous goodness attached to them? Education might, but some suffer lost earnings from going to school that they will never recoup. What about water and air quality? There are sunk costs in pollution that we could say one would suffer loss in remedying.

Kaldor Criterion

A second method of dealing with welfare is slightly less demanding: Should we not accept a policy if those in the community benefiting from the policy compensate those who lose by the policy, especially if the winners or beneficiaries still have some gain left over?

Consider this example. If the strict private goods only requirement were not relaxed (libertarianism), we would never get such goods as pristine ocean beaches. One finds it extremely difficult to slice up pieces of the ocean in order to allocate maintenance responsibilities to protect the beach. Moreover, nature's ways in forcing erosion and so on would make such coercion folly. Will one person maintain the beaches? Not by the table of benefits, especially when those benefits are held down by the inability to divide the resource or exclude others from its use.

But should the beaches be maintained? If costs equal the expense of maintaining the beaches and benefits equal the sum of everyone's perception of betterment, common sense would tell us yes. For example, in the following illustration, what would the Pareto criterion tell us if the cost were shared equally by all individuals?

Individual	Benefit	Cost	Condition
A	$ 3000	$ 2000	Better off
B	$ 3500	$ 2000	Better off
C	$ 2000	$ 2000	No worse off
D	$ 3000	$ 2000	Better off
E	$ 2500	$ 2000	Better off
Total	$14000	$10000	

The Pareto criterion—at least one is better off and no one is worse off as a result of a public program—supports a program, in which costs are shared equally, of $10,000. As the illustration above shows, that program would make no one worse off—even C—and at least one person, and in this case A, B, and E, would be better off. A $10,000 program passes muster.

The $10,000 program, however, provides greater benefits to some than to others (see the table below). The surpluses range from $1500 for B to $500 for E.

Individual	Benefit	Cost	Surplus
A	$ 3000	$2000	$1000
B	$ 3500	$2000	$1500
C	$ 2000	$2000	0
D	$ 3000	$2000	$1000
E	$ 2500	$2000	$ 500
Total	$14000	$9000	

We might say that the $10,000 version of beach cleanup is less equitable than it is efficient. Defining productivity as a balance between equity and efficiency, we want to find the program that would achieve both. The Kaldor criterion is meant to suggest a way to find that program.

Recall the Kaldor criterion provides for winners compensating losers in a given situation. Without assuming any losers, however, we can still create a Kaldor-like result, as the situation below suggests. To ensure that the winners bore their fair share of the costs and still stood to reap some gain, the maximum project would have to be $13,999. We can compute this amount by distributing the costs in the same way as the original surpluses so that one person gains $1 of surplus while all others have benefits that equal their costs.

Individual	Benefit	Cost	Surplus
A	$ 3000	$ 2999	$1
B	$ 3500	$ 3500	0
C	$ 2000	$ 2000	0
D	$ 3000	$ 4000	0
E	$ 2500	$ 2500	0
Total	$14000	$13999	$1

This distribution of costs and benefits underlies the progressive tax structure and redistribution of income programs that guided the construction and maintenance of the American version of the welfare state for some 50 or more years. More to the point of this chapter, however, the Kaldor criterion underlies the measurement of productivity and, especially, cost-benefit analysis. Cost-benefit analysis, like the Kaldor criterion, argues that as long as the benefits exceed the costs of a project, the project should go forward.

Voting

The problem with cost-benefit analysis and with the Kaldor criterion is the determination of benefit. In a country that values individualism and decentralized decision making, we assume that each person can value a policy alone. The sum of those values becomes the public welfare. However, that makes it difficult to calculate individual benefits. Instead, the political system, and specifically the voting system, takes care of that.

But what vote should be required? Unanimity, majority rule, three-fourths, two-thirds, plurality? The answer lies in the analysis of voting by legislative bodies. Following Buchanan and Tullock (1962), the analysis falls on the interaction of two variables: (1) the loss of value that occurs when we do not include in any decision each individual's calculation of his or her own benefit that would result from the implementation of a given project and (2) the cost of making an effort to ascertain each individual's preference.

As an alternative to the price system as a method of determining what and how much of a public good to produce, voting applies in finding the expected cost to the individual and to the group or public, which the individual alone can calculate, of implementing a public project. How much effort to exert in finding these individual preferences, or, specifically, in determining when we can feel sure we have solicited the opinions of enough people and when enough people desire a project to warrant its implementation, constitutes the basis of voting analysis.

Voting analysis demands that we know individuals' preferences toward a project. Obviously, 100% voting participation resulting in a consensus decision on the project would guide decision makers in making a valid decision. The first variable in voting analysis, therefore, is the probability of violating the Pareto criterion as we depart from unanimous consent. Such a problem occurs in sampling as well as in choosing majority rule over consensus.

Nevertheless, gaining unanimity has drawbacks, not the least of which is the cost entailed in cajoling participation and informing voting. The counterbalance to total participation and consensus is the cost that both would entail. The more closely we near total participation and consensus in voting, the higher the cost of the voting process. The lower the cost of the voting process, the less likely we will have valid facsimiles of the voters' preferences; that is, majority votes of whatever number of voters may not be valid expressions of the total population's preferences even though such an election may cost less than any method we could use to secure unanimity.

Obviously, the appropriate system of voting involves trading off the cost of exclusion against the cost of the election, a calculation easier than it looks. We seldom have single issues in which individuals have two choices and perfect information about them both. Rather, we have a continuous stream of issues about which individuals have varying levels of intensity of preferences.

It can be shown through studies of public opinion that our knowledge of and attention paid to issues faced by members of Congress is relatively low—over the 10,000 or so measures members see in every session, we, as voters, probably know something— anything at all—about less than 1% (100) and have intense preferences about even fewer, say 0.1% (10). We probably have full and complete knowledge of even less, say 0.01% (1), if that.

Also, the intensity of preferences among voters tends to form a regular pattern. Very few voters feel intensely about an issue either way. The vast majority, the middle, have no feeling about an issue at all and probably do not find the issue itself salient.

Such arrays of preferences yield themselves to vote-trading or logrolling as well as coalition building. In cases where we have public provision of goods, we have all the conditions for bargaining: costly participation, isolated issue salience, and unclear estimates of who benefits through policies and by how much.

Overspending

In cases where we have public provision of goods, we have conditions for overspending, say Buchanan and Tullock (1962), or underspending, says Downs (1960).

Consider an example Buchanan and Tullock offer as support for the idea that logrolling tends to create more expenditure than would ordinarily be the case if economic efficiency controlled. Consider the case of 100 farmers in a locality, each of which is served by a separate access road that requires maintenance. Maintenance of a specific road must be passed by a majority of voters and, if passed, is financed out of general tax revenues levied equally on all farmers. If each road's maintenance is voted on separately and no logrolling takes place, no road improvements would pass under general tax financing. Each road improvement benefits only one person but the cost is borne by several.

Suppose vote-trading agreements can take place. In order to have his road repaired, each farmer must agree to support the road repairs of 50 other farmers in order to get the 51 votes required for his own. The benefit to this farmer is the benefit of having his own road repaired. The cost to him of the agreement is his share of the repairs to be done on the 50 other roads he agrees to support. In the general case, each of the farmers will attempt to secure an agreement with 50 other farmers and the agreements will probably be overlapping since all 100 farmers want to get their own roads repaired. In the end each farmer will have secured agreement to have his road repaired. In determining the level of road repairs on each road, the benefit to the farmer whose road is being repaired is weighed against the costs of 50 farmers of repairing it. The costs incurred by the other 49 farmers not included in that particular agreement are neglected. Overall, the cost to all farmers will exceed the benefits from the chosen level of repairs in each road. The logrolling process will have resulted in overexpenditure.

Underspending

Anthony Downs (1960) demonstrates the opposite case, the case for spending less than would be necessary. If we consider the same example above but substitute higher education for road repair, we might find that the calculation of benefits each farmer made would result in undervaluing the public expenditure. Arguments, except for the agricultural experiment station, the cooperative extension service, and the college of agriculture at the state land grant university, would probably tend toward belittling most benefits and accentuating higher education's costs. In the end, higher education might be underfunded, given some notion of adequate or efficient funding, and the entire government budget made smaller than economic efficiency might otherwise dictate.

Summary

Allocation may be approached through cost-benefit analysis or through logrolling. Cost-benefit analysis is that allocation principle in which a project is selected if the costs and benefits are weighed and the result makes the society better off. The problem with cost-benefit lies in the implementation of the sharing of benefits in such a way that those who bear most of the costs get enough of the benefits to offset their losses.

Logrolling—using the political process to allocate—examines a project in the context of all projects on the agenda for study at one time. The supporters of a project, ultimately, get their way only because they trade favors with supporters of other projects, with the result a sharing of costs and benefits so that both sets of supporters, as a whole, are better off. The problems with logrolling tend to be those related to overspending, a condition supporters of logrolling think is a function of viewing the needs of the individual as greater than the needs of society. That is, those who favor cost-benefit analysis, and who believe logrolling results in overspending, tend to be those who favor the right of the individual to reach her goals in competition with others, without government's help. Those who favor logrolling rather than cost-benefit analysis see the needs of society as paramount, at least those needs that in the end, make society's benefits greater than society's costs.

Allocation, Organization, Analysis—Micro and Macro: An Introduction

Cost-benefit structures[5] drive project-by-project or budget-by-budget decisions. At the micro or project level, an analyst delves into the preferences for that project versus its cost. At the macro or budget level, decision makers must cope with combining, into some meaningful whole, projects that have overcome micro-level constraints. The systematic aggregation of micro decisions is not truly a macro decision. In reality, budgets are constructed from both micro views and from some systematic macro view—often call ideology or even political platform—that details how the entire basket of public goods should be chosen. This section describes both levels of analysis and describes practical ways the two levels may complement each other.

Micro Cost-Benefit Analysis

To begin a cost-benefit analysis, one has at least one project[6] that can be studied. In this case, the concept is straightforward: determine benefits and costs; then find the ratio of dollar-quantified benefits, at their current value, to dollar-quantified costs, at their current value (B/C). If that ratio is greater than 1, the analysis suggests that the project should be considered for inclusion in the jurisdiction's budget.

The concept, as just outlined, includes two major ideas that influence the analysis: the notion of measuring benefits and costs and the idea of measuring them at their current value. Measuring benefits and costs involves estimating, forecasting, and costing them, all difficult to do in the public goods sector. The second, calculating benefits and costs at their current value, requires knowledge of preferences about the time value of money.

---

[5]We follow Schmid's organization (1990) here, and the distinction is made for simplicity's sake only.

[6]In preparing analyses, project alternatives may need to be explored (Vogt, 1975). One alternative may involve a decision of whether a capital project is the best solution to a given problem. Perhaps an increase in the operating budget may allow fuller utilization of existing facilities, eliminating the need for investment. An example of such a decision might be the alternatives of constructing a more efficient sewage treatment plant or hiring additional operators to staff the existing facility. Another alternative may be a replacement-no replacement decision. These sorts of decisions may utilize cost-benefit analysis.

Uncertainty and the Measurement of Costs and Benefits

Measuring costs and benefits involves carefully estimating both the obvious and not-so-obvious elements that a project will entail, forecasting changes that will occur and affect these elements over time, and costing the elements properly, that is, in both accounting and economic terms. This section describes the hazards of estimating, forecasting, and costing.

Estimating. The first element of measurement is estimation. Estimation deals with the type of cost or benefit to be counted and costs and benefits that are real or pecuniary types, tangible or intangible, as well as direct or indirect benefits. First, real costs and benefits are those that have a real or absolute consequence for society as a whole. That is, on balance the cost or benefit to society was not one in which the cost to one group of individuals was offset by the benefit to another group of individuals. The cost or benefit was not merely redistributed—as a pecuniary cost or benefit would describe—but an absolute change in the well-being of society as a whole.

Second, tangible and intangible costs and benefits describe the difference between those that can be priced or for which society can agree relatively easily on a price and those that cannot. A tangible cost benefit to many is a project such as a dam, with its measurable construction costs and irrigation, flood control, and recreation benefits. An intangible cost might be the endangered species that is destroyed as a result of the dam's displacement and destruction of the species's habitat.

The last type of cost and benefit that must be confronted in estimating the numbers that feed the cost-benefit analysis is the direct-indirect contrast. Direct costs are those immediately apparent from the project. In the dam example, both tangible costs and tangible benefits illustrate this idea. The indirect or secondary costs from the dam's construction might include poorer or better drainage in streams and marshes that fed the undammed stream, greater air and noise pollution as a result of recreational equipment used on reservoirs created by the dam, and even climate changes that result from large bodies of water replacing water flows.[7]

In each case, the analysis would not be complete without considering the pecuniary, intangible, and indirect costs and benefits of a project. Most analyses suggest this to be difficult and controversial.

---

[7]A cost that is both direct and indirect is operating cost. The escalation of energy costs has caused more emphasis to be placed on life-cycle costs. Not only do capital projects affect the budget through initial costs, most have long-term, and sometimes substantial, impacts on future operating budgets, making it necessary to analyze present capital investments in light of estimated future operating costs. For example, it may be cheaper to construct a public building utilizing one kind of construction. The cheaper construction method may, however, result in higher energy and maintenance costs over the life of the building. A present worth analysis may reveal that the more expensive method is cheaper in the long run.

Moreover, a level of maintenance is often assumed in life-cycle costing. The level of maintenance depends on the productivity of the labor force, including adequate pay for the members of the labor force, adequate training, high morale, and materials budgets sufficient for upkeep. Some of these are intangibles.

Decision makers must determine if the budget can accommodate the higher initial expense of the most cost-effective plan. In other words, it may not be possible financially to construct the most inexpensive building (expressed in life-cycle costs) due to higher initial capital requirements and current budget constraints. Such an exercise prevents surprise as operating costs mount once the facility's construction is complete.

Forecasting. The policy problems and consequences of forecasting are often not based on political differences. Since no forecaster can know the future and, instead, must monitor various data sets, judgments must be made about what to consider important enough to follow closely, what is novel, and what is a trend. One's assumptions, built not only through political views but also through organizational and professional effort, guide one to search for answers to all three questions (Pierce, 1971, p. 53). Thus forecasting has great interpretive potential. Likewise one can influence the course of events. If one's view is substantially influential, the guidance this forecast provides can influence the course of events (Pierce, 1971, p. 41). As Klay (1985) has pointed out, however, what one wants to see can happen. Views do become self-fulfilling prophecies.

Many different classification schemes exist to understand forecasting as a rational exercise. Quantitative methods are those depending on empirical data and in which theories play a central role. Qualitative methods also may come into play. Forecasters may have only a fuzzy understanding of their theories' production under various conditions. Finally, forecasters may combine both forms, implicitly reflecting organization biases; a forecaster may even reason backward from a desirable conjectured state of affairs to data and assumptions necessary to support the conjecture (see Dunn, 1981, p. 195).

Quantitative Methods. Quantitative methods are those forecasting methods involving data and mathematical analysis. These quantitative methods fall into two basic categories: time-series analytical methods and causal models.

1. Time-series analysis. A time series is a sequence of observations of phenomena of interest. Usually these observations are spaced at specific and constant intervals. For example, the expenditures of a state government would form a time series when these expenditures, or a specific class of expenditures (the variable), were measured over a period of years. Analysis of a time series involves describing the source of the sequence of realizations, the factor generating the time series. The simplest method of forecasting time series assumes that present trends may be extrapolated. The basic methods used for extrapolation are least squares and other forms of regression analysis. Simple regression requires that a relationship between two variables exists and that enough history describing this relationship be accessible to determine quantitatively the degree to which movement in one variable may be predicted by movement in the other. Yet, decision makers doubt that what lies ahead will have repeated the past. Many discredit regression techniques that try to find linearity where none exists.

2. Causal models. A model consists of explicitly stated relationships among variables which portray an abstraction of some phenomenon such as taxes and economic growth. Most models build on history but, in addition, elaborate theoretical relationships, such as that involving the curvilinear relationship among productivity, tax rates, and revenue yields illustrated earlier.

Forecasting models range from relatively simple judgmental models to highly complex econometric models.

1. Judgmental models. A judgmental model is a method of economic analysis that is relatively unstructured and informal. The forecaster generally does not use mathematical equations to represent the economy, but relies instead on any information that seems useful—information about future investment intentions and upcoming political events, judgments and hunches of people familiar with economic events, and other considerations not explicitly a part of the national income accounts framework.

2. Econometric and mathematical models. An econometric model, at the other extreme, is a system of analysis in which the economic system of a country is represented by a complex system of statistically estimated mathematical equations. The number of equations that are needed to adequately represent the economy depends on the number of actors that are to be considered. The larger the number of equations, the greater the number of subtle economic variations that can be accounted for by the model.
3. Policy analysis with models. The same model can be used for policy analysis as well as for forecasting. To investigate any specific set of possible government actions, the policymakers simply insert the change into the model and solve to find out what the impact of the action is likely to be. In periods of inflation, the figure for taxes might be raised and expenditures lowered. In periods of depression, the opposite actions might be taken to determine the effect actual policies of this type might have.

An econometric model allows the government to predict the effects of a policy action before enacting it. The quality of the model depends on the accuracy with which it can predict these values. The distinguishing feature of econometric models is, in summary, an attempt to depict the economy by a set of statistically estimated mathematical equations. Particular emphasis is placed on having as many variables as possible explained within the system of equations, on the use of hard economic data, and on the simultaneous solutions of the model without the introduction of other considerations.

Qualitative Approaches.   Qualitative forecasting methods are those in which subjective estimation predominates. Such methods have greatest utility in murky or confusing areas of activity, those areas where our knowledge of the relevant variables and the patterns of interaction among these variables may not be well developed. Often qualitative methods' loudest partisans are those who reject *a priori* reasoning or positive theory.

The most basic qualitative forecasting technique is the judgmental forecast. Using judgment, individuals create a relatively unstructured and informal process. Those people with information relevant to the phenomena being considered essentially pool that knowledge and make educated guesses about the future. Hunches and intuition play a large role in the outcome of a judgmental forecasting process.

The Delphi technique is a well-known form of judgmental forecasting (Brown and Helmer, 1962). To employ this method, one empanels a group of experts. These experts respond to a sequence of interrogations in which their responses are communicated to each other. Specifically, their responses to one questionnaire are used to produce a subsequent questionnaire. Any set of information available to some experts and not others is passed on to the others through this sharing process. This information, the method envisions, sharpens judgment among experts and focuses attention and forecasts.

Brainstorming is another information gathering technology, one useful in aiding judgment and forecasting future events (Osborn, 1953). This method follows a very disciplined format. Criticism of any source of information or of the information provided is banned. In fact, farfetched ideas are encouraged as an aid to eliciting a large number of practical ideas. The quantity of data is emphasized. The first step in the process—the generating phase—rests primarily on creativity. The second phase is a winnowing-out phase in which individuals evaluate ideas generated earlier. The third phase builds on the best ideas surviving the second phase by focusing attention on synthesizing these best ideas. Finally, the evaluation phase forces the elimination of all but the best idea or forecast.

Finally, many organizations employ the nominal group technique (Delbecq et al., 1975) to forecast future events. A nominal group is a group composed of the pooled outputs of randomly chosen individuals who have worked alone.

Problems in forecasting. Forecasting in government is hardly ever the prerogative of only one group. Intergroup effort, in fact, describes what takes place when both legislative and executive bodies cooperate, of course (Kamlet et al., 1987), but such effort is also required among different offices within the executive branch (Pierce, 1971).

Common to all whose task is forecasting is ambiguity. Seldom is there a clear definition of cause-effect relationships. Seldom less is there agreement about what one wants to happen. Thus forecasting is often a judgmental process—especially influenced by forecasters' social construction of reality.

To understand the judgmental process, and thus revenue forecasting, it is necessary to understand the elements that interact to construct cause-effect relationships and desired outcomes. The interaction among actors in forecasting, as in all other organizational and judgmental exercises, assumes that all want stability; all participants interact and confine behavior in ways to trade stable expectations about behavior.

Explaining reality construction solely as an economy of social interactions is incomplete. March and Olsen (1989, p. 62) suggest that the market centers on bias:

> Although there seems to be ample evidence that when performance fails to meet aspirations, institutions search for new solutions, changes often seem to be driven less by problems than by solutions. . . . When causality and technology are ambiguous, the motivation to have particular solutions adopted is likely to be as powerful as the motivation to have particular problems solved, and changes can be more easily induced by a focus on solutions than by a focus on problems. Solutions and opportunities stimulate awareness of previously unsalient or unnoticed problems or preferences.

All parties to making judgments have a solution in mind. Judgment in a collective choice situation is a matter of convincing other parties of the connection between a preferred solution and the problem at hand.

The argument about one's preferred solution may be easier to make when the party realizes the importance of sequential attention. Parties to the making of judgment have limited time and limited willingness to devote more than a fair share of that time to a given judgment call. Any party realizing the limited time problem can choose to focus attention, or not, on a given solution.

One's ploy may well be to focus on the aspect of the problem that a given solution seems most capable of resolving. Or one's time may best be spent in characterizing a problem as one that a favorite solution has always been chosen by the group to use. In fact, Brunsson (1989: p. 5) has argued that it is possible to sustain a coalition among members who have what appear to be strictly inconsistent objectives because of sequential attention: "By adroitly applying technology and expertise, [executives] can manage the assumptions and judgments which must be made to combine . . . forecasts in some reasonable way and predict . . . change."

The recognition of biases, and the understanding that differences may be useful, underscores much research in judgment making (Wright and Ayton, 1987). That is, differences create a healthy skepticism about others' views and assumptions, bringing them out in the open (Golembiewski and Miller, 1981). Research by Klay (1983, 1985) and Ascher (1978) suggests that airing such differences may reduce overreliance on outdated core assumptions or "assumption drag," in forecasts, improving their accuracy.

Costing. Finally, cost-benefit analysts must cope with the assignment of some quantitative value to the stream of costs and benefits. This has special difficulty in the public goods sector, since markets have not "priced" these goods due to market failures in either rivalry or divisibility. Three specific costing problems bedevil analysts: estimating shadow prices, final prices, and opportunity costs.

First, the cost of a project or the benefit of it may often be estimated by analogy. Some equivalent market may exist for a project, somewhere; that equivalent is employed as the basis for costing out the elements of the project for analysis. The problems of finding such a shadow or of using the most nearly correct one still create problems.

Second, the lack of a shadow price leads to additional problems. That is, most public goods tend to be oriented toward outcomes rather than mere outputs. Outcomes are extremely hard to envision, much less estimate in dollar-denominated consequences. For example, street sweeping and cleaning are often touted as popular programs, even though they have no meaningful outputs (pounds of garbage collected, raves from residents) but definite outcomes. "Clean streets" has a meaning all its own and is an end in itself. Such an end-in-itself is hard to measure for cost-benefit analysis.

Third, a project without a shadow price always carries an opportunity cost that might be measurable and meaningful for analysis. The opportunity cost of any project is the cost and benefit of another project foregone to proceed with the present one. The true cost of any project, therefore, is the cost (and benefit) of the most obvious substitute. Clean streets may carry the cost of an opportunity, such as a rat amelioration program, foregone. The illustration also suggests the problem of lack of adequate quantifiability in opportunities foregone, the biggest problem in calculating costs.

Summary. Problems abound in estimating, forecasting, or costing project elements for analysis. Estimating costs and benefits accurately requires knowledge that far exceeds that available to an analyst. Forecasting demands an objectivity and a knowledge of theoretical relationships far beyond that normally expected of economics and social observers. Costing public programs has special difficulties in that few analogous, meaningful, or quantifiable projects exist on which to base estimates.

Valuation over Time and by Different Selection Criteria

The selection of projects through cost-benefit analysis is commonly derived from an investment theory utilizing comparisons between a stream of costs and a stream of benefits *measured at their current value.* Generally, these comparison are made on the basis of one or the other of two calculations, net present value (NPV) or internal rate of return (IRR).

NPV measures future streams of costs and benefits by "netting" or subtracting current value costs from current value benefits. A variation of this measure is the more popularly known ratio of current value costs to current value benefits. The criterion for selection in the former is a positive number; the criterion for the ratio is a number greater than unity (1).

A second method of selecting a project is to determine its rate of return (IRR). This calculation suggests that projects whose current value benefits exceed their current value costs by a given rate or percentage are better than those that do not.

The difference between NPV/CB ratio and IRR is in the former's discrimination in favor of large numbers. That is, IRR corrects for extremely large differences in scope among projects. IRR is more appropriately applied at the macro level where projects compete against other projects than at the micro level where a project's benefits compete against its costs.

Discounting. Nevertheless, the calculation of NPV and the CB ratio depend on establishment of current value costs and benefits. Current value costs and benefits are also known as discounted elements.

Discounting is based on a preference for the time value of money. For example, if given the choice between $100 now and $100 a year from now, most people would prefer to have the $100 now.[8] If forced to wait, we would want the year-from-now choice to be equal in value to the $100 today alternative. The amount that would make the $100 a year from now equivalent in value to the $100 today alternative is our preference for the time value of money. Some of us prefer more under some circumstances than others. To illustrate: in exchange for the delay in getting the $100, such as when we lend money to a college student daughter to buy an automobile in return for the promise to repay it, we would want to have compensation for the delay. What would the time preference be?

The calculation of time value may shed light on finding preferences. Consider that if you put $100 in a bank at 5% interest, you would have $105 in a year, if interest is compounded annually. The future value of that $100 (the amount it would be worth in one year) is $105, or:

$$\text{Future value of } \$100 = \$100 \times (1 + 0.05)$$
$$= \$105$$

A sum of $100 at the present time is equivalent to $105 next year at a 5% interest rate. A person's choosing not to put money in the bank tells us that the $100 sum we have today is equivalent to an amount next year of at least $105 and maybe much more. If the person feels that having $100 today and $105 one year from now are equivalent, then the 5% interest rate represents the time value of money—of waiting one year for the money. The 5% interest rate measures the willingness to trade $100 today (present value) for $105 one year from now (future value).

If we know the interest rate that reflects the tradeoff to the citizens of a community between $100 in benefits today versus some greater level of benefits in later years, we can convert the value of the future benefits into their present day worth. Two examples illustrate the need to know the present value of future benefits. In the first case, many governments often buy fleets of automobiles for their police forces and for many other departments. The government's decision makers face the quandary, should we buy or should we lease the automobiles? Present valuing the terms of the lease is the only true way to compare, on financial terms, the buy-versus-lease alternatives.

In a second case, governments often sell bonds in the market place to finance capital improvements such as roads and bridges. These bonds will be redeemed with principal payments the government will make annually over a period of years. The bond financings are, more often than not, competitively bid. Investment banks bid on bonds by offering an interest rate for each annual principal payment, ordinarily. If a bond financing covered a redemption period of 10 years, an investment bank would often bid on each of 10 annual payments or maturities. The government decision maker who evaluates the competing bids must calculate the present value of each principal payment on which the bank submitted a bid because, presumably, the interest rates the banks bid were different, leading to different total amounts of interest the government would pay.

[8]To those like Henny Youngman, this is "nem di gelt" or take the money: "Don't believe all the baloney people tell you about what they'll do for you tomorrow. Take the money" (Youngman, 1990).

Essentially, we calculate the present value in the opposite way we calculate interest earnings or future value. That is, if the formula for the future value of a sum of money is

Future value = present value × (1 + interest rate)

the formula for finding present value is solved by algebra (dividing both sides of the equals sign by the term (1 + interest rate) to get the formula

Present value = future value/(1 + interest rate)

In other words, if we know any two terms—future value, interest rate, or present value—we can find the third. And if we know the future benefits of a project with any certainty at all, as well as the interest rate, we can find the present value of the project.

We should note one fact about terminology related to the time value of money. The rate used to calculate future value is best thought of as an interest rate; most of us are familiar enough with that process through savings accounts and like investments. However, the rate used in present value calculations is known as the *discount rate* because the value of a benefit we receive at some future time is smaller today by comparison because we deduct an amount to compensate us for the delay. In other terms, we deduct from the future value by a factor that relates time and the discount rate.

Projects often begin to have benefits much later than 1 year after they have been built. The construction of a project, for example, may take 3 years. The benefits, while forecast to be a certain amount, may have to be adjusted because of the delay. The adjustment would be done in the same way as three separate 1-year present-value calculations. That is, if the present value of a forecasted benefit of $1000 (at 5%) for 1 year were

Present value = $1,000/(1 + 0.05)
= $952.38

then the present value for the second year would be

$952.38/(1 + 0.05) = $907.03

and the present value for the third year would be

$907.03/(1 + 0.05) = $863.84

The formula may be simplified by

$$\text{Present value (of \$x over 3 years at 5\%)} = \frac{\text{future value}}{(1 + 0.05)^3}$$

Thus, by cubing the discount factor (1 + 0.05), we calculate precisely as we did by the long method formerly.

Annual Costs and Benefits. Many projects have costs and benefits continually over a period of years. In other words, these projects have a benefit (or cost) stream. To find the total value of the stream from this succession of periods, we add terms to the basic formula for present value that we looked at earlier. If a project had annual benefits for n years, we would use the following formula:

$$\text{Present value} = \text{annual value} \times \frac{[(1 + \text{discount rate})^n - 1]}{\text{discount rate}(1 + \text{discount rate})^n}$$

Consider the following example. If a city were offered \$1800 for a piece of property today that it was leasing to a business for 5 more years at \$300 a year with the option of purchase at the end of the 5-year period for \$500, which would you advise the city leaders to choose? Using an interest rate of 5%, let's consider the two alternatives.

1. The lease

   Annual benefit = \$300
   One-time benefit = \$500

   $$\text{PV annual benefit} = 300 \times \frac{[(1.05)^5 - 1]}{0.05(1.05)^5}$$
   $$= \$1,299$$

PV one-time benefit = $\$500/(1.05)^5$
$$= \$392$$
   Total benefits = \$1299 + \$392
   $$= \$1691$$

2. The sale.
   The sale, theoretically at least, would take place today; therefore its present value is \$1800.
3. Comparing the two alternatives:
   Lease/purchase = \$1691
   Sale   = \$1800

We would probably advise the city to sell the property. Of course, the difference is small because, above all, we are dealing with rather small sums. Yet, if the differences were small even with bigger numbers, other considerations would be called into play to decide the question, such as the disposition of the property—given other city policies—if sold; the reliability of payments by the present lessor; other plans the city might have for adjoining property, and so on.

The city's main advantage in knowing the present value of the lease is the ability to compare directly the value of a sale and the value of the lease. These types of calculations make comparisons meaningful, since the cash flow from the lease—[(5 ×) \$300 + \$500] = \$2000—might have led decision makers to believe that the lease's value was more than it actually was.

Macro Cost-Benefit Analysis or Portfolio Construction

On a project-level evaluation of benefits and costs, the net present value idea has some merit. Certainly, one hesitates to spend taxpayers' money on projects whose worth cannot be shown readily. However, selection problems occur when the comparison is between projects of unequal size or projects of unequal economic or useful lives, as well as when an entire budget of projects is being selected. We find two strategies normally used to overcome these selection problems: a scheduling strategy and a strategy to construct portfolios.

Cost-Benefit Analysis without Constraint

First, capital projects are also often submitted with no expenditure ceiling specified. Consequently, more projects are submitted than can be funded. Prioritization is necessary to achieve the required cutbacks.

Prioritization is frequently achieved by scheduling. Scheduling helps alleviate waste by insuring construction of facilities required initially, that is, before primary construction. For example, sewers will be scheduled for construction prior to building a street, so that it will not be necessary to cut new pavement during sewer construction.

A danger of prioritization by scheduling is that rarely are projects completely eliminated. More often they are postponed and placed further down the schedule. As projects stay on the schedule for several years there can be a maturation effect; they may become *bona fide* projects with funding, even though they logically do not have a high priority.

Prioritization requires review to insure the project relates to the overall goals and policies of the jurisdiction. "Projects must be weighed in light of their contribution to programs which, in themselves, are not of equal rank. We emphasize that the project contribution-to-the-program approach, rather than the departmental or functional approach, should dominate thinking" at this level say Moak and Hillhouse (1975: p. 200).

Marginal Rate of Return Analysis

A second approach to cost-benefit analysis, one that overcomes the scheduling problem, employees marginal analysis in selecting productive projects. This method has greatest utility when projects are quite different in scale or useful life.

Marginal analysis requires three steps. First, a range of discount rates is evaluated to determine the likely field of opportunity costs for projects such as those being evaluated. Second, the analyst determines the internal rate of return for the entire set of projects and discards those that fall below the opportunity costs of capital. Third, the preferred choice is selected by finding that project that has the highest internal rate of return for the employment of capital.

Finding the Range of Discount Rates and Opportunity Costs.   Determining opportunity costs of projects provides the information one needs to discount future costs properly. That is, to be systematic in judging the value of public projects, the projects must be compared not only to the population of candidate *public* projects, but also to all investment opportunities, public and private. In this way, the economic efficiency of all institutions is preserved.

An opportunity's cost is the cost of a project foregone. That is, if one chooses one project over another, the true value of the choice is the value foregone to gain it. Consider the example of desserts. If we forego one that weighs in at 1000 calories for one that has 100 calories, we value the one we chose at its 10:1 savings rate. The one we chose is 10 times the value of the one we did not choose.

In this same sense, public projects compete with private sector projects. If we decide to spend money on public capital projects, we forego the economic benefits of leaving the money in the private sector, where, presumably, it generates other types and distributions of economic growth.

Since we cannot grasp the long-term costs and benefits of collective goods very well, the opportunity cost gets fixed as a discount rate by which we judge what costs and benefits we do know. We measure costs and benefits and discount this stream by the opportunity cost of capital.

Many consider the market to have done this costing for us, at least in constructing a range of opportunity costs for portfolio purposes. The difference between the tax-free yield on municipal bonds and the taxable yield on these bonds or on corporate bonds of equal risk of default might serve as the floor in our range. The yield on federal long-term yields might be our range's ceiling.

Why these? If the opportunity cost of capital is value foregone, the small difference in the former represents such a comparison. The tax exemption represent the subsidy or cost of pushing investment dollars from private to public sector. These bonds would not be sold, or the projects they finance built, we assume, if they had to be offered at market rates.

The top of the range is that market rate that attracts capital. The federal government's long-term taxable bond rate is such a rate.

Determining the Internal Rate of Return of the Projects. Instead of determining a cost-benefit ratio, many analysts follow the private sector practice of solving for the rate of return on investment, or the *internal rate of return* (IRR). Having discovered this internal rate, analysts discard those projects whose rates are less than the opportunity cost of capital—the floor of rates.

Consider the example of a project with an initial outlay of $20,000, annual costs of $10,000, and annual benefits of $13,000, all of which are paid or received at the end of the fiscal year. The projected life of the project is 10 years, and there is no residual benefit at the end of the project. This project's costs and benefits are represented with the following cash flows:

Year	Costs ($)	Benefits ($)
1	−30,000	+13,000
2	−10,000	+13,000
3	−30,000	+13,000
4	−10,000	+13,000
5	−30,000	+13,000
6	−10,000	+13,000
7	−30,000	+13,000
8	−10,000	+13,000
9	−30,000	+13,000
10	−10,000	+13,000

To find the IRR, we determine that discount rate at which the net current value (discounted costs and benefits) are zero. In the table below, we show four possible discount rates and the net current values for the cash flows above.

	Discount rate (%)			
	5	10	15	20
Project A	4118	253	−2334	−4088

Given the numbers that appear in the table, the discount rate of 10.41% brings the discounted benefits and costs into equality. That is, the net costs and benefits are almost zero.

The internal rate of return of a given set of cash flows (outflow in payments for construction and such, inflow in benefits received) is that discount rate at which the current value of the inflow equals the current value of the outflow. Finding the IRR is a matter of eliminating all those discount rates at which the two flows are not equal.

Take, for illustration, three projects with unique cash flows each over ten (10) years.

Project	Capital costs ($)	Annual costs ($)	Annual benefits ($)
A	20,000	10,000	14,000
B	30,000	10,000	15,000
C	50,000	17,000	25,000

With computers, it is possible to program to find the rate, since hunting for it is time consuming and tedious.

Project	Discount rate (%)			
	5	10	15	20
A	11,839	6396	2684	103
B	10,037	3450	(993)	(4038)
C	14,155	3702	(3328)	(8127)

Just as large numbers may make projects less practical, even though benefit-cost ratios make them look better, projects that have large internal rates of return also may not be practical. This may be so in limited budget situations particularly. For example, a budget with a limit of $15,000 simply cannot afford any of the projects, no matter what their IRR. Not only does the internal rate of return calculation limit the population of possible projects to those that exceed the minimum rate or the opportunity cost of capital, but, obviously, it also limits projects to those that a government can afford.

Selecting Projects by Their Marginal Rates of Return   The actual method of choosing a portfolio of projects that have internal rates higher than the minimum is by determining marginal rates of return among those that have not been weeded out already. This method operates on the principle that each additional dollar invested in a project should have at least the same, if not a higher, rate of return than the last. We would first employ the minimum acceptable rate criterion to projects to weed out those projects that alone could not produce a rate of return great enough to justify taxation to finance it. Then we would ask which combination of projects yields the highest marginal rate of return.

Taking the projects just described, and established a 7% minimum acceptable rate,[9] arriving at net current values and benefit-cost ratios comes first. The net current values and ratios are displayed below.

Project	Capital required	Current value at 7%	B-C ratio	IRR
A	20,000	9,403	1.11	20.2%
B	30,000	7,081	1.07	13.7%
C	50,000	9,460	1.06	12.4%

Then the process requires finding the differences between any and all projects. The marginal analysis method requires comparison between successively larger projects—between one project and another with larger capital requirements—and not the other way around (Gohagan, 1980, pp. 209–211).

In our example, our process requires moving from project A to project B (and on to project C) or from project A to project C. We ask whether it is justifiable to spend additional capital to mount a larger project. The marginal additions are portrayed below.

Marginal increase	In capital	Annual costs	Annual benefits	MIRR
From A to B	10,000	0	1000	0%
From A to C	30,000	7000	11000	7.06%

The analysis suggests two facts. The first is that there is no additional benefit to be gained by investing in project B rather than project A. However, because we set the rate of return floor at 7%, the move from A to C would be justifiable, since the $30,000 extra, invested in what we presume to be a popular project, would return at least that minimum. As a result of our analysis, the marginal internal rate of return calculation would suggest project C to be the most productive use of the public's money.

Portfolio Construction

A third approach to cost-benefit analysis deals with the most productive combination of projects by using investment portfolio approaches to choice. Finding this combination is the subject of capital budget deliberations. How does one build a portfolio?

Constructing a portfolio requires three steps. First, we set the minimum rate of return for capital. Second, we determine the marginal internal rate of return for each project or combination of projects over each other project or combination. Finally, we choose that combination that exceeds our minimum rate by the greatest margin.

Setting the Minimum Rate. In our last example, we set the minimum rate at 7%. We will be using the same data; however, let's make the hurdle a higher one (10%), since we will be dealing with large net current values as the following table reveals:

[9]This is a fairly low rate. As of this writing, municipal bond rates are in this range.

Project	Capital	Annual benefits ($)	Annual costs ($)	NPE 10% ($)	B/C 10%
A	20,000	14,000	10,000	6396	1.08
B	30,000	15,000	10,000	3450	1.04
C	50,000	25,000	17,000	3702	1.02
A + B	50,000	29,000	20,000	9847	1.06
A + C	70,000	39,000	27,000	10,098	1.04
B + C	80,000	50,000	27,000	7152	1.03

Determining Marginal Rates for All Combinations. As with the last group of projects, we will determine marginal rates, but with the portfolio approach, we will also combine projects and calculate IRR and MIRR for these combinations as well. For an illustration of this with our project data, see the table below. In it we report only the largest capital projects. The marginal rate of return is the rate of return on the extra capital invested in projects with higher capital requirements. In the A + C versus A + B example, the A + C required $20,000 more capital than A + B; therefore, the marginal rate is the rate of return on that extra $20,000.

Project	Marginal B/C	Marginal IRR
A + C over A + B	1.00	10.41%
A + C over C	1.08	10.24%
B + C over A + C	0.68	0.00%

Choosing the Best Combination. The criterion for choice is based first on total current value, then marginal benefit-cost ratios, and finally the marginal internal rate of return. In setting up the last comparison, we took only the portfolio with the highest total current value, A + C with $10,098. Then we compared it to those projects just smaller in capital requirements to determine whether the expenditure of the extra money was justified. The extra $20,000 resulted in at least equal costs and benefits when compared to the combination of A + B and a positive benefit-cost ratio when compared to project C. Each of the MIRR measures—that compared to A + B and that compared to C—was greater than the 10% hurdle we set up. We conclude that the extra $20,000 was a justifiable expenditure on these measures.

If A + C is a justifiable project, what about the next one, B + C, which requires larger amounts of capital? Is the extra $10,000 expenditure justifiable when we select B + C over A + C? According to the chart, it is not. The extra $10,000 represents substantially greater costs than benefits (a marginal benefit cost ratio of 0.68). Also, the extra capital brings no return at all.

We conclude with the choice of a simple portfolio of projects A and C. The total current value of benefits and costs was a positive $10,098. The marginal gain over the next lowest capital cost alternative was above the minimum rate of return we established, as well.

An Illustration

To test the assumption that the marginal internal rate of return method will provide the best guide to projects to select, consider five projects for which we may compute the rates of return, and then select the best portfolio, using experience as a guide. The illustration can suggest some of the important steps actually used in considering which projects are apparently in the best interest of a public agency to fund.

The choice among the projects in the illustration concerns the best use of $250,000 in state funds for an economically and socially destitute but politically sensitive area of a state. The five project choices are briefly described below:

1. A transportation project. A wooden trestle bridge, having an estimated economic life of 25 years, would cost $80,000 for initial construction and would need annual maintenance costing $4000. The wooden bridge would have to be rebuilt after 25 years, which would require a 1-month closure to traffic. The wooden bridge would be built in an area subject to flooding, one in which the "100-year flood" probabilities indicate some likelihood of a flood that would destroy the bridge up to three times during a 50-year period. There would be intangible, tourism-related, benefits to such a structure.
2. A transportation project. A steel replacement bridge, constructed on the same site as, but instead of, the wooden bridge, would have a 50-year economic life. The initial cost would be $160,000 with annual maintenance of $2000. The bridge would be invulnerable to the 100-year flood.
3. A jobs training program. The journeyman training program would recruit 100 trainees per year for 6 years, 50% from the hard-core unemployed and 50% from nonunion construction workers (who now make $8000 per year). The trainees would enter a 4-year training program. Once in, students would be paid $7000, and upon successful completion would be hired at $14,000. A trainee dropout rate of 10% per year could reasonably be anticipated; graduated journeymen would face an average 10% unemployment rate. Administrative costs for the program would be $100,000 per year.
4. A jobs training program. The clerical training program would also recruit 100 trainees per year over a 6-year period. The trainees would enter a 1-year program and be place in jobs that paid $7000 upon successful completion but receive nothing while training. Ninety percent of the trainees would come from the hard-core unemployed. Administrative costs for the program would be $100,000 per year.
5. An urban renewal project. The redevelopment project covers a 100-block area of an urban area and involves land purchases, resident relocation, redevelopment and improvements, public facilities, and administrative costs. The total of tangible costs equals $4.6 million. The total of tangible benefits equals $3.7 million. However, planners and proponents suggest large intangible benefits.

If given the problem, an office of budget analysts would be asked to use the internal rate of return method to establish relative worthiness and the marginal rate of return method to help identify components of the best mix. They would also be asked, specifically, to include the managerial implications of the portfolio, especially those related to fraud and abuse, and the political implications of various distributions.

Four major sets of findings emerge from this illustration of the practice of cost-benefit analysis, as it would probably be considered by a group of state budget analysts. First, the cost-benefit analysis can be swayed by both the assumptions built into the projects as well as assumptions projected, by the analyst, on to the study. For example, many would question the low dropout rate in the training programs, and this assumption is crucial to the benefit stream. Also, the analysts could easily disagree over the forecast unemployment rate, with those otherwise favoring the project forecasting a lower unemployment rate than graduate trainees would face in future job markets.

Second, intangibles tend to play a large part in the analysis of social infrastructure programs such as the urban renewal project. Arguments backing the inclusion of intangibles point toward all manner of benefits from redevelopment—from better health of residents to pride in community. Hard-headed numbers analysts deprecate these measures and discard this project from their portfolios.

Third, analysts would point out the fraud potential of the projects and add this factor into their analyses. Of these projects, urban renewal would be the consensus choice of the project most prone to abuse. Training programs are thought to be abused but able to be quarantined from such a problem by good management, itself an intangible cost.

Fourth, analysts would suggest that a short-term bias pervades analysis. This short-term bias affects judgments about training programs particularly, since their benefits and social consequences may not be apparent for a generation or more. The short-term bias is also manifested in the consumption-orientedness of the analytical approach. Conservation or patrimony benefits—as opposed to those from immediate consumption— often are difficult to envision, much less measure, due to their intergenerational quality.

Finally, undergirding all of the analyses is the constant presence of political considerations. In other words, what would "sell" politically, analysts always wonder. Despite its advantage in IRR terms, would a *wooden* bridge be politically as well as physically vulnerable? Could the bridge be explained in the face of conventional opposition, much less justified in the battle for funding by interest groups representing other proposals?

Some analysts would point out that a cost-benefit analysis imputes values and demands to individuals without actually verifying them. The value of a bridge, for instance, is, essentially, the individual's opportunity cost of traveling the next best route. However, no one ever asks an individual whether that is the route she would take or whether he would take that trip at all if there were no bridge. Some analysts would mention that the analysis only skirts politics when the political process is the only true gauge of what real individuals want or are willing to tax themselves to finance.

Politics, in the form of equity, also becomes an issue. Cost-benefit analysis is not particularly sensitive to the way in which income is distributed in society. The cost-benefit analyses here would tend to infer the same amount of value to rich and poor individuals. Also apparent is the method's conservatism: when used with the five alternatives here, the method tends to minimize the need for government intervention on behalf of the poor.

Despite the large number of caveats made to an otherwise quantitative analysis, analysts generally agree that there are serious public policy implications in undertaking a project that is not rational with respect to tangible costs that exceed benefits, particularly in times of fiscal austerity. The number of biases that emerge in analyzing the costs and benefits of a range of projects—fraud potential, short-term returns, consumption overwhelming conservation, tangible items to measure—suggests the extreme conservatism of the method. Yet the influence of fiscal austerity is revealing. It suggests that the political environment for tax policy, the willingness of individuals to pay taxes, and the civic mindedness of taxpayers serve to condition analysts to the need to be conservative in the assumptions and use of bias in analysis. Presumably, times other than fiscal austerity might prompt different analytical procedures.

Conclusions Regarding Cost-Benefit Analysis. This illustration has revealed that the internal rate of return method of cost-benefit analysis alone would not guide seasoned analysts in their choice of an optimal portfolio. A large number of other considerations, both managerial and political, guide judgment over and above quantitative techniques. However surprisingly, analysts would probably find that the internal rate of return calculation actually plays a large role—that it is not sound, "not rational," to select a project in which tangible costs exceed benefits. It would not be surprising, moreover, to find that analysts are loath to project their own political leanings or their social philosophies on the analysis, that they are content instead to act conservatively, in hopes that the political process would take over where they left off in creating an equitable, as well as efficient, portfolio.

Conclusions Regarding Other Facets of Linear Strategies. To follow a linear logic for investment, advocates have urged the use of applied microeconomics (Wetzler and Petersen, 1985). Wetzler and Petersen argue (1985, p. 8) strategy's inherent potency in helping one choose between capital markets and internal sources of financing. More broadly, decision makers actually have two concerns related to financing—whether to borrow money to pay for the project or pay for it out of operating revenues and, if borrowing is involved, what financing technique to use.

To borrow or not for a capital investment has often been answered in equity terms. The payback of borrowed funds spreads the burden across all generations who use the facility, implying a sort of user fee for the facility in the form of taxes that are then earmarked for debt repayment.

As for the use of operating funds, the burden is borne by those in the generation paying taxes until the facility is paid for. If the tax system is proportional or even progressive, this might be somewhat equitable; however, many view local tax systems as regressive.[10] This suggests that pay-as-constructed methods penalize one generation and poorer economic groups.

The use of operating revenues has important frugality arguments—no interest payments—as well as others in which financial management is crucial. For example (Smith, 1990), pay-as-constructed financing from operating revenues is appropriate when high interest rates are not offset by high inflation rates. High inflation—which might make real interest rates negative—and elastic revenues affected by high inflation would offset high interest rates and make borrowing appropriate. In addition, windfalls in the form of intergovernmental assistance or one-time events may permit operating revenue financing. Finally, in stable growth areas where capital expenditures are fairly consistent, budgeting can incorporate these investments.

Conclusions about Putting Linear Strategies to Use in Everyday Management. The linear model of strategy tends to blend applied microeconomics with planning and management for finance officers. Yet it fails to deal with two everyday phenomena in public financial management: mandated dependence, and conservatism with regard to financing tools.

---

[10]Economists traditionally view local sales tax based or property tax based revenue systems as regressive. Both tend to penalize those who spend the largest proportion of their incomes on consumption (either house or retail goods). Generally, this group is the poorest economic group. For more discussion on this, as well as views to the contrary, see Stiglitz (1988).

The ability to act in strategic ways assumes the independence to do so. Mandated programs and spending tend to create problems for a government strategic actor. Less discretion inhibits strategy building. In a survey of financial managers and teachers (Miller et al., 1987), we asked them the degree to which a major indirect mandate—federal government borrowing—inhibited action by the organizations to which they belonged. These data are portrayed in Table 1.

Since a large number of the respondents in our sample felt that federal borrowing would have a negative impact on their organizations, we infer that borrowing has a tendency to create organization dependency, a negative financial trend in this case. Such a dependency, then, would mitigate the effect of a strategic planning and management program based on a linear logic.

We also asked respondents about their knowledge and willingness to use prominent (and legal, at the time) tools of economic development strategy: general obligation bonds, revenue bonds, leasing plans, private purpose bonds, and advance refunding strategems. The reaction to the use of these methods emerges in Table 2.

As the table portrays, the agreement about appropriate tools and uses tends to decline quite amazingly as the conservatism of the method decreases. General obligation bond borrowings elicit broad agreement with nothing else approaching this level of acceptance. Private purpose financings, at the time of the survey, had great notoriety; now this notoriety has given way to codified limits on its use. Yet the limited capacity to employ the technique underlies a contemporary reading of reaction to the technique.

To summarize these findings, we understand financial managers to be buffeted by those who advocate advanced management techniques based on a linear logic. Yet conditions outside their control tend to inhibit strategic action. Moreover, understanding of strategy's tools, at least in the area of economic development and infrastructure rehabilitation, has its own limits; financial managers are not yet ready to chance the necessity to defend themselves against charges of profligacy.

General Conclusions Regarding Linear Logic in Capital Investment Strategy. We now place cost benefit analysis within the even larger body of literature characterizing all linear strategies in government, whether they deal with investment or other public policies. This review forms a critique of economics or, more specifically, rational choice

Table 1   U.S. Government Borrowing as an Inhibiting Effect on Financial Manager's Organization

[To respondents] "As a professional, your opinion has value. Please indicate your agreement or disagreement by circling the appropriate number in the scale immediately following [the] statement."

"The rate of growth of the national debt will affect the financial condition of my employing organization."

Response	Number	Percent of total
Strongly agree	307	37.3%
Agree	215	26.1%
Somewhat agree	129	15.7%
Somewhat disagree	64	7.8%
Disagree	61	7.4%
Strongly disagree	35	4.2%

Table 2 Willingness to Use Prominent Tools of Strategic Financial Management ($N = 824$)

[To respondents] "Please indicate which of the following instruments you believe government should or should not use as a long-term financing tool."

Instrument	Government Should Use	Government Should Not Use	Not familiar
Revenue bonds	701	45	20
General obligation bonds	701	45	28
Leasing	556	113	85
Advance refunding	469	173	116
Private purpose financing	436	255	59

theory, since this body of thought underlies the techniques, metaphors, and rhetoric associated with both cost benefit analysis and linear strategy.

The Maximizing Behavior of Government Actors and Agencies. The fundamental principle of economic reasoning states that "bureaucratic officials, like all other agents in society, are motivated by their own self interests at least part of the time" (Downs, 1957, p. 2).

In parallel fashion, political actors seek advantage for both themselves and their constituents and tend to maximize gain and minimize loss. Both bureaucratic and political actors reach their targets through a maze of rules, communication and coordination rules for bureaucratic officials and voting rules for political actors. The world within which behavior bends around rules is an unpredictable one, and gaining greater certainty about the acquisition of advantage may offset in part the size of the advantage itself. The actors, therefore, constantly calculate what is literally a risk-return relationship, given their preferences for different kinds of advantages to begin with.

Economic Decision Making. Economic decision making tends to be deductive and because of that has an elegance given to mathematics-like precision in detailing "proof" as well as an other-worldliness in which few argue its practicality.

The idea of looking at the world in terms of "decision" instead of some other concept, say sovereignty (another abstraction but one loaded with ideology) or resource problems (topical, practical ways of dealing with phenomena), is tribute to economists following a "scientific" approach to studying the world.

Decisions cut across all of mankind's activities; they occur every minute of every day and cover everything from the mundane to the spiritual and especially the sensible. Dimensions of decisions seem to cover all bases: psychological, political, remunerative, making the decision a truly fundamental element of life.

Having based microeconomics or the theory of the firm on the idea that firm owners maximized, economics could assert something called "optimal decisions." These decisions were based on the thinking of a group of philosophers called "logical positivists."

Logical positivism started in early twentieth century Vienna and became known through the work of A. J. Ayer (1936). Positivists hold that only two kinds of statements have meaning: (1) those that are true merely because of the definitions employed (all bachelors are unmarried), and (2) those that could be shown to be true or shown to be false by some possible sense experience, such as a scientific experiment (water changes from a liquid to a gaseous state as greater heat is applied). If it cannot be verified by scientific means (empirically verifiable), the statement loses meaning. Thus, the statement "there is a God" or "Jane loves Dick" has no meaning.

Logical positivists, not to take it too far, argue that there can be no meaning attributable to that "known" independently of experience. In fact Ayer himself said (1936, p. 721), "[T]he admission that there were some facts about the world that could be known independently of experience would be incompatible with one fundamental contention that a sentence says nothing unless it is empirically verifiable." Ayer and his fellows ran into mathematics—not verifiable independently but the truths that are certain and necessary.

Others had tried to square the two. John Stuart Mills, for instance, had argued that mathematics cannot be proved universally true until we have seen all of the cases. Natural sciences and mathematics, he said, were very similar; their truths are probably so, but we have no guarantee—there may be an exception.

So what happens when there is found an exception to a mathematical statement? Suppose, for instance, that we accept as probably true the statement that 2 times 5 equals 10 and, when we count 5 pairs of objects, we find 10 objects. Then once we count and do not find 10 objects. In such a case, we would say (a) we were wrong to suppose there were 5 pairs to begin with, or (b) an object was taken away when we were not looking, or (c) the counting was wrong. We would explain the phenomena so that it fit the facts, but 2 times 5 would still be 10.

In effect, there is logic and mathematics on the one hand and there is observation and experience on the other. Or as Kant would have it, a synthetic proposition depends on what we see—its validity is determined by the facts of experience—and an analytic proposition is valid solely because of the definitions of the symbols it contains.

Consider a brief example (Ayer, 1936). A statement such as "There are ants which have established a system of slavery" awaits experience for confirmation or falsification. However, a statement such as "either some ants are parasitic or none are" depends solely on "either," "or," and "none" and acquires truth independently of experience. The truth of the matter is we know nothing about parasitic ants after reading the last statement, but we could, through observation, know something about slavery among ants from the first statement. Analytical statements have no factual content. No experience will ever refute them.

There is no lack of use here, in any case. Because, as Lincoln reasoned through the problem of what to do with rebellious Southerners after the War Between the States, (1) all Southerners are rebels, (2) all Southerners are Americans, therefore (3) all rebels are Americans.

These statements are tautologies, obvious truths, internally so. The tautological form holds through all analytical propositions: if P implies Q, and P is true, Q is also true.

Still analytical propositions do not increase knowledge, they are a priori knowledge. In even more direct terms, as Herbert Simon (1976) would say, they are values.

Simon based his thinking on roughly the same analytic-synthetic distinction. Decision making in administrative contexts stems from a set of premises, value premises and factual premises. Roughly, people, having defined the situation in a certain way (provided for themselves the value premise), readily choose the one best way to act (ascertain the facts and choose the optimal way).

However, Simon went on to show that the latter may not be so. As a matter of fact, individuals in administrative contexts have less than full knowledge of or capacity (time, resources) to gather the facts. Rather than optimize, people *satisfice,* or choose the first satisfactory alternative, given their value premise.

Economics steps in via cost-benefit analysis, using logical positivism, in two ways. First, economists argue that given the value premise, and ignoring the individual who is about to make a choice, one can judge, from the external situation, behavior optimally adapted to the situation. Cost-benefit analysis can provide a standard of optimality against which competing alternatives may be judged.

Second, economists also argue the need for aids to calculation that will help individuals, suffering with bounded rationality, cope with complex situations. Thus, cost-benefit analysis can uncover masked or hidden facts or even suggest ways to limit one's boundaries to insight.

These aids to calculation form a class of analytical methods that evaluate the economic or the choice—aspects of given decisions. Others are *utility theory*, which examines the relative worth of various alternatives measured subjectively and generally incorporating probability and the decision makers' attitudes toward risk; *cost-effectiveness analysis*, a measure of the relative efficiency of various technologies in achieving an already decided maximum result; and *cost-benefit analysis*, a measure of the relative efficiency of projects economically—"are the intended effects worth the cost?"

The cost-benefit analysis approach has its limits in government decision making, as the hypothetical five-project budget analysis above suggested. That is, cost-benefit analysis is often used to justify *ex post facto* a position already taken; the most significant factor in cost-benefit analysis is often its sponsor. Cost-benefit analysis tends to neglect the distributional consequences of a choice. The method systematically undervalues projects that improve the distribution of wealth and systematically overvalues projects that exacerbate economic inequality. In the Kaldor terminology, cost-benefit analysis would recommend a course of action that could potentially allow the winners to compensate the losers so that no one is worse off, but the method does not guarantee that the winners *will* compensate the losers.

Over and above the operational problems with cost-benefit analysis and, by extension, linear strategies based on economic reasoning, there are intangibles of fundamental importance that cost-benefit analysis cannot conceive. There is, for example, a moral significance in the duties and rights of individuals and of government in relation to the individual that is not comprehended in the measurement of consequences alone. Related to this idea, certain rights such as due process cannot be conceived simply because they are processes valued for themselves rather than outcomes.

Cost-benefit analysis has been blamed for damaging the political system. Some argue that politics is superior to analysis because of the wider scope of ideas and concepts that the people practicing politics can fathom. Others argue that analysis enfranchises unelected policy analysts and disenfranchises those who do not understand, do not believe, or cannot use analysis to make their arguments to government. Such a situation creates a loss of confidence in government institutions.

To return to cost-benefit analysis's basis in economics, others argue that that basis, insofar as it describes or prescribes government action, is flawed. That is, cost-benefit analysis assumes that there can be no market failure. There are always opportunity costs and shadow prices with which public sector goods can be valued. Research suggests, however, that markets are not perfectly competitive, that that lack of competition leads inevitably to failure, and that public goods are produced to remedy that failure. Without a way to value public goods, therefore, cost-benefit analysis fails to inform the decision making process.

Defending analysis, on the other hand, a simple economic idea—that any alternative must be judged in terms of other alternatives—lends support. Proponents of cost-benefit analysis argue that there is no alternative to cost-benefit analysis, none as explicit or systematic. In fact, cost-benefit analysis's formalized, explicit nature allows the public to hold its public officials accountable to a larger extent than under "normal politics and management." Systematic analysis is less likely to overlook an important fact or consideration that, when placed in an adversarial process such as politics, may lead to the determination of the public interest far sooner than mere impressionistic surmise.

The controversy over the use, misuse, or lack of use of analysis often pits those who believe in government against those who see the market as the predominantly positive force in society. Typically, what cost-benefit analysis overlooks is what most pro-government-action proponents find government most useful in providing—equity. Pro-market proponents argue that government intervenes for spurious reasons and, in doing so, creates more problems than it solves, certainly leading to less rather than more economic efficiency.

Summary

We have defined capital investment in terms of both equity and efficiency in this section. We have also shown that the Kaldor criterion for allocating government services fulfills that criterion in theory. In demonstrating the Kaldor criterion, we have demonstrated cost-benefit analysis and have elaborated most of its important technical facets. In doing so, we demonstrated that cost-benefit analyses rely on comparisons made among programs at the suborganization, then organization, then interorganization levels and that the outcome of these comparisons is the construction of portfolios of investments. The technology that might be used to improve these comparisons, and thus improve productivity, we argued, could be borrowed from portfolio construction models in business investment practice, since they too are based on cost-benefit analytic principles.

We further argued the heuristic, if not the absolute determinative value of this technology. Moreover, we demonstrated, through a small illustration, that cost-benefit analysis is a crucial learning tool in understanding policy problems. Nevertheless, the illustration revealed the limited nature of this technology in that analysts use other, different criteria in making final choices. These other, different criteria, often more heavily weighted than cost-benefit analysis, include managerial feasibility and a project's tendency toward encouraging fraud and abuse.

In the end, we classed cost-benefit analysis with other methods of thinking that follow a linear strategy and are basically deductive in nature. These methods ignore intuition, feeling, and other means of informing decisions. While practical in a limited way, the analytical methods underlying cost benefit analysis are often self-defeating. Especially inappropriate to government productivity, the methods defy reality, an administrative reality that must reconcile plural views, each of which describes more than monetized utility, in allocation policy choices.

NONLINEAR MODELS OF CAPITAL INVESTMENT STRATEGY

While optimization has substantial support among those who argue that capital investment should follow certain lines of thinking, other models that reflect what is actually done also exist. One of these other models is a nonlinear, as opposed to a linear, model. The nonlinear model is based on the notion of competition, a phenomena spanning zero sum games—we win to the same degree that our competitor loses—and nonzero sum games—we win but our competitor does not necessarily lose (Rapoport, 1960, p. 130–139). A nonlinear strategy also employs tactics that involve principles of surprise (paradox) or deterrence (making the hinted-at the obvious), all used in ways that reverse the way we normally view strategy (Luttwak, 1987), whether that strategy involves war-making or capital investment.

Nonlinear strategies differ in several regards from linear strategies, as the diagram below reveals. First, they differ in origin. Nonlinear strategies tend to emerge as multiple, competing centers vie for advantage. Linear strategies develop from a simpler, usually centralized structure. Second, they adapt in different ways. Nonlinear strategies tend to adjust in reaction to various conditions as they develop competitively. In economics, such would be called "price taking." Linear strategies permit much more initiative—are proactive—in setting conditions, as would exist under monopolistic (price making), rather than competitive, conditions. Third, each operates under unique circumstances. A nonlinear strategy is one in which the environment has a great deal of uncertainty but in which there is at least a known payoff for every risk. The environment for linear strategies is much more certain, with little risk ever having to be considered in decisions.

Linear strategies	Nonlinear strategies
1. Forthright goal setting	1. Gaming strategies that employ paradox and surprise
2. Centrism	2. Polycentrism
3. Price makers (monopoly)	3. Price takers (pure competition)
4. Stable, information rich environments	4. Unstable, risky environments

A nonlinear strategy can underlie capital investment in one major sense: a competitive market exists among communities in seeking taxpayers (Porter, 1985, 1980). That is, communities in a metropolitan area (or states in a region), offering various residential and industrial locations, may compete to optimize their own residents' housing values, through zoning, schools, or other programs, or to reduce the costs of doing business in the trade or industrial locations they offer. Capital investments, in such a competitive market, seek to realize a rate of return large enough to entice high-income residents to move in or stay rather than to leave. Investment decisions also encourage preferred businesses and industries to reduce their costs by relocating to the community or remaining, if already there. Localities compete, and *defeating* or *outrunning* other communities and organizations may be the best way to optimize home values, encourage trade, reduce manufacturing costs, and satisfy all concerns while developing a sturdy tax base.

Three lines of research support thinking about nonlinear strategies: that by Tiebout (1956), Peterson (1981), and Schneider (1989).

Tiebout and "Voting with Your Feet." The Tiebout idea of markets for local goods includes derivatives of the buyers and sellers of the "real" market. Buyers are community residents, as well as businesses and industries, who locate there. They pay for this location choice through taxes.

The location choice is a summary decision. Based upon preferences and costs, the location, according to Tiebout, is a rational purchase made by *mobile* buyers or buyers who could take advantage of a better opportunity if they could find it.

The local governments, public authorities, and decision makers are the public goods sellers confronting buyers. Their decisions provide the bundle that buyers find attractive and on which buyers' location decisions are based. Localities' decisions are aimed toward providing an attractive bundle at a fair price to a market that they have focused on as their niche.

Sellers get feedback, and buyers provide it, when they enter or exit a market as appropriate. Sellers may decide that certain public goods are not their forte, and buyers may decide that a particular bundle is not to their liking on the basis of cost or substance. In such cases, sellers then exit.

For example, a mass transit program may be proposed for a community. Some public officials, acting as sellers, may find that mass transit appeals to a group not important to their strategy for the future. Residents, acting as buyers, may feel that a bundle of services including mass transit is not useful to them or too costly or both. Sellers exit the competitive mass transit market, and buyers exit the community that provides it.

Peterson and Strategic Budgeting. Such niches, and product selection by the community—based as it is on bundle selection by sellers and buyers—leads naturally to strategic budgeting. That is, community decision makers decide to spend tax revenues in ways that futher develop their competitiveness in the niche they have selected.

The foremost proponent of this route to budgeting, Peterson (1981) proposes three categories of expenditures—development, redistribution, and allocation—the levels of which are manipulated to entice or discourage various buyer groups. Development expenditures support growth and include streets, utilities, and other infrastructure items. Redistributive expenditures are usually social welfare, health, or hospital expenditures that trasfer tax revenues from high-income groups to provide a safety net for low-income groups. Allocational expenditures are those related to general administration and are housekeeping expenditures.

Strategy dictates that communities encourage the most attractive groups of buyers or residents. In some cases, the community may find affluent buyers the most attractive; in others, a heterogeneous mixture of groups is attractive. In the former case, these buyers may want indirect or group benefits. Thus more budget for developmental and less for redistributive expenditures, holding allocational spending constant, emerges as a valid strategy of an affluent (or a wanting-to-become affluent) community. For a heterogeneous community, some balance between developmental and redistributive expenditures must be found, keeping in mind the tendency for redistributive expenditures to drive out developmental ones as well as the affluent taxpayers who are paying for redistributive expenditures.

Competition, of course, exists in providing the most attractive balance of expenditures at the least cost to taxpayers. For example, upscale communities compete for high-income residents whose consumption patterns attract upscale retailers. These retail businesses bear the tax burden that permits greater developmental expenditures (and reduces the relative burden on residents' properties), in turn making the locality more attractive to upscale residents.

Schneider and the Competitive City. The competition among cities has permitted greater scrutiny of actors, constraints and strategies in an effort to determine how nonlinear strategies emerge.

Actors and Interests. Residents want to insure the flow of dollars into the community's coffers without increasing their own tax bills. Strategies to achieve this trick include shifting the burden of taxes to the business sector or to taxpayers outside the community, increasing intergovernmental aid, or reducing expenditures.

Firms want to reduce their costs and increase profits. Reducing costs may include reducing taxes. Increasing profits may be brought about by increasing the income of a firm's clients or markets—by assuming the burden of their taxes—making them larger buyers of the firms goods and services. The differences among industries are great. National and international industries face much greater competition, making price important. Regional firms may be less interested in lowering costs and more in creating quality markets. The former, therefore, may be interested in lower taxes; the latter may tend to support greater taxes, of which they are willing to accept the burden, as long as these taxes support developmental expenditures to entice affluent buyers to locate in a particular community. These businesses may be able to shift the burden of taxes through price increases to the parts of their markets outside the jurisdiction, with such methods as mail order business.

Bureaucrats may want larger budgets or, even more simply, more utility, defined as greater flexibility or slack that larger budgets and other factors influence. Slack may be created, in fact, by adding the number of workers as well as or instead of salaries that a larger budget would imply. However, departments with large capital (developmental) expenditures may collide with departments with larger redistributive expenditures. The former departments' strategies would seem to jibe with strategies for winning the intercommunity competition for more affluent buyer markets, but who wins the bureaucratic wars is not so clear.

In fact, bureaucrats' choices depend for their realization on the strategic positions they hold in the collective choice process. Clearly, planners set the basic assumptions about development, influencing future decisions about appropriate projects and groups to be rewarded. Public works chiefs decide what sequence and even what priorities projects will have in a multiyear framework. These same chiefs implement plans, forcing substitutions and change-orders that have a significant effect on outcomes, as well. Finance officers have a say in what the government can afford and in how and when existing plans may be financed. City managers, having citywide welfare in mind, use the power of triage to close down facilities to optimize those the locality can afford. The officials often act in less than consensual fashion, and their strategic positions allow them to construct vetoes over others' choices.

Politicians want reelection (Downs, 1957, 1967), and, to that extent, satisfying enough voters to win reelection is their chief aim. Attracting a majority is a matter of keeping services to some level that permits keeping taxes low. Thus Schneider argues (1989, p. 35), "politicians benefit from improving their community's tax base, since this allows more demands to be satisfied within a given tax rate."

Schneider's research supports Peterson's strategic budgeting of developmental expenditures, in the main. Residents that want low tax bills, firms that want higher-income markets, bureaucrats that want greater slack and have the position to attain it, and politicians that want the support of residents for reelection may be viewed as determining a competitive strategy that defeats other affluent communities and impoverishes communities whose strategies promote redistribution.

Constraints. The constraints that tend to affect politicians and bureaucrats are those related to partisanship. That is, partisanship (Key, 1949) or strong political party organization (Jones, 1981) sometimes increases the size of government as those who vote demand government provided services, increasing the size of budgets, work forces, or both. Nonpartisanship may have the opposite effect.

Others, however, see the size of government influenced less by party organizations than the decision rules bureau officials follow in determining service (Lineberry, 1977).

As argued above, for example, a city manager's position in the choice process and the decision rule of triage can determine whether and what is eliminated or kept in the city budget, influencing the size of the budget.

With these constraints, therefore, what strategy tends to follow? Schneider's reading of the evidence (1989, pp. 37–38) leads to the following:

> Democrats are less likely to oppose bureaucratic demands for services and hence Democratic control of local governments would lead to larger local governments. . . . Furthermore, in reformed cities, bureaucrats are supposedly more responsive to the demands of the middle class for less spending and lower taxes. . . .

Highly Democratic communities seem likely to follow a strategy aimed at higher taxes than would reformed cities. Yet, reformed cities without large middle classes demanding lower taxes may follow the same strategy. Apparently, only reformed cities in which the middle and upper classes set tax relief as the top priority would follow a strategy of developmental spending policies in the interest of being competitive in the market for affluent residents and high tax paying businesses (Peltzman, 1980).

The federalist governmental structure in the United States and the capitalist economic system may also explain capital investments made by local governments. Likewise, local decision makers optimize residents housing values by reducing expenditures to hold down taxes. This may be done by constructing infrastructure with money from intergovernmental transfers or from capital markets.

So far then, economic determinism and residents' or consumer sovereignty prompt capital investment strategies. Far more needs to be known about a locality, decision makers, and the decision rules they follow when elected or appointed to office and delegated the authority to invest. Far more needs to be known about flexible, local finance structures, which are responsive to the very different, sometims contradictory imperatives dictated by corporate, consumers', and residents' concerns.

AMBIGUITY AND OPPORTUNISTIC LOGIC IN CAPITAL INVESTMENT STRATEGIES

There are other views on capital investment that deny its strategic elements and argue its deterministic nature. Some point out that the larger, national economy may determine capital investment decisions far more than local initiative (Peterson, 1981). Industrial location decisions, for instance, may result from national and regional market considerations rather than local amenities; the fiscal impact of these "foreign" decisions then forces local capital investments.

How? At the most fundamental level, these national decisions push governments to pursue development policies to accomodate these national movements and to control their consequences. First of all, a national firm's industrial location decisions prompt local land development succeeded by local land improvements, including transportation amenities, water systems, and waste treatment facilities. Development and improvements then prompt changes in land use patterns, which have implications for a considerable number of capital items that governments take the responsibility to provide, such as items to support fire services, police services, schools, and parks. Thus, any local discretion at these stages usually revolves around making land available, zoning those parcels appropriately, and handling the consequences.

The consequences of these development decisions require capital investment for education and training, child care, and health care. To some extent in a few of these areas and to a greater extent in others, these investments, originally a private sector responsibility, have become a public one (Castells, 1977; Harvey, 1973, 1982). If these services are not provided, a different, far more dire set of consequences develops.

All of the local initiatives that might take place to force national firms' decisions in one way or another tend to be constrained by capital markets to whom local officials turn as fiscal stress grows. For example, should a local community have small but inelastic revenues, as most do, and face the choice to zone to keep a piece of land vacant for possible future business development rather than immediate housing development, the resulting revenue loss can determine the outcome. That loss of revenue may be the difference in the ability to afford another needed asset. The same problem exists for communities that want to entice development with amenities. Which amenities do which firms want or need; can communities afford to simply guess? Will the firms locate for the amenities communities can provide even if they do not know for sure which firms are even looking?

Therefore, the decision to locate an industry in a particular place and the government's decision to invest in a particular asset might be more randomly related than consciously so (Pagano and Moore, 1985). It is this randomness, as well as the consequential decisions that follow, that create a pervasive ambiguity when we refer to capital investment. Thus, capital investment might be thought of as opportunistic, taking advantage of situations as they appear at the time, rather than strictly linear or even nonlinear.

What is ambiguity and how do opportunistic strategies relate? In a web of organizations, a decision is an outcome of the convergence of several relatively independent "streams," each stream produced by one of the organizations in the web (Cohen and March 1986, p. 81). A decision is a product of *contextual rationality* or the tendency of people, problems, solutions, and choices to be joined by relatively arbitrary accidents of timing rather than by their relevance to each other.

The accidents of timing emerge, and what we think of what happened is an "interpretation." There is no such thing as a right interpretation; one's interpretation of an event that was created through the random interaction of variables is usually a matter of opportunism in rationalizing that event in an appropriate and favorable way after the fact (Daft and Weick, 1984; Cohen, March and Olsen, 1972). Opportunistic strategies make fact out of accident and plausibility out of happenstance, and they permit at least primitive organizing to emerge.

Interpretations are born out of metaphors that are carried around in leaders' heads to rationalize their methods of making choices as well as the choices themselves; what leaders use in hindsight to portray events springs from a metaphorical view of the world they hold. For instance, Cohen and March's study of university governance (1986) produced seven such metaphors that they found university presidents to impose on their organizations and their work. These metaphors are adapted to government organizations and portrayed in Table 3.

Each metaphor carries with it a reasonably independent method of management and resource allocation decision making. For example, the first five in Table 3 tend to be linear, strategic metaphors, whether a lone autocrat or a democratic process forces a decision. The competitive market metaphor underlies nonlinear strategy.

The anarchy metaphor is different still. It provides that the leader be the catalyst who brings together independent streams of only partially interested parties in choice situations that make use of superior information. The university president (1974, p. 39)

Table 3   Metaphors of Strategy

---

1. *Plebiscitary autocracy metaphor*. An autocrat makes all decisions on behalf of the organization until such time as a plebiscite is called for to ratify the autocrat's performance. The autocrat serves at the overwhelming approval of the electorate or abdicates. Decisions to be made are technically complicated relative to the amount of time and knowledge available to organization members, and the variance of objectives among participants is so small that small amounts of time and interaction may make up for it.

2. *Collective bargining metaphor*. Assuming fundamentally conflicting interests within the organization, citizens, managers, politicians, and other interested parties resolve conflicts by resorting to bargaining, often through representatives, using formal "contracts" and social pressure for enforcement.

3. *Democratic metaphor*. The organization can be viewed as community with an electorate of organization members and clients. Major decisions are made by resorting to voting, and votes are swayed by promises of one sort or another.

4. *Consensus metaphor*. To achieve agreement organization members resort to some procedure, including discourse and assembly, which have typically relied on those with high interest and large amounts of time for involvement and participation. Unanimity is possible because of the relative lack of both interest and time among organization members.

5. *Independent judiciary metaphor*. Authority is bestowed by some relatively arbitrary process—birth, cooptation, revelation—on a group of current leaders. This method assumes that "there are substantial conflicts between the immediate self-interests of current constituencies and the long run interests of future constituencies" (Cohen and March, 1986, p. 84). It is possible to train a judge to recognize the long-run interests and to convince constituencies to accept judgments made in this way.

6. *Competitive market metaphor*. Government organizations provide a bundle of goods and services in a free market. All needing these goods and services select among alternative providers and choose those that come closest to serving perceived needs.

7. *Anarchy metaphor*. The organization's members make autonomous decisions. Resources are allocated by whatever process emerges but without explicit accommodation and with explicit reference to some superordinate goal. Decisions produced in the organization are a consequence produced by the system but intended by no one and decisively controlled by no one. The statistical properties of a large number of these autonomous decisions are such that they will reliably produce jointly satisfactory states.

Source: Cohen and March (1986, pp. 81–84).

"gains . . . influence by understanding the operation of the system and by inventing viable solutions that accomplish . . . objectives rather than by choosing among conflicting alternatives." Subtle adjustments in the form of managing unobtrusively, giving more time, exchanging status for substance, facilitating opposition participation, overloading the system, and providing many opportunities in which problems, participants, solutions, and choice situations come together, work to the catalyst's interest in making choices (1974, p. 209–211).

Organizations, according to Cohen and March (1986), vary in the metaphorical requirements they have. Variance in most regards is a matter of the amount of attention the organization members can give a choice situation as well as the flow of problems and solutions involved. The patterns underlying the apt application of a metaphor might be a matter of how independent, exogenous, and rapid the flow of the streams of problems, solutions, participants, and choice opportunities might be.

The application to investment strategy's unique problems follows these premises. Capital investments represent simultaneous flows of information through various choice structures. Picture an ecology of games (Long, 1958) as an appropriate way to suggest the various interpretations involved. One's problem is another's solution. Many solutions—indicated by the number and type of participants on a given day—swamp the number of problems. Moreover, the number of choice opportunities—times in which a formal decision should be rendered—may vary from time to time. As Long (1985, p. 58) illustrates,

> [A] particular highway grid may be the result of a bureaucratic department of public works game in which are combined, though separate, a professional highway engineer game with its purposes and critical elite onlookers; a departmental bureaucracy; a set of contending politicians seeking to use the highways for political capital, patronage, and the like; a banking game concerned with bonds, taxes and the effect of the highways on real estate; newspapermen interested in headlines, scoops, and the effect of highways on the papers' circulation; contractors eager to make money by building roads; ecclesiastics concerned with the effect of highways on their parishes and on the fortunes of the contractors who support their churchly ambitions; labor leaders interested in union contracts and their status as community influentials with a right to be consulted; and civic leaders who must justify the contributions of their bureaus of municipal research or chambers of commerce to the social activity.

Each agenda and each choice opportunity are related by chance, making the outcome predictable only through random association.

March and Olsen's model illustrates two points that need to be kept in mind in discussing opportunistic investment strategy. The first is the contextual nature of decisions and, especially, the role of timing in decision results. That is, a decision is not made in the abstract but in the context of actual people interpreting events on a given day and determining an outcome with the information they have at the time and the metaphor they use to define the problem and to structure the problem-solving process.

The second idea relates to the role of institutions (Kaufman, 1960; Selznick, 1957). Permanent procedures and organizations make the randomness associated with contextual decision making a little easier to understand. Institutions provide stability where none may exist otherwise. Institutions also epitomize enduring values and attachments that members recall as they make decisions. With these values, and the procedures that go with them, institutions act as homogenizing influences, helping gain conformity in an otherwise fragmented system of attachments and work.

Applying Contextual Rationality and Anchoring Institutions to Capital Investment

Understanding the role of institutions in capital investment may seem difficult in the face of ambiguity. In fact, a few institutions have become issues themselves[11] because they had too much control over ambiguity.[12] The purpose of this section,[13] then, is to shed

[11]By some calculations, public authorities, for example, issue and manage between one-fifth and one-fourth of all long-term municipal securities. Given present forecasts, the 1990 total would suggest a market of some $25 billion. They are attacked (Walsh, 1978) for having too much responsibility and too little accountability, which in this case may mean too little ambiguity.

[12]For work on the Washington Public Power Supply System, see Leigland and Lamb (1986); for work on sidestepping the normal political accountability mechanisms with public authorities in order to build public facilities, see Bennett and DiLorenzo (1983), Henriques (1982), and Walsh (1978).

[13]This section is based on a paper delivered at the annual meeting of the American Political Science Association, Washington, DC, September 2, 1988. I thank Robert T. Golembiewski and W. Bartley Hildreth for their comments.

light on the institutions that thrive on ambiguity, how these institutions operate, and, most important of all, how and what opportunistic strategies public organizations use to budget and finance capital projects.

We turn next to a brief overview of the argument our observations lead us to make, followed by (1) an explanation of the form of institutionalization that takes place to permit opportunistic strategies to emerge; (2) a description of the process of mobilizing bias that underlies opportunistic strategies; and (3) a classification of capital investment strategies that provide opportunities to mobilize bias, construct reality and rationalize ambiguous events.

Institutionalization

Financing strategies emerge from a set of people who form a team; this semipermanent institutional form has responsibility for formulating and implementing the major parts of the investment strategy. Formulation tends to involve some form of bargaining among team members, with bargaining positions developed over long periods of network—team members and their multiple contacts—development through direct and indirect contact (Miller, 1985; Hildreth, 1986, 1987; Sbragia, 1983). Strategy implementation may best be described as the mobilization of bias through the classification of information. Classification emerges out of the efforts of those directly involved in the sales and the larger network of market participants of which they are a part.

Such a description of reality suggests something far different than a principal-agent model of strategy formulation suggested by both linear and nonlinear forms of capital investment strategy (Eisenhardt, 1989). We argue here that investment team members have different goals, and the outcome of their effort is more likely to be a least common denominator of these different goals than a rational pursuit of the issuer's end.

The basic assumption made in this argument is that each organization represented on the team pursues a goal suited to that organization's survival and success. In this research, we use an interorganizational network model that behaves as a political economy. Under some conditions, which we outline, the network members' stability or experience with each other becomes a major factor in the network's success. That experience, in turn, depends on the various bargains struck within the network. These bargains, in turn, reflect the larger pattern of interaction among network members and the outside world.

This approach also provides an alternative view to linear and nonlinear strategies, showing that capital investment is much more of a bargain struck among peer organizations. In fact, the amalgamation of positions after the bargain is hard to reconcile with prior positions, along strictly means-ends terms. Rather, the appropriate framework might go beyond such simple views to incorporate this network bargaining.

Principal and Agent Models

The myth of agency in conventional strategy formulation lies in the believed relationship between budgeting and debt financing; that belief forms the ideal for practice in communities,[14] and it has led reformers to point their efforts in the wrong direction.

The foremost proponents of the myth and of conventional public sector financing strategy, Wetzler and Peterson (1985), portray it as a rational process, as in Table 4. That

---

[14]See the recent action by the State of California regarding this ideal linkage, which they legislated into practice (Walters, 1990).

Table 4 Conventional (Linear) Strategic Choice Process for Capital Projects

Step	Description
1. Examine the environment	Examine locality's competitive position (e.g., industrial location)
2. Assess the current situation	Determine current condition of public goods or enterprises (e.g., infrastructure)
3. Set goals	Determine public goods or enterprises to be developed
4. Identify the alternatives	Identify debt instruments and investment vehicles, interest rate cycles, markets, and tax policies in effect or pending
5. Analyze alternatives via return on investment	Determine the savings or earnings per dollar committed by considering the capital project's lifetime costs and benefits *as well as* the costs of financing by the various means surveyed
6. Select optimal alternative	Choose the time and method of financing

Source: Wetzler and Petersen (1985).

is, strategy requires principals formulating strategy (managers) to choose among projects of different rates of return and levels of risk, in order to exploit targeted capital markets, which will, through time, convert resource and tax-base contributions to a higher performing portfolio of assets. This is very much what we described a the linear logic underlying some forms of capital investment strategy, in earlier parts of this chapter.

The strategy may be formed by employing agents (financial advisors, legal counsel, accountants, and other consultants). These agents provide the analyses of what measures will connect the project to a capital market that can finance it in return for the promise to repay implicit in a stream of revenue directly, indirectly, or not at all connected to the project itself.

Network Models

On the other hand, the strategies that emerge in financing capital improvements may actually result from substantial interaction among many parties, all of which have relatively insular views about the specific strategic and tactical moves to be made to insure success in financing. In fact, it is the insularity, the individual positions parties bring to the bond sale team, that makes bargaining, rather than mere computation, possible.

That bargaining may be the only accountability mechanism available, and it is one the agency myth overlooks. That is, the agency myth forces the reformer to blame public managers and to promote efforts to rein them in. The network approach can argue the benefits of bargaining in forcing team members to stabilize their relationships in order to achieve efficiency and, under certain circumstances, the public interest.

In the description of actual roles and behaviors in strategy formulation and implementation here, we discuss the market making efforts that go into creating a bond sale, then show how information is pooled, classified, and interpreted by this team through bargaining. The bargaining involves not only those directly involved in market making—the team—but also an even larger network of important decision makers that includes credit rating agencies, competing issuers of debt, and, ultimately, bond buyers, all of whom we describe and relate to one another in the next sections.

Strategy implementation, which we describe in the following section, involves three activities: (1) building a network, the structure behind the strategy; (2) mobilizing bias, giving purpose and direction to the strategy; and (3) determing the opportunistic strategies used in capital investment themselves.

The Structure behind the Strategy: A Network Model of the Bond Sale Team

If we consider the team-focused rather than the issuer-dominated framework as reasonable, we confront initially the lack of a workable concept. Public and private sectors relate bilaterally most often, as in buyer-seller relations. In multilateral relations, most conceptions, such as the Triple Alliance/Iron Triangle (Freeman, 1965; Cater, 1964), tend to be too simplistic or, as with issue networks (Heclo, 1978), irrelevant.

More recently, the concept of interorganizational networks has enjoyed revival and gained greater attention (Aldrich, 1979; Tichy et al., 1979). By a network, we mean the "totality of all the units connected by a certain relationship" (Jay, 1964, p. 138).

A network is constructed by discovering all the ties that bind a given population of organizations (Aldrich and Whetten, 1981). Typically, organization ties may be classified as organization-sets (Evan, 1966)—those organizations with which a focal organization has direct links—or action-sets (Barker and Jansiewicz, 1970)—a group of organizations that have formed a temporary alliance for a limited purpose—or both. The obvious difference between the two—organization- and action-sets—lies not just in the unit of analysis but in the more important concept of network stability, bearing in mind its consequences as well.

Network Stability and Its Consequences

Stability evolves through the work of linking-pin organizations, which have extensive and overlapping ties to different parts of a network. The links may be thought of as, functionally, communications channels between organizations, resource conduits among network members, and even models to be imitated by other organizations in the population. Thus, an accounting firm might channel information about a reporting standard from rating agencies to bond issuers; the firm might direct clients to financial advisors the firm's members respect as a result of previous bond sales; or the firm itself, through one or more of its many services, might serve as a model for a municipal finance office.

All organizations within a network are linked directly or indirectly, and stability depends on the strength of these links. Aldrich and Whetten (1981, p. 391) hypothesize:

> The ultimate predictor of network stability is the probability of a link failing, given that another has failed. This, in turn, is a function of the probability of any one link failing and two network characteristics: the duplication of linkages and the multiplicity of linkages between any two organizations.

Such hypotheses find confirmation in the literature on public management. Landau (1969) argued that redundancy tends to ensure performance. Golembiewski (1964) has argued that duplication works, in symbiotic interrelationships, to prevent the exercise of vetoes by powerful subunits.

Finally, the major result of stability is a greater willingness to take risks and greater adaptability. Richly joined networks provide for greater opportunity for trial and error and for the spread of innovation (Aldrich, 1979: 282; Terreberry, 1968).

Assume a simplistic situation, momentarily, a small network consisting of a financial advisor, an accounting firm, and a law firm (Lemov, 1990). The three are richly joined in the following ways:

1. The law firm acts as corporation to the other two organizations.
2. The accounting firm audits the transactions of the other two organizations; moreover, auditors have been recruited and have joined the financial advising firm from time to time as principals.
3. The three organizations are active in the new-issue market for municipal securities with all other possible participants, and they serve together on a team for a bond sale for public authority issuer A.

Authority A becomes the beneficiary of knowledge about changes made by Congress in tax laws relating to municipal debt, about specific needs for information by rating agencies, and new debt structures that may be designed to appeal to specific segments of the market. The richly joined network untimately results in locality A's ability to adjust to complex and changing environments.

Now consider a more complex example. Assume that among a population of law firms that act as bond counsel, the firms tend, as a matter of each's ideology, to differ in their approach to interpreting the law as it regards various creative capital financing structures, some firms being indulgent, others strict. Assume, furthermore, that in a population of accounting firms asked to forecast the revenue stream that would generate principal and interest payments for various creative capital financing structures, some firms would tend to be liberal, others tight. Finally, assume that among a population of financial advisors, the same sort of variation would exist among opinions about the applicability and marketability of debt structures.

Random selection of a combination of these firms by an issuer would yield a team advising the issuer to take a particular course of action, one in which the knowledge each advisor had, as well as the expectation each had of the other's interpretation and its effect on the market for the issue, would play a part. The result would produce a bargain in which a security configured in a unique way was rated and sold.

Now assume a second random selection of firms by an issuer and a second sale. What knowledge does the second team have about the configuration of the first security? What keeps the second team from relying on an incorrect interpretation of what the first team did? What keeps the second sale from "missing the market"?

The situation is somewhat like the cobweb economists use to explain market instability and sellers' imperfect knowledge. As portrayed (see Heilbroner and Thurow, 1984, pp. 126–127) in Fig. 1, a commodity supplier provides quantity OA, but under conditions of supply and demand at the time could sell OA for price OB. The next year, the supplier ensures that on-hand quantities equal that demanded the year before but finds under the same supply and demand conditions price OD. The result is a spiral of sorts. Yet if conditions change as the two graphs show, the spiral could be successively more beneficial (Fig. 2, left) or it would be successively more explosive (Fig. 2, right).

The upshot of the random selection notion with which we began is that, without gaining experience, the randomly selected team has as great a chance of exploding as spiraling into an equilibrium.

On the other hand, given learning that a stable network would produce, a team, not selected at random, might have a better chance of understanding the same market because members need less time to learn what to expect of each other—since they have duplicate ways of understanding each other—and more time to understand conditions in the market, whether changing or not.

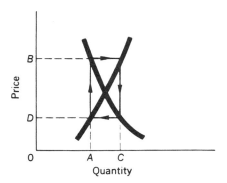

Figure 1 The cobweb. See text for the explanation. If expectations and information remain unchanged, producers will go on chasing their tails forever.

The Evidence

Evidence supporting the idea of stable networks comes in three parts: that from the Washington Public Power Supply System (WPPSS) bond default, from a recent episode in the saga of the New Jersey Turnpike Authority (NJTA), and from a case of a technical default in a midwestern city's Recycle Energy System (RES).

WPPSS

Noting the detailed analyses of the power supply system's default (Leigland and Lamb, 1986; Myhra, 1984; Jones, 1984), two causes of the default bear out facets of the exploding cobweb. First, Leigland and Lamb (1986) characterize the responsibility-taking of individuals—from WPPSS, bankers, bond counsel, and various subcontractors—as absent, stemming from a network significantly lacking cross checks of the incentives to challenge assumptions the others made. For example, they point out (1986, pp. 207–208):

> From the outset, top executives assumed that policy planning (particularly the assessment of demand for the plants) was the job of the board, public utility districts, and the regional planning system; that project management was the job of private contractors, particularly the architect-engineers; and that quality assurance was the job of the Nuclear Regulatory Commission. The board left planning to the Bonneville Power Administration and regional utility groups. Simply assuming that top management could effectively run the organization, the board occupied itself almost exclusively with details, such as individual change order approvals, without looking at the broader implications involved. . . . During the financing of the WPPSS projects, bond salesmen and analysts attached disclaimers to published reports on the WPPSS bonds to avoid responsibility for statements that were sometimes little more than good promotional copy. Underwriters and financial advisers concentrated on selling bonds at increasing interest rates leaving WPPSS the responsibility of understanding and solving the underlying problems that were undermining its creditworthiness. Bond fund managers and institutional investors carefully reviewed legal opinions to reassure themselves that all responsibility for WPPSS debts would rest squarely with the project participants.

In addition, the bond rating agencies could claim, as a reason for ignorance of problems besetting the system and impending default, as did one (Blumstein, 1983, p. 24F), "I react to information that's given to us."

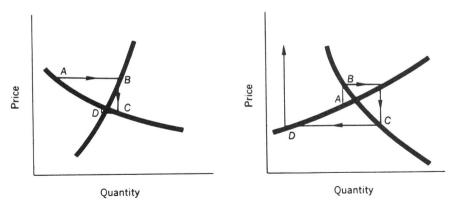

Figure 2 Stabilizing and explosive cobwebs. The cobweb on the left spirals into an equilibrium and the one on the right "explodes." The reason in both cases lies in the position and shape of the supply-and-demand curves. If supply and demand are favorable, a cobweb can lead to stability, if they are wrong, instability can result.

The lack of responsibility ultimately led to the "tar baby syndrome" or what Jones (1984) called vector politics. As the system's problems began to attract public attention on a broader, national scale, "everyone involved with WPPSS quickly became afraid of being associated with, and even more, responsible for, those problems—of being stuck to the tar baby" (Leigland and Lamb, 1986, p. 209). The tar baby appeared even stickier when it became known that some Congressional bailout effort was underfoot. To Jones (1984, p. 72), "numerous participants in the [process] all pulled hard to represent their separate interests and the resulting absence of compromise left no alternative to default. . . . Default was the result of vector politics."

The technical causes also point out the exploding consequences of decisions the system managers made. Myhra (1984) argues the exploding effect of the capitalized interest financing plan. The strategy involved issuing bonds that would pay for interest on earlier issues of bonds. This plan, often thought also to be a proximate cause of the New York City fiscal crisis (Morris, 1980, pp. 128–139), led to inverted pyramidiing in which larger and larger bond issues had to sell to pay for old interest, new construction, and new interest. As the issues grew larger, the creditworthiness of each one became more questionable since no new revenue-generating capacity had come on stream through power plants.

NJTA

The political controversy arising in the NJTA case involved a presumed advantage in issuing bonds before the deadline imposing new rules under the Tax Reform Act of 1986. In this case, the NJTA had reversed a policy of issuing bonds for repair, upkeep, and general, incremental improvement of the New Jersey Turnpike. Reacting to the limits placed on arbitrage and other matters in the Act (Watson and Vocino, 1990), the Authority and its bankers planned a major expansion of the highway, including widening the road through environmentally sensitive wetlands and large urban areas. The bankers proposed one large bond issue, which could be invested over the decades-long life of the construction project.

The glaring problem, and the politically explosive issue, involved the amount of planning that had been completed at the time of the bond sale. Later, observers noted that no environmental impact study had preceded the bond issue, and no consultation with environmental regulators or urban groups had taken place. Rather the bankers' view of the act's consequences had led to a rapid inventory of possible projects to justify the issue size, which had, in turn, prompted grander visions of the scope improvements could entail, in turn, again prompting a larger bond issue size through estimated construction savings and interest earnings.

Midwestern City RES

In the case of the Recycle Energy System (Hildreth, 1988), there exists the contrasting case of a stable network whose rich links promoted responsibility-taking for the common good. The RES was instituted as a public authority the principle purpose of which was the construction and operation of a steam-generating operation that burned solid waste. A state agency issued tax-exempt debt on the RES's behalf, securing repayment flow control ordinance agreements with the city and county,[15] tipping fees from solid waste haulers, and "take or pay" contracts with steam heat customers.[16] Revenues did not meet projected totals and a technical default was declared.

The important facts in this case, however, related to the "workout," the effort by those involved to get the revenue/repayment stream restarted and the default ended. Hildreth (1988) outlines the major participants and their survival strategies: the midwestern city, nominally the operator of the plan and guarantor of some of the bond payments as well as issue of some of the bonds; the bond counsel who had worked for the midwestern city for some 30 years and also counsel to the state agency issuing the bulk of the bonds; the trustee whose legal authority and commonsense role could lead to a conflict—ministerially declare the default and litigate or prudently plan to reach the objective of both issuer and bondholder; and the institutional investors whose primary interest was in getting the principal and interest to which their investment entitled them even if the city and state had to enact draconian tax measures to do it.

The rich links, however, prevented the wholesale cut-and-run that survival instincts promoted. Institutional investors, prompted by the midwestern city mayor's good faith efforts, pressured the bond trustee to act prudently rather than ministerially. The bond counsel added the ability to influence the state agency to go along with a carefully thought-through process of guaranteeing full payment to investors.

The Model

By combining elements of the bond deal with our hypotheses, we can build a model. From this model, we may draw conclusions on which to base advice for municipal bond issuers in forming teams.

Recall that the process of issuing debt involves four steps. Initiation of a sale rests

---

[15]According to Hildreth (1988, p. 10), "To ensure an adequate supply of refuse, both the city and county agreed to enact ordinances requiring that all solid waste collected in their respective jurisdictions be disposed of at the RES after payment of the required tipping fee."
[16]Again, according to Hildreth (1988, p. 10), "The contracts included 'take or pay' provisions: the contract customers paid for the contracted level of steam even if they did not use the steam."

on the choice of the market. Which investors will/should buy the securities? Tax laws, the economic cycle, and the habitual purchasing practices of individuals and institutions combine in reasonably predictable ways to encourage accurate choices.

The second step in the process involves structuring an issue to confront two problems: the predilections of the market chosen and the capacity of the issuer. The structure directly connects the market with disclosure.

The third step, then, is disclosure of the issue and the issuer: what facts will be disclosed, and, more importantly, what interpretation will be presented for these facts, whether in the OS alone or in the OS and to the ratings agencies.

The final step is the sale, at which time all parties decide the price of the issue. The sale confirms the assumptions made by the team about the structure of the issue and the level of demand for the quantity provided. In viewing the sale another way, it becomes a confirming piece of information about where the sale fell on the cobweb. If the guess about supply and demand resulted in a spiral inward, we can say the team "learned."

Learning and Expectations

Consider what factors might encourage "learning." Our hypothesis suggests that the number of links among members of the team leads to stability, and stability, in turn, leads to learning and adaptation. We use an expectations approach to understand richly linked organizations in the bond team context. That is, each member of the bond team must be guided in each one's assigned task by expectations of the behavior of others. The financial advisor cannot select a market unless the advisor can expect to have counsel's positive legal interpretation of the structure that would most logically follow the selection of that market. Likewise, the advisor cannot select a market without the expectation that the CPA will interpret the various issuer capacities in such a way as to support the structure the market suggests. No decision made by any member of the team, in the end, can be made in a vacuum, without the knowledge of what the other members are likely to do. Otherwise, the decisions made by the members form an endless iteration—a loop—in which market choice forces structure but is confounded by disclosure leading to a new market and a new structure and interpretations wedded to the previous structure, confounding this new market and structure.

Rich Links among Team Members

One solution to the problem of expectations is a richly linked network of organizations. Rich links lead to knowledge of likely behavior under varying circumstances. Assumptions at extremely general levels are shared or at least made widely known through large numbers of activities in which the linked organizations jointly participate. Rich links also provide multiple avenues for testing of expectations under widely varying conditions. For example, legal interpretations a bond counsel is likely to submit may be expected based on the legal interpretations the bond counsel has traditionally issued in the capacity of the corporate counsel, as the earlier illustration depicted.

Rich Links and Learning

If rich links lead to shared expectations of behavior, these links contribute to learning. Consider the argument for specific types of teams in municipal finance. The negotiated rather than the competitive sale invites the sort of stability and exploitation of existing rich links among potential members of a team. Negotiated sales require the issuer to choose precisely those members who have apparently "learned" the market as well as each other in terms of the market. A negotiated sale provides an opportunity to choose the market (especially when the sale is privately placed), opening the way or creating the need for innovation (craftwork rather than routine technology) in the type of issue structure chosen. The negotiated sale also provides incredible overlap and duplication in the work involved.

Such rich links and the opportunities provided by the negotiated sale invite learning. Stigler (1961) indicated that buyers and sellers accumulate information from their experience in the marketplace that allows them to obtain more favorable conditions in each successive transaction. More specifically, Bland (1985) found that issuers using multiple, negotiated sales received more favorable terms through each successive sale up to a certain point. He concluded (p. 236): "Local governments with previous bond market experience are capable of assembling a management team that can negotiate an interest rate comparable to what the most sought after competitive issues obtain."

To recap, a network's being stable or unstable depends on the wealth of links among its members. The greater the stability, the greater the opportunities for learning. The greater the amount of learning, the greater the chance for innovation and adaptation.

Efficient Markets

Finally, we turn to the notion of efficient markets, the broader goal of all participants in the sale of municipal securities. An efficient market is one that allocates scarce capital among competing uses, and assigns appropriate prices (interest payments to the issuer and bond prices and yields to the investor) to structures at particular levels of repayment capacity. Under what conditions does network stability lead to market efficiency?

The answer lies in the reiteration of our model with one significant addition. Network stability develops through duplicative links among organizations in a network. Rich links open opportunities for learning. Learning leads to greater adaptability. Greater adaptability, of course, leads to better guesses about which market to choose under what conditions. Moreover, adaptability helps shape disclosure, telling what to disclose to what market to provide its participants evidence of levels of risk and levels of reward.

Summary

In this section, we have depicted the strategic capital financing process as something more than the issuer-dominated activity researchers and public policymakers would have us believe. We argue that the process is much more a network activity that thrives when that network of participating organizations retains a large amount of stability. Such permanence allows the network to learn and its members to expect particular types of behavior from each other. More imporantly, the network creates a dependence, especially for finance officers, who require the reality construction that the network can provide.

Each member of the bond team must be guided in each's assigned task by expectations of the behavior of others. The financial advisor cannot select a market unless the advisor can expect to have counsel's positive legal interpretation of the structure that would most logically follow the selection of that market. Likewise, the advisor cannot select a market without the expectation that the CPA will interpret the various issuer capacities in such a way as to support the structure the market suggests. No decision made by any member of the team, in the end, can be made in a vacuum, without the knowledge of what the other members are likely to do. Otherwise, the decisions made by the members form an endless iteration—an exploding cobweb—in which market choice forces structure but is confounded by disclosure leading to a new market and a new structure and interpretations wedded to the previous structure, confounding this new market and structure. In short, an efficient and accountable process is one in which scarce capital is allocated among competing uses, and the issuer receives favorable interest costs and investors obtain desirable bond prices and yields. Gaining an efficient and accountable process rests on realizing networks with rich links among its members.

Mobilizing Bias

We have considered here the team involved in the sale of municipal securities, a fairly large group of experts involved in either of two types of sale: guaranteed debt and nonguaranteed debt (for this distinction, see Sharp, 1986). Guaranteed debt is that which the full taxing power of a governmental unit supports. Nonguaranteed debt is usually secured by the repayment capacity of a revenue stream, such as a sales tax or fees from the sale of water. Guaranteed debt sales have become ever more tightly regulated by state constitutions and legal codes; in addition, federal law allows both banks and investment banks[17] to underwrite (bid for or purchase) these securities.

As a result, these securities have become homogeneous, commoditylike instruments, requiring little distinction among advisors in their structuring. They rely for distinction on the creditworthiness of their issuers, as interpreted by rating agencies, and the point in the business cycle at which they are sold.

Ambiguity and Risk

A nonguaranteed debt sale has become the place where advisors may actually use their creative talents. Because revenue streams may lack history as a basis for forecasting, "the market" must rely on an advisor to depict their earning capacity. Legal interpretations may also be required. Moreover, the market itself has to be analyzed to determine likely purchasers of the securities both initially and in the secondary market.

Such ambiguity comes in at least four forms and is normally depicted as "risk." First, economic risk entails the ups and downs of the business cycle and the effect of those changes on interest rates. Second, legal risk may involve accurately depicting local, state, and federal law regarding securities offerings as well as foreseeing the strategic necessity to forestall litigation or, at the very least, unfavorable court judgments. Third, market risks reflect the sources of demand for municipal securities, and these sources of demand have become increasingly narrow for tax-exempt securities but far broader (and more volatile) for taxable municipal bonds (Petersen and O'Brien, 1988; Petersen et al., 1987). Fourth, the default risk is best known and is the calculated potential of a borrower to repay principal and interest in a timely manner.

The bond sale team's major responsibility lies in coping with these risks. The team does so by mobilizing bias, by identifying, exchanging, and classifying the bases for ambiguity and the coping mechanisms appropriate to them that are formed out of team members' biases. These biases respond to concerns of those outside the immediate circle of bond sale team participants, avoids opposition inside and outside, and advances each member's own interests. We discuss this mobilization of bias as three stages: (1) or-

---

[17]For the difference in banks and investment banks, see the discussion of the Glass-Steagall Banking Reform Act of 1933 distinctions in Horvitz (1981) and the distinctions related specifically to present underwriting opportunities in Dale (1988).

ganizing responsibility for sensing risk and opportunity, (2) exchanging this information, and (3) classifying it in ways that dictate action.

Information and Sensing

The ambiguity or risk that attaches to a municipal securities offering leads to both strategic and tactical necessities. Most of these can be classed as coping mechanisms for dealing with uncertainty (Miller, 1985) or, more simply, efforts at pooling available information. The issuer forms a team to pursue a securities offering, and this team pools information.

The team in a nonguaranteed debt sale forms out of three basic groups of advisors: those whose efforts are made toward informing the issuer of the market and of the economic conditions constraining the offering, those who inform the underwriter/investor of the law, and those who inform the issuer and the bondbuyers of the financial condition of the issuer.

On Economic and Market Risk. The financial advisor usually leads the effort to inform the issuer of economic and, especially, market conditions. The financial advisor determines how broad a market can be attracted to a sale and when the sale might take place to minimize interest costs or what might be done to negotiate a private placement. The determination of the market leads directly to the structuring of the security, influencing fundamentally its various features (see Hildreth, 1986, 1987; Moak, 1982; Lamb and Rappaport, 1980). The financial advisor may also be the underwriter—the buyer of the securities from the issuer for resale—if the sale is a negotiated one between issuer and underwriter, rather than a competitive one or a private placement.

On Legal Risk. The bond counsel leads the effort to inform the structuring of the security in terms of applicable law for the underwriter/issuer. Many regard bond counsel as the primary representative of investors, assuring them that the issuer will not default on an obligation by pleading legal defects in the procedures used to authorize or issue the bonds. Yet Petersen observes (1988, p. 4) that "additional roles of bond counsel in preparing transactions for market and [for] disclosure are extensive, flexible, and subjects of professional debate." Very clearly, one such additional role is that of creative thinker, assuring one and all that new financing techniques are not buried by the means and ends of traditional financing (Section on State and Local Government Law, 1987, pp. 8–25). Such roles blur the traditional view of the counsel as an overseer for investors, and, as a way to add focus, the bond counsel may be assisted by counsel for an underwriter in a negotiated sale as well as counsel for any other party, including the issuer, if the structure's complexity demands it.

On Default Risk. Third, the auditor or accounting specialist (CPA) informs the team members and potential bondbuyers of the issuer's financial condition, in terms of the structure of the security. For example, the CPA reports the issuer's financial status, as depicted through financial reports. If the revenue stream underlying the security must be forecast, the CPA may also verify the assumptions and calculations made to confirm the stream's contribution to the issuer's ability to repay principal and interest. While others, such as consulting engineers, management specialists or other experts may join in the pooling of information on the issuer's financial status or the project being financed, the CPA remains the primary data source for determining default risk.

Exchange of Information

The pooling of information that will be used later in characterizing the risk of the issue comes through consultation and advice, disclosure, and interview and inspection.

Consultation and Advice. Foremost among the expected traits of the financial advisor, bond counsel, and CPA is that of consultant. Looking at a vast number of important projects and the impenetrable future of the market for debt, the issuer relies on these sources of expertise. Yet these advisors must rely on each other as well, since the risks each deal with have implications for those of the others. To illustrate with the most obvious, the CPA's study of default risk has much to say about the financial advisor's opinion about timing of the sale: the greater the default risk, the greater the wait for periods of high market demand for securities of all levels of quality. Likewise, legal advice will confine the range of permissible debt structures, and that will, in turn, limit the market potential of the issue from the financial advisor's point of view.

The Public and Press. Information provided to reduce interest rate, market, legal, or default risk may also come from the larger public, including the press. Certainly, the financial press has a great deal to say about default risks, as experience with the Washington Public Power Supply System suggests. However, this press, as well as contact in more direct ways, serves to publicize and realize new debt structures, interest rate cycles, and litigation issues. This larger world of everyday securities practice, therefore, poses its own information constraints and opportunities for the bond sale team.

Disclosure. While the information and advice from financial and legal advisors comes with contact, and credit ratings may result from interviews and on-site inspections conducted by these agencies, the primary vehicle for information exchange is a process called disclosure. Therefore, economic and market information are implied, legal information is directly opined, and financial condition information related to default risk is analyzed in the process of disclosure among team members, between the team and the credit rating agency, and among the team, credit-rating agencies, intermediaries, and investors.

The three separate areas of information are disclosed primarily through the production of a document, the official statement (OS). The OS is both official—the issuer's authorization of all interpretations made on its behalf by the team members—and a "direct exposition of information concerning the offering" (Petersen, 1988, p. 5).

Other items of disclosure usually emerge in annual financial reports that are becoming common among issuers. These establish trends beyond those elaborated in the OS as well as providing information to secondary market traders in years subsequent to the initial issue.

In summary, the disclosure of the structure of the security and the legal status and repayment capacity of the issuer present the market with essential data regarding risk and reward. With these data, theoretically, the new-issue market for municipal securities may achieve efficiency by allocating scarce capital among competing uses, assigning appropriate prices (interest payments to the issuer and bond prices and yields to the investor) to structures at particular levels of repayment capacity.

Classification of Information.

Actually, however, the new-issue market must depend on classifications of these data that will permit interpretation. With the data collected and pooled through disclosure, the various parties classify it in straightforward ways, forcing interpretation. Three significant methods of classification usually emerge: the offering's structure, the legal class of the issue, and the credit rating.

The Offering's Structure. The debt structure may vary in terms of economic condition or budget requirements.

Structure and Interest Rates.   The economic conditions prompting a particular debt structure usually require attention to the sale date, and that date is a matter of long-range rather than short-range planning. With the average business cycle over the last 135 years lasting 3 years from peak to peak (see Table 5) the optimum sale date is one in which the peak of the cycle has passed and a contraction is in progress. Therefore, predicting the peak of a cycle is a means of forecasting the sale date at which interest costs will be lowest.

Predicting the peak of a cycle has its problems. For example, no cycle has ever lasted the same length of time as any other, as Table 5 also portrays. Most of the time the structure must adjust to the vagaries of the yield curve, a process illustrated in Fig. 3.

Table 5   U.S. Business Cycles

Business cycle reference dates		Duration (months)	
Trough	Peak	Contraction (trough from previous peak)	Expansion (trough to peak)
December 1854	June 1857	—	30
December 1858	October 1860	18	22
June 1861	April 1865	8	**46**
December 1867	June 1869	**32**	18
December 1870	October 1873	18	34
March 1879	March 1882	65	36
May 1885	March 1887	38	22
April 1888	July 1890	13	27
May 1891	January 1893	10	20
June 1894	December 1895	17	18
June 1897	June 1899	18	24
December 1900	September 1902	18	21
August 1904	May 1907	23	33
June 1908	January 1910	13	19
January 1912	January 1913	24	12
December 1914	August 1918	23	**44**
March 1919	January 1920	**7**	10
July 1921	May 1923	18	22
July 1924	October 1926	14	27
November 1927	August 1929	13	21
March 1933	May 1937	43	50
June 1938	February 1945	13	**80**
October 1945	November 1948	**8**	37
October 1949	July 1953	11	**45**
May 1954	August 1957	**10**	39
April 1958	April 1960	8	24
February 1961	December 1969	10	**106**
November 1970	November 1973	**11**	36
March 1975	January 1980	16	58
July 1980	July 1981	6	12
November 1982		16	?

Note: Numbers in bold face indicate periods of expansion or contraction that occurred during wartime. Source: National Bureau of Economic Research, as cited in *The Wall Street Journal*, November 5, 1990.

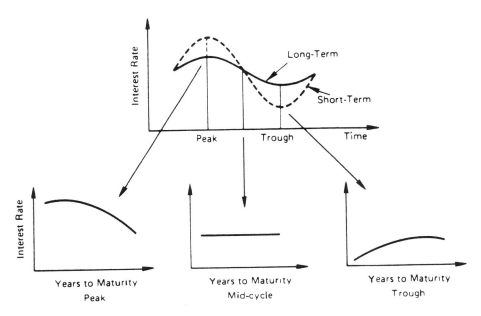

Figure 3 Interest rate and yield—curve patterns over the business cycle.

Experience (and almost every money and banking textbook) reveals that short-term interest rates are a product of and an influential agent in business cycles. As economic expansion takes place, as Fig. 4 portrays in the upper graph, short-term interest rates (1 month to 20 years) rise relative to long-term rates (21–30 years). As economic contraction takes place, these short-term rates fall in relation to longer-term ones.

To some extent supply and demand for money can help explain the phenomena. In expansions, firms find demand for their goods and services increasing and try to borrow money to expand and meet such demand. These firms effectively bid up the price (the interest rate) of a relatively fixed supply of money, as shown on the lower left graph in Fig. 3. The reverse occurs as a contraction takes place; less demand for goods and services reduces a firm's need to borrow to expand, as in the Fig. 3 graph on the lower right. Midway between peak and trough, demand and supply for money balance, and short-term rates nearly equal long-term ones as firms refinance short-term loans with longer-term ones (paying off short-term ones increases the money supply, borrowing long-term decreases it), as the lower middle graph reveals.

For issuers of debt, obviously, troughs have advantages for borrowing. If revenues permit, timing sales for troughs yields lower interest costs. Such countercyclical policies may not be feasible, however, so structuring an issue to take advantage of the yield curve may present the best alternative. At expansionary peaks, selling middle- to long-term debt may yield lower interest costs than would short-term debt, while troughs provide the opportunity for lower costs through shorter-term debt.

Structure and Issuer Budget Requirements. Besides the classification of information in terms of interest rates, the bond team categorizes strategies in terms of the issuer's budget constraints. The issuer's budget for debt service may guide the development of debt-structuring strategies that account for the cash flow requirements or cash available.

Three serial bond repayment patterns have wide use: equal annual maturity serial

Table 6 Maturity Patterns for Serial Bonds that Consider Budgetary Timing

Year	Equal annual maturity			Equal annual debt service			Irregular maturity (level total)			
	New principal	New interest	New total	New principal	New interest	New total	Existing debt	New principal	New interest	New total
1	$ 40,000	$ 2,000	$ 80,000	$ 25,000	$ 1,250	$ 65,000	$40,000	$ 5,000	$ 250	$ 85,000
2	40,000	2,000	78,000	25,000	1,250	63,750	40,000	5,000	250	84,750
3	40,000	2,000	76,000	25,000	1,250	62,500	40,000	5,000	250	84,500
4	40,000	2,000	74,000	30,000	1,500	66,250	40,000	5,000	250	84,250
5	40,000	2,000	72,000	30,000	1,500	64,750	40,000	5,000	250	84,000
6	40,000	2,000	70,000	30,000	1,500	63,250	40,000	5,000	250	83,750
7	40,000	2,000	68,000	30,000	1,500	61,750	40,000	5,000	250	83,500
8	40,000	2,000	66,000	35,000	1,750	62,250	40,000	10,000	500	88,250
9	40,000	2,000	64,000	35,000	1,750	63,500		50,000	2,500	87,750
10	40,000	2,000	62,000	40,000	2,000	66,750		50,000	2,500	85,250
11	40,000	2,000	60,000	40,000	2,000	64,750		55,000	2,750	87,750
12	40,000	2,000	58,000	40,000	2,000	62,750		55,000	2,750	85,000
13	40,000	2,000	56,000	45,000	2,250	65,750		60,000	3,000	87,250
14	40,000	2,000	54,000	45,000	2,250	63,500		60,000	3,000	84,250
15	40,000	2,000	52,000	50,000	2,500	66,250		65,000	3,250	86,250
16	40,000	2,000	50,000	50,000	2,500	63,750		65,000	3,250	83,000
17	40,000	2,000	48,000	50,000	2,500	61,250		70,000	3,500	84,750
18	40,000	2,000	46,000	55,000	2,750	63,750		70,000	3,500	81,250
19	40,000	2,000	44,000	60,000	3,000	66,000		75,000	3,750	82,750
20	40,000	2,000	42,000	60,000	3,000	63,000		80,000	4,000	84,000
Total	$800,000	$40,000	$1,220,000	$800,000	$40,000	$1,283,500		$800,000	$40,000	$1,697,250

bonds, equal annual debt service patterns, and irregular maturities in which the budgeted debt service from existing as well as new issues are leveled. These patterns are illustrated in Table 6.

The three patterns serve different budget purposes. The equal annual maturity pattern spreads repayment over the life of the facility, matching what is paid to what amount of the useful life of the facility is exhausted. This strategy makes sense in ensuring that the facility is paid for at the same rate as it is used. The strategy also ensures that the community residents who gain the benefit of the facility pay for it. That is, those using the facility in year 20 pay for their fair share of its cost just as do those using it in year 1.

The equal annual debt service and irregular maturity (level total) make predictable, if not exactly even, calls on budgets. Such level debt service makes budgeting more stable since the amount budgeted changes very little from year to year.

In addition to the various level debt structures, issuers may accelerate retirement of bonds, create blocks of term bonds, and set up sinking funds for retirement of term bonds. These strategies are portrayed in Table 7.

A revenue-producing facility that exceeds revenue productivity forecasts can illustrate accelerated retirement. Having more funds on hand than anticipated, a public enterprise, such as a toll road, might choose to retire bonds rather than invest in short-term securities. Bond indentures, however, govern accelerated retirement so that bondholders can anticipate the actual yields and prices of these bonds when initially offered.

Combining a serial bond issue such as those in Table 6 and a term bond feature may increase attractiveness to certain investors. For example, if in the equal annual maturity column in Table 6 the maturities in years 16–20 were "blocked" together to mature in year 20 as one (a single serial maturity or a term bond of $160,000), the issuer might create greater buyer interest due to the particular yield curve of the time, one in which significant differences in the yield of years 16–19 and year 20 prevailed.

Finally, to budget for these blocks or for a term bond in general, sinking funds often present advantages. The issuer simply contributes amounts to an investment fund before the maturity date of the block or term bond. These amounts are invested to yield the differences between the contribution and the principal and interest required to be paid the investor upon maturity. While federal tax reform has limited the utility of some of these sinking funds, the term bond/sinking fund approach has obvious budget appeal, since it can reduce budget commitments.

Table 7 Major Derivative Forms of Serial Bond Structures

Accelerated maturity	Serial bonds that are supported by revenues that may exceed minimum needs and therefore may be used to retire bond maturities earlier than anticipated. The acceleration may be mandatory or optional.
Block term bonds	Serial issues may contain a group of smaller, term bonds covering 5-year periods; that is, all serials from the 16th to the 20th year of an issue may be grouped together and mature together at the end of the 5-year term, in year 20.
Sinking fund bonds	An issue of term bonds may be retired through contributions to a fund that, when invested, accumulates the funds necessary to retire the issue or "sink" the debt. The sinking fund may be either optional or mandatory, although arbitrage regulations severely limit the utility of these funds.

Structure and the Tax Classes Affecting the Market Strategy of the Issuer. While interest rates influence those who have an interest in buying municipal securities, much concern also exists in specifically what well-known classes of bondbuyers want. Most of these concerns relate to tax-exempt income and the favorability of federal, state, and local tax law in encouraging these purchases. The major classes of bond buyers are shown in Table 8.

Recalling the three goals of investing as safety, liquidity, and yield, we can recognize the part that a tax-exempt investment will play in forming an investment decision by individuals, fire and casualty insurance companies, and commercial banks, the traditional mainstays of the municipal market.

For individuals, all these goals are served. The tax bracket of the individual determines the actual tax-equivalent yield, but an individual in the highest tax bracket, 31%, could receive a 10.1% yield if purchasing a 7% coupon bond.[18] The yield is comparable to the best corporate securities, each of which's principal is relatively safe. With the advent of mutual funds, even liquidity may be achieved.

For insurance companies, yield, and to a lesser extent safety, are important. For these insurance companies, premium income, in a period of low underwriting losses, can gain a high yield with lower-grade, long-term revenue bonds. In any case, the investment of funds set aside for reserves against losses demands yield as well as safety. Such investments increase the yields for insurance companies for the same reason as individuals and preserve the safety required of these reserves. Federal tax reform has had a large impact on the attractiveness of tax-exempt securities to insurance companies, but one observer notes that "with more profits to shelter and fewer options, property and casualty insurance companies should be good customers for tax-exempts" (Petersen, 1987, pp. 3–11).

For commercial banks, federal tax reform efforts have reduced demand for tax-exempt income (yield) considerably. Except for "public purpose" bonds or nonprofit organization bonds issued by government units in annual amounts less than $10 million, banks will gain less income from municipal securities than from taxable, corporate ones. Public purpose bonds are those already well known: general obligation bonds and nonguaranteed or revenue bonds in which private sector involvement represents less than 10% of the use of the bond proceeds. Nonprofit bonds are those for public authorities generally as well as universities and hospitals and governmentally owned airports, docks and wharves, and solid waste facilities. In the case of both public purpose and nonprofit bonds sold by small, under-$10 million a year issuers, commercial banks may deduct from their taxes 80% of the interest they earn.

Classification of Information through the Credit Rating. The ultimate classifier of information on municipal securities, and that pertaining to risk, comes from credit rating agencies. By considering the security's structure, the legal interpretation affixed to it, and

Table 8   Classes of Municipal Securities Customers

Individuals	Tax-exempt income; risk-free investment
Fire and casualty insurance companies	Risk-free investment; long-term yields; some tax-exempt income
Commercial banks	Tax exemption in certain cases

---

[18]The formula is (coupon) (1 − marginal tax rate) or, as in the example, 0.07 (1 − 0.31), or 10.1%.

the financial status of the issuer—as well as relevant economic and mangerial information—the agencies determine, essentially, the likelihood that the issuer will repay principal and interest as scheduled.

When referring to the credit rating agencies, we refer to three such organizations: Standard and Poor's Corporation, Moody's Investors Service, and Fitch Investors Service. Standard and Poor's (S & P) is a division of McGraw-Hill and is the most diversified of the three agencies, providing credit ratings as only one among many information services. Moody's is the oldest, largest, and a part of Dun and Bradstreet. Fitch is the smallest, newest, and is independent.

Each's process is basically the same. The issuer submits information relating to the financial, economic, and organizational condition of the issuer. More specific information is submitted on the debt being sold. In the view of an expert in these agencies, their use of this information is to establish "credit quality, the liklihood that bonds will pay interest and principal in full and on time" (Petersen, 1988, p. 8).

When the agency receives the information, the agency begins a review process that is basically comparative in nature. The process for S & P is reproduced in Fig. 4.

The analyst, given the issuer data, initially compares them to those in S & P's own database, which consists of revenue, expenditure, and debt statistics on all previous issues rated by S & P.

These data ara analyzed and presented to a rating committee. The committee includes the analyst and others expert in the particular region and type of financing. The rating committee members, almost all of whom are senior to the analysts, also use their experience for comparing the issuer they are rating with others.

Finally, each agency assigns a rating symbol indicating credit quality. These symbols are compared in Table 9. The speculative debt issues are those from Ba/BB to D. Investment grade debt is that rated from Baa/BBB up to Aaa/AAA.

What credit ratings relate to is a corporate secret held closely by the ratings agencies, although ratings' correlates are a matter of regular conjecture, argument, and even research. The agencies indicate that ratings are a mixture of quantitative analysis, subjective views, and judgment (Standard and Poor's Corporation, 1989). Research on Moody's ratings suggests the predominant importance of the total economy—a variable largely out of the control of a local decision maker attempting to increase creditworthiness (Carleton and Lerner, 1969; Horton, 1970; Bahl, 1971; Rubinfeld, 1973; Morton, 1975–76; Michel, 1977; Aronson and Marsden, 1980; Farnham and Cluff, 1982). One researcher, using Moody's ratings, observed

> Only economic variables show any real discriminating ability. The largest taxpayer and 10 largest taxpayers variables, which are intended to measure the concentration and dependence of the local economy, are significant. Unemployment shows the expected pattern, although only bonds rated lower than A exceeded the national average. Estimated full value of the tax base per capita showed a mild trend. The estimated full value of the tax base, by the way, was computed utilizing statistics on sales price/assessment ratio published by the Bureau of the Census in its quinquennial Census of Governments, rather than the statutory assessment ratio. Finally, change in population showed a surprising and disturbing trend, with the fastest growth being highly correlated with lower rating. (Willson, 1986, pp. 20–21)

Creditworthiness, it seems, may be a condition determined by national economic trends. Moreover, the wealth of data required by the agencies, as well as the local decision making control of financial management that this implies, may not guide ratings.

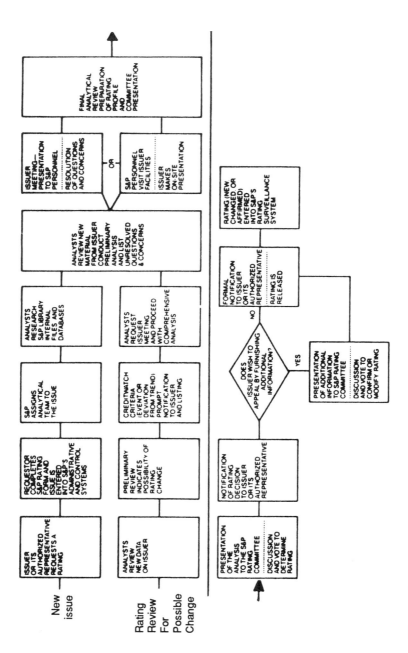

Figure 4 S & P municipal debt rating process.

Table 9 Bond Rating Symbols and Meaning

Moody's	S&P	Fitch	Meaning
Aaa	AAA	AAA	Highest quality; extremely strong ability to repay principal and interest
Aa	AA	AA	High grade; margins of protection are not as large; long-term risks somewhat larger
A,A-1*	A	A	Upper medium grade; adequate security; susceptibility to impairment
Baa,Baa-1*	BBB	BBB	Medium grade; neither highly protected nor poorly secured
Ba	BB	BB	Have speculative elements
B	B	B	Lack characteristics of desirable investment
Caa	CCC	CCC	Poor standing
Ca	CC	CC	Speculative in a high degree; default probable
C	C	C	Bonds for which interest not now being paid
Con	D	DDD,DD,D	Default; payment in arrears

Note: The hyphenated ratings of A-1 and Baa-1 used by Moody's indicate those credits are considered to be the better quality credits in the respective categories. An added plus or minus sign attached to Standard & Poor's and Fitch ratings indicates that a credit is considered to be in the upper or lower segment of the rating category.

The effect of the ratings on borrowing costs is substantial, nevertheless. Consider the analysis of two issues, one rated AA and one A (or Aa and A, in using Moody's ratings symbols). These issues and their costs appear in Table 10. Clearly, the two issues will have radically different costs, the A costing about 10% more for the project.

For investors, the ratings signal the amount of risk in timely payment of principal and interest, but not when to sell to avoid risk. For this reason, bond salespeople routinely warn investors not to smugly ignore the news in hopes that the ratings agencies are correct. For instance, *The Wall Street Journal* portrayed the price of Massachusetts bonds over a period of time before and after S & P and Moody's downgraded the bonds' rating. This timeline appears as Fig. 5. The price, on the strength of news reports concerning financial problems and budget stress, fell continuously from January 1 to May 17, 1989.

Table 10 Issuance Costs for a Revenue Bond, Comparison of Costs by Rating

Cost	AA Rated	A Rated	Difference
Construction costs	$10,000,000	$10,000,000	$ 0
Less: Interest earned during construction at 5%	502,543	502,543	0
Net construction costs	9,497,457	9,947,457	0
Capitalized interest	1,618,081	1,728,759	(110,678)
Reserve fund at 5%	1,107,751	1,119,064	(11,313)
Bond discount	15,300	18,548	(3,248)
Cost of issuance	100,000	100,000	0
Principal amount	12,238,589	12,363,828	125,239
Total interest over financing life	11,316,948	12,179,335	862 387
Total financing cost	$23,555,537	$24,543,163	$(987,626)

Source: Aguila and Holstein (1989, p. 39).

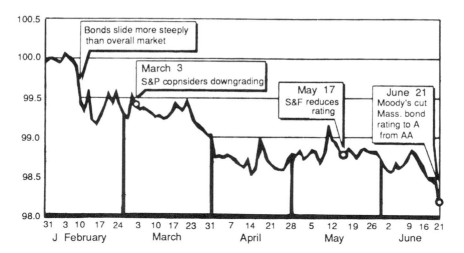

Figure 5   Track Massachusetts bonds. Price of Massachusetts general obligation relative to Bond Buyer 40-bond price index; daily data, Jan. 31, 1989 = 100.

S & P then reduced the rating, but Moody's, the last of the two agencies to reduce the rating, waited until June 21, after the price had fallen by almost a full two points.

Bond analysts have recommended that investors take a very close and skeptical view of ratings agencies. "In many cases, by the time a rating has been lowered on a given credit, you've already lost the bulk of your money," the *Journal* quoted a tax-exempt fund manager (Herman, 1989, p. C1). The *Journal* continued, "In fact, when a rating service finally gets around to downgrading an issue, that may be a good time to buy."

In summary, this outline of activity involved in implementing capital investment strategies has deliberately highlighted the range of discretion involved in a team's attempt to participate in an efficient market. Such discretion must exist to take account of the vast uncertainty with which an issuer must contend. The team must often guess, but at all times it must develop strategies that cope with phenomena that are dynamic and unpredictable. The next section illustrates these coping strategies.

Opportunistic Strategies for Capital Investments

There are an infinite number of variations[19] among financing strategies from which communities may choose when funding capital improvements, and most cities can find

[19]While we talk about financing strategies primarily as borrowing strategies, that is not the broadest picture one could paint.

One strategy involves an all-borrowing policy utilizing current revenues to finance debt incurred as the result of bonds issued to fund capital improvements. An all-borrowing approach is appropriate when inflationary increases exceed the interest that is paid on long-term debt.

A capital reserve strategy uses funds saved in a investment account, with the investment earnings applied to the project cost. This strategy is useful when inflation is not particularly high or when the project can be deferred for a period of time.

Several strategies are combinations of other strategies, including a partial pay-as-you-go plan whereby a portion of the project is paid utilizing current revenue or capital reserves and the balance is funded by bonds. Another combination might be referred to as a pay-as-you-spend plan.

(continued)

one that fits their own unique legal, economic, financial, and political constraints. How then do they choose?

Despite the fact that managers do not have values that permit innovation, outright devotion to innovation occurs and rather comprehensive innovations take place every year.[20] The answer, we argue, lies in the idea advanced earlier that managers themselves do not decide what reality is; if they did, their values would tend to limit their innovativeness. Instead managers participate with others in constructing a reality that many managers find particularly useful. This reality is constructed specifically to cope with an uncertain environment outside the organization; the innovations constructed create stability, in line with managers' values perhaps, while still promoting innovation.[21]

This section offers proof of innovation in its description of the ways state and local government financial managers reacted to uncertainty in their capital financing activities over the last fifteen years.[22] The period has had a breathtaking volatility when viewed from its end. Merely reciting the financial condition of New York City at the beginning and the end of the period—near default in 1975, embarking on major service increases and capital improvements with large surpluses in 1985, entering a period of fiscal stress in 1990—perhaps portrays the bust-to-boom-to-bust character of many, if not all, state and local governments during this period. The rest cover all bases: boom to bust (Phoenix), still busted (Detroit), and bust to boom (Dallas).

As a matter of surprise to no one now, the period witnessed some of the greatest instability among prices, interest rates, and markets in this century. For example, prices increased at rates in the double digits for the first time since the period following World War II. Interest rates on long, municipal bonds took a leap into double digits for the first time since The Bond Buyer began keeping records. As both cause and effect, the distinction among credit market participants, especially the issuer and the intermediary, became obscure (Petersen, 1981). Since the rate instability period following 1975, the market has witnessed one of the longest periods of relative stability in the century.

The reaction by issuers over the 15 year period may be described in terms of coping strategies (Hickson, et al, 1971, p. 217), prevention, absorption, and information.

Preventive strategies reduce the probability of shocks occurring so that resources flowing to the organization do not vary widely.

Absorption strategies adjust to events by making a given financial system operate within new and changing confines. Offsetting the effects of variations in resources,

---

Particular phases of the project, such as engineering, land acquisition, and constructions are financed from current capital resources. Engineering could be financed for the first year, land acquisition the second and third year, and construction the fourth or fifth year. Such an approach allows flexibility as resources can be accumulated for the anticipated larger construction phase over the 4-year engineering and land acquisition phase, or alternatively, debt can be issued the fourth year to fund the construction cost.

[20]In fact, two programs have done a great deal to show the substantial regularity and depth of these innovations: that at Rutgers University (National Center for Public Productivity, Department of Public Administration) and LOGIN, Norris Institute, as well as that at Harvard University's John F. Kennedy School of Government.

[21]This section is based in part on Miller (1985).

[22]The period roughly date from the publication of one U.S. Advisory Commission on Intergovernmental Relations study of note (Patton, 1975), and covers about 15 years, from 1975 to 1990.

particularly the ravages of inflation and interest rate increases, shock absorbers exist to hedge against change, to adjust to the variations in interest rates, and to level consumer demand.

Information strategies deal with uncertainty in capital investment by forcing a reinterpretation of reality by the strategizing organization or by the larger world. This often entails reinterpreting the agenda of issues that frame the need for investment (Kingdon, 1984). Agenda setting in the strategy formulation process encompasses the simple act of identifying a problem, thereby setting in motion the apparatus for solving it. The apparatus involves various institutional arrangements that act to aggregate resources.

This section catalogs each coping strategy, briefly noting and explaining it.

Coping by Prevention

Prevention efforts have attempted to forestall uncertainty. Generally, managers aim these efforts at reducing the probability of shocks occurring so that resources flowing to the organization do not vary widely. State and local financial managers have followed four basic strategies to prevent excessive variability: diversifying, merging, leveraging, and securitizing.

Diversification

Diversification, in state and local governments, has applied primarily to revenue sources. The search for alternative revenues to the property tax at the local government level and to the income tax at the state level has become one of the clearest trends of the last decade.

The results of the search for alternatives have yielded a trend: user fees and other benefit-based revenues have become a major area of growth for local governments. At the local government level, the trend toward benefit-based revenues has moved from a ratio of charges to taxes of about one-quarter in the early 1970s to one-third to one-half in the late 1980s (U.S. Bureau of the Census, 1989). Predictions based on that rate of growth suggest that that ratio will exceed one-half, or that communities will derive about a third of own-source revenues from user fees by the early 1990s.

Others disagree. In fact, some suggest the proportion will actually decline as the growth in expenditures for traditional user fee financed services stabilizes (Academy of State and Local Government, 1984). The atomizing or special district movement, however, may synthesize the two—numbers of activities financed by charges will grow, and demand for these activities may grow as well.

States have diversified to a lesser extent than simply raising taxes. Nevertheless, so-called "sin" taxes have gained intense scrutiny and debate among state level financial managers. Cigarette taxes, especially, have risen in the face of federal tax cutbacks.

Merger

Two major types of horizontal mergers and a form of vertical merger have entered the scene to provide much preventive potential for financial managers.

Horizontal Mergers. Annexation, the first type of horizontal merger, reports the U.S. Bureau of the Census, has fallen but still remains the merger technique of choice in the South and West (U.S. Bureau of the Census, 1980).

Horizontal mergers with the private sector have gained a great deal more notice as well as notoriety. "Privitization" of public functions has a substantial following and applies to almost any activity in which former public functions are shared with private sector or profit-oriented groups. There are at least seven major forms of horizontal merger through privatization.

1. *Equity kickers (Wall Street Journal, 1982).*[23] In several instances, the government has demanded an equity position in the project as well as the yield from the security financing the project. This has been true especially in short-lived industrial development bond financings in which cities have acted as issuers.

    However, the equity position has also become a negotiating object when cities have formed partnerships with private parties in using federal funds for redevelopment purposes. The City of Chicago, for example, demanded an equity position in a downtown hotel development project, in the form of a share of future earnings attributable to the improvements funded by city participation. Other cities exhibiting Chicago's behavior include:

    a. Louisville, KY. Louisville will receive 50% of the cash flow (after the developer gets a 15% return on his equity) and 50% of the future appreciation in a hotel project in return for aiding a development company with financing for a $50 million project.

    b. San Diego, CA. In a $200 million project downtown, including retail space, office space, and a hotel, the city and the developers agreed that the developer would lend the city $4 million, interest free, for 4 years to assemble a parcel of blighted acreage. The developer then would buy the land for $1 million. In return, the developer will pay the city 10% of rental income in excess of the base rent for 50 years along with 31% of the parking revenue.

    c. New Haven, CT. New Haven transformed an old brass mill into a research facility. The city created a nonprofit corporation as developer and sold the project's tax breaks to investors through limited partnerships to raise project equity. Construction financing was a no-interest loan from federal community development block grant money. Permanent financing came from construction unions' pension funds. To meet pension law requirements, the city persuaded the state of Connecticut to guarantee the first mortgage. An urban development action grant helped underwrite a second mortgage.

2. *Tax increment financing.* Unlike revenue streams due to increased sales or rental of facilities, tax increment financing creates a stream of revenue from the increased value of property and from the resulting taxes on that property after development financed by tax increment securities.

    The method relies, first, on a calculation of old and new property values. The issuing entity must establish a base year and value property in that base or pre-development year. The entity must also decide the allocation of base-year valuation and tax among those other entities relying on the property tax, such as school boards. Next, the entity estimates the value of the property during and after construction and redevelopment and through the immediate future.

    With these estimates, the entity creates a revenue stream from the incremental difference in postdevelopment tax revenues. The stream relies on the difference between redevelopment era property valuation and base-year valuation, multiplied by tax rates and subtracted from base-year allocations due other taxing entities.

    The financing method has its opponents. Much opposition arises from competing taxing jurisdictions. These jurisdictions, in effect, face a static tax base for the term of the repayment period.

    Defenders argue that tax increment financing reduces the likelihood of further tax base erosion. Moreover, they add, redevelopment adds jobs and activity that may work to increase the value of property in other areas, where houses of workers and

[23]One of several unpublished, in-house briefing papers from Rauscher Pierce Refsnes, Inc., a Phoenix, Arizona regional investment bank, which form the survey of financing tools reviewed in this paper.

businesses servicing these workers exist and form the property tax base on which all jurisdictions' tax bases rely.

3. *Private-public partnerships.* With tax-exempt leverage lease financing, private part-nerships assure production of capital goods. Using such a financing plan, a taxable third party builds and owns a facility. The third party, acting as lessor, leases the facility to an operator, including in the lease the cost of maintenance, repair, and insurance.

   The jurisdiction, in turn, enters into a service contract with a lessee/operator. The service contract secures the builder's loan; the loan comes from tax-exempt revenue bonds, but the builder contributes 20–40% of the purchase price. Revenues from the facility's customers to the city would service the contract.

4. *"On behalf of" issuers.* Assuming congenial state and local law, issuers can create nonprofit corporations that act as issuers "on behalf of" the original issuer, usually a state, county, school board, or city. The authority for the creation of an "on behalf of" issuer rests in federal law. Generally, the government entity forms the corporation for the purpose of leasing real property or equipment from the corporation. The corporation issues bonds of other securities. The lease payment stream from the government to the corporation acts as the underlying security.

5. *Sale and leaseback.* Using an "on behalf of" issuer, a jurisdiction can remove certain assets, but also liabilities, from its books. A city with a facility wholly owned might decide to create a "municipal assistance corporation" (MAC), an "on behalf of" issuer that might buy the facility and lease the facility back over a period equal to the facility's "useful" life. The MAC then would sell securities based on the lease payments the city pledged.

6. *Annuities and pension plans* (Yacik, 1985). Jurisdictions now shift their pension liability to the private sector through tax-exempt borrowings. For example, Essex County, NJ, sold general obligation bonds to purchase an annuity contract from Metropolitan Life Insurance Company, which, after Metropolitan invests the bond proceeds, will be obligated to pay out $10 million more in pension benefits. Thus the county issues bonds totalling $48 million, and will pay, over the life of the bonds, principal and interest of $94.9 million. Metropolitan will fully fund the pension system with $105.8 million.

7. *Tax-exempt leasing* (Vogt and Cole, 1983). A tax-exempt lease resembles the "on behalf of" issuing corporation technique. In a tax-exempt lease/purchase agreement, the government entity, as lessee, signs an agreement with a bank, investment bank, or leasing company, as lessor. The lessor raises funds through a lender or investor to pay for the objects covered by the lease. In return, the lender receives a security interest in the equipment, all rights and title under the agreement, and a stream of lease rental payments (principal and interest), of which the interest is tax-exempt. Due to the size of the transaction, more than one lender may participate. Certificates of participation can be issued, allowing lenders to share in a proportionate amount of the stream of the rental payments.

Vertical Mergers. While intergovernmental sharing of responsibility, especially that involving federal aid, continues to diminish, state aid to local governments in all forms actually may have increased. Most important are new structures, such as:

1. *Equipment loan funds* (The Bond Buyer, 1983). Several states and counties have issued bonds to fund equipment loan pools for hospitals or other nonprofits or departments within governments. These programs loan funds on an intermediate-term

basis, but the value lies in spreading the financing costs of the bonds over a number of equipment users. Credit-enhancement techniques allow merger of smaller or weaker credits to stronger ones.

2. *Bond banks* (Forbes and Petersen, 1983). The larger, unlimited object version of equipment loan funds is the bond bank. Public financing authorities, which pool capital financing for government entities into single, large bond issues, came into being around 1970 in the state of Vermont. By pooling obligations, the issue attracts more interest, spreads underwriting costs, and lowers rates. Evidence exists, however, to show, at least superficially, that the cost of the bond bank is more than made up by reduced interest costs and earnings from bond proceeds investment.

3. *Other forms of state assistance* (Forbes and Petersen, 1983). States also provide assistance to communities in marketing bonds. California's Health Facilities Construction Loan Insurance Program insures local revenue and general obligation bonds that finance health facilities' construction and comply with state health plans. In addition, the Michigan Qualified School Bond Fund operates a revolving loan fund to provide emergency assistance to school districts in meeting debt service.

The State of Texas commits royalties from state oil extraction sales to secure local school board bonds. The royalties suffice to back up the creditworthiness of large bond issues from all areas of the state, yielding an AAA rating.

Minesota's Board Guarantee Fund insures any local general obligation bond issue. State law allows the state to levy a special property tax on a locality, if default occurs.

Leveraging

With newer revenue sources based on an income stream, similar to an annuity, a government can leverage these streams, or borrow based on them by using them as pledges of collateral. Such approaches amount to simple revenue bonds; however, newer methods, in which various revenue streams act together as "leverage," provide the potential for new and more reliable sources of capital financing funds.

Cross-Source Leveraging (Bayless, 1985). One of the best examples of leveraging various revenue streams occurred in New Jersey recently. Through the New Jersey Turnpike Authority, the state's Transportation Trust Fund will gain $12 million a year to restore transportation infrastructure. The state's three toll roads earmark a portion of revenues for the trust, a combined total of $25 million yearly over a 20-year period to service and repay the bond issues financing repair work.

Those contributions will be highly leveraged: Every dollar contributed by the toll roads could be used to raise another $5, then matched nine times over by the federal government. The legislature appropriates funds and combines them with the annual contributions from the state's toll roads and a portion of the gasoline tax. This revenue stream guarantees the necessary work and provides for debt service on bonds.

Securitization

Traditionally, communities have financed limited-benefit capital improvements through pledges of receivables. For example, paving a residential street often has depended upon the willingness of the residents to pledge monthly repayments for the work. If the pledges emerged, the local government issued bonds with that revenue stream securing it.

Private sector borrowers call this procedure "securitization of assets." Involving an illiquid loan or lease agreeement, the securitization process transforms the asset into a liquid security.

Virtually any asset with a payment stream and a long-term payment history is an eventual candidate for securitization. State and local government lease agreements, that is, any fee-based service, produce such streams and histories. As a result, their capitalization might rest on securitization of the payment stream.

Likewise, capital improvements capable of "exclusion" or unit benefit analysis, might submit to "securitization." Capital goods usually defined as "public goods," such as streets, sidewalks, and even fire stations and police precinct houses (where fire calls and police calls may be defined as exclusive services), could become candidates.

The reverse could work financially. Regulatory fees for pollution control, where the entity pays regularly based on its emission level, could act as securitization for the capital facilities that might ameliorate the problem.

In addition, cities might benefit by private corporations' greater liquidity. A vendor using receivables-backed securities might offer better than the usual trade terms. Liquidity would not be affected because the receivables would be sold. Cities would get better terms because repayment forms a receivable of a given length susceptible to securitization. A city's cash flow could improve, providing it with the foundation for cash management and investment.

According to some sources (Shapiro, 1985; Sloane, 1985), bankers have begun to look at securitizing other kinds of assets. Beyond assets with a payment stream and a payment history, which can be tracked over a sufficient period of time, "The next generation is an asset that doesn't have a predictable cash flow associated with it. And it might not have any cash flow associated with it except when it's sold." Examples include commodity-backed agreements in which one could pledge or sell a group of assets to back securities: for instance, natural resources, site improvement incentives, zoning abatements, and more abstract forms of assets such as the aesthetics of the community or the quality of the school system as they affect business location.

Summary

The prevention of uncertainty through design of systems that increase the potential pool of resources and the willingness to use the resources have marked state and local government finance. Diversification and merger have gained new life. New techniques, such as leveraging and securitizing, have future value. Yet present needs require a great deal of absorption of uncertainty.

Coping by Absorption

Action during a period of uncertainty often occurs as absorption activities. Absorbing uncertainty means adjusting to it by making a given financial system operate within new and changing confines. Offsetting the effects of variations in resources, particularly the ravages of inflation and interest rate increases, uncertainty absorption tactics and strategies used by state and local government financial managers come in several forms. At least four groups of shock absorbers exist: hedging techniques to "insure" against inflation; new inflation- and interest rate-sensitive debt products; new advance refunding routines for adjusting existing debt to the variations in interest rates; and leveling demand efforts by which issuers find new bondholders.

Hedging to Absorb Uncertainty

Hedging involves the use of futures or options contracts or both to anticipate movements in interest rates. Futures contracts are agreements to deliver or receive cash or securities at a specified time or place.[24]

[24]See Fabozzi and Zarb (1981).

Options give investors the right, but not the obligation, to buy or sell something, such as a futures contract or a security, at a specified time or place.

Hedging Strategies

Hedging strategies have developed as futures and options markets have offered new products. Basic hedging involves the purchase of a futures contract, or an opinion on a physical or futures contract, to guard or "lock in" an interest rate.

Absorbing Uncertainty with New, Rate-Sensitive Debt Products

The fastest growing, and the most often used, method of absorbing uncertainty today has emerged as "creative capital finance" activities. The nature and type of these "creative" techniques have changed as quickly as the volatile trends affecting both borrowers/issuers and lenders/securities holders. These techniques span all dimensions that exist to describe capital financing: short- and long-term, interest-sensitive and -insensitive, borrower-tilted and lender-tilted, general and specific use oriented, and relatively more tax weighted versus less.

Six techniques have attained widespread use over the past 15 years: stage financing, commercial paper, floating-rate bonds, put-option bonds, guarantees, and stepped coupons.

Stage Financing. To respond to an expected population growth and service demand life cycle of a growth area, stage financing creates a fixed amount of debt service capacity that a governmental unit can maintain over a period of time. For example, a unit may decide to set its tax stream at a fixed mill levy for debt service purposes. In many cases this will be an average rate, seemingly high in the initial stages of growth, but low in the later ones. This millage devoted to debt service permits the unit a borrowing capacity great enough in the early stages to anticipate growth and service demand. The millage devoted to debt service in the later stages is not so great that undue burdens are placed on a stagnant or even declining revenue base.

Tax-Exempt Commercial Paper (Klapper, 1980). Tax-exempt commercial paper, an unsecured, tax-exempt loan with a shorter than 1 year maturity, offers another opportunity to limit exposure in a period of volatility. Interest rates on commercial paper follow the short-term debt market and, generally, fall below taxable Treasury bill rates. A commercial paper program requires refinancing of existing issues upon maturity. Because paper is unsecured, a letter of credit from a bank normally backs the program.

Floating-Rate Bonds. Floating- or variable-rate financing has emerged because chaotic conditions in the municipal bond market reduced reliance on traditional, long-term, fixed-rate issues. Investors who witnessed bond interest rates fluctuating between 5½% and 14¼% over the 5-year period from September 1977 to January 1982 had little demand for a bond bearing a fixed rate for 20–30 years. Yet the majority of city issuers prefer to finance for as long a term as possible.

The interest rate on variable rate bonds for each interest payment period is not fixed at the time of issuance but instead will "float" or adjust as market conditions change. As such, the rate is tied to an index or a market indicator reasonably sensitive to market conditions.

Pricing strategy is by far the most important factor in structuring and marketing variable rate securities. The strategy relies heavily on some index thought to mirror trends in competing investments of similar risk and maturity. The index provides a time series that can be compared to the interest rates of existing short- and long-term, tax-exempt and taxable securities over a relatively long period of time. The interest rate indices run the gamut from London Interbank Offered Rates (LIBOR) to federal securities rates to indices set by banks for their own customers.

The variable rate has obvious attraction. The issuer borrows in the short term market at a rate generally 2–4% lower than the traditional, long-term market rate.

"Put option" bonds. A bond carrying a put option allows the bondholder to sell the bond back to the issuer on a given number of days notice. Superficially, the "put" evens the sides, giving the bondholder a method of seeking the advantage the issuer always has had with a "call" feature.

The put option allows the holder of any bond to demand that the bond be purchased by a remarketing agent on a given day by presenting the bond to the remarketing agent on that day or upon notice specified on the bond. The bondholder receives the principal amount (par value) plus accrued interest, if any, to the date of purchase. The remarketing agent finds a new buyer for the bond sold back by the old buyer exercising the put.

If the remarketing agent cannot remarket a bond, a trustee draws on a "liquidity facility," a letter of credit or other liquid financial guarantee of payment usually provided by a bank, to pay the principal and accrued interest. Generally, put options carry with them the need for further guarantees of payment, generally a letter of credit.

The put feature allows issuers to sell long-term bonds with yields close to those on short-term issues, because the notice period required before the bond is put, in effect, acts as the bond's maturity. Issuers can save as much as 3% on the interest rate they must pay. The put feature first appeared on issues in 1980 and has gained popularity as interest rates have become volatile.

Third-Party Financial Guarantees (Forbes and Petersen, 1983). Default by the Washington Public Power Supply System in 1983 has created a desire by borrowers and lenders to "guarantee" the payment of principal and interest on bonds. Essentially, borrowers buy an insurance policy to guarantee payment to bondholders in case of default. Along with the guarantee comes the insurer's AAA credit rating that acts to lower the borrower's cost.

Bond guarantees come in several different forms. First, there are strictly defined insurance policies covering the principal and interest on long-term, fixed-rate issues, such as general obligation and revenue bond issues.

Second, surety bonds are used when the guarantor has no license for municipal bond credit insurance or, for other legal reasons such as state regulations, cannot issue insurance outright. Practically, surety bonds differ very little from insurance.

Third, banks issue letters and lines of credit. Letters of credit generally fit new types of financings carrying "put" features.

Fourth, layered guarantees provide a mix of security features that no bank can provide alone. Industrial development bonds (IDBs) issued by a tax-exempt entity on behalf of a private company may be small and the issue relatively unknown outside its locality. The anonymity and accompanying fear of default on the part of bond buyers may be alleviated somewhat by a letter of credit.

The size of the issue may be less a problem if issues are combined. A first layer of security provided by a multitude of unknown issuers, companies, and banks can get added security by another layer of security, for instance, a large regional bank's letter of credit. A third layer of security may be needed, however, if the regional bank has no credit rating that the individual investor can rely upon. Therefore, a rated bank, of which there are only a handful in the United States, may provide another letter of credit, relying on the financial well-being of the regional bank. With the third letter of credit, the issue could receive a AAA rating, and the letter-of-credit issuers share the risk of default.

Finally, a variety of interest rate swaps, segmented market penetrations, interest rate caps and floors, and secondary market deals have appeared.

Stepped Coupons (Forbes and Petersen, 1983). A stepped coupon bond uses maturities in which the coupons are "stepped" upward to increase yields over the life of the issue. All of the bonds may yield 7% in one year, for example, and 10% the next. The security looks like both a short-term and a long-term issue; moreover, the investor has some protection from interest-rate volatility.

The rate-sensitive debt instruments and financing techniques discussed here were developed in direct response to the volatile interest rates encountered throughout the last 10 years. When rates fall and stabilize, however, governments take advantage of the condition by "locking in" the lower rates through an advance refunding.

Absorbing Uncertainty through Advance Refunding

The concept of refinancing an existing indebtedness is a long-established practice utilized not only by state and local governments but also by corporations and individuals to reduce interest costs. New, relatively lower interest rate debt replaces debt issued at relatively higher interest rates.

Advance refunding programs, most frequently, are used to reduce debt service costs, with the most common refunding process involving issuing the refunding bonds at an interest rate that is lower than the rate of the refunded bonds. However, an advance refunding may also be employed to restructure debt payments or to update overly restrictive bond indenture covenants. Therefore, refunding has several characteristics: (1) it is a "clean" swap of the outstanding bonds with the refunding bonds; (2) outstanding bonds would immediately cease to have any pledge of revenues; (3) the yearly debt service reduction may, if desired, begin immediately; and (4) the holders of the outstanding bonds would have, as security for the outstanding bonds, a portfolio of qualifying securities.

Arbitrage and Escrowed Municipal Bonds. A new, and potentially more useful advance refunding technique developed in the early 1980s has increased the savings and uncertainty absorption potential available to state and local governments. The method employs the floating rate and put option debt features we have already discussed, but it also includes investment in municipal bonds. The new technique requires two innovations. First, the refunding bonds are sold at floating rates with put features. The bond proceeds then are invested in fixed-rate, tax-exempt municipal bonds, which in the late 1970s had reached unusually high levels.

While a variable-rate refunding bond reduces debt service, an escrow of fixed-rate municipal securities multiplies these savings. Assume that a refunded bond at, for example, 8.5% is matched against a refunding bond with a variable rate of averaging 6.5%. Future debt service is reduced by the difference. Next, since the old, refunded bond may not be able to be called until a first call option point, for instance 5 years from now, the refunding bond proceeds can be invested. An investment in municipal bonds at about 8.5% could yield substantial savings. The 2% savings on debt service would be added to the 2% earnings on the municipal bond investment.

Therefore, escrowed municipal bonds and variable-rate refunding bonds with put option accrue considerable savings in a volatile market. Moreover, no restrictions exist to prevent an issuer from borrowing at a tax-exempt floating rate and investing the proceeds at a tax-exempt fixed rate.

The use of rate-sensitive instruments in both general obligation and advance refunding situations provided governments a way to absorb the uncertainty, even shock, of interest rate increases to unusually high levels. However, giving debt instruments rate sensitivity also made them more competitive and helped attract new bondbuyers. Increasing the demand for debt instruments, moreover, had unique potential to absorb uncertainty by leveling or stabilizing demand.

Leveling Demand through New Bond Buyers

One major source of variation that state and local governments had to absorb in the last decade lay in changes in demand due to changes in types of bondholders. In fact, as banks and insurance companies, due to tax law changes and their own low profits (U.S. General Accounting Office, 1983), stopped buying bonds, individuals and households started. Significant new forms of securities have emerged to take advantage of these new buyers, such as unit trusts, zero-coupon bonds, bonds with warrants, and book-entry procedures for accounting for bond interest and principal payments as well as ownership.

Unit Trusts.   Fixed, diversified portfolios of long-term municipal bonds have entered the market to appeal to individual investors and households. One marketer describes their appeal as aimed to "income oriented people in their mid-50's or older. They fall into the top income tax brackets. They want a tax-free stream of income, and a packaged product appeals to them" (Vartan, 1985).

Unit trusts come in several forms. For instance, they may carry insurance. They may allow a double (or even triple) tax exemption because the trusts hold same-state securities and sell to investors in that state.

Mutual Funds.   Both closed-end funds, operating like units trusts, and open-end funds now exist to pass on tax-exempt income to individual investors. The basic difference between mutual funds and unit trusts is the funds' management, or its ability to buy and sell bonds for the portfolio continually to achieve higher returns, rather than merely buying a portfolio one time and holding it to maturity.

Several different types of funds have emerged to expand the municipal market. Closed-end funds have a finite size; open-end funds may expand as demand changes. Some of both are oriented to short-term municipals, others to longer-term municipals oriented toward safety, yield, or both.

Zero-Coupon Bonds.   Zero-coupon bonds are debt instruments sold at significant discounts from their face values with no annual interest payments. Over the life of the bond, the increased value is the original discount offering price compounded semiannually at the original yield.

The zeroes are aimed at individual investors facing volatility in the economy. Specifically, the investor can "lock in" the yield desired with a zero-coupon bond, ultimately benefiting if prevailing interest rates fall. The investor, nevertheless, gambles. If prevailing interest rates rise above the zero's yield, the zero-coupon bond falls in price.

Bonds with Warrants.   A bond with a warrant attached allows the purchase of additional bonds. The entitlement to purchase additional bonds carries what amounts to a "reverse call" option on the security. If prices on bonds rise (when interest rates fall), the reverse call would have a high value, and this potential entices bondbuyers.

Book Entry of Bond Certificates.   Like the Federal Reserve System's electronic book-entry system for U.S. Treasury and other federal agency securities, law now allows municipal issuers to alleviate the paperwork involved in offering genuine engraved bond certificates to bondholders. The paperless system registers all long-term securities, as federal law now mandates,[25] and utilizes electronic transfer of funds (Petersen and Buckley, 1983). Such a book-entry system, offered by many bank trust departments, establishes the ownership and records the trades in new issues. An audit trail for tax purposes, as well as a record of interest coupon and principal payment, now exists.

The initial test and evidence of bond buyer enthusiasm for book entry (and lack of resistance to having anything other than the genuine article in hand) came with the state of Utah's successful sale of a $10 million general obligation issue in July 1984. The state of Massachusetts sold $140 million a month later using a similar book entry system.

Summary

The uncertainty absorption activities of state and local government financial managers have led to the use of hedging programs to deal with interest rate risk exposure; new financial instruments that move with the changes in interest rates but also allow bondholders the opportunity to sell the security if necessary; advance refunding programs to convert relatively high interest rate debt service to lower rates as interest rates fall; and programs that entice an ever-larger group of investors into the market to maintain demand.

Coping by Information

Not only does the network political economy play a major part in the social construction of reality through the imagery of prevention and absorption activities. The communications and rituals of debt management add their part as well. In this section, I briefly describe additional sources of reality construction, in the consideration of information activities. That is, from activities that act to reinterpret the agenda of work or the roles of those involved, additional dimensions of a reality network members can agree on are constructed.

A third method of dealing with the ambiguity of project finance has emerged as a reinterpretation of the agenda of issues (Kingdon, 1984). Agenda setting in the policymaking process encompasses the simple act of identifying a problem, thereby setting in motion the apparatus for solving it. The apparatus involves various institutional arrangements that act to aggregate resources.

The last, full national issue-attention cycle neared its waning moments at the beginning of the 1975–1990 period that I have chosen for study. That is, the civil rights/urban disorders cycle of the late 1960s had exhausted itself to be replaced by the fiscal crisis, and, now, by the infrastructure crisis.

The fiscal crisis actually combined two issues, city financial emergencies and tax limitation. The financial emergency side began with New York City's 1975 crisis. The tax limitation movement was ignited by the passage of an expenditure "cap" law in 1976, ultimately spreading with California's Proposition 13 in 1978.

In a sort of policy dialectic, the fiscal crisis gave way to a new issue-attention cycle of the 1980s, infrastructure problems and their repair and replacement. Fiscal crisis solutions tended to lead ultimately to proposals for higher taxes. Tax limitation and antigovernment solutions barred the rise in taxes. In the standoff or vacuum, the opportunity arose for resetting the agenda.

[25]The Tax Equity and Fiscal Responsibility Act of 1982 (P.L. 97–248, 96 Stat. 595).

With the opportunity for agenda-setting came the opportunity for someone or some group not on either side to synthesize the proposals. Infrastructure provided the obvious candidate for synthesis, and public financial managers and investment bankers became the obvious issue entrepreneurs. The direct consequence of the fiscal problem was the declining facilities cities faced. At the heart of the tax limitation/antigovernment movement was the question of redistribution of wealth.

The infrastructure movement could solve both sides' greatest fear: that economic problems were not getting solved. Economic problems of cities might not get solved through infrastructure replacement, but the multiplier effect of government spending on infrastructure would have an ameliorative effect (and those standing for election might have something to distribute). Economic problems of individuals might not be solved by infrastructure, but the new emphasis might produce productivity improvements and spark economic expansion (and to the middle class blunt the redistribution of wealth carried on through social programs).

Likewise, infrastructure joined heretofore sparring institutions. Infrastructure repair could join federal departments: Transportation for roads, bridges, and mass transit; Housing and Urban Development for general purpose development and public administration professionalism; and Environmental Protection for sewer and water systems. These departments, with infrastructure dominating the agenda, might appear to be doing what they intended—something "new," "innovative," or "pioneering"—even if it involved the most standard, traditional, and mundane of activities and dealt with mere "upgrading of existing services." The infrastructure issue would also get the departments out of the "social engineering" morass and make managers responsive to the rising Frost Belt coalition of public officials.

The trick of getting infrastructure off and running in the face of tax limitation movements and federal budget contraction turned out to be financing. Who would pay for such a massive group of construction projects? Direct taxation or pay-as-you-go as well as direct federal aid having been eliminated, the only alternatives left were long-term debt. Seeing such a demand, investment bankers and financial managers literally reshaped public capital financing as well as short-term cash management.

The entire "rebuilding America's cities" movement, as well as the budding "good schools" movement, represent agenda setting of a high order. Forces at work have reshaped the policy agenda, focusing direct attention on an issue other than tax limitation and blurring the deflate-the-government debate. The essential truth, however, lies in the notion that public financial managers have coped with uncertainty by information strategies, by seizing the initiative and resetting debate on policy in such a way that uncertainty may be absorbed, adjusted to in traditional, agreed-upon ways.

Imagery

If reaction to risk captures the spirit of the decade, agenda setting images give that spirit color. Six images have prominence.

1. *The administrative state.* In the beginning of the period, the notion of an administrative state clearly signified the success financial managers had partially achieved and for which they continued to strive. Large social and community development efforts from Model Cities to Community Development Block Grants made financial managers overseers of a larger and larger dominion.

2. *Besieged.* Threats to dominion erupted quickly and violently. Fiscal calamities in New York City and Cleveland, crises brought on by the initial tax resistance

movements in California and Massachusetts, the growing willingness of the courts to allow personal liability of public officials (and later government liability and antitrust action against government activities), and finally the energy crisis itself placed the government manager in the role of incompetent administrator and the financial manager in that of besieged servant. The financial manager's perseverance had to grow to take on the additional role of major actor in austerity drives or cutback management.

3. *The magic touch*. If, however, the manager became something of a goat, he or she retained some of the magic associated with finance: managers, in a time when revenues were precious and tax increases rare, became known as prudent and successful investors, providing, at times, the equivalent of a year's property tax millage increase in interest income from idle funds investments, while reducing the cost of borrowing through novel, consumer-oriented financings. The innovations, aided by federal budget deficits drawing in foreign capital, created enough new resources that when they were added to remaining public funds, they helped end stagnation and spark a major economic renaissance in many states and localities, giving financial managers the image of magicians.

4. *Financial intermediaries*. Not wanting to leave the job without completing it, financial managers did something about the shrinking resource base itself. Early on, studies confirmed the first major movement created from tax limitation, the increased reliance on user charges, or the creation of revenue streams based on exhaustible, excludable services. The market force reliance also generated the impetus for removing barriers to investment with idle funds. Moreover, new bond financing techniques created the means to give the state and local industrial and economic base some diversity. The financial manager became a financier, the state or local government a financial intermediary.

5. *Risking scandal*. Scandal followed and has created problems for both capital financing and cash management. Overuse, some call scandalous misuse, of private purpose financings by some has led to curtailment of several types of economic development efforts for lack of adequate financial tools.

6. *Strategic thinker*. In each case of scandal, however, new products have appeared and roles have changed so that, substantially, the financial manager has become a strategic manager of risk. The last role promises to alter radically the skill level of those in the profession presently and place greater emphasis on sophisticated practice of the financial manager's fiduciary responsibility.

Reaction to Uncertainty

This chapter has discussed the reaction to uncertainty played out by finance officers in the 1975–1990 period. The reaction has taken the form of administrative notions called "coping" (Hickson, et al, 1971). Based on a theory of power in organizations, coping suggests where power lies. Those who can cope with the critical contingencies facing the organization, the theory goes, wield power. In this period, finance officers have apparently coped in direct ways through prevention and absorption and in more fundamental and indirect ways by helping to reset the policy agenda to preserve initiative and to guard the financial resources of government.

The nagging question remains: did financial managers cope or did they grow dependent on the networks that aided the effort? If dependent, the question about power focuses attention on those central to coping outside government, the financial advisors and their ability to help financial managers construct a coping imagery to overcome fiducial values.

The actors themselves deserve attention. The catalog that follows deals with financial managers' reactions to change over the decade. The catalog deals first with new products and processes, briefly noted. Then we review legislation affecting changes and sometimes spurring further change. Finally, we attempt to forecast future changes in the roles of the players in both cash management and capital project financing.

Revolution in credit markets

Changes occurring in the municipal credit market in the 1980s have created forces that may very well remake the complexion of the field of play. The changes affect the three major legs of the stool of the market: borrowers, states, and cities, as well as their creations entitled to the tax exemption; lenders, commercial banks, institutions, such as fire, casualty, and life insurance companies, and households; and intermediaries, such as investment banks and their fellow travelers, bank trust departments, bond counsel firms, credit analysis firms, and insurance companies.

Borrowers

Tax legislation through the 1980s has created a sharply defined group of borrowers in the tax-exempt market. Eliminating much of the burgeoning private purpose or industrial development bond borrowing demand, Congress has prompted greater use of a number of existing and long used methods of financing public goods. For instance, the nonprofit corporation explicitly designed to buy and thus provide cash flow to support public goods and their borrowings exists to a greater extent than ever before. Tax-exempt leases transform what could have been long-term borrowing objects to simple 1-year appropriable items. Third party and cofinancing operating under the guise of privatization of production of public goods could operate to reduce insistence upon public goods produced by governments.

At the same time, insistence by federal policy that major federally backed capital projects in states and communities be paid for, in part at least, by these local governments has created a vast new area of demand for credit. In all, tax reform has appeared at a time of extreme reluctance of governments to carry large long-term debt burdens, leaving short-term burdens to be refinanced from year to year. Thus, the demand for long-term funding for direct government-produced public goods has decreased at the same time that tax reform has mandated a decrease in the use of the publicly financed private project as a tool of economic development.

Lenders

Among those buying municipal securities, municipal bond funds for individual households as well as institutions have developed at a rapid pace. Besides the dilution of risk presented by any individual bond issue, the bond funds serve as a new source of capital by remarketing to a larger and relatively less sophisticated group of investors.

The new source of capital compensates for relatively less interest in municipal securities by banks due to federal tax reform and the normal cyclical swings in earnings of insurance companies and banks. The emergence of new types of securities marketed to individuals has encouraged the development of a vast deep pocket of capital for municipal securities.

Intermediaries

The changes affecting both borrowers and lenders directly pale in comparison to those changes affecting intermediaries and their compatriots and indirectly borrowers and lenders anyway. Beginning with the least earth-shattering, tax reform mandates the registration of municipal securities. Registration creates additional tasks for a bank trust department and additional fees for either bondholders or municipal borrowers to pay. However, the advent of the central depository and registration agent and the computerization of recordkeeping and other housekeeping duties creates the opportunity for communities to undertake the registration and paying agent functions themselves.

Additionally, the creation of the zero-coupon municipal security, which, in effect, is sold at a discount to accrete to full value rather than bear interest, eliminates the paying agent duty and instead provides the borrower's accountant the job of ensuring the existence of the accreted amount. In such a case the bank—one of the several participants in the bond issuance process—becomes a relatively less important participant and eventually a party not necessary to the process.

The credit rating agency, always powerful as analyst and handholder for the uninformed bond buyer, may be on the way to extinction. The risk of loss, by which the credit-rating agency creates a role in divining, now may be covered in all but the most obviously unrisky situations by bond insurance on the risk of default. Several such agencies now exist and more are sure to follow this group in supporting a lucrative line of business. The insurance agencies receive a gilt-edged rating by the credit rating agencies and bequeath this rating to the issues their insurance underwriting supports, in exchange for a fee and following rudimentary analysis of the terms and conditions of the issue and a superficial analysis of the borrower's financial condition. Thus analysis and the role of the analyst are replaced by the market.

Finally, change has affected the heretofore pivotal player, the fiscal agent/ underwriter. Presently, intense competition and state law have created a power struggle among firms for traditional lines of business, general obligation and traditional revenue bonds. In general obligation bond cases, state law often requires the separation of financial advising or fiscal agency—preparing an issue for market—from underwriting. In such a case, the competition for financial advising has become intense.

A cycle whereby greater numbers of firms compete, prices for services fall, rates of return to these firms fall, and shakeouts occur has come full turn. In many cases, financial advising for general obligation bond work has become a free service provided a client in exchange for rights to underwrite other issues the client has the legal authority to award without competitive bidding. In still other cases, state law requires that bond counsel, rather than an investment banker/financial advisor, substantially complete all work on an issue prior to marketing. If the shakeout cycle has substantial validity, the result of the shakeout holds either promise or warning for borrowers.

Should the shakeout result in only firms with large capital or most talented and thoughtful staff members remaining, perhaps the cycle will produce innovative substitutes for the tax-exempt general obligation bond, such as the greater reliance on coproduction and the ultimate, the taxable municipal security. Firms having two staffs, one working the tax-exempt side and the other the taxable side, both in the fixed-income department, could realize economies, and the community could benefit from the breathtaking innovation taking place in corporate securities marketing.

The warning provided by the shakeout cycle theory, however, has equal validity. That is, the shakeout results in fewer firms, all of which do what has been done traditionally, charging higher prices. The wild card in this scenario probably, as always, lies in federal income tax law. Present movements to restrict advance refunding, to further tighten arbitrage regulations that communities follow to gain the tax exemption, and to keep low the capital gains tax rates for individuals, may result in less use of tax-exempt securities.

The shakeout extends beyond the financial advising role investment banks play to the underwriting role as well. The creation of and greater reliance on bond insurance, particularly for more exotic financings for which investment banks command high prices, also has the effect of contracting spreads on underwritten securities.

Why should a community pay a spread *and* an insurance premium? In such a case, the community must decide the price for the expertise that exotic financings require and what price the risk entails for underwriting. The other risk feature that underwriters traditionally bear relates to interest-rate volatility. Will the issue be priced correctly when resold? Again, insurance exists to hedge the risk, nominally, already in municipal bond index futures contracts.

Underwriters, within reasonable tolerances, can reduce losses, and even gain, on the purchase of preset prices. In the case of both insurance against outright borrower default and contracts hedging price changes, the underwriter faces less risk than ever before, allowing a contraction of the spread as never before. The narrowing of the spread reduces the profit for investment bankers and the incentive for brokers and traders, mitigating the potential for talent and insight to progressively gravitate toward either of these jobs.

Is the investment banker doomed? Probably not. Communities, in the short run and probably the long run, will not acquire the expertise to be able to market and sell securities. No one but investment bankers and traders will have the expertise or the gall to devise strategies to profit from confusion and complexity, given the present tools for designing issues and the speed of innovation. Nevertheless, the investment banker as now known and appreciated may soon cease to exist.

This exploration of the future leads one to be able to conclude, not for the first time, that the present intermediaries will no long exist one day. The conclusion, however, will probably fail for two simple reasons. The first is a matter of concern to public administrators: government cannot recruit and retain the talent necessary to reduce the cost of government, at least the cost of government borrowing. Of course, if government borrowing ceases to exist, through privatization, the contraction of government functions, or the sale of assets, the expertise has no value anyway. Second, the investment banking function will continue because of the need to produce the innovations that keep borrowing costs low, whether these innovations concern new ways of marketing fixed-income securities or new ways to contract government functions.

Conclusions and Summary

This section of the chapter has discussed the reaction to ambiguity finance officers have had in the 1975–1990 period. The reaction has taken the form of administrative notions known as "coping." In that decade, finance officers coped in direct ways, through prevention, absorption, and information.

The question still remains: Did financial managers cope or grow dependent? Coping suggests a more knowledgeable and sophisticated profession than existed before 1975. Coping also suggests a deep understanding of the capital financing process, the political process that underlies it, and the credit markets that support it, subjects about which most research suggests finance advisors are somewhat less than completely knowledgeable.

If not coping but the more likely case of dependence, the question focuses attention on those central to coping outside government, the financial advisors. Financial advisors may be leading government financial managers into what amounts to greater ambiguity, to a casinolike world where puts and floaters, hedges and straddles, and arbitrage and speculation contribute to the creation of debt for the sake of creating debt.

The evidence in the section of the chapter lends credence to the explanation advanced earlier that managers themselves do not decide what reality is; if they did their values would tend to limit their innovativeness. Instead, managers participate with others in constructing a reality that many managers find particularly useful. This reality is constructed opportunistically to cope with an uncertain environment outside the organization; the innovations constructed create stability, in line with managers' values perhaps, while still promoting innovation.

Capital Investment in Communities Revisited

This chapter has surveyed three major approaches used in structuring, Formulating, and implementing strategies that pertain to capital asset production in communities. The conventional approach to this form of strategy resembles classic rational decision making in its singleminded insistence on clear priorities and in its employment of cost-benefit analysis.

However, we outlined two other, counter, approaches. The first, a nonlinear or competitive approach, describes what economists have either portrayed or projected onto suburban communities who vie among themselves for better quality tax bases.

The second, an opportunistic approach to strategy, pertained to communities who face more uncertain environments. Such communities also have decision makers and interested parties who are randomly related, have unclear goals, and who interact to make choices irregularly. Such a high degree of ambiguity creates vacuums of one sort or another and opens the way for opportunism by all involved.

REFERENCES

Academy of State and Local Government (1984). Local alternatives to the property tax: User charges and nonproperty taxes, in Becker, Stephanie, "Local Finance: A Bootstraps Operation" *Intergovernmental Perspective* 10 (2): 20.

Adams, C. T. (1988). *The Politics of Capital Investment: The Case of Philadelphia.* Temple University Press, Philadelphia.

Aguila, P. R. Jr., and Holstein, C. L. (1989). The cost of a rating downgrade. *Government Finance Rev., 5*(1):38–39.

Aldrich, H. E. (1979). *Organizations and Environments.* Prentice-Hall, Englewood Cliffs, NJ.

Aldrich, H. E., and Whetten, D. A. (1981). Organization-sets, action-sets, and networks: Making the most of simplicity. In P.C. Nystrom and W. H. Starbuck (eds.), *Handbook of Organizational Design,* Vol. 1, Oxford University Press, New York.

Aronson, J. R., and Marsden, J. R. (1980). Duplicating Moody's municipal credit ratings. *Public Finance Q., 8*(1):97–106.

Aronson, J. R., and Schwartz, E. (1987). Capital budgeting. In J. R. Aronson and E. Schwartz (eds.), *Management Policies in Local Government Finance;* International City Management Association, Washington, DC, pp. 400–421.

Ascher, W. (1978). *Forecasting: An Appraisal for Policy-Makers and Planners.* Johns Hopkins University Press, Baltimore.

Ayer, A. J. (1936). *Language, Truth and Logic.* Alfred A. Knopf, New York.

Bahl, R. W. (1971). Measuring the creditworthiness of state and local governments: Municipal bond ratings. *Proc. Natl. Tax Assoc.,* (September):600–22.

Barker, L. J., and Jansiewicz, D. (1970). Coalitions in the civil rights movement. In S. Groennings, E. W. Kelly, and M. Leiserson (eds.), *The Study of Coalition Behavior,* Holt, Rinehart and Winston, New York.

Bayless, P. (1985). A fast-lane financing. *Institutional Investor 19* (January): 253–254.

Beal, F., and Hollander, E. (1979). City development plans. In F. S. So, I. Stollman, F. Beal, and D. S. Arnold (eds.), *The Practice of Local Government Planning,* International City Management Association, Washington, DC, pp. 153–182.

Bennett, J. T., and DiLorenzo, T. J. 1983. *Underground Government: The Off-Budget Public Sector.* Cato Institute, Washington, DC.

Bland, R. L. (1985). The interest cost savings from experience in the municipal bond market. *Public Admin. Rev., 45:*233–237.

Blumstein, M. (1983). The lessons of a bond failure. *New York Times,* (August 14): Business (Section 3): 1, 24.

The Bond Buyer (1983). Innovative financing. *The Bond Buyer* (August 1): 11.

Bozeman, J. L. (1984). The capital budget: History and future directions. *Public Budgeting and Finance, 4*(3):18–30.

Brown, B., and Helmer, O. (1962). *Improving the Reliability of Estimates Obtained from a Consensus of Experts.* Rand Corporation, Santa Monica, CA.

Brunsson N. (1989). *The Organization of Hypocrisy.* John Wiley, Chicester, England.

Bryson, J. M. and Roering, W. D. (1988). Initiation of strategic planning by governments, *Public Administration Review, 48:* 995–1004.

Buchanan, J. M., and Tullock, G. (1962). *The Calculus of Consent.* University of Michigan Press, Ann Arbor.

Carleton, W. T., and Lerner, E. M. (1969). Statistical credit scoring of municipal bonds. *J. Money, Credit and Banking,* (December):750–64.

Castells, M. (1977). *The Urban Question: A Marxist Approach.* MIT Press, Cambridge, MA.

Cater, D. (1964). *Power in Washington.* Vintage, New York.

Chandler, A. D. (1962). *Strategy and Structure: Chapters in the History of the American Industrial Enterprise.* MIT Press, Cambridge, Massachusetts.

Cohen, M. D., and March, J. G. (1974). *Leadership and Ambiguity.* McGraw-Hill, New York.

Cohen, M. D., March, J. G., and Olsen, J. P. (1972). A garbage can model of organizational choice. *Admin. Sci. Q., 17*(1):1–25.

Cohen, M. D. and March, J. G. (1986). *Leadership and Ambiguity: The American College President, 2nd ed.,* Harvard Business School Press, Cambridge, MA.

Clausewitz, C. B. (1956). *On War,* Vol.1, trans. J. J. Graham, Barnes and Noble, New York.

Crecine, John P. (1967). *Government Problem Solving.* Rand McNally, Chicago.

Daft, R. L. and Weick, K. L. (1984). Toward a model of organizations as interpretation systems, *Academy of Management Rev. 9:* 284–295.

Dale, B. (1988). The grass may not be greener: Commercial banks and investment banking. *Econ. Perspect., 12*(6):3–15.

Delbecq, A. L., Van de Ven, A. H., and Gustafson, D. H. (1975). *Group Techniques for Program Planning: A Guide for Nominal Group and Delphi Processes.* Scott, Foresman, Glenview, IL.

Downs, A. (1957). *An Economic Theory of Democracy.* Harper & Bros., New York.

Downs, A. (1960). Why the government budget is too small in a democracy. *World Politics, 12*(4):541–563.

Downs, A. (1967). *Inside Bureaucracy.* Little, Brown, Boston.

Dunn, W. N. (1981). *Public Policy Analysis.* Prentice-Hall, Englewood Cliffs, NJ.

Eisenhardt, K. M. 1989. Agency theory: An assessment and review. *Acad. Manage. Rev. 14*(1):57–74.

Evan, W. M. (1966). The organization-set: Toward a theory of interorganizational relations. In

James D. Thompson (ed.), *Approaches to Organizational Design,* University of Pittsburgh Press, Pittsburgh, PA.

Evered, R. (1983). So what is strategy?, *Long Range Planning, 16* (3): 57–72.

Fabozzi, F. J. and Zarb, F. G. (1981). *Handbook of Financial Markets.* Dow Jones-Irwin, Homewood, IL.

Farnham, P. G., and Cluff, G. S. (1982). Municipal bond ratings: New results, new directions. *Public Finance Q., 10*(4):427–455.

Forbes, R. W. and Petersen, J. E. (1983). State credit assistance to local governments, In Petersen, J. E. and Hough, W. C., eds., *Creative Capital Financing for State and Local Governments.* Municipal Finance Officers Association, Chicago: 225–235.

Freeman, J. L. (1965). *The Political Process.* Random House, New York.

Freeman, R. E. (1984). *Strategic Management: A Stakeholder Approach,* Pitman, Boston.

Gilbert, D. R., Jr., Hartman, E., Mauriel, J. J., and Freeman, R. E. (1988). *A Logic for Strategy.* Ballinger, Cambridge, MA.

Gohagan, J. K. (1980). *Quantitative Analysis for Public Policy.* McGraw-Hill, New York.

Golembiewski, R. T. (1964). Accountancy as a function of organization theory. *Account. Rev., 39*(April):333–41.

Gordon, L. A., and Pinches, G. E. (1984). *Improving Capital Budgeting: A Decision Support System Approach.* Addison-Wesley, Reading, MA.

Harvey, D. (1973). *Social Justice and the City.* Johns Hopkins University Press, Baltimore.

Harvey, D. (1982). *The Limits to Capital.* University of Chicago Press, Chicago.

Heclo, H. (1978). Issue networks and the executive establishment. In A. King (ed.), *The New American Political System,* American Enterprise Institute, Washington DC.

Henriques, D. (1982). *The Machinery of Greed: The Abuse of Public Authorities and What to Do about It.* Princeton University Press, Princeton, NJ.

Heilbroner, R. L., and Thurow, L. C. (1984). *Understanding Microeconomics,* 6th ed. Prentice-Hall, Englewood Cliffs, NJ.

Herman, T. (1989). Downgrading the credit-rating services. *The Wall Street Journal,* June 23:C1.

Herson, L. (1957). The lost world of municipal government. *Am. Polit. Sci. Rev., 51*:330–345.

Hickson, D. J., C. R. Hinings, C. A. Lee, R. E. Schneck, and J. M. Pennings (1971). A strategic contingencies theory of intraorganizational power, *Administrative Science Quarterly 16*: 216–229.

Hildreth, W. B. (1986). Strategies of municipal debt issuers. Paper presented at the National Conference of the American Society for Public Administration, Anaheim, CA.

Hildreth, W. B. (1987). The changing roles of municipal market participants. *Public Admin. Q., 11*(3):314–341.

Hildreth, W. B. (1988). The anatomy of a municipal bond default. Unpublished manuscript, Public Administration Institute, Louisiana State University.

Horton, J. (1970). Statistical determination of municipal bond quality. Working paper no. 69–3. Federal Deposit Insurance Corporation, Washington, DC.

Horvitz, P. M. (1981). Commercial banks. In F. J. Fabozzi and F. G. Zarb (eds.), *Handbook of Financial Markets,* Dow Jones-Irwin, Homewood, IL.

Jay, E. J. (1964). The concepts of "field" and "network" in anthropological research. *Man* 64:137–139.

Jones, L. R. (1984). The WPPSS default: Trouble in the municipal bond market. *Public Budgeting and Finance,* Winter:60–77.

Kaldor, N. (1939). Welfare propositions of economists and interpersonal comparisons of utility. *Econ. J.,* (September): 549–552.

Kamlet, M. S., Mowery, D. C., and Su, T. T. (1987). Whom do you trust? An analysis of executive and congressional economic forecasts. *J. Policy Anal. Manage., 6*(3):365–384.

Kaufman, G. G. (1986). *The U.S. Financial System: Money, Markets and Institutions.* Prentice-Hall, Englewood Cliffs, NJ.

Kaufman, H. (1960). *The Forest Ranger: A Study in Administrative Behavior*. Johns Hopkins University Press, Baltimore, Md.

Key, V. O. (1940). The lack of a budgetary theory. *Am. Political Science Rev. 34*(6): 1137–1144.

Kingdon, J. W. (1984). *Agendas, Alternatives and Public Policies*. Little, Brown, Boston.

Klapper, B. (1980). Municipal commercial paper. *Standard and Poor's Perspective* (September 17): 1.

Klay, W. E. (1983). Revenue forecasting: An administrative perspective. In J. Rabin, and T. D. Lynch (eds.), *Handbook of Public Budgeting and Financial Management*, Marcel Dekker, New York.

Klay, W. E. (1985). The organizational dimension of budgetary forecasting: Suggestions from revenue forecasting in the states. *Int. J. Public Admin. 7*(3):241–265.

Lamb, R., and Rappaport, S. P. (1980). *Municipal Bonds: The Comprehensive Review of Tax-Exempt Securities and Public Finance*. McGraw-Hill, New York.

Landau, M. (1969). Redundancy, rationality, and the problem of duplication and overlap. *Public Admin. Rev., 29*:346–358.

Leigland, J., and Lamb, R. (1986). *WPP$$: Who Is to Blame for the WPPSS Disaster*. Ballinger, Cambridge, MA.

Lemov, P. (1990). For municipal bonds, it's not a plain vanilla world anymore. *Governing*, June:52–58.

Lineberry, R. (1977). *Equality and Urban Services*. Sage, Beverly Hills, Ca.

Long, N. (1958). The local community as an ecology of games, *Am. Political Science Rev. 64*: 251–261.

Luttwak, E. N. (1987). *Strategy: The Logic of War and Peace*. Belknap Press, Harvard University Press, Cambridge, MA.

MacMillan, I. (1978). *Strategy Formulation: Political Concepts*. West Publishing, St. Paul, MN.

MacMillan, I. (1983). Competitive strategies for not-for-profit agencies. *Adv. Strategic Manage., 1*:61–82.

March, J. G., and Olsen, J. P. (1989). *Rediscovering Institutions: The Organizational Bias of Politics*. Basic Books, New York.

Michel, A. J. (1977). Municipal bond ratings: A discriminant analysis. *J. Financial Quant. Anal.,* (November):587–598.

Miller, G. J. (1985). Coping with uncertainty. *Int. J. Public Admin. 7*(4):451–495.

Miller, G. J., Rabin, J., and Hildreth, W. B. (1987). Strategy, values, and productivity. *Public Productivity Rev., 11*:81–96.

Mintzberg, H. and McHugh, A. (1985). Strategy formation in an adhocracy, *Administrative Science Quarterly 30*: 160–197.

Moak, L. L. (1982). *Municipal Bonds: Planning, Sale and Administration*. Government Finance Officers Association, Chicago, IL.

Moak, L. L., and Killian, K. (1964). *A Manual of Suggested Practice for the Preparation and Adoption of Capital Programs and Capital Budgets by Local Governments*. Municipal Finance Officers Association, Chicago.

Moak, L. L., and Hillhouse, A. M. (1975). *Concepts and Practices in Local Government Finance*. Municipal Finance Officers Association, Chicago.

Morris, C. R. (1980). *The Cost of Good Intentions*. McGraw-Hill, New York.

Morton, T. G. (1975–1976). A comparative analysis of Moody's and Standard and Poor's municipal bond ratings. *Rev. Business Econ. Res.,* (Winter):74–81.

Musgrave, R. A., and Musgrave, P. B. (1980). *Public Finance in Theory and Practice,* 3d ed. McGraw-Hill, New York.

Myhra, D. (1984). *Whoops!/WPPSS*. McFarland, Jefferson, NC.

Neuhauser, P. E. (1988). *Tribal Warfare in Organizations: Turning Tribal Conflict Into Negotiated Peace,* Ballinger, Cambridge, Massachusetts.

Niskanen, W., Jr. (1971). *Bureaucracy and Representative Government*. Aldine, Chicago.

Osborn, A. (1953). *Applied Imagination: Principle and Procedures of Creative Thinking*. Scribners, New York.

O'Toole, J. (1985). *Vanguard Management*, Doubleday, New York.

Pagano, M. A., and Moore, R. J. T. (1985). *Cities and Fiscal Choices: A New Model of Urban Public Investment*. Duke University Press, Durham, NC.

Pareto, Vilfredo (1906). *Mannuala Economica Politica*, trans., Ann S. Schweier, Ann S. Schweier and Alfred N. Page (eds.) New York: A. M. Kelly.

Patton, J. N. and Hempel, G. H. (1975). *Understanding the Market for State and Local Debt*. U. S. Advisory Commission on Intergovernmental Relations, Washington D.C.

Peltzman, S. (1980). The growth of government, *J. of Law and Economics 23*: 209–87.

Petersen, J. E. and Buckley, M. P. (1983). *A Guide to Registered Municipal Securities*. Municipal Finance Officers Association, Washington, D.C.

Petersen, J. E. (1987). *Tax Exempts and Tax Reform: Assessing the Consequences of the Tax Reform Act of 1986 for the Municipal Securities Market*. Government Finance Officers Association, Chicago.

Petersen, J. E. (1988). Information flows in the municipal securities market: A preliminary analysis. Unpublished manuscript, Government Finance Research Center, Government Finance Officers Association, Washington, DC.

Petersen, J. E., and O'Brien, J. L. (1988). *Euromarket Financing for State and Local Governments*. Government Finance Officers Association, Washington, DC.

Petersen, J. E., O'Brien, J. L., and Harrison, J. (1987). *Offshore Financing for State and Local Governments*. Government Finance Officers Association, Washington, DC.

Peterson, P. E. (1981). *City Limits*. University of Chicago Press, Chicago.

Pierce, L. D. (1971). *The Politics of Fiscal Policy Formation*. Goodyear, Pacific Palisades, CA.

Porter, M. E. (1980). *Competitive Strategy: Techniques for Analyzing Industries and Competitors*. Free Press, New York.

Porter, M. E. (1985). *Competitive Advantage: Creating and Sustaining Superior Performance*. Free Press, New York.

Quinn, R. E., and Cameron, K. S. (1988). *Paradox and Transformation: Toward a Theory of Change in Organization and Management*. Ballinger, Cambridge, MA.

Rapoport, A. (1960). *Fights, Games and Debates*. University of Michigan Press, Ann Arbor.

Ring, P. S. and Perry, J. L. (1985). Strategic management in public and private organizations: Implications of distinctive contexts and constraints, *Academy of Management Review 10* (2): 276–286.

Rubinfeld, D. (1973). Credit ratings and the market for general obligation municipal bonds. *Nat. Tax J., 26*(1):17–27.

Sbragia, A. M. (1983). Politics, local government, and the municipal bond market. In A. M. Sbragia (ed.), *The Municipal Money Chase: The Politics of Local Government Finance*. Westview, Boulder, Co.

Schmid, A. A. (1990). *Benefit-Cost Analysis: A Political Economy Approach*. Westview, Boulder, CO.

Schneider, M. (1989). *The Competitive City: The Political Economy of Suburbia*. University of Pittsburgh Press, Pittsburg.

Scott, M. (1969). *American City Planning since 1890*. University of California Press, Berkeley.

Selznick, P. (1957). *Leadership in Administration*. Row, Peterson, Evanston, IL.

Sloane, L. (1985). New securities tied to assets. *New York Times* (July 20): 32.

Sharp, E. (1986). The politics and economics of new city debt. *Am. Political Sci. Rev., 80*:1271–1288.

Shapiro, H. D. (1985). The securitization of practically everything. *Institutional Investor 19* (May): 197–202.

Simon, H. A. (1976). *Administrative Behavior*, 3d ed. Free Press, New York.

Schultz, S. K. (1989). *Constructing Urban Culture: American Cities and City Planning 1800–1920.* Temple University Press, Philadelphia.

Smith, B. (1990). The pay-as-you-go-concept in municipal financing. *Government Finance Rev.,* 6(3):22–24, 48.

Standard & Poor's Corporation. (1989). *S & P's Municipal Finance Criteria.* McGraw-Hill, New York.

Steiss, A. W. (1975). *Local Government Finance.* Lexington Books, Lexington, MA.

Stigler, G. J. (1961). The economics of information. *J. Political Econ.,* (July/August):706–738.

Stiglitz, J. E. (1988). *Economics of the Public Sector,* 2d ed. W. W. Norton, New York.

Summers, H. G., Jr., (1987). When is a bad road good? A review of Strategy: The Logic of War and Peace by Edward N. Luttwak. *New York Times Book Rev.,* (August 30):22.

Swiss, James E. (1991). *Public Management Systems: Monitoring and Managing Government Performance.* Prentice-Hall, Englewood Cliffs, N. J.

Tiebout, C. M. (1956). A pure theory of local expenditures, *J. of Political Economy* 64: 416–424.

Terreberry, S. (1968). The evolution of organization environments. *Admin. Sci. Q. 12:*590–613.

Tichy, N. M., Tushman, M. L., and Fombrun, C. (1979). Social network analysis for organizations. *Acad. Manage. Rev.,* 4:507–519.

U. S. Bureau of the Census (1980). *Number of Inhabitants,* PC80-1-A, Chapter A, Superintendent of Documents, U. S. Government Printing Office, Washington D.C.

Vartan, V. G. (1985). Tax-exempt trusts flourish. *New York Times* (August 22): 31.

Vogt, A. J. (1975). Capital planning and budgeting for local government. *Popular Government,* 41(Fall):12–13.

Vogt, A. J. (1977). *Capital Improvements Programming: A Handbook for Local Officials.* Institute of Government, University of North Carolina, Chapel Hill.

Vogt, A. J. and Cole, L. A. (1983). *A Guide to Municipal Leasing.* Municipal Finance Officers Association, Washington D.C.

Wacht, R. F. (1987). *A New Approach to Capital Budgeting for City and County Governments,* 2d ed. (Research Monograph No. 87). Business Publishing Division, College of Business Administration, Georgia State University, Atlanta.

Wall Street Journal (1982). Cities getting part of profits for giving aid to developers. *Wall Street Journal* (September 29): 27.

Walsh, A. H. 1978. *The Public's Business: The Politics and Practices of Government Corporations.* MIT Press, Cambridge, MA.

Walters, D. (1990). Governor Deukmejian of California signs bill to implement long range capital planning. *MuniWeek,* October 8:29.

Watson, D. J., and Vocino, T. (1990). Changing intergovernmental fiscal relationships: Impact of the 1986 Tax Reform Act on state and local governments. *Public Admin. Rev.,* 50(4):427–434.

Wetzler, J. W., and Petersen, J. E. (1985). The finance officer as public strategist. *Government Finance Rev.,* April:7–10.

Wildavsky, A. (1988). *The New Politics of the Budgetary Process.* Scott, Foresman, Glenview, IL.

Willson, S. R. (1986). Credit ratings and general obligation bonds: A statistical alternative. *Government Finance Rev.,* 2(3):19–22.

Wortman, M. (1979). Strategic management: Not-for-profit organizations. In Dan E. Schendel and Charles W. Hofer (eds.), *Strategic Management: A New View of Business Policy and Planning,* Little, Brown, Boston.

Wright, G., and Ayton, P. (1987). *Judgmental Forecasting.* Wiley, Chichester, England.

Yacik, G. (1985). A new use for an old bond. *The Bond Buyer* (May 28): 10.

Youngman, H. (1990). "Nem di gelt" (Take the money). *New York Times* (July 31):A19.

Zald, M. N. (1970). Organizational Change: The Political Economy of the YMCA, University of Chicago Press, Chicago.

Appendix A

A Primer on Gross National Product Concepts and Issues

A study by the staff of the U.S. General Accounting Office. Reprinted from GAO Report 66D-81-47, April 8, 1981.

CHAPTER 1

INTRODUCTION

The national income and product accounts, summarized by the gross national product (GNP), are among the most important and widely used Federal economic statistics. The accounts, which collectively provide a broad overview of economic activity, are one of several economic accounting activities of the Department of Commerce's Bureau of Economic Analysis (BEA). Other national economic accounts compiled by BEA measure the Nation's wealth, international payments, interindustry economic activity, and regional economic activity. BEA supplements these various measurements by analyzing business cycles and trends. Since the national income and product accounts provide comprehensive measures of the Nation's current economic output, they are the most widely used of all the national economic accounts.

Subsequent revisions to the published GNP have on a few occasions drawn complaints from economic policymakers who claimed that the preliminary estimates had misled their analysis of needed actions. On other occasions, although not as critical, revisions to GNP gave a somewhat different picture of the state of the economy. Policymakers use GNP and related measures in making decisions which affect billions of dollars of the Nation's output and associated jobs, purchasing power, and allocation of resources.

WHAT ARE THE NATIONAL INCOME AND PRODUCT ACCOUNTS?

The national income and product accounts are a means of measuring the Nation's annual output of final goods and services at their market value. The accounts register the economy's output of finished goods and services and the incomes which flow to resource owners from their contribution to output. The accounts thus present for the Nation's economy the sort of information contained in a business' profit and loss statement or a household budget. They balance the flow of income earned against the flow of spending on the economy's output of goods and services.

The national income and product accounts consist of five interrelated accounts. The national income and product account summarizes total economic activity. It relates the market value of the year's final output (GNP) by type of purchaser to the earnings of those contributing to output by type of income. The remaining four accounts highlight activity in the economy's major sectors. The personal income and outlay account, which focuses on the total households in the economy, relates income received by source of income to how they were disposed. The government receipts and expenditures account relates the revenues of all governments by source to government spending by type of outlay. The foreign transactions account summarizes output and income flowing to and from foreigners. The gross savings and investment account relates savings from the year's income available for financing capital formation to investment spending.

These five accounts are interrelated because (1) entries in the household, government, foreign, and saving and investment accounts are the basic entries comprising the summary measures of GNP, national income, and other components in the national income and product account and (2) the four accounts which the national income and product account summarizes also have interrelating entries among themselves. An illustration of the accounts' inter- relationship is shown on the following page. For example, the basic GNP components of personal consumption expenditures, gross private domestic investment, net exports of goods and services, and government purchases of goods and services in the national income and product account are also key components in the other four accounts. GNP thus represents total spending by the institu- tional sectors represented in the accounts on the economy's output of final goods and services.

Charges against GNP, the income side of the national income and product account, is also composed of items appearing in the other four accounts. These include the basic national income components relating to employee compensation, proprietors' income, rental income of persons, corporate profits, and net interest income. Other items, which will be discussed later, are required to balance the GNP measure in the account. Definitions of national income and product components are provided in appendix I.

GNP and charges against GNP are alternative measures of the economy's gross output. GNP is the total spending of consumers, businesses, governments, and foreigners on the economy's output of finished goods and services. Charges against GNP is the sum of incomes earned during output's production plus other costs incurred during the production process.

The two measures are ways of observing the economy's output, first, as output's market value, and second, as the cost of pro- ducing output. In other words, GNP and charges against GNP are two views of the economic coin from its opposite sides. This may be better understood if the value of one item is considered. For example, the market value of an automobile registered in GNP is its retail price. The automobile's value is also registered in charges against GNP as the employees' compensation, rents, inter- est, profits, indirect taxes, depreciation and other economic costs of producing the automobile. The automobile's retail market value--retail price--should cover all costs incurred during its production and distribution and associated profits. Thus the automobile's retail value included in GNP should equal the incomes earned and other claims against the automobile's value that are included in charges against GNP. Applying the same reasoning to the sum of goods and services produced in the economy, the value of total product, or GNP, should equal the value of all claims against total product.

The national income and product account framework, shown on page 5, reflects the identity between total product's value and the sum of charges against its value. GNP, on the account's product side, is total product's value measured as total spending. Charges against GNP, on the income side, is the sum of all earned income and other claims against total product. Primary among these are business transfer payments, indirect business taxes, and capital consumption allowances.

The account thus presents a snapshot of the economic process of buying and selling. The incomes persons earn for selling productive services are either spent, saved, or taxed away by government. The portion spent satisfies personal wants. The portion saved is invested directly or flows through financial intermediaries and finances investment wants. The portion taxed away is spent by government to satisfy collective wants. The act of producing the goods and services to satisfy these wants, on the other hand, provides the demands for productive resources like land, labor services, and capital services. Those providing these services are remunerated in rental payments, wages and salaries, profits, and interest payments. These incomes provide the means to satisfy the personal, investment, and collective wants viewed in GNP.

The flow of economic activity captured in the account's framework is summarized in two major independent aggregates-- GNP and national income. GNP is gross output in that it includes the value of capital goods depreciated during output's production. National income is the sum of earned incomes or the value of claims against GNP by those contributing to its production.

The GNP and national income estimates for 1980 measured at annual rates are about $2.6 and $2.1 trillion, respectively. The levels of the Nation's economy--GNP, national income, and constant dollar or real GNP--since 1929 are shown in appendix II.

BEA estimates the two sides of the national income and product account independently. Individual analysts estimate values for the individual product side and income side components. These estimates are then summed to obtain the totals for GNP, national income, net national product, and charges against GNP. The difference between the estimates of GNP and charges against GNP is the statistical discrepancy which is entered on the account's income side.

INTERRELATIONSHIP OF THE
NATIONAL INCOME AND PRODUCT ACCOUNTS
1978
(BILLIONS OF DOLLARS)

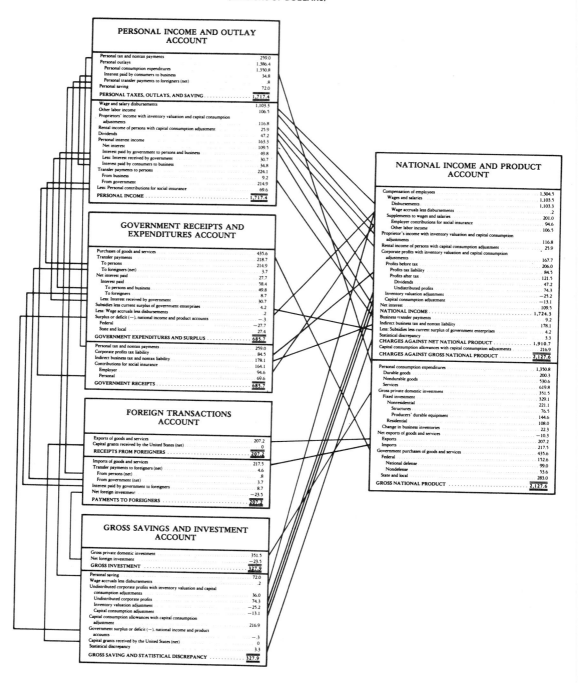

PERSONAL INCOME AND OUTLAY ACCOUNT

Personal tax and nontax payments	259.0
Personal outlays	1,386.4
Personal consumption expenditures	1,350.8
Interest paid by consumers to business	34.8
Personal transfer payments to foreigners (net)	.8
Personal saving	72.0
PERSONAL TAXES, OUTLAYS, AND SAVING	**1,717.4**
Wage and salary disbursements	1,103.3
Other labor income	106.5
Proprietors' income with inventory valuation and capital consumption adjustments	116.8
Rental income of persons with capital consumption adjustment	25.9
Dividends	47.2
Personal interest income	163.3
Net interest	109.5
Interest paid by government to persons and business	49.8
Less: Interest received by government	30.7
Interest paid by consumers to business	34.8
Transfer payments to persons	224.1
From business	9.2
From government	214.9
Less: Personal contributions for social insurance	69.6
PERSONAL INCOME	**1,717.4**

GOVERNMENT RECEIPTS AND EXPENDITURES ACCOUNT

Purchases of goods and services	435.6
Transfer payments	218.7
To persons	214.9
To foreigners (net)	3.7
Net interest paid	27.7
Interest paid	58.4
To persons and business	49.8
To foreigners	8.7
Less: Interest received by government	30.7
Subsidies less current surplus of government enterprises	4.2
Less: Wage accruals less disbursements	.2
Surplus or deficit (−), national income and product accounts	−.3
Federal	−27.7
State and local	27.4
GOVERNMENT EXPENDITURES AND SURPLUS	**685.7**
Personal tax and nontax payments	259.0
Corporate profits tax liability	84.5
Indirect business tax and nontax liability	178.1
Contributions for social insurance	164.1
Employer	94.6
Personal	69.6
GOVERNMENT RECEIPTS	**685.7**

FOREIGN TRANSACTIONS ACCOUNT

Exports of goods and services	207.2
Capital grants received by the United States (net)	0
RECEIPTS FROM FOREIGNERS	**207.2**
Imports of goods and services	217.5
Transfer payments to foreigners (net)	4.6
From persons (net)	.8
From government (net)	3.7
Interest paid by government to foreigners	8.7
Net foreign investment	−23.5
PAYMENTS TO FOREIGNERS	**207.2**

GROSS SAVINGS AND INVESTMENT ACCOUNT

Gross private domestic investment	351.5
Net foreign investment	−23.5
GROSS INVESTMENT	**327.9**
Personal saving	72.0
Wage accruals less disbursements	.2
Undistributed corporate profits with inventory valuation and capital consumption adjustments	36.0
Undistributed corporate profits	74.3
Inventory valuation adjustment	−25.2
Capital consumption adjustment	−13.1
Capital consumption allowances with capital consumption adjustment	216.9
Government surplus or deficit (−), national income and product accounts	−.3
Capital grants received by the United States (net)	0
Statistical discrepancy	3.3
GROSS SAVING AND STATISTICAL DISCREPANCY	**327.9**

NATIONAL INCOME AND PRODUCT ACCOUNT

Compensation of employees	1,304.5
Wages and salaries	1,103.5
Disbursements	1,103.3
Wage accruals less disbursements	.2
Supplements to wages and salaries	201.0
Employer contributions for social insurance	94.6
Other labor income	106.5
Proprietor's income with inventory valuation and capital consumption adjustments	116.8
Rental income of persons with capital consumption adjustment	25.9
Corporate profits with inventory valuation and capital consumption adjustments	167.7
Profits before tax	206.0
Profits tax liability	84.5
Profits after tax	121.5
Dividends	47.2
Undistributed profits	74.3
Inventory valuation adjustment	−25.2
Capital consumption adjustment	−13.1
Net interest	109.5
NATIONAL INCOME	**1,724.3**
Business transfer payments	9.2
Indirect business tax and nontax liability	178.1
Less: Subsidies less current surplus of government enterprises	4.2
Statistical discrepancy	3.3
CHARGES AGAINST NET NATIONAL PRODUCT	**1,910.7**
Capital consumption allowances with capital consumption adjustments	216.9
CHARGES AGAINST GROSS NATIONAL PRODUCT	**2,127.6**
Personal consumption expenditures	1,350.8
Durable goods	200.3
Nondurable goods	530.6
Services	619.8
Gross private domestic investment	351.5
Fixed investment	329.1
Nonresidential	221.1
Structures	76.5
Producers' durable equipment	144.6
Residential	108.0
Change in business inventories	22.3
Net exports of goods and services	−10.3
Exports	207.2
Imports	217.5
Government purchases of goods and services	435.6
Federal	152.6
National defense	99.0
Nondefense	53.6
State and local	283.0
GROSS NATIONAL PRODUCT	**2,127.6**

HOW IMPORTANT ARE THE NATIONAL INCOME AND PRODUCT ACCOUNTS?

The national income and product accounts' primary uses are to analyze the performance of the Nation's economy and provide a framework for predicting future economic activity and the impact of Federal policies. Limited use has been made of the statistics beyond that of an analytical nature. Legislative proposals introduced in the 96th Congress would have further expanded its use beyond that of an analytical tool to limiting Federal spending and triggering Federal assistance to State and local governments. Those initiatives were not enacted but point to potential uses beyond that of an analytical nature.

Executive branch uses

The accounts help Federal policymakers pursue the goals of the Employment Act of 1946--full employment, price stability, and economic growth. Federal economists use the accounts for short term fiscal, monetary, and wage-price policy analysis for managing the Nation's employment and anti-inflation goals and analyzing long term demands for skilled labor and financing for capital formation. Major Federal users include the Council of Economic Advisors, the Federal Reserve Board, the Office of Management and Budget, and the Departments of the Treasury and Commerce.

Various other Federal agencies also use the accounts in analyzing and forecasting particular areas and aspects of the Nation's economy. These include the Departments of Agriculture and Housing and Urban Development, the Department of the Interior's Bureau of Mines, and the Department of Labor's Bureau of Labor Statistics (BLS).

Although the analytical uses of the accounts are primary, additional uses are being made. The Trade Act of 1974 (P.L. 93-618) specifies the use of annual GNP estimates in determining limitations on preferential treatment extended to countries exporting goods to the United States. The GNP implicit price deflator is used as a component in the inflation adjustment factor in the Natural Gas Policy Act of 1978 (P.L. 95-621) and the Crude Oil Windfall Profit Tax Act of 1980 (P.L. 96-223) for determining the ceiling price on certain types of natural gas and the windfall profits on crude oil, respectively. The implicit price deflator--a byproduct of the GNP estimate--is a ratio of current dollar to real GNP which is discussed in chapter 6.

Congressional uses

Several congressional committees, including the Joint Economic, House Ways and Means, Senate Finance, and House and Senate Budget Committees, and the Congressional Budget Office use the accounts for evaluating the economy's performance, analyzing fiscal policy impacts, and analyzing the impact of proposed legislation. Proposed legislation in the 96th Congress would have further extended the use of GNP beyond that of an analytic tool and could have generated concern about what it represents and how well it does so. Federal spending would have been affected by the definition and accuracy of GNP.

NATIONAL INCOME AND PRODUCT
ACCOUNT FRAMEWORK

INCOME SIDE	PRODUCT SIDE
Compensation of Employees	Personal Consumption Expenditures
—Wages and salaries —Supplements to wages and salaries	—Goods —Services
Proprietors' Income with Inventory Valuation and Capital Consumption Adjustments	Gross Private Domestic Investment
—Farm —Nonfarm	—Structures: residential and nonresidential —Producers' durable equipment —Change in business inventories
Rental Income of Persons with Capital Consumption Adjustments	Net Exports of Goods and Services
Corporate Profits with Inventory Valuation and Capital Consumption Adjustments	—Exports —Imports
—Profits before tax: profits tax liability and profits after tax —Inventory valuation and capital consumption adjustments	Government Purchases of Goods and Services
	—Federal: national defense and nondefense —State and local
Net Interest	
NATIONAL INCOME	
Business Transfer Payments	
Indirect Business Tax and Nontax Liability	
Less: Subsidies less Current Surplus of Government Enterprises	
Statistical Discrepancy	
CHARGES AGAINST NET NATIONAL PRODUCT	
Capital Consumption Allowances with Capital Consumption Adjustment	
CHARGES AGAINST GROSS NATIONAL PRODUCT	GROSS NATIONAL PRODUCT

One proposed amendment to the Employment Act of 1946, H.R. 2314, would have limited Federal outlays in the President's Budget to equal the Council of Economic Advisor's estimated Federal receipts. The receipts would have been based on real economic growth using real GNP estimates as part of the formula for the calculation.

Another proposed bill, H.R. 4610, would have limited Federal outlays to a specific percentage of GNP for the last complete calendar year occurring before the beginning of the fiscal year. Fiscal year 1982 spending, for instance, would have been limited to 23 percent of calendar year 1980's GNP.

Lastly, H.R. 7112 proposed an antirecession assistance program for aid to State and local governments to be triggered by two consecutive quarterly declines in real GNP and real wages and salaries. Allocation of funds to States and local governments were to be based in part on the aggregate real wages and salaries component.

Private sector uses

In addition to the Federal uses, GNP data are widely used in various economic and business research and analysis activities in the private sector. The business community uses are largely for investment and marketing decisionmaking. Non-Federal users include State and local governments, businesses, professional and labor organizations, academicians, and economic forecasting and research organizations.

National income and product account
components are equally important

Although GNP is the most widely known of BEA's national income and product statistics, no one national income and product account output or income measure can be singled out in terms of its importance to policymakers and other users of the data. While GNP may indicate to users changes in overall economic activity, the component measures like personal consumption expenditures, producers' durable equipment, Federal government spending, or corporate profits will indicate changes within the economy's sectors that give rise to changes in gross output and earnings. In addition, measures like producers' durable equipment and the change in business inventories may also reflect shifts in business expectations of future economic activity.

Gross domestic product is becoming an
increasingly important output measure

In addition to the various national income and product estimates noted above, BEA prepares estimates of gross domestic product. Gross domestic product, as distinct from GNP, is the market value of goods and services produced by labor and property located in the United States. This measure excludes rest-of-the-world production, that is, incomes originating outside the United States to its residents' net-of-income payments to foreigners.

Due to the rapid growth of the rest-of-the-world sector in recent years, gross domestic product is becoming more widely accepted in the United States as an economic indicator. It is already the primary output measure used by most other countries which have been characterized by a larger rest-of-the-world sector than has the United States economy.

THE DEPARTMENT OF COMMERCE'S ROLE IN
MEASURING NATIONAL ECONOMIC ACTIVITY

The Department of Commerce compiles the national economic accounts and estimates the Nation's GNP and related measures on an ongoing basis under the authority of the Department of Commerce Act (15 U.S.C. 171, 175, and 1516). The Act stipulates that the Secretary of Commerce shall control the gathering and distributing of statistical information relating to commerce. It also provides that the Secretary may call upon other Federal agencies for statistical data and may collate, arrange, and publish such data as he sees fit.

The Department of Commerce first became involved in national income measurement in response to a Senate resolution of the 72nd Congress in 1932. The resolution provided for estimates of the origin and distribution of the national income for the years 1929, 1930, and 1931. These data were to satisfy information needs for developing Federal fiscal policies and economic legislation.

The first estimates of GNP were prepared by the Commerce Department during World War II. These estimates were useful for determining the allocation of the Nation's resources to support the war effort and for evaluating the related inflationary impact. The framework of thinking represented by GNP provided a tool for assessing the economy's productive capacity and provided a means for determining how much production of consumer goods, war goods, and basic supplies was feasible. The Department's GNP and national income estimates were also used to analyze the impact of war production on the demand for goods and services and prices.

GNP and national income were first incorporated into the national income and product accounts in 1947. Since that time the Department has revised and refined the accounts.

The Department of Commerce's economic statistics analysis and related activities are handled by BEA. Under the policy direction and general supervision of the Department of Commerce's Chief Economist, BEA is divided into four broad areas including the national economic accounts, national analysis and projections, regional economics, and international economics. The preparation, development, and analysis of the national income and product accounts is the responsibility of the National Income and Wealth Division within the national economic accounts area.

GNP's true cost is not reflected in BEA's budget. In fiscal year 1980, BEA was appropriated $15.6 million and 472 permanent positions. The National Income and Wealth Division was funded $2.3 million and 76 permanent positions for that fiscal year for its national income and product accounts activities. However, since the accounts depend upon the output of many statistical collection activities in the Federal government, the Division's budget data do not reflect the accounts' true annual cost. In fact, most of the data are collected for other purposes; the accounts are a relatively inexpensive byproduct. If all of the data used to estimate the accounts were collected solely for that purpose, the accounts' cost would probably be in the hundreds of millions of dollars.

OBJECTIVES, SCOPE, AND METHODOLOGY

Our objectives were to (1) provide the Congress and the public a basic understanding of the GNP and related measures, their data sources, and how they are compiled, (2) identify issues concerning the development and reporting of GNP, and (3) act as a catalyst to focus attention on matters requiring further study.

Our effort was limited to the national income and product accounts with specific emphasis on the GNP. We did not consider other economic accounts or other activities of BEA during this effort except insofar as they concerned the national income and product accounts.

Information presented in this study was obtained through interviews with officials of BEA, the Bureau of the Census, and the Office of Federal Statistical Policy and Standards, Department of Commerce; the Council of Economic Advisors; the Federal Reserve Board; the Treasury Department; and BLS, Department of Labor. Information was also obtained from relevant studies evaluating the accounts and their data base and other national accounting literature and documents. Especially important studies recommending improvements to the accounts were the Report of the Advisory Committee on Gross National Product Data Improvement (1977) and the Report of the National Accounts Review Committee of the National Bureau of Economic Research (1957).

CHAPTER 2

NATIONAL INCOME AND PRODUCT

THEORY AND ESTIMATION CYCLE

Measuring the Nation's economic output is a massive undertaking because of the economy's complexity and the many data sources BEA uses to compile the measure. The usefulness and limitations of national income and product data are better appreciated after what will be measured and how it can be measured are defined. This chapter discusses how BEA measures the Nation's output through its estimation and revision process and identifies the varying data sources used for the initial and revised GNP and related estimates.

DEFINING THE NATION'S ECONOMIC OUTPUT

The Nation's output measured as national income and product provides a gauge of the economy's performance and can be interpreted as a yardstick of the country's material well-being. GNP summarizes the Nation's annual output of final goods and services at their market value on the product side of the account as the sum of personal consumption expenditures, gross private domestic investment, government purchases of goods and services, and net exports. On the income side of the account, charges against GNP summarizes the value of total claims against output. National income measures the income earnings of resources used to produce output as the sum of employees' compensation, proprietors' income, rental income, corporate profits, and net interest.

Deciding what to include and what to exclude from an output measure requires distinguishing between economic and noneconomic production. The criterion for this distinction generally is whether an activity is to be reflected in the market place, either as an input to or as the final sale itself. Dishes washed by a domestic servant involve a market transaction and therefore are included in economic output whereas dishes washed by a household member are excluded.

Exceptions to the market rule exist. BEA believes that certain items must be included in GNP because their exclusion would distort the measure of productive activity. These items include imputations 1/ for the rental value of owner-occupied houses, food and fuel produced and consumed on farms, and services rendered without charge by financial intermediaries, such as free banking services.

Several other distinctions for measuring the Nation's output exist in addition to the distinction between economic and non-economic production. Total output should include only those market transactions which represent final output, current year's output, and actual value added.

In measuring national output, final products are distinguished from intermediate products. Final products are defined as those products which once purchased are not resold except as used goods. Intermediate products are defined as goods purchased for resale or for inclusion into the final product. The value of intermediate products like the flour sold to bakeries and the steel sold to automobile manufacturers are included in the bakers' and automobile manufacturers' production costs and thus are included in the market prices of bread and automobiles. If the values of such intermediate products sold by the flour and steel mills are included in the Nation's output, they will be double counted, once at the intermediate stage and once again in final output. To avoid this problem of double counting, national income estimators value only final products. Intermediate products are included in national output only where they represent inventory

---

1/Process of developing estimates for missing or incomplete data.

investment. In the example noted above, the change from the prior
year in steel inventories carried by the automobile manufacturer
from the previous year would be counted in that year's current
output.

In measuring national output a distinction is also made
between transactions involving current production and transactions
involving previous years' output. The value of a used car, for
example, is excluded from the measurement, but the seller's markup
is counted. This distinction is made because used cars and other
used goods were part of some previous year's output where the
products were initially marketed and counted.

A final distinction made in defining national output is that
between transactions concerning actual production or valued added
and those which involve strictly paper transactions. The value
of financial transactions such as the ownership transfer of stocks
and bonds do not represent production and thus are excluded from
output. However, the cost to persons and government of transferring financial assets, that is, the commissions paid by the consumer is included in the output measure.

OUTPUT'S DOLLAR VALUE IS MEASURED

The Nation's output can conceivably be measured by either
counting the volume or the dollar value of the volume of goods
and services produced during the year. The dollar value approach
is the accepted approach because counting the total number of
dissimilar goods and services produced using the volume approach
would yield a figure with no useful meaning. Furthermore, since
the value approach takes into account the relative market value
of different products, the problem of weighting different products'
relative value in a volume index is avoided.

The value approach has problems associated with its use,
however, specifically during periods of changing prices. During
such periods a dollar output measure registers both production
and price changes. To isolate changes in real output, the market
value measure is converted to a constant dollar or real output
measure by removing the impact of price changes. The accuracy
of the price measures used, primarily components of BLS' consumer
price index (CPI) and producer price index (PPI), will therefore
be reflected in the real output measure or real GNP.

The value of the Nation's output is measured in two ways
which conceptually should result in the same dollar value figure.
In practice, however, they do not. The two approaches are (1)
expenditures on final product and (2) incomes earned. BEA uses
both in measuring output. The expenditure and income approaches
are used to estimate product side and income side measures, respectively, in the national income and product account framework
as shown on page 5.

The expenditure approach provides a relatively timely means
to arrive at estimates of quarterly and annual national output.
For the product side expenditures on final products and changes
in inventories are summed to obtain GNP. This is feasible since

finished products' prices include materials' and intermediate
goods' costs and value added during production. The sum of
expenditures on final products therefore provides a measure
for the portion of total output sold. The value of the portion
of output not sold to final users, that is, the change in business
inventories, is added to or subtracted from final sales to obtain
gross output. GNP thus equals final sales plus inventory change.

The income approach is taken to arrive at quarterly and
annual charges against GNP on the income side of the national
income and product account. National income and other related
charges against GNP are measured as totals of income and nonincome charges against output incurred during production. Since
the sum of unit production costs and profits are theoretically
equal to a product's price and since GNP is conceptually the
market value of final products, it follows that the sum of incomes
earned during production and other charges incurred during production which are reflected in product prices should equal GNP.
Using the income approach the incomes accruing to the owners
of resources used in production as wages and salaries, rents,
interest, and profits are summed to obtain national income.

Other charges against production that do not represent
earned income, which are reflected in product prices, are included on the income side to arrive at charges against GNP.
Indirect business taxes and business transfer payments are
charges against output which are reflected in product prices
but do not represent income of productive resources. These
are added to national income to arrive at charges against net
national product. Capital consumption allowances are amortized
nonincome production costs that are reflected in product prices.
They are adjusted to replacement value and added to charges
against net national product to arrive at charges against GNP.
Subsidies, on the other hand, are deducted because they are
regarded as payments to elicit productive services and hence
are included in earned incomes, while the subsidized products
are included in output measured as final demand at market value.

Statistical discrepancy

Using the expenditure and income approaches to estimate
GNP results in two partially independent figures which differ,
even though in theory the two should be equal. In practice the
two approaches do not yield the same results because the data
sources are different and subject to error. This difference
is shown on the income side of the national income and product
account framework as the statistical discrepancy, as shown on
page 5. The discrepancy measures the excess of product or income.
It has no meaning as an output measure but has been used to a
limited degree as a measure of error as discussed in chapter 3.

FREQUENCY OF NATIONAL OUTPUT
ESTIMATES AND REVISIONS

BEA produces quarterly and annual GNP, national income, and
related national income and product account estimates. The

quarterly estimates are computed at an annual rate to make them
comparable to previous annual estimates by showing what the year's
estimate would be if the remaining three quarters had the same
level of activity as the quarter being measured. At the end of
the calendar year, annual estimates are prepared by averaging
the quarterly estimates for the year. In preparing the estimates,
BEA does more than simply gather data. The estimating process
which involves the use of judgment is discussed in chapter 6.

Any single preliminary quarterly or annual GNP figure is
subject to at least seven revisions. Revisions are necessary
to incorporate subsequently available and revised source data
and changes in definitions and methodologies.

Preliminary estimates of GNP and related account components,
except for national income, are first prepared for each calendar
quarter about 2 weeks (15 days) after the quarter's end. Approximately 6 weeks (45 days) after the quarter the preliminary estimates are revised, incorporating firmer data from monthly and
quarterly source data series. At the time of this first revision,
quarterly national income estimates are initially prepared.
Another revision of the quarterly estimates is done around
10 weeks (75 days) after the quarter with the exception of the
fourth quarter of each year. The reason for this exception is
the source data used to estimate corporate profits is available
a month later than for the first three quarters.

After the calendar year, in mid-January, the revised (75-day)
estimates for each of the first three quarters and the preliminary
(15-day) estimate for the year's final quarter are averaged to
obtain the preliminary annual estimate. This annual estimate
is revised twice during the following 2 months at the same time
as the final quarter's 45-day revision in mid-February and again
in mid-March at the same time as the final quarter's 75-day revision. During this period the only previous year's quarterly estimate to be revised is that for the fourth quarter.

The first full set of detailed estimates for the calendar
year are published in July following the reference year. The
data are presented formally in the national income and product
accounts' format. Also in July the year's quarterly estimates are
again revised. The calendar year's annual estimates are subsequently revised two more times during July of the following 2
years. The year's quarterly estimates are again revised twice
more at the same time as the two annual revisions. With preparation of the 5-year benchmark estimates from Census' quinquennial
economic censuses, the annual and quarterly estimates for the
calendar years since the last benchmark year are revised and are
revised again for the last time with the next benchmarking. The
chart on the following page illustrates the timing of the quarterly
and annual estimates and revisions. .

WHAT DATA SOURCES ARE USED TO MEASURE THE ECONOMY'S HEALTH?

The national income and product account is constructed from
numerous general, administrative, and regulatory statistical series

collected by Federal agencies and private organizations. The specific data programs used to estimate the product and income sides
differ for the differently timed quarterly and annual estimates.

Product side of the national income and product account

     The product side of the national income and product account
is based on a variety of data reflecting changes in the value of
final sales and business inventory holdings of goods and services.
Although several Federal agencies and private organizations provide
data for the quarterly GNP estimates, the Census Bureau is the
major single data source. Census data on manufacturers, retail
and wholesale trade, construction, foreign merchandise trade,
and State and local governments can comprise up to 60 percent or
more of the dollar value of quarterly GNP as shown on the table
on page 16.

     The revised quarterly and first annual estimates of GNP are
derived mainly from the same statistical programs and source
agencies as the preliminary estimates. These later estimates,
however, employ data based on survey responses that are more complete than the advance release of the survey data used to prepare
the preliminary estimates.

     BEA's second and third revised annual GNP estimates are based
upon more detailed data obtained from the Census Bureau, Internal
Revenue Service and other Federal agencies. These include annual
survey data on retail trade, manufacturers, housing, and detailed
expenditures and receipts of State and local governments and administrative data on professional services, medical services, and
regulated industries.

     The GNP benchmark estimates, which serve as a reference point
for other estimates because they are constructed with the firmest
data, are based primarily on BEA's quinquennial input-output table.
This table is produced from the Census Bureau's economic censuses

NATIONAL INCOME AND PRODUCT ACCOUNT
REVISION SEQUENCE

	REFERENCE QUARTER QUARTERLY ESTIMATES	REFERENCE YEAR ANNUAL ESTIMATES
Monthly and Quarterly Available Source Data and Revisions	**Preliminary 15-Day Estimates** **Revised 45-Day Estimates** **Revised 75-Day Estimates** **Revised w/1st Formal Estimate**	**Preliminary Mid-January** **Revised Mid-February** **Revised Mid-March** **1st Formal July Estimates**
Annually Available Source Data and Revisions	**Revised w/2nd Formal Estimates** **Revised w/3rd Formal Estimates**	**2nd Formal July Estimates** **3rd Formal July Estimates**
Economic Censuses Annual Source Data	**Revised w/Benchmark Revision**	**Benchmark Revision**

NATIONAL INCOME AND PRODUCT ACCOUNT
PRODUCT SIDE — PRIMARY DATA SOURCES

Component	Percent of GNP (a) (b)	Quarterly and 1st Annual Sources	2nd and 3rd Annual Sources
Personal Consumption Expenditures	63.4		
Motor Vehicle and Parts	4.9	Motor Vehicle Manufacturers Association/ R.L. Polk & Co.	Motor Vehicle Manufacturers Association/ R.L. Polk & Co.
Gasoline and Oil	2.5	Ethyl Corp./BLS	Ethyl Corp./BLS
Other Goods	28.0	Census	Census
Housing Services	9.8	BEA	Census
Electricity	1.3	Edison Electric Institute	Edison Electric Institute/Census
Natural Gas	.7	American Gas Association	American Gas Association
Telephone	1.0	Federal Communications Commission	American Telephone and Telegraph Co.
Private Hospitals & Sanitariums	2.6	American Hospital Association	American Hospital Association/ Department of Health and Human Services
Other Services	13.5	Census/BEA/BLS/Regulatory agencies	Internal Revenue Service Department of Health and Human Services/Department of Education/BEA/BLS/Census/ Securities and Exchange Commission/ Department of Transportation/ Regulatory agencies
Gross Private Domestic Investment	16.4		
Fixed Investment	15.8		
Nonresidential	10.7		
Structures	3.8		
Buildings, utilities & farm	3.2	Census	Census
Oil and gas well drilling and exploration	.6	American Petroleum Institute	American Petroleum Institute
Other	.1	American Telephone and Telegraph Co./ Interstate Commerce Commission/ Federal Power Commission	American Telephone and Telegraph Co. Interstate Commerce Commission/ Federal Power Commission
Producers Durable Equipment	6.9		
Motor Vehicles	2.0	Motor Vehicle Manufacturers Association/ R.L. Polk & Co.	Motor Vehicle Manufacturers Association/ R.L. Polk & Co.
Aircraft	.1	Census	Census
Other	4.7	Census/BEA	Census/BEA
Residential Structures	5.1	Census/National Conference of States on Building Codes and Standards	Census/National Conference of States on Building Codes and Standards
Change in Business Inventories	.6		
Nonfarm	.6		
Manufacturing and Trade	.5	Census/Department of Energy	Census/Department of Energy
Other	.1	FTC/Department of Energy	Internal Revenue Service/Department of Energy
Farm	.0	Department of Agriculture	Department of Agriculture
Net Exports of Goods and Services	-.3		
Exports	10.0		
Merchandise	7.0	Census	Census
Other	2.9	BEA	BEA
Imports	10.4		
Merchandise	8.4	Census	Census
Other	1.9	BEA	BEA
Government Purchases of Goods & Services	20.5		
Federal	7.3	Treasury Department/Defense Department/ Office of Personnel Management	Federal Budget/Office of Personnel Management
State and Local	13.2		
Compensation of employees	7.2	BLS	Census
Structures	1.8	Census	Census
Medical vendor payments	.8	Department of Health and Human Services	Department of Health and Human Services
Other	3.3	BEA	Census
GROSS NATIONAL PRODUCT	100.0		

Note a — 1978 fourth quarter GNP estimates.
    b — Total and subtotals may not add due to rounding.

NATIONAL INCOME AND PRODUCT ACCOUNT
INCOME SIDE – PRIMARY DATA SOURCES

Component	Percent of GNP (a) (b)	Quarterly Sources	1st Annual Sources	2nd and 3rd Annual Sources
Compensation of Employees	61.4			
Wages and Salaries	51.9			
Federal	3.6	Office of Personnel Management/ Defense Department	Federal Budget	Federal Budget
State and Local	6.4	BLS	Census/BLS	Census/BLS
Other	41.9	BLS/Department of Agriculture	BLS/Department of Agriculture	BLS/Interstate Commerce Commission Department of Agriculture
Supplements to Wages and Salaries	9.5			
Employer Contribution for Social Insurance	4.4	BEA	Department of Health and Human Services / Various Federal Agencies	Department of Health and Human Services
Old Age Survivors Disability, and				
Hospital Insurance	2.4			
State Unemployment Insurance	.6			
Federal Civilian Employment Retirement	.3			
State & Local Employees Retirement	.8			
Other	.3			
Other Labor Income	5.0	Various Federal agencies and private organizations	Various Federal agencies and private organizations	Internal Revenue Service/ Various Federal agencies/ private organizations
Proprietors' Income with Inventory Valuation and Capital Consumption Adjustments	5.5			
Farm	(c)	Department of Agriculture	Department of Agriculture	Department of Agriculture
Nonfarm	(c)	BEA	BEA	Internal Revenue Service
Rental Income of Persons with Capital Consumption Adjustments	1.1			
Rental Income	(c)	BEA	BEA/Census/Department of Agriculture	BEA/Census/Department of Agriculture
Capital Consumption Adjustments	(c)			Internal Revenue Service
Corporate Profits with inventory valuation and Capital Consumption Adjustments	8.0	FTC (d)/Federal Reserve Board/ Comptroller of Currency/Federal Deposit Insurance Corporation/BEA/ Department of Energy/ Public Sources	Public and trade source	Internal Revenue Service
Net Interest	5.0	BEA	Various Federal Agencies	Internal Revenue Service
NATIONAL INCOME	81.0			Various Federal Agencies
Business Transfer Payments	.5	BEA	BEA	Internal Revenue Service
Indirect Business Tax and Nontax Liability	8.2	Treasury/State	Federal Budget/Treasury/Census	Federal Budget/Internal Revenue Service/Treasury/Census
Less: Subsidies less current surplus of Government Enterprises	– .2	Treasury/Postal Service/Department of Agriculture/Commodity Credit Corporation	Federal Budget/Treasury/Commodity Credit Corporation/Census	Federal Budget/Treasury/Commodity Credit Corporation/Census
Statistical Discrepancy	.2			
CHARGES AGAINST NET NATIONAL PRODUCT	89.8			
Capital Consumption Allowances with Capital Consumption Adjustment	10.2	BEA	Department of Agriculture/BEA	Internal Revenue Service/Department of Agriculture/BEA
CHARGES AGAINST GROSS NATIONAL PRODUCT	100.0			

Note: a – 1978 fourth quarter GNP estimates.
    b – Total and subtotal may not add due to rounding.
    c – Detailed data not available.
    d – FTC corporate profit data–quarterly financial reports–not available to prepare preliminary estimates.

data and from various data used to compile the nonbenchmark annual estimates. The input-output table provides Census-based commodity flow estimates of personal consumption expenditures and of the producers' durable equipment component of gross private domestic investment. Benchmark estimates for the remaining components of gross domestic investment, net exports, and government purchases are based on a more indepth analysis of data used for the annual estimates and the introduction of previously unavailable source data adjustments.

Income side of the national income and product account

BLS, the Federal Trade Commission (FTC),and the Department of Agriculture are the major data sources for estimating the income side of the quarterly national income and product account as shown on the table on the following page. BEA's quarterly national income estimates incorporate data from BLS' 790 program on employment and earnings to estimate private and State and local government wages and salaries, the FTC's Quarterly Financial Report to estimate corporate profits, and the Department of Agriculture's farm income data. Other national income quarterly sources include Department of Defense data, used to estimate military compensation, and Office of Personnel Management data, used to estimate Federal civilian payrolls.

The remaining income components are based on data from several sources. Nonfarm proprietors' income is estimated using monthly indicators of activity in each major industry. To estimate employer contributions to social insurance, the appropriate tax rate for each major program is applied to the corresponding monthly wage and salary aggregate. Other labor income is computed using contribution rates applied to monthly employment data. Appropriate tax rates for major programs are applied to corresponding monthly sales estimates for indirect business taxes. Subsidies are based on various budget documents. Net interest is based on movements in interest rates and estimated levels of business borrowing and personal saving. The inventory valuation adjustment is based on the monthly PPI. Business transfer payments, rental income, and capital consumption allowances with capital consumption adjustments are based on past trends.

The first formal annual estimates of national income, since data from annual surveys are not yet available, rely on some of the same data sources as the quarterly estimates but include some new data sources. These include wage and salary data from BLS' 202 program, the Department of Health and Human Services' data on employers' social insurance contributions, public and trade source data on corporate profits, and Census' data on State and local government payrolls. Additional data sources also include more recent Department of Agriculture estimates of farm income and financial regulatory agencies' reports on net interest.

The second and third annual revised estimates of national income incorporate data from the Internal Revenue Service's Statistics of Income program. BEA uses this information from a sample of tax returns to revise the annual estimates of corporate profits, interest income, proprietors' income, and rental income. New data from the Annual Housing Survey used for the rental income estimates

and various data on employers' contributions for health and life
insurance for estimating supplements to wages and salaries also
become available. Revised annual estimates of the items reconciling national income to GNP are derived from the Internal Revenue
Service's income data, the Treasury and Agriculture Departments,
the Federal Budget, and Census's surveys of State and local governments.

In addition to several new data sources, many of the same
data sources from which the annual income measures are estimated
are used to benchmark the income side of the account. Data used
in the benchmark year estimates, however, are more complete and
fully analyzed than when the annual estimates were first compiled.
The new data sources include the Decennial Census of Housing used
for the rental income estimates, Internal Revenue Service data
for corporate profits and unreported business income, BEA survey
data on income from foreign investment, and the quinquennial Census
of Governments data on indirect business taxes and government
employee compensation.

DISSEMINATING THE DATA TO ITS USERS

The national income and product accounts data, notably GNP,
are made available to users through several Department of Commerce
and BEA vehicles. The most widely circulated, Commerce's monthly
"Survey of Current Business," provides preliminary and revised
quarterly estimates of GNP and national income and their major
components. This publication, with a 15,000 monthly circulation,
also provides (1) tables detailing monthly data for each of the
economy's sectors, (2) the formal annual accounts published
every July for the most recent and three previous years, (3) current and constant dollar estimates of GNP and national income, and
(4) other national economic measures including their subcomponents.

In addition to the monthly Commerce publication, GNP estimates
are made available through earlier BEA releases of the data. About
1,000 GNP press releases, widely quoted by the news media, are
distributed monthly. About 100 public and private users who
want the data as soon as possible subscribe to BEA's national
income and product account mailgram service, and another 100
major users in government and the private sector receive copies
of the detailed account tables from BEA when the estimates are
released.

National income and product data are also reproduced in
the Joint Economic Committee's "Economic Indicators," the "Federal Reserve Bulletin," and Commerce's "Business Conditions
Digest." Numerous private concerns also reproduce these data.
Most important are economic consulting firms that provide data
bank services such as Data Resources Inc., Chase Econometrics,
Wharton EFA, and Townsend-Greenspan Inc.

ISSUES FOR CONSIDERATION

Our work on the national income and product accounts surfaced
several broad issues. While these issues should be considered,
they should not be construed to be all-inclusive. The issues

that we have developed and present in the following chapters are:

--How important are accurate and reliable national income and product estimates, how accurate are they, how accurate can they be, and how accurate should they be?

--Are the accounts' source data reliable, complete, and timely, and are source data improvement efforts adequate and needed?

--How and to what extent do BEA's estimation procedures affect the accounts' accuracy?

--Are the accounts' concepts, classifications, and frequency adequate for present-day uses?

Chapters 3 and 4 address the first issue while chapters 5, 6, and 7 address the remaining issues, respectively.

CHAPTER 3

GNP'S ACCURACY IS UNCERTAIN

AND THE LEVEL NEEDED UNDETERMINED

The national income and product accounts, and in particular GNP, given its important economic policymaking uses, should be reasonably accurate and consistent in representing national output and income levels and changes. BEA contends that for short term policymaking uses accurate and consistent quarter-to-quarter changes are more important than an accurate level of GNP. Due to the lack of precise error measures, how well the accounts do this, however, is uncertain. Although BEA attempts to assess the reliability of its estimates by examining past revisions, economic policymakers do not know how accurate current national income and product estimates are and therefore risk proposing inappropriate policies. Nevertheless, due to political influences, differing economic theories, and other economic data which may enter into policy decisionmaking, the impacts of policy errors resulting solely from inaccurate national income and product estimates are difficult to identify.

METHODS USED IN DETERMINING GNP ACCURACY

The problem of judging the accuracy of national income and product measures has persisted for as long as the Commerce Department has been preparing estimates of the Nation's income and output. In 1933 Simon Kuznets, who prepared the initial 1929-32 Department of Commerce national income estimates, noted that the estimates were deficient because the measure's different constituent parts were liable to errors of differing character which were therefore not comparable or addable. BEA officials have reaffirmed that error measures cannot be provided for a good reason--the total error in the underlying source data cannot be measured.

Nevertheless, attempts have been and are being made by BEA and others to assess GNP's accuracy by analyzing the revisions, evaluating the statistical discrepancy, and using expert judgement.

BEA analyzes quarter-to-quarter changes in the GNP for provisional (the preliminary and first revised estimates which are subject to further revision) and later revised estimates. BEA publishes this information in its GNP press release. The GNP revision record is published to provide guidelines for assessing the likely size of the current quarterly estimates' revision. BEA's analysis shows that from 1964 to 1978 the average revision, disregarding plus and minus signs, in quarter-to-quarter percent changes in GNP and real GNP at annual rates from the preliminary to first July estimates was 1 percentage point. However, this method, rather than indicating the amount of error in the estimates, indicates only the probable size of future revisions to the early estimates. The following table shows the amount of the revisions and quarter-to-quarter percent changes for the preliminary and first July quarterly GNP estimates for the years 1977 through 1979. For the 3-year period, the average revision in quarter-to-quarter percent changes from the preliminary to the first July estimates was 0.8 of a percentage point. The limitations of analyzing the revisions as a means of assessing GNP reliability will be further examined in the following chapter.

REVISIONS AND QUARTER-TO-QUARTER PERCENT CHANGES IN
PRELIMINARY AND FIRST JULY QUARTERLY GNP ESTIMATES
1977-1979

Year/ Quarter	Preliminary Estimate	First July Estimate	Amount of Revision	Percent change in GNP from previous quarter	
	----------billions----------			Preliminary	First July
1977 I	$1,792.5	$1,806.8	$ 14.3		
II	1,869.0	1,867.0	- 2.0	4.3	3.3
III	1,911.3	1,916.8	5.5	2.3	2.7
IV	1,965.1	1,958.1	- 7.0	2.8	2.1
1978 I	1,992.9	2,011.3	18.4	1.4	2.7
II	2,076.9	2,104.2	27.3	4.2	4.6
III	2,141.1	2,159.6	18.5	3.0	2.6
IV	2,210.8	2,235.2	24.4	3.2	3.5
1979 I	2,265.6	2,340.6	75.0	2.4	4.7
II	2,327.2	2,374.6	47.4	2.7	1.4
III	2,391.5	2,444.1	52.6	2.7	2.9
IV	2,455.8	2,496.3	40.5	2.6	2.1

Source: Estimates of preliminary and first July GNP from Survey of Current Business

The size of the statistical discrepancy resulting from estimating GNP as total expenditures and gross income is also used to evaluate possible error in the estimates. A smaller discrepancy suggests that less error is contained in the various component estimates than a larger discrepancy. However, a small discrepancy may also result from offsetting errors in both sides of the national income and product account. Since the same source data is used in parts on both sides of the account and since BEA's efforts to con-

COMPARISON OF THE STATISTICAL DISCREPANCIES FOR
45-DAY AND FIRST JULY QUARTERLY GNP ESTIMATES
1977-1979

Year/ Quarter	45-day Statistical Discrepancy		First July Statistical Discrepancy	
	Amount (billions)	Percent of GNP	Amount (billions)	Percent of GNP
1977 I	$9.2	.51	$3.4	.19
II	-0.7	-.04	3.7	.20
III	2.2	.11	7.1	.37
IV	-3.6	-.18	4.8	.24
1978 I	-6.7	-.34	3.0	.15
II	0.9	.04	2.3	.11
III	3.0	.14	3.9	.18
IV	3.9	.18	4.1	.18
1979 I	2.1	.09	5.8	.25
II	-0.5	-.02	0.7	.03
III	7.9	.33	2.8	.11
IV	4.0	.16	-0.7	-.02

Source: Amounts of statistical discrepancies from Survey of
Current Business

tain the discrepancy may result in added estimation errors, it
is an imperfect error measure. The following table shows a comparison of the 45-day and first July quarterly estimates' statistical discrepancies for the years 1977 through 1979.

GNP accuracy can also be assessed by using expert judgment
in evaluating the measure's data sources and methodology. Knowledge of source data quality and the methods used provide a basis
for judging the relative strengths and weaknesses of the individual
components of GNP. Four data traits generally used in judging the
individual components are:

--Straightforward data responses, like the value of a store's
sales, are more likely to be accurate than those requiring
respondent calculations, like average monthly electric
power cost.

--Reported data is more reliable when respondent recordkeeping
is adequate, that is, when data collection procedures are
consistent and complete.

--Total universe data are more accurate than sample survey
data, and large samples provide more accurate data than
small samples.

--Estimates that require adjusting source data to conform
to national income and product definitions, like business
inventories, may be less accurate than components based
on data not requiring such adjustments.

Applying the four data traits in a given analysis always
involves subjective judgment; therefore, any assessment, even an
expert one, may be incorrect. The data traits are used to provide
guidance, not hard and fast rules. In addition, the lack of an
up-to-date handbook on data sources and methodology has hampered
the use of judgment in evaluating GNP. Evaluations using these

four data traits have been used to varying degrees by those whose studies we cite in the following chapters. They use this method coupled with an examination of the revisions and statistical discrepancy, rather than using an assessment based strictly on expert judgement.

INACCURATE GNP ESTIMATES HAVE OVERSTATED AND UNDERSTATED ECONOMIC ACTIVITY

Although a 1 percentage point average revision in quarterly changes in GNP expressed at annual rates may give the appearance of overall reliability, from the late 1940s through 1977 revised quarterly national income and product estimates showed the provisional estimates could have adversely affected appraisals of the economy's performance on eight occasions. Preliminary GNP estimates overstated the severity of the recessions of 1948-49, 1953-54, and 1957-58. Preliminary and first revised GNP estimates for 1965 understated the strength of the economy's expansion during that year. Preliminary and first revised estimates of the corporate profits component of national income for 1969-70 understated the impact of the 1969-70 recession on business incomes. Preliminary and revised quarterly GNP estimates for the second and third quarters of 1971 overstated the economy's recovery from the 1969-70 recession. The 1973 changes in nonfarm inventories and farm income estimates were understated and therefore understated the seriousness of the coming recession. Lastly, GNP estimates for 1975-76 understated the economy's expansion as measured by later revised estimates.

Causes of inaccurate estimates

The causes of these inaccurate provisional national income and product estimates can in most instances be traced to source data problems. Available information indicates this to have been the case for the revisions that occurred for 1965 and afterwards and highly likely to have been the principal reason for the revisions prior to 1965.

The upward revision of the 1965 GNP estimates which had understated the economy's expansion was the result of two influences, according to a BEA official. First was the incorporation of upwardly revised Census estimates of business investment spending and the change in business inventories coupled with better data on State and local government purchases. Second, the August 1965 benchmarking of the estimates changed the weights for the various detailed components in such a way as to have an upward influence on GNP.

The 1971 downward revision ($7 billion for 1969 and $5.9 billion for 1970) of the corporate profits component of national income for 1969 and 1970 arose, according to BEA officials, because BEA lacked adequate information to adjust early reported corporate book profits to an estimate of taxable corporate income. The initial estimates were based on corporate book profits reported to shareholders. The revised estimates were based on Internal

Revenue Service tabulations of taxable corporate income. BEA's provisional estimates were made assuming that the taxable income measure and the book profit measure, after certain adjustments, would show fairly parallel movements, as they previously had. However, in 1969 the two measures diverged, reported book profits increasing and taxable income declining. The early book profits data thus misled BEA's estimators.

The 1972 downward revision of GNP for the second and third quarters of 1971 ($3.1 and $7.4 billion) resulted from Census revising estimates for key source data programs, according to BEA. Census had developed new estimates of construction activity, retail sales, and retail inventories. These data all indicated less expansion in the economy than the earlier Census estimates used in compiling GNP.

BEA's 1974 upward revision of nonfarm inventories for the fourth quarter of 1973 ($6.5 billion) and first quarter of 1974 ($6.6 billion) was due mainly to the revision of data on nonfarm inventories. Census data on manufacturing and trade inventories reported at book value were revised for the third month of the quarter and made available after the 45-day GNP estimates were introduced. In addition, BEA introduced an adjustment for a bias between the monthly manufacturing and retail trade inventory series and annual surveys that become available later. The adjustment was subsequently justified and is now made on a current basis and should not cause further problems.

The understatement of 1973 farm income ($8.8 billion) resulted from the lack of current data on farmers' expenses. The estimates of farm income which are trended from annual level projections and historical relationships failed to reflect conditions that occurred in 1973.

The 1977 upward revision of 1975 and 1976 GNP ($12.5 and $14.9 billion) was due to Census revising data pertaining to personal expenditures on services, nonresidential construction, producers' durable equipment, and inventories.

Examples of the effects of misleading estimates on users

Relatively large revisions to preliminary GNP estimates appearing during critical phases in the business cycle, when economic policy options are being planned and implemented, can mislead assessments of the economy's performance and therefore mislead policy decisions. According to Council of Economic Advisors officials, who use the preliminary estimates, this occurred as a result of estimates released for 1965 and 1973-74. On the other hand, Federal Reserve officials said they have not been affected by GNP revisions.

The growth of real GNP for midyear 1965 as reported late in that year indicated the economy to be growing at a 5.5 percent annual rate. Later estimates for the same period showed the economy to be growing at an 8 percent annual rate. Arthur Okun, a member of the Council of Economic Advisors during the period, later complained that had the growth of GNP been more precisely reported,

the Johnson Administration would have foreseen the inflationary
impact of the escalating defense expenditures and proposed a tax
increase earlier than it had. 1/ Such a tax increase if enacted,
accordingly, might have curtailed total spending in the economy
sufficiently to have contributed to a noninflationary economic
policy at the time.

Arthur Burns, a former Council Chairman, also acknowledged
the difficulties the faulty 1965 GNP data created for Federal
policymakers. He, like Okun, claimed that the erroneous data
had understated the economy's inflationary propensity. 2/

Inaccurate estimates of the change in business inventories
component of GNP during 1973 and 1974 also misled Federal policymakers' assessment of the economy. Alan Greenspan, also a former
Council Chairman, claimed that the preliminary inventory data
failed to indicate the nature of the 1974-75 recession. 3/
According to another Council official, the revised inventory data
for the period which was released in July 1974 resulted in the
Council changing its economic forecast and policy recommendations
"overnight." As a result, he said the Council is now cautious
about acting on any single release of the estimates.

Federal Reserve Board officials claim not to have been
affected in their policies by large revisions. Since they independently analyze much of the same information that enters into
GNP, they anticipate GNP changes. As a normal practice, if the
GNP estimates do not look as anticipated they wait for more information before making policy decisions. They and other major Federal users of the estimates we contacted expressed no overall
dissatisfaction with the estimates' accuracy.

Inaccurate national income and product estimates may affect
the Nation's economy. Due to the number and complexity of economic
and political factors which affect economic policy decisions and
the economy, it is difficult to determine how inaccurate estimates
may affect the level of output, incomes, employment, and prices
in the economy. Nevertheless, the impact of inaccurate and misleading data can, in general, be outlined. Data which misleads
economic policies and business decisions can exact costs in
terms of idle or misallocated resources.

1/Arthur M. Okun, The Political Economy of Prosperity (Washington, D.C.: The Brookings Institution, 1970), pp. 68-69.

2/Arthur F. Burns and Paul A. Samuelson, Full Employment
   Guideposts and Economic Stability (Washington, D.C.:
   American Enterprise Institute for Public Policy Research,
   1967), p. 34.

3/Alan Greenspan, oral remarks, Conference on Income and
   Wealth, National Bureau of Economic Research, Washington,
   D.C., 4 May, 1979.

HOW MUCH ACCURACY IS NEEDED?

GNP cannot be measured exactly. The estimates should, within reason, accurately represent the trend of and turning points in economic activity to avoid the chance of misleading economic policies. The estimates should accurately represent changes in the structure of the economic process which give rise to changes in the economy's output and income. However, how precise these data can be or must be to be adequate for economic policymaking uses is uncertain.

Department of Commerce guidelines for the release of economic indicators state that revised data should be presented so that average differences between preliminary and revised figures are small relative to average changes in the series. How this policy might apply to the GNP estimates is not specified. However, summary measures for the quarterly GNP estimates for 1977 through 1979 presented on page 22 show

--an absolute average difference, disregarding plus and minus signs, between the quarter-to-quarter percent change in GNP measured by the preliminary and first July estimates of 0.8 of a percentage point,

--an average quarter-to-quarter change in GNP measured by the first July estimates of 3.0 percent, and

--the absolute average difference of 0.8 to be about 27 percent of the average quarterly change of 3.0 percent in the first July estimates.

The timing and intensity of economic fluctuations affects the associated data needs of policymakers for accurate national income and product data. Studies questioning accuracy and reliability which are the focus of the following chapter presented conflicting views of the estimates' overall reliability in the past. One of the analysts claims that maintaining past error rates in future estimates will not be sufficient for future analysis and policymaking needs.

CHAPTER 4

STUDIES DIFFER ON GNP'S

RELIABILITY FOR POLICYMAKING USES

Because of the lack of precise error measures, alternative means have been used to evaluate the reliability of current quarterly GNP estimates. The primary means used to assess the estimates' reliability include examining the revisions and judging the quality of the source data from which the GNP components are compiled. According to national accounts experts, neither of the methods used alone provide a complete assessment of the estimates' reliability, but in combination the methods provide an overall view. This chapter will focus on the major studies of GNP revisions and the following will consider source data quality.

Three major studies, 1/ using mostly the 45-day and later revised GNP estimates, present conflicting views of the estimates' overall reliability. Two studies found the current estimates adequate for economic policy decisionmaking while the third found the estimates unreliable enough that they could have misled policymakers throughout the 1947-61 period. The periods covered by these studies range from 1947 through 1961 and 1971. No subsequent major examinations of the revisions have been performed.

REVISIONS TO GNP ESTIMATES PROVIDE PARTIAL INSIGHT INTO ERROR

Part of the error contained in BEA's initial GNP estimates is removed through the revision process. BEA's estimation procedures include revising the GNP estimates as more complete data become available after the estimates are initially released. This procedure permits incorporating source data presumed more accurate than previously available data into the GNP time series. The revised estimates thus should be more accurate than the initial estimates. Furthermore, the difference between the initial and the revised estimates should provide a measure of the amount of error contained in the initial estimates. However, since the revised estimates may also contain error, the amount of the revision is only a partial error measure.

Summary statistical measures of the amount of the revision between initial and revised GNP estimates over a period of several years indicate the average and the range of revision that can be expected in the current estimates and may identify particular components needing improvement. These measures used alone, however, will not indicate the extent of error contained in any single release of current GNP estimates. Furthermore, since the measures are summary figures, they tend to give the appearance of accuracy over periods of relative economic stability when it is easier to predict changes in incomplete source data series used in the early estimates. The three studies discussed below each used such summary statistical measures in their evaluations.

1/George Jaszi, "The Quarterly National Income and Product Accounts of the United States, 1942-62," in Studies in Short-Term National Accounts and Long-Term Economic Growth, ed. Simon Goldberg and Phyllis Deane, Income and Wealth, 11 (New Haven: International Association for Research in Income and Wealth, 1965) pp. 100-187. Allan H. Young, Reliability of the Quarterly National Income and Product Accounts of the United States, 1947-71, U.S. Department of Commerce, Bureau of Economic Analysis Staff Paper No. 23 (Washington, D.C.: National Technical Information Service, July 1974); Rosanne Cole, Errors in Provisional Estimates of Gross National Product (New York: National Bureau of Economic Research, 1969).

EXAMINATIONS OF THE REVISIONS PRESENT CONFLICTING VIEWS

The three major studies judged the reliability of the national income and product data, and GNP in particular, primarily by comparing early released estimates to later revised estimates. 1/ Two of the studies' authors are associated with BEA. George Jaszi and Allan Young performed their studies while with BEA and are its current director and deputy director. Rosanne Cole performed her study with the National Bureau of Economic Research, a nongovernmental research organization, and is now with International Business Machines. More recently she served as a member on the Advisory Committee on GNP Data Improvement which we discuss in chapter 5.

In analyzing different estimates for similar periods, the three evaluators differed in their conclusions on the accuracy of the data for policy users. Jaszi and Young found the estimates to be adequate for economic analysis and policymaking uses while Cole concluded that the preliminary and 45-day revised GNP figures were erroneous enough that they could have misled economists using GNP as an indicator of the severity of contractions and the strength of expansions in the economy. She further concluded that the estimates, when used for economic forecasting, impaired the accuracy of the forecasts. Young did acknowledge the need for improved estimates for future uses which if not brought about would hamper policymaking and economic theory improvements. The three evaluators did agree that error in the GNP estimates has been reduced over the years since 1947, the initial data period used in their studies.

George Jaszi compared the 1947-61 quarterly changes in the 45-day national income and product estimates with the latest available revised estimates in his 1963 study of the quarterly estimates. He computed overall summary measures of quarterly percent changes in GNP, national income, and their components. Jaszi found the 45-day estimates understated the quarter-to-quarter change in GNP as measured by the revised estimates by 11 percent. The average absolute error, that is, regardless of positive or negative sign, was 35 percent of the absolute change in the later estimates. In addition, he found that 8 percent of the total number of directional changes, that is, from an increase to decrease or vice versa, in quarterly GNP differed for the 45-day series compared to the revised estimates.

Allan Young analyzed the GNP revisions in 1974 for the period 1947-71 and also looked at the subperiods 1947-63 and 1964-71. Young used basically the same method as Jaszi. His analysis of

---

1/The error measures cited from these studies are not directly comparable to BEA's analysis of the revisions noted on page 21. Aside from the different time frames and the differently timed estimates analyzed, the 1 percentage point on page 21 refers to the average revision of quarterly changes in GNP while the 11 and 35 percent measures noted in Jaszi's study and those noted in Young's analysis are average revisions of quarterly changes taken as a percent of the average quarterly change measured by the revised estimates.

the earlier period 1947-63 used the 1958 benchmark estimates that
were released in 1965 which were not available at the time of
Jaszi's study as the basis for comparing the quarterly changes.
For the 1947-63 period, he found the 45-day GNP estimates understated the average quarterly change in GNP in the latest estimates
by 15 percent. He measured absolute average error in the early
estimates as 43 percent of the absolute change in the latest estimates, and he found 12 percent relative directional misses between
the series.

Young found the estimates for the 1964-71 period improved
considerably. He found the 45-day estimates of quarterly GNP
change understated the latest available estimates by 8 percent
and the absolute average error in the 45-day estimates as 13 percent of the absolute average change in the revised estimates.
He found no directional misses. However, the 1964-71 period was
a period of relative economic stability compared to the 1947-63
period, thereby making the estimation process for the period easier.

Young's analysis of the GNP subcomponents for 1964-71 found
several subject to large revisions. He found the 45-day estimates
of quarterly change to either understate or overstate later estimates. On the product side, large changes included nonresidential
structures (-26 percent), residential structures (-17 percent),
producers' durable equipment (+12 percent), and nondefense Federal
expenditures (-23 percent). On the income side, the earlier estimates of unincorporated business and professional income (-37
percent), farm income (+59 percent), rental income of persons
(-39 percent), and corporate profits (+43 percent) were indicated
as being the most erroneous.

Rosanne Cole's 1969 analysis focused primarily on the 45-day
GNP and related major components for the 1947-61 period. Although
she considered the same period as Jaszi and analyzed the same
estimates as Young for 1947-63, her error measures cannot be directly compared to those of the two earlier studies. Her basis
for comparing 45-day and revised GNP estimates was the 1958
benchmark estimates released in 1965 which were not available
when Jaszi did his study; the benchmark data was used by Young.
Furthermore, her techniques for measuring error used the dollar
amount of revisions and quarterly changes rather than the quarterly
percent changes used by Jaszi and Young.

For the 1947-61 period Cole found that the 45-day GNP estimates understated the latest available estimates by an average
of $600 million. She measured the absolute average error in the
45-day GNP estimates at $3.2 billion.

Cole also found that:

--BEA's preliminary GNP and major component estimates were
   considerably more accurate than forecast estimates for
   the same period from the private sector.

--The revision process was effective in reducing errors
   contained in initial estimates, and error in the initial
   estimates had reduced over time.

--Preliminary and 45-day estimates understated the extent
of expansions in the economy and overstated the extent
of contractions throughout the period examined.

--Estimates of the value of nondurable goods, producers'
durable equipment, new construction, change in business
inventories, Federal spending, and net exports were the
most erroneous GNP components.

In summary, the three major studies present conflicting views
of the GNP estimates' overall reliability and differ in their
conclusions on the accuracy of the data for policy users. The
three evaluators do agree that error in the GNP estimates has
been reduced over the years covered by their studies and one noted
that there remains a need for improved estimates for future uses.

CHAPTER 5

RECOMMENDATIONS OF THE ADVISORY COMMITTEE

ON GNP DATA IMPROVEMENT: DO THE

BENEFITS JUSTIFY THE COST?

The accuracy and reliability of the national income and product estimates are affected by the quality of the data with which
they are compiled and the procedures used to estimate the components. A recent evaluation of the underlying data base performed
by independent national accounts experts found many areas in need
of improvement and recommended many changes. However, implementation
of the improvements recommended in the experts' 1977 report has
fallen behind schedule. It also appears that the need for the
improvements in terms of improved economic decisionmaking ability
has not been adequately demonstrated.

ADVISORY COMMITTEE FORMED TO
EVALUATE UNDERLYING GNP SOURCE DATA

Motivated by substantial revisions to GNP estimates in the
early 1970s, the Statistical Policy Division of the Office of Management and Budget--the predecessor to the Office of Federal Statistical Policy and Standards, 1/ Department of Commerce--estab-

---

1/The Office of Federal Statistical Policy and Standards is the
general statistical coordination agency of the U.S. Government.
Its work consists of planning priorities for the statistical
system's development, facilitating efficient methods for meeting
data users' needs, reducing burdens imposed on respondents, and
acting as a liaison among the various Federal statistical agencies.
The Paperwork Reduction Act of 1980 (P.L. 96-511) transferred the
Office's functions to the newly created Office of Information and
Regulatory Affairs within the Office of Management and Budget
effective April 1, 1981.

lished an advisory committee in 1973 to evaluate the quality and
timeliness of the underlying data used to prepare the national
economic accounts and to recommend improvements to the data. The
Advisory Committee on GNP Data Improvement's official assignment
was to focus on the statistical shortcomings of the GNP estimates,
the most widely known measure of the economic accounts.

The advisory committee was formed because the Statistical
Policy Division wanted an outside evaluation of data problems which
were the most pressing along with feasible solutions. This was the
first such comprehensive study of the underlying data used to estimate the accounts. The last outside review of the national economic accounts by an advisory committee was made in 1957 by the
National Accounts Review Committee, which we discuss in chapter 7.
That committee concentrated on the conceptual issues of the accounts.

Six nongovernmental national accounts experts were selected
as committee members. Included were Daniel Creamer of the Conference Board, Rosanne Cole of International Business Machines
whom we noted in chapter 4 as conducting a study of the revisions,
Edward Denison of the Brookings Institution (now with BEA),
Raymond Goldsmith of the National Bureau of Economic Research,
Alan Greenspan of Townsend-Greenspan Inc., and John Kendrick
of George Washington University. The committee also had a working
staff of four.

The advisory committee's evaluation of the source data base
used to compile the estimates appears to be a broad and detailed
study of the reliability and coverage of the data. The committee
looked at the complete data base used for estimating GNP and its
individual subcomponents.

The advisory committee's study and subsequent report 1/ in
1977 focused primarily on the data needs for the quarterly,
annual, and 5-year benchmark, and constant dollar GNP estimates.
The committee recommended about 150 data improvements to more
than 20 Federal agencies to be implemented over a 6-year period
at an estimated cost of roughly $25 million in 1976 prices. The
total cost was based on very elementary estimating techniques,
including considerable reliance on rules of thumb. To allow for
underestimation, the cost estimates were increased by 50 percent
to arrive at the $25 million. The objective of the recommendations
was to improve the accuracy and timeliness of the national income
and product estimates by improving the underlying data at a
reasonable cost.

FINDINGS AND RECOMMENDATIONS
OF THE ADVISORY COMMITTEE ON
GNP DATA IMPROVEMENT

The advisory committee's findings and recommendations address
problems involving the coverage and detail of specific areas of

----

1/U.S. Department of Commerce, Gross National Product Data
  Improvement Project Report (Washington, D.C.: GPO, 1977).

economic activity provided by source data programs and the accuracy and timely provision of the data. Other recommendations regard the frequency at which BEA provides its estimates and accompanying documentation of estimation procedures and reliability analysis. The recommendations generally pertain to the data used to estimate quarterly and annual GNP and national income and the quinquennial input-output table used in benchmarking the estimates. Improvements to data sources from which farm sector, rest-of-the-world (exports and imports), and constant dollar estimates are prepared were recommended separately, but nevertheless those data are used to compile the quarterly, annual, and benchmark estimates. The table on the following page shows the number of recommended improvements by type, estimates affected, and status.

Quarterly nonfarm data

BEA's 15-day and 45-day quarterly estimates of current and constant dollar GNP, current dollar national income, and their component estimates are the most important of the national accounts data for short term Federal macroeconomic fiscal and monetary policymaking uses. Based on its evaluation of the data underlying these estimates, the committee recommended 41 improvements. Fourteen would improve the data programs' accuracy, 13 their coverage and detail, and 11 the timeliness that the data are available. Major programs found problematic include Census' surveys of monthly retail trade, selected services receipts, and manufacturers' shipments, inventories, and orders; BEA's plant and equipment survey; and BLS' 790 program. If implemented, the recommendations directed at these and other statistical programs are expected to improve the accuracy of the quarterly estimates.

Examples of problems the committee identified with the nonfarm monthly and quarterly surveys were:

--Census' Monthly Retail Trade Survey failed to produce consistently accurate initial estimates of the level and change in retail sales and estimates of retail inventories.

--Census' Monthly Selected Services Receipts Survey failed to provide reliable initial estimates of consumer services and did not adequately cover private education services.

--Census' Survey of Manufacturers' Shipments, Inventories, and Orders deficiencies reflected the lack of a full probability sample for small firms and inadequate reporting of defense orders.

--BEA's Plant and Equipment Survey problems included the lack of a full probability and updated sample.

--BLS' 790 survey of company-reported payrolls and employment had poor response rates, lack of sample updating, and inadequate processing of survey data.

SCHEDULE OF THE ADVISORY COMMITTEE ON GNP DATA IMPROVEMENT'S

RECOMMENDATIONS BY TYPE, ESTIMATES AFFECTED, AND STATUS a/

ESTIMATES AFFECTED	TOTAL	ACCURACY	COVERAGE/ DETAIL	TIMELINESS	METHODOLOGY/ DOCUMENTATION	FREQUENCY
Quarterly Nonfarm						
Total	41	14	13	11	1	2
Not Implemented	23	9	8	6	0	0
Implemented	12	4	4	1	1	2
Partially Implemented	6	1	1	4	0	0
Annual Nonfarm						
Total	22	2	12	5	3	0
Not Implemented	20	2	11	5	2	0
Implemented	1	0	0	0	1	0
Partially Implemented	1	0	1	0	0	0
Benchmark						
Total	38	2	30	1	5	0
Not Implemented	26	2	19	1	4	0
Implemented	10	0	10	0	0	0
Partially Implemented	2	0	1	0	1	0
Farm						
Total	19	1	15	3	0	0
Not Implemented	16	0	14	2	0	0
Implemented	3	1	1	1	0	0
Partially Implemented	0	0	0	0	0	0
Constant Dollar						
Total	21	3	12	2	4	0
Not Implemented	13	3	7	1	2	0
Implemented	6	0	3	1	2	0
Partially Implemented	2	0	2	0	0	0
Rest-of-the-World						
Total	14	5	9	0	0	0
Not Implemented	14	5	9	0	0	0
Implemented	0	0	0	0	0	0
Partially Implemented	0	0	0	0	0	0
Total b/						
Recommendations	155	27	91	22	13	2
Not Implemented	112	21	68	15	8	0
Implemented	32	5	18	3	4	2
Partially Implemented	11	1	5	4	1	0

a/Based on GAO's analysis of the committee's recommendations and information provided by the Office of Federal Statistical Policy and Standards as of February 1980.

b/Does not include 11 recommendations made on the Federal Reserve Board's flow-of-funds accounts.

Annual nonfarm data

Since BEA's annual estimates are used as control totals for estimating the quarterly figures, improving the coverage, accuracy, and timeliness of annual source data would also improve the quarterly estimates. The advisory committee recommended 22 improvements to data programs used for the annual estimates. It recommended 12 coverage and detail, 5 timeliness, and 2 accuracy improvements to annual data. Major programs affected by these recommendations include Census' surveys of retail trade, wholesale trade, manufacturers, State and local governments, and a proposed survey of nonprofit organizations; BLS' 202 program; and a proposed FTC survey of annual corporate profits.

Examples of weaknesses the committee found with the annual nonfarm data were:

--Data from Census' Annual Retail Trade Survey, Wholesale Trade Survey, and Government Finances program and BLS' 202 program were not being provided in time for the first annual estimates.

--Data from Census' Annual Survey of Manufacturers were not provided in adequate detail by industry for annual updating and determining the distribution of goods in the input-output table.

--Existing data on income and expenditures of nonprofit organizations were limited in coverage and detail; therefore, a Census annual survey of these organizations was proposed.

--Existing data on corporate profits are inadequate and not timely; therefore, an FTC annual survey of corporate profits was proposed.

Benchmark data

Since the current quarterly and annual estimates are extrapolated from the benchmarks which for major GNP components are derived from the input-output table, improving the 5-year benchmark estimates would also improve the accuracy of the current GNP estimates. The advisory committee recommended 38 improvements to input-output and benchmark data. Thirty of the improvements relate to coverage problems, 5 to methodology and documentation, and 2 to accuracy. These recommendations are largely directed at the Census' economic censuses which are conducted every 5 years. Improving the quality and timeliness of the data coming from these programs should improve the quality and timeliness of the input-output table and likewise the benchmarks. The censuses cover manufacturers, retail trade, wholesale trade, services, construction, transportation, governments, and mining and materials.

To provide more detailed measures of economic activity in the benchmark years, the committee recommendations included expanding the coverage of the censuses to include all activity in each census field. It also recommended that the Census conduct censuses of the real estate industry and nonprofit organizations to further expand the coverage of economic activity.

Farm, constant dollar, and rest-of-the-world data

    In addition to the many data sources used to compile the
nonfarm domestic economy output and income measures, the advisory
committee separately examined data sources relating to the farm
sector, prices, and exports and imports. The committee recommended
19 improvements to farm data, mostly involving the coverage of
Department of Agriculture's statistical programs on farm output
and income. The committee found that the farm programs inadequately covered the agricultural sector for GNP use, particularly
quarterly measures of income from crop and livestock operations.
The committee further recommended 21 improvements to the constant
dollar estimates' source data programs, mostly coverage, primarily
affecting BLS' CPI and PPI programs and Census construction
prices. The price indexes, while found generally good, need
to be expanded to fill gaps and, in some instances, redefined
to be consistent with the GNP subcomponents. It recommended
14 improvements concerning exports and imports, mostly affecting
the coverage of Census and BEA data programs on merchandise
trade, transport, and travel. The committee found data programs
covering merchandise exports, travel, and transport suffering
from poor response and inadequate coverage.

HAVE THE ADVISORY COMMITTEE'S
RECOMMENDATIONS BEEN ADEQUATELY
CONSIDERED AND IMPLEMENTED BY
THE AFFECTED AGENCIES?

    Implementation of the 1977 Advisory Committee on GNP Data
Improvement's recommendations has not proceeded as planned. The
committee, working with the agencies, developed a 6-year program
for implementing the recommended improvements. The latest available data, as of February 1980, show that 32 recommendations have
been implemented and 11 partially implemented. Although current
updated information is not available, an Office of Federal Statistical Policy and Standards official told us that few changes
have been made since February 1980. Eighteen of the 56 improvements scheduled to be implemented during 1978 and 1979 had been
implemented. Several additional improvements directed at 1977
economic censuses were implemented before the commission's work
was completed. The number and February 1980 status of the recommended improvements by agency are shown on the following page.

    The committee's recommendations are directed mostly at the
Federal agencies responsible for collecting the data. The Federal
agencies' acceptance of the recommendations is strictly at their
discretion; however, implementing many of the improvements is
subject to the budget process. Implementation of the recommendations is being coordinated by the Department of Commerce's
Office of Federal Statistical Policy and Standards.

    Acceptance and implementation of the improvements to the
statistical programs do not hinge on any one factor. Cost,
response burden, and feasibility of implementation are prime
factors. Statistical improvements which can be easily implemented,
impose little or no additional burden on respondents, and incur
minimal budget increases are readily being implemented. For

NUMBER AND STATUS OF THE ADVISORY COMMITTEE ON GNP DATA
IMPROVEMENT'S RECOMMENDATIONS BY FEDERAL AGENCIES

Federal Agencies	Number	Status	
		Implemented	Partially implemented
Department of Commerce			
Census Bureau	65	13	2
Bureau of Economic Analysis	27	8	1
Office of Federal Statistical Policy and Standards	5	1	
Industry and Trade Administration	1		
Department of Defense	4		
Department of Labor			
Bureau of Labor Statistics	11	1	2
Other	2		1
Department of the Treasury			
Internal Revenue Service	6		1
Comptroller of the Currency	2		1
Other	3		
Department of Agriculture			
Economics and Statistics Service	18	3	
Department of Health and Human Services	5	2	1
Interstate Commerce Commission	2		
Federal Reserve Board	4	1	1
Federal Home Loan Bank Board	1	1	
Office of Management and Budget	1	1	
Federal Energy Administration	1		
Federal Power Commission	1	1	
Federal Trade Commission	3		
Securities and Exchange Commission	1		
Federal Deposit Insurance Corporation	2	—	1
Total Federal Agencies	165	32	11
National Bureau of Economic Research a/	1		
TOTAL b/	166		

a/Non-governmental private research organization.
b/Includes recommendations for the Federal Reserve Board's flow-of-funds statement.

those not meeting these conditions, the additional funding requirements compete with other higher priority demands on the
Federal budget. This results in more stringent tests in justifying the data improvements for which the benefits are difficult
to quantify. For example, improvements for Census' economic
surveys slated for fiscal year 1980 were declined funding by the
Congress due to (1) Census' inability to show the improvements
to be realized and (2) the already high cost of the 1980 census.
The Congress also rejected funding the data improvements which
were included in Census' fiscal year 1981 funding request. Additionally, several other Federal agencies have cited increased
burden on respondents as the reason for rejecting the recommended
improvements.

ARE THE GNP DATA IMPROVEMENTS REALLY NEEDED?

Determining whether or not the advisory committee's recommendations should be supported and implemented hinges on assessing
the relative benefits and costs of implementing them. The total
costs of implementing the improvements are presently unknown and
the benefits which could be realized are uncertain. With an
awareness of GNP's policymaking importance, the advisory committee
considered the benefits of implementing the recommendations to
have a high payoff relative to their cost. BEA, the producer of
the estimates, and major Federal users of the data, especially
the Council of Economic Advisors and the Federal Reserve Board,
generally feel that the improvements would produce more accurate
estimates and should be implemented. On the other hand, data
source agencies vary in their willingness to increase statistical
budget requests and to additionally burden respondents; therefore,
some may prefer not to implement the recommended improvements.

Benefits which could result from implementing the recommendations appear to be plentiful. More accurate source data with
improved coverage and provided in a more timely manner to BEA
would improve the accuracy of the GNP estimates and should aid
economic and business analysis and decisionmaking. The improvements
should also add to the quality of the individual statistical programs and thus benefit all users of the data series. The benefits
from implementing the recommendations would thus spill over to
improve the quality of a large part of the output of the Federal
statistical system.

The qualitative nature of the committee's recommended improvements makes the benefits received difficult to measure.
A dollar value is not readily apparent for improved understanding of the economy or better economic and business decisionmaking.

The costs of implementing the recommendations would be easier
to estimate than the benefits. Even though the $25 million cited
in the committee's report is a rough estimate of cost to improve
the data, firmer cost data can be obtained. Respondents likewise
can reasonably determine the dollar cost of answering statistical
inquiries.

Problems similar to those encountered in assessing the
benefits and costs of implementing the recommendations are

encountered in assessing the effects of not implementing the recommendations. Since several variables may enter into policy and decisionmaking, it is difficult to assess how using less than the best statistical information will affect policies and decisions. Equally difficult is the task of valuing output and income losses due to inadequate information.

CHAPTER 6

IMPACT OF BEA'S METHODS ON

THE ACCURACY OF NATIONAL INCOME

AND PRODUCT DATA IS UNCERTAIN

While inaccuracies and gaps in the source data affect national income and product data's accuracy, procedures used by BEA may also have an impact. However, how much and to what extent the procedures affect accuracy is uncertain. BEA states that its methods are selected to minimize error and are deemed to be the most satisfactory based on past experience, knowledge of the data, and consistency of results. These methods include procedures to (1) benchmark the data every 5 years, (2) measure quarterly and annual changes during the intervening and subsequent years, (3) estimate the individual components, (4) seasonally adjust the quarterly measures, and (5) provide constant dollar GNP estimates. The judgment of BEA officials also enters into the estimation process and may influence the estimates.

With the lack of a complete and up-to-date handbook of methods (the last such publication was in 1954), detailed information on BEA's present estimating methodology is not readily accessible to users. The Advisory Committee on GNP Data Improvement recognized this as an overriding need and recommended the preparation and publication of a new handbook detailing concepts, sources of data, estimating methodology, and their limitations. Although BEA has described its estimation methods in the 1954 publication and in various subsequent "Survey of Current Business" articles and staff papers, these efforts apparently do not satisfy user needs. The advisory committee cited users' frustration on the need to know the actual procedures. BEA is currently working on the updated handbook which it expects to complete in 1982.

BENCHMARKING AND THE QUARTERLY AND ANNUAL ESTIMATION PROCESS

The GNP, national income, and related component benchmark measurements are the result of efforts to actually measure the level of the Nation's income and product every 5 years. Current quarterly and annual estimates are extrapolated or projected on the basis of current information beyond the benchmark measures. The later revised estimates are interpolated or inferred on the basis of information from mostly the same data sources between two benchmark measures.

Benchmark measurements

The GNP, national income, and related component benchmark measurements are built up from voluminous statistical information pertaining to the value of economic production. Benchmark measures for the major GNP components of personal consumption expenditures and producers' durable equipment are derived from the quinquennial input-output table. The table is based on detailed production data provided by the economic censuses which are conducted every 5 years. The benchmark measures for other GNP and national income components are valued from various source data.

The input-output table is a matrix in which the flow of output is traced through intermediate production stages until it is tranformed into finished producer and consumer commodities. For each industry the disposition of output to intermediate use and final demand is tabulated. Since GNP is total final demand, the input-output table provides a suitable means for deriving the value of the Nation's output of final goods and services.

The method used in preparing the input-output table is called the commodity flow method. It is the most sophisticated and complex means of measuring gross industry output. Measuring output using this method requires detailed information from suppliers, manufacturers, wholesalers, and retailers on the cost of goods purchased for resale and the total cost of resources employed in output's production and distribution. This information is used to provide an analysis of the distribution of each industry's output among other industries and final consumers and producers.

The input-output analysis provides benchmark totals for the detailed GNP components of personal consumption expenditures and producers' durable goods purchased. These estimates are also used to establish the weights for the detailed categories of personal consumption expenditures and producers' durable equipment which are maintained from one benchmark to the next. The accuracy of the benchmarks, therefore, will affect the accuracy of all quarterly and annual estimates for subsequent and intervening nonbenchmark years.

Other GNP components, construction expenditures, government purchases, and net exports, are benchmarked directly from the input-output table but do not utilize commodity-flow techniques, except for the detailed breakdown. These components are valued using data from the economic censuses and sources used for quarterly and annual estimates.

Benchmark estimates for charges against GNP, the income side of the national income and product account components, are not derived from the quinquennial input-output table; they are valued from the same data sources used for the annual estimates. This procedure of estimating the two sides as independently as possible permits the statistical discrepancy to be derived as a residual which signals possible estimation errors.

Quarterly and annual estimation process

Quarterly and annual estimates of GNP, national income and their components are prepared as changes over time from and between the benchmark levels. Current levels of quarterly and annual GNP and national income are extrapolated from the most recent benchmark level. Quarterly and annual levels for years between established benchmark years are interpolated. These methods, used in conjunction with BEA's revision procedures are used to develop the continuously updated national income and product time series.

How BEA develops its quarterly and annual national income and product estimates can be explained by an example of how a GNP time series might be developed. Assuming that benchmark estimates exist for 1947 through 1977 for years ending in the numbers 2 or 7, this set of seven benchmark estimates can be used as a base for estimating quarterly and annual GNP for the period 1947 through the most recent year and quarter. The estimates for the years and the quarters between the benchmarks will be interpolations of the benchmarks while estimates for the years after 1977 will be extrapolations of the 1977 benchmark.

Available information from monthly, quarterly and annual statistical series that reflect consumer purchases of goods and services, construction, producers' purchases of equipment, government purchases of goods and services, and exports and imports of goods and services would be appropriate for estimating the annual and quarterly GNP. However, since this information would be less detailed and complete than that used to prepare the benchmark estimates, rather than use it to determine GNP's level, it would be used to determine annual and quarter-to-quarter percent changes from the seven established benchmark estimates. The annual changes between any two benchmark years and the quarterly changes between two annual estimates would be interpolated using information on economic activity during the particular years and quarters. The annual changes since the most recent benchmark estimate, 1977, and the quarterly changes since the most recent annual estimate would be extrapolated using appropriate available information. This example in very summary fashion describes how BEA produces its national income and product account time series.

BEA does not estimate quarterly and annual GNP, national income, or other related components in aggregate form as the above example may suggest. Various data are used to extrapolate or interpolate changes in the detailed subcomponents of these measures. For example, Census retail trade data is the extrapolator for retail sales of various consumer goods which are a component of personal consumption expenditures. The component estimates are summed to obtain GNP and related totals.

BEA's process of benchmarking every 5 years and interpolating and extrapolating during the intervening and subsequent years produces a time series reflecting business cycle fluctuations. A disadvantage of the process, however, is that errors made in the benchmarks will be interpolated and extrapolated to the other years' estimates. Errors made in preparing the annual estimates will be interpolated or extrapolated to the quarterly estimates.

ESTIMATING AND ADJUSTING THE
NATIONAL INCOME AND PRODUCT COMPONENTS

Extrapolation, interpolation, and revision characterize the process used to prepare the national income and product time series. Preparing the particular quarterly and annual estimates, however, involves many procedures for estimating the various sub-components' extrapolators or interpolators. Adjustments are also made to remove seasonal and price impacts from the data. The procedures used in estimating the various components, especially the quarterly estimates, are described in detail in the "Report of the Advisory Committee on Gross National Product Data Improvement" and a BEA staff paper "Quarterly GNP Estimates Revisited in a Double Digit Inflationary Economy." These estimates are prepared using data from various sources. We listed primary sources on pages 16 and 18 of this report.

Precisely. how the many procedures and adjustments used to estimate quarterly and annual GNP may affect the estimates' accuracy is uncertain. According to BEA, adjustments are made and standard procedures are not always relied on in order to improve accuracy. On the other hand, experts acknowledge that components requiring adjustments are potentially less accurate than those based directly on reported data.

Estimating the individual components

There are many detailed procedures for estimating the individual components and subcomponents which are aggregated to arrive at the total GNP and related estimates. The following examples indicate some of the procedures used.

Source data for the various subcomponents may differ in character and therefore are applied differently in the estimation process. Census retail trade data, for instance, is reported at current dollar value and likewise used. On the other hand, the extrapolator BEA uses for quarterly automobiles sales is reported in units sold and is converted to retail value by multiplying it by the average unit value of new cars. Similar to automotive sales, the extrapolator for quarterly wages and salaries is estimated using BLS' 790 program data on employment, earnings, and hours worked.

The basic data used to estimate the components may also be adjusted to (1) account for items valued by other means or (2) conform to BEA's concepts. An example of using alternative means to value items is the estimate for consumer goods. BEA uses Census retail trade data for most of the consumer goods, but values the automobile, gasoline, and oil sales' portion using other data; therefore, their value is deducted from the Census retail trade total used to estimate the value for other consumer goods. In conforming to BEA's concepts, an example is the distinction for the distribution of automobile sales among consumers and businesses. Automobiles sold to consumers are placed in the personal consumption expenditures component and those sold to businesses are placed in the producers' durable equipment component. While the adjustments noted appear to be fairly simple, there are others that are complex and require detailed steps to be performed.

Certain nonmarket activities included in the accounts have values which cannot be directly measured as defined. Such values, like the services of owner-occupied housing, are estimated from related information. GNP includes eight imputed items which amount to roughly 9 percent of its value. The principal imputations are the rental value of owner-occupied housing, the value of food and fuel produced and consumed on farms, food furnished employees, and free services provided by financial intermediaries. Figures for the value of owner-occupied housing, for instance, are estimated with housing stock data from the Decennial Census of Housing, the Annual Housing Survey, and the CPI for residential rents.

Seasonal adjustments

Seasonal adjustment is designed to remove seasonal impacts from monthly and quarterly series to highlight business cycle changes and trends. Each quarterly GNP component is seasonally adjusted individually by using seasonally adjusted source data to estimate them. Census and BLS adjust their data series before BEA receives the data and BEA adjusts the data from its surveys as well as many other data obtained from various sources.

The Census Bureau, BLS, and BEA use the X-11 Variant of the Census Method II Seasonal Adjustment Program. The method generally involves estimating seasonal adjustment factors which are applied to monthly or quarterly data to eliminate the seasonal component of total monthly or quarterly variation in a time series. The adjustment factors which are periodically revised are based on past experience of seasonal activity in a series. They are estimated using moving averages of time series data to isolate fluctuations due to the time of the year.

BEA's analysis of seasonally adjusted quarterly GNP suggests that seasonal adjustment contributes to the error in quarterly GNP. It found the seasonal adjustment factor revisions a major contributor to the size of the GNP revisions. It concluded that since the process of seasonally adjusting data introduces error into the source data, seasonal adjustment constrains efforts to improve the national income and product estimates' reliability. Revised seasonal factors, however, are necessary to account for changing patterns in seasonal behavior.

Constant dollar estimates

A final principal adjustment made to the GNP data involves developing constant dollar or real GNP estimates. This adjustment is done to eliminate the effect of price changes on the GNP time series. During periods of inflation, or its less common opposite deflation, this adjustment is important because it removes the impact of price changes from the current dollar value measure of output.

Constant dollar GNP estimates are typically developed by dividing the subcomponents of the major GNP components by the appropriate detailed consumer or producer price indexes. For example, the furniture and household equipment category of personal consumption expenditures is deflated by the BLS' CPI for furniture and bedding. 1/ A byproduct of this process is the implicit price deflator which is derived as the ratio of current dollar to real GNP.

BEA's procedure of estimating real GNP by deflating the GNP subcomponents, as opposed to GNP in total, picks up both changes in real output and changes in output's composition. The implicit price deflators calculated for each of the subcomponents also reflect changes in spending patterns. This procedure thus results in output measures which show how the value of output would have changed over time had prices remained unchanged.

In addition to elements affecting the quality of the current dollar estimates, the constant dollar estimates are affected by the quality of the price indicators used in the deflation process. Inaccurate price measures will result in inaccurate real GNP estimates. Furthermore, the price data must account for quality changes in products which will also affect the real GNP measures. Many studies on the effects of quality changes on prices have been done, and BLS adjusts many of its detailed price series for certain types of quality change.

Besides the real GNP estimates produced by BEA, the only other current major comparable measure of change in the physical volume of output is the Federal Reserve Board's monthly index of industrial production. The index is confined to the output of factories, mines, and utilities which comprise a major portion of total output as defined by GNP. The index's current estimates are derived using physical volume of output data and electric power inputs to industries and employee hours, both adjusted for productivity change. Similar to GNP, the index is benchmarked to the economic censuses.

While there are differences between the two measures, that is, concept and data sources, comparative analyses have been made of the movements of the two series. The comparisons, although performed on an irregular basis, have shown the two series to

---

1/The rationale behind the method of deflating GNP is based on the conceptual definition of GNP as a measure of the market value of current output. The market value of GNP is the total quantity of goods and services produced times their prices. Deflating GNP to some base year's prices is to value the current quantity of output in the base year's prices. This is done by dividing current dollar GNP by a price index which measures price changes from a base period to the current period.

be generally parallel measuring change, but in a few instances there were substantial differences. As a result, the advisory committeee on GNP Data Improvement recommended that the two agencies jointly analyze the two output measures and explain the differing movements between the series publicly.

BEA OFFICIALS' JUDGMENT IN THE ESTIMATION PROCESS

Although the procedures outlined above may suggest that estimating GNP, national income, and related components simply involves plugging numbers into established formulas, judgment also enters into the estimates, especially the current estimates. Since judgment is used during the estimation process primarily to fill gaps in missing source data, considerable judgment is used in the current estimates. For instance, out of 44 key data series entering into preliminary quarterly GNP estimates, 31 of the series data for the third month of the quarter are source data projections prepared by BEA. For the second month of the quarter for the same preliminary estimates the number of projected series reduces to 10. For the first month, only 2 series are projected. The projections are made available to the public on request, and BEA officials stated that from this information judgments made by them can be determined.

Judgments made by estimators responsible for the particular GNP and related component estimates are reviewed twice during the estimation process. The National Income and Wealth Division Chief reviews the component estimates and compiles the data into the GNP and charges against GNP framework. He reviews the component and total estimates for their reasonableness, consistency, completeness, and the size of the statistical discrepancy. BEA's Director also reviews the estimates prior to their release. During these two reviews information assumptions used and judgments made are presented. However, according to BEA, the reviews rarely result in the estimates being changed.

BEA views the process of estimating current GNP as a mixture of science and art or standard procedures and judgment which should be used flexibly since the economy and available data sources are subject to change. Since the preliminary GNP, national income, and related component figures are based on incomplete and preliminary data on economic activity with judgment compensating for the data gaps, the figures, rather than being actual measurements, are truly estimates of the current situation. BEA notes this characteristic of its preliminary estimates in its GNP press release.

In addition to the use of judgment during the GNP estimation process, judgments of BEA officials are further reflected in the estimates. BEA officials are responsible for selecting the national income and product accounts' concepts and classifications and for selecting the methods and data sources used to estimate the accounts.

CHAPTER 7

UNRESOLVED ISSUES OF NATIONAL

INCOME AND PRODUCT CONCEPTS,

CLASSIFICATIONS, AND ESTIMATION FREQUENCY

What national income and product should measure is a subject that has been debated for some time. Controversy over how national output and income should be defined evolved with the development of national accounting and modern economic theory during the 1930s. More recently issues involving national income and product concepts have reappeared in studies of the national accounts. How much detail the accounts should provide and how often the measures should be presented also continue to be questioned.

The last broad review to look at the accounts' conceptual aspects was done in 1957 by the National Accounts Review Committee of the National Bureau of Economic Research at the request of the Office of Statistical Standards, the Office of Federal Statistical Policy and Standards' predecessor. The latest review of the accounts, that of the Advisory Committee on GNP Data Improvement, completed in 1977, as covered in chapter 5, dealt primarily with the underlying data used to produce the national income and product estimates rather than what the concepts should be.

Besides the 1957 Review Committee's study 1/, the National Bureau of Economic Research has subsequently held periodic conferences (in 1971, 1973, 1974, and 1979) which have further dealt with the issues. In addition, individual national accounts' experts have studied the issues.

Controversy over measuring national output has occurred because the experts differ on output's definition for measuring national income and product. These differences do not address the statistical accuracy of GNP as defined and measured by BEA, but rather seek to change what is being measured. National accounts experts outside of BEA are not unanimous in their support of what changes should be made. The major unresolved issues of national income and product concepts, classifications, and frequency are presented in this chapter.

NATIONAL ACCOUNTS REVIEW COMMITTEE
CREATED TO EXAMINE AND EVALUATE THE
NATIONAL ECONOMIC ACCOUNTS

The National Accounts Review Committee was established by the National Bureau of Economic Research, a nongovernmental eco-

---

1/National Accounts Review Committee of the National Bureau
  of Economic Research, The National Economic Accounts of the
  United States: Review, Appraisal, and Recommendations
  (Washington, D.C.: GPO, 1958).

nomic research organization, at the request of the Bureau of the Budget's Office of Statistical Standards to undertake a review of the national economic accounts. The review's objective was to provide a thorough examination and evaluation of the accounts and to make recommendations for improvement, with specific emphasis on the conceptual matters that would serve Government and private users more effectively.

The review committee's 1957 study of the national economic accounts of the United States included the national income and product accounts, the international balance of payments statement, the flow-of-funds statement, the input-output table, and the national balance sheet. The committee made 29 broad recommendations to improve the national economic accounts. Twenty-one of the committee's broad recommendations directly or indirectly pertained to the national income and product accounts. Recommendations were made affecting the accounts' basic data, structure, definitions, detail, and frequency.

BEA has made major changes to the national income and product accounts as recommended by the review committee. It has simplified the accounts' structure, expanded the detail of the quarterly and annual current and constant dollar estimates, increased the estimation frequency of the constant dollar estimates, and integrated the national income and product accounts with the input-output table, the flow-of-funds statement and other economic accounts.

Although the National Accounts Review Committee's 23-year-old study was the last broad review of conceptual issues, subsequent examinations have been made of the accounts' concepts and classifications. 1/ The changes to the accounts considered in subsequent examinations are more radical than those recommended by the 1957 review committee and could, if adopted, affect the definition and use of the GNP and other national income and product components. These studies which incorporate other experts' research in national accounts are the basis of the following discussion of national income and product conceptual issues.

CONCEPTUAL CHANGES COULD IMPAIR GNP AS A
PRODUCTION MEASURE

The GNP has only limited usefulness in assessing real long term economic growth and economic well-being according to some national accounts experts because GNP as presently defined excludes nonmarket production, the services of household and government durable goods, and intangible investment from the accounts. The distinction presently made between intermediate and final products

---

1/Nancy Ruggles and Richard Ruggles, _The Design of Economic Accounts_ (New York: National Bureau of Economic Research, 1970); F. Thomas Juster, "Alternatives to GNP as a Measure of Economic Progress," in _U.S. Economic Growth From 1976 to 1986: Prospects, Problems, and Patterns,_ 10 (Washington, D.C.: GPO, 1977), pp. 12-24.

in the national income and product account also limits GNP's usefulness, and according to one economist the exclusion of much of
the subterranean activity in the accounts' framework presumably mis-
represents the measure of economic activity. Changing the accounts'
scope to include these items, however, would alter the market
activity character of GNP.

Nonmarket production

     Some economists believe nonmarket production of households
could improve GNP's usefulness. Household operation and maintenance
and personal care activities performed by household members, while
never recorded in market transactions, affect their physical welfare
and thus according to many economists should be included in the
measure of economic output. Including such nonmarket production
would entail measurement problems and would impair GNP, national
income, and related components as measures of activity in the
Nation's product and resource markets. Since activities performed
by household members do not involve market transactions and the
setting of prices, the value of these activities cannot be directly
measured. Including them in GNP would therefore require that their
values be estimated from other related data. This added imputation
in the accounts could weaken it as a measure of market activity.
However, estimates of the value of nonmarket production would not
affect GNP's present concept if they were presented as addendum
items in the accounts which users then could add to or subtract
from GNP as they see fit. BEA presently has a program underway
to develop such measures.

Services of durables

     Including value of services provided by consumer and govern-
ment durable goods could, like nonmarket household production,
improve GNP's usefulness. The value of consumer durable goods
purchases is presently measured in GNP. However, since these
goods yield services for years after they are purchased, many
economists feel that the value of these services, beyond the original purchase price, should also be included in GNP. One example
would be the services provided by a washing machine. Only the
machine's purchase price is included in GNP if it is purchased
by a consumer, while for a commercial laundry's purchase both
the machine's purchase price and the revenues received from its
use are counted in GNP. As with nonmarket production, the value
of such services from household durables cannot be directly measured; they have no market value and would have to be imputed.
This imputation could impair GNP as a measure of market activity.
In addition, the imputed flow of services from government capital
formation, such as structures or durable equipment which provide
services for years beyond the year they were purchased, is a
desired addendum to GNP. It would present problems similar to
measuring the services of household capital.

Intangible investments

     Spending on intangible investments is another area that
economists feel should be included in measures of capital formation in the accounts. Expenditures on items like education,

health care, and research and development are presently represented as current production. Since these types of expenditures are similar to tangible capital investment in that they contribute to future output, some national income experts feel that they should be reclassified as capital formation and that the flow of services from such spending should be imputed to current output.

Reclassifying household, business, and government expenditures on intangible investments within the accounts should not have any overall effect on the GNP measure, but imputing the value of the flow of services from such spending to current output would alter GNP. Like other imputations the imputed flow of services from intangible investments would add another component to the accounts which would not be based directly on reported data. The added imputation could weaken GNP as a measure of activity in the Nation's marketplaces.

Furthermore, imputing the flow of services from intangibles would probably also entail estimation problems. Because the benefits from education, health care, and research and development expenditures may never be realized, determining how to value the services presents a problem. In the present accounts, the benefits of such spending are included in the output and income measures as they are realized.

Intermediate and final goods distinction

Another area of controversy involving the accounts which affects GNP as a measure of economic growth and economic well-being is the distinction between intermediate and final goods. Presently, the distinction between intermediate goods and final goods is clearly defined for business output. This distinction, however, is not made for the government and household sectors.

Many government services, rather than being supplied to final users, are supplied directly to businesses. Since these services represent inputs to business output, they are intermediate goods rather than final output. Including the services in government spending and then also including in GNP the full market value of business products, the prices of which are presumed to cover the tax cost of providing the government services, thus amounts to double counting the services value. For this reason, the handling of government spending in the accounts has been the subject of discussion among economists since their inception. This controversy has not been resolved due to the lack of a feasible means of estimating what proportions of government spending directly benefits businesses versus that which benefits final consumers.

Some economists also feel that certain household expenditures should not be included in GNP because they are a cost of earning a living, similar to the expenses associated with operating a business. Such expenditures include transportation, clothing, and food costs associated with individuals going to work and earning a living. Although estimating these expenses should not present a difficult measurement problem, the desirability of excluding particular living costs from GNP remains questionable. For analytical purposes the total spending of households, in general, is a more useful indicator of the economy's performance than household spending less certain living costs.

Subterranean economy

Many activities occurring in what has been referred to as the subterranean economy do not enter into GNP. For the purpose of our discussion, the subterranean economy includes illegal and legal incomes which are not reported. Illegal activities include such areas as gambling, prostitution, narcotics trafficking, loan sharking, business theft, and white collar crime. Legal activities such as barter and other income that are not reported or underreported for tax purposes would also be included in the subterranean economy.

As presently defined, GNP excludes income from illegal activities but includes income from legal activities in the subterranean economy. According to BEA, illegal transactions are omitted from GNP primarily because there is no feasible method of estimating the extent of such activities. The GNP concept does include income from legal activities in the subterranean economy but all such income cannot be measured. BEA does make adjustments for underreported taxable legal income in GNP, but it does not have sufficient information to adjust for unreported legal income.

Estimates of the size of the subterranean economy vary widely. For 1976 the subterranean economy was estimated to range from $100 to $369 billion, 1/ which amounts to 6 to 21 percent of that year's GNP. For 1976 BEA roughly estimated that $6 to $10 billion--about 1/2 of 1 percent of GNP--was missed from its GNP estimates as a result of unreported legal income.

Excluding a large part of the subterranean transactions from official output and income statistics has been noted to misrepresent activity in the economy and bias economic decisionmaking. 2/ Effects of this exclusion include: overstated effective tax rate calculations; understatement of the rate of economic growth; and erroneous ratios of savings and consumption to income. These distortions are thus great enough to mislead economic policy prescriptions.

Due to the difficulty of collecting data on unreported legally and illegally earned taxable income, roundabout means must be used to estimate the size of the subterranean economy. The questionable accuracy of these estimates, like other imputed items, would increase the likelihood of error if they were included in GNP.

CLASSIFICATION CHANGES COULD IMPROVE GNP'S
USEFULNESS BY PROVIDING GREATER DETAIL

Aside from changes in the accounts discussed above that would alter the GNP's conceptual definition, changes to how the data is

---

1/Peter Gutman, "Statistical Illusions, Mistaken Policies,"
   Challenge, Nov.-Dec. 1979, pp. 14-15.

2/Ibid., pp. 16-17.

presented could enhance the accounts' usefulness without affecting the GNP concept. However, according to BEA officials, GNP's usefulness would be improved only if accuracy were not unduly impaired. Two major changes that reviewers of the accounts have recommended involve the presentation of the value of the output of nonprofit organizations and the presentation of government spending. Both these changes in presentation would require additional data.

The accounts could be improved if services provided by nonprofit institutions were measured separately. Currently the output of nonprofit institutions providing services to households is included in the services component of personal consumption expenditures along with services provided households by the business sector. Recognizing that activity among nonprofit institutions differs from businesses in that such institutions do not operate under the profit motive, critics of the accounts claim that services provided to households by nonprofit institutions, such as hospitals, colleges and universities, unions, and trust funds, should be presented in a separate classification.

Expanding the level of detail and presentation of government purchases also would improve the accounts' usefulness. Presently, in the detailed accounts, Federal and State and local government spending is classified by type (services, structures, etc.) and function (defense, education, etc.), but information about purchases of goods and services by product group is not available on a current basis. This information, which would be useful for analyzing the impact of changes in government spending on industries, is, however, planned for future presentation.

QUALITY IMPROVEMENTS WOULD MAKE MONTHLY GNP FEASIBLE

BEA estimates GNP and national income and related components quarterly (at annual rates) and annually. BEA has been estimating monthly personal income since 1938 and recently began estimating monthly disposition of personal income including personal consumption expenditures and its deflator. Although many users would like to have GNP estimated monthly, an interagency committee of the Office of Management and Budget has determined that source data quality and timeliness are inadequate for accurate monthly GNP estimates. However, should the quality and timeliness of key data programs on construction, producers' durable equipment, inventories, foreign transactions, and government spending improve, monthly GNP, like monthly personal consumption expenditures--a major GNP component--may become feasible.

CHAPTER 8

FOCUSING ATTENTION

ON GNP ISSUES

Prior efforts in addressing the issues surrounding the GNP's accuracy and reliability, methods, and concepts have brought changes to the estimates. Most notable are the efforts of the Advisory Committee on GNP Data Improvement and of the National

Accounts Review Committee. Nevertheless, issues and problems concerning the estimates still exist. Our study identifies several broad issues and some specific concerns with the GNP estimates centering on the accuracy and reliability of the estimates and the methods and concepts used. We hope that this study will act as a catalyst to focus attention on matters requiring further study.

The current state of the economy demands that Federal policymakers, those in the Congress as well as the executive branch, have reasonably accurate data on which to base decisions affecting the country's welfare. The GNP and related national income and product component estimates are a key part of this data base. Their importance would be difficult to overemphasize.

The National Accounts Review Committee noted in its 1957 report that national economic accounts estimates and projections are necessary for the formulation of successful economic policies, just as accounting information is necessary for the intelligent operation of a business firm. Although the national economic accounts, and more specifically the GNP and related components, are not the only ingredient necessary for successful economic policies, data which are statistically inaccurate and conceptually inadequate can result in badly designed economic policies. Poorly designed policies can result in wasted or misused resources and serious inflation.

Given the widespread impact which policymaking uses of the estimates may have on the Nation's economy, their accuracy and reliability are of obvious concern. The lack of precise error measures for the estimates--even though there are valid reasons why they cannot be provided--limits users' and researchers' capability to judge how accurate the estimates are and should be. Alternative means have been used to evaluate the reliability of the estimates, but no conclusive agreement was apparent, as we noted in chapter 4 on the studies of the revisions.

With the lack of precise error measures, the need to improve the underlying data sources is difficult to demonstrate. Improvements to the data sources that input into GNP should make the data more accurate and reliable. But, to complete the discussion, information is also needed on how good the estimates need to be and what reliance is presently placed on them.

Another pertinent issue is the estimation procedures used in developing the GNP and related estimates. The procedures used to estimate the detailed components and adjust source data are selected by BEA to improve the estimates' accuracy. Adjusting the underlying source data and using judgment in the estimation process, however, may increase the opportunity of introducing error into the estimates. Detailed up-to-date information on BEA's methods is presently not available in a comprehensive handbook. To understand the estimates' limitations users need to know the actual procedures used and how these procedures might impact on the estimates.

Aside from the issue of statistical accuracy, the relevance of the accounts' concepts and classifications to users' needs is also of consequence. The GNP measure is used to indicate both the economy's performance and the national well-being. Redefining GNP to improve it as a measure of economic well-being, however, could detract from its usefulness for purposes of analyzing the market economy's performance. Improving GNP as a well-being measure need not impair GNP as a measure of economic performance. Information needed to assess well-being could be presented as a supplement which could be added to or subtracted from GNP to suit particular users' needs.

The aforementioned issues are the results of our limited study of the national income and product accounts and are not presumed to be all-inclusive. Given the size and complexity of the accounts we are not certain if the questions surrounding the issues can ever be fully answered. Our intent in this study is to draw attention to this highly technical and complex subject, focus attention on the issues, and encourage others to express their views.

NATIONAL INCOME AND PRODUCT COMPONENT DEFINITIONS

Business transfer payments	Income of persons from business for which no goods or services are received in return. Such items include consumer bad debts, corporate gifts to nonprofit institutions, and personal injury payments to persons other than employees.
Capital consumption adjustment	Difference between depreciation reported at historical cost for tax purposes and depreciation at replacement cost based on the estimated service life of the asset.
Capital consumption allowances	Estimates of wear and tear, obsolescence, destruction, and accidental losses of physical capital at their historical cost. Capital consumption in the accounts includes depreciation charges by businesses and nonprofit institutions, depreciation of owner occupied dwellings, and accidental damage to fixed business capital. Depletion of natural resources are not included.

Charges against gross national
   product

Cost incurred and profits
earned in the production
of gross national product.

Compensation of employees

Income accruing to employees
as remuneration for work. It
is the sum of wages and salaries and supplements to wages
and salaries, such as employer
contributions to social insurance, private pension, health
and welfare funds, and injury
compensation.

Corporate profits

Earnings of corporations organized for profit. Profits are
reported without deduction for
depletion and exclude capital
gains and losses. Earnings
are adjusted for inventory valuation and capital consumption.

Government purchases

Goods and services purchased
by the three levels of gov-
ernment--Federal, State, and
local--and gross investments
of government enterprises.
Purchases include compensation
of government employees, construction expenditures on highways, bridges, and schools, and
purchases of equipment, supplies, and services.

Gross national product

Expresses in dollars the market
value of goods and services
produced by the Nation's economy within a specific period
of time, usually for a calendar
year or a quarter of a year
at an annual rate.

Gross private domestic
   investment

Fixed capital goods purchased
by private business and nonprofit institutions and the
value of the change in the
physical volume of inventories held by private business.
Purchases of dwellings are
included as fixed capital.

Indirect business taxes
   and nontax liability

Tax liabilities paid by business, other than employer
contributions for social insurance and corporate income
taxes. Sales taxes, excise
taxes, and real property

taxes paid by business are the principal types of indirect taxes. Nontax liability represents business payments for fines, copyrights, royalty payments, and penalties.

Inventory valuation adjustment

Gains or losses included in book profits due to differences between replacement and original cost of goods taken out of inventory.

National income

Total earnings of labor and property from the production of goods and services.

Net exports

Exports less imports of goods and services. Exports are part of national production and imports are not, but imports are included in the components and are therefore deducted.

Net interest

Excess of interest payments made by the domestic business sector over its interest receipts plus net interest received from abroad.

Net national product

Gross national product less capital consumption allowances with capital consumption adjustment, which are deducted from gross private domestic fixed investment to express it on a net basis.

Personal consumption expenditures

Goods and services purchased by individuals and nonprofit institutions which render services principally to individuals. The value of food, fuel, clothing, rent of dwelling, and financial services received in kind by individuals is also included. The rental value of owner-occupied dwellings is included, but the purchase of the dwellings is classified as gross private domestic investment.

Proprietors' income

Earnings of unincorporated
business--proprietorships,
partnerships, and producers'
cooperatives--from their operations. Capital gains and
losses are excluded and no
deduction is made for depletion. Supplementary income
from rental property to individuals is included in the
rental income component.

Rental income of persons

Earnings of individuals from
renting real property, such
as a house, store, or farm.
Also included are the im-
puted rental value of owner-
occupied dwellings and royalties from patents, copyrights,
and rights to natural resources.

Statistical discrepancy

Amount by which gross na-
tional product differs from
charges against gross na-
tional product. It arises
because both estimates are
made independently by a
methodology subject to error.

Subsidies less current
  surplus of government
  enterprises

Subsidies are monetary grants
provided by Government to
business. Current surplus
of Government enterprises is
the excess of sales receipts
over operating costs. Such
enterprises include the U.S.
Postal Service, the Commodity
Credit Corporation, and the
Tennessee Valley Authority.
These are distinguished from
other Government activities
by the fact that they are
financed by the sale of a
product or service rather
than through general taxes.

Appendix B
The Macroeconomic Effects of Deficit Spending: A Review

K. Alec Crystal *City University, London, England*

Daniel L. Thornton *Federal Reserve Bank of St. Louis, St. Louis, Missouri*

Reprinted from The Review, *Vol. 70, No. 6 (1988), published by the Research and Public Information Department of the Federal Reserve Bank of St. Louis.*

FOLLOWING the Keynesian Revolution in macroeconomics, a large number of economists argued that deficit spending was required to achieve two of the stated national economic objectives: full employment and a high rate of economic growth.[1] Society was thought to benefit from deficit spending because of the reduction in lost output and because the economy would achieve a higher rate of growth.

This view of deficit spending has been challenged increasingly over the years. A sizable number of economists now believe that deficit spending has little effect on employment and output, especially in the long run, and that it primarily results in a redistribution of output, either within the private sector or as a transfer of resources from the private to the public sector.[2] Support for this viewpoint has produced a growing concern about the potentially harmful effects of deficit spending and the size of the public debt.[3]

The existence and magnitude of the benefits from deficit spending have important implications for the public policy debate. Presumably, the decision to incur deficits is affected by the public's belief about whether deficits provide benefits to some individuals at little or no cost to others, or whether they merely redistribute income. Hence, a central issue in the debate over deficit spending is whether, and to what degree, it can be used to produce net benefits for society as a whole. The purpose of this paper is to examine some of the arguments and evidence on whether deficit spending yields net benefits to society.

DEFICIT SPENDING: SOME KEY TERMS

The phrases "deficit spending" and "fiscal policy" are not necessarily synonymous. While deficit spending is a particular fiscal policy action, not all

---

[1]One of Keynes' initial arguments was that saving would exceed investment at a level of output consistent with the full employment of labor. That is, the U.S. savings rate was too high. The view that the budget should be in persistent deficit was termed the "new fiscal policy." To see how opinions about deficit spending have changed in two decades, compare the deficit discussions in Levy (1963) with those in Levy, et. al. (1984).

[2]The once-common view that the market economy cannot sustain full-employment equilibrium has given way to the

concept of the natural rate of unemployment. For a discussion of these issues, see Modigliani (1986b), Blinder (1986) and Laidler (1988).

[3]For a discussion of the potential harmful effects of the public debt, see Bruce and Purvis (1986), Barro (1987) and Levy, et. al. (1984).

fiscal policy actions produce or involve deficits.[4] For example, the government could devise a policy whereby expenditures and taxes are changed by the same amount. This well-known "balanced budget" operation affects aggregate demand, because the change in government expenditures affects aggregate demand more than the change in taxes, but does not affect the deficit.[5]

Despite the balanced-budget multiplier, the stance of fiscal policy today is often associated with, and frequently measured by, the size of the federal budget deficit.[6] Thus, in this article, deficit spending and the stance of fiscal policy will be treated as synonymous. Furthermore, since they both produce the same qualitative shift in aggregate demand, no distinction will be made between deficits that arise from increases in government spending and those that result from tax reductions.

Cyclical and Structural Deficits and Discretionary Fiscal Policy

It is important to differentiate between "cyclical" and "structural" deficits when examining the effects of policy changes on the economy. Tax revenues rise during the expansion phase of the business cycle and fall during the contraction phase; in contrast, certain government expenditures (e.g., unemployment compensation) fall during expansions and rise during contractions. These counter-cyclical components of the

deficit—the so-called automatic stabilizers—are intended to smooth cyclical swings in income.

The structural deficit, on the other hand, reflects discretionary fiscal policy actions.[7] It is the part of the deficit that is invariant to the phase of the business cycle. Chart 1 presents measures of the actual and cyclically adjusted budget deficit. Although these measures depart substantially at times, generally they move together. While the analysis in this paper applies equally well to cyclical and structural deficits, from now on the discussion will focus solely on structural deficits.

THE NET BENEFITS FROM DEFICIT SPENDING

The effectiveness of deficit spending depends on two factors: the slope of the aggregate supply curve and the extent to which deficit spending shifts the aggregate demand curve. These factors are discussed in detail in latter sections of the paper. In this section, we present some general notions underlying the view that society can be a net beneficiary from deficit spending.

The initial popularity of using deficit spending to increase output was based on the belief that the market economy is unable to sustain aggregate demand at a level consistent with full-employment output. This idea of persistent unemployment is illustrated in chart 2 which shows a gap between actual and "potential" real output.[8] The

---

[4]There is a well-known caveat to this statement. Government tax rate changes are not neutral. The government may change certain marginal tax rates and simultaneously alter government expenditures to produce no net effect on aggregate demand, all other things constant. The ultimate effect on aggregate output, however, need not be neutral; the non-neutrality of the tax rate change could produce changes in aggregate supply.

Such analysis underlies much of the recent work by Auerbach and Kotlikoff (1987) and Kotlikoff (1988). Consequently, they have challenged the usual convention of associating deficit spending with fiscal policy. For example, Kotlikoff (1988), pp. 489–90, states that ". . . fiscal policies can matter a lot, but deficits may nonetheless tell us nothing useful about the true stance of fiscal policy." They argue that, within their life-cycle model, the labels "taxes" and "spending" are arbitrary. For them, a tight fiscal policy occurs when a larger burden of "government consumption" is borne by current rather than future generations.

[5]Aggregate demand increases because the marginal propensity to spend of the public sector (1) is greater than the marginal propensity to spend of the private sector (<1). If the private sector's marginal propensity to spend is large, the difference between the marginal propensities will be small and so, too, will be the effect of tax-financed expenditures on aggregate demand.

[6]It is common to measure fiscal action by the full-employment budget surplus or deficit. For a discussion of this, see Carlson (1987) and Seater (1985).

[7]See de Leeuw and Holloway (1983) for a detailed discussion of these concepts and Fellner (1982) for a critique of these measures. For a discussion of these concepts and a breakdown of the deficit, see Erceg and Bernard (1988).

[8]There is an issue, not taken up here, about the extent to which such unemployment is "involuntary." According to the usual textbook definition, involuntary unemployment occurs when individuals are willing to work at the market wage but are unable to find employment; that is, when there is an excess supply of labor at the market wage rate. If the market is competitive, the wage rate should fall to eliminate the involuntary unemployment. Hence, nearly all theories of involuntary unemployment require some form of nominal or real wage rigidity.

In early Keynesian models, involuntary unemployment was due to nominal rigidities in wages. This explanation requires real wages to fall when output rises. Empirical evidence, however, suggests that real wages are pro-cyclical. Recently, research by "New Keynesian Economists" suggests that persistent under-employment equilibria and involuntary unemployment can result from nominal price rigidities in the output market because of monopolistically competitive firms, and because of rigidities in real wages due to "efficiency wages." See Blinder (1988), Mankiw (1988), Rotemburg (1987), Prescott (1987), The New Keynesian Microfoundations (1987) and the cited references.

Chart 1
Actual and Cyclically Adjusted Budget
Surplus/Deficit

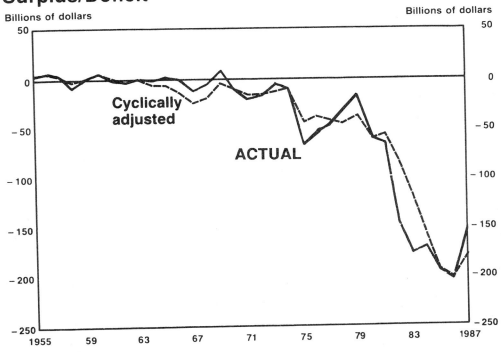

Billions of dollars

Billions of dollars

Chart 2
Actual and Potential GNP

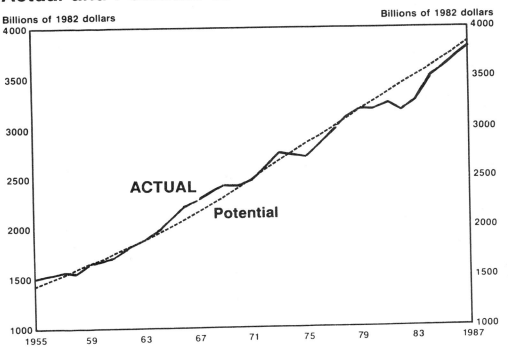

Billions of 1982 dollars

Billions of 1982 dollars

potential path of real output usually is associated with some full-employment rate of unemployment. Periods in which real output falls below its potential represent episodes of persistent excessive unemployment. If the economy is prone to periods of prolonged unemployment due to deficient aggregate demand for goods and services, the government could run a sustained deficit to make up for the deficiency. If successful, this deficit would keep output closer to its full-employment potential. Moreover, on average, real output growth would exceed the rate that would otherwise occur.

Deficit Spending and Capital Accumulation

Deficit spending could have a secondary effect on the rate of economic growth. Production of real output (y) is related to factor inputs, labor (N) and capital (K), via a production function, that is, y = f(N,K). The marginal products of both labor and capital are positive: for any quantity of capital (labor), output increases as more labor (capital) is used. The growth of the labor force is often considered synonymous with population growth, which is determined in part by factors that are independent of economic considerations. The size of the capital stock, on the other hand, is usually assumed to be related to economic factors. The higher the rate of capital formation (investment), the higher the rate of economic growth.

Firms determine the most profitable level of output and, simultaneously, the optimal capital/labor ratio. Because of the nature of capital goods, the decision to acquire capital is based (among other things) on expectations of output growth. If the market economy is subject to prolonged periods of unemployment and slow growth because of insufficient demand, expectations for output growth and investment will be lower than if these periods did not occur. If deficit spending raises the path of real output over what it would achieve otherwise, investment and, thereby, potential real output growth should rise even higher. Thus, de-

ficit spending could produce a higher rate of actual and potential growth because of increased capital formation.[9]

Deficits and Symmetric Business Cycles

The gains in output discussed so far are predicated on the assumption that cyclical swings in output around its potential path are asymmetric: cyclical downturns are longer and more pronounced than cyclical upturns. Since we are assuming that cyclical swings are due to variation in the demand for goods and services, this means that increases in the demand for goods and services are less frequent and smaller than decreases. If, on the other hand, fluctuations in aggregate demand around potential output are symmetric, periods during which output is above or below the potential path also will be symmetric.[10] This is illustrated by path 1 in figure 1 and by the aggregate demand and supply curves in figure 2. Given the slope of the aggregate supply curve, symmetric variation in aggregate demand produces symmetric movements in output about the potential level, y^*. On average, there are no "net output" gains to be achieved from deficit spending *over the cycle*. Periods of deficit spending when the economy is below the full-employment path would be matched by periods of budget surplus when output is above the path, so the budget would be balanced over the cycle and the average output level would be the same as with no fiscal action.

Society still may benefit, however, if the government runs deficits during the contraction phase of the cycle and surpluses during expansions. A cyclically balanced budget could stabilize aggregate demand and reduce the variability in output; this is illustrated by path 2 in figure 1.[11]

The Benefits From Stable Output

More stable output could reduce the risk associated with capital investment and, as a result, increase investment.[12] Consequently, the capital

---

[9]Achieving a higher rate of economic growth was part of the fiscal policy agenda during the 1960s. See Levy (1963).

[10]Recently, Sickel (1988) has investigated the asymmetry of the business cycles. He tests for both the "steepness" and "deepness" of post-World War II cycles and finds evidence that cyclical troughs are deeper than cyclical peaks.

[11]This discussion implicitly assumes that deficit spending does not alter the path of y^*, i.e., that deficit spending merely dampens the cycle.

[12]Many authors merely assert that there are benefits from more stable output growth without identifying these gains, e.g.,

Modigliani (1986a), (1986b) and Bossons (1986). At other times explanations of these gains sound hollow. For example, Bruce and Purvis (1986), pp. 60–61, argue for the benefits of avoiding a cyclical downturn by stating that "a government deficit will provide some stimulus to the economy and hence help reduce *the dead-weight costs of unemployment that would have occurred in the absence of the deficit.*" In the case where the government runs a surplus in order to prevent an economic boom, they argue that the surplus helps "avoid the *dead-weight costs that again arise because the economy is away from its long-run equilibrium.*" (Italics added.)

Figure 1
Symmetric Swings in Output

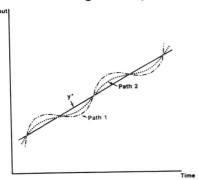

Figure 2
Symmetric Swings in Output and Aggregate Demand and Supply

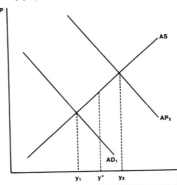

stock would increase, as would the level of potential output.[13] The economy would then achieve a higher rate of growth than otherwise.

Additional benefits could arise if more stable output growth results in more stable consumption. Economists usually argue that people maximize the utility of their consumption over some planning horizon and that the utility gains from increased consumption are smaller than the losses from equally probable decreases in consumption.[14] Even if the distribution of shocks to income and, therefore, consumption are symmetric, the distribution of utility gains and losses will be asymmetric. Consequently, the expected utility of consumption rises as income is stabilized.

The Benefits from Stabilizing Nominal GNP

There are additional benefits from stabilizing aggregate demand if cyclical movements in nominal GNP are symmetric, but cyclical movements in real output are asymmetric. That is, the aggregate supply curve is more steeply sloped above potential output as in figure 3. In this case, random variation in aggregate demand would produce larger changes in real output below the potential output level than above it. Of course, the change in nominal spending above and below potential output must be the same if variations in aggregate demand are symmetric about the natural rate. Stabilizing discretionary fiscal policy reduces both inflation and unemployment over the cycle and, thus, the cost of lost output associated with unemployment *and* the cost of inflation.[15]

Finally, deficit spending could yield net benefits if it merely offsets downward shifts in aggregate demand. For example, assume that cyclical swings in real output are symmetric so that there are no output gains on average over the cycle from stabilizing aggregate demand. Deficit spending still could result in net output gains for society, if de-

---

[13]The issue is whether the growth rate of real output is made *permanently* higher. Certainly, if economic stabilization policy merely causes the level of real output to be higher but does not affect the rate of real output growth permanently, there would still be a period immediately following the enactment of stabilization policy in which the observed rate of real output growth would exceed the full-employment growth rate.

[14]That is, the utility function is concave. Such gains from economic stabilization have been suggested by New Keynesian economics. See Rotemburg (1987), p. 83. To illustrate this point, assume that consumption is a random variable that is uniformly distributed on the closed interval 1 to 2, and let the utility of consumption be the simple concaved function, $u = C^5$. In this case, the expected value of utility is 1.22. Now assume that income and, hence, consumption are more variable, but

with the same expected value. Specifically, assume that consumption is now uniformly distributed on the closed interval 0 to 3. In this case, the expected value of utility of consumption is reduced to 1.15. Hence, reducing the variability of consumption increases the expected (average) utility of consumption. Of course, consumption may fluctuate much less than output over the business cycle if the life-cycle or permanent income theories of consumption are correct.

[15]The costs of expected inflation are in terms of its effects on long-term bond markets, the misallocation of productive resources and its effects on regulations. The casts of unexpected inflation are primarily in terms of its redistribution of wealth. For a discussion of these costs, see Leijonhufvud (1987) and the references cited there.

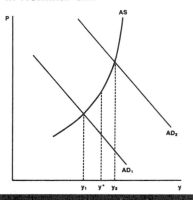

Figure 3
Asymmetric Swings in Output
but Symmetric Swings
in Nominal GNP

ficits were incurred when aggregate demand was weak, but surpluses were not incurred when aggregate demand was strong. Of course, in this case, the level of government debt would rise, both over the cycle and over time.

CRITICISMS OF THE ALLEGED BENEFITS OF DEFICIT SPENDING

As we have seen, the gains from deficit spending consist of reducing "lost" output due to reduced employment, increasing the growth rate of real output or stabilizing output and consumption. To achieve these gains, deficit spending must shift the aggregate demand schedule and the aggregate supply curve must be upward-sloping, at least in the short run. If the aggregate supply curve were vertical, shifts in the aggregate demand schedule would not affect output. Consequently, there could be no output gains from offsetting shifts in aggregate demand. Of course, if the aggregate supply curve were positively sloped, deficit spending would be effective only if it succeeds in shifting the aggregate demand curve. Attacks on the efficacy of fiscal policy have focused, therefore, on

the slope of the aggregate supply curve and the ability of deficit spending to shift aggregate demand.[16]

Asymmetric Cyclical Variation in Output

Both the Great Depression of the 1930s and the rise of Keynesian economics, with its emphasis on underemployment equilibrium, led to the acceptance of the notion that the market economy is neither able to sustain a full-employment level of output nor able to move back to it quickly when aggregate demand failures occur.[17] Prior to Keynes, it was commonly believed that output would naturally move to the level consistent with no involuntary unemployment. While shocks to either aggregate demand or supply might cause temporary periods of unemployment, resources were thought to be sufficiently mobile and wages and prices sufficiently flexible that the economy would return to its full-employment equilibrium fairly quickly.

Keynes argued that the economy might remain permanently below its full-employment level because of insufficient aggregate demand and market imperfections.[18] This below-full-employment equilibrium requires an upward-sloping aggregate supply curve. Typically, it was also argued that the aggregate supply curve would become steeper around the full-employment level of output, like the aggregate supply curve in figure 3.

The Phillips Curve

The Keynesian view was strengthened by the discovery of what appeared to be a stable long-run empirical relationship between the rate of inflation and the unemployment rate; this relationship was called the Phillips Curve.[19] If unemployment was too high (relative to the full-employment rate), policymakers could achieve a permanent increase in output by increasing aggregate demand through deficit spending. The cost would be a permanent increase in inflation. The extent of the cost is determined by the slope of the Phillips Curve. The closer income was to its full-

---

[16]This applies to monetary policy as well.

[17]For an interesting discussion of Keynesian and classical economics, see Blinder (1986), Laidler (1988), Eisner (1986) and Niehans (1987).

[18]There is a problem in defining "persistent" unemployment and establishing if and when it differs from cyclical unemployment. Many economists argue that there is no such thing as persistent unemployment because the market economy eventually

will adjust to the point at which the labor market clears. Keynes himself almost certainly believed this to be true in the long run; however, he regarded the long run to be too long for the adjustment to be left to market forces alone. His much-quoted defense of his view was that ". . . in the long run we are all dead."

[19]This apparent empirical regularity was first discovered by Phillips (1958) who used wages and unemployment.

employment level, the steeper the slope and, consequently, the higher the inflation rate. Presumably, without deficit spending, the economy would be stuck permanently below the full-employment level of output.

The Natural Rate Hypothesis and Rational Expectations: A Counter View to the Phillips Curve

The view that the economy could remain permanently at underemployment equilibrium was challenged by the Natural Rate Hypothesis.[20] It reintroduced the once-prevalent argument that the economy eventually will return to its full-employment equilibrium. That is, the Natural Rate Hypothesis implied that the long-run Phillips Curve is vertical at the natural rate of unemployment.

The implications of the Natural Rate Hypothesis were enhanced by the rational expectations revolution, which argued for the same conclusions, albeit along different theoretical lines. Rational expectations models of the business cycle showed that systematic stabilization policies could not affect real output permanently in markets populated by "rational" individuals.[21]

Both theories argue that the employment rate will tend toward its natural rate; consequently, demand management policies will be unable to keep the unemployment rate below the natural rate in the long run. The natural rate of output, y_n, is determined solely by the level of employment N_n, consistent with the natural rate of unemployment, given the stock of capital K. That is,

$$y_n = f(N_n, K).$$

Since demand management policies have no lasting effect on employment or the capital stock, they have no effect on the natural rate of output. In effect, these theories make it less likely that there will be asymmetries in the business cycle, thus, eliminating the possibility of permanent gains in net output from deficit spending. Unless shocks to demand or supply are asymmetric, on average, cyclical downturns need be no more pronounced nor of longer duration than cyclical upturns.[22]

The Natural Rate Hypothesis asserts that the long-run aggregate supply curve is vertical at an output level consistent with the natural rate of unemployment. It does not assert, however, that the short-run aggregate supply curve will be vertical at this level of output.[23] Hence, accepting the Natural Rate Hypothesis does not imply that society cannot benefit from appropriately timed and implemented deficit spending; however, it limits significantly the benefits that society can receive from deficit spending. As discussed previously, society benefits only if deficit spending reduces cyclical swings in output or nominal GNP.[24]

CAN DEFICIT SPENDING SHIFT THE AGGREGATE DEMAND SCHEDULE?

Even when the aggregate supply curve (short- or long-run) is upward-sloping, deficit spending will have little effect on output or prices if the increase in aggregate demand that it produces is largely offset by a deficit-induced decrease in private spending, that is, if deficit spending fails to change aggregate demand.

Competition for Credit—Indirect Crowding Out Through Interest Rates

When the government runs a deficit, it issues government debt.[25] Thus, the demand for credit increases relative to the supply. All other things

---

[20]See Friedman (1968) and Phelps (1967).

[21]Neither the Natural Rate Hypothesis nor many rational expectations models give rise to involuntary unemployment as defined in footnote 8. Many rational expectations models, however, give rise to cyclical movements in the natural rate of unemployment. See Fischer (1977), Taylor (1988) and McCallum (1986). For a list of other factors that could cause the unemployment rate to change without involuntary unemployment, see Blinder (1988).

[22]In chart 2, "potential" output is defined arbitrarily. Consequently, persistent unemployment can exist by definition. This applies to estimates of "potential" GNP as well as cyclically-adjusted deficits, etc. See Fellner (1982) and de Leeuw and Holloway (1982) for a discussion of this point.

[23]Also, it does not say explicitly what the level of the natural rate is. See Carlson (1988) for a discussion of the level of the natural rate.

[24]Actually, in such models, deficits can provide benefits in the absence of stabilizing output. These benefits come from smoothing taxes over the cycle. Public finance theory asserts that variation in tax rates across goods or activities results in welfare losses under most conditions. Consequently, it would be more efficient to run deficits and surpluses over the business cycle rather than balance the budget annually by altering tax rates. See Bossons (1986) and the references cited there.

[25]In models with a government budget constraint deficits are often financed directly through money creation. Given the current institutional structure, however, the government must initially issue debt even if it is subsequently monetized. See Thornton (1984a). See Thornton (1984b) for a discussion of and evidence on debt monetization.

unchanged, this causes interest rates to rise, reducing private expenditures in interest-sensitive sectors of the economy. Hence, the increase in aggregate demand associated with the deficit could crowd-out private expenditures indirectly by affecting interest rates.[26] Since investment spending is one of the most interest-sensitive components of spending, analysts often argue that deficit spending might retard the rate of capital formation and, hence, economic growth.[27]

Deficit Spending and the Trade Deficit

Assuming that deficit spending increases the demand for credit, its effect on interest rates depends on whether the economy is "open" or "closed." In the preceding example, we implicitly assumed that the economy was closed so that the government ran a deficit by borrowing from the private sector. In an open economy with a floating exchange rate and perfect capital flows, the results would be somewhat different.[28]

An increase in the budget deficit puts upward pressure on domestic interest rates. This leads to inflows of financial capital and an appreciation of the exchange rate. This appreciation, together with the higher domestic demand, is associated with a current account deficit in the balance of payments. In effect, the government deficit is financed by a larger trade deficit.[29] The economy may gain in terms of higher short-term consumption, but at a cost of an increase in external debt.

The decline in private expenditures is affected through higher interest rates, a larger trade deficit or both. In any event, the result is the same: the group that gains directly from deficit expenditures does so at the expense of those who lose, with little or no net increase in aggregate demand. The only difference is that those who gain directly are more readily identified than those who suffer indirect losses through higher interest rates or increased foreign claims on U.S. assets.[30]

Ricardian Equivalence

Another argument, referred to as the "Ricardian Equivalence Hypothesis," holds that deficit spending cannot shift the aggregate demand curve.[31] The closed-economy conclusion that deficit spending does not crowd-out private spending directly implies that government debt is net wealth to society. In other words, when the government issues debt to purchase goods and services, the holder of the debt views it as an asset; but the taxpayer does not view it as a liability (or, at least, views it as a smaller liability). That is, individuals believe that they will not have to pay current or future taxes to service or retire the debt.

---

[26]This problem cannot be solved by monetizing the debt. The increased rate of money growth will result merely in a higher rate of inflation and, hence, higher nominal interest rates. Many advocates of countercyclical fiscal policy view this as one of the most serious drawbacks to deficit spending. See Modigliani (1986b).

[27]This argument ignores how the deficits are spent. Recently, Heilbroner (1988) has argued that deficit spending is necessary to finance the purchase of public capital, that is, infrastructure. Other economist (for example, see Sturrock and Idan (1988)) argue that the real burden of deficits comes only when they are used to finance current consumption. This does not establish the desirability of deficit spending; it merely asserts that spending for infrastructure capital may increase the rate of economic growth, depending primarily on the relative productivity of the factor resources in the two sectors and on the productivity of public versus private capital.

The idea that such expenditures should be financed by deficits rests largely on the long-lived nature of capital goods. Since these capital goods provide services over a number of years, it is argued that public sector capital goods should be financed by borrowing just as businesses or households finance their acquisition of durable goods. In the case of businesses, however, debt service is financed out of the increased earnings that the capital goods are expected to provide. In the case of households, deficit financing is used to better match the desired consumption with expected future income. Hence, households, too, expect to service the debt through higher incomes. No similar increased earnings necessarily accrues from the acquisition of public capital. Income will increase only if the marginal product of public capital is larger than that of private capital. This is a difficult point to establish. Proponents of this view point to the productivity gains that could accrue from public expenditures on education and the like; however, these services could be provided by the private sector. Hence, this argument is about the appropriate role for government and public goods. See Aschauer and Greenwood and Aschauer (1988a, b and c) for a discussion of the benefits from social infrastructure expenditures. Hence, the only real argument for deficit financing of such expenditures is that it would equalize their costs and benefits across generations. This implies, however, that the increased indebtedness that such expenditures necessitate will eventually be retired through increased taxes unless the infrastructure acquired is infinitely lived.

[28]The assumption of perfect capital flows means that domestic real interest rates could not rise above world levels without inducing an inflow of financial capital from overseas. For a situation in which there is no expectation of exchange rate changes, this means that domestic and foreign nominal interest rates must be equal.

[29]See Mundell (1963). This result assumes no change in monetary policy to accommodate the deficit.

[30]In this model, the real market value of government debt is part of society's net wealth. In the closed economy model, at the natural rate of unemployment, the increase in wealth resulting from the increase in nominal debt due to deficit spending is just offset by a decline in wealth due to higher prices, interest rates or both. In the open economy model, it is offset by a reduced stock of national wealth due to increased claims by foreigners on U.S. assets.

[31]Technically, Ricardian Equivalence argues that, for a given level of government expenditures, aggregate demand will not change as the government switches from tax to bond financing. As O'Driscoll (1977) points out, Ricardo was merely offering this as a theoretical possibility and did not himself believe it.

Ricardian Equivalence, on the other hand, asserts that public and private debt are perfect substitutes. Individuals believe that they or their heirs will have to pay taxes equal to the deficit-financed expenditures, so an increase in present value of the expected future taxes just equals the current deficit.

At the macroeconomic level, Ricardian Equivalence implies that deficit spending will not be associated with increases in real interest rates, output, prices or the trade deficit.[32] Consequently, the Ricardian view yields a radically different notion of the national debt. For those who believe in the benefits of deficit spending, the national debt, which is the accumulated deficits, should be viewed as a blessing, not a curse. For those who believe in Ricardian Equivalence, deficit spending merely results in a redistribution of income and the national debt represents the cumulative amount of this net transfer.

Can Discretionary Fiscal Policy Be Successfully Implemented?

There is also an argument against the usefulness of deficit spending that is independent of its ability to shift aggregate demand. It is critically dependent, however, on the Natural Rate Hypothesis and on whether shifts in aggregate demand caused by other factors are temporary or permanent. It has been suggested that policymakers do not have the information needed to offset shifts in aggregate demand to stabilize output.[33] This argument is usually couched in a discussion of the lags in economic policymaking. For fiscal policy, the most important of these are the "recognition" and "implementation" lags. The recognition lag is the time between when a need for corrective action arises (an exogenous shift in aggregate demand) and when policymakers recognize the need. The issue is simply whether policymakers know where the economy is in the business cycle at any particular point in time.

The implementation lag is the time between when the need for corrective action is recognized and when policymakers take action. Thus, even if policymakers are quick to recognize that the demand has shifted, by the time they react to the situation, it may have changed and the need for corrective action may have vanished.

This argument is presented graphically in figure 4a. Assume that the Natural Rate Hypothesis holds and that the short-run aggregate supply curve is symmetric around the level of output consistent with the natural rate of unemployment. Assume further an exogenous decrease in aggregate demand, shifting it from AD to AD'. Now if policymakers did not react to the shift in demand immediately, the process of adjustment toward the natural rate would begin; the price level would decline and the quantity of output demanded would increase. Once policymakers reacted to the problem by increasing deficit spending, they would shift the aggregate demand curve upward, bringing output back to its natural-rate level.

If the shift in aggregate demand were temporary, a delay in policy might actually exacerbate the situation if deficit spending coincided closely with the return of aggregate demand to its former level. This is illustrated in figure 4b, where the simultaneous increase in deficit spending and the return of aggregate demand to its former level shift aggregate demand to AD".

Of course, if the decline in aggregate demand were permanent, the timing of policy would be less important. Deficit spending eventually would move the economy back to the natural rate; the timing of the policy action would determine only how quickly deficit spending moved the economy back to its full-employment potential. Of course, the economy would move back eventually to full employment even without deficit spending.

Demand or Supply Disturbances

Another problem is that policymakers must be able to differentiate between demand- and supply-side disturbances. Recently, some have suggested that business cycles can be explained solely by supply-side disturbances. Indeed, some "real business cycle" models have successfully produced cyclical swings in output that mimic real world data. Whether all cyclical swings in economic activity can be explained by such models is the subject of intense debate. Nevertheless, to the extent that some cyclical swings are the result of supply-side shocks, fiscal policy can succeed in stabilizing output only by exacerbating movements in prices (or it can help stabilize the price level only by exacerbating movements in output).

---

[32]Analysts frequently argue that Ricardian Equivalence must be invalid because the necessary microeconomic conditions for its validity are so stringent that they cannot possibly be satisfied. For example, see Buiter (1985). Also, see McCallum (1984).

[33]It is argued that inappropriately timed policy might destabilize the economy. See Friedman (1968).

Figure 4
The Timing of Changes in Fiscal Policy

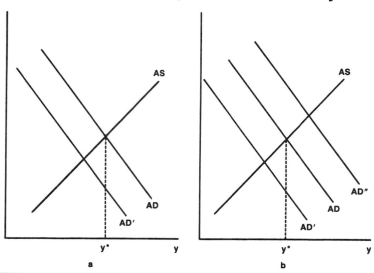

Consequently, policymakers must know not only where in the business cycle the economy is at any point in time, but whether its position was caused by a shift in aggregate demand, aggregate supply or, perhaps, simply the cyclical dynamics of the economy, unrelated to exogenous disturbances in either aggregate demand or supply. In short, some would argue that the information required to use discretionary fiscal policy effectively is simply too great.

WHAT IS THE EVIDENCE?

Assessing the evidence on discretionary fiscal policy is difficult. Effective discretionary fiscal policy implies that output should be more stable and suggests that perhaps the rate of real output growth should be higher on average when fiscal policy was used aggressively. It also suggests that deficit spending should be positively correlated with interest rates, prices (or inflation) or trade deficits.

A number of large-scale econometric models suggest that fiscal policy has significant short-run and, in some cases, long-run effects. Estimates of reduced-form models, however, typically show no long-run effects of deficit spending and, often, only weak short-run effects.[34] Hence, such models essentially substantiate the Natural Rate Hypothesis. These studies are subject to considerable controversy because of the difficulty in finding commonly accepted variables that reflect discretionary changes in fiscal policy and the continued controversy over reduced-form estimation.

The greatest challenge to the orthodox view of deficit spending comes from the Ricardian Equivalence Hypothesis.[35] Macroeconomic evidence from three recent surveys is largely consistent with the Ricardian view.[36] In general, there is no statistically significant relationship between structural deficits and interest rates or inflation, or between the budget and trade deficits.[37] These results are bolstered by work that shows a high negative correla-

---

[34]One of the earliest of these was the Andersen-Jordan equation. See Andersen and Jordan (1968).

[35]See Barro (1987), Bernheim (1987) and Aschauer (1988a). For more recent studies which report results consistent with Ricardian Equivalence, see Evans (1988), Koray and Hill (1988) and Leiderman and Razin (1988).

[36]The microeconomic evidence yields mixed results.

[37]Barro (1987) reports that he finds a statistically significant correlation between government deficits and the trade deficit only if 1983 is included.

tion between public and private savings.[38]

The Evidence on Stabilization

One commonly cited piece of evidence that demand management can stabilize the economy is a comparison of the volatility of U.S. output, unemployment and industrial production, before and after World War II. The fact that the pre-war series are more volatile than the post-war series has been cited as evidence of both the inherent instability of unmanaged capitalism and the success of demand management policies in stabilizing the economy.

There are several criticisms of this evidence. First, pre- and post-war data vary in terms of a quality and uniformity. Indeed, some argue that the excessive pre-war volatility of the commonly used series on unemployment, GNP and industrial production is due to various quirks in their construction.[39]

Second, even if the post-war economy is more stable, this may be due to other changes in economic fundamentals, not to discretionary fiscal policy per se.[40] Furthermore, even if fiscal policy is responsible for the apparently more stable post-war economy, this may be the result of increased relevance on the automatic stabilizers, not to discretionary fiscal policy.

Also, post-war real output growth in the United States is below its pre-war growth. The discrepancy is even larger if the Depression years are omitted.[41] Moreover, there has been a secular rise in the unemployment rate. These adverse movements roughly coincide with a secular rise in the U.S. structural deficit.[42] Hence, if the more stable post-war economy is used as evidence on the success of fiscal policy, the associated slower output growth and higher unemployment must be considered the costs of stability.

CONCLUSION

This paper has examined the theoretical arguments about the wisdom of deficit spending. The once-prevalent Keynesian approach, which concludes that such gains clearly exist, has come under attack. Increasingly, both theoretical innovations and empirical evidence suggest that modern economies are not well characterized by the Keynesian view. Support for the Natural Rate Hypothesis, which argues that deficit spending has no effect on the equilibrium level of output and employment in the long run has grown. If this hypothesis is valid, the gains from deficit spending result from stabilizing output around the level consistent with the natural rate of unemployment. Such an effective use of deficit spending, however, imposes information requirements on policymakers that are unlikely to be attained.

In general, empirical evidence on the effects of deficit spending is sparse and, for the most part, ambiguous. Most persuasive is the growing macroeconomic evidence, consistent with Ricardian Equivalence, that deficit spending has no long-run effect. The challenge for those who argue that deficit spending merely redistributes income and that stabilization policy will likely hurt is to explain phenomena like the Great Depression. Through adherents to both extreme Keynesian and extreme rational expectations views (and everything between) usually are able to rationalize historical events on their own terms, the Great Depression is as likely to be seen as an example of what bad policy can create as it is of what good policy can eradicate.

REFERENCES

Andersen, Leonall C., and Jerry L. Jordan. "Monetary and Fiscal Actions: A Test of Their Relative Importance in Economic Stabilization," this *Review* (November 1968), pp. 11–24.

---

[38]Of course, in a closed economy with output unchanged, the public sector deficit must equal the private sector surplus. Other studies of consumption have tried to determine whether government debt is net wealth, e.g., Tanner (1979) and Kochin (1974). Again, the results are consistent with the Ricardian Equivalence Hypothesis.

[39]See Romer (1986a, 1986b, 1986c and 1988). Romer's evidence has been challenged by Weir (1986) and Lebergott (1986).

[40]Pre- and post-war real output series for the United Kingdom, Germany and Italy show significant decreases in the variability of real output of a similar order of magnitude as that of the United States. The pre-war standard deviations of annual output growth for the United States, United Kingdom, Germany

and Italy were 6.61, 3.98, 6.10 and 4.79, respectively. The post-war standard deviations were 2.83, 2.00, 2.45 and 3.49. In all cases, the decline in variability was statistically significant at the 5 percent level. The data were obtained from Liesner (1985).

[41]The growth rate of real output from 1869 to 1938 was 3.1 percent, from 1945 to 1983, 2.7 percent, and from 1965 to 1983, 3.7 percent. These growth rates were calculated from data in Gordon (1986).

[42]The unemployment rate averaged 4.5 percent in the 1950s, 4.8 percent in the 1960s, 6.2 percent in the 1970s and 7.7 percent in the 1980s, respectively.

Aschauer, David. "The Equilibrium Approach to Fiscal Policy," *Journal of Money, Credit and Banking* (February 1988a), pp. 41–62.

_____. "Is Government Spending Stimulative?" Federal Reserve Bank of Chicago Staff Memoranda SM 88-3 (1988b).

_____. "Public Spending and the Return to Capital," Federal Reserve Bank of Chicago Staff Memoranda SM 88-2, (1988c).

Aschauer, David A., and Jeremy Greenwood. "Macroeconomic Effects of Fiscal Policy," *Carnegie-Rochester Series on Public Policy* (Autumn 1985), pp. 91–138.

Auerbach, Alan J., and Laurence J. Kotlikoff. "Evaluating Fiscal Policy with a Dynamic Simulation Model," *The American Economic Review* (May 1987), pp. 49–55.

Barro, Robert J. "The Ricardian Approach to Budget Deficits," Henry Thornton Lecture, City University Business School, London, November 1987.

Bernheim, B. Douglas. "Ricardian Equivalence: An Evaluation of the Theory and Evidence," NBER Working Paper No. 2330 (July 1987).

Blinder, Alan S. "The Challenge of High Unemployment," *The American Economic Review* (May 1988), pp. 1–15.

_____. "Keynes After Lucas," *Eastern Economic Journal* (July-September 1986), pp. 209–16.

Bossons, John. "Issues in the Analysis of Government Deficits," in John Sargent, ed., *Fiscal and Monetary Policy* (University Toronto Press, 1986), pp. 85–112.

Bruce, Neil and Douglas D. Purvis. "Consequences of Government Budget Deficits," in John Sargent, ed., *Fiscal and Monetary Policy* (University of Toronto Press, 1986), pp. 43–84.

Buiter, William H. "A Guide to Public Sector Debt and Deficits," *Economic Policy: A European Forum* (November 1985), pp. 14–79.

Carlson, Keith M. "How Much Lower Can the Unemployment Rate Go?," this *Review* (July/August 1988), pp. 44–57.

_____. "Federal Fiscal Policy Since the Employment Act of 1946," this *Review* (December 1987), pp. 14–30.

de Leeuw, Frank, and Thomas M. Holloway. "The High-Employment Budget and Potential Output: A Response," *Survey of Current Business* (November 1982), pp. 33–35.

Eisner, Robert. "The Revolution Restored: Keynesian Unemployment, Inflation and Budget Deficits," *Eastern Economic Journal* (July-September 1986), pp. 217–21.

Erceg, John J., and Theodore G. Bernard. "Federal Budget Deficits: Sources and Forecasts," Federal Reserve Bank of Cleveland, *Economic Commentary* (March 15, 1988).

Evans, Paul. "Are Consumers Ricardian? Evidence for the United States," *Journal of Political Economy* (October 1988), pp. 983–1004.

Fellner, William. "The High-Employment Budget and Potential Output: A Critique," *Survey of Current Business* (November 1982), pp. 26–33.

Fischer, Stanley. "Long Term Contracts, Rational Expectations, and the Optimal Money Supply Rule," *Journal of Political Economy* (February 1977), pp. 191–205.

Friedman, Milton. "The Role of Monetary Policy," *The American Economic Review* (March 1968), pp. 1–17.

Gordon, Robert J., ed. *The American Business Cycle: Continuity and Change,* NBER (University of Chicago Press, 1986).

Heilbroner, Robert L. "The Importance of Red Ink: How I Learned to Love the Deficit," *The New York Times,* September 4, 1988.

Kochin, Levis A. "Are Future Taxes Anticipated by Consumers?" *Journal of Money, Credit and Banking* (August 1974), pp. 385–94.

Koray, Faik, and R. Carter Hill. "Money, Debt, and Economic Activity," *Journal of Macroeconomics* (Summer 1988), pp. 351–70.

Kotlikoff, Laurence J. "What Macroeconomics Teaches Us about the Dynamic Macro Effects of Fiscal Policy," *Journal of Money, Credit and Banking* (August 1988, Part 2), pp. 479–95.

Laidler, David. "Taking Money Seriously," *Canadian Economic Journal* (forthcoming).

Lebergott, Stanley. "Discussion," *The Journal of Economic History* (June 1986), pp. 367–71.

Leiderman, Leonardo, and Assaf Razin. "Testing Ricardian Neutrality with an Intertemporal Stochastic Model," *Journal of Money, Credit and Banking* (February 1988), pp. 1–21.

Leijonhufvud, Axel. "Constitutional Constraints on the Monetary Powers of Governments," in James A. Dorn and Anna J. Schwartz, ed., *The Search for Stable Money: Essays on Monetary Reform* (University of Chicago Press, 1987).

Levy, Michael E. *Fiscal Policy, Cycles and Growth* (The Conference Board, 1963).

Levy, Michael E., et. al. *Federal Budget Deficits and The U.S. Economy* (The Conference Board, 1984).

Liesner, Thelma. *Economic Statistics: 1900–1983* (The Economist Publications Ltd., 1985).

Mankiw, N. Gregory. "Recent Developments in Macroeconomics: A Very Quick Refresher Course," *Journal of Money, Credit and Banking* (August 1988, Part 2), pp. 436–49.

McCallum, Bennett T. "Are Bond-financed Deficits Inflationary?: A Ricardian Analysis," *Journal of Political Economy* (February 1984), pp. 123–35.

_____. "On 'Real' and 'Sticky-Price' Theories of the Business Cycle," *Journal of Money, Credit and Banking* (November 1986), pp. 397–414.

Modigliani, Franco. "Comment on R. J. Barro, 'U.S. Deficits Since World War I,' " *The Scandinavian Journal of Economics,* Vol. 88, No. 1 (1986a), pp. 223–34.

_____. *The Debate over Stabilization Policy* (Cambridge University Press, 1986b).

Mundell, R. A. "Capital Mobility and Stabilization Policy under Fixed and Flexible Exchange Rates," *The Canadian Journal of Economics and Political Science* (November 1963), pp. 475–85.

The New Keynesian Microfoundations: "Discussion," in *NBER Macroeconomics Annual 1987* (1987), pp. 114–16.

Niehans, Jurg. "Classical Monetary Theory, New and Old," *Journal of Money, Credit and Banking* (November 1987), pp. 409–24.

O'Driscoll, Gerald P., Jr. "The Ricardian Nonequivalence Theorem," *Journal of Political Economy* (February 1977), pp. 207–10.

Phelps, Edmund S. "Phillips Curves, Expectations of Inflation, and Optimal Unemployment Over Time," *Economica* (August 1967), pp. 254–81.

Phillips, A. W. "The Relation Between Unemployment and the Rate of Change of Money Wage Rates in the United Kingdom, 1861–1957," *Economica* (November 1958), pp. 283–99.

Prescott, Edward C. "Comment," *NBER Macroeconomics Annual 1987,* pp. 110–14.

Romer, Christina D. "Is the Stabilization of the Postwar Economy a Figment of the Data?" *The American Economic Review* (June 1986a), pp. 314–34.

_____. "Spurious Volatility in Historical Unemployment Data," *Journal of Political Economy* (February 1986b), pp. 1–37.

_____. "New Estimates of Prewar Gross National Product and Unemployment," *The Journal of Economic History* (June 1986c), pp. 341–52.

_____. "World War I and the Post War Depression: A Reinterpretation Based on Alternative Estimates of GNP," *Journal of Monetary Economics* (July 1988), pp. 91–115.

Rotemberg, Julio J. "The New Keynesian Microfoundations," *NBER Macroeconomics Annual 1987*, pp. 69–104.

Seater, John J. "Does Government Debt Matter?: A Review," *Journal of Monetary Economics* (July 1985), pp. 121–32.

Sickel, Daniel E. "Business Cycle Asymmetry: A Deeper Look," unpublished manuscript, Board of Governors of the Federal Reserve System (1988).

Sturrock, John, and George Iden. "Deficits and Interest Rates: Theoretical Issues and Empirical Evidence," Congressional Budget Office Staff Working Paper (1988).

Taylor, John B. "Aggregate Dynamics and Staggered Contracts," *Journal of Political Economy* (February 1980), pp. 1–23.

Tanner, J. Ernest. "An Empirical Investigation of Tax Discounting," *Journal of Money, Credit and Banking* (May 1979), pp. 214–18.

Thornton, Daniel L. "The Government Budget Constraint with Endogenous Money," *Journal of Macroeconomics* (Winter 1984), pp. 57–67.

_____. "Monetizing the Debt," this *Review* (December 1984b), pp. 30–43.

Weir, David R. "The Reliability of Historical Macroeconomic Data for Comparing Cyclical Stability," *The Journal of Economic History* (June 1986), pp. 353–65.

Appendix C
Why Do Forecasts Differ?

Stephen K. McNees *Federal Reserve Bank of Boston, Boston, Massachusetts*

Reprinted from the New England Economic Review, *Jan./Feb. 1989, Published by the Federal Reserve Bank of Boston. This article is based on a chapter from* Econometric Model Comparison, *L. R. Klein (ed.), New York: Oxford University Press (1989).*

Experts typically have a wide variety of views on the future economic environment. Insofar as their views are based on explicit, systematic methods of assessing economic information, we can say forecasts differ because forecasters use different models. However, even if everyone used the same model, all forecasts would not be identical. First, most models are conditional; the predicted outcome depends on the specific input assumptions a forecaster uses to solve the model. A single model can generate an infinite number of forecasts, depending on what assumptions are made. Second, forecasters have different beliefs about the degree to which the predictive value of all information can be fully captured by a formal model. Some econometricians place their faith solely in their model and regard judgmental adjustments of their models as "unscientific" and more likely than not to be counterproductive. Other forecasters, typically those whose models have evolved, or even dissolved, are more open to the possibility that special events that cannot be formally modeled from historical data can still have predictive values. Differences in these attitudes affect the extent to which mechanically generated forecasts are modified.

Most forecasts, in other words, reflect a complex interaction among three elements: (1) a model, (2) the conditioning information or input assumptions used to generate a model forecast, and (3) the model user's attempts to incorporate extra-model information through judgmental adjustments.

Unfortunately, little is known about the relative importance of these elements. This article addresses three kinds of questions:

(1) What are the relative roles of the model and the modeler in generating a forecast? To what extent do forecasts reflect judgments by the forecaster in the form of input assumptions and judgmental adjustments?

(2) Why do ex ante forecasts differ? Clearly, different forecasters use different models. In addition, individual forecasters adopt different as-

sumptions about future macroeconomic policy and economic developments in the rest of the world. Forecasters also have different philosophies about how much to override the mechanically generated model results with their own judgment. Do these differences in assumptions and adjustments increase the dispersion of forecasts, exaggerating differences among models, or do they decrease the dispersion of forecasts, masking larger differences in what the models would predict on the basis of a common set of assumptions and adjustments?

(3) What are the sources of forecast errors? Do modelers' adjustments help or hurt forecast accuracy? When, in particular, have they helped and when have they hurt? Does lack of knowledge about future input variables impair forecast accuracy? Or, as some previous research indicates, can modelers somehow compensate for the deficiencies of their models through judicious choice of forecast assumptions?

A project designed to shed some light on these questions has been undertaken under the auspices of the Model Comparison Seminar, chaired by Lawrence Klein and sponsored by the National Bureau of Economic Research supported by the National Science Foundation. The initial stage, starting in early 1986, has been the collection of relevant data, a laborious and time-consuming part of the project. The following results are a preliminary report on an ongoing effort. The conclusions, based on the limited experience so far, must be regarded as highly tentative. Any success that has been achieved should be largely credited to the modelers who participated in this exercise.

I. An Overview

This article compares model solutions based on different sets of conditioning information. In general, a model can be thought of as a conditional statement about the relationship between inputs (Xs) and outputs (Ys), or $Y = f(X)$.

The most frequently observed model solution, the ex ante published forecast, or $(Y^{P,i})$, is the model solution based on the individual forecaster's expected values of the input variables (EX) and any judgmental adjustments (Ad) he chooses to make.

(1) $Y^{P,i} = f(EX^i) + Ad^i$.

The mechanically generated forecast, $Y^{m,i}$, is the solution of the model based on the individual modeler's input assumptions and a fixed, predetermined rule for adjustments based on the pattern of recent residuals,

(2) $Y^{m,i} = f(EX^i) + Rule^i$.

A comparison of the published and mechanical forecasts, (1) and (2), measures the importance for Y forecasts of the non-routine adjustments made in generating the published forecast.

The conditional model forecast, $Y^{C,i}$, is the model solution based on a common input assumption, $E\bar{X}$, as well as the rule,

(3) $Y^{C,i} = f(E\bar{X}) + Rule^i$.

Note that the individual modeler has no influence on the conditional model forecast, above and beyond that of constructing the model and the explicit adjustment rule. A rule, once it has been formalized, can properly be regarded as part of the model, as some models already include some form of residual adjustment in their estimation procedures. A comparison of the conditional model forecast and the mechanical forecast, (2) and (3), constitutes a measure of the role of the modeler's individual input assumptions relative to common assumptions. In fact, models employ many different kinds of input assumptions, a matter pursued more fully below.

The ex post forecast, $Y^{ep,i}$, is the model solution based on the actual values of the input assumptions, X, which are of course not observed until after the forecast period has ended.

(4) $Y^{ep,i} = f(X) + Rule^i$.

A comparison of the conditional model forecast and the ex post model solution, (3) and (4), reveals the importance of the knowledge of the actual values of the input variables relative to the common values that were assumed before the fact. The difference between the ex post model solution and the actual historic outcome will be regarded as the model error, the discrepancy between the actual value of Y and the value that the model indicates conditioned on the actual historic input information.

In summary, comparisons of model solutions based on varying sets of input information provide measures of the relative importance of the various factors that are blended together to generate a model-based forecast: the judgmental adjustments, the modeler's assumptions, and the model per se.

II. Model Adjustment Procedures

Most forecasters adjust their mechanically generated, "pure model" results to try to account for a multitude of considerations outside of their formal model or its inputs. These factors can range from the mundane—for example, the incoming high-frequency data indicate that the forecast of lower-frequency data is likely to be wrong—to the purely subjective—the results look "unreasonable" for no stated reason—to the nefarious—the results are manipulated to induce the forecast user to adopt a certain course of action. Because the rationales for these adjustments are seldom documented, different commentators characterize adjustments in different ways.

Conceptually, forecasters could be asked to document their motives for each adjustment and these could be categorized to assess the extent to which the adjustments are "scientific," that is, grounded in theory or evidence. Because the object of this exercise is to compare models rather than various forms of judgment, for the purpose of this exercise the participants decided to permit only adjustments that could be written down explicitly in the form of a predetermined rule based on observed residuals. Each modeler was permitted to devise the rule for his own model, or even a different rule for each equation in the model, but it was agreed that the rules, once adopted, would not be changed over time. With no room for individual discretion, once these adjustment rules were formulated, adopting this convention amounts to redefining the model as the model plus the appended adjustment rules. Except for published forecasts, all forecasts examined below employ the adjustment rule and no adjustments.

III. Input Assumptions

Even if there were only one model, it would be a challenge to understand how that model performed and the inputs used to generate forecasts with that model. In fact, because there are numerous alternative models and one wishes not only to understand each but to contrast and compare them, comparisons must confront the fact that model outcomes (Ys) are conditioned on the assumed values of the input variables (Xs) used to solve the model. This fact poses a dilemma: (1) On the one hand, Ys based on *any* Xs other than their actual values cannot be compared to the actual Ys to assess the model's accuracy. Counterfactual values of Xs can either increase or decrease discrepancies between the model solution and the actual outcome. To isolate the performance of a model defined as a conditional statement, the model must be solved with the actual Xs.

Ex ante forecasts intermingle the quality of the model with the skills of the model user in selecting future values of input assumptions. A clever model user may compensate for a deficient model by judicious choice of inputs. A foolish model user could confound even a perfect model by providing unreliable inputs. Ex ante forecast accuracy therefore does not provide a clear comparison of models as conditional statements. This is the reason why early model comparisons focused on ex post simulations, where none of the error can be attributed to counterfactual Xs. (2) On the other hand, different models are conditional on different, non-overlapping, sometimes even logically inconsistent, input information sets. Due to these differences in their "degree of exogeneity," comparisons of ex post simulations can be difficult to interpret. Models that require large amounts of input enjoy an informational advantage from the actual values of these additional variables in an ex post simulation.

Each forecast reflects a complex interaction among the model, the input assumptions, and the forecaster's judgmental adjustments.

The first step in this exercise was to examine the input assumption (or "exogenous variable") set of each participating model. That examination confirmed that models differ greatly in the informational input they require. Even when all models embody the same broad concept, such as "monetary policy" or economic growth outside the United States, typically each model uses a different specific measure of that concept. Complete standardization would therefore require supplementary procedures for reconciling alternative concepts and measures. Without building a supermodel to encompass all individual models, complete standardization across fairly similar models is virtually impossible. When different models adopt logically inconsistent assumptions, standardization becomes literally impossible.

Despite such differences, all of these models contain similar types of input assumptions.[2] For example, all participating models employ some assumptions about fiscal and monetary policy. The most obvious standardization of input assumptions is to solve each model on a common set of policy assumptions. With regard to fiscal policy, all models were constrained to follow common paths of nominal federal expenditures and were requested to introduce no changes in the tax code beyond those that had already been legislated.

Standardization for monetary policy was more difficult because of the lack of a consensus on the appropriate instrument to represent monetary policy. Rather than attempt to resolve this long-standing controversy, forecasts were generated under two alternative monetary policy assumptions—a given path of M1 and also a given path of short-term interest rates (the federal funds rate, or, for some models, identical changes in the Treasury bill rate).

All these models are also conditioned on input assumptions about economic developments in the rest of the world (ROW). These models vary greatly in the extent to which their external sectors are developed and disaggregated. A complete model of the world economy might require information on ROW macro policies, and perhaps the world price of oil, providing extensive linkages between these and the U.S. economy. At the other extreme, some models were developed essentially as closed models of the U.S. economy, excluding all these linkages and treating only real exports and import prices as input variables. The appropriate standardization for the world model would require other modelers to develop the additional linkages between foreign economies and the U.S. economy. This could be expected to change the character of these models. In order to "let the models be models," standardization for the ROW was made on the basis of the "lowest common denominator"—the closed economy model with the least-developed external sectors. Specifically, the closed economy forecasts are all based on the same assumptions about the path of real exports and the import price deflator. Auxiliary assumptions were provided on the world price of oil, ROW real growth, and ROW inflation rates to help the more open economy models conform to the common external assumptions.

This exercise did not attempt to standardize across all input assumptions but only for two different, important types of assumptions: macroeconomic policy and external sector. Extending the notation introduced earlier, the published forecast ($Y^{P,i}$) becomes:

$$(1a)\ Y^{P,i} = f\ (EP^i,\ EX^i,\ EO^i) + Ads^i.$$

Here EP^i, EX^i, EO^i are, respectively, the individual forecaster's policy assumptions, external sector assumptions and other input assumptions. The mechanical forecast becomes:

$$(2a)\ Y^{m,i} = f(EP^i,\ EX^i,\ EO^i) + Rule^i.$$

The conditional model forecast now consists of two parts:

The open economy forecast,

$$(3a)\ Y^{o,i} = f(E\overline{P},\ EX^i,\ EO^i) + Rule^i,$$

and the closed economy forecast,

$$(3b)\ Y^{c,i} = f(E\overline{P},\ E\overline{X},\ EO^i) + Rule.$$

A comparison of the mechanical forecast with the open economy forecast, $(2a) - (3a)$, measures the impact of the individual modeler's macro policy assumptions relative to the common assumption. A comparison of the open economy forecast with the closed economy forecast, $(3a) - (3b)$, illustrates the importance of the individual modeler's treatment of the external sector relative to the common assumption. Even the mechanical model solution with common policy and external sector assumptions depends on the modeler's assumptions about other input variables. It, like all ex ante forecasts, does not isolate the role of the model as a conditional statement. The model is isolated only in an ex post simulation:

$$(4)\ Y^{ep,i} = f(P,\ X,\ O) + Rule,$$

when P, X, and O are actual values.

In principle, any values could be used as the common core input assumptions. In fact, some combinations of input variables may be economically or politically infeasible. One way to try to avoid such inconsistencies would be to employ one individual's assumptions as the common ones. This would ensure that the common assumptions were consistent in at least one individual's eyes. In this case, the common input assumptions imposed on the models were a simple average among several forecasters, only some of whom participated in this project. Under this approach, the results measure the impact of an individual modeler's assumptions relative to "the" consensus view that is prevailing among forecasters generally.

IV. The Preliminary Results

The array of data collected so far is a rich one, covering 21 variables, each over an eight-quarter horizon for as many as eight models under as many as six sets of input assumptions. Some models participated in the early rounds, but subsequently dropped out for a variety of reasons. Other models joined the project after the first two rounds had been completed. The results presented here cover the five models that participated in the six sets of forecasts conducted in 1987 and early 1988. The results focus on two of the most important variables, the real GNP growth and the inflation rate, over three horizons—the first year, the second year, and the first two years.

Recall that the models were simulated under two alternative representations of monetary policy—a common M1 path and a common short-term interest rate path. The dispersion among the real GNP forecasts was smaller under the common M1 assumption than under the common interest rate assumption, while the dispersion of the inflation rate forecasts was about the same. The rest of this article deals only with the common interest rate path representation of monetary policy, because one of the regularly participating models does not contain an M1 variable.

The results are grouped into three sections—forecast dispersion, forecast decomposition, and error decomposition—that correspond to the three questions posed in the introduction to this article.

Forecast Dispersion

The answer to the question "Why do forecasts differ?" depends critically on the variable of interest. For example, while real GNP forecasts differ primarily because the underlying models differ, mechanically generated model predictions of the inflation rate based on common assumptions are somewhat more similar than published inflation rate forecasts. (See table 1.) This result reflects the differential impacts of individual forecasters' assumptions relative to common "consensus" assumptions and adjustments of their model forecasts.

Forecasters' choices of external assumptions have had a negligible impact on the dispersion of their real growth forecasts but a major impact on the dispersion of their inflation rate forecasts. This reflects both the diversity of opinion about future import prices and the different sensitivities across models to changes in import prices.

In contrast, the individual forecasters' choices of policy assumptions had a fairly small impact on the dispersion of their inflation rate forecasts over a two-year horizon, but a major impact on the dispersion of their real GNP forecasts. This result can be interpreted as illustrating the modeler's role as an implicit reaction function or policy rule that tends to push real

Table 1

Sources of Forecast Dispersion
Ranges, Annual Growth Rates

	(1) 1st Year	(2) 2nd Year	(3) Two Years
Real GNP			
Closed	3.4	3.6	2.7
Policy	2.8	3.4	2.5
Mechanical	2.6	2.5	1.8
Published	1.3	2.6	1.4
Inflation Rate			
Closed	1.7	2.3	1.8
Policy	2.6	3.0	2.8
Mechanical	2.9	3.3	3.1
Published	2.0	2.4	2.1

Closed: Mechanical forecasts with common policy and external sector assumptions.
Policy: Mechanical forecasts with common policy assumptions.
Mechanical: Mechanical forecasts with individual assumptions.
Published: Forecasts with individual assumptions and adjustments.

GNP back toward a satisfactory path. Specifically, if a model exhibits particularly weak (strong) real growth, the modeler is likely to employ more stimulative (restrictive) macroeconomic policy assumptions in his forecast. It is interesting to note that the implicit policy rule emphasizes stabilizing real GNP growth, not the inflation rate, at least over a two-year horizon.

The forecasters' adjustments virtually always work to make the forecasts more similar. Their importance is relatively large for the dispersion of inflation rate forecasts and of real GNP forecasts in the first, though not the second, year of the forecast period. This tendency of convergence toward the consensus may reflect a greater reluctance to rely on the model as the model deviates further from the consensus. The consensus view, for example, may be the most likely outcome and the model an indicator of the most likely deviation from the mode. For real GNP, the tendency to adjust the forecast toward the consensus reinforces the unifying impact of individual policy assumptions, so that published forecasts are far more similar than mechanical model forecasts based on common assumptions. For the inflation rate, the unifying adjustments serve to offset the diverging impact of individual external sector assumptions, so that the dispersion of published forecasts is about the same as the dispersion of standardized model forecasts.

Table 2

Importance of Three Forms of Forecasters' Judgment

Mean Absolute Change (Percentage Points)

	Real GNP			Inflation Rate		
	External Sector Assumptions (1)	Policy Assumptions (2)	Adjustments (3)	External Sector Assumptions (4)	Policy Assumptions (5)	Adjustments (6)
First Year						
Model 1	.7	.2	.4	.5	0	.9
Model 2	.3	1.0	1.1	.4	.8	1.1
Model 3	.3	1.1	0	.8	.1	0
Model 4	1.5	1.1	.7	.6	.5	.8
Model 5	.4	.2	.8	0	0	.6
Mean	.6	.7	.6	.5	.3	.7
Second Year						
Model 1	.9	.3	.6	.4	0	.9
Model 2	.1	1.2	.9	1.0	1.1	1.8
Model 3	.6	.3	0	.9	.2	0
Model 4	1.4	.9	.8	.7	.5	1.5
Model 5	.8	.3	.7	.1	0	.9
Mean	.8	.6	.6	.6	.4	1.0
Two Years						
Model 1	.8	.3	.4	.4	0	.9
Model 2	.2	.7	.6	.7	.9	1.5
Model 3	.2	.7	0	.8	.1	0
Model 4	.4	.4	.6	.7	.5	1.2
Model 5	.5	.2	.7	.1	0	.7
Mean	.4	.5	.5	.5	.3	.9

Forecast Decomposition

These data also help to measure the relative roles of the model and the modeler in generating a forecast. In table 2 the modeler's role is decomposed into three parts: the impact of external sector assumptions, measured as the difference between the forecast based on common policy assumptions and the forecast based on common assumptions for both policy and the external sector; the impact of policy assumptions, measured as the difference between the forecast based on common policy assumptions and the one based on the modeler's individual policy assumptions; and the impact of adjustments, measured as the difference between the published and mechanical forecasts. We focus on the mean *absolute* differences rather than the mean differences to avoid equating a forecaster who never makes adjustments

(for example, model 3) with a forecaster whose upward adjustments just happen to be as large as his downward adjustments. The results vary by both model and variable. For real GNP over a two-year horizon, adjustments were most important for models 4 and 5, policy assumptions for models 2 and 3, and external sector assumptions for model 1. For these five models taken as a group, each of these three forms of modeler's judgment is roughly equally important for each of the forecast horizons examined.

For the inflation rate, adjustments have the largest impact on the forecasts of four of the five models. The only exception was model 3, which was never adjusted and where the external sector assumptions were the most important form of judgment embodied in the inflation forecast. Differences in policy assumptions had relatively little impact on the inflation rate forecasts, except for model 2.

Combining the information on forecast dispersion with the information on the impact of assumptions and adjustments suggests a stylized description of the forecasting process: (1) When different models are solved initially with "consensus" values of external sector and policy assumptions, real growth forecasts differ by more than 3 percentage points and inflation rate forecasts by less than 2 percentage points. (2) When the modelers impose their individual assumptions, real growth forecasts converge (reflecting a real-growth-stabilizing implicit policy rule) but inflation rate forecasts diverge further. (3) Judgmental adjustments are imposed to narrow forecast dispersion, offsetting the divisive impact of individual assumptions on the inflation rate and reinforcing the converging impact on real growth forecasts.

The mean absolute deviation of the published real GNP forecasts from the average or "consensus" published forecast is about half as large as the deviation of "pure model" forecasts based on common assumptions. In contrast, the mean absolute deviation of the published inflation forecasts from the consensus forecast is about the same as the deviation of "pure model" forecasts based on common "consensus" assumptions. The net effect of the individual modelers' assumptions and adjustments is to draw their real GNP forecasts together—the forecasts are more similar than the models. The *net* effect is essentially nil for their inflation rate forecasts—the dispersion among published forecasts is similar to the dispersion among models, once the role of the individual modeler has been minimized.

Over this period the models, as a group, based on common consensus assumptions, generated higher forecasts of both real growth and inflation rates than the published forecasts. About half of the difference was due to adjustments, the other half due to the individual modelers' non-consensus assumptions.

Error Decomposition

All of the preceding information describes the evolution of individual ex ante forecasts and the dispersion of those forecasts. We have seen how the forecasters' judgments affect their forecasts and the disparity among forecasts. This section describes two forecast periods for which the actual outcome is now known. This enables us to examine not only how judgments affect the forecasts but also whether they aid or impair the accuracy of the forecast.

Chart 1 shows the quite general tendency to overestimate real GNP from 1986:I to 1987:IV, especially early in the period. For models 1 and 3, the extent of overestimation was greater with the actual values of exogenous variables than with any set chosen ex ante. The forecaster's own ex ante assumptions led to slightly better forecasts than did imposing consensus assumptions. For model 2, the overestimation was worse with the common, ex ante assumptions and less with the forecaster's individual assumptions than with their actual values. For models 1 and 2, the published, adjusted forecasts were less accurate than the mechanically generated forecasts.

Chart 2 shows forecasts of the deflator for personal consumption expenditures over the same period. The ex ante forecasts from models 1 and 3 tended to underestimate the price level. The ex ante forecast of model 2 was quite accurate. Using the actual values of the exogenous variables, the model 1 forecast remained too low, the model 2 forecast started to overestimate, and model 3's forecast became highly accurate. The proprietor of model 2 was able to offset his model's deficiencies to give "the right forecast for the wrong reasons." In contrast, model 3's ex ante error was solely attributable to the modeler's ex ante choice of assumptions; the model as a conditional statement was on track.

Individual modelers' assumptions and adjustments draw their real GNP forecasts together, while the net effect is virtually nil for their inflation rate forecasts.

Charts 3 and 4 graph the ex ante forecasts, ex post simulations, and actual data for the period from 1986:III through 1988:II. Chart 3 shows that all these forecasts tracked real GNP fairly closely. While the ex post forecasts of model 1 were somewhat better than its ex ante forecasts, the ex post forecasts of model 3 were somewhat worse. The adjustments to models 1 and 2 improved their forecasts, particularly early in the period.

Chart 4 shows the inflation forecasts over the same period. Ex ante, model 1 forecasts were quite accurate, the forecasts of models 2 and 3 were too low. However, with actual values of the exogenous

Chart 1   *Forecasts of Real GNP,*
                            1986:I to 1987:IV

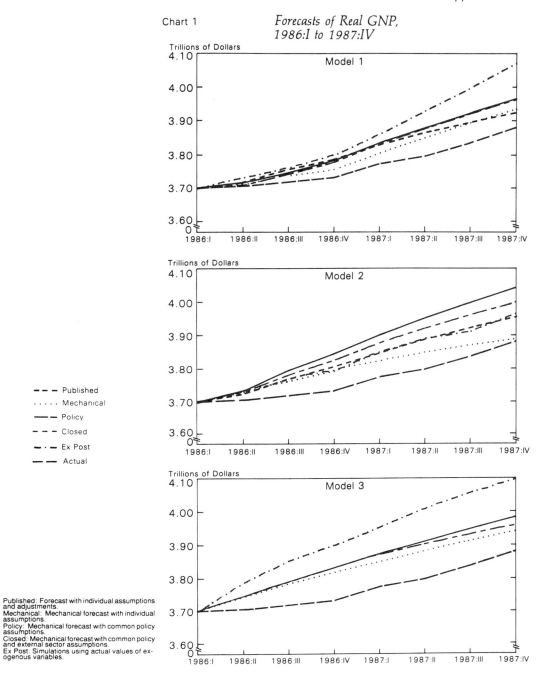

- – – Published
- · · · · Mechanical
- —— Policy
- – – Closed
- –·– Ex Post
- —— Actual

Published: Forecast with individual assumptions
and adjustments.
Mechanical: Mechanical forecast with individual
assumptions.
Policy: Mechanical forecast with common policy
assumptions.
Closed: Mechanical forecast with common policy
and external sector assumptions.
Ex Post: Simulations using actual values of exogenous variables.

Chart 2   *Forecasts of the Personal Consumption Deflator 1986:I to 1987:IV*

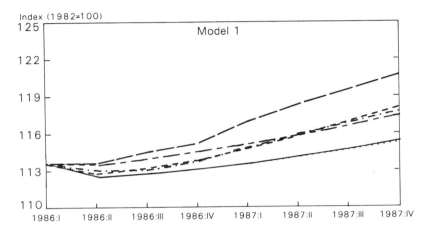

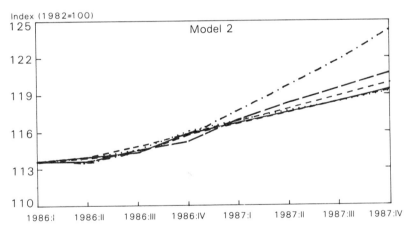

Published
Mechanical
Policy
Closed
Ex Post
Actual

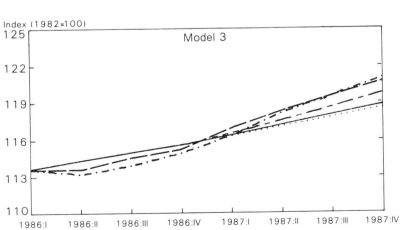

Note: See chart 1 for explanation of key.

Chart 3   *Forecasts of Real Gross National Product,*
               1986:III to 1988:II

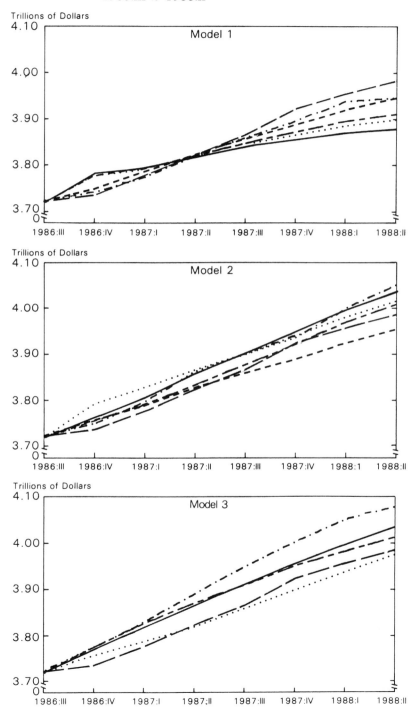

Note: See chart 1 for explanation of key.

Chart 4 *Forecasts of Personal Consumption
Deflator 1986:III to 1988:II*

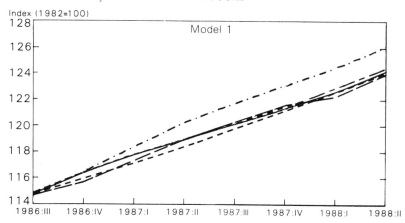

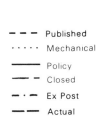

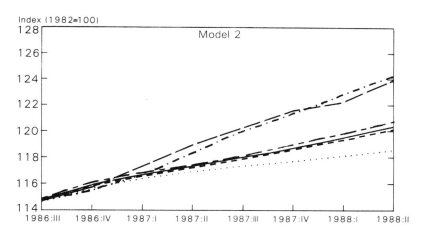

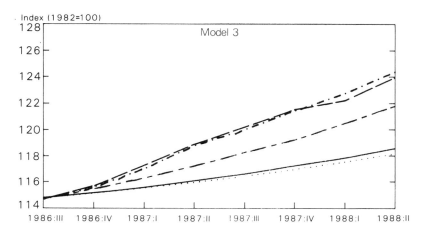

Note: See chart 1 for explanation of key.

variables, the forecasts of models 2 and 3 were quite accurate and model 1's forecast was slightly too high.

V. Summary and Conclusions

The article opened by posing three questions. This conclusion summarizes the limited evidence that has been presented.

(1) Although the importance of judgment adjustments varies among individual models, for the models as a group the choices of macro policy assumptions and external sector assumptions, relative to consensus assumptions, are as important to real GNP forecasts and nearly as important to inflation forecasts as are modelers' judgmental adjustments (table 2).

(2) The reason for the dispersion among forecasts depends critically on the variables analyzed. The differences between the modeler's individual policy assumptions and the consensus assumptions tend to narrow differences in real GNP forecasts. Differences between individual and consensus external sector assumptions tend to increase the disparity among inflation forecasts. Model adjustments seem to narrow the dispersion among forecasts of both real GNP and the price level.

(3) Judgmental adjustments can either help or hurt. This evidence shows instances of both "good" judgment and "bad" judgment, depending primarily on which forecast period is examined. The adjustments hurt the real GNP forecasts of models 1 and 2 in the first forecast period, but helped in the second period, especially for model 2 in the short term. Adjustments had little impact on the inflation forecasts. The sole exception is for model 1 in the first round, when adjustments improved the inflation forecast at the same time they hurt the real GNP forecasts. This evidence is not consistent with the widespread belief that mechanically generated forecasts are wildly inaccurate compared to adjusted forecasts. It is consistent, however, with the view that judgmental adjustments can either help or hurt. Other evidence, covering longer periods, does suggest that adjustments do tend to help on average over time, but very little is known about when adjustments are likely to hurt and when they are likely to help.

(4) Consensus ex ante assumptions do not necessarily produce a more accurate forecast than individual assumptions. Two very different concepts of a model coexist. To some, the main virtue of using a model is that it gives the same answer to a precise question regardless of who poses the question. A

model can be viewed as a disembodied system or formula like the laws of the natural sciences, totally independent of who uses it. From this perspective, there is no particular reason to believe that the person who built a model will necessarily be more skilled in formulating ex ante assumptions to generate a model-based forecast. If the model and the forecast assumptions were totally independent, there is no particular reason to think the model builder's individual assumptions would produce a more accurate forecast than any other feasible set of assumptions, such as the consensus assumptions.

Others tend to think of models, at least in a forecasting context, as tools the forecaster can use to enhance his skills. Just as not all craftsmen use the same kind of tools and not all athletes use the same brand of equipment, the performances of the model and the modeler are not independent and the two must be viewed as a team. Under this view, a model builder is in the best position to know the particular characteristics of his model and would, therefore, be especially capable of selecting ex ante assumptions to generate more accurate forecasts. Any externally imposed assumptions, such as the ad hoc consensus assumptions, would be less likely to be compatible with a specific model.

The evidence provides some insight into which of these perspectives is the more fruitful. Fortunately, these data are fairly clear across models and forecast periods. Unfortunately, the results differ depending on which variable is examined. Individual assumptions tend to produce more accurate real GNP forecasts than the common or consensus assumptions, reflecting perhaps the forecasters' implicit policy reaction function which attaches major importance to stabilizing real GNP. In contrast, the common consensus assumptions tended to produce more accurate inflation forecasts than the modeler's own individual assumptions. This result is more consistent with the traditional view of a model as independent of the model user. The individual's unique knowledge of the model is not particularly helpful for generating accurate inflation forecasts, at least over a two-year horizon.

(5) Model (ex post) accuracy versus forecast accuracy cannot be predicted on the basis of the evidence presented here. Forecast errors may either overestimate or underestimate the deficiency of a model viewed as a conditional relationship between input and output variables.

The input assumptions chosen ex ante to generate a forecast are bound to be counterfactual. To the extent that the actual assumptions enhance accuracy, the forecast error overstates the deficiency in the conditional model. In practice, much evidence suggests that the counterfactual (ex ante) assumptions work to offset model deficiences—that ex post model solutions, those based on actual input assumptions, are typically inferior to the ex ante forecast. These results are consistent with the view in Lucas (1976) that conditional models are flawed but that the model users can somehow offset these model deficiencies and generate reliable ex ante forecasts.

The limited evidence on this issue presented here is extremely mixed. For model 3, the ex post forecasts of real GNP were distinctly inferior to the ex ante real GNP forecasts, but the inflation forecasts were clearly superior. For model 1, the ex post real GNP forecasts were distinctly inferior in the first forecast but somewhat superior in the second period,

when ex post inflation rate simulations were inferior to the ex ante. The results for model 2 are even more ambiguous, except for the inflation rate in the second forecast period where the ex post simulation was more accurate than the ex ante forecasts. This evidence, in other words, does not provide support for either extreme position on the relative accuracy of ex post and ex ante forecasts.

As noted at the outset, these conclusions are based on a very limited number of observations and may well not hold in the future. The experiment is an ongoing one, to try to determine under what circumstances the conclusions hold and when they do not. In addition, future research on this topic should examine more variables and perhaps include more models. Much more experience will be required to understand why forecasts differ and to evaluate the reasons for their differences.

---

[1] The five models participating were those of Data Resources, Inc. of Lexington, MA; Fairmodel, Macro Inc.; Center for Econometric Model Research, Indiana University; Research Seminar in Quantitative Economics, University of Michigan; Allen Sinai at The Boston Company Inc.

[2] Using what appears to be a more heterogeneous group of models, Wallis et al. (1986) argue that differences in the degree of exogeneity are of little practical importance for comparisons of models of the United Kingdom's economy. Accordingly, they consistently find differences in exogenous variable assumptions account for little of the differences among forecasts.

References

Evans, Michael K., Yoel Haitovsky, and George I. Treyz. 1972. "An Analysis of Forecasting Properties of U.S. Econometric Models." In *Econometric Models of Cyclical Behavior*, Bert G. Hickman, ed. New York: National Bureau of Economic Research.

Haitovsky, Yoel, and George I. Treyz. 1972. "Forecasts with Quarterly Macroeconomic Models, Equation Adjustments, and Benchmark Predictions: The U.S. Experience." *Review of Economics and Statistics*, vol. 54, August, pp. 317–25.

Lucas, Robert E., Jr. 1976. "Econometric policy evaluation: a critique." In *The Phillips Curve and Labor Markets* (Carnegie-Rochester Conferences on Public Policy #1), K. Brunner, and A. H. Meltzer, eds. New York: American Elsevier, pp. 19–46.

Wallis, K. F. ed. 1984–87. *Models of the UK Economy: A Review by ESRC Macroeconomic Modelling Bureau*, vols. 1–4. New York: Oxford University Press.

Appendix D
Value-Added Tax Issues for U.S. Policymakers

A study by the staff of the U.S. General Accounting Office. Reprinted from GAO Report GGD-89-125-BR, Sept. 15, 1989.

WHAT IS A VALUE-ADDED TAX?

Multistage tax

A value-added tax is a tax on the value added to a product or service at each stage of the production and distribution process. The tax is collected on the difference between a business' sales and purchases. For example, if a business buys $100 worth of material and equipment and produces a product or service that sells for $150, its value added is $50. The value-added tax is not designed as a tax on business; it is a tax on consumption[1] that is collected throughout the production and distribution process.

Consumption taxes in the United States

A value-added tax is similar to the retail sales and excise taxes used in the United States. The primary difference between a value-added tax and a retail sales tax is the collection point; a retail sales tax is collected only at the point of sale to the ultimate consumer. A value-added tax is levied at each stage of the production and distribution chain.

A value-added tax differs from excise taxes in terms of the tax base as well as the number of collection points. Excise

---

[1]There are value-added tax systems that include investment goods in addition to consumption goods and services in the tax base. These value-added taxes are rarely used by industrialized countries. For the rest of this report, we will discuss only the consumption value-added tax. Other forms of consumption tax, in addition to the value-added tax, are retail sales and consumption expenditure taxes. For a detailed discussion of these alternatives, see Choosing Among Consumption Taxes (GAO/GGD-86-91, August 20, 1986).

taxes are targeted to specific products, whereas a value-
added tax covers a full range of products and services.
Excise taxes are also collected at only one point--generally
at the point of manufacture. The federal government now
levies numerous excise taxes on a wide assortment of products
and services. The taxes on alcoholic beverages, cigarettes,
and motor fuels raise the majority of federal excise tax
revenues.

VALUE-ADDED TAX AS A REVENUE RAISER

A federal value-added tax has tremendous potential for
raising tax revenues. Its value base can be as large as the
consumption component of the gross national product. The
Congressional Budget Office (CBO) has estimated that a
comprehensive 5-percent value-added tax could raise about
$125 billion annually, while one that exempted food,
housing, and medical care could yield about $72 billion. CBO
estimates are based on the projected 1992 tax base.

From discussions with value-added tax experts and a review of
the literature, it appears that many countries originally
introduced a value-added tax on a revenue neutral basis,
later transforming it through rate or base increases to
produce additional revenue. However, according to a 1989
report on consumption taxation by the Organization for
Economic Cooperation and Development (OECD), value-added tax
revenues in most countries have not increased any faster than
any other revenue source. For some examples, see Figure I.1.

**Figure I.1: Value-Added Tax as
Percentage of Total Tax Revenue, 1976
and 1985**

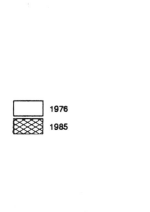

1976
1985

Source: Value-Added Tax: International
Practice and Problems, Alan Tait,
International Monetary Fund, 1988.

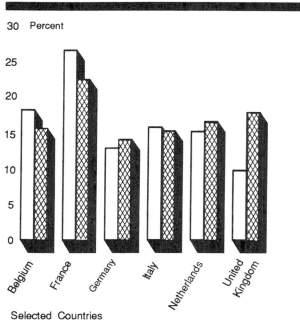

30 Percent

25

20

15

10

5

0

Belgium   France   Germany   Italy   Netherlands   United Kingdom

Selected Countries

HOW A VALUE-ADDED TAX IS CALCULATED

There are two primary methods for calculating a value-added tax--the invoice or tax-credit method and the subtraction method.[2]

Tax-credit: This is the primary method used throughout the world. With this method, the value-added tax is calculated separately for each purchase or sale and included in the price at each stage of the production and distribution system. It is shown separately on all invoices. For the tax period, the taxpayer subtracts the total value-added tax paid on purchases from the value-added tax charged on sales. The difference is the net liability to the government.

The tax-credit method allows great flexibility in the design and use of a value-added tax, enhancing its ability to respond to a variety of tax policy goals. To the extent this flexibility is used, however, the tax would be more complex both in terms of administration and compliance. In the remainder of this report, we refer to a tax-credit method value-added tax, unless otherwise indicated.

Subtraction: For the subtraction method, the tax is calculated once during the reporting period on the total business activity of the taxpayer. It is simply the total value of sales minus the total value of purchases multiplied by the tax rate. The essential characteristic of the subtraction method is that a firm can calculate its value-added tax from its normal books of account. No additional records are required. On April 1, 1989, Japan introduced the only subtraction method value-added tax at a 3-percent rate.

The subtraction method is simple to calculate but may not be fully compatible with certain design features of the tax. For example, should policymakers decide to alleviate regressivity by using multiple tax rates, the subtraction method for calculating the tax will not work properly.

COUNTRIES THAT HAVE ADOPTED
OR CONSIDERED THE TAX

Value-added taxes are widely used throughout the world. Forty-seven countries have introduced a value-added tax over the last 3 decades, including all 12 of the European

---

[2]For additional information on the two methods and the ability to address key tax policy issues under each, see Tax-Credit and Subtraction Methods of Calculating a Value-Added Tax (GAO/GGD-89-87, June 20, 1989).

Economic Community (EEC) member countries and 18 of the 24
OECD member countries. Japan is the most recent OECD member
to adopt a value-added tax.

A number of countries, including Canada, South Africa,
Poland, Thailand, and Iceland, have considered proposals for
introducing a value-added tax. For example, Iceland has
considered for 10 years the introduction of a value-added
tax. It currently has a 25 percent retail sales tax. This
rate of tax has apparently caused concern because the tax
collection responsibilities lie entirely in the hands of
retailers. Suspected tax evasion is one of the primary
reasons for considering a value-added tax. Introduction of
the tax has been delayed, in part due to concern about
administering tax refunds under the system proposed to offset
the regressivity of the tax.[3]

Canada has considered some form of a consumption tax since
June 1987. Recently, the Canadian federal government
outlined a multistage goods and services tax proposal that
is similar to a value-added tax. The proposal was included
in the government's budget for the 1989-90 fiscal year and
will replace the current Canadian manufacturer's sales tax.
The multistage tax will be set at 9 percent and will apply
to a very broad base, including most goods and services sold
throughout Canada. It is expected that legislation to
implement the new tax will be introduced in the Canadian
legislature before the end of 1989, with implementation
scheduled for January 1, 1991.

INTERNATIONAL MOVEMENT TOWARD VALUE-ADDED TAXES

Countries have introduced a value-added tax for different
reasons, depending on their pre-existing tax system and on
whether they were members of the EEC. Adoption of a value-
added tax is a necessary condition for membership in the EEC.
The EEC adopted the value-added tax to replace turnover taxes
as a means of decreasing trade and other economic distortions
among its members. The turnover tax is a tax on sales that
does not allow an offset for taxes paid on purchases. The
result is a tax on a tax.

As its first major step toward tax harmonization, in April
1967, the EEC instructed member states to replace their
existing national consumption tax systems with a value-added

---

[3]Taxes are regressive if low-income families pay a larger
proportion of their income in taxes than do high-income
families. Taxes are progressive if the result is reversed.

tax. Since then the EEC has moved forward with a second
stage of tax harmonization that is much more controversial.
It is attempting to require member countries to standardize
their value-added tax systems to two rates by 1992.

A broad tax reform movement was another major reason for
governments adopting a value-added tax. A revenue-neutral
approach was used by many countries, which often involved
using a value-added tax to increase revenues from general
consumption taxes in order to cut income taxes (Norway, New
Zealand, Austria). Other countries recognized that a
multiplicity of ad hoc sales taxes at different rates was
inefficient both administratively and economically. They
moved to a value-added tax to consolidate and modernize their
tax structures (Chile, Haiti, Hungary, and Korea).

COUNTRIES NOT USING A VALUE-ADDED TAX

A few industrialized countries do not have a value-added tax
system. These include the United States, Switzerland, and
Australia. All but the United States have some type of
broad-based national consumption tax.

Switzerland has a single-stage sales tax that is paid in
most cases at the retail level. The government's proposals
to replace the sales tax with a value-added tax were rejected
by referendum in 1977 and 1979. Other reform proposals have
since been made, but the government has not taken further
actions.

Australia has a wholesale sales tax. In 1985, the
government proposed moving to a retail sales tax. According
to a 1989 OECD report, the government took the view that
administration and compliance costs of a retail sales tax
would be lower than a value-added tax and that the advantage
of a value-added tax in combating tax evasion was
overstated. Further, the government had estimated that it
would take 12 months longer to introduce a value-added tax
than a retail sales tax. However, these retail sales tax
proposals were dropped and reforms were made to the existing
sales tax instead.

MAJOR ARGUMENTS FOR A VALUE-ADDED TAX

Economically neutral

A tax is said to be "neutral" if it does not change the
relative prices of goods and services. If it is assumed that
an economy operates most efficiently when all decisions are
made on the basis of market prices, tax neutrality is a

desirable attribute. A value-added tax preserves neutrality
between capital and labor by taxing the value added by each
factor equally; thus, it creates no incentive for businesses
to substitute one factor for the other. A single-rate value-
added tax also preserves neutrality among goods and services.
However, a value-added tax containing exemptions and multiple
rates is not neutral; lightly taxed or exempted goods and
services are given a price advantage.

Large and predictable revenue source

A federal value-added tax has tremendous revenue potential.
Its base can be as large as the consumption component of the
gross national product. Even allowing exemptions for
necessities and certain industries and groups, each
percentage point of a value-added tax has been estimated to
produce $14 to $15 billion, at least over the range of rates
estimated by CBO. Since consumption spending does not
fluctuate as much as income, a consumption tax would be a
more stable source of revenue than an income tax.

MAJOR ARGUMENTS FOR A VALUE-ADDED TAX

Potentially self-enforcing

Much has been written about a value-added tax being "self-
enforcing." This is predicated on the credit/invoice method
of calculating the tax, in which taxpayers who buy goods or
services for use as inputs in a business activity have an
incentive to obtain an invoice that accurately documents the
tax paid. Without an invoice, the taxpayer cannot claim a
credit for taxes paid against total tax liability. Invoices
allow tax administrators to track taxes owed the government.

Despite this administration advantage, the value-added tax
has not been a perfectly self-policing tax among EEC
countries. It has been reported that various forms of value-
added tax evasion have occurred within the EEC. However, the
full impact or significance of this evasion varies among the
countries, depending upon their tax enforcement activities,
rate structures, and the level of their value-added tax rate.

Not biased against saving

A value-added tax, incurred only when money is spent, is not
biased against saving, while an income tax is said to have
such a bias. Under an income tax, when a family saves more
its tax burden increases, due to the tax on interest. A
consumption tax, such as a value-added tax, has no such bias
since the tax burden does not depend on when funds are
spent, only if they are spent. Value-added tax advocates

claim that by increasing saving the tax would stimulate economic growth. There is no clear consensus as to whether a value-added tax would increase the private sector savings rate in the United States, let alone by how much.

MAJOR ARGUMENTS OPPOSING A VALUE-ADDED TAX

Regressive

Most economists regard the value-added tax as a regressive tax because lower income people use more of their incomes for consumption than higher income people do. The degree to which a value-added tax is regressive depends on the time period over which the regressivity is measured. The value-added tax always appears more regressive when taxes on annual consumption are compared with annual income. If we compare taxes on lifetime consumption with lifetime income, the degree of regressivity is reduced.

Money machine

Some claim that a value-added tax hands government an instrument for enlarging its role and scope. They cite Europe's experience in the 1970s and 1980s when value-added tax rates were increased. They point out that government revenue shortfalls can be met by simply increasing the value-added tax rate. The broad base of a value-added tax allows it to generate large amounts of revenue with small percentage rate increases. This could create a temptation to increase public expenditures.

New tax system for United States

Most industrial countries that have a value-added tax had some earlier experience with a broad-based consumption tax. However, the United States has never had this type of tax at the federal level. To introduce a value-added tax in the United States would require time and start-up costs for new systems, regulations, forms, instructions, and taxpayer education. In addition, the value-added tax would add to the compliance burden of millions of businesses.

Intrudes upon state tax base

State and local jurisdictions that impose sales taxes have a natural opposition to a tax on consumption at the federal level. The federal government has made only limited use of taxes on commodities. States and localities use this tax base extensively. States are concerned that even a low-rate value-added tax could inhibit expanded state use of this tax base in the future.

KEY VALUE-ADDED TAX POLICY ISSUES

A set of key policy issues exists surrounding the design and operation of a value-added tax. These issues include how to deal with the tax's regressivity, the impact of the tax on a country's international trade position, the administration and business compliance aspects of the tax, and the impact of the tax upon state and local tax systems.

KEY POLICY ISSUES: REGRESSIVITY

The value-added tax is considered a regressive tax. Controversy exists, however, over the degree of regressivity and the best method of compensation. In practice, various alternatives have been selected by tax policymakers throughout the world to adjust the distributional impact of a value-added tax. We identified four techniques or alternatives:

1. Multiple tax rates tax necessities at a rate lower than the standard rate and/or luxuries at a higher than standard rate. Also included is the use of zero rating on certain goods and services. Under zero rating, no taxes are collected on sales, but taxes paid on purchases used in production can be claimed as a credit.

2. Exemptions from the value-added tax base include certain items that are considered necessities, such as food, shelter, and health care.

3. A tax credit that is based on estimates of value-added tax paid could be credited against consumption taxes or income taxes.

4. Government transfer payments, such as Social Security, food stamps, or other social benefit programs, could be increased to reflect the tax. Some governments use a portion of value-added tax receipts to increase social program benefits.

KEY POLICY ISSUES: REGRESSIVITY

Option 1: Multiple rates

A recent International Monetary Fund (IMF) report indicates that most countries with a value-added tax use multiple rate systems. It says multiple rates arose in Europe out of a concern that value-added taxes would otherwise be too regressive. Many countries provide a reduced rate for

<u>Table I.1:</u>

<u>Value-Added Tax Rates for EEC</u>
<u>Countries as of January 1987</u>
(Rates in percent)

Country	Standard rate[a]	Rates lower than standard	Rates higher than standard
Belgium	19	1,6,17	25,33
Denmark	22	–	–
France	18.6	2.1,4,5.5,7	33.3
Germany	14	7	–
Greece	18	6	36
Ireland	25	0,2.4,10	–
Italy	18	2,9	38
Luxembourg	12	3,6	–
The Netherlands	20	6	–
Portugal	16	8	30
Spain	12	6	33
United Kingdom	15	0	–

[a] All country rate structures apply a zero rate for exports.

Source: OECD, "Consumption Taxation," January 1989.

necessities. Some also impose increased rates for luxury items. Table I.1 shows that 6 EEC countries use higher rates for luxuries, and 11 countries use reduced rates for necessities.

One of the drawbacks of using multiple rates is that the regressivity offset is not well targeted since a low tax rate on necessities benefits anyone who consumes the good, whether rich or poor. The use of multiple rates also causes administration and compliance problems. Multiple rates require complex regulations to classify goods for each rate. For example, is a chocolate-covered cookie a candy (luxury) or a food product (necessity)? Lastly, multiple rates raise the cost of keeping sales records, especially for small retailers who deal in goods covered by different rates.

Option 2: Exemptions

Exemption is a method for removing firms or goods from the value-added tax system. If a firm is exempt, it does not have to collect any tax or turn over any revenue to the government. While it is not faced with any costs of complying with the tax, an exempt firm gets no rebate on any value-added taxes paid on its purchases from other firms. As a result, an exempt firm will be faced with paying the tax itself or passing it on to purchasers without an accompanying credit.

Countries can exempt goods or services because they are
thought to have a particular value to society as a whole, or
in an attempt to reduce the burden of the tax on low-income
families. For example, 7 countries exempt original art; 12
countries exempt museums; and most countries exempt
educational services, medical services, and rental housing.
There are two problems with using exemptions to address
regressivity: (1) since the exemption usually occurs at the
retail level, all of the tax on previous stages remains; and
(2) any tax relief that is granted goes to all purchasers of
the good, rich or poor.

Option 3: Refundable tax credit

Some value-added tax experts believe that problems with the
regressivity of a value-added tax can best be handled through
the use of a refundable tax credit. The amount of the credit
could be based upon the average amount of value-added tax
paid by a low-income individual or household. Taxpayers may
offset this credit against any income tax liability. Those
who pay less income tax than the amount of the credit,
including those whose income is so low that they do not
currently file an income tax return, would receive a refund
from the government. In this way, the regressive
distribution of the value-added tax burden is offset. New
Zealand uses the refundable credit approach. Also, as of
October 1987, seven states in the United States used this
approach to lessen the burden of state sales taxes upon the
poor.

There are some operational drawbacks to the use of a
refundable tax credit. These include concerns about
designing a credit system that takes into account the
personal circumstances of families and individuals, including
family size, special medical circumstances, and regional cost
of living differences. Also, a system of refundable tax
credits would give rise to a large increase in the number of
people who must file tax returns to claim the credit. This
may cause a large number of people to file tax returns who
otherwise would have no need to file.

Option 4: Social expenditures

Some tax experts believe that it would be easier to
compensate for the regressivity of a value-added tax by
altering the country's social transfer programs. Low income
benefit transfer payments such as Supplemental Security
Income, Food Stamps, Aid to Families with Dependent Children,
or other benefit transfer programs might be used. The
countries of Sweden, Denmark, and Norway use social transfers
to compensate for the distributional effects of a value-added
tax.

One of the drawbacks to using this alternative is that not all low-income individuals and families receive social transfer payments; therefore, the use of social transfer payments would not completely alleviate the burden of the tax on low-income families and individuals. In addition, if all transfer payments, including Social Security, were adjusted, some families with incomes substantially above the poverty level would also benefit.

KEY POLICY ISSUES: INTERNATIONAL TRADE

There are value-added tax supporters who believe that adopting a value-added tax would improve the competitiveness of U.S. industry in international trade. The General Agreements on Tariffs and Trade allow countries using indirect taxes, such as a value-added tax, to rebate the tax on goods being exported and impose it on imports. Such adjustments cannot be made for direct taxes, such as corporate and individual income taxes. However, rebating the tax on exports is not equivalent to subsidizing exports, and imposing the tax on imports is not penalizing imports. The adjustment is needed so imports are not favored in competition with domestic products bearing the value-added tax and for exports to compete with foreign goods not bearing the tax. Without such adjustments, imports would have a price advantage over domestic goods, and exports would have a price disadvantage in foreign markets.

Value-added tax proponents also believe that U.S. foreign competitiveness would improve if a value-added tax replaced part or all of a direct tax like the corporate income tax. Whether such a tax substitution would improve the economic position of U.S. industry abroad depends, in part, on whether the corporate income tax is reflected in prices paid by consumers. If removing part of the tax (through the substitution of a value-added tax) lowers the prices of goods produced by U.S. corporations, the U.S. trade balance might improve for a time. However, most economists, trade, and tax experts believe that any such improvement would be short term and, in the long run, negated by adjustments in exchange rates or the rate of inflation. In general, they do not believe that the U.S. balance of trade problems are affected by the composition (mix of direct and indirect taxes) of the U.S. tax system. Thus, they maintain that the value-added tax should not be enacted in the hope of improving the U.S. balance of trade.

KEY POLICY ISSUES: BUSINESS COMPLIANCE

One of the most important factors affecting costs to both the government and business is the complexity of the value-added tax. Depending upon how the tax is structured and what business a firm is engaged in, the accounting requirements to comply with a value-added tax can be complicated. With multiple rates and exemptions, a firm would have to record separately purchases and sales of items taxed at different rates or exempted. One published study reported that multiple tax rates have been estimated to increase the cost of administering the tax by, on average, 50 to 80 percent. Most of this increase would be due to increased business and government personnel costs.

Some studies have reported that for larger firms, the value-added tax does not appear to impose an unusual accounting burden and that it adds relatively little to a firm's costs (less than 1 percent of a firm's total sales). For smaller operations (for example, small retailers), the accounting and administration requirements may be more burdensome. One tax authority suggests that the accounting costs for smaller businesses may increase 20 percent under a value-added tax.

Some countries exempt businesses from the value-added tax on the basis of sales being less than a certain amount. This is the practice in most countries in the EEC and some countries in Latin America. The advantage of this system is that it reduces tax administration costs with little revenue loss by eliminating the smallest traders from the tax. A drawback is that larger firms may feel discriminated against, and this may influence their attitude toward voluntary compliance.

Another method for dealing with small businesses is called the "forfait," in which the small business and the government determine the amount of the business' sales. Once a sales level is agreed to, a value-added tax liability is established. In most circumstances it appears this type of system requires a large amount of administration resources for relatively little revenue.

KEY POLICY ISSUES: ADMINISTRATION

Much of what is known about administering a value-added tax comes from the experience of EEC member countries. The main issues of value-added tax administration concern identifying taxpayers, processing returns, controlling collections, making refunds, auditing taxpayers, and levying penalties.

Before a value-added tax is enacted, authorities must decide which government agency ought to administer the value-added tax. Most EEC countries placed value-added tax administration responsibility in the agency handling the income tax. This was done for two primary reasons. First, the information collected while administering the value-added tax would assist income tax enforcement. Second, the personnel skills needed to administer the value-added tax closely resemble those needed to administer the income tax.

According to a 1989 OECD report, in only 3 of its 18 member countries are value-added taxes and income taxes managed by totally separate governmental entities. For example, in the United Kingdom, the customs department, not the income tax department, manages the value-added tax. In nine other OECD countries, the same tax inspector oversees both taxes, and in the remaining six the taxes are managed by the same department but within separate divisions. OECD reported further that two of the six countries with separate divisions currently are implementing changes to integrate value-added tax and income tax management.

An administration problem within most EEC value-added tax systems involves deciding what will be exempt. Because of valuation difficulties banking, financial services, and insurance are generally exempt from the value-added tax. In addition, and for a variety of reasons, many countries exempt cultural, educational, medical, and postal services, non-profit organizations, rental or leasing of real estate, and the purchase of buildings that are not newly constructed.

Administration costs

Another lesson learned from Europe is that the difficulty of value-added tax administration increases with the complexity of the rate structure and the tax base, as well as with the number of taxpayers. Literature on administration costs indicates that the simpler the value-added tax system, the lower the administration costs.

OECD reported administration costs as a percent of revenues for 12 countries. These costs ranged from 0.32 percent to 1.09 percent, with the Scandinavian countries (Denmark, Finland, Norway, and Sweden) having the lowest ratios. The Scandinavian countries have simple, single-rate, broad-based systems. However, they also have some of the highest value-added tax rates, which should bring in more revenue and could explain some of the apparent efficiency.

U.S. value-added tax cost estimates

There have been two studies of the costs of administering a value-added tax in the United States: both are by IRS, one published by the Treasury Department in 1984 and an unofficial IRS staff study in 1986. Although the assumptions of the two studies differed, both reports arrived at an annual cost of administering a value-added tax of

approximately $700 million. Both reports developed annual
staffing and cost estimates for a single-rate value-added tax
with 20 million taxpayers. Neither study incorporated the
cost of the Customs Service, which would be a necessary
component in dealing with the value-added taxation of goods
and services crossing our borders.

Additional aspects limit the studies' usefulness in
estimating the cost of introducing various designs of a
value-added tax. The Treasury study appears to assume that a
new infrastructure would be created to administer a value-
added tax. The other study suggests that administration
could be, in part, combined with the existing income tax
system. There is insufficient detail in the studies to
determine the basis for the estimates or to allow a
comprehensive examination of how different assumptions affect
the level of administration costs. If the value-added tax
that is enacted differs substantially from what was assumed
in the studies, there is little in these studies that would
be helpful for estimating the administration costs.

KEY POLICY ISSUES: STATE CONCERNS ABOUT A VALUE-ADDED TAX

State governments are concerned about the enactment of a
federal value-added tax. Forty-five states now have a broad-
based consumption tax in the form of a retail sales tax.
Historically, states have received a significant portion of
their tax revenues from sales taxes. If the federal
government enacted a tax, it would add a second layer of
consumption taxation that businesses in those states would
have to calculate and collect.

State officials are concerned that the imposition of a value-
added tax by the federal government would make it more
difficult to increase state sales tax revenues. If the
federal government adds taxes to the same items as the state
taxes, state officials believe it will be more difficult to
raise tax rates. They are concerned, further, that a federal
consumption tax would pressure the states to alter their tax
bases to conform with the federal tax base. There is also a
concern expressed in the literature that evasion of state
taxes will increase if sales are subject to a high combined
federal/state rate.

Another concern of state officials is about the burdens that
would be placed upon businesses that must charge two taxes on
each sale they make. A second consumption tax would increase
business compliance costs, but by incorporating certain
administration features the federal government might be able
to reduce these costs. One option would be to impose a
single tax and divide the collections between the federal
and state governments.

MAJOR CONTRIBUTORS TO THIS REPORT

GENERAL GOVERNMENT DIVISION, WASHINGTON, D.C.

Lynda D. Willis, Assistant Director, Tax Policy and
  Administration Issues
William Trancucci, Evaluator-in-Charge
Tom McCool, Economist
Mary Phillips, Evaluator

EUROPEAN OFFICE

Patricia Foley Hinnen, Evaluator

RELATED GAO PRODUCTS

GAO has issued a number of reports pertaining to value-added
taxation. These reports are:

Tax-Credit and Subtraction Methods of Calculating a Value-Added
Tax (GAO/GGD-89-87, June 20, 1989).

Choosing Among Consumption Taxes (GAO/GGD-86-91, August 20,
1986).

The Value-Added Tax--What Else Should We Know About It?
(GAO/PAD-81-60, March 3, 1981).

The Value-Added Tax In The European Economic Community
(GAO/ID-81-2, December 5, 1980).

ABBREVIATIONS

CBO	Congressional Budget Office
EEC	European Economic Community
IMF	International Monetary Fund
IRS	Internal Revenue Service
OECD	Organization for Economic Cooperation and Development

Appendix E

Pros and Cons of a Separate Capital Budget for the Federal Government

Charles A. Bowsher   *Comptroller General, Washington, D.C.*

Reprinted from GAO Report PAD-83-1, Sept. 22, 1983.

OBJECTIVES, SCOPE, AND METHODOLOGY

Because of recent interest in the idea of a separate capital budget, the Chairman and Ranking Minority Member of the Senate Committee on Environment and Public Works asked us to examine the advantages and disadvantages of the Federal Government using such a budget. The committee's request for this analysis and for an explanation of our previously stated position serves as the basis for this report.

We clarify the basic needs a separate capital budget would serve, present and analyze the potential advantages and disadvantages of using a separate Federal capital budget, and then consider three options for improving information on capital expenditures within the current unified budget.

When analyzing the advantages and disadvantages of a separate capital budget for the United States, one must examine its hypothetical attributes because the Federal Government has never used such a system. Thus, such an exercise could be highly speculative were it not for the controlled use of evidence and arguments that have bearing on this issue. Ideally, comparative data might be used in lieu of historical experience. Capital budgeting in the State and local governments and in the private sector might serve to exemplify the sorts of opportunities and drawbacks its adoption by the Federal Government would provide. Analogies cannot be pushed too far, however, especially when the differences between existing capital budgeting systems and that of a potential Federal equivalent are greater than the similarities. Comparative analysis, then, can help us to identify important budgeting practices but cannot determine their appropriateness in the Federal setting. Among the practices that emerge from the examination of existing dual budgeting systems are debt financing and the depreciation of capital assets and balanced operating budget requirements. Appendix IV contains a discussion of these.

In the absence of relevant historical data, other approaches
must be used. All budgeting systems are designed to serve specific purposes. Among the most basic of these purposes is the
allocation of resources, using a process and corresponding documentation that allows the allocation to be sufficiently visible
to permit effective decisionmaking and oversight. So, when analyzing the advantages and disadvantages, we focused part of our
analysis on the question, would it be easier to allocate Federal
resources under a separate capital budget or the current unified
budget?

In developing an alternative to a separate capital budget,
we further divided the purposes of the budget into two parts to
direct our analysis. First, a Government's budget and its supporting documentation should fully disclose both the costs and
the purposes of programs. Second, the display and analysis of
capital expenditures within the context of the current unified
budget should facilitate congressional decisionmaking and
oversight. The options considered represent differing levels of
commitment to augmenting the treatment of capital in the budget.

The visibility of decisions within any capital budgeting
system is highly dependent on the definition of capital assets it
employs. Also, how Federal capital assets are defined directly
affects whether or not there will be a budget surplus or deficit. To illustrate this effect, we constructed a simplified
model of a hypothetical Federal capital budget. The work of
Maynard Comiez in his 1966 study, "A Capital Budget Statement for
the U.S. Government," based on an earlier version prepared for
the Bureau of the Budget (now the Office of Management and Budget), provided us with the basic analytical orientation we
adopted in dealing with consequences of how capital is defined.
Our hypothetical capital budgets are based on data from the
President's budgets for fiscal years 1981, 1982, 1983, and 1984
and are discussed in greater detail and displayed in appendix V.

Notwithstanding the non-empirical character of our topic, we
did consult relevant literature and data bases. To learn about
existing capital budgeting systems, we reviewed diverse published
materials on planning, budgeting, and accounting practices. Our
experience, knowledge, and judgment about the Federal policymaking process have been used to assess the relevance of comparative information and analyses. Some of our data comes from a GAO
capital budget report, 1/ for which over 100 in-depth interviews
were conducted with officials in four States, four counties, four
large city governments, and four corporations.

As a quality control measure, we provided our findings and
conclusions to outside experts in the fields of budgeting, eco-

_____

1/U.S. General Accounting Office, "Federal Capital Budgeting: A
   Collection of Haphazard Practices," (PAD-81-19, February 26,
   1981).

nomics and public policy. Our analysis of the issues contained in this report has been refined on the basis of their comments.

LIMITATIONS

We did not study the detailed process, specific resource implications, nor the overall economic implications of producing and using a separate capital budget. Moreover, we looked at the effect on the computation of the deficit of only a limited number of definitions of capital investment and did not consider a separate Federal capital budget in light of specific balanced budget proposals. Were such a proposal to become enacted into law, its implications for capital investments would have to be evaluated with reference to its specific provisions. In the final analysis, the net benefits of costs of separating the budget into a capital and current portion is subject to empirical analysis. But, as we have stated earlier, evidence and experience on the use of a dual budget for the Federal Government does not exist and therefore cannot be examined empirically. One alternative, which could be the subject of a future study, would be to use a simulation experiment examining the budgetary, policy, and economic implications of using a separate capital budget. In our judgment, however, similar insight may be available from students and practitioners of budgeting and the public policymaking process.

Also, we did not study the specific steps and problems of making a transition from the current unified budget to a dual budget system, if the latter were adopted by the Federal Government. Clearly, such a transition would be a complicated process that would require the cooperation of leaders and policy officials in both the Congress and the executive branch.

ADVANTAGES AND DISADVANTAGES OF A SEPARATE FEDERAL CAPITAL BUDGET

Measured in terms of the dollars it spends or lends for capital assets, the Federal Government can be said to play a major role in our Nation's public facilities. Measured in terms of those assets directly managed through federally run programs, that role is considerably smaller. The Federal Government directly or indirectly finances or encourages billions of dollars worth of capital acquisitions over which it has minimal or no control. Federal grants-in-aid, loans, loan guarantees, and tax expenditures (revenue losses attributable to provisions of the Federal income tax laws encouraging certain activities) constitute sources of funds and incentives for acquiring capital assets whose ownership and management is controlled by State and local governments, businesses, and private individuals. Regardless of how successfully these organizations and individuals have controlled federally financed assets, the accountability to the U.S. taxpayer requires that a Government budget fully disclose how economic resources are allocated to meet a legislatively defined range of needs. The display of capital asset resource allocations in a separate capital budget is one way of employing descriptive categories and analytical discussions to provide a maximum amount of meaningful information to both citizens and decisionmakers. However, whether or not a separate Federal capital budget is the best way to handle capital investment decisions is a question open to debate. The adoption of a separate Federal capital budget has a number of advantages and disadvantages. Some of them are discussed in the following sections.

ADVANTAGES

The advocates of a separate Federal capital budget believe that if a separate Federal capital budget were adopted, it would provide a way for allocating capital investment dollars in a manner consistent with Federal policy and program objectives, even though ownership of capital assets is vested in non-Federal sectors. They also believe that it is a highly desirable vehicle for tracking and controlling the allocation of capital investment resources.

They argue that such a budget would

--serve as a national strategy for coordinating the many Federal capital investment programs and assessing their effect on public facilities and on public and private sector capital formation,

--help focus public attention on the amount and condition of capital assets owned and/or financed by the Federal Government,

--help change public perceptions of the relationship between long-term borrowing for capital assets and its effect on the Federal debt,

--help provide a way to distribute the costs of long-term capital projects equitably among present and future users through depreciation or some other adjustment formula.

Serve as a national investment plan

In the same way that it serves State and local governments, Federal decisionmakers would find that a capital budget establishes a useful planning process because it would focus on proposed long-term projects, their estimated costs, and their anticipated national benefits. Capital outlay information is available now in Special Analysis D of the unified budget, but not in sufficient detail for planning and analyzing proposed policy.

To a large extent, we are simply not aware of the full scope and nature of the Federal Government's contribution to public facilities and other capital investments. Diverse methods of financing, while useful in tailoring programs to meet policy objectives, tend to obscure the dimensions of the Federal role, especially when they do not result in measurable direct outlays from the Treasury, as is the case with tax expenditures and loan guarantees. 1/ While a separate capital budget would not necessarily resolve this problem, it could improve both the disclosure and planning of the various types of more direct Federal outlays used for capital investment purposes. At present, these are not fully reported in the various documents of the unified budget. Direct Federal programs, grants-in-aid, and direct loans are all employed to finance capital investments but are not always clearly identified as doing so. A separate Federal capital budget could require a more disciplined presentation of the scope and magnitude of Federal capital investments than currently exists within the unified budget. Such information is an important prerequisite for planning the acquisition of capital assets and for timing complex capital projects.

Until a more satisfactory solution is proposed, the more indirect spending could be handled in a special analysis of the budget that distinguishes whether these methods facilitate capital or current expenditures.

Focus attention on Federal assets and their condition

A capital budget would help focus public attention on the Government ownership and/or financing of assets that produce long-term benefits. As in the private sector, Government managers commonly make capital expenditures because they expect a future return in the form of increased services, benefits, or income for citizens. These capital expenditures represent collective investment and increase the Nation's assets. The value and stream of benefits derived from these assets decrease, however, if they are not adequately maintained. Also, the costs of owning and using capital assets increase over time. Thus, maintenance is a critical component of long-term capital investment strategy.

Presently, reliable information on the condition and maintenance costs of Federal capital assets is not available govern-

---

1/Tax expenditures and loan guarantees, for example, are not direct outlays from the Treasury. It is difficult to assess how much capital investment can be attributed to these two vehicles of financing on the basis of information provided in the current unified budget. Nevertheless, tax expenditures provide powerful and, in large measure, uncontrollable (entitlements) incentives for private investment in a diversity of capital assets. At the same time, they represent sizeable amounts of revenue foregone by the Federal Government. Loan guarantees also make the purchase of capital assets possible without the need for direct Federal expenditures. In addition, they influence private credit markets in ways not fully described in the unified budget.

mentwide. A separate capital budget would provide a stimulus
for acquiring this needed data. It would also help to illuminate
the degree of Federal responsibility being assumed for maintaining
assets financed by grants-in-aid and loans but owned and managed
by State and local governments. Bridges, highways, and waste-water
treatment facilities are among the capital assets built with substantial Federal funding but whose maintenance costs fall on the
budgets of State and local governments.

Change the public's perception of debt financing

Given the long-term benefits provided by capital assets, a
case is sometimes made for treating a Federal deficit incurred to
acquire these assets differently from one incurred for current
expenditures. Borrowing to finance current expenditures requires
extended payments for present benefits. Although there may be
sound economic reasons for doing so, this practice makes it appear
that the Government is spending beyond its means. In contrast,
using long-term debt to finance capital projects requires extended
payments for extended benefits. Such borrowing exchanges the extended repayment of loaned monetary assets for the future services
of tangible capital assets. Thus, deficits resulting from borrowing to acquire capital assets is accompanied by an increase
in the Nation's assets. A separate capital budget could be used
to highlight the distinction between the two forms of debt and
shape public awareness of the Federal deficit's composition as
well as its absolute magnitude. Nonetheless, we believe that an
inflexible rule requiring the debt financing of capital assets
is not a necessary or useful requirement of a separate capital
budget.

Increase intergenerational equity

It is often claimed that a separate capital budget that employs debt financing of capital assets contributes to increased
equity between those who pay for and those who use these assets.
If the life of the loan used for a capital acquisition approximates the service life of the asset acquired, then each generation pays for the amount of capital it actually uses. However,
debt financing of capital assets could occur without the need
for a separate capital budget.

DISADVANTAGES

Whatever benefits a separate capital budget might provide,
serious practical problems are associated with its adoption by
the Federal Government. Opponents of this budget system argue
that it has the potential to

   --impose constraints on countercyclical fiscal policy meas-
     ures if capital investment were financed by long-term
     debt;

   --require what may be extensive and costly changes in the
     current Federal budget process with little direct evi-
     dence of the potential benefits from doing so;

--introduce greater complexity and increased opportunity
for manipulation into the framework of budget categories
because of the need to define and decide what should
be classified as a capital asset and, if required, how
that asset should be depreciated;

--shift the focus of the budget away from broad questions
of resource allocation to meet functionally defined
national needs to narrower questions of public investment and how it is to be financed.

Constrain countercyclical fiscal policy

The effect a separate capital budget would have on Federal
fiscal policies used to counter short-term swings in the economy
depends on the specific characteristics that are built into a
dual budget system, such as how capital and operating expenditures are separated, whether or not assets are depreciated,
and how capital assets are financed.

Although there is no technical requirement that restricts
the acquisition of assets by debt financing alone, the assumption
that the adoption of a separate Federal capital budget would require this method to be used is what gives credibility to claims
about its effects on fiscal policy. Three reasons might be advanced to justify this assumption: (1) debt financing would be
desirable for increasing equity between those who pay for and
those who use capital assets; (2) debt financing capital expenditures would smooth the fluctuations in large Federal outlays;
(3) a separate capital budget might be adopted along with a balanced budget requirement, which would require balancing current
expenditures with current tax receipts and financing capital outlays through long-term debt.

The actual validity of the three reasons is less important
than their persuasiveness in linking debt financing with the
adoption of a separate Federal capital budget. If such a link
were successfully made, then the consequences of debt financing
for fiscal policy should be closely examined.

Were the Federal Government to use long-term borrowing for
the bulk of its capital expenditures, the flow of one type of
Federal outlay would be made independent of short-term changes
in economic conditions. To a greater extent, capital acquisitions
would be planned and financed to meet long-term capital needs,
not to play a role in the short-term stabilization of the economy.
Insulating capital outlays from serving the requirements of fiscal
policy would necessarily increase the burdens on expenditures from
the operating budget, tax policy, and monetary policy to act as
instruments of overall economic policy. If a balanced operating
budget were also a requirement of an adopted dual budgeting system, the corresponding constraints imposed on current outlays
and tax receipts would make the task of stabilization even more

reliant on monetary policy. 1/ How these potential consequences
are viewed depends on the amount of Federal economic stabilization deemed both necessary and desirable.

Disrupt the budget process

The adoption of a separate capital budget is quite likely
to unpredictably disrupt the existing budget process. A dual
budget would more than likely require some changes in institutional structure, shifts in responsibility, and modifications
of the budget cycle's timing. The need to relate aggregate debt,
tax, and spending limits to two separate budgets--capital and
operating--would introduce greater complexity into the already
complicated budget process.

Changes in the current budget process resulting from the
adoption of a separate Federal capital budget could only be justified if these changes produced substantial benefits. To assess
the benefits and costs of moving away from the current unified
budget, the capital budgeting experiences of non-Federal organizations would have to be examined so that a baseline for comparison could be established. Private businesses and State and local
governments can provide us with information on the successes,
failures, and operational characteristics of their capital budgeting systems. (See appendix IV.) However, all of these non-
Federal organizations function within the market system and in an
economic environment regulated in a variety of ways by the Federal Government, and many are recipients of substantial Federal
resources. This makes it questionable whether any of them would
serve as a relevant example. To accurately predict the benefits
of capital budgeting for the Federal Government on the basis of
private, State, and local experiences would require assumptions
of comparability that ignore these important differences.

Complicate budget categories

Establishing a dual budgeting system requires the ability to
distinguish between capital and operating expenditures and
assumes that it is possible to clearly and unambiguously define
capital assets. But, even among those public and private sector
organizations that use capital budgets, no definitions of capital
assets are universally accepted. In appendix V we illustrate how
alternative definitions affect the size of the operating budget
surplus or deficit. Whether or not the Federal operating budget
were in balance would depend upon what is included in the definition of capital. Although any budgeting system can potentially

---

1/These comments refer to the fiscal policy choices available to
   Federal decisionmakers under differing sets of requirements for
   the functioning of a dual budgeting system. In the absence of
   legislative changes to the contrary, the automatic stabilizers
   of the economy, such as unemployment insurance and the taxation
   of large marginal increases in profits, would still continue to
   operate.

be subject to manipulation and while strong oversight and accounting controls can minimize the occurrence of abuse, the complexity associated with defining Federal capital assets remains.

The problems of definition also interact with the question
of how capital assets, once defined, should be treated within a
dual budgeting system. More specifically, should Federal capital
assets be subject to depreciation, how should it be handled in
the budget, and what are the consequences of doing so? 1/

Shift the purpose of the budget

The primary purpose of the unified budget is to allocate
resources based on policy decisions made by the President and the
Congress. To reflect the major areas of the Government's responsibility, budget authority and outlays are organized in accordance with 17 functional categories designed to present the costs
of policy choices without regard to the jurisdictions of specific
Federal agencies. Although the yearly flow of Federal resources
is a necessary concern of the budget process and is expressed in
the budget documents, of even greater significance is the way
those resources meet the basic needs of society and the economy
as categorized in functional terms. The overriding objective of
policy is to ensure that these diverse needs of society are considered in making budget decisions.

A dual budgeting system could result in treating policy and
functional needs as secondary to the type of expenditure--capital
investment or operating expense. Capital and current expenses
present different technical problems to a resource manager and,
consequently, could be separated to ensure optimal financial
treatment of each. With a separate capital budget, the acquisition of assets could be more carefully managed, but the policy
implications of financial decisions could be blurred. The allocation of resources for capital is not separable, in a policy
sense, from the host of related operating expenditures with which
it is joined to execute Federal Government programs.

A functional breakdown of expenditures in the unified budget
presupposes that the primary policy goal of the budget--the satisfaction of different types of needs in society through the
allocation of resources--will take precedence over the specific
technical means used to achieve it. The possible financing of
social and other non-capital programs with current revenues or of
financing capital acquisitions through long-term debt has little
bearing on how each type of expenditure is judged in policy
terms. Programs are viewed as a unified whole regardless of the

---

1/Depreciation (the method of allocating the net cost of a
tangible capital asset over the estimated useful life of the
asset in a systematic and rational manner) of Federal capital
assets is being addressed in a separate GAO study and will not
be discussed in detail in this report. (See p. 28 for a discussion of business depreciation practices.)

mix of capital and non-capital resources required for their
implementation. In contrast, unless programs are wholly capital
or operating, a dual budget dissects the individual programs by
their operating and capital segments. Since these parts would
appear in two separate budgets, capital assets' contribution to
achieving either program goals or broader functional goals may be
obscured.

Although it might be feared that capital assets would obtain
a disproportionate share of total outlays under a dual budgeting
system because of the special attention they would receive, specific conditions must exist for this to be a likely consequence.
A separate capital budget does not in itself encourage a preference for capital items over the operating portion of the budget.
Its execution, however, is often regulated by procedures that may
have this result. Were a dual budget governed by the stipulation
that the receipts and outlays of its operating portion be balanced, then capital outlays might appear relatively more attractive in the absence of any other constraints. The financing of
capital acquisitions through long-term debt would in large measure exempt capital outlays from the direct budget balancing
requirements imposed on current outlays. However, large increases in debt-financed capital investments would eventually impose
indirect burdens on the operating portion of a dual budget
system. A requirement to charge debt service (interest) and depreciation of capital investments to the operating budget would
increase current outlays in step with increases in capital investment. Additional revenues or reduction of operating costs
would then be required to keep the operating budget in balance.

OPTIONS FOR PROVIDING CAPITAL INVESTMENT INFORMATION
WITHIN THE UNIFIED BUDGET

Any budgeting system used by the Federal Government should
disclose the full range of government programs and their associated costs, indicate the purposes and needs these programs are
intended to serve, and suggest the nature and size of budgetary
commitments that extend beyond a single budget year. These
criteria and the desire to increase the information on Federal
capital investments that is available for making budget decisions
do not automatically entail adopting a separate capital budget.
Many of the disadvantages of a dual budgeting system presented in
our analysis might be avoided by considering alternative displays
of budget information more closely tailored to the nature and
range of Federal responsibilities. The following three options
describe proposals for increasing the comprehensiveness with
which Federal capital expenditures can be examined.

OPTION 1: DISPLAY CAPITAL INVESTMENTS
SEPARATELY IN A RESECTIONED UNIFIED BUDGET

The need for more comprehensive information on the size and
composition of Federal capital investments can be partially satisfied by collecting and prominently displaying capital investment

data in the unified budget. Although the format in the budget documents would be altered, the fundamental purposes of the unified budget would still be served. Specifically, the budget functional categories used to aggregate outlays and budget authority across agency lines could continue to show how Federal policies serve national needs.

A primary focus of this option is to establish separate sections in the budget that are devoted to the display and discussion of capital investments. This kind of treatment of capital investments parallels that afforded to Federal credit programs for each function in the newly instituted credit budget. (See table 1.)

Table 1

Credit Programs--General Government
(in millions of dollars)

	Actual 1982	Estimate 1983	1984	1985	1986
Direct loans:					
Loans to U.S. territories (loans made by FFB):					
Net outlays	-18	a/	a/	a/	-1
Outstandings	66	65	65	64	64
Federal buildings fund (loans made by FFB):					
New obligations b/	12				
Net outlays	8	-9	-10	-10	-11
Outstandings	522	513	504	493	48
Total, direct loans					
New obligations	12				
Net outlays	-11	-9	-10	-11	-12
Outstandings	588	579	569	588	546
Guaranteed loans					
Federal building fund:					
Net change	-35	-19	-20	-22	-21
Outstandings	674	655	635	613	592
Total credit budget (new obligations and new commitments)	12				

a/$500 thousand or less
b/These are commitments made by the agency to guarantee loans that the FFB will disburse. In effect, they are commitments for off-budget direct loans, and are counted as such in the credit budget. Policy responsibility for these loans rests with the guaranteeing agency.

Source: Budget for fiscal year 1984.

Option 1 proposes a capital investment display similar to the credit budget. Modifications to the credit program example would be necessary to accommodate the various capital investment financing mechanisms or incentives: direct Federal outlays, grants-in-aid, loans, guaranteed loans, and tax expenditures.

Only those tangible physical assets traditionally identified
as capital items--because of the long-term benefits they provide--
would be included in these proposed sections of the unified budget.
To the maximum degree possible, budgetary data on capital investments would distinguish the amounts associated with different
financing mechanisms. Thus, displays would identify direct Federal
programs, grants-in-aid, direct loans, loan guarantees, and tax
expenditures. Best available estimates would be employed in those
cases where actual budget authority and outlay figures could not
be provided.

All of the proposed sections of the budget are designed to
convey a better sense of the distribution and future implications
of Federal capital investments than is currently possible. Projections 5 years beyond the current budget year, or even longer,
would help to identify the direction and levels of Federal capital
investments and could aid in planning the commitment of resources.
Such planning might also include assessing the maintenance and
operational costs associated with the acquisition of capital
assets. The expectation that capital investments will provide
a long-term stream of benefits presupposes the long-term commitment of resources for proper maintenance.

Resectioning the budget to enhance its treatment of capital
investment would directly affect the presentation of the President's budget proposals found in the primary budget document.
More specifically, the following would be altered: Part 3, Budget
Programs and Trends; Part 5, Meeting National Needs: The Federal
Program by Function; and Part 9, Summary Tables. In Part 3, the
addition of a new section discussing Federal capital investment
policy in an overall sense and the inclusion of summary tables
projecting long-term investment and other trends would facilitate
the planned use of scarce resources.

The new section in Part 3 could be aggregated and analyzed
in many different ways, depending upon the perspective one wishes
to take and which elements of the budget one wishes to emphasize.
We suggest a table (see table 2) and discussion of four broad
areas: defense and international, domestic programs, retirement
and insurance, and interest. Such a presentation would display
these broad "programs" by investment type and current activities
and would provide a broad perspective for policy analysis. Actual
and proposed budget authority and outlays for capital investments
and current activities by function (see table 3) could appear in
a new comprehensive table in Part 9.

More detailed new information on Federal capital investments
could appropriately be placed in Part 5 of the budget. This part
examines the range of Federal programs categorized by budget
function. It is also the location of the tables that already display Federal credit activities, which, as we noted previously,
serve as a precedent for handling capital investments suggested
here.

In Part 5, the discussion of each functional area of Federal
responsibility begins with a National Needs Statement. We propose

Table 2

Analysis of Defense and International, Domestic
Programs, Retirement and Insurance Programs, and Interest
by Investment-Type and Current Activities
(billions of dollars)

	Budget Authority			Outlays		
	1981	1982	1983	1981	1982	1983
Defense and international						
Physical assets	$ 53.9	$ 73.9	$ 98.7	$ 39.7	$ 46.9	$ 62.2
R&D	18.6	22.3	26.6	17.0	20.6	24.7
Loans	14.6	6.4	6.1	5.1	4.8	5.5
Current activities	131.1	147.5	164.1	120.1	139.0	155.1
Offsetting receipts	−11.1	−12.8	−14.4	−11.0	−12.8	−14.4
	207.1	237.3	281.1	170.8	198.5	233.1
Domestic Programs						
Physical assets	31.9	29.5	26.9	37.0	34.2	28.9
R&D	17.3	16.2	16.4	17.0	17.3	16.7
Loans	3.7	4.6	3.1	1.4	2.0	1.6
Current activities	153.7	131.1	111.3	138.2	138.4	123.0
Offsetting receipts	−24.2	−31.7	−33.1	−24.2	−31.7	−33.1
	186.0	149.7	124.6	169.4	160.2	137.1
Retirement & Insurance						
Current activities	291.4	333.0	349.3	282.8	321.1	340.1
Offsetting receipts	−18.7	−21.6	−21.3	−18.7	−21.6	−21.3
	272.7	311.4	328.0	264.1	299.5	319.4
Interest (current)	96.6	117.4	134.8	96.6	117.4	134.8
Offsetting receipts	−13.0	−16.6	−20.4	−13.0	−16.6	−20.4
	83.6	100.8	114.4	83.6	100.8	114.4
Total	749.4	799.2	848.1	687.9	759.0	804.0
Undistributed off-setting receipts	−31.0	−33.7	−46.2	−30.7	−33.7	−46.4
Total	$718.4	$765.5	$801.9	$657.2	$725.3	$757.6

adding a specific reference to capital investment needs to the
statements concerning each of the functional areas, for which this
is a relevant consideration. (See figure 1.) No such reference
would be necessary, for example, in the case of Interest, functional code 900.

To present data on capital investments for each applicable
budget function, separate displays could be used for two broad
categories based on financing methods that have different characteristics. The first category would include direct Federal pro-

Table 3

Analysis of Investment and Current Activities
by Function
(billions of dollars)

	Budget Authority			Outlays		
	1981	1982	1983	1981	1982	1983
050 National Defense						
Investment	$ 72.2	$ 95.9	$124.9	$ 56.6	$ 67.4	$ 86.7
Current	110.8	123.8	139.2	103.8	120.9	135.5
Offsetting Receipts	- .7	- .9	-1.1	- .7	- .9	-1.1
Total	182.3	218.9	263.0	159.7	187.4	221.1
150 International Affairs						
Investment	14.9	6.7	6.5	5.2	4.9	5.7
Current	20.3	23.7	24.9	16.3	18.1	19.6
Offsetting Receipts	-10.4	-11.9	-13.3	-10.4	-11.9	-13.3
Total	24.8	18.5	18.1	11.1	11.1	12.0
250 General Science, Space, and Technology						
Investment	6.5	7.0	7.8	6.3	6.9	7.6
Current	.1	---	---	.1	.1	---
Offsetting Receipts	---	---	---	---	---	---
Total	6.6	7.0	7.8	6.4	7.0	7.6
270 Energy						
Investment	7.1	6.6	4.4	10.4	8.2	4.7
Current	1.5	1.6	1.6	1.6	1.5	.9
Offsetting Receipts	-1.9	-3.3	-1.6	-1.9	-3.3	-1.6
Total	6.7	4.9	4.4	10.1	6.4	4.0
300 Natural Resources and Environment						
Investment	8.4	8.4	8.2	10.7	10.8	9.7
Current	5.1	5.1	4.7	5.1	5.2	4.8
Offsetting Receipts	-2.4	-3.5	-4.6	-2.4	-3.5	-4.6
Total	11.1	10.0	8.3	13.4	12.5	9.9

grams, grants-in-aid, and direct loans, all of which are included
in the budget totals and result in expenditures whose magnitude,
at least in principle, is subject to computation. (We recognize,
of course, that there will be problems in estimating the proportions of grants-in-aid that are actually capital-related.) The
second category would include loan guarantees and tax expenditure
Loan guarantees for capital investment purposes represent a contingent liability for the Federal Government. Direct outlays
from the Treasury result only in those instances when recipients

Figure 1

National Needs Statements
Contained in Part 5 of the Budget

TRANSPORTATION

National Needs Statement:

- Maintain a safe, reliable, and efficient transportation system to meet the needs of commerce and the public, with maximum reliance on the private sector and, secondarily, on State and local governments.

The Federal Role in Meeting the Need:

- Assist the States in developing and maintaining a highway system capable of providing for interstate commerce and the national defense.

- Provide capital assistance to repair and modernize existing mass transit systems, especially in large cities, while operating subsidies are phased out.

- Encourage the development of self-sufficient, cost-effective rail systems for freight and passengers.

- Provide safe and reliable management of the air space and of facilities within which the aviation system operates.

- Facilitate a safe, reliable, and efficient marine transportation system.

Source: The Budget for fiscal year 1983.

Option 1 would add a statement on capital investment similar to this for each functional category having significant capital investment activity. In the 1983 budget, such a statement appeared only in the Transportation function. In the 1984 budget, the format for national needs statements has been modified and shortened.

of federally guaranteed loans default on repayment. Tax expenditures constitute the conscious relinquishment of tax revenues to encourage certain types of expenditures by private businesses and individuals. They are not included in the budget totals and are not subject to the controls of the appropriation process. Because the ultimate cost to the Federal Government of both loan

guarantees and tax expenditures is sufficiently difficult to calculate with accuracy, capital investment data in the second category could only be based on best available estimates.

Although capital investments could be displayed separately
in the budget, such information must be aggregated from data
derived from individual appropriation accounts. These accounts
are included in the Budget Appendix, but data displayed within
them do not currently lend themselves to aggregate presentations
a resectioned budget would require. OMB instructions (OMB Circular A-11, July 1982) for preparing budget estimates recommend how
to deal with capital investment in the program and financing
(P&F) schedules. Section 32.2 provides that direct Federal capital investment will be shown separately from current operating
expenses in the "program by activities" section of the P&F schedules if the amounts are material. Otherwise, they will be
included in operating expenses without identification. Amounts
reported in P&F schedules will be consistent with the amounts
reported for the corresponding classification categories for Special Analysis D. Where capital investments are shown separately,
the side headings "Operating expenses" and "Capital investment"
will be used.

Identification of Federal capital investments at the appropriation account level would be facilitated if detailed displays
of information were more frequently and consistently presented.
This is currently not the case. Some accounts clearly distinguish between operating and capital, and others make no distinction at all. Sections on "capital investment" either display an
aggregated dollar amount for all capital activities or use highly
specific descriptive categories. Many of those accounts that
make no distinctions do, in fact, finance capital investment, as
indicated in the object classification displays.

Another difficulty with the existing presentations of capital investment in the program and financing schedules is that
there is no distinction between capital and operating costs funded through Federal grants-in-aid. (See table 4.) We have previously discussed displaying by budget function the aggregate
capital investment that is funded through direct Federal programs, direct loans, and grants-in-aid. Consistent treatment of
capital investment would also require displaying information on
the percentages of grants used for capital investment purposes.
Such information could be provided in displays for individual
appropriation acounts as well as in summary tables. In the
absence of hard data, estimates of the relative proportions of
capital and operating costs funded by grants-in-aid would be useful. Also, it would be desirable to obtain more reliable information that distinguishes between the capital and operating components of grants for previous budget years in the column that
presents actual as opposed to estimated outlays.

The separate display of capital investment in the unified
budget should be carried out uniformly and consistently in all
those sections of the budget documents to which the distinction
between capital investments and operating expenditures applies,

Table 4

Urban Mass Transporation Fund
Program and Financing (in thousands of dollars)

Identification Code 69-1119-0-1-401	1982 Actual	1983 Est.	1984 Est.
Program by Activities:			
Direct Program:			
Urban Discretionary Grants	1,707,705	1,608,000	---
Urban Formula Grants	1,348,884	1,236,000	300,000
Nonurban Formula Grants	74,320	70,000	51,500
Formula (block) Grants	---	---	1,973,500
Interstate Transfer Grants	567,483	365,000	380,000
Washington Metro	---	240,000	230,000
Research and Training	63,470	59,520	51,700
Administrative Expenses	25,533	28,566	29,666
Social Research	278	500	300
Waterborne Demonstration	1,277	777	---
Commuter Rail Operating Subsidies	367		
Total Direct Program	3,789,267	3,608,363	3,016,666
Reimbursable Program	58,394	123,268	3,000
10.00 Total Obligations	3,847,661	3,731,631	3,019,666
Financing:			
11.00 Offsetting Collections From: Federal Funds	-58,394	-123,268	-3,000
17.00 Recovery of Prior Year Obligations	-59,852	---	---
Unobligated Balance Available, Start of Year:			
21.40 Appropriation	-835,484	-663,410	-621,213
21.49 Contract Authority	-33,733	---	---
22.40 Unobligated Balance Transferred From Other Accounts	---	---	---
Unobligated Balance Available, End of Year:			
22.40 Appropriation	633,410	621,213	269,713
24.49 Contract Authority	---	---	---
25.00 Unobligated Balance Lapsing	8,630	---	---
Budget Authority	3,532,238	3,566,166	2,665,166

Nonurban Formula Grants--Provides transit operating and capital grants on the
basis of a formula to areas with populations below 50,000. In 1984, funds for
this program are provided within the new formula grant program.

Source: Appendix to the Budget for fiscal year 1984.

Option 1 advocates that capital and operating components of grants be distinguished. No such distinction is currently made in this sample.

including the individual appropriation account information as well as the summary tables.

OPTION 2:   PREPARE A NEW INFRASTRUCTURE AND CAPITAL INVESTMENT ANALYSIS

A new "infrastructure and capital investment analysis" is one way of providing capital investment data within the current budget. In addition to its prospective role for presenting aggregate data on Federal capital investment, it could also be used to reveal some of the policy implications of current capital investment levels. To ensure that this approach has adequate visibility in the budget documents, it could include a descriptive analysis in Part 3 of the budget--Budget Program and Trends --and tabular budget data in a new special analysis.

The descriptive analysis in Part 3 of the budget could discuss Federal capital investment policy and policy changes, programs, trends, and major problem areas. Two new special analysis tables could be prepared, one covering investment in existing assets and the other covering investment in new additions to public facilities.

For existing assets, the first analysis (see table 5) could show the past year's outlays, current year estimates and budget year estimates at current policy levels, and budget year outlays under the administration's proposed policy.

Table 5

Special Analysis __

Current Level Capital Outlays for Existing Inventory by Function and Program (millions of dollars)

	Current Level			1984
	1982	1983	1984	Proposal
400 TRANSPORTATION				
401 Ground Transportation				
Highways	xx	xx	xx	xx
Mass Transit	xx	xx	xx	xx
Railroads	xx	xx	xx	xx
Subtotal	xxx	xxx	xxx	xxx
402 Air Transportation				
Airways and Airports	x	x	x	x
403 Water Transportation				
Marine Safety and				
Transportation	x	x	x	x
Ocean Shipping	x	x	x	x
Subtotal	xx	xx	xx	xx
404 Other Transportation	x	x	x	x
TOTAL	xxx	xxx	xxx	xxx

Table 6

Special Analysis __

Current Level Outlays for New Capital
by Function and Program
(millions of dollars)

	1982	1983	1984	1984 Prop.	Addition to Inventory 1984	1989
400 TRANSPORTATION						
401 Ground Transportation	xx	xx	xx	xx	xx	xx
Highways	xx	xx	xx	xx	xx	xx
Mass Transit	x	x	x	x	x	x
Railroads	x	x	x	x	x	x
Subtotal	xxx	xxx	xxx	xxx	xxx	xxx
402 Air Transportation						
Airways and Airports	x	x	x	x	x	x
403 Water Transportation						
Marine Safety and Transportation	x	x	x	x	x	x
Ocean Shipping	x	x	x	x	x	x
Subtotal	xx	xx	xx	xx	xx	xx
404 Other Transportation	x	x	x	x	x	x
TOTAL	xxx	xxx	xxx	xxx	xxx	xxx

The second analysis (see table 6) would cover additions to the existing stock of assets. It would show investment for the past year, the current year, and the budget year under current policy; budget year investment under the administration's proposed policy; and expected additions to the capital stock. Thus, this analysis and the one on existing public facilities would enable policymakers and decisionmakers to determine whether to expand the capital stock or to maintain the existing capital stock according to national needs and policy.

Both of the proposed analyses could be prepared using the budget functional format that is designed to relate Federal policies to the satisfaction of national needs. Major programs would follow the functional categorization. This would allow the decisionmakers to focus on areas of investment priorities and allocation of scarce budgetary resources. It would also be possible to distinguish between direct Federal investment where assets are owned and maintained by the Federal Government and those investments that are not owned and maintained by the Federal Government.

Preparing infrastructure and capital investment analysis tables would require the agencies to prepare and maintain an

inventory and condition assessment against which projected spending authority and outlays could be judged. In this regard, certain complexities would have to be resolved; capital investment
is not quite analogous to providing beneficiaries with a constant
stream of services. Capital projects have discrete life cycles:
There will always be new starts, ongoing efforts, completions,
and disposals of existing assets. Also, Federal investment in
capital assets involves both outlays for assets owned and maintained by the Federal Government and grants to State and local
governments for assets owned and maintained by them.

Examining capital investment for physical assets already in
the inventory and new assets to be acquired in relation to a
level of existing activity provides no sense of how well national
needs in this policy area are being served. Although existing
qualitative and quantitative information on national investment
requirements is imperfect, enough data could be made available to
produce a descriptive analysis along with a gross characterization of the budget's effect. Preparing and presenting data on
national capital needs would also provide an important incentive
to improve and expand data bases that characterize the number,
description, and condition of Federal capital assets.

Adequate capital investment inventories and condition
assessment information would be available to assist Federal decisionmakers in addressing the difficult but unavoidable problems
that scarcity and budgetary constraints impose upon them. Generally, the concepts, procedures, and the data for this alternative
are not developed or readily available. Such items as the compatibility of data in data bases and how to treat grants versus
direct Federal investments would have to be overcome to make this
a viable alternative to a separate capital budget. Despite the
wealth of information that would be available to assist decisionmakers in making informed decisions, it may take considerable
effort, time, and money to fully carry out this option.

OPTION 3: IMPROVE THE SPECIAL
ANALYSES OF THE BUDGET

The collection of better data on Federal capital investments
and their display in the Special Analyses, which constitute a
companion volume to the President's budget proposals, is a third
option. It is the easiest to carry out but has less potential
impact than the other two. This option would entail revising
Special Analysis D, "Investment, Operating, and Other Federal
Outlays," to display information in a format that would be of
greater use to decisionmakers. It would also require that an
improved version of the Special Analysis on "Federal Public Works
Activities" be reinstated. (It was deleted from the budget documents after 1974. See table 7.)

Special Analysis D could become an appropriate vehicle for
disseminating information on Federal capital investments. It is
part of the existing budget documents and is published in conjunction with the formal budget. It is prepared by the staff of

Table 7

Table 0-9. FEDERAL PUBLIC WORKS ACTIVITIES (in millions of dollars) By Major Function and Agency						
	Budget Authority			Outlays		
Function, Agency, and Program	1972 Actual	1973 Estimate	1974 Estimate	1972 Actual	1973 Estimate	1974 Estimate
Civil Public Works						
Natural Resources and Environment						
Department of Agriculture:						
Soil Conservation Service:						
Flood prevention and watershed protection:						
Direct work	0.3	0.4	0.4	0.3	0.4	0.5
Grants	103.1	116.8	65.9	80.0	102.1	82.4
Forest Service: Roads, research, recreational, and other facilities a/	202.4	94.7	79.2	157.7	209.1	152.1
Department of Defense--Civil:						
Corps of Engineers--Civil:						
Flood control, navigation, and multi-purpose projects with power	1,077.2	1,281.5	933.3	1,054.7	1,114.5	1,006.7
Trust funds	18.4	19.7	18.4	19.5	20.0	19.0
Grants	1.2			1.2		
Department of the Interior:						
Bureau of Land Management:						
Roads and other facilities:	21.1	12.1	8.8	15.9	15.1	17.9
Bureau of Outdoor Recreation:						
Grants for recreation facilities	147.2	105.0	28.9	42.7	72.9	92.4
Office of Coal Research: Demonstration plans	12.5	25.0	28.3	1.8	15.7	24.5
Bureau of Sport Fisheries and Wildlife: Facilities	7.2		6.9	5.0	8.2	5.8
National Park Service: Parkways, roads, buildings and utilities a/	127.0	44.8	23.5	51.0	59.7	69.9
Bureau of Reclamation:						
Irrigation and multiple-purpose projects with power a/	277.0	348.1	203.8	240.6	349.6	298.8
Small irrigation projects:						
Grants	b/	1.6	3.1	2.2		2.9
Loans	11.4	18.8	13.6	11.2	20.0	15.1
Power transmission facilities:						
Bonneville Power Administration	87.4	89.7	93.8	90.2	82.3	89.8
Southwestern Power Administration	0.9	0.7	0.5	2.6	1.7	0.6
Office of Saline Water: Facilities	0.3	0.3		0.4	0.4	

a/Includes amounts from trust funds.
b/Less than $50,000.

Source: Special Analysis O, Budget for fiscal year 1974.

Option 3 would restore an improved version of this special analysis.

the Office of Management and Budget, which has the built-in capability to analyze current Federal spending in the capital investment area as well as direct access to the data necessary to describe the dimensions of the Federal role. Unfortunately, Special Analysis D is currently an after-the-fact presentation based on the President's budget proposals that have already been made. It could be, along with a Federal Public Works Special Analysis,

of value to the Congress and the public in assessing Federal
investment activity.

In our previous report, "Federal Capital Budgeting: A Collection of Haphazard Practices" (PAD-81-19), we indicated some of
the deficiencies of Special Analysis D. 1/ Although OMB has made
some modifications to the analysis, addressing some of our concerns, the data displayed in this analysis do not constitute full
disclosure of Federal capital investment activities.

As it is currently published, Special Analysis D distinguishes between current and investment-type outlays and further
subdivides them between civil and national defense programs. The
examination of investment-type outlays proceeds by using such
categories as loans, construction and rehabilitation of physical
assets, acquisition of major equipment, commodity inventories,
conduct of research and development, conduct of education and
training, etc. OMB made improvements beginning with the 1984
budget presentation to include new summary tables for major public physical capital investment to display the historical trends
both in current and constant dollar amounts. They have also
included an addendum to include the capital investment activities
of off-budget agencies. Despite these improvements, the categories of capital investment in the summary tables do not consistently parallel the lines of responsibility for decisionmaking in
the Congress (see also p. 26). Also, the concept of investment
used in Special Analysis D goes well beyond the more limited
notion of physical capital that we are discussing here.

One of the primary purposes of the President's budget is to
describe our national objectives and the costs of their attainment. The budget itself, as distinguished from Special Analysis
D, displays actual and projected expenditures using 17 broad
functional categories. These budget functions provide a way for
grouping together related programs without regard to the patterns
of agency responsibility for their execution. They represent a
viable choice for displaying information on capital in Special
Analysis D in a way that would be consistent with the policymaking categories being used by the Congress. Knowing what the Federal Government spends on capital items for national defense,
energy, transportation, natural resources and environment, community and regional development, and other functional areas gives

---

1/The limitations noted in our report included the (1) inaccurate
   portrayal of the magnitude of capital investment activity because outlays from one category are netted against the receipts
   from the same category, (2) failure to include the financial
   activities of off-budget agencies, (3) inadequate representation of total capital stock because capital outlays are displayed for only 3 fiscal years, (4) inconsistent definition of
   physical capital, and (5) misleading treatment of programs in
   which the recipients have discretion over the use of funds for
   capital or operating purposes.

us an important perspective on our current priorities and increases our knowledge about potential future costs.

Although using the budget function categories to display capital information would improve Special Analysis D, other limitations remain to be addressed. In particular, its utility for decisionmaking and oversight is constrained by two practices noted earlier: the net reporting of appropriation account receipts (offsetting collections) and the handling of disbursements whose use is at the discretion of the recipient (general revenue sharing and block grants). Both practices lead to the reporting of data that may incorrectly state the magnitude of Federal activity in the categories in which it is recorded. OMB Circular A-11, "Preparation and Submission of Budget Estimates," gives the following directions:

> In the case of some grants-in-aid programs (such as community development block grants), the recipient jurisdiction has discretion between using funds for current or investment-type purposes. In such instances, all of the outlays for grants are to be recorded in the category where the majority of the funds are anticipated to be used. (July 1982, A-2)

Notwithstanding the difficulties in tracing the use of discretionary funds, OMB's reporting instructions to the executive agencies magnify the inaccuracies in agency data submissions. If over 50 percent of a grant were anticipated to be used for capital investment purposes, 100 percent of the grant would be included in a capital investment category within Special Analysis D. The error attributable to miscategorization in such an instance could constitute up to 49 percent of the total funding of the grant. Although the optimal remedy for this problem would be the institution of better estimating procedures to determine the patterns of Federal grant utilization, a temporary measure might be considered. Recording outlays for broad-based grants whose primary expected use is capital in nature as 75 percent capital, 25 percent operating, reduces the maximum possible error due to miscategorization to 25 percent.

The second part of this option relates to public works, which represents a major component of Federal capital investment activity. Public works covers a wide variety of projects that collectively contribute to the building of public infrastructure, those core structures and facilities upon which both the public and private sectors of our national economy are based.

A special analysis, "Federal Public Works Activities," last appeared as a part of the budget for fiscal year 1974. The discontinued analysis contained a very useful compendium of tables designed to describe the character and magnitude of the Federal public works role. In particular, table 0-9 was very useful for assessing the range of Federal activities because it presented data by major function and agency. We believe that this type of budget presentation is crucial to maintaining informed congressional decisionmaking on public works.

In our draft report we stated that even if Special Analysis
D·were revised appropriately, the importance of information on
Federal public works activities calls for its separate treatment
in a restored special analysis along the line of the analysis
discontinued after 1974. According to OMB, the special analysis
was discontinued because sufficient information was available in
Special Analysis D and the increasing complexity of the budget
process required elimination of marginal--but useful--analyses.
However, at the time the public works special analysis was discontinued, Special Analysis D was in a different format and provided more information than it currently does.

Special Analysis D has been modified and now has summary
tables of Federal outlays for major physical capital investment.
OMB has also prepared and made available more detailed data in a
series of tables not included in the budget documents. This
series of tables includes direct Federal capital investment for
defense and non-defense activities and grants to State and local
governments since 1941. The defense and grants data are generally presented on a functional and major program basis, whereas the
non-defense direct investment tables are based on the Special
Analysis D categories of construction and rehabilitation and
acquisition of major equipment. We believe that if OMB continued
to make improvements to the data supplied by categorizing it all
on a consistent functional and major program basis, including a
greater level of detail from the old public works special analysis, and packaging it as a new public works analysis, significant
improvements in information would be available to the executive
branch for planning and budgeting and to the Congress for authorizing and funding capital investment programs.

WEIGHING THE OPTIONS

All three options are designed to remedy the inadequate
presentation of capital information within the unified budget
framework. None of them incurs the disadvantages that we have
indicated to be associated with adopting a Federal dual budget
system. None of them requires the depreciation or the debt
financing of capital assets, two attributes usually associated
with a separate capital budget. Beyond these similarities,
however, are important differences that should not be obscured.

The proposal to resection the unified budget to distinguish
between capital investment and current Federal programs and obligations is an option that would affect the budget formulation
process within the executive branch. Resectioning facilitates
the careful consideration of spending aggregates for capital
investment and current programs as the President's budget proposals are being prepared. These focal points would also serve to
sharpen the congressional response to the Presidential budget
initiatives by increasing the visibility of each type of outlay.
Thus, the major advantage of this option is that it presents
capital outlays in both aggregate and as components of individual
programs for use in budget debates and in decisionmaking at all
levels.

An infrastructure and capital investment analysis could require an inventory and condition assessment of the existing infrastructure. Based upon this information, both current levels of effort and the proposed levels could be compared. Such an analysis would greatly enhance the Federal decisionmakers' information upon which critical decisions must be made. However, the development of the data bases by the agencies to support such analyses would probably be time-consuming and expensive.

Modifying Special Analysis D and preparing a new Special Analysis on Federal Public Works Activities are stopgap measures. Although the information these special analyses could provide would strengthen the ability of the Congress to perceive overall dimensions of the Federal capital investment role, their timing and largely descriptive nature limit their potential usefulness for policymaking.

EXISTING CAPITAL BUDGETING PRACTICES

Many organizations are bound by operational or legal constraints that dictate the use of capital budgets. Businesses, for example, must separate current expenses from capital outlays to determine net profit or loss. Most State and local governments distinguish between capital and operating expenses because they are required by law to present balanced operating budgets. Often, businesses and governments use capital budgets as plans for determining the need for and nature of capital assets, as well as their cost, timing of acquisition, and methods of financing. The Federal Government, however, treats capital asset outlays in the same manner as current operating expenses because it is not bound by any of the constraints that would require it to separate the capital and operating portions of the national budget.

BUSINESS ACCOUNTING AND CAPITAL BUDGETING PRACTICES

Business accounting practices are designed to portray accurately the magnitude of the firm's current operations, the value of its assets, and the extent of its indebtedness. Creditors, stockholders, and government agencies require information concerning these three factors. Consequently, businesses typically report data on their revenues, expenses, profits, tax liabilities, assets owned, depreciation, and equity and bond issues. Many of these data and the structure of the budget and financial statements in which they appear are not relevant to many of the purposes and responsibilities of the Federal Government.

Unlike the Federal Government, business firms usually do not deduct total capital outlays from current revenues in computing a "bottom line." Rather, capital expenses are shown as a series of operating charges representing the annual depreciation of capital assets and the cost of borrowing. Businesses charge depreciation in order to allocate proportionately the investment costs of depreciable assets to each accounting period during which the asset

was used in the production of goods and services and to recognize
the decline of service potential. Annual depreciation for tax
purposes is determined using the Internal Revenue Code. 1/ Depreciation for accounting purposes may be determined on a basis
more consistent with the estimated life of the asset.

Many businesses draw up separate capital budgets that show
large capital outlays scheduled to be made in future years, the
proposed means to finance them, and their expected benefits.
In this regard, the purpose of the capital budget is to help
evaluate the need for and nature, cost, and timing of acquiring
and financing long-lived assets. This is similar to the capital
budgeting practices of State and local governments.

STATE AND LOCAL GOVERNMENTS' ACCOUNTING AND CAPITAL BUDGETING PRACTICES

State and local governments use capital budgets as plans for
acquiring and financing capital items. Frequently, capital items
are distinguished and separated from the operating budget because
of a legal requirement to balance operating budgets. However,
they are not identical to business models. Generally, strict
business-type accounting methods are not used. Usually, except
for self-supporting enterprise funds, State and local governments
do not draw up business-type balance sheets of assets and liabilities, nor do they provide an estimate of asset depreciation.
This makes it impossible to compute their net worth or determine
whether their stock of assets is increasing or decreasing. Where
depreciation is used, the productive life of an asset is often
defined the same as in business accounting practices.

Capital budgets have become an essential part of the financial plans of State and local governments. Although the definition of capital varies substantially, many capital budgets summarize each capital item's need, cost, method of financing, and,
in some cases, its anticipated contribution to the community.
Used in this way, the capital budget is a good way of displaying
proposed capital projects--such as schools, sewer and water systems, public parks, and the like--and focusing the public's
attention on a very important segmet of government operations.

Capital budgets have also become an effective means of
carrying out the long-term projects of State and local governments. For the purpose of obtaining borrowed funds, capital
budgets are indispensable because State and local governments

   --often operate under legislative constraints that restrict
     borrowing and taxing ability (mandatory debt ceilings,
     requirements to balance the budget, limitations on tax
     rates and what can be taxed), and

1/Sections 167 and 168 of the Internal Revenue Code guide this
   determination. However, accelerated tax depreciation schedules
   do not correspond to the actual service life of an asset based
   on physical wear and tear and/or technological obsolescence.

--must meet solvency criteria set by investment bankers to gain access to financial markets. 1/

Separate budgeting for capital and operating expenses can and has caused coordination problems for State governments. One State developed its capital budget independent from its operating agencies. This resulted in the construction of facilities that were unplanned and even unwanted by the agencies that had to operate them. However, many States are recognizing this oversight and are improving their capital planning techniques. Operating and capital budgets are now often contained in the same document or handled as companion documents within a coordinated timetable. The recognized interdependence of capital assets and their operations has increased this type of coordination.

Many of the reasons that a capital budget is useful to State and local governments do not apply to the Federal Government. These include the fact that the Federal Government

--does not need a capital budget to preserve its credit rating and obtain access to the financial market;

--is not, in its ability to borrow, affected by asset acquisition, as in the case of municipal governments; and

--is not subject to the solvency criteria investment bankers enforce on local governments.

Instead, the Federal Government makes capital investment decisions within the boundaries set by aggregate debt limits, spending ceilings for each of the functional areas within the budget, and targeted levels of taxation. Collectively, these components of the budget process provide a major means of discipline for fiscal policy.

CAPITAL BUDGETING CONCEPTS AND THEIR IMPLICATIONS

How capital items are defined determines the percentage of total outlays that can be included in a capital budget. Varied definitions of capital assets can affect the respective sizes

----

1/Between 1972 and 1977, debt financing of State and local capital outlays declined from slightly over one-half to slightly over one-third of totals for this type of expenditure. There has been a corresponding, although not uniform, increase in reliance upon Federal grants-in-aid for capital financing, which in 1977 reached a 21 year high of 47 percent. Users fees, short-term debt, and accumulated reserves are also sources of capital investment funds. See U.S. Department of Commerce, A Study of Public Works Investment in the United States, April 1980, vol. I, ch. 4.

of capital and operating budgets and directly influence the size of the Federal deficit.

WHAT IS A CAPITAL EXPENDITURE?

Because there is lack of agreement on what should be classified as capital, organizations use various classifications. Different organizations using different definitions of capital items and capital budget totals showing large fluctuations from year to year complicates assessing the real costs of capital investment. Comparing yearly totals may be misleading because of irregular rates of new acquisitions or major rehabilitation of capital assets, and totals aggregated for more than one organization may be misleading because of the varying capital investment definitions used by different organizations. Under a dual budget system, it is often argued that the operating budget shoul• be balanced, and thus the incentive is strong to define capital as broadly as possible.

Generally, businesses define capital expenditures according to accounting principles and tax regulations. However, there is still some variation among businesses as to what is counted as a capital item. As a matter of prudence, State and local governments restrict capital expenditures to tangible assets, but their definitions of this term also vary widely.

For the Federal sector, limiting the definition of capital to federally owned non-military tangible assets would be very restrictive. Less than 6 percent of Federal outlays (see p. 35) are in this category. Using this definition would give only a partial picture of the Federal Government's contribution to asset formation. The Federal Government plays various roles in stimulating capital investment. It directly builds and maintains infrastructure, such as bridges and roads, and helps State and local governments do the same through grants-in-aid. The Federal Government also helps individuals and businesses with capital investments by making direct loans and by guaranteeing loans obtained from private sources. Frequently discussed but probably the least direct stimulus to capital investment provided by the Federal Government is the use of tax incentives, such as tax credits and accelerated depreciation allowances.

Direct Federal programs, grants-in-aid, loans, loan guarantees, and tax expenditures have diverse effects when they contribute to the building of infrastructure and the stimulation of private sector capital formation. It is difficult to identify the scope and intensity of the Federal role even in those areas where that role seems to be the most straightforward. Although direct Federal programs and grants-in-aid, for example, often produce highly visible public facilities--highways, mass transit systems, waste-water treatment plants, and the like--the benefits of these projects for the private sector of the economy are often unmeasureable. Not only do private corporations depend upon public facilities for the conduct of commerce and industry, but their own decisions to invest in new capital may be influenced--

in some cases decisively--by Federal investments either projected
or current.

Notwithstanding the virtues of adopting a broadly based
definition of capital investment, it is important to note the
potential pitfalls in doing so. Any departure from defining capital investments in terms of tangible assets clears the way for a
wide range of expenditures, each possessing a legitimate claim to
be classified as developmental or capital forming. The problem
is: where does one stop? Exactly what should be called capital
is a policy choice and depends on how the Congress chooses to use
the budget. Keeping a capital budget free from manipulation requires a precise and consistently used definition of capital. 1/
It is worth noting, however, that unified budgets can be similarly abused through the use of off-budget items.

Alternative definitions

Assets are defined as "probable future economic benefits obtained or controlled by a particular entity as a result of past
transactions or events." 2/ But, classifying an item as an asset
does not solve the problem of defining which items to capitalize. Tangible assets run the range from supplies to buildings,
yet no one would dispute treating supplies as current and
buildings as capital expenditures. What is not clear is how to
treat the assets that fall between these extremes.

Deciding which assets to capitalize is largely a matter of
judgment and depends on the asset's life, value, and frequency of
procurement. To place an asset in the capital category, it must
have a service life longer than the fiscal period, usually 1
year. Beyond this, the distinction between operating and capital
items lies in the perceived role of an item in relation to other
items being classified and, generally, whether the item is a re-

---

1/New York City is a prime example of how a capital budget can be
manipulated. GAO has conducted several reviews (PAD-77-1, GGD-
78-13, and GGD-80-5) of New York City's fiscal crisis. These,
as well as a study entitled The Future of New York City's
Capital Plant, prepared by the Urban Institute, showed that New
York included in its capital budget many expenditures that, in
strict municipal accounting terms, are generally operating
costs. These included funds for manpower training and vocational education, code enforcement, repair programs, purchase
of motor vehicles, and lease payments. By listing these expenditures as capital, the City removed them from a severely constrained operating budget and made them eligible for bond
financing. In fiscal year 1975, which was the onset of New
York's fiscal crisis, these expenditures exceeded 50 percent of
the capital budget.

2/Financial Accounting Standards Board, "Statement of Financial
Accounting Concepts No. 3," December 1980.

curring or non-recurring expenditure. What would be considered a capital item for a small municipality might be regarded as too insignificant to be similarly classified by a large city, a State, or the Federal Government. Furthermore, most of the time only non-recurring expenditures are considered capital.

Despite the inherent problems of classification, specific criteria for defining capital must be established before a capital budget can be used at the national level. For the Federal Government, criteria could take numerous forms, such as the nature of the asset, the asset's ownership, or the asset's relationship to accomplishing agency and program goals. Using these criteria, it is necessary to determine whether the definition of capital

--should be restricted to only tangible assets or broadened to include research and development expenditures and financial assets,

--should include only civilian assets or also military assets,

--should include only federally owned assets or also those assets totally or partially financed by the Federal Government but not federally owned, or

--should be restricted to those major items needed to accomplish an agency's primary mission as opposed to those items that provide administrative support.

Whether or not capital investments used for defense purposes should be included in a capital budget raises an issue meriting closer attention. Defense assets are often highly specialized in the purposes they serve, may be highly expendable for the same reason, and may also be subject to rapid and unpredictable technological obsolescence. It is commonly believed that defense assets are not productive in the same way as are the capital assets of the private sector or of Federal civilian agencies. These grounds could be used to justify excluding defense investments from a capital budget.

One way of arguing for including defense assets in a capital budget is to consider which of these assets are potentially transferable for civilian Federal or private sector use. Only transferable defense assets would then be capitalized. The primary difficulty with this approach is the arbitrary assumption upon which it is based. Many capital assets, regardless of the sector of society that uses them, are highly specialized, vulnerable to premature deterioration and subject to technological obsolescence. When private sector or civilian Federal assets are considered in these terms, little justification would seem to exist for no longer regarding broad categories of "rapidly depreciable" assets as capital investments. Insofar as an asset has a projected useful life in excess of 1 year and is expected to deliver a stream of future benefits, a cogent argument can be made for treating it as capital. So viewed, defense assets can be regarded quite appropriately as capital investment, although there may be other reasons for their exclusion from a capital budget.

HOW CAPITAL EXPENDITURES ARE DEFINED CAN AFFECT THE FEDERAL OPERATING SURPLUS OR DEFICIT

A number of advocates and opponents often assume that if the Federal Government had a dual budgeting system current expenditures would be kept in balance with annual receipts, while capital expenditures would be handled through debt financing. This being the case, how capital is defined affects the size of the operating budget deficit or surplus. To illustrate this point, we have developed five different definitions of capital, applied them to the Federal budget, and determined to what extent the resulting operating expenditures would be covered by total receipts. These definitions of capital range from a very narrow definition that includes only federally owned civil tangible assets to a very broad one that includes civil and defense physical assets, research and development, and education and training outlays. (See table 8.) Although capital can be defined in many ways, we restricted ourselves to five.

If a separate capital budget were adopted and there were a requirement to balance the operating budget, priorities should be established regarding payment of outlays. Under a dual budgeting system, payment of operating outlays can take precedence over making capital expenditures. Under these circumstances, total annual receipts are first targeted to meet operating expenditures. A combination of the current budget surplus, if any

Table 8

Cumulative Percentage of Capital Outlays
Based on Different Definitions of Capital

Model Number	Definition of Capital	Cumulative Percentage of Total Budget Outlays			
		1979	1980	1981	1982
1	Civil: Construction and rehabilitation and acquisition of physical assets	5.8	5.5	4.9	4.2
2	Plus: Defense construction and rehabilitation and acquisition of major equipment and other physical assets	11.8	11.2	10.9	10.9
3	Plus: Civil research and development	14.7	13.9	13.5	13.0
4	Plus: Defense research and development	17.2	16.4	16.1	15.7
5	Plus: Civil education and training	22.3	21.0	20.1	18.6

exists, and long-term debt is then used to finance capital outlays. This practice makes the definition of capital very important in determining both the size of the operating budget and the
degree of reliance upon debt financing.

Because no uniform criteria for defining capital are used,
organizations can classify a wide range of items as capital. We
developed the five budget models based on different definitions
of capital to illustrate how the budget totals are dependent on a
particular definition. Initially, we divided the unified budget
into its operating and capital components, based on each model's
definition of capital. To do this, we extracted the actual outlay figures for fiscal year 1979 through 1982 from Special Analysis D based on the definitions of capital shown in table 8. For
example, capital is defined in model number 1 as civil tangible
physical assets.

Capital outlays are calculated by combining the data
displayed in Special Analysis D in the civil construction and
rehabilitation of physical assets category with those in the
acquisition of major equipment category. Each subsequent definition of capital we describe is cumulative. In other words, each
definition includes not only the categories of items for that
particular definition of capital but also the categories used in
the previous definitions.

Once the capital outlay totals for all 4 fiscal years and
each definition of capital were determined, we subtracted the
capital outlay total for each fiscal year from the unified budget
total of that year to determine operating outlays. Finally, we
subtracted operating outlays from total receipts to determine the
deficit or surplus. As is shown in table 9, the operating budget
picture changes as the definition of capital changes. For example, the fiscal year 1982 operating outlays exceed total receipts
by $79.8 billion for model 1 (civil construction and rehabilita-
tion and acquisition of physical assets). If defense physical

Table 9

Effect of Removing Capital Items from the Federal Budget
on the Deficit or Surplus for 1979-1982
Five Definitions of Capital a/

Fiscal Year	Actual Budget Deficit/Surplus	Model Number				
		1	2	3	4	5
1979	-27.7	0.8	30.2	44.4	56.6	82.0
1980	-59.6	-28.0	4.9	20.5	35.1	61.3
1981	-57.9	-25.8	13.9	31.1	48.0	74.2
1982	-110.6	-79.8	-31.0	-16.2	3.6	25.2

a/We did not include loans and financial investments or commodity
   inventories programs in our definitions of capital type items.

capital (model 2) is also subtracted from the operating budget the deficit is reduced to $31.0 billion. If civil and defense research and development is subtracted, there is a $3.6 billion surplus that can be applied to a portion of capital outlays. This surplus grows to $25.2 billion when human capital (model 5, civil education and training) is subtracted from the operating budget.

Appendix F
How Changes in Fiscal Policy Affect the Budget: The Feedback Issue

Reprinted from a special study by the Congressional Budget Office, June, 1982.

SUMMARY

Federal tax cuts or spending cuts are often discussed as though they were simple subtractions from revenues or outlays. Their effects are estimated on the assumption that they make no difference in the performance of the national economy. It is widely recognized, however, that tax and spending changes may cause changes in the economy, which in turn may affect budget revenues and outlays through "feedback effects." Satisfactory estimates of the overall budgetary impacts of tax or spending changes are, however, not always available to the Congress.

This paper develops estimates of feedback rates for different tax and spending changes in order to illustrate their rough magnitudes and the number and importance of the issues that are involved. The estimates are derived with the assistance of several econometric models.[1] Emphasis is given to differences in the estimated feedback rates for four different tax and spending changes: reductions in personal income tax rates, in corporation tax rates, in federal purchases of goods and services, and in federal transfer payments. Two special tax measures are considered

---

1. As it turns out, there is significant variation among the results from different models. While this fact itself is evidence that the state of available knowledge about feedback effects is uncertain, it provides little guidance as to their likely magnitudes. Accordingly, the paper develops illustrative "model consensus" estimates for each policy change, and discusses some of the sources of uncertainty.

separately: provisions governing special-purpose tax-exempt bonds
such as industrial revenue bonds, and reductions in the special tax
rate on capital gains.

How Feedback Effects Work

When feedback effects are ignored, the impact of a 10 percent
cut in tax rates is given by the change in effective tax rates
multiplied by the level of taxable income anticipated for that
year. This is called the "static" impact.[2] The change in tax
rates may, however, stimulate changes in working and spending by
households and in hiring and investing by firms, among other
economic effects. These impacts may increase Gross National
Product (GNP) and taxable incomes, and therefore tax receipts. The
increase in receipts is directly related to the tax cut, and is
therefore known as the "revenue feedback effect" or "revenue
reflow" of the cut. The feedback effect at least partially offsets
the static budget impact, leading to an actual impact on budget
revenues that is a combination of the two separate parts.

The change in the behavior of the economy may also cause
changes in budget outlays. Changes in unemployment affect unemployment compensation and other categories of transfer payments,
while changes in inflation have impacts on programs that are
indexed to the price level. Outlays for interest on the federal
debt may change because of changes in interest rates and in federal
borrowing that may be caused by the policy change. All of these
induced responses in outlays together make up the "outlay feedback
effect." This effect, together with revenue feedbacks and the
static impact, constitutes the overall effect of the policy change
on the budget.

When Should Feedback Estimates Be Used?

Static budget impact estimates are valuable for many purposes. Such figures provide useful information on the quantity of

---

2. Both static and feedback estimates are sensitive to the under-
    lying economic forecast. If the particular monetary and fiscal
    policies that are assumed in making the economic forecast are
    not actually put in place, then both the forecast and the
    budget estimates that are based on it can be inaccurate. For
    this reason, close attention to the assumptions underlying a
    given set of budget estimates is important.

resources that the federal government allocates to different uses and on the magnitude of the impulse that the budget gives to overall economic activity. Incorporating feedbacks is important only when interest centers on the overall impact of a given tax or spending proposal on the budget deficit. Even then, however, trouble can sometimes be saved by using static impact estimates during some stages of discussion. Since all budget policy changes may entail feedbacks, and since such changes are usually considered in groups, it saves time to consider individual proposals in terms of static impact estimates and to incorporate feedbacks only when the outline of an overall package of proposals becomes known. At that point, proposals thought to have similar feedback rates can be combined.

Estimating Feedback Effects

One way to generate budget estimates that include feedbacks is to develop an entirely new economic and budgetary forecast on the basis of each tax or spending proposal that comes under consideration. This procedure is cumbersome, however, given the numbers of budget policy changes that are typically discussed during a legislative session. A more practical alternative that is developed in this paper is to generate simple "feedback rates" expressing the percentage of the static budget impact of a given type of policy change that is offset by feedbacks in a given year. A tax cut with a static revenue loss of $10 billion and a feedback rate of 40 percent, for example, would cause a net increase in the federal deficit of $6 billion; the other $4 billion would be offset by feedback effects. Negative feedbacks, conversely, represent cases in which the feedbacks <u>reinforce</u> the static deficit impact of a policy change, instead of offsetting it.

ECONOMIC IMPACTS OF CHANGES IN FEDERAL FISCAL POLICY

There is considerable controversy and uncertainty regarding the economic impacts of changes in federal fiscal policy. Traditional theories have been severely criticized from a "supply side" point of view for taking insufficient account of the effects of fiscal policy on the available supplies of work and savings, and of possible changes in the structure of the economy in recent decades. Another important line of criticism, the "rational expectations" point of view, holds that traditional analytic approaches pay insufficient attention to the expectations of workers, employers, and other economic agents regarding the future course of the economy.

The estimates presented in this paper are largely based on traditional and, to a lesser extent, "supply side" analysis. Few "rational expectations" approaches to short-term quantitative policy analysis like that discussed in this paper are available, largely because adherents of this point of view are less concerned with short-term analysis, and because some argue that current techniques for quantitative analysis are highly unreliable.[3] Since alternative points of view to those taken in this paper are possible, however, the estimates presented here are far from definitive.

Outlay and Revenue Feedback Rates

A range of estimated feedback rates is shown in Summary Table 1 for each of four different budget policy changes assumed to have taken effect on October 1, 1981. The changes consist of reductions in individual income tax rates, in corporation income tax rates, in federal purchases of goods and services, and in federal transfer payments to persons. In fiscal 1982, for example, the figures suggest that between 6 and 22 percent of the static revenue cost of a cut in personal tax rates may be offset by induced increases in revenue. Increases in outlays for interest and other programs, however, may amount to as much as 6 percent of the static revenue loss, and like the static loss these outlay changes increase the deficit rather than reduce it. As a net result the revenue and outlay feedbacks taken together may offset between 2 and 23 percent of the static deficit impact in 1982. The estimates assume that the Federal Reserve follows a "partially accommodating" policy of holding the path of nonborrowed reserves unchanged, perhaps allowing both interest rates and the money supply to vary somewhat in response to the budget policy change.

Estimates of each feedback rate vary widely among econometric models, largely reflecting technical differences in the models. Much of the variation is contributed by the estimates of outlay feedback rates, which reflect induced changes in spending for interest, transfer payments, and programs that are "indexed" to the price level. These rates are, however, consistently negative be-

---

3. For discussion of these points, see Robert Lucas, "Econometric Policy Evaluation: A Critique," in Karl Brunner and Allan Meltzer, eds., The Phillips Curve and Labor Markets (North Holland, 1977), pp. 19-46, and Stanley Fischer, ed., Rational Expectations and Economic Policy (University of Chicago Press, 1980).

SUMMARY TABLE 1. RANGES OF FEEDBACK RATES FOR FOUR FISCAL POLICY CHANGES ESTIMATED FROM ECONOMETRIC MODELS ASSUMING THAT MONETARY POLICY IS PARTIALLY ACCOMMODATING[a] (By fiscal year)[b]

	1982	1983	1984	1985	1986
Reductions in individual income tax rates					
Total	2 to 23	8 to 31	6 to 35	-5 to 34	-23 to 43
Revenues	6 to 22	20 to 39	28 to 46	31 to 59	31 to 81
Outlays	-6 to 0	-15 to -8	-27 to 12	-42 to -15	-60 to -20
Reductions in corporation income tax rates					
Total	-11 to 13	-6 to 27	-7 to 69	-14 to 113	-26 to 146
Revenues	-9 to 16	2 to 34	10 to 70	13 to 105	12 to 129
Outlays	-6 to -1	-11 to -3	-17 to -1	-28 to 8	-38 to 17
Reductions in federal purchases					
Total	27 to 48	33 to 62	31 to 68	39 to 74	26 to 75
Revenues	26 to 46	37 to 61	54 to 71	60 to 89	59 to 104
Outlays	-3 to 2	-12 to 0	-23 to -3	-29 to -5	-37 to -7
Reductions in federal transfer payments					
Total	2 to 20	3 to 25	8 to 29	-5 to 28	-23 to 39
Revenues	7 to 19	16 to 35	31 to 42	37 to 56	38 to 76
Outlays	-6 to 1	-15 to -9	-23 to -13	-42 to -17	-39 to -21

a. The econometric models that were used to generate these estimates are those of Chase Econometrics, Inc.; Data Resources, Inc. version US81C; Evans Economics, Inc.; and Wharton Econometric Forecasting Associates, Inc. version 6.1.

b. Percentage of static budget impact offset by feedback effects. Negative sign denotes feedbacks that reinforce static impact, rather than offsetting it. Figures for revenues and outlays may not sum to those for total feedback rate because "revenue" and "outlay" figures shown may be drawn from different models, while each "total" figure is based on revenue and outlay estimates from the same model.

cause of the large impact of each policy change on interest payments on the federal debt. Interest outlays change by relatively large amounts because changes in budget policy affect both the amount of federal borrowing and the level of interest rates. A tax cut, for example, may increase both federal borrowing and interest rates, while a spending cut does the reverse. According to the estimates presented in this paper, changes in interest payments almost always reinforce the static impact on the deficit, and they always dominate other outlay feedbacks. These estimates, however, are heavily dependent on the "baseline" levels of interest rates. Should rates fall from the relatively high levels that were assumed in this study, the magnitudes of interest outlay responses to changes in policy could be significantly smaller.

The strongest revenue feedbacks, for economic reasons that are explored in the text, appear to be those from changes in federal purchases, followed by those for changes in personal tax rates and changes in transfer payments to persons, which appear to be approximately the same. Estimates of revenue feedbacks for changes in corporation income tax rates are highly uncertain, but they appear to be the lowest from any of the different policy changes, at least during the first two years after enactment.

In absolute terms the figures for cuts in purchases suggest that revenue feedbacks offset roughly one-quarter to one-half of the static budget saving of a cut during the first year after enactment, an amount which rises above one-half by the third year and even higher in the fifth. The revenue feedbacks for reductions in transfers and in individual income tax rates are slightly below these levels: a third to half of the static revenue loss is recouped in revenue feedbacks by the third year, and perhaps as much as 80 percent by the fifth year. The revenue feedback figures for reductions in corporation income tax rates, finally, are too widely divergent to permit useful inferences to be drawn.

Summary Table 2 shows "model consensus" feedback rate estimates for each different policy change. These figures were developed using CBO's Multipliers Consensus Framework.[4] They largely reflect the quantitative inferences that have just been described. The estimates for a personal tax cut, for example,

---

4. The Multipliers Consensus Framework was developed as a means of reconciling varying results from different econometric models by averaging certain "key" parameters of those models. For a detailed description, see Appendix C of this report.

SUMMARY TABLE 2. "MODEL CONSENSUS" FEEDBACK RATE ESTIMATES FOR DIFFERENT FISCAL POLICY CHANGES ASSUMING THAT MONETARY POLICY IS PARTIALLY ACCOMMODATING (By fiscal year)[a]

	1982	1983	1984	1985	1986
Reductions in individual income tax rates					
Total	11	13	12	10	5
Revenues	19	37	45	50	57
Outlays	-8	-24	-33	-40	-52
Reductions in corporation income tax rates					
Total	-2	13	25	28	20
Revenues	8	26	40	48	42
Outlays	-10	-13	-15	-20	-22
Reductions in federal purchases					
Total	25	33	29	21	18
Revenues	30	49	57	61	68
Outlays	-5	-16	-28	-40	-50
Reductions in transfer payments to individuals					
Total	11	13	13	10	9
Revenues	19	37	46	52	59
Outlays	-8	-24	-33	-41	-50

a. Percentage of static budget impact offset by feedbacks; negative sign denotes feedbacks that reinforce static impact, rather than offsetting it. Detail may not sum to totals because of rounding.

suggest that 19 percent of the static revenue cost is offset by
revenue feedbacks in 1982, and 57 percent in 1986, though negative
outlay feedbacks reduce the overall feedback rates in each of these
years. The revenue feedback rate estimates for cuts in corporation
income tax rates are the smallest from any of the policy changes.

The Importance of Monetary Policy

There is some uncertainty about how monetary policy might
behave in response to changes in tax or spending policy. The estimates presented above assume that the Federal Reserve would allow
both interest rates and the money supply to change somewhat in the
face of a fiscal policy change—an assumption called "partial
accommodation" that has been satisfactory in the past. The Fed's
1979 announcement that it intends to control the money supply more
closely raises the possibility, however, that the money supply
might change little or not at all—a "nonaccommodating" monetary
policy—while interest rates might be affected more strongly. If
this happened, feedback rates for budget policy changes might be
significantly reduced from the levels shown above. This is shown
in Summary Table 3, which shows feedback rate estimates from simulation of each of the policy changes discussed above on two econometric models, assuming that the Federal Reserve follows a nonaccommodating policy. The revenue feedback rates are reduced and the
negative feedbacks from outlays for interest are increased relative
to the levels for a "partially accommodating" monetary policy. The
figures reflect a stronger likelihood that a tax cut, for example,
may increase the deficit by more than the static revenue loss estimate, principally because of the strong increases in interest
rates, and therefore in budget outlays for interest, that the tax
cut may cause.

Are Strong Feedback Effects Necessarily Good?

It is tempting to conclude that high feedback rates of tax
cuts are a positive factor, on the grounds that the static revenue
costs of such tax cuts are misleadingly high. A large part of this
revenue feedback, however, may result directly from increases in
inflation that may be caused by the tax cut. Inflation is especially efficient at producing new federal revenues: increases in
wages and profits reflecting inflation swell the tax base and also
push individual taxpayers into higher tax brackets. When the revenue feedbacks of cuts in personal tax rates are recomputed on the
assumption that the tax cut causes no change in inflation, the
estimated revenue feedback rates are reduced substantially.

SUMMARY TABLE 3.   RANGES OF FEEDBACK RATES FOR FOUR FISCAL POLICY CHANGES ESTIMATED FROM ECONOMETRIC MODELS[a] ASSUMING THAT MONETARY POLICY IS NONACCOMMODATING (In fiscal years)[b]

	1982	1983	1984	1985	1986
Reductions in individual income tax rates					
Total	-4 to 22	-22 to 14	-36 to 1	-48 to -16	-57 to -43
Revenues	4 to 22	5 to 29	6 to 32	7 to 35	10 to 34
Outlays	-8 to 0	-27 to -14	-41 to 31	-55 to 51	-68 to 77
Reductions in corporation income tax rates					
Total	-1 to -11	0 to -5	-17 to -6	-36 to -14	-43 to -27
Revenues	-9 to 4	2 to 15	10 to 11	5 to 13	8 to 12
Outlays	-5 to -1	-15 to -7	-28 to -16	-41 to -27	-50 to -40
Reductions in federal purchases					
Total	3 to 44	-12 to 47	-24 to 45	-42 to 33	-45 to 14
Revenues	16 to 41	17 to 49	21 to 56	17 to 59	25 to 57
Outlays	-12 to 2	-30 to -2	-45 to -12	-59 to -26	-70 to -43
Reductions in federal transfer payments					
Total	-3 to 20	-23 to 15	-31 to 3	-44 to -16	-52 to -43
Revenues	5 to 19	3 to 26	7 to 30	7 to 34	10 to 35
Outlays	-8 to 1	-26 to -11	-38 to -28	-51 to -50	-61 to -78

a.   The econometric models that were used to generate these estimates are those of Data Resources, Inc. version US81C; and Wharton Econometric Forecasting Associates, Inc. version 6.1. Other models were not used because of technical difficulties in analyzing nonaccommodating monetary policy on those models.

b.   Percentage of static revenue loss offset by budget feedback; negative sign denotes feedback that reinforces static deficit impact, rather than offsetting it. Conversion of results to Unified Budget accounting basis was done by CBO.

CHAPTER I.   INTRODUCTION

What is the overall effect on the federal budget of a given change in tax rates or federal spending? Can tax cuts pay for themselves by stimulating new surges of taxable economic activity? Do matched tax and spending cuts leave the deficit unchanged? These frequent questions concern the "feedback" or "reflow" effects of tax and spending changes.

Federal spending and taxes play such a large role in the economy that changes in them are likely to stimulate significant changes in spending, working, investing, and other kinds of economic behavior. These in turn may affect taxable incomes and tax revenues and change certain budget outlays that are sensitive to fluctuations in the economy--impacts that are known as the budgetary "reflow" or "feedback" effects of a change in fiscal policy. Estimating feedback effects for different types of fiscal policy change makes it possible to convert static impact estimates into estimates of the actual net effect on the budget.

WHEN SHOULD FEEDBACK ESTIMATES BE USED?

Static budget impact estimates are valuable for many purposes.   They convey useful information on the quantities of resources that the federal government devotes to different uses, and on the magnitude of the impulse to the economy that the federal budget entails. They also contain incomplete but useful information on both the overall budget impact of a proposal and on its distribution, which is valuable because it is less controversial and uncertain than are net-of-feedback estimates. Finally, since most changes in budget policy entail feedbacks, and since such changes are normally considered in groups, use of static instead of net-of-feedback estimates can often save trouble. In many cases the feedbacks of one program change will be offset by those of others, implying that efforts spent on computing feedbacks for each separate proposal will have been wasted.

When interest centers on the overall deficit impact of a change in tax or spending policy, however, feedback effects must be considered.   One way to incorporate feedbacks in budget estimates is to make an entirely new economic forecast on the basis of each budget policy proposal, together with forecasts of the resulting levels of federal revenues and outlays. This procedure may often be cumbersome, however, given the number of policy proposals that typically come under consideration during a legislative session. A more practical alternative is to develop simple rules for converting static impact estimates into net impacts. Different policy changes with similar feedback rates per dollar of static budget impact can be grouped together before the rules are applied, permitting the net budgetary impact of a program to be estimated relatively easily.

This paper sets forth the issues associated with the feedback question together with illustrative estimates of the feedback rates for different fiscal policy changes based on simulations of econometric models. Efforts are made to show how much these estimates might be affected by changes in underlying conditions. Chapter II gives a brief overview of the economic and budgetary factors that underlie feedback effects. Chapter III discusses in detail the feedback effects of four important types of budget policy change using quantitative estimates from simulations of various econometric models.

The economic and budgetary impacts of policy changes that affect the economy as a whole--like cuts in personal or corporate tax rates--may differ from those of changes that focus on only a small part of the economy. Appendixes A and B develop estimates of the feedbacks from two such special provisions--reduced tax rates on capital gains, and the federal tax exemption for the interest on certain bonds such as industrial revenue bonds. Appendix C, finally, provides technical data relevant to feedback rate estimation, and briefly describes the feedback-estimation procedures used by the Congressional Budget Office (CBO).

The revenue feedback rates of cuts in federal spending, on the other hand, represent <u>reductions</u> in revenues. These may offset at least some of the static reduction in the deficit brought about through spending cuts. In these cases, however, a large part of the revenue feedback may reflect reductions in inflation, so the revenue feedback effects of reductions in spending are not entirely undesirable. Moreover, since spending cuts may cause significant reductions in outlays for interest, as reflected in their outlay feedback estimates, they may cause a substantial overall reduction in the deficit.

CHAPTER II. HOW FEEDBACK EFFECTS WORK

The effects of changes in budget policy are estimated with the aid of economic forecasts. The static impact of a cut in personal tax rates, for example, is calculated by multiplying the change in effective rates by a forecast of taxable income made without taking the tax change into account. But the change in tax policy may be expected to stimulate the economy, changing gross national product GNP, taxable income, employment, and other factors. The budget feedback effect is estimated from increases in expected tax revenues and changes in the forecasts of other budget components that are sensitive to increased economic activity.

Changes in fiscal policy may exert feedback effects through their effects on the demand for goods and services and on the supplies of labor and other inputs to the process of production. Tax cuts and spending increases, for example, may cause GNP to expand through these channels, and may thus increase taxable incomes and tax revenues. The reverse may be true of tax increases or spending cuts. The result is a set of revenue feedbacks that may at least partially offset the static impact of the policy change.

Fiscal policy changes can also cause feedback effects through induced changes in budget outlays. A tax cut or spending increase may increase employment, reducing outlays for unemployment compensation and other programs that provide "transfer payments." The reverse may be true of tax increases or spending cuts.

Other feedback effects are more complex. A tax cut may increase the rate of inflation by raising the demand for goods and services. The increase in inflation would increase budget outlays for programs like Social Security that are "indexed" to the price level. This feedback effect working through increased outlays would increase the deficit and thus <u>reinforce</u> the static deficit impact of the fiscal policy change.

A final significant feedback impact of changes in tax or spending policy works through changes in interest payments on the federal debt. A tax cut or spending increase, for example, may increase interest rates in the financial markets at the same time that it forces the government to issue more debt to cover the budget impact of the change. Both the increase in debt and the higher interest rates are likely to cause budget outlays for interest to increase. This is also generally a negative feedback, reinforcing the static deficit impact of the policy change.

ESTIMATING FEEDBACK EFFECTS

This paper presents illustrative estimates of the feedback effects of several important types of change in federal spending and tax policy. In each case, the estimated budget impact is described in terms of its feedback rate—the percentage of the static budget impact of a given policy change that is offset by feedback.

The net result reflects the overall impact of the policy change on the budget. For example, a tax cut that has a feedback rate of zero increases the deficit by an amount equal to its static revenue loss estimate, while a cut with a positive feedback rate of 100 percent has no impact on the deficit--it is "self financing" in that its feedback effects offset its static revenue loss entirely.

The process of estimating revenue feedback effects can be broken down for analytic convenience into five steps:

o Estimating the static impact of a given policy change;

o Estimating the impact of the change on GNP, unemployment, inflation, and interest rates;

o Estimating the response of various components of taxable income to the change in GNP;

o Estimating the effective tax rates applicable to these changes in taxable incomes; and, finally,

o Estimating feedbacks involving changes in budget outlays using direct estimates of the responsiveness of outlays to changes in unemployment, inflation, and interest rates.

Technical issues associated with these analytic steps, and CBO's estimating procedures, are discussed in Appendix C.

Estimating Static Budget Impacts

The static budget impacts of changes in federal spending policy are normally estimated by CBO, while those for changes in tax policy are usually estimated by the staff of the Joint Committee on Taxation. In each case, estimates are made using a single, standard economic forecast. This forecast assumes a particular set of economic policies and is generally not adjusted to reflect the economic impacts that the change in policy may have.[1]

---

1. Both static and reflow estimates are sensitive to the underlying economic forecast; a given estimate is accurate only if the forecast is. One important reason for which a given budget impact estimate can be misleading is that the economic policy that was assumed in making the economic forecast may not actually be put in place. For example, as the discussion below will show, budget impact estimates based on a forecast assuming a relatively liberal "accommodating" monetary policy may be inaccurate if the actual monetary policy is tight or "nonaccommodating." Similarly, estimates made assuming that certain fiscal policy changes have already been enacted will be inaccurate if those changes are not made. For these reasons it is important to pay attention to underlying assumptions when using "static" or "reflow" estimates.

Economic Impacts of Changes in Fiscal Policy

As the next chapter points out, there is much controversy and uncertainty in the analysis of the economic impacts of changes in federal fiscal policy. This implies that any quantitative estimate must be regarded as tentative, since it is based on a particular economic point of view.

According to the traditional economic analysis that underlies much of the discussion in this paper changes in federal tax rates and spending levels may affect GNP by causing changes in aggregate demand and in the amounts of labor and savings that are supplied. The initial GNP impacts of these changes may then be augmented through the action of multiplier effects.[2]

Cuts in individual income tax rates may exert impacts on GNP by increasing taxpayers' disposable incomes, which may increase their demand for goods and services (if no offsets occur) and consequently increase GNP. In addition, cuts in tax rates may increase the willingness of individuals to work and save, and this may increase GNP by increasing the supplies of labor and capital, two important inputs to the process of producing GNP. Most analysts and model builders, however, believe that these effects are small. Initial increases in GNP that may occur through these channels may be augmented through "multiplier" effects as recipients of new income from the increases in production spend some of this increase, causing GNP to expand still more. Firms may, in addition, expand their investment, motivated partly by the new supplies of individual saving and partly also by a need to expand their productive capacity to meet the increases in consumer demand that they foresee as a result of the tax change.

Cuts in business taxes, such as reductions in statutory corporate tax rates, may induce firms to expand their investments because the tax cut reduces the after-tax cost of funds and increases business cash flow. The increases in investment may in turn cause larger increases in GNP, first through the multiplier

---

2. For a detailed discussion of traditional views of the ways in which tax and spending changes affect the economy, see Congressional Budget Office, Understanding Fiscal Policy (April 1978). For different points of view, see Norman B. Ture, "'Supply-Side' Economics and Public Policy," testimony presented to the Joint Economic Committee, U.S. Congress, May 21, 1980, and Stanley Fischer, ed., Rational Expectations and Economic Policy (University of Chicago Press, 1980).

effects described in the previous paragraph, and, after some time has passed, through their effects in expanding the stock of capital that can be used in producing GNP. As the next section will show, however, estimates of both the magnitude and the timing of increases in investment in response to business tax cuts are especially uncertain.

Reductions in federal purchases of goods and services such as outlays for payroll costs may cause GNP to fall by reducing the demand for goods and services. The ultimate reduction in GNP may be larger than the cuts in federal spending themselves because of multiplier impacts.

Reductions in transfer payments to persons, such as Social Security or unemployment insurance benefits, may reduce GNP through channels much like those for changes in personal tax rates. The disposable incomes of recipients are reduced, and this may reduce their demand for goods and services. Cuts in transfers may also have effects on the supply of labor if they affect the attractiveness of extra work for their potential recipients.

Changes in Taxable Incomes

The federal revenue impact of the changes in economic activity described above cannot be estimated without first calculating the resulting changes in the tax base. Since most federal revenue is derived from income taxes, this means that the impacts must be estimated for three taxable income aggregates: wages and salaries, corporate profits, and taxable nonwage personal income (unincorporated business and farm profits, rental income, dividends, and personal interest income).[3] Changes in wages and salaries are taxed under the individual income tax and the payroll taxes for Social Security and unemployment insurance. Nonwage personal income is taxed under the individual income tax, and corporate profits before tax under the corporation income tax.[4] Certain

---

3. The behavior of the different components of the tax base in response to a change in GNP is discussed in more detail in Appendix C and in Congressional Budget Office, "A Model of Taxable Incomes for Forecasting and Analysis," unpublished technical paper, 1981.

4. Parts of nonwage personal income are subject to tax under the self-employed provisions of the Social Security tax, while dividends, because they are counted under both nonwage personal income and corporate profits before tax, are taxed under both the corporation and the individual income taxes.

other sources of federal revenue, such as excises and customs duties, respond more directly to GNP itself, while others, such as the windfall profits tax and Federal Reserve profits, have specialized bases.

Tax Rates Applicable to Changes in Taxable Incomes

A final step in determining the feedback effects of changes in federal fiscal policy on federal revenues is estimating the tax rate that applies to the change in each component of the tax base, as well as the timing patterns according to which the resulting federal revenues are reflected in the Unified Budget. Different rates apply to different parts of the tax base. Moreover, some of these rates can be expected to change in response to changes in the economy, including those caused by federal fiscal policy.

Budget Feedbacks Working Through Changes in Outlays

Changes in federal fiscal policy may exert feedback effects on the budget not only through changes in revenues, but also through impacts on budget outlays that are responsive to changes in the economy. This is true regardless of whether the initial policy change involves taxes or outlays. In particular, changes in employment caused by the policy change have impacts on transfer programs; changes in prices cause changes in programs that are legally or effectively indexed to inflation such as Social Security, federal pensions, Medicare, and others; and changes in interest rates and in outstanding debt change the interest paid on the federal debt.[5] Changes in interest payments can be quite large, as the estimates presented in this paper show. However, they are quite sensitive to the assumed "baseline" level of interest rates; should interest rates fall from their early 1982 levels, the sensitivity of interest outlays could change.

ARE STRONG FEEDBACK EFFECTS ALWAYS GOOD?

It is tempting to conclude that policy changes having strong positive feedback effects are especially attractive because they

---

5. For discussions of the effects of economic variables on federal budget outlays, see Congressional Budget Office, Base-line Budget Projections: Fiscal Years 1982-1986 (July 1981), pp. 53-58; and Frank de Leeuw et. al., "The High-Employment Budget: New Estimates, 1955-80," Survey of Current Business (November 1980), pp. 13-43.

have relatively small impacts on the budget deficit. To the extent that the revenue loss from personal tax cuts is offset by revenue feedback, for example, economic changes that may be achieved through the policy change, such as increases in economic growth, appear to be without cost in terms of lost revenues.

Such arguments can be misleading, however, because they may overlook certain economic costs of these policy changes in order to focus more narrowly on the federal budget effects. Expansionary fiscal policies such as tax cuts or spending increases may produce strong revenue feedback effects because they may increase the rate of inflation, which (until tax indexing is introduced in 1985) will increase revenues relatively strongly by pushing individual tax-payers into higher tax rate brackets. Thus, the strong revenue feedback effects of such policy changes result in part from un-desirable economic effects—increases in inflation. A second reason why budget policy changes with strong feedbacks are not necessarily desirable is, of course, that feedbacks apply to both increases and decreases in tax rates or spending levels. Just as strong feedbacks imply that relatively little <u>increase</u> in the deficit may result from some tax cuts or spending increases, they also mean that little <u>reduction</u> in the deficit may be achieved when spending is cut or taxes raised.

THE IMPORTANCE OF MONETARY POLICY

The impact of changes in fiscal policy on the economy and the budget depends critically on the behavior of monetary policy. The Federal Reserve's response may determine whether the fiscal policy change causes, at one extreme, a small short-run impact on GNP, unemployment, and prices, together with a large change in interest rates; a relatively large economic impact with little or no change in interest rates at another extreme; or something in between. In the longer run, too, the relationship between the stances of fiscal and monetary policy can have significant implications for important economic magnitudes such as productivity and inflation.

Because of these economic effects, budgetary feedback effects are quite sensitive to the stance of monetary policy. In particu-lar, as the estimates in the next chapter will show, if changes in fiscal policy are accompanied by strict Federal Reserve efforts to control the money supply, relatively sharp changes in interest rates may result. These may cause federal outlays for interest on the debt to fluctuate strongly enough to dominate other feedback effects.

CHAPTER III. FEEDBACK RATES FOR SELECTED FISCAL POLICY MEASURES:
EVIDENCE FROM ECONOMETRIC MODELS

This chapter provides feedback estimates for each of four
major types of fiscal policy change: reductions in individual income tax rates, reductions in corporation income tax rates, reductions in federal purchases of goods and services, and reductions in
federal government transfer payments to persons. Estimates are
given of feedback rates over several fiscal years for each type of
change, together with a discussion of the degree of uncertainty
associated with each estimate. The procedure is to derive ranges
of estimates based on simulation results from various econometric
models, together with "model consensus" estimates developed at CBO.

Uses of Econometric Models

Econometric models are collections of statistical equations
expressing economic relationships in quantitative terms. These
collections of equations are designed to replicate the actual
economy so as to show how the economy and the budget deficit would
be affected by particular events, such as a hypothetical tax or
spending cut. Because several different reactions occur simultaneously in response to any policy change, a framework of different
equations is needed that can be solved simultaneously, taking into
account and reconciling these conceptually separate but nevertheless simultaneous events.

While models are useful for estimating the likely magnitudes
of the economy's responses to changes in policy, they also raise
many problems. Neither the economic theories on which models are
based nor the statistical techniques used in translating theory
into concrete form are sufficiently developed to prevent different
models from generating divergent estimates of the same economic
magnitude. One reason among many is perhaps that the structure
of the economy is changing in ways that statistical relationships
based on historical data do not recognize. For such reasons,
results from any given model must be used critically.

Modeling Alternative Views of How the Economy Works

In recent years, conventional ideas about how government
policies affect the economy have undergone extensive criticism.
One set of criticisms from a "supply-side" perspective has been

based on the view that government tax and spending policies exert their major effects on the supply of labor and savings, rather than on aggregate demand as in traditional analysis. A second critical view, from a "rational expectations" point of view, also focuses on supply, but its main emphasis is on the role of policy in relation to workers' and employers' expectations of the future course of the economy.[1]

The analysis presented in this paper is based on traditional and, to a lesser extent, supply-side analysis. Rational expectations discussion is not presented, mainly because it is intended more for long-run analysis than for the short-run purposes of this paper, and because few quantitative rational expectations models are available. Indeed, some rational expectations economists have expressed grave doubts about the accuracy of current methods of quantitative policy analysis.[2] Because alternative approaches are possible, however, the estimates presented in this paper are far from definitive.

The Importance of Initial Conditions

The estimates presented below are based on the assumption that the specified policy changes go into effect on October 1, 1981. The initial economic conditions are therefore those that were in effect on that date. The economic conditions that exist when a fiscal policy change takes effect have an impact, of course, on its feedback rate. If the unemployment rate is relatively high, for example, the likelihood that a stimulative policy change such as a tax cut will generate increases in inflation may be reduced. The level of interest rates is also important to the feedback rate. Since most fiscal policy changes affect the amount of new federal debt that must be issued and financed, interest rates help determine the amount by which outlays for interest respond to the policy change.

---

1. For discussion of these points of view, see Norman B. Ture, "'Supply Side' Economics and Public Policy" testimony presented to the Joint Economic Committee, U.S. Congress, May 21, 1980; and Herschel I. Grossman, "Rational Expectations, Business Cycles, and Government Behavior," in Stanley Fischer, ed., Rational Expectations and Economic Policy (University of Chicago Press, 1980), pp. 5-22.

2. See Robert Lucas, "Econometric Policy Evaluation: A Critique" in Karl Brunner and Allan Meltzer, eds., The Phillips Curve and Labor Markets (North Holland, 1977), pp. 19-46.

The feedback estimates presented below reflect economic and budgetary conditions prevailing in the fall of 1981, and as projected at the time. These include high levels of interest rates, and moderately high unemployment rates. Projections made then did not include the recession of 1981-1982, with its higher level of unemployment and slightly lower level of interest rates. Should those levels be sustained, the feedback rate estimates would need to be adjusted accordingly. The projections also did not include the significantly higher federal budget deficits that are expected currently. These imply that feedback effects working through interest on the federal debt may be noticeably stronger than in the estimates reported in this paper.

Feedback Rates for Combined Proposals

The estimates presented here are for specific policy changes made in isolation. The figures for a cut in individual income tax rates, for example, assume that no other tax or spending changes are made at the same time. In fact, however, various tax and spending changes are usually put into effect at the same time. The feedback rates for such combined policies may be expected to differ from the sum of the individual rate estimates presented here, although there is no reason to believe that the differences would be large. Similarly, the feedback rates for policy changes that are the same as the isolated changes shown here, but of a different size, may be expected to differ.

The Estimation Period

A final caveat concerns the length of the period for which the estimates are made. Estimated feedback rates are given for each policy change for a five-year period, 1982-1986. Because the models on which these estimates are based are meant for use in more short-term contexts, however, the estimates for the later years, 1984-1986, should be regarded as especially uncertain. These figures are presented because a multiyear planning horizon is important, but they really represent only educated guesses.

REDUCTIONS IN INDIVIDUAL INCOME TAX RATES

Table 1 shows estimated feedback rates from different models for a 3 percent reduction in the levels of individual income tax rates, leaving bracket widths and all other provisions unchanged. Feedback rates show the percentage of the direct revenue loss caused by the tax change that is offset by reductions in the

TABLE 1. ESTIMATED FEEDBACK RATES FOR A 3 PERCENT REDUCTION IN INDIVIDUAL INCOME TAX RATES ASSUMING THAT MONETARY POLICY IS PARTIALLY ACCOMMODATING[a] (By fiscal year and model number)

	1982				1983				1984				1985				1986			
	1	2	3	4	1	2	3	4	1	2	3	4	1	2	3	4	1	2	3	4
Total	14	8	23	2	31	19	16	8	35	18	6	11	34	27	-5	9	29	43	-23	4
Revenues	18	14	22	6	39	35	29	20	46	43	33	28	49	59	36	31	49	81	37	31
Outlays	-5	-6	0	-5	-8	-15	-13	-12	-12	-25	-27	-17	-15	-32	-42	-21	-20	-38	-60	-27
Interest	-6	-7	-6	-3	-12	-19	-18	-8	-16	-27	-30	-13	-20	-31	-43	-16	-23	-32	-60	-19

Note: The change is assumed to take effect on October 1, 1981. Results are drawn from simulations on the econometric models of Chase Econometrics, Inc. (Model 1); Data Resources, Inc. version US81C (Model 2); Wharton Econometric Forecasting Associates, Inc. version 6.1 (Model 3); and Evans Economics, Inc. (Model 4). Budgetary estimates from models using a National Income Accounts accounting basis were converted to a Unified Budget accounting basis by CBO.

a. Given as the percentage of static revenue loss offset by budget feedback; a negative sign denotes feedback that reinforces the static deficit impact rather than offsetting it. Detail may not sum to totals because of rounding.

deficit occurring through feedback effects. The calculations assume that the tax change takes effect on October 1, 1981, and that the Federal Reserve holds the nonborrowed reserves of the commercial banking system unchanged from their baseline path.[3] As the discussion in Chapter II pointed out, this represents a "partially accommodating" monetary policy because it allows the money supply to increase automatically as a result of the tax cut as banks borrow monetary reserves to support expansion of checking accounts and other components of the money supply. Partially accommodating monetary policy permits larger changes in GNP, and larger budget feedbacks in response to changes in federal fiscal policy, than an alternative monetary policy that holds the path of the money supply fixed. The consequences of a "nonaccommodating" monetary policy with a fixed money supply path are discussed more fully below.

The results show that there is significant variation among models in feedback rate estimates, especially later in the projection period. The range of variation is smaller for feedbacks involving changes in revenues alone, however, than for those involving changes in both revenues and outlays. This is partly because outlay feedbacks are heavily influenced by changes in interest on the federal debt, which are variable from model to model for reasons that will be explored below.

The revenue feedback rates differ significantly from model to model. Generally, the figures suggest that between roughly one-tenth and two-tenths of the static revenue loss from the tax cut may be recouped through induced increases in revenues during the first fiscal year after the tax change, and that roughly one-third to one-half of the static revenue loss may be recovered in later years. In the last year of the forecast period, the figures for one model even suggest that revenue feedback may be as high as 81 percent.

---

3. The "baseline" forecast on which these and subsequent simulations are based includes the 23 percent individual income tax rate cut as well as other tax and spending provisions passed by the Congress during the summer of 1981. The baseline underlying the simulations of the Wharton model differs from those in the other models in that it includes the 1981-1982 recession. For this reason, minor differences in the estimated feedback rates in the Wharton model may occur relative to the levels they would have if estimated on a baseline comparable to those used in the other models.

The "supply-side" model of Evans Economics, Inc., generally exhibits the lowest revenue feedback rates. Tax rate cuts in this model reduce the growth of wages; this holds down nominal income growth, and with it the growth of tax revenues.[4]

Considering feedbacks that occur through changes in outlays as well as revenue suggests a less optimistic, and still less precise, view of the overall impact of the tax cut on the deficit. Outlay feedbacks increase the deficit, reinforcing the impact of the static revenue loss rather than offsetting it as revenue feedbacks do; this is shown by the negative sign on the estimated outlay feedback rates shown in the table. The main cause of the net deficit-widening impact of the outlay feedbacks is the extra interest on the federal debt that the tax cut makes necessary: since the tax cut may raise interest rates and also make it necessary to issue new federal debt, outlays for net interest increase, more than offsetting reductions in transfer payments and other outlay programs that may be caused by the tax cut. The projected outlays for interest are quite sensitive to the assumed "baseline" levels of interest rates, however. Should interest rates fall significantly from their current levels, these estimates of interest feedback effects could prove to be too high.

The ranges of outlay feedback estimates show, moreover, that estimates of the change in interest payments are more uncertain than those of other feedback components. This is because interest payments are determined through a more complex process than the others. Unlike other feedbacks, for example, the change in interest payments during a given year depends directly on the other feedbacks during that year (because they help determine how much new debt must be financed); it also depends on feedbacks during all other years since the tax change took place (because these help determine how much new debt that needs to be serviced this year was issued during those years); and it depends directly on the "baseline" forecasts of both the federal debt and the levels of interest rates. Each of these factors plays a role in making the feedback rates for changes in interest very different in different models. Tests of the sensitivity of overall feedback rates to the assumed

---

4. The way in which this phenomenon has been embodied in the Evans model has come in for especially strong criticism. See Stephen Braun, "Discussion of the Evans Paper," in The Supply-Side Effects of Economic Policy: Proceedings of the 1980 Economic Policy Conference (St. Louis: Federal Reserve Bank). For more discussion, see "Those Disappearing Reflows" in Evans Economics, Inc., Analysis (September 4, 1980).

path of the Treasury bill rate, for example, show that the feedback rate might vary by as much as 32 percentage points by 1986 for every percentage point difference in the interest rate forecast during the projection period.

Underlying Changes in Economic Behavior

What change in the economy does the tax cut cause in order to produce the feedback effects shown here? Table 2 shows the induced changes in nominal GNP and in taxable incomes, which have to do primarily with revenue feedbacks, and the changes in the rates of inflation, interest, and unemployment, which determine feedback occurring on the outlay side.

Impacts on GNP and Taxable Incomes. The change in GNP that occurs in response to the tax change amounts to slightly less than the static revenue loss from the tax cut in the year of enactment,

TABLE 2. ECONOMIC IMPACTS UNDERLYING BUDGET FEEDBACKS SHOWN IN TABLE 1 FOR A 3 PER billions of dollars unless otherwise noted)

	1982				1983			
	1	2	3	4	1	2	3	4
GNP	6.6	6.3	6.6	4.0	12.7	12.1	8.6	8.4
Wages and salaries	2.3	2.7	1.6	1.5	5.1	5.6	3.5	3.8
Nonwage personal income[a]	1.3	1.5	1.5	0.3	2.9	3.5	3.2	0.1
Corporate profits before tax	3.4	2.0	3.8	1.4	5.1	3.4	3.0	2.9
Inflation rate (GNP deflator, percent)	0.0	0.0	0.04	0.03	0.05	0.0	0.06	0.04
Treasury Bill rate (percentage points)	0.20	0.17	0.07	0.10	0.25	0.19	0.09	0.06
Unemployment rate (percentage points)	-0.07	-0.05	-0.10	-0.01	-0.16	-0.10	-0.09	-0.02
Static revenue loss (fiscal years)	8.3	8.6	8.4	9.2	8.6	9.5	8.8	9.6

NOTE: The change is assumed to take effect on October 1, 1981. Results are drawn from sumulations on the econometric models of Chase Econometrics, Inc. (Model 1); Data Resources, Inc. version US81C (Model 2); Wharton Econometric Forecasting Associates, Inc. version 6.1 (Model 3); and Evans Economics, Inc. (Model 4).

but rises through the "multiplier" process described in Chapter II to roughly 1.5 to 3 times the contemporaneous static revenue loss by 1986. Wages and salaries rise in most models at first by less than half the change in GNP, but by 1986 they rise to approximately half the contemporaneous GNP change. The change in corporate profits, on the other hand, exhibits a pattern that varies from model to model. The change in nonwage personal income, finally, generally rises as a fraction of the change in GNP. This pattern is due largely to increases in interest rates, which increase personal interest income. As a result of these changes and the tax rates that apply to the separate components of the tax base, the overall effective tax rate relating the increase in calendar-year GNP stimulated by the tax change to increases in fiscal-year revenues varies between 14 and 28 percent in 1982, and 22 and 25 percent in 1986.

All models except the Evans agree that the tax cut causes a reduction in the unemployment rate, an increase in interest rates,

CENT REDUCTION IN INDIVIDUAL INCOME TAX RATES (By calendar year and model number; in

1984				1985				1986			
1	2	3	3	1	2	3	4	1	2	3	4
17.5	16.8	11.1	12.5	21.5	26.5	13.5	16.2	25.6	41.1	15.6	17.5
7.7	8.1	5.1	5.9	10.2	12.9	16.5	7.0	12.8	19.9	7.7	6.2
5.0	5.1	4.9	0.3	7.3	6.8	7.0	0.7	10.1	9.1	9.5	0.9
5.0	4.1	2.8	3.8	4.0	6.4	2.6	4.7	2.7	9.5	2.2	5.6
0.08	0.08	0.08	0.05	0.07	0.12	0.08	0.06	0.10	0.10	0.07	0.07
0.29	0.13	0.12	0.07	0.32	0.09	0.19	0.10	0.34	0.04	0.26	0.10
-0.18	-0.10	-0.06	0.02	-0.17	-0.10	-0.03	0.02	-0.15	-0.20	0.00	0.05
9.6	10.5	9.5	10.0	10.6	11.7	9.9	11.2	11.6	12.9	10.0	12.3

a. Nonwage personal income is the sum of farm proprietors' income, nonfarm proprietors' income, rental income, personal interest income, and personal dividend income.

TABLE 3.   "MODEL CONSENSUS" FEEDBACK RATE ESTIMATES FOR A 3 PERCENT
           REDUCTION IN INDIVIDUAL INCOME TAX RATES ASSUMING THAT
           MONETARY POLICY IS PARTIALLY ACCOMMODATING[a] (By fiscal year)

	1982	1983	1984	1985	1986
Total	11	13	12	10	5
Revenues	19	37	45	50	57
Outlays	-8	-24	-33	-40	-52
Interest	-12	-29	-38	-43	-49

Note: The change is assumed to take effect October 1, 1981.
        Estimates are on a Unified Budget accounting basis; figures
        are based on estimated economic impacts of the tax change
        drawn from simulation on CBO's Multipliers Consensus Frame-
        work, which are then fed through CBO's outlay- and revenue-
        estimating models. For a description of these procedures,
        see Appendix C.

a.   Given as the percentage of static revenue loss offset by budget
     feedback; a negative sign denotes feedback that reinforces the
     static deficit impact rather than offsetting it. Detail may
     not sum to totals because of rounding.

and an increase in inflation. The Evans model, unlike the others,
projects that the unemployment rate rises in response to the tax
cut as more persons enter the labor force without finding employment. Despite the reductions in transfers that are caused by
declining unemployment rates, all models show a net negative outlay
feedback rate reflecting increases in interest and, in some cases,
an increase in outlays for indexed budget programs.

    Table 3 gives "model consensus" feedback rate estimates for a
3 percent individual income tax rate cut assuming a partially
accommodating monetary policy.[5]   These show revenue feedbacks

---

5.   The consensus estimates were developed using CBO's Multipliers
     Consensus Framework as revised through the addition of new
     procedures for determining the behavior of prices, real output,
     and employment. Results from the Evans model have not been
     incorporated in the "consensus" estimating procedure mainly
     because of severe criticisms that have been made of the model,
     such as that cited in footnote 4. For a description of the
     elaborated Multipliers Framework, see Appendix C.

rising from 19 percent in 1982 to 57 percent in 1986, and outlay feedbacks from -8 percent to -52 percent in those same years.

The Impact of Inflation on Revenues

How much of the changes in nominal GNP and taxable incomes shown in Table 2 represent increases in prices alone? Although the changes in inflation rates shown in Table 2 seem modest, even these small changes are sufficient to imply that a large part of the increase in nominal GNP stimulated by the tax change is due to induced increases in prices. Because of the interaction between inflation and the progressive income tax, moreover, an even larger fraction of the resulting revenue feedback is due purely to inflation. Figure 1 compares the feedback estimates given in Table 3 with those that would result if the tax cut caused no increase in prices over what they would have been anyway.[6] The revenue feedbacks would be reduced significantly from their 1986 level of 57 percent given in the consensus feedback estimate in Table 3 to only 36 percent. Although these figures are not shown, the overall feedback rate estimate in 1986 would be reduced even more sharply because smaller revenue feedbacks during the earlier years would necessitate issuing more federal debt, which would increase outlays for interest. These results indicate that strong positive feedback rates, which seem desirable for cuts in tax rates, may largely reflect undesirable increases in inflation.

Alternative Monetary Policy Assumptions

There is some uncertainty about how the Federal Reserve might react to a shift in fiscal policy such as a cut in personal tax rates. The Fed has historically been concerned to a varying degree with controlling both the level of interest rates and the level of

---

6. These estimates are derived by holding the GNP deflator at its "baseline" level during each year and using this revised deflator to recompute the levels of nominal GNP that occur after the tax change. This is equivalent to assuming that the response of real GNP to the tax cut is the same as in the "consensus" result, but that prices are unaffected. Corresponding changes in the components of taxable income are computed by applying the same shares to this change in GNP that were observed in the actual simulation underlying Table 3. In computing budget impacts, finally, the elasticity of the individual income tax to taxable income was held at the relatively low level applicable when the only source of "bracket creep" is changes in worker productivity.

Figure 1.

Revenue Feedback Rates for a Reduction in Individual Income Tax Rates

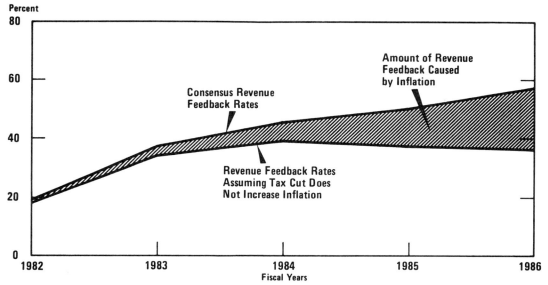

Percent

the money supply, both of which come under pressure from a fiscal policy change. If the Fed were to hold the path of nonborrowed reserves unchanged, as has been assumed in the simulations presented above, both interest rates and the money supply might rise somewhat under a cut in personal tax rates. Consequently, this policy of "partial accommodation" would permit the tax cut to have bigger GNP impacts and feedback effects than a "nonaccommodating" policy, which might not allow the money supply to change at all while interest rates rose substantially. A policy of "full accommodation," on the other hand, would hold interest rates constant while both the money supply and GNP would respond quite strongly.

While partial accommodation has proved a satisfactory assumption about Federal Reserve behavior in the past, the Fed's announced policy since October 6, 1979, has been to put much heavier emphasis on control of the money supply. There is still, however, widespread uncertainty about how far the Fed will actually allow money and interest rates to respond to changes in fiscal policy and other factors that put upward pressure on interest rates.[7] There is also widespread debate as to whether the Fed should continue this policy.

---

7. See, for example, Michael Hamburger and Burton Zwick, "Deficits, Money, and Inflation," *Journal of Monetary Economics*, vol. 7 (1981), pp. 141-50.

TABLE 4. ESTIMATED FEEDBACK RATES FOR A 3 PERCENT REDUCTION IN INDIVIDUAL INCOME TAX RATES ASSUMING A NONACCOMMODATING MONETARY POLICY[a] (By fiscal year and model number)

	1982		1983		1984		1985		1986	
	2	3	2	3	2	3	2	3	2	3
Total	-4	22	-22	14	-36	1	-48	-16	-57	-43
Revenues	4	22	5	29	6	32	7	35	10	34
Outlays	-8	0	-27	-14	-41	-31	-55	-51	-68	-77
Interest	-9	-6	-28	-20	-43	-34	-57	-51	-70	-74

Note: The change is assumed to take effect on October 1, 1981. Estimates were made from simulations on the econometric models of Data Resources, Inc. version US81C (model 2); and Wharton Econometric Forecasting Associates, Inc. version 6.1 (model 3). Other models are not included because of difficulties in analyzing nonaccommodating monetary policy on those models. Budgetary estimates from models using a National Income Accounts accounting basis were converted to a Unified Budget accounting basis by CBO.

a. Given as the percentage of static revenue loss offset by budget feedback; a negative sign denotes feedback that reinforces the static deficit impact rather than offsetting it. Detail may not sum to totals because of rounding.

The reduced feedback rates that may obtain if the Fed does stick to its emphasis on controlling the money supply are illustrated in Table 4, which shows feedback rate estimates from two econometric models for a simulated personal tax cut identical in all respects to that considered above, except that the response of the Federal Reserve is assumed to be nonaccommodating rather than partially accommodating as before.[8] The revenue feedbacks are smaller than those shown in Tables 1 and 2 for the alternative

---

8. That is, the path of M1 was assumed to be held fixed, rather than the path of nonborrowed reserves. Two of the models used in estimating feedbacks under partially-accommodating monetary policy are excluded from the estimates in Table 4 because it has not been possible as yet to make estimates for nonaccommodative monetary policy on these models.

monetary policy option. The negative feedbacks from increased outlays for interest on the national debt, moreoover, are stronger, both because interest rates rise further and because, with smaller revenue feedbacks, the amount of new debt on which interest must be paid is larger. As a result, the overall feedback rate is more likely to be negative. This implies that if taxes are cut while the Federal Reserve holds to a predetermined money supply path, the deficit may be increased by more than the static revenue loss estimate of the tax cut.

Revenue Feedback Through Reduced Tax Evasion

Would reductions in personal tax rates raise tax revenues by reducing tax evasion? While it is likely that the answer to this question is "yes," so little is known about this behavior that reliable estimates cannot be made. The subject is important enough, however, that some attention to the magnitudes involved is worthwhile.

The Internal Revenue Service has estimated that the amount of unreported income in 1976 was between $100 and $135 billion, or 6 to 8 percent of official GNP. Of this, $75 to $100 billion--4 to 6 percent of GNP--consisted of unreported but otherwise legal income, such as tips, cash retail receipts, and expense accounts, while the remainder, $25 to $35 billion, was estimated to be from illegal transactions such as gambling, racketeering, and prostitution.[9] Published statistics on GNP include an estimate of unreported production. The income that this production generates, however, is still missing from the tax base, so while estimated GNP is not affected by the unreported economy, actual tax receipts are.

The IRS has estimated that the loss in 1976 tax revenues from this unreported income was $19 to $26 billion. Preliminary IRS figures for the revenue loss in 1981, moreover, suggest that it has grown substantially, to perhaps $95 billion.[10] If a reduction in

---

9.   Internal Revenue Service, Estimates of Income Unreported on Individual Income Tax Returns, U.S. Treasury Department publication 1104 (9-79) (September 1979).

10. This figure implies that unreported production has grown significantly as a percentage of GNP. See "Statement of Roscoe L. Egger, Jr., Commissioner of Internal Revenue, before the Subcommittee on Oversight of the Internal Revenue Service, Committee on Finance, U.S. Senate," March 22, 1982. This estimate takes account of the fact that, according to the IRS report, most persons who fail to report legal income have relatively low incomes and marginal tax rates. This implies that a lower tax rate applies to this income than to taxable personal income as a whole.

income tax rates could return a significant portion of reported income to the tax rolls, then the feedback rate of the tax cut might be increased significantly. Of course, no change in tax rates would cause all unreported income to be reported, so the increase in taxes would be a small fraction of this figure.[11]

While no reliable estimates of the sensitivity of tax evasion to changes in tax rates are available, the potential impact on budgetary feedback rates can be illustrated by noting that the estimated revenue loss from unreported GNP is roughly equal to the static revenue loss from a 30 percent cut in individual income tax rates in 1982. If a 30 percent tax cut was enacted, and if it reduced the amount of unreported GNP by only one percent, this would increase the feedback rate of that tax cut by one percentage point. Thus, even a modest percentage reduction in unreporting of GNP in response to tax rate cuts could have a noticeable impact on feedback rates.

Legal Tax Avoidance

The amount of tax avoidance through legal tax sheltering, as opposed to the illegal tax evasion described above, is clearly quite large. How much of this activity would disappear in response to reduced marginal tax rates has not been estimated. The response might, however, be large enough to affect tax revenues, and consequently the feedback rates estimated in this paper, significantly. As with tax evasion, published GNP statistics would not be likely to be affected.

REDUCTIONS IN BUSINESS TAX RATES

Reductions in business taxes generate budget feedback by improving business cash flow and the after-tax rate of return on new capital goods, thereby stimulating business investment. While there is general agreement about this broad proposition, the magnitudes of the investment responses and budget feedbacks are highly uncertain. Most econometric models take the same general approach, but their conclusions about the likely magnitudes of the effects

---

11. Economic theory postulates that a tax evader, in deciding whether to report an extra dollar of income, would weigh the extra income to be gained by nonreporting against the extra penalty he might incur, together with any increase in the probability of getting caught and having to pay the penalty.

vary widely, as the results in this section show.[12] Moreover, if
certain arguably reasonable modifications of these models are made,
the results vary still more.[13]

These arguments are meant to show that there is unusual
uncertainty about the feedback effects of any particular business
tax change.   There is still more uncertainty, however, about
whether the range of estimates for a particular plan accurately
reflects the range for business tax changes generally.   It is
possible that the range of estimated effects for a different
proposal would itself be quite different.   A change whose benefits
are distributed among firms in a different pattern, for example,
can be expected to have different investment effects because firms
in different industries vary considerably in their sensitivity to
tax changes.[14]   Some programs, in any case, like the Accelerated

---

Since neither the extra penalty nor the extra risk of getting
caught is very sensitive to the amount of tax evasion for most
persons involved, evaders might reduce their tax evasion relatively sharply in response to a reduction in tax rates.
Reduced tax rates would cut the benefit from extra evasion,
while the risk attached to extra evasion would stay the same
(unless IRS enforcement was simultaneously reduced).   Some
would argue, however, that these considerations apply mainly
to persons considering becoming tax evaders.   Once the skills
are acquired, they may be used indefinitely unless the benefits are reduced quite sharply.

12. For a survey of the ways in which investment decisions are
     treated in different models, see R. Jeffery Green, "Investment
     Determinants and Tax Factors in Major Econometric Models," in
     George M. Von Furstenberg, ed., The Government and Capital
     Formation (Ballinger, 1980).

13. Robert S. Chirinko and Robert Eisner, "The Effects of Tax
     Parameters on the Investment Equations in Macroeconomic Econo-
     metric Models," U.S. Treasury, Office of Tax Analysis Paper 47
     (January 1981), and Chirinko and Eisner, "The Effects of Tax
     Policies on Investment in Macroeconometric Models: Full Model
     Simulations," U.S. Treasury, Office of Tax Analysis Paper 46
     (January 1981).   For a rejoinder, see Allen Sinai and Otto
     Eckstein, "Tax Policy and Business Fixed Investment Revis-
     ited," Data Resources, Inc., unpublished paper (February 16,
     1981).

14. Clopper Almon and Anthony J. Barabera, "Investment in Producer
     Durable Equipment 1976-1990," in George M. Von Furstenberg,
     ed., Capital, Efficiency, and Growth (Ballinger, 1980).

Cost Recovery System implemented in 1981, involve changes that are so large relative to experience that any projection of their effects on investment is extraordinarily uncertain.

Another complication is that the static revenue loss is different for different types of business tax cuts. Broadly speaking, the static loss from a reduction in statutory corporation tax rates varies with the current level of corporation profits, while that for changes in the investment tax credit varies primarily with the current levels of investment and profit. The loss from changes in depreciation provisions, finally, varies primarily with profits and cumulative investment after the tax change takes place.

Table 5 shows budgetary feedback rates for a 3 percent reduction in the levels of statutory corporation income tax rates based on simulations of four econometric models. The change is assumed to take effect October 1, 1981, and the policy of the Federal Reserve is assumed to be partially accommodating.

The variation from model to model in the estimates in Table 5 is even wider than that shown earlier for reductions in individual income tax rates. Nevertheless, most of the estimates suggest that revenue feedback rates are lower early in the five-year projection period than are the corresponding rates for personal tax cuts shown in Table 1. This is because of the relatively long time that is required before business investment responds to a tax change in these econometric models. As time passes, however, the revenue feedback rates for the business tax cut rise to levels generally equal to, or even greater than, those for the personal tax cut. As in the case of personal income tax cuts, some of the deficit-closing impact of this revenue feedback is offset by negative outlay feedbacks. Most models suggest, however, that the overall feedback effect helps narrow the deficit.

Underlying Changes In Economic Behavior

Table 6 shows the changes in GNP and taxable incomes underlying the feedback rate estimates in Table 5, as well as the changes in interest rates, unemployment, and inflation. The figures for the Wharton model reflect the possibility that reductions in corporation tax rates might initially reduce prices relative to what they would be without the tax cut. Consequently, nominal GNP would be reduced despite a slight increase in real GNP accompanying expanded demand for investment goods. This might come about because firms, given an increase in after-tax profits per dollar of sales, could reduce the markup over labor and materials costs that they use in setting prices. The models are far from unanimous,

TABLE 5. ESTIMATED FEEDBACK RATES FOR A 3 PERCENT REDUCTION IN CORPORATION INCOME TAX RATES ASSUMING THAT MONETARY POLICY IS PARTIALLY ACCOMMODATING[a] (By fiscal year and model number)

	1982				1983				1984				1985				1986			
	1	2	3	4	1	2	3	4	1	2	3	4	1	2	3	4	1	2	3	4
Total	10	1	-11	13	23	26	-6	27	34	69	-7	30	45	113	-14	24	42	146	-26	22
Revenues	16	6	-9	14	34	33	2	31	46	70	10	37	58	105	13	36	58	129	12	40
Outlays	-6	-5	-1	-1	-11	-6	-8	-3	-12	-1	-17	-8	-14	8	-28	-12	-16	17	-38	-18
Interest	-6	-5	-6	-3	-11	-10	-18	-7	-14	-8	-30	-10	-17	1	-38	-12	-18	13	-46	-15

Note: The change is assumed to take effect on October 1, 1981. Results are drawn from simulations on the econometric models of Chase Econometrics, Inc. (Model 1); Data Resources, Inc. version US81C (Model 2); Wharton Econometric Forecasting Associates, Inc. version 6.1 (Model 3); and Evans Economics, Inc. (Model 4). Budgetary estimates from models using a National Income Accounts accounting basis were converted to a Unified Budget accounting basis by CBO.

a. Given as the percentage of static revenue loss offset by budget feedback; a negative sign denotes feedback that reinforces the static deficit impact rather than offsetting it. Detail may not sum to totals because of rounding.

however, in predicting that a reduction in prices and nominal GNP might come about in response to a corporation tax cut. The other models predict a more conventional outcome in which increased demand for investment goods causes prices to rise instead. In these cases, nominal GNP rises strongly because of increases in prices as well as in real GNP fueled by increases in investment.

The behavior of taxable incomes varies with that of nominal GNP. Where prices are predicted to fall in response to the tax change, wages and salaries and nonwage personal income fall as well, while corporate profits increase. In models in which prices are predicted to rise, on the other hand, the pattern of changes in the components of taxable income is more like that experienced in response to a cut in personal tax rates: corporate profits, wages and salaries, and nonwage personal income all rise, but the change in wages and salaries generally rises as a percentage of the change in GNP, while the reverse is true of the change in corporate profits. Subsequently, however, the percentage increases in wages and in nonwage personal income grow relative to that of corporate profits. Partially as a result, the effective tax rate on the change in GNP is between 22 and 34 percent in 1982, and 19 and 36 percent in 1986.

The responses of the rates of unemployment and interest are closely related to the price and real GNP effects mentioned above. Unemployment is projected to fall slightly in response to increases in real output, while the response of interest rates is less clear. Interest rates increase in most models.

"Model consensus" feedback estimates for reductions in statutory corporation tax rates assuming a partially accommodating monetary policy are shown in Table 7. The estimates are smaller than those for personal tax cuts; the revenue feedback rates reach 48 percent in 1985, while increases in outlays offset about half of the revenue feedbacks.

Feedback Rates Under a Nonaccommodating Monetary Policy

Table 8 shows feedback rates for a 3 percent cut in corporation tax rates assuming that the Federal Reserve follows a nonaccommodating policy of holding the path of the money supply rigidly fixed. All other assumptions are identical to those underlying Table 6 and 7. As in the case of personal tax cuts, the revenue feedback rates are reduced relative to the levels in Tables 5 and 7, and negative outlay feedbacks for interest appear more likely to be sufficiently strong to dominate all other feedbacks. As a

TABLE 6. ECONOMIC IMPACTS UNDERLYING BUDGET FEEDBACKS SHOWN IN TABLE 5 FOR A 3 PER in billions of dollars unless otherwise noted)

	1982				1983			
	1	2	3	4	1	2	3	4
GNP	2.0	0.7	-0.5	2.4	4.0	4.0	-0.1	4.6
Wages and salaries	0.5	0.4	-0.6	1.0	1.4	1.9	0.1	2.4
Nonwage personal income[a]	0.0	0.4	0.2	0.3	0.0	1.0	0.8	0.7
Corporate profits before tax	1.4	0.3	-0.5	1.2	2.9	1.5	-0.1	1.6
Inflation rate (GNP deflator, percent)	-0.05	0.0	-0.09	0.03	0.05	0.0	-0.02	0.04
Treasury Bill rate (percentage points)	0.09	-0.01	0.00	0.03	0.09	-0.07	0.01	0.05
Unemployment rate (percentage points)	0.00	0.00	-0.02	-0.02	-0.03	0.00	-0.06	-0.04
Static revenue loss (fiscal years)	3.4	2.6	1.9	2.8	3.9	3.0	2.4	3.5

NOTE: The change is assumed to take effect on October 1, 1981. Results are drawn from sumulations on the econometric models of Chase Econometrics, Inc. (Model 1); Data Resources, Inc. version US81C (Model 2); Wharton Econometric Forecasting Associates, Inc. version 6.1 (Model 3); and Evans Economics, Inc. (Model 4).

a. Nonwage personal income is the sum of farm proprietors' income, nonfarm proprietors' income, rental income, personal interest income, and personal dividend income.

result, the possibility exists that a cut in corporation tax rates might increase the deficit by an amount greater than its static revenue loss estimate.

REDUCTIONS IN FEDERAL PURCHASES

Table 9 shows feedback rates based on different econometric models for a $10 billion reduction in federal purchases of goods and services effective October 1, 1981, assuming that the Federal Reserve follows a partially accommodating monetary policy as de-

CENT REDUCTION IN CORPORATION INCOME TAX RATES By calendar year and model number

1984				1985				1986			
1	2	3	3	1	2	3	4	1	2	3	4
6.9	8.7	0.5	6.6	9.4	13.4	1.2	9.7	10.4	18.0	2.3	12.0
2.7	4.3	0.6	3.6	3.9	6.9	1.3	5.3	4.7	7.5	2.1	7.3
0.4	1.5	1.4	1.0	0.3	1.4	2.1	1.5	-0.08	0.9	3.1	2.0
4.5	2.6	-0.1	1.7	6.1	3.4	-0.4	1.8	6.5	3.9	-0.8	1.7
0.00	0.04	0.02	0.04	0.08	0.08	0.05	0.04	0.03	0.03	0.06	0.04
0.11	-0.13	0.03	0.05	0.12	-0.17	0.04	0.08	0.15	-0.21	0.07	0.09
-0.06	-0.08	-0.07	-0.05	-0.07	-0.10	-0.08	-0.06	-0.06	-0.10	-0.06	-0.05
4.8	3.1	2.7	4.3	5.6	3.3	3.3	5.1	6.5	3.4	4.1	5.8

TABLE 7. "MODEL CONSENSUS" FEEDBACK RATE ESTIMATES FOR A 3 PERCENT REDUCTION IN CORPORATION INCOME TAX RATES ASSUMING THAT MONETARY POLICY IS PARTIALLY ACCOMMODATING[a] (By fiscal year)

	1982	1983	1984	1985	1986
Total	-2	13	25	28	20
Revenues	8	26	40	48	42
Outlays	-10	-13	-15	-20	-22
Interest	-10	-13	-25	-31	-33

Note: The change is assumed to take effect on October 1, 1981. Estimates are on a Unified Budget accounting basis; figures are based on estimated economic impacts of the tax change drawn from simulations on CBO's Multipliers Consensus Framework, which are then fed through CBO's outlay- and revenue-estimating models. For a description of these procedures, see Appendix C.

a. Given as the percentage of static revenue loss offset by budget feedback; a negative sign denotes feedback that reinforces the static deficit impact rather than offsetting it. Detail may not sum to totals because of rounding.

TABLE 8.   ESTIMATED FEEDBACK RATES FOR A 3 PERCENT REDUCTION IN
           CORPORATION INCOME TAX RATES ASSUMING A NONACCOMMODATING
           MONETARY POLICY[a] (By fiscal year and model number)

	1982		1983		1984		1985		1986	
	2	3	2	3	2	3	2	3	2	3
Total	-1	-11	0	-5	-17	-6	-36	-14	-43	-27
Revenues	4	-9	15	2	11	10	5	13	8	12
Outlays	-5	-1	-15	-7	-28	-16	-41	-27	-50	-40
Interest	-5	-5	-16	-18	-29	-30	-41	-38	-50	-46

Note: The change is assumed to take effect on October 1, 1981.
        Results are drawn from simulations of econometric models of
        Data Resources, Inc., version US81C (model 2); and Wharton
        Econometric Forecasting Associates Inc., version 6.1 (model
        3).   Other models are not included because of difficulties
        in analyzing nonaccommodating monetary policy on those
        models.   Budgetary estimates from models using National
        Income Accounts accounting basis were converted to a Unified
        Budget accounting basis by CBO.

a.   Given as the percentage of static revenue loss offset by budget
     feedback; a negative sign denotes feedback that reinforces the
     static deficit impact rather than offsetting it.   Detail may
     not sum to totals because of rounding.

scribed above.[15]   Purchases of goods and services include spending
on the federal payroll, defense procurement, highway construction,
and the like.   In fiscal year 1981, purchases accounted for 33 per-

---

15.   The static budget impact of the assumed spending cut in fiscal
      year 1982 is $10 billion.   In subsequent years the static size
      of the cut is assumed to represent the same percentage of
      baseline federal purchases as in 1982.   Accordingly, the
      static budget impact changes over time, as is shown in the
      last line of Table 8, and varies from model to model with the
      baseline forecasts of purchases in those models.   "Partially
      accommodating" monetary policy in this context, as above,
      means a policy of holding the path of nonborrowed reserves
      unchanged.

TABLE 9. ESTIMATED FEEDBACK RATES FOR A $10 BILLION REDUCTION IN FEDERAL PURCHASES OF GOODS AND SERVICES ASSUMING THAT MONETARY POLICY IS PARTIALLY ACCOMMODATING[a] (By fiscal year and model number)

	1982				1983				1984				1985				1986			
	1	2	3	4	1	2	3	4	1	2	3	4	1	2	3	4	1	2	3	4
Total	48	39	43	27	62	40	47	33	68	31	47	48	74	43	39	64	75	65	26	68
Revenues	46	42	41	26	61	52	49	37	71	54	56	61	78	72	60	89	82	96	59	104
Outlays	2	-3	2	2	0	-12	-2	-4	-3	-23	-10	-13	-5	-29	-21	-25	-7	-30	-33	-37
Interest	-4	-6	-4	-3	-9	-18	-13	-9	-11	-27	-23	-13	-13	-31	-31	-15	-13	-31	-40	-17

Note: The change is assumed to take effect on October 1, 1981. Results are drawn from simulations on the econometric models of Chase Econometrics, Inc. (Model 1); Data Resources, Inc. version US81C (Model 2); Wharton Econometric Forecasting Associates, Inc. version 6.1 (Model 3); and Evans Economics, Inc. (Model 4). Budgetary estimates from models using a National Income Accounts accounting basis were converted to a Unified Budget accounting basis by CBO.

a. Given as the percentage of static budget saving offset by budget feedback; a negative sign denotes feedback that reinforces the static deficit impact rather than offsetting it. Detail may not sum to totals because of rounding.

cent of federal spending using a National Income Accounts accounting basis. Since a cut in purchases reduces GNP in these models, the feedback represents lower tax revenues and increases in transfer payments that partially offset the direct reduction in the deficit caused by the spending cut.

The feedback rates in fiscal year 1982 range from 27 to 48 percent, meaning that between 27 and 48 percent of the deficit-reducing value of the reduction in purchases may be lost in 1982 because of feedbacks that tend to widen the deficit. By fiscal year 1986 the feedback rates in the different models vary widely, ranging from 26 to 75 percent.

Revenue feedback rates are generally higher than these overall figures, suggesting that revenues might fall by about half the size of the spending cut by the second year after its enactment. Both the revenue feedback rates and the overall rates, moreover, are generally higher throughout the forecast period than those for personal tax cuts shown in Table 1. This is because cuts in feder-

TABLE 10.   ECONOMIC IMPACTS UNDERLYING BUDGET FEEDBACKS SHOWN IN TABLE 9 FOR A $10
            model number; in billions of dollars unless otherwise noted)

	1982				1983			
	1	2	3	4	1	2	3	4
GNP	-14.5	-16.4	-12.7	-14.3	-21.8	-18.1	-15.7	-25.5
Wages and salaries	-6.0	-9.9	-3.5	-8.2	-10.3	-11.3	-6.4	-17.8
Nonwage personal income[a]	-0.6	-2.3	-2.0	-0.9	-2.5	-3.8	-3.9	-2.6
Corporate profits before tax	-7.9	-3.0	-7.6	-3.3	-8.9	-2.6	-6.1	-4.0
Inflation rate (GNP) deflator, percent)	-0.10	-0.05	-0.05	-0.08	-0.13	-0.04	-0.09	-0.17
Treasury Bill rate (percentage points)	-0.30	-0.26	-0.06	-0.20	-0.38	-0.27	-0.07	-0.29
Unemployment rate (percentage points)	0.30	0.15	0.14	0.19	0.41	0.20	0.21	0.31
Static budget saving (fiscal years)	9.8	9.8	9.8	9.8	10.6	9.8	9.6	10.5

NOTE: The change is assumed to take effect on October 1, 1981. Results are drawn from sumulations on the econometric models of Chase Econometrics, Inc. (Model 1); Data Resources, Inc. version US81C (Model 2); Wharton Econometric Forecasting Associates, Inc. version 6.1 (Model 3); and Evans Economics, Inc. (Model 4).

al purchases have stronger effects on GNP per dollar of static budget impact in the models used in this exercise than do cuts in taxes.

Underlying Economic Factors

Table 10 shows the changes in GNP, taxable incomes, and other economic factors that underlie the feedback rate estimates given in Table 9. The figures show a reduction in GNP ranging from roughly two to more than four times the static impact of the spending cut in 1986. As time passes a larger and larger share of the change is reflected in wages and salaries and nonwage personal income. This pattern of change in the components of the tax base corresponds generally to those observed for the tax cuts discussed above, as well as to the analytic considerations that are described in Appendix C. The effective tax rate on the change in GNP is between 18 and 32 percent in 1982, and 20 and 26 percent in 1986.

BILLION REDUCTION IN FEDERAL PURCHASES OF GOODS AND SERVICES (By calendar year and

	1984				1985				1986		
1	2	3	3	1	2	3	4	1	2	3	4
−28.8	−20.8	−18.6	−38.7	−35.6	−30.5	−23.2	−52.8	−42.3	−44.5	−28.4	−63.1
−14.3	−13.2	−8.9	−27.6	−18.5	−18.1	−11.4	−37.8	−22.8	−25.1	−14.1	−44.8
−4.4	−4.7	−5.6	−4.7	−6.5	−6.3	−7.5	−6.2	−8.7	−8.0	−10.0	−7.2
−9.5	−2.5	−4.9	−6.0	−9.0	−5.0	−4.8	−7.0	−7.9	−7.9	−4.4	−6.8
0.16	−0.04	−0.13	−0.20	−0.10	−0.07	−0.14	−0.26	−0.16	−0.17	−0.10	−0.30
−0.40	−0.22	−0.10	−0.29	−0.39	−0.13	−0.15	−0.29	−0.37	−0.07	−0.22	−0.26
0.41	0.13	0.23	0.34	0.37	0.18	0.20	0.32	0.31	0.20	0.15	0.22
11.5	10.2	9.0	11.2	12.4	11.1	9.3	11.8	13.3	12.1	10.1	12.4

a. Nonwage personal income is the sum of farm proprietors' income, nonfarm proprietors' income, rental income, personal interest income, and personal dividend income.

The spending cut reduces inflation and increases the unemployment rate in all models. The effects of the increase in unemployment on budget outlays are more than offset, however, by the decrease in outlays for interest, part of which is due to the fall in interest rates shown in Table 10.

"Model consensus" feedback estimates for a reduction in federal purchases assuming a partially accommodating monetary policy are shown in Table 11. They show the overall feedback rate varying from 25 percent in 1982 to 18 percent in 1986. For revenue feedbacks alone, the figures are 30 percent in 1982 and 68 percent in 1986.

Feedback Rates Under a Nonaccommodating Monetary Policy

Table 12 shows feedback rates for a $10 billion reduction in federal purchases assuming that the Federal Reserve follows a non-

TABLE 11. "MODEL CONSENSUS" FEEDBACK RATE ESTIMATES FOR A $10 BILLION REDUCTION IN FEDERAL PURCHASES OF GOODS AND SERVICES ASSUMING THAT MONETARY POLICY IS PARTIALLY ACCOMMODATING[a] (By fiscal year)

	1982	1983	1984	1985	1986
Total	25	33	29	21	18
Revenues	30	49	57	61	68
Outlays	-5	-16	-28	-40	-50
Interest	-9	-25	-34	-40	-45

Note: The change is assumed to take effect on October 1, 1981. Estimates are on a Unified Budget accounting basis; figures are based on estimated economic impacts of the spending change drawn from simulations on CBO's Multipliers Consensus Framework, which are then fed through CBO's outlay- and revenue-estimating models. For a description of these procedures, see Appendix C.

a. Given as the percentage of static budget saving offset by budget feedback; a negative sign denotes feedback that reinforces the static impact on deficit rather than offsetting it. Detail may not sum to totals because of rounding.

TABLE 12. ESTIMATED FEEDBACK RATES FOR A $10 BILLION REDUCTION IN FEDERAL PURCHASES OF GOODS AND SERVICES ASSUMING A NON-ACCOMMODATING MONETARY POLICY[a] (By fiscal year and model number)

	1982		1983		1984		1985		1986	
	2	3	2	3	2	3	2	3	2	3
Total	3	44	-12	47	24	45	-42	33	-45	14
Revenues	16	41	17	49	21	56	17	59	25	57
Outlays	-12	2	-30	-2	-45	-12	-59	-26	-70	-43
Interest	-14	-4	-33	-13	-48	-24	-61	-36	-72	-48

Note: The change is assumed to take effect on October 1, 1981. Results are drawn from simulations on the econometric models of Data Resources, Inc. version US81C (model 2); and Wharton Econometric Forecasting Associates, Inc. version 6.1 (model 3). Other models are not included because of difficulties in analyzing nonaccommodating monetary policy on those models. Budgetary estimates from models using a National Income Accounts accounting basis were converted to a Unified Budget accounting basis by CBO.

a. Given as the percentage of static revenue loss offset by budget feedback; a negative sign denotes feedback that reinforces the static deficit impact, rather than offsetting it. Detail may not sum to totals because of rounding.

accommodating monetary policy of holding the path of the money supply rigidly fixed. All other assumptions are identical to those underlying the results in Tables 9 to 11. As in earlier estimates, the assumption of a tighter monetary policy results in lower revenue feedback rates, more strongly negative outlay feedback rates due to changes in interest rates, and a stronger likelihood that the overall feedback rate estimate will be negative. This implies that if monetary policy is nonaccommodating, reducing federal spending might narrow the deficit by an amount greater than the static estimate of budget savings.

REDUCTIONS IN TRANSFER PAYMENTS

Feedback rates are shown in Table 13 for a $10 billion reduction in transfer payments to persons, effective October 1, 1981, and assuming that the Federal Reserve follows a partially accommodating monetary policy.[16] Transfer payments cover such programs as welfare, Social Security, and unemployment compensation; in fiscal year 1981, they accounted for 42 percent of federal spending, using a National Income Accounts accounting basis. The feedback rates range between 2 and 20 percent in fiscal year 1982, and -23 to 39 percent four years later, in fiscal 1986. Like the feedback rates in Tables 9 and 11 for reductions in federal purchases, these feedbacks reflect reductions in tax revenues and increases in some outlays that are stimulated by the cut and serve to offset some of the deficit-reducing effects of cutting transfers. The feedback rates for reductions in transfers, however, are lower than for reductions in purchases, implying that more deficit-reducing progress can be made per dollar of outlay reduction by cutting transfers than by cutting purchases. The reason that feedbacks are weaker for transfer payments than for purchases is that, according to these econometric models, the demand effects of cuts in purchases are stronger because they affect GNP more directly. The models on which these estimates are based do not include supply-side impacts from reductions in transfers, such as the effects of greater incentives to work.

Underlying Economic Factors

The induced changes in GNP and in other economic variables that underlie these feedbacks are shown in Table 14. The table shows a drop in GNP as a result of the spending cut amounting to less than the static size of the cut in 1982, and about 2 to 3 times the static cut in 1986. The drop is reflected in corporate profits as well as wages and salaries, although, as with other policy changes, wages and salaries take up a larger share of the change in GNP later in the estimation period. The inflation rate falls noticeably, and the unemployment rate rises. The effective tax rate is 19 to 25 percent of the change in GNP in 1982, and 21 to 26 percent in 1986. This increase reflects "bracket creep" and

---

16. Like the cut in federal purchases, the static impact of the cut in transfers is assumed to grow over time so that it always represents the same percentage of federal transfers in the "baseline" forecast in each model.

TABLE 13. ESTIMATED FEEDBACK RATES FOR A $10 BILLION REDUCTION IN FEDERAL TRANSFER PAYMENTS TO PERSONS ASSUMING THAT MONETARY POLICY IS PARTIALLY ACCOMMODATING[a] (By fiscal year and model number)

	1982				1983				1984				1985				1986			
	1	2	3	4	1	2	3	4	1	2	3	4	1	2	3	4	1	2	3	4
Total	10	8	20	2	25	20	16	3	29	18	8	10	28	25	-5	20	25	39	-23	18
Revenues	14	14	19	7	33	35	26	16	42	41	31	31	45	56	37	50	46	76	38	56
Outlays	-5	-6	1	-5	-9	-15	-10	-13	-13	-23	-23	-21	-17	-31	-42	-30	-21	-37	-61	-39
Interest	-6	-7	-6	-4	-13	-19	-19	-9	-17	-27	-32	-14	-21	-32	-48	-18	-24	-34	-65	-21

Note: The change is assumed to take effect on October 1, 1981. Results are drawn from simulations on the econometric models of Chase Econometrics, Inc. (Model 1); Data Resources, Inc. version US81C (Model 2); Wharton Econometric Forecasting Associates, Inc. version 6.1 (Model 3); and Evans Economics, Inc. (Model 4). Budgetary estimates from models using National Income Accounts accounting basis were converted to a Unified Budget accounting basis by CBO.

a. Given the percentage of static budget saving offset by budget feedback; a negative sign denotes feedback that reinforces the static deficit impact rather than offsetting it. Detail may not sum to totals because of rounding.

TABLE 14. ECONOMIC IMPACTS UNDERLYING BUDGET FEEDBACKS SHOWN IN TABLE 13 FOR A $10
          number; in billions of dollars unless otherwise noted)

	1982				1983			
	1	2	3	4	1	2	3	4
GNP	-6.3	-7.2	-7.5	-3.6	-13.3	-13.6	-9.1	-9.0
Wages and salaries	-2.1	-3.0	-1.7	-1.6	-5.3	-6.1	-3.7	-5.3
Nonwage personal income[a]	-1.4	-1.8	-1.6	-0.3	-3.1	-4.2	-3.5	-0.4
Corporate profits before tax	-3.3	-2.2	-4.4	-1.3	-5.4	-3.8	-3.1	-2.9
Inflation rate (GNP) deflator, percent)	-0.05	-0.00	-0.03	-0.04	-0.05	-0.05	-0.06	-0.07
Treasury Bill rate (percentage points)	-0.25	-0.21	-0.09	-0.14	-0.30	-0.24	-0.10	-0.15
Unemployment rate (percentage points)	0.06	0.05	0.14	0.03	0.16	0.10	0.17	0.08
Static budget saving (fiscal years)	9.8	9.8	9.8	9.8	10.6	10.9	9.6	10.4

NOTE: The change is assumed to take effect on October 1, 1981. Results are drawn
       from sumulations on the econometric models of Chase Econometrics, Inc. (Model
       1); Data Resources, Inc. version US81C (Model 2); Wharton Econometric Fore-
       casting Associates, Inc. version 6.1 (Model 3); and Evans Economics, Inc.
       (Model 4).

scheduled increases in Social Security taxes, which more than offset the 1981 tax rate reductions in these models.

"Model consensus" feedback rate estimates for cuts in transfer
payments assuming a partially accommodating monetary policy are
shown in Table 15. These figures show revenue feedback rates rising from 19 percent in 1982 to 59 percent in 1986; outlay feedbacks
varying from -8 percent to -50 percent in the same years; and, as a
result, the overall feedback rate varying from 11 percent in 1982
to 9 in 1986.

Nonaccommodative Monetary Policy

Table 16 shows feedback rate estimates for a $10 billion
reduction in federal transfer payments to persons assuming that the

BILLION REDUCTION IN FEDERAL TRANSFER PAYMENTS TO PERSONS (By calendar year and model

1984				1985				1986			
1	2	3	3	1	2	3	4	1	2	3	4
-18.5	-18.2	-11.4	-17.5	-23.0	-28.3	-14.0	-25.8	-27.6	-43.2	-16.9	-31.7
-8.2	-8.6	-5.5	-11.4	-11.1	-13.4	-7.3	-17.4	-14.1	-20.6	-9.2	-21.8
-5.3	-6.1	-5.3	-1.2	-8.0	-8.4	-7.4	-1.8	-10.9	-11.0	-9.9	-2.2
-5.5	-4.4	-2.5	-5.0	-4.5	-6.7	-1.9	-6.0	-3.2	-9.7	-1.1	-5.6
-0.08	-0.04	-0.09	-0.09	-0.07	-0.08	-0.10	-0.13	-0.06	-0.14	-0.09	-0.15
-0.35	-0.21	-0.14	-0.19	-0.39	-0.16	-0.20	-0.21	-0.42	-0.11	-0.28	-0.22
0.20	0.10	0.16	0.14	0.20	0.18	0.12	0.16	0.17	0.20	0.08	0.13
11.5	12.0	9.8	11.2	12.7	13.4	9.4	12.1	13.9	14.9	9.4	13.2

a. Nonwage personal income is the sum of farm proprietors' income, nonfarm proprietors' income, rental income, personal interest income, and personal dividend income.

Federal Reserve holds the path of the money supply fixed--a policy of nonaccommodation. All other assumptions are the same as those underlying the estimates in Tables 13-15. As in earlier estimates, the assumption of monetary nonaccommodation reduces revenue feedback rates and makes overall feedback rates more likely to be negative, again suggesting that the cut in spending, by reducing outlays for interest, might reduce the deficit by more than the static estimate of budget savings.

CONCLUSION

The range of feedback rates that is suggested by different models for each type of policy change makes clear that such estimates are quite uncertain. This is especially true of estimated rates for business tax cuts: the corporation income tax cut, for example, is the only case in which the econometric models used in this exercise gave conflicting results regarding the direction of the impact on nominal GNP. There is still more uncertainty about whether the estimated range for other business tax cuts would be similar.

Despite the variation in feedback rates, there are clear differences in the estimates for different tax and spending changes, as reflected either in the relative sizes of the consensus feedback rate estimates for different policy changes or in the estimates drawn from different econometric models. Cuts in federal purchases appear initially to have the strongest feedback rates in terms both of overall feedbacks and of revenue feedbacks alone. The estimates of revenue and outlay feedbacks together imply that these effects may offset as much as half of the static budget impact of cuts in federal purchases by the third year of enactment. Considering

TABLE 15. "MODEL CONSENSUS" FEEDBACK RATE ESTIMATES FOR A $10 BILLION REDUCTION IN FEDERAL TRANSFER PAYMENTS TO PERSONS ASSUMING THAT MONETARY POLICY IS PARTIALLY ACCOMMODATING[a] (By fiscal year)

	1982	1983	1984	1985	1986
Total	11	13	13	10	9
Revenues	19	37	46	52	59
Outlays	-8	-24	-33	-41	-50
Interest	-12	-29	-37	-45	-50

Note: The change is assumed to take effect on October 1, 1981. Estimates are on a Unified Budget accounting basis; figures are based on estimated economic impacts of the tax change drawn from simulation on CBO's Multipliers Consensus Framework, which are then fed through CBO's outlay- and revenue-estimating models. For a description of these procedures, see Appendix C.

a. Given as the percentage of static budget saving offset by budget feedback; a negative sign denotes feedback that reinforces the static deficit impact rather than offsetting it. Detail may not sum to totals because of rounding.

revenue feedbacks alone suggests that the offset is even higher, and may approach a dollar-for-dollar level after several years have passed.

Cuts in transfer payments and in individual taxes appear to have slightly smaller feedback effects of roughly equal magnitude. Considering outlay and revenue feedbacks together suggests that tax and transfer cuts have feedback effects of less than half their static budget impacts during the entire forecast period. When revenue feedbacks are considered alone, the feedback rates are slightly larger, but are still well below those of cuts in purchases. Cuts in corporation income tax rates, finally, are harder to predict because they are more uncertain than other feedbacks. The consensus estimate is that revenue feedbacks from across-the-board corporation tax cuts approach 40 percent after three years when investment responses are felt. Overall feedback rates are lower mainly because of increases in interest outlays.

In the case of each policy change, the estimates of revenue feedbacks alone vary less from model to model than do the estimates of outlay and revenue feedbacks combined. This is due to the sensitivity of outlay effects, which consist largely of changes in interest payments, and to the differences between models in "base-line" forecasts and in estimates of other feedbacks. The qualita-tive implications of the outlay feedback estimates reported in this chapter are nevertheless important: changes in outlays for interest on the debt that are occasioned by cuts in spending or in taxes can be large, especially after several fiscal years have passed, and especially at current high rates of interest. With tax cuts, for example, the interest on the increased debt that the government must issue to cover the net revenue loss from the cut can swamp other outlay feedback effects.

It would be tempting to conclude that the relatively high revenue feedback rates reported in this chapter for cuts in taxes make such tax cuts nearly "costless" in terms of revenues after several years. In most models, however, large parts of these revenue feedbacks are brought about by increases in inflation caused by the tax cuts. Increases in prices swell taxable income and increase the effective rate of the personal income tax. When both of these factors are discounted, estimated revenue feedbacks are reduced significantly.

The estimated feedback rates for cuts in personal income tax rates that have been presented in this chapter do not take explicit account of potential reductions in tax avoidance that such cuts might bring about. While estimates of the sensitivity of tax avoidance to cuts in tax rates are not available, the impact on estimated feedback rates could be significant.

TABLE 16.   ESTIMATED FEEDBACK RATES FOR A $10 BILLION REDUCTION IN
FEDERAL TRANSFER PAYMENTS TO PERSONS ASSUMING A NONAC-
COMMODATING MONETARY POLICY[a] (By fiscal year and model
number)

	1982		1983		1984		1985		1986	
	2	3	2	3	2	3	2	3	2	3
Total	-3	20	-23	15	-31	3	-44	-16	-52	-43
Revenues	5	19	3	26	7	30	7	34	10	35
Outlays	-8	1	-26	-11	-38	-28	-51	-50	-61	-78
Interest	-9	-6	-29	-21	-42	-35	-55	-55	-66	-79

Note: The change is assumed to take effect on October 1, 1981.
Results are drawn from simulations on the econometric models
of Data Resources, Inc. version US81C (model 2); and Wharton
Econometric Forecasting Associates, Inc. version 6.1 (model
3).   Other models are not included because of difficulties
in analyzing nonaccommodating monetary policy on those
models.   Budgetary estimates from models using a National
Income Accounts accounting basis were converted to a Unified
Budget accounting basis by CBO.

a.   Given as the percentage of static revenue loss offset by budget
feedback; a negative sign denotes feedback that reinforces the
static deficit impact rather than offsetting it.   Detail may
not sum to totals because of rounding.

APPENDIX A.   SPECIAL CASES OF BUDGETARY FEEDBACKS: REDUCED TAX
RATES ON CAPITAL GAINS

Chapter III discussed the feedback effects of changes in major
federal fiscal policies that have a broad impact on the economy.
The economic and budgetary issues can be quite different, however,
for policies that affect smaller segments of the economy.   Two
examples are taken up in this and the following appendix: special

provisions governing taxation of capital gains, and special-purpose tax-exempt bonds.

Capital gains income receives preferential treatment under the federal income tax law.[1] Low capital gains tax rates are thought to increase investment and risk taking, and to allow existing investment capital to flow from one asset to another in response to changing economic rates of return.[2]

Proposals are often made to reduce capital gains tax rates further as means of maintaining or increasing these desirable investment effects. In evaluating the consequences of these proposals for federal revenues and the deficit, it is necessary to consider not only their static revenue costs, which assume no changes in economic behavior, but also the new revenues that such cuts might produce by stimulating new taxable sales of capital assets. Investors who previously had been deterred from selling these assets by the level of the capital gains tax rate may find it advantageous to sell after the rate is reduced.[3] These realizations generate new revenue--revenue feedback--through the capital gains tax, thus reducing the overall revenue cost of such tax cuts.[4]

---

1. Individual taxpayers may exclude 60 percent of net long-term capital gains from taxable income, so the marginal tax rate on capital gains for a given taxpayer is 40 percent of the marginal rate on income from other sources. Taxation of capital gains for corporations is similar.

2. Another reason for lower capital gains tax rates is to reduce the burden on a taxpayer that occurs when a capital gain accruing over several years is realized, requiring the taxpayer to pay tax at progressive rates on several years' income all in one year.

3. For detailed statements of the theory of this "locking-in effect," see Charles C. Holt and John P. Shelton, "The Lock-In Effect of the Capital Gains Tax," National Tax Journal, vol. 15 (December 1962), pp. 337-52; and Beryl W. Sprinkel and B. Kenneth West, "Effects of Capital-Gains Taxes on Investment Decisions," Journal of Business, vol. 35 (April 1962), pp. 122-34.

4. Capital gains tax cuts may also have broader feedback effects through their impacts on business investment, GNP, and employment. These impacts are extraordinarily hard to estimate. Moreover, most current interest centers on the more narrowly-defined feedback effects discussed here. For these reasons, the broader feedback effects are not analyzed in this appendix.

Capital gains tax reflows have become quite controversial even though few reliable studies of their magnitude have been available.[5] Recently, however, two new studies of the possible magnitudes of such revenue effects have been published permitting detailed analysis of arguments about feedback. This appendix summarizes the evidence contained in these studies.[6]

HOW TAX CUTS INDUCE CAPITAL GAINS REALIZATIONS

The level of capital gains tax rates partially determines whether it is worthwhile for holders of assets with accrued capital gains to realize these gains, pay the capital gains tax liability, and reinvest the proceeds in higher-yielding assets. As capital gains tax rates are reduced, the rate of return on alternative assets that is required for such transactions to be worthwhile becomes lower.

A capital gains tax cut should stimulate a surge of new realizations in the first year or so after the cut, representing all the gains which had accrued before the tax cut but which only became worthwhile to realize after the cut took place. After this marginal stock of accrued capital gains is depleted, new realizations should settle at a level determined by the stocks of accrued gains on assets with various rates of return, and by the frequency with which rates of return on alternative assets rise high enough rela-

---

5. For a typical exchange, see "The Impact of the 1978 Capital Gains Tax Cut," Tax Notes (January 12, 1981), pp. 57–58.

6. One eagerly awaited source of evidence was a forthcoming Treasury Department study of the feedback caused by the capital gains tax cuts in the Revenue Act of 1978. While the Treasury paper had been rumored to contain evidence that capital gains feedbacks are very strong, these reports were circulated while the study was in its very early stages. The study was not available at the time of this writing.

    The study was required under Section 533 of the Revenue Act of 1978, P.L. 95-600. The act established a deadline for its release of September 30, 1981, although in May 1982 the report had still not been issued. For an unofficial account, see "Large Unlocking Effect from '78 Gains Cut," Tax Notes (February 23, 1981), p. 382. The act increased the fraction of net long-term capital gains that may be excluded from taxable income from 50 to 60 percent.

tive to those on assets with accrued gains to make it worthwhile to convert these gains. How often this will occur, what assets will be involved, and how much tax revenue will result is difficult to determine. On the basis of theoretical reasoning it seems probable that the rate of realization will be increased by the tax cut. Accurate estimation, however, requires detailed financial analysis and equally detailed data on the tax rates of wealthholders and on the assets that they own in different years. Existing data are not adequate for a fully satisfactory analysis.

EVIDENCE FROM 1973 INCOME TAX RETURNS

Without sufficient data to analyze the capital gains realization problem precisely, analysts have had to make do with approaches tailored to the available information. One such approach is the analysis of data on capital gains realizations of different taxpayers in the same year, which is published periodically by the Internal Revenue Service.[7] Such figures permit inferences to be made about the influences of different tax rates on realizations using formal statistical procedures to compare the realizations of taxpayers with different tax rates, while taking account of other relevant personal characteristics such as age and income from sources other than capital gains.

An analysis of this type by Joseph Minarik suggests that the response of high-income taxpayers to changes in tax rates may be strong enough to increase their net tax payments, but that this is not true of all taxpayers (see Table A-1).[8] Overall, according to

---

7. Most recently the IRS published 1973 Statistics of Income, Supplemental Report: Sales of Capital Assets Reported on Individual Income Tax Returns (November 1980).

8. These estimates are reported in Joseph J. Minarik, "Capital Gains" in Henry Aaron and Joseph Pechman, eds., How Taxes Affect Economic Behavior (The Brookings Institution, 1981), pp. 241-77. Minarik's approach represents an improvement on one developed in an earlier study by Feldstein and associates. See Martin Feldstein, Joel Slemrod, and Shlomo Yitzhaki, "The Effects of Taxation on the Selling of Corporate Stock and the Realization of Capital Gains," Quarterly Journal of Economics, vol. 94 (June 1980), pp. 777-91; and Joseph J. Minarik, "The Effects of Taxation on the Selling of Corporate Stock and the Realization of Capital Gains: Comment," Quarterly Journal of Economics (forthcoming).

TABLE A-1. ESTIMATED RESPONSIVENESS OF TAXPAYERS WITH DIFFERENT AMOUNTS OF DIVIDEND INCOME TO CHANGES IN CAPITAL GAINS TAX RATES (Percentage increase in realized capital gains per percentage reduction in tax rates)

Dividends (1973)				
$3,000–10,000	10,000–20,000	20,000–50,000	50,000	Average
0.76	0.79	1.08	1.27	0.79

SOURCE: Joseph J. Minarik, "Capital Gains," p. 263.

TABLE A-2. ESTIMATED CHANGES IN TAX LIABILITY RESULTING FROM 1978 CAPITAL GAINS TAX REDUCTION (1973 income levels; returns with dividend income $3,000 or more only)

Adjusted Gross Income (dollars)	Change in Tax Liability (percent)
0 – 2,500	−98.0
2,500 – 5,000	−9.1
5,000 – 7,500	−8.4
7,500 – 10,000	−1.7
10,000 – 15,000	−2.0
15,000 – 20,000	−2.1
20,000 – 25,000	−2.5
25,000 – 30,000	−1.4
30,000 – 50,000	−3.2
50,000 – 100,000	−3.7
100,000 – 200,000	−6.1
200,000 – 500,000	−11.1
500,000 – 1,000,000	−16.5
1,000,000 and Over	−20.9
Average	−5.8

SOURCE: Joseph J. Minarik, "Capital Gains."

Minarik's results, taxpayers appear to respond to reductions in tax rates by increasing realizations but not by enough to eliminate any revenue loss from the tax cut.

Minarik has analyzed the revenue implications of the capital gains provisions in the Revenue Act of 1978 using the estimated realization responses reported above. His results are reported in Table A-2. The most important estimate is that capital gains realizations should increase by approximately 0.79 percent for each percentage-point reduction in the capital gains tax rate. Since a 1.00 percent response would be needed to offset entirely and permanently the static revenue loss from the tax cut, this estimate suggests that the increase in realizations is strong enough to eliminate most, but not all, of the static loss. CBO estimates very roughly that these figures imply an overall loss of $1.4 billion in calendar year 1979 tax liability as a result of the capital gains provisions of the 1978 act.[9]

EVIDENCE FROM REALIZATIONS IN DIFFERENT YEARS

The Minarik study is forced by a lack of information to neglect the role played by the accrued stocks of capital gains and the behavior of rates of return on alternative assets. Another study by Mai N. Woo uses data on total accrued gains in different years to attempt to remedy this problem.[10] On the basis of a relatively simple analysis involving only the effective capital gains tax rate and the stock of accrued gains in different years, Woo concludes that the response of realizations to a tax cut should be quite strong in the first year after the cut, but significantly smaller later on because of the depletion of the stock of accrued gains that is caused by the initial surge of realizations. When applied to the 1978 capital gains tax rate cut, Woo's analysis suggests that the cut should have caused an overall increase in capital gains tax revenue of $0.24 billion in calendar 1979, and

---

9. On the basis of recent IRS figures cited below, Minarik's estimate appears quite accurate. See Joseph Minarik "Did the 1978 Capital Gains Tax Cuts Pay for Themselves?" Tax Notes (April 5, 1982).

10. Mai N. Woo, "How Far Can Gains Tax Rates Be Cut Without Loss of Revenue?" Tax Notes (May 11, 1981); and Mai N. Woo, "A Time-Series Analysis of the Lock-In Effect of Capital Gains Taxation in the United States," unpublished doctoral dissertation, Georgetown University (Spring 1981).

smaller (but still positive) net revenue gains in subsequent
years. Because of the depletion of the stock of gains caused by
the 1978 cut, however, Woo concludes that enactment of further cuts
in capital gains tax rates would be unlikely to raise overall
revenues.

The Woo study makes an important contribution by analyzing the
influence of the stock of accrued gains on the response of realizations to a tax cut. Like the Minarik paper, however, it unavoid-
ably excludes from consideration other factors that play a role in
determining realizations, such as the behavior of rates of return
on alternative assets and income from sources other than capital
gains.[11]

CONCLUSION

While the Minarik and Woo studies disagree over the precise
revenue implications of the 1978 capital gains tax cut, they agree
that the "unlocking" response should not have been large enough to
raise significant amounts of new revenues, as had been argued in
earlier studies.[12] This broad conclusion seems to derive support
from preliminary Internal Revenue Service data on realizations
after the 1978 tax cut, which show a reasonably strong realization

---

11. Woo excludes from consideration many factors that may influ-
    ence capital gains realizations while retaining only the ones
    that she believes are "relevant and dominant"--the marginal
    tax rate and the stock of accrued capital gains. Many other
    variables are also relevant, however, and their exclusion can
    bias the measured influence of the included variables because
    the excluded and included factors are unlikely to be statisti-
    cally independent, and because some serial correlation may
    result. Projected levels of capital gains tax revenue that do
    not take these variables into account, moreover, can be quite
    inaccurate. Examples of variables that Woo did not consider
    but which are potentially important are income from sources
    other than capital gains, capital losses on other assets and
    accumulated capital loss carryover, and yields on alternative
    assets.

12. See Feldstein, Slemrod, and Yitzhaki, "The Effects of Taxation
    on the Selling of Corporate Stock and the Realization of
    Capital Gains."

response in the first year but a decline during the second year.[13] (The precise revenue implications of this response remain to be determined by the Treasury Department.) The Minarik and Woo studies both suggest, moreover, that further cuts in capital gains tax rates like that implicit in the general individual income tax rate cut enacted in 1981 are unlikely to be net revenue raisers.

APPENDIX B.   SPECIAL CASES OF BUDGETARY FEEDBACKS: TAX-EXEMPT BONDS

During the past 20 years, the Congress has allowed state and local governments to issue bonds that are exempt from the federal income tax. These bonds are used to finance investment in pollution control, home mortgages, student loans, general industrial development, and other programs that extend beyond the public activities traditionally financed by state and local tax-exempt bonds. The cost to the federal government of these bonds has grown rapidly; the revenue loss is estimated to total $4.6 billion in fiscal year 1982 (see Table B-1). Critics of these programs argue that these costs are excessive, while supporters counter that conventional static revenue cost estimates ignore the budget feedbacks from induced increases in investment and GNP. As a result, the budget feedbacks associated with tax-exempt bonds have become quite controversial.

Measuring the feedback effects of tax-exempt bonds is difficult because the underlying economic relationships are complex. This appendix summarizes the economic interactions that underlie these feedbacks and develops estimates of their size. The discussion is intended to clarify the issues associated with this topic rather than to encourage wider use of revenue feedbacks in evaluating individual budget programs like tax-exempt bonds. The usefulness of revenue calculations for such small budget programs is limited by the fact that all budget programs may have feedbacks, as was illustrated in Chapter III. Calculating the feedback implications of particular programs like tax-exempt bonds is useful only if these differ significantly from those of other programs. Otherwise, different budget items may be compared on the basis of their static

---

13. Noreen Hoffmeier, "Preliminary Income and Tax Statistics from 1980 Individual Income Tax Returns," <u>SOI Bulletin</u> 1,3 (Winter 1981-82), p. 5.

TABLE B-1. REVENUE COST OF TAX-EXEMPT SPECIAL PURPOSE BONDS (By fiscal year; in billions of dollars)

	1982	1983	1984	1985	1986
Industrial development bonds	1.6	2.2	2.8	3.4	4.2
Pollution control bonds	0.8	1.0	1.1	1.2	1.3
Housing bonds	1.5	1.9	2.2	2.5	2.6
Student loan bonds	0.1	0.1	0.2	0.3	0.3
Hospital bonds	0.6	0.8	0.9	1.0	1.1
Total	4.6	6.0	7.2	8.4	9.5

SOURCE: Joint Committee on Taxation, Estimates of Federal Tax Expenditures for Fiscal Years 1982-1987, 97:2 (March 8, 1982).

budget implications alone, in confidence that the feedback implications of a dollar's direct budgetary effect in one program is roughly the same as that in another. This saves the trouble of making repeated estimates of feedback effects, many of which involve complex calculations and are highly uncertain.

ECONOMIC EFFECTS OF TAX-EXEMPT BONDS: THE CASE OF INDUSTRIAL REVENUE BONDS

New issues of tax-exempt industrial revenue bonds (IRBs) totaled $8.4 billion in 1980, and are projected to reach $21.0 billion by 1986. These bonds are issued by state and local government agencies at below-market interest rates reflecting the tax savings available to holders.[1] The proceeds are made available to private firms, which bear the interest costs. Effectively, these firms have

---

1. For a detailed discussion of industrial revenue bonds, see Congressional Budget Office, Small Issue Industrial Revenue Bonds (1981).

borrowed on the private financial market at tax-subsidized rates of interest.

The tax subsidy to these firms' borrowing costs represents a reduction in their overall cost of capital. This may lead to increases in their desired stock of capital, giving rise to increases in investment and consequently in GNP, provided that new savings become available to finance the added investment. Increases in GNP, in turn, imply increased tax revenues and changes in budget outlays—budget feedback effects.

The critical issue in this chain of economic responses to the issuance of IRBs is whether or not savings increase, permitting increases in overall investment to go forward. There are two reasons for believing that such increases may occur. If there is some initial unemployment, expanded investment plans may themselves stimulate increased saving. Firms planning new projects order new equipment or hire construction firms, and the increased wages and profits that result give rise to increases in saving. Moreover, the "multiplier" effects discussed in Chapter II may expand incomes and savings further.[2] Even if there is no significant initial unemployment, however, an increase in saving may occur as a direct result of the tax exemption for interest on the new IRBs. The tax exemption represents an increase in the after-tax rate of return to saving, and this may induce individuals to increase the fraction of their current incomes that is saved, expanding the total supply of savings. On the other hand, if few unemployed resources are available and if the sensitivity of the savings rate to the after-tax rate of return is low, investments may be financed by savings attracted away from other projects; in that case, there may be no net increase in investment.

Unless the increase in saving that is stimulated by the tax exemption is large enough to finance the entire increase in outstanding IRBs, there is likely to be an increase in the interest rates on other borrowing instruments that will partially choke off new investment. Under these conditions, some of the funds invested

---

2. This process does not go forward if the federal government offsets the expansionary effects of the increase in IRB supplies with increases in other taxes or reductions in other spending programs. One reason that the government might have for doing so is that it may have an overall target for the budget deficit as part of its fiscal policy strategy. Such a target would imply that increases in IRB supplies would be matched with decreases in other programs to offset the deficit-widening effects that their tax-exempt status entails.

in new IRBs must be attracted away from other financial assets--
other tax-exempt bonds, partially or fully taxed bonds, bank
accounts, corporate stocks, mortgages, or other assets. When this
happens, interest rates on these alternative financial assets may
rise, increasing the cost of investment and at least partially offsetting the original investment-stimulating effects of the expansion
in IRB supplies.

ESTIMATING FEEDBACK RATES FOR IRB TAX EXEMPTIONS

Revenue feedback effects for removal of the tax exemption for
interest on IRBs can be estimated in a three-step process representing reversal of the effects of IRB issuance as described above. The
first step is to calculate the increase in the cost of capital that
withdrawal of the tax subsidy implies for eligible firms, and the
consequent decrease in their desired stock of capital. The second
step is to estimate the corresponding path of decreases in investment, and consequently of changes in GNP and other economic variables. The final step is to calculate revenue feedback effects on
the basis of these economic changes.

Effects on the Cost of Capital and Desired Capital Stock

The cost of IRB financing for eligible firms can be estimated
by multiplying the interest rate on alternative means of finance by
the average marginal tax rate of holders of IRBs. The result, the
effective after-tax interest rate on alternative financial instruments, is the rate of interest that must be paid on IRBs in order to
make them at least as attractive as taxable issues. Since CBO estimates the average marginal tax rate of holders of IRBs to be 30 percent, the interest cost of financing with IRBs may be 30 percent
lower than the cost of alternative means of finance.[3] Eliminating
new supplies of IRBs increases financing costs to affected firms by
this amount.

Assuming that there is no offset to this 30 percent interest
increase in the form of reductions in other financing costs--as was
done in making these estimates--results in a relatively large estimate of the ultimate impact on investment and GNP. This is equivalent to assuming that there is a relatively large decrease in saving
in response to reductions in IRB issues. This is an exaggerated
figure given current estimates of the responsiveness of saving to

---

3. For details on CBO estimates of IRB financing costs, see <u>Small
   Issue Industrial Revenue Bonds</u>.

changes in its rate of return.   The actual decrease in saving and increase in financing costs for firms are likely to be smaller.

Assuming a full 30 percent increase in borrowing costs does not, however, imply that the increase in the overall cost of capital for eligible firms would be a full 30 percent, since the cost of capital includes depreciation and the costs of other financing instruments that are not affected by the change.   A standard approach to estimating the after-tax cost of capital, taking account of such factors as marginal tax rates, tax depreciation allowances, and investment tax credit rates, suggests that a 30 percent increase in borrowing costs may imply only a 0.3 percent rise in the cost of capital.   This in turn is estimated to imply a 0.3 percent reduction in the desired stock of capital for firms eligible for IRB finance.[4]

Impacts on Investment, GNP, and the Budget

The magnitude of the budgetary effects of these decreases in desired capital depends critically on how fast firms are assumed to reduce their investment in response to the decrease.   Evidence from studies of business investment behavior suggests that it may take as little as five years for firms to carry out a change in desired investment, but that taking account of various complications in investment behavior increases this estimate to 30 years or even more.[5]

The implications of different assumptions about these investment periods for budget feedback effects are illustrated in Tables B-2 and B-3.   These tables show the estimated impacts on investment and GNP and the estimated budgetary feedbacks of eliminating all

---

4. This estimate is a consequence of the assumption that firms' production technology exhibits a unit elasticity of substitution between labor and capital.   These and other technical factors used in developing these estimates are described in detail in Small Issue Industrial Revenue Bonds, Appendix F.

5. A relatively low five-year estimate of this time period is in Peter K. Clark, "Investment in the 1970's: Theory, Performance and Prediction," Brookings Papers on Economic Activity (1979:I), p. 86.   Higher estimates are in Allen Sinai and Otto Eckstein, "Tax Policy and Investment Behavior Revisited" (Data Resources, Inc., 1981).

TABLE B-2.   EFFECTS OF ELIMINATION OF NEW ISSUES OF INDUSTRIAL REVE-
NUE BONDS EFFECTIVE JANUARY 1, 1982, ASSUMING INVESTMENT
RESPONSE REQUIRES FIVE YEARS (By fiscal year; in
billions of dollars)

Change in	1982	1983	1984	1985	1986
(1) Investment[a]	-0.02	-0.28	-0.82	-1.48	-2.08
(2) GNP[a]	-0.40	-0.72	-1.86	-3.92	-5.05
(3) Revenues	-0.07	-0.15	-0.36	-0.58	-0.84
(4) Static revenue gain	0.47	0.97	1.49	2.04	2.62
(5) Net revenue gain ((4)+(3))	0.40	0.82	1.13	1.46	1.78
(6) Feedback rate (in percent) ((3)÷(4))	15	16	24	28	32

SOURCE: CBO estimates.
a. Calendar year change.

increases in IRB supplies effective January 1, 1982.[6]   Table B-2
reflects the assumption that a period of only five years is needed
for all reductions in investment that are required to implement each
decrease in the desired stock of capital, while Table B-3 assumes

---

6.   These estimates are constructed by first estimating the increase
in the aggregrate capital stock implied by a 1 percent increase
in the desired capital stock of firms using IRB financing. This
was done by multiplying the percentage increase in desired capital for eligible firms by the ratio of the increase in IRB supplies in each year to total business fixed investment in that
year, and then applying this factor to the projected level of
the total business capital stock.   The timing patterns of the
increases in investment were taken from those reflected in simulations of investment-expanding tax changes on the Data
Resources, Inc., econometric model.   The increases in GNP induced by each increase in investment were deduced using CBO
estimates of the investment/GNP multiplier, and of the rates of
return to, and depreciation of, changes in the capital stock.
These increases in GNP were then translated into taxable incomes
using the percentages of actual GNP represented by each component of taxable income in1980.   The final feedback estimates
were calculated using CBO's revenue-estimating models.   The
estimates differ from earlier CBO estimates cited in <u>Small Issue
Industrial Revenue Bonds</u> because of refinements in estimating
technique and changes in the economic outlook.

TABLE B-3.   EFFECTS OF ELIMINATION OF NEW ISSUES OF INDUSTRIAL REVE-
              NUE BONDS EFFECTIVE JANUARY 1, 1982, ASSUMING INVESTMENT
              RESPONSE REQUIRES FIFTEEN YEARS (By fiscal year; in
              billions of dollars)

Change in	1982	1983	1984	1985	1986
(1) Investment[a]	-0.01	-0.12	-0.35	-0.62	-0.88
(2) GNP[a]	-0.38	-0.42	-0.88	-1.47	-1.98
(3) Revenues	-0.07	-0.10	-0.18	-0.26	-0.34
(4) Static revenue gain	0.47	0.97	1.49	2.04	2.62
(5) Net revenue gain ((4)+(3))	0.40	0.87	1.31	1.78	2.28
(6) Feedback rate (in percent) ((3)÷(4))	14	10	12	13	13

SOURCE: CBO estimates.

a.   Calendar year change.

that the period is 15 years.   In fact, as the references cited in
footnote 5 point out, the period may be much longer.   The tables
show that the budgetary feedback rates fall as the investment period
is assumed to grow longer.   This is because the reduction in investment occurring each year because of a given decrease in IRB supplies
is less with the longer investment period.

With the assumption of a 15-year investment period, the revenue
feedback as a percentage of the static revenue gain from eliminating
new issues of IRBs is 13 percent in 1986, 19 percentage points less
than the 1986 figure assuming a five-year investment period.   CBO
has not made estimates of the feedbacks that might occur on the out
lay side of the budget.   Given the estimates for general business
tax cuts presented in Chapter III, however, it is likely that these
would show reductions in outlays due mainly to reductions in interest on the debt: since the revenue feedbacks only partially offset
the static revenue gain, eliminating the program reduces the budget
deficit and permits a reduction in federal borrowing.   This reduces
outlays for interest on the debt, contributing an outlay feedback
effect that helps reduce the deficit.

The estimates of feedback effects for a general business tax
cut shown in Chapter III suggest that different estimating techniques result in different estimates.   The same is true in the con-

text of the estimates shown here for decreases in the supplies of
IRBs. It is unlikely, however, that different estimating techniques
would produce higher feedback rates, since the assumptions used in
developing these figures were chosen deliberately to produce the
highest likely feedbacks. In particular, as has already been
pointed out, these estimates assume a strong saving response to
changes in IRB supplies, reflected in the assumption that no offsetting changes in other interest rates were assumed to occur. In
addition, a relatively high degree of responsiveness of desired
capital to changes in its cost was assumed, the investment period
was assumed to be shorter than in some estimates, the percentage
reduction in the cost of capital from IRB finance was overestimated
by assuming that all IRB-financed investment is in structures (which
have a relatively low depreciation rate), and the importance of tax-
exempt financing in the debt structures of investing firms was
deliberately overstated.[7] The overall stance of fiscal and monetary
policy, finally, was assumed to be flexible enough to allow any
budgetary implications of changes in IRB supplies to be realized.

APPENDIX C. TECHNICAL ISSUES IN FEEDBACK ESTIMATION AND CBO ESTI-
           MATION PROCEDURES

As the introduction pointed out, the economic analysis of the
budget feedback process can be broken for analytic convenience into
four distinct stages: the measurement of the response of such
variables as GNP, prices, interest rates, and employment to a
change in budget policy; the determination of the resulting
behavior of wages, profits, and other parts of the tax base; the
estimation of induced changes in effective tax rates; and the
determination of the response of budget outlays to induced changes
in interest, unemployment, and inflation rates.[1] The procedure in
the first stage is already well documented: it is detailed in

---

7. These assumptions are discussed in more detail in Small Issue
    Industrial Revenue Bonds, Appendix F.

1. In fact the different parts of the analysis are not independent
    and should be considered as a whole. Beyond its convenience as
    an aid to understanding the analysis, however, the description
    in terms of separate parts corresponds to the separate contri-
    butions to CBO's quantitative estimates by different groups of
    specialists. A detailed discussion of CBO's estimating proce-
    dures is presented in this appendix.

earlier CBO publications as well as in various macroeconomics text-books at all levels.[2] The analysis involved in the other three stages, however, is not as well known. For that reason, this appendix describes the technical issues involved in each of these stages. This discussion is followed by a brief description of CBO's procedures for carrying out the corresponding quantitative analysis.

RESPONSES OF TAXABLE INCOMES TO CHANGES IN FISCAL POLICY

When economic activity (real GNP) changes because of a change in federal tax or spending policy, taxable incomes respond in characteristic ways.[3]

Wages and salaries normally change at first by a percentage smaller than the percentage change in GNP. This is typically because firms do not change the number of workers, or the number of hours worked, promptly when their production changes. Rather, they normally keep some excess labor available to permit them to increase production easily when demand rises. If the change in economic activity turns out to be long lasting, however, employment and wages gradually adjust so that they change by approximately the same percentage as GNP does after a period of roughly two years.

Profits and dividends, for their part, change initially by a greater percentage than GNP. This is simply a consequence of the fact (cited above) that wage changes lag behind changes in GNP; profits, which are what is left over after wages are paid, expand or contract to make up the difference. However, there appears to be a difference in the degree of sensitivity of the profits of corporations and unincorporated businesses: corporate profits are more volatile with respect to changes in GNP than are the profits of unincorporated businesses.[4]

---

2. See, for example, Congressional Budget Office, Understanding Fiscal Policy (April 1978); and William J. Baumol and Alan S. Blinder, Economics: Principles and Policy (Harcourt Brace Jovanovich, Inc., 1979), pp. 163-96.

3. The generalizations reported in this section are based on William Nordhaus, "The Falling Share of Profits," Brookings Papers on Economic Activity, 1974, 1, pp. 169-218; Congressional Budget Office, "A Model of Taxable Incomes for Forecasting and Analysis," unpublished working paper (1981); and Frank deLeeuw, Thomas Holloway, Darwin Johnson, David McClain, and Charles A. Waite, "The High-Employment Budget: New Estimates, 1959-80," Survey of Current Business (November 1980), pp. 31-32.

    <u>Personal interest income</u> is related more closely to the behavior of interest rates and the stock of interest-bearing assets than to that of profits. Expansionary changes in federal tax or spending policy may increase both the stock of assets and the level of interest rates (and conversely for restrictive policy measures), so interest income is initially quite sensitive to changes in policy.

    These generalizations about the changes in different components of taxable incomes <u>as percentages of their baseline levels</u> permit other generalizations about these changes <u>as percentages of the change in GNP</u>. Since wages and salaries normally represent a relatively large fraction of GNP (about half), the small percentage of their own former level by which wages and salaries initially change in response to a change in fiscal policy represents a significant fraction of the change in GNP. Corporate profits are normally a small fraction of GNP (about 10 percent), so the large percentage of their former level by which profits initially change in response to a change in fiscal policy represents a smaller percentage of the change in GNP. Roughly speaking, then, the change in GNP may initially give rise to equal changes in corporate profits and in wages and salaries--somewhat less than half the change in GNP. As time passes, the change in profits declines toward a percentage of the change in GNP about equal to the normal fraction of GNP represented by profits--about 10 percent. Meanwhile the change in wages and salaries rises to about half the GNP change.[5]

---

4. The reasons for this difference are not obvious. It may be that it is easier to lay off workers in unincorporated enterprises, and that in very small businesses entrepreneurs also perform labor. Profits may therefore represent a steadier share of income.

5. Certain modifications to these generalizations must be made for particular changes in federal policy. Changes in federal purchases that involve payrolls have larger effects on wages and salaries, and smaller effects on profits, since in such cases nearly the entire direct GNP effect of the policy change is reflected in wages and salaries. Liberalization of depreciation allowances reduces reported profits directly, since tax-allowable depreciation is one item deducted from gross business income before arriving at taxable profits. Changes in Social Security tax provisions, finally, may ultimately affect wages and salaries relatively strongly, since firms treat their Social Security tax payments as part of the total compensation of labor, and may reduce direct wage payments to compensate for increases in the employer share of Social Security taxes. It may take several years, however, for this pattern to emerge. The more immediate effect may be an increase in prices.

TAX RATES APPLICABLE TO CHANGES IN TAXABLE INCOMES

A final step in determining the revenue feedback effects of changes in federal fiscal policy is estimating the tax rates that apply to the changes in each component of the tax base, as well as the timing patterns according to which the resulting federal revenues are reflected in the Unified Budget. There are differences in the rates that apply to different parts of the tax base. Moreover, some of these rates can be expected to change in response to changes in the economy, including those caused by fiscal policy.

The Individual Income Tax. The effective marginal tax rate applicable to changes in wages and salaries and nonwage personal income under the individual income tax depends on the extent to which those changes reflect increases in prices alone as opposed to increases in aggregate real income. This is because increases in aggregate real income often reflect increases in the number of taxpayers while income increases representing inflation alone are more likely to accrue to existing taxpayers. If in the first case the new taxpayers have average income close to that of existing taxpayers, the tax rate applicable to the aggregate increase in taxable income is close to the existing average tax rate. Increases in income accruing to existing taxpayers, however, are taxed at these taxpayers' highest current rates; moreover, if the increase in income is sufficient to push these taxpayers into higher tax brackets, it is taxed at still higher rates.[6] In either case, the tax rate applicable to an inflation-induced increase in aggregate

---

6. Inflation also affects the effective individual income tax rate in ways that are harder to predict if it increases the wages that taxpayers receive at rates that differ from the rates of increase for items that they deduct from taxable income. If the prices of deductible items rise significantly faster than current wage rates, the effective marginal tax rate on wages and salaries can fall since taxpayers' deductions will rise. This sort of difference in rates of increase appears to have raised the effective individual income tax rate on adjusted gross income substantially in 1972–74 since wages rose faster than deductions during that period. See David Greytak and Richard McHugh, "Inflation and the Individual Income Tax," *Southern Economic Journal*, vol. 45 (July 1978), 168–80.

income is significantly higher than the existing average rate.[7]
CBO estimates that the individual income tax rate applicable to
increases in wages and salaries and in nonwage personal income
reflecting increases in aggregate real income alone in 1982 would
be approximately 17 percent. For increases reflecting inflation,
the estimate is higher--roughly 24 percent. Because of the
combined effects of inflation and the recently-enacted cut in
personal tax rates, both rates should fall slightly over the next
two years before nearly leveling off in 1985 because of the
indexing provisions of the 1981 tax bill.

This tax rate determines the accrual of tax liability under
the individual income tax. These revenues appear in the Unified
Budget on a slightly different schedule because of delays in withholding and remittance of estimated payments, and because of the
final settlements that take place during the January-June period of
each year. As a result of these considerations, CBO currently
estimates that 75 to 76 percent of individual income tax liability
accruing during a given calendar year is recorded in budget
receipts during that same fiscal year, with the remaining 24 to 25
percent recorded the following fiscal year.

Payroll Taxes for Social Insurance. The overall marginal tax
rate on aggregate wages and salaries is increased by contributions
to Social Security. The wages and salaries of all workers except
federal and some state and local government employees are taxable
under the Social Security tax at a flat rate of 13.4 percent up to
a limit of $32,100 per worker in 1982.[8] In future years the
statutory limit will increase automatically, roughly according to
the rate of wage inflation lagged by two years; the statutory tax

---

7. For further discussion of these points, see Congressional
   Budget Office, "Bracket Creep and the Elasticity of the
   Individual Income Tax," unpublished working paper (1981); and
   Frank deLeeuw, Thomas Holloway, Darwin Johnson, David McClain,
   and Charles A. Waite, "The High-Employment Budget: New
   Estimates, 1955-80," Survey of Current Business (November
   1980), pp. 13-43.

8. Participation of state and local governments in the Social
   Security system is optional. Seventy-two percent of all state
   and local government workers are covered.

rate is scheduled to increase as well.[9] For calendar year 1982, CBO estimates that the effective marginal tax rate relating changes in Social Security tax liabilities to changes in aggregate wages and salaries is approximately 11 percent. Seventy-two percent of liabilities accruing during a given calendar year are estimated to flow into Unified Budget receipts in the same fiscal year, while the remaining 28 percent are received the following fiscal year.

The Corporation Income Tax. CBO estimates that an effective marginal tax rate of 36 percent applies to increases in corporate profits before tax in 1982. While the statutory marginal tax rate is 46 percent, the effective rate in recent years has been lower because part of any increase in corporate profits accrues in nontaxed forms such as tax-exempt interest income, or is offset by deductions of state and local taxes paid or carryovers of losses from other years. Moreover, increases in taxable profits also tend to be associated with increases in the dollar magnitudes of credits

---

9. This tax structure means that the effective Social Security tax rate on aggregate wage and salary income may fall temporarily when wages are increased by inflation, because a greater percentage of some workers' incomes is lifted above the taxable limit, which is not affected until two years later. When aggregate wage income is increased by increases in employment, on the other hand, the aggregate effective tax rate will be roughly unchanged if the wages of the newly employed are roughly the same as those of existing workers. The indexing formula states effectively that the amount of taxable wages per worker in a given year will be given by the ratio of total taxable wages in the first quarter of the year two years earlier to total taxable wages in the first quarter of the year before that. This ratio times the previous year's taxable wage base gives the new base. See Social Security Bulletin: Annual Statistical Supplement, 1976, p. 23. For more on the effects of changing economic conditions on Social Security revenues, see Congressional Budget Office, Paying for Social Security: Funding Options for the Near Term (February 1981), pp. 15-18; and John C. Hambor, "An Econometric Model of OASDI," U.S. Department of Health, Education, and Welfare, Social Security Administration Working Paper No. 10 (November 1977).

claimed against tax, such as the investment tax credit and the foreign tax credit.[10]

Because the accounting and tax payment systems of corporations are complicated and long drawn out, CBO estimates that only 50 percent of a change in corporate tax liability accruing during a given calendar year appears in Unified Budget receipts in the same fiscal year; 48 percent appears the following fiscal year, and 2 percent the year after that.

Other Federal Revenue Sources. The remaining sources of federal revenues are indirect taxes (excise taxes, including the windfall profits tax, customs duties, and estate and gift taxes), and miscellaneous receipts, which consist largely of profits returned to the Treasury by the Federal Reserve banks. Among these, customs duties and excises other than windfall profits tax receipts vary with changes in GNP such as those caused by changes in fiscal policy, and therefore contribute to feedback. CBO estimates that the effective tax rate relating customs and excise tax liabilities to GNP is approximately one percent. This effective rate is expected to decline slightly in future years under the impact of recent Multilateral Trade Negotiations on customs duties. Federal Reserve profits, finally, vary with interest rates and various economic factors determining the size of the Federal Reserve System's portfolio of Treasury debt instruments. 1982 Federal Reserve profits are estimated to change by approximately 0.8 billion for every one percentage point change in the Treasury bill rate. CBO estimates that 75 percent of Federal Reserve profits and indirect tax liability for a given calendar year appear in the Unified Budget in that fiscal year, while the remaining 25 percent is received in the following fiscal year.

Overall Effective Tax Rates

Taken together, the information developed here on the behavior of income shares and marginal tax rates permits inferences to be

---

10. The rule of thumb used here and based on these tendencies in recent experience is highly uncertain. When the economy is emerging from a recession and more corporations than usual have been suffering losses, the effective tax rate may be lower because of larger loss carryovers. The behavior of credits such as the investment tax credit is variable, depending on factors such as investment behavior and the profitability of operations overseas. The effective tax rate is also sensitive to the distribution of profits across corporations, which differ in their individual tax rates.

drawn about the overall effective tax rate that applies to changes in GNP that are stimulated by fiscal policy changes. For GNP changes that are substantially "real"--that is, that do not result from induced increases in inflation--the effective overall marginal tax rate may be roughly 21 percent in the first year after the fiscal policy change takes effect (1982). If on the other hand the GNP change results entirely from induced increases in prices, implying that a higher income tax rate applies to wages and salaries and nonwage personal income, the overall tax rate on GNP is closer to 26 percent in 1982. The actual rate will be somewhere between these extremes in the first year, depending on how much real GNP and prices change in response to the change in fiscal policy. In subsequent years, moreover, the rate might change because of the action of several factors, such as changes in the share of the impact on GNP that is purely "real" as opposed to inflationary; reductions in personal income tax rates, and increases in Social Security tax rates scheduled under recent legislation; the ongoing effects of "bracket creep" before indexation is implemented in 1985; and the decline in the share of the change in GNP going to profits in favor of wages and other shares that are taxed at different rates, as described above.[11]

RESPONSES OF BUDGET OUTLAYS TO CHANGES IN UNEMPLOYMENT, INFLATION, AND INTEREST RATES

Impacts of Changes in the Unemployment Rate. The main outlay impact of changes in the unemployment rate is through the Unemployment Compensation program. Increases in unemployment expand outlays as more workers become eligible, and the average benefit increases because newly unemployed beneficiaries have higher wage histories. For 1982, CBO estimates that outlays for Unemployment Compensation change by about $5 billion for each percentage point by which the unemployment rate changes in the same year. Smaller

---

11. At least two other complications attend this calculation. The tax rates cited here are those determining the accrual of tax liability. These accruals are not reflected immediately in receipts by the federal government because liabilities are only paid off after a lag which is as long as two years in the case of the corporation income tax. The figures do not reflect changes in receipts of earnings from the Federal Reserve System, which contribute noticeably to changes in overall federal receipts, although in ways which are hard to quantify at this general level.

increases occur in outlays for food stamps and other "transfer payment" programs whose beneficiary populations rise.[12]

Outlays Indexed to the Inflation Rate. Several outlay programs are indexed by law so that they increase automatically when prices increase.[13] The principal examples are Social Security and federal employee retirement. Other programs, like Medicare, Medicaid, and unemployment compensation, are indirectly indexed because outlays rise automatically with the prices of the services that they finance, or because of increases in the wage histories of beneficiaries. If a change in fiscal policy increases or decreases the rate of inflation, outlays for these programs are increased or decreased relative to the levels projected at baseline inflation rates. CBO has estimated most recently that a one-percentage-point increase in the inflation rate during 1982 would add $0.5 billion to outlays for automatically and indirectly indexed programs in 1982.

Interest on the Federal Debt. Fiscal policy changes affect federal outlays for interest on the debt by changing market interest rates and federal borrowing. These feedbacks work against most other feedback effects. A tax cut, for example, increases both interest rates and federal borrowing, and this increases outlays for interest. This feedback works to increase the deficit, thus offsetting the other feedback effects of the tax cut. The magnitude of these negative feedbacks can be substantial, as is shown in Chapter III.

CBO'S ESTIMATING TECHNIQUES

CBO's procedures for estimating budgetary magnitudes involve the joint efforts of the Fiscal Analysis Division, which is responsible for economic forecasting; the Budget Analysis Division, which carries out forecasts of budget outlays on the basis of economic forecasts as well as other data; and the Tax Analysis Division, which develops the corresponding forecasts of revenues. Entirely new forecasts of the levels of economic and budgetary magnitudes

---

12. For further quantitative discussion of these and other spending programs discussed in this section, see Congressional Budget Office, Baseline Budget Projections: Fiscal Years 1982-1986 (July 1981), pp. 53-58.

13. Other programs are often increased, not automatically, but at the discretion of the Congress. Such programs are not included in this discussion.

are developed two or more times per year according to the requirements of the Senate and House Budget Committees. At other times,
estimates of changes in economic and budgetary variables that might
be caused by specified changes in policy or in economic conditions
are made using special procedures within each division. These procedures were used to develop the "model consensus" feedback estimates presented in this paper.

The Multipliers Consensus Framework

The Multipliers Consensus Framework maintained by the Fiscal
Analysis Division is a facility for reconciling diverse estimates
from different economic models of the economic response to changes
in budgetary policy. The approach is an algebraic procedure for
averaging key components of fiscal policy "multipliers" in different large-scale econometric models. This framework is currently
geared to generate "consensus" nominal GNP impacts from the
econometric models of Chase Econometrics, Inc; Data Resources,
Inc.; and Wharton Econometric Forecasting Associates, Inc.[14] The
associated impacts on real GNP and the GNP deflator are estimated
by a newly-developed "consensus" procedure that has recently been
added to the framework,[15] while the impacts on interest rates and
taxable incomes are estimated using a consensus procedure representing an extension of the original "Multipliers" approach.

These procedures were used in generating consensus estimates
for this report of the economic impacts of the changes in indivi-

---

14. For detailed description of the "Multipliers" framework, see
    Congressional Budget Office, The CBO Multipliers Project: A
    Methodology for Analyzing the Effects of Alternative Economic
    Policies (1977). While CBO has been using the Evans Eco-
    nomics, Inc., model as well as those mentioned in the text,
    this model has not been incorporated in the "Multipliers"
    framework because of technical difficulties with the current
    version of the model; for an account of these problems, see
    Albert Ando, "Discussion of the Evans Paper," in The Supply-
    Side Effects of Economic Policy, Proceedings of the 1980 Eco-
    nomic Policy Conference, Federal Reserve Bank of St. Louis
    (May 1981), pp. 103-112. Another commercial model that is in
    use at CBO, the Townsend-Greenspan model, has not yet been
    incorporated in the "Multipliers" framework because it is
    quite new.

15. See Congressional Budget Office, "Real-Price Decomposition of
    Nominal GNP Changes," unpublished technical paper (1981).

dual income taxes, federal purchases, and federal transfer payments to persons. In the case of each policy change, the static impact on a National Income Accounts basis was estimated within each full-scale econometric model.[16] These impacts were then averaged, and the result was used in generating economic impacts using the Multipliers Consensus Framework and associated procedures as described above.

The economic impacts of the cut in corporation income tax rates studied in this report were not estimated using the formal consensus framework, since the economic response to a cut in business tax rates is quite different from those of other changes in budget policy. For this policy change, the impact on real GNP was taken to be the average of those estimated by the two full-scale econometric models that were judged to have the most reasonable overall response patterns (those of Chase Econometrics, Inc., and Data Resources, Inc.). The GNP deflator was assumed to be unaffected by the policy change, while the changes in interest rates and taxable income shares were generated by the procedures described above.

Estimated Outlay Impacts

Once the estimated economic impacts of changes in budget policy were computed, the corresponding changes in budget outlays were estimated by the Budget Analysis Division.

The impacts of projected changes in the inflation rate were accounted for using current baseline projections of spending levels in relevant programs together with the statutory scheduling of price adjustments, where applicable. Estimated outlay impacts of projected changes in unemployment rates were computed using current baseline projections of benefit levels of unemployment compensation, Social Security, food stamps, and other programs in which the

---

16. As is noted in Chapter III, the static impact of the personal income tax rate cut was generated in each model by multiplying the cut in tax rates by the baseline forecast of the tax base in that model. The static impacts of the cuts in purchases and in transfers in each model were estimated by cutting spending by $10 billion during the first fiscal year, and by an amount during each subsequent year that represented the same percentage of spending in the model's "baseline" forecast as did $10 billion during the first year. This procedure implied that the static impact of each cut was estimated to grow over time.

eligible population is sensitive to the unemployment rate, together with econometric estimates of the sensitivity of these eligible populations to the aggregate unemployment rate. Estimates of outlays for net interest were based on a current baseline projection of new federal financing and refinancing together with projected baseline levels of interest rates. Forecasted changes in interest rates and in overall deficits were also incorporated, together with projected timing patterns and maturity structures for the resulting federal financing needs. Account was also taken of changes in outlays for student loans and other programs that are sensitive to interest rates.[17]

Estimated Revenue Impacts

The revenue impacts of the four budget policy changes were estimated by the Tax Analysis Division using estimated impacts on taxable income shares, interest rates, prices, and other economic variables developed by the Fiscal Analysis Division as described above. The estimates were made using a simple accounting framework that applies the Tax Analysis Division estimate of the appropriate effective marginal tax rate to the estimated changes in each taxable income component. These figures are then combined with timing factors reflecting the accrual of receipts under the Unified Budget. This procedure accounted for revenues collected under the individual and corporation income taxes as well as the payroll taxes for social insurance. A similar procedure applying effective tax rates to nominal GNP as a whole accounted for revenues accruing from federal excise taxes and customs duties, while changes in the earnings of the Federal Reserve banks were estimated as a function of projected levels and changes in Federal Reserve holdings of Treasury debt and interest rates.[18]

---

17. For quantitative aspects of these estimating techniques, see Congressional Budget Office, Baseline Budget Projections: 1982-1986 (July 1981), pp. 17-22.

18. For discussion of the magnitudes of revenue effects estimated using these procedures, see Congressional Budget Office, Baseline Budget Projections: Fiscal Years 1982-1986 (July 1981), pp. 33-35.

Appendix G
Budget Issues: State Practices for Financing Capital Projects

A study by the staff of the U.S. General Accounting Office. Reprinted from GAO Report AFMD-89-64, July, 1989, pp. 6–22.

INTRODUCTION

We have been examining the concept of capital budgeting as a step in strengthening financial management within the federal government. We have reviewed various aspects of this issue.[1] Last year, we released an exposure draft (Budget Issues: Capital Budgeting for the Federal Government, GAO/AFMD-88-44, July 1988) which proposes restructuring the unified budget into operating and capital components.[2]

Most states have had experience with capital budgeting and related financing techniques. In our 1986 study of states' capital budgeting practices, 37 of 45 states responding indicated they had some form of a capital budget. Furthermore, 21 states replied they used long-term borrowing to finance capital assets. According to the U.S. Bureau of the Census, the 50 states spent over $34.5 billion in 1986 on capital assets.

The federal government, on the other hand, has limited experience using a capital budget as a decision-making tool during the budget process. Its unified, cash-based budget treats outlays for capital and operating activities the same. This should not be the case. Capital outlays, whether they are for buildings or loans, produce future streams of benefits to the government or the economy. The benefits may be cash flows, facilities to carry out government operations, or other such economic returns. Although the current budget provides a comprehensive report

---

[1] Budget Issues: Capital Budgeting Practices in the States (GAO/AFMD-86-63FS, July 15, 1986); Capital Budgeting for the Federal Government (GAO/T-AFMD-88-3, December 8, 1987); and Budget Reform for the Federal Government (GAO/T-AFMD-88-13, June 7, 1988).

[2] The term "capital budget" is not universally defined. In our capital budget proposal, we define a capital budget as that part of the unified budget which segregates capital revenues and investments from the operating budget's revenues and expenses. Capital revenues and capital investments are excluded from the calculations of the operating budget's surplus or deficit, but the operating budget is charged for depreciation.

of cash receipts and outlays, it does not distinguish between expenditures for capital investments and current operations.

While our previous work provides an overall framework for capital budgeting at the federal level, a number of issues must still be resolved prior to implementing a capital budget within the unified federal budget. One of those issues concerns developing specific procedures for defining and identifying capital assets. A second issue is how capital acquisitions should be financed. A third issue, which has generated congressional interest, is whether borrowing maturity can or should be linked to the life of the capital asset. We examined how the states budget for and finance capital investments. Their experiences could provide useful information to the Congress, OMB, and federal departments and agencies as they evaluate and discuss the concept of implementing a capital budget for the federal government.

Objectives, Scope, and Methodology

The principal objectives of this study were to (1) identify the criteria states use for defining a capital asset and the procedures they use in developing their capital budgets, (2) identify the methods states use to finance capital assets, and (3) determine the extent to which states link borrowing maturities to the useful life of a capital asset.

To achieve our study objectives, we reviewed related books, articles, and other published reports, including prior GAO reports, for information on state budgeting practices for financing capital assets. In addition, we selected nine states for detailed study.

In selecting these states, we used our 1986 report (Budget Issues: Capital Budgeting Practices in the States, GAO/AFMD-86-63FS, July 15, 1986) which identified 19 states that (1) used long-term borrowing for financing capital assets and (2) linked borrowing maturities to asset life. From these 19 states, we wanted to select states which were responsible for a majority of the capital expenditures. For the 19 states, we reviewed (1) the amount of the state's total capital outlays, (2) the state's capital outlays as a percentage of total state expenditures, (3) the amount of the state's long-term debt, and (4) the percentage of the state's capital outlays financed by long-term debt. For our current study, we wanted to determine whether and, if so, how the states directly link borrowing maturities to asset life.

As a result of considering the above criteria, we selected a judgmental sample of 8 states for study—Florida, Georgia, Illinois, Kentucky, New Jersey, New York, Pennsylvania, and Virginia. These 8 states accounted for 73 percent of the capital expenditures made by the 19 states in our 1986 survey. In addition, we selected Colorado because it not only uses a capital budget, but it also responded to our 1986 survey that it does not link long-term borrowing maturities to asset life. Colorado also identified long-term borrowing as its largest source of revenue for capital expenditures. In addition, Denver, Colorado, is the home of the National Conference of State Legislatures, where we obtained valuable information for this study.

In each of the nine states, we interviewed various state officials to obtain information regarding their capital budgeting approach and process and to gather data on their respective state's debt. We also used U.S. Bureau of the Census data on capital expenditures if the information we obtained from the individual states was not presented in the format necessary to complete our review.

The results of our review are presented in the following three chapters. Chapter 2 describes the criteria states use for defining capital assets and the procedures they use in developing their capital budgets, and it also provides specific details on the nine states in our survey. Chapter 3 discusses the states' general methods of financing capital projects. Chapter 4 examines whether there is a linkage between the financing method or borrowing maturity and a capital asset's useful life.

STATE BUDGETING FOR CAPITAL ASSETS

A majority of the 50 states use a capital budget, segregating capital and non-capital expenditures. Furthermore, most states have established (1) criteria for defining capital assets and (2) specific capital budgeting procedures. The nine states we reviewed all use a capital budget and most have defined capital assets and developed capital budgeting procedures.

Defining Capital Assets

Capital assets are often defined as those intended for long-term use or possession. They are relatively permanent in nature, and they are not intended for resale. Usually, they are classified into general groups, such as land, buildings, and equipment. The general classifications represent many types of capital projects which cover various functions such as medical and educational facilities, prisons, parks and recreation, general public buildings, airports, and highways.

Table 2.1: States' Capital Expenditures,
Fiscal Year 1986

Dollars in billions

	All states	Nine states in GAO review
Highways	$20.4	$6.8
Education	5.1	1.2
Natural resources	1.1	0.3
Hospitals	0.8	0.3
Correction	1.6	0.4
Parks and recreation	0.4	0.1
Public buildings	0.4	0.2
Health	0.3	0.2
Police	0.3	0.1
Airports	0.2	0.1
Other	3.9	2.1
Total	**$34.5**	**$11.8**

Source: U.S. Bureau of the Census State Government Finances in 1986.

In fiscal year 1986, the 50 states reported that they spent about
$34.5 billion on capital projects. Table 2.1 provides the 50 states' capital
expenditures by function, according to the U.S. Bureau of the Census.
The table also includes the capital expenditures made by the nine states
included in our study. Because most states in our study presented their
expenditures by departmental or cabinet structure rather than listing
them strictly along functional lines, we used the Census Bureau's data
on capital expenditures.

According to the National Council of State Legislatures, there are seven
states which have no specific written definition for a capital asset. In
the nine states we visited, most have developed strict definitions for
determining what constitutes a capital asset, while others have only
general and broad criteria. The criteria each of the nine states uses to
define capital assets are discussed below. For purposes of the following
discussion, the terms capital asset, capital project, and capital items are
used interchangeably, depending on the state's choice of terminology.

Colorado - A capital asset is any nonstructural improvement to land
such as land-grading, drainage, roadways, or sewers, which costs more
than $100, but less than $5,000; any alteration or repair which costs
more than $100, but less than $15,000; and any equipment, furniture,
etc. with a useful life over 1 year, which is continuously used, and

which costs $100 to $50,000. Projects such as site purchase or development, major repairs or renovations, building construction or equipment purchases which cost more than $50,000 are considered capital construction.

Florida - A fixed capital outlay is real property (land, buildings, appurtenances, fixtures and fixed equipment, structures, etc.), including additions, replacements, major repairs, and renovations to real property which materially extend its useful life or improve or change its functional use. Also, it includes the capital outlay necessary to furnish and operate a new or improved facility.

Georgia - This state's budget office determines what constitutes a capital asset. It bases its decision primarily on an estimated useful life determination of proposed capital projects. The life of the capital asset or project should equal or exceed 5 years. Additionally, the project must be "bondable," that is, market conditions are favorable for selling bonds, and bond ratings will not be adversely affected.

Illinois - This state's budget office also determines, at its discretion, what constitutes a capital asset. It relies on the project's bondability in determining whether it can be classified as capital. For bonding, projects must meet certain criteria, including: the project is of a durable nature; the project is not subject to inherent risk of failure or intended to fulfill temporary needs; expenditure of funds must appreciably increase or enhance the interest of the state; the state must have a direct interest; and project expenses must exceed $25,000.

Kentucky - Capital projects are any construction item, or any combination of capital construction items necessary to make a building or utility installation complete which are estimated to cost $200,000 or more and major items of movable equipment estimated to cost $50,000 or more.

New Jersey - This state defines capital projects as any undertaking proposed to be funded by general obligation bonds, or by an appropriation in the annual capital budget. They include the acquisition of land and the purchase of construction and equipment which exceed $50,000.

New York - Capital projects are any projects which would be financed through debt issuance by the state, funded by an appropriation from the Capital Projects Funds, or funded by an appropriation from the Capital Projects Budget Bill. Capital projects are those involving the acquisition, construction, demolition, or replacement or major repair of a fixed asset.

Pennsylvania - Capital projects include any building, structure, facility, or physical public betterment or improvement; any land; any furnishings, machinery, apparatus, or equipment for any public betterment or improvement; or any undertaking to construct, repair, renovate, improve, equip, furnish, or acquire any of the foregoing, provided that the project is designated in a capital budget as a capital project. The project or equipment must have an estimated useful life in excess of 5 years and an estimated cost in excess of $100,000.

Virginia - Capital items include real property acquisitions; new construction greater than 5,000 square feet or greater than $75,000; improvements to existing facilities greater than $200,000 or resulting in operating costs greater than $15,000; and equipment, if financed through revenue bonds. The detailed descriptions and criteria for property and improvements, plant and improvements, and equipment are provided in state budgeting procedure guidelines.

How States Budget for Capital Assets

A prior GAO report[1] on capital budgeting issues reported that 37 of 45 states responding said they have a distinct capital budget where capital capital amounts are reported separately. The report also provided the following information about the states that responded:

17 states maintain separate capital and operating budgets,
13 states combine capital and operating amounts into an overall budget total, and
7 states use various other procedures to report capital.

In November 1987, the National Conference of State Legislatures completed a study, Capital Budgeting and Finance: The Legislative Role, regarding the legislative role in the capital budgeting and finance process for the states. One of the recommendations the study made to the states was that the "executive branch should be required to submit to the legislature a single capital budget that includes all capital requests for the forthcoming budget period, by priority, across agencies, presented by funding source." The study's authors favor a single and separate capital budget request because they believe that

presenting all capital requests, arranged by proposed funding source, in one separate document enhances the examination of alternative financing mechanisms for various projects and

---

[1]Budget Issues: Capital Budgeting Practices in the States (GAO/AFMD-86-63FS, July 15, 1986).

- showing all requests in one place and ranking them allows legislators to better consider the trade-offs among different projects across state agencies.

Because capital budgeting practices in the nine states we visited vary from state to state, it would be very difficult to call any one state typical. Some states are more centralized than others, with greater decision-making on capital projects within the governor's office. On the other hand, some states are strong legislatively and use legislative committees to establish priorities.

For example, in Florida, Kentucky, and New Jersey, all state agencies are required to prepare a capital facilities plan every year. In Florida and Kentucky, the governor's office reviews and consolidates the plans before submitting them to the legislature. In New Jersey, the state's Office of Management and Budget is charged with coordinating the agencies' plans. The final plan is then presented to the State Capital Planning Commission which develops and maintains, on an ongoing basis, short- and long- range capital spending plans and makes final recommendations to the Governor for inclusion in the annual state budget. In contrast, Colorado has a permanent legislative committee, known as the Capital Development Committee, which is charged with ranking capital construction projects in order of importance for annual recommendation to the Joint Budget Committee.

All nine states we visited maintain distinct capital budgets, but only five combined the capital and operating budgets into one overall budget. For instance, as part of its annual financial report, Kentucky prepares combined general purpose financial statements showing sources of revenue, including proceeds from bond sales, and overall expenditures, including those for capital projects. In addition, the financial report provides more detailed statements for individual funds such as the general fund, special revenue funds, and federal funds. One of these individual funds is the capital projects fund. According to Kentucky's annual financial report, the capital projects fund accounts for financial resources appropriated by the General Assembly for the acquisition, construction, or renovation of major capital facilities, and for the acquisition of major equipment, other than items financed by proprietary funds, certain trust funds, and university and college funds.

Similarly, Illinois' state budget provides summary statements indicating general uses for all appropriated funds. However, the budget also provides detailed financial data for all the state's departments, agencies, and programs. The capital program is included in the budget report as a separate program. It provides information regarding the sources of capital funds and a description of all current and proposed capital projects.

METHODS OF FINANCING CAPITAL ASSETS

States finance capital assets primarily through the use of current revenues and long-term debt. In a 1986 GAO survey,[1] 29 of the 37 states who
responded that they used a capital budget indicated that one of their
primary funding sources for financing capital assets was current revenues (state revenues and intergovernmental funds from the federal government and local governments). Similarly, 21 of the reporting states
indicated that long-term borrowings were also a primary source of funds
for financing capital assets.

Current Revenues

Current revenues consist of state revenues and intergovernmental
funds. State revenues are collected primarily from taxes, current
charges, and miscellaneous general revenues. Taxes constitute the largest segment of state revenues, with sales and gross receipts taxes,
income and license taxes being the major kinds of taxes.

Miscellaneous general revenues comprise the second largest type of
state revenues. These revenues include interest earnings, rents, royalties, lottery net income, donations, and fines and forfeitures.

Current charges are the third largest type of state revenues. States
receive these revenues from the public for performing specific services
benefitting the person charged, such as rents and sales from furnishing
commodities or services, and intergovernmental transfers.

In addition, states receive intergovernmental funds. These funds include
federal funds and funds from local governments. The federal funds are
frequently grants for physical capital investments, such as highways or
community and regional development projects. The funds from local
governments are for shares in the financial support of state-
administered programs, reimbursements for services performed or
expenditures made for them by the state, payments on debt service of
state debt issued for their benefit, and repayment of advances and contingent loans extended to them.

In some of the nine states we visited, current revenues fund most capital
expenditures, with a majority of those revenues provided by the federal
government. In Georgia, a state official told us that the state's 1988 projected capital outlays would be about $900 million. Current revenues,

---

[1]See footnote 1 in chapter 2.

including state revenues of $180 million and federal funds of $315 million, would finance 55 percent of the total capital expenditures. The federal funds were earmarked for Georgia Department of Transportation projects.

In Virginia, the 1987 capital budget program was projected at $343 million. Except for $36 million of long-term debt, the program was financed entirely from current revenues. For the 1987-88 fiscal year, New York planned capital outlays of $2.2 billion. Approximately 50 percent, or $1.1 billion, would be derived from current revenues. Of that portion, federal funds would comprise 62 percent.

In six of the states that we visited, lottery revenue is used to support specific programs. Pennsylvania, for example, primarily uses its net lottery revenues for programs in its Departments of Aging or Public Welfare. However, some states are beginning to use lottery revenues for capital projects. For instance, Colorado's 1988-89 budget has dedicated lottery proceeds to finance $16.5 million in capital projects.

We also found that state governments use current revenues for lease payments in order to finance capital projects. Leasing is a capital financing mechanism that allows a state to pay for the purchase or use of a facility or equipment in installments rather than all at once. State governments use leasing as an alternative to bond financing or full cash payments.

There are several types of leases. The two more common forms are operating leases and capital leases.

An operating lease is a short-term rental agreement where the state leases an asset for only a fraction of the asset's useful life. As the lessee, the state uses the asset in return for regularly scheduled rental payments, which are classified as current expenses. The lessor, normally a manufacturer or vendor, provides the asset in return for the agreed-upon payments. The lessor is usually responsible for maintenance, insurance, and taxes. These responsibilities enable the lessor to claim the tax benefits of ownership.

A capital lease, also known as a lease-purchase agreement, is one where the ownership of the asset normally transfers from the lessor to the lessee at the end of a lease term. This agreement establishes periodic payments divided into both principal and interest, and a date when title to the asset may transfer, if the lessee meets all contractual requirements. A capital lease may involve a single item or multiple items.

States reported they use leasing instead of borrowing for several reasons:

- A state is unable to enter the bond market with a new issue because it has reached its legal debt limit.
- A state is unable or unwilling to enter the bond market because of high interest rates.
- The need for voter approval on bond issues makes leasing more attractive.
- The useful life of an asset or changing technology makes issuance of long-term bonds an inappropriate financing mechanism. Lease agreements are typically 4, 6, or 8 years, whereas long-term bonds are normally for 10 years or more.

Some of the nine states we visited use leases extensively. Florida leased nearly $400 million worth of equipment in 1986. Kentucky leases $35 million to $40 million a year in small equipment. Similarly, Colorado's state agencies had issued about $26 million in lease-purchase agreements through 1985. New York planned to issue about $426 million of lease-purchase debt to finance about 20 percent of its 1987-88 capital program.

Debt Financing

States use a combination of short-term and long-term debt to finance capital expenditures. Short-term debt consists of interest-bearing debt payable within 1 year from the date of issue, such as bond anticipation notes, bank loans, and tax anticipation notes and warrants. States use short-term debt mostly in anticipation of tax receipts; it is seldom used to finance the start of capital projects.

Long-term debt, however, is the most frequently used debt financing tool for capital assets. In 1988,[2] we reported that the use of long-term debt by the 50 states increased, in aggregate current dollars, from about $19 billion in 1961 to over $212 billion in 1985. During the 1981-85 period, state debt grew at an annual rate of 12 percent.

There are two major forms of long-term debt—full faith debt and nonguaranteed debt.

Full Faith Debt

When a state issues full faith debt, it promises to repay the debt using, if necessary, its taxing powers to obtain the needed funds. Full faith debt

---

[2]Budget Issues: Overview of State and Federal Debt (GAO/AFMD-88-11BR, January 27, 1988).

is generally issued in the form of general obligation bonds. A distinction does exist between general obligation bonds payable from unlimited taxing powers, and those where the power to tax for debt repayment is subject to some kind of limitation. In either case, the bondholders rely on the state government to take whatever action is necessary to ensure repayment. For this reason, general obligation bonds generally have lower interest rates than nonguaranteed debt.

The states we visited finance varying portions of their capital projects with general obligation bonds. In New York, new general obligation debt totaling $365 million was planned to finance about 17 percent of the 1987-88 capital plan. Georgia was planning on issuing $405 million of general obligation bonds to finance 45 percent of its $900 million capital program.

Another category of full faith debt is zero coupon bonds. These bonds are offered at a discounted rate and are payable at maturity at their full par value. Of the nine states in our review, Illinois was the only state that was using this financing method. The state is calling the bonds "General Obligation College Savings Bonds," and they are issued in denominations which have maturity values in $5,000 multiples. Illinois' first zero coupon bond issue in 1988 was for about $93 million. Officials indicated that they sold out immediately and probably could have sold about three times the state's initial issue.

Debt Limitations

Most states have constitutional or statutory debt limitations to prevent state and local government fiscal mismanagement and to protect the interests of bondholders. One common form of debt limit restriction is placing a limit on the dollar amount of the debt the state may incur. This amount is either given as an absolute value or as a flexible limit, such as a percentage of the state's revenue receipts or a percentage of the assessed value of the state's property tax. For example, Pennsylvania's constitution establishes a debt limit at 1.75 times the average of the state's annual tax revenues for the previous 5 years. In Georgia, the constitution restricts borrowing to 10 percent of the previous year's net revenue. At the other extreme, Colorado's constitution prohibits the state from issuing any full faith and credit debt.

A second type of debt limit restriction requires that debt be issued only for certain public purposes. Generally, those purposes must be related to capital projects. In Florida, for example, the state constitution states that state bonds pledging the full faith and credit of the state may be issued only to finance or refinance the cost of state fixed capital outlay projects.

A third type of debt limit restriction is one that requires voter approval in order to exceed certain dollar limits for debt or to simply issue any debt. In Kentucky, there are no constitutionally imposed limits on debt, but all debt financing must have prior approval by the state's General Assembly, which sets the limits on the volume of bonds issued. In Florida, full faith and credit bond issuance is generally subject to voter approval.

Nonguaranteed Debt

Nonguaranteed debt is payable solely from a specific pledged source, as opposed to general obligation bonds, where the full faith and credit and taxing power of the issuing state are pledged for the repayment of the debt. Nonguaranteed debt is financed primarily through revenue bonds. They are secured by user fee repayments (revenue generated from the project itself) or earmarked revenues. In case of default, the issuing state does not have a legal liability to pay the debt from general tax revenues. Its liability only extends to the specific revenue pledged to repay the debt. In fiscal year 1986, state nonguaranteed debt represented over 73 percent of all long-term debt for the 50 states.

The principal advantages of revenue bonds over general obligation bonds are that they normally do not require voter approval, and they generally are not subject to constitutional or statutory debt limitations. Other advantages are the capital projects are usually paid for by user fees, and bond issuers can adjust their rate structure to keep up with inflation and pay operating costs. The major disadvantage is that revenue bonds are issued for a long time period in order to provide a safe margin for covering costs and debt charges. This extended maturity increases the bond interest rate.

There are three broad categories of revenue bonds. Government enterprise bonds, the traditional category of revenue bonds, are used to borrow funds for constructing or improving facilities, such as utilities, airports, and bridges. In such instances, utility payments, landing fees, and bridge tolls provide revenues to fund the debt service.

Public bonds for private purposes are issued to support activities such as housing, economic development, construction, industrial pollution control, student loans, or other activities. The private beneficiaries of the bonds' proceeds repay the debt through lease payments or other kinds of periodic payments which cover debt service over the life of the bonds.

A third category of revenue bonds, government lessee bonds, differs from the previous two types in that repayment is usually from taxes, not revenue-producing activities. In these cases, one state entity with borrowing authority issues bonds and uses the debt proceeds to acquire facilities for another state entity. The two entities enter a lease agreement which requires the entity using the facility to make lease payments to the entity that issued the bond. The lease payments are usually funded by tax revenues and are used to liquidate the debt.

Revenue bonds are issued by a state or public authority. For example, Florida's state government had $605 million in revenue bonds outstanding at the end of fiscal year 1987. These bonds financed roads, bridges, and other capital projects and will be paid from revenue sources other than state taxes. In Kentucky, which has not issued any general obligation bonds since 1965, revenue bonds are used to finance capital projects. These bonds are secured by revenue from the projects financed, not the full faith and credit of the state or state taxes.

In addition, revenue bonds may also be issued by a political subdivision of a state, referred to as a "public authority." A public authority is a public bond-issuing entity generally established by statute to finance public facilities that have not or cannot be financed by an existing state agency or that can be better financed by an authority. Authorities usually do not have taxing power, but accomplish their financing with revenue bonds.

There are several different types of public authorities. Some authorities are established to finance public projects that can be repaid with user fees. Others are set up as building corporations to issue debt for constructing state offices and other facilities and repay the debt from leases to the state. A third type of authority provides an interest subsidy (tax-exempt status) to a private activity defined as being in the public interest (for example, health facilities authorities).

The actions of a public authority can affect a state's credit, regardless of whether the authority's issues are backed by the state. Furthermore, public authorities are viewed by some as a means of "back-door financing" because they are normally beyond the control of voters and legislators.

In the nine states we visited, we found that such authorities are used to finance specific projects. For instance, New Jersey has 13 public authorities, which had outstanding debt of almost $15 billion at the end of 1986. On August 31, 1987, five Illinois state authorities had outstanding debt totaling over $700 million. Colorado also makes extensive use of public authorities, and their cumulative indebtedness as of 1985 was nearly $3 billion. New York has 29 major authorities which had $24.1 billion in outstanding revenue and nonrecourse bonds at the end of 1986.

Another type of nonguaranteed debt is "moral obligation bonds." Typically, these bonds are issued by state agencies under legislation that implies that the state will secure the debt if default is threatened. Usually, the issuing agency must establish a debt service fund from bond sale proceeds. The agency will then use income from its normal sources to meet debt service costs as they become due. However, if this income is not sufficient to meet costs, money is advanced from the debt service reserve fund to make payments. The state, in turn, may then make appropriations to restore the debt service fund.

Moral obligation bonds are not enforceable against the legislature, and the legislature has the legal right to elect to forego such payments. On the other hand, it is assumed that, because the state legislature authorized such debt under these terms, it incurred a "moral obligation" to meet the revenue shortfalls needed for debt service. New York's public authorities, for example, had $15.4 billion in moral obligation bonds outstanding at the end of September 1986.

As stated above, state debt limits do not apply to nonguaranteed debt, because state debt limits are either silent on the issue, and such debt is generally not considered a legal obligation of the state, or specifically exclude this type of debt from constitutional limitations. As a result, nonguaranteed debt is occasionally used to circumvent or avoid a state's debt limit requirements. Indeed, officials in several of the states we visited indicated that they relied heavily on nonguaranteed debt, partly because it was easier to issue since they did not have to follow the states' legislative limitations regarding debt.

LINKAGE BETWEEN BORROWING MATURITY AND ASSET LIFE

The nine states we visited generally do not directly link the financing method and borrowing maturity to a capital asset or its useful life. It is sometimes held that linking debt maturity to estimated asset life assures that those who benefit from the asset will be the ones who help pay for it (through their annual taxes used for debt service). However, the states we visited link the type and maturity of the financing more directly to factors other than asset life, such as prevailing market conditions, the states' desire to achieve the best economic results, the need to maintain a high quality bond rating, legislative limitations on the type and amount of debt, and other considerations.

In our review, Kentucky was the only state that attempts to match an asset's useful life to the financial life of its debt. In that state, useful life is determined according to capitalization and depreciation procedures. User agencies advise the financing agency and the budget office of the useful life based on their maintenance and obsolescence experience. However, there are no written state guidelines for determining useful life.

Two of the nine states—Pennsylvania and New York—statutorily require that the life of the project be longer than the project's financing. Although their laws require that the bond life be shorter than the project life, market conditions and the need to keep interest rates as low as possible actually determine the life of bonds issued for capital projects in these two states. Virginia state officials said that financing terms are designed to provide the best economic result for the state and are not tied directly to the individual asset. However, these officials added that financing is not undertaken where the life of the asset would not at least match or exceed the term of the financing.

Generally, we found that the nine states we visited do not link borrowing maturity to a specific asset's life. In Pennsylvania, for example, there is no attempt to associate a specific type of financing with specific assets. Debt issues are usually influenced by general bond market conditions, and they are tied to state programs rather than to specific capital assets. In Georgia, general obligation bonds are the only long-term financing used. According to a Georgia budget official, many factors influence the decision to finance certain assets with debt. These factors include overall fund availability, amount of other commitments or agency requests, market factors, the useful life of the assets, the specific nature of the assets being financed, the size of the bond package, and the legislative attitude about bonds.

Although the nine states generally are not linking borrowing maturity to asset life, some states are using a form of financing known as certificates of participation, where specific assets or a pool of assets are used to secure the debt. The certificates are usually issued for a relatively short period of time, normally 5 years. More importantly, they are not a full faith and credit obligation of the state because the capital assets financed are security for the certificates.

New Jersey is one state that uses certificates of participation, primarily to finance equipment purchases. The state is consolidating all outstanding equipment lease purchase agreements under certificate of participation arrangements. In 1987, for example, New Jersey issued certificates of participation which would give the certificate holders a proportionate share of lease payments that would be made for certain items of equipment, such as computers and helicopters. The certificates' security is the equipment itself, which is specified in detail in the offering prospectus.

Florida also uses certificates of participation, but its process varies somewhat from New Jersey's. Florida's certificates are being used to create a financing pool which can be drawn down as needed for equipment acquisition. However, the certificates' security remains the equipment itself or more directly the "program rental" that will be paid by state agencies for the equipment's use. The equipment that can be acquired under Florida's program is described as "computers, copiers and office equipment, office automation/word processing equipment, typesetting equipment, tractors, telecommunications or telephone system equipment."

New York is also using certificates of participation. However, it imposes a statewide limit of $160 million. The governor recommends that agencies use certificates of participation for funding the installment or lease purchases of real and personal property.

Index